THE WARS OF WATERGATE

ALSO BY STANLEY I. KUTLER

The American Inquisition (1982)

Privilege and Creative Destruction:
The Charles River Bridge Case (1971, 1989)

Judicial Power and Reconstruction Politics (1968)

EDITOR

American History: The View from Abroad (1986)

The Promise of American History:
Progress and Prospects (1982)

Looking for America, 2 vols. (1975, 1980)

John Marshall (1973)

The Supreme Court and the Constitution:
Readings in American Constitutional History (1969, 1977, 1984, 1990)

New Perspectives on the American Past,
2 vols., with Stanley N. Katz (1969, 1972)

The Dred Scott Decision: Law or Politics? (1967)

THE WARS OF WATERGATE

THE LAST CRISIS OF RICHARD NIXON

STANLEY I. KUTLER

W · W · NORTON & COMPANY

NEW YORK · LONDON

For Jeff, David, Susan Anne, Andy

and

Sandy

Copyright © 1990 by Stanley I. Kutler

First published as a Norton paperback 1992 by arrangement with
Alfred A. Knopf, Inc.

All photographs credited to the *Washington Star* are copyright
by the *Washington Post* and reprinted by permission of the D.C.
Public Library.

Library of Congress Cataloging-in-Publication Data

Kutler, Stanley I.
  The wars of Watergate: the last crisis of Richard Nixon / Stanley I. Kutler.—1st ed.
    p. cm.
    1. Watergate Affair, 1972–1974. 2. Nixon, Richard M.
(Richard Milhous), 1913– . 3. United States—Politics and
government—1969–1974. I. Title.
E860.K87 1990
364.1′32′0973—dc20   89-43351
                                                          CIP

Printed in the United States of America

ISBN 0-393-30827-8
W. W. Norton & Company, Inc.
500 Fifth Avenue, New York, N.Y. 10110
W. W. Norton & Company Ltd
10 Coptic Street, London WC1A 1PU

1 2 3 4 5 6 7 8 9 0

At the coming of the seventh month, when the people of Israel were in their towns, all the people gathered as one body in the square in front of the Water Gate. They asked Ezra the scribe to bring the book of the Law of Moses which the Lord had enjoined upon Israel. On the first day of the seventh month, Ezra the priest brought the Law before the assembly, both men and women, and all who could understand; and he read from it, facing the square in front of the Water Gate, from early morning till noon.

NEHEMIAH 8:2-3

PREFACE
TO THE NORTON PAPERBACK EDITION

Watergate is both living and contested history. Richard Nixon and many of the combatants remain committed to writing and interpreting history as they wish it to be. As we commemorate the twentieth anniversary of the Watergate affair, the interests of contemporary participants and observers dominate historical attention. Books and articles regularly appear, breathlessly revealing "new" accusations or conspiracies, designed to relieve the accusers of their own culpability and point the way to different villains. In *Scandal*, Suzanne Garment recently observed that "[w]e are still mesmerized by each new theory or fragment of information related to Watergate."

Recently, for example, a group of President Nixon's former aides concocted new accounts of the break-in story. In *Silent Coup*, which is described as the "John Mitchell book," after one of Nixon's aides who was deeply involved in the break-in and the cover-up, the principal characters seek to exonerate Nixon and themselves. Now, two decades later, they implicate John Dean as initiating the Watergate burglary and the subsequent cover-up in order to protect his particular interest. The book rests on hearsay evidence, much of which involved altered stories by participants or was elicited by leading, suggestive questions. Meanwhile, the well-documented record, including taped conversations and sworn testimony, was cast aside, dismissed as if it were the product of some totalitarian system of justice. Pleas at the bar of history require more than unsubstantiated finger-pointing.

From another side, various factions or persons who contributed to the fall of the Nixon Administration continue to compete for preeminence. Prosecutors, various congressional groups, and journalists naturally seek recognition for their roles in exposing and punishing wrong-doers. In this work, I have tried to assess each fairly and to recognize that each contributed to the mosaic that makes for the history of Watergate.

The search for "Deep Throat" continues to fascinate. But as more documentary materials are released, the media's role in uncovering Watergate diminishes in scope and importance. Television and newspapers publicized the story and, perhaps, even encouraged more diligent investigation. But it is clear that as Watergate unfolded from 1972 to 1974, media revelations of crimes and political misdeeds repeated what was already known to properly constituted investigative authorities. In short, carefully timed leaks, not media investigations, provided the first news of Watergate.

Many of the current concerns tend to trivialize Watergate, and reduce it to a conspiracy involving a burglary or to a modern-day version of *The Front Page*. The affair involved a bitter struggle for power and for its limits; in that sense it had enormous political and constitutional implications for its time—and ours.

Of course, no one has a greater stake in Watergate revisionism than Richard Nixon. As I have suggested, since his resignation Nixon has been engaged in his final campaign, his campaign for history. His efforts continue, with yet another memoir published in 1990 which tries to reduce much of the Watergate story to "myths." Most critics dismissed his claims as diversionary or deceptive. Although Watergate formed only a small fraction of Nixon's latest work, that story monopolized the media's attention. The point, of course, is that Nixon cannot escape his history. Despite various "comebacks" and "recoveries" since 1974, he has been unable to shake loose from the Watergate quagmire. For it is Watergate and the unprecedented spectacle of a presidential resignation that distinguish Nixon's uniqueness and significance in American history. Watergate remains his burden and legacy.

My warmest thanks to my old friends at the House of Norton for publishing this edition.

Stanley I. Kutler
January 1992

CONTENTS

Photographic inserts of 16 pages and 8 pages will be found
　following text pages 208 and 432, respectively

ACKNOWLEDGMENTS

My debts accumulated in the writing of this book are enormous. But it is a pleasure to thank various institutions and individuals for their extraordinary cooperation.

The University of Wisconsin Foundation administers the E. Gordon Fox Fund, which has supported my research and writing for the past decade. That support, coupled with additional funds from the Graduate School at the University of Wisconsin, significantly lightened my task. The staffs of various research centers and libraries offered me unfailing courtesy; in particular, I must note the conscientious professionals at the Nixon Archives and in various branches of the National Archives.

Large and small favors came from Stuart Applebaum, Allen Arrow, Tadashi Aruga, M. Carlota Baca, James M. Banner, Michal R. Belknap, William C. Berman, Paul Blustein, the late Beatrice Braude, Ellen Kuniyuki Brown, Thomas Charlton, R. Taylor Cole, Robert Dallek, Elias Demetracopoulos, Philip A. Dibble, Father Robert Drinan, Elaine Edelman, Leon Epstein, Kelly Evans, Susan Falb, David Frohmeyer, Eric Glitzenstein, Patti Goldman, Fred Graham, Otis Graham, Gerald Gunther, William Hammond, Han Tie, William Hanchett, Jonathan Hart, James Hastings, Robert Henderson, Seymour Hersh, Bernard Hollander, J. Woodford Howard, Richard Jacobson, Victor Jew, Barbara Jordan, Harold Kaplan, Robert Kastenmeier, David Kepley, Judith Kirkwood, Harold Koh, Richard Kohn, David Konig, Benedict Leerburger, Wolfgang Lehmann, Liu Xu-yi, Steve Lynch, Tom McCormick, Richard McNeill, Michael McReynolds, Pauline Maier, Marilyn Mellowes, Martha Minow, Tom Mooney, Charles Moser, Jeanne Oates, William Proxmire, Henry Reuss, Donald Ritchie, Martin Ridge, Morris Schnapper, Stanley Schultz, David Shapiro, Father Don Shea, David Shepard, Geoffrey Shepherd, Diane Sherman, Dianne Smith, Aviam Soifer, John Stennis, Carl Stern, Mary Ternes, Steve Tilley, Jay Topkis, David Ward, Peter Weil, David Wigdor, Graham Wilson, Michael Wreszin, the late Tim Wyngaard, and Jerome Zeifman. Harold Hyman and Leonard Levy, truly distinguished historians and longtime friends, especially encouraged me at very crucial moments.

A special thank-you to the anonymous source who, in 1973 or 1974, referred to Watergate as the "War of the FBI Succession."

Willard Hurst and Richard Sewell have again generously extended their editorial talents, moral support, and friendship to me. As always, they have saved me from gross errors, bad judgment, and dreadful writing. They are not responsible, of course, for anything I have done contrary to their counsel.

The wait was worth it, but I finally have had my chance to work with Ashbel Green, vice president and senior editor at Alfred A. Knopf. He saved me from numerous lapses of good taste, not to mention good sense. (He may also be the only book editor able to share memories of the glory days of the Cleveland Indians.) Castle W. Freeman, Jr., provided magnificent copy-editing, while Jenny McPhee and Melvin Rosenthal shepherded me through the book's production.

Dan Bailey, my incomparable research assistant, did everything from checking a citation to deciphering and helping me master the White House tape transcripts; moreover, he labored strenuously to make sure that I would sound fair in Oshkosh. Susan Bissegger, Joe Ehmann, Dan Ernst, Ellen Goldlust, David Gordon, and Henry Wend also provided research support. Anita Olson valiantly made sense out of many confusing taped interviews. Susan Dewane is Management masquerading as a Secretary. John Wright— what can I say? *Agent extraordinaire, agent provocateur; sans lui, le déluge.*

My mother, as always, has taken a keen interest in my labors. Through his time of terrible troubles, my brother always managed to ask, "How's your work?" I have often thought of my late father, who taught us: "A liar is worse than a thief." My wife, Sandra Sachs Kutler, and my children, Jeff, David, Susan Anne, and Andy, who contributed in unique ways, like to see their names in print. This book is for them for all the reasons.

S.I.K.
Madison, Wisconsin
August 10, 1989

PREFACE

Some fifteen years after Richard Nixon resigned as President of the United States, Watergate remains contested history. Nixon and his partisans still proclaim his innocence, or they dismiss the affair as a minor stumble when measured against his great achievements, or they minimize his responsibility by comparing his sins to similar sins of his predecessors. Nevertheless, apologists and their opponents can agree on the importance of the case: there is no account, no judgment, no history of Nixon without Watergate.

While Watergate is a familiar story for those who were involved and who remember it, for many others today it is merely a word or symbol, dimly recalled or barely and imperfectly understood. This book is addressed to these varied audiences. The perspective of time and the evidence contained in once-unavailable documents add new dimensions to the familiar story of Watergate. The French historian Jules Michelet suggested that history is the "action of bringing things back to life." But as we revitalize "things," we also must comprehend them; otherwise the memory will disappear, and we will have learned only to forget.

I hope this book will be a reminder of the importance of most of the characters and the seriousness of the events it describes. Watergate was more than a burglary at the Democratic National Committee headquarters in June 1972, more even than the political and legal consequences of that act. The ensuing drama, culminating in Richard Nixon's resignation in August 1974, was rooted in the tumultuous events of the 1960s in the United States and abroad, and in the personality and history of Nixon himself, going back to his first presidential term and earlier. Since his resignation, Watergate has echoed loudly in our public life. In its time, and since, Watergate raised weighty issues of governance, especially concerning the role of the presidency and its relation to other institutions in the governmental apparatus.

And yet, though Watergate has implications that go to the heart of our political and constitutional system, Richard Nixon unquestionably stands at the center of that larger story as well. He must be acknowledged as one of a handful of dominant political figures in the United States for more than a quarter-century, but controversy persistently followed and fueled his long public career, making him one of the most divisive personalities in our recent public life. By Nixon's own assessment, Watergate was essentially one more episode in a series of wars and clashes with long-despised enemies. "I had thrown down a gauntlet to Congress, the bureaucracy, the media, and the Washington establishment and challenged them to engage in epic battle," he noted in his memoirs. Nixon thrived on conflict, conflict that ineluctably resulted from a lifetime of accumulated resentments, both personal and political.

The Watergate break-in parted the veil on the Nixon Administration's dubious tactics—the "White House horrors," as former Attorney General John Mitchell called them. The fury of the response led eventually to the second serious attempt in our history to impeach a president. Despite the vast power and resources of his office, Nixon eventually found himself involved in an inescapable struggle, unable to turn adversity into opportunity as he had done so often throughout his career. Watergate proved fatal to his political life and undoubtedly will haunt his historical reputation. History will record a fair share of the significant achievements of Nixon's presidency, but Watergate will be the spot that will not out.

Although Nixon is the leading actor in the Watergate drama, this book is neither a biography nor a full-length account of his presidency. He has had a generous number of biographers, and undoubtedly their interpretations will provoke as much heat and division as Nixon himself did throughout his career. His Administration's programs and policies deserve, and they are receiving, careful attention. *The Wars of Watergate,* however, focuses on the indelible reasons for his downfall and disgrace. Watergate dominated Richard Nixon's presidency. We cannot disentangle Nixon's domestic and foreign activities either from his unremitting warfare against real and imagined enemies at home or from the weighty burden of self-knowledge about his role in the Watergate cover-up. These consumed him, eventually resulting in a fatal self-inflicted wound.

In the end, Nixon offered his own eerie, albeit unintended, insight into his downfall: "[N]ever be petty," he told loyal members of his Administration as he departed the White House on August 9, 1974, and "always remember, others may hate you, but those who hate you don't win unless you hate them, and then you destroy yourself." It was just such corrosive hatred, however, that decisively shaped Nixon's own behavior, his career, and eventually his historical standing. The net result was a wholly unprecedented testing of the American political and constitutional system, in which Richard Nixon and Watergate are forever entwined—figures and events truly unique and unforgettable.

THE WARS OF WATERGATE

PROLOGUE

TRIUMPH AND FOREBODING: ELECTION NIGHT 1972

The victory was spectacular. Richard Nixon, who had contested two of the closest elections in American presidential history, was overwhelmingly re-elected on November 7, 1972. Save for Massachusetts and the District of Columbia, Nixon swept the Electoral College vote and captured over 60 percent of the popular vote. It was to be his last electoral campaign; "[M]ake it the best," he had told his Chief of Staff, H. R. Haldeman, in September. Nixon's triumph rivaled Franklin D. Roosevelt's in 1936 and Lyndon Baines Johnson's in 1964; and like them, President Nixon would quickly discover that the electorate's mandates were neither absolute nor irrevocable.

From the outset, the enormous victory was not quite satisfactory to Nixon or his family. The President's daughters, Tricia and Julie, petulantly complained that Democratic candidate George McGovern had not conceded gracefully enough, describing his congratulatory message as 'cold and arch,'' presumably because he had expressed the "hope" that the President would provide peace abroad and justice at home. Nixon himself, for all his outward satisfaction, privately found his joy muted on Election Day night. His reasons ranged from the banal to the serious.

The President worried that a temporary cap on his tooth might fall off if he smiled too broadly. He fretted about having to confront another Democrat-dominated Congress and at his inability to end the Vietnam war. He felt more sadness than relief at having fought his last election campaign. Most of all, Nixon would remember, he felt "a foreboding" that dampened his enthusiasm. Perhaps, he later mused, "the marring effects of Watergate may have played a part." On election eve, he had noted in his diary that Watergate was the only "sour note" of the moment. "This," he admitted, "was really stupidity on the part of a number of people."[1]

The President's Press Secretary had smugly labeled the incident a "third-rate burglary" after police captured five men within the national headquarters of the Democratic Party at the Watergate office complex on June 17, 1972. At the time, the event had sounded only a minor discordant theme in the campaign, barely acknowledged outside Washington. The President and several close aides nevertheless had cause for concern. They realized that an inquiry into the Watergate affair might link the White House to the burglary and its aftermath, and expose a pattern of unethical and illegal conduct condoned and encouraged by the President himself. Nixon later claimed that "when the President does it, that means that it is not illegal."[2] He knew better.

On election night, therefore, when celebration was in order, Nixon nursed festering grievances. His public image clashed with what he knew to be reality, and he reacted, in anger, resentment, and perhaps even fear, as he had so often done in the past. Within hours, Haldeman asked for resignations throughout the Administration, quickly dampening the joy of the President's loyal supporters. The signs of Nixon's overwhelming victory had been apparent for months. Yet during that time, and in the immediate aftermath of the election, the President rubbed old wounds and planned revenge on his "enemies." Magnanimity, generosity, and tolerance simply did not exist in his political vocabulary. He spurred his chief aides to find men to direct the Federal Bureau of Investigation, the Central Intelligence Agency, and the Internal Revenue Service who would do his personal bidding and fill his personal political needs. On September 15, 1972, he called White House Counsel John W. Dean III to the Oval Office and told him to "remember all the trouble" the President's foes had caused. "We'll have a chance to get back at them one day," Nixon promised, adding that he intended to utilize the FBI and other agencies to harass his political antagonists. Nixon also thanked his young aide for his work in containing the Watergate affair. At the time, he undoubtedly never considered that enemies and friends alike eventually would hear their conversation, which he himself had taped.[3]

The re-election, then, produced nothing but contradictions. Where confidence should have abounded, confusion reigned; instead of joy, resentment surged through the White House; and whereas "peace abroad and justice at home" should have dominated the President's concerns, the "sour note" of Watergate was to echo through the remainder of Richard Nixon's presidency. Still, victory did, naturally enough, generate a measure of optimism, and some in the President's entourage looked forward to four more years of achievement. As Nixon began his new term on January 20, 1973, he presented his chief aides and Cabinet members with a four-year calendar inscribed: "The Presidential term which begins today consists of 1,461 days—no more, no less. . . . . [T]hey can stand out as great days for America, and great moments in the history of the world."

The cloud of Watergate and the unknown mocked that note of optimism. On Christmas Day 1972, James McCord, indicted for his role in the Watergate burglary, ominously threatened to implicate the White House. Presidential speechwriter Patrick Buchanan had warned Nixon that Watergate was a growing problem, although he probably did not realize the extent of the President's own involvement. Meanwhile, Leonard Garment, a White House aide and former law partner of Nixon's, had his own sense of foreboding. Quoting José Ortega y Gasset, he wrote: " 'We do not know what is happening, and *that* is what is happening.' "[4]

Richard Nixon knew.

OF TIME
AND THE MAN

DISCORD, DISORDER,
AND RICHARD NIXON

BOOK ONE

I

BREAKING FAITH: THE 1960S

The Age of Watergate witnessed the nation's most sustained political conflict and severest constitutional crisis since the Great Depression. Attention centered first on the role of the Committee to Re-elect the President in the break-in at the Washington headquarters of the Democratic National Committee. The burglary at the Watergate complex not only raised questions about the integrity of the political process, but eventually made an issue of the President's personal role in the event and its aftermath. And subsequent revelations uncovered what Nixon's key political lieutenant, former Attorney General John Mitchell, characterized as the "White House horrors"—the numerous instances of officially sanctioned criminal activity and abuses of power, as well as obstruction of justice, that had preceded and followed the Watergate break-in.

These events all fall under the "generic term of 'Watergate'," as Congress labeled them in a 1974 law. History is disciplined by context, and the Watergate affair cannot be bounded by the flurry of events from the burglary on June 17, 1972, to the President's resignation on August 9, 1974. Watergate involved the political behavior of the President and his men, and the critical assault on their authority, that began during Nixon's first term. Some of that behavior, and some of that critical assault, had its roots in the tumultuous events of the 1960s.[1] The struggles in that decade over civil rights and over the control of the cities, and above all over the war in Vietnam, brought dramatic divisions and violence to American society and resulted in the destabilization of both civil and social institutions. Furious protests swirled initially around President Lyndon Baines Johnson, a symbol of and a scapegoat for the nation's ills and anxieties. A tidal wave of political and media criticism eventually swept Johnson from the White House, discredited, despised, and desperately searching for historical vindication.

Richard Nixon promised the nation in 1968 that he would "bring us together." But during his watch, the divisions persisted and even widened. He, even more than Johnson, became a focal point for the furies and frustrations that wracked American society. "Watergate" increasingly defined his Administration, and it provided the "sword," as Nixon himself characterized it, for dissident interests to use in successfully mounting their challenge to vested power and authority. Nixon had unfortunately inherited a vastly weakened and increasingly vulnerable presidency. That institutional crisis, together with his own political past, which made him one of the most divisive figures in America, culminated in his unprecedented resignation as President.

We must also look to Nixon's long public career to explain his conduct as President. His personality, his lengthy tenure in the political arena, and his behavior in prominent events of the previous quarter-century clearly conditioned much of his presidency. Those years were ones of preparation for his ambition; they also molded and shaped those special qualities that anticipated the disaster that befell him. With Richard Milhous Nixon's election to the presidency in 1968, the times and the man came together—and Watergate was the result.

John F. Kennedy heralded a new public perception and involvement with the presidency, personalizing it with carefully crafted mannerisms. His vigor, wit, and candor quickly captured the imagination of the nation, despite his razor-thin margin of victory in 1960. The young President appealed to the nation's emerging youth, forcefully identifying with their hopes and aspirations. Americans found themselves riveted to the President as the center of public life, particularly as the media emphasized the glamour and vitality of Kennedy, his wife, and his family.

The underside of the Kennedy years—the President's extramarital affairs, his compromises with segregationists, his ineffectiveness in dealing with Congress, his Administration's plots to assassinate foreign leaders, and the growing combat involvement in Vietnam—was either hidden or studiously ignored. Kennedy and his advisers skillfully managed to convey the impression of a leader who was at once a liberal and a conservative, a hard-line anticommunist and a statesman genuinely committed to new directions for reducing Cold War tensions.

Kennedy's assassination in Dallas in November 1963 elevated him instantly to demi-sainthood, leaving both his admirers and his enemies to vent their wrath and frustrations on his successor. Kennedy's death began a mystique that grew through much of the 1960s, a mystique which, however distorted, haunted Lyndon B. Johnson. There was no escape for Johnson. Beginning with his surprise selection as John F. Kennedy's running mate in 1960 and continuing through Johnson's sorrow-laden succession in 1963 and Robert F. Kennedy's challenge in 1968, the Kennedys hung like a brooding omnipresence in Johnson's sky, alternately shaping and paralyzing his presidency.

When Johnson, on assuming the presidency, said, "Let us continue," he meant to realize the fallen Kennedy's promise of renewed energy and purpose in government. Johnson understood the need to assuage the sense of national grief, yet he instinctively sensed as well the opportunity to capitalize on the memory of the late President to attain desirable political results and create his own memorial. Within days, Johnson revitalized his coalition-building talents and organized a new national consensus on behalf of long-standing and innovative liberal agendas. Like the creatures entering Noah's Ark two by two, they called or came to the White House: Harry Truman and Dwight Eisenhower, Martin Luther King, Jr., and George Wallace, Senators Mike Mansfield and Everett Dirksen, the heads of the AFL–CIO and the National Association of Manufacturers, and then, of course, the world leaders—all anxious to gain the new President's ear while he, just as eagerly, worked to bring them aboard *his* ship. Kennedy's promises had stalled on the two shoals of civil rights legislation and tax-cutting. Johnson would not just jawbone, but deliver.

Deliver he did, and at a frenzied pace for the next six months, dazzling friends and dismaying foes. The Kennedy New Frontier program faded into memory as Johnson stamped his own Great Society brand on a breathtaking cascade of legislation. By the time of the 1964 presidential election, he had secured both the Tax Reduction and Civil Rights acts. New laws and new ideas abounded—urban mass transit, clean air, wilderness preserves, manpower retraining, and a variety of antipoverty measures. Lyndon Johnson had apparently never met a constituency he disliked.

The tax and civil rights laws appeared to assure Johnson's historical reputation. Both had seemed hopelessly elusive during Kennedy's short tenure; Johnson, however, moved deftly and surely through the familiar congressional jungle and emerged with his original goals largely intact. As Senate Majority Leader in the 1950s, Johnson had repeatedly frustrated his liberal allies with what seemed to them an all-too-ready acceptance of half-loaves. But not during the halcyon early days of his presidency. The tax cut, co-opted in part by Keynesians from orthodox Republican doctrine, ensured a further takeoff for the reigning prosperity. Johnson's civil rights legislation induced a national orgy of self-congratulation and raised hopes for a new era of peaceful racial relations. The Supreme Court's invalidation of segregation ten years earlier at last had a legislative imprimatur and the blessing of a Southern President.

On every front, Johnson commanded and directed a succession of triumphs. The opposition—what there was of it—was in total disarray. "I am a fellow that likes small parties," Johnson quipped, "and the Republican party is about the size I like." The President's power was immense, almost absolute. "He's getting everything through the Congress but the abolition of the Republican party," James Reston wrote in the *New York Times,* "and he hasn't tried that yet."

And yet, despite Johnson's triumphs, a White House aide noted, "something was wrong, drastically wrong." Johnson himself acknowledged that his support was "like a Western river, broad but not deep." Kennedy loyalists nipped at the President's heels, snickered at his Texas roots and mannerisms, claimed he was succeeding only because of sympathy for the martyred Kennedy, and, most of all, complained about something they called "style." The Pedernales did not flow through Camelot.

For the Kennedy-Arthurians, Johnson was the Black Knight, not fit to sit at the Round Table. Their contempt was publicly apparent, and the media dutifully reflected their mood. Jack Kennedy had been a favorite of press and television reporters as he successfully charmed and wooed them, despite his Administration's candid advocacy of news management. Mocked, even shunned, by his supposed allies, President Johnson yearned for love and acceptance from those who counted most—the people. But a wary, even hostile, media made gaining the public's affection a formidable task. Camelot, described by a British observer as an "idiotic Tennysonian fantasy" concocted by adoring Kennedy admirers in the media, symbolized the "resentful escapism" that bedeviled Johnson.[2]

The President had some tattered robes that lent substance to the criticism of his detractors. His successes paradoxically reinforced all the negative images of him as a wheeler-dealer, a conniving hustler, and a manipulator cloaked in deceit and secrecy—images that had haunted Johnson pitilessly throughout his career. Questions centered on the personal fortune he and his wife had amassed during his years of public service, particularly in the government-regulated television business; his association with Billy Sol Estes, a shady entrepreneur who lavishly supported Texas politicians, including Johnson; and, most harmful of all, the corrupt dealings of his Senate aide and protégé, Bobby Baker. The President insisted he hardly knew Baker—"one of the great whoppers of American political history," as Johnson's former Press Secretary described it.[3]

The master politician could not elude the questions and innuendoes regarding his moral character. The United States' growing involvement in Indochina was intractable and unpopular enough, but Johnson's lack of moral authority compounded the difficulty. The result was tragic for him, and for the nation.

President Johnson eagerly anticipated the 1964 election as a personal referendum, a plebiscite offering him a ticket of admission to the White House in his own right rather than as an "accidental president"; 1964 would release him from the Kennedy bondage. His wish seemed to be granted. Whatever his personal merits, Lyndon Johnson was lucky—blessed, it might seem—in having an opponent that year who politically and emotionally terrified a substantial part of the American electorate. The President's triumph over Senator Barry Goldwater rivaled Franklin D. Roosevelt's landslide victory in 1936. Johnson's victory was total, absolute, and, like so much else about him, excessive. The staggering dimensions of his election, with 61 percent of the popular vote, certainly gave him an exaggerated sense of his mandate. Ironically, however, the very scale of his victory served to heighten suspicions of him.

Barry Goldwater, the junior Senator from Arizona, had captured the Republican nomination on the strength of a dedicated, resourceful organization, and because of his appeal as a genuine political alternative. He also promised to "get tough" with the "international Communist conspiracy." In May 1964, Goldwater urged greater American involvement in the war in South Vietnam. Specifically, he called for the bombing of supply routes in the North. When told that the dense jungle cover hid many of the trails, he suggested the possibility of "defoliation of the forests by low-yield atomic weapons." Two months later, Goldwater said that victory in Vietnam was assured if the military were given a free hand.

No matter the outcome in 1964, Goldwater had sparked a movement to make conservatism respectable, and it proved to be a movement that would not roll over and die as political pundits insisted it must or should. Yet Goldwater's moment of triumph also sealed his fate. When he told his loyal followers at the San Francisco Republican Convention in July that "extremism in the defense of liberty is no vice [a]nd . . . moderation in the pursuit of justice is no virtue," many Americans regarded him as a moral monster commanding a pack of fanatics totally alien to the American mainstream.[4] Actually, Goldwater's words had a noble quality, but the context distorted the message into something sinister.

Goldwater's hopes for upsetting the President in the 1964 election rested on his ability to persuade voters of Johnson's moral defects. That image was ready-made and exploitable, but Goldwater could not overcome his own, larger negatives. Americans realized Johnson's shortcomings, yet planned to vote for him. "Johnson leaves me cold, but I am going to ring doorbells for him," said a St. Louis optometrist—hastily adding: "Goldwater is beyond belief." Pollster Samuel Lubell described a Dayton, Ohio, precinct where nearly one-fourth of those who intended to vote for the President questioned his fundamental honesty. The eloquent voice of the Very Reverend Francis B. Sayre, Jr., of the Episcopal cathedral in the nation's capital, a grandson of Woodrow Wilson, seemed to speak for many Americans. He deplored the "sterile choice" confronting the electorate, a choice between "a man of dangerous ignorance and devastating uncertainty" and "a man whose public house is splendid in its every appearance, but whose private lack of ethic must inevitably introduce termites at the very foundation."[5]

The 1964 election seemed simple enough, with its apparent ideological conflict. But in truth, the clash was more complex, pitting Republican ideological concerns against Democratic programmatic agendas. One side had ideology without program; the other, programs largely devoid of any coherent philosophical scheme. Neither proved wholly satisfactory in the 1960s— and the problem continued to especially plague the Democrats for the next two decades. Following the election, a Maryland housewife thought the country was domestically "mixed up." She bemoaned the lack of direction. "I think it's very, very confused. People have lost the old rules and values by which they lived, and they haven't got any new ones to substitute."[6]

The President was not "mixed up"; if anything, the election puffed his well-endowed ego. Press Secretary George Reedy noted the change. American elections, Reedy observed, had "elements of sanctification," but Johnson had advanced the concept "to one of deification." The President's natural wariness—even fear—toward the press turned to contempt. "I've been kissing asses all my life and I don't have to kiss them anymore," he declared. As for holding press conferences, Johnson instructed Reedy to "tell those press bastards of yours that I'll see them when I want to and not before."[7]

The 1964 campaign was a referendum on the welfare state, now three decades old. It also focused on the issues of war and peace, particularly highlighting the ominous developments in Southeast Asia. Johnson had a veritable monopoly on the peace corner. Speaking in Eufaula, Oklahoma, on September 25, he could not resist gilding the lily: "There are those that say you ought to go North and drop bombs, to try to wipe out supply lines, and they think that would escalate the war. We don't want our American boys to do the fighting for Asian boys. We don't want to get involved . . . with 700 million people and get tied down in a land war in Asia."[8] In the meantime, Barry Goldwater was the candidate who reputedly wanted to "lob one into the men's room in the Kremlin."

Johnson promised "peace for all Americans," yet he repeatedly emphasized that what his predecessors and Congress had defined as vital national and world interests demanded an American presence in South Vietnam, as well as in Korea, Japan, Taiwan, Thailand, and the Philippines. In other ways as well, his private actions did not match his public prudence. During the election campaign, Johnson approved numerous secret operations throughout Southeast Asia, including air operations against the North. On October 1, National Security Adviser McGeorge Bundy sent the President a memo acknowledging the probability that American forces would be engaged in "some air and land action in the Laotian corridor or even in North Vietnam within the next two months."[9]

Johnson's victory inevitably produced claims of a "mandate." But as always in American politics, the question was, "Mandate for what?" For endorsing the President's legislative record? Probably. For advancing the Great Society? Possibly. For sustaining the Gulf of Tonkin Resolution authorizing presidential retaliation for attacks on American personnel in Vietnam? Yes—at least, if such attacks were overt. For keeping American boys out of Asian wars? Certainly. Ironically, LBJ's campaign rhetoric regarding the war established an image of apparent deception that would plague him in the years to come, as he led the nation deeper and deeper into the Vietnam quagmire.

The Gulf of Tonkin incident, early in August 1964, and Johnson's subsequent dealings with Congress, eventually shaped that image of deception more than any other event of his presidency. The congressional resolution authorizing Johnson to retaliate against North Vietnamese attacks never escaped the smell of presidential duplicity. Whether Johnson used the occasion to fulfill longstanding plans for wider American involvement in the war, as Senator J. William Fulbright later believed, or whether the resolution resulted from the President's fear that Goldwater and the Right would preempt him on the issue of standing up to Communism—or both—the Tonkin Gulf Resolution was a watershed not only for the Vietnam war but for the relationship between the executive and legislative branches for the next decade.[10]

What happened in the Tonkin Gulf on the nights of August 2 and 4 remains to this day somewhat cloudy. What is certain is that the Administration neither fully understood what had occurred nor reported the "incidents" fairly and fully. In January, Johnson had approved military plans for covert activities against North Vietnam—"dirty tricks," as they were known. By early summer, these operations increased as South Vietnamese resistance deteriorated.

On the night of August 2, three Vietnamese PT boats attacked the American destroyer *Maddox*. The destroyer sank one. Intercepts of enemy radio traffic showed that the North believed the Americans had coordinated action with the South Vietnamese. Defense Secretary Robert McNamara later testified that the incident occurred thirty miles out to sea, when in fact the vessels had been only thirteen miles from shore. McNamara also denied any coordination, insisting that *Maddox* had been on a routine patrol mission. For the moment, Johnson and his advisers decided not to escalate the action but vowed to maintain naval operations in the Gulf despite warnings from the naval commander on the scene that they constituted "an unacceptable risk." The Pentagon ordered *Maddox* and another destroyer, *C. Turner Joy*, back into action on August 3. The next night, the commander radioed that North Vietnamese intercepts showed that the enemy believed the destroyers were preparing to attack their bases. Again, what happened is in dispute. The destroyers signaled that enemy boats were attacking; whether they had been sighted on radar or had actually attacked remains in question. No matter, the President left no doubt of his resolve to retaliate.

But Johnson needed congressional acquiescence—for political, hardly constitutional, reasons. The pressures of the pending election, combined with his innate political caution, dictated that he seek congressional cooperation. By the evening of August 4, Johnson had secured promises of support from the leadership for both retaliation and a resolution authorizing executive initiatives. And that night, carrier-based aircraft attacked North Vietnamese naval stations and an oil depot on the Gulf, even while Pentagon wireless operators were still seeking details of the attacks on the American destroyers.

Johnson prevailed on his Senate friends to secure the necessary resolution. Fulbright, Chairman of the Foreign Relations Committee, steered the measure through—to his eventual regret. The Senator persuaded himself that the resolution would fend off Goldwater's hawkish appeals and that a limited American military response would set the stage for serious negotiations between the warring Vietnamese parties and the United States. Years later, Fulbright realized that Johnson had ordered the destroyers back into action to provoke an " 'excuse' which would allow him to retaliate militarily and, later, to play upon the 'chauvinism' of the Congress."[11]

Senator Gaylord Nelson (D-WI) pressed Fulbright the hardest. Nelson urged his colleagues to accept an amendment limiting the American role in Vietnam to "aid, training assistance, and military advice." Fulbright told Nelson that he agreed with the sentiment and was confident that the President shared the same view. But, responding to Johnson's prodding, Fulbright went on to say that amendments would only complicate the congressional process and send the wrong message to Hanoi. The Gulf of Tonkin Resolution, he insisted, was "harmless"; privately, he told colleagues that it offered the best opportunity "to pull the rug out from under Goldwater." Only Senators Wayne Morse (D-OR) and Ernest Gruening (D-AK) resisted Fulbright's pleadings. Strangely, as the nation turned against the war in 1968, both were defeated and shunned as the proverbial messengers of bad tidings. (Meanwhile, Johnson ordered the FBI to investigate Morse's Oregon supporters.) That same year, Fulbright's committee staff amassed damning evidence of the Administration's duplicity. But as George Ball later noted, "if it wasn't Tonkin Gulf, it would have been something else."[12]

Johnson carried the Gulf of Tonkin Resolution in his pocket, readily showing it to visitors who questioned his policies. He treated it as a blank check for congressional support, although Congress's support was not unlimited, and in time, Johnson *and* the presidency paid high interest for its use. The Gulf of Tonkin incident and its aftermath planted the seeds for a decade of discord and estrangement between the presidency and Congress over Vietnam policy.

Johnson's smashing victory in 1964 swept a swollen Democratic majority into control of Congress. The Democrats gained 37 seats in the House of Representatives, giving them a 295–140 majority. In the Senate, with a 68–32 margin, the Democrats had nearly the same proportional control. The previous Congress had given the President much of what he had asked for in response to his considerable bargaining skills and out of sympathy for the martyred Kennedy. But this was very much Johnson's Congress. Many newly elected representatives came from districts which were only marginally Democratic, or which Republicans had lost because of Goldwater's liabilities. These representatives (many of whom served only one term) naturally looked to Johnson for leadership and guidance. He provided both in abundance.

Washington had seen nothing like it since the Hundred Days of the New Deal. "Johnson's Congress" compiled a staggering legislative record. The sweeping, almost revolutionary, Voting Rights Act and the long-sought Medicare program headed the list. Congress also created the National Endowment for the Humanities, the National Endowment for the Arts, the new Department of Housing and Urban Development, and the Arms Control Agency. It passed clean-air, clean-water, and highway-beautification measures to preserve the environment. It allocated new and enlarged grants for federal research on heart disease, cancer, and stroke, as well as a raft of new programs for the President's "War on Poverty," including provisions for rent subsidies, manpower training, and Operation Head Start.

Ironically, however, as the President fulfilled the leading items on the liberal agenda, much of the liberal coalition began to desert him. The year after his sweeping victory, 1965, was an ambivalent period. The President's legislative achievements deserved admiration, yet discordant notes filled the air. The summer witnessed outbreaks of violence in the black urban ghettos. Campus protests blossomed, questioning what had seemed to be sacred values of educational authority. Sappers penetrated the American Embassy in Saigon, protesters publicly burned draft cards, and that winter saw the first organized antiwar rally in Washington. By December, air strikes over North Vietnam had become routine, dropping tons of bombs—and yet they seemed only to strengthen the enemy's resolve. By the end of the year, 200,000 Americans were in Vietnam.

Polls consistently reflected a widespread dislike for Johnson. Critics complained about his "lack of style," notwithstanding a grudging respect for his achievements. But Johnson damaged himself by his actions more than by his manner. First, the war had escalated dramatically. The retaliatory raids had developed into a full-scale air war on the North, designed, as General Curtis LeMay said, to bomb it "back to the Stone Age." Marines landed at Danang in March 1965, allegedly to protect American planes and pilots but actually with combat orders. Johnson was now haunted by his promises not to send American boys to fight Asian wars, and their false notes heightened the latent suspicions of his style and character. The heady successes of the 1964 election and in Congress afterward magnified those perceived traits of wheeling and dealing, deception, and furtiveness that clung to the President's reputation like barnacles.

The notion of a "credibility gap" in the Administration symbolized the growing unease. In a speech at Johns Hopkins University on April 7, 1965, the President called for "unconditional discussions" for peace and outlined a scheme for a TVA-type development project for the Mekong River valley in Southeast Asia. Typically, a flurry of activity followed the speech to offer an impression of reality. Johnson pressured World Bank President Eugene Black to head the project and promised him full support and a blue-ribbon panel to help implement the scheme. It never happened: no project, no panel, no support. Six weeks later, David Wise described the President's "credibility gap."[13] Johnson's tall Texas tales—that his grandfather fought at the Alamo, for example—no longer amused; instead, they appeared as part of a dangerous pattern underlining the reality that Johnson would not— or could not—tell the truth.

Johnson ordered his doctor to say that he drank only bourbon (a good American drink) when Washington circles knew he favored Scotch. He justified military intervention in the Dominican Republic by insisting that the rebels had beheaded people and that the American ambassador had been fired upon—none of which was true. Secrecy abounded regarding presidential nominations, budgets, travel plans, and programs. The President thus assured the limelight for himself, as only he could announce or authorize what was to be. If the press discovered a pending presidential appointment, Johnson sometimes would reverse his plans out of what seemed to many to be sheer perversity. The dean of Washington columnists, Arthur Krock, charged the President with "evasive rhetoric" whenever he escalated the war. One writer, who elaborated on the credibility gap and described Johnson as "one of the ablest Presidents this country has produced," said that Johnson could be even better "if he would stop getting wounded every time a reporter or editorial writer takes issue with him on some point." Johnson's actions and thin-skinned reactions only widened the chasm between himself and the press.[14]

At the outset of his administration, Johnson had ostentatiously cultivated the press, hoping to emulate Kennedy's success with reporters. He dispatched a special plane to bring James Reston of the *New York Times* to the President's ranch on Christmas 1963. He bragged about having columnist Walter Lippmann to dinner. But when Lippmann turned hostile toward the Vietnam adventure, the President pointed to his repeated errors and delighted in salacious jokes about him. Other journalists described it as "the war on Walter Lippmann." After the President courted reporters with a high-speed drive across his ranchlands, he became infuriated when they wrote about the adventure, including a description of Johnson sipping a cup of beer while driving. Johnson craved personal attention, and then objected when press accounts depicted his behavior as grotesque or undesirable.[15]

Johnson's war policies and his reactions to his critics generated geometric leaps in the form and intensity of the opposition. American presidents, Washington and Lincoln included, have rarely been immune from vicious, mean-spirited criticism. But the fury against Johnson seemed unprecedented. English journalist Henry Fairlie was appalled: "I have found nothing more strange than the way in which American intellectuals take pleasure in reviling President Johnson." He could not understand their "fastidious disdain for the man, . . . a slob," as someone described him to Fairlie. Cartoonists had a field day depicting the Gargantua-like figure, with his homeliest features heavily exaggerated. The biting, even cruel, satirical play *MacBird* was a favorite on elite campuses.[16]

The net result of his bad press was that Johnson responded with an equal measure of contempt. Worse, he retreated into an ever-shrinking shell of friends and advisers in the White House. Unwilling to confront hostile receptions, he became a virtual prisoner in Washington, increasingly under siege. Johnson's seclusion was ominous. Even at the nadir of his popularity, Harry Truman still moved freely about Washington, taking his morning walk down Pennsylvania Avenue, accompanied only by a few Secret Service agents. Aides urged President Johnson to travel, believing he could generate a counterwave of sympathy. Reportedly, the Secret Service and Johnson himself rejected the advice.[17]

American presidents in the twentieth century have generally had good relations with the press. Within that relationship, however, presidents consistently have tried to manage the reporting of their administrations. And although the relationship of press and president is inherently adversarial, it usually has been governed by mutual respect and trust. All that changed dramatically with Lyndon Johnson. Betraying his typical frustration, he once lashed out at the press: "Somebody ought to do an article on *you,* on your damn profession, your First Amendment." Perhaps he could not understand the media. He certainly could not control them as he would have liked. "[A]ll you guys in the media. All of politics has changed because of you," he lamented.[18] The media, in other words, set the agenda and, for that reason, they were fair game for Johnson's manipulation—if he could manipulate them.

At the end of his administration, Johnson touched on the disastrous state of affairs between himself and the press. He acknowledged that a presidential relationship with the media inevitably would be like a "lover's quarrel," but one that nevertheless was healthy so long as both sides acted with "respect for each other's purposes." Johnson realized what had happened during his tenure: "I would be less than candid if I failed to say that I am troubled by the difficulties of communicating with and through the press."

It must have galled Johnson and his aides to compare their media relations to his predecessor's. When Kennedy was accused of "news management," Press Secretary Pierre Salinger candidly defended the practice on both national-security and self-interest grounds. Editorial reaction was sharp and pointed, yet Kennedy maintained extremely cordial and close relations with the press. One Johnson assistant envied and resented Kennedy's success. Johnson had "no physical glamour to carry him through when the news was bad. He was a high-pressure salesman," Harry McPherson wrote, "always trying to get his foot in the door, frequently arousing—in professionally skeptical men who had spent their working lives listening to the apologies of politicians—an incredible resistance."[19]

The ever-growing hostility alarmed and saddened some reporters. The *New York Times*'s White House correspondent, Max Frankel, told the President's Press Secretary that it was "most painful for me to see my President being cut up." Frankel complained that Johnson and his staff had fostered the bitterness, but he also acknowledged that both sides had lavished excessive attention "on the most petty aspects of policy and personality." Why, he said, "must we all punish each other so strenuously on things that don't [count]?" UPI's White House correspondent, Merriman Smith, whose son had been killed in Vietnam, told his colleagues that Johnson was "the object of some of the worst vilification—even obscenity—that I've seen or heard in more than 25 years on the White House assignment."[20]

The problem was serious, and went beyond simple matters of personal tastes and preferences. The credibility of the President—and, in effect, of the United States government—was on the line. The battles with the press, George Reedy noted, became battles with important segments of the public. The distrust and vilification both impaired the President's standing and confirmed many prevailing negative images of his leadership. The President worried that the attacks only weakened his hand abroad. "Why should Ho Chi Minh believe me when the newspapers and the broadcasters in my own country won't believe me?" he asked one correspondent. Perhaps there was a touch of paranoia in that statement, and yet it had a certain painful truth.[21] The circle was vicious—for the President, the presidency, the press, and the national interest.

Johnson's well-worn habits of secrecy produced the appearance and reflected the actual practice of deception. His efforts to conceal his thoughts
and intentions only incensed an increasingly hostile media and further weakened his public standing. Secrecy was his familiar means of control. He told
reporters during the 1964 campaign that "if you play along with me, I'll
play along with you. . . . If you want to play it the other way, I know how
to play it both ways, too, and I know how to cut off the flow of news."
Ironically, as a sympathetic observer noted, "the very qualities and experiences that had led to his political and legislative success were precisely those
that now operated to destroy him."[22] He was accustomed to resolving conflict; tolerating it was totally alien to him. The problem was that Lyndon
Johnson was no longer operating in the friendly, close confines of the United
States Senate.

The Vietnam war seared the Johnson Administration and scarred American
society for decades. The war neither started with Johnson—as he ceaselessly
reminded the nation, invoking the venerated Eisenhower and the martyred
Kennedy as the war's patron saints—nor ended with him. "I didn't get us
into Vietnam. I didn't ring up out there and say, 'I want some trouble,' "
he told a campaign audience in Louisville in 1964.[23] But Johnson wove the
war inextricably into the fabric of American politics and society. The Vietnam venture raised fundamental questions about the course of American
foreign policy; eventually, however, those questions spilled over into more
basic domestic considerations of presidential authority and power. The result
was a politics of turmoil and upheaval that did not abate for nearly a decade
and witnessed the unexpected departures of two presidents.

In retrospect, Johnson complained that "that bitch of a war" took him
away from "the woman I really loved"—his Great Society. The war ruptured
the nation, sparking unprecedented anger and resistance to government policies. The President and his advisers, however, stuck to their chosen position, determined to justify the conflict as a defense of the national interest.
In the end, however, both success abroad and consensus at home eluded
them. Demoralized, even a bit bewildered, Johnson said in 1968 that the
only difference between Kennedy's assassination and his was that he was
"alive and it has been more torturous." The war "cut the arteries of the
LBJ administration," wrote a sympathetic aide. It nearly cut the nation's as
well.[24]

Johnson struggled to preserve his relationship with "the woman he loved,"
despite the incessant demands of his "bitch." During his last years in office,
with inflation soaring nearly out of control, and with the budget deficit at a
then-astronomical $25 billion, he finally accepted some restraints on Great
Society spending in exchange for a tax surcharge. Valiantly—and success-

fully—he struggled for a new civil rights bill that among other things prohibited discrimination in the sale and rental of housing.[25] But despite that
success, the drive for the Great Society was over. The pressures for a wider,
more expensive war prevailed after 1965. Curiously, the counterpressures
for peace only accelerated the war effort as the President desperately tried
to bring Hanoi to the peace table.

The decision to commit American forces in the Vietnam war, and the
subsequent conduct of the war, remain controversial. But the passage of time
has not eroded contemporary judgments of friend and foe alike that Lyndon
Johnson failed miserably to exercise his vaunted leadership and political
skills. He failed to tell the nation that sacrifice was inevitable; he failed to
prepare the nation for the protracted war that flowed from his limited pursuit
of war aims; more significantly, he failed to inform the nation why it was at
war. He committed American men and arms, but he failed to commit the
American people to that war.

And he knew better. Clark Clifford, one of the few men Johnson held in
awe, warned in July 1965 that the war was futile. "I don't believe we can
win in South Vietnam," he said. "If we send in 100,000 more men, the
North Vietnamese will meet us. If North Vietnam runs out of men, the
Chinese will send in volunteers. Russia and China don't intend for us to win
the war." Clifford urged that we get out "honorably." Otherwise, he warned,
"I can't see anything but catastrophe for my country."

However valued Clifford may have been, the President soon made it clear
that opposition to his policies was a luxury at home and a boon to the enemy.
He was sure, he said, that our soldiers did not "think we should enjoy the
luxury of fighting each other back home." But most of all, he heaped scorn
on his critics and blithely appealed to patriotic abstractions. "There will be
some Nervous Nellies and some who will become frustrated and break ranks
under the strain," the President remarked. There would be those who would
"turn on their leaders and on their country and on our fighting men. There
will be times of trial and tensions in the days ahead that will exact the best
that is in all of us."[26]

Johnson's patriotic homilies were inadequate. George Washington, at Valley Forge in 1778, warned that whoever built upon patriotism as a sufficient
basis for conducting a long and bloody war "will find themselves deceived
in the end." Such a war, Washington insisted, could never be sustained by
patriotism alone. "It must be aided by a prospect of Interest or some reward.
For a time, it may, of itself push Men to action; . . . but it will not endure
unassisted by Interest." Nevertheless, Johnson and his advisers "wrapped
themselves in the flag," decrying the "Nervous Nellies" who opposed the
war. Deception and self-delusion alike pervaded the Johnson Administration's conduct of the war.

Vietnam was not prominent in the first months of the Johnson Administration. The problem still fit into the pattern of continuity with the Kennedy policies. In a telephone conversation on March 2, 1964, Johnson told Senator Fulbright that he would follow Kennedy's course, and the Senator enthusiastically concurred. If Johnson had any doubts, certainly Fulbright allayed them. The Senate's foremost foreign-policy spokesman rejected any proposals for negotiations with the North until the American and South Vietnamese bargaining positions had been strengthened. Whether the United States chose to expand the conflict "one way or another," or confined itself to bolstering the South, he said, required "a continuing examination by responsible officials in the executive branch." But the Senator's basic position was simple and blunt: the United States should "continue to defend its vital interests with respect to Vietnam." [27]

That general view had substantial support in early 1964, however imprecise the perception of "vital interests." The popular media offered no significant opposition. Reporters who would later win Pulitzer Prizes for their criticism of the war were at this point proposing an enlarged commitment. Until late 1967, public-opinion polls consistently demonstrated widespread support for Johnson's policy, which ostensibly steered a middle course between total war and withdrawal. There is also evidence that the steady escalation in the period after 1964 had solid public approval. [28] The margin of public support and approval, however, had to be balanced against a steadily growing opposition that reflected deep divisions within American society.

Vietnam had historically been a difficult problem. The Chinese and the French had failed to understand, let alone master, the area. American policymakers had little to guide them besides the well-worn Cold War principle of keeping the dominoes from tumbling, and an unshakable belief that an aggressive Communist China was manipulating its North Vietnamese puppets. Critics who thought the President had not prosecuted the war adequately operated on these premises. Richard Nixon, in a March 1965 speech, argued that the Vietnam war really was a war with China, with all of the Pacific Rim and Asia at stake. Nixon called for bombing in the North and more aid to the South. [29]

Little sophisticated analysis was applied to what was a complex situation. The policy that emerged was more the product of default and inertia than of design. Johnson's challenge to present "viable alternatives" to his policies went unanswered by those increasingly uncomfortable with the drift of events.

The policy of a limited, contained American involvement in Vietnam was doomed to frustration. Eventually, policy-makers and the country faced the hard choices of expansion or withdrawal. The concept of limited war was consistent neither with the President's personality nor with the temperament of the American people. The outcome of the Korean War, a decade earlier, had never been understood or accepted; for Vietnam, the American people eventually demanded total victory or withdrawal. Curiously, Johnson himself on occasion recognized the difficulties. He was acutely aware of Harry Truman's experience with public opinion and the Korean War. In his January 1965 message to Congress, Johnson warily warned that "we may have to face long, hard combat or a long, hard conference, or even both at once."

The truths and realities of Vietnam were hard to understand; they were even harder to explain. Johnson's concern for ensuring his popularity left no space for such frankness. Thus, much of the expanding American commitment occurred amid secrecy that in turn was a handmaiden to deception. For four years, the Johnson Administration carried out an extensive air war in Laos, hidden from most of the Congress and the public.[30] Laos typified the Administration's working combination of secrecy and deception rather than candid explanations of policies and goals. The subsequent cost of that style proved terribly high.

The intractability of the Vietnam war, and Johnson's conduct of it, undermined his cherished preference for consensus-building. The war's frustrations inevitably produced a swelling chord of domestic dissent. For Johnson, there was no response except to harden his position. His view of consensus "had come to mean balancing existing forces rather than bending them into new shapes." Imaginative solutions were cast aside as the President desperately sought public approval, even if securing approval required dissembling and the stifling of dissident views. Johnson had hoped that if he had "to turn back I want to make sure I am not in too deep to do so." By 1967, however, he was deep in the Vietnam "mud." "We face more cost, more loss, more agony," he reported in his 1967 State of the Union message. The result was that the master of crafty, pragmatic politics now emerged as a rigid ideologue, seemingly unresponsive to emerging political realities.[31]

The pressures on Johnson came in equal measure from those who wanted to "win" the war and those who wanted to end American involvement—"hawks" and "doves" were the simple labels given the players. The doves—largely the liberal intelligentsia—were more articulate and vocal than their adversaries, yet less effective in influencing the President. University campuses and classrooms, political journals, and literary magazines offered convenient forums for denouncing Johnson as a "preternatural villain, a monster who had seized on domestic liberalism as a cover for his stupid (or cunning, depending on the writer's needs) intervention in Vietnam." In time, the President and these critics passed the realm of dialogue and descended into shrill, often insulting, characterizations of each other's views. Johnson responded with more bitterness, more isolation, more bombs, and more insistence that he was right and that history would vindicate him.[32]

Criticism from hawks seemed less overt; yet it may have had more impact. Goldwater's 1964 position sparked enough fear and trembling in Adminis-

tration circles to contribute to the first significant escalation of the war. Johnson kept a wary eye on the right wing—the "great lurking monster," as he once characterized it. An aide revealed that Johnson feared merciless attacks from conservatives if he left South Vietnam destabilized. The Left, he was certain, could be contained or more easily satisfied; a Right that capitalized on his foreign-policy failures, however, might well imperil his cherished Great Society.

The military represented an uncertain quantity to Johnson. Was there possibly another Douglas MacArthur lurking in the wings? Admiral Thomas Moorer, a member of the Joint Chiefs of Staff, grumbled at the restraints the President had imposed on the use of military power and his close superintendence of that use. Moorer advocated an amphibious assault on the North, or even just the credible threat of one. The North, he realized, could deploy most of its troops in the South without having to fear any strike against its home terrain. "They didn't believe it at first, and then, finally, they came to the conclusion that we were really that stupid," Moorer later complained.

Lady Bird Johnson, the President's wife, afterward recalled that the major pressure came from such congressional conservatives as Senators Russell, Stennis, Byrd, and Thurmond—"people demanding that we get this thing over with by dropping the deadliest of bombs." The President listened to them. He was used to accommodating his former Senate cronies as if he were still Majority Leader. And then in Green Bay, Wisconsin, in February 1968, Republican candidate Richard Nixon must have sent a chill down Johnson's spine when he sounded the same note, insisting that the only effective way to force Hanoi to the bargaining table was to "prosecute the war more effectively."[33]

Johnson was described by a contemporary as "king of the river and a stranger to the sea."[34] He was a clever navigator of the congressional stream, paddling deftly through its pools and eddies, ever alert for the occasional sandbar. But in the open sea of foreign policy, with its shifting, almost imperceptible currents, its swells and tempests—there he was out of his depth. He could not be the master he wished to be, and this only embittered and frustrated him more. What he knew best did not apply in these unpredictable waters. International politics was not domestic politics writ large.

The concern over Johnson's policies in Southeast Asia eventually went beyond his personality, raising the issue of the nature and power of the presidency itself. That power had come a long way from the pristine handiwork of the framers of the Constitution. The history of presidential power is a history of aggrandizement; the transformation of the office in the twentieth century alone has been remarkable.[35] Economic dislocation, global wars, and the assumption of world leadership have focused power in the presidency, and with it the rapt attention of a fascinated, often adoring, public.

The expansion of presidential power was by and large welcomed and approved, and perhaps nowhere more eagerly than in the liberal and academic communities. Richard Neustadt, a former presidential aide and a leading student of the institution, suggested that the new powers and responsibilities of the modern presidency dictated a new constitutional view. By 1964, the old constitutional partnership between executive and legislative branches on the crucial questions of war and peace had been modified by new technology. The president, Neustadt argued, was the only one in the system "capable of exercising judgment under the extraordinary limits now imposed by secrecy, complexity, and time." The president must be the man in charge; he must, Neustadt concluded, "stretch his personal control, his human judgment, as wide and deep as he can make them reach."

One of Neustadt's critics noted that such behavior ordinarily would reflect "excessive, even pathological, vanity and opportunism." Neustadt wrote largely to applaud John F. Kennedy's self-image as president, the image Kennedy sought to project both within government and in the public arena. But Kennedy never really fulfilled his own image. Johnson, however, made it living, striking reality—and found that the celebrants of a strong presidency no longer were so certain or so forthcoming in their approval.[36]

In his maiden speech to the Senate in March 1949, Lyndon Johnson had warned that the modern president, with his "virtually unlimited powers of influence," and the unchecked power of his aides, represented "a force well-nigh irresistible." Senator Johnson, of course, saw all this as potential tyranny, and with a typically exaggerated rhetorical flourish, pictured the Senate as offering, if necessary, "the precious last-ditch fighters for freedom against a tyrannical president." Sixteen years later, he confidently asserted that he need not have the concurrence of Congress for his actions in Vietnam. "The authority of the president is very clear and unquestioned without a resolution," he said. "The Commander in Chief has all the authority that I am exercising." And a year later, in July 1966, he told a crowd that his election meant that while many could advise and a few had to consent to his policies, only he had "been chosen by the American people to decide." He was that "force well-nigh irresistible."[37]

Executive power once seen as beneficent was now perceived as arrogance, as the war and criticism of it steadily expanded in tandem. Johnson loved the limelight, often demanding it from others more deserving. But suddenly he found himself an unwanted center of attention as the situation in Vietnam deteriorated. At issue now were *his* war, *his* mounting casualties, *his* inadequate or misguided bombing raids, and *his* soaring inflation. Just as Johnson had exaggerated his power, critics equally exaggerated his responsibility for their frustrations.

The war effort itself, of course, was a casualty of the growing dissent. Equally important, perhaps, there was widespread questioning—most significantly, from the liberal forces in America—of a presidency that perhaps was too unbridled, too unchecked, and just too powerful.[38] The longstanding public unease and disquietude with Johnson took on added dimensions. He had rapidly expended the huge political capital he had gained in 1964. Now he was perceived as a man who had both lost control and was out of control. The combination was fatal.

The first month of 1968 portended the "continuous nightmare," as Johnson later characterized the final year of his presidency. It was, he said, "one of the most agonizing years any President ever spent in the White House."[39] By then, he interpreted assaults against the United States as personal humiliations, even when his fault was minimal or the enemy's victory dubious. On January 23, 1968, North Korea—perhaps North Vietnam's prototype in Johnson's eyes—seized the USS *Pueblo*, a highly sophisticated spy ship. One week later, the North Vietnamese and their Viet Cong allies unleashed the Tet offensive. No matter who might have been the immediate or long-range military victor of the Tet engagements, the sight on American television screens of an enemy assault in the courtyard of the American Embassy in Saigon only deepened public frustration with the war.

Perception was taken as reality, and the perception throughout much of the world and in the United States was that the United States and its South Vietnamese ally had been mortally humiliated. Tet actually resulted in severe losses for the enemy once American troops struck back with a counteroffensive. But the North Vietnamese boldness and audacity belied repeated assurances from Johnson and General William Westmoreland that the war was being won. Tet's most conspicuous casualty was the President.[40]

At best, the Vietnam war was difficult to explain or understand; Tet stands out as one of the more complex moments. It simply could not be treated definitively with each successive day of a journalist's deadline. The sight of Viet Cong troops swarming through the American Embassy compound was indeed stunning and unforgettable, but it may have been more symbol than substance. The television reporter from Saigon who had negotiated that precious ninety seconds from his network could not explore much below the surface sensationalism. Even if he had, chances are his words would not have correlated with the spectacular film of fire fights in the embassy's courtyard. The ultimate reality for the President and his advisers was that three of every four Americans received their news in this way.

Tet truly was a media event. Journalists hastily praised the enemy offensive for its discipline, organization, and success—judgments not necessarily in accord with reality. Later studies demonstrated that the North Vietnamese and their Viet Cong allies had not executed their plans very effectively and that, in fact, American and South Vietnamese troops had fought well. Without doubt, the media's "major distortion of reality—through sins of omission and commission— . . . helped shape Tet's political repercussions in Washington and the administration's response."⁴¹ Meanwhile, television showed a South Vietnamese police chief publicly executing a Viet Cong guerrilla in another shocking image which generated widespread revulsion.

The antiwar movement gained its apostolic benediction on February 27, 1968. CBS anchorman Walter Cronkite—oft cited as the "most trusted man in America"—journeyed to Vietnam following the Tet offensive to survey the war's progress. His judgment was emphatic and stunning: "It seems now more certain than ever that the bloody experience of Vietnam is to end in a stalemate." Johnson allegedly told his Press Secretary that if he had lost Cronkite he had lost "Mr. Average Citizen." Cronkite in effect put his imprimatur on a rising feeling that the war was no longer worth the effort. Clearly, the public was no longer in a mood to tolerate Johnson's handling of the struggle. While national support for the war stayed at about the 45 percent level between November 1967 and March 1968, approval of the President's conduct sank to an abysmal 26 percent.⁴² Tet, it seemed, *was* his fault.

Late in 1967, Minnesota Senator Eugene J. McCarthy decided to challenge President Johnson in the forthcoming spring primaries. What at first seemed like nothing more than a quixotic gesture soon offered a channel for the public's growing disaffection with the President. Everything about McCarthy seemed ambivalent: his liberal commitments, his interest in being a senator, and even his sincerity in challenging the President. But the mistake was to take him at less than his word. Whatever his original intentions in entering the primaries, McCarthy proved to be a formidable David in the classic confrontation against Goliath.

McCarthy may have fashioned himself in the mold of Thomas More, ready to risk disfavor with the King rather than submit to his heresies. McCarthy's importance in the days following Tet, however, lay not in offering any stark contrast to Johnson—indeed, the Senator opposed unilateral withdrawal— but rather in the fact that he dared to confront the President and publicly question his authority. The anti-authoritarian mood of that "Age of Aquarius" gave McCarthy an aura and legitimacy for the disaffected and alienated. His detachment and deliberately muted criticisms served him well (at least until June) and struck many as refreshingly cool, given the overheated political climate. McCarthy moved quietly but emphatically against an imperious ruler and his obsequious retainers. The Senator's bold proposal to dismiss General Lewis Hershey, the Selective Service Director, and J. Edgar Hoover, the seemingly untouchable head of the Federal Bureau of Investigation, suggested some new direction, different from the long-prevailing course of hallowed institutions.

New Hampshire's Democratic governor readily dismissed McCarthy, stating that the Senator would get barely 5 percent of the primary vote in his state. Perhaps that is all he would have garnered if he had been perceived only as an antiwar candidate. But Tet changed the campaign. Public resentment ran high because of the embarrassment of that debacle, and the resentment was shared by supporters of the war as well as opponents. Now Johnson was the man "who could neither pacify the ghetto, speak the plain truth, lick inflation, nor above all end the war."[43]

The Tet backlash focused attention in early March on the New Hampshire primary, the nation's first. The results shocked the nation. Hawks joined doves, Republicans crossed over—and McCarthy captured 42 percent of the vote, and the majority of the state's delegates. Whether McCarthy was David or Thomas More was questionable; but he had unquestionably embarrassed the President of the United States.

Invigorated by his New Hampshire "victory," McCarthy moved on to Wisconsin, which was far less politically ambiguous than New Hampshire. The old Progressive tradition, the high level of political activism, and a longstanding tradition of suspicion toward foreign adventures quickly made McCarthy the frontrunner in the state's primary. McCarthy's appeal to his Wisconsin neighbors transcended the war issue. More than anyone else at the time, McCarthy recognized the deeper issue of presidential power and its abuse—an enormously sensitive subject in a state with deep-seated distrust toward public officials. He suggested that presidential candidates acknowledge the limitations of power. Most of all, he twitted Johnson for personalizing the office. "A President should not speak of 'my country' but always of 'our country'; not of 'my cabinet' but of 'the cabinet,' because once the cabinet is appointed, it becomes something different from the man who may have nominated these persons, even from the Senate which confirms them in office." In more playful moments, McCarthy sarcastically noted the President's references to "my helicopters," or "my troops." Johnson's conception of the office was wrong, McCarthy stressed. The office "belongs not to the man who holds it but to the people of this nation."[44]

With less than a week to go before the Wisconsin election, Johnson's supporters in the state predicted McCarthy's overwhelming triumph. Projected estimates for the Senator ranged as high as 65 percent of the vote. Meanwhile, the swelling opposition to the President encouraged Senator Robert F. Kennedy to announce his own candidacy. Ironically, the immediate effect was to create bitter divisions in the anti-Johnson and antiwar camps.

The Tet surprise, the New Hampshire rebuke, the prospect of repudiation in the Wisconsin primary, the new reality of the ever-present Kennedy threat, the inability to get Hanoi to the bargaining table, the rebelliousness of Congress—to name only the most obvious factors—projected a different image of the President, one of Gulliver harassed by an army of Lilliputians. And they seemed about to topple him. Physically ill and worn, obsessed with the fear of a second heart attack, demoralized by his failure to win the hearts and minds of Americans, Johnson announced his withdrawal from the presidential race in a March 31 televised address. "I shall not seek, and I will not accept, the nomination of my party for another term as your President." The President also announced a partial bombing halt, stressing a desire to avoid partisan entanglements for the sake of "the presidency" and the opportunities for peace; but he fooled very few. The political system had mastered him—not the other way around—as his editorial and public support dropped sharply, and key supporters drifted away or opposed his policies. The primary results portrayed a painful truth: the President was not very widely loved, and worse, he was judged a failure. He may well have rationalized his withdrawal as giving him an opportunity to gain, as Doris Kearns has written, "more control over and more love from history—the only constituency that really mattered in the end."[45]

The President's withdrawal was cloaked in typical, albeit understandable, secrecy. The day after announcing it, Johnson insisted that his action had been long planned and had nothing to do with his declining political fortunes. Nevertheless, it seemed—and again, the perception was important— that media and street politics had, for the first time, driven a president from the White House. Johnson acknowledged as much when in a speech to broadcasters in Chicago on April 1, he blamed the failure of the war on the media which had fostered and marshaled unfair opposition to that war and his policies.[46]

Johnson's decision to withdraw provoked a great outpouring of affection and goodwill (even though the lingering skepticism was such that a sizable portion of the media and the public doubted whether he really was through as a candidate). He was, as he so often reminded the people, "the only president you've got." Images of November 1963 and his healing force, as well as his inspiring legislative *tour de force,* briefly flashed on the scene. The President's popular approval rating soared from 36 to 49 percent. For the first time in many months, the White House mail came overwhelmingly from friendly correspondents.[47] Yet little warmth or depth characterized the response; there was mostly numbness. The war had deeply divided the American people, and those who supported and opposed it at last could agree: it was best for the President to go. The momentary rush of good feeling certainly did not usher in a new era; rising social tensions and the events of the electoral season soon rekindled and unleashed almost boundless furies.

The nation had rejected Johnson as it had few other sitting presidents. He was perceived as a man who had misled, maybe even willfully deceived, the American people. To achieve his aims, he had attempted to suppress countervailing forces and institutions; his imperiousness and arrogance had led him to ignore dissident voices, outside and inside the White House, and had provoked the unprecedented protests that rent the land. Johnson's failure to accommodate or temper those protests eventually isolated him and left him no alternative but to leave the presidency—and to leave it largely in disgrace.

Johnson's decision was both exhilarating and disturbing. The critics of the war and of the growing excesses of presidential power could take great satisfaction in Johnson's departure. The "voice of the people" had been heard; democracy had been served. But few pondered the implications for the nation and the presidency. Johnson's presidency lay in ruins—confused, demoralized, and pervaded with bitterness. The presidency itself, battered from without and distorted from within, had suffered enormously. And worse was yet to come.

II

MAKING MANY NIXONS: 1913-1965

The Democratic presidential primaries dominated the nation's attention in 1968. Lyndon Johnson's withdrawal opened the way for Vice President Hubert Humphrey, a longtime claimant for the party's honor who now was cast in the dubious position of Johnson's surrogate. Eugene McCarthy and Robert Kennedy intensified their campaigns, vigorously competing for the same constituency to gain the nomination. Meanwhile, Alabama's segregationist governor, George Wallace, emerged as a wild card, pointing his own message to a wholly different quarter of alienated America. Despite talk of the wholesomeness of intra-party squabbling, the chemistry of the Democratic Party's struggle offered a prescription for disaster, and even tragedy.

Lyndon Johnson had been embarrassed in the New Hampshire primary and defeated in Wisconsin, but for Richard Nixon, both elections amounted to a coronation. His chief rival, George Romney, withdrew from the field before the New Hampshire balloting, in large measure humiliated by his own ineptness. Nixon carefully worked to preempt the center and thus dominate his party; yet the fringes represented real threats. Nelson Rockefeller may not have been a viable alternative, but he retained the capacity to make life difficult for Nixon—as he had for a decade. And now, from Nixon's own California base, newly elected Governor Ronald Reagan staked his claim to the still-substantial Goldwater legacy in the Republican Party and offered every indication that his made-for-media style would expand it. Reagan's threat was formidable, yet it was not quite his time. "Nixon's the one," the campaign slogan proclaimed. So he was.

* * *

Richard Nixon in 1968 had been a familiar figure on the American political scene for two decades; still, characterizing him generated contradiction more than consistency, confusion rather than clarity. Descriptions of Nixon recorded in those years leave us with many Nixons. When Nixon emerged as "the one" for the 1960 Republican presidential nomination, General Lucius D. Clay confidently predicted that he would be "the leader of the Conservative forces." New York's middle-of-the-road Senator Kenneth Keating described Nixon as "pretty much my brand of Republican"; while liberal Republican Arthur Flemming, Eisenhower's Secretary of Health, Education, and Welfare, labeled Nixon as "a genuine, progressive Republican."[1] Eight years later, people spoke of a "New Nixon" as if to underline not only the "Old Nixon" but the multifaceted image that had prevailed for so long.

Portraying Nixon demands a *Rashomon*-like approach if one is to understand those varied images he projected, and the society and constituencies that stimulated and responded to him. The varieties and vagaries of biographies have left us with a portrait of a deeply troubled man, insecure and sometimes tottering on the brink of mental instability; and yet we can also discover a cool, rational man, totally in command of his emotions and reconciled to his destiny. We have been given a cold, impersonal, awkward man; and yet we also have portrayals of a compassionate personality, inwardly and outwardly expressing the Quaker values instilled in him as a child. For some, Nixon vacillated between being sanctimonious and supercilious; others saw stoicism and strength in his character.

Richard Nixon is a controversial figure in any historical assessment of the postwar era of American history. His place will vary with the passage of time, running a gamut of estimates. But for now, Nixon certainly ranks with the two Roosevelts, Woodrow Wilson, and Dwight Eisenhower as a dominant, influential, and charismatic figure of the twentieth century.

Nixon's legions of detractors and enemies must confront that reality. They must accept that for those who love and admire Nixon he was an an inspiring personality. His impact on his party was similar to that of Adlai Stevenson in the 1950s. Liberals and intellectuals found themselves uplifted by Stevenson's appearance on the national scene in 1952. He offered them a refreshing contrast to the crass partisan politics of Harry Truman (who had not yet been discovered as a neo-folk idol) and a languid, entrenched, self-satisfied Democratic Party. Stevenson's eloquence and candor revived a wave of political emotion that had been largely subdued since Franklin D. Roosevelt's death in 1945.

Nixon had achieved similar success on the other end of the political spectrum. What a contrast he offered to the defeatism of Thomas Dewey and the dour negativism of Robert Taft! He was a winner (though not always) and a fighter (except at the end). He was dedicated to dissipating the fears that substantial numbers of Americans had regarding Communism and governmental control of the economy. Significantly, his support declined appreciably when his presidential policies seemed to contradict those goals.

For his supporters, Nixon's enemies and causes generated substantial passion and sympathy for him. After all, a good part of this country despised what New Dealer and accused Soviet spy Alger Hiss symbolized. Who can gainsay a popular basis for Nixon's defeat of Helen Gahagan Douglas for the Senate in 1950? H. R. Haldeman, a young Californian in 1952, found Nixon exciting, a man "fighting against odds and the establishment, and winning." For those who loved and admired him, Nixon's investiture as Crown Prince in 1952 confirmed the emergence of the real "Modern Republicanism."

Nixon could evoke a range of views from one and the same observer. Walter Lippmann, never one to bind himself to consistency as a virtue, painted a variegated landscape of opinions of Nixon over the years. Lippmann described Nixon's 1952 "Checkers" speech (which defended his use of certain campaign contributions) as "the most demeaning experience my country has ever had to bear." He found it "disturbing," and "with all the magnification of modern electronics, simply mob law." As President Eisenhower campaigned for re-election four years later, Lippmann remarked that the President "unites the country and heals its divisions. This is precisely what Nixon does not do. He is a politician who divides and embitters the people." More in sorrow than in heat, Lippmann described Nixon's 1962 California gubernatorial defeat as that of "a politician who does not have the confidence of moderate men." But in 1968, Lippmann had joined the converts to the notion of a "New Nixon," acknowledging a "new Nixon, a maturer, mellower man who is no longer clawing his way to the top, . . . who has outlived and outgrown the ruthless politics of his early days." The humiliation of Nixon's resignation six years later reduced Lippmann to analyzing the stars, and not the man. Arthur Schlesinger asked Lippmann if Nixon had been the worst president in history. "No, not the worst," Lippmann replied, "but perhaps the most embarrassing. . . . Presidents are not lovable. They've had to do too much to get where they are."[2]

All that layering, all that complexity, all that elusiveness, beggars attention. Ronald Steel once remarked that Nixon was like the Ancient Mariner, forever tugging at our sleeve, anxious to tell his story. But if we are to understand and explain Richard Nixon and what he did, we, too, are compelled to tell it again and again.

"I was born in a house my father built." So begin the memoirs of Richard Nixon. This pointed opening illustrates his humble beginnings and his strong sense of familial community, and offers a twentieth-century analogue to being born in a log cabin. Any view of Nixon, friendly or unfriendly, comes down to a Horatio Alger–style political story. It is a model for the notion that truly any "ordinary" American boy can grow up to be President of the United States. Accounts of few other modern presidents emphasize their humble beginnings as elaborately as does Nixon's. The detail, candor, and repetition invite comparison to tales, both mythical and factual, of the young Abe Lincoln. For his admirers, in his early years Nixon (like Lincoln) "managed to stand out in one way or another." For them, of course, Nixon emerges in this picture as an exceptionally gifted young man, destined for greatness, while others find dark forebodings of the sinister, erratic behavior that later characterized his career.[3]

The mature Nixon loved to claim "firsts." Appropriately, he was the first child born in Yorba Linda, a farming community thirty miles inland from Los Angeles. Born on January 9, 1913, Richard was the second son of Frank and Hannah Nixon. Frank had migrated from Columbus, Ohio, where he had been a streetcar motorman. In Southern California, he tried a variety of jobs, including carpentry, working a citrus ranch, and finally, opening a gasoline station and general store in Whittier. At one juncture, apparently, Frank passed up a chance to buy a site that later turned out to be valuable oil property, provoking endless family laments thereafter over a missed opportunity to be rich.

Frank Nixon had a hot temper and was known to be severe in disciplining his children. He came from a long line of "tough, strait-laced, Bible-pounding Methodists," but when he married Hannah Milhous in 1908, he easily moved his allegiance to his wife's Quaker faith. Throughout his political life, Richard invoked his parents' memory. The imagery usually centered on his father as a fighter, a scrapper, a man who took on an essentially hostile world that seemingly conspired against him. He portrayed his mother, however, as a strong, quietly assertive, but always effective woman. Richard eagerly sought his mother's love and approval, especially as he had to cope with her three-year absence when she desperately nursed her tubercular oldest son, Harold. Those family struggles have provided ample grist for the psychohistorians, and Richard Nixon himself has hinted at some large meanings. In his memory, Hannah Milhous Nixon emerged as the center of the family, giving it cohesion and stability. In Quaker terms, Richard probably understood his mother as guided by an "inner light"; publicly, he described her as a "saint." As his parents were different, Richard responded to them in different ways through the years, always acknowledging their special legacies to him.[4]

Richard's high school years in Whittier were notable for his interest and accomplishments in debate and dramatics. He had hoped to attend college in the East—not the last time that he sought to escape Southern California for some sort of salvation in the nation's more prestigious power centers. Nevertheless, Whittier College provided him with ample, treasured rewards, offering him a history professor who imparted to his students the Progressive tradition he had learned at the University of Wisconsin, and another who stressed Christian humanism. Despite his parents' steadfast Republicanism, Nixon's early thinking had, in his words, "a very liberal, almost populist, tinge."

But his real interests at Whittier, again, lay in debate and dramatics—and football. Always a second-stringer, Nixon nevertheless reveled in his football exploits. Whatever influences the Progressive historian and the Christian humanist exerted on Nixon paled next to those of his memories of his revered coach, Wallace ("Chief") Newman, who was of Indian descent. Newman, Nixon recalled, had no tolerance for Grantland Rice's sentimental credo that how one played the game mattered more than whether the game was won or lost. "Show me a good loser, and I'll show you a loser," Nixon remembered Newman as saying. More important, Nixon gratefully remembered Newman's influence in imparting a competitive spirit and a determination to come back after a defeat.[5]

Richard finally realized his ambition to go east when he received a scholarship in 1934 from the newly established law school at Duke University. Here he found himself on a faster track, and even at first overwhelmed by what he had to memorize and master. But a classmate gave him a variant on Chief Newman's competitive advice: "You don't have to worry," the fellow student said. "You have what it takes to learn the law—an iron butt." Nixon learned law; he also learned about Southern views toward race and the Civil War, which he thereafter referred to as the "War Between the States."

During his stay at Duke, Nixon first realized that "it was time to bring the South back into the Union"—a point he emphasized as part of his "Southern Strategy" in 1968. He also learned something of politics, getting himself elected president of the Student Bar Association. Eventually, however, he discovered barriers to his ambitions, as when he failed to land a job in a New York law firm and unsuccessfully applied for an appointment to the Federal Bureau of Investigation.[6]

Nixon decided to go home to California. Whatever its shortcomings for him, Whittier provided a safe haven. He returned in 1937 and settled into a career as a typical small-town lawyer—not, however, without some controversy over his ability and even his ethical behavior.[7] The next year, he met a young new teacher at Whittier High School, Thelma Catherine Ryan, better known as Pat. She was nearly a year older than Richard (born on March 16, 1912, not St. Patrick's Day, as Nixon once claimed in a speech). Pat, too, was interested in dramatics, and the couple seemed to share a number of other mutual interests. They were married in 1940. By that time

Richard had established himself fairly well in Whittier, was active in community affairs and Whittier College activities, and had even dabbled in politics. He claimed that local Republican leaders approached him about running for the state assembly, but the war intervened. A few months earlier, he later recalled, he had welcomed the outbreak of the Russo-German War, believing that it would lead to Hitler's defeat. Despite his apparent lively interest in politics, Nixon, by his own admission, had no particular anti-Soviet or anticommunist feelings at this time.[8]

The war gave Nixon his long-awaited opportunity to seek his fortune in the East. Thanks to a recommendation from a Duke professor, he received a post in the newly created Office of Price Administration. Now, he later remembered, he could go to Washington "and observe the working of the government firsthand." The job also satisfied his mother, who thought he could work for the government and not totally compromise his pacifist Quaker principles by joining the armed forces. If this represented some inner conflict between Nixon's religious and family past and his future vision of himself, the future won. After only a few months as a junior lawyer in the OPA's tire-rationing division, in August 1942 Nixon secured an appointment to the Navy's Officer Candidate School at Quonset Point, Rhode Island. The brief tenure with the OPA left its mark; Nixon later claimed that he learned a great deal about bureaucratic logrolling (from a future Truman aide) and about bureaucrats' obsession with their own power.[9]

Nixon learned more about the mysteries of bureaucracy after he received his commission, when he was assigned to the Naval Air Station in Ottumwa, Iowa. At first, he thought he would spend his entire war service in the Midwest, but he eventually was accepted for sea duty and sent to the South Pacific. In 1944, he served as a transport-control officer on New Caledonia and Bougainville. He experienced some Japanese shelling of his base, saw some air-crash victims, and by his own account had a great deal of success at the poker table. Poker may have honed some worthwhile political skills, but his "combat experience" and his officer status gave him a political winning hand and ample chips to play it.[10]

Whatever significance emerges from Nixon's early years results to some extent from reading history backward, from reading deeper meanings into earlier events that may or may not anticipate later ones. In that vein it is clear that after 1946, Richard Nixon became a public man. His history thereafter is a matter of record, and consists of conscious and unconscious deeds, as well as both calculated and accidental incidents, that together form a complex mosaic of explanation of the man and his actions.

Nothing shaped the basic historical perception of Richard Nixon more than his first campaign for public office, in 1946. Shortly after the end of the war, a Whittier banker wrote to Nixon, then in Baltimore awaiting demobilization, asking if he were interested in running for Congress. With no

apparent prospects in sight, Nixon promptly expressed interest and offered
to begin campaigning by the first of the year. But he had misunderstood the
query; his friend was only seeking prospective candidates who would be
scrutinized by a "Committee of One Hundred." The committee consisted
of conservative Republican businessmen and professionals passionately committed to defeating the incumbent congressman. Nixon appeared before
the group (in his naval uniform), assailed the New Deal, and promised "a
platform of practical liberalism." The committee promptly chose him in
preference to a Pomona furniture-store owner.[11]

Jerry Voorhis, the Twelfth District incumbent, was no ordinary congressman. First elected in 1936 in the Roosevelt landslide, he had managed to
retain office in a marginal district through careful attention to his constituents' needs and his support of liberal public legislation that nevertheless
appealed to rural conservatives. Voorhis became an expert in such matters
as rural electrification and farmers' cooperatives. Now, after ten years in
Washington, he was well regarded by liberals and conservatives alike, and
he had attracted a good deal of attention from the national press. In his most
recent term, Voorhis had given his name to Public Law 780, which required
organizations controlled by foreign governments to register with the Department of Justice. Communist-front groups were Voorhis's obvious target;
indeed, the West Coast edition of the *Daily Worker* bitterly complained that
"Voorhis is against unity with Communists on any issue under any circumstances."[12] In all, Voorhis was an entrenched incumbent, active on a wide
front of popular legislative activities, and a man who had diligently nurtured
close ties with his constituents. He was a model anticommunist liberal.

For a variety of reasons, 1946 was a Republican year, and California's
Twelfth District race in that year was special. The political novice, totally
unknown outside Whittier, trounced the five-term Congressman by more
than 15,000 votes out of a total of 115,000. Richard Nixon later claimed
that the contest was between "a well-known New Dealer and a conservative
Republican." Voorhis lost because "that district was not a New Deal district," Nixon contended.[13] But Nixon had promised his benefactors "a platform of practical liberalism," and that is largely what he offered during the
campaign. The New Deal in 1946 was still fighting ground, bitterly contested
by conservative Republicans. In his campaign, Nixon dutifully alluded to
the dangers of governmental control of economic life, yet he hammered
away most strongly on the need for jobs for veterans, a position that hardly
illuminated any ideological difference. The Republican candidate neither
walked nor talked like a "conservative Republican." Nixon, who had
emerged from Whittier College as a self-confessed "liberal," nowhere stated
in 1946—nor ever acknowledged—any rejection of the New Deal's basic
recovery, relief, and reform measures. At Duke, Nixon had been known for

his enthusiastic support of Supreme Court Justices Brandeis, Cardozo, and Stone, who distinguished themselves at that time for their support of the New Deal. The simple ideological confrontation that Nixon described for his maiden campaign explains nothing.

It was Nixon's style and language that distinguished this campaign and set the tone for the search for the historical Nixon. For Nixon's defenders, his campaign against Voorhis amounted to a typical effort by an "out," free to attack his opponent's record and to promise change. By this logic, Voorhis, the "in," had "only one positive theme": his seniority and experience. The implication is that he was "soft," and incapable of confronting the challenge of his "buzz-saw opponent"; but the ultimate "softness" charge centered on the claim that Voorhis was a tool of the "Communist-dominated" Political Action Committee (PAC) of the Congress of Industrial Organizations (CIO).

In the first public debate between the candidates, Voorhis denied having sought and received support from the labor PAC. But Nixon countered with a report from Southern California unions recommending that the PAC endorse Voorhis. Apparently, Voorhis realized that for many of his constituents Sidney Hillman and other CIO-PAC leaders seemed like some alien, sinister force, and he issued a tortured statement saying that he long had cherished support from organized labor but repudiated any from the CIO-PAC. He acknowledged the possibility that the Communist Party exercised "inordinate if not decisive influence" in the CIO. It was not enough. Nixon hammered at the theme that Voorhis had loyally voted for the CIO-PAC programs, and he talked obliquely about "lip-service Americans" and high officials "who front for un-American elements." Nixon also emphasized his military service, indirectly underlining Voorhis's civilian status. As for the charge that voters received anonymous phone calls denouncing Voorhis as a Communist, Nixon's supporters thought it possible that such calls were designed to hurt Nixon "by making him appear guilty of vicious tactics."[14]

Critics have denounced Nixon's campaign for its smears and innuendoes. For example, his attacks on Voorhis's labor connections emphasized the PAC's "Communist principles and its huge slush fund." Nixon's leaflets described him as "the clean, forthright young American who fought in defense of his country in the stinking mud and jungle of the Solomons," while Voorhis remained "safely behind the front in Washington." The campaign, Nixon's detractors have contended, represented only techniques and tactics, with no ideological substance whatever. He displayed here a rhetorical skill he eventually mastered, one of leveling a charge even while self-righteously denying he would ever do so.

The evil genius behind Nixon's campaign supposedly was Murray Chotiner, a Southern California political public-relations man who had worked

for Senator William Knowland and the conservative wing of the Republican
Party. Chotiner believed that a candidate could be packaged and merchan-
dised to the public as a commodity. Nixon's debate training and speaking
skills, combined with his youth and war record, provided a perfect match
for the Chotiner formula. Technique dominated, and substance was immaterial—all "a calculated part of the synthetic image that [Nixon] with the
help of his financial backers contrived." Voorhis had not in fact been endorsed by the CIO-PAC; a local group had merely recommended doing so.
No matter. Nixon had "learned how to employ the various devices of the
half-truth, the misleading quotation, the loose-jointed logic, that were indispensable in the creation of the BIG DOUBT." [15]

The contrasting portraits are clear. For some, Nixon was the returning
war hero determined to rid America of its un-American elements; he was
vigorous, aggressive, and, above all, resourceful. For others, the Nixon of
1946 marked a new beginning in the commercialization and packaging of
political candidates; as for the man himself, he was perceived as manipulative, exploitive, opportunistic, even deceptive and dishonest. For both proponents and detractors, however, Nixon was now a man to be reckoned
with.

Nixon's victory over Voorhis gave him some measure of national visibility,
but nothing was as extraordinary as his meteoric emergence as a national
public figure during his freshman term in Congress. Timing and events operated in his favor. Nixon coveted a seat on the House Labor Committee,
and he was duly rewarded by the victorious Republicans. But they also selected him for the Committee on Un-American Activities, for reasons that
are somewhat uncertain; membership on the committee had not been considered a plum assignment. Nixon claimed that Speaker Joe Martin asked
him to serve as a personal favor and to help reverse the dubious reputation
the committee had acquired through the years. "[I]t was an offer I could not
very well refuse," he later recalled almost apologetically, adding that he
accepted only reluctantly. It was also true, however, that Nixon had discovered the Soviet threat and the corresponding link to internal subversions,
both topics within the purview of the Un-American Activities Committee. [16]
That offered an opportunity he could not refuse.

Nixon participated in the preparation of the Taft-Hartley labor law, and
he publicly debated the merits of the bill with John F. Kennedy, a freshman
Representative from Massachusetts and fellow Labor Committee member.
In addition, perhaps as repayment for his favor to Martin, the Speaker selected Nixon as one of nineteen congressmen to participate in a select committee—chaired by Christian Herter, a future Secretary of State—formed to
determine the foreign-aid needs of war-torn Europe. According to Nixon, a
poll revealed that three-fourths of his constituents opposed any aid package,

and he received warnings not to be seduced by eastern Republicans and the siren calls of Europeans. Nevertheless, he eventually supported the Marshall Plan, invoking Edmund Burke's classic injunction that representatives must vote their conscience, not the whims of their constituents. [17]

But it was Nixon's service on the Un-American Activities Committee that catapulted him to national prominence. The committee persisted in its controversial ways, warmly applauded by those who believed the nation in imminent danger from internal subversion and international Communism, and roundly condemned by civil libertarians, by those who saw the committee exclusively serving the interests of the Republican Party and the business community, and by those, who, from a variety of motives, believed that the preservation of world peace required cooperation with the Soviet Union. There was little middle ground; similarly, Nixon's chosen role defied neutrality.

As a member of the committee, Nixon rode the crest of the anticommunist hysteria that paralleled the heightening conflict of the Cold War. When an American Legion member in San Francisco wrote to ask whether "Communist art" (a typical mural of the 1930s, depicting proletarian themes) could be removed from the San Francisco post office, Nixon solemnly replied that a Republican president and Congress would "make a thorough investigation" of such art and would remove any of it found to be "inconsistent with American ideals and principles." [18] Post office art, of course, was small change when stacked against the most sensational charge of the day: that Soviet intelligence had penetrated the Democratic administrations of Roosevelt and Truman as a result of betrayals by high officials. After nearly ten years of making what seemed to be altogether implausible charges of like character, the Un-American Activities Committee found a receptive public. And Richard Nixon proved its most skillful member in exploiting the opportunity.

Early in 1947, the committee treated the nation to an early version of guerrilla theater when it spent months trying to prove that a small band of Hollywood screen writers had injected Soviet and Communist propaganda as wholesome values in some films. The hearings revealed a variety of Hollywood civil wars, but only the notoriety of the accused gave the sessions some public credibility. Charges of subversion and spying in high places in Washington presented another matter altogether. Whittaker Chambers, ex-Communist, ex-Comintern agent, and then a highly placed editor of *Time* magazine, appeared before the committee in August 1948 and repeated charges he had made earlier to FBI investigators and others. Chambers's most sensational moment came when he testified that a ring of Soviet sympathizers had infiltrated the government. The most prominent member of the group, he claimed, was Alger Hiss. Hiss was then working for the Carnegie Endowment for International Peace, but as a ranking State Department official he had accompanied Roosevelt to Yalta in 1945 and choreographed the San Francisco Conference that inaugurated the United Nations that same year. By 1948, Yalta was a synonym for "sell-out," even treason for some critics. Hiss was made to order for the moment. He was many things, but above all, he served to focus many hatreds: Harvard Law School graduate, New Deal bureaucrat, eastern-oriented internationalist. In his subsequent public appearances, he struck many as haughty and arrogant, and thus only confirmed their visceral reactions.

The Chambers–Hiss confrontation became the first of Nixon's famous "Six Crises." His own description of the affair, as well as that of his supporters, portrayed him as a relentless prosecutor, convinced of Chambers's truthfulness and Hiss's perjury. Hiss's subsequent conviction, of course, only reinforced the picture. Inevitably, Nixon's enemies long nursed grievances against him for his role in the case. An extensive study of the case, one decidedly hostile to Hiss, contended that Nixon was not the "cool, confident and decisive" investigator he had long claimed to be; instead, a "combination of accident, good luck, inside information, fear, and panic" best characterized Nixon's first crisis. Subsequently, Pat Nixon asked the committee's chief investigator, Robert Stripling, who had persuaded Chambers to provide the famous "pumpkin papers," to "allow Dick to take credit for breaking the case."[19]

Whatever the historical judgment on the Hiss affair, it firmly established Richard Nixon's reputation and prominence. Few forgot his role; he certainly never did. As the Watergate crisis deepened a quarter-century later, Nixon repeatedly advised his aides to read the Hiss chapter in *Six Crises*, his first memoir. Presidential assistant Charles Colson later testified that he may have read it fourteen times; it was, he said, "a benchmark" for ongoing matters of current interest.[20] Ostensibly, Nixon sought to impart lessons on fighting and persistence in his book; could he have forgotten that his version of the tale exposed lying and corruption in high places?

First, Voorhis. Then Hiss. And all in such short order. In two congressional terms, Richard Nixon had spectacularly captured headlines and national attention. And there was more to come.

California Democratic Senator Sheridan Downey signaled that he would not run for re-election in 1950. Downey represented what had been the party's dominant conservative wing, but it had steadily diminished in numbers and influence. His withdrawal opened the Democratic primary to a bitter ideological confrontation between Manchester Boddy, editor of the Los Angeles *Daily News*, and Representative Helen Gahagan Douglas. Boddy equally condemned Governor Earl Warren's liberal Republicanism, Democratic New Dealers, and Douglas, his party's apparent favorite. Douglas regularly identified with liberal causes in the Democratic Party and left-wing concerns outside of it. The primary, which was bitter and ugly, set the tone for the general election.

Boddy bluntly charged that Douglas associated with a subversive "clique of red hots," and that her voting record followed that of Vito Marcantonio, a New York Representative openly sympathetic to the Soviet Union and Communist causes. Douglas's votes against aid to Greece and Turkey seemed to give some credibility to the charges. Even so, however, she captured nearly 50 percent of the primary vote, holding Boddy to only 30 percent. The remainder went to Nixon, as California law permitted crossover filings. (Douglas received 13 percent of the Republican primary vote.)

The red-baiting and ugly accusations that tarnished the primary merely sounded an overture. The Nixon-Douglas campaign included Nixon's first references to Secretary of State Dean Acheson's alleged appeasement of Communism, and it marked his public endorsement of Senator Joseph McCarthy's tactics of smearing Democrats allegedly "soft on Communism." Nixon's campaign literature depicted Douglas as "the Pink Lady," and his staff circulated pink sheets comparing her voting record to Marcantonio's. Nixon had support from the notorious anti-Semite Gerald L. K. Smith and from the China Lobby supporters of the deposed Chiang Kaishek. In November, the young Republican Congressman scored a smashing victory, besting Douglas by more than 600,000 votes. And with that, the nation first heard of "Tricky Dick."

Even pro-Nixon accounts of the campaign concede that the campaign was "the most hateful" California had experienced in years. The notable difference in the two camps, according to a Nixon admirer, "was in the adroitness and calmness with which Nixon and his people executed *their* hyperbole and innuendo."[21] Adroitness and calmness; hyperbole and innuendo. By whatever description, the Nixon-Douglas campaign became a new standard for measuring negative campaigning—and for the winner's partisans and foes alike to use in measuring their man.

Nixon's accomplishments as Senator stand in almost inverse proportion to the immense expenditure of energy in the 1950 campaign. His tenure was notable only for the further visibility it gave him, a visibility that led to his nomination for the vice presidency in 1952. The notoriety of his campaign victory, along with his growing reputation, made him much in demand as a speaker at party gatherings. A friendly biographer identified Nixon as a "Republican meld of Paul Revere and Billy Sunday," preaching the party's gospel and warning of the dangers of the Democratic hordes.[22]

The Senator had some identification with his party's internationalist wing, largely through his role on the Herter Committee, but that seemed uncharacteristic. His work on the House Labor Committee, his prominent role on the Un-American Activities Committee, and his campaign rhetoric seemed to align Nixon comfortably with the party's conservatives. When he announced for the Senate in November 1949, he denounced the Democratic Party for its "phony doctrines and ideologies," and for offering "the same old Socialist baloney."

But Senator Robert A. Taft—"Mr. Republican," as he was known, a man universally acknowledged as head of the party's conservative wing—had little regard for his California colleague. At one point, he described Nixon as "a little man in a big hurry," with "a mean and vindictive streak."[23] Taft's candor and bluntness were characteristic of the man, but his failure to cultivate Nixon cost him dearly. Senator Nixon resolutely supported the delegate claims of Taft's rival, General Dwight Eisenhower, at the 1952 Republican Convention, a procedural move that eventually cost Taft the nomination.

Nixon's selection as Eisenhower's running mate is cloaked in ambiguity and obscurity. Clearly, Eisenhower's advisers, led by Thomas E. Dewey, saw Nixon as a vigorous young man, ideally fit to carry the burden of a partisan campaign while leaving the General above the main battle lines, thereby preserving his statesman-like image. Nothing came to Richard Nixon without controversy, however. Pledged to support the candidacy of Earl Warren as California's favorite son, Nixon seemed all too eager throughout the convention to abandon Warren and provide the necessary support to give Eisenhower his margin of victory. Warren and his friends thereafter bore a grudge against their fellow Californian.

The 1952 campaign decisively pushed Nixon into national prominence. Partly because of their reluctance to attack Eisenhower, a popular national hero, the Democrats concentrated much of their fire on Nixon. For perhaps the first time in American history, the question of the suitability of a vice-presidential candidate as a potential president became a major issue.

Nixon slashed away at the Democrats, promising that a Republican Administration would expose corruption and clean up "the mess in Washington," rid the nation of domestic subversives, and reverse the Truman-Acheson policy of containment of Communism, which, he charged, was tantamount to appeasement. In late October, he attacked President Truman and presidential candidate Adlai Stevenson as "traitors to the high principles" of the Democratic Party. "Traitors" was the operative word; "party" was unimportant, for in his next statement, Nixon claimed that Democrats had tolerated and defended Communists in government. Nixon's supporters knew the value of what he *seemed* to be saying. He did not call Secretary of State Dean Acheson a "pink," but he referred to "Acheson's color blindness—a form of pink eye toward the Communist threat in the United States."

Nixon attacked Adlai Stevenson for testifying as a character witness for Alger Hiss. He conceded that doing so was Stevenson's right, maybe even his duty, but he then expressed outrage that Stevenson had never condemned Hiss's treachery. The fact was, however, that Stevenson had done so, and he responded with contempt for Nixon—"the brash young man who aspires to the Vice-Presidency." Stevenson loathed Nixon and his "flexible convictions." The Democratic nominee had hoped for a campaign of "elevating national discussion." But, blaming Nixon, he complained that the nation heard a systematic presentation of "innuendo and accusations aimed at sowing the seeds of doubt and mistrust." More tellingly and more cuttingly, Stevenson derided Nixon as a comic figure, describing him as the "kind of politician who would cut down a redwood tree, then mount the stump for a speech on conservation."[24]

Nothing in the campaign generated more controversy than the revelation that Nixon had a secret fund maintained by supporters for his personal use. The fund itself soon became unimportant, as many other politicians (including Stevenson) had similar arrangements. More important, and ever more memorable, was Nixon's defense of the fund, highlighted by his quintessential performance in his "Checkers" speech. However commonplace such funds, Nixon's gave the Republicans special problems. Pledged to clean up that mess in Washington, the Republicans now found themselves in a dilemma. Eisenhower talked about the necessity for being as "clean as a hound's tooth," and the party's high command gave serious consideration to dropping Nixon from the ticket. Eventually, Eisenhower's campaign strategists decided to give the vice-presidential candidate an opportunity to explain his situation to the public.

The Republicans bought a half-hour of television time from NBC. The speech was unforgettable. Nixon defended his fund, but then quickly switched to a homily about his wife's "Republican cloth coat," drawing a contrast to the mink-coat scandals that had beleaguered the Democrats. He counterattacked with an assault on Stevenson's fund; he praised Eisenhower; and finally, he urged his audience to let the Republican National Committee know whether he should remain on the ticket. But the most remarkable moment in Nixon's speech came when he acknowledged that he had received one gift after his nomination—"a cocker spaniel dog, Checkers," for his daughters. And "whatever they say," the candidate declared in his most serious tones, "we are going to keep her." How could the Democrats take that dog from those little girls? For many, Nixon had reached a new low; but Middle America—and the Republican leadership—loved the speech. Eisenhower said, "You're my boy," and publicly read an effusive telegram from Hannah Nixon guaranteeing her son's integrity and honesty. Nixon remained on the ticket—and Checkers remained with the family.[25]

The Nixon Fund crisis, however, put a damper on the Eisenhower-Nixon relationship from the start. Eisenhower, openly antipathetic toward professional politicians, never seemed comfortable with his Vice President. For his part, Nixon glimpsed Eisenhower's instinctive dislike for hard, quick, firm decisions. He had told Eisenhower during the fund crisis that the General had to "shit or get off the pot," and determine whether Nixon should continue on the ticket. "The great trouble here is the indecision," he added.[26]

The General's indecisiveness aroused Nixon's contempt, a feeling that he openly expressed in other moments of frustration and disappointment with Eisenhower. He brusquely dismissed Eisenhower's penchant for avoiding and minimizing conflict. Nixon did not subscribe to the myth that a man had to be noncontroversial and liked by all; he simply did not believe in that " 'togetherness' bullshit." Nixon's position as Vice President inherently compounded the ambiguities surrounding the relationship with Eisenhower. At one point, Nixon complained to some journalists that Eisenhower saw him only as a political animal and would not, for example, care to listen to him on defense matters. "You've got to realize," Nixon observed, "that a Vice President is in a very special position, a difficult position."[27]

For the next eight years, Nixon functioned as Eisenhower's partisan campaigner and political lightning rod, roles hardly calculated to win him awards for popularity or amiability. In apparently unintended irony, Eisenhower and his key aides had Nixon do much of the negotiating on Capitol Hill that led to the Republicans' cooperation in the Senate censure of Senator Joseph McCarthy. In 1954, whether on his own or by direction, Nixon hinted at American intervention in the critical battle then raging in Vietnam, at Dienbienphu. That same year, Nixon carried the party's water in a desperate but unsuccessful attempt to maintain the Republican majorities in Congress. Meanwhile, as Eisenhower remained above criticism, the Democrats concentrated their attacks on Nixon. The Vice President always managed to touch the rawest of nerves. Mentioning Secretary of State John Foster Dulles by name, he remarked: "[I]sn't it wonderful, finally, to have a Secretary of State who isn't taken in by the Communists, who stands up to them?"

Either from despair or in self-pity, after the 1954 elections Nixon talked about leaving politics at the end of the presidential term. Perhaps he sensed that Eisenhower and his immediate entourage wanted to drop him. The President scattered hints that Nixon might want to consider a Cabinet office, allegedly because it would give him better experience and visibility for a run at the presidency. Harold Stassen, then regarded as close to the President, publicly led a "dump Nixon" campaign in 1956, contending that Nixon endangered Eisenhower's chances of re-election. Given, however, the great unlikelihood of anything at all endangering Eisenhower's chances, there are reasonable grounds for suspecting that more than Harold Stassen figured in this episode.

Nixon would never be president, Eisenhower believed; he told Republican National Chairman Leonard Hall that "people didn't like him." Hall promised to "get Nixon out of the picture willingly." Eisenhower—who was taping the conversation—told Hall to proceed, and when Hall failed, he (Hall) reported that he "never saw a scowl come so fast over a man's face."

Many years later, the President's younger brother, Milton, left no doubt about Ike's feelings. Had Nixon been "a more sensitive man," he would have taken the hint and resigned from the ticket. "But he wanted to be there," Milton Eisenhower recalled. "He thought this was his chance to be President."[28]

In any event, the effort to drop Nixon failed to get off the ground—if only because Eisenhower refused to act decisively. Vice President Nixon kept his spot on the ticket and again bore the brunt of Democratic assaults in the 1956 campaign. But this time there was a new twist. Eisenhower had suffered a massive heart attack the year before. The Democrats were blunt: the vice presidency, Adlai Stevenson warned, was insurance; if the Republicans were re-elected, the nation would go "uninsured" for four years. On election eve, Stevenson went even further: "every piece of scientific evidence that we have, every lesson of history and experience," he said, "indicates that a Republican victory . . . would mean that Richard M. Nixon would probably be president of this country within the next four years." The election was for the living, however, and no such warning could overcome Eisenhower's enormous reservoir of popularity. The President's health, however, remained problematic; he suffered two more serious illnesses in his next term, including a stroke. Eisenhower generously gave Nixon the power to determine if the President were disabled. Perhaps that act measured some of Eisenhower's faith in Nixon's ability, particularly because the nation really had no effective constitutional or legislative standards for determining presidential disability.[29]

Early in 1959, President Eisenhower dispatched Nixon to Moscow to open an American exhibit. Relations between the superpowers were then particularly precarious, largely because Soviet leader Nikita Khrushchev had threatened to force the Western allies from Berlin. Khrushchev also was aware of American U-2 spy plane overflights of Russia, and he felt provoked by a congressional resolution decrying the plight of the "captive nations" of Eastern Europe. The result was a tense confrontation, resulting in harsh exchanges between Nixon and Khrushchev. Their "debate" in Moscow is vital, for Nixon hagiographers and demonologists alike. Some, like Nixon himself, have seen it as one of his great crises, one in which he mastered and demonstrated vital leadership qualities. His detractors argue that the encounter demonstrated both Nixon's lack of competence and his immaturity. The same debate has been joined over his behavior the year before: on what should have been a routine Latin American tour, violence erupted against Nixon and his party in Lima and Caracas. Then, too, sharp differences of opinion had surrounded his role. Some saw Nixon as a cool, tough individual who had "stood up for America," while others argued that Nixon had needlessly provoked the Latin American crowds and ignored warnings from on-the-scene diplomats. But that was South America. In Moscow, Nixon was in *the* enemy's house—slightly redesigned to include a model American kitchen.

At the outset of his trip, Nixon clearly perceived its domestic potential. Before he left, he rejected State Department speech drafts, telling his military aide that he never wanted his speechwriters to insert any endorsement of "peaceful coexistence"—and promised to dismiss any staffers who suggested that approach. Nixon objected to the phrase as the State Department's "Acheson line," though one would have been pressed to remember such a phrase from Secretary Acheson's lips. Nixon had his own stamp to put on things, as he repeatedly stressed the notion of "peaceful competition" when he spoke in the Soviet Union.

Khrushchev regarded Nixon as the spokesman for the American right wing and the champion of an aggressive, belligerent stance toward the Soviet Union. The Soviet leader seemed determined to display his own brand of belligerency. The two visited the U.S. exhibition, in Moscow's Sokolniki Park, and Khrushchev used the occasion to dismiss the products on display (Polaroid cameras, Pepsi-Cola, IBM computers, Singer sewing machines) as gimmicks. The two men taped a discussion for American television, but Khrushchev used the occasion to denounce U.S. foreign policy. Most observers agree that Nixon emerged somewhat shaken. At that point, William Safire, working as a public-relations man for one of the exhibitors, persuaded the two men to look over a "typical American kitchen." There Nixon recovered his composure and responded a bit more effectively to the Soviet leader's barbs. The two played one-upmanship over which country was "ahead" in different areas. And that essentially constituted the famous "Kitchen Debate," "standing up" to the Russians and personifying what *Time* magazine called a "disciplined vigor that belied tales of the decadent and limp-wristed West." In Nixon's view, Khrushchev was trying "to bully" him and the only way to win his respect was to resist and demonstrate his own commitments. Milton Eisenhower, who was accompanying Nixon (largely as watchdog for his brother), was unimpressed.[30]

At the end of his tour, Nixon spoke to the Soviet people on nationwide television. The first draft of his speech was belligerent, and clearly for American consumption. The U.S. ambassador urged him to tone it down. "You are the first American Vice President to address the Soviet people. You've got to make sure you are not the last," he said. Nixon was "upset, terribly nervous and high-strung" from the situation, and according to Milton Eisenhower, he drank six martinis before dinner. Nixon solicited opinions on his speech, and then, Eisenhower noted, he used "vulgar swear words and everything else in this mixed company." Altogether, the President's brother thought Nixon "a strange character."[31]

The Vice President, however, never doubted his success. The media widely reported the Kitchen Debate, portraying Nixon as the man who "had stood up to Khrushchev." Nixon had in one sense elevated his California style to the international arena, and the supposedly hostile media had credited him with a triumph. Some, however, saw the trip as confirming that Nixon could never successfully negotiate with the Soviets. The net result—as was often the case for Nixon—was a grab bag of pluses and minuses.

The succession was Richard Nixon's. As the Eisenhower presidency wound down, Nixon emerged as the only serious contender for the Republican nomination. That was the easy part.

The contest for the presidency consisted of two campaigns. The first involved Nixon's long, painful pursuit of Dwight Eisenhower's blessing. The second was against his opponent, John F. Kennedy, a onetime friendly rival, but now a formidable obstacle. Nixon's problems with Eisenhower were psychologically simple and classic. Developing a working relationship of mutual respect could not come easily, given the age difference between the two men and Eisenhower's accomplishments and prestige. Kennedy was another matter altogether. Nixon was only a few years older than Kennedy; they had entered public life together in 1946. Politically, they were peers. But Kennedy was many things that Nixon was not, much to Nixon's envy. Kennedy had those links to the eastern bastions of power and intellectuality that Nixon himself had courted with limited results; Kennedy was wealthy, with a successful, even appealing, family; and finally, Kennedy exuded an easygoing affability and charm that obviously contrasted to Nixon's shyness and public awkwardness.

Nixon just barely won the first campaign, but he lost the one that really counted. And it was so close: Kennedy won with a popular margin of 113,000 votes out of more than 68 million cast. Nixon was devastated. "Of the five presidential campaigns in which I was a direct participant," Nixon recalled, "none affected me more personally. . . . It was a campaign of unusual intensity." And it was bitter: "[T]he way the Kennedys played politics and the way the media let them get away with it left me angry and frustrated."[32] Through the following years, the memories of "the Kennedys" and "the media" festered in Nixon like an angry boil. The memory was Nixon's nemesis. It periodically engulfed him, diverted him, and led him to rash, ill-considered action—eventually with tragic results.

The Eisenhower–Nixon relationship offers a veritable playground for psychohistorical speculations. The essential elements are enough to show that Eisenhower's behavior undoubtedly heightened Nixon's periodic anxieties and doubts about their relationship and his own future. But the experience also demonstrated Nixon's special qualities of resilience and fortitude.

His relations with the President had been at stake, or at least at issue, since the slush-fund episode of 1952. The public speculation surrounding Eisenhower's desire for a new running mate in 1956 fueled Nixon's insecurities. At that time, Eisenhower referred to Nixon only in "generally cold and indifferent" terms; he told a speechwriter that Nixon "just hasn't grown [and] . . . I just haven't honestly been able to believe that he *is* presidential timber." A few years later, Ike, referring to Nixon, complained to his secretary that "it is terrible when people get politically ambitious." He also told her that he could not understand how a man such as Nixon could have so few personal friends. The secretary summed up the views of Eisenhower's closest associates (views that might well have been Ike's as well): the President, she wrote, "is a man of integrity and sincere in his every action. . . . [E]verybody trusts and loves him. But the Vice-President sometimes seems like a man who is acting like a nice man rather than being one."³³ Those were private remarks. Perhaps in that cloying, close world of Washington, the Vice President heard about them. But the public statements, whether cryptic or garbled, deeply injured Nixon politically; we can only speculate as to their personal effect.

If Nixon was Eisenhower's preferred heir, the President hardly made that perfectly clear. Eisenhower nursed fantasies that the Republican Party would rise above simple political considerations and choose a candidate for his achievements and intellectual skills—men such as his Secretary of the Treasury, Texan Robert Anderson, or even his brother, Milton. The President had numerous objections to Nelson Rockefeller, the apparent alternative to Nixon. At one point, Eisenhower told a press conference that the Republicans had numerous "eminent men, big men" who could succeed him. Eisenhower would not identify them, but as if suddenly remembering who was going to gain the nomination, he lamely stated that he was "not dissatisfied with the individual that looks like he will get it."³⁴ With such endorsements, the Vice President needed no enemies.

After the Republican Convention, reporters pressed Eisenhower as to Nixon's role in the Administration. Ike insisted that Nixon had taken an active part in discussions, had expressed his opinions openly, and when asked, had offered numerous recommendations for decisions. Reporters persisted, asking the President for a specific instance of a Nixon proposal that the Administration had adopted. Eisenhower snapped: "If you give me a week, I might think of one. I don't remember." Fittingly, the news conference ended on that note, giving the remark an air of finality.³⁵ Nixon never escaped its apparent meaning.

The campaign itself strained this already delicate relationship. An Eisenhower biographer has perceptively noted that Nixon's emphasis on his experience and participation in the Administration inadvertently reinforced the notion that Eisenhower reigned but did not rule. Furthermore, Nixon needed the Republican Party far more than did Eisenhower. Consequently, he made the usual concessions and compromises to attain measures of party support. This included appeasing Rockefeller on reducing defense spending and other issues. The press dubbed the Nixon-Rockefeller agreement the "Compact of Fifth Avenue," but Barry Goldwater angrily denounced it as the "Munich of the Republican party." The President complained to Nixon, saying that it might be difficult for him to support a platform that failed to wholeheartedly endorse his Administration. Near the end of the campaign, Ike was frustrated by Nixon's apparent indecisiveness in giving the President an expanded schedule of speeches. "Goddammit," he told staff members, "he looks like a loser to me!" Eisenhower campaigned vigorously at the end, but the general consensus was that it was too little, too late.[36] His late intervention has been variously blamed on his own inertia, his wife's adamant opposition to his campaigning, and Nixon's tardiness in asking for the President's aid. More than two decades later, Nixon omitted any chapter on Eisenhower in *Leaders,* his reminiscence of prominent world leaders he had known.

The Kennedy-Nixon debates highlighted the 1960 campaign. These so-called "Great Debates" were neither great nor real debates. To compare them—as contemporaries did—to the Lincoln-Douglas debates of 1858 only mocks history and trivializes political discourse at its best. The 1960 debates offered a preview to an unsuspecting America of the years to come, when style, format, and media, rather than issues and substance, would prevail in political campaigns. Communications theorist Marshall McLuhan learned vastly more from the Kennedy-Nixon exchanges than did the electorate.[37]

In retrospect, Nixon, Eisenhower, and Nixon's supporters regarded the decision to debate Kennedy as misguided, and, of course, fatal. But Nixon fancied himself at the time as the skillful forensic competitor; debate was his turf. After all, he had challenged Jerry Voorhis to the debate platform and immediately put his opponent on the defensive. His debater's skills had proven effective in his campaign against Helen Gahagan Douglas, and the "Checkers" speech represented a classic illustration of rhetorical technique. The temptation to debate again must have been compelling. Besides, by debating Kennedy, Nixon could demonstrate being "on his own."

The story of the four debates is familiar. The first apparently damaged Nixon, perhaps irreparably. He appeared without make-up, highlighting his famous "five o'clock shadow." He recently had been ill, and the combination made him appear haggard, nervous, and ill-kempt, particularly next to the handsome, neatly groomed, coolly poised Kennedy. Perhaps even more damaging, a reporter resurrected Eisenhower's remark that he would need a week to think of Nixon's contributions in the White House. Nixon stumbled through an understandably lame response.

Interestingly, those who heard the first debate on radio thought Nixon had done quite well. But Nixon recognized his basic mistake—and long before Marshall McLuhan: "I had concentrated too much on substance and not enough on appearance."[38] The Day of the Package had arrived in American politics.

In subsequent debates, Nixon seemed polished and informed. During the third encounter, on October 13, 1960, Nixon satisfied his rightist constituency when he berated Kennedy's apparent unwillingness to defend the Chinese Nationalist–held offshore islands of Quemoy and Matsu. In the finale, on October 21, Nixon managed to reach out in the other direction and cast Kennedy as the adventurist Cold Warrior. He chided the Senator for his proposal to assist anti-Castro elements, noting that the charters of both the United Nations and the Organization of American States prohibited such intervention in Cuban internal affairs. If we followed Kennedy's policy, he warned, "we would lose all of our friends in Latin America, we would probably be condemned in the United Nations, and we would not accomplish our objective."[39] At that moment, of course, Nixon was privy to the Eisenhower Administration's efforts to organize military intervention in Cuba. In any event, his remarks were profoundly prophetic.

The third debate also revealed much about the comparative styles of the candidates. A reporter asked Senator Kennedy if he would apologize to the Vice President for former President Truman's blunt remarks as to where Nixon and the Republican Party "could go." Kennedy at first appeared taken aback, but his face quickly betrayed a wry amusement. No, he wouldn't apologize; and it was a little late in the day to persuade the seventy-six-year-old Truman to change his "particular speaking manner." Perhaps, Kennedy playfully countered, Mrs. Truman could deal with the problem. It was Kennedy's moment, but Nixon clumsily groped for one of his own. The Vice President solemnly intoned that a president or former president had "an obligation not to lose his temper in public." One must think of the mothers and children who were in the presence of presidential candidates; America, said Nixon, needed a man to respect. He was "very proud that President Eisenhower restored dignity and decency and, frankly, good language to the conduct of the presidency of the United States." And if elected, Nixon promised, he would maintain the dignity of the office. Parents would be able to tell their children: "Well, there is a man who maintains the kind of standards personally that I would want my child to follow."[40] Fourteen years later, when Nixon's tapes revealed his own salty vocabulary, the hypocrisy of his comments about Truman and Eisenhower finally triumphed over their banality.

Kennedy's election hurt Nixon deeply. Its close outcome inevitably led to second-guessing of might-have-beens or should-have-dones. But the answers were painfully concrete for Nixon. First, he believed that Chicago Mayor Richard Daley and the Democratic organization in that city had stolen the election to give Kennedy the important state of Illinois. Periodic tidbits through the years have lent credence to the possibility. A Kennedy confidant has recorded that Daley telephoned the Democratic candidate on election night, saying: "With a little bit of luck and the help of a few close friends, you're going to carry Illinois." But the charges have remained just that. It is important to note that the Illinois election board, dominated four-to-one by Republicans, did not hesitate to certify Kennedy's election. Furthermore, whatever the truth of the Illinois situation—and opinion is decidedly divided—the fact is that Illinois alone would not have given Nixon an Electoral College majority.

Richard Nixon believed (or chose to believe) that the 1960 election had been stolen from him. Supporters and friendly biographers generally have praised him for not challenging the outcome, thus sparing the nation a great deal of anguish and difficulty. But Nixon's outward magnanimity and graciousness masked his faith in the relativeness of political morality. Privately, he seethed over Kennedy's tactics and behavior. A dozen years later, President Nixon repeatedly invoked the behavior of others to defend his own actions.

The loser's rationalizations in 1960 were vintage Nixon. He believed that Kennedy had unfairly exploited his intelligence briefings to raise the issue— and promise—of military intervention in Cuba. The Kennedys also had blatantly exploited the Catholic issue. (Actually, Kennedy's approach to the problem of his religion was also a favored Nixon device; turn a negative to one's own advantage.) The Kennedys had lavished money and other favors in the right places. But most of all, Kennedy had seduced the media, which gave him excessive and favorable attention largely at Nixon's expense. The Kennedy camp had "bred an unusual mutuality of interests that replaced the more traditional skepticism of the press toward politicians," Nixon later wrote. In less personal reasoning, Nixon also pointed to other factors that contributed to his loss: the recession, the U-2 affair and the failure of the Paris Summit in 1960, and the CIA's mishandling of the alleged "missile gap." Years later, as President, Nixon regularly berated CIA Director Richard Helms and the agency for giving Kennedy advice on Soviet missile strength which the Democrat had exploited.[41] Nixon was not alone in such judgments. But they offered small comfort at best: defeat was still defeat.

The letdown must have been excruciating. A few weeks before he left office, the Vice President fulfilled his constitutional duty by formally counting the electoral votes in the Senate and declared Kennedy the victor. Nixon was gracious in performing this function as the first Vice President since 1861 to confirm his opponent's victory. That seemed to be his last hurrah. "I found that virtually everything I did seemed unexciting and unimportant by comparison with national office," Nixon later wrote. Ironically, the Kennedy Administration's disastrous Bay of Pigs adventure brought Nixon briefly back into the national limelight, but given his own identification with anti-Castro policies, his public statements mostly were confined to the usual bland recommendations for nonpartisanship in foreign policy.[42]

Once again, Nixon returned to his native California following a failure to "make his fortune" in the East. Not for the last time did he return in shame. He accepted a partnership in a California law firm, but only for its promised income, not for its challenges. After fourteen years in public life, Nixon and Nixon-watchers alike seemed uncertain, even confused, over his future course. Certainly, he remained a public figure. Almost from the moment of his defeat, speculation centered on whether Nixon would challenge California Governor Edmund G. ("Pat") Brown in 1962. The reasoning was simple: Nixon had to have a political base if he were to maintain any leadership role in the party and the nation.[43] But the reasoning was flawed: Brown was fairly popular, with a long record of state electoral success, and he had done a creditable job as governor. Most important, Richard Nixon knew precious little about the special problems confronting state governments, particularly in the burgeoning principality of California.

The California gubernatorial campaign in 1962 had a surrealistic quality. Nixon's familiar campaign methods seemed irrelevant, if nothing else. Californians confronted enormous problems and challenges peculiar to their rapidly expanding society. Water, education, land use, environmental controls, roads, and, of course, taxes—these were the issues. Nixon's references to his experience with the National Security Council, his exchange with Khrushchev, his visits to Latin America and other places throughout the world—all this provided no insight into controlling smog or allocating scarce water resources. Brown was expert and knowledgeable about state issues, and he defeated the former Vice President. Brown's margin of victory was only a bit more than a quarter-million out of six million votes; nevertheless, given his national prominence, Nixon had been outclassed, even humiliated.

The humiliation led to Nixon's extraordinary post-election press conference—which he promised would be his last. The morning after his defeat, Nixon had his Press Secretary read his concession statement. Reporters asked why Nixon did not publicly read the statement himself. Watching the proceedings on television, Nixon decided to confront those he regarded as his longtime antagonists. Nixon berated the reporters, charging that they had treated him unfairly. He "recognized" the media's "right and responsibility" to give a candidate "the shaft" if they opposed him, but he insisted they still had a responsibility to provide coverage of what the candidate said. Unlike "other people" (that is, President Kennedy), Nixon said he had never canceled a newspaper subscription. But seemingly it was the end:

"You won't have Nixon to kick around anymore, because, gentlemen, this is my last press conference."

The event may have been contrived; in the end, it proved Nixon to be alive and well. As soon as it was over, he told his young campaign aide, H. R. Haldeman: "I finally told those bastards off, and every goddamned thing I said was true." Haldeman has recalled Nixon as "delighted."[44] At last he had used the media; his performance was the news, not his defeat. California television stations replayed filmed coverage of the press conference several times throughout the day and evening. Audiences watched and watched again with almost morbid fascination. Nationally, ABC News offered an instant analysis entitled "The Political Obituary of Richard Nixon." But ABC used Alger Hiss as a commentator—and that itself quickly became the news, even creating a backlash of sympathy for Nixon. With or without Hiss, ABC, along with those other media pundits who cogitated about the political death of Richard Nixon, would have been better advised to read the story of Lazarus.

If the repetition of pattern means anything, Nixon-watchers might have divined more meaning in his next move. Once again, Nixon faced east, as if sensing that his fortune and destiny were there and not in his native western wilderness. In May 1963, he announced that he would join the distinguished New York law firm of Mudge, Stern, Baldwin, and Todd—now to become Nixon, Mudge, Rose, Guthrie, and Alexander. The firm announced that Nixon would concentrate on labor law, a rather unlikely prospect unless the firm thought that several years on a congressional labor committee more than fifteen years earlier gave the new partner special expertise.[45]

It was somewhat late in the day for Nixon to seriously assume a full-time career as a Wall Street lawyer. The Nixon literature generally attributes his move to a wish for financial security and to satisfy his family's needs, especially its desire that he abandon politics. But a fifty-year-old man, in the prime of life, who had come so close to the pinnacle of his ambition, simply could not abandon the very life that sustained him. Nixon may not have liked the last shuffle or two, but he liked the game.

Nixon's real value to his new law firm was the prospect that he would lure clients who, unlike California voters, would covet his international connections and reputation. Still, Nixon needed to make some mark as a lawyer. Appropriately, he soon found a case that allowed him to do so and had the added advantage of national prominence—the case even gave him the limelight of a Supreme Court appearance. In 1966, he represented the plaintiff in an invasion-of-privacy suit against *Life* magazine. Nixon lost the appeal, largely on First Amendment grounds, but he advanced some telling arguments on behalf of individual privacy. Reports generally praised his performance before the Justices. Leonard Garment, Nixon's law partner and chief of litigation in the firm, had prevailed in the case in the lower courts. For the appeal, Garment worked closely with Nixon on the preparation of the briefs, and the two spent a great deal of time together in the office and on planes discussing the First Amendment. "He worked like a horse and learned the law," Garment recalled, comparing Nixon's effort to starting "athletic life by doing the Olympic decathlon." Perhaps moral victories meant little to Nixon, however. He told Garment that he never wanted to hear of the case again, and he did not mention it in his memoirs. Nixon also told Garment he never would be permitted to win "against the press."[46]

Politics never strayed far from Nixon's thoughts. He realized that he had little claim on the Republican presidential nomination in 1964. The California debacle was still fresh in memory, underlining an emerging theme: Nixon was a loser. Nixon also may have believed that Kennedy would be too popular to overcome. In the event, 1964 belonged—especially after Kennedy's assassination—to the growing polar forces in the Republican Party: Barry Goldwater and Nelson Rockefeller. Goldwater's eventual nomination alienated many within the party, but Nixon proved to be the loyal soldier. (He scoffed at Eisenhower's stumbling and indecisive endorsement of Goldwater, privately calling Ike a "senile old bastard.") Nixon introduced Goldwater at the Republican Convention and forthrightly supported the Arizonan. More important, Nixon paid special attention to the needs of other Republican candidates. After the election, Nixon dutifully touched base with President Johnson, congratulating him on his victory and also taking the occasion to urge support for an official residence for the Vice President. Johnson, in turn, urged Nixon to join him in mobilizing national unity. "You can do much," he told Nixon, "in making that unity a firm reality."[47] Nixon wasn't about to become a nonpartisan unifier. It was time to restock the political capital for Nixon's inevitable claim to an inheritance denied—or stolen, as he believed. After Goldwater's rout in the 1964 election, someone had to pick up the Republican pieces. Nixon was there.

III

"BRING US TOGETHER": 1965-1968

Richard Nixon's years in political limbo thinly veiled a calculated "long march" in his ongoing quest for the presidency. The journey began in the ashes of his agonizing defeat in 1960; the California debacle proved only a temporary setback and, given the events of 1964, a most fortunate one for Nixon. New York became his Yenan, the base from which he mounted carefully orchestrated operations designed to gain his cherished objective. As befitted his isolation and weakness, Nixon first staged a series of guerrilla forays, meanwhile carefully planning the sustained drive that would eventually award him the ultimate prize.

The march quickened as Nixon beat the campaign hustings for the 1966 congressional elections. A little luck and a lot of ineptness on the part of his enemies spurred the pace. As Nixon prepared for a trip to Waterville, Maine, to campaign for Republican candidates, a CBS reporter interviewed him and recorded the predictable remarks: Johnson was growing unpopular; the 1964 election had produced an exaggerated Democratic victory; and Republicans would make significant gains in the November elections. At the same time, the *New York Times* ran a feature on Nixon. It was too much for the increasingly harassed and ever-thin-skinned Johnson. When asked about Nixon's remarks, he denounced him as a "chronic campaigner . . . who never did really recognize what was going on when he had an official position in the government." Walter Cronkite promptly gave the former Vice President an opportunity to respond on the CBS evening news broadcast. Thanks to Johnson, Nixon was news.[1]

Nixon smelled blood and reverted to form. He stepped up his attacks on the President's Vietnam policies, contending that the war could last another five years and cost more casualties than Korea. While he repeatedly said that he would not attack Johnson personally—only his policies—he referred to the President as "that master political operator in the White House," who used the eighty-ninth Congress as his "lapdog." Johnson "barks and it barks," Nixon said. "He tells it to roll over and it rolls over. He tells it to play dead and it plays dead. In fact, he doesn't even have to pick it up by the ears." The President's staff replied in backgrounders to reporters that Nixon talked out of both sides of his mouth, one moment advocating escalation of the war, the next talking about peace. His complaints about Johnson's peace efforts, they said, were "dirty pool," reminiscent of Nixon's earlier allegations that Truman and Speaker Sam Rayburn were traitors. The staffers adroitly contrasted Nixon's attacks with the loyal support for the President tendered by Eisenhower and Republican Senate leader Everett Dirksen.[2]

The Republicans made significant gains in the 1966 elections, substantially trimming Democratic majorities in both houses. And suddenly, Nixon was back. With the party's polar wings at odds, and their leaders, Goldwater and Rockefeller, equally contemptuous of one another, Nixon emerged as the preeminent party spokesman. He campaigned in more than sixty congressional districts. The *Washington Star* reported that "his standing with the Goldwaterites is very good indeed, and though he is disliked he is not completely unacceptable to the moderates." Nixon even received a little help from Eisenhower, who offered a belated explanation of his famous 1960 remark. He privately told Nixon that he "could kick" himself "every time some jackass brings up that goddamn 'give me a week' business. Johnson has gone too far." Eisenhower then issued a public statement, flatly contending that any suggestion or inference that he "at any time held Dick Nixon in anything less than the highest regard and esteem is erroneous."[3] An attack from Johnson, a blessing from Eisenhower, an interview with Cronkite; truly Nixon's cup was filling.

For the next year, Nixon ran the old-fashioned way, beating the political bushes, touching base with party officials and contributors who would influence primaries and delegate selections. The apparent purpose was to aid and build the party; Richard Nixon himself, of course, was the primary beneficiary. The march was now the race.

Johnson's withdrawal in the spring of 1968 resolved Nixon's future. But the future of the war itself and the nation's political leadership remained unsettled and in doubt. The *Washington Post,* a Johnson supporter, praised the President's "personal sacrifice in the name of national unity," and thought him entitled "to a very special place in the annals of American history and to a very special kind of gratitude and appreciation." Gratitude for what? For the promise of a presidential campaign "of less divisiveness and less bitterness than the one the country had expected." The metaphors swirled in editorial ecstasy: "The President" had "lanced the boil of faction and opened the abscess of partisanship on the body politic," the *Post* concluded; his "moving declaration" had restored "unity."[4]

But LBJ's lame-duck actions only magnified frustrations with the war. When he announced his withdrawal as a candidate in March 1968 and promised his best efforts to the peace process, approximately 486,600 Americans were in South Vietnam. By August, the President had authorized a troop level of 545,500. Johnson talked of massive peace efforts, and his new Defense Secretary, Clark Clifford, advocated what later came to be called "Vietnamization"—that is, enlarging the Army of South Vietnam, equipping it, and giving it sole responsibility for the defense of the country. And yet the reality of the war hardly changed a ripple, accentuating the President's image as a manipulator and deceiver. Most of all, the unity that the *Washington Post* had predicted would be the consequence of Johnson's withdrawal remained elusive and illusory.

Unity was not the only casualty. Johnson's command of power steadily diminished. Johnson understood power: "I know where to look for it, and how to use it," he said. But by the spring of 1968, there was little for him to use. The President's own faults and shortcomings only partially explained his declining position. The Vietnam war, it must be remembered, was not the only cause for alienation and disaffection in American life. The rebellions in the northern black ghettos and in the white South, and among educated, middle-class young whites, as well as various other causes ranging from ecology to gay liberation, had little connection with Johnson's lack of "style" or his conduct of the war. Altogether, the prevailing unrest was, as law professor Alexander Bickel noted, "an extraordinarily sustained experience of civil disobedience and conscientious objection."[5] Probably no regime could have survived, let alone turned back, such powerful tides.

America seemed to be coming apart, and its President appeared so powerless, so unable to master events. The assassination of Martin Luther King, Jr. sparked a new wave of urban riots in New York, Chicago, Newark, Baltimore, and saddest of all, in Washington, D.C. Looting was widespread, and police responded quickly and with decisive force, as if sensing a new mood that demanded such a reaction. The sight of flames in the nation's capital, only blocks from the White House and Congress, offered another blow to the Administration's pride and reinforced its appearance of isolation. What was worse, the flames seared the consciousness of significant portions of the nation, spelling new trouble for powerholders. Protests had been heard in the land for nearly three years; but now, new

voices of counterprotest emanated from what, unscientifically but not without reason, would be dubbed the "Silent Majority."

The important, sustained revolution came from within the ranks of what
had been the dominant political coalition. The "risen" middle class, the
blue- and white-collar workers, and ethnics who had nourished the growth
of the Democratic majority, now found themselves unhappy with the young
protesters who were the new cohabitants of its political home. The protesters' challenges to cherished views of the American way of life, the criticisms of what was wrong with America, left the "old-fashioned Democrats"
confused, shaken, and above all frightened, especially as events took a violent turn. Whatever their own disenchantment with the Vietnam war, they
hardly identified themselves with the public expressions of outrage by disaffected groups. A political alliance between protesters and conventional
Democrats simply was improbable. The latter had little sympathy for the
blacks and dispossessed who, in their minds, had not worked to achieve the
American Dream. Their disdain, even contempt, for the alienated young
campus radicals was as powerful. After all, these were the spoiled, pampered, comfortable children of those above—or even their own ungrateful
offspring.[6]

America had changed. The long-familiar assets that historically had characterized American society—vast space, mobility, available and abundant
capital for technological development, sophisticated communications techniques, "grassroots democracy"—now emerged as liabilities. Their negative effects multiplied and rippled into waves of irritation and mutual distrust
that threatened the harmony and delicate balance of American life. Perhaps
the pluralist wars that raged just beneath the surface of life no longer could
be contained.

The counterrevolutionists questioned long-prevailing liberal dogma that
crime, poverty, and other social disorders reflected cultural and social
wrongs. The standard liberal response to social ills was money, programs,
and empathy—"bleeding hearts" and "doing good," in the terms of unfriendly commentators. The same simplistic, one-sided approach is precisely
what the Silent Majority also questioned, as they saw cities in flames, order
and authority flouted, and the cherished realities and symbols of flag and
institutions treated with contempt. Enough. Poverty and unemployment could
be deplored, yet the prevailing liberal sympathy for the aggrieved seemed
somehow disproportionate to other realities. Wasn't there a place for condemning anarchy and lawlessness as well? Richard Nixon thought so.

As the 1968 primary season wound down, and as he had imposed his own
moratorium on discussions of the war, Nixon turned to the "law-and-order"
theme. He scoffed at Johnson's Great Society programs. Money, he insisted,

had not solved the problem of crime. We needed more police and more money for them, less "soft" Supreme Court decisions, an Attorney General who would enforce the law, more wiretapping—in short, more support for the "peace forces" and less sympathy for the "criminal forces." Nixon never strayed far from that theme.[7] Meanwhile, black militant H. Rap Brown called violence "as American as cherry pie," only compounding the liberal dilemma and further legitimating Nixon's law-and-order demands.

Alabama Governor George Wallace's presidential campaign in 1968 was a twofold blessing for Nixon. First, during the primaries, Wallace divided the Democrats. His third-party candidacy guaranteed some erosion of Democratic strength. Better yet, Wallace's stridency on the war (particularly after he selected as his running mate Air Force General Curtis LeMay) and on domestic issues gave Nixon a golden opportunity to preempt the middle. But one had to divine the calculus of the middle. After King's assassination, Nixon advisers hotly debated whether he should attend the funeral services. His law partner Leonard Garment reportedly remarked: "Things have come to some pass when a Republican candidate for President has to take counsel with his advisers about whether he should attend the funeral of a Nobel Prize winner." Nixon eventually went, but he did not march behind the mule-drawn wagon bearing King's body—*that* presumably was no place for a centrist candidate. Still, Nixon would periodically thereafter rebuke those who had suggested he attend the funeral, complaining that it had been "a serious mistake" and almost cost him the South.[8]

The political earthquakes that divided the Democrats left the Republican Party mostly untouched. The party's internal fratricide of four years earlier now seemed to be history, largely because the conservative faction dominated. But the conservatives lacked a candidate of their own, and Nixon soon had the field to himself. It seemed so easy, perhaps even boringly so.

George Romney served as Nelson Rockefeller's surrogate in 1968. Rockefeller himself no longer seemed viable as a candidate, since the entrenched Goldwaterites remained implacable toward him. As president of American Motors, Romney had made a name for himself as a gadfly to the Detroit automobile establishment, successfully challenging their pet marketing and design notions. He parlayed his entrepreneurial success into a political one, twice winning election as governor in the Democrats' Michigan stronghold. He was "Mr. Clean," a man whose integrity and moral rectitude went unchallenged. Romney seemed a perfect alternative to the tarnished images of "old pols" such as Johnson and Nixon. But any candidate of the time had to come to terms with the Vietnam war, and that proved Romney's undoing.

In a casual interview with a local Detroit radio station, Romney remarked that he had been "brainwashed" by his military hosts when he had visited South Vietnam. No doubt, Romney had been misled, perhaps even deliberately deceived, as others had been before and would be after him. The remark seemed true to the man: candid and blunt, yet betraying a long-suspected naïveté. If Romney could be brainwashed by our own military, how could he withstand other, more pernicious, attempts to influence him? "Brainwashing" was a poor choice of words, conjuring up images of Korean prisoners of war who had displayed a fatal weakness when confronted with a trying situation. Somehow, the media managed to convey the image of Romney as an inept, incompetent, perhaps even clownish figure. He was through. His explanations fell flat, and he announced his withdrawal even before the New Hampshire primary balloting. Richard Nixon had a clear field.

Party leaders steadily gravitated toward Nixon. Republican Senate leader Dirksen regarded Nixon as a party loyalist—"kosher" was his improbable description. Even Eisenhower proved malleable to Nixon's will after all the years. The former President had offered to endorse Nixon but proposed waiting for the opening day of the Republican Convention. Nixon pressed Ike for an earlier statement and got it on July 17. Eisenhower praised Nixon in the predictable fashion, but he added a personal note on a copy of his prepared text that he sent his Vice President: "Dear Dick—This was something I truly enjoyed doing—DE."[9]

Nixon's greatest tactical success came not from any actions of his own but from the Democrats' fratricidal warfare. Johnson's withdrawal left the putative dragon slayer, Eugene McCarthy, still in the field. But McCarthy would not accept his role as a Kennedy spear-carrier and get out of the way of the engine of history. Robert Kennedy, LBJ's readily imagined foe, now became Nixon's very real one when he entered the race. And then there was Vice President Hubert Humphrey, eagerly trying somehow to repudiate his President and yet succeed him. His formula was the "politics of joy," a slogan that rang hollow amid the growing casualties in Vietnam, the state of siege and open rebellion in major American cities and universities, and the gloominess and defeatism pervading an Administration he was obligated to defend. Joy somehow seemed perverse.

Much of the Democrats' primary brawling at first was left to McCarthy and Kennedy, since the Vice President had entered the race too late to qualify for the elections in most states. In May, McCarthy surprised Kennedy with a decisive victory in Oregon, thus piercing the Kennedy aura of invincibility. The Democrats' nomination really was settled in the California primary a few weeks later, and in a surprising, tragic manner. Kennedy edged McCarthy in the balloting. But the evening's results were dramatically reversed in the early morning hours when Sirhan Sirhan, a frustrated Palestinian nationalist, assassinated the New York Senator in the Ambassador Hotel in Los Angeles. Assassination for a second Kennedy, and for the second prominent American figure in two months, paralyzed the nation, with grief for Kennedy's partisans and with shock for others, appalled again by the convulsive violence that wracked the society. The mourning and sadness scarcely disguised the fact that Humphrey had been the primary political beneficiary.

When the Republicans gathered in Miami for their convention in August, Nixon's well-oiled machine projected an impression that the convention was merely a coronation ritual. After all, Nixon was the "people's choice," as the primaries had shown; since Romney's withdrawal, no candidate had seriously challenged him. But the Miami convention closely resembled the pro-Goldwater gathering in San Francisco four years earlier, and the thunder on the right was ominous. For many delegates, Nixon was a choice, yet not one that enraptured either their hearts or their minds. Conservatives desired a rollback of the liberal welfare state and realized all too well that Nixon had often opportunistically supported it. The 1968 platform reflected their will as it reaffirmed the preceding one in a call for a conservative counterrevolution. Nixon simply was not "the one" for those fully committed to such views.

By 1968, Barry Goldwater lacked credibility as a national electoral candidate, but the Republican Right now had Ronald Reagan, then in his first term as California governor and a rising star on the political scene. After years on the lecture circuit, attacking big government and promoting free enterprise, Reagan had gained national prominence with a last-minute television speech on behalf of Goldwater in 1964. Two years later, he parlayed his newfound fame into a rout of Governor Pat Brown. Reagan had promised a reduction in spending, lower taxes, and an end to campus disruptions. He delivered on none of his promises, but his popularity and appeal remained undiminished.[10] And Reagan bore no loser image; after all, *he* had defeated Brown. Nixon had a real problem.

From practically the moment of his election as governor in 1966, Reagan had been publicly coy about seeking the presidency. His lieutenant governor, Robert Finch, who had been Nixon's personal assistant during the 1960 campaign, remembered that during the state election, Reagan's staff was not yet prepared for the presidential game. But "twenty minutes after" he was elected, Reagan's supporters turned their attentions to the big prize. They thought Finch would support him, but he remained loyal to Nixon.[11]

The Reagan people had an informal alliance with the Rockefeller forces, one characterized by cynicism and convenience. The New York governor believed that to stop Nixon and gain the support of a deadlocked convention for himself necessitated giving Reagan running room. Such thinking was futile, naïve, and downright dangerous—unless the allegedly "liberal" Rockefeller actually preferred Reagan to Nixon. Many Nixon delegates reportedly were prepared to bolt to Reagan after an obligatory first-ballot declaration for the former Vice President. The Texas delegation had voted 41–15 for Nixon, but supposedly the figures would have been reversed in Reagan's favor on a second ballot. The real danger to Nixon came from Southern delegations, ones deeply committed to the conservative agenda. Reagan clearly had gained some momentum in Miami, particularly after the Nixon camp had let it be known they would seriously consider various liberal Republicans for the vice presidency.

For some time, the Nixon camp had worked out the outlines of what came to be known as the "Southern Strategy," whereby, first, Southern convention delegates would be corraled, and ultimately, Southern electoral votes sealed for the candidate in November. Such a strategy entailed close alliances with prominent Southern political leaders. South Carolina Senator J. Strom Thurmond, a former Democrat who led the "Dixiecrat" revolt against Harry Truman in 1948, was the key figure. Nixon assured Thurmond of his opposition to school busing to achieve racial balance and promised to restore "local control" over education—a code phrase for reversing or at least limiting the process of desegregation that had been underway since the Supreme Court had declared "separate but equal" facilities unconstitutional in *Brown v. Board of Education* in 1954.

Thurmond was Nixon's most important operative at the Miami convention. He moved among the Southern delegations, affirming his satisfaction with Nixon's stand on the busing and school issues. Equally important, he repeated what Nixon had told him in Atlanta on June 1: Nixon pledged "to appoint Supreme Court Justices who will respect the Constitution rather than rewrite it." Nothing had reassured Thurmond more about Nixon, according to Thurmond aide Harry Dent. Thurmond also conveyed word to the delegates that Nixon had promised to consult him on the selection of a vice-presidential candidate, one who would be "acceptable to all sections of the party." Fellow conservatives William Rusher and Phyllis Schlafly warned Thurmond and his aides to get their "pound of flesh" from Nixon, including written commitments on certain issues involving the South and national security.[12] Thurmond, however, maintained his trust in Nixon and his commitment to him. John C. Calhoun, the great antebellum Southern political theorist and Thurmond's ancestral political godfather, would have rejoiced when the South in effect realized Calhoun's cherished notion of a concurrent veto.

The Nixon lines held at the Republican Convention, and he gained his first-ballot victory, with 692 votes. But the combined total of his opposition was 641. It was not his last close call of the electoral season.

After his nomination, Nixon selected his running mate in a largely conventional manner. He chose Maryland Governor Spiro Agnew, a onetime

Rockefeller supporter who had faced down black militants in the Baltimore riots following King's assassination in April. Agnew's presence on the ticket apparently satisfied Nixon's Southern allies, but it would eventually cause him no end of problems—in the campaign and beyond.

For Hubert Humphrey and the Democrats, the convention in Chicago was a disaster. The McCarthy forces remained adamantly opposed to the Vice President. The Kennedy delegates, with Senator George McGovern as their front man, were determined to assert their priorities and distance the party from the Johnson Administration. Meanwhile, Lyndon Johnson stayed in the White House, seemingly irrelevant to the convention. In fact, he still exerted enough power to ensure a platform that in no way repudiated his presidency or his current policies, especially regarding the war. The result was an impossible situation for Humphrey. As he entered the race, he predicted that "Johnson's not going to make it easy."[13] Given his position within the Administration, and given Johnson's residue of power, Humphrey simply could not build bridges to the party's detached wings.

The Democratic Convention proceedings eventually became a sideshow to the turmoil in Chicago's streets. Day and night, national television audiences watched confrontations between demonstrators and the Chicago police that seemed reminiscent of newsreel accounts of political rioting in Europe in the 1930s and elicited feelings that could be shared by Right and Left alike. If this were the "democratic process" at work, it did the Democrats little good. Indeed, the Chicago street battles only reinforced the fears and forebodings of that "Silent Majority." The very success of certain elements in the old Democratic coalition only alienated them from the outraged protests in Chicago.

At the convention itself, a last-minute attempt to reincarnate Camelot with Senator Edward Kennedy fell victim to Kennedy's inertia and deteriorated into a comedy of errors as the "new pols" clumsily imitated "old pols" in wheeling and dealing. Humphrey easily captured the nomination on the first ballot, with more than four hundred votes to spare for a majority. But the convention would not record the usual unanimous vote for the candidate. The McCarthy forces left the convention with candles and departed for a funeral march through downtown Chicago. The next day, McCarthy addressed his loyal followers as "the government in exile." The anger and activism in the streets had turned to contempt. One demonstrator held aloft a sign reading: "There Are Two Sides to Every Question—Humphrey Endorses Both of Them."

A few weeks later, George Wallace formally launched his American Independent Party. Talk persisted of a fourth-party candidacy for McCarthy.

Humphrey was surrounded. The polls showed him trailing Nixon by more than fifteen points and ahead of Wallace by only five. Among the press and public there was enough contempt to allocate equally among the candidates. Comedian Dick Gregory thought that Humphrey looked like the man who would buy a used car from Nixon, and Wallace looked like one who would steal it.[14] Still, reports of the Democrats' demise were premature, if only because Richard Nixon remained a dubious commodity.

The Nixon and Humphrey campaigns carried on, isolated from each other and from reality. Whatever the substantive shortcomings of the Kennedy-Nixon debates in 1960, they offered some appearance of engagement, of confrontation, allowing each candidate to offer a public test of himself while pitted against his adversary. None of that occurred in 1968. One candidate talked of a politics of joy, the other of unity. One was unreal, while the other offered unity on terms precisely opposite to the expressed needs and demands of those who had broken the national consensus. The Republican candidate broke new ground with a "made-for-media" campaign, largely avoiding longwinded orations, relying instead on clever thirty- or sixty-second commercials and using carefully screened public audiences for "grassroots" question-and-answer sessions. The Democratic candidate meanwhile ran perhaps the last traditional campaign in American presidential elections, featuring large rallies of the party faithful whom he addressed with hortatory stemwinders, desperately hoping to create a bandwagon psychology. Nixon shielded himself from intimacy with working journalists; Humphrey desperately sought it, but not necessarily to any advantage. (Some reporters confided to one another that they preferred Nixon: his victory would mean Key Biscayne presidential vacations rather than Minnesota ones.[15]) The campaigns to some extent reflected the different personalities of the candidates. But in fact, money—its abundance and its scarcity—dictated the differing strategies.

Nixon's campaign had been pointed at the alienated American "middle" since the primary season. The arrangement with Thurmond and other southerners sealed the course. The candidate's surface talk of unity thinly disguised a blatant appeal to darker forces. Tape-recorded conversations with convention delegates revealed Nixon's instinct for the expedient positions on the war, the role of the courts, open housing, gun control, and desegregation. In brief, Nixon chose to exploit the divisions in American society, carefully calculating what he thought was the winning position. The danger was apparent; eventually, as a leading editorial voice warned, he would have "to consider what kind of country he would then have to govern and whether he, or any man, could govern it effectively."[16]

Just after his nomination, Nixon told reporters that he would "barricade" himself "into a television studio and make this an antiseptic campaign." He was as good as his word. The campaign was a seamless web of public-relations tactics. Nixon carefully avoided discussions of hard issues, darting especially around the vexatious Vietnam war. One aide later observed that the staff had tired of balloons and rallies and yearned for "issue-oriented drop-bys," but he admitted that they produced few "because we were short on ideas." Nixon and his handlers sought only to enhance his image as the man who would reassert traditional American values, while seeking to paint his opponent as one who had tarnished those values.

The "selling" of Nixon in 1968 is central to understanding the campaign. Nixon's advisers knew they had to use television to his advantage to avoid past mistakes. Marshall McLuhan had written in 1964 that Nixon's 1960 television appearances had been disastrous. The Vice President's "sharp, intense image" had contrasted unfavorably with Senator Kennedy's "blurry, shaggy texture." The Richard Nixon of 1960 was all wrong for the medium, McLuhan argued. Nixon was too anxious to sell himself, perhaps too pushy. His staring, dark eyes, McLuhan thought, gave him the image of a "railway lawyer who signs leases that are not in the interests of the folks in the little town." Television typecast Nixon, making him all too obvious and leaving nothing to the viewer's imagination.[17] Nixon's entourage thoroughly absorbed the McLuhan lessons. "[T]elevision would have to be controlled," wrote one Nixon media adviser. He would need men around him "who knew television as a weapon" and could exploit it to portray "Richard Nixon, the leader, returning from exile." Image was all. Even Nixon's chief speechwriter understood. He urged experimentation with film and television techniques in order to pinpoint "those *controlled* uses of the television medium that can *best* convey the *image* we want to get across." Words and ideas fruitlessly engaged the voters' intellect, writer Ray Price argued; better to work on their emotions, which "are more easily roused, closer to the surface, more malleable."[18]

What had to be sold was a "New Nixon," something new for the media to project, something new for people to consider. Nixon's advisers pushed hard on the idea. Leonard Garment described himself as a lifelong Democrat who had found Nixon abhorrent. "But he's changed," Garment insisted to reporters. "The years in exile have made him a better man, a more thoughtful and compassionate man." Journalists, thus briefed, received an interview (more like an audience) with the candidate, who then would dutifully portray the New Nixon, impressing those who came with his new, serious views, betraying none of the stereotypical negative images so familiar to media people who had been close to him. The *New York Times* assigned a reporter full time to Nixon in late 1967. He diligently cultivated the Nixon staff, convincing them that he saw Nixon with "a fresh eye." In one of his first stories, he announced that the familiar "Red-baiting Nixon" was gone, and the New Nixon represented "a walking monument to reason, civility, frankness."

The new package was also offered in a newly humanized flavor. Nixon appeared on the popular television program *Laugh-In,* revealing that he could make fun of himself. His participation was calculated and marked the absorption of another McLuhan lesson. In 1963, Nixon had chatted and played the piano on a popular talk show. Instead of the "slick, glib, legal Nixon," McLuhan observed, "we saw the doggedly creative and modest performer." That kind of touch, McLuhan believed, might well have altered the 1960 results.

More hostile critics, such as writer Norman Mailer, admittedly found Nixon "less phony," agreeing that he had moved away from his earlier drives of "total ambition and total alienation from his own person" to a point of partial conciliation with himself. Mailer thought Nixon a blur, going in and out of focus between something true and something false, but now carefully correcting the "phony step." Mailer missed the point; becoming a blur was the ultimate McLuhan "message."

In a carefully contrived television question-and-answer session with a popular football coach as host, Nixon showed his own special way of dealing with the old/new dichotomy. To great applause from his studio audience, he urged Americans to ask "which Humphrey" they now faced. The Republican candidate acknowledged himself as a "new Nixon," older, wiser, and aware of a new, changing world. But there was, too, an "old Nixon," firmly wedded to his belief in "the American system." Thus he offered "new ideas for the new world," but as for his belief "in the American view and the American dream, I think I am just what I was eight years ago."[19]

Perhaps there was no New Nixon—just new perceptions. Howard Phillips, a militant conservative who had idolized Nixon since his teen years, believed that the man never really changed. Speaking in the last days of the Nixon Administration in 1974, as he issued a "conservative manifesto" calling for the President's resignation, and at a time when talk of a New Nixon had faded and the Old Nixon appeared very much restored, Phillips said: "Throughout his public career, Mr. Nixon has always tried to please his audience, seeking their confidence and admiration by becoming the man he thinks they want him to be. The changing perceptions of Nixon—the New Nixon, the Old Nixon, the statesman, the strategist—do not reflect a change in the man but in the audience to which he is at any moment appealing." When the imagery was contrived, Ray Price understoo." what was necessary: "It's not the man we have to change, but rather the *received impression.*"[20] In short, the changes in Nixon really amounted to smoke and mirrors. What was new was an outwardly restrained Nixon—a "cool" man to match the media needs his handlers so respected and understood, and which, together, they would master in this campaign.

* * *

The war that had consumed much of American life and energy for three years festered like an open wound. Nixon's great achievement through that fateful year of 1968 was that he skillfully skirted the issue and moved to his more comfortable law-and-order terrain. With Wallace in the race, Nixon easily seized the "moderate" ground.

During the New Hampshire primary campaign, Nixon repeatedly pledged "to end the war and win the peace in the Pacific." But when Humphrey and reporters pressed him to reveal his "plan," Nixon deflected the questions, insisting that he would not reveal his bargaining position in advance. Finally, he commissioned a speech on the subject but privately told the writer that "there's no way to win the war. But we can't say that of course. In fact, we have to seem to say the opposite." The Nixon camp scheduled the speech for radio delivery the evening of March 31, when Johnson announced his intention not to run again. The prepared text proposed subduing Hanoi by offering Moscow some vaguely conceived "mutually advantageous cooperation." But when Nixon learned of Johnson's plan to address the nation the same night, he canceled his own speech. The President's efforts at negotiation gave candidate Nixon the perfect excuse for declining to offer his own views. *He* would not undermine "the American position," and therefore would say nothing.[21] A few days later, he polled nearly 80 percent of the Wisconsin Republican primary vote.

With the war on ice as a political issue, Nixon deftly turned to the profitable and resonating issues of domestic peace and effective governance. America was in trouble, he said, "not because her people have failed, but because her leaders have failed. And what America needs are leaders to match the greatness of her people." This political leader recognized no malaise, no inner failings or contradictions in the American system; that kind of negativism was not for Richard Nixon.

Nixon strategists assembled an array of devastating statistics demonstrating skyrocketing crime and violence in America since 1960: murder up 34 percent, assault 67 percent, narcotics violations 165 percent, and home burglaries 187 percent. Nixon chided Attorney General Ramsey Clark, quoting him as having said that the crime level had risen "a little bit, but there is no wave of crime in this country." Nixon sensed that the nation thought otherwise. The lesson was clear: the nation could no longer afford such leadership as it had with Johnson and Humphrey. The first order of business for President Nixon, he promised, would be a new Attorney General, "to restore order and respect for law in this country." Nixon conceded that law enforcement was primarily a local responsibility, but he pledged that his Administration would create the necessary "public climate" in order "to win the war" against crime.

Most important, Nixon argued that the family, the church, and the school

were the effective sources of moral civic order. Admittedly, the familiar
institutions had fallen short, but Nixon implied that the present Administration had failed to provide them with the necessary encouragement and support.

Nixon recognized in crime and morality a basic concern of the unorgan-
ized, inarticulate segments of society. More crucially, he acknowledged their
existence. Accepting his party's nomination on August 8, Nixon pointedly
decried the new wave of political protest. He insisted that a president must
listen not only to the "clamorous voices," but also to the "quiet voices."
He promised to go beyond the "wail and bellow of what too often passes
today for public discourse" and find the "real" sentiments and purposes of
the people. Here was the unheeded "great, quite forgotten majority—the
nonshouters and the nondemonstrators, the millions who ask principally to
go their own way in decency and dignity, and to have their own rights
accorded the same respect they accord the rights of others." There was no
law and order when the courts weakened the "peace forces as against the
criminal forces." However commendable it was that judges dedicate themselves to the great principles of civil rights, they must also recognize, Nixon
said, "that the first civil right of every American is to be free from domestic
violence." It was time, he urged, "for some honest talk" about the problem
of order.

The code language was not so subtle when Nixon complained about and
promised to end the plague of "unprecedented racial violence." The Humphrey camp recognized Nixon's target, and the Democratic candidate soft-
ened his talk about "justice"—the generic word for the demands of the
disaffected and deprived—and struggled to offer voters some balance between reform and stability. On October 2, Humphrey promised to ensure
order and end the nation's turmoil. "As President, I would stop these out-
rages at whatever cost." Still he dodged Nixon's contention that poverty and
crime had no relationship.[22]

The Silent Majority had found its voice. Nixon shrewdly transformed the
prevailing preoccupations with war and race into the ever more appealing
concerns of order and civility. In his special way, he conveyed the message
that he was for those virtues, virtues that had been emasculated or disdained
by his opponents. He seemed to promise to "do something" about the
present crisis. It did not hurt Nixon that on the very night the Republicans
balloted to nominate him in Miami, local blacks rioted and four died.

Nixon's retreat into silence on the war issue further distanced him from
potentially hostile, dangerous media contacts. The CBS reporter covering
him would finally get a moment alone with the candidate as the campaign
plane was descending. Then in two minutes he would have to hasten to his
seat for landing. The tactic was well known by accompanying journalists,

who labeled it the "three-bump interview." Reporters repeatedly pressed Nixon with shouted questions about his "plan" for peace, but got no response. Media people knew that there was no plan, but they were in their "let's be fair to Nixon" mode. In other words, a reverse-intimidation situation existed. Seventeen years later, Richard Nixon finally admitted that he had no plan, that his program for peace was only campaign talk.[23]

Peace, even the immediate expectation of peace, might well have favored Humphrey and the Democrats. On September 30, Humphrey made his minibreak from Johnson's control. In a televised speech from Salt Lake City, he offered to stop the bombing of North Vietnam if the enemy offered some evidence that it would restore the demilitarized zone separating the two Vietnams. However qualified his position, Humphrey immediately was perceived as the candidate willing to halt the bombing. By October, negotiations seemed to promise some breakthrough toward peace, one that would be accompanied by a bombing pause. Nixon shrewdly anticipated such a move, saying he would not object if the end of the bombing produced some change in the North Vietnamese position—a stance not much different from Humphrey's. Nixon hinted that political opportunism was at work in the negotiations. On October 27, he appeared on *Face the Nation* and charged that attempts at peace negotiations were linked to an effort to elect Humphrey. Reporters quickly pointed out that Nixon had ended his self-imposed moratorium on discussing peace negotiations in the campaign. After doing precisely that, Nixon of course denied it. On the last day of the month, President Johnson told congressional leaders that he would stop the bombing and that peace talks would resume in Paris on November 6. Nixon's suggestion that political cynicism prompted the Administration's action received support, as more than two-thirds of the telegrams sent to the White House after the President's announcement were critical in one way or another.[24]

The last-minute Vietnam developments, accompanied by cooling passions among the warring Democrats, dramatically chipped away at Nixon's earlier lead. Nixon had enjoyed a fifteen-point Gallup poll advantage over Humphrey in mid-September. By Election Day, they were almost dead even. Nixon had gained nothing in nearly two months. He commanded a 43 percent rating in the September poll, and that is the percentage he received on November 6. All the imagery, all the contrivances of his campaign organization, changed nothing.

The election outcome uncannily mirrored the ambiguity so characteristic of Richard Nixon. He had won; that was for certain. But the closeness of the result underlined the deep divisions within the nation. Nixon won with a plurality of less than a half-million votes. He had captured 43.4 percent of the vote, while Humphrey had finished with 42.7 percent. (George Wallace attracted most of the remainder. Nixon, in his memoirs, expressed a belief that Wallace's votes would have gone mostly to him and thus would have effectively given him an overwhelming mandate.) Nixon had lost almost 2.5 million votes from his 1960 total. Even more striking was the fact that only 61 percent of the eligible voters turned out in 1968, a decline of 3 percent since 1960. Division was not the only malaise: apathy, even cynicism, pervaded the electoral process.

This time, however, the pain of defeat belonged to someone else. Richard Nixon knew Hubert Humphrey's private anguish as no one else could. Perhaps in Humphrey's case the might-have-beens and could-have-beens were even more sharply etched than they had been for Nixon in 1960. Humphrey must have winced at his recollection of Johnson's 1964 remark, "I just knew in my heart that it was not right for Dick Nixon to ever be President of this country." His heart and mind had apparently changed by four years later, for the President did precious little to help his ostensible heir apparent.

Nixon cleverly exploited the delicate relationship between Johnson and Humphrey. The Republican candidate met Billy Graham in Pittsburgh on September 8 and asked him to deliver a confidential message to the President. Nixon passed the word that he would never embarrass the President after the election, that he would continually seek his advice, and that he would ask Johnson to undertake special missions to foreign countries. He assured the President that when the Vietnam war was settled, he would give Johnson a major share of credit and do everything to ensure the President's place in history. A week later, Graham delivered the message and recorded that the President warmly appreciated and was "touched" by Nixon's gesture. His last words were that he intended "to loyally support" Humphrey, but if Nixon were elected, he would "do all in my power to cooperate with him."[25]

A year after the election, Humphrey chastised himself for not having maintained his identity and for not having held fast to his own beliefs and principles. "I ought not to have let a man who was going to be a former President dictate my future," he wrote to a friend. Some close to Johnson believed that LBJ expected Nixon to win and that his "opinion of his Vice President was . . . not very high." So Johnson deserted Humphrey, whom he often professed to love and admire. Nixon, the implacable enemy of Johnson's friends Truman and Rayburn, somehow was deemed the more deserving, the more reliable beneficiary. Johnson, for his part, thought it a miracle that Nixon's election did not set off major demonstrations.[26]

The counterrevolution of 1968 had partially succeeded. But it was not the one set in motion by the Left earlier in the decade. America was lurching rightward. The revolt inspired by the Left against the war turned into a challenge against established authority in general. Those dismayed by the turn of events, shocked as they were by the pervasive turmoil and near anarchy, drifted to Nixon, convinced that he offered a respite. Perhaps as many as 97 percent of black voters supported Humphrey, but the Democratic candidate captured only 35 percent of the white vote. Three of every ten white voters who had supported Johnson in 1964 voted for either Nixon or Wallace in 1968. Humphrey received nearly 12 million fewer votes than Johnson had in 1964.[27] There is no explanation for the reversal other than the volatile political-social climate. Nixon's campaign positions in 1968 differed little in programmatic content from Goldwater's in 1964; Nixon simply offered a moderate front and less provocative rhetoric. Americans voted against social disorder and, they hoped, for social peace. Liberalism seemed routed. The hammer blows from both the Left and the Right had left it discredited and in disarray. Only the Right now could command respectability and votes. That right-wing breakthrough in 1968 prefigured the next four presidential elections.

Just after noon on November 6, Humphrey conceded defeat, and Nixon followed with his victory speech to the nation. He delivered paeans of praise for his rival and his predecessor and pledged anew to fulfill his promised goals. But there was one new tone. At the end of his remarks, he recalled a teen-age girl in Deshler, Ohio, who held up a sign saying "Bring Us Together." And that, the President-elect added, "will be the great objective of this administration at the outset, to bring the American people together." His Administration would be an open one, bridging the gap between the parties, races, and generations.

It was a disingenuous pose, given the calculated campaign strategy of bringing *some* Americans together while deliberately exploiting divisions elsewhere; even the homily was wrapped in deception. The young girl, daughter of a Methodist minister, had actually held a much more partisan sign, one really befitting the Nixon appeal: "LBJ Taught Us, Vote Republican!" The child reflected the nation's volatility and mercurial political allegiances more than anything else, for her real choice had been Robert Kennedy.[28] Ambrose Bierce once described the American president as "the leading figure of a small group of men of whom—and of whom only—it is positively known that immense numbers of their countrymen did not want any of them for president." "None of the above" may really have been the electorate's choice in 1968.

Oppositions do not win elections; governments lose them. That, coupled with a perverse retaliation against the excesses of Lyndon Johnson—*ressentiment*, the French call it—squeezed Nixon to power. Perhaps Nixon's long-awaited triumph was a negative one, one in which people essentially voted against the opposition and the past. Nevertheless, the victory and power were his, freely won and freely given by those who chose to participate. That verdict could not be denied.

* * *

John Bartlow Martin, a veteran political journalist and speechwriter for
Democratic candidates since Adlai Stevenson's first presidential campaign,
suddenly found himself thinking the unthinkable during the last month of
the 1968 presidential campaign. Hubert Humphrey's candidacy did not give
Martin much heart, but he found it unbearable to "imagine Richard Nixon
in the White House." "I thought Nixon a thoroughgoing scoundrel, a hollow
man, a master of deceit, and, considering his and Joe McCarthy's campaign
against Stevenson in 1952, a real menace to civil liberties." Martin berated
fellow liberal Arthur Schlesinger, who refused to help Humphrey: "All
right," he said, "you can abstain if you want, but you're going to help elect
Richard Nixon." In the early morning hours of November 6, as Nixon's
razor-thin victory margin became apparent, Martin had perforce to "imagine Richard Nixon in the White House." He was not alone in his misery.
Eugene McCarthy, who in his own indirect way had contributed to Nixon's
victory, evoked poetic images for his lament: "It is a day for visiting the
sick and burying the dead. It's gray everywhere—all over the land."[29]

Nixon's narrow triumph and his decline in the polls prior to Election Day
reflected his innate capacity for survival. He had survived eight grueling
years as Eisenhower's Vice President; he had survived the heartbreaking loss
of the presidency in 1960; he had survived the humiliating defeat in the 1962
California gubernatorial campaign; he had survived the 1968 primary season
and the convention—largely by default, but also by his resolve and stamina;
and through a combination of perseverance, luck, and the self-inflicted
wounds of his opponents, he had survived the electorate's close decision on
November 5. Survival is success of its own sort; but now Nixon needed
success to survive.

BOOK TWO

FIRST TERM, FIRST WARS

IV

"THE MAN ON TOP"

As Richard Nixon prepared to take office, he felt like a long-deprived heir ready at last to assume his rightful estate. He was serene. He had waited through an eight-year apprenticeship, a hairline defeat, and then another eight years in a political purgatory. Perhaps, he reflected, the "wilderness years" had been good, giving him needed time for education and growth. What had he learned? "I knew," he later wrote, "what would *not* work. On the other hand, I was less sure what *would* work." Nevertheless, he had "definite ideas about the changes" he thought necessary. "As 1968 came to a close, I was a happy man," Nixon recalled.

But Nixon's serenity belied alternating moods of anger, suspicion, and hostility, moods that eventually governed his behavior as president and guided the conduct of those who served as the instruments of his feelings. The politics of *ressentiment* had elected him in 1968; his own resentments flowed generously within his political and philosophical juices. "Fight," "battle," "enemies"—these are key words in the Nixon vocabulary, amply reflected in his tapes and memoirs. Life was conflict, not accommodation. Enemies, he believed, fought his good intentions; enemies must be confronted, contained, and eventually defeated.

Enemies lurked both without and within the governmental apparatus. Nixon had longstanding grievances against the "liberals," whom he identified chiefly within the media and among intellectuals. Officially, they were entangled with the Democratic-controlled Congress and what he believed to be a bureaucracy still dominated by the "old New Deal crowd." Nixon alternately despised and feared Washington's "iron triangle"—legislators, bureaucracy, and lobbyists—but he altered the geometric design with a fourth side: the media. He channeled enormous intellectual energies and emotional drives against "the establishment," his own "iron square."

Nixon assuredly had a fair share of real enemies. A good deal of the working media did not like him; the Democratic leadership in Congress had nursed resentments of their own for nearly two decades; and indeed, some bureaucrats (quite naturally) preferred their own vested interest, however archaic, to presidentially desired policy changes.

But the times were special. The militancy of the antiwar movement had not abated in the slightest with the election, and for good reason: the war itself had not abated. Rather, during the first two years of the Nixon Administration, it broadened. For those within the Administration, from the President on down, outside agitation—whether it came from antiwar activists, environmentalists, or civil rights advocates—mirrored the hostility within and contributed to both a sense of isolation and a feeling of "us" against "them." Several years later, in a rambling conversation with his aide John Ehrlichman, the President bitterly assaulted environmentalists. He thought them "overrated," and that they served only the "privileged." Their issue, he said, was just "crap," and for "clowns," and "the rich and [Supreme Court Justice William O.] Douglas." The tensions, from both sides, only further poisoned the political air.

Nixon and his associates personalized the opposition, and again not without cause. The resistance and civil disobedience of the 1960s confronted a system which some considered evil and intolerable. Much of that activism was condoned by politicians, intimidated intellectuals, and the media. Nixon's election, for them, constituted a self-fulfilling prophecy, justifying more opposition, more disobedience. The whole business was circular, as Alexander Bickel observed: "Men who are loudly charged with repression before they have done anything to substantiate the charge are apt to proceed to substantiate it."[1]

Various Administration officials reflected on the times and their feelings. Ehrlichman flatly denied any notion of White House paranoia toward antiwar demonstrations. Others have testified to the contrary. Admiral Thomas Moorer, Chairman of the Joint Chiefs of Staff, deeply resented the demonstrations. He remembered the "tension" because of the war, the opposition, and the media. The President himself acknowledged that "I was a paranoiac, or almost a basket case with regard to secrecy," fearing that leaks would jeopardize diplomatic negotiations or even reveal the precariousness of the military situation in Vietnam.

William Ruckelshaus was in the Department of Justice in October 1969 when tens of thousands of demonstrators converged on the capital. Ruckelshaus had a well-earned reputation as a moderate man and was hardly a presidential sycophant. But he recalled the tear gas that drifted from the streets into the Attorney General's office ("so much you could hardly speak") and the buses surrounding the White House for security purposes: "My Lord," he said, "you don't have to be paranoid to say everything ain't working just swimmingly here." The net result of the demonstrations, according to Ruckelshaus, was that they provoked extreme reactions on the other side as well. However justified the civil disobedience, the counter-reaction, he thought, "inevitably" would go beyond what good judgment considered appropriate. White House aide Jeb Stuart Magruder later testified to the alternate feelings of frustration and anger among the President's men. The President's opponents, Magruder contended, failed to appreciate his efforts to end the war on his often-articulated basis of "peace with honor." Their resistance created "frustration and a feeling of impotence"; consequently, Magruder admitted, the President's men grew more callous toward their enemies, whom they saw committing illegal acts with the approval of a large portion of the American public.[2]

Wars historically impose enormous strains on the Constitution, and the Vietnam war proved no exception. The Administration's responses to antiwar activists (wiretapping), demonstrators (mass arrests), and leaks from Administration operations (more wiretapping and illegal break-ins of private offices to obtain ostensible evidence) reflected a government threatened from without and besieged from within. Nixon's oft-declared insistence that he would not be the first American President to lose a war to a large degree inspired his Administration's behavior and justified it to him and his loyal supporters.

Nixon's first term often is viewed as a successful one—after all, the American voters enthusiastically endorsed it in 1972. A decade after the President's resignation, some historians and journalists, following Nixon's lead, sparked a burst of revisionism that ranged from a view of Watergate as but a blip on the continuum of both American and Nixonian history, to a full-blown public declaration of rehabilitation by some members of the media the ex-President had once fought so bitterly. Nixon's historical reputation, it was argued, would stand or fall on his policy achievements, and some commentators argued that his domestic triumphs far outstripped those in foreign policy.[3]

Nixon himself claimed little in the way of legislative achievement. To be sure, he lacked LBJ's congressional majorities, not to mention his standing and skill with Congress. Nixon's own party, moreover, was badly divided on legislative goals. When the President pushed an affirmative-action program, Senate Republican leader Dirksen warned that Nixon would split the party if he insisted on the law. "[I]t is my bounden duty to tell you," Nixon remembered Dirksen as saying, "that this thing is about as popular as a crab in a whorehouse." The most famous Nixon proposal was the Family Assistance Plan (FAP), a promising welfare-reform proposal pushed by Daniel P. Moynihan and other academic experts. But this project floundered amid Left-Right legislative and White House pressures. In the end, Nixon himself abandoned the idea, and FAP died aborning.

Similarly, he vetoed the Comprehensive Child Development Bill in late 1971, with a strident ideological message that was designed to appease conservatives embittered by the President's decision to visit China. Perhaps Nixon's most prominent domestic move was the imposition of wage and price controls in 1971, although years later he devoted several pages of his memoirs to repudiating that same policy.[4]

Foreign policy, of course, offers a weightier argument for Nixon's leadership qualities. Here the President was in his favored milieu. In the years following World War II, Congress had tended to accord presidents preeminence in foreign-policy matters. Thus Nixon had greater opportunities to act in this area than he did in domestic policy. Certainly, his move toward rapprochement with China was a major historical achievement—whatever his mixed motives and his own past efforts and commitments toward isolating the Chinese. Visiting China in 1972, he toasted the event as "the week that changed the world." Perhaps he exaggerated, but his trip did in fact change the relationship between two great nations, and, as Nixon noted fifteen years later, the move showed that through cooperation between the two nations, "the world *can* be changed—and changed for the better."

His moves toward détente with the Soviet Union are especially intriguing; ironically, their long-range success and wisdom have earned Nixon extraordinary enmity from many of those who otherwise loyally supported him. Finally in the survey of his foreign policy, the Vietnam war proved to be no less a burden for Nixon than it had been for Johnson. Nixon promised to withdraw American troops, gain the release of prisoners of war, and secure "peace with honor" while preserving the integrity of South Vietnam. American soldiers came home, along with the POWs, but only after losses in men and matériel that almost matched those suffered under Johnson. The resulting North Vietnamese takeover of all of Indochina confirmed much of the contemporary skepticism and contempt for Nixon's vaunted "peace with honor."[5]

The public achievements of Nixon's first term are scattered. They merit historical recognition, but have little to do with what always will make Nixon unique: his resignation in disgrace, amid ever-mounting scandals. The revelations that followed the break-in at the Watergate offices of the Democratic National Committee headquarters in June 1972 pierced the curtain that had masked the seamy side of the Administration for almost four years.[6] Therein lay the origins of the tragedy that engulfed Richard Nixon and the nation.

* * *

John Mitchell, Nixon's 1968 campaign manager and the first of his five Attorneys General, testified in 1973 about the "White House horrors," a term he applied generically to a range of political "dirty tricks" he considered far more disturbing than the Watergate break-in. Mitchell's comment was pointed at roguish presidential aides who he believed had misled and badly advised the President. Other contemporaries referred to the staff more charitably, characterizing them as the "Beaver Patrol," dutifully parceling out "Mickey Mouse" missions. The sarcastic veneer of that judgment barely concealed the reality that Richard Nixon commanded the patrol and dictated its missions.

The Nixon presidency marked a further evolution in the style and life of the White House. Since the Eisenhower years, it had come increasingly to resemble a monarchical court. Former Johnson aide George Reedy accurately portrayed that development and uncannily anticipated its continuance. White House life, Reedy wrote, basically served the material needs of the President, from providing the most luxurious means of travel to having a masseur constantly present. But, more important, he was treated with kingly reverence. "No one speaks to him unless spoken to first. No one ever invites him to 'go soak your head' when his demands become petulant and unreasonable." Reedy's master was well known for his almost compulsive drive for micro-managerial control which paralyzed initiatives and innovations from others. In Johnson's White House, presidential aides seemingly existed to carry out the leader's whims and decrees and, in time-honored fashion, they were to have a "passion for anonymity."[7]

Nixon's conception of his role varied only slightly from Johnson's. That same drive for control, that same intensity of involvement across a wide spectrum of activities, from the most global and profound to the most localized and petty, characterized Richard Nixon's behavior. For many, Nixon's staff, especially Haldeman, his main "gatekeeper" (as the President characterized him), and Ehrlichman, served as scapegoats, as the "bad Germans," to explain the darker side of the Nixon Administration. Senator Dirksen had complained of having to work through the White House's "Berlin Wall"—meaning Haldeman and Ehrlichman. House Republican leader Gerald Ford likewise excoriated these aides for their apparent view that Congress existed "only to follow their instructions, and we had no right to behave as a co-equal branch of government." But Ford later conveniently discovered that such attitudes were not exclusively held by presidential aides. As President himself, Ford savored his prerogatives; Congress, he complained, had disintegrated as an organized legislative body.[8]

The idea that his sinister aides transformed the newly minted Nixon of 1968 back into the old, familiar Nixon apparently has its source in accounts of the campaign. Nixon's media advisers claimed that he lost his large lead over Humphrey when Haldeman came more directly into the fray. Rose Mary Woods, Nixon's personal secretary since 1951, and long regarded as the "fifth Nixon," later—after the Watergate revelations—complained: "It was all warm and friendly until . . . Bob Haldeman arrived."[9]

Harry Robbins Haldeman had stood outside the Los Angeles television studio where Nixon made his "Checkers" speech in 1952. The twenty-six-year-old advertising account executive sent a note into the studio, offering to help in the campaign, but he was refused. The rebuff showed that Senator Nixon had something to learn about gratitude, for Haldeman's father had contributed to Nixon's $18,000 "slush fund." Haldeman's grandfather, who had made a fortune in the plumbing-supply business, had co-founded the Better American Federation of California, an early anticommunist organization. Following the 1952 election, Haldeman continued his career in advertising, handling accounts as diverse as Disneyland and Black Flag insecticide. He finally gained a place in the Nixon camp when he signed on to work in the 1956 re-election effort. Robert Finch, then Nixon's Chief of Staff in all but name, was impressed, and made Haldeman the chief advance man in the 1960 campaign. Haldeman opposed Nixon's pursuit of the California governorship but loyally coordinated the effort when it was decided upon. While John Mitchell managed Nixon's presidential bid in 1968, Haldeman maintained proximity to the candidate and quietly assumed the lion's share of power. After the election, he commanded the transition arrangements and eased into the role he occupied until the end of April 1973.

For several of the Nixon campaigns, Haldeman had enlisted the services of his college friend John D. Ehrlichman, who had been practicing real-estate law in Seattle. Ehrlichman, too, served an apprenticeship as a Nixon advance man, but in 1968 he worked closely with Haldeman. Quite naturally, he followed his friend into the White House, where he first served as Counsel to the President, and later as head of the Domestic Council. Ehrlichman, far more than Haldeman, worked with the President on substantive policy matters.[10]

Haldeman and Ehrlichman's detailed notes of their constant meetings with the President faithfully recorded Nixon's wishes and complaints—not, however, without occasional sarcasm or astonishment at his behavior. At one point during their repeated visits to the Oval Office in the 1972 campaign, Haldeman scratched a note to Ehrlichman: "Why did he buzz me?" Like a schoolchild answering a passed message, Ehrlichman sketched several sarcastic answers in his inimitable style: "He had an itchy finger." "Also there was a chair unoccupied." "Also he has been talking about not just reordering the chaos, and he would like you to understand that point."

In general, however, the two aides dutifully gave their President the loyalty that they demanded of others in his name. "There shouldn't be a lot of leeway in following the President's policies," Ehrlichman said in 1972. "It should be like a corporation, where the executive vice presidents (the cabinet officers) are tied closely to the chief executive, . . . [and] when he says jump they only ask how high.'' Critics of Haldeman and Ehrlichman regularly complained that they were not men of ideas, that they pursued power as an end in itself. Richard Whalen, who had written speeches for Nixon in 1968, was a conservative with firm ideological and policy convictions. Whalen was appalled at the lack of values and philosophy in the President's key aides, and he winced when Ehrlichman announced that the President was only interested in what was "feasible and tactically shrewd.'' Whalen eventually realized that Ehrlichman was no different from the others; he served as a functionary, carrying out the role and duties designed by Richard Nixon. CIA Director Richard Helms, too, understood the role of the President's aides; as for Nixon himself, Helms considered him "the original loner.''[11]

"We had a strong, tight-knit team with a passion for anonymity,'' Haldeman said rather disingenuously, nearly fifteen years after he left the White House. But unlike Johnson, Nixon did not demand anonymity from his aides; their visibility served him conveniently and well, especially in diverting heat and attention from himself. Visibility and independent power are quite different things, however. Both primary aides have offered ample testimony that they had executed the President's wishes, not invented them. Their self-effacement was self-serving, to be sure. But Robert Finch came to the same conclusion. He insisted that the Richard Nixon of 1960 obviously was not the Richard Nixon of 1968 through 1972. Finch, who saw Haldeman in a role he once had, at first thought that "they"—Haldeman and other White House aides—"were constantly changing Nixon." But Finch reluctantly concluded that "they" were but an extension of Nixon's own personality. And Harry Dent, another White House aide, who ranked just below Haldeman and Ehrlichman, and who disliked Haldeman intensely, scoffed at the notion that Nixon could not control his subordinates. "I know from whence every order came. . . . You couldn't be around without knowing that everything came from one well, one spring." Egil Krogh, a particular Nixon favorite, concurred.

Nixon had the message, and in Haldeman he had his medium. William Safire, who savaged Haldeman in his account of his White House years, well understood Haldeman's role: *"Haldeman organized the dissemination of the President's thinking; . . . . Haldeman organized the execution of the President's orders,"* Safire wrote. Haldeman even had a verb for his function—"game planning." His memos came in a cascade, "game planning" Vietnam, prisoners of war, and Clement Haynsworth's Supreme Court nomination. By "Game Planning we will attempt to co-ordinate total Administration activities toward producing the maximum possible results from any of the key objectives that the President feels requires special attention and an all-out effort," the Chief of Staff told his subordinates.

The President's daughter admitted that "my father wanted Bob Haldeman to be the sole conduit to him." Hardly an admirer of Haldeman's, however, she added that he "seemed to want that even more." Nixon depended "mightily" on his Chief of Staff, and he did not want to hear criticism of Haldeman. According to Julie Nixon Eisenhower, her father "closed his eyes to Haldeman's occasional overstepping" of his bounds and allowed his aide to isolate him. Her account reads like a historical novel depicting a powerless medieval king manipulated by supposedly inferior feudal barons. Ultimately, however, the President's daughter conceded that Haldeman's "occasional overstepping" reflected "what the President wanted."

A decade earlier, Nixon had acknowledged the difficulty, even the impossibility, of certain administrative functions. For those, he said, "you need a son-of-a-bitch in it." Such was Haldeman's position, and both men realized what was required. Haldeman readily acknowledged his role: "I'm his [Nixon's] buffer and I'm his bastard. I get done what he wants done and I take the heat instead of him." Haldeman later recalled that early in the Administration, he lost his "passion for anonymity" when he appeared on television to denounce congressmen who had criticized the President's Vietnam policy, accusing them of "consciously aiding and abetting the enemy." But he made that statement, he revealed, "at the president's orders."[12]

Haldeman displaced Rose Mary Woods as the President's most important assistant, an act that Haldeman's detractors often cited to illustrate his grasping for power. But the directive that elevated Haldeman came from Nixon. Haldeman's notes for his September 19, 1971 meeting with the President record Nixon as saying: "When Rose gets back—reevaluate her job. 80% of her time making calls." The next day, Haldeman dictated an action paper as follows: "When Rose Woods gets back we should reevaluate her job. She should shift to a use of her time that is more externally productive. Approximately 80% should be spent making phone calls. She should be checking things like congratulations to the staff people and outside people. . . ." Given her experience with the President, Woods must have recognized who had demoted her.[13]

Knowledge was control, and it extended even to what did not happen. Early in the first term, the President conveyed to Haldeman his "uneasy feeling" that many of his directives for action were ignored when the staff thought them unreasonable or unattainable. "I respect this kind of judgment," Nixon remarked. But, he added, "I want to know when that kind of decision is made." He instructed Haldeman to keep a checklist indicating what action had been taken, "and particularly I want to know when the action that I have ordered has *not* been taken." Two years later, the President told Haldeman to let friendly reporters and commentators know that "I am very persistent in checking to see whether my orders are carried out."[14]

Alexander Butterfield, a Haldeman aide who monitored the paper and staff flow to the President and set his schedule each day, saw the President as much, if not more, than Haldeman did. Testifying to the House Judiciary Committee in 1974, Butterfield coolly described Nixon's conduct of his office.[15] Butterfield's detailed testimony amply corroborated Harry Dent's general observation that in the last analysis Nixon was the master in his house.

The President's day began with Patrick Buchanan's news summaries, running usually from sixty to eighty pages and including a listing of recent happenings and notice of attitudes toward the President and his policies throughout the nation. Nixon made marginal comments, directing Haldeman or Ehrlichman to take note, or even commanding sudden, dramatic (and often unattainable) changes, such as telling Kissinger to cut American forces in the Philippines by 80 percent in six months. Butterfield regularly saw the President's personal memoranda to his staff, and he described approvingly their attention to detail. Nixon was concerned about whether curtains were open or closed, on which side of the room the staff should place state gifts to visiting dignitaries, the table and entertainment arrangements for social dinners, whether and when salads should be served, whether the Secret Service should salute and sing during the playing of the "Star-Spangled Banner," what aides had what photographs of former presidents in their offices, the comments of visitors on White House paintings, and whether or not to move the tennis courts. He very much wanted to know where his people were and what they were doing. He instructed Butterfield to institute a program requiring Cabinet members to clear travel plans through Butterfield's office. "[A]ll of these things are understandable," Butterfield remarked at one point. They were, he noted, "typical of a thoughtful and careful and well-disciplined man, . . . highly interested in detail." Such a man was unlikely to give *carte blanche* to mere gatekeepers.

Nixon gave lip service to delegating work on details, but he qualified this by asserting personal control over "matters . . . where I have particular competence and where my decision rather than anybody else's can make the big difference." Thus he prescribed the order of seating and serving at dinners and told Haldeman he wanted all musical selections for state dinners cleared with him. He ordered an Army choir to sing for a congressional dinner, later adding that he knew Leonard Garment and others did not approve of such entertainment, preferring instead "some offbeat modern ballet such as that utterly disgusting group we had from New York." Nixon wanted to know when a baseball player hit his five-hundredth home run so he could properly congratulate him; he dictated a memorandum requesting a waste basket for the washroom off the Oval Office; and he ordered precise word limits on speeches prepared for him. In the spring of 1972, he gave a great deal of attention to "his" gift of a blue Lincoln Continental to Leonid Brezhnev. "For Ford [Motor Company], of course, it would be a pure business deal in any event since they are negotiating with the Russians for putting in a plant," Nixon told Haldeman. The Chief of Staff dutifully repeated the language verbatim as he delegated the problem to one of his own aides.[16]

The Haldeman directives, whether written memos or shouted instructions to awed subordinates, are legendary for their authoritativeness. Even when the staff characterized them as "Mickey Mouse" orders—such as harassing a senator who had said something critical about the President the day before—they knew, as Dent remembered, that the instructions really came from the President. The authority was Nixon's, that "one well, one spring," as Dent said. Butterfield vividly recalled how Haldeman regularly emerged from the Oval Office with his yellow legal pad, reading directives to others or going to his "dictating machine [to] spit out instructions to the staff members." Presidential commands, both important and trivial, were often formulated as the President sat alone at night in his Executive Office Building hideaway or in the Lincoln Room in the White House residential quarters. Nixon "was unquestionably the decision maker," Butterfield insisted, "and those decisions would normally be brought down in the morning on the yellow pad." Dent's former secretary corroborated the technique. Haldeman had taken the woman for his own staff. Her job: to type Nixon's memos, either handwritten or left on a Dictabelt from the previous evening. Haldeman then turned them into "his" instructions, often repeating the President's language precisely.[17]

Butterfield admired Haldeman as a friend and patron, and as his immediate superior, but he had no illusions about the role of the Chief of Staff. Haldeman was only "an implementer," who did "nothing without the knowledge of the President"; "he was not a decision maker," Butterfield later told House and Senate investigators. "Haldeman's preoccupation [was] . . . to see that things went in accordance with the President's likes and dislikes." To that, Haldeman was "dedicated . . . in a very selfless way." Inadvertently, Butterfield confirmed the danger that Reedy had sighted four years earlier. The President's staff, Butterfield thought, sometimes mirrored his personality too readily, and even accentuated his weaknesses rather than compensating for them. Julie Eisenhower was a bit more delicate: "loyalty was demanded of all, not judgment."

Sometimes, the staff might create an illusion of self-sufficiency when there was none. In a reflective mood, Butterfield thought "that may have happened" in the Nixon White House. Charles Lichenstein, a sometime aide and ghostwriter, thought that Nixon had a devastating tendency to isolate himself from possibly critical assistants. "This inability to draw on good, skilled people is an inadequacy in Richard Nixon," he said, and sadly added that he was at a loss to explain it. Vice President Spiro Agnew was contemptuous of the sycophantic quality of Nixon's staff. Whatever directives came from Nixon, via Haldeman and Ehrlichman, generally were followed, an Agnew aide added, largely because the staff had no principles of their own. Harry Dent, on the other hand, remembered that he and others would simply ignore some of the more outrageous or silly orders. Stephen Bull, who also worked in the Oval Office and later assumed many of Butterfield's duties, thought that Haldeman occasionally ignored Nixon's instructions or allowed others to ignore them. Bull thought that Haldeman was merely an "extension" of the President on policy matters, but that he managed the staff on his own. Finally, Communications Director Herbert Klein recognized that Haldeman operated with "the full concurrence and encouragement of the President."[18]

Butterfield portrayed Richard Nixon as a man utterly consumed with his position. Intending his comments as complimentary, Butterfield described Nixon's total dedication and involvement. "He was preoccupied with the Presidency . . . with his place in history, with his Presidency as history would see it." Remarkably, Butterfield anticipated the essence of Nixon's memoirs and his second "long march"—that is, his search for rehabilitation following the disgrace of his resignation. That kind of man, with that kind of preoccupation with detail, never openly subscribed to managerial theories of loose delegation.

When Nixon delegated authority, he often would use two men for essentially the same task, but he would work them in different ways. Haldeman had a shrewd perception of Nixon's different uses for men such as John Ehrlichman, Charles Colson, and himself. "Most of us operated in watertight compartments, unaware of what Nixon was ordering our colleagues to do," Ehrlichman wrote. Murray Chotiner, who had worked with Nixon since 1946, told White House Counsel John Dean that the President did not like his aides to share information he had provided them, thus encouraging an aura of secrecy and a sense of compartmentalization. Henry Kissinger, hardly a neophyte in understanding administrative dynamics, similarly acknowledged the careful compartmentalization of information in the Nixon White House.

Compartmentalization ensured fragmentation of power, precisely what Nixon desired. (Of course, the technique was not new; Franklin D. Roosevelt was a past master at such administrative dealings.) In 1972, for example, Nixon appointed John Mitchell as his ostensible campaign director; at the same time, Haldeman directed a good share of the operation from the White House. Haldeman's task was chiefly to audit Mitchell's activities, but according to Dent, all this was in order for Nixon to keep control. At one point, Mitchell wanted Dent as his assistant, but the President sent Haldeman's aide, Jeb Stuart Magruder. "Things didn't happen around *that* White House willy-nilly," Dent insisted. "The man on top was on top."[19]

The top man had elaborate procedures for ensuring that his staff briefed him fully and across an incredible range of subjects, as Butterfield explained. The concerns for presidential briefings sometimes went to ridiculous lengths.

In March 1971, Garment was working mainly as house advocate and monitor
of civil rights, ethnic, and intellectual affairs. He told Henry Kissinger that
"a confidential source"—probably a secretary or a congressional aide—had
provided a copy of the remarks that a delegation of black congressmen would
make to Nixon about the continued bombing in Indochina. Curiously, Garment asked Kissinger to provide background material, so that the White
House staff could properly brief the President for his response. The request
seemed improbable. What could the delegation possibly say that would ne-
cessitate such activity and concern on the part of the President? After all,
this President was supposed to be expert on foreign and military policies.

The White House staff simply feared the consequences if the President
stumbled. Kissinger realized that staffers never knew which Nixon they would
encounter: the "idealist[ic], thoughtful, generous" one, or the "vindictive,
petty, emotional" Nixon. One was "a reflective, philosophical, stoical
Nixon, but its obverse was an impetuous, impulsive, and erratic one." Kissinger claimed that he could recognize an "impulsive instruction," and
thought it wise to have the "reflective Nixon" go over it before taking any
action.[20] The observation is instructive for its insight into personality; more
important, it demonstrates a president in command—with whatever personality was momentarily dominant in his psyche.

Nixon diligently struggled to create the illusion that he had broadly delegated authority to experts throughout the government. The creation of his
Cabinet is a case in point. He introduced his designated department heads
on national television on the evening of December 11, 1968. The President
presented his nominees one by one, assuring the country that these were
independent thinkers and declaring that not one of them "agrees with me
completely on everything." He insisted he did not want a Cabinet of "yes
men" and each officer, he promised, "will be urged to speak out" on the
great issues. As Secretary of State he selected his claimed friend William
Rogers; actually, Nixon harbored deep resentments against Rogers. "Inef-
fectual, selfish, and vain," was how he characterized the Secretary in private. Rogers in turn could not, as Elliot Richardson observed,
"psychologically bring himself to subordinate himself to Nixon." When
Nixon made the appointment, he and Henry Kissinger already had worked
out a plan for bypassing the State Department in making foreign policy.

The President-elect also named George Romney to Housing and Urban
Development—Romney, his former foe in the primaries, for whom Nixon
had nothing but personal and intellectual contempt, having once compared
him to Harold Stassen. Within five years, Nixon had a new Cabinet. When
his Administration began to disintegrate in 1973, he promised to make greater
use of his Cabinet and deal directly with the heads of the departments.[21] He
never did.

"I've always thought this country could run itself domestically without a

President," Nixon said in 1967. "All you need is a competent Cabinet to run the country at home. You need a President for foreign policy; no Secretary of State is really important; the President makes foreign policy." This oft-repeated remark implied that Nixon really had little interest in domestic affairs and was prepared to allow a "competent Cabinet" to run its own course. Nothing was further from the truth. In his eyes, the Cabinet was only an extension of Richard Nixon and the Oval Office; he well realized how domestic affairs intersected with political and public-relations considerations which in turn vitally affected his public standing. As a result, Nixon intimately involved himself in overseeing Cabinet activities, once again using his trusted staff to determine and protect his interests. His interests, as usual, were political and personal rather than those of substantive policies.

Three days after the outset of the Nixon Administration, Harry Dent complained that some Cabinet members had not been "giving enough weight to political considerations." Jeb Magruder described the blunt manner in which he or Charles Colson would tell a Cabinet officer: "Mr. Secretary, we're sending over this speech that we'd like you to deliver." Cabinet officers basically were "useful spokesmen when we wanted to push a particular line—on Cambodia, on [Supreme Court nominee Harrold] Carswell, or whatever." Another staffer warned Cabinet officers to "rethink" their positions if they wished to say anything critical about the President or his policies, for they served at the President's pleasure, and "they should know that it is the President's intentions and the President's program that count and not what some cabinet member or undersecretary thinks." White House aides had to "readjust the compasses of political appointees" lest any develop proprietary interests and err by speaking of "my department" or "my program."[22]

The fate of Interior Secretary Walter Hickel, the former governor of Alaska, gave the lie to the President's public call for independent thinking. White House staffers such as Magruder thought Hickel to be "one of the most long-winded and egocentric men" in Washington—and soon vented those feelings to the media. One man's longwindedness, however, was another man's concern for allowing departments "to develop policy for those activities under [their] control." Hickel bristled at the White House interference and the prospect of doing nothing except waiting for "marching orders to be issued by the Executive Mansion."

Hickel went public with his criticism during the Cambodia invasion in the spring of 1970, urging the President to break away from his White House isolation and his dependence on his subordinates. The President conveyed a clear message that it would be "a good idea" for Hickel to return to Alaska and run for governor. Hickel ignored the warning. Five months later, Nixon ordered an audit of the Interior Department, specifically looking for excessive spending by the Secretary on his office remodeling and his travels. On

Thanksgiving Eve, the President saw Hickel and asked for his resignation. Hickel wanted to know if that was to be effective on the first of the year. "That's effective today," Nixon replied. Later, when Robert Finch, in charge of Health, Education and Welfare, similarly tried to move the President in a different direction, his fate was no different from Hickel's, albeit a little less harsh. Finch was invited to serve in the White House as a presidential assistant, but he soon discovered he had no access to Nixon. "My utility was so badly diminished," he recalled, "I thought I had better get out. I did."[23]

Henry Kissinger, who worked within both the White House and the Cabinet, saw the President's relations with his Cabinet as psychologically complex. He thought "students of psychology" could explain why every President since Kennedy trusted his immediate aides more than his Cabinet.[24] The answer, of course, lies in presidential perceptions of political and personal needs, the need to enhance his image and power, as well as to protect his public standing. The Nixon White House staff was particularly attuned to those requirements. Simple gestures were weighed with political consequences always in mind. In March 1969, a staff aide proposed that the President stop in Atlanta on Good Friday on his way to Florida and meet privately with Mrs. Martin Luther King, Jr. More than a gesture was involved, for it was suggested that the President then go on television and talk about nonviolence in the context of Easter week. The act, it was believed, would improve the Administration's relations with blacks and defuse black militants' calls for violence.

The visit to Mrs. King seemingly had support across a wide ideological spectrum in the Administration: Leonard Garment, Arthur Burns, Richard Kleindienst, Herbert Klein, and Patrick Buchanan. In fact, however, Buchanan reached the President through another door, reminding him of the political consequences of such a visit in terms of the constituency that Nixon had carefully cultivated in the 1968 campaign. "It would outrage many, many people who believe Dr. King was a fraud and a demagogue, and perhaps worse. Dr. King is *one of the most divisive men in contemporary history*—some believe him a Messiah, others consider him the devil incarnate." Buchanan knew which he believed. King's background, he reminded the President, "was a sordid one, if we can believe our friends in the Bureau." Haldeman and Ehrlichman similarly advised against the move. The President and his immediate entourage went directly to Key Biscayne for his vacation.[25]

Just after the turn of the new year, 1969, Daniel P. Moynihan, a Democrat who had agreed to serve as a presidential aide ("Unlike so many liberal academics, Moynihan was free of professional jargon and ideological cant,"

Nixon recalled), told the President-elect that his task was clear: "To restore the authority of American institutions." Moynihan worried that the United States might be in a position analogous to that of the Weimar Republic in the 1920s—in danger of collapse as a result of assaults from the extremes. Restoring unity—"bringing us together"—was essential to preventing that collapse. Unfortunately, as even his admirers admitted, Richard Nixon made his famous promise of unification "just once, never before, nor after." William Safire, one of the President's speechwriters and often identified with Nixon's "good side," told his chief on Armistice Day 1970: "The war is ending. Let's turn on the lights."[26] But all the wars were not over for Nixon; he still had need of the dark. Even in the first term, life in the White House demonstrated an enormous preoccupation with imagery and with the exploitation of social divisions for immediate political gain. That first term uncannily reflected the style and process of the 1968 campaign.

At the outset Nixon recognized that he had to adopt "complex political strategies" to secure his program. He was determined to be an "activist President in domestic affairs. . . . I was prepared to use the first year of my presidency to knock heads together in order to get things done." The "complex political strategies" included public-relations operations and a preoccupation with "the opposition." Safire complained about the obsession with "PR," apparently directing his pique toward Haldeman and his advertising-agency minions who filled the West Wing of the White House. But the obsession was Nixon's; as always, Haldeman was merely the instrument. In an earlier memo to his aide, the President emphasized "PR" activities. Henceforth, every Monday, he wanted a week's projection of major opposition attacks, "so we can plan our own statements with those in mind." Nixon demanded to "be informed as to what action has been taken and, if action is not taken, why the decision has been made not to take it." Earlier, it was the President—not Haldeman—who ordered that all editorials and "column plays" be sent daily to the appropriate White House staff members.[27]

Nixon was unhappy with the public response to his June 1969 meeting with South Vietnamese President Nguyen Van Thieu and his announcement that he would withdraw 25,000 troops from South Vietnam. Admittedly, the media found the news "most welcome," but Nixon categorized the reaction as "what else is new?" He blamed his staff for a failure to follow through on his efforts. Alexander Butterfield, who spent most of the day at the President's side, conveyed Nixon's dissatisfaction to White House aides, including Herbert Klein, who was supposedly in charge of dealing with the media. "*All* of us," Butterfield told them in a memo, "failed to provide that massive exploitation action which is so vital (essential) to the achievement of our political and other goals." He asked Klein and another aide for written responses. The matter was most urgent.[28]

The White House had a special staff to deal with the public-relations aspects of policy problems—the "ten o'clock" and "five o'clock" groups—whose sole function was to create a favorable flow of news for the President, timed to fit noon and evening news deadlines. By mid-1971, with little more than a year remaining before the next presidential election, the public-relations groups seemed concerned that the nation did not view the President as "being *personally involved* in domestic issues." One staffer thought it important that the President, not Attorney General Mitchell, speak out on drugs; that President Nixon, not the Environmental Protection Agency's William Ruckelshaus, talk about pollution; and again, that President Nixon, not Secretary of the Treasury George Shultz, discuss the economy. Ehrlichman and Haldeman agreed that the President must be more involved—or, at least, more visible—in domestic matters. Haldeman stressed "the real issues like economy & drugs," not "the phonies like health & environment." Ehrlichman thought that the President had overlooked the need for "credibility, compassion and humanity." Not so, Haldeman retorted: "We may be failing to get them across; we are sure as hell not overlooking them."[29]

In October 1969, Nixon instructed Haldeman to have his speechwriters work out a statement of his philosophy. It "would be worth some work and effort by our PR group," the President thought. Haldeman directed Safire to deal with the details. Safire had been frustrated since the campaign by his inability to establish a coherent overview of Nixon's political philosophy. At the moment, he was trying to write a rationale for the President's "New Federalism" program, a term Nixon had casually dropped at the National Governors' Conference in September. Now, ten months into his presidency, Nixon wanted someone to develop his philosophy. Safire's observation was revealing, however inadvertent: "Strange, fitting a philosophy to the set of deeds, but sometimes that is what has to be done."[30]

The President periodically pressed his aides for a "manifesto of the Nixon programs for progress." But his need for a coherent philosophy paled in comparison to his constant concern for his image. Haldeman's notes typically recorded presidential self-advertisements: "Nixon superbly qualified for summitry experiences, does home work, tough, strong, . . . met more [heads] of govt—conciliatory, subtle, knows the subject." In a March 1970 memo, Nixon told Haldeman: "On another subject, RN's effectiveness with small groups, on toasts, etc., might be a theme to have Klein, Ziegler, *et al* get out as they talk to people for background purposes." The same day, Nixon asked his aide to have the "PR group" consider whether "New Majority," rather than "Silent Majority," should become the Administration's slogan. En route from California to Washington one day, the President dictated more than a dozen memos to Haldeman and Ehrlichman regarding things for them to do in the public-relations sphere. He consistently laid out "themes" for his aides and surrogates to pursue, such as his own "come-back," his effectiveness in using television, and his being the only twentieth-century president (excepting Theodore Roosevelt, Wilson, and Hoover) who "completely writes a major speech."

The President was determined to project himself as the man in charge. At the outset of his Administration, he admonished Ehrlichman to refute media commentators who described the Nixon regime as "government by committee." "Of course, as you know," Nixon told Ehrlichman, "nothing could be further from the truth." He urged him to "get across the point that RN provides very positive direct leadership to the Cabinet committees." Later, he pressed Ehrlichman to mount "a more effective public relations campaign" that would demonstrate the President's leadership in combatting crime. Nixon thought John Dean would be the ideal man to carry out the task.[31]

After two years in office, the President remained dissatisfied with the White House's public-relations efforts. In March 1971, he thought that he needed a "full-time PR man to really convey the true image." This most serious of men worried about a need for humor and color in his talks. Above all, he wanted to be portrayed as having warmth and passion; what he wanted, of course, was love and affection from the nation.

Nixon prodded Haldeman to arrange a "private" gathering of his men at Blair House in March 1971 at which they would discuss what Haldeman described as the Administration's "principal flaw": its failure to secure proper credit for the President's achievements. The gathering was not so private, in fact, for Haldeman arranged to have it taped. The Chief of Staff presided, speaking from notes prepared by Charles Colson. But the un-doubted star of the evening was Treasury Secretary John Connally, then at the height of his standing with the President. Connally exhorted the others to do more for the President. Nixon himself might as well have been speaking when Connally said: "[Y]ou have a President who is a hell of a lot better President than he's getting credit for being. Secondly, he's doing things for which he receives not only no credit, but no attention." Connally stirred his audience most when he urged that someone do something about the President's awkward thrusting up of his arms and giving the V-for-Victory signal with his fingers. The other presidential aides thought Connally was the only one who could tell Nixon to stop the gesture.[32]

The quest to shape the President's image as he wanted it continued throughout the Nixon presidency, amid success and amid disaster. In the days of the "global village," of course, public relations are an inevitable aspect of politics. But in this case it may have come too late. The nation knew Richard Nixon after his more than two decades in public life; its perception of him had long since crystallized. Shortly after he attended the Blair House gathering, Leonard Garment told Ehrlichman he thought it futile to project the President as anything other than what he was. Instead he suggested that the President simply continue to act responsibly, and with a little luck, he would persuade voters in 1972 on the critical issue: "Has the President managed the corpus of Presidential trust through four incredibly difficult years so that it is not impaired?"[33] Unfortunately, the President and his campaign advisers had far more complicated and grandiose plans for persuading the electorate.

The perception which Nixon and his staff had of the Cabinet involved a conviction that its officers were captives of their own bureaucracies. "We don't need an army of bureaucrats," the President told Haldeman in 1971. Nixon's tones were more bellicose in a complaint to Ehrlichman in April 1973: "We have no discipline in this bureaucracy. We never fire anybody. We never reprimand anybody. We never demote anybody. We always promote the sons-of-bitches that kick us in the ass." A few weeks earlier, Ehrlichman recorded a typical Nixon expression: "Burocracy [sic] fighting us." The President and his aides were by then under increasing fire as a result of Watergate revelations; indeed, Ehrlichman would resign in less than two weeks. But the sentiments were familiar ones for Nixon in other contexts. From the earliest biography to his own memoirs, Nixon repeated a set refrain about his own experience as a bureaucrat in the Office of Price Administration in 1942. That service "disillusioned" him about the bureaucracy, revealed the "mediocrity" of civil servants, and taught him about the "old, violent New Deal crowd" that was out "to GET business" and used government for that purpose. He deplored bureaucratic waste and "empire-building." The refrain became an article of faith. As Vice President, he often talked about removing entrenched New Dealers and Democrats who threatened Republican goals.[34]

Venting hostility toward the bureaucracy has, of course, always been a convenient safety valve for political frustration. "What is a bureaucrat?" Senator Alben Barkley mockingly asked in 1948. "It is a Democrat who has some job a Republican wants." At a meeting in August 1970, Senator Barry Goldwater berated the President for not having control of the government. Goldwater insisted that Nixon had not changed governmental policies in accordance with his 1968 mandate, and urged prompt firings and transfers. Two years later, a young White House aide bitterly complained that the President did not run the bureaucracy: "the civil service and the unions do. It took him three years to find out what was going on in the bureaucracy."

John F. Kennedy's aide and biographer, Arthur M. Schlesinger, Jr., recalled many instances of his and Kennedy's frustration in getting the bureaucracy to respond to policy directives. Schlesinger claimed that he spent three years unsuccessfully trying to persuade the State Department to stop using outmoded references to the "Sino-Soviet Bloc." More generally, he observed that "the President used to divert himself with the dream of establishing a secret office of thirty people or so to run foreign policy while maintaining the State Department as a facade in which people might contentedly carry papers from bureau to bureau." (Ironically, that was precisely the system that Nixon and Kissinger installed.) Schlesinger saw the problem in broad institutional terms: "Kennedy, who had been critical of the Eisenhower effort to institutionalize the Presidency," Schlesinger wrote, "was determined to restore the personal character of the office and recover presidential control over the sprawling feudalism of government."

Finally, Schlesinger almost despaired "of making the permanent government responsive to the policies of the presidential government." In fairness, he admitted that the problem cut two ways: "The aggressiveness of the White House staff no doubt compounded the trouble"; furthermore, "White House meddling struck some of the pros as careless intrusion by impulsive and ignorant amateurs."[35]

Bureaucracy had thrived amid the putatively hostile, antibureaucratic Republican atmosphere of the 1950s. In fact, the relaxed *laissez faire* managerial style that characterized much of the Eisenhower Administration heightened the power, even autonomy, of the government's components. The Kennedy and Johnson presidential assistants changed that, as Schlesinger observed, haranguing bureau chiefs, demanding action and movement in the President's name.

Nixon and his entourage placed a premium on loyalty from below. In this, their expectation was no different from that of other administrations—and it probably was similarly fruitless. Various instances that involved the Nixon Administration's insistence on bureaucratic loyalty only further exposed a general pattern of behavior. When the Pentagon eliminated the position of a prominent "whistle blower" as an "economy measure," Butterfield was elated. He told Haldeman that while the man was "no doubt a top-notch cost expert, . . . he must be given very low marks in loyalty; and after all, loyalty is the name of the game." When several lower-level State Department officers quietly circulated an internal memorandum protesting the Cambodian invasion in 1970, Alexander Haig, then Kissinger's deputy, demanded that the men "be separated" or be reassigned "to field duties where they may be subjected to the kind of discipline that seems to be missing from their Washington assignments." The President himself complained that "lower echelons" of the State and Defense Department bureaucracies had "deliberately" attempted to sabotage his policies. He asked his closest advisers "to give consideration as to how we can get better discipline with the bureaucracy." Through it all, of course, Nixon disclaimed any desire to "censor" the views of others.[36]

The White House staff moved beyond occasional intrusions and oversight procedures directed toward the bureaucracy by seeking direct and operational control of policy-making, often at the price of creating a parallel system of personnel and activity. Kissinger's expansion of his role as National Security Adviser is the most obvious case, although by 1973 John Ehrlichman's Domestic Council had developed the same tendency. When Nixon spoke to Richard Kleindienst after Kleindienst became Attorney General, the President's "talking points" paper noted: "From time to time I'll give you *policy guidance* through the Domestic council staff. I expect it to be complied with; if you object to it I expect to hear back from you *at once* via the same channel. I won't have subtle diversion of my instruction by a dissenting bureaucracy." The President also emphasized that he would insist on having "reliable men," cleared by the White House, in subordinate positions. The "administrative presidency," born and nurtured in previous administrations, matured significantly in the Nixon years.[37]

Richard Nixon and his advisers were convinced that the bureaucracy was another form of the enemy within. The opposition controlled Congress, the bureaucracy's natural ally. The two quite naturally resisted Nixon policies, which threatened the programs of one and the existence of the other. Contemporary studies did show a high degree of ideological hostility to the Nixon Administration in the upper strata of the civil service. As a practical matter, however, bureaucrats under Nixon did what they always did, even when not ideologically hostile to the Chief Executive: they fought for position and a share of power and often settled on the basis of mutually satisfactory group bargains.[38] That was not the game favored by the President and his men. And as the White House staff grew, that bureaucratic structure, with its own subunits, confronted the myriad of established bureaucracies scattered throughout the government, giving a new dimension to jurisdictional warfare.

The tale of the Huston Plan offers a variety of insights into Nixon's desire for personal control of matters he considered sensitive, the Administration's plans for the bureaucracy, and the latter's counterattacks. Perhaps most important of all, the story offers a revealing indication of the Administration's contempt for constitutional limitations.

The Huston Plan bore the name of Tom Charles Huston, a second-echelon White House aide. Huston, a former national leader in Young Americans for Freedom, was a deeply committed right-wing ideologue who sometimes signed his memos "Cato the Younger." He proposed to gather all domestic intelligence activities under his direction in the White House. According to fellow aide John Dean, Huston believed the government would surely fall if it did not deal harshly with the revolutionaries who were determined to destroy it.[39] Reflected in the plan was a combination of White House frustration at the alleged inefficiency of the intelligence community with a desire to have that community focus on activities that affected the Administration's political concerns.

Tom Huston wrote the details, but the CIA Director had no illusions about their ultimate source: the plan, Richard Helms said, was "basically Richard Nixon's doing, and he called it the Huston Plan." The idea logically followed from Nixon's law-and-order campaign theme in 1968. For some, providing order meant putting an end to protest, demonstrations, and dissent—whatever the constitutional legitimacy of those political activities. That conviction was rooted in a longstanding American belief, first heard in response to political protests in the late 1790s and continuing through the Cold War, that dissent was necessarily something nourished abroad to foment subversion and hence destruction at home. James Madison once lamented that "the loss of liberty at home is to be charged to the provisions against dangers, real or pretended, from abroad."

Nixon himself, of course, was not unfamiliar with such notions. Throughout the years of antiwar activism, a theme of the response from the Right was that the protests were inspired and fueled in Moscow, Hanoi, or Peking. J. Edgar Hoover, in his forty-fifth year as Director of the Federal Bureau of Investigation when Nixon assumed office, already had in place COINTELPRO, an elaborate program of infiltration and disinformation against the so-called New Left. Still the protests mounted, eventually provoking the President to demand greater efforts to discredit the dissidents.

As a Nixon aide throughout the protests of the 1960s, Tom Huston shared the President's concerns. In February 1970, he first proposed fundamental changes in the procedures for handling internal-security matters. He suggested separating the collection and evaluation of intelligence from the formulation of policy based on that intelligence. In short, Huston recognized that as a result of the commingling of those functions, "responsibility is divorced from authority and . . . roadblocks are institutionalized." Vested bureaucratic interests had their own agendas, often quite different from those of the President. Huston frankly thought that "the bureaucracy must be treated as the enemy; . . . in the pursuit of facts one must be prepared to harass, brow-beat, do whatever is necessary to get the desired information. On the other [hand], in the formulation of policy, the bureaucracy must be courted and treated gently."

Huston pushed hard for an interagency working group, "chaired by the White House," to coordinate intelligence in the internal-security area. Huston told Egil Krogh, another young lawyer concerned with law-and-order issues, that the "President's interest" in discrediting Students for a Democratic Society, the Black Panthers, and other activist groups simply was not being served by the Department of Justice—which meant the FBI. Krogh agreed, telling Haldeman that Justice was "almost blind to opportunities which could help us." Krogh thought that Huston should be sent as a "special assistant" to Mitchell to review internal-security matters and recommend political courses of action to the Attorney General. Perhaps then, Krogh added, the Department of Justice might "work for the President."

Huston devised his interagency scheme, to be directed by a White House staff man, with a "clear and unequivocal Presidential mandate" for "decisive leadership" in order to provide the President "with the best and most timely intelligence possible." It was a self-directed job description. Properly, he protected the President, suggesting that Nixon merely brief the heads of intelligence agencies orally, thus eliminating "whatever risk might attach to putting on paper the President's concern in this area."[40]

On June 5, 1970, Nixon met with the directors of various intelligence agencies: the FBI, the CIA, the Defense Intelligence Agency, and the National Security Agency. He criticized their overlapping activities and jurisdictions, and he demanded that they reorganize to provide him with one informed body of opinion on domestic political intelligence. He named Hoover as Chairman of the group—first among equals, so to speak—and installed Tom Huston as "staff director." Perhaps the President was aware of Huston's experience in Army Intelligence; more likely, he had been impressed with Huston's earlier performance in prodding the Internal Revenue Service to audit Administration enemies. He had known Huston for five years and undoubtedly trusted him to carry out his intentions. Another participant in the June 5 meeting found the President clear: "We must develop a plan which will enable us to curtail the illegal activities of those who are determined to destroy our society."

The selection of Hoover was a paradox, for the Huston Plan in some measure had its origins in White House dissatisfaction with the Director's performance; indeed, some believed that he was at best an anachronism. Helms thought that Hoover's lack of aggressiveness in recent years had prompted the President to have the White House assume operational control of domestic intelligence activities.[41] Perhaps Nixon and his aides thought that by naming Hoover chairman they could coopt him.

Nixon and Hoover had been both tacit and overt political allies for more than two decades and were social friends as well. Following his election, Nixon told Hoover that he was to have "direct access" to the Oval Office, and that Attorney General–designate John Mitchell—supposedly Hoover's superior—had been so informed. A few weeks later, LBJ told Nixon that he must depend on "Edgar" to "maintain security." Put your "complete trust" in him, Johnson advised. Nixon needed little prompting, for he had forged a close bond with Hoover since his service on the House Un-American Activities Committee in the 1940s. Hoover had kept up the contact, providing Nixon with information throughout the latter's "wilderness years."

Shortly after he took office, Nixon asked Hoover to investigate his own longtime political mentor, Murray Chotiner.[42]

By 1969, however, Hoover struck some Nixon staffers as an outmoded relic, a bureaucrat stubbornly clinging to his place, afraid to move in new directions. Ehrlichman, for example, complained of the poor quality of FBI investigations and even had the audacity—he claimed—to return FBI reports to Hoover when he considered them inadequate. Hoover, for his part, registered shock at White House requests that he considered unwise and even dangerous. Much of the difficulty probably was due to Hoover's declining energies; he preferred to consolidate his empire and not open it to further assaults. Hoover no longer could be counted on to meet CIA or White House demands for actions that, if carried out and subsequently revealed, might have irreparably harmed his beloved Bureau. Consequently, he refused requests for mail openings, break-ins, wiretaps, and campus infiltrations.

Hoover's finely attuned political antennae remained intact; indeed, they operated far better than those of the White House. Given the heightened judicial and public consciousness of the importance of maintaining rigorous constitutional standards, Hoover recognized that the operations favored by the White House threatened problems for the President—and not least of all, for "his" Bureau and for himself. Techniques that infringe on traditional rights, he told Helms, "must therefore be scrutinized most carefully."

Huston's implicit instruction was to bypass the recalcitrant Hoover and provide an intelligence-gathering apparatus that would serve the President's will more effectively. Huston was aided by the ambitious William Sullivan, third in the FBI's hierarchy and a possible successor to the Director. When the various intelligence directors met to consider the President's request for a reorganized domestic intelligence effort, Hoover said that he believed the President wanted "a historical study" of intelligence operations and present security problems. Huston smelled a Hoover ploy of delay and obfuscation. "We're not talking about the dead past," the President's aide said, "we're talking about the living present." Huston got his plan (with Sullivan's help), including the creation of a permanent interagency committee to develop new intelligence policies, and including a range of surveillance activities such as mail openings, burglaries, and infiltration. "The President loves this stuff," Mitchell told John Dean, adding, however, that it really was unnecessary, presumably because such activities already were in place.[43]

The new domestic intelligence committee needed an aide who would serve as the President's liaison, much in the fashion of Henry Kissinger at the National Security Council. Tom Huston was the obvious choice, but he had made a dangerous enemy for himself. He was not the first man whose ambitions outstripped J. Edgar Hoover's vision of what must be.

When the Huston Plan went to the President in July, Hoover managed to insert numerous footnotes disassociating the FBI from the plan's proposals. The fact that he challenged the report on civil liberties grounds must have stunned White House officials. Hoover noted that mail openings were illegal, that the FBI opposed "surreptitious entry," and that military agents were prohibited from engaging in domestic intelligence operations. Hoover feared that "jackels" [sic] of the press and the American Civil Liberties Union would discover the operations and embarrass the Administration. He flatly opposed allowing a presidential aide to coordinate domestic intelligence activities "in the same manner as Dr. Henry Kissinger."

The plan was dead, despite Huston's bitter fulminations to Haldeman. Nixon knew Hoover: if the plan proceeded, it would be only a matter of time before the press became aware of the Administration's expanded operations. The President protected himself in classic fashion; he approved the plan, he said, but insisted that Huston sign the necessary orders. Helms, for one, believed that Nixon fully supported the plan but would never do so openly. The various intelligence chiefs responded to Huston's name with scorn and ridicule, scoffing at Nixon and Haldeman, who "didn't have the guts" to sign the directive for the plan themselves. There was no way that intelligence officers would carry out such bold proposals on the basis of Huston's signature.

Hoover was more direct: he warned Mitchell that he would insist on the President's signature for any activity that might be illegal. Mitchell saw the danger and informed the President. Two weeks after his initial approval, Nixon ordered the plan scuttled. And in the meantime, Hoover remained free to conduct the "dirty war" against subversion, in a fashion not too different from that proposed by Huston, but on J. Edgar Hoover's terms.

Hoover's victory only heightened the White House antagonism toward him. Ehrlichman concluded that Hoover was an "embarrassment" and gave Nixon a report written in the fall of 1971 by G. Gordon Liddy, another aide, concluding that Hoover should resign. Nixon thought the memorandum "brilliantly argued," and agreed that Hoover must go. The President confronted the Director in a White House meeting in October and obliquely hinted, "as gently and subtly as I could," that he feared attacks on Hoover from outside critics would increase and force him to leave under pressure. Nixon had a talking paper, proposing that Hoover become "a consultant to the President," with his own office, car, and driver, after the 1972 elections. Hoover understood the hint and let the President know he would be glad to step aside—any time the President so asked. Nixon appreciated the master stroke: it was the same tactic he had used on Dwight Eisenhower during the fund crisis in the 1952 election. Richard Nixon, the champion of law and order, could hardly ask the Director of Law and Order to resign.

Perhaps the President was not a "good butcher," as he later remarked about another situation; perhaps, too, he remembered how and why Hoover refrained from publicizing possibly embarrassing information. Nixon later acknowledged that the meeting was a "strike-out," for him. Certainly it was not for Hoover, who walked away with his empire and throne more secure than ever. Apparently Nixon had some concern regarding Hoover's disloyal subordinate William Sullivan, as he suggested to Ehrlichman that they give him "a judgeship or something as [the] price for silence." Sullivan, however, died from a gunshot wound, apparently self-inflicted, shortly after the Huston Plan was exposed two years later.

There was also a reward for Huston, for a year later the President appointed him to the Census Bureau Advisory Committee on Privacy and Confidentiality.[44] The irony was probably unintentional.

Hoover died shortly after the defeat of the Huston Plan, in May 1972. Nixon returned from the funeral, announced that the new FBI building would be named in Hoover's honor, and ordered the Acting Director, L. Patrick Gray, to bring Hoover's files to the White House. It developed that they were gone; supposedly, Hoover's secretary got there first.[45]

With Nixon, Hoover won his usual battles over his prerogatives and authority, but the nation lost the constitutional war. Although the Huston Plan was officially abandoned, its measures were used in a variety of forms, the most extreme being the creation of the Special Investigative Unit, more familiarly known as the "Plumbers." Ostensibly established to determine the source of new leaks from inside the Administration, the Plumbers graduated to "black bag jobs" and illegal entries. The linkage between the official scuttling of the Huston Plan and the Plumbers is curiously mixed. Some argued—most notably, William Sullivan—that killing the plan led to the creation of the Plumbers, to mounting similar enterprises, and thus, to Watergate. Ehrlichman said that the inability of the White House to get rid of Hoover necessitated finding "other ways of doing things." Huston heatedly denied that his plan offered a model for the Plumbers and other Watergate-related enterprises, yet he conceded that if Hoover had gone along with the plan, the Administration would have never had to do its own "black-bag jobs."[46]

Public revelation of the failed Huston Plan in May 1973 contributed to the President's deteriorating public standing, and Senator Sam Ervin used it with great effect to describe the "Gestapo mentality" of the White House. Several months earlier, in February 1973, the President nostalgically yearned for the helping hand of J. Edgar Hoover. Nixon told John Dean that he was certain Hoover would have protected him. "He would have fought. That was the point. He would have defied a few people. He would have scared them to death. He had a file on everybody," the President remarked, rather wistfully.[47]

V

"I WANT IT DONE, WHATEVER THE COST."

ENEMIES, PLUMBERS, TAPS, AND SPIES

As 1970 drew to a close, Richard Nixon, as was his custom, prepared a list of goals for the future and made random notes that left tracings of his moods. His writing offered an idealized version of himself and his Administration, a view he ardently sought to impose on the nation, his entourage, and history.

Nixon wrote about his programs to end the Vietnam war, to attain arms control or to increase the defense budget, to restore law and order, to implement a scheme for revenue-sharing, and to "restore pride in America." His agenda, he believed, could be fulfilled only if his staff presented the "facts" about him, such as:

1. The success of Cambodia—President's courage
2. The "open" White House
3. Dignity and respect—at home and abroad
4. Effective handling of Press Conferences—TV
5. Warmth in personal relations with staff & people
6. Handling of world leaders
7. Takes attacks by Press et al—without flapping
8. Hard work
9. Listens to different views

A week later, sitting in the Lincoln Room at night, Nixon wrote about his need for a "definite image." His introspection led him to prepare a catalogue of traits and self-descriptions, one which he undoubtedly wanted projected on his behalf: "compassionate, humane, fatherly, warmth, confidence in future, optimistic, upbeat, candor, honesty, openness, trustworthy, boldness, fights for what he believes, vitality, youth, enjoyment, zest, vision, dignity, respect, a man people can be proud of, hard work, dedication, openmindedness, listens to opposing views, unifier, fairness to opponents, end bombast, hatred, division, moral leader, nation's conscience, intelligent, reasonable, serenity, calm, brevity, avoid familiarity, excitement, novelty, glamour, strength, spiritual, concern for the problems of the poor, youth, minorities, and average persons." All this seemed to represent the image for a "visible presidential leadership." His prefatory theme was "don't let them dominate the dialogue."[1]

For much of Nixon's first term, he and his aides labored to portray him as the President he believed himself, or desired, to be. And to a great extent, that was the President that the media reported and projected. Richard Nixon had his detractors and perennial critics, but neither they nor the American public had any sense or proof of a darker side to him or to the acts of his Administration. That "underside," as J. Anthony Lukas aptly described it, operated silently, and unmistakably pointed toward the disintegration of the Nixon presidency.

The Huston Plan involved structural arrangements that would impose the President's personal direction on fragmented bureaucracies. There was more to the plan than power for power's sake, however. The plan and its formulators, encouraged by the President, reflected a concern for neutralizing, and in a few cases destroying, political opposition. The White House view of its "enemies" eventually lengthened to include not only antiwar activists but also those who operated within the traditional framework of political conflict. The Huston Plan was only one corner of a more general design for dealing with political enemies of all kinds. Enemies would be fought by intervening directly in the government's bureaucratic machinery and using it—or, as often was the case, the fight would bypass the usual channels to implement illegal operations.

Less than three months into the first term, John Ehrlichman had hired John Caulfield, a former New York City policeman, to establish a White House "investigations unit." Caulfield had been a Nixon bodyguard in 1968, and Haldeman assigned him to Ehrlichman after the election. Caulfield's ostensible job was to serve as liaison with the Secret Service and local police units, but he eagerly plunged into the task of investigating Senator Edward Kennedy and the Chappaquiddick accident of 1969, in which Kennedy drove a car into the water, drowning a female companion. Caulfield's first recommendation about the case was to exploit Kennedy's delay in reporting the accident as precluding the prompt administering of last rites, thus damaging

Kennedy among Catholics. Ehrlichman had earlier prodded Harry Dent to have reporters friendly to Nixon question Kennedy for his views on busing, compulsory integration, amnesty for war resisters, and student revolts. Given Nixon's obsession with the Kennedys, the President was eager to learn more about the Chappaquiddick incident. In August 1969, Nixon told Ehrlichman that Kissinger had some "fascinating" information on the subject, and the President told his aide to have the story checked out and "properly exploited."[2] The concern with Kennedy was only the most obvious White House pursuit of its "enemies."

In August 1971, White House Counsel John Dean prepared a rationale for developing and maintaining what came to be known as the "enemies list." The memo, Dean later claimed, was prepared at the request of Haldeman and Ehrlichman. This may well have been true, but Dean was not without his own enthusiasm for the task. The idea of the enemies list was, as Dean put it, to "maximize the fact of our incumbency in dealing with persons known to be more active in their opposition to our Administration." More bluntly, this involved the use of "the available federal machinery to screw our political enemies." No "elaborate mechanism" or "game plan" was needed, Dean said. Key staff members (Colson, Dent, Buchanan) could provide names. Then the "project coordinator" would determine how the White House "can best screw them." He would, of course, have "access to and the full support" of top officials throughout the Administration. Dean thought that Lyn Nofziger (another White House aide) would "enjoy" being project coordinator, but he warned that there must be "support at the top."

Within a month, Charles Colson provided a modest list of twenty names. Senator Edmund Muskie's chief fundraiser and the AFL-CIO's political director headed the list. Colson also included a top aide to New York Mayor John Lindsay—"a first class S.O.B."; black Congressman John Conyers—who had a "known weakness for white females"; Daniel Schorr of CBS—"a real media enemy"; actor Paul Newman—who was involved in "Radic-Lib causes"; and Maxwell Dane, who headed an advertising firm that "destroyed Goldwater in '64."

While Dean thought it worthwhile to add a few names every so often, he urged that the enemies list be kept "within reasonable bounds." But the number quickly grew to over two hundred as others in the Administration chimed in with their favorite enemies, now taking in institutions as well as individuals. Included were not only obvious political opponents, such as Kennedy, Muskie, and Senator Walter Mondale, but also the presidents of leading universities and foundations, the National Education Association, and, for some reason never determined, the National Cleaning Contractors. Movie stars, newspaper columnists, television newsmen, and even football quarterback Joe Namath made the list that would in time be considered an honor roll. Dean later told Senate investigators that the enemies list was merely "an exercise" which he had no intention of acting on, although he contended that Haldeman and Colson used it. Some time later, Alexander Butterfield complained to Dean that several people had come to a White House function despite being on the "Do Not Admit Under Any Circumstances" list—suggesting that Dean had a role as enforcer of the list.[3]

Colson later insisted that he had no knowledge of an "enemies list," only a roster his office compiled in order to keep undesirables away from White House functions. That comment was at odds with Dean's original memo, however, as well as with subsequent events. It also was at odds with a larger folder among Colson's papers, entitled "Blacklist." The file revealed that Colson had his own "enemies list" well underway before Dean launched his. Colson included businessmen, entertainment personalities, labor leaders, political figures, academics, and organizations. He had a record of people who had attended a certain Democratic fundraiser. A Colson aide prepared her own "Bad Guys List" but later eliminated some names as "not that bad." Tom Huston offered his own roll, headed by "Think Tanks." Colson ordered his staff to garner the names of those who signed ads against the Vietnam war, and he added to the enemies lists one of his antagonists in the Teamsters Union, a group for which he ardently lobbied.[4]

Haldeman selected a number of people on the various lists for IRS audits and other forms of harassment. *Washington Post* lawyer Edward Bennett Williams was targeted. Williams at first regarded the attention as a "badge of honor"; on more sober reflection, he realized how dangerous it was to have the "President of the United States obsessed with the idea of wreaking some kind of revenge against me." The IRS audited him for three consecutive years.

Nixon later candidly acknowledged his own involvement in such harassment. He "hit the ceiling," he recalled, when he learned that the IRS had audited John Wayne and Billy Graham. He told his aides: "Get the word out, down to the IRS, that I want them to conduct field audits of those who are our opponents, if they're going to do in our friends." He immediately suggested Democratic National Chairman Larry O'Brien as a target.[5]

The White House staff followed the President's command with a vengeance. On July 1, 1969, a call from Huston to the IRS Commissioner's assistant resulted in the creation of the Special Services Staff (SSS) at the IRS, a group that would, as Huston suggested, investigate dissident, leftist political organizations. Patrick Buchanan thought that the IRS should investigate the liberal political activities of such bodies as the Ford Foundation and the Brookings Institution. In a memo to Nixon on March 3, 1970, Buchanan argued that the foundations' tax exemptions created an "institutionalized power of the left" to "succor the Democratic party."

By September 1970, the SSS had compiled information on more than 1,000 institutions and 4,000 individuals. Other staffers, however, remained dissatisfied and urged the IRS to widen its net. Intelligence organizations within the Justice Department, the Secret Service, and the military added another 2,000 groups and 4,000 individuals for the IRS to study. The White House strongly believed that IRS commissioners could not be trusted to carry out its will and assigned John Caulfield to work with Vernon Acree, the IRS Assistant Commissioner for Inspection, to stimulate activity. Dean at one point passed on instructions that Caulfield should secure an audit of a newspaper reporter who had written a series of stories on the activities of presidential crony Bebe Rebozo. But Dean failed to persuade the IRS to investigate presidential candidate George McGovern's staff and contributors.

At Colson's suggestion, Dean also directed Caulfield to investigate the tax-exemption status of a number of liberal lobbying groups. Colson thought it wrong to grant exemption to those who "lobby against the Government." In fact, Colson meant the Administration; he had no intention of invoking similar measures against foundations or corporations that criticized general government policies. White House pressure probably resulted in the denial of tax-exempt status for the Center for Corporate Responsibility in May 1973. Caulfield surreptitiously gained access to IRS internal reports and passed word to Dean that there had been no purposeful harassment of John Wayne or Billy Graham, whose audits had prompted a special presidential complaint. Meanwhile, the President was particularly interested in expediting the IRS's investigation of the tax returns of Alabama Governor George Wallace's brother.[6]

The White House worked hard on IRS Commissioner Johnnie Walters, diligently seeking to make him subservient to its political needs. Haldeman told Dean in 1971 that he should discuss IRS investigative matters with Walters and Treasury Secretary John Connally. Dean later prepared a memorandum for Haldeman, based on information provided by Caulfield, outlining the Administration's criticisms of and expectations for Walters and the IRS. Caulfield complained that IRS was "a monstrous bureaucracy . . . dominated and controlled" by Democrats. The Service had been too "unresponsive and insensitive" to the White House. Commissioner Walters, Caulfield noted, appeared "oversensitive" in his concern that IRS actions might be labeled political. That had to change, Dean said. Specifically, Dean told Haldeman that Walters "must be made to know that discreet political actions and investigations on behalf of the administration are a firm requirement and responsibility on his part. We should have direct access to Walters for action in the sensitive areas and should not have to clear them with Treasury." Finally, the inevitable rationale: the Democrats "used [IRS] most effectively. We have been unable." Caulfield had also urged that Dean be given "access and assurances" that Walters would accomplish what was expected.[7]

As his first term ended, the President continued to complain about the unresponsiveness of the IRS. He believed that the IRS had leaked his own returns in 1952, and he remembered his own tax audits in 1961 and 1962—harassment, he called them. He told Ehrlichman in August 1972 that he had not pursued his opponents with tax audits because he had "no mandate." But for the next term, things would be different, he promised. He wanted, he said, full control of subcabinet officials in the IRS and the FBI, as well as the Treasury and Justice departments. He instructed Ehrlichman to remove all IRS appointees after the election. A month after his re-election, the President harped on the same themes and suggested that John Dean work directly on some sensitive tax cases, ones that Treasury Secretary George Shultz was reluctant to pursue.[8]

President Nixon and his men also considered direct action, less subtle and including physical force, against "enemies." During antiwar demonstrations in Washington in May 1971, Haldeman told the President that Charles Colson would use his connections with the Teamsters' Union and hire some "thugs" to attack the protesters. Haldeman's enthusiasm was unmistakable: "Murderers. Guys that really, you know, that's what they really do. Like . . . the regular strikebusters-type and all that . . . and then they're gonna beat the [obscenity] out of some of these people. And, uh, and hope they really hurt 'em." Nixon enthusiastically chimed in: those "guys" would "go in and knock their [the demonstrators'] heads off." His contempt was obvious: "These people try something, bust 'em," he added. Haldeman also emphasized the public-relations concern, noting that the television networks had shown some "good footage" of the unruly mobs. Nixon was anxious that the demonstrators be caught attacking the flag or carrying one upside down. Haldeman was pleased that the convicted ringleaders of the 1968 Chicago demonstrations had been involved in the current protests. "Aren't the Chicago Seven all Jews?" the President asked. (They were not.)

The two men had a wide-ranging discussion of political "dirty tricks" that various aides had organized. Haldeman mentioned that Dwight Chapin, the President's appointments secretary, had been in touch with "a guy that . . . we're going to use . . . for the campaign next year." The man—undoubtedly Donald Segretti—already had worked against Senator Muskie, then considered to be Nixon's most likely opponent in 1972. Nixon and Haldeman were particularly pleased and amused by Colson's attempts to disrupt Muskie's campaign. Haldeman, with obvious relish, reported that Colson had "got a lot done that he hasn't been caught at." Nixon and Haldeman laughed throughout the exchange. But in that compartmentalized White House world, Haldeman was equally glad to report that "we got some stuff that he [Colson] doesn't know anything about, too."[9]

Walter Bagehot, the astute nineteenth-century British commentator on government and constitutionalism, said that there are arguments for having a royal court and there are arguments for having a splendid court, but there could be no argument for having a mean court.

Richard Nixon knew how Vietnam policy leaks had plagued the last years of Lyndon Johnson's presidency. Nixon recalled Johnson as first "frustrated, then angered, and, finally, nearly obsessed by the need to stop them." The description aptly describes Nixon's own subsequent behavior: "I soon learned that his concerns were fully justified," Nixon wrote. Within five months of taking office, Nixon recalled, he counted at least twenty-one major news stories apparently derived from National Security Council leaks. The subject of leaks infuriated the President, especially after the publication of the Pentagon Papers in June 1971. "You're going to be my Lord High Executioner from now on," Nixon told Haldeman then. The President instructed his aide to order a loyalty test for every State Department employee, an instruction that Haldeman immediately placed on the "no-action-ever" list he kept in his mind. Charles Colson reported the President as saying: "I don't give a damn how it is done, do whatever has to be done to stop these leaks and prevent further unauthorized disclosures; I don't want to be told why it can't be done. This government cannot survive, it cannot function, if anyone can run out and leak whatever documents he wants to. . . . I want to know who is behind this and I want the most complete investigation that can be conducted. . . . I don't want excuses. I want results. I want it done, whatever the cost." [10]

Haldeman assigned Caulfield to find the source of leaks to columnist Jack Anderson. Caulfield uncovered possible links to Anderson from Senator Hugh Scott, the Republican leader, and his staff, as well as from some people in the Office of Management and Budget. When OMB Director George Shultz complained about the investigations, they stopped. Caulfield recommended to Haldeman that "an overt firing" of a person responsible for leaks would be a valuable deterrent. [11]

The President's concerns had some validity, of course. Leaks pertaining to bargaining positions in negotiations with foreign countries certainly could weaken the government's posture. Not all leaks are dangerous, however: what is inimical to the concern of the powerholders is not necessarily inimical to or inconsistent with the national interest. The revelations of the "secret bombing" of Cambodia were a case in point. But the Nixon Administration betrayed a concern for secrecy that transcended immediate issues of policy. In and out of office, Richard Nixon consistently was preoccupied with his place in history. To him, the control of information and documents was then—and continued to be—essential for ensuring a satisfactory standing at the bar of history. Perhaps nothing illustrated this better than the 1971 episode involving the White House's response to the publication of the Pentagon Papers.

On Sunday morning, June 13, 1971, the *New York Times* carried a front-page photograph of the President and his daughter Tricia, standing together in the Rose Garden following her wedding ceremony. The other side of the page carried the first installment of the ''Pentagon Papers,'' a 7,000-page document commissioned by Robert McNamara, Defense Secretary under Kennedy and Johnson. The study traced the origins of the American involvement in Vietnam and offered significant insight into decision-making processes in the foreign-policy and military establishments. Nothing better revealed how secrecy had served the cause of deception than the revelations in these papers. Melvin Laird, Nixon's Secretary of Defense, told the President that 98 percent of the Pentagon Papers could be declassified. But Nixon responded that ''the era of negotiations can't succeed w/o secrecy.''

Some Nixon staffers thought the publication harmless to their own interests and embarrassing only for the previous administration. Charles Colson immediately assigned his friend Howard Hunt the task of going through the papers to find unfavorable material on leading Democrats. Colson hoped that the papers would offer an opportunity to tie ''our political opposition into the enemy camp.'' A few days earlier, HUD Secretary George Romney made a public statement that he thought the government had a tendency to overclassify documents. Colson was infuriated and complained to Ehrlichman, demanding that Romney be reprimanded at a Cabinet meeting.[12]

The President later agreed with Colson. In September, he told Haldeman that the opposition had an interest in forgetting the papers, but ''ours is to play it up.'' Apparently, Colson had convinced him by then that the papers could be used to inflict political damage on the opposition. But when the newspapers first published the Pentagon Papers, Nixon (and Kissinger) knew better. They were aware that the publication of such secrets imperiled their own operations and created a precedent that could come back to haunt the protection of their own secrets. However tempting the political advantage of exposing chicanery in the opposition, Nixon realized that he ran the risk of exposing such deceptions as he also believed necessary for the pursuit of his own policies. Certainly, a major issue raised in the Pentagon Papers concerned deception and what one of their authors described as ''the crucial question of governmental credibility.'' Credibility was crucial for the current Administration at this moment especially: for the first time, a Gallup poll revealed that Americans wanted the war over ''even at the risk of an eventual Communist takeover of South Vietnam.''[13] Credibility was indeed at stake, since Nixon, as President, had increased the country's investment in the war.

The *Washington Post* soon joined in publishing the Pentagon Papers. Shortly afterward, Daniel Ellsberg, a former National Security Council operative with links to the CIA, was revealed as the source of the massive leak.

Ellsberg, once a hawk in the Kennedy and Johnson years, had turned against the war. Two weeks after publication of the papers, he acknowledged his complicity in their release. That admission put the issue of the war—its necessity, its wisdom, as well as its morality—squarely at the center of public attention.

John Ehrlichman later contended that Henry Kissinger fanned the President's passion on the Pentagon Papers issue. For Nixon, Ellsberg was a liberal antiwar intellectual who had leaked secrets; Kissinger, to be sure, shared those perceptions. But certainly, the President needed little guidance from Henry Kissinger. Nixon told Ehrlichman at one point that he would go "an extra mile to defend the security system to reassure China and friendly governments." Both Nixon and Kissinger realized the personal danger if any president lost control over classified documents and allowed them to be used to smear his predecessors. Moreover, for Nixon the whole incident was personal. "The *Times*'s decision to publish the documents," he later wrote, "was clearly the product of the paper's antiwar policy rather than a consistent attachment to principle."[14]

The topside of the Administration's response involved an attempt to obtain a court order enjoining the newspapers from continued publication of the Pentagon Papers. The strategy succeeded for a few weeks, as a lower court granted a temporary order and the Supreme Court sustained it pending further arguments. The Court immediately heard lawyers from both sides, however, and in a nearly unanimous opinion lifted the injunction and allowed the newspapers to proceed with publication. Significantly, the Court decisively rejected Solicitor General Erwin Griswold's argument that the release of the papers would affect lives, the recovery of Vietnam prisoners of war, and the peace process. Those considerations, he argued, had "such an effect on the security of the United States that [they] ought to be the basis of an injunction in this case." The Justices thought not, but their surface unanimity masked deep feelings. Some, like Justice Hugo Black, in what proved to be his final judicial opinion, bitterly assailed the Administration and the courts for permitting even a temporary injunction. Chief Justice Warren Burger dutifully defended the Administration, however, and Justice Byron White expressed biting contempt for Ellsberg's action and urged that the government prosecute him under the ordinary criminal statutes.

The Solicitor General had no opportunity to see the Pentagon Papers themselves, but after consulting with the State and Defense departments, he knew he had "no possible basis for objecting to the publication of the overwhelming proportion" of them. Griswold thought it a mistake to pursue the injunction proceedings, but he did not push this view hard, for he believed that Mitchell and Assistant Attorney General Robert Mardian had strong pressure from Nixon to proceed. "[I]t was plain to them," Griswold recalled, "that that's what the top man wanted. . . . [K]nowing Mr. Mitchell,

I knew that meant Nixon. [Mitchell] wouldn't take any decision from Ehrlichman or Haldeman or some of those people." Griswold thought that the case "came out exactly as it should." Eventually, the Administration brought criminal charges against Ellsberg (against Griswold's recommendation), but the proceeding ended in a mistrial—ironically, because of the Administration's own illegal behavior.[15]

One of the more bizarre by-products of the Pentagon Papers affair was a plan either to raid or to firebomb the Brookings Institution and to pilfer papers there belonging to Leslie Gelb and Morton Halperin, former National Security Council aides. These papers allegedly represented a Pentagon Papers analogue for the Nixon years. The Brookings plan has been described by three people: Ehrlichman, Dean, and Caulfield. All agreed that Charles Colson pushed the idea, but all asserted that Nixon inspired it. Caulfield testified that he talked to Colson after Colson had discussed the subject with "certain people" in the presidential entourage. Dean claimed that Nixon had demanded he obtain the Gelb-Halperin papers, and he also learned from Egil Krogh that White House people thought Dean had "some little old lady" in him because of his reluctance to go along with the plan. Dean claimed credit for thwarting the plan, but his rival John Ehrlichman insisted that he had blocked it. Only later, Ehrlichman wrote, did he learn that Nixon knew about the plan. Colson and Nixon, he claimed, had few secrets between them, but in his memoirs Colson never mentioned the subject. Meanwhile, John Dean was not so passive. He gave Krogh copies of the Brookings tax returns and proposed to "turn the spigot off" by revoking some of the institution's government contracts.[16]

The Pentagon Papers affair had a substantial impact. It energized the press and endowed it with a new confidence and sense of legitimacy, given its clear triumph over governmental secrecy. Claiming almost a co-equal status with governmental institutions, the media managed to identify themselves collectively as the people's paladin against the impersonal, devious forces of government. This constituted a further weakening of an already precarious popular faith in the efficacy of government and heightened the Administration's already substantial suspicions of the media. Thus, the Pentagon Papers incident intensified the adversarial relationship between the Administration and the media, a relationship that was to deteriorate still more sharply. These developments, together with a failure of the courts to provide the desired protection and relief demanded by the Administration, led directly to one of the most fateful decisions of the Nixon presidency: the creation of the Plumbers.

The Plumbers synthesized the concern of the White House for controlling and disciplining the bureaucracy, as well as its willingness to utilize illegal methods and abuses of power for doing so. The President himself left no doubt on this score. After the Pentagon Papers had been leaked in June 1971—almost exactly a year after Hoover had frustrated the grandiose Huston Plan—Nixon "wanted someone to light a fire under the FBI in its investigation of [Daniel] Ellsberg, and to keep the department and agencies active in pursuit of leakers. If a conspiracy existed, I wanted to know," Nixon wrote, "and I wanted the full resources of the government brought to bear in order to find out. If the FBI was not going to pursue the case, then we would have to do it ourselves. . . . I wanted a good political operative who could sift through the Pentagon Papers as well as State and Defense Department files and get us all the facts on the Bay of Pigs, the Diem assassination, and Johnson's bombing halt. . . . I wanted ammunition against the antiwar critics, many of whom were the same men who, under Kennedy and Johnson, had led us into the Vietnam morass in the first place." (Apparently Henry Kissinger did not hear the President. He later solemnly stated that "from the beginning Nixon thought it improper to place the blame for the Vietnam war on his predecessors.")

Haldeman and Colson heard the President's rage against leaks. John Ehrlichman also knew what the President wanted: "If we can't get anyone in this damn government to do something about the problem that may be the most serious one we have, then, by God, we'll do it ourselves," Nixon said. In 1969, he ordered Ehrlichman to establish "a little group right here in the White House. Have them get off their tails and find out what's going on and figure out how to stop it."

And thus the President of the United States called into being the Plumbers, a group specifically created to do what J. Edgar Hoover would not do without the validation of Nixon himself. According to Harry Dent, Lyndon Johnson told Nixon to rely on Hoover to cope with enemies within; but Hoover had failed his longtime friend Nixon. Five men connected to this group would go to jail for a specific crime committed in fulfillment of the President's wishes. One of them, Egil Krogh, later recalled being told by Ehrlichman (another of those convicted) that the President suggested he read the Hiss chapter in Nixon's book *Six Crises*. Dutifully carrying out the assignment, Krogh concluded that the President wanted him to proceed "with a zeal comparable to that he [Nixon] exercised . . . in investigating Alger Hiss." The President's wish, he added, "fired up and overshadowed every aspect of the unit's work." Krogh later said that Ehrlichman repeatedly instructed him that the President considered the unit's work "a matter of the highest national security and that I was under no circumstances to discuss it."[17]

Before his eventual recantation, Krogh publicly took a benign view of his task. The *Washington Post* first revealed the existence of the Plumbers in December 1972. A month later, Egil Krogh appeared before a Senate committee considering his nomination as Undersecretary of Transportation. The Plumbers, he said, had been organized merely to prevent unauthorized disclosures of classified information. His job consisted of developing "relationships" with other departments "to define the objectives of our work." The senators were passive and cordial; no one asked Krogh about methods and results. Ehrlichman, who served as the link between the President and the Plumbers, testified that the unit was established "to stimulate" the various executive departments to better control leaks and to "bring to account" the various security offices in sensitive agencies and get them to do a better job.[18]

There is no evidence, however, that the Plumbers either attempted or accomplished such goals; instead, their tasks centered on covert activities. Working under Ehrlichman, Krogh and David Young supervised the unit's operations, with an office in Room 16 of the basement of the Executive Office Building. Krogh, a lawyer and an Ehrlichman protégé from Seattle (he viewed Ehrlichman as a "father-figure"), had served in the White House in a variety of posts, chiefly centering on the Administration's antidrug measures and on District of Columbia affairs. Young had served with Kissinger as a Rockefeller retainer, and the two worked together on the National Security Council before Ehrlichman peremptorily recruited Krogh for his own needs.

Besides Krogh and Young, the unit's experienced operatives were E. Howard Hunt and G. Gordon Liddy, who had served intermittently in the CIA and the FBI respectively. Both were right-wing ideologues who had neither political nor moral qualms over using illegal methods against those they regarded as enemies of the state. Colson thought Liddy "excellent" and Hunt "very useful." He told Ehrlichman that Krogh had "a good investigative mechanism."

The Plumbers' most notorious venture involved Ehrlichman's verbal instructions to Krogh in mid-July 1971 to determine the causes, sources, and ramifications of the Pentagon Papers leaks. (The group's quaint name was coined when one member, David Young, told his mother-in-law that he was plugging leaks of sensitive information. She thought it was nice to have a plumber in the family.) The White House did not trust Hoover for the investigation because of his close relationship with Daniel Ellsberg's father-in-law; Young later confirmed the White House's belief that the "regular investigative agencies" were not completely reliable. Ehrlichman also told Krogh that the Administration would not use the CIA, because its jurisdiction was legally limited to operations abroad, and this was a domestic matter. (A somewhat exceptional adherence to scruples given the President's entanglement of the CIA with the Huston Plan and the collection of domestic intelligence. In fact, the CIA did get involved in the Plumbers' operations, by aiding its notorious alumnus Howard Hunt.) Krogh subsequently testified that his group had information that Ellsberg had accomplices in leaking the Pentagon Papers and that the Soviet Embassy had a copy of the papers prior to their publication. Ellsberg thoroughly commanded the Plumbers' attention, even to the point where their task became one of discrediting him as an antiwar spokesman rather than developing effective measures to protect national security.

Charles Colson had also been meeting with the President, Krogh, and Ehrlichman regarding Ellsberg. Colson saw Ellsberg as a target of opportunity to accomplish numerous goals. "To paint Ellsberg black is probably a good thing; to link him into a conspiracy which suggests treasonous conduct is also a good thing, but the real political payoff will come only if we establish that there is . . . a 'counter government' which is deliberately trying to undermine U.S. foreign policy and the U.S. position in the world and that it is the President who stands against this 'counter government,' " Colson told Ehrlichman. Colson could not resist the opportunity to link Ellsberg to the political opposition—"the enemy camp." Beyond that, Colson wanted to exploit the Pentagon Papers to discredit Kennedy and Johnson. He reported to Ehrlichman that Hunt was gathering "facts" regarding the "key targets," just as he had earlier done in an attempt to implicate President Kennedy in the assassination of South Vietnamese President Diem.[19]

Krogh meanwhile had received information that the FBI had interviewed Ellsberg's former psychiatrist, Dr. Lewis Fielding. The CIA had provided its own psychological profile of Ellsberg—much to the later regret of Richard Helms, who thought it necessary at that time to appease the President—but someone in the White House group decided that there might be more to learn about Ellsberg's behavior if Fielding's office could be raided to secure information. Young later told investigators that if they could get more data on Ellsberg's conduct, they could "discredit him as a nut." After much "soul-searching," Young joined Krogh in recommending action. Permission was granted to "engage in covert activity"—in other words, to burglarize Fielding's office and obtain his notes on Ellsberg. Ehrlichman signed off—with the President's knowledge, he later insisted. When Nixon and Ehrlichman had their last official meeting on May 2, 1973, the President asked if he, Ehrlichman, had known about the Fielding break-in earlier. Ehrlichman noted that he silently nodded, and Nixon replied: "If so, it made no impression." Colson indirectly supported Ehrlichman's claim that Nixon knew. Colson assumed, he testified, "that John Ehrlichman wouldn't take something like that upon his own shoulders."

In his memoirs, Nixon said he could not recall giving authorization for the Fielding break-in, but he acknowledged that "I cannot rule it out." He added that the break-in was not as wrong or as excessive as what Ellsberg did in copying and releasing the Pentagon Papers in the first place. Krogh, for his part, denied that he had any specific instructions from the President but acknowledged that Ehrlichman relayed the President's wishes—drawing a distinction that is anything but distinct. Krogh met with the President and Ehrlichman on July 24, 1971, a day after the *New York Times* revealed the Administration's "fallback" position in the pending Helsinki Strategic Arms Limitation (SALT) talks. Nixon was "deeply troubled," Krogh recalled, and demanded extensive polygraph tests throughout the government. He told Krogh that further leaks would not be allowed and made Krogh "feel personally responsible" for carrying out this assignment.[20]

In any event, the Fielding operation yielded nothing, leaving only destruction in the doctor's office to cover the burglary. Liddy and Hunt wanted to raid Fielding's apartment, but Krogh recommended against it. Ehrlichman agreed and ordered all such covert activity ended. After the incident became public in early 1973, the White House insisted repeatedly that the break-in was required by considerations of "national security." But Special Prosecutor Leon Jaworski later scoffed at the notion and demanded that the White House produce proof, not slogans. Ehrlichman desperately tried to persuade incoming Attorney General Elliot Richardson in April 1973 (as Ehrlichman himself was leaving the White House) that the President did not want Richardson to intrude into the "national-security" area. "I am confident," Ehrlichman told Richardson, "that this will seem to be an ephemeral thing."

David Young thought he was doing right for the President and the country, but he later feared that his action had prejudiced "national security beyond recognition." For his part, Krogh sadly acknowledged that the Fielding break-in "represented official Government action" and "struck at the heart" of government's responsibility to protect individual rights. In later years, after serving a jail sentence for his role in the event, Ehrlichman called this break-in the "seminal Watergate episode"; Krogh considered it far more significant than the Watergate break-in for demonstrating the Administration's commitment to illegal activities. Before that, however, Krogh recommended Liddy for a salary increase, and in December 1971 successfully supported him for the position of Legal Counsel to the Committee to Reelect the President.

At his trial for his part in the Fielding break-in, Ehrlichman testified that he considered the operation was an appropriate, "legal, conventional investigation"; the notion of an illegal break-in, he said, "didn't enter my thought process." He thought the act conventional because it was what the FBI regularly did. At the time of the break-in, however, Ehrlichman was not so distant and removed. Writing to Colson on August 27, 1971 regarding the "Hunt/Liddy Special Project #1," Ehrlichman said: "On the assumption that the proposed undertaking by Hunt and Liddy would be carried [out] and would be successful, I would appreciate receiving from you by next Wednesday a game plan as to how and when you believe the materials should be used." That "game plan" had nothing to do with national security;

instead, it was designed simply to discredit Daniel Ellsberg and the antiwar movement.

When Attorney General Richardson reviewed the Fielding operation in May 1973, he immediately recognized that it would be impossible to make any public distinction between it and the Watergate break-in. Both events, he realized, involved Hunt and Liddy, both were illegal, and both could be traced to the White House. He favored prompt disclosure if "the trail" led no further than Krogh and Young. Richardson had good reason for making that qualification. Charles Colson, who had consulted with the President on the project, pressed Richardson for an immediate dismissal of Ellsberg's court case. The presiding judge had requested affidavits from Hunt and Colson, and Colson feared they "would disclose [the] White House role and RMN[']s role." No wonder, then, that Richardson considered the "likelihood that [the] trial would lead further."[21] The information had already been relayed to the presiding judge in Daniel Ellsberg's criminal trial in April 1973, and the next month he declared a mistrial. The trail of "White House horrors" began to unfold. The Plumbers offered a vital link to Watergate, perhaps even a fatal one.

In one of the most shadowy episodes of the Nixon presidency, the art and practice of surveillance was turned against the Administration itself, a development that only heightened its sense of isolation and confirmed its belief in the strength of its enemies within. The episode centered on Yeoman Charles Radford's dual role—spying on the Administration for the Joint Chiefs of Staff, and allegedly leaking secrets to a journalist. The affair was uncovered in December 1971, but it remained sealed from public view until 1974.[22]

In December 1971, newspaper columnist Jack Anderson published language from several secret National Security Council memoranda regarding the Indo-Pakistani War and a possible American tilt toward Pakistan. Anderson subsequently received the Pulitzer Prize for his revelations. Several days later, Admiral Robert O. Welander, a Joint Chiefs liaison officer with the NSC, identified his assistant, Yeoman Radford, as the source of Anderson's material. Welander claimed that only he and Radford had access to the same documents. Both men often accompanied Kissinger and his deputy Alexander Haig on trips abroad (Radford was in the entourage during Kissinger's first secret trip to China) and worked near their offices in the White House. The White House ordered the FBI to tap Radford's telephone, hoping to uncover his ties to Anderson. Instead, the wiretap disclosed that Radford had been pilfering documents from Kissinger and the NSC files and turning them over to the Joint Chiefs of Staff. Radford eventually confessed that he had stolen perhaps a thousand documents from NSC files and burn bags and then delivered them to Welander, who served as middleman for Admiral Thomas Moorer, Chairman of the Joint Chiefs. Radford steadfastly denied he had leaked to Anderson.

The Radford revelations did not point to vague, shadowy "enemies" without—that is, the usual suspects: liberals, antiwar activists, media. Now, the enemy was within, an enemy thought to be an ally. Egil Krogh undoubtedly reflected insider thinking. He saw Radford's revelations as "an extremely serious matter." The *Seven Days in May* scenario of a military coup crossed his mind. "It was a question whether there was an actual move by the military into the deliberations of the duly-elected and appointed civilians to carry out foreign policy." Ehrlichman, David Young, and others, Krogh remembered, regarded the matter "extremely seriously at the time." Krogh also noted that the incident had never been disclosed in its entirety. One of his reasons for hesitating to reveal the Plumbers' role when that operation was uncovered in 1973 was that he feared it would inevitably lead to the unraveling of the Moorer-Radford affair.[23]

Military dissatisfaction with foreign and military policies obviously had been festering throughout the Vietnam war. Moorer bitterly remembered what he regarded as foolish and soft policies toward North Vietnam. His successor as Chief of Naval Operations, Admiral Elmo R. Zumwalt, Jr., came close to accusing Nixon and Kissinger of treason and Kissinger of being a Soviet sympathizer. He thought that Nixon's foreign-policy aide was eager to make any deal with the Soviets. Zumwalt flatly accused "the President, Henry Kissinger," and a few subordinates of deliberate deceit and concealment of policies—regarding détente, SALT, the Vietnam war, military strength levels—that were "inimical to the security of the United States."[24]

Moorer later testified at public hearings in 1974 and in interviews that he had no need of Radford's materials, claiming he regularly saw all top-secret NSC memoranda. He thought that Radford had conjured up the spying allegations as a smoke screen to divert attention from the fact that he had leaked to Anderson. He also believed that the affair fueled the White House's "paranoia." To be sure, someone—the President? Ehrlichman?—had ordered a Department of Defense investigation of Radford and one within the White House carried out by the Plumbers. Those reports remain buried.

The only public discussion of the Radford affair came in a desultory Senate Armed Services inquiry in 1974, artfully managed by Senator John Stennis (D–MS) to produce the least possible information. None of the principal investigators testified. Senator Stuart Symington (D–MO) wanted Ehrlichman called as a witness, but Stennis dodged on this. Defense Department Counsel J. Fred Buzhardt filed a report on the affair, but none of it was discussed. The hearing, in sum, dealt with few substantive issues, although several interesting tidbits filtered out. For example, Admiral Welander tes-

tified that Haig had arranged his meeting with David Young, indicating Haig
had knowledge of the Plumbers. (Curiously, according to Ehrlichman, Young
thought Haig was behind the whole spying effort.) At one point, Ehrlichman
prepared a confession for Welander to sign, but the admiral refused.

In the end, Welander was transferred to sea duty, and Radford was sent
to a coastal station in Oregon. Secretary of Defense Melvin Laird implemented these decisions, claiming to be following Buzhardt's recommendations. The President certainly had an interest in the outcome of the affair.
He thought it "too dangerous to prosecute Radford," seeing the yeoman as
"a potential time bomb that might be triggered by prosecution." Nixon
knew that Radford had been transferred and kept under surveillance which
included the use of wiretaps. "It worked," Nixon said; "there were no
further leaks from him." Moorer received no punishment; in fact, the next
year, Nixon reappointed him to another term as Chairman of the Joint Chiefs.
When knowledge of the Radford affair became public in 1974, some thought
that Nixon had blackmailed Moorer into supporting his arms-control agreements. The reappointment, it was said, amounted to Nixon's taming of the
military. The President also was anxious to keep the Joint Chiefs from being
too closely allied with Defense Secretary Laird, long an object of suspicion
among Nixon's aides.[25]

Curiously, Nixon in retrospect thought that Radford's leaks to Anderson
constituted the most important single element of the affair. That was also
the aspect that he stressed at the time. Bizarrely, in 1975, the Watergate
Special Prosecution Force considered the possibility that Colson had ordered
Howard Hunt to assassinate Anderson. At the time of the Radford affair,
David Young ordered a Defense Department investigator to prove that Jack
Anderson had had a homosexual affair with another Nixon enemy. The investigator refused, and Young became furious. "Damn it, damn it, the president is jumping up and down and he wants everything and we're always
telling him everything can't be done," Young reportedly said. (Eighteen
months later, that same investigator, who knew a great deal about internal
spying within the Administration, demanded consideration for the position
of FBI Director, raising concerns in the White House that it was being
subjected to blackmail.) Nixon himself was strangely silent about the military's role in the Radford affair.

Altogether, this lurid affair remains shrouded in mystery. Senator Symington thought it had more to do with "national embarrassment" than
with national security. Its significance and links to other events tantalize.
John Mitchell interviewed Moorer for the President. The admiral insisted
that he was innocent of any wrongdoing, and Mitchell believed him. In later
years, however, Mitchell took a more sinister view of events. He was convinced, for example, that Moorer had deceived him and that Alexander Haig,
Kissinger's deputy, "was involved in it." In a conversation with Ehrlichman

on December 23, 1971, the President instructed his aide: "Don't let K[issinger] blame Haig." Nixon emphatically wanted Kissinger kept out of the affair, and while he talked about prosecuting Radford and Welander, he apparently said nothing about reprisals against the military chiefs. Mitchell also thought that Nixon "knew a lot more about it at the time than I knew, and he decided to roll with it." Why did the military spy on the NSC? Mitchell surmised that the Joint Chiefs were concerned about the President's defense policies, his attempts to get Pentagon spending under control, the SALT negotiations, and the China opening which was about to take place. David Young thought the Radford affair important in understanding Watergate. Did he fear that the military, if implicated, would reveal the existence of the Plumbers? Why did the President and his aides fear that Laird would use the Radford material to gain power over the Joint Chiefs?[26]

A curious, shadowy business, this was. Most of the White House principals acknowledged the dismay it engendered in the Oval Office and among the President's aides. Now, they truly were victims; again, however, the enemy remained elusive.

As Daniel Ellsberg's trial in Los Angeles came to an end in March 1973, the Department of Justice disclosed that the FBI had overheard Ellsberg in telephone conversations originating in the house of Morton Halperin, then a Kissinger consultant in the National Security Council. Acting FBI director William Ruckelshaus further revealed that Halperin's phones had been tapped between 1969 and 1971, but he confessed that the Bureau's records of the taps had been missing since mid-1971. At that point, Judge Matthew Byrne suspended the trial. In fact surveillance had extended far beyond the Halperin tap: twelve other NSC aides plus four reporters—for CBS, for the *New York Times,* the *Washington Post,* and the *London Sunday Times*—also had been bugged as part of an operation designed to plug leaks from the National Security Council.

On May 9, 1969, the *New York Times* exposed the "secret" bombing war in Cambodia. Nixon and Kissinger were furious. The President considered the leak to the *Times* part of the organized conspiracy to destroy his presidency. Years later, Kissinger concurred and recalled that few administrations "faced a more bitter assault on their purposes, a more systematic attempt to thwart their policies by civil disobedience, or a more widely encouraged effort to sabotage legitimate and considered policies by tendentious leaks of classified information in the middle of a war."[27]

After the latest leak, Mitchell, following a request from Nixon and Kissinger, quickly authorized the FBI to carry out electronic surveillance on reporters and some NSC staffers. J. Edgar Hoover apparently voiced some concern from the outset, realizing the potentially harmful fallout if it were revealed that the FBI had eavesdropped on newsmen. He insisted on written authorization and ordered all records kept out of regular FBI files. Meanwhile, Kissinger aide Colonel Alexander Haig served as liaison between the NSC and the FBI. Kissinger and Haig together went to FBI offices to read the wiretap logs.

Kissinger complained to Assistant FBI Director William Sullivan that he felt besieged by the leakers in the NSC. "It is clear," he complained, seemingly without irony or guile, "that I don't have anybody in my office that I can trust except Colonel Haig here." (Kissinger meanwhile had other aides auditing Haig's actions.) He also said that the hard-line policy on Vietnam favored by the President and himself was being undermined by others "high in the administration." Kissinger then added the names of several other newsmen to be wiretapped and expressed his gratitude for the FBI's help.[28]

The Nixon Administration eventually found itself in a civil war, one vitally affected by the brewing War of the FBI Succession. The wiretap logs and records soon became hostage to bureaucratic ambitions. In 1971, Hoover and Mitchell disagreed over who had authorized the taps. After Justice officials threatened a congressional investigation, Hoover reportedly countered with a threat to expose the operation. Assistant Attorney General Robert Mardian then secured the wiretap logs and summaries from Sullivan. Mardian met with Nixon in the President's retreat at San Clemente, California, on July 12, 1971, and explained the problem. The President ordered him to give the logs and records to Ehrlichman for safekeeping. Mardian kept them in the Justice Department for a while, but the President's decision was reaffirmed at a White House meeting on October 8 between Nixon, Mitchell, and Ehrlichman, and the records were delivered to Ehrlichman.

Sullivan, as he had before in the Huston Plan proceedings, had labored to cultivate his White House relationship in order to nurse his ambitions as Hoover's successor. But Sullivan's action in cooperating with Mardian was the final straw for Hoover, and the Director demanded and received his resignation a few weeks later. Sullivan had supported the Administration's widening interests in using the FBI for secret political purposes; curiously, Hoover, an old hand at this sort of thing, sensed the shifting political winds and seemed to realize it was time to solidify the FBI's public image. The President, for his part, was sad that the surveillance had been fruitless: "Unfortunately," he lamented, "none of these wiretaps turned up any proof linking anyone in the government to a specific national security leak." Clarence Kelley, Hoover's successor, similarly acknowledged that the wiretaps never uncovered anyone who had leaked secrets. Unhappily for Nixon, after admitting he approved the tap on Morton Halperin, a Kissinger aide, he became the first president ordered to pay damages—a $5 award, meant to be symbolic—to a private citizen for acts committed by the Chief Executive while in office.[29]

In his inaugural address, Nixon had promised that the government would listen to the people. The promise had been kept, but in a very different sense.

The taps of National Security Council aides and journalists were designed to ensure the Administration's control over the flow of news and the formation of policies. But wiretapping was also a basic tool of the plan to maintain surveillance over potentially subversive domestic elements, particularly antiwar and civil rights activists. The efforts were extensive and violated both the letter and spirit of the law.

White House surveillance proceeded on many fronts. Los Angeles Mayor Sam Yorty encouraged the President to believe that Communists were behind the prevalent campus unrest. Nixon arranged for Yorty to meet with Attorney General Mitchell to discuss intelligence gained by Los Angeles Police Department undercover agents. Ehrlichman's investigator, John Caulfield, proposed in early 1969 that new military inductees be used as undercover campus agents. As part of some undefined "larger game plan," Alexander Butterfield, operating from the Oval Office, instructed Egil Krogh to have the FBI determine the precise connections between antiwar groups and the North Vietnamese and international organizations.[30]

The Nixon Administration had inherited an Army Intelligence operation that since 1965 had collected information on domestic civil disturbances. Using more than a thousand plainclothes officers, the Army aimed to be better informed on political conditions as preparation for riot duty. The preparedness principle acquired its own imperatives, including compiling dossiers on thousands of politically active Americans whether in antiwar, civil rights, white supremacist, black power, or liberal organizations. The Army's agents gathered newspaper clippings, attended public meetings, and took notes and photographs. Other agents were infiltrated into groups in covert attempts to disrupt their activities. Officers inevitably assembled lists of prominent activists in a variety of movements, but the lists also included congressmen and senators. Army Intelligence fed the information into computer banks at Fort Holabird, Maryland, and then disseminated it to Army posts at home and abroad. On one level, the intelligence reports were a gossipy newsletter, but there was, of course, a more pernicious side to them.

When the Nixon Administration took office in 1969, the Army's civilian leadership attempted to curb the intelligence program and favored transferring its duties and records to the FBI. Someone in the Pentagon had not received the proper signals from the White House, however. Deputy Attorney General Richard Kleindienst and the FBI urged the Army to continue its intelligence activities. Some intelligence officers had their doubts about the wisdom and validity of the program, but most enthusiastically supported it. In January 1970, Army Intelligence Captain Christopher Pyle exposed the operation as part of the Nixon Administration's widening attempt to counter domestic political dissent.[31]

A year later, Senator Sam Ervin's Subcommittee on Constitutional Rights investigated the use of federal data banks and found itself drawn into questions about the Army's program. Assistant Attorney General William Rehnquist boldly defended the program as part of the President's authority to use the Army to enforce the laws and suppress rebellion. The basic, broad question of the legitimacy of a government's surveillance of its own people really was at issue between Ervin and Rehnquist. The Senator thought that such activity had a chilling effect on the exercise of First Amendment rights. Rehnquist disagreed: "I do not believe it violates the particular constitutional rights of the individuals who are surveyed." He conceded that there was a great deal of waste of taxpayers' money in such projects, but he refused to raise the issue to the level of a constitutional violation. Surveillance itself was no vice, Rehnquist argued. He cited *Tatum v. Laird,* a case challenging the Army's program, which was then pending in the Court of Appeals. Rehnquist thought that the plaintiffs had wrongly sought an injunction to prevent the executive branch from gathering intelligence. He spoke of a 1949 "Delimitation Agreement" which, he argued, gave the Army authority to act as it had. That document has not surfaced, but a 1969 agreement clearly prevented the Army from surveillance of persons other than its officers and civilian employees.[32]

Some twenty months later, in the summer of 1972, the pending case had moved to the Supreme Court. Ervin put in an appearance to argue against the government's policy, describing the Army's action as a "cancer on the body politic." Chief Justice Burger led a five-man majority which specifically followed Rehnquist's formulation that the mere existence of governmental surveillance activities was not a violation of First Amendment rights. Rehnquist, now an Associate Justice, refused to disqualify himself in the case, claiming—in the face of his public testimony—that he had no personal knowledge of the case itself. He also insisted that he had never acted in an advisory role for the government in the case. Rehnquist's vote, of course, was crucial; a tie vote would have sustained the lower-court ruling against the government. Fourteen years later, in 1986, Rehnquist faced the issue again during hearings on his nomination to be Chief Justice of the United States Supreme Court. He reiterated that he had "no recollection" of participating in the formulation of Army surveillance or intelligence policies. But earlier testimony from the Army's General Counsel clearly contradicted Rehnquist. The Senate Judiciary Committee also obtained a 1969 Rehnquist memo stating that the Army "may assist" in collecting intelligence on antiwar protesters. At the time, Rehnquist had engaged in extensive negotiations with the Army and had worked out an agreement that involved the Army, the Justice Department, and the President. Rehnquist's failure to recollect his work was the failure of a highly intelligent lawyer, concerning policy matters that directly involved his office, and about which he had been queried on three official occasions.[33] Had the plaintiff's lawyers in the *Tatum* case pursued discovery proceedings, William Rehnquist might well have been a defendant.

The Army's domestic intelligence-gathering program was inherited, but the Nixon Administration had its own contributions to make in the area. Shortly after he assumed office, Attorney General John Mitchell authorized the FBI to engage in electronic surveillance of a black militant group, the Black Panthers, and of various campus antiwar dissidents, most notably the Students for a Democratic Society. Prevailing Supreme Court doctrine held that if a trial judge in any relevant case learned of illegal surveillance, he must then order the records turned over to the defense. In the Chicago Conspiracy trial in 1969, flowing from the disorders at the Democratic Convention the year before, the government had wiretap records obtained by former Attorney General Ramsey Clark. Mitchell, without acknowledging the existence of such records, submitted an affidavit contending that the President had the constitutional power to wiretap "to gather intelligence information concerning those organizations which are committed to the use of illegal methods to bring about changes in our form of government and which may be seeking to foment violent disorders." The judge concluded that the taps had no relevance to evidence introduced in the trial.

Mitchell's assertion was bold and sweeping, but the court did not pass on its validity. The Omnibus Crime Control Act of 1968, Title III, from which he claimed authority, only acknowledged presidential power to use electronic surveillance to protect the nation from foreign attack and spying and to prevent the overthrow of the government by force or other unlawful means. Nevertheless, Mitchell, according to a former Justice official, claimed an executive power independent of that granted by Congress.[34]

The same questions of presidential power arose the following year in a case in Michigan, where the government brought indictments against a group of "White Panthers" for a conspiracy to bomb a CIA office in Ann Arbor. On October 5, 1970, defense lawyers filed a routine motion to compel the government to disclose whether it had obtained wiretap information on the defendants. If it had, the defense motion requested a hearing to determine whether such evidence tainted the government's case. More than two months later, the government lawyers responded with an affidavit from Mitchell, claiming that the wiretaps were "necessary to protect the nation from attempts of domestic organizations to attack and subvert the existing structure of the Government." In January 1971, District Court Judge Damon J. Keith ruled for the defense and ordered the government to produce the wiretap transcripts. Government lawyers, joined by Assistant Attorney General Mardian, appealed to the Sixth Circuit Court of Appeals to overrule Keith, but the higher-court judges upheld their colleague. The Supreme Court granted certiorari in June. The case now took on the paradoxical title *United States v. United States Court for the Eastern District of Michigan*, but is more simply known as the Keith Case.

The government formulated its basic position in the Court of Appeals, contending essentially that the President had the responsibility to safeguard the nation's security against subversion: "This power is the historical power of the sovereign to preserve itself." A supplementary memorandum added: "The power at issue in this case is the inherent power of the President to safeguard the security of the nation." The government cited no constitutional language in support of its position and alluded vaguely to a few cases that the Court of Appeals found inappropriate.

In the Keith Case, the government strikingly ignored the Steel Seizure Case of 1952, though this was the leading case on inherent presidential powers. There, the Supreme Court had rejected President Truman's claims of inherent powers to nationalize the steel mills because of the Korean War emergency. The Court of Appeals in the Keith Case thought it odd that the President of the United States should claim the sovereign powers of George III, whose authorization of indiscriminate searches and seizures had been a vital issue in the Revolutionary Era.

When the Keith Case moved to the Supreme Court, the government's brief avoided any broad construction of "inherent powers"; Solicitor General Griswold thought that opening that topic "would just irritate the Court." Griswold appeared in the courtroom, but he was convinced the government would lose. Mardian presented the oral argument and maintained that the President's power "may be gleaned from the Constitution as a whole," which he was sworn to protect. The defense responded that the Constitution involved a "legal fabric woven by the founding fathers and by this Court to protect our fundamental liberties. One might think," they added, "in reading the Government's brief, that we had no pertinent history to help resolve this profound question." Again, the defense compared the President's position to that of George III.

The Supreme Court's eight sitting justices affirmed the lower court in the Keith Case. Justice Lewis Powell, a recent Nixon appointee and a onetime public supporter of the Administration's wiretap program, spoke for the Court. Chief Justice Burger concurred in the result, and Justice White in the judgment. Nixon's other recent appointee, William Rehnquist, recused himself, apparently because he had helped draft the government's earlier briefs.

The Keith ruling actually was quite narrow. Powell specifically avoided confronting the inherent-powers issue, relying instead on the proposition that the government's concerns did not justify departing "from the customary Fourth Amendment requirement of judicial approval prior to initiation of a search or seizure." The Court acknowledged that the President had a constitutional role in maintaining domestic security but insisted that that role be exercised "in a manner compatible with the Fourth Amendment." The case was a stunning rebuke to the Administration. Characteristically, the President complained in its aftermath that he was misunderstood: the Nixon Administration had reduced wiretaps by 50 percent from the all-time high under Robert Kennedy.[35]

The Supreme Court announced its decision in the Keith Case on June 19, 1972, only two days after the Nixon Administration's buggers had proceeded to another operation on their agenda, one that would help to focus the issues more clearly—and fatefully for the President.

VI

THE POLITICS OF
DEADLOCK

NIXON AND CONGRESS

Richard Nixon's assuming office marked the first time since Zachary Taylor's election in 1848 that a first-term president failed to meet a Congress controlled by his own party. The Democratic majority, however, represented only part of the problem. Nixon confronted a Congress sympathetic to ideological and institutional forces increasingly resistant to presidential wishes.

In recent decades, Congress had assumed its own characteristic institutional identity, one that added a dimension to the concept of separation of powers. Committed to a large number of programs through its natural links to the bureaucracy that administered them, Congress eventually developed its own agenda, often at odds with presidential desires, whether the president was a Republican Eisenhower or a Democratic Kennedy. Presidents struggled with this ever-burgeoning congressional will. The Vietnam war magnified the conflict, as differences sharpened over both domestic and foreign priorities.

Richard Nixon's first term focused and dramatized those conflicts. Issues that had been muted, or even stalemated, erupted into open, bruising conflict between 1969 and 1972. The President and Congress clashed over a variety of problems, including reorganization of the executive branch, impoundment of appropriated funds, Supreme Court appointments, and finally, the war in Southeast Asia. The President won some of these skirmishes and lost others; but by 1972, he and Congress viewed each other with mutual animosity. That feeling, and those skirmishes, poisoned the relationship of executive and legislative branches and set the stage for the fateful war of the second term.

The task of accommodation between the branches of government is not easy, requiring tact, mutual respect, bargaining, and a willingness to share power. Manipulation is inevitable, to be sure, but generally occurs within the bounds of courtesy and compromise. Franklin D. Roosevelt's "Hundred Days" in 1933 is often cited as a standard for demonstrating modern-day presidential leadership, but a close examination of the legislative process in this case reveals, as in so many others, that partnership between President and Congress which must prevail in American political life.

John F. Kennedy remarked after two years in office that "Congress looks more powerful sitting here than it did when I was there in the Congress." Nixon apparently never shared that insight. During the interregnum between November 1968 and his inauguration the following January, he reportedly never discussed legislative strategy with the aides he had appointed to deal with Congress. He even refused to prepare a State of the Union message— in reality, his legislative program—just after taking office. From the start, then, Nixon and his White House staff followed the path he had laid out in a 1968 campaign talk: the magic of the President and the People, working together, would fulfill the nation's needs. Richard Nixon's experience in both the legislative and executive branches for fifteen years must have made him mindful of political reality. Nevertheless, he directed his staff toward a policy that alternated contempt for Congress with a belief that, through the borrowed techniques of advertising and public relations, the White House could sell its program directly to the public and so make Congress irrelevant.[1]

Nixon was determined to be an "activist President in domestic affairs." He would not, he said, later be accused of having been too cautious. Confrontation with Congress was the order of the day; but contempt pervaded the President's orders: "I thought it was absurd for members of Congress to complain that the executive branch had stolen power from them. On the contrary," Nixon wrote, "modern Presidents had merely stepped into the vacuum created when Congress failed to discipline itself sufficiently to play a strong policy-making role."[2]

Nixon's confrontational style invites comparison with the Administration he served as Vice President. Eisenhower had his share of conflicts with Congress, but a public veil of goodwill and cooperation shrouded their encounters. He governed during his first two years with a slim Republican majority in Congress; during the next six he faced ever-increasing Democratic majorities, often dominated by Lyndon Johnson, who had his own insatiable ambitions. Recalling the slight Republican majority in Congress in 1953, Eisenhower said that "I knew from the beginning that noisy, strong-armed tactics would accomplish nothing, even if I were so inclined." He cultivated numerous lines of communication with congressional leaders and urged his Cabinet members to develop friendly contacts in Congress. Nixon, in contrast, thought that such familiarity only made Cabinet secretaries sub-servient to congressional wishes.

Eisenhower proudly described his close working relationship with Senator Robert Taft, his erstwhile rival for the presidency. "Legislative leaders of both parties were my friends," he wrote. Despite some acrimony and seri-ous differences, Eisenhower never questioned the motives of the opposition. Nixon, on the other hand, thought that liberals had "deluded" themselves and acted "dishonorably" in opposing his Anti-Ballistic Missile program. The measure passed by one vote, but when it did, Nixon credited his staff for corraling votes rather than acknowledging congressional cooperation, especially from the conservative wing of his own party.[3] *Fight* and *battle* again prevailed as Nixon's leading metaphors.

In foreign-policy matters, Eisenhower respectfully regarded Congress's role, whether consultative or formal. He carefully touched congressional bases during the tense moments surrounding the French collapse in Vietnam in 1954, the Formosan Straits crisis in 1955, the Suez invasion in 1956, and the civil war in Lebanon in 1957. Nixon, on the other hand, discussed his Cambodian invasion plans with Congress in 1970 only after the decision had been reached. His memoirs make no mention of congressional advice on SALT, the Indo-Pakistan War, or other major issues regarding his foreign policy.[4] The omission reflected the reality of a divisive condition between President and Congress that steadily worsened throughout the Nixon years.

As he prepared for the campaign of 1972, President Nixon told his aides to instruct friendly congressmen to make daily speeches noting the number of days that had passed without congressional action on his programs. Nixon thought doing so would be an "effective needle in the Democratic leader-ship" and that it would provide the "groundwork for our major attack" on Congress. Cynicism alternated with contempt. "I don't think Congress is supposed to work with the White House—it is a different organization, and under the Constitution I don't think we should expect agreement," H. R. Haldeman told a reporter.[5] Such was the monumental ignorance of the gov-ernmental and political processes that pervaded the Nixon Administration's five-year relationship with Congress.

We cannot calibrate precisely the relative strength of the presidency when Lyndon Johnson stepped down in January 1969. He had squandered a for-tune in goodwill and trust in the years since his landslide victory in 1964.

Presidents had left office before in disgrace or in low esteem, but the prestige of the office itself had quickly revived. Special combinations of man and times—a Franklin D. Roosevelt or a Dwight D. Eisenhower—followed the unpopular tenures of Herbert Hoover and Harry Truman. The nation waited in 1969 to see what it had chosen.

It soon became clear that the election had not stilled any of the nation's civil strife; most significantly, Nixon's installation as President only widened the chasm and conflict between the executive branch and Congress. Moreover, that conflict had taken on a new character in recent years.

The constitutional separation of powers has always had a special appeal for those wary of unbridled power. Some have also found virtue in the partisan (and sometimes ideological) division between the presidency and the legislature which, when Nixon took office, had been commonplace since the end of the Roosevelt era. This tension served as an informal extension of constitutional checks and balances. The philosophical split between President and Congress had its modern origins in the formation of an ideological alliance between conservative Democrats and Republicans as a counterweight to what they regarded as the excesses of Roosevelt and the New Dealers. That coalition blossomed with almost concurrent-veto power in the Truman Administration. Yet the alliance was mostly negative, simply serving to block or hamper presidential initiatives. Curiously, the reverse situation prevailed in the 1950s. Liberals from both parties united and used their influence in the bureaucracy and Congress to prevent rollbacks from the gains of the New Deal era. And despite the Eisenhower landslide in 1956, Democrats retained control of Congress.

Liberal presidents seemed most victimized by the opposition of Congress—which by the 1960s had a fashionable tag: "The Deadlock of Democracy." The longstanding conservative congressional coalition maintained control of such traditional levers of congressional power as committee chairmanships, and from such bases often dictated the course of events. Liberal activists and scholars deplored the situation, particularly as John F. Kennedy's tax-reform and civil rights proposals stalled in Congress. For liberals, the conservative ideological alliance had little virtue, and the resulting stalemate menaced both the general welfare and national security.

A distinguished political scientist, James MacGregor Burns, summarized the deadlock-of-democracy notion in a book by that title in 1963. Burns had impeccable liberal credentials. *The Lion and the Fox*, his scholarly account of Franklin D. Roosevelt's presidency, presented Roosevelt as a classic model of the forceful activist leader, confirming and amplifying the view of him held by generations of admirers. In a 1959 campaign biography, Burns anointed Kennedy as the designated heir to the Roosevelt tradition, offering him in sharp contrast to Eisenhower's supposedly passive rule. But the promising young candidate had not responded to the challenge as Burns had hoped. In *The Deadlock of Democracy,* Burns chided Kennedy for his failures in leadership, but he concluded that the President's shortcomings derived as much from structural, constitutional traditions as from personal qualities and style.[6]

Burns's essential theme was that the furious pace of modern social change and the imperative demands of foreign and military situations required timely, effective governmental action. He believed that we had allowed the Madisonian system of checks and balances to thwart and fragment "leadership instead of allowing it free play within the boundaries of the democratic process." The result was a political system divided along both partisan and institutional lines—and, all too often, a paralysis of governmental will and power.

Concern with the executive/legislative deadlock evoked different concepts of representative government. For the proponents of an activist presidency—or the "plebiscitary" presidency—Congress was antediluvian, or at best obsolete. No one dared to advocate its abolition, but the activist argument worked hard to square the circle, calling for congressional recognition of the national will as embodied and expressed in the presidential program. Traditional beliefs in a conglomeration of individual constituencies, representing a myriad of interests chosen throughout the nation, now were eclipsed by a unitary vision of a President who could divine and then represent the true national will.

Johnson's mobilization of power and his activist leadership of diverse congressional groups followed the liberal prescription. The results provided liberals with some measure of satisfaction: provisions for tax reform, civil rights, Medicare, and other items in the litany of the liberal platform. Despite those victories, however, Johnson's regime did not work out as promised. The Vietnam war dampened the spirits of many liberals, and the Great Society seemed much less great by 1966. Liberals needed the healing balm of older articles of liberal faith, such as Lord Acton's dictum: "Power tends to corrupt, and absolute power tends to corrupt absolutely." Some even began to think small and retreated to the Jeffersonian maxim that the government governs best that governs least. Liberals seemed confused and at sea. Some believed that Lyndon Johnson had corrupted the faith only momentarily; others began to question the established wisdom of the need for a strong presidency.

Richard Nixon never seemed cut out for conformity to the traditional Republican concept of a limited, passive president, despite his reflexive assaults on Roosevelt and on Truman's exercise of power. As he campaigned for the White House in 1968, his antidote for the battered presidency and the paralysis of national will was a more activist presidency. In a radio address on September 19, Nixon promised to revitalize the presidency—in short, to lead. He went so far as to criticize Johnson, of all people, as too passive.

"Let me be very clear about this: The next President must take an activist view of his office," Nixon declared. "He must articulate the nation's values, define its goals and marshal its will." He promised to be what Americans had been accustomed to: a personal president, one who would have a "special relationship, a special trust" with the people, who would not "paper over disunity," and who would have "an open, candid dialogue with people" so as to "maintain his trust and leadership." Nixon went on to add another dimension, promising to "bring dissenters into policy discussions," to "invite constructive criticism not only because the critics have a right to be heard, but also because they often have something worth hearing." Keeping that promise would have been unprecedented for the kind of activist president Nixon described—but it was, of course, good rhetoric in the divided political scene of 1968.

The Nixon speech sounded as if it had been crafted by speechwriter Theodore Sorensen in the Kennedy style. Nixon spoke of presidential involvement in the "intellectual ferment" of the time. He recognized that "the lamps of enlightenment are lit by the spark of controversy." The President, Nixon noted, was both "a user of thought" and a "catalyst of thought." He talked of attracting "the ablest men" to his Cabinet, and he promised "a reorganized" executive and "a stronger White House than any yet put together." Finally, there was a Kennedyesque call for elevation of the crusade: "Our cause today is not a nation, but a planet—for never have the fates of all the people of the earth been so bound up together."

Nixon's crusade was to be one for the "President and people together"—or, he concluded, "it won't be done at all." That conclusion underlined the fact that the candidate never mentioned Congress in his scheme of governance; he offered no recognition of shared power whatsoever. The omission hardly represented a new approach, but it was a departure for a Republican; old-guard stalwarts who still blanched at the name of Roosevelt must have shuddered at Nixon's words, unless they believed that he did not mean them.

Nixon's omission flew in the face of political realities that unfolded after his election. The Democrats retained decisive margins in both houses of Congress. Resentful over the imperial ways of Johnson, one of their own, as president, they hardly seemed inclined to abandon their share in governance.

Not for the last time, Richard Nixon effectively united his enemies. His legislative program, such as it was, soon was hopelessly mired in the congressional labyrinth. The situation raised images of the Kennedy years, but now liberal activists and scholars could not rail against a "deadlock of democracy" that thwarted Richard Nixon. In a deft maneuver, however, the President simply made their message his own.

Almost two years to the day after his campaign address omitting mention of Congress, Nixon himself confronted the deadlock of democracy that had plagued John F. Kennedy. But while JFK had responded with stroking and appeasement, the new President preferred a frank recognition of the gulf between him and Congress. In a September 11, 1970 message, Nixon berated Congress for its failure to act on his "reform" proposals. He conceded that the system of traditional checks and balances made "stalemate" inevitable and the exercise of power "difficult." But the nation now faced important and momentous issues that demanded greater cooperation between the branches. Congress, he bluntly charged, had failed to respond at all to his initiatives. In a "mood of nostalgia and partisanship," Congress had devoted too much energy "to tinkering with programs of the past while ignoring the realities of the present and the opportunities of the future." For Nixon, "the good repute of American government" itself was at stake.[7]

Lest any misunderstand the President's intention to confront Congress and to maintain his alliance with "the people," Vice President Agnew, on a political speaking tour in the West the day before, told his audience that the nation faced a "deadlock of democracy." Agnew had other touches, reminiscent of the vintage "Old Nixon" style, circa 1954: "Will America be led by a President elected by a majority of the American people or will we be intimidated and blackmailed into following the path dictated by a disruptive radical and militant minority—the pampered prodigies of the radical liberals in the United States Senate?" Nixon appropriately described Agnew as "the perfect spokesman" to reach the Silent Majority.[8]

Nixon and Agnew's provocative remarks uncannily replicated the standard liberal litany of presidential stewardship. No one yet referred to an "imperial presidency." Instead one spoke of the presidency (as Theodore Roosevelt had) as "a bully pulpit," or as an educational platform, or of the President as a steward for all the people. The notion of an aggressive, outspoken presidential leader who dealt in intimate, personal terms with "the people" and derided the obstructionism of a Congress dominated by backward-looking vested interests had become a twentieth-century article of faith in the American liberal political catechism. That faith rested on Theodore Roosevelt's concept of a president free to do anything except what was expressly prohibited in the Constitution. Now Nixon was telling the people the same thing. In Alexander Bickel's well-chosen metaphor, Richard Nixon caught the liberals bathing, and walked off with their clothes.[9]

Whether Nixon could take on the mantle of that faith, however, and whether he could exercise it, remained to be seen. His enemies had powerful appeals of their own, demanding an end to the Vietnam war, the restoration of economic well-being, and a pacification of domestic disorder. The appeals and the enemies alike were formidable. At this stage, to see matters as grave was not just paranoia; for President Nixon, there was an all-too-real enemy within in the form of Congress.

Nixon operated, as usual, in ambivalent fashion in meeting the difficulty.

At the outset of his term, he expressed a willingness to reach out to Congress for ideas and to work in a conciliatory spirit. In early March 1969, Nixon told Haldeman that he was impressed with the number of good ideas of congressmen, ideas whose "imagination and emotion" he contrasted favorably with the "routine" ones originating "from our White House and Cabinet teams." Not responsible to any voting constituency, staff and department officials often were out of touch and became "pretty ingrown and incestuous intellectually." Yet Nixon had no interest in "massaging" congressmen on "their pet ideas"; instead, he hoped to add "a little more imagination and ingenuity" into "our own executive organization." He complained that "we are simply too busy fielding the balls that are being knocked our way." Presidential Assistant Alexander Butterfield reported in July 1969 that Nixon considered it necessary to "continue (at least for the time being) working with the Democratic Congress in as friendly a way as possible, . . . that pressing our programs on Congress in a more forthright, uncompromising fashion would be a little premature at this time." But Butterfield also noted that the President recognized "that we should definitely reconsider this strategy around the end of September or early October."[10]

"Watch what we do, not what we say"—John Mitchell's famous remark about the Administration's civil rights policy—was a favorite slogan of the day. During Nixon's first term, executive–legislative relations were governed as much as anything else by the President's avowed promise "to knock heads together."

In 1803, President Thomas Jefferson matter-of-factly reported to Congress that he had not spent a $50,000 appropriation for Mississippi River gunboats because "the favorable and peaceful turn of affairs . . . rendered an immediate execution of the law unnecessary."[11] Thus began the history of presidential impoundment of duly authorized funds. Impoundment had always posed practical constitutional problems, but these seemed of minor consequence until the Nixon Administration (with an important precedent from the Johnson years) transformed an occasional practice into a special test of wills with Congress. For Nixon, the exercise of impoundment also became part of his constitutional responsibility. In a January 31, 1973 press conference, he announced "the Constitutional right for the President of the United States to impound funds[,] and that is not to spend money, when the spending of money would mean . . . increasing prices or increasing taxes for all the people, that right is absolutely clear."

It was not, however, "absolutely clear." No constitutional language specified such authority. One favorite argument supporting impoundment was that the Constitution required the President to "take care that the laws be faithfully executed." From this, the idea developed that if an appropriation contravened the purposes of other statutes, the President had discretionary power to ignore it, thus harmonizing conflicting legislative objectives. Without doubt, Nixon escalated impoundment to a new level of "magnitude, severity, and belligerence," wrote Louis Fisher, the leading authority on the subject.

Jefferson's successors occasionally invoked his precedent, but usually as a discrete action rather than a considered, consistent policy. Following World War II, Presidents Truman, Eisenhower, and Kennedy used the power of impoundment to control defense spending and to resist crass, interest-group legislation serving the luxuriant demands of what later came to be called the military-industrial complex. The practice dramatically changed in 1966 when President Johnson announced that he would not spend $5.3 billion in appropriated funds for various domestic programs. He justified his action as necessary to curb the inflationary pressures created by dramatically accelerated war expenditures. Attorney General Ramsey Clark at the time provided a formal opinion justifying impoundment on the grounds that "an appropriation act in itself does not constitute a mandate to spend."[12]

Johnson in effect framed his own constitutional question and provided an answer to suit his needs. Previous opinion within the executive branch usually had run the other way. FDR's Attorney General, Homer Cummings, told him in 1937 that without legislative sanction, a presidential order withholding expenditures "would not be binding." A Kennedy legal aide told the President in 1961 that aside from defense appropriations, impoundment "in the civilian area is not customary and of doubtful legal basis." And Nixon's Assistant Attorney General William Rehnquist substantially repudiated Clark's extravagant view of impoundment powers and contended that the President was "not at liberty to impound in the case of domestic affairs" that had no relation to national-defense or foreign-policy considerations. But President Nixon's actions, and the statements of his aides in the next four years, significantly undercut Rehnquist's opinion.

When Nixon took office, Congress provided him with authorization to impound $6 billion from previously approved funding bills. In effect, Congress gave the President discretionary power to do what LBJ had done on his own. In allowing impoundment, the Democrats seemed inclined to prevent Nixon from preempting the spending and inflation issues. But politics had many faces, and the Democrats later found themselves obligated to defend and expand public projects beneficial to their traditional constituencies. In 1970–71 they did not confer further discretionary power, but the President nevertheless withheld nearly $13 billion. Senator Sam Ervin (D–NC) assembled his Subcommittee on Separation of Powers in March 1971 to engage in a colloquy with Administration officials on impoundment. Ervin typically tried to preempt the strict constitutional position. The Constitution's framers, he insisted, intended that the President execute "all laws" duly passed by Congress, "irrespective of any personal, political, or philosophical views he might have." Ervin denied that the President had any discretionary authority as to what laws would or would not be executed. "Yet," he said, "by using the impoundment technique, the President is able to do just that."[13]

The hearings curiously enhanced the Administration's position. First, Office of Management and Budget Director Caspar Weinberger effectively undermined Rehnquist's narrow construction and insisted that the President could impound funds to reconcile conflicting congressional goals—for example, impoundment enabled the President to enforce the national-debt limitation law. Weinberger had his own view of strict construction to checkmate Ervin. Impoundment, he said, would "insure that overall the will of Congress is maintained." Ervin responded with a bill requiring the reporting of all impoundments. It narrowly passed the Senate but died in the House. The Administration skirted the constitutional issues and lobbied against the Ervin bill on the grounds that it would substantially increase the workload of the Office of Management and Budget.[14]

Congressional inertia on impoundment amounted to benign acquiescence, which in turn emboldened the Administration to expand impoundment actions. Cost-cutting activities most often involved programs that the White House wanted eliminated and replaced with state initiatives financed by revenue-sharing measures. Altogether, Nixon impounded more than $18 billion in his first term.[15] Unlike the impoundments of his predecessors, none of his involved defense expenditures; the impounded funds consistently affected pet pork-barrel projects and traditional liberal causes. Impoundment became an instrument serving preferred presidential policies, policies that aided fiscal restraint and at the same time frustrated congressional wishes.

On the eve of the Administration's thumping electoral approval in late 1972, the President offered his most powerful challenge. On October 18, Congress had overridden the President's veto of new amendments to the Federal Water Pollution Control Act, one of the most comprehensive and expensive environmental laws in American history. The measure clearly was popular, and the veto was overridden 247–23 in the House and 52–12 in the Senate. The legislation set new standards for water-quality control and authorized over $18 billion in grants for the states to construct new waste-treatment plants. When the President vetoed the bill, he announced that if Congress overrode his action, he still would refuse to spend the appropriated money. In his veto message of October 17, Nixon threw down the gauntlet: "I have nailed my colors to the mast on this issue; the political winds can blow where they may." The day after, Nixon and Ehrlichman agreed that the "solution to pollution is not dilution of the dollar." Nixon insisted that the act contained discretionary powers for spending and that he meant to use them. On November 22, Nixon acted true to his word and directed

Environmental Protection Agency Administrator William Ruckelshaus not to spend the appropriated funds.

Again, Congress responded with hearings. This time, a joint *ad hoc* subcommittee of the Judiciary and Government Operations committees met to consider impoundment. The tension between the executive and legislative branches on this issue had sharpened dramatically since the previous hearings in 1971. Ervin was more indignant; perhaps his growing involvement with a Senate resolution to provide hearings into the financing of the 1972 election campaign heightened his irritation. The Administration responded with a renewed confidence in the President's constitutional powers. Deputy Attorney General Joseph T. Sneed repudiated Rehnquist's earlier narrow view and claimed a broad constitutional mandate for impoundment of funds by the President. Any restriction on impoundment, Sneed testified, would deprive the President "of a substantial portion of the executive power vested in him by the Constitution." Sneed also flatly rejected the Rehnquist memorandum of 1969 as "far too restrictive" of executive power as conferred by the Constitution.[16]

Nixon himself acknowledged the problem as one of public image rather than of constitutionalism. He told John Ehrlichman that they were "cold, efficient, good managers." He said he would provide compassion and care for the hungry and poor, but yet he opposed the passion for spending.[17] Impoundment, for him, was good management and gave him the high ground of responsible fiscal policy. Then, too, impoundment left his opponents isolated and scattered, anguished when their pet programs were affected but silent and acquiescent at other times. Sam Ervin's defense of constitutional niceties offered a rare outburst of principled concern.

The President's challenge to the new pollution controls introduced a new wrinkle to what had been a kind of stylized game between the executive and legislative branches, a game that had been confined to the politics of defense spending. Clearly, the constitutional process had run its prescribed course: Congress had passed a bill; the President had vetoed it; and Congress had overridden the veto. The bill was law, even without a presidential signature. The President, however, had no interest in "faithfully executing" it.

During the summer of 1974, the House Judiciary Committee considered whether the President's impoundment activities constituted grounds for impeachment. Committee staff lawyers admitted that the historical record on impoundment offered a certain basis in precedent for Nixon's actions. Furthermore, they conceded that the President's position could be rationally deduced from both constitutional powers and specific statutes. Perhaps, the staff report stated, an "unjustified, sustained and deliberate refusal" by the President to execute spending statutes might be cause for impeachment, but not every temporary "abrasion . . . need lead to the impeachment of a President."[18]

What went unacknowledged was the historical fact that Congress traditionally had acquiesced in particular uses of impoundment and indeed had found the device useful for its own policy purposes. Still, the fact that impoundment had risen to the respectability of being considered grounds for impeachment measured the furies Richard Nixon aroused in Congress.

Since Theodore Roosevelt, presidents regularly have promoted plans to reorganize the executive branch. Franklin D. Roosevelt's elaborate Executive Reorganization Plan in 1938 marked a significant breakthrough in the modern organization of the presidency, and each of his successors expended some effort in this area. Harry Truman, hoping to create a bipartisan consensus, named former President Herbert Hoover to direct elaborate studies of executive operations and make recommendations, many of which were adopted. At that time, of course, the sprawl and size of executive operations were relatively new and hence more tractable. All presidential plans for reorganizations were motivated in part by a desire for increased administrative efficiency, as well as by a desire to fulfill presidential political and personal ambitions.

In Richard Nixon's case, the struggle to centralize executive-branch decision making in the White House clearly highlighted his reorganization proposals. Nixon made it "too apparent that reorganization was about power." The consequent political embarrassments of his Administration, centering as they did on the abuse of power, ultimately made Nixon's "reorganization planning itself a suspicious enterprise."[19] However laudable their goals, Nixon's plans not only appeared to enhance his own power, but did so at the expense of congressional prerogatives and the vested interests of Congress's bureaucratic constituents.

Early in 1969 Nixon asked Congress to renew presidential authority for proposing reorganization schemes, and Congress promptly complied. The President appointed an advisory commission headed by Roy Ash, president of a prominent corporate conglomerate and a defense contractor. In its first report, the commission focused on overall management responsibility and suggested a need for new organizational arrangements in the President's own office.

The task of centralizing authority was not easy. Forty years earlier, Herbert Hoover had recognized the roadblocks: any reorganization proposal, he warned, "enlivens opposition from every official whose authority may be curtailed or who fears his position is imperiled by such a result; [and] of bureaus and departments which wish to maintain their authority and activities."[20] The barriers had not fallen; if anything, they had become more formidable.

The evidence of Nixon's commitment to executive-branch reorganization is compelling. William Safire noted the President's frustrated response to a memo telling him that a particular proposal could never work its way through the bureaucratic maze: "govt doesn't work," the President wrote. "We're going to reorganize the government come hell or high water," he told Nelson Rockefeller in 1971. But Leonard Garment recognized the dangers of making a "lunge at the private parts . . . of all the different establishments in Washington." And there was ambivalence on the issue in the White House itself. Three months later, as the President's staff was engaged in one of its periodic assessments of how best to sell the President to the public, an aide remarked that "the public could care less" about reorganization. The aide recommended leaving the subject to one specialist, "but not one minute of Presidential time ought to be put against it. Unless we want to make it *the* issue, then the President will have to spend all his time on it." Haldeman pithily wrote in the margin: "Never!" Nixon, of course, was no stranger to political realities. In early 1971, he told his Cabinet that his reorganization proposals could not get very far "because [of] too many vested interests. Vested interests will be stronger, in a sense, than we are."[21]

In 1970, the Ash Commission presented a reorganization plan which replaced the fifty-year-old Bureau of the Budget with the Office of Management and Budget (OMB) and created the Domestic Council. The OMB emphasized newly created management and supervisory roles and established the agency as the President's principal arm for managerial functions. The plan transferred functions previously exercised by the Budget Bureau and its Director to the President, who would delegate them to the OMB Director—and presumably could recall them to himself. The OMB would assist the President in the budget's preparation and carefully audit its execution, and it was given greater influence on the framing and acceptance of legislative or administrative actions. The OMB also could evaluate program performances across agency lines and thus carry out an additional mandate to improve interagency cooperation. Predictably, some Cabinet members objected to the new arrangement, seeing the OMB as diluting their influence within their own departments—which, of course, was precisely the point.[22]

The other major feature of the 1970 plan involved the creation of the Domestic Council, a proposal that inevitably aroused greater congressional concern than OMB had, for it threatened operations of executive agencies that had close ties with congressional committees and staff. The Administration regarded the Domestic Council as a twin to the National Security Council. Its task was to coordinate and integrate both complementary and contradictory policies emanating from the departments of Treasury; Interior; Agriculture; Commerce; Labor; Health, Education and Welfare; Transportation; and Housing and Urban Development. The council was intended to focus on broad policy formulation in order that the President and his White House staff could have immediate influence on the various departments.

Chet Holifield (D–CA), Chairman of the House Committee on Government Operations, was skeptical of the plan, fearful that Congress could not scrutinize the functions of the Domestic Council; in addition, he noted that its head would be a "political appointee," not confirmed by the Senate—that is, with no ties to the Congress. The President subsequently named John Ehrlichman to head the Domestic Council, and the aide soon confirmed the fears of both Cabinet and congressional critics. Ehrlichman seemed less interested in broad policy formulation than in making the council into an operational agency. By all accounts (except Ehrlichman's, of course), the Cabinet became increasingly isolated, even irrelevant, as contacts increased between the White House and middle-level bureaucrats.[23]

The 1970 reorganization plan made its way through Congress during the uproar over the President's actions in Cambodia, thus heightening suspicions of presidential aggrandizement of power. But at the time Nixon still had sufficient respect to overcome congressional opposition. His lobbyists deflected criticism as they emphasized the President's right to manage his "organizational household," and the plan went into effect.[24]

What a difference a year made. By 1971, the sharpening clashes over Vietnam policy and domestic issues, particularly spending, and the President's assault on Congress in the 1970 elections, had heightened the nascent antagonism between the two branches. Early in the year, Nixon's reservoir of good will had largely evaporated. In March, the President submitted a series of new reorganization bills. The centerpiece was a reorganization of the executive departments that focused on domestic affairs. The measure proposed reducing to four the sprawling Cabinet offices charged with domestic affairs, and developing them along functional lines: departments of National Resources, Community Development, Human Resources, and Economic Affairs. Whatever the merits, the plan died aborning.

Nixon's public declaration, both in his January 1971 State of the Union speech and in his message accompanying the submission of the reorganization plans, stressed the need to change the framework of government to make it more responsive. In January, he predictably attacked "bureaucratic elites in Washington" who acted as if they always knew what was best. Two months later, he complained that governmental power was "exceedingly fragmented" and so diffuse as to create countervailing policies. These "fragmented fiefdoms," he bluntly stated, had a "hobbling effect . . . on elected leadership and, therefore, on the basic principles of democratic government."

The "fragmented fiefdoms," however, had powerful allies in the subcommittee structure of Congress. There, individual congressmen, and their personal and committee staffs, had a substantial stake in the *status quo* that they would not lightly surrender. Bureaucratic self-defense coupled with congressional self-interest, amid heightening suspicions of presidential intentions, combined to defeat Nixon's 1971 reorganization plan.[25] The system that so frustrated the President remained largely intact.

Studies of presidential administration and executive organization typically stress that Nixon's reorganization schemes were common to modern presidents. Nixon may well have been more determined than his predecessors to offer new, definitive answers to the problems of governance in the twentieth century. Still, his failure to give effect to reform had much in common with the failures of other presidents, for they too directly confronted the entrenched, fragmented forces in the government. Such an interpretation stresses the failures of reorganization itself, not this President's character flaws. Nixon's abortive reorganization schemes, the argument continues, prevented him from gaining his desirable managerial goal of control. From this same analysis, however, flowed an easy rationalization for the Plumbers, the attempts to politicize upper civil service positions, and the misuse of the Internal Revenue Service.

Those abuses of power certainly represented rationalizations for control and effective management, but they had less to do with governmental efficiency than with advancing the personal interests and political stature of the President. The grandiose charts and plans for streamlining government are difficult to separate from the Administration's internal perceptions of "enemies," including a bureaucracy that in the President's mind frustrated his programmatic goals because of its ideological hostility—thus justifying a purge that often took on "the air of a vengeance crusade." While nominal Democrats may have dominated the career bureaucracy, no inexorable logic dictated the conclusion that they deliberately sabotaged Nixon's policies for ideological reasons.[26] In the final analysis, it appears, reorganization aroused suspicions that each plan was another Nixon Administration design for confrontation and presidential aggrandizement—and at the expense of Congress.

President Nixon's battles with the Senate over Supreme Court nominees offered the most vivid constitutional, partisan, and institutional confrontations of his first term. The confirmation struggles exposed a mutual contempt between the President and Congress, and the results kindled new bitterness on the part of the President, a bitterness that flowed over into other areas and colored his relationship with Congress for the remainder of his presidency.

In the Dred Scott decision in 1857, the Supreme Court of the United States defended the right of slaveholders to take their chattels to the territories. The ruling provoked bitter division in the nation, and political aspirants assailed the Court, promising a reversal of the controversial decision. Abraham Lincoln, in his famous 1858 senatorial campaign against Stephen A. Douglas, said that the decision had wrongly interpreted the Constitution, and he forthrightly opposed it. "Somebody has to reverse that decision, since it is made, and we mean to reverse it, and we mean to do it peaceably."[27] Lincoln's meaning was clear: "We"—the Republicans—would win at the polls, appoint Supreme Court Justices who thought differently from those who handed down the Dred Scott decision, and reverse the decision "peaceably." In fact, Congress ignored the decision once the South seceded, Lincoln's Supreme Court appointees never applied it, and Union armies effectively reversed it. History has been kind to Abraham Lincoln.

Richard Nixon attacked the Supreme Court in his 1968 campaign for its alleged coddling of criminal forces, and he promised to appoint Justices who would favor "law and order." Nixon's opponents were appalled by his assault on the Court, which they perceived as a nonpolitical institution. They criticized him for his demagoguery and for his attacks on a largely defenseless institution and charged that he ignored the true, underlying causes of crime and violence in the nation. To some degree, however, a significant part of the electorate believed that the Court's decisions had undermined police authority and had fostered contempt for the law. In any event, Nixon's promise to appoint Supreme Court Justices who reflected his own philosophical beliefs was hardly new in history.

When Chief Justice Earl Warren notified President Johnson in June 1968 of his intention to retire "solely because of age," many greeted the news with some skepticism. Warren's announcement seemed like a cynical ploy. Well known was Warren's longtime animosity toward Richard Nixon, dating back to California days and particularly to Nixon's role in abandoning Warren's favorite-son candidacy for the presidency in 1952. When Johnson announced his nomination of Associate Justice Abe Fortas as Warren's successor, skepticism multiplied, as suspicions spread that both Johnson and Warren had somehow connived to prevent the possibility that Richard Nixon might name the fifteenth Chief Justice of the United States.

Fortas carried enormous handicaps. Nominated for Chief Justice by a retiring, unpopular president, he symbolized the most advanced liberal views of the Warren Court, positions that only enhanced his vulnerability, for they were the focus of the political assault on the Court in that time of unrest. Fortas's activities also gave rise to serious doubts about his ethical behavior and standards. The Justice's role as an untitled presidential adviser was well known; perhaps that, coupled with the possible realization that his personal activities might be subjected to unwanted scrutiny, contributed to Fortas's initial reluctance to accept Johnson's nomination to the Court in 1965. Reports of his continued White House involvement regularly circulated in Washington. For his part, Fortas refused to fully acknowledge the extensive work he did for Johnson, a role that overshadowed and potentially conflicted with his judicial position.[28]

Whatever Warren's purposes or Johnson's motives, the President again could not shake his well-known image as a wheeler-dealer. As he submitted Fortas's name to the Senate, Johnson also nominated fellow Texan Homer Thornberry to Fortas's place on the Supreme Court. Thornberry, then a federal judge, had been a popular member of the House of Representatives, with close ties to the dominant Southern leadership but with a voting record that gave him solid links to other Democrats. Clearly, the President hoped to gain support from Southern Democrats and conservative Republicans for a package deal. He persuaded Republican Senate Leader Dirksen to support Fortas in exchange for some political favors. Senator Richard Russell (D–GA), leader of the southerners and a great power in the Senate, reportedly told the President: "I will support the nomination of Mr. Fortas for Chief Justice, but I will enthusiastically support Homer Thornberry." But the ploy did not work.

Michigan Republican Robert Griffin led the opposition and focused on Fortas's fee of $15,000 for a series of university lectures and some other instances of alleged greed and shadowy dealings. A former Fortas law partner had raised the cash for the lecture fee from persons who might have future dealings with the Court. The opposition also made much of Fortas's role as a presidential adviser, claiming that the Justice and the President had violated the sanctity of separation of powers. A Republican filibuster succeeded: on October 1, the Senate voted 45–43 on a motion to close debate, fourteen votes short of the two-thirds necessary to proceed to the nomination.[29] It was a staggering, embarrassing result for both Fortas and his patron.

Earl Warren's status now was in limbo. As it became clear that Fortas could not be confirmed, Warren gave a rare interview, emphasizing that he had told President Johnson that he would retire "at your pleasure." Asked whether this meant Johnson's pleasure or that of the "office of the presidency," Warren grinned and cryptically urged his interviewer "to read the letter." Whatever he meant, the public perception was that the Chief Justice intended to retire. Nixon, however, took no chances. After taking office, he sent William Rogers to visit the Chief Justice to work out the precise timing of his departure, and they agreed that Warren would step down in June. With that, Nixon instructed Attorney General John Mitchell to begin the search for a successor.[30]

Apparently Nixon gave some consideration to promoting Associate Justice Potter Stewart, a moderate Republican. But, given the President's campaign talk about changing the Supreme Court, Stewart's promotion was unlikely despite his fair degree of opposition to some of the same Warren Court rulings that rankled conservatives. Stewart later claimed that he did not want the Chief Justice's job, calling it a "lousy" one, fine for "someone who wants the highest title he can get, but it adds nothing to the best job in the world, that is, being a justice."[31]

The "highest title" was not altogether unappealing, however, for Warren Earl Burger, judge of the federal Circuit Court of Appeals for the District of Columbia. The D.C. Circuit was generally then regarded as the bastion of judicial liberalism and activism. In scholarly and Washington legal circles, its members were often as well known, and sometimes more highly regarded, than the Justices of the Supreme Court. Headed by the controversial David Bazelon, the D.C. Circuit Court helped shape many of the provocative doctrines more familiarly known as products of the Warren Court. The Circuit Court judges were like-minded and rendered decisions marked with a high rate of agreement. Court-watchers knew, however, that Warren Burger stood out as the exception who proved the rule. Burger, a former Assistant Attorney General, had been appointed to the Circuit Court by Eisenhower in the late 1950s. He consistently took issue with his liberal colleagues, often sarcastically berating what he considered their activism, elitism, and excessive concern with the rights of defendants at the expense of social order. In 1967, *U.S. News & World Report* published excerpts from some of Burger's dissents and speeches, emphasizing his law-and-order themes. The article caught the attention of then-candidate Richard Nixon, and he used some of the ideas in his presidential campaign. Impressed with Burger's "moderate conservatism," Nixon nominated Burger as Chief Justice on May 21, 1969.[32]

It was an adroit move. The President avoided any charge of cronyism or political payoff. Instead, Nixon selected a man with judicial experience and one who fulfilled his campaign pledge to appoint judges mindful of the "peace forces." Typically, the President could not resist a jab at the ideological opposition. Introducing Burger to a national television audience, the President emphasized his nominee's "unquestioned integrity throughout his public and private life"—an obvious reference to Fortas's problems, which had received even more publicity since his failed nomination the previous year. Despite doubts on the part of those who had closely studied Burger's opinions—doubts that were both ideological and intellectual—the nomination had little difficulty in the Democratic-dominated Senate, and Burger was confirmed a month later.

The day after the nomination, the President called in reporters to discuss his ideas about Supreme Court Justices. Nixon said that he would have an "arm's-length" relationship with Burger—again, a dig at Fortas. But he focused his remarks on his own philosophy as a "strict constructionist." What had once been a clearly understood term in scholarly discourse about the Constitution now became a pliant phrase, grist for political exploitation and manipulation. Politicians who railed against the Warren Court's expansive views of civil liberties appropriated the slogan as their own. The criticism dripped with irony. A generation earlier, "strict construction" had been the liberals' rallying cry against alleged conservative excesses in construing the

Constitution to invalidate modern liberalism. Moreover, Justice Hugo Black, often credited for leading the modern Court's libertarian drives, always insisted that he was a strict constructionist; his opinions, he contended, merely enforced the protective language of the document.

Black's definition in its own way departed from the original understanding of the term. In the early nineteenth century, strict construction was advocated by those who opposed what they regarded as the overly broad interpretations of the Constitution by Chief Justice John Marshall. But at that time, Marshall was regarded as the consummate conservative. His opponents, particularly Thomas Jefferson (who on occasion found it convenient to discard his own notions of strict construction), were the liberals of their day. Nixon's response to the Supreme Court's decision in 1962 prohibiting prayer in the public schools underlined how useless the public discourse over strict construction had become. Asked for his reaction, Nixon said that he had "no intention of criticizing" the ruling. In the next breath, however, he complained that the Court had "followed its usual pattern of interpreting the Constitution rigidly."[33]

If the Burger nomination was a political and personal triumph for the President, his next offerings were disastrous. Perhaps nothing with the exception of the ever-growing interinstitutional conflicts of the Vietnam war so poisoned the relations between Nixon and Congress as the Senate's rejection of his successive nominations of Clement Haynsworth and G. Harrold Carswell to the Court. A failure to confirm a presidential nomination is rare enough, but for it to happen with two successive nominees was truly extraordinary. The Senate's action resulted from its differences with the President over political objectives and philosophy, but it also must be viewed from the perspective of the Fortas rejection in 1968 and the circumstances surrounding his resignation the next year.

Fortas's confirmation hearings exposed doubts about his integrity, doubts that lingered as a ticking time bomb. Several months after his nomination as Chief Justice failed, a *Life* magazine article charged that Fortas had accepted improper fees and had intervened with a federal regulatory agency in behalf of a former client whose foundation he served as a paid consultant. And Department of Justice investigators reportedly turned up more incriminating evidence. The *Chicago Tribune* disclosed on May 14 that the department had sent word to Fortas that he had "been extended unusual courtesy" because of the need to respect the Court, but he also was reportedly told by someone in the department that the courtesy was not "openended." Fortas was threatened with release of the information unless he resigned from the Court. As the pressure intensified against Fortas, Attorney General Mitchell visited Chief Justice Warren and briefed him on the department's evidence; shortly afterward, Fortas submitted his resignation. Mitchell and his aides carefully orchestrated a press campaign that fostered the impression of a very substantial case against Fortas. In fact, they did not have an airtight case, as one aide later admitted.

The Republicans' glee at Fortas's downfall was undisguised, but that reaction disturbed some Administration supporters. Court of Appeals Judge Warren Burger, for example, told the President that Republicans should consider points of "basic fairness" as well as the political consequences that such behavior could have for future Supreme Court nominees. He warned Nixon that the "suppressed rage" of Fortas's supporters "will likely assert itself and your nominee may become *their* 'whipping boy.' "[34] The next nominee—coincidentally, Burger himself—emerged unscathed, but his prophecy soon proved correct.

Fortas's resignation sparked presidential aide Pat Buchanan's talent for convoluted political maneuvers. Buchanan told the President that Mitchell had hinted that the charges regarding Fortas were "only a part" of what might be revealed against other Justices. Perhaps the President was about to reap a bonanza. But Buchanan warned that Nixon's first nominee must not be perceived as "Nixon's Fortas." Instead, Buchanan offered a scenario whereby Associate Justice John Marshall Harlan—widely respected by all sides—would be elevated to Chief Justice as an "interim Pope," while the President selected the "most able, most brilliant" appellate judge as Associate Justice. Buchanan's endgame envisioned two triumphs for the President: first, Nixon would gain the prestige of a Harlan nomination, but also Harlan's age and his physical infirmity meant that Nixon might name two Chief Justices in his first term.[35]

The President's selection of Burger had obvious political motivations. His next choices for the Court offered payment on his obligation to key Southern supporters, particularly Senator J. Strom Thurmond, to appoint a man from the South—presumably a judge who would be less amenable to pressures to uphold desegregation measures. On August 18, 1969, Nixon nominated Clement F. Haynsworth, who had spent the past twelve years on the Fourth Circuit Court of Appeals and who was, like Thurmond, a South Carolinian. By now, the Fortas affairs—both in 1968 and in 1969—had provoked deep resentment among Senate Democratic liberals. The Haynsworth nomination and its apparent link to Nixon's vaunted "Southern Strategy" only exacerbated their hostility. But Haynsworth had just enough vulnerability as a Supreme Court nominee to enable the senators to rationalize their opposition on more than political or ideological grounds.

"The President particularly wants to see us scoring points on Haynsworth in the South. He has been pushing me on this," presidential aide Harry Dent reported. Dent had been a Thurmond assistant, and he was a primary Nixon advisor on politics, particularly Southern politics. But the appeal to the South only gave Northern liberals increased determination to defeat Haynsworth's nomination. Senator Birch Bayh of the Judiciary Committee led the opposition, focusing on two points. First, there was some question of Haynsworth's personal ethics, as it was discovered that he had ruled in a case involving a company in which he owned stock. Second, some of his decisions in labor and civil rights cases aroused opposition from powerful constituencies to which Senate liberals had intimate, perhaps even dependent, links. While Haynsworth had significant support from liberals who knew him or who had studied his work, they were isolated and eventually overwhelmed by the concerted lobbying of organized labor and civil rights organizations.[36]

As the opposition developed, the President counterattacked in his own way. He accused senators of "character assassination" and vigorously defended Haynsworth. Instead of defending the judge's record and invoking his respectable list of supporters, Nixon emphasized presidential prerogative and threw down the gauntlet to the liberal opposition. Haynsworth's conservative philosophy was precisely what Nixon wanted: "I think the court needs balance and I think the Court needs a man who is conservative." Meanwhile, Dent's staff diligently investigated Senator Bayh's own financial dealings and his ties to organized labor. They also urged Republican Whip Robert Griffin (who had organized the filibuster on the Fortas nomination) to mute his opposition to Haynsworth. When Senator Edward Brooke (R–MA)—the only black in the Senate—hinted that he would vote against Haynsworth, Nixon wrote him to defend the judge's racial views and civil rights record. He regretted Brooke's statement, but even more he regretted that Brooke "felt compelled to publicize the difference between us." Griffin and other Republican senators urged the President to withdraw the nomination, but he steadfastly refused.[37] On November 21, seventeen Republicans joined a 55–45 majority to reject Haynsworth.

For the first time since 1930, the Senate had turned down a presidential nomination to the Supreme Court. The Haynsworth defeat demonstrated the fragility of Richard Nixon's congressional support only one year after his election. Likewise, it demonstrated the reality that the opposition's power necessitated some finesse, some accommodation on the part of the Administration. What was *not* needed was further confrontation. Betraying his pique, even his contempt, for the Senate action, however, Nixon announced that he would invoke the same criteria for his next Court nominee. In fact, he did not. Instead, he offered a caricature of a Southern conservative, resulting in a humiliating defeat and a decisive break in his congressional relations.

G. Harrold Carswell was born in Georgia and attended law school there, but after an unsuccessful campaign for the state legislature, he moved to Florida. Carswell converted to the Republican Party in the 1950s, and Eisenhower appointed him U.S. Attorney and then a federal district judge. President Nixon promoted Carswell to the Fifth Circuit bench shortly after he took office. In that brief honeymoon period, the Senate did not scrutinize nominations very closely, particularly when they involved apparently routine judicial promotions. Florida Governor Claude Kirk suggested Carswell as a Supreme Court nominee to Nixon in May 1969, endorsing him as "a man for all 'regions.' "

The immediate response to Carswell's Supreme Court nomination seemed favorable; most of the President's Republican opponents in the Haynsworth affair quickly indicated that they would have no difficulty supporting a Southern nominee. The "Carswell Game Plan," as devised by White House aide Lyn Nofziger, oozed confidence. Nofziger quickly had taken action "to nullify wrongful racist charges," which some critics, he said, had raised against the nominee. Assistant Attorney General William Rehnquist, who had a part in Carswell's selection, insisted that there was "nothing else in Carswell's background to worry about." He had devised a brief, "The Case for Judge Carswell," for distribution to key aides. Finally, Rehnquist would be available to write speeches for Senator Roman Hruska (R–NB), a key Administration supporter on the Judiciary Committee, and he would provide some "attack material" for Nofziger's use.[38]

Within a few days, however, civil rights groups denounced the nomination, pointing out incidents of Carswell's rudeness toward black attorneys, the substantial number of his rulings against civil rights advocates, and the high rate of reversal of his opinions by the Fifth Circuit. Opponents also unearthed a 1948 statement in which Carswell said that "segregation of the races is proper and the only practical and correct way of life in our states. I have always so believed and I shall always so act." The nominee promptly went on national television and repudiated the statement. Unfortunately, prompt investigations showed that strong racial biases continued to pervade Carswell's personal affairs and judicial decisions long after the 1948 statement.

The hearings by the Senate Judiciary Committee brought forth an array of witnesses who denounced Carswell as racist, antilabor, and hostile toward women's rights. Leaders and scholars within the national legal community severely criticized the appointment, one witness declaring that Carswell's record was distinguished only for his "persistent refusal to make the law an effective shield for black people claiming elemental rights." Yale Law School Dean Louis Pollak (a former Supreme Court clerk) struck the dominant chord when he charged that Carswell had a mediocre record and "the most slender credentials of any man put forward [for the Court] in this century." The response of the Administration was lame and became a classic. During the Senate debate in March, Senator Hruska confronted Pollak's charges and said that there "are a lot of mediocre judges and people and lawyers. They are entitled to a little representation, aren't they, and a little chance?" The bitterness was all too apparent: "We can't have all Brandeises and Cardozos and Frankfurters and all stuff like that there," the Senator went on. Although Hruska denied that Carswell was mediocre, the damage was done.

The President put it a bit more elegantly when he said that Carswell's 1948 statement did not concern him, but that the nominee's twelve-year judicial record was sufficient—"a record which is impeccable and without a taint of any racism, a record, yes, of strict constructionism [in] . . . the interpretation of the Constitution and . . . the Court needs [that] . . . kind of balance." Privately, the President was seething. In a White House meeting with key aides on March 26, 1970, he said that he never wanted Republican Senators Case, Goodell, Mathias, Percy, and Schweiker in the White House, complaining that they were not supporting him on this or any other issue. He was bitter about the lack of concerted effort on Carswell's behalf from the Justice Department. Mitchell, he said, was "on the line," and apparently, he was not satisfied with Rehnquist's work. Ehrlichman reported that the President said the Assistant Attorney General was "not a nutcutter." Someone in the group—Nixon or Haldeman—saw the handwriting on the wall: "we'll prob[ably] lose it."[39] Two weeks later, despite intense White House pressure on Republicans, the Senate rejected the Carswell nomination, 51–45.

The President responded with a display of public anger nearly comparable to his dramatic "last press conference" in 1962. He turned the charges of bias around and accused the detractors of both Haynsworth and Carswell of "vicious assaults" on the nominees' intelligence, integrity, and character. They had been falsely accused of racism. Strip away the hypocrisy, the President said, and what was left was that both men had been rejected for their legal philosophy of strict construction, "and also the accident of their birth, the fact that they were born in the South." With a bow to his Southern supporters, the President reluctantly concluded that the Senate, "as presently constituted, will not approve a man from the South who shares my views of strict construction." That was the political challenge to the Senate, as well as an emotional appeal to the South.

But Nixon also contended that his "constitutional responsibility" of appointment was frustrated by senators who wished to impose their philosophical views on the process. The Senate, he insisted, had violated the proper constitutional arrangements for appointments—and for personal reasons. With vintage self-pity, Nixon rhetorically asked whether he would be "accorded the same right of choice in naming Supreme Court justices which has been freely accorded to my predecessors of both parties." In this the President simply was wrong: the Senate had rejected twenty-four Supreme Court nominees—nearly a fourth of the total number of justices in American history until that time. The framers had a specific intention in their requirement of Senate "advice and consent" to nominees. Alexander Hamilton wrote at the time of the adoption of the Constitution that "the possibility of rejection would be a strong motive to care in proposing.'' Nearly twenty years after the Haynsworth and Carswell votes, a more popular president than Nixon realized the virtue of consulting in advance the Senate leadership before proposing a nominee.[40]

The President subsequently nominated Judge Harry Blackmun of the Eighth Circuit Court of Appeals. Some senators worried that the nominee would prove only a twin to his fellow Minnesotan, Chief Justice Burger, but Blackmun's record appeared competent and workmanlike. Above all, it generated little controversy. Republican Senator Robert Dole complained to the President about naming a second Minnesotan and another nominee in his sixties, but he went along with the nomination.

The President had his own way of saving face in the Blackmun nomination. He told Haldeman to have somebody like Senator Hruska praise the nomination as that of a man who shared the same constitutional philosophies as Haynsworth and Carswell. ''This line,'' Nixon said, must have the ''highest priority with our whole Congressional and PR staff.'' He wanted it known that Blackmun was to the right of the other candidates on law and order and ''very slightly to the left only in the field of civil rights.'' He did not want the nomination in any way to appear as a concession to liberals or to indicate that he ''was forced to back down by the Senate and name a liberal or even a quasi-liberal.'' This project, he instructed Haldeman, had ''the highest urgency.''

Meanwhile, Justice Potter Stewart counseled the President to meet Blackmun, to understand what kind of man he had nominated. The President had not seen Haynsworth or Carswell, and Stewart thought unfamiliarity had led Nixon to mistake the quality of the men. Stewart forcefully reminded the White House that it is the President, not the Attorney General or his staff, who appoints Supreme Court justices.[41]

Whatever Nixon's motives in naming Blackmun, the judge was confirmable, and the Senate unanimously approved his nomination. Ironically, Blackmun produced the Nixon Court's most controversial decision with his 1973 *Roe v. Wade* abortion opinion, one that since has been the important rallying point for conservative advocates of ''strict construction.''

One week before the Senate rejected Carswell in April 1970, House Republican leader Gerald Ford leveled a variety of allegations concerning ethical and judicial improprieties against Associate Justice William O. Douglas, long the darling of liberals. Ford asked for a special committee to investigate the charges and determine whether they merited an impeachment. Ford intended that his proposal go to the conservative-dominated House Rules Committee, but the Democrats, in a parliamentary maneuver of their own, introduced an impeachment resolution, thus ensuring jurisdiction for the Judiciary Committee, which had a heavy representation of northern liberals.

Ford's timing was hardly coincidental. A newspaperman friendly to Ford, who later became his Press Secretary, described the move as a White House-inspired attempt to retaliate against Senate liberals for the defeat of Haynsworth and Carswell, and contended that Ford had been "tricked" into making the move. Nixon himself asked J. Edgar Hoover to brief Ford on Douglas. The Justice Department provided Ford with material for his original speech and subsequent ones. Ford later stated that the Justice Department gave him "leads" but then refused further cooperation. Yet he admitted periodic contact with Will Wilson, an Assistant Attorney General, and one of his staff acknowledged that Ford's office had help from a middle-level Justice official who ran the names of some Douglas associates through the computer files. Ford at one point complained to White House aide Bryce Harlow that the IRS would not furnish him with information on Douglas "unless there is a *special* Presidential directive requiring that this material be provided." Harlow told one of his assistants to follow through, "because there is some growing indication, involving Justice as well as IRS, of a low level bureaucratic attempt to frustrate a full-fledged investigation." In other words, the White House wanted a serious investigation but once again allegedly found itself thwarted by a recalcitrant bureaucracy. Later, however, Wilson complained that "Ford took the material we gave him and screwed it up. Ford blew it."[42]

Ford's blunderbuss charges made it relatively easy for Judiciary Committee Chairman Emanuel Celler and Douglas's counsel, former federal judge Simon Rifkind, to dismiss them as partisan and frivolous. Even if there had been merit and seriousness in the allegations, the clumsy, obvious hand of the White House and the Justice Department would have only lent an air of political vendetta to the proceedings. The whole affair backfired for the Administration (and for Ford personally); worse, it left a legacy that four years later came back to haunt Richard Nixon.

In his opening salvo against Douglas, Ford raised the question of what constituted an impeachable offense. "The only honest answer," he responded, "is that an impeachable offense is whatever a majority of the House of Representatives considers [it] to be at a given moment in history; conviction results from whatever offense or offenses two-thirds of the other body considers to be sufficiently serious to require removal of the accused from office." Impeachment, Ford later argued, was a "protective," not a "punitive," device. It was meant to protect the nation from official misdeeds and need not involve criminal offenses, he said.[43] Ford had a good deal of history on his side supporting those arguments, history that he and the President conveniently repudiated in 1974.

White House staff workers blamed Attorney General Mitchell and his department for badly advising the President on Supreme Court matters. Particularly critical was John Ehrlichman, who constantly sniped at the Attorney General. But the appointments and confrontations served a variety of presidential political needs, including appeasing the South and publicly challenging congressional liberals. By late 1971, with two new nominations to submit and an election only a year away, the Administration could no longer afford mistakes.

Ehrlichman had his protégé Egil Krogh devise procedures to tighten the White House grip and influence on Court nominations, primarily at the expense of the Justice Department. Krogh told Ehrlichman that the President could not again "play catch up ball with a nomination." Conceding initial selection and checkout procedures to Justice and the FBI, Krogh suggested that a White House unit be established to oversee the proceedings—with John Ehrlichman at the helm. Krogh devised roles for the President's key men in securing future nominations: Clark MacGregor and William Timmons to handle Congress, William Safire to deal with the press, Charles Colson to brief various interest groups, and John Dean to coordinate the others. Krogh urged that David Young, his fellow Plumber—whom Krogh called "the one independent mind, very facile and penetrating"—should be heavily involved. Krogh also did not trust the FBI. He proposed "CIA-type debriefings" of two to three days for leading Court candidates, particularly emphasizing "*demeanor* evidence." Finally, if the President submitted two nominations, the more difficult one should go first, Krogh wrote. Subsequently, someone—presumably Krogh—devised a questionnaire for candidates, including queries regarding their financial net worth, psychiatric background, family relations, possible "guilt by association," knowledge of "enemies," life-style, and specific positions on civil rights, criminal procedure, wiretapping, the right of privacy, subversive activities, and church–state relations.[44]

The White House knew that numerous members of the Court were in precarious health. Shortly after his sharp attack on the Nixon Administration for its attempts to censor the press in the Pentagon Papers case, Justice Hugo Black became gravely ill. He submitted his resignation in September 1971. A week later, Justice Harlan, nearly blind and debilitated by bone cancer, also resigned. It was a golden opportunity for the President, but he came perilously close to opting for mediocrity and confronting the Senate once more.

Nixon now found himself pressured from an unexpected quarter. His wife publicly stated that she was pushing for the nomination of a woman. "I'm talking it up," she told reporters. "If we can't get a woman on the Supreme Court this time, there'll be a next time." When her husband submitted two male nominees, Pat Nixon "strongly" told the President that he should have named a woman. "With exaggerated weariness," according to his daughter, the President cut off the conversation, telling her: "We tried to do the best we could, Pat."[45] Indeed, there had been serious consideration of a woman. The 1971 nominations witnessed a sharp struggle between those in the

White House who sought to exploit immediate political advantages even if doing so occasioned further conflict with the Senate, and those who tried to persuade the President to act for long-term political advantage and his historical reputation. Pat Buchanan argued for quick nominations "to head off mounting lobbies of women, blacks and labor." He pressed hard for a southerner, asserting that Senator Edmund Muskie (the Democrats' leading presidential contender) would have difficulty explaining away three antisouthern votes, especially if the nominee were a congressman.

Buchanan had a candidate: Richard Poff, a Virginia Representative, a member of the House Judiciary Committee, and highly respected among congressional southerners and conservatives. Poff had a problem, however: he had long ago signed the so-called "Southern Manifesto," counseling resistance to the Court's 1954 desegregation decision. Buchanan found that tantalizing, thinking that an "impeccable" nomination such as Poff's would generate a Senate "mini-rebellion." It would be a bitterly divisive issue for the Democrats: "either they kick their black friends in the teeth, or they kick the South in the teeth." As long as the Administration nominated "qualified strict constructionists," then the Democrats were "on the hook." Buchanan also urged the President to reject Irving Kristol's suggestion of University of Chicago President Edward Levi as a nominee. Buchanan thought there was no mileage in the President's nominating a Jewish candidate; instead, he urged Nixon to find "the most brilliant and qualified Italian-American strict constructionist . . . and then name play up his Italian background—and let the Democrats chop him up, if they want." Sectional wars, partisan wars, ethnic wars—they were all grist for Buchanan's assault on Democratic senators.

Leonard Garment weighed in with his own political calculus. He thought that time was not of the essence; what was important was for the President to choose wisely and avoid a prolonged fight. Garment's immediate concern was scuttling Poff. Poff's views on race, women, and ethnics offered obvious rallying points for the Administration's well-entrenched and vocal foes. The President needed Senate support for other items on the agenda; why needlessly antagonize? Garment appealed to Nixon to encourage an "open discussion" of candidates and to avoid "surprises." Such discussion, he believed, would prevent possible embarrassment and indicate the Administration's seriousness in finding the best-qualified nominees.[46]

Buchanan pursued the President's heart; Garment went for his head. Meanwhile, the Administration's internecine battle over Supreme Court nominees had become public, and Poff withdrew (probably in accord with White House wishes) to avoid a protracted battle. The President and his aides gave some consideration to nominating a Senator, hoping to simplify the confirmation procedure. Apparently, Howard Baker (R-TN) was given an informal offer. In a more cynical vein, to annoy liberals Nixon let it be known that he was considering Senator Robert Byrd (D–WV).

Garment's views did not immediately prevail; instead, a variety of sources pushed the candidacies of Mildred Lillie and Herschel Friday. Lillie was a Superior Court judge in Los Angeles who first had been touted to Nixon by Mayor Sam Yorty. The President had two of his aides convey the suggestion to Mitchell. Apparently the Attorney General believed that it constituted an endorsement, or at least an idea to be taken seriously. Assistant Attorney General Rehnquist certainly treated Lillie seriously and defended her judicial record.[47] Friday was a Little Rock lawyer, known to Mitchell from their work together as municipal-bond attorneys. Beyond these vague links, neither candidate had much by way of recommendation; indeed, the American Bar Association indicated to Mitchell that it would not be able to endorse either Friday or Lillie. (Perhaps Lawrence Walsh, head of the ABA committee on Court candidates, remembered his public embarrassment when the committee endorsed Carswell.)

With the Lillie and Friday nominations, the Administration stood at the brink of another political and public-relations disaster. If the nominations were made, and without ABA support, the likelihood was that the Senate again would reject the President's choices. This time, however, confrontation was avoided. Just before the ABA decision became a matter of public record, on October 21, 1971, the President nominated Lewis Powell, a Richmond, Virginia, lawyer and a past president of the ABA, and Assistant Attorney General Rehnquist.

Powell's nomination won widespread acclaim, giving the lie to Nixon's earlier charge that the Senate would not confirm a southerner. Powell had a reputation as a conservative, an able lawyer, and a strict constructionist, but he also had gained praise for his role, as school-board chairman, in peacefully desegregating the Richmond public schools. He impressed the Senate Judiciary Committee with his balanced views. The government, he said, had a right to protect itself against potential insurrectionaries, but it must avoid injuring or arresting innocent people. He conceded that wiretapping could be justified at times, but he assured the committee that he would oppose "indiscriminate" use of it.

Nixon's problem this time was with a displaced Wisconsinite who had moved to Arizona. Enough was known about William Rehnquist to tab him as a conservative ideologue. His views on desegregation became suspect following the revelation of a memorandum he had written while clerking for the late Justice Robert Jackson in the early 1950s. Rehnquist claimed that the memo merely summarized different "legal" views of segregation, not his own. There were also questions about his advice to the Administration on the civil rights status of antiwar demonstrators. Rehnquist refused to discuss these matters, claiming attorney-client privilege. Senator Birch Bayh urged Nixon to waive the privilege. Inasmuch as Rehnquist supposedly shared the President's judicial philosophy, the Senator insisted it was important that Rehnquist enlighten the Senate on those views. Bayh's position cannot have been new to Rehnquist. Writing in 1959, largely in protest against the civil rights views of the Warren Court, Rehnquist himself had called on the Senate to do a better job of determining the judicial philosophy of Supreme Court nominees. "The only way for the Senate to learn of these sympathies," he said, was to make proper inquiries during the confirmation process.

The President refused to waive attorney-client privilege, and Rehnquist did not discuss with the Senate committee his judicial philosophy. Nixon later happily recalled that he picked Rehnquist for his philosophy. He was particularly impressed with Rehnquist's appearance before the Senate Judiciary Committee. "Demolished them," Ehrlichman noted, although Nixon also had earlier called Rehnquist "a clown."[48] Rehnquist was confirmed on a 68–26 vote.

The Powell and Rehnquist appointments to the Supreme Court were Nixon's last. Yet he had hopes of more. In late 1972 he instructed Ehrlichman to tell Burger to "nudge" Justices Douglas and Thurgood Marshall, both reportedly in ill health. A few months later, the President thought he should replace Burger, given that the Chief Justice was getting on in years. If Burger wanted more government service, Ehrlichman was instructed to tell him that "we'll find something worthy of you."[49] Nothing came of either idea.

Nixon's battles with the Senate over Supreme Court nominations offered a vivid example of his determination to change national priorities without interference or challenge by Congress. Despite the Democratic majority in the Senate—perhaps even a liberal ideological majority—Nixon boldly confronted that power. He would have had no difficulty had he initially nominated Justices with the qualities of Powell or Blackmun. These men were hardly liberals, yet their personal characters were unimpeachable and their legal records worthy of broad support. Rehnquist's well-known rightist views proved no handicap when weighed against his intellectual and legal capabilities. Nixon's early nomination of lesser candidates showed his contempt for both the Senate's political sensibilities and its constitutional role, as well as his contempt for the Court as an institution. How else to explain the nominations, even the serious consideration, of a Carswell, a Lillie, a Poff, or a Friday? Those names might have provided some short-range political mileage for Nixon, but their obscurity belittled the Court's significance as an institution, and their mediocrity only signaled the President's willingness to devalue the Court's role in the governmental apparatus.

* * *

The struggles with Congress over the Supreme Court, over executive-branch reorganization, and over impoundment of allocated funds contributed to the ever-growing tension between the President and Congress. These battles were important, yet they were sometime things, occasioned by momentary considerations or needs. By contrast, the persistence of the Vietnam conflict, and the widened battles at home over that war, colored both the day-to-day and long-term relations between the two branches. Johnson's tarbaby became Nixon's, and as with his predecessor, President Nixon's perception of American interests abroad poisoned his own fortunes at home. In his 1968 campaign, Nixon had recognized that the United States must extricate itself from the war. Yet questions of how and when proved as explosive and intractable as the war itself.

Public protests against the Vietnam war mounted at the outset of the Nixon Administration, but after the fatal shootings of student demonstrators at Kent State and Jackson State Universities in May 1970, and the bombing at the University of Wisconsin in August 1970, some of that pressure abated. Not so in Congress, however.

Thanks largely to the growing realization that President Johnson had interpreted the Gulf of Tonkin Resolution as a blank check for conducting the war on his own terms, Congress had grown increasingly suspicious of executive policy. Nixon's lament about Congress's denial of the "free hand" in Supreme Court appointments that had been given to his predecessors might have rung truer regarding Vietnam and foreign policy. The traditional liberal faith in a strong presidency had particularly underlined the need for broad presidential powers in foreign policy; Americans looked to their presidents to play the leading role for the United States in world affairs.

Now, for a variety of reasons—a realization of its rightful role, a response to public pressures, a distrust of Richard Nixon—Congress began to assert itself in foreign-policy concerns after a long period of quiescence. The ingredients were all in place for fateful clashes.

Congress's customary behavior had permitted an extravagant growth of executive war powers. Perhaps Congress had been overwhelmed by a "cult of executive expertise"; perhaps there was a residue of guilt left over from the Senate's 1919 rejection of the League of Nations and American international responsibilities; or perhaps, as a Senate committee suggested in 1969, Congress found itself "unprepared" to assert its constitutional role as the United States suddenly found itself in a new and dangerous world after 1945.[50] In any event, for better than a generation, presidents generally dealt with tame, pliant congresses in foreign-policy matters. The frustrating obstacles Congress regularly had imposed on presidential domestic policies simply were absent in foreign affairs. With cause, Richard Nixon thought he had a "free hand" in the international arena.

Henry Kissinger's interest in defending his actions and those of the President inevitably conflicted with his scholarly, historical detachment. In a rare moment, however, detachment prevailed as Kissinger clearly stated the ironic, tragic nature of the conflict between the President and Congress over foreign policy. The Vietnam debate, Kissinger later wrote, "represented a flight into nostalgia," a notion that America had somehow lost its way and desperately needed to recover its moral purity. Kissinger dismissed the confusion and debate over the war as an expression of self-indulgence that "opened the floodgates of chaos and exacerbated . . . internal divisions." Kissinger admitted that Nixon compounded the bitterness with an ample dose of his own. Convinced that he confronted a hostile conspiracy, Nixon responded with anger toward critics of his withdrawal plans, and toward what he saw as a lack of concern with the fate of innocent populations of Indochina. He also deplored the radical opposition to his foreign policy, marked by firebombings, thefts of classified information, incitements to draft resistance, and leaks of sensitive documents. Typically, the President charged that "intellectuals" and opponents of the war such as the *New York Times* thought they were "doing God's work." Nixon criticized in general terms the media, the "eastern establishment," and "Congress v. us," particularly singling out Senators Fulbright and Mansfield, respectively the Chairman of the Senate Foreign Relations Committee and the Senate's Majority Leader.[51]

Congress signalled its shifting mood toward control of foreign policy only months after Nixon assumed power. The Senate overwhelmingly approved the "National Commitments Resolution" on June 25, 1969, a statement designed to reassert Congress's role in committing American armed forces to the defense of other nations. Such action, the Senate said, "results only from affirmative action taken by the legislative and executive branches." Nixon criticized the proposal as unduly tying the President's hands. That was precisely the intent of the Senate: 45 senators who had voted for the Gulf of Tonkin Resolution in 1964 supported the 1969 action.

Nixon sensed the new mood. Just a few weeks earlier, he attacked critics of American foreign policy as "neo-isolationists." Yet several months later he effectively neutralized his critics with his response to the massive protests in October 1969. In a national television address, he appealed to the "Silent Majority," confidently asserting that they outnumbered the protesters and supported his goal of "peace with honor." North Vietnam, he insisted, could not defeat or humiliate the United States; "only Americans can do that." Three hundred representatives and fifty-eight senators signed a resolution supporting the President's Vietnam policies. The favorable response to the speech—his public-approval rating jumped to 68 percent—convinced Nixon that he now would have two years to complete a plan for a phased withdrawal of American troops, with the resulting "Vietnamization" of the war.[52]

The President had hoped to stave off public and congressional critics as the nation realized the wisdom of his plan. But six months later, his action ordering American forces into Cambodia to attack North Vietnamese and Viet Cong sanctuaries rekindled the opposition. Public protests cascaded throughout campuses and cities. Nixon responded on May 1, 1970, with a Pentagon speech attacking campus demonstrators as "bums" living a protected, sheltered life while "the kids" in Vietnam "stand tall." The remarks prefaced more violence, including the fatal shooting of students at Kent State University in Ohio. A week later, the President visited protesters at the Lincoln Memorial in the middle of the night, hoping to explain his policies in a direct, unprovocative manner. Public protests thereafter subsided somewhat, but more in fear of further violence than because of agreement with the President.[53]

The real change in attitude toward Vietnam was in Congress. On June 24, 1970, the Senate repealed the Gulf of Tonkin Resolution, 81–10. Nixon had not relied on that measure as overtly as Johnson; nevertheless, the vote was powerfully symbolic and a portent of congressional resistance. Nixon understood this. He wanted "our friends" to "fight [the repeal] vigorously," although he thought it "completely irrelevant as far as this Administration is concerned." Still, he was concerned that repeal of the historic resolution "might be detrimental to American foreign policy abroad since it could well be misunderstood." Republican Senator Jacob Javits of New York said that Congress must find the means to establish its authority at the outset of military hostilities—a cue for what was to become the War Powers Act of 1973. Representative John B. Anderson (R–IL), one of the Republican leaders, complained that the President had too much "initiative and responsibility" for deployment of American troops abroad; this was not, he said, the intent of the Constitution.[54]

The President counterattacked, instructing Cabinet members to defend the Cambodian action with direct attacks on Congress. Presidential surrogates emphasized the President's need to protect American troops and called upon Congress not to "stab our men in the back." Congressional resistance, it was suggested, gave the enemy "aid and comfort," encouraging them "to kill more Americans." If Congress voted against the war, the directive continued, then it "must assume responsibility" for the lives of American troops, "rather than leaving such responsibility, and the decisions connected with it," to the President. Finally, Congress must be held accountable "for an ignominious American defeat if it succeeds in tying the President's hands through a Congressional appropriation route."[55]

By June 1971, with the war and diplomatic negotiations both dragging on wearily, congressional restlessness gave rise to a gesture of rebellion. As part of a defense-authorization bill, Congress called on the President to terminate military operations in Indochina and provide for withdrawal within nine months, subject to the release of prisoners of war. In a bold fashion of his own, Nixon said he would ignore the proviso, since it did "not reflect my judgment about the way in which the war should be brought to a conclusion," adding that he considered the statement "without binding force or effect." The next year a federal court repudiated the President: "No executive statement denying efficacy to the legislation could have either validity or effect," the court's decision said, and the court characterized Nixon's statement as "very unfortunate."[56]

But the war continued, and the President planned to end American participation on his own terms. He also turned his attention to the war critics. Noting the correlation of their criticism and North Vietnamese resistance to his peace proposals, the President proposed an all-out attack on the critics, reminiscent in style and tone of his earlier political campaigns. He wanted his opponents accused of "playing politics with peace." He claimed that he had "done everything but offer surrender to the enemy." The critics, he charged, "want the United States to surrender to the Communists. They want to turn South Vietnam over to the Communists. . . . They want the enemy to win and the United States to lose." In a more positive vein, Nixon emphasized the necessity for negotiation and, correspondingly, the need for closing ranks. But he preferred "the attack line" to the positive one. Attack, he said, was more effective because it tended "to keep the critics from getting out too far and also because it simply makes more news. We have often failed in the past in these PR efforts because we simply have not had colorful enough attack lines and have not followed up on them. I do not want us to make that mistake this time," Nixon said. He told his aides to press leading Republicans to use these themes, and to find "a good, hard-hitting newspaper editorial" for broad circulation to friendly editors. Finally, he directed the staff to emphasize that Senators Muskie, Humphrey, and Kennedy "got us into the war [and] are now trying to sabotage Nixon's efforts to get us out." The President also had difficulties on the Right and in his own house. Vice President Agnew urged that there be no deal with North Vietnam unless it cleared all of its troops out of the South. "Unreasonable," the President told Ehrlichman.[57]

Nixon realized that Congress was the domestic battlefront, not the universities or the streets. But his assault was ineffective, and Congress responded in its own fashion. At the opening of the new Congress in 1973, Senate Majority Leader Mansfield told the Democratic caucus that the war must end. He did not know if it could be done through the legislative route, but he did "know that the time is long since past when we can take shelter in a claim of legislative impotence. We cannot dismiss our responsibility by deference to the President's." Apparently Mansfield's remarks anticipated Nixon's growing vulnerability and offered an opportunity for Congress to take the initiative. Soon, characterizations of congressional "impotence," "acquiescence," and "passivity" lost their earlier applicability. As the Senate Select Committee opened its hearings on the conduct of the President's 1972 re-election campaign, a House Foreign Affairs subcommittee began its own inquiry into the Constitution and war powers. Representative Spark M. Matsunaga (D-HI) offered a keynote: Vietnam's great lesson, he said, pointed out the need for "definite, unmistakable procedures to prevent future undeclared wars."[58] Months later, the War Powers Act of 1973 was law. Whatever its ambiguity, it offered a coda to the long struggle between the branches of government over Vietnam policy, and it signalled a new era in executive-legislative relations.

"Let's face it, most Americans today are simply fed up with government at all levels," Nixon said in his 1971 State of the Union message. The remark reflected frustration at his inability to gain congressional support for his program; it was an extension of the "deadlock" theme he had propounded in the 1970 midterm elections. The election results had changed nothing to alter the President's view of congressional relations. The attack on "government" was an oblique attack on Congress, and hence an attack on the Democratic Party as the party and paladin of government. Nixon's war on Congress would continue.

Modern presidential-congressional relations have a checkered history. Some observers have been critical of an altogether too compliant Congress. Carl Vinson, who first arrived as a Georgia Congressman in 1914, sadly lamented in 1973 that Congress was a "somewhat querulous but essentially kindly uncle who complains while furiously puffing on his pipe but who, finally, as everyone expects, gives in and hands over the allowance, grants the permission, or raises his hand in blessing, and then returns to his rocking chair for another year of somnolence broken only by an occasional glance down the avenue and a muttered doubt as to whether he had done the right thing." Indeed, even Richard Nixon could be a beneficiary of that kindly old uncle. Congress passed the Economic Stabilization Act in 1970, which gave the President sweeping authority to regulate wages and prices—a domestic equivalent to the Gulf of Tonkin Resolution, as one writer remarked.[59]

Still, the pattern of deadlock was real. More important, Congress had begun to resist and question executive authority, an authority that some believed relied too much on deceit and bullying. In facing those resentments, Nixon again had to grapple with a dubious legacy from LBJ, but his own actions contributed to an ever-widening gulf filled with mistrust, suspicion, and ill will between the White House and Congress. Nixon believed that government could work better, but only with changes in structure and direction. His rejection of traditional political accommodation in the legislative process, as well as his notions of change and effectiveness, clashed with those who believed in the status quo—or who distrusted Richard Nixon. They perceived his design as one that deliberately sought to devalue or weaken other institutions in order to strengthen his own influence and power. Perhaps the President believed that the 1972 campaign could change all that. For his second term, perhaps he could win a smashing victory, capture that ever-elusive mandate, and exercise power with an ideological majority in Congress that would enable him to imprint his stamp on other institutions.

The American people voted in 1972 to retain Richard Nixon for the usual mixture of positive and negative reasons. They also voted to retain a Congress dominated by Democrats. Nixon knew that this meant more confrontation and acrimony. The conflict went on and even escalated to include the President's urging his staff to order the IRS to audit every member of Congress. For Nixon, Congress was a hopelessly archaic institution that mindlessly resisted innovation both in other branches of government and in itself. He promised that by the end of his second term, he would "blast" Congress for having prolonged the Vietnam war by encouraging the enemy in hard bargaining. Nixon had no fear of challenging Congress. The nation, he believed, was indifferent to the question of which branch was supreme, although he warned his aides to be aware of seeming arrogance. Still, in an interview published after the election, he promised that he would move decisively in his second term. To his White House staff the President said: "There are no sacred cows. We will tear up the pea patch."[60] Even as he spoke, however, it was too late.

Richard Nixon admired Woodrow Wilson perhaps more than any other of his twentieth-century predecessors. As a professor, Wilson had studied and analyzed congressional power, drawing lessons that he usually applied with great skill as President. But tragically—some might say willfully—President Wilson failed to make the necessary bargains and accommodations to secure acceptance of his cherished League of Nations in 1919. On the League, he would have his way absolutely, or not at all. Strange, given Wilson's own axiom that the American system rejected absolute power anywhere: the tact and mutually beneficial bargaining that had characterized Wilson's earlier dealings with Congress gave way to direct confrontation in the vain hope that the American people would deliver a referendum vindicating him. It never came. Strange, too, that the same lesson seemed lost on Wilson's admiring pupil, Richard Nixon.

VII

MEDIA WARS

In December 1968, on the eve of his presidency, Richard Nixon solicited his speechwriters for a research paper recapitulating "the typical opposition smears of Richard Nixon back through the years, including the more vicious press comments." The staff ignored this particular request and according to William Safire, one of the writers, denied Nixon and his men the opportunity to "rub each other's sores"—a favorite Nixon phrase. There were plenty of sores to rub. Five years later, as his Administration began to unravel, Nixon described some reporters as snobs and offered a familiar refrain to one visitor: "I've earned their hatred." The hostile press was, he said, "all wrong on Hiss." Alger Hiss had provided Nixon with national attention, but Nixon knew the price. "[The Hiss-Chambers case] left a residue of hatred and hostility toward me—not only among Communists but also among substantial segments of the press and the intellectual community," he wrote in 1962. Anticommunism eventually lost some of its political appeal, but intellectuals and the press remained formidable adversaries, another vital link in Nixon's chain of enemies.[1]

Nixon had both an instinctive, visceral hatred of the news media and a compulsive desire to manipulate and tame them. At times, they were an enemy; at other moments, useful instruments to be played for political and public-relations gain. Richard Nixon and his aides spent much time attempting to master both drives. The Nixon Administration mounted an unprecedented, transparent assault on the media and individual reporters; yet that Administration, like others, went to extraordinary lengths to cultivate the press. And for good reason: the media had become an essential component in the task of governance in late-twentieth-century America. Mastery of it, or at least maintaining its goodwill, became a recognized, desirable prize as presidents sought to reach and shape public opinion and to build constituencies for their programs and future campaigns.

The news media have fostered and promoted a cult of presidential personality. Presidents make easier copy than such less sharply defined, more impersonal institutions as Congress, the courts, or the regulatory agencies. The President makes news; he *is* news. For many Americans, the President is the government of the United States. The problem for a president, therefore, is not visibility—that he has in abundance—but controlling that visibility to show himself in the best possible light.

Usually, the relationship between press and President has been relatively easy and friendly, and the media have normally been deferential. But because Richard Nixon believed the relationship to be adversarial and hostile, both by the nature of American government and because of his personal views, the problem became a fixation for him. His longtime friend and media adviser, Herbert Klein, acknowledged that "there was no organized conspiracy in the White House, but mistrust of the press was strong and ever present."

Klein had worked for Nixon since the 1950s as a press-relations specialist. After the 1962 gubernatorial defeat in California, Klein returned to San Diego, where he became the editor of the *Union,* the Copley chain's flagship newspaper. Klein rejoined Nixon for the 1968 presidential campaign. He soon recognized the ominous signs that the "New Nixon" had new extensions—Haldeman, Ehrlichman, Colson, Mitchell—to reflect and carry out some of his darker designs. It was a side of Nixon that Klein remembered and disliked. While Nixon shifted power to a new set of aides who would be close to him, however, he also found places for such older retainers as Klein.

Nixon and Haldeman installed Ronald Ziegler as Press Secretary. This was apparently a conscious move to diminish, certainly to subordinate, the position. Ziegler had been a Disneyland guide and a Haldeman aide in an advertising agency. Not to name a working reporter for the post marked a dramatic departure for a new Administration, although LBJ had done the same late in his presidency.

Herb Klein may have realized that Nixon intended to bypass him for his obvious role as Press Secretary, or he may have hoped the President had some more important job in mind for him. In any case, Klein proposed the creation of a wholly new White House post: Director of Communications, with himself as the obvious candidate. Klein's scheme provided that the

Director of Communications would report directly to the President, attend Cabinet meetings and other White House staff gatherings, and serve as the President's liaison to the newspapers and television networks. Klein envisioned an official in touch with network executives, anchormen, publishers, and leading columnists. Day-to-day news and briefings would be left to Ziegler. Significantly, Klein did not provide that the Director of Communications would direct Ziegler's office; he wisely sensed that would be the domain of the President and Haldeman. For Klein, however, it was a fatal omission in terms of his authority and effectiveness.[2]

The choice of Press Secretary, even the creation of a Communications Director, were somewhat immaterial. Nixon, determined as always to be the "man in charge," often demonstrated that *he* would decide what information the White House dispensed. For example, in November 1970, he prepared an elaborate ten-page memorandum for Haldeman, dictating answers to questions submitted for a later, "intimate, spontaneous" interview.[3]

In anticipation of the 1960 campaign, Nixon had told his staff that the only way to change the media was "not to cooperate with them." Ten years later his aides prepared memoranda listing various reporters "who should receive special treatment." On March 2, 1970, Nixon dispatched to Haldeman a flurry of directives relating to the press. In one, he called for "an all-out, slam-bang attack on the fact that the news people are overwhelmingly for Muskie, Kennedy, any liberal position. . . . I want a game plan on my desk." The same day he told Haldeman to arrange a private session with *Time* magazine correspondent Hugh Sidey. "Leave the time open so that I can talk to him as long as I feel it is worthwhile." Two years later, however, Nixon wanted Sidey "cut off in as effective a way as possible." The President directed his staff to treat the media with "the courteous, cool contempt which has been my policy over the last few years." Yet he took the trouble to write to another reporter, "I always will appreciate your objective coverage of my activities over the years," and at Nixon's direction, Haldeman privately pressed Time-Life executives to restrain their writers from going "beyond . . . normal objective criticism."[4]

Thus the President's mood toward the news media vacillated, usually in response to momentary externals. He perceived the media as a mixed bag of friendlies and unfriendlies. They were like any other interest group—to be courted and wooed as occasion dictated and to be fought when necessary.

The problem of Nixon's relations with the media, as the President often saw it, was not his, but theirs. He was delighted when Henry Kissinger turned the tables on James Reston's question as to why Nixon did not get along better with the press. Kissinger suggested to Reston that maybe the fault lay with the press. Nixon directed Haldeman to get a friendly columnist to explore the theme. Shortly afterward, however, the *New York Times* published the Pentagon Papers, and Nixon was in a frenzy. He told Haldeman

that "under absolutely no circumstances" was anyone in the White House
to give an interview or respond to any queries from the *Times*—"unless I
give express permission (and I do not expect to give such permission in the
foreseeable future)."

Nixon's suspicions and need for control of the press often came together.
Around the period of his banishing the *Times*, the President complained
to Haldeman that "K[issinger] went to L.A. *Times* again—*Why?*" A year
later, he ordered *Time* and *New Republic* White House reporters Hugh Sidey
and John Osborne excluded from receiving White House news summaries
and cut off from interviews. Nixon claimed to have unimpeachable evidence
that both reporters had said derogatory things in circles "where you really
find out what the people think—the Georgetown cocktail parties." Nixon
was livid. "There is no appeal whatever—I do not want it discussed with
me any further," he told Haldeman. He ordered Haldeman to crack down
on White House "prima donnas"—Kissinger?—who continued to give interviews.[5]

The relationship between Nixon and the media was not confined to hostility and conflict, however. The media form a vague, amorphous entity,
difficult to define precisely or clearly understand. Nixon's papers reveal a
steady torrent of his familiar diatribes against the press. No doubt they were
genuinely felt. Yet leading journalists—from press lords, to television executives, to working reporters—moved easily in Nixon's company and Administration circles. That kind of familiarity resulted in a press bonanza
that newspaper owners had been unable to reap from Lyndon Johnson's
Administration.

Competition from television, along with burgeoning costs, had resulted in
the steady closings of major newspapers, particularly in the large metropol-
itan areas. New York City, which once had boasted as many as twelve dai-
lies, was down to three by the 1970s. Typically, large cities had a morning
and an afternoon paper, with the latter generally lagging because of its head-
to-head competition with evening television news. The mounting economic
woes in newspaper publishing dictated cooperative ventures, in which competing newspapers merged their printing facilities and business offices. One
of the net effects was to create local monopoly situations in printing classified advertising. In response, the government brought antitrust proceedings,
winning in the lower court in 1965 and in the Supreme Court four years
later. Meanwhile, the newspapers sought support for a legislative exemption
from the antitrust laws, which would allow them to combine and so survive.

In June 1969, the Nixon Administration's new Assistant Attorney General
for the Anti-Trust Division, Richard W. McLaren, testified against the proposed Newspaper Preservation Act. The Democratic-dominated Judiciary
subcommittee appeared pleased with the Administration's position, but the
White House had yet to hear from its friends. Richard Berlin, President of

the Hearst Corporation, had neither hostility toward the newly elected President nor any compunctions about asking him to support the antitrust exemption. Berlin spoke of the matter as one of "common interest to both you and me," and gently reminded the President that "important publishers and friends of your administration" needed the exemption. "All of us look to you for assistance." Berlin spelled it out a bit more bluntly for McLaren. He told him that the affected newspaper publishers almost unanimously supported Nixon in 1968. "It therefore seems to me," Berlin said, "that those newspapers should, at the very least, receive a most friendly consideration." Finally, Berlin complained that the publishers had "become the victims and the targets" of a dated, narrow economic philosophy.

The friends Berlin spoke of represented the publishing chains of Hearst, Scripps-Howard (which controlled United Press International), Cox, Knight, Newhouse, and Block. While the exemption involved only a few of their newspapers, these chains combined reached forty million readers. Berlin's message came through loud and clear. Congress passed the Newspaper Preservation Act in 1969, and the President promptly signed it. The law inevitably facilitated the growth of more newspaper monopolies—and higher advertising costs. Nixon ignored advice from the Justice Department. Democrats, he knew, opposed the bill, and those who favored it, he said, "are for the most part on our side."

He was right. Despite Nixon's steady assaults on their integrity, their quality, indeed even their patriotism, most newspapers throughout the United States consistently gave him a high level of support. In 1972 the major chains supported Nixon and largely suppressed Watergate news, while four years earlier, a third of the Hearst and Cox newspapers and half of the Scripps-Howard chain had backed Hubert Humphrey. In the 1972 election, these chains unanimously endorsed the President.[6]

Writings on the news media alternatively have interpreted the Vietnam-Watergate years as marking the development of a new form of advocacy journalism that inevitably led to an adversarial relationship with power-holders or as years in which cooperation remained at the core of government-media relations, but in which the adversary elements became the most visible and vocal. In varying degrees, both interpretations accept the idea that government officials view the media as a natural enemy. Some emphasize governmental attempts to manipulate and intimidate, while others stress the use of the carrot and co-optation. The Nixon Administration, like all others, used a bit of both.

Whatever interpretation is taken, clearly the 1960s profoundly transformed the White House's relationship with the media. Until that time, the White House press corps resembled a club, observing certain rules and amenities

that lent an air of formality, privilege, and amicability to their relations with
the Administration. Unofficial but clear lines of mutual respect existed and
were well known. White House service was a plum assignment for reporters,
and they usually stayed for a long time.

The relationship changed. Perhaps it was a matter of style, as journalists
began to speak more and more of themselves as professionals. Competition
between print and electronic communications heightened the pressure for
the dramatic, the sensational, and the instant in the "news." The media's
concern was for the moment, and that made it more difficult for government
officials to work in obscurity and with regard for the long view. Journalism
was history with a 5:00 P.M. deadline.

The times themselves fostered a critical, cynical regard on the part of the
press for official statements and policies. For many journalists, the Vietnam
war operated on a level where reality clashed with the creation of official
illusions, even deceptions. The 1960s brought reporters a heightened perception that the interest of government was too easily identified with the
interest of a political man, an interest that then could be rationalized as in
harmony with the public's. Again, Richard Nixon had inherited an unwanted
legacy of media skepticism; but once more, it was a legacy to which he
brought his own special baggage.

Press attacks on the presidency were not new, of course. Truman and
Johnson, in recent years, had suffered enormously, but Nixon thought he
was uniquely victimized. Revealing both his phobia and his self-pity, he told
a correspondent in March 1971: "It is true that of all the Presidents in this
century, it is probably true, that I have less, as somebody has said, supporters in the press than any President." Nixon thought it was important
not to be captured by the Washington "elite crap." He scorned the Washington press and party scene, noting that "I'm one of the most hated"
presidents by the Washington establishment—particularly the media. He
thought this amusing because "they know I'm one of them, but I'm not
captured by them." Nixon never shared the confidence and luxury of Dwight
Eisenhower's observation at his first press conference that "I don't see that
a reporter could do that much to a President, do you?"[7] The times and the
President had changed.

Four years after what had seemed to be a humiliating defeat in the California
gubernatorial election, a defeat followed by the famous "last press conference," Nixon saw the reversal as fortunate. "California served a purpose,"
he said, "The press had a guilt complex about their inaccuracy. Since then
they've been generally accurate, and far more respectful." He acknowledged
that he had been too "serious" about the press, but "now I treat it like a
game." For the next several years, Nixon purposefully preyed upon that

guilt. The "game plan"—to use a term favored by the President and his courtiers—was designed to put the media into a "let's be fair to Nixon" mode. Nixon's 1968 victory gave him the power and resources to settle old scores and to turn the media to his advantage.[8]

Nixon deliberately sought to foster a public perception that he cared not a whit for his image, even while he anxiously reached out for public support and acceptance. In March 1971, he appeared for a two-hour interview on the *Today* television program. Emphasizing the "enormous responsibilities" of the presidency, Nixon insisted that the Chief Executive "must not be constantly preening in front of a mirror, wondering whether or not he is getting across as this kind of individual or that." He had no truck with the public-relations types "constantly riding me, or they used to in the campaign, and they do now. 'You have got to do this, that, and the other thing to change your image.' I am not going to change my image, I am just going to do a good job for this country." The facts were otherwise. Nixon was constantly concerned and preoccupied with image; and it was the President himself, not "spinmakers" and public-relations men, who set the agenda for this concern. Just prior to his *Today* appearance, Nixon told Haldeman that it was time to use a "full-time PR man to really convey the true image of a President to the nation."[9]

Five days after his inauguration, Nixon had advice for the "Five O'Clock Group," a task force created to manage the news flow. He told Ehrlichman that he wanted someone to do "an effective job on the RN come-back theme. Some way I just don't feel we have adequately presented this case and that we have generally been too defensive on our whole PR approach." Ten days later, he reminded his staff that he wanted the "best, brief, affirmative" comments about his inaugural address "properly distributed." The President even supplied some quotes. He also suggested projects for the Five O'Clock Group, such as an organized letters-to-the-editor campaign and calls to television stations. He thought this would give campaign volunteers a continued involvement and that it would give him "what Kennedy had in abundance—a constant representation in letters to the editor columns and a very proper influence on the television commentators." Nixon had a detailed plan for the letters campaign, suggesting that individuals express enthusiasm for the "RN crime program in Washington, the RN press conference technique and the Inaugural, and the general performance since the Inauguration." Letters also had to be written when columnists and editorialists "jump on us unfairly." He cautioned against sending a public "blunderbuss memorandum" to hundreds of people; instead, he suggested "a discreet but nevertheless effective Nixon Network [be] set up." The President repeatedly urged that the staff mount an organized letter-writing campaign. He suggested that Kissinger, Buchanan, Safire, and Moynihan describe their work in personal letters to "15 or 20 or maybe 50 people" across the country.

By November 1969, Nixon was urging that there be no letup in that campaign. Apparently, he thought that the public-relations group had been too content following Nixon's earlier world trip and the moon landing, "when we [were] . . . doing rather well in public opinion."

The President recognized the need to monitor and counterattack criticism. Paul Keyes, a speechwriter and formerly the writer of a leading television humor program, had suggested to Nixon that television entertainment programs be monitored for deliberately negative comments about the Administration. Keyes specifically targeted the *Smothers Brothers* program on CBS. Apparently, the President saw one sequence in which the comedians said that they found nothing to laugh about when considering the news about Vietnam or the cities but then added: "Richard Nixon's solving those problems," and "that's really funny." The President was not amused. He wanted such programs monitored, and he wanted supporters to write objections to the producers, stressing that the criticisms were ill-taken, "particularly in view of the great public approval of RN's handling of foreign policy, etc. etc." He told Ehrlichman "ad infinitum" that Kennedy's people regularly did this.

Nixon's repeated emphasis on justifying his image concerns with Kennedy precedents offered a familiar refrain, but it also underlined his conviction that he confronted unique opposition. He instructed Haldeman to emphasize in his "PR activities" the fact that the Nixon Administration "had unprecedented opposition of the press but also that we had an opposition Congress to work with which has been the case for the first time in a President's first term since Buchanan [*sic*]."[10]

The modern President and the media have a symbiotic relationship. The President carries a publicity train in his wake; he needs a flow of information to his public constituency. Media workers are conduits, sometimes allowing free flow, sometimes selecting, sometimes adding their own gloss. Meanwhile, White House announcements and printouts gush like a torrent, inundating the recipients with more information than they or their reading and viewing public can possibly absorb. Every presidential remark, every move, is recorded and logged for the historical record. The presidential annals also are dispensed for immediate consumption—often to the point of trivialization.

President Nixon's China trip is a case in point. During his first visit in 1972, Nixon made the obligatory trip to the Great Wall. Like others before and since, he found it awe-inspiring. Ron Ziegler told a friendly reporter that the President would have a comment if asked what he thought of the Great Wall. Perhaps the reporter thought this was to be a historic moment. He dutifully posed the question. Nixon indeed was ready with a detailed response praising the wall. But at the end, he solemnly noted: "I think that you have to conclude that this is a great wall." Correspondents carefully recorded the remark. Just in case any of them missed it, the White House Traveling Press Office Xeroxed copies and distributed the statement. Perhaps Nixon wasn't sure of himself, for he turned to Secretary of State William Rogers and asked for confirmation of the Wall's greatness. Rogers readily agreed. But the President needed to check one more source: he asked the reporters, and like a well-rehearsed chorus they replied, "Yes, Mr. President."[11]

The media are not always so in accord, especially among themselves. Obvious partisan, even ideological, differences characterize them. Then, too, the print and television media are vastly different in form, quality, and appeal. Television's focus on images, of course, sets its products apart from newspaper and radio reports of the news. A *New York Times* account of a presidential or governmental action might use 2,000 words; even the wire-service story, which typically dominates the nation's newspapers, might carry 600–800 words. Television meanwhile will offer perhaps several sentences. All three accounts probably will rely on an official handout, but television will use the officially prepared summary points, while newspapers might print more explanation. Nothing sinister here; nothing more than the costs and demands of network time and the abiding fear of displaying a mere "talking head" dictate television's choice of news. They simply are in the nature of the medium. What also has been inevitable is the steady growth of television's dominant position as the chief medium for offering news. No wonder, then, that President Nixon and his aides focused much of their attention on the networks and their reporters.

The manner of news manipulation attempted by the Administration pointedly recognized the media's vulnerabilities in laziness and the lack of resources to probe for deeper meanings to events. Haldeman instructed his aides that every presidential statement should be accompanied with a summary. He was blunt as to the purpose: "We will get better coverage if we write the press' story for them, and . . . we should always do this rather than leave it up to them to find the salient points in our release." Years later, Haldeman blamed the press for "an obsession" with covering every aspect of White House affairs, which in turn caused the President and his staff to respond in detail, thus making it appear that the White House was "obsessed with getting all this out." Original sin was in the eye of the beholder.[12]

Dealing with television involved the more rewarding prize, and the easier task. First, government regulation complicated relations between the Administration and the television industry. Spiro Agnew's famous Des Moines assault on the media only made the implicit threat of oppressive regulation more explicit. Second, the Administration could focus its efforts more with television than with newspapers, as it could negotiate directly with the few important network executives.

After the *New York Times* commented on his "bitter" response to the Senate's rejection of his nomination of G. Harrold Carswell to the Supreme Court, Nixon told Haldeman that he had received scores of letters from people who had seen him on television and did not think that he appeared at all bitter. "This had led RN to the conclusion," the President told Haldeman, to have all future press conferences televised. Nixon thought "the TV guys will like it and the press guys will shape up a little better." He recognized that television reporters must be more restrained, tied as they were to the image they displayed on the screen.

In this particular instance, the President was anxious to make public certain facts of his travel costs. He thought that it would be best to give the story exclusively to one of the network reporters. "Obviously, a major television coverage would be more important than having it appear in some column or even on a wire service," he told Haldeman. Nixon respected television. When the President directed the staff to monitor such entertainment programs as that of the Smothers brothers, he noted that this was a far more important activity than sponsoring letter-writing campaigns in newspapers. Nixon had confidence in using television; his effectiveness was "remarkable," a Haldeman aide reported, in words that again probably came from the President himself.[13]

The presidential press conference has come to be the most visible point of public contact between presidents and the media. It is often said that this is the closest American approximation to the British parliamentary practice of periodically questioning government ministers. The comparison pales. The British system is institutionalized and works on a regular basis, operating between assumed equals in status, if not quite in power. All questioners are members of Parliament, standing in deference to their monarch but not to the Prime Minister. The questioners stand forth openly as political opponents, with the opportunity to coordinate and focus a series of questions designed to secure political advantage for themselves. Above all, parliamentary examination is a vital component of ministerial accountability. Presidential press conferences simply have lacked those qualities of tradition and institutionalization.

Presidents have met the press in a variety of ways. Theodore Roosevelt occasionally talked to a reporter or groups of reporters, sometimes with a public design, other times on a social basis. Woodrow Wilson conducted the first regular press conferences and inaugurated conferences as fairly routine White House functions. Wilson knew the importance of cultivating working reporters. At his first press conference, in March 1913, he told a group of them: "I feel that a large part of the success of public affairs depends on newspapermen—not so much on the editorial writers, because we can live down what they say, as upon the news writers because the news is the atmosphere of public affairs." Wilson told the reporters that their duty was to inform Washington officials of what the country was thinking and not to emphasize what Washington was thinking. Wilson's initial optimism with regard to press relations molded a pattern for his successors. "I sent for you," he told the reporters, "to ask that you go into partnership with me, that you lend me your assistance as nobody else can." Bring the "freight of opinion into Washington," he said, and we will "try and make true gold here that will go out from Washington." It was a noble beginning, but the transcripts reveal little substantive information being exchanged in Wilson's press conferences.[14]

Wilson requested that the press not quote him directly, fearing that he might make a momentary error of fact or grammar. His immediate successors, Harding, Coolidge, and Hoover, held irregular conferences distinguished by the requirement that reporters submit written questions in advance. That practice, like much else in the presidency, changed with Franklin D. Roosevelt in 1933.

Roosevelt, like Wilson, believed that if he made page one, the editorial pages were of minor consequence. FDR's first press conferences in 1933 (fashioned after those he had held as Governor of New York) marked a new stage in presidential relations with the press, one in which the President personally assumed control to manage the news flow. FDR largely succeeded, through a combination of charm, guile, cajolery, and flattery. He was, a recent biographer noted, "a picture of ease and confidence." Without television to convey a visual image of himself, the President nevertheless portrayed himself to the press—and hence to the public—as "unprecedentedly frank, open, cordial, personal."

More than any of his predecessors, Roosevelt recognized and realized the potency of the press conference as a forum for projecting the image he desired. Like his predecessors, Roosevelt met casually with individual reporters or small groups to suggest a story—either to press something that interested him or to send up a "trial balloon."[15] FDR made the mold, and the working press was his for the next twelve years.

President Truman held both scheduled and impromptu sessions with the press, though hardly the number conducted by FDR. In the Truman Administration, reporters accompanied the President on his early morning walks along Pennsylvania Avenue, questioning and conversing with him to gain morsels of information. But like FDR, Truman punctuated many of his answers with pithy "no comments," as well as friendly and unfriendly banter. The press long had been accustomed to numerous restraints during the Roosevelt presidency, particularly deferring to the President's privacy (rarely

describing his serious physical handicap) and to the need for wartime secrecy. During a few early vacation trips with Truman, however, the press
thought it important to report that he played poker and drank bourbon,
signalling a new era in media concerns. Truman responded heatedly when
reporters attacked his family. He once jabbed his finger into a reporter's
abdomen, cursed, and called him a liar for reporting that the President's
wife and daughter had returned from Missouri in a private railroad car. In
fact, they had paid for a compartment and waited in turn for the diner. The
reporter apologized. Truman regarded the media as hostile and adversarial;
furthermore, he rarely used his relations with the press to sell or publicize
his Administration's ideas and programs.[16]

Dwight Eisenhower, like Roosevelt with radio, adapted well to the new
technology of television. The President allowed the new medium to record
his press conferences. Eisenhower was experienced in accommodating the
media and turning them to his advantage. In his first press conference, he
praised the role of reporters and went out of his way to thank them for their
past kindnesses. Eisenhower held 193 press conferences in his eight years
in office, far more than any other president, before or since. Sophisticated
audiences often responded contemptuously to the President's jumbled syn-
tax, his rambling, "often inappropriate or impossibly confusing answers,"
and his confessions of "I don't know." But his style was effective, and the
press conferences contributed to Eisenhower's continuing extraordinary popularity. Eisenhower cultivated good relations with reporters, regularly inviting them to cook-outs during his vacations, playing golf with them, and
treating them as "quasi members of his staff." Occasionally, he might betray some anger or annoyance at a particular incident involving the press,
but he never permitted or fostered open antagonism.[17]

John F. Kennedy went one step beyond Eisenhower when he established
the live television press conference. Handsome, witty, informed, articulate,
Kennedy, like Roosevelt, had found his natural forum. Television favors
glamour, and for many Americans Kennedy rivaled the appeal and allure
generally associated with popular entertainers. Victorious by less than 1
percent of the popular vote in 1960, the President saw his approval ratings
steadily rise in the next three years, largely as a result of the captivating
image he projected. The President carefully prepared for his press conferences. His command of detail, his witty observations, his occasional playful
self-mockery, hardly were spontaneous. When reporters asked him to respond to the Supreme Court decision forbidding officially prescribed prayers
in public schools, the President coolly remarked that he welcomed the decision. With calculated wit, he expressed the hope that Americans now would
pray more at home and in the churches, places more appropriate than public
schools. The press conference had moved a long way from the casual treatment of Wilson's early days.

Reporters liked Kennedy and generally respected his privacy. Still, he proved as thin-skinned as his predecessors when criticized. He once ordered a newspaper subscription canceled after the paper published hostile articles, and his staff regularly berated reporters who printed leaks. When the Defense Department press officer talked imprudently about the government's right to "manage news," and its "inherent right to lie" to save itself if faced with nuclear disaster, for example, he aroused inevitable protests. Nevertheless, press and President understood each other in the Kennedy years. Asked in 1962 what he thought of the press, JFK responded typically: "Well, I am reading it more and enjoying it less [laughter] . . . but I have not complained, nor do I plan to make any complaint. . . . I think they are doing their task, as a critical branch . . . and I am attempting to do mine."[18]

By the 1960s, the Age of McLuhan had arrived: style rivaled substance—as Lyndon Johnson painfully learned. For Kennedy, a podium and microphone were natural appendages, and he treated his live press conferences as part of a day's ordinary work. President Johnson, by contrast, seemed only awkward, ill at ease, out of place, and, on the whole, unhappy with press conferences. Close observers of Johnson always emphasized his effectiveness in individual or small-group settings; the formal address or the probing eye of the television camera made him appear wooden, even contrived, thus raising questions of credibility. Perhaps he tried too hard to appear sincere. Certainly, the Kennedy image dogged Johnson throughout his presidency. The metaphor of the "credibility gap" eventually developed a life of its own. And with that, Johnson's relations with the media fell on hard times.

Richard Nixon, as always, inherited much from Kennedy and Johnson—in this case a variety of precedents and attitudes governing the relationship between the President and the media. Whatever the precedents, personal predisposition was paramount. Roosevelt, Eisenhower, and Kennedy all realized the usefulness of press, television, and radio, but they also appeared to have a genuine fondness and respect for reporters and the media. Too much had happened in Richard Nixon's public life before 1969 for him to share those feelings. No doubt, a good part of the media responded in like fashion. Nixon, as should be clear, was not the first president to perceive a hostile press, but perhaps no other president saw hostility more clearly and consistently, or chose to combat it so passionately.

Nixon's attitude toward the press was demonstrated first in his shunning it. The President averaged less than seven press conferences a year. Kennedy and Johnson averaged twenty-two and twenty-six, respectively; Gerald Ford and Jimmy Carter—perhaps reflecting a new wariness—averaged sixteen and fifteen.

Press conferences are not as spontaneous as they seem. The live televised proceedings dictate careful preparation on the part of the President, including briefings and even rehearsals. Good staff work usually ensures that there are no surprises. The likely questions are obvious and generally are confined to issues of the moment. Nixon complained to Haldeman that the staff received too much credit for his answers. He wanted it understood that the President's responses were his alone. He demanded more recognition for his role and less for the staff. "If we cannot find staff people who are willing to work on that basis, I, of course, will have to do more work myself, which would be self-defeating," he complained. Yet Nixon could graciously thank staffers for their help in preparing him.[19]

Given their numbers and differences, reporters at press conferences have no opportunity for coherent questioning. Thus control of the event usually belongs to the President. His problem is to guard against the infrequent slip of the tongue, the inadvertent remark. Nevertheless, control can on occasion slip from his hands: witness Nixon's experience on June 1, 1971. A reporter raised a question regarding alleged civil liberties violations surrounding the mass police arrests of the May Day antiwar demonstrators that year. (Charges already had been dropped against more than two thousand arrested individuals.) Nixon's reply focused on the danger of the demonstrations to the government, ignoring the civil liberties question. What followed was unusual, as one reporter after another rose to bore in on the same issue, pressing hard on the question of improper police tactics. Nixon evaded them, finally finding a "safe" reporter who invariably strayed from the pack to ask irrelevant, obscure questions. She did not disappoint him in this case, dropping the dangerous line of questioning to inquire about a surplus of telephone poles in Vietnam. The President, visibly relieved as the press conference quickly returned to its familiar anarchy, nevertheless realized the danger. He did not hold another televised press conference for nearly thirteen months.[20]

By that time, Nixon already had attempted to evade any hostility in the forum. Claiming Roosevelt and Eisenhower as precedents, he told his staff in June 1969 that he would stop "calling on those who are trying to give us the hook." He ordered Ehrlichman to compile information on those reporters who are "out to get us and which ones are either neutral or friends." He told Ehrlichman to ignore the objections of Klein and Ziegler. "This is my decision and I intend to follow it up." Angered by increasing criticism from prominent columnists, he directed Klein to: "1. Get some tough letters to these guys from subscribers. 2. Be sure they are cut off."[21] Nixon's ideas were as petty and petulant as Kennedy's cancellation of a newspaper subscription, but in Nixon's case, the behavior was not an isolated episode. Indeed, those impulses fueled a considered policy of harassment, intimidation, and confrontation.

America and its presidents had changed vastly from a half-century earlier. Perhaps few changes were more dramatic and telling than those in the relationship between presidents and the press. Calvin Coolidge, known for his silence, actually was quite talkative off the record. He had a kindly, warm attitude toward the press and once apologized because reporters "had to" spend summer vacations with him. On one occasion, Coolidge went to elaborate lengths to congratulate the newspapermen for their "constant correctness" in reporting his views; he was amazed that "very seldom . . . any error creeps in." Coolidge also noted that they had been "very helpful to the country in coming to a comprehension of what the Government is trying to do, how it is trying to function, what efforts it is making to benefit the condition of the people."[22] Richard Nixon never was known to invoke Calvin Coolidge as any kind of media role model.

In October 1969, Nixon pushed Haldeman for "that hard list" of media workers that would allow the Administration to concentrate on friends. Get the list, he told Haldeman, and then "get in Klein, Buchanan and Ziegler and give them their marching orders." Three months later, the President told Haldeman he wanted to give Medals of Freedom to "outstanding people" in the press, including—"hold your hat," Nixon said—Walter Lippmann. Nixon thought the move would have a "great effect" and wanted the idea checked "with the PR types." By January 1971, a Haldeman aide had developed a "friendlies list" of over eighty men and women in the media, ranging across the political spectrum from William Buckley to Sam Donaldson.

Most Nixon memoranda on the subject of the press, by contrast, focused on what he called "activity in the counterattack field." He wanted to keep abreast of editorial and columnists' comments, "so that I know what we must do to counteract whatever effect they may be having on public opinion." He was convinced that "a solid majority" of 60–65 percent of the press corps began "with a strong negative attitude toward RN." While occasionally they "will throw us a bone[,] their whole objective in life is to bring us down." Being less antagonistic in response only encouraged them, Nixon believed, continuing an established refrain that intimidation brought positive results. The object was to force hostile reporters to show "fairness" in order to maintain their credibility.

Johnson had mistakenly "slobber[ed] over them with the hope that [he] could 'win' them. It just can't be done." Indeed, Nixon was proud of the fact that he had not allowed the press to filter his ideas to the public. "This is a remarkable achievement," an aide said—undoubtedly quoting the President himself.

By March 1970, the time had come for the Administration's "all-out, slam-bang" attack on his enemies in the news media. "Now I want this done," Nixon told Haldeman. "I want a game plan on my desk. I will give you until Wednesday in order to have it—Wednesday afternoon which I usually reserve to myself is a very good time to discuss this. A game plan to do something about this."

The President's anger focused in a particularly vicious manner in November that year, when Haldeman, at Nixon's direction, called J. Edgar Hoover and asked for "a rundown on the homosexuals known and suspected" in the Washington press corps. Hoover confirmed he had the material and noted that he would not need to make any specific investigation. The Director sent the files to the White House.[23]

Just as Nixon delegated duties in his press wars, so, too, did Haldeman. The best-known "game plan" that emerged was the brainchild of Haldeman's primary aide in the early days, Jeb Stuart Magruder. Magruder was thirty-five, young and restless, eager and ambitious. He had come to the White House more through chance than design. A Korean War veteran and a graduate of Williams College, Magruder had had a mixed career as an IBM employee, a paper-products salesman, and a management consultant, and had held junior-executive posts with supermarkets and department stores. Interspersed with these jobs, he participated in political campaigns as a Republican volunteer, first in Illinois for Nixon in 1960 and then for Goldwater in 1964, as well as in some local races. In 1968, Magruder worked for Bob Finch in Nixon's California campaign, but he soon realized that Finch was *passé* in the Nixon camp and that power really rested with Mitchell and Haldeman. After the election, Finch offered Magruder a place in the Department of Health, Education and Welfare, but the young man thought the job a dead end, and by then he had little respect for Finch. Magruder undoubtedly knew that something bigger could be had. He had caught Haldeman's eye, thanks to a mutual friend who worked in public relations. In August 1969, Haldeman and Magruder met in San Clemente, and Haldeman had his man. It was a perfect match: Magruder was pliant, reliable, and obedient. In time, Haldeman dispatched Magruder to Herb Klein as the "Deputy" in the White House Office of Communications, and fatefully, in 1972 he became Mitchell's "Deputy" at the Committee to Re-elect the President. Klein was my "nominal boss," but Haldeman was his "real boss," Magruder acknowledged.

In late fall 1969, the dutiful Magruder received Haldeman's distillation of Nixon's marching orders guiding the Administration's retaliation against the media, and he responded with a plan calculated to appeal to every Nixon prejudice. In his "Rifle and Shotgun" memo of October 17, 1969, Magruder urged that the Administration stop "shotgunning" its critics with disorganized calls and protests; instead, he proposed a more precise "rifle" approach. For example, he suggested that newly installed Federal Communications Commission Chairman Dean Burch should monitor the networks' fairness; that the Justice Department's Anti-Trust Division should investigate the networks ("the possible threat of antitrust action I think would be effective in changing their views"), that the IRS should be used against the networks and reporters ("a threat of an IRS investigation will probably turn their approach"); that the Administration should play favorites with the media; and that the Republican National Committee should organize a campaign of protest letters to the news media. There was hardly an original thought to the memo. Incredibly, Magruder later claimed that his "memo was a failure because it suggested that Richard Nixon change his attitude toward the press, and that, as I came to realize, was not to be."[24] In fact, the "Rifle and Shotgun" memo was pure Nixon; the President could not have written it better himself. And Magruder underestimated his effort, for it soon bore fruit.

Several weeks afterward, the President delivered a national television speech, explaining his Vietnamization policy of turning the war over to the South Vietnamese, and expressing confidence that he had the support of the "Silent Majority." Nixon had made a favorable impact, according to the instant polls. Still, there was anger and annoyance in the White House with the usual network "analysis" following the speech, commentary that contained a few negative remarks, such as those by Ambassador W. Averell Harriman. Sores had to be rubbed.

The President continued the metaphor when Pat Buchanan prepared a savage attack on the networks for their lack of fairness and balance. "This really flicks the scab off, doesn't it," the President told William Safire—and then added to Buchanan's text a few tough lines of his own. It was a rare speech, going through only three drafts, but basically retaining Buchanan's "white-heat vitality," Safire remembered. The speech, eventually delivered in Des Moines on November 13, 1969, marked the unleashing of Spiro Agnew as Nixon's bulldog against the press. Herb Klein was "astonished" when he received an advance copy—not because of its content but because he considered it a "sneak attack" on his own authority. Despite the unfavorable network "instant analysis," Klein had received ample supportive comments from editors and broadcasters for the President's Silent Majority talk, and he worried that the Agnew speech might shatter that fragile support.[25]

Believing he could preempt criticism, Klein sent out copies of the speech to various news bureaus and the networks. Why and how the networks responded as they did remains unclear, but all three decided to broadcast the Vice President's speech live and in its entirety. It was an extraordinary, unprecedented decision. Perhaps the President was right: contempt, attack, and fear offered the right weapons for intimidating the media.

The Agnew speech in Des Moines had been nurtured in the darker moments of the Goldwater candidacy in 1964. The Vice President offered the nation, particularly its heartland, a conspiracy theory that blamed the anti-Nixon bias of the media on an Eastern liberal establishment. "A small group of men, numbering perhaps no more than a dozen anchormen, commentators, and executive producers, settle upon twenty minutes or so of film and commentary that's to reach the public. . . . [They] live and work in the geographical and intellectual confines of Washington, D.C., or New York City. . . . They draw their political and social views from . . . one another, thereby providing artificial reinforcement to their shared viewpoints." It was time, he said, to question the power of this "small and un-elected elite." Given the government's role in regulating the broadcast networks, Agnew's threat was only thinly veiled: "the people," Agnew warned, "are entitled to a full accounting of [the networks'] stewardship."

Agnew had struck the sensitive nerves of the media and liberal intellectuals, but he also won the hearts and minds of those who already believed the notions he espoused. They responded with passionate support for the Vice President. Antisemitic letters constituted 11 percent of one network's mail, while tirades against blacks made up another 10 percent. In an ABC poll, 51 percent of the respondents agreed with Agnew.

The President was elated. But his aide Charles Colson—a self-described "original 'hard-line' paranoid on the press"—thought matters might get out of hand and urged Haldeman to ask the President to restrain Agnew. Haldeman and speechwriter Ray Price, perhaps sensing overkill, did so, but to no avail. Nixon ordered more speeches from Buchanan for the Vice President. A week later, Agnew told a Montgomery, Alabama, audience that the networks needed representation from "a broader spectrum of national opinion." Pat Nixon reportedly worried that Agnew had gone too far and that his attacks would provoke further media counterassaults. They certainly provoked ridicule. "If I went on the air tomorrow night and said Spiro Agnew was the greatest American statesman since Washington, Jefferson, Madison, Adams and Hamilton . . . the audience might think I was biased," NBC's David Brinkley told an audience. "But he wouldn't'."[26]

Agnew's frontal assault resembled more a fusillade of cannon than Magruder's carefully aimed rifle, but others in the Administration were using more precise weapons. For all his outrage at Agnew's speech, Herb Klein himself had called local stations the day of Nixon's Silent Majority speech to ask if there would be editorial comment. Klein claimed he called for "sampling" purposes; others noticed the move's chilling effects. After the networks' commentaries on the speech, FCC Chairman Dean Burch asked for transcripts of the remarks. Network executives claimed that Klein and Ziegler asked them to supply details of future commentaries. A member of the Subversive Activities Control Board, a nearly moribund agency (according to Klein, the board member "apparently needed something to do"), took it upon himself to ask local stations for samplings of their news coverage and editorials regarding Administration policies.

A few days after Agnew's talk, Klein appeared on *Face the Nation,* and said that Agnew's charges raised "a legitimate question." Ritualistically voicing objections to governmental "participation" in such questioning, he said that in "any industry—if you look at the problems you have today and you fail to continue to examine them, you do invite the government to come in." Klein quickly added, "I'd like not to see that happen," but too late. Few listened to the disclaiming tag line, and Klein found himself lumped with Agnew and Burch as persecutors of the media. What was wrong was the identification of the persecutors. The President had sponsored Agnew's speech, and it was later revealed that Colson instructed Klein to have Burch make the request of the networks. Colson rarely acted on his own initiative; his deeds, like Haldeman's and Ehrlichman's, correlate with his notes of his regular meetings with the President. At the end, Klein best understood that there really had been no victors.[27]

Several months later, in July 1970, the Administration continued its efforts at intimidation after CBS introduced a series entitled *The Loyal Opposition.* Democratic National Committee Chairman Lawrence O'Brien appeared on the show and scored the Administration for its alleged failures in fighting the war on crime, in stimulating the economy, in advancing civil rights, and in ending the Vietnam war. In September, Colson visited various network presidents to complain about their companies' anti-Nixon bias, and in a memo to Haldeman he bragged about his success. "The harder I pressed them," he wrote, "the more accommodating, cordial and apologetic they became." Colson was convinced that the executives were "very much afraid of us." His memo became public during the Senate's Watergate investigation. Network executives contended that Colson had exaggerated their eagerness to oblige. What was not in dispute was the fact that the Administration had dispatched an envoy to voice its complaints directly to the news media. Moreover, the chosen representative was not Herb Klein, who had folded "liaison" with the media into his job description; instead, it was Charles Colson, a man known for his rough tactics and his closeness to the Oval Office—the same man who had flown to New York to congratulate *New York Times* pressmen engaged in a wildcat strike to protest the printing of an antiwar ad, an action that Klein acknowledged had "antagonized even the strongest Nixon friends in the news corps."

Although the President reflexively continued to talk about his enemies in the media, White House officials believed that their assault had had positive effects. The way to change opinion, Nixon told Haldeman, "was to make it less unfashionable to be with us."[28] The campaign fit Nixon's personal, proven formula for contempt and intimidation, to force the "enemy" to bend over backward to appear fair—the same tactic that worked in the 1968 campaign.

Sometimes the Administration's attacks on newsmen had both comic and chilling overtones. Most television reporters were treated benignly compared to their brethren in the print media. But CBS correspondent Daniel Schorr seems to have been singled out for special attention. Allegedly on the grounds that Schorr was being considered as Assistant to the Chairman of the Council on Environmental Quality, Haldeman requested an FBI check of his background in August 1971. The FBI questioned Schorr himself as well as the CBS Washington Bureau Chief and officials in the CBS New York headquarters. Sometime after answering questions, Schorr asked that the check be terminated, telling the FBI that he was not interested in any government position. After receiving a preliminary report, the White House also asked the FBI to stop, claiming it did so on its own because it no longer was interested in hiring Schorr. Ziegler also said that the report had been destroyed. The whole affair was bizarre. Schorr, of course, as the President subsequently admitted, was not being considered for any position. "We just ran a name check on the son-of-a-bitch," the President told aides. Haldeman later acknowledged that it was a "fair assumption" that the President would use any unfavorable material.[29]

Schorr's tale is notable for the Administration's clumsiness and heavy-handedness. John Hart, Schorr's CBS colleague, was victimized by a process far more subtle, and perhaps more pernicious. He, too, had caught the President's eye. Hart, Nixon told Haldeman, had been "a violent, anti-Administration commentator for years."

Hart had spent six months in South Vietnam in 1966–67. He then returned to the United States and covered Robert Kennedy's 1968 primary campaign. After Kennedy's death, he was assigned to Nixon for the nominating convention. He followed Nixon through the campaign but then became host on the network's *Morning News*. During that stint, Hart went to North Vietnam in September 1972. In Hanoi, he realized that his hosts staged events for him and carefully supervised his schedule. Despite repeated requests, he could not see American prisoners of war. Still, Hart went on reporting and filed twenty-two stories in a three-week span. His reports were earmarked for Walter Cronkite's *Evening News* broadcasts, but unknown to Hart while he was abroad, Cronkite stopped carrying them at about midpoint.

Hart was convinced that the bombing of the North was fruitless and would not change the fanaticism of the North Vietnamese, whom he labeled "Calvinist Communists." When he returned, he planned to do a documentary on his visit, but Richard Salant, head of CBS News, "cross-examined" him at length over his inability to get more information on the POWs and his failure to report more unfavorably on the North. Instead of doing a documentary, Hart appeared on only a few late-night spot reports. He believed that he had lost the confidence of his bosses. He later realized that he had covered the story as a journalist, not as an "American journalist." One of his colleagues emphasized how important it was to preface or conclude his reports with reminders that "these people were Communists."

On October 16, 1972, Hart received a letter from Frank Shakespeare, Director of the United States Information Agency—on official stationery and with a franked envelope—complaining about his lack of objectivity. Shakespeare specifically cited Hart's reports from North Vietnam of having heard "frequent laughter," praising the people's "richness of hospitality," describing the full attendance at a Catholic mass, noting the display of "forgiveness" toward American pilots, filming bomb-damaged hospitals and churches, and describing North Vietnam's Premier Pham Van Dong as a man of "energy and wit." "Where, John, was the balance?" Shakespeare demanded. Why hadn't Hart talked about the invasion of the South, the refugees in the South, the dictatorship in the North, the North Vietnamese troops in Cambodia and Laos? Why did Hart thank his hosts for their hospitality and kindness? Shakespeare's assault wavered between being comical and sinister. He berated Hart for being "technically factual" while not playing it "straight." There was no fairness, he thought; indeed, Shakespeare thought it wrong to report at all from the enemy's capital. Why, Shakespeare concluded on a chilling note, was Hart so careful not to criticize the Hanoi government?

The same day the Internal Revenue Service wrote to Hart, saying that his tax returns would be examined. When he later called the IRS as requested, they told him they had never notified him that they would scrutinize his returns.

Hart also responded to Shakespeare, sending him complete transcripts of his broadcasts and politely noting that he regarded the criticisms as serious. Indeed, they were, Shakespeare retorted—and the transcripts, he said, left him only "puzzled and depressed." He charged that Hart had offered a "skewed impression" of both North Vietnamese and American actions.

Meanwhile, Richard Salant wrote to Shakespeare, defending Hart. Whatever Salant's immediate support, however, Hart received less as time went on. At one point, Salant reportedly told him he needed "rehabilitation." Was Salant under pressure? Perhaps Shakespeare, a former CBS vice president, still had influence at the network. Certainly, Shakespeare's belief in the bias of television news could be traced back to the 1968 campaign. In any event, frustrated with his lack of work, Hart left for NBC in 1975.

John Hart later interviewed Charles Colson, who admitted that he had been in contact with CBS executives regarding the correspondent's broadcasts. Colson recalled that the White House was "up the wall" over the reports. He told Hart that he "was bitching and moaning" to the network's leaders, "and they were kissing my ass." Hart's conclusion was obvious: the Administration's pressures had played havoc with his position at the network, which was never the same afterward.[30]

Jeb Stuart Magruder's memo on influencing the news media suggested that the Anti-Trust division of the Justice Department be used to intimidate broadcasters. In April 1972, the Justice Department filed suit against the networks, claiming they had monopolized the production of prime-time entertainment programming. The networks responded that the suit was without merit and would have the effect of turning control of television programming over to advertising agencies and motion-picture producers. The timing of the suit seemed to fit the Administration's ongoing antimedia drives and seemed particularly appropriate to the onset of the 1972 campaign.

The Anti-Trust Division had a longstanding concern with various network practices, particularly the networks' attempts to control original productions for their programming schedules. Would they broadcast only programs which they had produced or in which they had a financial stake, or would independent, outside producers have access to programming slots? Clearly, the networks preferred to use their own shows as much as possible, but how much of that pattern of preference constituted monopoly? Enough, apparently, to satisfy the Anti-Trust Division. It had been investigating the questioned network practices since the 1950s, years before Magruder's memorandum and wholly apart from the Nixon Administration's political agenda. Herb Klein and other Administration officials realized the downside potential of the suit. But the Anti-Trust people had their way—undoubtedly supported by key Administration officials who could only see an upside to the controversy.

The networks predictably based their case on political reprisal and demanded access to Nixon's papers in order to substantiate their charges. As the litigation unfolded, however, the defendants found that the government could not make the President's papers available, and on November 26, 1974, a federal judge dismissed the suit without prejudice. But once the papers could be perused for evidence, Attorney General William Saxbe reinstituted the action several weeks later. The case dragged on, and eventually, in May 1980, the networks signed consent decrees limiting their control over production and agreeing to change their practices. In short, the allegations of antitrust violations had merit.[31]

That the government's suits against the networks in 1972 might have merit was a fact overshadowed by the powerful evidence of the Administration's hostility toward the media. That image was the message. The suit, not the accompanying recitation of charges and evidence of network management wrongdoing, was what made an impact.

The Nixon Administration's war on the media was more than image, however. In October 1972, before real assaults distracted him, the President directed his aides not to talk to the *New York Times,* the *Washington Post, Time,* or *Newsweek*—the *Los Angeles Times* still was acceptable, but that soon changed—and to exclude their reporters from social functions. Heavy artillery was also put in play. In the heady days following the President's November 1972 electoral triumph, Clay Whitehead, the Director of the White House Office of Telecommunications Policy, boldly called on local television stations to refuse to carry "biased" news accounts from the networks. He warned local managers that dissemination of news involved their greatest responsibility; in this light he asked whether "station licensees or network executives [would] take action against this ideological plugola?" The question was more than rhetorical: failure "to correct imbalance or consistent bias from the networks" would make local broadcasters "fully accountable" at license-renewal time.[32] As the President moved to his second term, he had every intention, it seemed, of continuing the media war.

Richard Nixon's presidency paralleled the rising importance of the media. As a young politician, and later as President, Nixon always understood the necessity of using the media for his success. Use meant control—control not only of the flow of information, but of the nuances and conclusions drawn from that information. Such total control was impossible, however, given the fragmentation and disparity among the media. And the inability to wield control only frustrated the President and alienated him the more.

Did the Nixon Administration conspire to discredit the press? Did the President and his aides foster the "us-against-them" mentality with respect to the news media that eventually boomeranged with such devastating results for the President in his second term? Did the President himself encourage and direct the campaign against the media? The President's friend and former aide, William Safire, long ago concluded that the answer to all the questions "is, sadly, yes."

In the best of times, Richard Nixon remembered. Following his re-election, he instructed Haldeman to work with Buchanan to prepare a monograph entitled "Things They Would Like to Forget." He remembered that commentators and columnists had solemnly predicted World War III at the time of the Cambodian invasion; that at the same time they had predicted the collapse of summit preparations; that they had predicted his defeat in 1972; that they were certain that George McGovern would capture the youth vote and that Nixon would "blow the lead." Thirteen years after he left the presidency, Nixon joined forces with McGovern's campaign manager to commiserate about the slings and arrows of the media. Journalists demand the right "to ruthlessly question the ethics of anyone else," Nixon told former Senator Gary Hart in 1987. "But when anyone else dares to question *their* ethics, they hide behind the shield of freedom of speech." The media leaders refused, he complained, "to make the distinction that philosophers throughout the centuries have made between freedom and license."[33] Time had not healed that old sore.

BOOK THREE

THE WATERGATE WAR

ORIGINS AND RETREAT
JUNE 1972–APRIL 1973

VIII

"WE SHOULD COME UP WITH ... IMAGINATIVE DIRTY TRICKS."

THE WATERGATE
BREAK-IN

Friday, June 16, 1972, was a fairly typical day for the President. He conducted a Medal of Honor ceremony in the White House Rose Garden, discussed welfare legislation with several advisers, met his Cabinet, and then received a visit from Mexican President Luis Echeverría. As he did routinely, Nixon held a long meeting with John Ehrlichman and a shorter one with Oval Office assistant Alexander Butterfield, and, on various occasions throughout the day, he met with his principal aide, H. R. Haldeman. That afternoon, he boarded his plane, the *Spirit of '76*, and flew to the Bahamas, accompanied by the Haldemans, Press Secretary Ron Ziegler, the White House doctor, and some press representatives. The President's friends Bebe Rebozo and Robert Abplanalp joined him there. They swam together, had dinner, and watched the movie *The Skin Game*.

Several hours later, in the early morning of the seventeenth, police arrested five men in the Watergate offices of the Democratic National Committee in Washington. A security guard discovered an apparent burglary in progress and notified the local police. When captured, the suspects had several cans of Mace, carried lock-picking devices, and wore surgical gloves. One had a portable radio receiver. The police also found camera equipment and telephone-bugging devices. Because of the possibility that the federal Interception of Communications statute had been violated, the D.C. police called in the FBI. Preliminary investigations on the scene led Bureau agents to believe that the burglars were in the process of installing the listening devices in the Democratic offices. Shortly after the arrest, an attorney showed up at police headquarters, stating that he represented the men in custody. The suspects, however, had refused to make any telephone calls, and the lawyer would not tell agents how he had learned of their arrest.

Four of the men in custody were identified as Cubans, although they gave aliases at first. They had with them when they were arrested $2,400 in cash, including thirteen new hundred-dollar bills. Later that day, FBI agents obtained warrants and searched the suspects' hotel room. They discovered a sealed envelope with a check written by E. Howard Hunt. Hunt's name, along with the notations "W.H." and "W. House," appeared in the address books of two suspects. Bureau records revealed that Hunt had been the subject of an inquiry a year earlier when he was hired for a White House staff position. Hunt's file also showed that he had listed Douglas Caddy, a local attorney, as a reference. Caddy was the same lawyer who had appeared at police headquarters, after—it was later discovered—Hunt and the wife of one of the defendants had called him. FBI agents further learned that the Cubans had previously been employed by the CIA.[1]

Investigators subsequently determined that the June 17 incident was the second illegal entry of the Democratic headquarters. Just after Memorial Day, a group of burglars had installed wiretaps and photographed documents. The purpose of the June 17 break-in, according to later testimony, was to rearrange the taps.

The suspects were arraigned in the afternoon of the seventeenth. Assistant U.S. Attorney Earl Silbert appeared for the government and asked the court not to grant bond, as the men had given false names and might flee the country. When asked for occupations, one of the defendants replied, "Anti-Communist." That day Richard Nixon, on vacation, talked on the phone several times with Haldeman, but mostly he spent time with his friends and saw another movie, *The Notorious Landlady*.

In Columbia, South Carolina, retiring presidential aide Harry Dent heard about the arrests on the evening television news. "It's all over," he told his wife. Instinctively, Dent figured out that the burglars must have had links to the Committee to Re-elect the President (CREEP)—and that, he well knew, meant Haldeman and the President. "I had seen enough of the Keystone Kop capers and Mickey Mouse stuff" during the first term, Dent remembered. The break-in, he thought, reflected "the lack of reality and the funny business that was going on in the White House." But another observer, Leon Jaworski, the President of the American Bar Association, was not "particularly perturbed" when he learned of the Watergate break-in, dismissing the incident as a typical political game.

What the FBI did not immediately learn was that Howard Hunt and G. Gordon Liddy, the then-counsel for the re-election committee, with another operative, had observed the whole arrest procedure at the Watergate from a room in a nearby hotel. One of those arrested, however, had a key to that room, and eventually police searched it and discovered that Hunt had been present.

By late afternoon of June 17, Bureau identification records revealed that the fifth burglar, booked under the alias of Edward Martin, really was James W. McCord, a onetime CIA employee. The FBI soon learned that McCord was chief of security for the President's campaign committee. They also determined that McCord had rented motel rooms opposite the Watergate and on the same level as the Democratic headquarters. Meanwhile, Assistant Attorney General Henry Petersen, head of the Justice Department's Criminal Division, ordered the Bureau's Washington field office to ask the CIA whether the suspects were then actively employed by the agency. Petersen also requested that all new information developed by the Bureau be furnished to him for passage to the White House.

Details quickly reached the White House. After breakfast on the morning of the eighteenth, the President and Rebozo flew to Key Biscayne, Florida. Nixon called his wife, his daughters (several times), Haldeman, Charles Colson, Henry Kissinger, and John Connally, then visiting in Australia. The President's logs did not record any conversations with John Mitchell, the Chairman of CREEP; Mitchell nevertheless announced that day that neither McCord nor the others had in any way operated in behalf of the campaign committee. Mitchell also complained that his office, too, had "security problems." In Key Biscayne, Nixon and Rebozo had dinner alone and then watched *When Eight Bells Toll,* a convoluted mystery that plunges the viewer into a maze of subplots. The President ended the day with a call to a professional golfer.[2]

Alexander Butterfield told FBI agents that Hunt had been a consultant for the White House on "highly sensitive confidential matters" less than a year earlier but had not been used since. But by June 19, agents had learned that Hunt had been a longtime CIA agent and that he had worked for the White House in late March, directly for Charles Colson. That day, the FBI requested permission to interview Colson. On June 23, less than a week after the arrests, FBI Acting Director L. Patrick Gray ordered the "highest priority investigative attention" for the Watergate case. Meanwhile, the President and Haldeman made a desperate gamble to curtail the Bureau's investigation and enlisted Gray and the CIA in their effort.

Monday morning, June 19, Ron Ziegler met reporters and refused to comment on what he dubbed a "third-rate burglary attempt." He warned that "certain elements" would try "to stretch this beyond what it is." Ziegler, of course, was his master's voice. Nixon's own reaction to the break-in and arrests was, as he later described it, "cynical, . . . a cynicism born of experience." Vote fraud and various dirty tricks were familiar stuff; "I could not muster much moral outrage over a political bugging," he wrote.

Some Republicans were concerned about the incident. Representative William J. Keating, a leading minority member of the House Committee on the Judiciary, indignantly wrote to FBI Acting Director Gray that "the specter of spying on political parties or candidates or office holders for political reasons should not be tolerated." Keating urged Gray to conduct a "thorough investigation" to restore public confidence in the political system.[3]

Ziegler's response to reporters' questions about the break-in underlined the growing publicity about the affair. The generic term "Watergate" eventually became synonymous with media leaks. From the outset, local Washington reporting, especially in the *Post,* closely tracked the FBI's work, relying primarily on raw Bureau reports. The media also reported repeated charges by Democratic National Committee Chairman Lawrence O'Brien that the White House and CREEP had been directly involved in the burglary. By the twentieth, Colson's and Hunt's names, as well as McCord's employment at the re-election committee, had become public knowledge. O'Brien called a press conference and announced that the Democrats had filed a $1 million damage suit against CREEP. Citing the involvement of Colson, O'Brien charged that the case had developed "a clear line to the White House."

Colson visited the President on June 20 and complained that newspapers had tainted him with guilt by association because of his links to Hunt—a man Colson later characterized along with Liddy as "good healthy right-wing exuberants." But Colson directed most of the conversation to assuring the President that matters seemed under control and typically suggested that the White House begin its own political offensive. Early in the exchange, Nixon, referring to "this thing here," remarked: "I, uh, I've got to, well, it's a dangerous job." Colson picked up the thread and commented that Haldeman was pulling "it all" together. "I think we've done the right things to date," he added. At one point, the President said that the break-in didn't sound like a very skillful job. "If we didn't know better, [we] would have thought it was deliberately b[o]tched." Apparently, Nixon had learned—and was satisfied—that those arrested simply had blundered, but their ineptness cued both men to imagine new conspiracies against the President. Colson and Nixon exchanged views on political espionage, and both agreed that the Democrats undoubtedly had someone spying on the President's re-election committee. Nixon remembered the theft and publication of the Pentagon Papers; he wanted an article commissioned and a speech given that would remind the country of those events. The President and Colson also discussed an advertisement that had appeared in the *New York Times* calling for the impeachment of the President. Colson thought it possible to trace another anti-Nixon ad to Senator George McGovern, which then would make "eavesdropping at the Watergate Hotel look like child's play." Meanwhile, Colson assured Nixon that "we won't let this one bug us." For himself, the President concluded that "I [will] just stonewall it."[4]

Nixon met reporters on June 22, telling them that the "White House has had no involvement whatever in this particular incident." On June 25, Lawrence O'Brien challenged the President and called for the appointment of a "special prosecutor of unimpeachable integrity and national reputation." He claimed that abundant evidence now existed linking the White House to the Watergate burglary. Six days later, John Mitchell announced his resignation as the President's campaign manager, claiming that he wanted to spend more time with his family. Before he left, however, Mitchell dismissed Gordon Liddy when he learned that the CREEP aide had refused to cooperate with the FBI. Within several weeks, the FBI found that Liddy had been employed by the White House and the Treasury Department for several years. Eventually, the Bureau also discovered that Liddy had worked for John Ehrlichman on "law enforcement matters." In fact, Liddy had been in the Special Investigations Unit, better known as the Plumbers. His colleagues had included Howard Hunt and several of the Watergate burglars. The Watergate break-in was part of a seamless web.

Richard Nixon took charge at a White House meeting with Mitchell and Haldeman on June 30. The President clearly wanted Mitchell's resignation. The conversation centered on the fear of "a potential problem"—Haldeman's oblique way of describing the possibility that Watergate might be linked to the White House. "The longer you wait the more risk each hour brings," he said. Nixon readily agreed. "Well, I'd cut the loss fast. I'd cut it fast. If we're going to do it I'd cut it fast." In short, Mitchell's departure could reduce the danger to the President. There was a cover for Mitchell, however. His resignation would be explained "in human terms"—family concerns, in other words—and woe to any reporter who questioned the President further on the subject. They would appear insensitive, Nixon said, and "look like a selfish son-of-a-bitch, which I thoroughly intended them to look like." For nearly a year, Nixon had regularly told staff people that the drinking and emotional instability of Martha Mitchell, the Attorney General's wife, had been responsible for her husband's bad judgments. Ten days before the resignation, Nixon claimed that he had called Mitchell to "cheer him up a bit." According to the President, his campaign manager was chagrined over the recent course of events and regretted that he had not policed his organization more effectively. The conversation established the foundation for a strategy that Nixon and his top aides pursued for nearly a year: John Mitchell would take the fall.[5]

In May 1974, with his grip on the presidency slipping, Nixon told a friendly reporter that "history will have to record whether I made the right decision in terms of the allocation of my time; my major error was not doing what many persons have appropriately criticized me for doing in previous campaigns—that was always running my own campaign.'' He indicated that if he had done so, he would have stopped the planned break-in.

Richard Nixon had a special knack for regretting or repudiating the opposite of what was true in order to obscure reality. So it was with the direction of the 1972 campaign. Nixon himself—not John Mitchell, not Clark MacGregor (the ostensible campaign chairman), and not the hierarchy at the Committee for the Re-election of the President—was the campaign manager in 1972. And as in most other matters, Haldeman was the loyal, efficient instrument of his wishes. Alexander Butterfield testified that for two years the President and his aides had directed the committee's operations. The leading figures in CREEP—Jeb Magruder, Hugh Sloan, Maurice Stans, Frederick Malek, MacGregor, and Mitchell—Butterfield acknowledged, were ''trusted'' White House aides. ''There is no question about that liaison,'' he said.[6]

The creation of the re-election committee reflected Nixon's determination to present a public image of nonpartisanship. The model for a separate campaign group may have had its origins in the 1952 Citizens for Eisenhower, an organization that consciously sought to convey the idea that General Eisenhower was above traditional political strivings. Nixon also sought, in establishing the committee to re-elect, to bypass the Republican National Committee so as to keep control of the campaign in his own hands. But, as always, image was basic: Nixon's committee enabled the President to avoid the aura of partisanship and professional politics.

Nixon repeatedly stressed to his aides that the 1972 campaign really was about patriotism, morality, and religion, and not material concerns such as taxes and prices. The ''movement,'' that is, the antiwar, civil rights, and environmental crusades, he confidently asserted, was finished, or, as he put it on another occasion, ''The Liberal Establishment Media May Have Had It.'' In any event, ''Square America'' was back. Nixon would forge a ''New American Majority'' for an across-the-board appeal against ''permissiveness'' and ''elitism.'' Confronted with a suggestion that the Administration consider adopting Truman's policy of pardoning draft evaders during the Korean War, Nixon scrawled on the memo, ''never.'' He wanted campaign surrogates to hold McGovern's ''feet to the fire'' whenever the Democratic candidate appealed for quotas, affirmative action, or other measures for special-interest groups. Nixon must have known he was on the right track when he learned on July 19 that George Meany and the AFL-CIO would not endorse McGovern.[7]

Haldeman's action memos for the campaign derived from notes taken at his daily meetings with the President or from presidential memoranda. The White House directed the campaign, not CREEP headquarters at 1701 Pennsylvania Avenue, and not Republican National Committee Chairman George Bush. Those organizations simply executed White House directives. Around September 1971, Haldeman summarized his presidential meeting notes on political activities: "Mitchell will deal only with Haldeman in the future. Haldeman will operate only as a conduit and not as a manager. This is a role that he will have to perform for the time being." The note was written as the President settled on John Mitchell as his purported campaign director. When Mitchell formally took the post in February 1972, Nixon, in a hand-written note, told him he was one of those "rare men," one of the "very few indispensable men," and the "man to run the campaign of 1972." Finally: "I can't pay you what you are worth. But if just plain 'thank you' will do—you have that a thousand fold (and Martha too!)[.]"

If Haldeman was the conduit from and to Mitchell, there is no question who was the intended party at the other end. During the peak months of the campaign, July through November 1972, Haldeman's meeting notes are pre-dominantly—perhaps 80–90 percent—concerned with campaign activities. One finds few direct orders regarding policy matters. As with everything else that touched him closely, the President kept a tight rein on his campaign and remained intimately involved. Equally clearly, the events that flowed from the Watergate break-in in the summer and fall of 1972 deterred him not at all in his quest for re-election and the overwhelming favor of American voters.[8]

In late 1971, Mitchell asked Harry Dent to work with him on the cam-paign. The two knew each other well from the 1968 election; together, they had worked to fashion and realize the "Southern Strategy." Dent was atten-tive to details and relished the role of political operative. He was a natural choice and was anxious to work with Mitchell. But Dent told Mitchell that it would never happen. Haldeman would never permit Dent to enter the campaign, preferring one of his trusted lieutenants to work at CREEP head-quarters. Dent thought Haldeman would select Magruder, but Mitchell as-sured him that the President had put the Attorney General in charge, and Dent was his choice. Two months later, Mitchell informed Dent that he had been vetoed and that indeed Magruder had been selected. Dent later learned that Haldeman had considered him too much of a "boy scout." Dent also knew that, as always, "it was the hand of Haldeman but it was the voice of Nixon." Nixon undoubtedly respected John Mitchell, but only Nixon him-self could command his political operations. "He trusted no one else to handle his politics," Dent observed.[9] Certainly, politics dominated the Pres-ident's daily discussions with his aides.

Haldeman's memos faithfully reflected the President's views that "RN" had matters well in hand. In a June 10, 1972, memo, Haldeman told other White House aides that the current North Vietnamese offensive only proved that the Communist infrastructure in the South no longer existed. The enemy "are absolutely at the end of their rope. The only possibility now is that they may try to stagger through to November, hoping that President Nixon will lose and they can get a good deal from the next Administration." Obviously, this was the line that the aides were to peddle to media sources.

Many memos reflected the President's concern for tactics rather than substance. On June 20—as the Democrats stepped up their attacks because of the Watergate break-in—Haldeman asked the staff to collect the worst "smear materials" about Nixon and develop a counterattack blaming the Democrats for the charges. Time and again, he relayed the leader's warnings against the most dangerous enemy: complacency. "There is no thought of coasting this election, or of just sailing through it. We are not taking anything for granted. The President considers this terribly important and is working like Hell and it will be an intensive campaign as far as Presidential activity is concerned." Then Haldeman warned against the appearance of nonchalance. In a message that floated through the White House, he said that the Vice President "should knock off golf and use of the White House tennis courts." (Typically, the suggestion was oblique, and Agnew apparently did not receive a direct order on the matter.) Nixon had only limited respect for his running mate. The President had told Haldeman that he wanted Agnew kept at "low key" so he did not become an issue. In August 1972, Haldeman parceled out campaign assignments and responsibilities for those close to the President, including Mitchell, MacGregor, Ehrlichman, Colson, Dent, and Connally.

There was concern over a campaign song. The President thought that it should be one with country-music performers. Haldeman wrote detailed suggestions for television commercials. As in so many other matters, the President involved himself in the most minute details. He discussed his choices of suit colors with Haldeman, convinced that he appeared best in light tones. He told Ehrlichman that bumper stickers were the most effective form of campaigning; he warned, however, that they should never be forced on a car owner. The President wanted his people to "co-opt" the American flag lapel button. He also insisted that the line on his campaign buttons be changed from "Re-elect the President" to "Re-elect President Nixon." But the word "re-elect" bothered him, fearing as he did that it might reflect upon himself as part of the establishment.

The attempted assassination of George Wallace during the spring primaries, and his subsequent paralysis, undoubtedly saddened the President. Nixon offered Wallace a plane with medical facilities to allow him to attend the Democratic Convention. Was there a political motive? "This would be done with no fanfare," Haldeman wrote, "and, of course, no obligation on his [Wallace's] part." A day later, Haldeman suggested that CREEP applaud Wallace for his strong stand on defense, contrasting the Southerner with those who sought to hurt the President in that area. Planting seeds of division in the opposition, of course, lay within the rules of the game.

Many presidential comments and Haldeman memos involved tracking the opposition. On September 16, Haldeman ordered a probe of the families of McGovern and Democratic vice-presidential candidate Sargent Shriver, just as there had been, he claimed, for Nixon's and Agnew's families. Such concern with the opposition persisted to the waning moments of the campaign. The day before the election, Haldeman asked an aide to get a "reading" of McGovern's final network broadcast. At the end, Nixon complained about "dirty attacks" and warned his aides to be ready for dramatic charges. Haldeman recorded notes from a late-night presidential telephone call in mid-October. "Have to ride the attacks out. Z[iegler], hardline it. They are throwing their big punch now." Nixon was enraged when McGovern stepped up his attacks by calling the Administration a "cutthroat crew, . . . a corrupt regime." Senator Edward Kennedy said he would investigate corrupt campaign practices; the President labeled the criticism as the "last burp of the Eastern establishment."[10] Meanwhile, the polls continued to show Nixon's insurmountable lead.

The President relished George McGovern as his opponent. He repeatedly stressed that McGovern was doomed, yet he appeared alternately amused by the Democrats' ineptitude and intrigued by the possibilities of arousing invective against his opponent. When Senator Thomas Eagleton, the Democrats' original selection as McGovern's running mate, admitted he had undergone electric-shock treatments for depression, Nixon preferred that Eagleton remain on the ticket. After he watched the Democratic Convention, including vice-presidential nomination speeches for Julian Bond and Martha Mitchell which delayed until 3:00 A.M. McGovern's acceptance speech, Nixon thought that the "scene had the air of a college skit that had gotten carried away with itself and didn't know how to stop."[11]

Nixon remembered that Barry Goldwater had never been able to rid himself of the albatross of ultra-right-wing supporters. He used a similar tactic against McGovern, who was saddled with left-wing allies, though Nixon complained that he would "not have the media cooperation" that LBJ had in tarring Goldwater in 1964. He wanted such radicals as Abbie Hoffman and Angela Davis publicized as McGovern supporters. He suggested to Haldeman and Colson that they get a prominent veteran's group or a labor leader or independent Democrat to write a public letter calling on McGovern to repudiate his radical backers. Nixon urged that his aides nail McGovern "to his left-wing supporters and [force] him to repudiate them or accept their support." The "media blackout" on this point, Nixon demanded, must be broken: "I consider this a top priority objective."[12]

Nixon doubtless considered McGovern dangerous to national security and the economy. Even worse, he regarded McGovern's nomination as a victory for Senator Edward Kennedy. Perhaps humorously, perhaps not, the President typed McGovern as a "sin-chaser." In a sense, he welcomed McGovern's assaults, for they made the challenger's anti-institutionalism the issue, not the President's record. Nixon meticulously collected information on Democratic defections, such as those of Connally and former Senator George Smathers, as well as the coolness toward McGovern on the part of AFL-CIO President Meany and Senate Democratic leader Mike Mansfield. Smathers assured the President that McGovern had alienated Democratic Senate stalwarts Richard Russell, Robert Byrd, and Herman Talmadge, who he said were anxious to avoid an endorsement. Warren Magnuson (D–WA) realized that McGovern's calls for reduced defense spending might be harmful to the Boeing Company, a key industry in his state. Nixon gleefully told Connally that Magnuson and Democrat Henry Jackson, the state's other Senator, realized how much the Administration's policies helped the aircraft industry in Washington. Secretary of the Treasury George Shultz reported to the White House in August that Meany thought McGovern "stupid" and a "dumb cluck." Through Shultz, Meany conveyed support to the President on specific issues.[13]

During the summer, the President occasionally expressed concern regarding Watergate. In late July and early August, he and Haldeman discussed White House Counsel John Dean's suggestion that Magruder be given immunity from possible criminal prosecution for his role in the break-in planning. In September, Nixon wanted the staff to do more checking on Lawrence O'Brien. In an allusion to Lyndon Johnson's embarrassing protégé, he also encouraged his aides to "run down [the] Bobby Baker stuff," apparently hoping to find Democratic scandals. Nixon's personal secretary, Rose Mary Woods, had telephoned Baker, the onetime LBJ aide who had been convicted for larceny, fraud, and tax evasion, to gain information about O'Brien and Senator Edmund Muskie. (Several days later, the President told Haldeman that Bebe Rebozo was going to see Baker, adding: "If he can help us we will help him"—presumably with a pardon, as Baker had been sentenced to prison in January 1971.) As a response to the Democrats' million-dollar suit against CREEP, Nixon urged Haldeman to go ahead with a countersuit alleging libels by O'Brien, but the President warned Haldeman not to get into "specific denials."

In the closing days of the campaign, the President discussed with Haldeman and Ehrlichman McGovern's hammering on the corruption issue. Nixon thought that the evidence linking the White House to the break-in was minimal. He complained, however, about the difficulty of proving a negative. Colson, Haldeman, and Ehrlichman agreed to push hard against the *Washington Post* after the newspaper admitted that it had erred in linking Haldeman to Watergate because of his control over some campaign funds. Yet

Haldeman told his colleagues that he was concerned about the possible incriminating testimony of the campaign treasurer, Hugh Sloan; Haldeman and Ehrlichman talked about "cutting losses." Six days before the election, the President told Ehrlichman to initiate conversations with journalist Theodore White, who had close ties to Nixon. White, as he had done for campaigns since 1960, was writing a history of this one, and Nixon wanted Ehrlichman "to make the record" on Watergate.[14]

The 1972 tactic of insulating Nixon from his campaign built on the practices of 1968, but now the Administration enjoyed the advantage of incumbency. The President rarely left the White House to campaign. Ceremonial Rose Garden appearances and other activities kept Nixon in the public spotlight, looking "presidential." One of the President's image makers remarked quite appropriately: "There is only one candidate in this election, not two. There is the incumbent. The President. Mr. Nixon. And then there is the only candidate, McGovern." Nixon remained in his protective cocoon, frustrating his opponent and the media alike. The "television end run," first deployed in 1968, now was perfected. "We're being finessed out of our boots," said one prominent newspaper reporter. "We're just sitting on the bench while the administration dribbles the ball past us."[15]

In spite of his dominating the campaign, the President periodically offered his usual complaints about the media. Haldeman told the staff that the campaign pitted the eastern media, the intellectual elite, and the academic community against the views and philosophy of Richard Nixon. The President undoubtedly liked to portray himself as waging a lonely war against that unholy trinity. "The point is to make this a mandate on the issues," Haldeman said, "not just the man. We need to pick up the wrong predictions of the media and build off of that."[16]

The White House simply refused to acknowledge Watergate publicly in any serious way. During one press briefing, Ron Ziegler responded with variations of "no comment" to some twenty-nine questions regarding possible Administration involvement in the break-in. Here and there, reporters began to talk about "stonewalling." Indeed, Nixon ordered Haldeman and Ehrlichman to stand firm against reporters—"*never* apologize," he said. Late in October, after CBS had devoted extensive attention to Watergate, the President complained at length to Haldeman. He ordered Kissinger to do nothing with the network for a week. Ziegler was not to talk to CBS reporters or to the *Post*. Colson upbraided CBS's top executives and succeeded in having the network reduce a promised follow-up program.

The media remained useful to Nixon as an instrument for manipulation as well as an object of public scorn. Kissinger was instructed to "play" the *New York Times*. When Senator McGovern appeared on ABC's *Issues and Answers* on October 22, the White House sent seven questions to the program's moderator. Although the moderator informed McGovern that the questions had come from the Administration, the point was that the moderator obediently asked them. Meanwhile, McGovern was unable to engage the President in a face-to-face debate.[17]

The President, of course, saw reporters, but whom and when and how were his choices. He constantly expressed concern about the possibility of being tripped up, of being trapped, of making mistakes, but his anxiety paled before the careful preparations to guard against such contingencies.

The Watergate break-in eventually exposed a whole array of campaign practices designed to disrupt or embarrass the political opposition, all of which commentators later summarized as "dirty tricks." Nixon recalled in his memoirs that he had "insisted to Haldeman and others . . . that in this campaign we were finally in a position to have someone doing to the opposition what they had done to us. They knew that this time I wanted the leading Democrats annoyed, harassed, and embarrassed—as I had been in the past." The rationale always centered on retaliation: "I told my staff that we should come up with the kind of imaginative dirty tricks that our Democratic opponents used against us and others so effectively in previous campaigns." He acknowledged that he ordered "a tail on a front-running Democrat" (without saying for what purpose) and directed that federal agencies' files be checked for suspicious or illegal behavior by Democrats. Again, Nixon's involvement was admittedly intensive—with the usual qualification: the President claimed that he had tried to keep himself and his staff out of politics as long as possible in 1972.[18]

Nixon's re-election organization and his management of it were firmly in place by 1971. The language of his memoirs inadequately conveys what became an obsession. Nixon always perceived himself as the victim in campaigns. He certainly had encountered rough opposition, but any implication that dirty tactics had been only on one side amounted to a new peak in self-pity. In fact, Nixon and Haldeman had been "convicted" of illegal campaign behavior long before. During the 1962 California gubernatorial campaign, they had established a bogus organization called the Committee for the Preservation of the Democratic Party in California. The Nixon finance committee supported the dummy group and mailed postcards to registered Democrats expressing concern for the welfare of the party under Governor Pat Brown. The cards failed to state that they had been paid for by the Nixon for Governor Finance Committee. The Democrats sued, and nearly two years later a Superior Court ruled that the mail campaign had been deliberately misleading. The judge, a Republican, found that the postcard poll "was reviewed, amended and finally approved by Mr. Nixon personally," and added that Haldeman similarly "approved the plan and the project." Supporting roles had been played by Ron Ziegler and Maurice

Stans. Earlier in the campaign, the Nixon staff had circulated cropped photographs of Brown and Nikita Khrushchev.[19]

Some of the "tricks" used for the 1972 campaign were amusing, but perpetrators like Donald Segretti (whose name means "secrets" in Italian) apparently could not distinguish sophomoric stunts (ordering unwanted pizzas sent to a Democratic rally) from underhanded personal attacks (manufacturing libels about the sexual preferences of candidates or forging letters in their names). CREEP provided a haven for spinning fantasy plots as well as for mounting sophisticated intelligence operations in the name of re-electing the President. Senator Edmund Muskie's chauffeur regularly reported to CREEP, which then transmitted the reports to Haldeman aide Gordon Strachan. Less than six months after the election, the nation listened to accounts of exotically named operations: Townhouse, Sedan Chair I, Sedan Chair II, Sandwedge, Gemstone, and other CREEP-inspired ploys, not knowing whether they offered parodies of bad spy novels or Keystone Kops at play.[20]

Sandwedge was a typical operation. Created by Ehrlichman's "private detective," John Caulfield, the plan involved creation of an organization to perform both "offensive intelligence and defensive-security" operations for the Nixon campaign. The former included penetration of the Democratic nominee's headquarters and entourage, a "black-bag" capability, surveillance of Democratic primaries, conventions, and meetings, and investigation and dissemination of derogatory information on a worldwide basis; the defensive operations included selection and supervision of private security for the Republican Convention, the maintenance of security at CREEP headquarters, security for the campaign staff, and measures to initiate party- or campaign-oriented investigations. The Sandwedge operation was to have a private business cover and thus avoid direct involvement with CREEP.[21]

The Watergate break-in had its origins in a plan called Gemstone, supposedly devised by Gordon Liddy. It included conducting surveillance and wiretapping of the Democratic National Convention, the use of call girls to compromise Democratic candidates, sabotaging the air conditioning system at the convention, and running security squads to mug and kidnap radical leaders who might demonstrate at the Republican Convention. John Mitchell reportedly listened to the proposal of Gemstone, puffed on his pipe, and told Liddy that it was "not quite what I had in mind" and that he was to devise more "realistic" and less expensive plans. The entry and bugging of the Watergate offices of the Democratic National Committee was the more realistic plan concocted by CREEP's "security" forces. Mitchell later ruefully reflected that he should have thrown Gordon Liddy and his entire plan out the window. As Attorney General—which he was until March 1972—Mitchell might have done better to arrest Gordon Liddy for his proposed conspiracy.

* * *

The Watergate break-in itself eventually diminished in importance as the nation discovered what John Mitchell labeled the "White House horrors" and the clear patterns of presidential abuses of power. The subsequent attempts by the White House to obstruct the investigation of the Watergate affair—the "cover-up," which itself led to more abuses of power—further detracted from the significance of the break-in. But if they seemed to diminish with time, the events of June 1972 rekindled the mood of cynicism and distrust toward officialdom that the Nixon Administration had inherited in 1969.

Inevitably, the generally received version of the Watergate break-in has attracted its share of skepticism. Traumatic national events generally do so. "Official" versions of events such as the Lincoln and Kennedy assassinations, the sinking of the *Lusitania,* the attack on Pearl Harbor, and the decision to drop the atomic bomb, for example, have evoked critical challenges, some verging on the paranoid, delusional, and absurd, others posing worthwhile questions for which there are no satisfactory answers.

At the time, the certainties of the Watergate break-in were three: the burglars were real; they had entered the office complex; they had bugging devices with them. The five perpetrators eventually were convicted for breaking and entering and for violating laws prohibiting unauthorized wiretaps. Hunt and Liddy were also found guilty. As the prosecutors developed their case, they discovered, as did subsequent investigations, that the seven men had important links to CREEP and the White House; in particular, all had received money from questionable campaign contributions. But what was the purpose of the break-in? Clearly, the operation was political. But what had been its end? For what specific gain had the break-in been planned?

One theory traces the break-in to a convoluted plot masterminded by Charles Colson. Colson involved Mitchell, Haldeman, and Ehrlichman in his scheme, so this account goes, but he later used them to take responsibility when the attempt failed.

Colson and his spymaster, Hunt, it is suggested, in effect usurped CREEP's Operation Gemstone for their own purposes. The plan's immediate objectives were Nixon's re-election, the elimination of George Wallace, and the isolation of the Left. By this theory, Colson and Hunt worked in their own way, financing Wallace's would-be assassin and planting left-wing literature in his apartment. With Wallace no longer a factor in the 1972 election and victory assured, Nixon's other aides signed off on Gemstone, abandoning the plan to bug Democratic headquarters, but Colson and Hunt continued to pursue it, for their own reasons. They planned the initial, successful, Watergate break-in to find or plant evidence linking the Democrats to left-wing radicals and to install phone taps. The second break-in, the one that was foiled, was to fix a faulty tap. Colson and Hunt also planned widespread violence for the Republican Convention which would be blamed on radical groups. Colson would use that violence as a pretext to persuade the President to call a state of emergency and declare martial law. When the second break-in failed, the plan collapsed. In the final scene of this suggested scenario, Colson and Hunt concealed their true objectives and managed to implicate the rest of the Nixon Administration.[22]

Arthur Kinoy, the lawyer who successfully challenged the Administration's broad claims for inherent presidential powers to wiretap without warrants, offered a second hypothesis to account for the break-in. Earlier in the spring, Kinoy had represented federal judge Damon Keith, who had ordered the Administration to disclose wiretaps in a case involving alleged White Panther members. Throughout the proceedings, the Justice Department attorneys had pressed luxuriant claims of inherent executive powers to wiretap. If the Supreme Court had accepted the government's position, the Administration would have had a perfect cover for wiretaps and "black" operations already underway or planned. The Watergate break-in occurred, Kinoy suggested, because the Administration was privy to the Court's adverse decision and someone ordered that the phone taps be removed before the Court gave its ruling, scheduled for announcement the Monday after the break-in. Why were so many men caught at Democratic headquarters if their mission was only to repair one faulty tap? Kinoy theorized that the burglars were removing equipment.[23]

More vivid convolutions appear when other theories link the CIA to the break-in. Two key players, Hunt and McCord, had been employed by the CIA, and other figures connected to the affair had tenuous or alleged ties with the Agency. The CIA role was given a certain *cachet* by Haldeman's endorsement. According to him, Nixon intensely disliked the CIA and its Director, Richard Helms. The animosity went back to the 1960 campaign. Nixon blamed the CIA for providing John F. Kennedy with inaccurate estimates of Soviet missile capabilities, thus enabling Kennedy to exploit a so-called "missile gap." Nixon also blamed the Agency for Kennedy's advocacy of armed intervention in Cuba after the CIA had briefed the Democratic candidate on its proposed Bay of Pigs invasion. When Nixon became President, according to Haldeman, the White House and the CIA often were at odds. Furthermore, the CIA, Haldeman believed, like the FBI, saw the proposed Huston Plan of 1971 as a "disembowelment" of its power and from that moment began to monitor the White House. Haldeman also endorsed Senator Howard Baker's 1973 comment: "Nixon and Helms have so much on each other, neither of them can breathe."[24]

Haldeman was no stranger to Nixon's hostility toward the CIA. A month before the break-in, the President told him that the Agency needed a "housecleaning''; its ''muscle-bound bureaucracy'' had ''completely paralyzed'' its brain. It had too many Ivy League and Georgetown types, Nixon claimed, rather than the kind of people recruited by the FBI. Nixon wanted a study made of how many CIA people he could remove through a reduction in force. Henceforth, in addition, he insisted that the CIA recruit applicants from schools whose presidents and faculty supported the war. Publicly, the Administration would rationalize the CIA dismissals as necessary budget cuts, but the President said, ''you . . . know the real reason and I want some action to deal with the problem.''[25]

Haldeman later argued that the CIA and the Democratic National Committee knew about the first Watergate break-in and that, singly or together, they sabotaged the second. He claimed that the Cubans, Hunt, and McCord remained on the CIA payroll. The CIA's animosity toward the Administration, its fear that after his re-election Nixon would move decisively to bridle its power, and its determination to protect an old ally, industrialist and financial manipulator Howard Hughes, Haldeman argued, explained the failure of the break-in.

Haldeman traced the initial motivation of the break-in to the obsession of Nixon and Colson with gaining derogatory information on Lawrence O'Brien, particularly regarding his ties to Hughes. Mitchell, Haldeman wrote in his memoir, was too cautious and politically astute to approve such an operation—implying, as Haldeman intended, that Nixon knew about the break-in in advance.[26]

Haldeman's later solicitude for Mitchell was apparently not at work in April 1973, when he, with the President and Ehrlichman, connived to implicate Mitchell as solely responsible for Watergate. And for all the fascination with Haldeman's projection of CIA mischief in the case, it is instructive to remember that he contended only that the CIA *sabotaged* the effort—in short, Haldeman acknowledged that the break-in originated from the President's camp.

Jim Hougan's book, *Secret Agenda,* fleshes out Haldeman's claims for a pervasive CIA role in Watergate. Hougan has established the most thorough reconstruction of the crime. As evidence of the CIA's involvement in the events of May–June 1972, Hougan traced the Agency's dealings back to Howard Hunt's roles in the Pentagon Papers case and the break-in of Daniel Ellsberg's psychiatrist's office. Throughout this period, Hougan argues, Hunt was a CIA operative and regularly reported on Administration doings, particularly the sexual peccadillos of various politicians.

Hougan claims that the second Watergate break-in had nothing to do with the original one, but instead occurred because Haldeman and John Dean possessed information that the Democratic headquarters had something to do with a call-girl operation, curiously involving both Democratic and White House officials. Hougan suggests that the prostitution ring was a CIA operation or was under the Agency's surveillance. Consequently, he argues, McCord, like Hunt still a CIA operative, deliberately sabotaged the second break-in to prevent its uncovering the call-girl ring. Other undercover CIA agents then played a prominent role in leading journalists to various aspects of the White House involvement in the break-in and thereby successfully covered up the Agency's role in the origins of the President's downfall, Hougan concludes. Hougan has ventured the most revisionist account of the origins of Watergate; his story, he insists, proved the common understanding of Watergate to be one based on "fraudulent history."[27]

Questions regarding the CIA appear in various segments of the Watergate story. The Agency's role, however, seems destined to remain shadowy. Such CIA principals as Helms, Deputy Director Vernon Walters, and future Director William Colby have adamantly denied any CIA role in initiating any Watergate events or in implicating the White House. But Assistant U.S. Attorney Earl Silbert charged, and Colby admitted, that the CIA had withheld cooperation with the investigation. What eventually emerged from the inquiries into Watergate—wholly apart from the events of the break-in and subsequent cover-up—was the CIA's changed relationship to other power centers in the government. Richard Nixon's entanglement with Watergate surely allowed the Agency to escape confrontation with a President apparently bent on tightening his own command and control of it. But at the same time, that escape ironically gave force to the concept and even the existence of congressional oversight of the CIA.[28]

Nixon had a longstanding interest in Lawrence O'Brien. O'Brien had been a Kennedy political operative, both in Massachusetts (where Charles Colson was an old adversary) and in national politics. Later, he faithfully served Lyndon Johnson. Nixon also knew that O'Brien had been retained by Howard Hughes as a secret lobbyist, although, unlike himself, the Democrat never had to answer politically for the link. Nixon bitterly resented continuing Democratic efforts to connect him to Howard Hughes, efforts which included a Kennedy Justice Department investigation in 1961 because of a Hughes loan to Nixon's family. Haldeman noted that when matters involved connections to Hughes, "Nixon seemed to lose touch with reality." Partly because of the Hughes connection, Colson maintained a large folder of materials on O'Brien, labeled "Political Statements by Lawrence F. O'Brien."

When George McGovern sought a vice-presidential candidate to replace Thomas Eagleton in the summer of 1972, the President advised his aides to say nothing of Eagleton's problem, but "then hit the successor all out—esp. if it's O'Brien." Ehrlichman and Nixon discussed O'Brien's taxes and a reputed loan from Hughes at some length on August 7, 1972, after Rose Mary Woods had called Bobby Baker for information on the Democratic

Chairman. Several weeks later, the President instructed Ehrlichman to get busy to "worry O'Brien," and to work through John Dean. In January 1971, Nixon told Haldeman that "the time is approaching when Larry O'Brien is held accountable for his retainer with Hughes." Perhaps, the President added, "Colson should make a check on this." Haldeman, however, ordered Dean to make a report. Word for word, he repeated the President's words.

Dean thought that the Watergate break-in had its origins in Nixon's obsessive desire to incriminate O'Brien. Magruder tentatively agreed some years later but then admitted he was uncertain. Haldeman firmly believed that Nixon's orders to Colson, which he had conveyed, made their way to Hunt and Liddy. More than that, as Haldeman wrote, "Nixon *knew* what had happened," as he repeatedly told Haldeman after the burglary that "Colson must have done it." [29]

Dean turned the O'Brien matter over to John Caulfield, Ehrlichman's in-house private detective. Caulfield found little on O'Brien, but he kept running into more details of the Hughes-Nixon connection and warned Dean that it might be dangerous. Nevertheless, the IRS began a tax audit of Robert Maheu, Hughes's ousted chief aide. Maheu retaliated with a leak to columnist Jack Anderson about a reported $100,000 Hughes payment to Nixon through Bebe Rebozo. Las Vegas journalist Hank Greenspun told Herb Klein that he had information the money had been used to furnish the President's San Clemente estate.

Stories regarding the Hughes-Nixon connection included a controversial loan to Donald Nixon, the President's brother, in late 1956 which purportedly resulted in a favorable IRS ruling for the Howard Hughes Medical Institute, and allegations of Donald's involvement with a convicted Hughes associate. The rumors began to mushroom early in 1972. Dean noted that Nixon particularly blamed O'Brien for sensationalizing the Administration's decision not to bring an antitrust prosecution against the International Telephone and Telegraph Company.

As a result, the President and Colson added pressure for more intelligence on O'Brien. Shortly afterward, Mitchell and Magruder approved the original break-in of Democratic headquarters, and Magruder enthusiastically pushed for improved bugs when the initial fruits proved insignificant.

At one point, Liddy allegedly was instructed to find out about O'Brien's "shit file" on Nixon as well as about the Hughes-O'Brien connection. According to this account, spelled out in a biography of Hughes, Nixon later told Haldeman his real reason for wanting to get O'Brien. That conversation occurred on June 20, but the biographer conveniently claimed that it was part of an erased 18½-minute segment of a taped conversation in the Oval Office. He also suggested that the CIA undermined the Nixon cover-up to protect its own links to the Hughes organization.[30] Such speculations had no evidentiary accompaniment.

Months after the break-in, Nixon still was preoccupied with "getting something" on O'Brien. On August 9, he informed Haldeman that the IRS had investigated the Hughes Tool Company and found payments to O'Brien, possibly during the time he served as Hubert Humphrey's reportedly unpaid campaign manager in 1968. Nixon had learned all this from Treasury Secretary John Connally, who urged the President to make use of the information as soon as possible. The problem was in forcing the IRS to publicize the payments; apparently, the agency had resisted doing so. Nixon expected Haldeman or Ehrlichman "to ride IRS." He wanted the agency to call O'Brien in for voluntary interrogation. If he refused, the IRS was to subpoena him—"before O'Brien stonewalls it."[31]

The so-called "Greek Connection" provides yet another theory for the Watergate break-in. Once again, there is a link to Lawrence O'Brien, and the motive may, like the O'Brien-Hughes theory, lie in G. Gordon Liddy's contention that the Watergate break-in *"was to find out what O'Brien had of a derogatory nature about us, not for us to get something on him or the Democrats."* James McCord also testified that the purpose of the June 17 break-in was "to do photocopy work of documents" as well as to install new listening devices. The story has its origins in a September 1968 campaign speech delivered by vice-presidential candidate Spiro Agnew. Agnew earlier had promised Elias P. Demetracopoulos, a Greek newspaperman who had escaped Greece shortly after an army coup in 1967, that he would maintain public neutrality toward the Greek Colonels' dictatorship; privately he relayed word that "my hopes are that we will see Greece in proper hands very shortly." But in response to a question at the National Press Club on September 27, Agnew strongly endorsed the regime and vigorously denounced the opposition as Communist-inspired and -dominated.

What had happened? According to Demetracopoulos, the Greek KYP—the intelligence service which had been founded by the CIA and subsequently subsidized by the Agency—had transferred three cash payments totalling $549,000 to the Nixon campaign fund. The conduit was Thomas Pappas, a prominent Greek-American businessman with close links to the CIA, the Colonels, and the Nixon campaign. (Agnew insisted that he "had absolutely no knowledge" of such money.) The charges that KYP money had come into the presidential campaign, with CIA knowledge, were circulated in the United States and in Greece. CIA Director Richard Helms commented with studied ambiguity: "Even if somebody suggests they would like to do it, I would insist that they don't tell me about it because that is dynamite." Such domestic activity grossly violated the CIA's 1947 charter. In 1987, an authoritative KYP official confirmed that the money had flowed from Greece to the Nixon campaign in 1968. Pappas had well-known ties to Nixon, and he was widely regarded as the man who had persuaded Nixon and Mitchell to put Agnew on the ticket, although Agnew later claimed that he disliked the businessman.[32]

Demetracopoulos arranged a meeting with O'Brien through former California Governor Pat Brown. He reluctantly provided Brown with sketchy information, fearing quite correctly that his telephone was bugged. (Later revelations proved that the FBI had tapped Demetracopoulos's telephone in this period.) Demetracopoulos saw O'Brien on October 19 and gave him the particulars of the cash transactions. During the meeting, it was suggested that the CIA be brought in to confirm the charges. But Demetracopoulos long had been *persona non grata* with the Johnson Administration, which had tried to block his entry into the country in 1967. LBJ already had resumed aid to the Greek Colonels at the time, and he was known to be infuriated with Demetracopoulos's lobbying activities against the military regime. He or the CIA may even have known that the Greek regime had planned to kidnap Demetracopoulos, according to the junta's ambassador to the United States. Two days after the O'Brien meeting, Demetracopoulos's lawyer received word that a deportation hearing was scheduled on October 23 for his client, but he managed to get a continuance.[33] After the meeting on October 19, Demetracopoulos had further telephone contacts with O'Brien and his aides, and they met again on October 26. O'Brien said that nothing could be done to alter the Administration's position, although he publicly denounced the Nixon-Agnew-Pappas-Greek connections.

Nixon's election set in motion a variety of events that brought Elias Demetracopoulos into the limelight—and made him a repeated target of Administration reprisals. John Caulfield sent a memo to Ehrlichman in October 1969 regarding the "Greek Inquiry." Demetracopoulos also remained under surveillance by the FBI, and probably by the CIA as well. In July 1971, Representative Benjamin Rosenthal (D–NY), Chairman of a House Foreign Affairs subcommittee, opened an investigation of the Administration's support for the Greek regime. Demetracopoulos appeared as a witness on the twelfth and denounced Thomas Pappas's connections, contending that he had been given extraordinary economic concessions for his support. In response to a question from Rosenthal, Demetracopoulos promised a detailed supporting memorandum, with documented material.

Following the open hearing, the U.S. Ambassador to Greece, Henry Tasca, sent a lengthy telegram to Secretary of State William Rogers and Attorney General John Mitchell, urging that Demetracopoulos be thoroughly investigated by the FBI. Tasca called him a "subsidized agent" and a "dangerous and mysterious enemy." The Ambassador regularly entertained Pappas, he was particularly close to the Greek regime, and Nixon had known him well since 1947. Within a few days after Tasca's telegram arrived in Washington, agents from the Internal Security Section of the Department of Justice questioned the subcommittee staff and secured a stenographic transcript of the hearing but did not get the detailed memorandum until after Demetracopoulos filed it on September 17. The agents advised the staff that Demetracopoulos had possibly been in violation of the Foreign Agents Registration Act. They also visited officials at the Greek Desk in the State Department, who urged them to make "any kind of case" against Demetracopoulos, whom they regarded as a "shady character and a troublemaker."

Representative Rosenthal announced that he would continue the investigation and perhaps call Thomas Pappas as a witness. Similar sentiments were expressed by Democratic members of the Senate Foreign Relations Committee. In fact, nothing happened. Pappas was not a man whom the Administration wanted to subject to public scrutiny. In December 1971, David Abshire, Assistant Secretary of State for Congressional Relations, assured various committee members that the department had no interest in persecuting Demetracopoulos, yet he vigorously defended Pappas's conduct. Abshire also apologized to Demetracopoulos, clearing his letter of apology with John Dean.[34]

But the harassment continued. In September 1971, Murray Chotiner, the longtime Nixon operative, had visited Demetracopoulos (they were on a first-name basis) and warned him that he could be deported if he continued to attack Pappas and cooperated in any investigation of the President's "friend," as Chotiner characterized Pappas. Months later, a close friend of both Demetracopoulos and Mitchell reported that at a luncheon, Mitchell spoke loudly of his intention to deport the Greek. "He is *furious* at you—and your testimony against Pappas. He kept threatening to have you deported!" she wrote Demetracopoulos.[35]

Thomas Pappas's links with the Nixon Administration became still stronger in the 1972 campaign as he solicited hundreds of thousands of dollars from businessmen. He also raised illegal funds from foreign sources. (Receiving foreign money apparently was not unusual for a Nixon campaign: Philippine President Ferdinand Marcos reportedly contributed in both 1968 and 1972.) Most important, Pappas figured heavily in discussions regarding the payment of hush money to the Watergate burglars. John Dean claimed that in March 1973 Ehrlichman suggested Pappas as a source of assistance. "Did you talk to the Greek?" Dean subsequently asked Mitchell. "Yes I have," Mitchell replied. "Is the Greek bearing gifts?" Dean asked, but Mitchell could not answer on the telephone at the moment.

Dean himself said he had talked to Pappas about the need for hush money. In a later conversation with the President, Pappas acknowledged that he was, as Nixon remembered, "helping, uh, uh, John's [Mitchell] special projects." Nixon also acknowledged that he had been told that Pappas had been "very helpful on the, uh, Watergate thing." How helpful? The Watergate Special Prosecutor later learned that Pappas had given Mitchell $50,000, ostensibly for "closing costs" on a real-estate loan. Pappas also admitted that he had been asked to contribute to help the defendants in the break-in. One memo in the prosecutor's files states that "some documentary evidence indicates that those involved in the cover-up may have expected funds for it from Pappas." One of the CREEP lawyers admitted to Dean that a Greek law firm actually was a CIA front and could channel some of the money to the defendants.[36]

Thomas Pappas had longstanding connections with the CIA and the Greek KYP; politically and economically, he supported the Greek junta. In 1976, Ambassador Tasca reportedly testified in executive session to the House Intelligence Committee that Pappas indeed had transferred funds from the KYP to the Nixon campaign committee in 1968. Pappas had powerful friends and real influence in the Administration. When the Colonels intervened in Cyprus in 1974, the Commander-in-Chief of the Greek Armed Forces claimed that Pappas brought a message from American officials to the KYP supporting the action.

Information derogatory to Pappas was also information derogatory to the Administration—as Elias Demetracopoulos found out throughout the Nixon years. What that information was exactly, and how much Lawrence O'Brien knew about it, might well have fallen into the category of intelligence that Liddy and his wiretapping team had to ascertain. Curiously, through both campaigns in 1968 and 1972, O'Brien did not seem anxious to exploit the information. Nevertheless, knowledge about O'Brien's knowledge of Demetracopoulos's intelligence, together with "derogatory information" about O'Brien's past dealings with Hughes, for example, might have offered the Administration some bargaining leverage with O'Brien.

In time, the Nixon Administration made Demetracopoulos pay dearly for what he had said. Columnists friendly to the Administration, such as James J. Kilpatrick, denounced Demetracopoulos as a fraud and suggested that he might be a Communist agent. (Kilpatrick, however, soon discovered that he had been misled and retracted every charge.) The FBI, the CIA, the State Department, and the Department of Justice all maintained files containing allegedly hostile information on Demetracopoulos—information that each agency eventually acknowledged was wrong. Significantly, the "Greek Connection" theory of Watergate caused the most anxiety for the longest period of time for the Nixon Administration, and the agencies that served it.[37]

Since the Watergate break-in clearly was a political intelligence operation, the insights of the *real* campaign director deserve mention. Richard Nixon never offered an explicit or implicit theory explaining the event. In his mem-

Richard M. Nixon, 37th President of the United
States, 1969 – 1974. (National Archives)

Spiro T. Agnew, Judy Agnew, Pat Nixon, and
Richard M. Nixon at the 1972 Republican
Convention in Miami. (National Archives)

The President and Vice President with the entire
Cabinet and other leading presidential advisers,
at the White House, November 1969. (National
Archives)

Vice President Agnew and President Nixon,
1971. (National Archives)

The President and his key aides, Henry Kissinger, John Ehrlichman, and H. R. Haldeman, in the Oval Office. (National Archives)

Nixon campaigning for George Bush in Texas, 1970. (National Archives)

Nixon, Attorney General John Mitchell, Press Secretary Ron Ziegler. (National Archives)

HEW Secretary Robert Finch (left) after his dismissal in June 1970, with his successor, Elliot Richardson, and the President. (National Archives)

Alexander Butterfield, Oval Office aide and custodian of the taping system, with Nixon. (National Archives)

Chinese Premier Zhou En-lai and Nixon, Beijing, January 1972. (National Archives)

Left: Charles Colson, presidential assistant. *Right:* Jeb Stuart Magruder, White House aide and Deputy Director of CREEP. (National Archives)

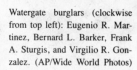

Watergate burglars (clockwise from top left): Eugenio R. Martinez, Bernard L. Barker, Frank A. Sturgis, and Virgilio R. Gonzalez. (AP/Wide World Photos)

James McCord, Watergate burglar, former CIA agent, and Chief of Security for CREEP, testifying before the Senate Select Committee. (*Washington Star*)

E. Howard Hunt, Watergate burglar, Colson aide, and former CIA employee. (*Washington Star*)

G. Gordon Liddy, CREEP employee and planner of the Watergate burglary. (*Washington Star*)

L. Patrick Gray, Acting Director of the FBI, 1972–1973. (*Washington Star*)

Richard Helms, former Director of the Central Intelligence Agency, testifying before the Senate Select Committee. (*Washington Star*)

Nixon with Thomas Pappas, "the Greek bearing gifts." (LAM)

OPPOSITE: *Top:* Patrick Buchanan. (National Archives) *Left:* Donald Segretti, convicted for campaign "dirty tricks" in 1972. (*Washington Star*) *Right:* Hugh Sloan, CREEP Treasurer, testifying in 1973. (*Washington Star*)

Federal Judge John Sirica, who presided over several Watergate trials. (*Washington Star*)

Assistant Attorney General Henry Petersen, who directed early phases of the Watergate investigation. (*Washington Star*)

White House Counsel John Dean in May 1973, after his dismissal by the President. (National Archives)

Leonard Garment (left), after his appointment as Counsel in May 1973, with Ron Ziegler. (National Archives)

Melvin Laird, Nixon, and Chief of Staff Alexander Haig after the forced resignations of Haldeman and Ehrlichman, June 1973. (National Archives)

White House aides with Presidential Counsel J. Fred Buzhardt. (National Archives)

Vice Chairman Howard Baker (left) and Chairman Sam Ervin of the Senate Select Committee, June 1973. (*Washington Star*)

Senate Select Committee Counsel Samuel Dash (left) and Senator Lowell Weicker, June 1973. (*Washington Star*)

Nixon and CBS correspondent Dan Rather in a heated exchange during a September 1973 press conference. (National Archives)

Nixon and Soviet leader Leonid Brezhnev on a Potomac cruise during a recess in the Senate hearings, June 1973. (National Archives)

oirs, he broke his explanation down to the "factual truth" (a literal description of the events of Watergate, events that could never be completely reconstructed), the "legal truth" (involving judgments about motives), the "moral truth" (which considered whether the White House's behavior was ethically wrong), and the "political truth." The political truth, he explained, was the total impact of all the other truths on the nation and the nation's judgment of Nixon and his Administration. On one point, of course, the President was firm and consistent: he had no prior knowledge of the break-in.[38] He never discussed his responsibility for instructing his aides to gather derogatory information on O'Brien or other political enemies, however.

As time passes, the Watergate burglars and the specifics of their plans and deeds will recede further from historical consciousness. The burglary itself—its planning, its flawed execution, and even its motives—ultimately must be seen as part of a behavior pattern characterizing the President and his aides that stretched back to the beginnings of the Nixon Administration. The Watergate burglary parted the veil that hid the "underside" of that government. Even if we should learn that the Administration was victimized by a CIA plot—even if we should learn the motive for the burglary—that would change nothing regarding our understanding of John Mitchell's "White House horrors." Nor would it mitigate the resulting inter-institutional conflicts and encounters, which raised profound constitutional and political questions, or the constitutional crisis generated by the Administration's behavior in the wake of the burglary. That behavior resulted in the special crimes of cover-up and obstruction by high Administration officials—up to and including the President of the United States.

The FBI quickly assumed primary responsibility for the investigation of the Watergate break-in. In fact, overall responsibility for the effort belonged to the Department of Justice, particularly to the Criminal Division. Assistant Attorney General Henry Petersen, a career government official, headed the division. He maintained contact with Acting FBI Director Gray and with the U.S. Attorney's office in Washington. U.S. Attorney Harold Titus turned the case over to his chief assistant, Earl Silbert. After Hunt and Liddy had been implicated, Titus directed two more assistants, Seymour Glanzer and Donald Campbell, to work with Silbert.

The FBI's investigation, and the U.S. Attorney's handling of the case, were later criticized as inept, unnecessarily cautious, and overly solicitous of the Administration.[39] Such criticism ignores the Administration's successful efforts to contain the investigation. Throughout the period, the White House directed a campaign of noncooperation, lies, and a tragic betrayal from within to effectively hamstring the FBI's efforts.

The prosecutors sought to learn more about the break-in as they attempted to immunize one of the burglars and offered James McCord a deal in exchange for his cooperation. Three months of investigation and the prosecutors' organization of evidence produced indictments on September 15 against the five burglars as well as Hunt and Liddy. Yet for six more months, the Administration successfully concealed facts and the involvement in the Watergate affair of a wide range of CREEP and White House officials, until such individuals as McCord, Magruder, and Dean decided to reveal the larger story out of their own self-interest.

From the very beginning, FBI efforts to move beyond the basic seven suspects met determined resistance. If agents interviewed White House officials such as Charles Colson, White House Counsel John Dean was present—and quarrelsome. When agents spoke to campaign officials, CREEP lawyers stayed in the room, often objecting to questions and interfering with the process. Earl Silbert counterattacked at one point by issuing grand-jury subpoenas to CREEP personnel so they could be questioned without attorneys present.

In a few cases, re-election committee employees made an effort to speak to investigating agents away from campaign headquarters. From one, FBI agents learned that a committee administrator had not been "frank" with agents and had diverted them from investigating substantive matters by providing leads to keep them "busy" with relative trivialities. Investigating agents simply could not corroborate other tips, such as one that important information had been destroyed.

The FBI's subsequent evaluation of its investigation acknowledged that it had been wrong to allow Dean to sit in during interviews and to clear all requests for information. But there had been no alternative: the investigatory procedure had been determined by FBI Acting Director Gray, who proceeded under White House orders. Furthermore, Gray had routinely submitted FBI investigative reports to Dean, which enabled the White House aide to keep abreast of the investigation. What also would be learned was that Dean had given Gray important evidence belonging to Howard Hunt, evidence that Gray would withhold and later destroy.

In their investigation of the re-election committee, Bureau agents logically focused on McCord's links, trying to determine who had hired him, what money was available to him, and who worked with him. The agents conducted more than sixty interviews at CREEP headquarters, but later revelations showed that those interviewed had lied and evaded questions, including Mitchell, Magruder, and Liddy's secretary. Robert Odle, the CREEP director of administration, waited ten months before revealing that he had hidden the Gemstone file from investigators. Agents had been told on several occasions in June 1972 that evidence had been destroyed, and specifically that Liddy had shredded documents, but they simply could not prove the destruction. Nearly a year later, Mitchell described for the Senate Select Committee the White House determination in "keeping the lid on and no information volunteered." Those interviewed had been coached to lie, and their testimony had been rehearsed.

Several hours after the burglary, Liddy turned up at a Washington golf course to see Attorney General Kleindienst. According to Kleindienst, Liddy said that Mitchell wanted the Attorney General to get the suspects out of jail at once. Kleindienst claimed he did not believe Mitchell would send such a message and publicly threatened to have Liddy arrested. But he told no one of the incident. The FBI later claimed that if it had known immediately of that episode, it would have more easily identified Liddy as an important actor in the events it was investigating, would have wasted less time on needless interviews at committee headquarters, and would have had reason to zero in early on Mitchell and Liddy. Perhaps, Bureau investigators later speculated, the cover-up might have been more quickly exposed. But even when FBI agents questioned Mitchell and various White House officials, they naturally "assume[d] that men of [such] stature would have no involvement," as Special Prosecutor Leon Jaworski said two years later.[40]

The President had a favorite word for the White House strategy: "stonewall."

IX

"WHAT REALLY HURTS IS IF YOU TRY TO COVER IT UP."

WATERGATE AND THE CAMPAIGN
OF 1972

September 15, 1972. Earlier that day, a federal grand jury had returned indictments against the five Watergate burglars as well as E. Howard Hunt and G. Gordon Liddy. A Justice Department spokesman described the investigation as "in a state of repose" and thought it "highly unlikely" that it would be extended. Following the President's suggestion, Republican Party officials demanded that the Democrats apologize for their allegations of White House wrongdoing in the break-in; campaign marching orders still came from the Oval Office. On September 14 Nixon had been pleased to learn that the indictments would be confined to lower echelons, and he was confident that the indictments would "obviate whitewash," as H. R. Haldeman noted. Meanwhile, the election campaign exhilarated Nixon. It was his tenth campaign—the last, he told Haldeman, so "make it the best."

Nixon met with Haldeman in the late afternoon of September 15. Watergate was very much on their minds, as was the young lawyer in charge of damage control. Haldeman congratulated himself on having designated John Wesley Dean III for that task. While Dean would not "gain any ground for us," Haldeman told the President, he would make "sure that you don't fall through the holes." Haldeman knew the way to Richard Nixon's heart. Dean, he noted, was "moving ruthlessly on the investigation of McGovern people, Kennedy stuff, and all that too." Altogether, Haldeman reported, Dean had turned out to be tougher than he had anticipated.

Such a performance apparently merited a presidential audience. It was close to 5:30 P.M. when the President summoned the White House Counsel. Nixon greeted Dean rather casually. "Hi, how are you?" "Yes sir," Dean responded. The President wasted no time in coming to the point: "Well, you had quite a day today, didn't you? You got, uh, Watergate, uh, on the way, huh?"[1]

September 15 was an important day for the President's growing involvement in the cover-up of any White House connection to the break-in. For John Dean, especially, it was a red-letter day, for now he was about to receive official recognition, even blessing, for his direction of the cover-up campaign. He had worked hard for three months to keep the President from falling through the holes. Dean thought he was on his way to the top. From another perspective, at another time, he saw his life that day as "touching bottom."

John Dean was thirty-two years old in May 1970 and working for John Mitchell in the Department of Justice when he met his friend Egil Krogh. Krogh, very much a White House insider, suggested that Dean join the presidential staff. The meeting and the invitation were probably not coincidental. Shortly before, Jeb Magruder had mentioned Dean's name to Haldeman. Magruder remarked in a memo that Dean was "an example of a sophisticated, young guy we could use." "*Absolutely*[.] Really work on this," Haldeman scrawled in the margin.

Several months later, White House telephone operators located Dean in a Washington restaurant and told him that Haldeman wanted to see him at once in California. Telephone operators, planes to pick up and quickly deliver people from one coast to the other—the heady stuff of power. Dean promptly left Washington for San Clemente. There he met Haldeman, and after a short chat the Chief of Staff offered him the post of White House Counsel. For Haldeman, Dean had perfect credentials: like his sponsor, Magruder, he was pliant, reliable, obedient, and consumed by insatiable "blind ambition." That same day Dean met the President, who formally offered him the position.[2] Despite the lofty title and its apparent responsibilities, however, Dean rarely saw Richard Nixon over the next two years.

Dean's modest experience typified the Nixon White House; the essential qualifications for important positions consisted of loyalty and subordination. Young, ambitious men who knew those values seemed to fill the bill quite well. Dean's résumé undoubtedly seemed just right to Haldeman. Born in Akron, Ohio, in 1938, Dean had graduated from Wooster College and the Georgetown Law School—no Ivy League taint to that pedigree. After he had applied unsuccessfully for a clerkship with District Judge John Sirica, Dean had worked in staff positions in Congress and the Justice Department. Richard Kleindienst, his immediate superior, learned to dislike Dean, yet acknowledged that he had performed with "great distinction." Kleindienst also claimed that he had warned Dean against moving to the White House, telling him that he would only be "a runner for Ehrlichman"; being "counsel to the President," he said, was only an illusion. But John Dean—the WASP Sammy Glick—was an adaptable young man: he would move from being John Mitchell's "boy" to become Haldeman's, not Ehrlichman's.

Curiously, Haldeman ordered no FBI check for Dean before elevating him to President's Counsel. Had he done so, he might have learned of Dean's dismissal from a Washington law firm for "unethical conduct." Dean had managed to persuade his former employer to soften that charge for Civil Service Commission records—much to the employer's later regret. But strange values dictated personnel matters in the Nixon White House. Haldeman once told Dean that the President liked Dean's clothes because they made him look "hippie" and offered a counterpoint to the Administration's conservative image. John Ehrlichman, however, had difficulty with Dean's style: Dean had worked for John Mitchell, wore Gucci loafers, and drove a Porsche sports car.[3]

Solicitor General Erwin Griswold, well acquainted with ambitious young lawyers from his days as Dean of the Harvard Law School, considered John Dean a "nice young man" but nevertheless "was astounded" when he heard of his appointment as White House Counsel. Griswold believed Dean unqualified by either ability or experience. The position, Griswold said, "required a more mature person, with the fiber and strength to stand up to the President and to other people in the White House, and to do it gracefully so that you avoid head-on collisions." Neither Nixon nor Haldeman included those qualities in their job description, however. Dean assumed some duties of former Nixon aide Clark Mollenhoff. Mollenhoff liked Dean, but he realized the new Counsel had not been installed as a "boat-rocker." Dean was "ambitious," Mollenhoff noted, but he quickly learned "that any daring acts should have the approval of the boss." Dean suffered from a fatal combination, Mollenhoff thought, of "ambition and his willingness to perform any chore in order to survive." Donald Santarelli, who worked with Dean on Capitol Hill and in the Justice Department, warned White House and Justice officials that Dean was self-serving and unprincipled but realized that Haldeman and Ehrlichman believed Dean to be ideal for he had no independent power or constituency.[4]

Dean succeeded Ehrlichman as White House Counsel when Ehrlichman inaugurated and chaired the Domestic Council. Perhaps Dean's most important early activities involved his work as a conduit for FBI and Secret Service reports to the White House regarding antiwar demonstrations. Essentially, however, Dean directed a small staff of lawyers to handle routine legal chores. He served as the White House checkpoint to guard against internal conflicts of interest. For example, Charles Colson wrote the Counsel to ask whether he could keep a Smithfield ham a lobbyist had given him. Dean said he could but suggested that Colson tell the friend not to give such gifts in the future. He considered whether Pat Buchanan's stock ownership in a Florida resort might constitute a conflict. He told Buchanan that he would appreciate "the opportunity to meet with you regarding your personal financial interests." The tone was both solicitous and aggressive. The new Counsel shrewdly sensed that handling what seemed to be the dull, routine matter of interest conflicts offered a key to advancement. He realized that by knowing a man's financial situation he could gain his confidence. And winning confidence, Dean knew, would bring more "business"—contacts and chores that would make Dean more visible and ever more valued.

A more amusing line of chores than tracking conflicts of interest required Dean to threaten action against any unauthorized uses of the presidential seal. Thus, he wrote to a book publisher demanding the removal of the seal from a novel that used the word "President" in its title. When the General Accounting Office requested White House records concerning flights involving officials and the President's family for campaign purposes and inquired about the extent of reimbursement for such travel by the Committee to Re-elect the President, Dean replied for Haldeman: such information "has traditionally been considered personal to the President" and not a matter for congressional inquiry. Dean invoked executive privilege to seal the flight manifests and logs.[5]

Dean ran his office as a private law firm, anxious and willing to accept business to build more business, even if some affairs were not official matters. Less than a month into his new position, he received instructions to rebut an attack by an obscure magazine on Vice President Spiro Agnew. Specifically, Dean was to recruit the IRS to make a tax inquiry. He also screened a pornographic movie entitled *Tricia's Wedding,* to determine whether he could initiate legal action against the producers. He worked with Tom Huston on the plan to coordinate domestic intelligence activities within the White House. He advised other White House aides on divorce matters and Filipino mess stewards on their immigration status. The Counsel's firm, and its founder, grew in stature. Dean was, Haldeman recalled, a "service facility" for White House employees.

When Dean first moved into the White House, he was assigned quarters next to the men's room. The flushing sounds of the plumbing carried rather easily; moreover, Dean's room had nondescript, military-issue furniture and badly needed painting. But Dean soon received important status symbols: copies of the President's daily news summaries, a Signal Corps telephone service with twelve lines, and more newspaper and magazine subscriptions than he needed. Haldeman's blessing had been secured; Dean was on his way.[6]

* * *

Dean's desire for visibility reaped big dividends following the Watergate break-in. The White House Counsel had just returned from a trip to the Orient, but at Ehrlichman's instructions he lost no time in talking to a variety of Administration principals regarding their knowledge of the burglary. Dean interviewed Colson, Magruder, Mitchell, Kleindienst, Liddy, and Gordon Strachan, a Haldeman aide. From Strachan, Dean learned that Haldeman had received logs from the wiretaps of the Democratic National Committee. If Haldeman were implicated, Dean realized, the President could not be far behind.

Dean's role in Watergate began, in his words, as that of a fact-finder. From there, he worked his way up to idea man, and "finally to desk officer." He met with involved officials, advised them, and made recommendations as to the disposition of evidence. He shuttled between the warring camps in the White House and the Committee to Re-elect the President. John Dean did not initiate the Watergate cover-up, but in time he came to be the orchestrator of the various disparate parties to the cover-up.

Others had roles to play as well. Jeb Magruder subsequently testified that "I do not think there was ever any discussion that there would not be a cover-up." Magruder later claimed that on June 19, he talked to John Mitchell and urged him to "cut their losses" and admit culpability. According to Magruder's version of events, Mitchell consulted Haldeman and Ehrlichman, who told him that things had to be kept under wraps. The implication here was that the White House feared exposure of "other things," such as the Plumbers, if they owned up to the break-in.[7]

The first step in the cover-up belonged to Mitchell and was taken several hours after the news of the burglars' arrest broke, when he denied any involvement by CREEP officials. On June 19 Colson urged that Howard Hunt's White House safe be confiscated. Mitchell suggested to Magruder that he "have a little fire" at his house with the Gemstone files. The next day, Haldeman ordered Gordon Strachan to "make sure our files are clean." Strachan promptly shredded numerous documents. Later that afternoon, Dean and his Associate Counsel, Fred Fielding, sifted the contents of Hunt's safe, finding evidence of more "dirty tricks," including an attempt to fabricate a direct link between President Kennedy and the assassination of South Vietnamese President Diem. The safe also contained memos between Colson and Hunt regarding the Plumbers. Dean informed Ehrlichman about the materials, and Ehrlichman told him to "deep six" them. Dean instead gave them to FBI Acting Director L. Patrick Gray.

Haldeman later expressed surprise when he discovered on June 23 that Dean was the " 'project manager' on the Watergate problem." He thought Ehrlichman was in charge, but "my crafty friend," as Haldeman characterized Ehrlichman, had managed to fade out of the picture for the current business. Ehrlichman hastily informed other relevant parties, such as Gray, that Dean had White House responsibility for an "inquiry" into the break-in. Ehrlichman scrambled for distance. In a telephone conversation with a reporter in August 1972, he claimed little knowledge about Liddy's "work product," yet a year earlier he had given Defense Secretary Melvin Laird a detailed report regarding Liddy's work in the Pentagon Papers affair.

"Almost by osmosis," Haldeman observed, Dean assumed command of the "project." In fact such an assumption of power was unlikely in a Haldeman-managed enterprise. White House aide Richard Moore, who befriended Dean and who saw him as a "schemer" but a "very disarming gentleman," refused to believed that Dean "initiated any activity that he thought unauthorized." Haldeman needed someone to manage the cover-up, Moore remembered. He knew that Leonard Garment would never be a party to that enterprise, and neither would Moore himself. Nor could Haldeman pick Colson, because he "would run away with it or blow it up." Dean was the "logical" man for the cover-up; "who else," Moore thought, "would he have turned to?" John Mitchell, too, knew that "somebody gave Dean a charter." Mitchell was bemused. "Who gave him the charter and put him on that course?" he asked, as he scoffed at Haldeman's seeming confusion.[8]

Henry Petersen of the Justice Department met Dean at the outset of the cover-up and bluntly told him that the investigation could not be shut down. Earlier, according to Kleindienst and Gray, Ehrlichman had ordered Petersen to terminate the Watergate investigation within forty-eight hours. "Screw you," Petersen reportedly replied. Petersen liked Dean and even confided in him, quite unsuspecting of Dean's role. Petersen later bitterly recalled that Dean had become the "linch pin" (a term Dean himself used) of the conspiracy, acting through Haldeman and Ehrlichman. He grudgingly recognized that Dean was a splendid choice to direct the cover-up. Because Dean had worked in Congress on the committee to reform the criminal laws, and because he had been in the Justice Department, Petersen said, "we trusted him. We thought he was one of us. He had a degree of rapport with us that an ordinary counsel who just came in out of the political hinterlands never would have had with the Justice Department." What we saw, Haldeman testified, summing up a commonly held view, "was a young man, unquestionably intelligent, unfailingly courteous, doing his job efficiently."[9]

Haldeman's characterization of Dean as the "project manager" of the Watergate cover-up was disinguous and uncharacteristically modest. Dean perhaps managed details, but the mission had been determined by others. John Dean did not decide that there would be a cover-up: that was determined by the President of the United States and his Chief of Staff. "The

President was involved in the cover-up from Day One," Haldeman later revealed—thus conceding his own involvement. After Nixon returned to Washington following the break-in, he learned on June 20 about Hunt and Liddy and their connection to CREEP, but he did not order Haldeman or anyone else to inform the FBI. That night, Nixon talked to Haldeman about raising money for the burglars and for the first time suggested bringing CIA pressure on the FBI to limit the investigation. Surely he was anxious to avoid any links between the burglars and the White House; but Haldeman also knew that Nixon feared any exposé of "other things," as the President often characterized certain White House activities and campaign "dirty tricks."

One of the President's June 20 meetings with Haldeman, according to the Chief of Staff, involved a public-relations treatment of Watergate to counterattack the criticism, as well as to deal with Nixon's fear that Colson had initiated the break-in from his White House office. How, the President asked, could his enemies "justify this [the break-in] less than stealing [the] Pentagon Papers?" That conversation, Haldeman claimed, was all or part of an 18½-minute tape segment subsequently erased—by the President himself, according to Haldeman.[10]

During the course of at least three meetings covering more than two hours on June 23, Nixon and Haldeman took steps to impose a blanket on the investigation and to cover up any links between the burglars, CREEP, and the White House. Their actions, in legal terms, constituted an obstruction of justice. In political terms, in the public's perception, the cover-up projected an indelible impression that Nixon personally was involved in the crime.

The President and Haldeman met on the morning of the twenty-third to discuss the FBI's widening investigation of the break-in. Haldeman reported that Dean had advised him and Ehrlichman that Gray could not restrain his agents. According to Haldeman, Mitchell had suggested that CIA Deputy Director Vernon Walters (a recent Nixon appointee) call Gray and tell him to "stay the hell out of this." Walters was to complain that FBI investigators were intruding into sensitive areas of CIA operations. Haldeman pushed the idea, confident it would work because the FBI was aware of the Cuban burglars' CIA links and could recognize that the affair might have national-security implications. Haldeman knew the FBI had traced the source of the burglars' money, and he realized that this would implicate the re-election committee. Nixon eagerly agreed on the need for containment. He ordered Haldeman to tell CIA Director Helms and Walters that the White House needed their cooperation. It was time to call in debts, Nixon said: "we protected Helms from one hell of a lot of things."

The President asked if Mitchell knew about the break-in. "I think so," Haldeman replied. "I don't think he knew the details, but I think he knew." The President wanted to find out what "asshole" devised the plans. He thought it might be Liddy, whom he described as "a little nuts." Interestingly, Haldeman thought that Mitchell had pressured Liddy for "more information" on the Democrats. The President's response was quite knowing: "All right, fine, I understand it all. We won't second-guess Mitchell and the rest." He was enormously relieved on one point: "Thank God," he declared, that Colson was not responsible.

Nixon was careful not to get too close; Haldeman would instruct Helms and Walters. But the President advised Haldeman to tell CIA officials that he feared the investigation would reopen questions involving the Bay of Pigs. Therefore it would be best if they told the FBI that for the good of the country the case should not be further investigated. "That's the way to put it, do it straight," the President said. The conversation drifted to a discussion of the McGovern campaign and homosexuals, to Herbert Klein's incompetence ("He just doesn't have his head screwed on," Nixon said), to his daughter Tricia's complaints about "labor thugs" booing at one of her talks, and to the President's advice to keep the campaign away from anything having to do with the arts ("The Arts you know—they're Jews, they're left wing—in other words, stay away").[11]

Nixon and Haldeman met briefly again just after 1:00 P.M. on June 23 to go over the "game plan." The President warned Haldeman, in asking the CIA to help quash the FBI's investigation, to avoid letting Helms and Walters "get any ideas we're doing it because our concern is political." But he quickly added, "I wouldn't tell them it is not political." In his memoirs, the President recalled only that he wanted the matter handled "deftly."[12]

An hour later, Haldeman returned to the Oval Office to report that Helms and Walters had agreed to help despite some uncertainty that the scheme would work. Haldeman reported that Gray already had informed Helms the day before that the Bureau thought it might have "run right into the middle of a CIA covert operation." Helms had assured him at the time that it had not. But as Haldeman relayed his conversation with Helms to the President, Nixon seemed less confident. He thought the FBI still could trace the money seized with the burglars, but Haldeman told him that the Bureau already had enough evidence to convict the burglars without worrying about the money.[13]

Helms remembered that he immediately thought Haldeman's concerns amounted to "baloney," but he did not know "what the baloney was." Gray himself testified that Helms told him on July 22, and again on July 27, that the CIA had no concern about the FBI investigation of the burglars' money. Helms claimed to be mystified about a current White House notion that an FBI investigation would uncover the Agency's "money-laundering" operation in Mexico; "we never used the term," he insisted. The CIA, Helms revealed, had no need to operate in such a fashion: "We could get money any place in the world. We ran a whole arbitrage operation. We didn't need to launder money—ever."[14]

The President also met with Colson and Ehrlichman at one point on that memorable June 23. According to Ehrlichman's notes, either the President or Colson put a fitting epitaph on the day: "Responsible administrations in a tough political year are born losers." [15]

The President capped his long day with a western gunslinger movie, *Hang 'Em High*. The story centers on a wrongfully accused man who promises to play by the rules but then disposes of his enemies one by one, convinced that he is an avenging angel.

Vernon Walters later claimed Haldeman and Ehrlichman had directly demanded that the CIA persuade Gray to halt the FBI investigation of the break-in, despite Helms's assurances that the Agency was not involved. After the White House meeting, Walters told Gray that he had been "directed" by White House officials to say that the FBI investigation jeopardized the Agency's covert operations. He checked again at the CIA and confirmed that the FBI's investigation in no way threatened the Agency's "assets," including operations in Mexico. But Walters made no effort to convey that information to Gray, who had dutifully carried out the order to cut back the investigation. Gray, in his later testimony, insisted he did not know that Walters and Helms had met with Haldeman, and swore Walters never mentioned "senior people at the White House." He thought Walters was speaking for the CIA.

A couple of weeks later, on July 6, the President telephoned Gray from San Clemente. Gray told Nixon that he and Walters believed that "people on your staff are trying to mortally wound you by using the CIA and the FBI and by confusing the question of CIA interest in, or not in, people the FBI wishes to interview." The President, Gray reported, paused slightly, and then urged Gray to continue his "aggressive and thorough investigation." After the call, Nixon advised Ehrlichman not to "raise hell" with Gray or Walters, adding that the White House could take the heat. But at another meeting later in the day, he told Ehrlichman that Gray and Walters were not to discuss Watergate any further with him. The President seemed to recognize that covering up for subordinates could only be harmful to him. He had told newly appointed campaign chairman Clark MacGregor the day before never to talk to him about Watergate. Distance was now important.

Nixon repeatedly recalled at the time that it had been because of a Democratic cover-up that "I got Truman"—an exaggerated reference to both Truman's and his own part in the Alger Hiss affair. Later, he said that Truman's role was "pure political containment," which was not a corrupt motive; otherwise, he insisted, Truman would have been impeached. He warned Ehrlichman again on July 8, however, that there could be no appearance of a cover-up—"not a whiff of it." But more than cover-up was on his mind. Nixon discussed Helms, Walters, the CIA, the Pentagon Papers controversy, the Bay of Pigs, and the Diem assassination—somehow connecting them all with an ongoing Watergate investigation. If the probe persisted, he said, "all will blow."[16]

The President later insisted that his efforts did not constitute a cover-up, because "my motives were not criminal. I didn't believe that we were covering any criminal activities." Five years after the event, he insisted that neither Mitchell nor any of his aides were involved, despite the public record of his June 23 discussions with Haldeman. Nixon finessed his directives to the FBI and the CIA with a convoluted linkage between the political interests of the Agency and his own: it would be best if the investigation did not uncover the role of a former CIA agent—Howard Hunt—who, incidentally, worked in the White House. Nixon thus rationalized that there had been no cover-up; the CIA was simply protecting one of its own agents "with a long history of distinguished service."

Not coincidentally, and straining for a note of altruism, Nixon said he "didn't feel at the time that any eroding of the strength of the President in the country . . . [or] his defeat in an election . . . would be in the best interest of the country." As he described his actions in his memoirs, he simply was "handling in a pragmatic way . . . an annoying and strictly political problem. . . . I saw Watergate as politics pure and simple. We were going to play it tough." As always, the justification was that he acted tit-for-tat: "I never doubted that that was exactly how the other side would have played it."[17]

"I was being set up by the President of the United States to take a fall." Thus Richard Helms made his assessment of the President's political tactics as the summer of 1972 wore on. But Helms was determined not to be the "goat" of the affair. Helms knew that Walters had been a longtime Nixon loyalist and that the President could have his way with him. Helms believed that Nixon intended to "embroil the Agency . . . and use the Agency as the cover for the cover-up." Although he later resisted further demands from the White House, however, Helms at first cooperated in allowing the Agency to be used accordingly. His resistance eventually cost him his standing with the President, and his cooperation exposed his treasured organization to unprecedented public scrutiny. The Watergate affair was a disaster for Richard Helms and the CIA.[18]

Nixon's "pragmatism" in approaching the cover-up often lost touch with practical reality. Meeting with Ehrlichman in San Clemente on July 10, he rambled about potential disruptions at both presidential nominating conventions. If he were in any danger, he wanted the Secret Service to make arrests, to book and charge people. Then the day after the election, he would issue a general pardon and cease prosecutions of those who provoked the demonstrations. But there was a *quid pro quo:* that pardon would be "a basis for pardon on both sides"—presumably meaning the Watergate burglars.[19]

Between the break-in and September 15, John Dean met with Nixon only once, when on August 14 he prepared an estate plan for the President's signature. But Nixon was aware of his Counsel's work in more immediate problems. In a press conference on August 29, he turned aside a suggestion that he appoint a special prosecutor. He pointed to the FBI's investigation, one by the House Banking and Currency Committee, and John Dean's "complete investigation" as ample evidence that "we are doing everything we can to take this incident and to investigate it and not to cover it up." Dean's investigation had satisfied him, Nixon insisted. "I can say categorically that his investigation indicated that no one in the White House staff, no one in this administration, presently employed, was involved in this very bizarre incident." Charitably, the President said that "overzealous" people often do wrong things in campaigns. But his charity had limits. "What really hurts" in dealing with wrongdoing, he remarked, "is if you try to cover it up."[20]

For Richard Nixon, Watergate at that time was a staff problem. The campaign and his opponent were subjects more to his liking, stirring his competitive juices. In a lengthy meeting with his aides on July 31, the President analyzed McGovern's record at length and outlined how he thought the campaign should proceed against him. Four days later, he discussed the possibility of checking McGovern's IRS files. But in September, the President allowed himself a rare moment of relaxation and believed the polls. He thought McGovern simply could not overcome the disaffection against him within traditional Democratic constituencies. Nixon instructed his staff to disregard McGovern, yet he solemnly criticized the Senator for having attacked J. Edgar Hoover after his death. A few days later, he was still expressing concern over McGovern's tax proposals, conceding they were quite clever. The President wanted his surrogates to keep hitting McGovern on taxes, higher prices, and recession. The McGovern budget, he insisted, was a fraud. Nelson Rockefeller, the President's old adversary, visited the White House on September 14, telling Nixon a sick joke about a Kennedy-Eagleton ticket: it would be "waterproofed and shockproofed."[21]

Richard Nixon claimed that his diary entry for September 15 only briefly alluded to the grand-jury indictment of the Watergate burglars. "We hope," he wrote at the time, "to be able to ride the issue through in a successful way from now on." For Nixon, this meant that the incident was of only minor concern to him and that the trial of the burglars would end the matter.

Earlier that day, he had talked confidently with Haldeman about the election, noting that "bugging isn't hurting." He seemed certain that the Democrats had overplayed the break-in as an issue and simply could not match the "Eis[enhower] father image" he had fostered. There was no one else for the electorate, Nixon told Haldeman.

The diary entry for September 15 also mentioned that the President had met John Dean that day, at Haldeman's suggestion, to thank him for his work. Haldeman acknowledged that Dean was "keeping track of all the different Watergate problems for us." Later, Haldeman told Senate investigators that he did not "congratulate" Dean "for the job he had done."²² But the written and taped records of that meeting betray the President's and Haldeman's sure knowledge of the real nature of John Dean's work on Watergate. Nixon hesitated not at all in speaking boldly and frankly in front of his young aide. Confidence on the part of all participants flowed through the conversation. Everything appeared well; indeed, the President seemed serene yet exhilarated.

Dean began the September 15 meeting by reporting that the press was playing the story just as expected. They had not exactly "whitewashed" the story, as Haldeman had thought; instead, they had reported it straight and seemed pleased that two White House aides had been indicted. Dean, Haldeman, and Nixon apparently believed that the indictment would end the affair. Clark MacGregor had demanded an apology from the Democrats who had been charging that the crime had been directed from high places in the Administration. The President knew they would not get one, but he had bigger plans. "[J]ust remember all the trouble they gave us on this," Nixon said. "We'll have a chance to get back at them one day."

He raised the question of the second bug in the Watergate offices and seemed fascinated by Dean's suggestion that the Democrats themselves had planted it. He wanted details of the FBI's doings and questions at the Democratic National Committee's offices. When told that Patrick Gray and his people were "pissed off" at O'Brien's charges that the FBI had been negligent, Nixon thought that would make the Bureau work harder and perhaps find that the Democrats had bugged themselves. Maybe it was small talk, but Dean told the President that the FBI investigation had been "really incredible" and was more thorough than that done following the Kennedy assassination. (Nixon later publicly quoted this almost verbatim.)

Haldeman was disgusted by the expenditure of resources in the investigation. "Who the hell cares?" he remarked. The President quoted Barry Goldwater to the effect that "everybody bugs everybody else." "Yeah," Haldeman said. "I bugged—" and his words trailed off as the President contended that he had been bugged in previous campaigns. Dean seemed fascinated by the intimacy of the meeting. Nixon claimed that he had proof that his 1968 campaign had been bugged, but he did not want to embarrass

LBJ—who, Nixon added, had bugged Humphrey. Nixon also said he did not want to reflect unfavorably on the Bureau.

The discussion turned to the Democrats' pending civil suit and their lawyer, Edward Bennett Williams. Haldeman hoped that the FBI would start questioning "that son-of-a-bitch" Williams. Dean reported that the case had been assigned to Judge Charles Richey, a Nixon appointee. Dean observed that the judge was not known for his intellectual qualities, and the President began to say something about the judge's "own stupid way." But he heard that Richey had talked to Kleindienst about the case, and that the judge had suggested that Maurice Stans file a countersuit for libel. A phone call from Clark MacGregor interrupted the proceedings. Nixon told MacGregor about Richey and ended the conversation on a note of black humor as he instructed his campaign chief not to bug anyone without his consent.

The rare opportunity for such intimacy with the President inspired Dean to inject real confidence into his report. "I think that I can say that fifty-four days from now that, uh, not a thing will come crashing down to our, our surprise." Nothing, he promised, would disturb the anticipated election results. Knowing that much more than the Watergate break-in might be at stake, Nixon remarked that the matter was a difficult "can of worms" and "awfully embarrassing." Still, he took the moment to praise Dean for a "skillful" job. Dean gave the President even more, describing his "hawk's eye" monitoring of the McGovern campaign for campaign violations. Dean knew how to ingratiate himself. "[T]his is war. We're getting a few shots and it'll be over," the President responded. "I wouldn't want to be in Edward Bennett Williams' . . . position after this election," he added. "A bad man," was Williams. Haldeman, too, played to the President: "That's the guy we've got to ruin." Nixon promptly agreed. "I think we are going to fix the son-of-a-bitch. Believe me. We are going to. We've got to, because he's a bad man," Nixon reiterated.

The mood was infectious. Dean was not there only to report on the cover-up. He, too, knew that the President loved to "rub sores." He told the others that he had been keeping notes on people who were emerging "as less than our friends." "Great," Nixon interjected. Dean warmed to the task. The present crisis was going to be over someday, and enemies would not be forgotten. The President sounded almost ecstatic. He told Dean that he wanted "the most comprehensive notes on all of those that have tried to do us in." Why was there so much opposition, he asked, when the election was not even close? The enemy, he concluded, was "doing this quite deliberately and they are asking for it and they are going to get it. . . . We, we have not used the power in this first four years, as you know." Dean knew better; nevertheless, he dutifully agreed. The President was unstoppable. "We haven't used the Bureau and we haven't used the Justice Department, but things are going to change now." It was Dean's turn to be ecstatic:

"That's an exciting prospect." The President still had a full head of steam: "Oh, oh, well, we've just been, we've been just God damn fools. . . . It's not going, going to be that way any more." He regretted that his campaign people had not attacked Democratic senators more effectively—"they're crooks, they've been stealing," he complained.[23]

Haldeman thought it was the right moment to note the irony of the fact that the White House had tolerated Dean's "damn regulations" about conflicts of interest. Dean could not resist a bit of oblique self-congratulation as he praised the White House staff for its careful compliance with his rules. Irony abounded.

Soon, Dean remembered his place and returned to the cover-up. He told the President and Haldeman that there might be a problem in coping with a pending investigation by the House Banking and Currency Committee, headed by Wright Patman (D–TX). Dean had arranged with the Cuban defendants' lawyers to visit committee members to warn that public hearings would jeopardize their clients' civil rights. Richard Nixon suddenly found himself on the other side from candidate Richard Nixon and the "peace forces." He suggested that the government should dismiss the criminal charges against the Cubans because, in Haldeman's words, of "the civil rights type stuff." Dean was his usual accommodating self. His staff, he told the President, already had been in contact with the American Civil Liberties Union on behalf of the accused. Dean later recalled the move was "supremely cynical," but he was primarily worried that Maurice Stans, Nixon's campaign finance director, might have to face questions from Patman. What about using Connally to pressure Patman, he asked? Or making better use of House Minority Leader Gerald Ford? Dean had one more card: he was convinced that the Banking and Currency Committee members themselves had not always complied with campaign-financing laws; perhaps it was time for the White House to play rough.

The President warmed to the conversation. He expressed contempt for the ranking Republican member of the committee and thought Ford should exert pressure on him. "Jerry's really got to lead on this," he insisted. He wanted Ford to make a public case for the rights of the defendants; for the President it simply was, as he said, a public-relations problem.

The conversation drifted in other directions, but Dean quickly revived the Patman situation. He thought it might be tragic if they let Patman "have a field day up there." He mentioned that one of the committee's junior Republicans, Garry Brown (R–MI), had asked Kleindienst whether an investigation might jeopardize the criminal case against the burglars. The President was pleased: he considered Brown smart and aggressive. He wanted Ford and Brown called in to work with Ehrlichman—"they ought to get off their asses and push it. No use to let Patman have a free ride here."

The President worried about Congressman Patman and his committee in one corner of his mind. In another corner, he was concerned about the impact of the entire affair—"one of those unfortunate things"—on his campaign or, even more, on his security in the White House. He needed reassurance, and Dean artfully provided it. The events "had no effect on you," he said. "That's the . . . good thing." Haldeman agreed, almost congratulating Dean for having prevented any linkage to the White House or to the President. Apparently satisfied, the President again shifted his concern to the civil rights of "these poor bastards"—the accused burglars. He decried the fact that the press already had convicted them. If the Watergate burglars had been communists or convicted multiple murderer Charles Manson, he said, the *Times* and the *Post* would have raised hell. Well, the *Post* was in for some rough times, Nixon exclaimed—"damnable problems," he said, such as not getting their television-station licenses renewed. The President seemed to be in his element at the meeting with Haldeman and Dean.[24] Dean left the Oval Office shortly after the remarks about the newspapers. He had his orders; he did not talk to the President again until February 28, 1973. The mood then would not be so confident.

Dean was certainly right when he told the President that Watergate had not affected the campaign. The information from the polls had been particularly striking on the day of his meeting with the President. Both the Gallup and Harris polls gave Nixon a 34 percent lead, with McGovern holding only 25 percent of the electorate. While some predicted that the Democratic Party would go the way of the dinosaur, McGovern campaign manager Gary Hart insisted that the prospects were improving and that the polls reflected a "cultural lag." He believed that McGovern was only 20 points behind. Less than two weeks later, pollster Louis Harris reported a "significant" change: Nixon's lead had "dropped" to only 28 percent. For Hart, that offered vivid proof of the electorate's "tremendous volatility"; for the President, such volatility could only confirm his confidence.

Meanwhile, media interest in the Watergate affair was almost nonexistent. Of the three television networks, only NBC assigned one of its Washington reporters full time to the story. Fewer than 15 of the more than 430 reporters in Washington news bureaus for different newspapers and media outlets worked exclusively on Watergate. The *Chicago Tribune* did not feature a Watergate story on its front page until August 27 and displayed the affair on its lead page only thirteen times—compared to seventy-nine and thirty-three for the *Washington Post* and *New York Times*, respectively. More than 70 percent of the nation's newspapers endorsed the President, while only 5 percent backed McGovern, further underlining the irony of Nixon's complaints about media treatment.[25]

* * *

Speaker of the House Carl Albert believed that Nixon lived "in constant torture" about the Watergate cover-up from the moment Wright Patman's Banking and Currency Committee began its investigation. Patman started something, Albert said, "that made Nixon's life a living hell from then on. He knew that this thing had been done, he knew that . . . there had been a cover-up and he had not stopped it. He was afraid all the time that they might find that out. So he must have had a life of real misery." House leaders knew that Patman was a formidable adversary; Albert and others had crossed swords with him many times. He was, Albert remembered, "about as tough as anybody in the House. He was fearless, absolutely fearless."[26]

Patman had a reputation as a loner, yet his base as Chairman of the Banking and Currency Committee gave him a place in the House's power structure. Crusty and cynical, Patman was one of the shrewdest of congressional barons. When Lyndon Johnson went to Washington, his father, Sam, had told him to watch and follow the Texas populist. Patman knew how to make waves. He arrived in Washington in 1931 and promptly challenged President Hoover with his support for the early payment of a bonus to World War I soldiers. Patman later led a revolt against some of FDR's early measures when he thought they undermined the essential need to pump money into the economy. He ruthlessly fought corruption, whether in the banking system or the political process. Wall Street bankers and presidents—from Roosevelt through Eisenhower, Johnson, and Richard Nixon—all gained his implacable enmity. One of Patman's aides remembered that "his attitudes were his own, and they weren't delivered every Monday morning by whatever interest group was before the committee." Although his unwillingness to compromise and "stroke" his colleagues underlined his reputation as a loner, others recognized that Patman had a "longer range view of things than some of us did."[27]

Four days after the break-in, Senator William Proxmire (D–WI) requested the cooperation of Federal Reserve Board Chairman Arthur Burns in seeking the name of the banks involved in issuing the cash found on the burglars. Burns refused. The next day, Patman seconded Proxmire's request, telling Burns that the "Executive Branch can't investigate itself." Burns again declined.

Meanwhile, federal attorneys revealed that Bernard Barker, one of the alleged burglars, had withdrawn $89,000 in cash from a business account to which it had been deposited in April from four checks drawn on a Mexican bank. Several other reports appeared in July and August about foreign contributions and a $25,000 deposit to Barker's account made by Kenneth Dahlberg, a GOP fundraiser. Banking and Currency Committee members raised questions about the foreign money involvement and the possible misuse of the banking system to transfer illegal funds. Henry Reuss (D–WI) urged Patman to have the committee staff look into the matter. Reuss argued that the importation and exportation of capital, the possible misuse of financial institutions, and illegal bank transfers of capital were proper inquiries for the committee. He did not want the burglars called as witnesses, for he was concerned with their constitutional guarantees against self-incrimination, but he reinforced what the FBI already had practiced: follow the money trail.

On August 17, Patman told Reuss that he would have the staff conduct interviews and gather available documents. Although the General Accounting Office had promised to cooperate with committee investigators, it notified the committee on August 22 that it would no longer do so. Patman quickly learned that GAO investigators had flown to Miami and discussed illegal campaign contributions with Maurice Stans. On the twenty-fifth, Patman promised to continue his investigation, and in a preemptive move he noted that although the White House undoubtedly would apply "extreme pressure" to his Republican colleagues, he hoped that their responsibilities would outweigh their partisan loyalties.

The next day, the GAO referred possible criminal violations to the Justice Department. Patman repeated Lawrence O'Brien's earlier call for a special prosecutor. He also wrote to the Comptroller General, questioning a bank charter hastily granted to two men found to have deposited money in Barker's account.

Patman was turning up the heat. Nixon responded with a rare move, a televised press conference from San Clemente on August 29. The first question, possibly planted, raised the idea of a special prosecutor—without mentioning Patman. Nixon used the occasion for a lengthy answer that did many things but failed to respond to the specific question. The President discussed the mishandling of campaign funds and then dismissed it as an issue, insisting that both sides were equally guilty of "technical" violations. Mostly, he focused on the various investigations of the break-in and insisted that "we are doing everything we can to take this incident and to investigate it and not to cover it up."

Congressman Patman meanwhile focused his attention on Maurice Stans, the CREEP finance chairman. On August 28, he asked Stans to allow the House committee's staff to interview him regarding a public report that he had criticized the GAO. The President had said in San Clemente that he would discharge anyone who would not cooperate in any Watergate investigation. Stans called Patman on August 30. He agreed to an interview but asked that a minority staff member be present and that no information be made public until he saw it. Patman agreed, and committee staff members questioned Stans that day. During the session, Stans received a call from the

President. Stans complained to Patman that the staff had bullied him. The next day, Patman asked Stans to clarify his comments regarding contributors and the Mexican money found in one of the burglars' bank accounts.

The Republican counterassault to Patman's investigation began on September 4. Representative Garry Brown protested the investigation and charged that the Banking and Currency Committee staff had acted improperly. Brown also contended that Stans should not have to say anything regarding testimony he had given to the grand jury investigating the burglary, as Brown demonstrated equal concern about the rights of the alleged burglars. His remarks were based on telephone calls and letters from the Department of Justice, many of which had been coordinated by the lawyers at CREEP.

Patman vigorously defended his actions. But the meaning of Brown's remarks was clear: Republicans would not cooperate in any investigation. The next day, at a committee hearing, Stans denied any knowledge when pressed by Patman's further questions. The Chairman called another meeting of the whole committee for September 14 and announced that he had asked Stans to appear. On September 11, Stans's lawyer declined the invitation, contending that his client's appearance would jeopardize the civil rights of the alleged Watergate burglars.[28]

The policy toward Patman's investigation was part of a larger pattern. Nixon's campaign manager dubbed Watergate a "synthetic" issue of "very minimal importance." John Mitchell repeatedly denied that he had any part in the affair. And an FBI official leaked word that "unless one of the people on the inside track comes through, we may never get this whole story." The Administration's "stonewalling" policy had paid dividends. Meanwhile, the nation and the world watched the more identifiable horrors of the Munich Olympic Games.[29]

Patman was furious. He told Stans's attorney that his client's refusal to appear amounted to "a high level decision . . . to continue a massive cover-up and to do everything possible to hinder a full-scale public airing of the Watergate case." He called this the "first political espionage case" in American history and warned that "it must not be swept under the rug."[30]

Coincidentally, the Banking and Currency Committee's staff report was ready the next day, and Patman submitted it to the full committee. The report focused on the extraordinary flow of contributions to the Nixon campaign on April 5, just two days before a new law requiring disclosure of campaign contributors took effect. Patman told his colleagues that the committee needed subpoena power in order to trace the sources of the burglars' money. He asked that the report be kept confidential—which it was not; Patman of course recognized the necessity for capturing public opinion as well as any experienced politician. Stans meanwhile labeled the report a "mess of garbage," filled with "deliberate falsehoods, misrepresentations and slanted conclusions."[31]

Patman and his staff believed that as the chief financier of the Committee to Re-elect the President, Stans was a key link between CREEP and the break-in. But Stans was an elusive witness. Lacking subpoena powers, Patman's committee could do nothing. Stans refused to testify, contending that the proceedings were "political" and designed to aid the McGovern candidacy. It would not be the last time that a Nixon supporter justified action on the grounds that the national interest required saving the nation from George McGovern. Stans also was confident that Patman did not have the support of his full committee.[32]

The Banking and Currency Committee assembled on October 3, with only one Democrat and one Republican absent out of thirty-seven committee members. Patman told the committee that the international transfer and concealment of campaign contributions might have financed "the greatest political espionage case" in American history and could not be ignored. Charges and allegations, he noted, reached "right into the White House" and other high places in the Administration. He complained that the White House had obstructed the staff's efforts. He scoffed at the concerns of "newly found converts to the cause of civil liberties," labeling their actions a "smokescreen to hide the real reasons" for thwarting the investigation. Patman wanted the facts out; then he was content to let the electorate decide on their import. The Administration, he charged, wanted the jury verdict first, the facts later. If they had their way, he warned, "they will shut the door, possibly for all time, on this sorry affair."

Stans's refusal to appear before his committee required Patman to ask the full Banking and Currency Committee for subpoena powers. Henry Reuss offered a motion to that effect, authorizing subpoenas to banks that had dealings with CREEP, to the telephone company, and to campaign contributors who allegedly had received governmental favors, as well as to specific individuals, some well known, and others who later would receive their moment in the sun—including John Mitchell, John Dean, John Caulfield, Fred LaRue, Jeb Magruder, Robert Mardian, Hugh Sloan, and Maurice Stans.[33]

Patman sensed that his committee had discerned a deep pattern of corruption. Those close to him recognized his outrage and anger. His finely tuned intelligence network alerted him to the White House's intense lobbying of the House Banking and Currency Committee, although he probably was not aware of the precise links that lobbying used. He knew that the Justice Department had publicly opposed further hearings on the break-in for fear of jeopardizing the defendants' rights and had reassured Patman's committee that the Justice investigation was proceeding well. But Patman did not realize that John Dean had been hard at work securing the information he had promised the President at their September 15 meeting. Eleven days later, Kenneth Parkinson, attorney for the CREEP Finance Committee and for

Stans, sent Dean a memorandum detailing the House committee members' campaign-finance reports and the political action committees which contributed to members' campaigns. Dean, it will be remembered, was convinced that the Banking and Currency Committee's members themselves had not wholly complied with the law. He promised the President that if anyone wanted "to play rough," the White House would not hesitate to respond in kind. Dean proposed nothing less than blackmail.[34]

Again, Representative Garry Brown spearheaded the Republican opposition. He attempted to wrest procedural control of the committee's hearings from Patman, but the Chairman ruled that members could comment on Reuss's motion to authorize subpoenas but not offer amendments. A Republican critic referred sarcastically to the "9:42" or the "10:18" rules, depending on the time the Chairman pronounced a judgment. Another complained that Patman had taken thirty minutes to explain the need for an investigation, while others had only five minutes each to reply. But the significant mischief came from within Patman's own ranks—from conservative Southern Democrats and from two northerners who were rather unlikely opponents.

Robert Stephens of Georgia was widely recognized as one of the Patman Committee's shrewdest horse traders. When the committee's ranking Republican yielded his time to Stephens, Patman was upset. Speaking for himself and two other southerners, Stephens stated bluntly that the staff report did not indicate any need for legislative change; rather it focused on the possibility of legal violations. Therefore, Stephens insisted, the jurisdiction belonged to the Justice Department. He acknowledged the committee's proper oversight role, but he thought any action premature pending court developments.

Benjamin Blackburn, a Georgia Republican, assailed Patman, charging that the Chairman had "prostitute[d] his committee for blatant political purposes." Blackburn wanted no part of a "witch hunt" that would endanger the rights of the burglars. But the real jolt for Patman came when Garry Brown yielded his time to two Democrats who consistently had supported the Chairman. Frank Brasco of New York endorsed Blackburn's remarks: "politics should stay out of justice." Richard Hanna of California complained that the committee had delayed action on a housing bill for months; clearly, then, it could not act properly on such short notice for the proposed investigation. The short time frame, he maintained, demonstrated that the proposal to use subpoena powers was "purely political," and he could not support the resolution. Another southerner tried to propose a substitute motion to subpoena documents but not witnesses, pending examination of the written materials. The effect, of course, was to delay matters, and Patman ruled the proposal out of order.

With Republicans holding firm, the Democratic defections made defeat of

Reuss's motion for subpoena powers inevitable. The vote was 20–15. As the meeting adjourned, a bitter Patman warned: "The fight is not over."[35]

Prying into campaign irregularities was, to be sure, a potentially embarrassing subject for a variety of individuals, especially during a campaign. But the reasons for the Patman Committee's impasses were less abstract and more personal. The committee's southerners openly disliked George McGovern. Their leader, Stephens, had close ties with the Administration. In the next six months, he received an extraordinary amount of patronage. Stephens had little interest in the civil liberties issue. When later asked if he were a civil libertarian, he replied that there was a club in Georgia with "a bad connotation—a civil liberties club." Another Banking and Currency Committee member, William Chappell (D–FL), was in a tight race for election that year. Before the committee's vote, he visited privately with the President and then had a photo session—an important move, given McGovern's immense unpopularity in Chappell's district. Perhaps more important, one of the Congressman's secretaries had signed a complaint in 1969 alleging that Chappell had forced her to kick back some of her salary. Chappell acknowledged a "technical error," and the Justice Department decided not to prosecute.[36]

When Brown yielded time to Brasco and Hanna, he probably knew what they would do. Although the northerners' defections were a surprise to Patman, they revealed the extent of Administration pressure. In 1974 Brasco was convicted for conspiring to take bribes, and Hanna similarly was found guilty for his role in the Koreagate scandal in 1978. Past illegal activities of both congressmen were known in the Department of Justice as of October 1972. Brasco had been the target of an investigation of alleged fraud and bribery activities since 1970. Late in 1973, John Dean told Senate investigators that John Mitchell had met with Brasco and a New York City Democratic leader to discuss Brasco's role in the House Banking and Currency Committee proceedings. Governor Nelson Rockefeller admitted that he had arranged a meeting at that time between Mitchell, Brasco, and the Democratic leader. Dean also claimed that Mitchell told him he had "assurances" that a New York Congressman would not appear at the crucial House committee meeting or would oppose Patman.

A House subcommittee revealed in 1978 that the Administration had information dating back to November 24, 1971, regarding Congressman Hanna's Korean connections. On that date, J. Edgar Hoover told Mitchell that Korean lobbyist Park Tongsun had made campaign payments to Hanna and that the money had originated with the Korean CIA. In another memo dating from early in 1972, Hoover reported that Hanna had actively solicited payments from Park. (Hoover's reports also went to Henry Kissinger, who nevertheless later insisted that he had no knowledge of the affair until 1975.)[37]

In the September 15 White House meeting with Haldeman and Dean, the

President told his aides that "the game has to be played awfully rough." After the House Banking and Currency Committee rejected the subpoena motion, the *Washington Post* reported that the Administration's "intense arm-twisting" was common knowledge. Congressman Reuss later remembered that the Justice Department had persuaded the committee's members to believe that it had the investigation thoroughly under control. Brown admitted the next day that he had worked closely with Justice, but he denied Patman's charges of intense White House pressure. "I would have to presume that the White House wouldn't want further attention paid to this. I'm not so stupid to have to be told," Brown said. In June 1973, however, he admitted he had been in contact with White House congressional liaison people, although years later he claimed to have advised them to "stay away." In July 1973, Brown expressed remorse for his role, saying that if he had known of the Watergate cover-up in October, he would have voted differently. The committee, he said, "probably should have gone ahead with the investigating."

Brown insisted throughout that he had had no contact with Dean or any representative of the President, adding that he began his opposition to Patman on his own. Representative William Curlin, Jr. (D–KY), was the most junior member of the committee. When Brown offered his public *mea culpas* in the summer of 1973, Curlin stated that "certain members of the committee were reminded of various past political indiscretions, or of relatives who might suffer as a result of [a] pro-subpoena vote." It was not clear whether he was talking about Brown, Stephens, Brasco, Hanna, or all of them. But Curlin pinpointed the Administration's role: "they really call in dues."[38]

The Administration further undermined Patman by associating him with Elias P. Demetracopoulos, whose opposition to the Greek junta had antagonized powerful elements in and out of the government. Administration sources informed Banking and Currency Committee members that Demetracopoulos had arranged a Wall Street speaking engagement (and fee) for Patman, and they showed wavering committee members leaked documents charging Demetracopoulos as a pro-Communist agent. Documents subsequently released showed that the FBI, acting on instructions, had searched Demetracopoulos's bank records to find evidence of ties to Patman. Chairman Patman knew of the smear campaign and warned Demetracopoulos, also noting that Hanna, his alleged friend, had been "bad-mouthing" him as part of the campaign to discredit both Patman and Demetracopoulos.[39]

House Minority Leader Gerald Ford's role in the Patman Committee affair later came under particular scrutiny. During Senate confirmation hearings on Ford's nomination as Vice President in November 1973, Senator Robert Byrd asked if Ford had acted to influence Republican members of the Patman Committee because he thought further investigation would be harmful to the President and the party. Ford said no, but during the White House meeting on September 15, the President had remarked that "Jerry's really got to lead on this. He's got to really lead." Dean also suggested that Stans brief Ford. A few days before the House committee vote, Ford wrote to Republican members urging them to attend the committee meeting "to assure that the investigative resolution is appropriately drawn."

Congresswoman Margaret Heckler, a member of the committee, stated that Ford had briefed her, relaying White House assurances that Hunt and Liddy alone had perpetrated the Watergate "caper." Ford charged that Patman had started a "political witch hunt" and offered his own assurances that no one in the White House or CREEP had been involved. He also met with other members of the Banking and Currency Committee—after the September 15 meeting, not before, as Ford first said—but he insisted that he had received no White House directions.

In its 1974 recommendations for impeachment proceedings, the House Judiciary Committee cited Richard Nixon for "obstruction of justice" because of the White House role in blocking the Patman Committee inquiry. But when Congresswoman Elizabeth Holtzman (D–NY) during the 1976 campaign asked the Special Prosecutor and the Department of Justice to re-examine Ford's role, both refused. Attorney General Edward Levi replied that "there is no credible evidence, new or old, justifying further investigation." Ford meanwhile blamed Dean for the allegation. "He's a little snake in the grass who'll say anything about anyone," Ford told his advisers in 1976.[40]

As the Patman Committee prepared to vote, George McGovern once again assailed the Nixon Administration, calling it the most corrupt in history. He blamed the President for hiding the truth of White House involvement in the Watergate affair. Wright Patman redoubled his efforts. He wrote to the GAO, urging that office to continue its investigation. More important, he wrote to District Court Judge John Sirica on October 4, complaining that Sirica's order forbidding discussion by government officials, defendants, or lawyers in the pending case against the Watergate burglars had been used by the Administration as an excuse to thwart other investigative avenues. The judge modified the order the next day, noting that he had not intended to affect congressional activity or news-media reporting. This ruling came too late for Patman, but perhaps not too late for Sirica to heed Patman's warnings. The Texan told the judge that the Justice Department had no interest in continuing the investigation, charging that high departmental officials had intervened with his committee, and he warned Sirica that they would use the judge's orders for their own "blatant political purposes."[41]

Patman still had some tricks up his sleeve. He scheduled a meeting for October 12, inviting Mitchell, MacGregor, and Stans to testify. CREEP chief counsel Kenneth Parkinson replied that he had advised his clients not to appear. Patman also invited Dean, but the White House Counsel declined, invoking executive privilege. Patman staged a "hearing" with empty chairs for the witnesses. He blamed the President "for the elimination of the people's right to know." The President and his campaign committee, he said, were determined to sabotage the two-party system, making for "a sad spectacle, a really sorry affair which must sicken anyone who really believes in our system of Government."

Patman, by now, was playing for the historical record. On October 31 he released the House Banking and Currency Committee's staff report linking CREEP officials to the burglars and charging that the White House had authorized the most effective "curtain of secrecy ever erected." Ford remained faithful to the Administration, demanding dismissal of the staff members. He derided the report and the Chairman for "last-minute smear tactics."[42] Just as predictably, the report had no influence on the electorate.

John Dean had his marching orders, but by the time of the Patman Committee's report he realized that preserving the cover-up and his own safety were inextricably linked. "We really need to turn Patman off," he told Haldeman. Although he felt a measure of self-satisfaction and pride in his work, Dean realized how easily matters could spin out of control. The same day Patman held his empty-chairs hearing, the *Washington Post* published stories about Donald Segretti's "dirty tricks" campaign. Dean did not think that Segretti had violated any laws, but he knew that Segretti would lead to inquiries about Haldeman, White House aide Dwight Chapin, and Nixon's personal lawyer, Herbert Kalmbach, and their questionable campaign-fund dealings. The President himself was aware at the time that Kalmbach had paid Segretti for his work.[43]

The Watergate "caper" had become a ball of yarn, slowly but steadily unraveling. Containment appeared increasingly difficult—cutting off loose strings would no longer do. Patman's inquiry accomplished nothing in the immediate sense, but its encounters with CREEP and the White House had some important consequences. Patman's pressure required that the cover-up be intensified and expanded, thus widening chances for error and eventual exposure. Meanwhile, Patman had perceived the cover-up. He was a formidable enemy, with a long memory and a penchant for settling scores. Several months later, he ordered his staff to share its materials and findings with Senator Sam Ervin and the newly created Senate Select Committee, named to probe 1972 campaign financing. Patman himself wrote to Ervin, urging that Dean be questioned closely on his interference with the House Banking and Currency Committee.[44] Finally, Patman's probe drove the Administration to a new level of provocation in its coercive relationships with congressmen, an illustrative lesson that did not go unnoticed.

The White House continued to search for vindication and the high ground. Late in September, Vice President Agnew remarked that "someone set up these people to have them get caught . . . to embarrass the Republican party." The President took his own civil liberties tack at an October 5 press conference. Questioned about the indictments of the burglars, Nixon recalled the furor he had once raised when he labeled California slayer Charles Manson guilty before he was tried. With apparent self-satisfaction and a just-perceptible grin, Nixon told reporters: "I know you would want me to follow the same simple standard by not commenting on this case."

The outcome in the Banking Committee investigation offered some vindication for Maurice Stans. He went about his task of fundraising seemingly oblivious to any impending disaster. Stans told the President on October 5 that a September fundraiser had netted between $6.5 and $7 million—50 percent more than had ever been raised in a single affair in political history.[45] Stans knew the President's penchant for "firsts."

For Stans, fundraising was a labor of love for a President he deeply admired; moreover, his perception of McGovern as a dangerous radical undoubtedly spurred his efforts. Who cared about Watergate? Public-opinion polls consistently confirmed the general impression that Watergate was a "Washington story." By a 70–13 margin, respondents in one survey thought the tapping of Democratic headquarters was merely a case of acceptable political spying, and by a 57–25 count they believed political spying was a common occurrence, particularly during the heat of a campaign. Only 18 percent of respondents believed that the President's re-election committee had received huge amounts of contributions from special interests and had concealed the amounts. "Who the hell cares?" Bob Haldeman had demanded in the September 15 meeting with the President and Dean—with justification.

The 1972 campaign ended with the President's victory margin settling at the point where the polls had all along predicted it. George McGovern's effort began in confusion and ended in disarray. The Administration successfully portrayed him as a bungler, a demagogue, and a radical. Richard Nixon and his campaign managers pursued Lyndon Johnson's 1964 prescription of isolating the opposition and persuading the nation that it had no real alternative to "four more years" of the incumbent.

McGovern frightened many and alienated more. The *Washington Post* coverage of Watergate and the campaign offered a case in point. Throughout October, Watergate news appeared on page one nearly every day, especially an ongoing story of Haldeman's suspected connection to a secret campaign fund. But in November, the situation changed dramatically; Watergate coverage virtually disappeared. Between November 4 and November 18, the *Post* published only one related story. The paper did not endorse Nixon, but it muted its editorial attacks. Clearly, McGovern was unacceptable to the *Post*, which repeatedly questioned his "aptitude for political leadership"—and by extension, his ability to govern wisely and well. Still, given Nixon's "darker side," the choice, the *Post* concluded. "was neither easy nor obvious."[46]

Nixon repeatedly had expressed concern over how his victory would be interpreted. He urged his aides to predict only a margin of 10 million votes and to establish that figure in the public mind, because he feared that commentators would think even a 15-million-vote margin "very" disappointing. After his victory, Nixon confidently told one of his chroniclers that the election had been settled the night McGovern was nominated. Probably that was true; still, the notes of the President's aides indicate that hardly a day passed without Nixon's analyzing what needed to be done to win.

The results of November 7 should have given him enormous pleasure. More than 47 million Americans voted for him, nearly 18 million more than had voted for George McGovern. The President swept every electoral vote save those of Massachusetts and the District of Columbia. He shattered familiar voting behavior patterns: 55 percent of blue-collar workers voted for him, 51 percent of union families, 37 percent of registered Democrats. Traditionally Democratic ethnics—Italians, Poles, Irish, and Jews—gave their votes to a Republican candidate in unprecedented numbers. (Eisenhower had never captured more than 23 percent of Democratic voters.)

Nevertheless, throughout the summer of 1972, Nixon had impressed upon his staff the need for "the most intensive campaign in history." He considered McGovern to be dangerous, and he was convinced that for the good of the nation, he must defeat his opponent decisively. The President consistently talked about the opportunity to forge a broad mandate. The campaign of 1972 was to be very different from the calculated divisiveness of 1968. Now, the President assiduously courted Democrats, labor, blacks, Jews, and the young, while expecting (quite correctly) that his 1968 constituency would remain with him if only because it had nowhere else to go.[47]

The President was anxious to know whether he had beaten Lyndon Johnson's 1964 margins—he had more electoral votes but a smaller popular percentage—and how he had done in the South. Unlike LBJ, Nixon failed to capture any working majority in Congress. Beguiled by the possibilities of winning all the states and surpassing LBJ's votes, the Nixon campaign focused on the presidential race and made little effort to create any coattail effect for lesser Republicans. The Democrats remained in control of Congress by margins of 57–43 in the Senate (up two), and 243–192 in the House (down twelve). Personally, Nixon spoke bitterly of his party. He remembered that in 1970 "I broke my ass for the party at considerable cost." As far as he was concerned, the Republican National Committee simply could be folded into the White House. He told Ehrlichman that he had never stood higher in public esteem, while the Republican National Committee had never stood lower. The fact is that in order to gain personal support Nixon willingly sidestepped giving support to Republican candidates. A year earlier, he told Ehrlichman, Mitchell, and Magruder that Democrats who had opposed the Mansfield Amendment, providing for a cutoff in support for the Vietnam war, were not to have "significant" Republican opposition. He told Senator George Smathers (D–FL) that he wanted leading congressional Democrats to support him or at least stay neutral while they concentrated on their own races.[48]

The President's erstwhile campaign manager had no doubts as to the meaning of the 1972 election. John Mitchell told the President that voters saw Richard Nixon as "the personification" of what they wanted in the office. Those voters might not have understood the "brilliance" of the President's foreign policy or all the "nuances of his economic policy," but somehow, Mitchell said, "they can perceive the total accomplishment and accept it as in their interest and in the interest of the USA." Nixon told Haldeman that this was a "brilliantly perceptive" thought. Mitchell also praised the President's understanding of the political forces in the nation. Finally, he touched on that favorite sore—"our friends in the media." They were wrong, Mitchell gloated: "Richard Nixon was the one" who really had hold of the national pulse. The President marked the passage and told Haldeman that it would be "good for a column."[49]

As usual, Nixon had his own special post-election analysis. Before and after the election, he told his aides that they should prepare a monograph entitled, "Dirtiest Campaign in History Against a President." Throughout the campaign he emphasized the need to expose and counterattack "smears"—a category in which he included any attacks regarding Watergate. He wanted the smears connected to similar attacks in the past to show that he had always been the victim, not the perpetrator. In his earlier campaigns, Nixon admitted, "RN hit hard on the issues, but never . . . rais[ed] questions about motives or patriotism, only about judgment." The President remembered his campaign against Helen Gahagan Douglas as "one of the cleanest" in history. Most important to Nixon, he wanted his aides, in publicizing the election, to emphasize that "RN Won It"—not that McGovern lost it or that the McGovern candidacy was tailor-made for an easy victory. He stressed the "overwhelming odds" he confronted—a hostile Congress and a Republican registration of only 25 percent of all voters, down from the 35 percent of the Eisenhower years. Then, too, he wanted "RN" praised for the "tough decisions" he had made, such as on Cambodia; the mining of Haiphong Harbor; the visit to China; his Supreme Court appointments; his Southern Strategy; his opposition to busing; his "standing firm on the patriotic theme"; his opposition to expanded welfare, marijuana, and amnesty—on the whole, "where RN took a strong position, he turned out to be right and some of the staffers turned out to be wrong." McGovern didn't lose the election, the President repeatedly insisted; "it was the case of RN winning the election."[50]

It was a triumphant moment for Nixon, Mitchell, and Haldeman. They savored it, and indulged themselves in flights of self-congratulation. For the President, it was the history he would write, and would want others to remember from the 1972 campaign. Nothing was said among the President and his men, however, of the dark secret that lingered between them.

Wright Patman was depressed. The Democrats seemed to be in disarray despite maintaining their hold on Congress. And George McGovern, their routed standard-bearer, was dismayed. Speaking at Oxford University two months after his defeat, McGovern remarked that he thought Congress would become ineffective and that Nixon was closer "to one-man rule than at any time in our history," and this, McGovern said, "by a president who is not popular." Petulant, paradoxical, and possibly correct. "After the disastrous reigns of three King Richards, England had been spared a King Richard IV," McGovern observed, but "we seem to have him—for four more years."[51]

However muted in the fall of 1972, the sounds of Watergate were to resonate from the outset of the President's new term. The talk of a "money trail," a "cover-up," and a "special prosecutor" barely played outside Washington during the campaign. They would soon become household words in America.

John Dean still had his tasks, busily trying to keep the ball of yarn tightly wrapped. His "firm" was esteemed in inner circles—and was ever more indispensable. "John Dean is handling the entire Watergate matter now," Haldeman told Colson in March 1973, "and any questions or input you have should be directed to him and to no one else." For the President, John Dean was "a superb young man." Later, others would, with anger and bitterness, argue that Dean had "organized and directed" the resistance to the Patman hearings, miraculously absolving anyone else of responsibility and culpability—the incontrovertible evidence of the Oval Office tapes notwithstanding.[52]

Dean had so established himself that in December 1972 he boldly sent out a revised job description for the office of President's Counsel. He listed approximately twenty routine tasks, including clearance of executive orders and proclamations; reviews of presidential appointees requiring Senate confirmation; "game planning" of confirmation hearings; recommending presidential pardons and clemency; solving military-justice problems; monitoring use of the presidential seal; overseeing the Nixon Foundation and Library; writing the President's estate plan; and the disposal of the President's papers. Then there were *ad hoc* assignments, such as preparing contracts for a film of the President's China trip, interviewing Supreme Court nominees, and conducting certain "special projects," including the handling of Watergate and Donald Segretti. Dean found it all a "mixed bag," but he boldly stated the unifying element in the Counsel's many jobs: the objective was to keep "the President and his people out of trouble or, if we arrive too late on the scene, getting them out of trouble."

Self-congratulations out of the way, Dean proposed a bold, wide-ranging reorganization of his office that would expand its functions and its staff. He wanted a mandate to handle and resolve questions of law, and he wanted to be charged with the formulation of all policies that affected the President or were incidental to the presidency. As Dean described it, his office would be inserted as an adjunct of Haldeman's, touching the flow of work in and out and maintaining overall responsibility for ensuring that legal decisions in the executive branch conformed to the President's policies and objectives.

Dean's *démarche* effectively gave him access and influence for almost any function in the executive branch. Only bits and pieces of the plan were implemented; the most important steps in reorganization were not. The turn of events in the next months doomed Dean's grandiose scheme. But it was a measure of his influence and standing that he proposed such an obvious reach for his own power—and apparently was in no way rebuked. Perhaps the young Counsel was a "service facility," as Haldeman later characterized him, but he was a highly valuable one.[53]

Dean, it will be remembered, barely saw the President during his first two years in the White House Counsel's office. His December 1972 memo redefining and expanding his duties was designed to give him a central role as the President's man. Had he succeeded in his primary role as the linchpin of the cover-up, his gambit might well have been an offer that neither the President nor Haldeman could have lightly refused.

"We want the air cleared," the President said at his August 29, 1972, press conference. "We want it cleared as soon as possible." With John Dean as his primary instrument, and aided by loyal congressional and executive-branch lieutenants, the President cleared some important hurdles, but the clouds lingered. John Dean had made good on his promise that nothing would interfere with the election results. He planned and executed the design for thwarting any legislative inquiry into the Watergate affair and possible White House involvement. That was the bottom line. But Dean acted on the wishes of the President, as expressed in their September 15 meeting. They were only words, only fantasies in which Nixon indulged himself, Nixon's defenders have argued. "At that time," a former aide noted, Richard Nixon was only "guilty of being a pain in the ass."[54] But the President talked tough, and his counsel promised he would "play rough" to stop Patman's inquiry. Words had become actions, and a "third-rate burglary" had escalated to real political hardball.

In March 1973, Colson told the President that Dean had "done a spectacular job. I don't think anybody could do as good a job as John has done." From the other side of the fence, Dean also received lavish praise when FBI investigators later acknowledged "that the President's most senior associates at the White House conspired for nine months to obstruct our investigation."[55] The President's Counsel had not yet fallen from grace. On September 15, 1972, John Dean had promised the President fifty-four days; he had delivered more.

X

"THE COVER-UP IS THE MAIN INGREDIENT."

A BLACKMAILER, A SENATOR, AND A JUDGE
NOVEMBER 1972–MARCH 1973

President Nixon's anticipated policies and personnel shifts for his second term dominated the post-election news. Watergate remained a back-page item in the nation's consciousness. Meanwhile, the new year stimulated Nixon's self-confidence. Fresh from his electoral triumph, privately noting the milestone of his sixtieth birthday, he looked back at milestones of the previous decades, finding significance in all years ending with the number 3. For 1933, he noted his college prize in extemporaneous speaking; 1943, his service in the South Pacific; 1953, his election as Vice President; 1963, his defeat for governor of California; and for 1973, his re-election as President. His fudging of the last three dates—the significant years actually ended in a 2—apparently did not bother him.

Nixon also jotted down some Ben Franklin–style aphorisms: "No man is finished—until he quits," he wrote. Blessed with his own good health, he listed older men he admired who had achieved much in their later years: Dwight Eisenhower, Charles de Gaulle, Yoshida Shigeru, Konrad Adenauer, Winston Churchill, and Zhou Enlai. Finally, he offered some stern injunctions to himself: "Live every day as if last—Never let a day go by w/out doing something useful—Think young."[1]

Despite the President's high spirits, within the inner circles of the Nixon White House Watergate slowly but perceptibly loomed larger. Pat Buchanan warned the President in early December 1972 that Watergate was not behind him. There was dissatisfaction "even among our staunchest friends," Buchanan wrote, "and calls for the President to clean house." Some of those closest to the President were admittedly "concerned," H. R. Haldeman recalled, about things that "we felt boded trouble." Leonard Garment was optimistic about the second term yet also feared the cloud of Watergate. People were beginning to come to him wondering whether they might have some legal problems—"no one would come and say this was a real serious problem," he recalled, "but there were different things."[2]

Mastery of the Watergate cover-up demanded ever-increasing time and resources. The cover-up begat more cover-up, enlarging so as to plant the seeds of its destruction. Meanwhile, the President's familiar enemies— Congress, the government bureaucracy, and the media—began to look beyond the White House version of Watergate as a "third-rate burglary." New wars seemed in the offing. For good reason, a channel of apprehension paralleled the confident course of the Nixon White House after the November election.

In the wake of his electoral triumph, Nixon was determined to seize the moment to reshape the government and bend it to his will. His dissatisfaction with personnel was not confined to his historic resentment toward the entrenched bureaucracy; it extended to the highest levels of government, including officials he himself had appointed. As the election approached and his victory seemed more assured, he speculated ceaselessly with his trusted aides on the days of reckoning that would follow the election. In this period, restructuring the government preoccupied the President more in his discussions with Haldeman and Ehrlichman than anything save the details of the campaign itself. He often quoted Benjamin Disraeli's description of William Gladstone as an "exhausted volcano," as if to ensure and underscore that such would not be his fate.

Richard Nixon persisted in thinking that everything would go well if he persuaded the nation of his positive achievements. It was, as always, "really a question of PR. Actually, we have done a number of things very well, but we have had an enormously difficult time getting it [*sic*] across." He warmly praised his foreign-policy achievements and various "goodies" in the domestic area, such as the fight on drugs and crime, and the nation's economic recovery. He told aides to seize three, at most four, major achievements "and put the PR emphasis on them virtually to the exclusion of others so that the Administration will be remembered for at least doing something *very* well rather than being forgotten because we did a number of things *pretty* well." Perhaps, Nixon suggested, he might offer action in dormant areas, such as women's rights ("just to take a way out example," he said) or enhancing the legacy of the national parks.[3]

"There are no sacred cows," the President remarked in an interview published just after his re-election. "We will tear up the pea patch." On

November 8, one day after the election, the President assembled the White House staff and Cabinet, thanked them for their efforts, said (again) "there would be no sacred cows," and talked vaguely about new directions and goals for a second term—reiterating that his government would not consist of "exhausted volcanoes." Thereupon, he left the room, turning the meeting over to Haldeman, who promptly demanded everyone's resignation. The intention was clear: there would be new directions and new managers, ones who would swear fealty to Richard Nixon. The program was summed up by a White House adviser active in what he called the "plot" to advance the administrative presidency and the President's power: the new team was "to take on the Congress and take over the bureaucracy."

The taste of triumph quickly soured for the Administration's celebrants and stalwarts as they contemplated the President's wholesale demands for resignation. The record showed one significant area of resistance. Richard Helms told his CIA deputy, Vernon Walters, that they would not submit the usual post-election courtesy resignations. Alexander Haig had assured Helms that he could continue for another year, until he reached retirement age. But Helms was forced to resign in late November and received the dubious prize of the ambassadorship to Iran. It was a time of revenge for the victorious President.[4]

The President's desire for loyal subordinates reflected his conviction that executive officers in each agency must respond to his focused policy concerns rather than conforming to the agency's inertia or its interest in aggrandizing its own power. As the second term approached, Nixon sensed that after four years, the more things had changed, the more they had remained the same. Congress, the bureaucracy, and the media, as always, "worked in concert to maintain the ideas and ideology of the traditional Eastern liberal establishment" that had animated the New Deal and the Kennedy-Johnson years. Just as he had in his 1968 campaign, he ignored or sought to bypass Congress to forge an alliance between himself and the New American Majority—his new label for the hitherto Silent Majority. Nixon was prepared to reform, replace, or circumvent institutions that had become "paralyzed by self-doubt." Government, like so much of American life, he believed, had become infected with a "fashionable negativism" and "underlying loss of will." Now, he would lead; he would "provide America with a positive and . . . inspirational example of leadership that would be . . . an impetus for a new rebirth of optimism." He told Haldeman that he was "going to wear the flag, come hell or high water."[5]

Charles Colson knew exactly what the President wanted. Just after the election, he forwarded private correspondence of Solicitor General Erwin Griswold to Ehrlichman to prove that Griswold "belongs in his overdue retirement." Colson also recruited New York labor leader Peter Brennan for the post of Secretary of Labor. In a three-hour meeting he "clarified" matters for Brennan. Colson warned him that he might have to defend Administration policies, in opposition to organized labor. Brennan assured Colson he would be a "team player" and would abide by Administration decisions. Colson "explained" the "pre-eminent" role of Teamsters' Union President Frank Fitzsimmons, implying that "Fitz" was not to have any trouble. Colson then told Brennan just who was in charge of the Labor Department: the President would appoint the Under Secretary and Assistant Secretary, and Brennan would clean out "holdovers, enemy bureaucrats and deadwood, replacing them with loyalists." Colson reported that Brennan, a Bronx Democrat, wanted to help the Republicans gain labor's "permanent allegiance."[6]

Ehrlichman's office offered some shrewd advice early in 1973 for reducing confrontational politics with Congress, quite in contrast to the long-prevailing style of the Nixon Administration. The basic strategy, it was argued, should be to "deinstitutionalize" conflicts and instead present them as confrontations between the President—elected as he was by over 60 percent of those voting—and the New Minority, deeply entrenched in Congress, the media, and the academic world. This so-called New Minority represented interests quite alien to those of Richard Nixon's New Majority and easily could be identified with those who served unlikable special interests—such as Senator Edward Kennedy on labor policies; Senator William Proxmire on banking affairs; Senators J. William Fulbright and Frank Church on dovish peace and defense policies; the broadcast networks and their personalities, including Walter Cronkite, Roger Mudd, Dan Rather, and John Chancellor; the *New York Times* and the *Washington Post*; the liberal foundations; and those with no "fixed address," such as Ramsey Clark.

The document marked a significant maturation from the reflexive anticongressional statements of the 1970 campaign and the crude, even boorish concept of "enemies lists." What it also represented was a recognition that the Administration had to respect and bargain with Congress. The Democrats remained in solid control; Republicans, meanwhile, were none too happy with Nixon's preoccupation with swelling his 1972 vote totals while failing to seriously contest more congressional races.[7]

Nixon told Haldeman shortly after the election that Congress would be "mean and testy," but he would keep it "off balance" by shifting personnel in and out of the White House and the executive agencies. The President later rationalized his action in poker terms, a metaphor much to his liking. He thought that the Democrats had "all four aces" in Washington: Congress, the bureaucracy, the media, and the lawyers and lobbyists. He was determined to keep the "fifth ace" for himself in the form of a vigorous opposition party.[8]

In an August 3, 1972, meeting with John Ehrlichman, the President talked of gaining control with new appointments in such areas as the Treasury, Internal Revenue Service, and Federal Bureau of Investigation. Nixon wanted all appointed Treasury officials, including the Commissioner of Internal Revenue, dismissed after the election and a Nixon loyalist installed as deputy to Treasury Secretary George Shultz.

The IRS post particularly interested Nixon. It was another "sore" he rubbed because he believed that the agency had harassed his family and friends. Repeatedly, he insisted to his aides that he wanted a Commissioner to faithfully do his bidding. In a "talking paper" prepared for the President's meeting with George Webster, a prospective IRS Commissioner, Nixon indicated that the post was "one of the most sensitive" jobs in government, and he expected Webster "to track" with Shultz on day-to-day matters and with Ehrlichman "on matters of political significance and sensitivity." The President also was to tell Webster to clean out entrenched "deadwood," and that he was to work with White House aides on this matter. At the last moment, however, Nixon chose not to tender the position.[9]

Richard Kleindienst's direction of the Department of Justice left the President annoyed and disenchanted—"RNK is a total waste," he told Haldeman a week after the election. A few days later, he instructed the Chief of Staff to call Mitchell and have him secure Kleindienst's resignation. But Mitchell reported back that the Senate Judiciary Committee leaders (and Nixon supporters), James Eastland and Roman Hruska, had advised the President to wait until "the situation was cleaned up"—presumably a reference to Watergate. Nixon then called in Kleindienst. They discussed wholesale dismissals of the Attorney General's subordinates, but Nixon insisted that the Criminal Division head, Henry Petersen, be "an exception." Still, the President maintained an ill-disguised contempt for his Attorney General, complaining that he had become "a creature of the department" and would not make satisfactory personnel changes. The Watergate affair may have forced Nixon to retain Kleindienst, yet he urged Ehrlichman and Dean to superintend Justice Department matters.[10]

The position of FBI Director figured prominently in the President's poker game. Few positions fascinated him and occupied his attention more, given his experience with the power and ways of J. Edgar Hoover. At a November 14, 1972, meeting, Haldeman, Ehrlichman, and the President discussed the possibility of appointing Washington, D.C., Chief of Police Jerry Wilson to head the Bureau and moving Acting Director L. Patrick Gray to the State Department as Under Secretary of State. Egil Krogh was also suggested for the FBI post, probably by Ehrlichman.

Filling the FBI slot and finding a job for Gray continued to be troublesome. The President seemed determined to place his loyal retainer—whether out of fondness or fear is not clear. On November 22, Nixon and Ehrlichman discussed Gray for the NATO ambassadorship or as head of the Office of Emergency Planning. John Mitchell apparently had advised the President not to send Gray's nomination as FBI Director to the Senate, and on November 30, the President instructed Ehrlichman to ask Kleindienst to submit four names for the President's consideration as Director. But two weeks later, Gray remained a possibility despite Kleindienst's warning that his nomination would provoke a bloody confrontation in the Senate.

Apparently, the President could not settle on a trustworthy FBI Director. Ehrlichman floated several suggestions, including Cook County (Chicago) Sheriff Richard Ogilvie and Federal District Judge Matthew Byrne (a Democrat). But Nixon seemed reluctant to abandon Gray. Kleindienst sensed the President's wishes and decided that Gray might not be perceived as too "political." It was important, the President warned, to name someone who would "survive EMK [Edward M. Kennedy]." Meanwhile, Watergate hung like a cloud. Kleindienst told the President at the November 22 meeting that John Mitchell's troublesome wife, Martha, had calmed down, and the President replied—not for the first or last time—that his friend could have prevented Watergate if he had not been distracted by her.[11]

Just after the new year, Nixon again was inclined to nominate Gray for the FBI post but worried whether he had the strength to withstand the inevitable fire. By mid-January, the President seemed to downgrade Gray's chances, thinking he always would be suspect as too much of a Nixon loyalist. Nixon indicated a preference for former Assistant FBI Director Cartha DeLoach, who had been the conduit for information from J. Edgar Hoover to Nixon. DeLoach was a highly respected professional with the weight of tradition and much of the FBI hierarchy behind him. But Nixon passed him over for reasons that are not apparent; perhaps he thought he could not wholly trust DeLoach to serve as he wished. By February 13, Nixon told Haldeman he was prepared to nominate Gray, but as the Bureau's second-in-command he wanted William Sullivan, Hoover's former deputy, a chief instigator of the abortive Huston Plan and apparently a Nixon loyalist. The Gray nomination went to the Senate on February 17. It was the President's most fateful and disastrous decision in this crucial period, for Gray's confirmation hearings offered the Democratic Congress an immediate opportunity to raise questions about Watergate.[12]

Nixon, Haldeman, and Ehrlichman discussed Watergate at length in early December 1972. They apparently agreed that Donald Segretti and his dirty-tricks campaign had no connection to the break-in. (Nixon later told John Dean that he thought Segretti was "clownish," and that he did not understand "how our boys [laughs] could have gone for him.") It was a time for lamenting. Mitchell had failed him, but Nixon wanted it known that he would stand by his own "loyal retainer [Dwight] Chapin" (who had recruited Segretti), even though Chapin was going to leave "voluntarily." Nixon noted that Haldeman's aide, Gordon Strachan, also must go—*"he knows everything,"* said Haldeman, and suggested that Strachan be given a good job to keep him quiet. Nixon himself laid out the Administration's counterstrategy to minimize the effect of embarrassing revelations. He wanted Dean to emphasize how demonstrators had sabotaged the President's campaign. McGovern, he said, must take responsibility, and he ordered his aides to prepare a list of disruptive events.[13]

On the subject of the Paris Peace Accords, recently completed with North Vietnam, the President was openly belligerent. He "took off his gloves," as he said, and in a January 31 press conference baited his longtime media critics regarding the Vietnam war. He bluntly charged that the leading peace advocates were the most outspoken critics of his efforts to end the hostilities. But Nixon was determined to have the last word: "as far as this administration is concerned . . . we finally have achieved a peace with honor. I know it gags some of you to write that phrase, but it is true." Meanwhile, Nixon told Henry Kissinger to emphasize to Joseph Alsop, a friendly columnist, "the lonely & heroic courage" of the President.[14]

Well aware of his own vulnerabilities, Nixon urged his aides to press the media to portray the Administration favorably and to expose his enemies' misdeeds. The President pushed Dean again in January to get hard evidence that his campaign plane had been bugged in 1968. He suggested that Dean secure details from DeLoach at the FBI. With that information, Nixon was certain that Lyndon Johnson could "turn all this off"—meaning that the former President could persuade his fellow Democrats to cease their attacks lest they embarrass him. Nixon instructed Haldeman to speak to Connally in an attempt to reach Johnson. Meanwhile, he wanted Dwayne Andreas, who had contributed heavily to both Nixon and Hubert Humphrey, to "go in & scare Hubert." Johnson died on January 22, two days after Nixon's second inaugural. In a post-election telegram, Johnson had promised that he would "do anything . . . to ease your burden and help you make a good president in the days ahead." The President had lost a possible ally, but one of doubtful influence at that point.[15]

The public bravado disguised the continuing cover-up, which had mustered the proverbial bodyguard of lies to protect the truth. Actually, there were two cover-ups: one to conceal the involvement of CREEP in the Watergate break-in, the other to protect the President. They eventually converged, ostensibly to "protect the presidency," as Nixon liked to say; what he meant, of course, was to protect himself.

Charles Colson dealt with one of the stickier parts of the cover-up as he negotiated with his friend and retainer E. Howard Hunt over the payment of "hush money." Hunt began calling Colson in October 1972, demanding that commitments be "honored," but the two did not talk until November, apparently just after the election, when Hunt boldly escalated his demands. The recorded call revealed the growing complexity of maintaining the cover-up. Colson's discomfort was obvious, and he repeatedly insisted that he knew nothing of Watergate and wanted to keep things that way, fearing that if he had any knowledge, he might have to perjure himself. "Which I'm afraid John Mitchell has already done," Hunt responded. Colson warily sought distance; "unknowing as I am," he claimed, "right now I don't know anything about the Goddamn Watergate." But Colson could not avoid Hunt's purpose in calling, as Hunt put it, "because of commitments, uh, that were made to all of us at the onset, [that] have not been kept." Hunt reported a good deal of "unease and concern" among the defendants over their expenses; the money, he complained, had come in "minor dribs and drabs." It was time, Hunt said, for the White House to "start to give, uh, some creative, uh, thinking to the affair." After all, "we're protecting the guys who, who were really responsible." The pressure was direct: it was time for "moves" to be made; "your cheapest commodity available is money," Hunt delphically said.

Colson desperately tried to avoid the issue of money. Instead, he wanted to talk about Watergate as plot. When he wrote his memoirs, Colson told Hunt, he would say that "Watergate was brilliantly conceived as an escapade that would, uh, divert the Democrats' attention from the real issues, and therefore permit us to win a landslide that we probably wouldn't have won." The remarks made no sense and were beside the point. Hunt, frankly, was blackmailing the White House, because of his role in the break-in and because he was "protecting" those "really responsible." Colson never replied to Hunt's demand for money, skirting it with the irrelevant observation that he knew that Hunt "never had a goddamn thing to do with this." The conversation concluded with maudlin commiseration over the suffering of their respective families because of the affair, and with a fanfare of patriotism. "Thank God," Colson said, that the country had Nixon for another four years. Hunt joined in the salute to the flag: "I've had a lifetime of serving my country, and in a sense I'm still doing it." "That's right," Colson replied. "Damn right."[16]

The Hunt-Colson conversation was elaborately reprised in a document sent to the White House shortly after the election, apparently by one or more Watergate defendants. The document threatened nothing less than blackmail. It stated fears on the part of the defendants that they had been abandoned and would be used as scapegoats. But the writer offered several items for consideration, including a reminder that the defendants had been involved in "highly illegal conspiracies . . . at the behest of senior White House officials." The warning was blunt: the Administration had been "deficient" in living up to its commitments for financial support and pardons. "To end further misunderstandings," the defendants set 5:00 P.M. on November 27 as a deadline for the White House to meet financial requirements and offer "credible assurances" that other commitments would be honored. "Loyalty," they said, "has always been a two-way street." Liddy, meanwhile, told Dean that he needed money for his lawyer.[17]

At times, the President seemed anxious for Colson to leave the Administration. He told Haldeman on November 15 that Colson "doesn't really fit" into the reorganization schemes he had in mind. Haldeman called Colson that day (claiming he was doing so without the President's knowledge) to say that Hunt's forthcoming trial would bring inevitable problems and implications for Colson. When that occurred, the President would not want to have to force his aides out; therefore, "you're needed outside *now,*" Haldeman said. He promised Colson that he would have a continuing relationship with the President, somewhat like that of Clark Clifford with Democratic presidents. Colson could set up a campaign firm within a law firm, and the President—determined as he was, according to Haldeman, to get politics out of the White House—would use Colson as the man for people to see on political issues. Haldeman suggested that Colson see Nixon and tell him this was what he wanted to do. "[B]e a big man," Haldeman said. But Colson stayed on for several more months; he apparently provided comfort and confidence for the President. He satisfied Nixon's "dark side," as Mitchell and White House aides Richard Moore and Harry Dent testified. Herb Klein also knew that Colson enthusiastically supported Nixon's "fantasies of vengeance."[18]

E. Howard Hunt's wife was killed in a United Air Lines jetliner crash near Midway Airport in Chicago on December 8. Her purse was found to contain more than $10,000 in cash, and she had taken out $225,000 in flight insurance, with no stipulated beneficiary. Two days later, Assistant U.S. Attorney Earl Silbert asked the FBI to determine if the money could be traced. Silbert discovered that Howard Hunt had been to Chicago the day after the crash in an apparent attempt to retrieve the money. The Bureau learned from relatives that Dorothy Hunt had flown to Chicago to complete a business deal. They investigated handwriting on one of the bills but could not positively identify it as coming from any of the defendants in the break-in case. The FBI insisted that it was not looking for evidence that the plane had been sabotaged—but in fact it was.

Given the times, suspicions were aroused, and some linked the crash to the Watergate case. Dorothy Hunt had traveled with an unusual amount of money. Talk circulated that allegedly she had the same CIA links as her husband, and there was shadowy talk of "hush money." In any event, the final report of the National Transportation Safety Board on August 29, 1973, found no evidence of "sabotage or foul play" in connection with the accident. Meanwhile, the White House was aware of Mrs. Hunt's importance in the cover-up. Three months after her death, Dean told the President that she "was the savviest woman in the world. She had the whole picture together," he said.[19]

On January 8, 1973, just days before the Watergate burglars' trial was scheduled to begin, Nixon and Colson had a ninety-minute conversation in the President's Executive Office Building hideaway. The two men had the burglars' forthcoming trial uppermost in their minds. The futility of the entire adventure embittered Nixon: "We didn't get a God-damn thing from any of it that I can see." That was water over the dam. The problem now was to "save the plan," as the cover-up often was called. Specifically, Nixon realized the necessity for Hunt's continued cooperation. Colson told the President that he had urged Hunt to plead guilty: "I think it's the right thing for him to do, Chuck," the President replied. He then volunteered that clemency was a real possibility. Hunt's wife was dead, he had a brain-damaged child, and he had given eighteen years of good service to the CIA. William Buckley, Hunt's good friend, could be persuaded to publish a column in his behalf. When Nixon admitted that he might have difficulty providing clemency for the other defendants, Colson was not concerned; their "vulnerabilities" were different. Indeed, Hunt was different. He was a man with secrets—especially concerning the break-in of Daniel Ellsberg's psychiatrist's office—and he could be a very "incriminating" witness. The others were expendable. Colson assured the President that Hunt and Liddy, "good healthy right-wing exuberants," as he was fond of calling them, could be trusted. "This is the last damn fifty miles," the President responded, rather cryptically.

Nixon knew that his aides had paid money to Hunt and the defendants, but he only worried about finding new donors for "hush money." "Goddamn hush money," the President complained, "uh, how are we going to [unintelligible] how do we get this stuff. . . ." In a February 14 conversation with Colson, he talked about maintaining the cover-up: "The cover-up is the main ingredient," he told Colson. "That's where we gotta cut our losses; my losses are to be cut. The President's losses gotta be cut on the cover-up deal." The day before, Nixon bluntly told Colson that the cover-up must be maintained: "When I'm speaking about Watergate," the President said, "that's the whole point of the election. This tremendous investigation rests, unless one of the seven begins to talk. That's the problem." But the President had confidence in his old friend John Mitchell, as he was pleased that Mitchell had "stonewalled it up to this point." Colson and Mitchell were adversaries, but Colson admiringly told the President in response: "John has one of those marvelous, ah, memories."

The cover-up had developed another layer, with new, determined efforts to thwart any possibilities of involving the White House and the President's closest aides. Nixon had some concern that Congress, with "its God-damn cotton-pickin' hands," might make trouble. Typically, Nixon saw the subject all in combat metaphor. He told Colson he knew it was "tough" for him, Haldeman, Ehrlichman, and the rest. But, he promised, "[W]e're just not gonna let it get us down. This is a battle, it's a fight, it's war and we just fight with a little, uh, you know, uh remember, uh, we'll cut them down one of these days." In March, both John Dean and Charles Colson advised the President to retain Colson as a consultant without pay in order to maintain a curtain of executive privilege around him.[20]

The President's conversations with Colson reflected the growing concern within the White House. On January 6, Senator Mike Mansfield had called for a full investigation of Watergate, by a select committee armed with proper funds, staff, and subpoena powers. The time had come, Mansfield said, "to proceed to an inquiry into these matters in a dispassionate fashion." The Senator thought that his North Carolina colleague, Sam Ervin, was the man to head such an investigation. Ervin's conservative credentials and his well-known constitutional scruples, Mansfield said, would "defuse" charges that such an investigation was a "vendetta." The question was not "political, it is constitutional," Mansfield declared. "At stake is the continued vitality of the electoral process."

The Senate and an invigorated press threatened the Administration's containment strategy. On February 25, the President told Haldeman and Ehrlichman to stay out of Watergate affairs and leave the field to Dean and Kleindienst. Three days later, Nixon talked to Dean about both senior aides' cooperating with the forthcoming Senate investigation, and yet he raised the 1968 bugging issue for the first line of counterattack. Interestingly, the President stressed the importance of appearing to cooperate with the investigation, anxious to avoid being perceived as recalcitrant, as Truman was in the Alger Hiss affair. Nixon was defensive once more about the press, complaining that L. Patrick Gray was often described as his "political crony." They had never met in a social situation, Nixon insisted. But the talk of Gray made the President nostalgic for J. Edgar Hoover. "[H]e'd have scared them to death. He's got [sic] files on everybody, God damn it," meaning, it seems, that Hoover would have called off the dogs for Nixon.

Dean's efforts earned him some time for extensive conversations with the President, beginning in February 1973. Ever ingratiating and accommodating, he suggested that Senator Edward Kennedy had pressured Mansfield to create the new Senate Select Committee. Surprisingly, Nixon rejected this line, although less than three weeks earlier he had told Haldeman that the whole affair was a Kennedy plot against him. Talking with Dean, the President reserved his greatest invective for the Republican senators who thought the Senate inquiry should be an objective, bipartisan affair. He considered Ervin a sham, scoffing at his reputed authoritativeness as a constitutional lawyer. He thought Ervin had totally "buffaloed" the designated committee Vice Chairman, Howard Baker; Ervin, he said, "is as partisan as most of our Southern gentlemen are. They, they, they are great politicians. They're just more clever than the minority [*sic*]. Just more clever!''

Nixon clearly was worried when Dean reported that Nixon's lawyer, Herbert Kalmbach, was being questioned by the U.S. Attorney. Dean earlier had told Haldeman that the prosecutors had subpoenaed Kalmbach's phone records. The President seemed particularly pleased that questions regarding "San Clemente and the like" had been covered by lawyer-client privilege and were out of bounds. But the landscape was strewn with mines. Nixon raised the question of clemency, asking whether Hunt and the others expected it within "a reasonable time." Dean thought so, yet he advised the President to tread cautiously because things could become quite "political" in the next six months. Nixon agreed.

He emphasized that Dean must get through to Kleindienst—he was the "man who can make the difference," Nixon said; moreover, Kleindienst "owes Mitchell" for his position. Finally, Nixon again raised the Hiss case and applied it in an odd, almost perverse way. He told Dean that Whittaker Chambers, Hiss's accuser, suffered greatly because he was an informer. Chambers, he thought, was one of the great men and writers of his time. Still, "they finished him. . . . [T]he informer is not wanted in our society. Either way, that's the one thing people do sort of line up against.''[21] Was that pointed advice for John Dean?

The trial of Hunt, Liddy, and the Watergate burglars began on January 10 in the U.S. District Court for the District of Columbia. Assistant U.S. Attorney Earl Silbert depicted the break-in as part of a well-financed, many-layered espionage and "special intelligence" operation against the Democratic Party, organized by the Committee to Re-elect the President. Silbert promised to offer evidence on the recruitment of spies, earlier attempts to bug McGovern's offices, the monitoring of telephone calls from the tap in the Democrats' Watergate headquarters, and, of course, the facts relating to the capture of the burglars and the activities of Hunt and Liddy. The defendants had been indicted on multiple counts of burglary, conspiracy, and interception of wire and oral communications. Silbert and his assistants had prepared their case carefully and confined it narrowly. The prosecutor realized that in other matters the liberal Circuit Court of Appeals had reversed decisions of presiding judge "Maximum John" Sirica to an unusual degree. Accordingly, Silbert framed his indictment with "shrewd parsimony," restricting himself to those offenses that appeared beyond dispute. "There was nothing to try," a former federal attorney later wrote.[22]

For his part, Howard Hunt realized that nothing could be gained in a trial. The defense attorneys had responded feebly to Silbert's presentation with the argument that the defendants had no evil motive, "no criminal intent."

That same day, Hunt offered to plead guilty to three charges, but Sirica promptly refused the offer, citing the strength of the government's case. The public, he admonished, must have "not only the substance of justice but also the appearance of justice." On January 11 Hunt pled guilty to all six counts. Patriotism was his last refuge. He had acted, he insisted, "in the best interest of my country"; he added that he had no knowledge of "higher-ups" in the conspiracy. Sirica released Hunt on $100,000 bail.

The four Cuban burglars similarly pled guilty on January 15 to all counts in the indictment. Responding to questions from Sirica regarding their actions, the burglars insisted that they had acted on behalf of Cuban liberation, and because they believed McGovern's election would lead to Communism in the United States. They continued to deny any knowledge of the sources of the large amounts of cash discovered in their possession at the time of the break-in. The *New York Times* reported that great pressure had been exerted on the defendants to plead guilty, but it named no sources.

McCord and Liddy nevertheless pressed their cases. Judge Sirica often interrupted from the bench, indicating his disdain for testimony that attempted to keep the conspiracy confined to the accused in the case. McCord's lawyer offered a "defense of duress," contending that his client thought it necessary to secure intelligence on the Democratic Party in order to protect CREEP officials from bodily harm; therefore, McCord broke a law, the lawyer said, to prevent a greater harm. Sirica brusquely called the argument "ridiculous," although he later noted that it might have carried more weight if the defense lawyer had been able to say that the former Attorney General of the United States had approved the operation. The jurors, too, were unimpressed. On January 30, after deliberating only ninety minutes, they returned guilty verdicts on all counts against McCord and Liddy. Three days later, Sirica set bail and could not restrain his skepticism. "I am still not satisfied that all the pertinent facts that might be available— I say might be available—have been produced before an American jury." He expressed the hope that the anticipated Senate inquiry might "get to the bottom of what happened in this case."[23]

Sirica's statement reflected his knowledge of parallel developments in the Watergate affair. Senator Mansfield was preparing for a debate on his resolution for an investigating committee, and he was carefully assembling the bipartisan support to give it the necessary element of credibility. On the day that Hunt offered his guilty plea, the Justice Department's Henry Petersen, still in charge of investigating the "Watergate Incident," assured Congressman Wright Patman that his office had closely followed the leads provided by Patman's staff and was "vigorously" pursuing "all evidentiary leads." That same day, Justice filed charges against CREEP for campaign-financing violations.[24]

* * *

Patman's earlier attempts to unravel the Watergate puzzle failed because of White House pressure, the distractions of the political campaign, and, not least, because his investigation was perceived as a partisan attempt to embarrass the President. In one respect it was indeed partisan: Republican members of the House of Representatives had no interest in discrediting their own national campaign. If the dominant Democratic congressional majority confronted Watergate as something more than politics-as-usual, then it would have to do so on higher ground. Attention to campaign practices and financing provided the ticket.

The stifling of Patman's investigation in October 1972 effectively took Watergate off the front pages. George McGovern desperately tried to exploit the issue. But the Democratic presidential candidate could not attract serious attention on more momentous matters; how, then, could he hope to arouse voter interest in what seemed to be a campaign peccadillo? His harsh comparisons to Teapot Dome sounded hysterical, even absurd.

In the wake of Nixon's smashing triumph, the verdict in the Watergate trial made little news. The lack of attention reflected the nation's lack of interest. When the burglars' trial began, newspaper reports treated it as a commonplace criminal event. The *New York Times* stories appeared in the inside pages. Howard Hunt's guilty plea briefly made the headlines, but attention quickly waned, despite Judge Sirica's dramatic attempts to uncover bigger news.

Watergate might have remained as the story-that-never-was had it not been for the determination of Mike Mansfield and Sam Ervin. Ervin played a crucial role in securing Senate passage of a resolution calling for the creation of a Select Committee to investigate illegal and unethical conduct in the 1972 presidential campaign. Mansfield, meanwhile, worked behind the scenes to marshal Democratic support for the resolution. He kept Ervin in the forefront, shrewdly using Ervin's political capital among Southern Democratic and Republican senators.

Mansfield gave Ervin command of the floor debate, signalling his intention that the North Carolinian chair the investigation. The conservative Ervin was respected on both sides of the aisle, his integrity was unquestioned, and he was widely known as a constitutional "strict constructionist." He had been regarded as Richard Russell's heir apparent for leadership of the Southern caucus. But the Senate's routine business did not interest him, and he had little taste for day-to-day political negotiations.[25] Two decades earlier, Ervin had served on the Select Committee that recommended censure of Senator Joseph McCarthy—an onerous assignment, but one that reflected the confidence of his colleagues. They also appreciated his wit. Supporting censure, Ervin invoked the wisdom of "Uncle Ephraim Swink," an "arthritic mountaineer," who described what the Lord had done for him: "Brother, He has mighty nigh ruint me."

The Senate's 77-0 support for Senate Resolution 60, creating the Select Committee, belied the two days of sharp partisan debate. This was a Democratic cause, but even within that camp the leading support came from polar opposites. Ervin may have had a somewhat exaggerated reputation as the Senate's constitutional authority; nevertheless, in all quarters he was respected for his decency and his sense of fair play. Democratic liberals might chastise him for his conservative views, but they respected him—and also, in view of senatorial club politics, they realized there was little mileage in attacking him. Senator Edward M. Kennedy's support for an investigation, however, struck many as part of a blood feud with Nixon. Had Kennedy, not Ervin, proposed Senate Resolution 60, the results might well have been different. Ervin scrupulously maintained a correct posture toward the President. At the outset, he found it "simply inconceivable" that Nixon might have been involved.[26]

The debate parodied the senatorial process, replete with stylized discourse that masked deep divisions and featuring occasional outbursts of sentiment, declamations of noble purposes—and blatant partisanship. The Republicans could only hope to hobble the investigation; they could not prevent it. Accordingly, they challenged the proposal for the Senate Select Committee on three counts: the numerical composition of the committee, the scope of the investigation, and the expenditures of the committee's $500,000 allocation.

Howard Baker led the Republicans and welcomed the idea of a Select Committee. Ervin's original proposal provided for a committee of five, with three seats earmarked for the Democratic majority. Baker proposed an additional Republican to divide the committee equally along partisan lines. Baker and his fellow Republican, Lowell Weicker of Connecticut, emphasized the need for nonpartisanship. "Partisanship [was] . . . a serious national problem," Weicker said; Alaska Republican Ted Stevens worried that the investigation would turn into a "political witch hunt." Ervin responded on historical and practical grounds, noting the danger of partisan tie votes. The Senate rejected Baker's amendment on a nearly party-line vote, 45-35. (In fact, an equally divided committee had directed Joseph McCarthy's censure inquiry. The Republicans had established a three-to-three division to avoid the onus of directing the castigation of one of their own.)

The scope of the investigation exposed partisan concerns. Baker politely queried Ervin on whether the Select Committee might, in the "spirit of a broad inquiry," look at other presidential elections. The Republicans wanted the committee to investigate the 1968 and 1964 elections, obviously to substantiate widespread rumors of Democratic skullduggery in those campaigns. Ervin sensed the Republican purpose but obliquely replied that such a diffuse effort could not be fulfilled given the committee's mandate to report

its findings within a year. He distinguished between investigating past rumors and current alleged criminal matters. Diverting the inquiry away from
the recent election, he warned, would be "as foolish as the man who went
bear hunting and stopped to chase rabbits."

But Florida Republican Edward Gurney pushed hard for a wider investigation, while characterizing Watergate as "one of those political wing-dings
that happen every political year." He thought Watergate had no influence
whatsoever on the election. John Tower (R-TX) suggested that Democratic
acceptance of the broader mandate would serve to defuse any charges of
partisanship. But Democratic lines held, and again the Senate turned back
the Republican challenge.

Republican frustration spilled out during a debate on the allocation of
Select Committee funds. Specifically, they wanted one-third of the available
funds to provide minority staffing. Democratic resistance, Stevens charged,
demonstrated the blatantly "partisan concept" of the committee. Ervin apparently realized that the Republican demand mainly was a face-saving gesture, and he agreed to the proposal. Baker and others consistently applauded
the idea of a Select Committee, but their remarks seemed more like gestures
than convictions. Senator Jesse Helms (R–NC) probably expressed his party's basic view when he said that the FBI and Patman investigations, and
the media coverage, demonstrated that "the Watergate situation has received
the closest and most penetrating scrutiny."[27] What the Republicans finally
voted for was more an expression of faith in Senator Ervin than of any real
desire for a Select Committee. In truth, however, they had little choice in
the matter.

The brief partisan flare-up over Watergate still did not kindle much public
interest. The *New York Times* covered the first day of the Senate debate on
page 36; news of the resolution's passage moved up four pages. After the
vote, Senator Baker visited Tennessee and asked a former campaign worker
to serve as the committee's Minority Counsel. The lawyer, Fred Thompson,
later admitted that he was barely aware of the Watergate story as it had then
unfolded.

But the White House was not oblivious. The creation of the Senate Select
Committee meant that the maintenance of the cover-up would have to be
expanded. The new dimensions, however, only increased the likelihood of
exposure. Administration resources proved to be limited, vulnerable, and
ultimately, incompetent.

The President realized the danger. On February 11, he told Haldeman that
they must discredit the hearings, reiterating the now-familiar theme that this
was a commonplace "political crime." He wanted it stressed that the focus
on Watergate was "all a *Kennedy* deal." A month later, Nixon wanted his
political aides to find a candidate to oppose Sam Ervin in North Carolina
and "nip at his heels."[28]

John Dean later revealed details of the Administration's strategy. While adopting a public posture of cooperation with the Select Committee, presidential staff would make every effort to restrain the investigation and "make it as difficult as possible to get information and witnesses." They would cultivate the media to expose the inquiry as partisan. "The ultimate goal," Dean admitted, was "to discredit the hearings and reduce their impact by attempting to show that the Democrats have engaged in the same type of activities."[29]

The Administration's response was instinctive and in character. The President's strategy toward Ervin remarkably paralleled that of Charles I regarding parliamentary opposition in seventeenth-century England. Charles "never was . . . more unfortunate than when he attempted at once to cajole and to undermine [Oliver] Cromwell," as Thomas Macaulay later wrote. Charles eventually lost his head and his crown. Richard Nixon's life was never at stake, of course, but neither he nor anyone else realized that his office was in jeopardy. He soon discovered that attempts to "cajole and undermine" Sam Ervin had risks of their own. The contempt shown by such aides as Ehrlichman, who had clashed with Ervin in January over executive privilege, had the added danger of irritating the Senator.

Ervin was formidable. He had the confidence of his colleagues, and consequently his power increased proportionately. At one committee meeting, Ervin summoned committee member Herman Talmadge (D–GA), then presiding at another meeting. The Georgian promptly came to Ervin's session, conferred with the Chairman, and left Ervin with his proxy.[30] In time, during the Watergate hearings, Ervin became a neo–folk idol. Ironically, he had been completely out of step with popular sentiments and causes of the past decade. His vaunted role as the Senate's constitutional expert contrasted with his paternalistic views on civil rights for blacks and equal rights for women ("blame fools"). He had uncritically championed presidential policy on the Vietnam war. Finally, he opposed Medicare legislation—much to his regret in his later retirement years.

Ervin's positions faithfully reflected his constituency. But the rhetoric and the abstract value of liberty that he regularly invoked served him well when Watergate emerged as a national concern. His uniquely Southern, cadenced English, and his use of a variety of homespun, Shakespearean, and Biblical allusions, made him an instantly popular television personality. But he often leavened his humor and theatrics with the sharp rhetorical skills of a shrewd Harvard lawyer—which he also was. Critics might have scoffed at him, but Sam Ervin, "country lawyer," well understood the nation's mystical constitutional bonds. The President and his staff grossly underestimated Ervin and his serious purposes.

* * *

During the early months of 1973, the White House constantly wavered between confidence and apprehension. Haldeman's aide Larry Higby told the Chief of Staff that Jeb Magruder had fairly well solved all his Watergate problems. Magruder would have no difficulty in court and was certain he would have only a minor role in the forthcoming congressional hearings. Several weeks later, however, the President sharply reversed his view of Congress. He instructed John Ehrlichman to be careful in writing veto messages and not to use "certain words [that] unnecessarily infuriate Congress[.]" Much of the post-election brazenness and euphoria had evaporated, and Nixon warily glimpsed the future.[31]

The mounting caution in the White House reflected the tension of maintaining the cover-up, an effort heavily dependent on the continued cooperation of the convicted burglars. The events surrounding their sentencing snapped the tenuous bonds that connected their interests to the White House. In a few short months, the shattered chrysalis of the cover-up revealed the knowledge and complicity of the "higher-ups" that the likes of Howard Hunt had so steadfastly denied weeks earlier.

Sam Ervin, however underestimated, was a known enemy. By contrast, the man who stood at the vortex of one of the decisive events of the Watergate affair was an unlikely, even surprising, choice for his historical role. Federal District Judge John J. Sirica caricatured the type of judge that candidate Richard Nixon loved. His courthouse nickname—"Maximum John"—virtually said it all. Sixty-nine years old in 1973, a veteran of the bench since 1957, when Eisenhower had appointed him (with the strong backing of Nixon supporters William Rogers and Leonard Hall), he was, by dint of seniority, the Chief District Judge.

Sirica was born in Connecticut to Italian immigrant parents. He moved around a great deal as a child but finally settled for life in the District of Columbia in 1918. He tried George Washington University Law School briefly when he was seventeen, dropped out for a year, did some boxing, and then re-enrolled at Georgetown Law School. He was, by his own admission, an incompetent student and unsure of himself when he graduated in 1926. "Incredible," was his own reaction to his successful bar examination. He drifted into a nondescript criminal practice, but the U.S. Attorney for the District, a former sparring partner, kept Sirica on his staff for over three years. The prosecutor was a Republican, and out of gratitude, Sirica adopted the same political affiliation. Sirica became quite active in local politics; indeed, that activity and his close friendship with Jack Dempsey seemed to be the highlights of his life before he became a federal judge. Perhaps his most fortunate move was one he did not make: his friend, Senator Joseph McCarthy, offered Sirica the position of counsel for his Senate investigating committee, but Sirica declined since he had just taken a partnership in a prominent Washington firm.[32]

From March 1973 onward, Judge Sirica was lionized in the media by liberals and conservatives alike. The image comforted; it also distorted. Some remembered Sirica as a man who badgered and castigated witnesses and lawyers, who had been reversed with alarming regularity by higher courts in important cases involving constitutional rights, and who lacked judicial temperament. "The worst thing about Sirica is his lack of interest," one prosecutor reported; a defense lawyer added that "the worst thing about Sirica is that he has absolutely no capacity for understanding people." In sum, the judge never had been a favorite of liberal crusaders or of those knowledgeable about local trial courts. Indeed, just before the Watergate trial opened, Sirica ordered a *Los Angeles Times* reporter to jail for contempt for refusing to surrender a tape recording of a potential witness in the case. The reporter remained in custody only two hours before the Circuit Court ordered him released. The *Washington Post,* later to become one of Sirica's most enthusiastic cheerleaders, bitterly attacked his action, concluding that "the First Amendment is in real trouble and so are we all."[33]

Sirica never was modest about how he came to the Watergate case. As Chief Judge, he assigned it to himself, but he claimed that his colleagues urged him to do so, portraying him (in his recall) as a paragon of objectivity: " 'Look, you are a Republican, you ought to take this case because we know you'll go right down the middle. If you appoint some judge who's been appointed by a Democratic president and something goes wrong, a hue and cry might go up. . . .' So it made sense" that he take the case, he concluded.[34] He said nothing about the obvious risk for a Republican judge perceived as favoring a Republican president. Yet Sirica had been Nixon's kind of judge. And until 1973, Richard Nixon had been John Sirica's kind of president.

Sirica had scheduled sentencing of the Watergate burglars for March 23. Three days earlier, James McCord delivered a letter to the judge's chambers that led directly to the unraveling of the conspiracy. Recognizing the possibility of a stiff sentence, and "in the interest of restoring faith in the criminal justice system, . . . [and to] be of help to you in meting out justice in this case," McCord told Sirica that pressure had been applied to have the defendants maintain silence; that perjury had occurred in the trial; that Watergate was not a CIA operation, but it involved other governmental officials; and that McCord wanted an opportunity to discuss the case at greater length with Sirica. The judge exuberantly told his clerk: "This is going to break this case wide open."

McCord's loyalty to the Administration had been questionable for several months. Apparently, he had been uneasy regarding attempts to link him most directly with the Cubans and thereby draw attention away from Hunt and Liddy. McCord also believed that the White House was anxious to blame the CIA for the break-in and would cite McCord as evidence for the notion. He wrote to his friend White House aide John Caulfield at the end of December, warning that "if Helms goes, and the Watergate operation is laid at [the] CIA's feet where it does not belong, every tree in the forest will fall. It will be a scorched desert," McCord warned.[35]

Richard Nixon knew in advance about McCord's letter to Sirica. The day it was delivered, the President told Haldeman that Dean and others were concerned about the convicted burglars' sentences and what Sirica might do. He knew that McCord did not want to go to jail and apparently had decided to talk. Haldeman realized the implications: McCord, he said, "would have a lot on Mitchell." The President replied as if he were unaware of the connection between the two. John Dean knew the implications: "The dam was cracking," he later said.

At the same moment, the hearings on L. Patrick Gray's nomination as Director of the FBI verged on disaster, with Gray about to admit that he had cooperated with Dean in seeking to limit the investigation of the break-in. The nomination also brought a confrontation with the Senate over executive privilege. The day after McCord sent his letter to Sirica, Dean told the President that there was "a cancer on the presidency." Still, the "containment" effort persisted. Howard Hunt received a $75,000 payment from a White House emissary. Kleindienst, probably acting on White House orders, publicly minimized McCord's charges and privately wrote to Sirica, chiding him for not sending McCord's letter through Department of Justice channels. But Assistant Attorney General Petersen knew, as well as the prosecutors did, that Kleindienst's complaint was beside the point: the case, to use a favorite Oval Office expression, was about to blow.

The President and Haldeman in their March 20 meeting did not see any particular problems for themselves or any other key White House figures, however. They believed that they had to focus on protecting Mitchell and CREEP officials, confident that the problems of campaign officials were not their own. Eight days later, Ehrlichman telephoned Kleindienst, conveying word that no White House people had *prior* knowledge of the break-in. Nixon wanted Kleindienst to keep him informed on developments in the case, particularly any information that involved White House officials. But he was concerned about Mitchell and the people at CREEP, Ehrlichman reported. "So am I," Kleindienst added. Ehrlichman relayed the President's demand for "a private communication" from Kleindienst if he learned anything about Mitchell.[36]

After reading the McCord letter in court on March 23, Judge Sirica turned to the sentencing of the other defendants. He had pondered the question for some time and became convinced that he could use his power to force cooperation from the defendants. Accordingly, he ordered maximum sentences, including six to twenty years for Liddy, thirty-five for Hunt, and forty for the Cubans, plus fines. (Sirica subsequently reduced the sentences for all except Liddy.) When he announced the sentences, Sirica minced no words: the defendants controlled their own fates. "I recommend your full cooperation with the grand jury and the Senate Select Committee. You must understand that I hold out no promises or hopes of any kind to you in this matter, but I do say that should you decide to speak freely, I would have to weigh that factor in appraising what sentences will be finally imposed in each case. Other facts will, of course, be considered, but I mention this one because it is one over which you have control."[37]

Sirica believed that McCord's letter and his own actions vitally affected events. "This case would never have been broken if McCord had elected to stand pat and had not written the letter to me," the judge wrote. Sirica thought that McCord's "trust" in him and the courts led to the letter. But McCord had hedged his bets and sent a copy of his letter to a *Los Angeles Times* reporter. Kleindienst dramatically noted that "future historians, in a more detached environment, might well conclude that the McCord letter was not only the turning point in Watergate but perhaps a turning point in modern civilization as well." Perhaps; but, in fact, the cover-up already had begun to fray in the Gray hearings then underway. In addition, the prosecutors still had not given up on their pressures to induce the Watergate defendants to cooperate, and they were questioning CREEP employees at great length. Finally, the Senate's investigators had begun to approach similar leads. Sirica knew that the prosecutors had planned to get convictions, grant immunity from further prosecution, and then bring back all the figures to the grand jury in hopes of amplifying their story. The prosecutors themselves deeply resented numerous reports that they had not attempted to bargain with McCord.[38]

Sirica's threat of maximum sentences skirted dangerously close to the precipice of forcing self-incrimination. The judicial precedents were mixed. An appellate court had vacated sentences in a drug-trafficking case because they trenched upon the defendant's right to avoid self-incrimination. "Mercy seasons justice," the court said, "but the quality of mercy is strained when its price is abandonment of the classic freedom against self-incrimination." Two years later, a Second Circuit Court ruling sustained broad discretion for the sentencing judge, including his right to consider matters inadmissible at trial. More to the point of Sirica's example, the court ruled that when a judge left open the possibility of sentence reduction if the defendant subsequently cooperated, any judicial reference to the defendant's silence was not a punishment for exercising self-incrimination. Ironically, the losing attorney in that case was Samuel Dash, the designated Majority Counsel for the newly created Senate Select Committee. Dash had recommended the precedent to Sirica, hoping that it might persuade the defendants to cooperate. He did so, he claimed, with great reluctance, believing as he did that the precedent abused the sentencing function. But legal and constitutional arguments, he noted, often come down to a cynical rationalization turning on "whose ox is gored."

Civil libertarians had their problems with Sirica, lauding his interest in gaining the full story but contending that his pressures upon the defendants raised serious civil liberties problems. One prominent lawyer thought Sirica had exceeded his judicial role, citing the American Bar Association canon that the only purpose of a criminal trial is to determine the guilt of the accused, and that the trial judge must not permit the proceedings to be used for any other purpose. George V. Higgins, a former Assistant U.S. Attorney, also chastised Sirica for stretching the bounds framed by the prosecutor and the indictments in the case. The other issues were not properly before him. "Under the rules," Higgins wrote, "he should not have messed with it." Meanwhile Kleindienst, for entirely different reasons, complained to the White House that Sirica was "really lousing this thing up."[39]

In White House conversations, Richard Nixon called the sentences "outrageous"; John Sirica himself was a "son-of-a-bitch of a judge" by the President's lights. Yet a month later, when he admitted the possibility that Watergate was more than a "third-rate burglary," the President praised Sirica as a "courageous judge," in an obvious attempt to mollify growing public restlessness. Just days before the sentences, Nixon offered a new anticrime program, providing the death penalty for a number of offenses, mandatory minimum sentences, and bail prohibitions in some circumstances. Typically, he condemned "soft-headed" judges.[40] Sirica's actions confused the President's categorical labels.

Nixon had no burning desire to determine whether in fact there was any involvement of "higher-ups" in the Watergate break-in; instead, he believed that the "main thing we have to get off our backs, of course, is the whole problem of political pressure." Two days after making that remark, he told Haldeman that "we simply wouldn't be able to govern" if the controversy escalated. Haldeman thought the opposition wanted to drive out the President's top aides in order to prove corruption in the White House, but Nixon steeled himself to support Haldeman and Ehrlichman against the mounting assaults. He had little choice; they were, after all, extensions of his own will. Yet he knew things had changed. Watergate no longer was a Washington story, and it would become worse if the defendants talked. He was concerned about the men in jail and about Haldeman, Ehrlichman, Magruder, and Mitchell. Writing in retrospect, and anxious to demonstrate his utter ignorance of Dean's activities, he recorded his greatest solicitude for Dean, who deserved "the most consideration because he was acting always as a counsel, giving his best advice and always avoiding anything which would smack of illegal or improper activities." But Nixon never strayed too far from self-concern. He feared the unknown: "I guess we're all a bit depressed," he wrote in his diary.[41]

The President and his closest White House aides had determined by then that John Mitchell must be a sacrificial lamb if the strategy of containing the revelations was to work. Such passiveness occasionally gave way to exhortation. "Stonewall it," "plead the Fifth Amendment," "cover up"—anything to "save the plan," he said defiantly. But in the next breath, he talked about his preference for "the other way"—in which his good friend John Mitchell would take the blame.[42]

The Oval Office was infected with confusion and ambivalence, blended with feistiness and belligerence. The President himself ran the gamut of those moods; his aides, as usual, reflected him. Sometimes Nixon and his men underestimated their adversaries and the dangers confronting them. But at bottom, the President recognized the peril. He instructed Haldeman to keep Dean working on the case. From the moment Senator Mansfield proposed a congressional investigation, Nixon was concerned. Dean, he said, should "try to turn it off."

The trickle of revelations about Administration wrongdoing rapidly had turned into a steady stream; "every day," John Ehrlichman complained, "the news was freighted with new accusations."[43] The President's "enemies" were massing. A bunker mentality soon pervaded the White House. Administration figures saw the situation in terms of a metaphor, if not a defense: several talked about circling the wagons around the White House. But the circle may have been closed too late. The enemies were already within; the defenses had been breached.

XI

"WE HAVE A CANCER WITHIN, CLOSE TO THE PRESIDENCY."

COVERING UP THE COVER-UP:
JANUARY–MARCH 1973

James McCord's letter to Judge Sirica tugged at the tightly wrapped strands of John Dean's improvised cover-up. Back on September 15, Dean had promised the President fifty-four days—until the election—free of trouble. He had delivered. But four months later, Howard Hunt was demanding more money; Senator Ervin's investigators were at work, following leads already established by the FBI, the grand jury, and the U.S. Attorney's office; more important, congressional hearings on Gray's FBI nomination were coming closer to unveiling Dean's involvement. And any questions about Dean, of course, eventually had to lead to his intimate dealings in the Oval Office.

At the beginning of March, Dean remained outwardly confident. When the White House insisted on sending Jeb Magruder to the Commerce Department with a new appointment, Dean told Secretary Frederick B. Dent that Magruder had no particular problems. He might have some "bad publicity" in the next few weeks, Dean wrote, but he did not believe it would last. Only two weeks later, on March 20, Dean told Richard Moore, the President's special counsel, that the cover-up could not be maintained much longer. Moore thought the situation had become like a "tumor"; "it's like a cancer," he told Dean. The next day, Dean reported to the President.

"I have the impression that you don't know everything I know," John Dean told Nixon. "In other words, I have to know why you feel that we shouldn't unravel something?" the President responded, as if knowing that his aide wished to release some of the pressure on the cover-up. The optimistic, even cocky, Dean of September 1972 had vanished; for him, the outlook was terribly grim. "We have a cancer within, close to the Presidency, that is growing," Dean reported. "It is growing daily. It's compounded, growing geometrically now, because it compounds itself." Dean thereupon launched into a long narrative of the origins of Watergate and the subsequent White House responses. But radical surgery lay in the distance. For now, the President and his aides launched a new cover-up, one to mask their earlier effort and also to find appropriate people "to take the heat."[1] Dean's pronouncement of March 21 was no surprise to Richard Nixon; he already had prepared for that new stage.

The innuendoes and rumors that had floated through Washington since the break-in ripened into substantial revelations during Gray's confirmation hearings in February and March. The situation was fluid, dictating even more defensive innovations by Dean, the cover-up ringmaster. The Senate Judiciary Committee's confirmation hearings began shortly after the President announced Gray's nomination as FBI Director on February 17. By the end of the month, Gray had acknowledged his direct contacts with the White House during the Watergate investigation, and his ambitions lay shattered.

The task of wisdom was to replace Gray; still, his nomination went forward. Gray was a disaster waiting to happen. His lack of any constituency, the hostility of old FBI hands, and his vulnerabilities as a witness given his early attempts to stall the Watergate investigation clearly foreshadowed difficulty for an Administration already besieged with troubles. Perhaps Gray's Watergate ties gave the President no alternative. Dean observed that Gray offered "no choice"; the Administration, he said, could not "afford an angry Pat Gray loose on the streets." The only thing worse than nominating Gray, Dean concluded, was not nominating him.[2]

The President's incessant concern for finding a new, pliant FBI Director curiously yielded nothing except to bring him back to Gray. Was Nixon concerned about the danger of not nominating him? Perhaps; but equally likely, the President stubbornly remained fixated on appointing subordinates absolutely loyal and dedicated to Richard Nixon. Gray fit the mold perfectly.

He had substantial credentials. Fifty-seven years old, from a railway worker's family, Pat Gray had attended Rice University on scholarship during the Depression. He then received another four-year grant to attend Annapolis and served as a submarine commander during World War II. The Navy selected Gray to attend George Washington University Law School, and he graduated with honors in 1949. As a legal officer, he served both the Joint Chiefs of Staff and the Secretary of the Navy. He had met Nixon in 1947, admired him greatly, and worked in the 1960 campaign. Shortly thereafter, Gray moved to Connecticut to join a law firm, but he left in 1968 to move into the new Nixon Administration as Executive Assistant to Robert Finch, whom Gray had met in 1960. In 1970 Gray transferred to Justice, where he became Assistant Attorney General for the Civil Division and later Deputy Attorney General. Most notably in this period, he directed efforts to prosecute antiwar protesters in Washington.

"The world's original patriot, with a strong boy scout tendency," a close friend and aide of Gray recalled. Nixon knew he would be loyal. Ex-submarine-commander Gray was a man trained to accept uncritically decisions of superior officers; those of the Commander-in-Chief, of course, were particularly beyond question. But Gray also had a conscience, a conscience that the Nixon people apparently never measured properly, if at all. He had been concerned over the propriety of the Justice Department's mass arrests of antiwar demonstrators and repeatedly expressed worry to friends about the effects of prosecution on the young defendants. Gray may never have fully fathomed the motives and ambitions of such presidential aides as Ehrlichman and Dean. Although he realized that he had been used by them since the break-in had occurred, he naively asked his own aide, a man with longstanding ties to Nixon himself, if such men would knowingly violate any laws.[3]

John Mitchell had first suggested Gray's name for the FBI post in the summer of 1971, amid the Administration's growing disenchantment with J. Edgar Hoover. Mitchell thought that Gray should be sent from his Justice Department post to the FBI as Hoover's deputy for about six months and then be nominated as Director. Ehrlichman and Nixon further discussed Gray at a meeting on October 25, 1971, both apparently believing that Hoover might agree to Gray as his successor.[4]

No doubt, Gray was the President's man. Nixon wanted changes in the Bureau; it had grown too ossified, too rigid, and above all, too much into a personal fiefdom. He wanted a Director and a Bureau more responsible to his own wishes, a laudable goal given Hoover's almost total unaccountability. Gray was the right man. Shortly after he became Acting Director, a White House operative suggested that Gray speak to the prestigious City Club in Cleveland during the forthcoming political campaign because of Ohio's electoral importance. Neither Nixon nor any president would have approached J. Edgar Hoover with such a "request." But there was a side to Gray that the President may not have anticipated; he opened the FBI's windows for the winds of change. Women, blacks, and Hispanics were actively recruited; younger people received more rapid advancement as older hands were encouraged to retire early; family wishes became a consideration in what once had been a capricious transfer system for agents; and Gray even explored the possibility of an FBI oversight board.[5]

Gray's positive achievements were quickly disregarded once the Judiciary Committee hearings disclosed that he had regularly submitted FBI investigative reports to Dean. He contended that Hoover had made a practice of providing reports of ongoing investigations; further, he thought that he was merely supplementing Dean's own investigation. In a conciliatory move, Gray offered to make the Watergate files available to the senators—an offer later vetoed by the White House. But more was to come. The committee learned that Dean took a week to turn over the contents of Howard Hunt's White House safe to the FBI (Gray thought nothing was "irregular" about this: "the President's got a rather substantial interest as to what might be in those papers," he said on March 6). The Judiciary Committee also secured affidavits from CREEP employees who had cooperated with the investigation, stating that their superiors knew almost immediately about their statements to the FBI. By March 13 the committee had heard enough and voted unanimously to invite Dean to testify. The Democrats indicated that Gray's nomination might be held hostage pending Dean's appearance. The next day, however, Dean declined to appear, although he agreed to accept written interrogatories.[6]

The President invoked executive privilege and adamantly opposed any public testimony by his aides. Speaking at his March 2 press conference, Nixon insisted that "no President" could ever allow his Counsel to testify before a congressional committee. Ten days later, he found an enlarged sanctuary in the separation-of-powers doctrine. He transformed separation and independence into unbridled autonomy, maintaining that the manner of exercising assigned executive powers is not subject to questioning by other branches. The fig leaf of executive privilege carried with it high moral purpose. Any questioning of presidential aides in effect impaired the President's "absolute confidence in the advice and assistance offered by the members of his staff." At another press conference several days afterward, Nixon conjured up a whole new doctrine of "double privilege" for John Dean: executive privilege plus lawyer-client privilege. In typical contradiction, Nixon insisted that Dean would be "completely forthcoming," unlike officials in "other Administrations." Watergate itself, he maintained, was a trifle—merely "espionage by one political organization against another." But in his memoirs, the President recalled that at that press conference, he suddenly realized: *"Vietnam had found its successor."*[7]

Gray kept in close touch with the White House throughout his nomination hearings. When he learned that the American Civil Liberties Union had submitted a statement to the Senate committee, protesting that the inquiry threatened the rights of potential defendants, the nominee was ecstatic. But he told John Ehrlichman in a taped March telephone conversation that "John Wesley"—Gray appropriated an almost reverential name for Dean—must "stand awful tight in the saddle and be very careful about what he says." Dean must say that he delivered everything developed by the White House investigation of the break-in to the FBI, Gray warned. All this he put on a note of knowing conspiracy: "I'm being pushed awfully hard in certain areas," he reminded Ehrlichman, "and I'm not giving an inch and you know those areas." In another conversation, Gray was bitter and sarcastic. He believed that Dean's claims for privilege were protected by "your god damn constitution," and then went on to complain because such protesters as the Berrigan brothers (Catholic priests active in the antiwar movement) had received kid-glove treatment. Finally, Gray assured Ehrlichman that he would tell the committee nothing more of their relationship than that they discussed "procedural" aspects of the investigation. Gray's records show that the two had had five telephone calls and two meetings. Ehrlichman was relieved to hear that no one asked whether he had initiated the meetings.

The Ehrlichman conversations confirmed Gray's instinct that he was in an adversarial position with the White House. What he did not believe then, and had great difficulty believing later, was that his good friend and patron, Richard Nixon, had ordered that relationship. But he did remember that John Dean had told him twice on June 21, 1972, at the outset of the investigation, that he, Dean, was reporting directly to the President. Dean, of course, exaggerated, but he was keeping Haldeman informed.[8]

The devious Ehrlichman quickly called Dean, and the two snickered about Gray's alleged toughness. His testimony, Dean said, "makes me gag." Ehrlichman wondered if Gray had called to "cover his tracks." He contemptuously dismissed Gray. Ehrlichman wanted Gray to just hang there; "let him twist slowly[,] slowly in the wind." Dean responded that those were exactly the sentiments of "the boss." The President, he claimed, had questioned Gray's ability to lead the Bureau, given the way he had conducted himself before the committee. The President himself decided that Gray was useless and expendable. Nixon told Dean on March 13 that Gray "should not be head of the FBI"; because of the hearings, Nixon added, "he will not be a good Director, as far as we are concerned."[9]

The low opinion of Gray within the President's immediate circle reflected frustration with his unwillingness to follow blindly White House directives. Dean complained to Nixon that too often Gray made "decisions on his own as to how to handle his hearings. He has been unwilling all along to take any guidance, any instruction." The President seemed mournful that not even Gray would give him the blind obedience he so desperately wanted. "He's stubborn," the President said, and "also he isn't very smart." In the next breath, however, Nixon allowed, "he's smart in his own way."[10]

If there were any doubts about Gray's fate, they were resolved on March 20 when he informed the Senate committee conducting hearings on his nomination that he had been ordered not to discuss the Watergate case any further. The White House sorely misgauged the determination of the senators, and Gray confronted an impossible situation.

Senator Robert Byrd, the Democratic Whip, bluntly warned the White House on March 19 that if Dean did not testify, Gray was doomed. Byrd proved to be a formidable antagonist, a rather ironic twist given his previous friendly relations with the President. On March 22, Byrd challenged Gray: was his first duty to the FBI or to the President?—a "tough question," as Gray characterized it. But he could not "evade" the fact that he took orders from the President. Gray even admitted he would continue to give Dean FBI reports if the President requested them. Byrd then elicited Gray's frank charge that Dean had lied when he had told FBI agents that he did not know whether Hunt had an office in the White House. Gray had broken contact with Dean by then, sensing that Dean had pushed beyond the bounds of propriety—and foolishly believing that the White House Counsel was an independent authority. Byrd's questions were devastating. They involved Gray's political speeches; his political uses of the FBI; his relations with the President, Dean, and other White House staff members; his conduct of the Watergate investigation; and his personal handling of evidence from Howard Hunt's safe.[11] The performance was a model of congressional interrogation— so incisive, in fact, that Byrd's substantive material and questions bore the mark of having originated in the FBI itself.

The White House's troubles were written all over the congressional walls. On March 27, three leading conservative Republican senators—James Buckley (NY), Norris Cotton (NH), and John Tower—implored the President and Dean to speak out and clarify matters. More liberal Republicans were alarmed. Minority Leader Hugh Scott (R–PA) complained that he was "deeply disturbed," and Marlow Cook (R–KY) thought the whole affair cast a "severe stigma on the Republican party." Gray's friend, Senator Lowell Weicker, the maverick Republican from Connecticut, demanded that Haldeman speak out. The Democrats, on the other hand, could afford a low profile. The President meanwhile authorized Scott to say in his name: "I have nothing to hide. The White House has nothing to hide."

But there was much to hide, and to borrow a favorite Nixon phrase, "losses had to be cut." The end mercifully came for Gray on April 5 when he asked that his name be withdrawn. This scenario had been contrived by the President. On March 27, Nixon had told Ehrlichman that Gray should come to the White House and say that lacking Senate unanimity and widespread trust, the President should withdraw his name and send another nominee in the same day. On April 4, the White House congressional liaison reported that Gray could not be confirmed. The Democrats, William Timmons warned, were anxious to vote out an unfavorable report on Gray in order to string out a floor debate and "kick him and the President around."

The next day the President directed Ehrlichman to have Gray make the public suggestion that his name be withdrawn. Suspecting that Gray had been sabotaged from within the Bureau, Nixon ordered it "cleaned out" at the top. Gray did his part, and the President's spokesman in San Clemente reported that Nixon had "regretfully" agreed to withdraw Gray's name. The presidential statement vigorously defended Dean's role and Gray's cooperation with the President's Counsel. When the President withdrew the nomination, he again obliquely assumed responsibility because of his orders to Dean to "conduct a thorough investigation." The President predictably lamented that Gray had been unfairly exposed to "innuendo and suspicion," thus unduly tarnishing his "fine record" and "promising future." A week later, Nixon instructed Ehrlichman to determine whether Supreme Court Justice Byron White might be interested in the FBI directorship. Perhaps he sensed that he would have to nominate a prestigious man, one independent of the President's will.

Gray was gone, the victim of the President's machinations and those of his aides, victimized also by Hoover loyalists in the FBI who eagerly leaked word of his activities. One of Hoover's closest retainers told the President's secretary that Pat Gray "was never the man for the job."[12]

On April 4, the day before Gray withdrew his nomination, Ehrlichman met with Judge Matthew Byrne, of the Federal District Court in Los Angeles. Kleindienst enthusiastically recommended Byrne, a Democrat, for the FBI directorship. Nixon liked the idea, and all agreed that Byrne should visit the President in San Clemente. At the moment Byrne was presiding over Daniel Ellsberg's criminal trial, but according to Ehrlichman the judge did not think it improper for him to discuss the FBI position while the trial was in progress. Kleindienst claimed that he warned Ehrlichman not to talk to Byrne. Ehrlichman's contemporary notes reveal that the President asked him to meet Byrne but not to discuss the pending case. Kleindienst did not believe that Ehrlichman fully informed Byrne of the purpose of the visit, and apparently no one else did either. Several weeks later, Byrne used the event as a basis for declaring a mistrial in the Ellsberg proceedings.[13] Byrne dropped out of contention for the FBI post, but once again, appearances of Administration wrongdoing dominated public memory.

The creation in early February of the Senate Select Committee investigating the 1972 campaign had caused barely a ripple of public attention. Reporters waited until near the end of the President's March 2 press conference to raise a rather polite Watergate question. But as John Dean's "containment" policy disintegrated against the backdrop of revelations unveiled in the Gray hearings, "Watergate" rapidly became a meaningful—and loaded—political term that spread across the nation, raising far-reaching political concerns. During March, White House reporters posed 478 questions to Press Secretary Ron Ziegler, who often seemed on the verge of tears or hysteria in his responses. "You don't have to accept this rationale," he snapped. "You can giggle if you like."[14]

The *Rockford* (IL) *Morning Star,* a Republican newspaper in America's heartland, in an April 2 editorial recognized the transformation of Watergate from an "imbecilic bugging" to "more and more a case of high level government dishonesty." The *Roanoke Times,* a prominent voice of Southern conservatism, had enthusiastically supported Gray's nomination on February 23, but as his role in a Watergate cover-up emerged, the newspaper concluded on March 22 that Gray was "not his own man; he is Mr. Nixon's, for that is what the White House insists on." That was enough for the newspaper to call for Gray's rejection.

No one better understood the shifting sands of public opinion than John Dean. He had determined that it was time for a direct, thorough discussion with the President of the United States. The President and his men had to confront their past—and their future.

Meanwhile the President had created a new layer to the cover-up. On March 12 he issued a blunt statement asserting the nature and broadening the power of executive privilege. Cloaking himself in precedents dating back to George Washington, Nixon argued that executive privilege was sanctioned by the Constitution's separation-of-powers doctrine and was necessary to protect internal communications of the executive branch regarding vital national concerns. He insisted that revelations of such communications threatened the candor of discussion and decision making. He pledged that executive privilege would not be invoked to prevent disclosures of "embarrassing information" but only to prevent disclosures harmful to the public interest.[15] The next day, however, the Senate Judiciary Committee challenged the President by "inviting" John Dean to testify at the Gray hearings.

Shortly after noon on March 13, Nixon met Dean and Haldeman to discuss new measures to divert attention from the Watergate affair. Dean described how potential witnesses might fare before the Ervin Committee, then scheduled to begin public hearings in two months. The three discussed asking William Sullivan to exploit his FBI connections for information on Democratic presidents' abuses of the FBI; they also speculated about a public-relations campaign to provide an appearance of openness and cooperation in any Watergate inquiry. The question of the President's cooperation—or pretense at cooperation—ran like a red thread throughout this meeting and the ones that followed over the next weeks. "I better hit now, . . . as tough as it is," Nixon told Dean. While it would be easier to "bug out," he preferred to "let it all hang out." The President knew he had to answer questions yet deny any White House complicity.

Nixon realized that Gray presented an immediate problem; his hearings had shaken the Administration's previously impenetrable calm. The President thought it might be best to delay the Gray hearings until after the Senate inquiry. In all probability, Gray then would be further damaged, thus giving the President an opportunity to withdraw the nomination. Clearly, Nixon by now had given up on Gray.

The Ervin Committee dominated the President's thoughts at the March 13 meeting. He asked Dean to summarize the potentially damaging witnesses. Dean thought that particularly vulnerable were Hugh Sloan, the CREEP treasurer, who had passed money to Liddy, and Herbert Kalmbach, Nixon's lawyer, who had provided hush money to the burglars. Nixon protested that Kalmbach, as his lawyer, merely handled some San Clemente property matters and his income tax—"he isn't a lawyer in the sense that most people have a lawyer."

At this point, Haldeman left the room; Dean, after all, had no surprising information for the Chief of Staff. The President and his Counsel then considered the Ervin Committee's likeliest targets. Nixon thought Mitchell and Haldeman to be the leading candidates; Dean added Ehrlichman to the list. The President particularly focused on the actions and knowledge of Haldeman's aides, knowing full well that whatever they knew or did in one way or another could be traced to Haldeman. But Dean said that the same people could be linked to Mitchell. The President seemed exasperated. "What a stupid thing. Pointless. That was the stupid thing." He then blurted: "[T]o think that Mitchell and Bob would allow, would have allowed this kind of operation. . . ." Mitchell *and* Bob, the President said; in time, he would have to disentangle the two. Mitchell was his *former* Attorney General, his *former* campaign manager, his *former* partner; Haldeman was here and now: he was too close. "The hang-out road's going to have to be rejected," Nixon concluded. Dean warned of a domino effect if people started to talk. "So there are dangers, Mr. President. I'd be less than candid if I didn't tell you the—there are. There's a reason for us . . . no—not everyone going up and testifying."[16]

Four days later, on March 17, the President returned to his recurrent theme that he needed a report from Dean on the Administration's investigation of Watergate, a report that would enable the President to go public, appear to be totally forthcoming, and affirm that the White House had no involvement in Watergate. Dean, however, was concerned over precisely that involvement, especially his own. He informed the President that he had been present when Mitchell, Magruder, and Liddy had discussed political-intelligence plans. Nixon saw no problem. His aides legally and necessarily had to discuss such operations because of the potential violence of the forthcoming political campaign. "We had to have intelligence . . . about what they were gonna do," he said. Indeed, given the necessity of such activity, the Administration could turn it to political advantage, the President perversely thought, since it had not used the FBI. "You can use them against demonstrations. But for political character [sic]," he solemnly stated, "the Bureau is never used."

When Dean told Nixon that Colson and Strachan (acting for Haldeman) had demanded more political intelligence, the President again seemed unperturbed. After all, he had repeatedly urged his aides to know the enemy and steal a march whenever they could. Again, Nixon acknowledged the vulnerability of Mitchell and Haldeman. But he always focused on the roles of others in planning or having knowledge of the break-in. On the surface, Nixon did not recognize that the deep involvement of the White House in the cover-up immediately following the break-in was the real problem. Or did he? Did he not realize that the task now was to cover up the cover-up— to "save the plan," as he often said? If that was to happen, sacrificial lambs would have to be prepared.

As the conversation concluded, Dean told the President about Ehrlichman's role in the break-in of the office of Daniel Ellsberg's psychiatrist. The President appeared stunned, even mystified, claiming that it was the first he had heard of the matter. "What in the world, what in the name of God was Ehrlichman having something [unintelligible] in the Ellsberg?" Nixon asked. Whatever the answer, the "hang-out road" now had to be even further circumscribed. Another key aide was vulnerable; another "horror" might be revealed. Furthermore, Dean told the President, the CIA had developed pictures Hunt had taken of Liddy in the doctor's office. Was the CIA, not exactly a reliable Nixon friend, wholly knowledgeable about that break-in? Perhaps not, but the Agency knew that Hunt had some illegal involvement. Here the President lost some of his aplomb, some of his sense of command. "It's irrelevant," he told Dean. Ervin had no business in the Ellsberg matter. Ervin had his "rules of relevancy"; "now what the hell has this got to do with it[?]"—meaning the Watergate break-in. More and more had to be contained, had to be covered up.[17]

It all proved too much for John Dean, who could cope no longer; the dominoes he had imagined had begun to totter. *He* had to let it all hang out. When Dean appeared in the Oval Office shortly after 10:00 A.M. on the morning of March 21, determined to share the growing problem with the President, Nixon tried to put him off until one o'clock that afternoon. Dean would not budge; he remained with the President for nearly two hours, and Haldeman joined them for approximately the last fifteen minutes. Immediately, Dean blurted out that the White House defenses had crumbled, and the "plan" had failed. Whatever the pending business, the President chose to listen to Dean, knowing that Dean was wavering in his commitment to the "plan."

Dean's recitation began with Haldeman's instruction that he establish "a perfectly legitimate campaign intelligence operation" at CREEP. John Caulfield first developed a plan, but Mitchell and Ehrlichman agreed with Dean that it was not suitable. Dean then suggested that they commission Gordon Liddy for the task. Liddy proposed several hare-brained and expensive schemes, which again were rejected, but he then enlisted Hunt as an ally. The two visited Colson who, in turn, pressed Magruder for action. Meanwhile Haldeman, through his aide, Gordon Strachan, similarly pressured Magruder for campaign intelligence. Magruder responded by turning to Mitchell and urging the campaign to authorize Liddy's plan to wiretap the Democratic National Committee. Mitchell agreed, and the fruits of the taps went to Strachan, who gave them to Haldeman.

Dean informed the President that Magruder ordered Liddy to make a second foray into the Watergate offices—and added that "no one over here knew that. I know, uh, as God is my maker, I had no knowledge that they were going to do this." The President, rather passive to this point, quickly began to question Dean on the extent of the Counsel's awareness of White House involvement. What about Bob Haldeman? the President asked. Dean carefully hedged, saying he did not believe the Chief of Staff "specifically" realized the source of the intelligence, although he charged that Strachan did. Haldeman knew of CREEP's "capacity" for illegal operations, but he "wasn't giving it specific direction."

Dean then turned to the events following the break-in, laughingly reminding the President that he was "under perfectly clear instructions not to really investigate this, that this was something that just could have been disastrous on the election if it had [*sic*], . . . and I worked on a theory of containment." However much Dean realized that his handiwork now was being undone, he spoke with pride of how well he had served the President. He described how he had monitored and even restrained FBI moves and noted his ability to secure grand-jury transcripts. John Dean had his own intelligence operation, which gave him a constant advantage. But there were blacker roles for him. Liddy had informed him that the Watergate defendants needed money for "living expenses." Herbert Kalmbach was enlisted to raise money, and he distributed it to the defendants through a committee and Hunt's lawyer. All that, Dean told the President, was "the most troublesome" thing, for it involved Haldeman, Ehrlichman, Mitchell, and also Dean himself in obstruction of justice. Again, Nixon was most concerned about Haldeman's involvement. Dean told him that Haldeman had authorized the use of a $350,000 cash reserve in his safe to pay the defendants. The President was not surprised, for he knew this from Haldeman himself. Dean carefully refrained from mentioning any presidential complicity in the obstruction of justice.

But the crunch had come, Dean told Nixon. The demands for living expenses had escalated into outright blackmail. Howard Hunt—that "romantic adventurer," as former CIA Director William Colby characterized him—had demanded $122,000 and threatened to destroy Ehrlichman if he did not get the money. According to Dean, Hunt passed the word that "I will bring John Ehrlichman down to his knees and put him in jail. Uh, I have enough seamy things for he [sic] and Krogh, uh, that they'll never survive it." The President asked Dean whether Hunt had referred to the Ellsberg break-in. Yes, Dean replied, Ellsberg "and apparently some other things." Nixon said he did not know of other things, although for at least four days, and probably more, he had certainly had knowledge of the break-in of Ellsberg's psychiatrist's office.

Dean focused on several key problems, particularly the vulnerability of the White House to continuing blackmail from the Watergate defendants, and officials' actions that compounded obstruction of justice. John Mitchell, he said, was "one of the ones with the most to lose." Meanwhile, Mitchell and his aide Fred LaRue were still trying to raise money from Nixon's longtime supporter, Thomas Pappas. The President already knew that. Money, however, seemed to be no problem. How much do you need, he asked Dean? A million dollars over the next two years, the Counsel replied. "We could get that," the President said. "[I]f you need the money, I mean, uh, you could get the money. . . . [Y]ou could get a million dollars. And you could get it in cash. I, I know where it could be gotten. . . . I mean it's not easy, but it could be done."

Throughout the discussion Dean talked of numerous problems and persons. Nixon apparently had little concern for sacrificing such pawns as Magruder, LaRue, Krogh, and Strachan. But Hunt concerned him deeply. Hunt was the "major guy to keep under control," he told Dean; Hunt knew much "about a lot of things." Dean added that Hunt could "sink" Colson; and Colson was too close to the President. "You've got to keep the cap on the bottle . . . in order to have any options," Nixon added. And then, rather wistfully, he remarked: "Either that or let it all blow right now." As if on cue, Dean interjected: "that, you know, that's the, the question." In other words, would the President resort to radical surgery, would he blow the cover-up and settle the affair once and for all?

It was not to be. Nixon backed away and asked Dean to tell him more about the problems of other principals. Dean tried to get back to "the question." He was concerned that the White House would now try to maintain the cover-up with blackmail money and perjury; then, "if this thing ever blows," Dean warned the President, "it'd be extremely damaging to you." Apparently Nixon did not appreciate the whole range of consequences, however, for he seemed to think that only "the whole concept of Administration justice" would be damaged. Whatever concerns he had for the "presidency" remained muted at this point. But Dean got him back on track, urging that he sit down with Haldeman, Ehrlichman, and Mitchell "to figure out how this thing can be carved away from you, so it does not damage you or the Presidency." Again, Nixon dodged the point, coming back to ask about Colson's role while reassuring Dean that he himself had no involvement in the plans for the break-in.

Dean reminded Nixon again of "soft spots" in the White House position and declared that he had no confidence "we can ride through this." He warned Nixon that aides were "pulling in," hiring counsel, and figuring " 'how do I protect my ass[?]'." Finally, Dean confessed that the Gray hearings had broken his own cover, and he no longer had the "facility" to handle things.

What was to be done? the President pleaded. Complete disclosure? "Isn't that the best plan?" Nixon asked. It was Dean's turn to dodge, for "complete disclosure" threatened him because of his role in the obstruction of justice. Dean wanted the President to ask for another grand jury, order the prosecutors to immunize witnesses, and sacrifice a few individuals. The lawyer-President seemed to have difficulty comprehending the point: "I don't see it. I can't see it," he said. He thought Dean simply had served as a proper President's Counsel; in any event, he seemed to think the matter could be handled easily enough. Suddenly, the President sounded satisfied with his prospects. "Sometimes it's well to give them . . . something, and then they don't want the bigger fish then." And just as quickly, he realized that blackmail money still would have to be paid—"it would seem to me that would be worthwhile," Nixon said. He speculated about clemency for the convicted burglars but dismissed the idea as politically untenable.

Both men sensed with sadness the inextricable web they had woven. Dean spoke of the "burden" on the second Administration. "It's something that is not going to go away, sir." Nixon agreed, but thought people might "get tired of it." No, anything would "spark it back into life," Dean said, and then pushed the President to consider action that would cut losses, "minimize the further growth of this thing," and stop the need to pay blackmail money. But after Dean raised the possibility of indictments for Haldeman (because of the break-in connection) and Ehrlichman (because of the Ellsberg case), Nixon sensed the greater danger to himself. It would be better, he said, "to fight it out, and not let people testify." Still, he knew there were "mine fields down the road." It was time, the President and Dean decided, for all of the key principals to meet to discuss future strategy—Haldeman, Ehrlichman, Mitchell, Dean, and the President.

Haldeman appeared near the end of the meeting. He and the President agreed that Colson—who alone rivaled Haldeman in access to Nixon's political confidences—could not be trusted to keep silent. Magruder was another weak link. Haldeman seemed worried and doubtful about maintaining the cover-up. But the President firmly believed that matters could be satisfactorily settled. Again, he said it would require a million dollars "to take care of the jackasses that are in jail." That could be arranged with no problems. Clemency, he knew, was another matter, and Hunt's patience was on the line, for Colson apparently had promised Hunt he would be out of jail by Christmas. Meanwhile, the President thought Dean had no choice but to pay Hunt. There was another course, however. Let Hunt and the others talk, the President said; "that would be the, the clean way," he added. Then he would order another grand jury, where the principals would testify but selectively employ "I don't recall" answers and the Fifth Amendment. The President liked to spin out hypotheticals: "How about a special prosecutor?" he asked.

The unmistakable pessimism that began the meeting resumed its grip at the end. The President, who usually summed up discussions, understood the matter very well. If Hunt talked, Ehrlichman, Colson, Mitchell, and others would fall. If the cover-up continued and eventually broke, "it'll look like the President"—Dean finished the point: ". . . is covering up." The risks were high, very high. Amazingly, the President believed that Dean could still take care of things. Dean, after all, had come up with the right plan before the election. He handled "it" just right; he "contained it." Now, the President said, Dean had to come up with another plan, one that would last four years. The Administration could not be "eaten away" for the remainder of its term. "We can't do it," he said with finality. Watergate was not a major concern, Nixon believed, but sadly, even prophetically, he added, "it will be. It's bound to be."[18]

The morning meeting adjourned with agreement on further talks among those at the center of the circled wagons: the President, Haldeman, Ehrlichman, and Dean. The four resumed the discussion at 5:20 on the same afternoon. Ehrlichman offered another circle metaphor: "you go round and round and you come up with all questions and no answers. Backed up where you were at when you started." Altogether, a sense of siege pervaded the discussion, heavily freighted with confusion and disarray among the principals. The President himself vacillated between tactics of delay (a presidential panel to investigate the matter), continued efforts at containment (payoffs, perjury)—or, he added (borrowing from General Ulysses S. Grant), they could "keep fighting it out on this ground if it takes all summer."

Dean remained anxious that everyone testify to the grand jury under immunity, assuming that in this fashion the facts would come out and those involved would suffer little damage. Ehrlichman apparently suspected that the "enemies" would want blood, as close to the top as possible—meaning his own. He opposed anything that might bring indictments for White House personnel. Ehrlichman proposed that the White House prepare several internal reports summarizing what the President knew about the scandal, turn them over to the Ervin Committee, and rely on Howard Baker to keep the investigation limited to a few specific issues. If any additional information appeared, the President could maintain he had been misinformed.

But Ehrlichman knew that the immediate problem involved Hunt. He favored continuing the pattern of containment and blackmail and ultimately giving Hunt a pardon. Nixon tentatively agreed, yet wondered whether Hunt might get clemency from the court if he talked. Dean warned the President that that was a real possibility; he outlined exactly the scenario that James McCord, not Howard Hunt, had initiated the day before. Dean then contemptuously sneered at those (Colson, Kalmbach, Chapin) who had hired criminal lawyers "to protect their own behinds . . . ; self-protection is setting in." Ten days later, Dean himself called a prominent criminal lawyer, disingenuously telling Haldeman that he needed someone to "figure out what everybody else's criminal liabilities are." [19]

Dean in effect reciprocated Ehrlichman's rejection of his grand-jury idea by leveling Ehrlichman's suggestion of preparing internal reports. Ehrlichman's plan had the virtue of most heavily implicating Dean; the President and his favored men apparently did not realize at that point that Dean would not let himself go down alone. Dean defended his grand-jury idea as the quickest way of dealing with the problem and probably the best way to protect the President. If the cover-up continued, after what the President himself described as "stonewalling," and if the case then "blew," the President was in real danger.

Dean's theory steered the discussion into the question of just who would go to jail. Awareness of possible criminal liability jolted the conversation back to the easiest course of all: continuing the cover-up. All agreed that Hunt must be paid, and the President offered to make a public statement promising cooperation with the Ervin Committee and an internal investigation to quiet growing concern. Dean warned, however, that these were merely stopgap arrangements, again stressing that the story would eventually become public knowledge. That route, Haldeman exclaimed, held out "a certainty, almost, of Magruder going to jail, Chapin going to jail, you going to jail . . . [and] probably me going to jail." Soothingly, the President responded: "I question the last two."

As the discussion trailed off, Nixon seemed to offer his closest attention to his young Counsel. For whatever reason, Dean was the only aide present who voiced concern about protecting the President. Naturally, he wanted to limit his own criminal liability, but Haldeman and Ehrlichman more blatantly expressed that concern for themselves. Dean, of course, had become a public target; because of the Gray hearings, he was far more exposed at the moment than the other two. Neither the press nor Senate investigators had focused as much on them as they had on Dean. Clearly, the two senior aides believed that continuing the cover-up and offering limited public statements presented their own best course. Dean sensed at this point that Haldeman and Ehrlichman ultimately might isolate him. After the meeting broke up, Dean told Richard Moore (who had urged him to speak to the President) that "all of a sudden my two friends, Haldeman and Ehrlichman, don't know anything about all of this." Dean also informed his associate Fred Fielding that he saw problems because others refused to admit their complicity.

Self-interest abounded at the meeting. The President operated on his own level. Typically, his backing and filling covered the range of options, as he probed the feelings of others and tried to find the most secure ground for himself. He talked about ending the cover-up, but he was unwilling to take the risk that entailed. Dean's strategy had its appeal to Nixon, but could this most distrusting of men trust others to fall on their swords for him? Familiar Nixon tactics sifted through these conversations: fostering division within his own ranks, and working to maintain the compartmentalization that was the essence of his style. Perhaps he believed that dividing and separating his counselors on tactics and strategy would keep them from uniting against him. But his calculations did not take into account the instinct for self-protection.[20]

On the night of March 21, 1973, two hours after his Oval Office meetings had ended, the President turned to a different compartment: Charles Colson, a man always ready with fresh intelligence and a singular point of view. Nixon appreciated Colson's special knack for "dealing" with things. In a telephone conversation that night, Colson eagerly reported to the President that he had met with Howard Baker's administrative assistant, who claimed "that Howard really wants to [be] with us totally." Baker wanted the President to know "that he wasn't getting off the reservation"—a statement repeated twice by Baker's man. The White House, the aide said, could ignore Baker's comments on the Senate floor critical of the Administration; "Howard regrets them," Colson reported. But Baker had to maintain his "credibility" with Ervin in order to negotiate effectively with him, hold him "at bay," and "control him." Baker had to "act like one of the Senate club," lest he destroy his effectiveness with Ervin. Baker's frustration stemmed from his desire to be the President's defender while appearing to be disinterested. Meanwhile, he complained that he had been unable to secure a good communication channel to the White House. The aide insisted that Baker wanted to help—to "go all the way and work with us and . . . defend you and the Republican Party." Baker took the Senate Select Committee assignment because he believed he could serve those causes. The President wanted to know whether Baker understood Ervin. According to

Colson, Baker thought Ervin bordered on senility and he was phony, and Baker had no respect for him.

Perhaps Ervin could be dismissed lightly, but the President sensed other dangers. "How about the [Ervin Committee's] Counsel—he is not senile. That is a problem there[,] isn't it?" Colson knew about Samuel Dash. No, Colson reported, Dash was not senile, and he was anxious to make a name for himself.

The President's problems, however, were more immediate than those posed by Ervin, Dash, and a Senate investigating committee. "What is your judgment as to what ought to be done now?" Nixon asked Colson. Colson assured the President that he was "not being hurt by this at all. This is a Washington story still. . . . I am convinced that is so." Nixon relayed Dean's concerns about the future, a cue for Nixon to praise Dean's "superb job here keeping all the fires out" and for Colson to laud his "spectacular job— I don't think anybody could do as good a job as John has done." Colson realized that Dean could be charged with obstruction of justice, but he planted an idea Nixon later adopted, that Dean had the double protection of executive privilege and lawyer-client privilege.

Colson's solution for the President's mounting woes was to appoint a "special counsel," someone with "impeccable credentials," "integrity," "standing before the Bar," "totally loyal" (to whom or what, Colson did not say), a "damn good lawyer," and "a highly respected guy." The President responded with some enthusiasm:

PRESIDENT: The ideal guy would be Fortas if he hadn't been involved.
COLSON: Well[,] he's bound and tied— . . . he would be very good.
PRESIDENT: He's what you need.
COLSON: Well—that's right. Another fellow that I thought about is
[J. Lee] Rankin [former Solicitor General]—he is highly respected.
PRESIDENT: [Judge Lawrence] Walsh.
COLSON: Yeah—Walsh.

The two men also talked of Hunt. The conversation was elliptical, yet both seemed to know the stakes. Nixon thought that Hunt had "problems if he does anything. . . . You know what I mean—he's . . ." Colson interrupted and said that Hunt would not "hang in where he is" unless something else was keeping him there. In the meantime, both knew they could expect trouble from Judge Sirica, who already had McCord's letter. But Colson was not fazed. The President thought it better to deal with the judge and a grand jury than with the Senate investigating committee. And yet, they both knew that it would be politically difficult to invoke executive privilege in the secret sanctuary of the grand jury. Nixon thought a "bland" public statement from him, citing ongoing investigations and like actions, would be worthwhile. Colson assured him that he was "in the right posture at the moment."[21]

* * *

That same night, the President taped his thoughts about the day—one he described as "relatively uneventful except for the, uh, talk with Dean." He recalled the reference to a "cancerous growth," Dean's discussion of his own criminal liability, the report that some of the aides were seeking their own lawyers, and Haldeman's concern that Magruder was a weak link. He recorded his judgment that Haldeman had made a terrible mistake in selecting Magruder, a man who lacked character when the "chips are down." Haldeman had made few mistakes, but Nixon said this was one case where his secretary, "Rose [Mary Woods,] was right." Nixon liked Dean's grand-jury idea, but he acknowledged that Haldeman and Ehrlichman, after discussing the idea between themselves, effectively vetoed the suggestion.

"I feel for all of the people involved here, because they were all . . . involved for the best of motives," the President recorded. He then reviewed the sequence of events that led to the Watergate bugging, focusing mainly on Colson's insistence that Magruder and Liddy gain useful information about the Democrats. And, also for the record, the President disingenuously noted that for the first time he learned that Ehrlichman had sent Hunt and his crew to check on Ellsberg. (Throughout this period, Nixon either feigned surprise when that subject was raised or justified the action in national-security terms.) Ehrlichman had told him that he himself "was three or four steps away" from involvement, but that Egil Krogh had a "problem." The President felt sorry for Krogh, who was only trying to do something "helpful." He also praised Dean for maintaining vigilance against "every loose end that might come out." John Mitchell would join further discussions in the morning, and the President hoped that his former law partner and Attorney General might have wisdom on "some sort of a course of action we can follow." Something had to be done, Nixon realized—"just to hunker down without making any kind of a statement is really, uh, too dangerous as far as the President. . . ."[22] The fragment trailed off, but the candor was exceptional. The "President," not the "presidency," was endangered.

"Uneventful," the President called his day—a rare understatement.

The March 21 discussions were an overture to the series of meetings that began the next day and continued into April. Much of that time was spent maneuvering John Mitchell and his CREEP aides into position to take responsibility for Watergate, leaving the White House entourage relatively immune. But that scenario had been devised before the President heard Dean's "cancer" exposé on the twenty-first. The evening before, Nixon and Haldeman met for more than an hour. They knew that McCord had offered to talk; accordingly, they mapped their own strategy.

Nixon realized that he would have to offer a public statement on what he knew and on what his aides did or did not do. But there were limits: "it isn't that we are afraid of facts, we certainly are afraid of publicity," he said. But he *was* afraid of facts—of the perjury that some had committed (Magruder, "that son-of-a-bitch") and the payments to Hunt and the other defendants. The President went on to curse the futility of the break-in. Colson had told him that he had "all sorts of stuff" on the Democrats, but it turned out to be "not a God damned thing," Nixon complained, more in disappointment than in criticism.

Haldeman thought that Dean's containment plan still could work. Liddy, "a little bit nuts and a masochist," could be relied on to keep silent, while others would do so because of the payments they would receive. Haldeman felt that the President's aides could be protected with executive privilege. Both Nixon and Haldeman believed that Ehrlichman posed a problem, however, not for what he knew about Watergate, but for the break-in of Daniel Ellsberg's psychiatrist's office. Haldeman suggested that key aides should prepare statements for publication in the *Washington Star,* but Nixon objected—"open[s] too many doors." He would issue a statement, perhaps a general one, expressing confidence in his staff and basing it on "the Dean report"—a nonexistent document to be conjured up when convenient. But both men were sensitive to the danger of saying that any truth was "the whole truth." "Never, never, never," the President emphasized. At this point Nixon acknowledged a dependence on Dean for making the right legal moves: "Dean's the expert here," he said. Nixon, supposedly the wise political veteran, relied on a thirty-five-year-old neophyte: the situation veered between the absurd and the tragic.

At one key point in their March 20 meeting, Haldeman shifted the conversation to his own fate. "What bothers me," he told the President, "is that I still think I'm being tarred in order to protect some other people." The press then was attacking Gordon Strachan and Dwight Chapin, both of whom were linked, correctly, to Haldeman. But the press wanted "bigger fish"—specifically, as Haldeman figured, Colson and Mitchell. No one, Haldeman knew, believed that Jeb Magruder had acted on his own to authorize Liddy and Hunt's activities. The President quickly covered for Colson, asserting his conviction that Colson had no prior knowledge of the Watergate break-in. Nixon and Haldeman both believed that Mitchell had an interest in maintaining the cover-up because of his own complicity in— or at least awareness of—the plan. "No question about that," Haldeman emphasized. The stage was set for Mitchell to play his part.[23]

Nixon and Haldeman resumed their conversation for nearly ninety minutes on the morning of March 22. First, Haldeman briefed the President on his use of $350,000 in campaign contributions to pay the defendants. Haldeman had directed Dean to channel the money to Strachan, who in turn gave it to Mitchell's aide and friend at CREEP, Fred LaRue. The money had been collected since 1968 and had initially been set aside by Haldeman for taking polls and surveys. Nixon argued that none of this constituted an obstruction of justice (as Dean had contended it did) and that the funds were not covered by the recent campaign-financing laws. The two connived at formulating alibis and explanations for the origins of the funds, but their use was the real question. Was it an obstruction of justice—was it blackmail—to pay the defendants? The President insisted that he would not be blackmailed: it was "right" to pay. "God damn it, the people are in jail, it's only right for people to raise the money for them. I got to let them do that and that's all there is to it. I think we ought to. . . . [W]e're taking care of these people in jail. My God, they did this for—we're sorry for them. We do it out of compassion. . . . What else should we do?" More a plea than a question, it seemed. But the bottom line was that the President agreed to blackmail payments.

And how would others be kept in line? Magruder could not be trusted— "he's not a Liddy type," Haldeman warned; "he's exactly the opposite," meaning, of course, that he might have much to say to the prosecutors. Haldeman complained that Magruder was a man "loaded with ego, personal pride, political ambition," as if berating himself for not having sensed or tempered those egregious qualities.

Hunt's threat to expose Ehrlichman's role in the Fielding break-in rankled. Whenever the subject arose, Nixon hesitated to speak of what he called the "Ellsberg affair" and acted uninformed. "[W]hat happened?" he asked Haldeman—and proceeded to get a report on the operation and its purpose as if this were the first time he had heard the tale. The sordid story only deepened the gloom about how the White House could deal with Hunt.

The conversation eventually settled on the paramount problem: how to "circle the wagons around the White House" and protect the President and his closest aides. Dean had told Haldeman that the only culpability of the White House was for its protection of CREEP officials. As if on cue, the President responded: "Mitchell, Magruder." Haldeman reiterated: "The White House has no guilt in the Watergate thing." The skids were greased for John Mitchell.

Mitchell's "awfully close to you," Haldeman said, as if to prod the President, but getting only a grunting "Yeah." In the terms of an old political saw, Haldeman was a man who "seen his opportunities and took 'em." Mitchell no longer was as close to the President as Ehrlichman, himself, and, now, Dean had become. Proximity was power and influence. Besides, Haldeman said, "Mitchell will find a way out." Still, he told Nixon, "you have to let them get to him, I think." Dean's strategy, Haldeman continued, forced Mitchell "to take the responsibility rather than allowing Mitchell to

hide under the blanket of the White House, which he's been doing." Dean
was certain that Mitchell could take care of himself, Haldeman reassured
the President. The President hesitated a bit: "They'll kill him. . . . They'll
convict him," he told his aide; but then he quickly charted a legal strategy
he believed would save Mitchell. Nearly five years of internecine struggle
by Haldeman and Ehrlichman against Mitchell had now come down to a
tactic redolent of betrayal.[24]

At 2:00 P.M. on March 22, the President assembled Haldeman, Ehrlichman,
Mitchell, and Dean and asked, "[W]hat, uh, words of wisdom do we have
from this august body on this point?" Rather sarcastically, Ehrlichman remarked that "our brother Mitchell" had brought some wisdom on the matter
of executive privilege. Mitchell seemed to sense his vulnerability and cautioned his erstwhile law partner that the more he waived executive privilege,
the less it was worth. He urged tough negotiations with Senator Ervin,
through Howard Baker, and he recommended organizing "a damn good PR
team" in order to avoid "a political roadshow." Given his vulnerabilities,
Ehrlichman heartily endorsed Mitchell's advice. Haldeman worried that any
testimony might indicate that "the President was involved"—certainly an
uncomfortable possibility for him, as well.

Mitchell also thought that the Ervin investigation could be contained, if
the White House preempted the field with its own account of events, based
on FBI documentation. Dean conceded the necessity of a report but warned
it would be difficult; no report from him could be "complete." Ehrlichman
observed, "it's a negative setting for us." The President nevertheless decided to dispatch Dean for a weekend at Camp David to write a report and
"carefully put down that this individual, that individual . . . were not involved." Dean and Mitchell feared such a report would compromise the
rights of the Watergate defendants; Ehrlichman and Haldeman thought not,
because it would deal only with White House involvement. Dean urged that
the report be submitted to Ervin but not be made public—as if in that time
of wholesale leaks, such a report would have remained confidential for long.
Losing touch with reality became contagious. If any "new development"
occurred, Ehrlichman thought the report would enable the President to say
later that he did not know, and he could "fire A, B, C, and D."

Who would testify before the Ervin Committee? Haldeman knew the committee wanted "big fish," meaning that he and Ehrlichman could not avoid
an appearance. He seemed confident they could handle things. Clearly, everyone appeared anxious to keep Dean away from the committee: his vulnerability was the vulnerability of all. There was talk of the lawyer-client
relationship to give him further protection.

The idea of a Dean Report took on a magical promise, for it would be the way in which the White House would say that John Dean had revealed everything. Nixon in particular envisioned the report as the ultimate defense barrier. His immediate aides concurred, perhaps more in wish than in thought. But Dean knew better:

PRESIDENT: You think, you think we want to, want to go this route now? And the—let it hang out, so to speak?

DEAN: Well, it's, it isn't really that—

HALDEMAN: It's a limited hang out.

DEAN: It's a limited hang out.

EHRLICHMAN: It's a modified limited hang out.

PRESIDENT: Well, it's only the questions of the thing hanging out publicly or privately.

DEAN: What it's doing, Mr. President, is getting you up above and away from it. And that's the most important thing.

PRESIDENT: Oh, I know. But I suggested that the other day and we all came down on, uh, remember we came down on, uh, on the negative on it. Now what's changed our mind?

DEAN: The lack of alternatives, or a body. (Laughter)

EHRLICHMAN: We, we went down every alley. (Laughter). . . .

The President thought the Dean Report indispensable, and "if it opens doors, it opens up doors, you know." When Ehrlichman sarcastically said that Mitchell was "sorry" he had sent the burglars in, the President joined in the little joke, and Mitchell responded, "[Y]ou are very welcome, sir." The resultant laughter sounded nervous, even hollow.

Deferentially, almost, the President thanked Mitchell and Dean for carrying a heavy load. Dean was singled out for a special presidential commendation. After all, he "put the fires out" and "almost got the damn thing nailed down" till past the election. Nixon wavered between confidence and cheerleading. More would come out, but "we will survive it," he assured everyone. "That's the way you've got to look at it." But he quickly added, "get the God damn thing over with." He reviewed the "game plan": hold the line on executive privilege, and make the Dean Report the framework for any outside investigations.

The President concluded the session by drawing his own historical lessons from the Sherman Adams episode in the Eisenhower Administration and from the Alger Hiss affair. Adams, who had been Eisenhower's Chief of Staff, had improperly accepted a gift from a friend and subsequently intervened in his behalf with a federal agency. Eisenhower commissioned Nixon to fire Adams, a chore Nixon later described with distaste, contending that Adams had not done anything to merit dismissal. (In truth, Nixon had urged Eisenhower to act decisively and dismiss Adams.)

The Adams and Hiss affairs ran like threads throughout the President's conversations in his moments of greatest adversity. But he skewed facts, and the lessons gleaned always seemed curious, even twisted. Nixon talked forcefully of the need that a president loyally support subordinates who make honest mistakes, strongly implying that he would stand by his men. As for Hiss, Nixon repeatedly argued that if he only had admitted his association with Whittaker Chambers and had not covered it up, thereby perjuring himself, and if Truman had cooperated and not stonewalled congressional investigators, nothing would have happened. Thus Richard Nixon interpreting history and applying its lessons: "I don't give a shit what happens," he defiantly told his men. "I want you all to stonewall it, let them plead the Fifth Amendment, cover-up or anything else, if it'll save the plan. That's the whole point."

Did Nixon then suddenly remember that Oval Office conversations were taped? Perhaps, for he quickly shifted gears. He preferred, he said, to "do it the other way." Tell it all now—before leaks, charges, and innuendoes made things worse. The guilty must step forward. But he was not yet prepared to push "the other way." Indeed, in the next breath, the President reverted to his conspiratorial ways. Work on Howard Baker, he urged. Mitchell complained that it was difficult to establish a liaison with Baker, for the Senator believed that his phone was tapped. Nixon was incredulous. Who would tap Baker? he asked, apparently secure in the belief that he had not done the like himself. He immediately answered his own question: Ervin. Perhaps Nixon believed that, but the talk really was trivial. The President's final order could not be clearer: "Again," he said, "you really have to protect the Presidency, too."[25] Not for the last time did Nixon bind the interest of the "Presidency" to that of the "President."

Three days after Judge Sirica read McCord's confessional letter in open court, the *New York Times* revealed that the former CIA agent had implicated White House and CREEP officials in the Watergate break-in and that there were hints and promises of further disclosures that would expand the stories of official wrongdoing. McCord had spoken to Sirica, to the federal prosecutors, and to Sam Dash, the recently appointed Counsel to the Ervin Committee. "Scot free—a hero," the President remarked bitterly. Bob Woodward, a *Washington Post* reporter, visited the President's Assistant Press Secretary on March 27, charging that Watergate involved a wider conspiracy than hitherto believed. He asked for an interview with the President to discuss the facts.[26]

That day, nearly a week after Dean's lengthy session with the President, the inner defense circle had been altered. Now, as Nixon considered his most crucial decisions, his Counsel was no longer present. Dean had been sent to Camp David to compose a report, but he knew that such a document would implicate everyone, from the President down. No Dean Report was written.[27] In Dean's absence, the President, Haldeman, Ehrlichman, and Ziegler decided that John Mitchell would serve the presidency and the President as he had never imagined.

Richard Nixon later mourned that he was not a "good butcher" (William Gladstone's first requirement for a Prime Minister); but, in retrospect, his work indeed resembled the deft cuttings of a skilled surgeon; Nixon knew precisely whom to cut and how. At the outset, he told his aides he did not want the staff dividing and accusing one another. "The point is [,] what's done is done. We do the very best we can, and cut our losses," he stated. Haldeman reported that Magruder was claiming that the entire intelligence operation had originated in the White House with Haldeman and Dean. Both Haldeman and Ehrlichman emphasized to the President that Dean had no such involvement and that Haldeman had pressed only for better intelligence, without providing specific instructions. Magruder already had lied to the grand jury and now seemed very eager to clear himself. But everyone knew that Magruder inexorably led to Mitchell.

Mitchell could solve everything. Haldeman reported a CREEP lawyer as saying that "Mitchell could cut this whole thing off, if he would just step forward and cut it off." For the moment, the President let the remark pass, but he knew that it was the only solution, and that securing Mitchell's cooperation would be difficult. He was sure Mitchell would never admit perjury or his role in the origins of the break-in and the cover-up, even if the prosecutors gave him immunity. Haldeman thought that Mitchell would be offered immunity only if the prosecutors believed he could lead them to the President. Mitchell was higher than anyone else the prosecutors had pursued. Indeed, he was "the big Enchilada," as Ehrlichman added.

The President suggested inviting Mitchell and Magruder for a talk. Perhaps Magruder could be persuaded to take sole responsibility. Nixon again resorted to his Hiss-Chambers touchstone experience. Hiss had been destroyed because he had lied; but Chambers, too, Nixon said, was destroyed because he had been an informer. What did that have to do with anything? It certainly did not offer Magruder any promising options; either way, if Nixon's history lesson was relevant, he would be destroyed. Still, they devised a script for Magruder to follow, whereby he would appear before the grand jury, gain immunity, and admit he had lied earlier of his own volition. John Dean, in fact, had coached Magruder in preparation for his perjured testimony.

But Nixon, Haldeman, and Ehrlichman realized the importance of protecting the President's Counsel. Magruder was only a "little fish" in the public eye; the President's inner circle knew they had to serve up a "big fish." They believed that the U.S. Attorney would grant Magruder immunity in order to get to Mitchell. Haldeman sounded gleeful: "The interesting thing . . . would be to watch Mitchell's face at the time I, I recommend to Magruder that he go down and ask for immunity and confess." Haldeman displayed boldness and confidence, and why not: Mitchell was the expendable, vulnerable one, not himself. Ehrlichman, perhaps a bit shrewder than Haldeman (and also more vulnerable and expendable), was not so certain that "the thing will hold together." That was after he made sure that the President was protecting *him* on the Ellsberg matter with a "national security tent over the whole operation." "I sure will," the President promised.[28]

Haldeman summoned John Dean from Camp David the next day. Dean had no report. Haldeman later said that this was because the document would have made "a tighter and tighter noose around John's neck"—a rather disingenuous remark for one who controlled Dean with a short leash. Dean sensed some important changes in his master. Haldeman wanted him to see Mitchell and Magruder to coordinate his story with theirs. Dean claimed that both men still wanted him to protect their stories, even after Mitchell admitted his complicity in the formulation of the break-in plans. Dean remained a useful go-between for the Oval Office and those outside. The day after the key March 22 meeting, Nixon told Ehrlichman that Dean had "done [a] superb job," given his heavy load.[29] Whatever his motivation—to save his skin, to save the President, to acknowledge the futility of more lying— John Dean knew that he could no longer contain the scandal. His circle had closed and he needed his own wagons. Dean hired a criminal lawyer.

Richard Nixon himself was running perilously close to the time when he must talk—or it might be too late. Barry Goldwater pleaded with the President—"a valued friend and leader"—to be forthcoming. It was time, he told Nixon on March 29, "probably past time, that you either make public disclosures yourself relative to the Watergate or allow some of your men to make statements themselves to clear up what I know to be lies and misstatements." Goldwater warned Nixon that prominent Republicans throughout the nation were uneasy and restless.[30] If Goldwater believed that the President and his men had lied, then indeed the President was in trouble. But Nixon preferred his own options: stonewalling, modified limited hang outs, sacrificial lambs. He remained confident that he could get his house in order as April approached. But truly, for him it became the "cruelest month."

XII

"WE HAVE TO PRICK THE GODDAM BOIL AND TAKE THE HEAT."

CUTTING LOOSE:
APRIL 1973

April found the embattled President and his staff confronted with mounting criticism and ever-more-formidable inquiries. On April 1, Senator Lowell Weicker of the Select Committee demanded that Haldeman explain his ties to the President's re-election committee. Three days later, Weicker admitted that he had no evidence of criminal involvement on Haldeman's part, but the implication had been planted. *Der treue* Gordon Liddy received an additional jail term for contempt of court because he refused to answer the Ervin Committee's questions, but news leaked that James McCord had had a great deal to say to Senate investigators, including particulars about the roles of John Mitchell, John Dean, Jeb Magruder, and Charles Colson in the Watergate incident. Weicker warned reporters that they had uncovered only a small fraction of what McCord had revealed and that they would miss significant stories if they focused exclusively on the Watergate break-in. Sam Ervin, meanwhile, made it clear that he would challenge the President's extravagant claims of executive privilege in order to gain the testimony of key White House aides. The trickle of Watergate news in March swelled into a rampaging stream.

Richard Nixon and his advisers faced inward. Critics—from both parties—dominated congressional commentary; the Senate investigation widened in scope; a Republican judge, noted for his admiration of Nixon, charged that the White House had covered up criminal activities; the Department of Justice and the U.S. Attorney's office carefully cultivated distance from the President; and that ever-familiar "enemy," the media, seemed determined to make prophecy out of Spiro Agnew's well-remembered criticism. Nixon's patterns of compartmentalization no longer were adequate; instead, he had to turn exclusively to his most intimate and loyal retainers—and decide how to use them in his own struggle for survival.

Haldeman was worried about his future. He and the President had nothing but contempt for Jeb Magruder, contempt and a dread that Margruder was weak and would drag others down. They feared that Magruder would break under pressure from the prosecutors. Nixon had asked John Ehrlichman to maintain watch over John Dean, who, in turn, was supposed to keep an eye on Magruder. Dean himself had had lawyers in touch with the prosecutors since April 5. Trust within the circle was cracking.

At the beginning of April, the President and his aides talked about Dean, describing him as "personally innocent." But on April 4, Nixon and Ehrlichman considered the possibility that if Dean testified, he might implicate Haldeman. "Splash," Ehrlichman noted in his minutes.[1]

Dean told Ehrlichman that Earl Silbert and the U.S. Attorney's office knew Magruder had perjured himself in earlier testimony to the prosecutors. Nixon and Ehrlichman obviously had prepared for this eventuality. Ehrlichman had suggested that Magruder simply tell Silbert he had "refreshed" his memory. On April 8 the President urged Ehrlichman to push Magruder in that direction. But events had overtaken plans. Dean had learned—undoubtedly from his lawyer—that the prosecutors had larger concerns: what higher authorities had initiated and approved the Watergate break-in? Dean's advice was "to let it flow"; Nixon and Ehrlichman agreed. Nixon tried to be confident about the security of the White House, telling Ehrlichman that if Magruder "pull[ed] the plug," he would do so on Mitchell, not Haldeman.[2]

Two days later Magruder and his lawyer began extended discussions with Silbert leading to a confession and a plea bargain. The deal was struck on April 14, but a day earlier, Haldeman delegated his top aide, Larry Higby—popularly known as "Haldeman's Haldeman"—to sound out Magruder. Magruder told Higby that the U.S. Attorney's office would get all the facts, but Haldeman, he assured Higby, would have "no problem." Mitchell, Dean, and Liddy had problems, but not Haldeman, Magruder insisted. Magruder seemed terribly anxious not to incur Haldeman's wrath, perhaps believing that he and the President might yet provide absolution. Higby drew the lines: "I've been on the periphery of this God damned thing and it—to my knowledge you never did talk to Haldeman about any of this kind of bullshit." Magruder frantically agreed—only afterward, he said, did he speak to Haldeman. Higby pressed hard. Did Liddy ever relay any instructions from Haldeman? Any indication that Haldeman "had ever seen anything?"

The President? "Shit [,] no," Magruder exclaimed, and hastily added that
he would not say anything "that will . . . implicate the President of the
United States in anything." Higby repeated the line of questioning several
times, probing again and again for any sign of weakness.[3]

Just in case Magruder changed his mind, Higby—and Haldeman—had his
promise on tape.

Magruder kept his word. His discussions with the prosecutors confined
Watergate matters to Mitchell and the CREEP operation, keeping the White
House free from involvement. Magruder's testimony provided the President
and his top aides with a new opportunity to contain the inquiry and ward
off any further assaults on their position. The very day that Magruder finished his negotiations with Silbert, Nixon, Haldeman, and Ehrlichman devised a convoluted plan to convince Mitchell to assume responsibility for
the whole affair.

Passing strange that on that same day Ehrlichman gave the President a
"report" paralleling Magruder's story, and minimizing the activity of the
White House in the initiation of the break-in or its subsequent cover-up.
Ehrlichman's version focused on John Mitchell and his zealous aides—
Magruder, Liddy, and various CREEP officials and lawyers—who had
"misinterpreted" White House requests (from Haldeman and Colson)
for intelligence, planned and executed the break-in, and then sought to cover
up their activities. Except for Mitchell's request to Dean that the White
House help raise money for the defendants, the report flatly stated, no Administration personnel had knowledge "of any specific acts of obstruction
of justice or sought to procure any person's testimonial silence."

Nixon must have been bemused, for he, of course, had long known of the
attempts to keep Hunt mollified. Ehrlichman's report minimized Dean's
role—although he well knew that Dean had played a large part in rehearsing
Magruder's earlier perjured testimony. He acknowledged that Dean was ready
to testify but he was confident he would confine his remarks to Mitchell and
Magruder. But Ehrlichman had misplaced his confidence. John Dean's conversations with the prosecutors broke the bounds shaped by Magruder's testimony and by those which Ehrlichman hoped to establish.[4]

The talks of April 14 began with a morning meeting of more than two
and one-half hours between the President, Haldeman, and Ehrlichman. The
tape recordings of the conversations at times appear disjointed. The transcripts have been cannibalized for a juicy tidbit here, a titillating curse there.
Interpreting the transcripts as showing hesitation or uncertainty in the Oval
Office would be an error, however. The transcripts reflect a consistent line
of discussion. Certainly, participants occasionally sounded unsure of matters, but that only mirrored the compartmentalization that Nixon generally
had imposed on his dealings with aides. The President himself always seemed
to know the correct answers, and throughout he established and maintained

the drift and tone of the conversations. In his most perilous moments, Richard Nixon remained the man on top.[5]

Nixon was determined to solidify his defensive position, a strategy that involved getting John Mitchell "out front." Ehrlichman and Haldeman suggested language that the President could use to steer Mitchell on the proper course. This was not unusual; providing words—"talking papers," in White Housese—always had been a part of their job. They knew what they needed; they also understood the President's needs—and wants. Ehrlichman and Nixon projected a dialogue for Ehrlichman to use when he confronted Mitchell:

EHRLICHMAN: We've got to think of this thing from the standpoint of the President and I know you [Mitchell] have been right along and that's the reason you've been conducting yourself as you have.

PRESIDENT: Right.

EHRLICHMAN: It's now time I think to rethink what best serves the President and also what best serves you in the ultimate outcome of this thing.

PRESIDENT: Right.

EHRLICHMAN: I think we have to recognize that you are not going to escape indictment—there's no way—and far better that you should be prosecuted on information from the U.S. Attorney based on your conversation with [him] . . . than on an indictment by a Grand Jury of 15 blacks and 3 whites. . . .

PRESIDENT: And the door of the White House—we're trying to protect it.

Ehrlichman proposed that he invite Mitchell to call the President to hear the word directly. But Haldeman, as if he were writing a movie about conspiracies, had a better idea. He would phone Mitchell and say that the President wished to speak to him. That would obscure any role for himself or Ehrlichman and make it appear that the President operated "unilaterally."

The three men knew that Mitchell would be difficult. Ehrlichman suggested that Nixon tell his friend that he could not remain in New York, pretending that "the thing" would go away. On two occasions, the President interjected "[T]here's nobody else that can do it"—meaning that only Mitchell could keep the affair contained. Only a week earlier, Nixon had been insisting to Haldeman that he wanted Mitchell to know he stood "firm" with him; now, Mitchell was the "real problem" and should take responsibility. Nixon allowed himself some self-pity—perhaps intended ultimately for Mitchell—lamenting the "impossible position" of the White House and the growing chorus of Republican criticism. Still, he carefully explored his options. Should they continue to stonewall it, take their chances with the Ervin Committee, or take any other step that might be better than "this cave-in"? Ehrlichman reassured him that the Mitchell "cave-in" was the only route. The President took the cue; he would tell Mitchell, "I think it is a lot better for us to be forthcoming before you are indicted."

The ever-calculating Ehrlichman found multiple advantages in Mitchell's sacrifice. If Mitchell were indicted, that would hamper the Ervin inquiry, for any testimony by White House people might jeopardize Mitchell's right in a subsequent trial. Mercilessly, Ehrlichman kept depicting Mitchell as incompetent and hopelessly mired in legal violations. He told the President about a pending indictment in New York, involving Mitchell and Maurice Stans and the receipt of a contribution from Robert Vesco, a financier with great legal problems of his own. The President characterized Mitchell's role there as "dumb."

Nixon knew about another case of which his aides had learned, and he wanted to hear more particulars. A Baltimore grand jury had been hearing testimony concerning Maryland building contracts and the bribery of public officials, including the former Governor, now Vice President, Spiro Agnew. Agnew's potential problems provided a welcome diversion. Haldeman reported that Agnew was "scared shitless," and had threatened to involve Mitchell as a recipient of illegal campaign contributions unless the White House helped him. (Agnew denied ever implicating Mitchell, who "was one of my closest friends," while Haldeman and Ehrlichman "were my biggest problems on the Nixon staff.") Nixon thought all Agnew's problems involved a Jewish crowd in Baltimore, but he found it unbelievable that Agnew would take money in his office, as had been charged. Haldeman and Ehrlichman confidently believed that the Republican U.S. Attorney (a brother of a Maryland senator) would not indict Agnew. But they seemed to enjoy the fact that he would be tarnished and perhaps take some heat away from the White House. "Thank God I was never elected Governor," the President said, as he referred to the bribery problems of another state official.[6]

Perhaps Richard Nixon saw Agnew as a pawn; neither then nor later did he understand that Agnew represented a built-in insurance policy against impeachment proceedings directed at himself. For the April siege, however, Agnew still had his uses. On April 25 the Vice President delivered a brief statement to reporters, reaffirming his "full confidence in the integrity of President Nixon," and urging that nothing be done to prejudice the rights of possible defendants.

The forthcoming Ervin Committee inquiry provided another diversionary moment during the lengthy morning meeting on April 14. Weicker by then had completely alienated the White House. Nixon bitterly resented Weicker's public criticisms, and he believed that Weicker was miffed because of the treatment of his friend Pat Gray. Apparently, Ehrlichman and Haldeman thought they had sufficient derogatory information to force Weicker off the committee, but Ehrlichman suggested waiting until the hearings started. Then they could embarrass the whole proceeding and, as Haldeman suggested, strike fear into other Republicans. Nixon suggested that his aides "stick it right to him," but also thought it would be better to fight Weicker, his slick public-relations techniques and all, as opposed to some "smart son of a bitch." Ehrlichman, meanwhile, remained confident that Howard Baker would safeguard the White House. A few days earlier, on April 11, he had told Mitchell that Baker continued to be guarded in his dealings, but really helpful.[7]

Ehrlichman had his own agenda. Mitchell, of course, was his primary target, but Ehrlichman thought that Dean, too, should be given an opportunity to serve the President in like fashion. He reminded Nixon of Dean's knowledge of the hush money, as well as several other links to the cover-up. Ehrlichman did not want Dean fired; if he remained as the President's Counsel, Ehrlichman believed that Silbert and the grand jury would be more respectful. The President then spoke carefully about Dean's role. He "only tried to do what he could to pick up the Goddamn pieces and . . . everybody else around here knew it had to be done. . . . Uh, let's face it. I'm not blaming anybody else . . . That was his job." But Ehrlichman noted that quite a number of White House people knew what Dean was doing—and even the President admitted his awareness. Nixon then thanked *both* men for arranging Dean's role in the way they had, for it showed "why the isolation of the President isn't a bad position to be in." Still, Dean was special for the President, even to the point of distinguishing him favorably from Mitchell. Back to the point: if Dean were fired for his wrongdoing, Ehrlichman emphasized, then Nixon would have to—"fire the whole staff," the President interrupted. Ehrlichman realized that Magruder was no problem, but Dean was a big time bomb. Ehrlichman knew that they must handle Dean with kid gloves; his solicitude, of course, was only self-serving.

Everyone had an agenda; appropriately, the President's was unique. He told his aides that he was convinced that no one wanted to hurt "the President." He welcomed that attitude "because it isn't the man, it's the Goddam office" that must be protected. Better, however, that others protect the office. He told Ehrlichman to call Mitchell and persuade him to take responsibility. Nixon may have sensed how much Ehrlichman relished the idea of telling Mitchell what he had to do. But it was not a time for ironic reflections. The President himself could not face Mitchell; indeed, he directed Ehrlichman to inform Mitchell that he considered it the "toughest decision he's made," tougher than Cambodia and the Christmas bombing together. Nixon waxed and waned as to the outcome. He sounded certain that Mitchell would resist, but finally realized that the former Attorney General must submit. Nixon closed by exhorting his troops: "We have to prick the Goddam boil and take the heat. Now that's what we are doing here. We're going to prick the boil and take the heat."[8]

* * *

Shortly after lunch on April 14, Nixon and Haldeman met briefly in the Oval Office. Haldeman finally had reached Magruder, who informed him that "it is all done now"—that he had decided to cooperate with the prosecutors. "[E]verybody involved here is going to blow," Magruder warned. Nixon had not yet told Mitchell of his decision, but he realized the bleakness of Mitchell's situation. "How the hell can John Mitchell deny it? He was right on the [unintelligible] spot," Nixon said. But now, in reality, Mitchell was beside the point. What would Magruder say about his relationship with the White House, specifically with Gordon Strachan and thus with Haldeman? Haldeman confidently believed Strachan would deny any knowledge that the reports he had received from Magruder came from illegal wiretaps. Magruder, however, had reported that the prosecutors had little interest in Strachan.[9] So far, so good—for the White House.

Meanwhile, John Mitchell appeared at the White House to meet Ehrlichman, who had been delegated to do the President's bidding. (Although Ehrlichman later expressed shock that Nixon had taped their meetings, he himself had regularly engaged in the practice, as he did on this occasion.) Ehrlichman and Mitchell played a cat-and-mouse game. "Poor John" Dean, the former Attorney General said. He'd gotten caught in the middle, and like others (presumably himself) had been simply "trying to keep the lid on" until after the election. Mitchell added that Dean had kept the lid on things even "worse, I think, than the Watergate business"—in an almost taunting reference to Ehrlichman's involvement with the Plumbers. Clearly, the President's men were at an impasse among themselves, each having sufficient knowledge to incriminate the others.

But Mitchell made his position clear. He would stay where he was. He had been "euchred into this thing" because he had not paid attention to the "bastards" who had been directed from the start by the White House. Thus, Mitchell, too, had decided to "stonewall"—a term he borrowed from the President. Ehrlichman so informed the President, adding that Mitchell had lobbed "mudballs" at the White House and refused to take any responsibility.[10]

Ehrlichman gave complete details of his talk at an afternoon meeting with Nixon and Haldeman. Mitchell implicitly had threatened Ehrlichman with his own knowledge of things. Mitchell opposed a special prosecutor but believed that the President needed Counsel to take Dean's place and suggested one of their former law partners. Meanwhile, Nixon bravely announced that he would not be intimidated by Mitchell's threats. "[T]hrowing it off on the White House isn't going to help him one damn bit," he said. Yet he realized that if Mitchell carried out his threat it would be "a hell of a problem for us." Interestingly, the President seemed equally, if not more, concerned that Colson might be indicted. Perhaps that would be too close for comfort, as he remembered Colson's promise of clemency to Hunt.

Clemency talk rang a bell for the President and his men. "There could be clemency in this case and at the proper time," the President said, "having in mind the extraordinary sentences of Magruder [who had not yet been sentenced]. . . . but you know damn well . . ." Haldeman finished the point: "It's gotta be down the road." During the morning session on April 14, the President seemed to promise "full pardons" for everyone. He also spoke of clemency for Magruder, provided he kept the White House distanced from his story.

Ehrlichman thought that it would be useful to get his report to Kleindienst to demonstrate the White House's cooperative spirit. Ehrlichman and Nixon spun a story claiming that the President ordered an investigation when McCord revealed his intention to talk. The two carefully coached and rehearsed each other. After a pause, the President asked whether Mitchell would be convicted. Ehrlichman thought he would be. Alone later with Haldeman, Nixon consoled his aide, berating Mitchell for trying to involve Haldeman. But as always, his feelings covered a wide gamut. Indignantly, he complained that Mitchell had let it all happen himself. But he was worried that Mitchell had said he knew of other things. The President was sure Mitchell would never go to prison. "What do you think about that as a possible thing—does a trial of the former Attorney General of the United States bug you?" he asked, as if thinking out loud. "This God damn case," he muttered.[11]

Shortly after 5:00 P.M. on that April 14, Ehrlichman returned to the Oval Office to report on his meeting with Magruder and his lawyers. It was as expected: Magruder would implicate Mitchell, along with Dean. He had given the prosecutors details of the extent to which Dean's coaching had led to his earlier perjured testimony. Nixon realized that Dean might be an enemy within, now that he found himself threatened. Magruder had warned that the prosecutors were hot on Dean's trail and that they remained interested in Haldeman's links to the wiretap intelligence. It was time to think the unthinkable: Would Haldeman, too, have to sacrifice himself? Briefly, the President speculated on Haldeman's resignation, perhaps expecting some help from his side. But Haldeman told him he would have to "figure out" that "crunchy decision" by himself.

At the end of the conversation the President cursed the growing official and public preoccupation with the Watergate story. "[D]ragging the God damn . . . thing out and dragging it out and being—and having it be the only issue in town," he complained to Ehrlichman. Get the "son of a bitch done," he said. Indict Mitchell and the rest; there would be a horrible two-week scandal, but he was sure they could survive. He thought the story might appear worse than Teapot Dome, but he saw a difference: no venality, no thievery, no favors. Still, he realized the seriousness of the picture if Mitchell were indicted. And then there was what he described as the vulnerability of others—he must have realized that these others included him—regarding the charges of obstruction of justice. On this front, he exhorted Haldeman and Ehrlichman to fight. After all, he said, "we were simply trying to help these defendants."[12]

Ehrlichman had a substantial body of information in his possession. Lest he ever have to face any charge as an accessory, he sought cover by unburdening himself to Attorney General Kleindienst—and undoubtedly testing Kleindienst's reaction to Mitchell's involvement. But when Kleindienst learned that Ehrlichman had been collecting information for several weeks, he delivered a warning: "Yours is a very goddamn delicate line as to what you do to get information to give to the president and what you can do in giving information to the Department, you know, to enforce the law." With undoubted sarcasm, Ehrlichman replied: "Well, you are my favorite law-enforcement officer." With that, Kleindienst, the President, and all his men prepared for the annual White House correspondents' dinner. The *Washington Post* won numerous awards that evening for its Watergate stories, articles Nixon considered libelous. Yet he noted the irony, as he said, that he had just "learned the facts" of the Watergate case.[13]

Before the dinner, Nixon dictated a long diary entry, summing up the extraordinary events of April 14. He expressed relief that "the loose cannon"—meaning Magruder—"finally has gone off." He regretted that "we" had not resolved the affair just after the elections. "I just wasn't watching it that closely then and nobody was really minding the store." Pity the good men who had acted with "the best of intentions, with great devotion and dedication," who were caught up in the affair. He berated himself for leaving too much to Dean and Mitchell. But not a word about how he had schemed to have Mitchell assume responsibility in order to keep the White House and "the presidency" secure. Finally, the inevitable self-pity: Nixon noted the good approval rating he had received in the polls, but he sensed that this was probably the last time it would appear so high, "unless we get a couple of breaks toward the end of the next year."[14] It never was to be.

The President could not let go. After the correspondents' dinner, he had telephone conversations with both Haldeman and Ehrlichman. Each man fit a special compartment of his concern. Nixon realized that Haldeman might have to be sacrificed because of his links with the fruits of the Watergate break-in, such as they were. Ehrlichman was an especially delicate problem because of his connections to the Plumbers. How long could that business remain under wraps?

Whatever empathy or relief the President expressed toward Magruder in his diary entry was forgotten as he told Haldeman that he just could not depend on Magruder. He seemed particularly anxious to establish the line that money payments to the defendants had not been intended to obstruct justice. He reassured himself that it would be the word of felons such as McCord and Hunt against the word of those who raised the money. But he worried that someone might have "some piece of paper that somebody signed or some God damned thing. . . ."—as if in fear that written or taped evidence would undermine the White House in some way. Alternate notes of confidence and defiance ran through the President's thoughts. He told Haldeman that they should consider telling the Ervin Committee that White House officials would testify in executive session or not at all.[15]

Several minutes later, the President called Ehrlichman. He discussed Haldeman's possible resignation, insisting he would be loath to have it. It would give an appearance of other wrongdoing; besides Haldeman had done many good things. "You don't fire a guy for a mistake, do you?" But what Nixon really wanted to know was how Ehrlichman planned to deal with Dean. By now he realized that Dean, not Magruder, was his greatest danger. The President was blunt in what he could offer Dean: "Look, he's gotta look down the road to, to one point, that, uh, there's only one man that could restore him to the ability to practice law in the case things still go wrong. . . . [H]e's got to have that in the back of his mind." Ehrlichman had to reach all those involved and get the "straight damn line" that "we raised money, . . . but, uh, we raised money for a purpose that we thought was perfectly proper." (When the White House prepared tape transcripts a year later, Nixon inserted at this point: "RN is referring to E[hrlichman], H[aldeman], [and] not to himself.") The President was beside himself: "[W]e weren't trying to shut them up, we just didn't, we didn't want 'em to talk to the press." That was "perfectly legitimate, isn't it?" he asked his former Counsel. Ehrlichman guardedly said he did not have a "perfect understanding" of the law relevant to the matter. Like a man anxious to establish an alibi, the President eagerly sought to ensure that everyone offered the same explanation for the payment of money to the defendants.

Ehrlichman knew that Kleindienst was talking to the prosecutors that very evening, and he expected to hear from him in the morning. The President thought Kleindienst could be intimidated and be made to understand that Mitchell was the primary target. Whatever loyalty Kleindienst felt toward Mitchell was beside the point. Both men thought that Kleindienst now would turn the case over to "the Dean," presumably Solicitor General and former Harvard Law School Dean Erwin Griswold.

But Kleindienst was not on the President's mind at the moment. John

Dean, and what he might do, clearly loomed larger the more Nixon dwelt on the subject. What was Ehrlichman going to do with him? The aide seemed reluctant to lean too hard. Nixon knew the route, however. Ehrlichman could tell Dean that "the President thinks you've . . . carried a tremendous load and . . . his affection and loyalty to you is [sic] just undiminished. . . . And . . . we can't get the President involved in this." Nixon suggested that Ehrlichman work on Dean for his role regarding obstruction of justice. He claimed that he felt better now that the story was breaking. "I don't want the Presidency tarnished," he said, "but also . . . I'm a law enforcement man. Right?" he asked. "Yep, and you've got to move on to more important things," Ehrlichman replied, offering one of his lengthier comments in the whole conversation.[16]

The President had belatedly recognized his weakest link. By then, Dean's lawyers had had several meetings with the prosecutors, and Dean himself had talked to them on April 8. At that early stage, Dean bargained hard for immunity, although both sides sensed that it might impair his credibility. Dean's conversations with the prosecutors at first centered on Magruder and Mitchell but then expanded to the roles of the President's aides, including information on the Fielding break-in. Only when Dean became convinced that he would be the scapegoat, and when the President began to ease him out of the case, did he escalate his charges to embrace the President. From the outset, the prosecutors worried about corroborating Dean's charges, but they rejected a suggestion to "wire" him for his White House meetings.[17]

Shortly after the President and Ehrlichman spoke late in the evening of April 14, Kleindienst finally learned about Dean's conversations. The containment operation was over; the domino principle now applied, and damage control was the order of the day.

At the White House correspondents' dinner that evening, Kleindienst received an excited call from Henry Petersen, who told his chief he had to see him at once. Earlier that evening, Harold Titus, the U.S. Attorney, and his aides, Earl Silbert, Seymour Glanzer, and Donald Campbell, had briefed Petersen as to the roles of Mitchell and Dean. Petersen had trusted Dean and had much respect for Mitchell; he was, Silbert remembered, visibly stunned and upset. At 1:00 A.M. on April 15, Petersen, accompanied by Titus and Silbert, recounted for the Attorney General the story Dean had given to them. Kleindienst listened for nearly four hours, distressed, distraught, but undoubtedly relieved as the prosecutors assured him that Dean had not specifically implicated the President in the cover-up. They all agreed that Kleindienst must see the President promptly.[18]

Kleindienst called Nixon at 8:00 A.M., and the President agreed to see him after the White House prayer service. Several hours later, Nixon informed Ehrlichman about the call and asked, in apparent innocence, who Titus and Petersen were. Ehrlichman was sure that Kleindienst would plead for a special prosecutor so that he could remove himself from the case and yet remain in office. Ehrlichman opposed the idea. The President agreed, thinking a special prosecutor would only mean "another loose cannon rolling around the deck." Both expressed some concern that Hunt might have alerted the grand jury about the Plumbers, and both again thought Colson might be exposed. Dean increasingly was on their minds, and both sounded fearful that he might have to cooperate in order to defend his activities.[19]

Nixon and Kleindienst met for seventy minutes in the Executive Office Building. Nixon listened calmly as Kleindienst related what he had heard from the prosecutors. He played Kleindienst like an instrument, explaining that Dean had been handling the investigation of the break-in while everyone else was preoccupied with the election. "But after the election," the President said, "I couldn't think what in the name of [expletive deleted] reason did they play around then?" Nixon had his excuses. He always had run his own campaigns, but the burdens of the presidency, including preparation for the Russian summit, had prevented that the past year. Then, after the election, he had been distracted by his involvement in the December bombing of Vietnam.

The President asked Kleindienst if *he* knew of the break-in or the cover-up. Defensively, the Attorney General denied any knowledge. Clearly, Kleindienst was sympathetic. He thought that there were two "overriding" considerations: "one is yourself and your Presidency and secondly is the institution." Both, he believed, had to be "protected and preserved by the institution of justice." Nixon carefully guided the Attorney General away from any immediate appointment of a special prosecutor and, in view of Kleindienst's close relationship with Mitchell, the two agreed to let Petersen handle matters.

Kleindienst was struck by the President's calm reaction to the news of Mitchell's complicity in the break-in. Petersen, who accompanied Kleindienst to another meeting with the President later that afternoon, recalled being "a little exasperated perhaps considering the man's station, perhaps even a little bit rude in consideration of the calm with which he accepted what I thought was shattering information." The President, of course, knew the facts, and he understood how Petersen had learned them. Later, Petersen bitterly chastised himself for not being skeptical or cynical enough. "Maybe people in power have different rules, but they certainly are not straightforward, certainly not honest. . . . I credited this guy with more character than he obviously had." Richard Nixon liked to give surprises; he did not relish receiving them.[20]

The President realized the importance of the appearance of justice. Although he had been persuaded against naming a special prosecutor, just after

his early meeting with Kleindienst he told Haldeman that he would accept
a special prosecutor to oversee the case through indictments, but not necessarily to prosecute. He said that he was leaning toward Charles Alan
Wright, a University of Texas Law School professor; earlier, he had suggested Circuit Court Judge Edward Lumbard to Kleindienst. Nixon and
Haldeman seemed to have their confidence rejuvenated. They no longer had
to manipulate Mitchell into a confession: he would be indicted, and, as "a
hell of a big fish," the President said, he would "take a lot of the fire out
of this thing on the cover up and all that sort." Haldeman readily agreed.
They also concurred with Secretary of State Rogers's contention that the
Ervin Committee would have to close down once indictments came forth.[21]

John Dean still had some White House cards to play. He called Haldeman
on April 15 to relay some messages to Nixon. Dean wanted the President to
understand that he remained loyal; "if it's not clear now, . . . it will become
clear," Dean said. He refused to meet Ehrlichman, but he would meet the
President at any time. Finally, he urged Nixon to counsel with Petersen,
"who I assure you does not want the Presidency hurt." Although Nixon
seemed unsure about Dean, Haldeman and most emphatically Ehrlichman
had turned rather sharply on him. Sometime in this period, Ehrlichman
suggested that Dean sign two letters to put in the President's hands, one
resigning, the other requesting a leave of absence. If Dean maintained the
cover-up and protected the White House, he would be on leave of absence
pending the outcome of his trial. Clearly, this was designed to entice Dean
with promises of future support if he remained loyal. Still, Ehrlichman could
not resist whacking away at Dean and the beleaguered John Mitchell. He
claimed to have told Dean not to bother with Hunt's payments, because he
no longer cared if Hunt went public on the Plumbers. That matter, Ehrlichman said, was covered by "national security." Furthermore, for the first
time Ehrlichman informed Nixon that he had urged Dean to reveal everything in the summer of 1972, but that Dean had refused, ostensibly because
doing so would hurt the campaign. Dean in fact, Ehrlichman argued, had
been protecting Mitchell.[22]

Nixon scheduled another meeting with Petersen for April 16. But the night
before, the President placed at least four calls to Petersen, obviously anxious
to establish a comfortable relationship in advance. Direct calls from the
President of the United States spanning fifteen minutes—and on such an
important matter—had to be heady stuff for Petersen, but the attention was
all manipulative on Nixon's part, for he used the opportunities to determine
what the prosecutors knew and how he might use that information to thwart
them.

From Petersen the President learned that Dean's lawyer thought it would
be a "travesty" if Haldeman and Ehrlichman were not indicted; without
that, he insisted, Dean would plead not guilty and go to trial. Clearly, Nixon

had to reach Dean. But he told Petersen he needed to see Dean because he wanted the whole truth, and he was "not going to screw around with this thing." Seven minutes later, Nixon called again, saying that Dean was in transit to the White House. He took the occasion to indicate his desire that Liddy cooperate. Why not? Liddy could only reinforce the case against Mitchell, a point that remained essential for the President. Within a half-hour, Dean met the President. He remembered later that Nixon asked him "leading questions which made me think the conversation was being taped." Specifically, he recalled Nixon's remark that his March 21 statement about raising a million dollars to sustain the cover-up had been merely a joke. Dean pointedly assured the President that he would not discuss national-security matters with the prosecutors. But most intriguing of all, Nixon emphasized that he first learned the facts of the break-in and cover-up during their March 21 meeting. Dean knew that the President was "posturing," but he still "couldn't tell which way he was going."

Nixon then called Petersen, claiming falsely that Dean was not in the room. The call was trivial and simply repeated Nixon's desire that Liddy talk. Apparently, he sought to impress Dean with his comfortable working relationship with Petersen. Two hours later—near midnight—the President phoned Petersen again. The relationship seemed to be becoming intimate. Nixon anxiously tried to give Petersen the impression that he was deeply involved in the case and interested only in pursuing the truth. "The main thing, Henry, we must not have any question, now, on this, you know I am in charge of this thing. You are and I am. Above everything else and I am following every inch of the way and I don't want any question . . . of the fact that I am . . . way ahead of the thing. You know," he emphasized, "I want to stay one step ahead of the curve." Petersen then revealed which principals would be questioned in the next several days. When the President slyly, almost parenthetically, asked about Haldeman and Ehrlichman, Petersen indicated that they might have to resign. He promised to give the President "all the facts with respect to them into a pattern." Unwittingly, but understandably, Petersen had informed the wrong man of his plans.[23]

The President's record for April 16 at first glance seemed frantic and disorganized, as if he had proceeded through the day on an *ad hoc* basis. But in fact Nixon was very much on top of matters. Meeting with such disparate principals as Haldeman and Ehrlichman on the one hand, and then with John Dean, followed by Henry Petersen, Nixon conducted a virtuoso performance of his own. Appropriating the ideas of others, feigning ignorance, expressing incredulity and bewilderment, manipulating subordinates for his own protection, and typically, concerned about the public-relations aspect of the case, the President struggled for survival. That he eventually failed is no adequate measure of his effort.

Nixon met with Haldeman and Ehrlichman briefly before seeing Dean at

10:00 A.M. He told them he would present Dean with two alternative letters, one offering resignation, the other a leave of absence. The latter was designed on the basis for establishing a bargain, a bargain that eventually would include presidential clemency or a pardon. The aides urged the President to turn on Dean and give evidence to Petersen if Dean refused to cooperate, but all of them knew that was empty talk. Nixon quickly turned the conversation to whether Dean might reveal the Plumbers' operations or any other bugging enterprises. Not to worry, Ehrlichman said: "They're all national security"—and Nixon quickly added: "privileged." But Ehrlichman soon learned that the prosecutors had informed Petersen of the Fielding break-in.

Nixon then asked his aides to give worst-case scenarios for their own problems but promised not to make "any God damn hasty decisions." The three also agreed that Dean had failed to provide a report and that Ehrlichman's report of April 14 was the one that broke the case. Finally, Nixon urged them to concentrate on "the PR thing." Incredibly, but typically, he wanted personal credit for the breaking revelations. As the men sought to coordinate their accounts, John Dean clearly emerged as the principal "enemy." Dean "stonewalled," he "shot down" White House attempts to make a clean breast of things in 1972, and "he dug in his heels." Haldeman and Ehrlichman desperately made the case against John Dean. Of course, Haldemen conveniently chose to ignore his control of Dean and his praise of the Counsel's work at the September 15, 1972, meeting with the President. The praise that all of them earlier had lavished on Dean was now a mere echo. Confident he was speaking for historical judgments that would applaud him, the President concluded the conversation: "I can say that the Watergate case has been broken."[24]

Haldeman and Ehrlichman passed Dean on their way out of the Oval Office, "laughing like college pranksters," Dean recalled, until they saw him. Dean realized they did not look like men who had been told to resign. When he sat down, the President immediately confronted him with the alternative letters that Ehrlichman, apparently, had prepared. Dean balked, insisting that Haldeman and Ehrlichman, too, must resign. The President then baldly lied, claiming that he had similar letters from them. Dean warned Nixon against believing that the aides had no problem. "I'm telling you, they do," he declared. Nixon then seemed to agree.

The President feared the damage Dean could inflict. Almost deferentially, he asked Dean how he could stay "one step ahead of this thing" and "what the hell can I say publicly?" Despite his disparaging Dean in the presence of his aides a few minutes earlier, Nixon apparently believed that Dean could still do magic for him. The conversation revolved around the President's knowledge of the Watergate break-in and when he gained it. Nixon once

more tried to sidestep the September 15 meeting, at which he had met Dean
and discussed the case and the cover-up: "Remember[,] I didn't see you
until after the election." Dean had his own deferential game: "That's right,"
he replied. Nixon instructed Dean that he could not claim executive privilege
on matters that involved "wrongdoing," but hastily added that the wiretap
policy involved national security and hence was privileged. Dean seemed to
look for some glimmer of hope. He emphasized that he had persuaded Magruder to come forth with the truth—ignoring the fact that he had first
coached him for perjury. In that fashion he could buttress Nixon's claim that
the White House broke the case.

Who was using whom? Nixon asked Dean to stress that the President had
fully investigated the case. "Shit, I'm not going to let the Justice Department
break this case, John." But he remembered the need to please Dean: "We
triggered the whole thing. You know what I mean? . . . You helped to trigger
it." Dean replied with his vision: "When history is written, . . . and you
put the pieces back together, you'll see why it happened. It's because I
triggered it. I, I put everybody's feet to the fire because it just had to stop."

The President's treatment included fatherly advice on truth-telling. "John,
I want you to tell the truth," the President said. "I have told everybody
around here, said, 'God damn it, tell the truth.' 'Cause all they do [when
they lie], John, is compound it." The experienced Nixon offered his advice,
resurrecting Alger Hiss's perjury. "[D]on't ever lie with these bastards,"
Nixon emphasized. He reminded Dean that right clearly could be distinguished from wrong, but when Dean agreed, the President added: "perhaps
there are gray areas."[25]

Shortly after noon, the President discussed public-relations questions, appropriately, with Haldeman, who also relayed some advice from presidential
aide Leonard Garment. Haldeman and Ehrlichman had little fondness for
Garment, and they had sniffed a bit when they earlier learned that he had
become involved in the case—another compartment for the President, it
seemed. Haldeman quoted Garment as advising the President that "you are
in possession of knowledge that you cannot be in possession of without
acting on." Garment also initiated a refrain he was to beat steadily for the
next two weeks: the President must make a clean cut of things and remove
Haldeman and Ehrlichman. No wonder Ehrlichman had urged the President
not to see Garment. The President was wary. Garment had briefed Kissinger
and Haig, clearly believing that he could help the President. "[W]hat the
hell did he do that for?" Nixon demanded. Nixon did not want Garment
involved in the day-to-day business of crisis management. Haldeman considered Garment "the panic button type," but sheepishly added, "that
doesn't mean he isn't right this time, incidentally." Garment had proposed
a dramatic gesture, such as a presidential television address, but Nixon dis-

missed the idea, certain it would only magnify what was still a minor story. Haldeman was not so sure. "We are going to have one hell of a time," he concluded.[26]

Garment's advice actually was more pointed. In a draft memo to the President (the ideas were conveyed, if not the actual language), he warned that saving the presidency and the President conflicted with the goal of saving Haldeman and Ehrlichman. The notion of a leave of absence was ambiguous and unacceptable; the media would close in and interfere *"grossly."* Leaves of absence would demonstrate that Nixon either loved or feared his aides, more likely the latter. Garment considered it "worthless" to deal with Haldeman and Ehrlichman: "They will never keep their word. They want to save themselves now." A "clean sweep," he told the President, was the only way to save his presidency.[27]

Outside the White House, others sensed the shifting fortunes and power of the President. Howard Phillips, Acting Director of the Office of Economic Opportunity, a prominent conservative dedicated to the dismantling of New Deal–Great Society programs, pleaded with Haldeman to continue the fight to abolish the legal-services aspect of the poverty program. "Everything Richard Nixon stands for will continue to be opposed at public expense, as we continue to subsidize advocates of busing, abortion, welfare rights, prison rights, gay liberation, lettuce boycotts, and the like, ad nauseam," Phillips complained. Republicans had won the election; why, he asked, should the President's opponents dictate policies? "We hold all the cards," Phillips said. But he did not see the President's hand.[28]

Senator J. William Fulbright, Chairman of the Committee on Foreign Relations, appeared on a television interview program on April 15, about the time Nixon was meeting with Kleindienst and Petersen. Fulbright grasped the President's growing weakness and the debilitating effects of Watergate more readily than Phillips. The Senator thought the scandal might provide an opportunity to restore balance between the executive and legislative branches by offering a focus on such questions as impoundment of appropriated funds, presidential war powers, and executive privilege. Still, Fulbright recognized that the President retained great authority. If he "decided to bomb Burma tomorrow, I don't know how we could stop him from it."[29]

For the next several weeks, Richard Nixon confronted a different challenge—this time in handling Henry Petersen, one of the pursuers, not one of the pursued. The President spoke to Petersen in intimate tones, seemingly open, cooperative at every turn, and eagerly solicitous of his advice. First, Nixon prodded Petersen to persuade Ervin to suspend his operation, suggesting that the hearings could not avoid jeopardizing the government's case against Mitchell and Magruder. He then moved to seal off another compartment; he told Petersen that he was to talk only to the President and no one else on the White House staff except special counsel Richard Moore. Nixon coyly asked whether he should accept Dean's resignation at once or wait until he made his deal with the prosecutors.

While asking for his advice, Nixon did not hesitate to urge Petersen to let the White House announce Magruder's cooperation with the Justice Department so the President could have proper credit for breaking the case. He also wanted "to keep ahead of the curve" by publicizing Petersen's role, but the latter thought that would reveal a lack of confidence in Kleindienst. Finally, the President asked for advice on his chief aides. Petersen urged that they leave, particularly Haldeman, who had knowledge of the break-in budget proposals. Nixon vehemently denied this—"all Mitchell," he said, and insisted that Haldeman had no campaign authority "whatever."

The conversation ended with the President's primary concern: what had Dean said about him? Petersen assured Nixon that Dean had turned only on Haldeman and Ehrlichman. Nixon then noted that the prosecution had a problem with what kind of deal to offer Dean. If he received more than others, the fact would sacrifice his credibility. More important, the President reminded Petersen to keep him posted of any further breaks.

Like the President, Dean still had hopes that things might work out in his favor. His charges against Haldeman and Ehrlichman had prompted Petersen to see Nixon. The resulting dialogue might have enabled the President to handle things favorably to himself—and to John Dean. But to think so was to cherish a naive hope; as Petersen later explained, "The Son of God could not have turned off that investigation in April 1973."[30]

Dean reappeared for another brief session with the President late in the afternoon of April 16th. Again, he urged Nixon to take the lead on breaking the story and relieve Haldeman and Ehrlichman. Dean told the President he would not be a scapegoat for the White House as Magruder had been for Mitchell. Nixon sparred tentatively with Dean, challenging his contentions that the President's aides had been guilty of an obstruction of justice. Dean reiterated that he found it "painful" to be the first White House aide to testify. "Just tell the truth," the President said, reassuringly. "That's right. That's what I am going to do," Dean replied.[31]

John Dean was history for the President, who now focused his energies on Petersen. Perhaps Nixon remembered Dean's March 21 characterization of Petersen as a "soldier," one who "believes in this Administration." Nixon called Petersen at nine that evening, again urging him to share information. He wanted grand-jury information, promising not to pass it on to anyone else—"because I know the rules of the Grand Jury." They discussed some particulars about potential defendants, but the President learned nothing really new. He ended as he began: "[I]f anything comes up, call me even if it is the middle of the night."[32] Henry Petersen had become the Henry Kissinger of Watergate Security Affairs.

By the end of the President's long weekend, the White House was in disarray. But Richard Nixon understood the worst-case scenario better than anyone else; therefore, in a curious way, once again he was in command. Following his initial talks with Petersen, Nixon realized that John Dean belonged to the prosecutors. There would be no aid and comfort from Dean's quarter. He would not, as he had told the President earlier, go to his fate alone. (On April 19, Dean's secretary telephoned reporters to make public his determination not to "become a scapegoat in the Watergate case.")

Haldeman and Ehrlichman, the President's most vital extensions, were not prepared to fall on their swords, either. They believed they had served the President and that he could and should save them. Nixon realized this, it appears. He understood the limits of their loyalty; they would not save him, but he could save himself. He would sacrifice Haldeman and Ehrlichman as readily as he had been prepared to offer John Mitchell. For the last two weeks in April, Haldeman and Ehrlichman underestimated the President's resolve. They joined him in finger-pointing sessions to lay the blame at the feet of others (Magruder, Mitchell, Dean, Gray), conjuring up explanations, skewing memories—all designed to rationalize their behavior and impugn that of others. The idea of "getting out in front of the story" disappeared in a wash of recriminations and excuses.

Richard Nixon had to save his presidency—and himself. He had engaged in a criminal conspiracy since June 1972 for that very purpose. Nixon had been prepared to sacrifice Mitchell, his good friend, former partner, and close adviser; Haldeman and Ehrlichman certainly could not be denied their opportunity to be used for so high a purpose. Leonard Garment's recommendation that Haldeman resign in order to allow the President to "move ahead of the game" undoubtedly lodged in Nixon's mind. He had a great deal of personal ambivalence toward Secretary of State William Rogers, yet throughout the years, he regularly turned to Rogers in delicate situations. He did so now. Rogers, too, said that the aides must resign. The President had his purposes in cultivating Petersen, who after all remained privy to the latest investigation news. When Petersen recommended that Haldeman and Ehrlichman resign, the President listened. He knew his aides had to go. Undoubtedly he was loath to dismiss them, but Richard Nixon's antennae of self-interest left him no choice. He realized this by April 16: for the rest of the month, however, he played out the string, hoping that his advisers would leave quietly and of their own accord.

The White House charade eventually cost the President dearly. Those crucial April days offered him opportunities to "get out in front" and take control of the situation, although in order to do so he would have had to expose his own involvement. At the time, the risk still was affordable for him. Watergate was breaking out of its Washington cocoon. Containment no longer was possible, but the President's public standing still gave him the benefit of the doubt.

Nixon recognized the growing seriousness of the problem. On April 17 he acknowledged that "major developments" had resulted from "intensive new inquiries" he had made into the affair. His Secret Service agent remembered that the President sobbed after his statement. Later that afternoon Press Secretary Ron Ziegler decisively transformed the story. Ten months earlier he had contemptuously dismissed any significance to the Watergate burglary. On April 17, with one unforgettable word, Ziegler declared all his previous remarks on Watergate "inoperative."[33] That dramatic concession clashed with Nixon's reluctance to act decisively in his own house. He had told Petersen that he was "so sick of this thing. I want to get it done with and over." But he did not. Richard Nixon prided himself on his decisiveness. Thoughout this period, he proudly referred to his firm, bold actions in Cambodia and the Christmas 1972 bombing in Vietnam. That President Nixon had disappeared by April 1973.

During a nearly two-hour session with Haldeman and Ehrlichman on the afternoon of April 17, the President discussed the implications of Petersen's charges. Haldeman insisted that he had done nothing illegal and that he had told Dean that the blackmail path was a dead end. He joined with Ehrlichman to lay the obstruction of justice on Dean's doorstep. Dean, they contended, had meant to protect his friend and original patron, John Mitchell. Charitably, Haldeman allowed that Dean might have worn himself to a "frazzle," "past the point of rationality." Desperately, Haldeman thought that Dean would not do anything "un-American and anti-Nixon." He was "an unbelievable disaster" for the White House; perhaps, too, the nation would find him unbelievable. Someone expressed a concern that Colson and Strachan would corroborate Dean in exchange for immunity. Finger-pointing was fully in style.[34]

Afterward, the President spoke to Ehrlichman on the telephone to prime himself for a meeting with Petersen. Nixon had rejected immunity for any of his top aides. Ehrlichman tried to stabilize the President's position on resignations. When Nixon asked if the agreed-upon policy was resignation on charges or indictments, Ehrlichman insisted that the procedure be suspension on indictment and resignation only on conviction. The President amended that formula to include resignation "on refusing to cooperate."[35]

Meeting Petersen afterward, Nixon shamelessly manipulated the Justice

official. The President asked if it were "legal" for him to know specifics—
for example, what charges the department would bring against Mitchell.
Petersen had little choice but to agree. After all, Richard Nixon had sworn
an oath to "take care that the laws be faithfully executed." How could he
be denied information? The President assured Petersen that he was "just
trying to do the right thing." Petersen dutifully replied, "Mr. President, if
I didn't have confidence in you—I wouldn't be here."

Petersen graciously gave Nixon details of the stories that Dean had told
the prosecutors regarding Ehrlichman, Gray, and the suppression of evidence. Nixon later discussed this with Ehrlichman. The President pressed
Petersen to cooperate in the effort to stop the Ervin Committee, again using
the pretext that the committee's activity might jeopardize Mitchell's trial. He
effectively persuaded Petersen at the time that his concern centered on the
need to bring wrongdoers to legal account. Nixon questioned the propriety
of granting Dean any immunity. (Without immunity, perhaps there was a
chance that Dean would limit his cooperation with the prosecutors.)

Most important, Nixon learned for certain from Petersen that Haldeman
and Ehrlichman would be named as unindicted co-conspirators, a fact that
confirmed his determination to separate himself from his aides. He told
Petersen that such a charge justified presidential dismissal. It was as if he
would use the weight of Henry Petersen and "the law" in order to stand
above his closest collaborators. He knew on April 17 what his course must be.
But he was desperate. At one point, Nixon thought Petersen signalled that
if Haldeman and Ehrlichman resigned, they would not be indicted. Petersen
quickly corrected the President. "Have a good day, Mr. President," Petersen said, as he left, apparently without intended sarcasm.[36]

One minute later, Nixon offered Haldeman and Ehrlichman some details
of his conversation. He told them that Dean's lawyers had promised to make
a case against the Administration. When talk of the senior aides' resignation
or leave of absence briefly surfaced, Haldeman aggressively argued that such
a course would not necessarily serve the President. Meanwhile, the two aides
were seeing a lawyer that afternoon. The three agreed on a statement regarding immunity, testimony before the Ervin Committee and executive
privilege, and the President's discovery of "serious charges." Ron Ziegler
knew that he would face hostile questions, but he agreed to state simply that
this now was the "operative" statement. "Don't [expletive deleted] on
Dean," the President cautioned Ziegler, apparently still hoping to cut a deal
in that quarter.[37]

William Rogers met the President shortly afterward. He agreed with Petersen that Haldeman and Ehrlichman would have to resign. Nixon went
through some proclamations of resistance, but clearly his mind was set. He
insisted that his aides were "not guilty of a damn thing"; their involvement
was "only tangential." Ehrlichman had had his domestic chores, and Halde-

man "was working with me at the time." They had no campaign connection, Nixon said disingenuously. He berated Mitchell for not "tending the shop." Mitchell, he contended, "was—in this whole thing—and frankly, Dean was handling it for the White House." But curiously, he admitted that "our people" were aware of Dean's connection—"we," as he also put it.

After Rogers left and Haldeman and Ehrlichman had returned to the Oval Office from their appointment with their lawyers, the President admitted "Dean had handled a lot of stuff well." Haldeman agreed, and Nixon thought he might have an opportunity to "make our deal or not with Dean within a week." He reminded his aides that Dean alone could sink them. Ehrlichman knew that flirting with Dean was futile, and he favored provoking Dean into a slanderous public statement. The President liked that. They then would get the "most vicious libel lawyer there is. I'd sue every [expletive deleted]. . . ." It was now clear between the three men that the aides had to go. Nixon filled his men with promises of a rosy future. He acknowledged that they would not be able to come back to government even if found innocent. But "you are not damaged goods as far as I am concerned." They would have jobs with his foundation—it would be "a hell of a big thing." Haldeman wanted funding to clear his name, and then would spend the rest of his life "destroying what some people like Dean and Magruder had done to the President."[38] The future would have many "sores to rub." But for the moment, Haldeman and Ehrlichman still thought they could turn the tide.

The next day, April 18, the President called Petersen to ask whether there was "anything I need to know today?" Petersen had nothing significant to report, but Nixon probed him on Dean's moves. It was as if he still had a glimmer of hope that his Counsel, who once had served so nobly, might yet contain and limit the investigation.[39]

Nixon met Ehrlichman on the afternoon of the nineteenth. He asked for a cold, objective assessment of the situation, "not in terms of Bob, in terms of the President." The President operated again in his separate compartments. Dean had left him confused. Nixon claimed he no longer knew what he had been told. But how could anyone question Dean on this? "We were all talking frankly," the President said, "that's why the counsel was sworn." But Nixon did not get an objective assessment; instead, the session ended with the now-familiar finger-pointing. He himself said that protecting Mitchell was the essence of the cover-up; "we weren't protecting the White House now, right?" Ehrlichman responded that "we" merely had protected the President's re-election, but added: "We didn't know what from." He agreed that the cover-up "was pure Mitchell."[40]

Late that afternoon, the President had a long session with Special Counsel

Richard Moore, who had close ties to Mitchell and had been on very friendly terms with Dean. Moore himself had just been subpoenaed by the grand jury, and the President seemed anxious to learn the extent of his knowledge of Dean's activities and the cover-up. At the outset of the conversation, Moore revealed that he had started smoking again during the campaign. "Goddamn campaign," the President responded, lost as he was in his own troubles. Moore acknowledged he had some awareness of a number of Watergate-related activities and the cover-up. But he agreed with Nixon that Dean repeatedly had said that no one in the White House had been involved. The President had his opening for more finger-pointing: "I'm afraid that our great, dear friend, John Mitchell is the culprit," he said. Then he painted Dean into the picture, falsely claiming that he had never spoken to Dean on Watergate-related business until after the election. Moore warned the President that Dean would make every effort to involve Haldeman and Ehrlichman, but Nixon countered that Haldeman had nothing to do with the break-in and wiretaps, while Ehrlichman's role with the Plumbers involved national security. The President oozed confidence on the Plumbers episode; no way, he believed, could he or his aides be brought to account on that issue.

How could the President end the affair? Moore tried to make him understand the seriousness of the cover-up and, above all, the need to satisfy public perceptions of truth and propriety. Nixon wanted to believe that the public would perceive Dean as a scoundrel; Moore saw it otherwise, even arguing that Dean had been fulfilling the dictates of the Nuremberg Doctrine by refusing to cooperate in official wrongdoing. Moore told the President that heads must roll: Haldeman, Ehrlichman, and he himself should go. That should satisfy the "vultures," he thought. Mitchell and Dean would be indicted, and Kleindienst, "a corrupt Attorney General," Moore noted. But he thought that the Democratic leadership, especially Mike Mansfield and Hubert Humphrey, would be satisfied. Nixon and Moore agreed that Mitchell should take responsibility. The President wanted Moore to talk to Dean, to get him in place, but Moore declined because of his own jeopardy.

Moore tried to assure the President that nothing "touches you." But Nixon worried about his conversations with Dean. He labored mightily to persuade Moore that the payments to the Watergate defendants were not an obstruction of justice, but Moore stood his ground. Nixon wanted reassurance that Dean would not attack him personally. Moore hesitated: "John's a strange fellow," he responded, "I don't know much about him." Dean had gone to three different schools, Moore noted, and he had had some ethical difficulty in his law firm (which the President seemed to know). "I don't know how much principle he has. . . . I have a feeling he will attack anybody . . . and say anything, at this point forward, if it suits his purpose," said Moore.

With that, the President reassumed his lofty posture, offering to get Dean immunity and letting him say anything. After all, Nixon said, "I understand it isn't me personally. It's the office we've got to protect." (That same day Nixon had told Haldeman that "it just irritates me when people like Garment and others come in here and say, the hell with people, the Presidency is bigger, and so forth.") The conversation with Moore ended on a totally different note, however, as Moore warned Nixon to be cautious in his dealings with Petersen.[41]

Earlier that day Haldeman told the President: "I did not know, and you did not know, and I don't know today, and I don't believe you do really, *what happened* in the Watergate case." Nixon readily agreed, but as Haldeman later recalled, his own statement was a classic—presumably a classic intended to construct a defense for the President and his men. That morning discussion apparently paved the way for the President's evening meeting with John Wilson and Frank Strickler, attorneys representing both Haldeman and Ehrlichman. The lawyers forcefully argued that the prosecutors could not have a very viable criminal case, and they urged the President to stand firm on behalf of their clients. Haldeman had warned that morning that "the President is going to be badly hurt by our stepping out." Nixon appeared to waver in his decision to force his aides' resignation, for the arguments seemed compelling. But Richard Nixon was a political man, not a legalist; he had to confront immediate political reality, not the law and the lengthy process of justice. Time enough for that later, he recognized.[42]

Nixon always was a man who knew his interest. Now he imagined favorable scenarios—that Dean would cooperate with the White House, for example, or that Mitchell would take complete responsibility. As late as April 25, Nixon still considered means of mollifying Dean. More likely than reclaiming Dean's allegiance, however, was that retaining Haldeman and Ehrlichman would provide a measure of protection. The President gave complete trust only rarely. Could he trust these men if they were on their own? They knew so much—and they knew there were records. Haldeman had helped to install the secret Oval Office taping system; Ehrlichman was aware of the system as well, though apparently he was not supposed to be. Indeed, on April 26 Ehrlichman urged the President to listen to his tapes to determine exactly what he had said to Dean. Ehrlichman reassured Nixon that he and Haldeman wanted no harm inflicted on the President or the office, but he thought impeachment might be conceivable—"on the ground that you committed a crime." Ehrlichman hastily added that he did not think Nixon had done so, but he suggested listening to the tapes.

Nixon had to get his men behind him. "What would you fellows answer[,] for example[,] if Dean testifies that there *was* a discussion in which I said Hunt's lawyer had to get paid off[?]" Ehrlichman responded, "Let's see what the tapes do." They then moved from Nixon's "central concern," as Haldeman characterized it, to the future of Haldeman and Ehrlichman. Ehrlichman fought like a tiger. Fire Dean, he urged. Haldeman should take a leave because of the charges, but Ehrlichman himself should stay on, because no serious charge had been leveled at him. Someone—the President, Haldeman, or Ehrlichman—bitterly assailed Dean and Petersen, somehow suggesting that Dean had blackmailed Petersen and thus would get immunity—a statement wholly opposite from Petersen's position. (On April 26, Nixon pathetically told Haldeman that Petersen was "all I got," after he learned that Haldeman's lawyers did not trust the Assistant Attorney General. Nixon thought that Petersen would "hold up." "[D]epends on how much Dean has on him, and he's got a lot," Haldeman responded.)

Ehrlichman warned that if he had to take leave, "I gotta start answering questions." Whether he was presenting a fact or a threat was not clear. "Let me ask you this, to be quite candid," the President responded. "Is there any way you can use *cash*?" Haldeman reacted with a blend of fury and sarcasm. They were being "drummed" out of office for their "supposed role" in payments to the defendants, and now the President offered them cash. "That compounds the problem," he told Nixon. "That really does."

The President persisted in lining up his alibis. "We have to remember what our, what the line, and the line has got to be." The others agreed that Dean now must be their primary target. The President should tell the nation that he could not operate the presidency under threat from the likes of John Dean, Haldeman said. Ehrlichman contributed his part: "The American people—you gotta go on the assumption that the American people want to believe in their President." Cover-up still was the order of the day, but now John Dean would be the scapegoat.[43]

Haldeman listened to the March 21 tape that afternoon and then gave an interpretation that would remain at the foundation of the President's defense. Nixon and Dean had discussed the White House's role in the break-in and the defendant's demands for money. Now, Haldeman proposed the following version: Nixon had asked leading questions; he was trying to "bust the case," and he did not know "whether to believe this guy [Dean] at this point." The President had also then realized that Hunt was blackmailing him on the Plumbers, but he no longer would support payments because he knew he could defend the burglary of Ellsberg's psychiatrist on national-security grounds. Haldeman was not sure that this interpretation of the March 21 record could be sustained—particularly if Dean had a different version of the conversation. "I just wonder if the son-of-a-bitch had a recorder on him," Nixon remarked. The two men had raised the possibility earlier in the morning. "I just can't believe that anybody, that even John Dean, would come into this office with a tape recorder." Few conversations in this period dripped with more irony.

The next day the President told Haldeman that they had to keep the Oval Office taping system secret. If the tapes became public knowledge, Nixon said, they should admit they made them, but only for "national security information"—which, of course, then had to remain secret. "You never want to be in a position to say the President taped it, you know. I mean taped somebody." Haldeman thought there was no need to worry—unless there were impeachment proceedings, which he considered out of the question. "My God, what the hell have we done to be impeached?" Nixon responded. Haldeman thought that if Dean taped the March 21 meeting, it would only show he was trying to trap the President, and his motives would be subject to scrutiny. Nixon praised his men for the protection they gave him, but laid down the alibi one more time: "I didn't know, you know. I mean I didn't. I deliberately got—the staff protected me from it for their credit[,] and I just wasn't getting involved."[44]

On the evening of April 25, Ehrlichman learned that his spirited defense of himself earlier that day had been for naught. Nixon called to relay the news that the Justice Department had notified the Ellsberg case's trial judge about the Plumbers; Petersen had finally decided to reject the President's earlier angry order not to "be messing in national security matters." Gently, but absurdly, Nixon told Ehrlichman that he had instructed Kleindienst to do everything possible to keep the news secret. Now, the President said, Ehrlichman had to take a leave of absence. Bad news exploded like Chinese firecrackers. Two minutes after Kleindienst called about the Plumbers, Nixon learned that the *New York Times* was about to reveal Pat Gray's destruction of the evidence from Hunt's safe linking Colson to the Plumbers—evidence Ehrlichman had suggested that Gray "deep six."

Nixon's last official conference with Haldeman ended with a tirade—against Dean, Ehrlichman, Alger Hiss, Sherman Adams, the usual enemies, and the violence that had been directed against *him;* it all spilled forth like a torrent. What went wrong? "I mean, we don't have any *investigators,* that's our *problem,* see," he said. This, as Haldeman later noted, from the man who created the Plumbers.[45]

Not all the bad news reached the White House. The prosecutors had learned from Anthony Ulasewicz, a former New York policeman, that he had been a courier for Herbert Kalmbach and had delivered cash payments to several of the Watergate defendants, including $154,000 to Howard Hunt.[46] With Ulasewicz offering corroborating testimony, John Dean's credibility increased significantly. So, too, did his vulnerability—as did that of his various superiors at the White House.

On April 27 Nixon spoke to Assistant Attorney General Petersen again. Published reports indicated that Dean had implicated the President. Petersen assured Nixon that he had instructed the prosecutors that they had no "mandate" to investigate the President; "we investigate Watergate," he told them.

He flatly told Nixon—and consistently maintained the position—that the House of Representatives had the responsibility for investigating the President of the United States. In short, only an impeachment inquiry was proper. But Nixon demanded that Petersen determine the source of the Dean story. Several minutes later, Petersen returned, reporting that the threat had come from Dean's attorney, and the prosecutors had no idea what he had in mind. They thought the lawyer had engaged in bombast as part of plea-bargaining.

Nixon was furious. He called in Ziegler and ordered the story refuted, claiming that Petersen had found it untrue. The anger compounded with mockery and self-pity. He told Petersen that he had "to maintain the Presidency out of this. I have got things to do for this country," Nixon said. "I sometimes feel I'd like to resign. Let Agnew be President for a while. He'd love it." One minute he said he did not want to hurt Dean; moments later he told Petersen he would fight Dean and refute any challenge. Nixon thought it would be fine to immunize Dean, but Petersen resisted because he believed an immunized Dean would lose credibility. Petersen's successful challenge on this score was crucial for maintaining Dean's standing as a public witness. Petersen told Nixon that immunity was the responsibility of the Department of Justice; the President's opinion would be "advisory only." He envisioned John Dean—co-defendant, not immunized witness—providing the key testimony against Haldeman and Ehrlichman. Richard Nixon did not own Henry Petersen; the Assistant Attorney General was not Henry Kissinger, after all.

Nixon pleaded for advice in dealing with Haldeman and Ehrlichman. The least painful course for him was that they take leaves of absence. But Petersen challenged the President: why did he think he could separate the two from Dean—because they were "loyal" to the last minute? Petersen considered the distinction between dismissal and leave illusory. Later, he testily remarked that "the President was poorly advised on the premises." But his suspicions were aroused. His wife, he told Nixon, had asked him whether he thought the President had been involved. He himself would resign if he thought so, he told her. Oblique as the implied request was, Petersen had asked the President the most important question of all. "Mr. President, I pray for you, sir," Petersen remarked, as if to reinforce his concern. And again, he urged Nixon not to distinguish Haldeman and Ehrlichman from Dean. He pleaded with him to be forceful and take action. He knew the President and others wanted the investigation shut down. Petersen had told his parish priest that he considered Watergate the greatest constitutional crisis since the Civil War, "and this guy [the President] is sitting there telling me I had to be fair to these people." Eight days earlier Petersen had assured the President of his "confidence" in him. Obviously, the past eight days had shaken Petersen's certain world. But Nixon refused to give him the direct answer he wanted. "We've got to get it out. . . . I have wrestled with it," was all Nixon could manage.[47]

Pat Gray's withdrawal of his nomination as FBI Director, on April 5, allowed him to stay in place pending the appointment of a successor. But the end for Gray came suddenly on April 27—probably before either he or the President intended, particularly in the light of Nixon's crisis involving the futures of his closest White House aides. The *New York Times* revealed that Ehrlichman and Dean had given Gray, then Acting FBI Director, the contents of Howard Hunt's office safe at a White House meeting on June 28, 1972. Dean reportedly said that the contents "should never see the light of day." Gray accepted the material after Dean assured him that it had nothing to do with the Watergate incident. He stored the papers in his house until July 3 and then brought them to FBI headquarters for destruction, claiming that he never examined them. Dean had informed the Justice Department of the incident in mid-April, after he had lost control of the cover-up and as he bargained for the best possible advantage for himself. Gray twice denied the charge but finally admitted it to Petersen. He acknowledged having burned the material, although he claimed he had never read it. Gray stood exposed as a perjurer, for he had testified earlier to the Senate Judiciary Committee that he was convinced Dean had made no effort to conceal Hunt's files.

The President heard the news while aboard Air Force One and ordered Ehrlichman to demand Gray's immediate resignation from the FBI. On that same flight, the President mused to Ehrlichman that 50 percent of him and Haldeman was worth more than 100 percent of any replacement. Nixon seemed to be offering a graceful exit, as he told Ehrlichman that he and Haldeman could continue to work on their files and ease things for their successors. Comfortingly, he added that Sherman Adams never had been indicted.[48]

The President—and the FBI—now desperately needed a leader who would be perceived as "Mr. Clean." He came in the form of William Ruckelshaus, a bright, highly respected, middle-level Administration official then serving as Environmental Protection Agency Administrator. Although he filled the bill, however, Ruckelshaus was not exactly what Nixon had in mind. The model remained J. Edgar Hoover—feared, loathed, respected, useful—but withal, too independent and too powerful. Nixon had no objection to the Hoover model, save for a proviso that the Director be *his* Director. The President instructed Ziegler to announce that Ruckelshaus was not being considered for the post on a permanent basis and would eventually return to the Environmental Protection Agency, at Ruckelshaus's own request. Nixon and Ehrlichman met immediately with Ruckelshaus. Following their session,

Ehrlichman went to his office for an FBI interview regarding his role in the break-in of the office of Daniel Ellsberg's psychiatrist.[49] The land mines seemed to be everywhere.

The Ruckelshaus appointment again rattled the FBI hierarchy. Not lightly did they accept the selection of a man who had led celebrations of Earth Day as head of the EPA while they had masterminded surveillance of the same event. The old guard was in near-mutiny, boldly sending a letter to the President urging consideration for "the highly qualified professionals with impeccable credentials of integrity within the organization itself." Ruckelshaus immediately ordered heads of FBI field offices to Washington to a meeting and reassured them that the Bureau would maintain independence. He thought that the disaffection rested only at the very top levels. When he took office, he realized the Bureau was "torn asunder," yet he did not think it was "falling apart." He found the institution as a whole quite strong, "so highly structured, with its assignments so clearly delineated, . . . [that] the institution itself was largely untouched outside of Washington." Ironically but appropriately, Ruckelshaus credited Hoover for the legacy of an effective, functioning FBI. Hoover's old aides, however, actively schemed for one of their own as Director. Louis Nichols, a former Associate Director who was close to the President, urged that Nixon personally approach Cartha DeLoach, a former top official, or ex-agent John Bugas, both then highly placed in the business world. In case the President still felt indebted to William Sullivan, his ally in the Huston Plan and Hoover's old nemesis, Nichols passed the word that Sullivan had had a nervous breakdown and also that he had opposed Nixon in 1968.[50] The War of the FBI Succession was more than a skirmish in the widening Watergate War.

When Ruckelshaus agreed to take the FBI post, he asked Nixon whether the President himself had been involved in the Watergate affair in any way. Nixon offered the respectful Ruckelshaus "a very convincing argument" that he was in no way implicated in any wrongdoing. That was the last time Ruckelshaus saw the President; but he was not the last to hear Nixon's "convincing argument" for his innocence.[51]

The Plumbers and the Gray revelations proved too much for Attorney General Kleindienst. On Friday, April 27, as Gray stepped down, Kleindienst decided to submit his resignation the following Monday. But Richard Nixon had other plans. On Sunday he summoned Haldeman and Ehrlichman to Camp David to demand their resignations. Five days earlier, Nixon had told Haldeman that he would consider asking him to take a leave of absence, but he would not demand his resignation. For his part, Ehrlichman had not expected such summary treatment and resisted, furious that he was lumped together with Dean. The President told each man separately that he prayed he would not awake; to Haldeman, he added that "I'm the guilty one," mentioning his giving free rein to Colson, his allowing Dean to maintain the cover-up, and his mistake in allowing Mitchell to run the campaign.

Despite his tearful appearance, the President knew his course. That weekend, he also called in Kleindienst and ordered him to submit his resignation at once. He wanted to announce the resignations of Haldeman, Ehrlichman, and Dean—and Kleindienst—as a package, to demonstrate his determination for a "clean sweep." Kleindienst argued it was unfair to link him to the others. Nixon recalled that "the poor beleaguered man" sobbed, yet the President told him that Elliot Richardson already had been selected to succeed him and, in fact, was in the next room. The firings were the "toughest thing I've ever done in my life," the President told Richardson. Nixon called Kissinger that evening, "nearly incoherent with grief," and told him that he needed him more than ever, to "help me protect the national security matters now that Ehrlichman is leaving." Kissinger spitefully, but correctly, regarded the remark as both "a plea and a form of blackmail."[52]

The President spoke to the nation the next evening, Monday, April 30. In retrospect, his words ring hollow. But at the time he projected a measure of confidence, and given his undoubted exhaustion from the events of the past few days, he displayed remarkable resiliency.

Nixon decided to admit no culpability for himself, a decision he later explained as a response to his growing fear of the nature of his enemies and opposition. In his memoirs, he acknowledged he had "thrown down a gauntlet to Congress, the bureaucracy, the media, and the Washington establishment and challenged them to engage in epic battle." If he admitted any vulnerabilities, he thought, his opponents would "savage" him. He believed he could portray events as "just politics." The resulting address was vintage Nixon. He blamed externals, extolled his record, and both praised and questioned the motives of others. He accepted responsibility as "the man at the top," a thinly veiled abstraction that he later admitted fooled no one. Nixon lied when he said he had no knowledge of events prior to March 21. He thought he could put Watergate behind him with "excuses," a style not unfamiliar to him. Later, he realized that "he could not have made a more disastrous miscalculation."[53] "Fatal" would have been more accurate.

Henry Kissinger had watched the President's April 30 television address and found it unconvincing. Worse, he thought, no one "could avoid the impression that he was no longer in control of events." The President had offered a similar judgment a few days earlier: "It's all over, do you know that?" he remarked to his Press Secretary. Nixon later realized that he had amputated both arms. Perhaps he could survive, he recalled, but the day left him "so anguished and saddened that from that day on the presidency lost all joy for me." He noted that he had written his last full diary entry on April 14. "Events became so cheerless that I no longer had the time or the desire to dictate daily reflections." But an anonymous aide fit the event into a familiar Nixon pattern: "For Nixon," he claimed, "the shortest distance between two points is over four corpses." Around this time, former aide Daniel Moynihan offered the President some curious comfort, suggesting that his men had not acted evilly but had brought on the "present shame" as a result of their "innocence." Somehow, Moynihan concluded their actions were analogous to the "innocence" of antiwar and antiestablishment demonstrators in "elite schools." "Extremely thoughtful," Nixon told Alexander Haig, who had moved into Haldeman's place.[54]

The bright prospects for the second term had dimmed. The high expectations for fresh ideas and personnel were strangled at the outset, virtually stillborn as the President and his closest aides grappled with the growing tentacles of Watergate. Their struggles were futile; in effect, by April 30 the presidency of Richard Nixon was over. The President told the nation in his television address that he wanted the 1,361 days remaining in his term "to be the best days in America's history." But Richard Nixon spent the next 465 days mostly fending off his "enemies," themselves once pursued, now the pursuers. To be sure, he had a few triumphs left to savor, but these would be in foreign lands, not his own. The President and Kissinger still worked for diplomatic glory, for the United States, and for themselves. But there was no Haldeman, no Ehrlichman, no Mitchell, no Dean to fend off Nixon's demons and antagonists and to cover the mistakes and misdeeds of his Administration. Indeed, several days after Nixon dismissed his aides, John Dean began to speak to the prosecutors in the Justice Department about the activities of "Mr. P" himself.[55] The President's personal fate had to be played out, but one suspects he knew what it would be long before others. Richard Nixon stood alone, naked to his enemies.

BOOK FOUR

THE WATERGATE WAR

DISARRAY AND DISGRACE
MAY 1973–AUGUST 1974

XIII

NEW ENEMIES

THE SPECIAL PROSECUTOR
AND THE SENATE COMMITTEE: MAY 1973

The April explosions gave no sign of abating as the calendar turned to May. The President's April 30 speech fueled charges of wider scandal and stimulated pressures for a wider investigation. Nixon's credibility was at stake. If Haldeman and Ehrlichman were among the "finest public servants" he had ever known, as he had said on the air, then why fire them?

The President now confronted the need to replace his staff, a need that required him to find loyal retainers, yet ones who would inspire public confidence. Having no alternative, Nixon also had to accept the appointment of a Special Prosecutor to plumb Watergate. Meanwhile, the Senate Select Committee prepared for a midmonth opening of its hearings, and its investigators pursued many witnesses already questioned by the U.S. Attorney, some of whom were now prepared to offer greater cooperation.

Nixon's position was deteriorating rapidly, and a sharp erosion of his public support undermined him even more. The Silent Majority or Square America—however he characterized it—had begun to question the President's behavior. In early April, a Gallup poll showed that the President had a nearly two-to-one approval rating, standing at 59 percent of respondents approving of his performance, 33 percent disapproving. The surveys for May 1–3 demonstrated a striking change, recorded at 48–40 percent approval/disapproval, with 12 percent now undecided. Ten days later, Gallup discovered the truly dramatic shift: 44 percent of respondents now approved of the President, while 45 percent disapproved. Reflecting the national erosion of confidence, Egil Krogh, under intense pressure for his role in the Field-

ing break-in, found the President's speech "unpersuasive." Krogh told Ehrlichman that Nixon was "on darn thin ice," and "in a helluva spot" for
not having investigated matters "vigorously."

Pat Buchanan pleaded with Nixon not to appease his opponents. This was
not the time, Buchanan warned, "to surrender all claim to the positions we
have held in the past"; instead it was a time for a "low profile and quiet
rearmament in this worthwhile struggle." He urged Nixon to take the offensive and not passively "suffer the death of a thousand cuts." Nixon responded that it would be useful to unleash Spiro Agnew or John Connally
to say that the President had been right in his handling of the Watergate
affair.

But would the President have the credibility and the public support that
Buchanan claimed for him? In early May, conservative political strategist
Kevin Phillips wrote in the newsletter he published that the "wheels of
government [had] ground to a substantial halt." Washington, he said, now
confronted the central questions: "1. Is the scandal going to get worse? and
2. Is *Richard Nixon* himself going to be involved? More and more people
believe that the answer to both is 'yes.'" President Richard Nixon had
moved into uncharted, dangerous territory.[1]

The President was demoralized, confused, and increasingly reclusive. A
year later, he recalled April 1973 as "about as rugged a period as anybody
could be through." At a Cabinet meeting on May 2, Nixon upbraided outgoing Attorney General Kleindienst because the FBI had sealed the office
files of Haldeman and Ehrlichman. Nixon had apparently forgotten that
he had directed that action. Frustrated and angry himself, Kleindienst defended the move and left the meeting. Meanwhile, Seymour Hersh of the
New York Times reported that six leading White House and CREEP officials—Haldeman, Ehrlichman, Mitchell, Dean, Magruder, and LaRue—
would be indicted.

Ron Ziegler offered an olive branch to the press. He contritely apologized
to the *Washington Post* and its reporters, who had pursued the Watergate
story most diligently. "In thinking of it all at this point in time, yes, I would
apologize to the *Post,* and I would apologize to [reporters] Mr. Woodward
and Mr. Bernstein." Ziegler pleaded that he had been "overenthusiastic"
in his earlier remarks.[2]

Haldeman, however, had some good news. The dismissed aide continued
to work in the White House, using his files (by then unsealed) to prepare for
his defense. Haldeman also listened to some Oval Office tapes and prepared
summaries for Nixon. In early June, he informed the President that Dean
had left no written records of the fateful March 21 meeting. Ziegler told
Nixon on June 4 that Haldeman's summaries did not indicate any presidential

cover-up. Nixon himself had signed out twenty-six tapes that day and then
listened to them on earphones for ten to twelve hours some days. Somewhat
reassured, the President returned to familiar topics: the failures and culpability of John Mitchell; and leaks, including those by "our Jewish friends—
even on our White House staff." Meanwhile, Nixon widened the circle of
those with knowledge of the secret tapes, apprising his new Chief of Staff,
General Alexander Haig (who informed Kissinger), his recently appointed
Counsel, J. Fred Buzhardt, and Stephen Bull, a young aide who had assumed
many of Alexander Butterfield's duties.[3]

On May 4, Nixon announced that General Haig would assume Haldeman's
duties on an "interim" basis. Haig already had moved into the post before
the announcement. The "interim" designation served only to mark time
before Haig could "retire" from the Army and assume his civilian position.
Some congressmen futilely challenged the legality of the appointment, since
Haig would serve the President while on active military duty. John Connally
was brought to the White House as an unpaid adviser, but his duties were
ill-defined, and he left soon thereafter. Buzhardt, General Counsel at the
Department of Defense, came to the White House on a "temporary" basis
as special counsel for Watergate affairs, supposedly with direct access to the
President. Buzhardt and Haig had been together at West Point and were
good friends. Buzhardt remained at the White House for the next fifteen
months, and he served as Haig's closest confidant.
 Circumstances gave Haig more influence with the President and far more
authority of his own than Haldeman had enjoyed, though Haig seems to
have performed less efficiently. Haldeman had rarely imposed his personal
beliefs on his job or acted on his own authority, but the times—and the
President's preoccupation with his own problems—had changed conditions,
and Haig did not hesitate to do so. Haig probably reduced the President's
affinity for compartmentalization of his affairs, more as a result of circumstances than of design. When Haig moved into his post, most of his potential
rivals had departed. After May 1, no Haldemans, Ehrlichmans, or Colsons
remained to serve the President in their special, independent ways. When
such rivals did emerge, as for example, the parade of various lawyers who
conducted the President's defense—Leonard Garment, J. Fred Buzhardt,
Charles Alan Wright, and finally, James St. Clair—they operated under the
shadow of Alexander Haig. St. Clair served the President during the darkest
hours of the impeachment crisis, yet he rarely saw Nixon alone. "It was my
responsibility," St. Clair recalled, "to keep General Haig fully informed.
To keep him fully informed was thus keeping the President fully informed. . . . [O]n occasion I reported directly to the President. Almost in
every case, General Haig was there."[4]

Vice President Spiro Agnew considered Haig "the de facto President" after he became White House Chief of Staff. Haig had cultivated extensive connections within the CIA, the FBI, and numerous other agencies throughout the government, Agnew wrote. More tellingly, he described Haig as "self-centered, ambitious, and ruthless"—in no other way could a man so quickly move from lieutenant colonel to four-star general and become the President's most important aide. Perhaps Nixon believed that Haig would serve in gratitude for his rapid promotion. Haig was a man who knew how to ingratiate himself for his own gain, however petty. In a lengthy "personal and confidential" memo to Haldeman in April 1971, Haig, then Kissinger's deputy on the National Security Council, pleaded for a place on the "A List" for the White House Motor Pool. Marshaling his arguments as if contending for a significant policy shift, Haig cited his long hours, his need to be on call "to put out one fire or another," his surrender of Army privileges (living quarters, car, personal aide, and a servant), and his family's need for a car ("so that family management can progress alongside White House management")—all this, Haig said, "would more than justif[y]" an automobile privilege.[5]

Haig's rise had been meteoric and had not been achieved without doubt and distaste on the part of his fellow military officers. He had graduated 214th in a class of 310 at West Point in 1947. He served on General Douglas MacArthur's staff for two years and subsequently experienced combat in Korea and Vietnam. The Army initially nominated several more-experienced colonels when Kissinger requested a deputy for himself as National Security Council adviser, but Kissinger insisted on Haig as a result of a recommendation by one of his own patrons. By the end of 1972, Haig had his four stars as a general "without the benefit of a single day in a military job since his command of a battalion . . . in 1967," as General Bruce Palmer wrote, and he had been jumped over 240 senior officers. In January 1973, Nixon nominated Haig to be the Army's Vice Chief of Staff to replace Palmer, although Haig's selection went against the recommendations of both outgoing Chief of Staff William Westmoreland and his successor, Creighton Abrams. After Haig moved to the Pentagon, the President provided him with a secure phone link to the White House, and Haig remained "deeply involved" in Administration affairs. Haig's connection only fueled resentment in the Pentagon.[6]

Until the Watergate crisis, Haig was a shadowy figure, yet one Nixon trusted in a special way. In the wake of the Joint Chiefs of Staff's spying on Kissinger and the National Security Council in 1971, the President directed that nothing be done to harm Haig. Haig was then Kissinger's deputy, although many suspected that he kept both White House and Pentagon officials apprised of Kissinger's activities. By early 1973, Nixon and his aides used

Haig as a counterweight to Kissinger. When General Brent Scowcroft moved into the National Security Council on January 1973, Haldeman told Haig to brief his fellow general and "totally level with him on the Kissinger problem," meaning the difficulty of working with Kissinger.[7]

White House staffers knew that Haldeman was the President's alter ego, but so was Haig in his way. Agnew found him "servile to those in the President's favor, overbearing to those outside the loop." He usefully served Nixon, a man who liked to "achieve results through indirection," Agnew added.

Yet Haig always seemed uncertain of his authority. According to Stephen Bull, Haig often would say, "I am the Chief of Staff" whenever challenged, "and I make all the decisions in the White House," repeating himself five or six times in the same situation. Bull, who served under both Haldeman and Haig, deeply believed that Haig served himself rather than the President. When, as Secretary of State in 1981, Haig appeared at the White House following the attempted assassination of President Reagan and proclaimed, "I am in charge here," many observers found him displaying a familiar pattern of behavior—characterized by Bull as a "very serious personality disorder." Haldeman, Bull recalled, never had to remind others of his authority, and Haig often expressed insecurity about himself vis-à-vis Haldeman. But then, one often was uncertain as to which Haig he encountered. The General was, recalled one official, "an *improvisateur* of a persona."

South Vietnamese President Nguyen Van Thieu remembered his meetings with Haig similarly: "When he is a general, Haig thinks like me," said Thieu. "When he is a special envoy of President Nixon, he does the job of a special envoy." Haig had a way of making himself indispensable, like Thomas Cromwell, who in a famous play described his role for Henry VIII: "I do things." Kissinger praised his deputy as a man who "disciplined my anarchic tendencies and established coherence and prudence" in the staff of "talented prima donnas." But Kissinger also recognized that Haig was ruthless; Haig, he remembered, "was implacable in squeezing to the sidelines potential competitors for my attention." Altogether, Kissinger concluded, a "formidable" man.[8]

Repairing staff damage, of course, had a high priority for the President. It was imperative that he appoint a new Attorney General who could command respect across the political spectrum. William Rogers pressed for Elliot Richardson, a man with proven skills and versatility with experience in both the Nixon and Eisenhower administrations. The President had anticipated Rogers's suggestion nearly a year earlier. One day before the Watergate break-in, Nixon told Ehrlichman to inform Richardson, then Secretary of Health,

Education and Welfare, that he would be one of the few Cabinet officials retained; in fact, the President told Ehrlichman, he might name Richardson as Attorney General.[9]

A Harvard Law School graduate, a former law clerk to Judge Learned Hand and Justice Felix Frankfurter, and a quintessential Boston Brahmin in appearance, manner, and commitment, Richardson epitomized all that the President despised, distrusted—and envied. But that same background, coupled with a respect for his integrity, now offered an irresistible appeal to the beleaguered President. Richardson had assumed the leadership of the Defense Department just three months earlier, after his stint directing HEW. He had no desire to leave the Pentagon, for he regarded his Cabinet job as equal in importance to that of Secretary of State. The President, Richardson claimed uneasily, had promised him that he would be a "counterweight" to Kissinger in mapping the Administration's geopolitical strategy. Furthermore, the prospect of an ongoing Watergate investigation promised much unpleasantness. But Elliot Richardson was widely regarded as a "good soldier," and the request to head the Department of Justice gave him an opportunity to add to his already substantial reputation as cooperative and reliable. When Richardson took the Pentagon post, for example, he literally begged the President to allow him to retain his longtime personal aide, conceding, however, that he would respect the President's wishes. Meanwhile, concerning the Watergate scandals, Nixon assured Richardson on April 29: "You've got to believe I didn't know anything."[10]

Perhaps because he sacrificed much in accepting the new post, Richardson took the opportunity to provide the President with some useful counsel. Watergate, he said, had created a crisis of confidence, but Richardson thought it might offer an opportunity to display the President's openness and magnanimous spirit. Richardson sensed that Nixon must curb his well-known proclivity for nursing grievances; above all, he believed, the President must realize that he had "arrived," that he had stature in the eyes of the people. "[Y]ou have *won*—not only won, but been reelected by a tremendous margin. You are the President of *all* the people of the United States. There is no 'they' out there—nobody trying to destroy you." But he remembered that the President sat mute, offering no expression of either agreement or disagreement.[11] Richardson's truth, as he saw it, simply did not fit Richard Nixon's perception of reality or his favorite guise of outsider. It was not a promising beginning. As it turned out, Richardson's five-month tenure in the Justice Department was framed by two weekends, on one of which the President proved to be a good butcher, and on the other, a bad one.

The President told Richardson at Camp David on April 29 that the Attorney General had "specific responsibility" to get "to the bottom of this." All guilty parties were to be prosecuted, "no matter who it hurts." He promised Richardson full access—"there will be nobody between you and me." But Richardson soon learned—much to his frustration—that the Haldeman and Ehrlichman "Berlin Wall" did not disappear with their departure. That wall had been erected and maintained by the President of the United States; his new staff members quickly adapted to a similar structure—and so did Richardson, who had almost no personal dealings with the President for the next five months. The President also instructed Richardson to "stand firm" on two points: first, presidential conversations must remain privileged; and second, there could be no intrusions "into [the] national security area." Otherwise, the President said, "I don't give a Goddamn what it is—Mitchell, Stans—anybody."¹²

Despite the turbulence of the Administration's changes, Richardson remained optimistic. The new Attorney General told John Ehrlichman that he would continue to have Richardson's "total respect." Richardson informed Ehrlichman that he wished he himself had not become "an instrument" in dealing with the affair, but he had not been "convincing enough" to the President. Ehrlichman, confident as ever, said he had no concern as to the outcome of events and believed the whole thing "ephemeral." "I have that feeling, too," replied Richardson. But as Richardson reviewed the Watergate affair and the Fielding break-in during the next few days, he had less reason to be so optimistic.¹³

By this time the demands for a Special Prosecutor had grown irresistible. In his Camp David discussion with Richardson, the President readily conceded the point, even projecting such possible candidates as John J. McCloy, the well-known adviser of presidents dating back to FDR; J. Edward Lumbard, a former U.S. Attorney and now Circuit Court Judge; and Richardson's former aide, Wilmot R. Hastings. Nixon had periodically discussed the idea of bringing an outside lawyer to the White House to deal exclusively with Watergate. He wanted a respected personality but also someone who was a "friend"; he needed, he told Ehrlichman, someone who would say that despite "all those Segretti projects, ... none of the White House people were involved. There are no other higher-up[s]." But Ehrlichman reminded him that he had a "Dean problem."¹⁴

Within days, Richardson's staff assistant prepared a list of potential Watergate Special Prosecutors which included Lumbard as well as several sitting, retiring, or former federal judges, notably David Peck, Lawrence Walsh, Henry Friendly, and Harold Tyler. Lumbard and Peck were the early favorites. But Lumbard indicated that no sitting judge should accept the position, and Peck was eliminated because he was a Republican. Cyrus Vance, John Doar, Albert Jenner, Warren Christopher, Alexander Bickel,

Paul Freund, Leon Jaworski, and Archibald Cox were on a list of 100 names compiled by May 11. From that the staff gave Richardson a short list of thirteen. The only full-time sitting judge on the list was Tyler, who was included chiefly because he indicated a desire to leave the bench, not because the staff considered him the most able candidate. Erwin Griswold weighed in with advice to Richardson, his former law student, suggesting that he appoint a "nonpolitical" Democrat like Christopher, Arthur Goldberg, Nicholas Katzenbach, E. Barrett Prettyman, or Simon Rifkind.

Richardson approached numerous people—exactly how many he could not later recall. One after another declined, including Leon Jaworski. The reasons varied: simple lack of interest, realization that the task would be difficult and complex, fear that the position could never have the necessary degree of independence. On May 14 the staff prepared to announce the selection of Judge Tyler, who had served in the Kennedy Justice Department. But the announcement stalled pending the preparation of guidelines for the responsibilities and independence of the Special Prosecutor, something the Senate Judiciary Committee had requested.

Richardson could not act promptly enough to suit Tyler, and the judge decided that he "could not wait much longer in light of my current burdens on the court." To Richardson, however, Tyler seemed unwilling, after all, to give up his seat. In any event, several days later, Richardson approached Harvard Law School Professor Archibald Cox, who less than a week earlier had been omitted from the staff's short list. Cox was "up front" regarding his independence, a subject that others only skirted. He readily indicated his interest, and on May 18, Richardson announced his selection.[15]

Richardson later claimed that no one "forced" him into making the appointment of a Special Prosecutor: "I was fully convinced it should be done." Yet he confronted a pointed appeal from the Justice Department's own prosecutors, who had reached a crucial stage of negotiations with witnesses and lawyers and urged that they be allowed to continue. On April 30, U.S. Attorney Harold Titus wrote to Richardson, in a letter signed by his three principal assistants, Earl Silbert, Seymour Glanzer, and Donald Campbell, stating the case. These men had directed the Watergate investigation from the outset—"we have guided the FBI, and we have handled the delicate difficult relationships with witnesses . . . and possible prospective witnesses such as Magruder and Dean." Their strategy of bargaining with and inducing certain witnesses to come forth had worked and now had reached a critical state. "We are in the driver's seat," they told Richardson, adding, "we have momentum." The prosecutors chose not to alert Richardson to the fullness of their case, but warned him not to require them to report to the President, because so much of his staff was involved. The President and the prosecutors alike, they feared, would be in an "impossible position."[16]

* * *

Richardson's confirmation hearing was so linked to the appointment of a Special Prosecutor that on May 21 the nominee brought Archibald Cox to the Senate Judiciary Committee. Committee members seemed particularly anxious to understand how each man perceived their upcoming relationship. Chairman James Eastland asked Cox whether he thought he could work amicably with Richardson. Cox was certain he would, but he amended the answer to underscore his own commitment to independence, which might mean his and Richardson's going separate ways. J. Strom Thurmond inquired about Cox's political affiliation. When Cox responded, "Democratic," Thurmond thought that this would be fine for public confidence. Even the President's warmest supporters found it convenient to have the Special Prosecutor come from the "other side."

Democratic Whip Robert Byrd asked the most questions, the tone of which should have indicated to the President that some traditional Democratic allies had grown uneasy. Byrd asked Richardson and Cox to discuss how they thought their relationship would evolve. Richardson acknowledged that he had conceded a great deal of discretion to Cox. Byrd asked Cox whether he needed still broader authority. No, Cox thought it was clear: "Let's face it, I think I will have the whip hand." And "you won't hesitate to use it?" Byrd asked. "No, sir," Cox firmly answered. If the Attorney General pressed him for information that he preferred not to give, then Richardson would be reduced to his "final statutory authority"—to fire the Special Prosecutor. How far would Cox go in the investigation—to the Ellsberg case, for example? "Even though that trail should lead, Heaven forbid, to the oval office of the White House?" Byrd queried. Cox was emphatic: "Wherever that trail may lead."

Byrd explored the Special Prosecutor's possible dealings with the President. Could the President demand a status report? Not if "I felt that it was against the interests of the investigation," Cox said. Could the Attorney General overrule him? No, Cox said, Richardson's only choice would be to dismiss him. Cox challenged the President's position on immunity, saying he would grant it to witnesses if he thought it proper. Finally, Cox said that the presidential claims of "executive privilege" involved an "appropriate role" for judicial determination. For himself, he expressed great skepticism regarding the doctrine. He told another Senator that executive privilege lay with the executive branch and not with individuals.

Senator John Tunney (D–CA) homed in on the meaning of "extraordinary improprieties," which was the proposed term for defining what would justify removal of the Special Prosecutor. The answers from both Richardson and Cox were as nebulous as the words themselves. Richardson thought the "public," expressing itself through the Senate, would have a good deal to do with firing any Special Prosecutor. Cox thought that if he were guilty of "extraordinary improprieties," he should be fired.

Several senators raised the delicate issue of Cox's cooperation with the Department of Justice investigators and prosecutors. Cox told Senator Philip Hart (D–MI) that he would review the status of the investigation and then make his own judgments and decisions as to procedures. Senator Edward Kennedy, perhaps as much Cox's patron as any senator, tried to stretch the guidelines and the Special Prosecutor's authority, though without much success. But he spurred Cox to assert that he would make his own staff appointments. Cox also told Kennedy that he expected to phase Henry Petersen out of the investigation. It would not be the last time that those who had pressed the case as far as it had come would be treated with a curious mixture of skepticism and derision.[17]

Richard Nixon publicly welcomed Richardson's selection of Cox and complimented his new Attorney General for demonstrating a "determination" to find the truth. "In this effort," the President said, "he has my full support." But the public words only veiled the President's wariness, even anger, over the appointment. One would be hard pressed to invent a more unacceptable choice than Cox, given Nixon's well-known defensiveness and animosity toward certain groups. Cox represented many of them: Harvard Law School professor, East Coast liberal, Solicitor General in the Kennedy Administration, and still a Kennedy loyalist. (Nixon may not have known that Cox's maternal great-grandfather, William Evarts, had defended President Andrew Johnson during his impeachment trial in 1868.)

Richardson, of course, was some of the same things as Cox, but the President undoubtedly regarded the new Attorney General as *his* Harvard man. Cox had voted for McGovern, and just two weeks before his selection as Special Prosecutor, he had criticized John Mitchell as "insensitive" toward civil liberties. When he was sworn in on May 24, Senator Edward Kennedy and Mrs. Robert Kennedy attended. Few events of the period left Nixon more bitter. Had Richardson searched specifically for the man the President could least trust, he would have selected Cox, Nixon wrote. "Unfortunately," as he put it, he had given Richardson "absolute authority" to select a prosecutor, and thus "put the survival of my administration in his hands," and Richardson in turn had given it to a "partisan viper."

Within days after he assumed office, Cox's appointments to positions in the Special Prosecutor's office raised further distress signals for the President. Cox first selected a Press Secretary, James Doyle, a prominent Washington newsman well known for his anti-Nixon views. He then chose two Harvard Law School colleagues for leading positions on his staff, following them with the staff appointment of James F. Neal, a forty-three-year-old

Nashville attorney who had been the U.S. Attorney in that area and Robert F. Kennedy's special assistant from 1961 to 1964. Seven of the Special Prosecutor's eight-person senior staff had held office in the Kennedy and Johnson administrations. More than half the lawyers who served in the Special Prosecutor's office had graduated from the Harvard Law School.

Cox's sweeping authority alarmed the Administration even more than his personnel. Richardson and Cox agreed on a charter, and on May 31, the Attorney General directed Cox to investigate all "possible offenses" of the Administration—not just those relating to the Watergate break-in, but including all other "allegations involving the President, members of the White House staff or presidential appointees." Nixon was "shocked and angry." Richardson assured Haig that the language referred only to the Watergate break-in and cover-up, but the President knew better. His doubts, resentments, and fears only magnified. His staff and supporters mirrored his mood. Within a few months, White House lawyers and the President's supporters were contemptuously referring to the Special Prosecutor's office as "Coxsuckers," or as "Cox's Army," one with "sharp ideological axes to grind." The Special Prosecutor's office appeared to them as nothing less than the vanguard for Senator Kennedy's march to the White House.[18]

Haig had called Richardson as early as June 19 to complain about Cox after the latter had told reporters he might subpoena the President. Weeks later, Haig told Richardson that the President "was very uptight about Cox" and "wants a line drawn." If Cox did not stay within the guidelines, Haig warned, they would "get rid" of him. Buzhardt expressed similar sentiments, according to Richardson.[19]

Perhaps Cox was the wrong man for the job. What he represented, and how he proceeded, undoubtedly exacerbated the situation. Henry Petersen, who naturally resented the transfer of the case from his own jurisdiction, thought Cox "ultra-liberal" and believed the post should have gone to "a less partisan man." The job required a man "with more detachment"; Cox's rectitude, Petersen thought, was "second only to God." Less than three months after Cox's appointment, Petersen bitterly described his resentment to the Senate Select Committee. "Damn it," he exploded, "I think it is a reflection on me and the Department of Justice. We could have broken that case wide open, and we would have done it in the most difficult circumstances. . . . That case was snatched out from under us when we had it 90-percent completed." By that time, Petersen realized how the President of the United States and his Counsel, John Dean, had so badly misled him. It was a frustrating conclusion to a worthy career.

The staff that Cox assembled underlined "prosecution" as the operative word in the formal title of the office: "Watergate Special Prosecution Force." Undoubtedly, public spirit motivated many of the men and women in the office. But they were also profoundly hostile to the President and his Administration. They operated according to the calculus and dictates of persons chosen to pursue alleged wrongdoers: with zeal, passion, and absolute certainty that their subjects must be guilty. Erwin Griswold, Cox's former Harvard dean, found himself under investigation by some of the young lawyers in the Special Prosecutor's office. In his interested assessment, most lacked "background or judgment." They often proceeded with "far more zeal than judgment." Griswold saw no "corruption in their motives," but he thought they often went "overboard" to show they were doing their duty."[20]

The Senate confirmation hearings reflected Richardson's and Cox's wariness toward one another. Their relationship may well have always been a little "uneasy," as William Ruckelshaus, who was close to both, remembered. They shared Harvard, clerkships with Learned Hand, and friendships with Felix Frankfurter, but Cox's political commitments and loyalties diverged immensely from Richardson's. Cox, a Kennedy loyalist, undoubtedly had contempt for Richard Nixon. Richardson had battled the Kennedys' grip on Massachusetts and had real loyalty to a President who had trusted him with a succession of high, important offices. Spiro Agnew later mocked the "didactic Richardson" as a man who "changed from a transparent toady to a sanctimonious lecturer on morals." Maybe Watergate transformed him a bit, but until the very end of his tenure, Richardson remained what he always had been: a steadfast, loyal retainer of his patron, the President of the United States.

Again unlike Cox, Richardson had been domesticated to the President's service and needs. He was a man with an ambition to serve, to accomplish something, both for himself and the nation. Some months earlier, when he had been appointed Secretary of Defense, Nixon had promised Richardson a voice in the making of foreign and defense policy. He never had it. Perhaps Richardson hoped, as he said, to get to "the bottom" of Watergate, and serve the nation and the President in that fashion. Again, the President seemed to promise him access to that route. Again, he never had it.[21]

Some of the criticism directed toward Cox and his staff implied that the Special Prosecutor heightened the conflicts leading to the political and constitutional crisis of October 1973. Nixon, so this analysis goes, never would have dared confront a different man, one immune to the accusation of partisanship—someone like John J. McCloy.

Archibald Cox later recalled that by spring 1973, "it became apparent that the Department of Justice was not investigating the charges as vigorously as the evidence then warranted." Indeed, it did appear to many that Richard Nixon's Justice Department could not be trusted to vigorously investigate and prosecute the mushrooming charges. Senator Sam Ervin offered more pointed criticism. Allowing for the prosecutors' difficulties in bargaining with Magruder and Dean, Ervin nevertheless remarked that "the prosecutors fell substantially short of prying open and presenting to the grand jury the truth respecting the Watergate affair." Ervin, too, certainly had his interest and place in history to defend. Solicitor General Robert Bork had a different interest. From his vantage point, he remembered, the regular prosecutors "would have made the case just as it was ultimately made." Bork dismissed as silly any notion that a case could be fixed. Too many people knew what was happening. If someone had tried "to bag a case," Bork believed the news would have leaked instantly; the fragmentation and rivalries within the Justice Department made it impossible for anyone "to fix" the case.[22]

The perception that the Justice Department's investigation was compromised was not without reason, but both Cox and Ervin knew better. The U.S. Attorney's office had in fact discovered the cover-up conspiracy and had broken the case by the time Cox took control, and before Senator Ervin's committee provided a public venting of what the prosecutors had learned.

The U.S. Attorneys' narrow construction of the criminal case against the Watergate burglars had aroused criticism and even suspicion of their motives. As the trial ended, Earl Silbert, frustrated by his inability to "turn" any of the defendants, told reporters that "there is no evidence of a wider conspiracy." He was right; but the rapid exposure of evidence in the next few weeks unfairly made him appear either incompetent or part of yet another cover-up. Later, critics such as Senator Ervin thought that if the prosecutors had pursued leads as far back as August 1972, they might have discovered the involvement of various White House aides, such as Strachan and Chapin—implying that that discovery might have led to Haldeman and the President. But as Ervin acknowledged, "hindsight is easier than foresight." The Senator, furthermore, failed to acknowledge John Dean's success in keeping the prosecutors at bay.

By the end of May, Henry Petersen had come under increasing attack, which touched the prosecutors themselves. Critics scoffed at Petersen's reluctance to impinge on executive privilege and probe conversations between Nixon and Dean. Petersen's view that the President could not be prosecuted was well known, as was his insistence that only the House of Representatives could consider incriminating evidence against him. Even the prosecutors themselves were a bit wary about Petersen, their superior. They advised Elliot Richardson as early as April 30 that Petersen should withdraw from the case. At that point, Silbert and his associates had discovered the extent of Dean's conversations with Petersen, and they realized that Petersen might himself have to be a witness in the case. Dean demanded that Silbert not tell Petersen of Dean's revelations regarding "Mr. P"—as Dean's lawyer referred to the President—quite simply because he was no longer sure of Petersen.[23]

By mid-May, the prosecutors had effectively sealed their case against the

President's men for their roles in the break-in and the cover-up. Harold Titus, Silbert's superior, wrote to Richardson on the fifteenth, describing the delicate state of the case. His aides had worked long and hard but had only begun to gain the necessary evidence to make their arguments. Just at this time, for example, Fred LaRue had corroborated Mitchell's role in the cover-up. Most important of all, the prosecutors had gained Dean's cooperation, without granting him immunity. Dean and his lawyer had bargained hard for immunity at the outset, when Dean had confined his incriminating remarks to Haldeman and Ehrlichman. Whether because he failed to gain immunity, or in a further gamble to do so, Dean later decided to implicate the President as well. But Silbert stood fast, as he understood throughout that if he granted immunity, both Dean and the prosecution would suffer a loss of credibility. Silbert, moreover, firmly believed that Dean was the ringmaster of the cover-up, the one who had "perverted the system."

In his May 15 letter, Titus worried that the Senate Select Committee hearings, scheduled to begin in two days, might irreparably harm subsequent trial efforts. Such publicity, he feared, might be so prejudicial as to affect the government's ability to select a fair and impartial jury. Titus hoped that somehow Richardson might persuade Ervin to give the prosecutors more time to complete their work. But Richardson had his own problems. He had yet to be confirmed—and Ervin served as a key member of the Senate Judiciary Committee—and he had not yet selected a Watergate Special Prosecutor. Hence it was "inappropriate" for him "to intervene at this juncture," Richardson told Titus. Once it became clear that the Senate hearing would proceed and that Richardson had no choice but to select a Special Prosecutor, Titus wrote back on May 18, for the record, saying that Richardson should be aware of "the totality of the current investigation." The major witnesses in the case had been interviewed at length, and most had appeared before the grand jury. A "key member" of the conspiracy had agreed to plead guilty without immunity. Titus meant Dean, of course, though he did not identify him.[24]

By then, the Watergate investigation was contested turf. Samuel Dash, the Senate Select Committee's Counsel, and his staff dismissed any attempts to restrain their efforts. Dash's staff divided when they heard Silbert's request that they tread carefully for fear of upsetting the indictments. The dominant voices simply refused to trust the prosecutors and insisted that the hearings proceed. Dash met Silbert in an attempt to settle their differences, but distrust on Dash's side, and Silbert's concern with protecting his case, doomed any attempts at cooperation. Dash was convinced that Dean was more willing to cooperate with the Senate than with the prosecutors. The Select Committee's workers, of course, had their history to make, but one knowledgeable staff member later conceded that "Silbert had broken the case—that's why

Dean and McCord came to us." Meanwhile, Cox indicated to Dash that he had doubts about the credibility and motivation of Dean. Cox knew at that point—quite correctly—that if Dean were the best witness, then the whole case rested on his credibility.[25]

Time flew like an arrow for Silbert and his colleagues. The Senate hearings opened on May 17, and Richardson appointed Cox the next day. The U.S. Attorneys' days in the case were numbered. Cox eased the transition in order not to lose the momentum of the case. The federal prosecutors briefed their successors at great length as to the evidence and prosecutorial theories they had developed. James Neal, who had gained the conviction of Jimmy Hoffa, was brought to Washington by Cox in late May, to prepare for prosecutions. Neal graciously complimented the prosecutors for their efforts. Silbert was ambivalent. The appointment of the Special Prosecutor deprived him and his associates of a proper share of public credit; still, he had grown weary of the unfair criticism and of maintaining proper procedures and fairness in the face of media pressures. Ultimately, he acknowledged that "the special prosecutor may be considered necessary for the appearance of justice."[26]

When the U.S. Attorneys surrendered control, they provided Cox with a detailed eighty-seven-page summary of their efforts. Silbert set down the basic nature of the misdeeds and criminal violations by White House aides, CREEP staff, CIA and FBI leaders, and Justice Department officials. At this point much of what they knew came from the testimony of Dean, Magruder, various CREEP workers, and the Plumbers' chief operatives, Krogh and Young. The charges were clear; what remained was to garner and assemble the evidence necessary to gain convictions.

At the end of his report, Silbert listed witnesses yet to be interviewed or presented to the grand jury. He named twenty-seven in all—number 27 being no less than Richard Nixon himself. "Were he not President," Silbert wrote, "there is no question but that President Nixon would have to be questioned about a number of matters." Silbert ticked off the President's post–break-in conversations with Haldeman, Ehrlichman, Helms, Walters—and most important, with Dean. Silbert had crossed the Rubicon in his trust of the President. Nixon's May 22 statement proclaiming his innocence, "rather than answering all the questions, raises a host of others," Silbert observed. An interview with the President, he suggested, "could be vital in determining the truth."

The federal prosecutors' report to Cox was a turning point for the President's fortunes. For the first time a duly constituted authority had officially raised the possibility of Nixon's own involvement in aspects of the criminal conspiracy. Ironically, the May 22 press conference statement of the President had raised the prosecutors' suspicions. ("I neither authorized nor encouraged subordinates to engage in illegal or improper campaign tactics.")

Nixon's lengthy discussion of the creation of the Plumbers, his relation to it, the 1969 wiretaps, the abortive Domestic Intelligence Reorganization (Huston Plan) of 1970, and the White House response to the Watergate break-in, indicated some presidential involvement. Though he steadfastly denied any criminal conduct or wrongdoing on his part, the President's admissions raised the possibility that he might not be the best judge of his own innocence. Nixon himself had conceded that different people "saw the same situation with different eyes and heard the same words with different ears."

The prosecutors no longer had the mandate, the time, or the resources to question the President. The case now belonged to Cox. But the U.S. Attorney's office also understood the problem of confronting the President of the United States: "obviously a matter of such extreme sensitivity, raising Constitutional questions." The buck was passed: "whatever steps are taken," they told Cox, "can only be by you."

If Archibald Cox had left Harvard Yard to take on the guise of Macduff and impose a well-deserved retribution on Macbeth, here was his opportunity. He refused. Cox was inclined to "lay off for now," as he noted on the U.S. Attorney's summary memo. The numerous, varied cast of the President's men who might be implicated in wrongdoing was imposing and challenging enough. Dirty tricks, campaign excesses, and possible criminal conspiracies seemed to offer a full table. The President himself? Dash suggested such a possibility to Cox at the same time Silbert's report did, but Cox simply responded that whatever his office learned would be passed on in his eventual report to Congress.[27] Cox believed (or preferred to believe) at this point, as did Henry Petersen and others in the Department of Justice, that presidential wrongdoing first required a response by Congress. In June 1973, the notion of a prosecutorial challenge to the President seemed best confined to the realm of black humor.

As the case passed to the Special Prosecutor, the U.S. Attorney's office provided Cox with their materials. Silbert and his colleagues would not reap the harvest of a year's intimate contact with the Watergate case and the growing ramifications of it; that glory would belong to others. On June 29 they wrote to Cox, renewing a request to withdraw from the case. They used the occasion to state the record of their long, arduous work. By mid-April their office had uncovered "the existence of a massive conspiracy to obstruct justice, the participants therein, and their motives." They broke Magruder, successfully pried information from Dean without immunizing him, discovered the Plumbers' operations, and gained several guilty pleas. Finally, the prosecutors realized that their separation from the case might seem to justify criticism of their work. "Such speculation is wholly unwarranted," they bluntly concluded. Cox replied graciously, acknowledging that they had suffered unfairly from adverse criticism and adding that he and his staff believed that the prosecutors had acted only in accord with their "honest judgment and in complete good faith."[28]

With that, Cox focused on completing his housekeeping chores for his new position and on expanding the investigation. He established his own channel to the FBI, designed to bypass the Attorney General and the Criminal Division of the Justice Department, a move that only reinforced public feeling that he had taken over a discredited investigation. Cox's chief aides urged him to turn his hoard of political capital into tangible assets as quickly as possible. The Special Prosecutor should provide for an appropriation for "a very sizable professional and support staff," adequate office quarters, and senior and middle-level staffers "while this issue is hot." He should demand access to presidential papers and information on CIA and FBI internal-security operations, and he should mount a challenge to the President's views on executive privilege. Ultimately, Cox's office boasted a staff of more than 150 persons, including a security group of 19. Cox paid close attention to staff dealings with the press. The problem was delicate. He could not afford to alienate so substantial an ally, yet he could not risk prejudicial publicity that might jeopardize any of his cases.[29]

Cox perceived that his task force had a substantial rival in the Senate Select Committee. The committee had been at its work for more than three months when Cox appeared on the scene. The day before Richardson announced Cox's appointment, the committee launched its public hearings. Cox quickly came to the same conclusion that Earl Silbert had reached: the committee's public hearings could well interfere with future prosecutions. Several days after Cox's appointment, Select Committee Counsel Sam Dash paid a courtesy call on his former professor. He offered Cox access to the committee's computerized files and asked what else he could do. "Disband," Cox said.

Senator Howard Baker later characterized Cox's attitude toward the Ervin Committee as preferring that "we go out of business." On June 4 Cox specifically asked Ervin to suspend the hearings until all trials had been held, in order to "promote our mutual goals." He thought that the hearings would impede investigations because witnesses would rather bargain than testify publicly; he worried that excessive publicity would undermine accepted standards for fair trials; he believed that grand-jury proceedings might better protect the innocent; and finally, he argued that dual investigations would result in confusing releases of bits and pieces of information.

Cox told Ervin that he feared his request might be construed as a cover-up, but Ervin recognized that Cox simply did not want the Select Committee in the field. What Cox desired, the Senator told his colleagues, was for the committee to delay "until the last ringing echo of Gabriel's horn trebles off into silence." Ervin and Senator Herman Talmadge argued that the committee had no power to delay, however, since it operated under orders from the full Senate.

When the Select Committee applied to Judge John Sirica for immunity for Magruder and Dean, Cox perfunctorily challenged the request, urging the judge to require private hearings for the witnesses or deny the committee access to them altogether. With intended irony, Dash invoked an argument Cox had made as Solicitor General in the Kennedy Administration, that courts could not interfere with congressional public hearings to protect pending criminal trials. Judge Sirica emphatically agreed with Dash and Solicitor General Cox.[30]

The Senate Select Committee prepared for more than three months for the public hearings. The White House did likewise, beginning with Ehrlichman presiding over a lengthy meeting in San Clemente in February to discuss the committee and White House moves. The participants agreed to delegate a liaison with Howard Baker, one directed by Dean. Ehrlichman assessed the committee and dismissed the Democrats as inevitably partisan. He told Dean that the name of Senator Daniel Inouye (D–HI) should be pronounced "Ain't no way," for "ain't no way he's going to give us anything but problems."

Shortly after the committee convened, Baker visited the President for a "totally off-the-record," "private" meeting and reported on the committee's early activities. Ervin, Baker commented, was "full of compliments"—it was not clear whether they were for Republican members or for the President. Nixon urged Baker to keep the investigation confined to the Watergate burglary, rule out hearsay evidence, and invoke the "Hiss rules," whatever those were. Several times over the next week, Nixon insisted that executive privilege not be compromised, but somehow he confused what he regarded as Truman's "cover-up" of the Hiss affair with a proper course of action for himself. Yet he proved willing to compromise, suggesting that his staff might answer written questions from the Senate committee. Discussions of the forthcoming hearings repeatedly evoked presidential soliloquies on his role in the Hiss hearing. As always, Nixon believed that he had earned "their" hatred because of that case. The "New York–Washington axis," he firmly believed, was out "to get" him.

The President directed that his aides guide Republican congressional leaders in establishing a firm defensive line against the committee. At one and the same time, he said that the issue must be "defused" and that he would not tolerate a cover-up. He wanted Kleindienst and Baker to work together to ensure executive sessions for White House personnel and thereby avoid confrontations over executive privilege. But in the Administration, confrontation often accompanied conciliation. Nixon wanted Ziegler briefed so that he could "kick the Ervin committee." Haldeman meanwhile would publicize examples of Democratic Party sabotage and violence during the campaign. By April 11 the President wished to know who would handle the "counter-attack" against the committee; he particularly wanted questions to be raised concerning Democratic campaign spending and practices. He instructed Ehrlichman to talk to their friends in the press and urge them to cease writing about the Administration's lack of cooperation with the committee. Nixon, however, underestimated the situation, confidently believing that Senators Baker and Edward Gurney would provide strong minority reports, thus reducing the heat. Still, he looked for a deal with Ervin whereby John Dean might testify in executive session.[31]

Charles Colson and Ehrlichman worked together to develop guidelines that might best protect the President's aides and his claims to executive privilege once the hearings commenced. John Mitchell contributed a bit to the discussions, as did Baker. Ehrlichman and Ervin negotiated at length—with their telephone conversations dutifully taped by Ehrlichman.[32]

The President trusted Baker and Gurney. But Lowell Weicker troubled him deeply. "What the hell makes Weicker tick?" Nixon asked Haldeman and Ehrlichman. "Nobody's been able to figure that out," Ehrlichman responded. Several days later, Ehrlichman asked Baker the same question.[33]

The White House thought that attacks on Dash might intimidate or delay the proceedings. Ehrlichman asked Gray to have the FBI check Dash's background. When Dash hired a chief investigator—a man distinguished for inventing a "bug" designed to simulate a martini olive—White House staff workers publicly complained that Dash had "compromised" the entire investigative process, despite the fact that the man had already been relieved. They also discovered that Dash had criticized Mitchell and that a Select Committee staff lawyer had criticized the Administration when he had been fired as head of legal services at the Office of Economic Opportunity. White House aide Ken Khachigian told Larry Higby that with enough pressure, they could force Dash's resignation and "throw the Ervin Hearings into chaos." But Khachigian was operating amid chaos—and did not know it. He gave his memo to John Dean, requesting approval and action; at the same time, Dean was negotiating with the prosecutors and preparing to talk to Dash.[34]

The most elaborate White House plans for coping with the Senate Select Committee involved its arrangements with Howard Baker. Baker had led the Republican opposition when the Senate authorized the committee in February. Despite senatorial courtesy, Baker's readily transparent attempts to narrow the scope of the investigation fooled few people. In the months prior to the public hearings, Baker regularly consulted with Nixon's chief aides, fought to contain the investigation, and argued in behalf of the President's tactics within the committee. He failed, notwithstanding his thinly disguised appeals for "fairness."

According to Dean, Baker requested an off-the-record meeting with the President in late February or early March, just after he selected Fred Thompson, a Tennessee campaign aide and a former U.S. Attorney, as the Senate Committee's Minority Counsel. White House congressional-liaison men had suggested other names to Baker, but Baker went his own way. Dean thought that Baker wanted to assure Nixon of his good intentions. The President's briefing paper—prepared by Dean or his aides—suggested that Baker prevent the hearings from becoming a "political circus" and that they be concluded quickly because they were nothing more than a "witch hunt." The President could assure the Senator that the White House had no prior knowledge of the Watergate break-in, and he could inform Baker that the Democrats had bugged Nixon's own offices in 1968. The paper also stressed that Dash was partisan and urged that the minority members of the committee treat him roughly. Finally, it was suggested that Baker meet with Dean to discuss committee matters, a ploy that would reinforce claims for executive privilege for Dean should he be called as a witness.

When Dean and Baker later clashed over this meeting in an executive session of the committee, Dean admitted that Baker had urged the President to waive executive privilege. But he insisted that Nixon believed he had Baker's commitment to aid the White House. Colson told the President on March 21 that Baker was eager to cooperate and that the Senator had signalled the President to ignore his public statements, as they were for "political" consumption. Baker met Kleindienst for secret consultations, and a Baker aide informed Colson that Baker hoped to "control" Ervin. Ehrlichman assured Nixon that Baker was "protecting us" regarding executive-session testimony by White House aides. Baker and Ehrlichman held lengthy discussions regarding television coverage of the hearings. They talked several times in late March and early April, and on several occasions, Baker spoke to the President.[35]

Baker and Thompson labored to ensure that the hearings would end by June and to keep them confined to the Watergate break-in, dirty tricks, and campaign financing. At a crucial May 8 executive session of the committee, Baker argued that the burglars (excepting McCord) and the arresting police officers should appear first, followed by Mitchell, Colson, Haldeman, and Ehrlichman. Dean would be last, thus enabling the others to avoid responding to his accusations. Baker also wanted senators to question witnesses before the committee counsels had their turn. Ervin would have none of it: "Well, my daddy used to say that if you hire a lawyer, you should either take his advice or fire him. Since we're not planning to fire Sam Dash, I suggest we take his advice."

Baker tenaciously opposed granting immunity to Dean, as requested by Dash. He faithfully echoed the emerging White House line: "I believe he is probably the most culpable and dangerous person in the Watergate affair." He complained that Dean and his lawyer had intimidated the committee. Again: "From what I hear, Dean is the principal culprit in this Watergate affair." Gurney readily supported him, but Weicker backed Dash's position, leaving Baker no choice but to go along rather than isolate himself. He asked that the record show his "grave concern." Senator Ervin, always mindful of senatorial courtesies, "suspected" that the White House tried, but unsuccessfully, to influence Baker.[36]

In the wake of the departure of Haldeman and Ehrlichman, with possible indictments facing them and other White House staffers, Pat Buchanan fretted over the forthcoming hearings, with "the Great Constitutionalist putting on his daily television show." He suggested that if the President revealed "all" the campaign's dirty tricks on both sides, and if he advocated campaign-financing legislation, he might abort the proceedings or at least defuse the revelations of what Buchanan called "a trick-a-day." By now, however, events and revelations had far outstripped the Administration's capacity for defensive, let alone counteroffensive, measures.[37]

On February 21, at the initial meeting of the newly formed Senate Select Committee, Baker offered what was to become a familiar homily on nonpartisanship. The inquiry, he said, should be a "Committee undertaking and not a Republican-Democratic undertaking." He urged his colleagues "to act as much as possible as a judicial body." The group approved Ervin's selection of the committee's Counsel, Sam Dash.[38]

The Democrats appointed Senate veterans to their four places on the Select Committee. They were low-profile legislators who did not project the fiery partisanship of an Edward Kennedy, and their publicity mills largely pointed to their home constituencies. Herman Talmadge, like his father before him, had long commanded the loyalties of his fellow Georgians. As Chairman of the Senate Agriculture Committee, he had important connections to conservative Midwestern Republicans. He retained only a few vestiges of Georgia populism, and he and his wife had social links to the Nixons. Daniel Inouye of Hawaii had been a risk-taker as a young Army combat soldier in Italy during World War II, but he had evolved into a cautious, discreet Senator whose caution and discretion had served his career quite well. Inouye's bland demeanor barely masked his contempt for the Nixon White House, however. Joseph Montoya was an amiable veteran of New Mexico politics. Throughout the proceedings, Montoya's staff prepared superb questions for him, many of which opened unexplored ground. But the Senator had neither the wit nor the energy to lead witnesses; instead, he preferred to squeeze

vague moral advice to the young from those accused of wrongdoing. Whatever their differences in background and temperament, all three Democrats
joined in unswerving support of Sam Ervin. His authority in the committee
was never in jeopardy.[39]

The Republicans lacked the Democrats' cohesiveness. They also had different reasons for serving on the committee. Howard Baker had both Senate
and national ambitions. Edward Gurney and Lowell Weicker actively campaigned to be on the committee. According to the Minority Counsel, Gurney
considered television his medium and argued that he would project a favorable image for the party. A Republican from a traditionally Democratic state,
Gurney had little modesty about his partisanship. He also had a problem
with a political slush fund of his own. Of the three Republicans, only Gurney
never indicated by appearance or substance anything less than absolute loyalty to Richard Nixon.

Weicker reportedly had been prepared to denounce the Republican leadership if he were denied a seat on the Senate Watergate Committee. During
the months of preparation for the hearings, the White House correctly perceived the Connecticut Republican as an adversary. The Senator's motives
are not easily discerned. He was a loose cannon, as the Administration had
feared. Dash never decided whether Weicker merely sought publicity,
whether he was conducting a personal vendetta against the White House, or
whether he pursued the investigation altruistically. Weicker immediately
sensed that the Minority Counsel was Baker's boy; he had a similar disdain
for Dash. Both Ervin and Baker had difficulty keeping Weicker from marching off the reservation. With Weicker on their side, the outnumbered Republicans had no chance for unity.

Throughout March and April Weicker became a familiar television figure,
particularly for his spirited defense of Pat Gray and then for his equally
spirited assault on the White House for its manipulation of Gray. But for
many, much of that anger appeared contrived to boost the political stock of
a first-term Senator who had captured only 38 percent of the vote in a three-
way race. Whatever Weicker's motives, however, his behavior to some extent
forced the Ervin Committee to operate more openly than the Administration
and Baker would have liked. The President's supporters, with some justification, condemned the steady stream of leaks and the committee's skillful
use of television as an ordeal, not as an investigative tool necessarily characterized by fair play. Weicker, however, insisted on openness. At the outset
he challenged his colleagues: "The most refreshing thing we can do is open
the doors and let the press come in so that even our meetings would be
public." Secrecy and concealment, he contended, had been the hallmarks
of the Watergate affair; he saw no reason for the investigators to operate in
the same manner.[40]

If Weicker's actions were complex, Baker's were nothing less than Byzantine. He developed back-channel lines to the White House, constantly sending word that Nixon was not to be misled by his public statements. Yet those statements were devastating, particularly Baker's relentless—but largely misunderstood—line: "What did the President know, and when did he know it?" Baker rarely sought to pursue the circumstantial evidence that he elicited from witnesses, and as a former prosecutor noted, he interfered when others tried to do so.[41] He projected extremely well on television, combining a boyish smile with the appearance of a diffident, nonpartisan pursuit of the truth. In the end, Baker served himself well: a Republican, he nonetheless emerged from a Democratic-dominated show with his reputation substantially enhanced. He subsequently parlayed that performance into the position of Senate Republican leader and gained national visibility as a presidential contender.

The Watergate hearings developed into a blend of education and extravaganza, and Sam Ervin was the undisputed impresario of both. When his White House critics called him the "Great Constitutionalist," they both mocked and honored his reputation. Ervin's constitutional views on some of the great issues of the day—on race, most notably—made him an unlikely paladin for any anti-Nixon venture. But the Administration's views on wiretapping, executive privilege, and separation of powers deeply offended Ervin's traditional, at times literal, understanding of the American Constitution. Whatever the depth of his constitutional knowledge or the extent of his commitments (and both were far greater than Ehrlichman and Buchanan would concede), Ervin unquestionably gave the lie to the Administration's litany that the Senate proceedings merely masked a vicious, determined effort of Democrats and liberals to destroy their archenemy, Richard Nixon. Ervin hardly qualified as a member of any New York–Washington axis. Any notion that he fronted for Edward Kennedy or liberals, or that he sought to destroy Richard Nixon's presidency, bordered on the absurd.

Nixon's aides only reflected his own attitudes toward Ervin. Shortly after his re-election, the President had Ervin on his mind, suggesting to Ehrlichman that some move be made to embarrass Ervin for the benefit of Jesse Helms, the Republican junior Senator from North Carolina. When Ervin asked Ehrlichman to waive a retirement-age requirement for an FCC commissioner, Ehrlichman coolly ignored him. After the creation of the Senate Select Committee, Nixon called Ervin one of four jackasses. In May 1973, North Carolina Republican officials confirmed that Haldeman had requested them to "dig up something to discredit Ervin and blast him with it." Ervin responded to a reporter that the statute of limitations had expired on his past indiscretions, and he no longer had the capacity to commit others.[42]

Sam Ervin had been a prime force in establishing the committee, and he easily dominated it. His Democratic colleagues gave him free rein. He hired Dash, a man with a considerable background in criminal law as a prosecutor and professor, who in turn assembled a formidable staff of lawyers and investigators. Dash, at forty-eight, was eighteen years older than Fred Thompson, his Republican counterpart. His experience in the Philadelphia District Attorney's office and as a trial attorney in the Criminal Division of the Department of Justice, and his prominence in academic circles, dwarfed Thompson's brief tenure as an Assistant U.S. Attorney in Tennessee with a few years in private practice. Ervin, Dash, and the majority staff simply overwhelmed the lesser—and divided—Republican forces. Ervin himself was splendid media copy; he used some of his own staff for the committee's work, and they skillfully leaked tantalizing and explosive information. From the start, the Senate Select Committee had the best of the White House when it came to public relations.

Congressional hearings in television's early days had attracted considerable attention. They did so both because their subject matter was dramatic— witness the Kefauver Crime Hearings and the Army-McCarthy Hearings— and because of skimpy competition from daytime network commercial programming. By 1973, however, daytime television was big business. Was Watergate of such compelling public interest as to justify coverage by the networks, entailing huge revenue losses? After the dramatic April 30 White House resignations, the television networks indicated a growing interest in the forthcoming proceedings. Broadcast executives pressed Dash for his schedule of witnesses. He disappointed them when he outlined his plan for building his case from lower-level officials before turning to the big names.[43]

A week before the hearings began on May 17, public television committed itself to live coverage, but the three commercial networks remained undecided. At the last moment, they chose to cover the first day's proceedings but to remain flexible thereafter. Network executives offered their own self-fulfilling prophecies. A CBS official feared that after a few days, the network would hear from "200,000 nice little old ladies whose favorite soap opera had been pre-empted by something called Watergate." By the second day of the hearings, the networks' lament was predictable. They complained that the hearings had attracted only 9.5 million viewers, down more than 4 million from their normal audiences. By the end of the first week, ABC and CBS revealed that their callers were speaking ten to one against live coverage. Most were angry: "We're sick of nothing but Watergate, Watergate." "Watergate is being shoved down our throats." "You're hurting the President." By the beginning of the second week, the networks reached an unprecedented agreement among themselves to rotate live coverage, ostensibly to satisfy "viewer discontent." The real discontent was in the boardrooms, since each hour of pre-empted programming lost the networks an estimated $120,000 in advertising revenues.[44]

The networks did gain the sensational interest necessary to lure audiences when James McCord testified on the second day of the hearings that the cover-up could be linked to "the very highest levels of the White House." On May 21, the Senate Foreign Relations Committee released memoranda written by Vernon Walters of the CIA, including one quoting Haldeman as saying several days after the break-in that it was "the President's wish" for Walters to talk to Gray regarding the investigation. Haldeman heatedly denied the allegation: "I can flatly say the President was not involved in any cover-up of anything at any time."

Nixon spoke for himself the next day. In a lengthy statement, he maintained that he had no prior knowledge of the break-in; that he had "no part in, nor was I aware of, subsequent efforts that may have been made to cover up Watergate"; that he knew of no offers of executive clemency; that his directive to Walters was meant only to protect covert CIA operations and that he never intended or attempted to involve the CIA in Watergate; that not until his own investigation had he learned of the break-in of Ellsberg's psychiatrist's office; and that he "specifically authorized" furnishing that information to Judge Byrne in California. While Nixon said he knew of the Plumbers, he denied approving or having knowledge of their illegal activities. "It now appears," he added, that some persons had "gone beyond" his directives and used national security as an excuse "to cover up any involvement they or certain others might have had in Watergate." Excessive zeal in behalf of the President and national security had become Nixon's basic defense line. But now the President's men were on their own. To underscore that point, the President reversed himself on executive privilege. He would not sanction such claims whenever testimony involved possible criminal conduct. A month earlier, on April 17, when the President publicly acknowledged his recognition of "serious charges" about the Watergate case, he had insisted emphatically that he "reserved" executive privilege and that it might be asserted regarding any questions raised during the hearings.[45]

The President's reversal on May 22 dramatically underscored his eroding position; nothing declined more sharply than his ability to challenge Congress. The irony of his situation must have tormented him. He repeatedly pressed his aides on President Truman's behavior, insisting that Truman had improperly asserted executive privilege both in the Hiss case and following allegations of corruption among his aides. While claiming that Truman had behaved wrongly, President Nixon had seemed intent on following that course. Did he remember Congressman Richard Nixon of California, who had challenged a presidential order on executive privilege in 1948, contending that it was wrong "from a constitutional standpoint or on the basis of the merits"? To allow such power, Nixon then argued—as Senator Ervin had contended for years—would prevent Congress from excercising its proper investigative authority.

The control of information and access to it were at the heart of the Administration's strategy. Typically, it coated its political problem with legal and constitutional protection—this time, until May 22, in the guise of executive privilege. In February and March, the President directed Ehrlichman and Dean to check the precedents for invoking executive privilege. He ordered that Republican leaders and "friendly columnists" be informed that executive privilege was not designed to cover up anything criminal and that he intended to cooperate fully with the Ervin Committee.

As late as April 10, Attorney General Kleindienst offered a spirited, feisty defense of the most luxuriant claims of executive privilege. He told a group of senators that presidential aides could not be compelled to testify before Congress for reasons "fundamental to our system of government." His authority rested in part on separation-of-powers doctrine, but more on the basis of customary precedents. Kleindienst, however, had a way of turning separation of powers into a doctrine of totally separate spheres utterly ignoring that necessary degree of cooperation and civility that makes the American system work. He told Senator Edmund Muskie that if the President commanded him not to appear before a congressional committee, that would be the end of the matter. "So our power to command is in the President's hands?" Muskie queried. Congressional power to get information was limited to commanding citizens, not the President, Kleindienst answered. Brusquely, he added: "You do not have the power to compel me to come up here if the President directs me not to[,] and even if you would attempt to compel me, I would not come here."

After the testy exchanges with Muskie, Ervin pressed the Attorney General and narrowed the question:

> Your position is the President has implied power under the Constitution to deny to the Congress the testimony of any person working for the executive branch of the Government or any document in the possession of anybody working for the Government?

Kleindienst sharpened the confrontation:

> Yes, sir, and you have a remedy, all kinds of remedies, cut off appropriations, impeach the President.[46]

The sardonic smile that played across Kleindienst's face barely masked the chip on his shoulder. "Impeach the President"—it was as if to say, Drop the atomic bomb. That exchange had occurred in April. Now, in May, such confidence, such arrogance was on the wane. Nixon's reversal on executive privilege signaled the retreat. The steady stream of his men before the Senate Select Committee left the doctrine in shambles, at least as far as Congress was concerned. The courts, indeed, provided one final forum for invoking the privilege, but that was for another day.

Meanwhile, references to impeachment no longer were viewed as black humor; indeed, the time for thinking the unthinkable rapidly was drawing close. Besides the Senate Select Committee, five other congressional committees were scrutinizing Administration behavior in areas as diverse as the sale of wheat to the Soviet Union, the settlement of an antitrust suit against ITT, and the domestic activities of the CIA. A New York grand jury handed down indictments on May 10 against John Mitchell and Maurice Stans for alleged campaign-law violations. Most important, Nixon now faced a two-front war—against the Senate Select Committee and the new enemy within, the Special Prosecutor. Events outpaced reactions. His ten-month-old containment policy had collapsed, and Richard Nixon stood at the brink of losing control of his own fate.

XIV

"WHAT DID THE PRESIDENT KNOW AND WHEN DID HE KNOW IT?"

THE SENATE COMMITTEE: SUMMER 1973

Sam Ervin gaveled the Senate Select Committee to order on May 17. On the same day, Elliot Richardson announced his guidelines for the Special Prosecutor post, but the limelight had shifted. A congressional inquiry takes on a particular coloration, all the more so when the events and personalities are as dramatic as those of Watergate. In such hearings, the lonely, isolated witness confronts a panel of interlocutors. The committee and its staff move steadily toward a well-defined goal, while all but the most cooperative and friendly witnesses resist that advance and provide information designed to limit their own culpability.

Part inquest, part inquisition, congressional investigations are subject to no restraints except those imposed by congressmen themselves. A committee applies the traditional judicial measures of due process according to its own sense of fair play and perceptions of what public opinion demands or will tolerate. In the heyday of the House Committee on Un-American Activities or of Senator Joseph McCarthy, witnesses had been subjected to interminable questions, each of which evoked incantations of the Fifth Amendment's prohibition against self-incrimination. The net effect only heightened public belief in the noble ends of the interrogators and the evil of the witnesses. The Senate Select Committee in the present case, acting according to its opinion of constitutional proprieties, as well with an eye on what would be politically acceptable, chose not to follow that particular form of humiliation. When the committee Counsel informed Ervin that a witness had decided to take the Fifth Amendment, the chairman found "no legislative purpose" in bringing him to a public session.[1]

Historically, congressional investigating committees have played a prominent role in spotlighting alleged wrongdoing in the executive branch and corruption in other aspects of American life. Individual and institutional interests of members of Congress inevitably blend with higher motives, thus creating a strange mixture of circus, morality play, exposé, and education. It was ever thus, beginning with a congressional inquiry into military adventures against Indians in the western lands during George Washington's Administration in the 1790s, and continuing through inquiries into the British burning of Washington in 1812, the Joint Committee on Reconstruction, the revelations of the money trust by the Pujo Committee in 1913, the machinations of World War I munitions dealers, Harry Truman's firing of General MacArthur, and whether organized baseball had violated the antitrust laws. History permeated the Senate Caucus Room, the site of the 1973 hearings and of the dramas of Teapot Dome, the Kefauver Crime Hearings, and the Army–McCarthy confrontation—the site, too, of the Senate's inquiry into censure proceedings against their very own Joseph McCarthy, an inquiry in which Sam Ervin had played a key role.

The formalities of the May 17 opening session barely concealed the personal and political postures of each senator. Sam Ervin was predictably apocalyptic; for him the Watergate break-in represented nothing less than an attempt to invade American homes and steal Americans' "most precious heritage: the right to vote in a free election." The Senator had his special concerns, notably impoundment of funds appropriated by Congress, and executive privilege, both of which he believed reflected the dangerous growth of executive power. In a more general sense, Ervin hoped that the probe would dissipate the growing public distrust and suspicion of government. The other Democrats, Herman Talmadge, Daniel Inouye, and Joseph Montoya, generally shared Ervin's concerns, and they gave him free rein in administering the committee.

For the Republicans, Howard Baker scrupulously reminded the committee that its task was to assemble facts and proceed toward remedial legislation on campaign financing. But Baker also acknowledged that congressional investigations have a myriad of purposes, not the least of which may be partisan. He reminded the spectators that from the outset he had advocated equal party representation on the committee. But, almost as if to disarm his fellow senators, he assured them that "this is not in any way a partisan undertaking but, rather, it is a bipartisan search for the unvarnished truth." Privately, Baker realized that scapegoats had to be offered, and he carefully distinguished between the campaign practices of political professionals at the Republican National Committee and the actions of the President's men. Was Baker suggesting that the party and its well-being were more important than the President? It was not clear; but in time, it would be. Baker's remarks keynoted themes that became a litany: Republicans would be serious and impartial throughout the hearings. Meanwhile, Baker maintained communications with the White House.

The fissures within the committee exposed themselves during the opening statements of Republicans Edward Gurney and Lowell Weicker. Gurney established himself as a Nixon loyalist and steered clear of the pieties that Baker had expressed. Key figures, Gurney argued, had been indicted and tried; others, whose conduct might have been questionable, had resigned. The only possible result from the hearings, he suggested, would be to destabilize the American presidency. "[T]he rocking of the boat by Watergate, its catastrophic effect upon the institution of the Presidency," was, said Gurney, a matter of real concern. By August, he complained that the hearings had damaged the government, the nation, and relations with other nations.

If Gurney wanted to close down shop, Weicker had only expansion on his mind. His metaphors hardly missed a political button. "A few men," he contended, "had gambled that Americans wanted the truth suppressed rather than the 'turbulence' of truth. And they were stopped a yard short of the goal by another few, who believed in America as advertised." The Watergate story, then, was not just one of breaking and entering and bugging, "but of the acts of men who—who almost stole America." The Republicans did not have a majority on the Senate Watergate Committee, but they certainly had diversity.[2]

Committee Counsel Samuel Dash decided to forgo drama for the first day and instead developed the foundations for his case. Dash's first witness, Robert C. Odle, the former director of administration for CREEP, described his organization and personnel. Odle testified that when he heard about the Watergate burglary, he told his associates that it could never happen at Republican headquarters because James McCord headed its security staff. Following Odle, Bruce Kehrli, the White House Staff Secretary, described its organizational structure and provided a list of persons transferred from the White House to the re-election committee. Baker asked Kehrli if any White House officials had instructed him as to his testimony. "I was encouraged to cooperate," Kehrli responded.[3]

McCord offered a mixture of fact and fancy in his testimony, especially when he described his motivation for revealing his story. He passionately affirmed his deep attachment to the CIA. He especially was eager to ridicule the White House attempt in June 1973 to use the Agency to thwart the FBI investigation, and he was equally anxious to repudiate any hint that the CIA had anything to do with the break-in. McCord would not, even at the cost of his freedom, "turn on the organization" that had employed him for nineteen years. The President's dismissal of CIA Director Helms convinced him that the White House had succeeded in establishing "political control" over the Agency. McCord compared the grab for control of the CIA and the FBI with Hitler's hegemony over his intelligence services.

McCord unwittingly provided a foundation for the Administration's defense when he explained why he thought the break-in was permissible. He noted that the operation had been approved by Mitchell as Attorney General, "the top legal officer of the U.S. Government," and by Dean, the President's Counsel. He knew that the Attorney General could approve wiretapping for national-security reasons. Whether this was a national-security operation was "a justification beyond which was known to me," as McCord put it. He believed that Mitchell had taken the matter "to higher authority and got a final approval from his superior." He admitted to Gurney that it was a "gray area," but the involvement of Mitchell and the White House proved decisive for him. "I realized the illegality under normal circumstances," said McCord, "but I also realized that the Attorney General can make matters legal by his signature on a piece of paper, or his oral authorization of it [*sic*]."

Much of what McCord related on May 18 had earlier been leaked. Perhaps he did his greatest damage when he discussed the pressures on him to remain silent, pressures that he traced to "the very highest levels of the White House." He cited discussions with Howard Hunt, his own attorney, and John Caulfield. Caulfield, in particular, had relayed several messages, including one that promised McCord executive clemency, care for his family, and a future job. He urged McCord to "get on track" and follow "the game plan." When asked why he was so long in coming forth, McCord replied: "Because it involved directly the President" and his own friend, Caulfield.[4]

His "friend" corroborated much of McCord's story. Caulfield acknowledged that he had lengthy discussions with Dean regarding McCord's silence and executive clemency. While neither Dean nor Caulfield ever spoke of the President's having promised executive clemency, both believed that clemency had been considered at "the very highest levels." But Caulfield testified that on the basis of his three years in the White House he knew "what the relations are," and in his mind, he "felt that the President probably did know" about the matter.

Caulfield acknowledged that "my loyalties . . . to the President of the United States" overrode his respect for the law. Ervin gently pressed the point, asking whether Caulfield had been "trying to protect" Nixon by carrying out a mission assigned by the President's Counsel. "Absolutely correct, Senator," Caulfield responded. The next witness, Anthony Ulasewicz, offered further corroboration as he described his role in relaying messages between Caulfield and McCord. Ulasewicz conceded that he had been an accessory to obstructing justice.[5]

The testimony of McCord and Caulfield revealed that Nixon would have vigorous support within the committee. When McCord offered the first intimation of White House involvement, Baker quickly interrupted to establish that McCord's belief was based on hearsay evidence that he had picked up from Gordon Liddy. Gurney similarly broke in to note that Caulfield was not working in the White House when he allegedly delivered the messages to McCord.[6]

Bernard Barker, one of the Cuban burglars, testified on May 24 that he thought the break-in would lead to the liberation of Cuba. He claimed that he looked for documents linking Cuban government contributions to Senators McGovern and Kennedy. By helping his friend "Edwardo"—E. Howard Hunt—who had participated in the 1961 Bay of Pigs operation and was a known friend of Cuban liberation, Barker and his colleagues hoped to persuade the White House to move against the Castro government. Barker painted a picture of a paramilitary operation, in which one never questioned the decisions of superiors and focused on a paramount goal. In that atmosphere, it made no difference whether he burglarized Daniel Ellsberg's psychiatrist or the headquarters of the Democratic National Committee. But Barker responded rather pathetically to Weicker's question whether he truly thought national-security matters could justify the break-ins. "I feel it was a proper justification for Ellsberg, and although not in the same degree, I feel it was a justification for Watergate," Barker said. "But quite frankly, I am just a human being. I get confused about all these things. I do not pretend to have all the answers, sir."[7]

The hearings adjourned for nearly two weeks to give the staff more time to prepare its case. But the committee's brief public doings added to the growing perception that Watergate was something larger than a break-in, larger even than a high-level cover-up. Acting FBI Director William Ruckelshaus spoke to the growing sense of national unease when he addressed the commencement ceremonies at Ohio State University on June 8. Ruckelshaus recognized the declining credibility of previously cherished institutions, from business to religion to education. "To our country's great misfortune," he noted, "the 'Watergate' has accelerated that process." Recent events had shaken public confidence in government, that most fragile of institutions. Ruckelshaus emphasized the necessity for maintaining faith that government could and would bring lawbreakers to account. He directly confronted those who wished to dismiss the affair as "politics as usual." To do so, he warned, only invited "cynical abuse" of the political process. Quoting Ralph Waldo

Emerson, Ruckelshaus concluded that "this time 'like all times is a very good one, if we but know what to do with it.' "[8]

When the sessions resumed on June 5, the committee focused on the structure of CREEP and the activities of key personnel. Former CREEP treasurer Hugh W. Sloan, Jr., testified that key campaign officials pressured him to cover up cash payments he had made to White House officials and to the Watergate burglars. Sloan admitted giving $250,000 to Herbert Kalmbach, the President's lawyer, and $350,000 to Gordon Strachan, Haldeman's aide. Liddy had requested $83,000, ostensibly to finance the activities of his break-in team. Sloan discussed the matter with the campaign finance chairman, Maurice Stans, who told him: "I do not want to know and you do not want to know" why Liddy needed money. Sloan described efforts by Magruder and LaRue to suborn his perjury if he were called to testify in the burglars' trial and said that Dean told Sloan's lawyer that Sloan could be a "real hero around here" if he took the Fifth Amendment. Less than a month after the break-in, Sloan resigned, futilely trying to establish some distance between himself and the other conspirators.[9]

Herbert Porter, the former scheduling director at CREEP, poignantly testified to the tremendous pressures on members of the "team" to "go along." Central Casting could not have provided a better actor than Porter to play the quintessential Nixon admirer who found himself betrayed and disenchanted. Porter testified that at Magruder's request, he secured $69,000 in cash from Sloan for Liddy's use and that at Magruder's request, again, he had lied to the FBI, the grand jury, and the burglars' jury as to the purpose of the money.

Baker used the occasion to explore Porter's motivation and thereby portray him as a misguided, youthful zealot. Why, Baker asked, didn't Porter try to stop activities when he concluded they were wrong and nonproductive? Porter offered an elementary lesson in group dynamics: "In all honesty," he replied, "probably because of the fear of group pressure that would ensue, of not being a team player." Porter then said that he was also moved by personal loyalty "to this man, Richard Nixon," a man whom he believed he had known longer than any other witness the committee would hear. With obvious emotion, Porter described meeting Nixon when Porter was eight years old, in 1948. The young boy proudly wore Nixon campaign buttons in that election and succeeding ones. His parents worked in Nixon campaigns. "I felt as if I had known this man all my life—not personally, perhaps, but in spirit," Porter stated. "I felt a deep sense of loyalty to him. I was appealed to on this basis." Baker would have none of it, claiming that he had known Nixon even longer, and that Porter's worst disservice to the President was "to abdicate his conscience." But Porter had the last word, saying that he believed the truth would provide "atonement" for him—regardless of the damage it created for those he so admired.[10]

Maurice Stans's testimony on June 12 was particularly dramatic because he was under indictment, along with John Mitchell, in a pending case in New York not related to the Watergate problem. He confirmed Sloan's testimony yet maintained that he had no prior knowledge of the break-in. He vigorously argued that he had followed the new campaign laws as best as he could, and with the advice of his committee counsel, Liddy. He offered insights into his money-raising activities and protested that prominent contributors had suffered unfairly because of the Watergate affair. Stans vehemently denied that political contributions had any *quid pro quo* connotations. He had admittedly persuaded the president of McDonald's, the fast-food chain, to give $250,000 to re-elect the President, but Stans had promised nothing in return; there was no connection, he insisted, between the contribution and legislation permitting the chain to pay below the minimum wage. No one challenged Stans. He pleaded for the committee to clear innocent individuals, such as Sloan and prominent contributors. For himself, he asked that the committee "give me back my good name."[11]

The testimony by Sloan, Porter, and Stans set the stage for Jeb Stuart Magruder, CREEP's deputy director and the designated go-between with the White House. Magruder's aide, Robert Reisner, earlier had provided key details of Magruder's work, including descriptions of planning meetings for questionable campaign activities that were held in the White House, the Justice Department, and Key Biscayne. Reisner testified that Magruder instructed him to inform Liddy of the final approval of his plans, including the plan for the Watergate break-in. Reisner described a wide range of clandestine activities, such as Colson's request for counterdemonstrations at J. Edgar Hoover's funeral, planting a "mole" in Hubert Humphrey's organization, and arranging for a woman to strip at the Democratic Convention. He acknowledged shredding documents for Magruder after the break-in. Reisner revealed that every Magruder document directed to Mitchell was duplicated for Haldeman and Strachan, testimony that both diminished Magruder and magnified the White House role in the campaign.[12]

Magruder had a grant of immunity from Judge Sirica. When he testified, what had been rumor for weeks was publicly stated before the committee by a key principal, as Magruder implicated Mitchell, Dean, LaRue, and Strachan in the planning and cover-up of the Watergate break-in. Magruder resisted citing Haldeman, although he recognized that Strachan's knowledge undoubtedly meant that Haldeman was aware of events. In his opening statement Magruder specifically asserted that the President had no knowledge of the cover-up attempts. When Inouye reminded him of his recent public declarations regarding the key roles of the President and Haldeman in campaign decision making, Magruder insisted that he had "no knowledge" of presidential participation in planning the burglary or in the subsequent decision to cover up any White House involvement.[13]

Magruder sought vindication when he pursued a thesis that the illegal activities could be justified because antiwar leaders themselves repeatedly broke the law. He confessed that he had lost "respect for the legal process simply because I did not see it working as I had hoped." Ervin contemptuously compared such attitudes to McCarthyism and took the occasion to condemn the Huston Plan and the various schemes for wiretapping and military surveillance of Administration opponents, charging that the same mentality fostered a preposterous notion that something might be gained by burglarizing the Democratic National Committee.

Republican senators and staff questioned Magruder at length, developing a line of attack that would make Dean the scapegoat for the whole affair. The Minority Counsel tried unsuccessfully to get Magruder to blame Dean for the hiring of Liddy. He then explored Dean's role in ensuring Magruder's perjury before the grand jury, particularly emphasizing Dean's desire to avoid implicating himself. Gurney asked Magruder whether it was possible that someone in Dean's position would meet alone and regularly with the President. "That would not have been in the normal pattern of events," Magruder noted. But, for Montoya, Magruder conceded that Dean acted under authority from Haldeman or Ehrlichman, and not on his own.

While Republicans concentrated on setting up John Dean, Ervin bore in on the President's connections to his aides. Magruder acknowledged that he knew for a certainty that Haldeman had the full story by January 1973. Was it not Haldeman's duty, then, to take that story to the President? Magruder never answered directly but he left the clear implication that Haldeman reported such things to the President. Magruder's careful yet evasive answers contributed to a slowly, almost inexorably, evolving impression: Richard Nixon knew more than he had publicly acknowledged.[14]

Two days after Magruder concluded his testimony, Soviet leader Leonid Brezhnev arrived in Washington for a summit meeting with Nixon. It was one day short of the anniversary of the Watergate break-in. Baker relayed to his colleagues a Soviet journalist's remark to an American reporter that Brezhnev was "concerned." Baker insisted that he was merely noting the fact and was not asking the committee to halt its proceedings—and then he did just that. Despite objections from Weicker, who thought that continuing the hearings might demonstrate the strength of the American system and the people's confidence in it, the committee suspended the public hearings. But news continued to filter out, as witnesses such as Kalmbach, Strachan, and Dean testified to the staff behind closed doors. The Soviets reportedly were "bewildered" by the growing allegations against the President. Nixon worried about Democrats and liberals, convinced, as always, that they were his enemies. Soviet journalists, however, spoke of a "right-wing plot" designed to discredit the President's détente policy.[15] "Left" and "Right" had lost their meanings. Moscow's rulers, of course, could not look kindly on any attempt to criticize or topple a leader.

John Dean began to provide some answers during a full week of intensive testimony. On Monday, June 25, with only a ninety-minute lunch recess, he read a 245-page statement over nearly seven hours, describing his role in the Watergate cover-up and his dealings with an extraordinary range of characters, headed, of course, by the President.

What the senators and the public saw was a young man accompanied by a striking blonde wife, himself handsome, impeccably dressed, articulate, dispassionate, seemingly self-effacing, and withal exhibiting a remarkable memory. Dean seemed the very model of a young man on the move. In fact, he was ruined, at least for the time being. His mind was not a tape recorder, as he told Gurney and Inouye, but he had an uncanny ability to recall whole passages of conversation, recollections eventually substantiated by tape recordings of Oval Office talks. Presidential aide Richard Moore had once suggested that Dean make a record of his meetings with the President. Why had he not done so? asked Inouye. "I thought they were very incriminating to the President of the United States," Dean replied in his fast, unemotional manner.[16] When he had finished his statement, the reality of a corrupt *apparatchik* dissolved Dean's surface images and, more important, the Nixon Administration's long-cultivated law-and-order image.

Dean portrayed the climate of opinion in the White House that nurtured deep antagonism toward political foes in the years before the Watergate break-in. Watergate, he said at the outset, was "an inevitable outgrowth" of an environment marked by "an excessive concern" over the impact of demonstrators, "an excessive concern" over leaks, and "an insatiable appetite" for political intelligence—all linked with "a do-it-yourself White House staff, regardless of the law." At the outset of his testimony, Dean depicted Nixon and staff as convinced, immediately following the arrest of the Watergate burglars, that they had been victimized by an elaborate Democratic-inspired conspiracy. He had been commissioned to "prove" this, but he testified that he "never found a scintilla of viable evidence indicating . . . a master plan."

Nixon and Haldeman, however, remained unconvinced, and throughout the summer and fall of 1972, they pushed repeatedly for more intelligence on the Democratic campaign. This prompted, Dean related, a variety of questionable and illegal actions, such as the attempts by Caulfield to gain derogatory information on Senator Kennedy and the operations by Liddy and his associates at CREEP. Dean acknowledged that he had been present, some time before the break-in, when Liddy offered Mitchell his master plan for damaging the opposition. Dean reported to Haldeman that he thought the whole scheme was "incredible, unnecessary, and unwise." Liddy's plans included bugging, mugging, kidnapings, and prostitutes. Dean informed Haldeman, and warned that the White House should not be involved. Haldeman agreed, Dean claimed.

The rest of Dean's testimony described the cover-up and his role in it. He revealed with uncanny accuracy the crucial September 15, 1972 meeting with Nixon and Haldeman. Dean had left that meeting, he remembered, with "the impression that the President was well aware of what had been going on regarding the success of keeping the White House out of the Watergate scandal." He then described his role in blocking the Patman investigation, the cash payments to the burglars and Hunt, the discussions of executive clemency, and the formulation of plans to perpetuate the cover-up throughout the Senate hearings. Finally, Dean recalled the extensive White House meetings throughout March and April 1973, again with surprising, intimate detail that magnified Nixon's personal role in events.

Dean vacillated between a rendition of events in which he described himself as a reluctant pawn of higher officials and a narrative that betrayed a determination and enthusiasm for doing an effective job of crisis management. His testimony clearly reflected his ambition, his desire to become an indispensable member of the "team," as he later characterized his behavior. Unlike Porter, Dean did not seem at all skittish about responding to peer pressure; he was eager to be a loyal "team player." His moment had arrived, and Dean described it with perhaps more pride than penitence.

Near the end of his grueling testimony, Dean described the President's contention that he had a tape recording of a meeting in which Dean allegedly had sought immunity in exchange for testimony against Haldeman and Ehrlichman. Dean denied the charge but urged the Ervin Committee to secure the tape of the whole meeting. The conversation, he contended, would portray the larger dimensions of the case, including Nixon's talk of hush-money payments and executive clemency. Dean did not know whether such a tape existed, but if it did he believed that it "would corroborate many of the things that this committee has asked me to testify about."

As he concluded his testimony, Dean described a phone call he received from the President on April 22, wishing him a Happy Easter. He knew what the approach was, a "stroking call." Eight days later, his secretary had told him that the wire services had reported that Haldeman and Ehrlichman were resigning and that Dean's resignation also had been requested. The committee had heard other witnesses who contritely confessed to their own wrongdoing and implicated others in singular transgressions. But John Dean was different. He had challenged the integrity and image of the Administration; more important, he had portrayed the Nixon White House as deeply entwined in illegal activities and the obstruction of justice. Dean's exposing the falsity of Nixon's sponsorship of any serious attempt to investigate Watergate was reminiscent of the remark of a critic of Freudian psychoanalysis who called it "the disease that presumes itself the cure."

White House aides were furious at Dean's testimony. Haldeman's assistant, Larry Higby, told the committee staff in a private session that Dean was "trying to save his ass and screw everyone else." Higby contended that people had talked to Dean believing that they were covered by lawyer-client confidentiality; now, Higby said, Dean used that information for his own advantage and to damage others. No one, however, understood the implications of Dean's testimony better than the President. During Dean's testimony, he listened to relevant tape recordings of his meetings with his former Counsel. According to Kissinger, Haig claimed that the White House found a tape that caught Dean in a misstatement. If that one tape were released, however, the President might have to release others, ones potentially damaging. Nixon knew that if even the least part of Dean's testimony was accurate, he was in serious difficulty. And he had to realize that Dean had rendered a far more accurate account of their dealings than he had. In the end, he understood, "it would make less difference that I was not as involved as Dean had alleged than that I was not as uninvolved as I had claimed."[17]

Dean said he honestly believed that the President did not understand the implications of his own involvement in the break-in and cover-up. Perhaps gratuitously, he expressed the hope that the President would be "forgiven" once the facts emerged. Dean may have hoped for a similar absolution for himself. But Committee Counsel Dash immediately challenged his contention that—as a lawyer and a "sophisticated man in politics"—the President did not realize the meaning of his actions. After Dean's detailed revelations of meetings such as that of September 15, he had no choice: the facts indicated that the President "would certainly have some appreciation of the legal problems involved; yes, indeed."[18]

Dean was fair game for the President's loyalists on the committee. Ervin had no intention of inhibiting them, and never interfered with their allotted questioning time. At one point, Gurney promised to be brief (he was not), but Ervin, following the Senate's stylized courtesies, told Gurney he was rendering "a real service to the committee and the country[,] and I don't want you to feel rushed at all." Dean, as Ervin well knew, would stay with his story; more time in the witness chair could only damage the Administration's case. Gurney selectively cited Dean's testimony to put the President in the most favorable light. But Ervin undid Gurney's efforts with a few review questions of his own. The most dramatic came when he asked Dean if the President had tried to discover the facts at any time between the break-in and the establishment of the Senate Select Committee. Dean recalled a moment after the election in which Haldeman asked him about the consequences for the White House if the President revealed all the facts. Indictments, Dean said—indictments for at least Haldeman, Ehrlichman, and himself. "That does not seem like a very viable option, does it?" Haldeman responded.[19]

The Democrats proved so accommodating that Inouye devoted his time to reading questions prepared by White House Counsel J. Fred Buzhardt (aided by Haldeman and Ehrlichman), questions so blatantly hostile that even Inouye's deadpan rendition could not disguise the intensity of the Administration's hostility toward Dean. The White House had assigned extra staff to Buzhardt, including Diane Sawyer and Larry Speakes, to "prove" that Dean had lied. Speakes later claimed that he concluded Dean had not lied, and had so informed Sawyer, but the effort to discredit Dean continued.

Inouye suggested that Buzhardt's questions might serve as an *in absentia* cross-examination of Dean by the President himself. Ervin never interrupted as Inouye followed the White House script, interspersed with a few clarifying questions and comments of his own, for more than an hour and a quarter. The White House framed its questions to place Dean at the center of the cover-up conspiracy to protect his patron, John Mitchell, and to advance his own importance and career. What had been imaginary scenarios concocted in the Oval Office by the President and his top aides in March and April now saw the light of day. Their net effect gave Dean an opportunity to reiterate, even reinforce, his story and thereby strengthen his public credibility—and ironically enough, to do so at the expense of the White House.[20]

In the afternoon of June 28, Howard Baker began his questioning. He conceded that Dean's testimony had been "mind-boggling," and that some of his allegations were "prima facie extraordinarily important." Baker said that he had no desire to test Dean; what he wanted instead was to plow over the ground and structure the testimony in order to have a "coherent presentation" to measure against the testimony of other witnesses.

With that, Baker went right to what had emerged as the "central question" from Dean's testimony: "What did the President know and when did he know it?" The Senator's question had nothing less than the purpose of impeaching Dean's importance as a witness. He asked Dean to structure his answer within three categories: direct, circumstantial, and hearsay evidence. Baker seemed confident that any complete answers to his basic question could only fall within the last or, at best, the second category.

Baker led the witness through different time frames for both the break-in and the cover-up to show that his knowledge was based only on circumstantial or hearsay evidence. Dean counterattacked with a memorandum he had prepared for the President's meeting with Baker to discuss the proceedings of the Senate Select Committee. For his part, Baker managed to establish that the meeting focused on his advice that the President waive executive privilege. Dean preserved his credibility and Baker his. But the moment disarmed Baker, and again the White House apparently suffered a net loss. After Dean's revelations, Baker seemed more muted, even more obsequious and deferential to Ervin, lavishing praise on his cooperativeness, sensitivity, and bipartisanship. "It has been a great privilege for me to learn from you and to go forward in this unpleasantness," Baker told his colleague.[21]

The discussion of White House maneuvers to discredit the Senate hearings also unmasked the Administration's hostility toward Lowell Weicker. The Connecticut Senator deftly used the moment to equate the attempts to smear him with the heavy-handedness of the "enemies list." He had a transcript of an Ehrlichman–Kleindienst March 28 conversation discussing the Senator's attacks on the White House. Weicker delivered what amounted to a stump speech, defending his credentials as a Republican and contending that Republicans did not commit illegal acts, did not view fellow citizens as enemies, and did not cover up crimes. It was stirring television, whether live or on the evening news. And again, it did not exactly make a profitable moment for the Administration.[22]

By Friday, June 29, John Dean had completed a remarkable week of testimony. The senators and the staff counsels had followed his prepared testimony with a variety of cross-examination, some friendly, some hostile, and some skeptical. Rumors abounded about Dean's sexual escapades, his misappropriation of funds, and his fears of homosexual attacks if he went to prison. Dean stood up to the challenges. "Truth," he confidently asserted, was his "one ally." At one point in his testimony, he confused the name of a hotel with a coffee shop, but when his critics tried to use this to derogate his truthfulness, they succeeded only in humanizing him. Throughout, Dean maintained his composure, his appearance of restraint, and above all, his consistency. He had painted a pattern that shaped the rest of the hearings—and the emergence of the case against the President. Few would dispute Dean's conclusion: "there was a terrible cloud over this Government."[23]

The committee adjourned for eleven days over the Fourth of July holiday period. Perhaps to regain the initiative, or to win sympathy, the White House chose to reveal at this time that the President had considered resignation. Julie Nixon told reporters on July 3 that her father had raised the subject as "devil's advocate," suggesting that his resignation might be best for the country. His family dutifully objected, contending that it would be "an admission of wrongdoing." Nixon thus projected both a grievance and a sense of hurt; more, there was the inevitable comparison to worse villains. His daughter attacked the media for portraying Daniel Ellsberg as a "hero," even though he "stole" documents and "broke the law" involving national-security matters.

This was not the first discussion of resignation to emerge from high-level circles. The day after the Senate hearings began, John Mitchell's wife told reporters that the White House was to blame for the scandal. Her husband, she contended, had only been protecting "Mr. President." She predicted that Nixon would resign or be impeached. "I think he'd be much wiser to resign," Martha Mitchell said. Mitchell himself told reporters afterward that he would not be a "fall guy." On June 6 a liberal Republican congressman began to read a speech in the House, charging that the President might have violated criminal laws, when a fellow Republican stopped the proceedings for lack of a quorum. A week later, a congresswoman suggested that the House of Representatives establish an impeachment inquiry.[24]

Meanwhile, Nixon urged his staff to seize the initiative. In a memorandum reminiscent of the public-relations concerns that had so preoccupied the President and Haldeman in the first term, he complained to Haig that "we have tried to get a point across using only one bullet [while] our opponents have been enormously effective in getting three or four rides out of the same story." He wanted more Cabinet officers and Republican senators to speak out in defense of his aides. Typically, he suggested a counterattack focusing on the Kennedy and Johnson administrations for their uses of the FBI and the military for wiretapping and surveillance activities and their use of the IRS for political purposes. But perhaps more important, Nixon wanted Elliot Richardson to rein in Archibald Cox and take him to task for conducting "a partisan political vendetta rather than [doing] . . . the job he was appointed to do—bring the Watergate defendants to trial at the earliest possible time." Richardson, the President feared, would "be a relatively weak reed in this respect."[25]

During the holiday recess, Nixon released a letter he had sent to the Senate committee, refusing to make presidential papers available or to testify himself. He had urged his staff to furnish "information pertinent" to the investigation, but he would not allow "public scrutiny" of his private papers. The Senate request that had elicited that response had been vague and, to some extent at that point, constituted a fishing expedition. Dean had described the President's habit of annotating daily news summaries, for example—words that sometimes in a vague sense implied a directive but often simply reflected his momentary responses. Those notes, Nixon insisted, in no way constituted a criminal act, and, more important, they had no bearing on the legislative concerns of a Senate investigating committee. As to whether or not he would testify, Nixon insisted that his doing so would offer "irreparable damage" to the separation-of-powers principle.

The Senate Select Committee met on July 12 to consider the President's position. Baker urged his colleagues not to confront Nixon, confident as he was that the President would eventually comply with the request because of other pressures. But the committee insisted on stating its position to the President, and Ervin allowed Baker to draft the letter. Baker suggested that Nixon meet with representatives of the committee to avoid "a fundamental constitutional confrontation between the Congress and the Presidency." When Ervin read the letter in open session and announced that it been sent in a sealed envelope, marked for the President's eyes only, the spectators laughed. Earlier, in executive session, Ervin spoke to the President on the telephone and described the substance of the letter. Throughout the call, Ervin insisted that "we are not out to get anybody." The Senator assured the President that he would be delighted to say that there was "nothing in the world to connect you with the Watergate in any way." Nixon told Ervin that he was ill with viral pneumonia and would be hospitalized. He added that he would meet the Chairman at some future date to discuss the impasse.[26]

Magruder and Dean had revealed themselves as foot soldiers, prepared to sacrifice themselves, though not in silence. They had implicated the President's closest and most important aides, and by indirection, Nixon himself. The President would not appear before the committee—there would be no subpoena—but others had no choice. John Mitchell testified for nearly three days. The cooperation so apparent in the Magruder and Dean testimony now evaporated, replaced by a public display of what the President himself had called "stonewalling." The printed record inadequately conveys Mitchell's behavior. His recalcitrance, his foggy, vague answers, his angry interruptions, and his snide, sarcastic remarks directed at the committee and at some of his own associates need to be seen and heard to be fully appreciated. His long pauses, his silent rejection of questions, and his facial expressions amply reflected his absolute contempt for the proceedings and his total loyalty to the President. That loyalty is the more remarkable in view of what Mitchell and the President both knew: Mitchell acted as he did despite Nixon's eagerness to make him a scapegoat just two months earlier.

The antagonism between Mitchell and the President's closest aides ran deep, especially in the case of Ehrlichman. Early in the Administration one White House staff member supposedly remarked that Mitchell believed only in his own advancement and that of his friends. Nixon's April meetings with Haldeman and Ehrlichman consistently betrayed hostility toward Mitchell on the part of the President's retainers. Ehrlichman complained that "M lies unsuccessfully," and told the President to stand by his immediate advisers and not move "a peg." Dean had testified about the "rather strained relationship" between Mitchell and Ehrlichman and the "longstanding competition" between Mitchell and "certain people" in the White House. The

White House memorandum and questions Inouye read to Dean implicated Dean for trying to protect his earlier patron, Mitchell. But shortly before Mitchell testified, Buzhardt said that the memo did not represent the White House position and that the President had not "reviewed" it, although he had been "briefed" on its contents. Shortly afterward, Mitchell's lawyer told reporters that the former Attorney General "definitely has no information implicating the President in the Watergate bugging or cover-up."[27] The White House disavowal of the memorandum and Mitchell's subsequent posture before the committee seemed more than coincidental.

Mitchell early on indicated how he would deal with the committee. When Talmadge asked him about his March 1972 testimony to the Senate Judiciary Committee that he had no "party responsibilities" while Attorney General, Mitchell tried to distinguish between party matters and the President's re-election campaign. Talmadge found that the record showed that Mitchell had been asked specifically about "re-election campaign responsibilities." Mitchell simply insisted that the question had been raised in the "context" of party matters. Talmadge was disgusted and brought forth CREEP memoranda illustrating Mitchell's campaign activities as far back as December 1971. "The public can draw their own conclusions," he said. The next day Ervin reminded Mitchell of his confirmation hearings in 1969, in which he pledged to be the President's legal, not political, adviser. Why had he not fulfilled that promise? Ervin asked. "Mr. Chairman," Mitchell answered, "that would have been my fondest wish. Unfortunately, it is very, very difficult to turn down a request by the President of the United States."[28]

In his own fashion, Mitchell revealed a great deal about the nature and character of the White House and the President's close aides. He vehemently denied Magruder's allegation that he had been involved in discussions regarding bugging the Democratic National Committee. "To the best of my recollection," Mitchell said, no targets had been discussed, and "to the best of my recollection," he had not suggested any. He admitted that Liddy's original plan for spying on and sabotaging their opponents was "beyond the pale" and that he had instructed him to return with detailed plans for dealing with demonstrators. But why didn't Mitchell throw Liddy out of his office? Dash asked. "Well, I think, Mr. Dash, in hindsight I not only should have thrown him out of the office," Mitchell somberly replied, "I should have thrown him out of the window." When Dash further queried why Mitchell did not arrest Liddy for conspiring to commit illegal acts while talking in the Attorney General's office, Mitchell wryly answered that it "would have been a very viable thing to do." He denied having seen any wiretap documents; Magruder's contention to the contrary was "a palpable, damnable lie."[29]

As Dash led Mitchell through his knowledge of the Huston Plan and the Plumbers' operations, Mitchell referred to these activities as the "White

House horrors." His remarks at this point effectively diminished the singularity and importance of the Watergate break-in and provided a window on the entire pattern of wrongdoing and abuse of power in the Administration. He bluntly stated that the cover-up really was designed to conceal the "horrors" rather than any aspects of the Watergate break-in. Watergate, in short, "did not have the great significance that the White House horror stories . . . had," Mitchell concluded. When Magruder told Mitchell that it would be best to "cut their losses" and acknowledge their role in the break-in, Mitchell replied that the White House could not allow that. Indeed, he told the committee substantially the same thing: "some" White House people had been involved in those adventures, and their "interests" dictated a cover-up strategy.

Mitchell subsequently listed the White House horrors for Talmadge: the Ellsberg psychiatrist's office break-in, the silencing of an ITT lobbyist, the forging of cables regarding the assassination of South Vietnamese President Diem, "alleged extracurricular activities in the bugging area," the planned firebombing of the Brookings Institution, "a lot of miscellaneous matters" relating to Chappaquiddick, "and this, that, and the next thing." Some of Mitchell's information, he said, had come from friendly White House staff workers who often enlisted his aid "to pour water on inflammatory requests," such as those involving political reprisals against Republican congressmen who occasionally strayed from the Administration line.[30]

More chilling, perhaps, was Mitchell's explanation of why he never informed Nixon of wrongdoing that had occurred. Talmadge particularly pressed him, reminding Mitchell that he had a special relationship with the President. "[W]hy on Earth didn't you walk into the President's office and tell him the truth?" Talmadge asked. The truth was not the issue, Mitchell said; rather, it was important not to involve the President in such things. Knowing Richard Nixon, Mitchell said, led the Attorney General to believe that he would "just lower the boom," and the result would be to hurt his re-election. Talmadge pressed further: was the President's re-election more important than his learning about the crimes, perjury, and obstruction of justice that lurked all about him? Mitchell: "Senator, I think you have put it exactly correct. In my mind, the reelection of Richard Nixon, compared with what was available on the other side, was so much more important that I put it in just that context." He later testified that he was certain that the President did not know about the Watergate cover-up.

Inouye raised the obvious question: why not tell the President after the election? By then, however, Mitchell worried that such matters might be "a detriment" to the second term. He told Baker that none of the crimes and "horrors" could match the importance of re-electing the President. "I still believe," he said, "that the most important thing to this country was the re-election of Richard Nixon. And I was not about to countenance anything that would stand in the way of that re-election." Mitchell, like the President, wanted to relive the 1972 campaign as the most effective way of deflecting the growing charges against the Administration. Despite Nixon's declining approval ratings, polls still showed that voters overwhelmingly preferred him to George McGovern. But when Ervin told Mitchell he had exalted the President's political fortunes above Nixon's responsibility to take care that the laws be faithfully executed, Mitchell displayed a rare glimmer of uncertainty as he acknowledged that that was a "reasonable" interpretation and, on reflection, "it is a very serious one."[31]

On Friday, July 13, committee investigators privately interrogated former Haldeman aide Alexander Butterfield in preparation for his public appearance. Butterfield was an important witness in setting the scene for testimony from Haldeman and Ehrlichman. The three men had attended UCLA together in the 1940s. Butterfield's and Haldeman's wives were best friends, and the two men were on good terms. Butterfield had served more than twenty years in the Air Force as a fighter pilot and a member of the jet aerobatics team, rising to full colonel. At Haldeman's invitation, he had joined the White House staff shortly before Nixon's inauguration in January 1969 and remained until March 14, 1973, when he resigned to become Administrator of the Federal Aviation Agency.

Butterfield's job was, in his own words, to see to the "smooth running of the President's day." He completely controlled the paper flow to the President, logging in memos, weeding out those which "the President did not have to see"—certainly a considerable responsibility. Butterfield and Haldeman shared the task of accompanying the President on domestic trips, mainly to direct the staff. (Haldeman monopolized the foreign excursions, apparently trusting Butterfield to oversee White House operations in his absence.) At 2:00 P.M. each day, Butterfield and his aides would map the President's schedule for the next day. Every presidential meeting required a briefing paper that included "talking points" for the President. Whoever prepared the paper generally would attend the meeting and then have responsibility for preparing a summary memorandum afterward, for both immediate and historical reference. Butterfield tracked those reports and ensured that they were completed. He also directed FBI investigations made on behalf of the White House. Although an FBI background check was normal procedure for nominating appointees, Butterfield acknowledged that he filled approximately eight requests for investigations of individuals who were not prospective appointees, including entertainers Frank Sinatra and Helen Hayes, and reporter Daniel Schorr. (Interestingly, Butterfield classified Schorr as a "non-appointee," indicating that the background check for job purposes was a ruse.)

Although relatively unknown outside Administration circles, and of a modest, accommodating demeanor, Butterfield nevertheless could act with an authoritative confidence. After the President and Ehrlichman had met with key Administration officials on tax policy in September 1972, Butterfield's aide asked Ehrlichman's assistant for a memorandum of the meeting for the White House records. The Ehrlichman man replied that Ehrlichman had said that there should be no report, because of the "sensitive nature" of the session. Butterfield personally replied: "Nothing is too sensitive— *really!* No one sees these except Dave Hoopes [his aide] & me . . . & neither of us *has* to read anything. We have K[issinger]'s memos on Mao, Chou, Brezhnev, etc. . . . —Haldeman's, Connally['s] meetings. Surely you can comply with this request. Just put memo in sealed envelope & mark it P[resident] & E[hrlichman] eyes only—if you want. But some written record is mandatory."[32]

Butterfield's decision to leave the White House apparently was his own. He told Senate investigators that the position no longer challenged him. Nixon initially asked Butterfield whether he wanted to join the State Department. The FAA was a second suggestion. Shortly after he left in March, Butterfield visited U.S. Attorneys Silbert and Glanzer to describe his tenuous connection to Haldeman's $350,000 fund for "political polling."

Three Senate committee staffers interviewed Butterfield on that Friday afternoon in July. He cooperated mechanically, aptly reflecting his White House functions. But except for Haldeman, the investigators would speak to no one with as intimate a knowledge of the President's day-to-day conduct. Since Dean's rather offhand remark that he thought his Oval Office conversations had been taped, the Ervin Committee's staff had routinely asked witnesses if they had any knowledge of such action. When asked whether he was aware of any taping, Butterfield forthrightly responded: "There is tape in the Oval Office. This tape is maintained by the Secret Service, and only three (3) Secret Service men knew about it initially . . . now four (4) know about it. The system was installed about 2½ years ago, I think—about at the 18-month point of Mr. Nixon's 1st term. . . . [T]he President is very history-oriented and history-conscious about the role he is going to play, and is not at all subtle about it, or about admitting it."

Butterfield told the committee staff that Nixon had directed him to have the Secret Service install and operate a voice-activated taping system. Besides the Secret Service operatives, only three other White House aides knew about it. Even the Director of the Secret Service Presidential Protective Division was unaware of its existence. Dean, he was certain, also did not know of it. The system had been installed in the Oval Office, the President's Executive Office Building retreat, the Cabinet Room, several private White House rooms, and the President's cabin at Camp David. "*Everything* was taped . . . as long as the President was in attendance. There was not so much as a hint that something should *not be taped."* Butterfield did not believe any transcripts existed, nor had Nixon (in Butterfield's tenure) requested any tapes for review. Butterfield believed that the President had no intention of depositing the tapes in the National Archives at the conclusion of his presidency.

The original report of the investigators noted that Butterfield had stated that he thought his revelation was "something you ought to know about in your investigation." But when Butterfield read the report, he protested, concerned as he was that some might think he had been "eager" to reveal the existence of the recording system. He had told the committee staff that he had not informed the U.S. Attorneys of the system because "they did not ask anything even closely related to this." He corrected the report to read that he knew that the President would not want the information known, but since he had been asked, he had "no choice but to answer. And, of course, there is only one kind of truth." He noted on the transcript that he had not said anything about the committee's "need" to know. "That," he said, "sounds as though I was *eager,* & I was not."33

Butterfield had assumed that the committee already had asked Haldeman and Higby about the tapes, and believed he was only corroborating what they had said. But apparently someone in high quarters had given Butterfield comfort after he had made the revelation, since in his public testimony he remarked that the tapes provided "the substance" for the President's future defense. For his part, Butterfield hoped that he had not "given away something" that Nixon had planned to use in support of his position.

John Dean, for one, was ecstatic over the revelation of the White House tapes. Alexander Butterfield, on the other hand, seemed distinctly unhappy with himself for having revealed them. Nixon later described himself as "shocked." He thought that "any staff member" would have raised executive privilege rather than reveal the system's existence.34

In those suspicious times, Butterfield aroused the darkest of suspicions. Minority Counsel Fred Thompson thought that Nixon, that shrewdest and most nimble of politicians, had deliberately instructed Butterfield to describe the taping system because, Thompson believed, it would allow the President to provide irrefutable evidence of Dean's culpability. Some suspected Butterfield of being a CIA agent, a charge Richard Helms later denounced as "ridiculous." "I didn't need Butterfield to spy for me," Helms remarked. Butterfield's motive was beside the point, however. His testimony changed the course of the hearings and redirected the conflict between Congress and Nixon. The tapes constituted the President's deepest secret. Less than three months earlier, Nixon had underlined their importance when he warned Haldeman that the tapes had to remain secret. "Have we got people that are trustworthy on that?" the President asked. "I guess we have," he said, providing his own response.35

Most important, the President's ability to defend himself and to be defended had shifted dramatically with the introduction of the White House tapes. Despite appearances, Howard Baker had been Nixon's most effective supporter on the Senate Select Committee. While Edward Gurney was a caricature of the Nixon loyalist, Baker *appeared* to be disinterested. His question regarding the President's knowledge, carefully repeated as it was, served to protect Richard Nixon. Who among those witnesses knew what the President knew, or when he knew it? Not many, and those who did seemed unlikely to answer. But the discovery of the tapes undid Baker's careful handiwork. The tapes made irrelevant his question to John Dean, "What did the President know and when did he know it?" Through the tapes, Richard Nixon himself could answer Baker, and in indelible words.

The President moved hastily to thwart the committee's attempts to gain access to the tapes. On July 16, he directed that no Secret Service agents give testimony regarding their protective or other White House duties. A week later, an obviously bitter Richard Nixon dispatched two letters to Senator Ervin which were read that day in the Senate Caucus Room. The first said that Nixon knew of no useful purpose for holding a meeting between the two. The second curtly rejected any access to the tapes. The "special nature of tape recordings of private conversations" was such, the President said, as to make the principle of confidentiality even greater for tapes than for documents. The tapes, he insisted, were "entirely consistent with what I know to be the truth and what I have stated to be the truth." Listening to them could only be confusing, for they were subject to interpretation against a wide range of other conversations and documents.

The sharp rejection distressed Ervin. He replied, expressing his love for the nation, his veneration of the presidential office, and his wishes for President Nixon's success—"because he is the only President this country has at this time." But the widening scope of Watergate had alarmed him. With obvious pain and emotion, Ervin described it as "the greatest tragedy" in American history—one even more profound than the Civil War, which at least had the redeeming qualities of sacrifice and heroism. "I see no redeeming features in Watergate," he concluded. Baker seconded Ervin's comments, apparently having decided that the President now had to do more than "stonewall." With that, the committee unanimously voted on July 23 to issue a *subpoena duces tecum* requiring the President to deliver the tapes to the committee.

Three days later, Nixon rejected the subpoena. Baker moved that the committee take the matter to the courts. There was no precedent, but the issue was joined, as Ervin noted, "whether the President is immune from all of the duties and responsibilities in matters of this kind which devolve upon all the other mortals who dwell in this land.'' The entire Senate voted to subpoena Nixon the following November. Lowell Weicker then suggested that the committee meet with the President to discuss the impasse, but Nixon again refused either to honor the subpoena or to talk to the senators. By December, Ervin was in despair. The President had convinced him "of his unrelenting purpose to hide . . . the truth respecting Watergate."[36]

Alexander Butterfield's public testimony had disrupted the carefully channeled flow of witnesses that the committee staff had charted. Following Dean's revelations of the cover-up and Mitchell's acknowledgment that CREEP had authorized operations by its ''security'' team, the next witnesses confirmed the implementation of the cover-up. Herbert W. Kalmbach, Fred C. LaRue, and Anthony Ulasewicz all testified after Butterfield to their varied roles in the payment of "hush money."

Kalmbach poignantly talked of his trust in Dean and Ehrlichman, who had repeatedly encouraged his money-raising efforts for the Watergate defendants. "The fact that I had been directed to undertake these actions by the No. 2 and No. 3 men on the White House staff made it absolutely incomprehensible to me that my actions in this regard could have been . . . improper or unethical." He described how Ehrlichman, a friend, specifically reassured him and told him that Dean had been authorized to direct him to raise money. All this gave the lie to Ehrlichman's portrait of a John Dean who operated on his own writ, without the knowledge of his superiors. In a taped telephone conversation, Ehrlichman assured Kalmbach that the money paid was only for "humanitarian" purposes. That call, not coincidentally, came just before Kalmbach testified to the grand jury and clearly reflected Ehrlichman's concern for the damage Kalmbach could do.[37]

LaRue's testimony was marked by confession and contrition: his actions, he said, were wrong "ethically and legally, . . . and I am prepared to accept the consequences." He described his delivery of cash payments, as well as his part in destroying records at CREEP. Like Mitchell, LaRue stressed the importance of re-electing the President, but with a sober sense of proportion markedly different from Mitchell's.

Damon Runyon might have written the script for Ulasewicz's testimony. The former New York policeman's comic descriptions of driving on the Washington Beltway, carrying a money changer for telephone calls, putting keys and envelopes in phone booths, lurking around corners, behaving in an exaggeratedly surreptitious manner, and delivering cryptic messages would have been the stuff of Broadway comedy except for the serious implications of his efforts. "Who thought you up?" Baker asked, much to the amusement of the audience. But Inouye soberly demanded to know whether Ulasewicz actually believed that he had delivered money for the legal defense of the Watergate conspirators. "Not likely," Ulasewicz admitted.[38]

Gordon Strachan, the key Haldeman staff assistant, established the relationship of Haldeman and CREEP and further described the workings of the Nixon White House. Strachan acknowledged at the outset of his testimony that his information would be "politically embarrassing" to himself and to the Administration, and he obliquely allowed that he had "closely associated" with confessed criminal elements. Blond-haired, well dressed, polite in demeanor, Strachan epitomized the dedicated young-man-in-a-hurry type embodied in many White House aides. He shamefacedly told Inouye that the White House staff had "an overwhelming and frequently inappropriate" sense of loyalty.

Near the end of Strachan's testimony, Joseph Montoya (as he often did) led the witness through a sackcloth-and-ashes expurgation of his sins. Were you "thrilled and enthused" about working in the White House? Montoya asked. "To be 27 years old and walking into the White House and seeing the President on occasion, and Dr. Kissinger . . . [is] a pretty awesome-inspiring [sic] experience for a young man," replied Strachan. Montoya then reviewed Strachan's "soldierly obedience" to his superiors and his "fall into the Watergate pit," all of which, he noted, provoked disappointment and disillusionment in younger people and affected their attitude toward public service. What advice could Strachan give them? "Stay away," he retorted, probably not offering quite the penitent statement Montoya desired.[39]

Strachan described Haldeman's vaunted efficiency, detailed the Chief of Staff's intimate involvement with campaign matters, and explained his use of Dean. He was certain that Dean disclosed his doings to Haldeman and never would have operated on his own. Perhaps not inadvertently, Strachan testified as to Dean's "remarkable facility" in remembering facts. Aside from attacking Magruder for continuing to perjure himself, Strachan carefully avoided incriminating anyone. He admitted that, just three days after the break-in, he had destroyed numerous memos regarding the campaign and Haldeman's links to it, but he denied that the contents reflected illegal activity. The material simply was "politically embarrassing." Strachan acknowledged that he had shredded documents at Haldeman's request but would not confirm Ervin's allegation that one of the memos described a "sophisticated intelligence operation" before the break-in.[40]

The committee moved closer to the Oval Office when Ehrlichman and Haldeman testified from July 24 through August 1. For the first time in the hearings, the committee confronted formidable adverse witnesses who had prepared well for their appearance and doggedly defended their actions and those of the President. As if by prearrangement, the two men switched their public personae before the Senate committee. Haldeman, generally portrayed as a cold, ruthless, and rude *fonctionnaire,* appeared as reasonable and courteous. Ehrlichman, often considered the more amiable and gracious, and less dogmatic, of the two, responded defiantly, even contemptuously, to the committee. His body language and facial expressions reflected disdain for the committee's intellectual and political qualities. He made no effort to disguise his low opinion of the senators and their staff.

Egil Krogh, one of the Plumbers, who regarded Ehrlichman as something of a father-figure, had described him as "an intensely proud, vain man," unable to tolerate being proven wrong on anything. Krogh saw Ehrlichman as the master of the "one-line putdown" and described him armed with a "razor-sharp wit" to skewer his antagonists. In later years, Ehrlichman acknowledged that his behavior before the Ervin Committee had been a tactical error: "I offered everyone an example of how not to do it."[41] When Ervin quoted a Biblical parable, Ehrlichman snapped back: "I read the Bible, I don't quote it." He used Sam Dash as a foil, alternately responding with mock amusement and outrage to Dash's questions, generally treating the interrogation as pedantic and simplistic. Tapping anti-intellectual currents, Ehrlichman would refer to Dash as "Professor," especially when (as often was the case) Dash would present a rather convoluted question. Altogether, Ehrlichman appeared as a man sometimes in error but rarely in doubt.

Ehrlichman and Haldeman figured to be the President's main line of defense. Yet White House Counsel J. Fred Buzhardt uncannily gauged their vulnerabilities. In a memo prepared for Nixon or Haig, Buzhardt expressed concern because of Ehrlichman's aggressive manner. He realized that Ehrlichman would wrap himself in the blanket of national security to defend his actions with the Plumbers and worried that this reliance upon the President's special role constituted danger for Nixon himself. Haldeman, on the other hand, had a "good demeanor," but he was known as an inveterate note-taker and thus would accentuate the President's "document denial problem."[42]

Ehrlichman's testimony underscored the Administration's basic defense: John Dean was a "vital link in a chain of delegation" who failed the President because of his desire to protect Mitchell and to cover up his own participation in criminal wrongdoing. In his opening statement, Ehrlichman challenged Dean's credibility on almost every point. With typical effrontery, he dismissed the description of the fear and paranoia that Dean had contended gripped the White House. The reality, Ehrlichman insisted, involved the need to have critical positions staffed by loyalists, the need to prevent

leaks that would jeopardize delicate negotiations, and the need to prevent the "terrorism" that reflected "a highly organized attempt to shut down
the Federal Government." Ehrlichman testified that the President was "not
paranoid, weird, [or] psychotic on the subject of demonstrators or hypersen-
sitive to criticism."

That defense was at odds with the analysis of Richard Nixon that Ehrlichman and Haldeman later offered in their memoirs. But in July 1973,
Ehrlichman consistently defended the President as a man determined to conduct foreign policy on his terms, who refused to be influenced or intimidated
by contrary opinions, and who initiated or considered activities including
the use of the Plumbers, wiretapping, and the Huston Plan to prevent anarchy and subversion. Any successful defense of Nixon, of course, absolved
Ehrlichman himself of culpability, but as Buzhardt realized, the game was
a dangerous one for the President.

Despite Ehrlichman's desire to discredit Dean—the "star witness," as he
scornfully described him—the committee's concern with Ehrlichman did not
go directly to Dean's testimony but centered on the nature of the Plumbers,
his own connections to that group, and the President's knowledge of their
operations. Ehrlichman labored to depict Nixon as a President bent on fashioning a foreign and defense policy tailored to the national interest, who
was thwarted and diverted from his mission by political enemies equally
determined to fulfill their agendas, and even to force upon him a foreign
policy "favorable to the North Vietnamese and their allies." Such political
expressions, Ehrlichman insisted, "were more than just a garden variety
exercise of the first amendment." Perhaps Ehrlichman was correct: clinical
judgments of paranoia were beside the point. The conflict centered, from
the White House perspective, on political divergence that was quite real.
The only overuse of the imagination may have been in the Administration's
perception of their foes' motivation, especially as it appeared in the more
sinister overtones of Ehrlichman's comments.[43]

Ehrlichman defended the break-in at the office of Daniel Ellsberg's psychiatrist, finding nothing "completely irrational" in the action. Even if the
deed had become public knowledge, he believed it could not have been
"seriously embarrassing" to the Administration. Why? First, it was "part
of a very intensive national security investigation" and second, the Plumbers
were operating under "express authorization" in carrying it out. In short,
the President had dictated the mission; and as a national-security matter, it
could not be questioned.

The actions of the Plumbers, Ehrlichman maintained, fit "well within the
President's inherent constitutional powers"—inherent powers that Ehrlichman confidently asserted were "spelled out" in the U.S. Code. Almost
unnoticed in his testimony was that Ehrlichman took issue with his old
antagonist John Mitchell, who had contended that the Plumbers represented

part of the "White House horrors" and that Nixon would have "lowered the boom" had he learned of them. But Ehrlichman could speak firsthand for the President, correctly recalling Nixon's contention that the Fielding break-in was "a vital national security inquiry," well within the constitutional functions of the presidency. Meanwhile, Ehrlichman, recognizing the specter of a criminal indictment, fenced with Dash over his own role in the Fielding burglary: he was not conducting a "covert entry" but a properly authorized "covert investigation" of the psychiatrist's offices. Still, the committee offered in evidence Ehrlichman's August 11, 1971, memorandum to the Plumbers' principals, Krogh and Young, approving a "covert operation" if done under their assurance "that it is not traceable."[44]

Ehrlichman strikingly contrasted the Watergate break-in with that of Dr. Fielding's offices. The former he dismissed as "dumb, shocking, irredeemable"—words similar to those used by nearly every Administration witness. That righteous indignation did not extend to the action against Ellsberg's psychiatrist. Ehrlichman's condemnation of the Watergate burglary in effect said, "I had nothing to do with it." His criticism was that it was "dumb," not wrong. But if Watergate was wrong because it was a burglary, then the same was true for the Fielding venture.

Ehrlichman's spirited defense abandoned the higher ground to those who would advocate a traditional notion of constitutional purity. None did that more effectively than Herman Talmadge. The exchange between the Senator and the witness offered one of the hearings' most unforgettable moments— and marked a decisive, irretrievable setback for the Administration. What had started with Ehrlichman's theoretical excursions into the higher reaches of inherent-powers doctrine had turned into a bald statement that the President might determine his own power, with no recognizable checks or accountability. Talmadge asked Ehrlichman to recall some fundamental principles:

Do you remember when we were in law school, we studied a famous principle of law that came from England and also is well known in this country, that no matter how humble a man's cottage is, that even the King of England cannot enter without his consent [?].

Ehrlichman stared across the table, eyebrows furrowed, jaw set, and replied:

I am afraid that has been considerably eroded over the years, has it not?

Talmadge never hesitated:

Down in my country we still think it is a pretty legitimate principle of law.[45]

Spontaneous applause from the audience left Ehrlichman momentarily stunned. The President's confident aide had touched upon a tender, treasured principle, one not as readily dismissed as the less well understood First and Fifth amendments.

Committee members also forced Ehrlichman into political dark corners when he attempted to equate the "defense fund" for the burglars with similar funds raised for political activists opposed to the Vietnam war. Ervin insisted that people in such cases openly gave money, knowing the purpose of the funds and believing the cause correct. Certainly, Ervin argued, those who contributed to the President's re-election campaign neither had knowledge of, nor probably would they have approved, payments to burglars. Ehrlichman hastily retreated to a discussion of his own lack of involvement in those payments. Weicker turned on Ehrlichman's defense of employing such "investigators" as Caulfield and Ulasewicz. Ehrlichman contended that the White House had a legitimate interest in unmasking unfit political figures, for example, those with drinking problems—a daring ploy to discredit unnamed senators. Weicker also raged at Ehrlichman for equating an FBI investigation, duly authorized by statute, with the free-lance techniques of Ehrlichman's private investigators.

Ehrlichman's defense of White House attempts to discredit the committee's hearings by reference to Ervin's partisanship virtually invited the North Carolinian to pose as the champion of constitutional liberty and nonpartisanship. Ervin refused to apologize for his criticism of what he regarded as the Administration's usurpation of constitutional powers, usurpation entailed by its claims to executive privilege, inherent powers, and rightful impoundment of funds. But he deftly noted that few Senate Democrats had supported the President more staunchly than he on economic and war issues, referring in particular to his recent vote against the War Powers Act because it encroached on the President's proper constitutional authority.

Ehrlichman offered a maze of detail, contradiction, evasion, and confrontation. He told the committee that as early as July 1972 the President had forbidden his aides to discuss executive clemency for the burglars, omitting mention of other times when Nixon openly considered the possibility. He lamely tried to explain away his instructions that Patrick Gray "deep six" the contents of Hunt's safe and his discussion of the FBI Directorship with Federal Judge Byrne. Repeatedly, almost desperately, Ehrlichman tried to steer the committee to his fundamental contention that Dean was the primary villain.[46]

Ehrlichman concluded his testimony on Monday, July 30, once more jabbing at the "falsity" of Dean's charges. In measured, confident words, he rejected Strachan's unduly flippant advice urging young people to stay away from Washington. Ehrlichman said he would give them a mission: "Come and do better. Don't stay away." Good people, he contended, must be attracted to fight for what is right, to fight against the "seat-warmers and hacks" who would dominate the field if it were abandoned. Finally, Ehrlichman heaped scorn on a Washington culture he truly loathed. If you worked for the executive branch, he said, Congress and the media would never "throw rosebuds." Washington was a place which rejected patriotism and family values, Ehrlichman said, implying that a kind of *kulturkampf* explained the Administration's vulnerability. The truth was there to be seen, he concluded; "preconception or partisanship" never would find it, as if to encourage doubt that the committee could do so. Ervin by this time had had enough of the witness. He left the chair and allowed Baker to offer the usual soothing parting words.[47]

Haldeman's demeanor contrasted sharply with that of his colleague. Friendly, smiling, and deferential almost to the point of unctuousness, Haldeman nonetheless conceded nothing by way of personal or Administration wrongdoing. His flat, undramatic tones made his appearance somewhat disappointing, but in this fashion, he offered a determined, tenacious defense, convinced as Ehrlichman was that the Administration had acted only out of necessity and for the national well-being. Haldeman directed a White House operation that worked as a "zero defect system." He proudly described working with "one of America's greatest Presidents, a President who had ended the Vietnam War and the cold war," who had opened dialogues with the Soviet Union and China, and who had returned power to the people with revenue sharing and governmental reorganization.[48]

Haldeman moved to seal off Richard Nixon from any responsibility for the matters under inquiry. He described a President who generously delegated authority so that he could spend his time on the important issues rather than closely superintending details, seeing everyone who wanted to see him, and reading everything sent to him. Haldeman's statement stood in stark contrast to his massive files of presidential memoranda devoted to details, often trivial ones.[49]

Haldeman firmly denied that there was any paralyzing fear in the White House of demonstrators and protesters, but he noted a "healthy and valid" concern for national and domestic security. Accordingly, Nixon designated Haldeman as his "lord high executioner" to deal with leaks in executive agencies. Haldeman described his approach to this task rather benignly as merely directing department heads to tighten security. The Plumbers went unmentioned. He flatly denied any knowledge of the Watergate break-in or the bugging of the Democratic National Committee, and he disclaimed any interest in intelligence-gathering operations by the re-election committee; whatever Strachan knew or did in these areas never touched him, Haldeman asserted.

If the senators wanted a villain, Haldeman thought that John Dean could accommodate them best. Dean was, he said, the "Watergate project officer" in the White House. He had authority to work on his own; his task was to keep Haldeman and Ehrlichman posted on developments, and through them, the President. Alas, Haldeman concluded, Dean "apparently did not keep us fully posted[,] and it now appears he did not keep us accurately posted." Haldeman pointedly reminded the committee that he, Ehrlichman, and the President were busily engrossed in "vital matters" in this period, and hence they made no attempt to get into the details, or to "take over" the Watergate case. The White House files again would impeach Haldeman's view of things, only this time the tapes would offer more than mute testimony to belie Haldeman's brazen denials.

Weicker pressed Haldeman on his attempts to smear McGovern and the Democratic Party for their alleged links to the "peace forces" and to Communist countries. Haldeman doggedly countered with allegations of Democratic sabotage of the Republican campaign, Democratic-organized demonstrations against the President, and Democratic plans to disrupt Republican meetings and rallies, as well as other misdeeds which he said he should exclude because of the "tender mercies" of the television audience. All these, he said, were documented instances or ones which he had observed.[50]

Ehrlichman had managed to skirt discussion of the White House tapes. For Haldeman, who acknowledged that he had supervised the installation of the recording devices, that was not so easy. Furthermore, he infuriated the senators when they learned that he had had access to the tapes and had taken them to his house as part of his preparation for his testimony. Ervin sarcastically noted as a "strange thing" that Haldeman could listen to the tapes but the committee could not. The presidency had not been destroyed, the Constitution had not collapsed, and the heavens had not fallen because Haldeman had heard the tapes. Surely then, Ervin thought, the committee could not cause any such calamity. Dash argued, without much success, that Haldeman had violated the terms of his subpoena by failing to turn the "documents" over to the committee as stipulated. If Haldeman could use them as he had, then, as some senators argued, they were, as the President claimed, no longer privileged.

The tapes were a trap for Haldeman. His answers to Baker regarding the March 21 meeting with Dean and the President concerning the unraveling cover-up formed the basis for a subsequent perjury indictment, as the tapes demonstrated a quite different story from the one Haldeman had rendered. The former Chief of Staff, however, confidently believed that the contents of the tapes would never become public knowledge.[51]

Haldeman concluded his testimony much as had Ehrlichman, affirming that good people should come to Washington to serve the nation. By indirection he, too, attacked the President's critics by urging people to understand the totality of the Nixon Administration's accomplishments and not to view its record through the "microcosm" of Watergate. Haldeman acknowledged that Watergate constituted a failure of some kind, but in a note that he would sound for years afterward, he expressed puzzlement and bewilderment as to what that failure was, why it occurred, and who was responsible for it.[52]

Haldeman's testimony took less than three days, and after Ehrlichman, the weary senators seemed grateful for his more direct responses. Sometimes, of course, Haldeman's denials only evoked incredulity, as in the case of his inability to explain why the re-election committee had decided to pay the burglars' expenses. Ervin found it hard to believe that political organizations had become "eleemosynary institutions." Still, the senators responded to Haldeman's seeming difference in like manner. Gurney may have taken matters to an extreme when he said that Haldeman had testified so fully on the key matters of the President's involvement in the break-in and subsequent cover-up that he could not "think of a single question" to ask the witness.

Curiously, at the end, John Wilson, Haldeman's lawyer, decided to do battle with Daniel Inouye. Inouye had irritated Wilson throughout, especially since the Senator had muttered into the microphone, "What a liar," in response to some of Ehrlichman's testimony. Wilson unsuccessfully sought to stop Inouye from introducing into the record a California court judgment against Haldeman for illegal activities in Nixon's gubernatorial campaign in 1962. He objected again when Inouye discussed a memo outlining reprisals against a Defense Department "whistle-blower," and once more when the Senator questioned Haldeman about White House containment tactics directed against the Senate Select Committee. Wilson hardly helped his efforts when he referred publicly to Inouye as a "fat Jap." The day after Haldeman's testimony, Ervin and Baker vied with each other to sing Inouye's praises as a war hero and valued member of the committee.[53] The Administration had lost another skirmish in the vital public-relations war.

After August 2, the committee heard from a variety of prominent witnesses, including Richard Helms, former CIA Deputy Directors Richard Cushman and Vernon Walters, L. Patrick Gray, Richard Kleindienst, and even E. Howard Hunt, who eagerly portrayed himself as a good soldier with a life imitating the spy novels he had written. Henry Petersen defended the Justice Department and the U.S. Attorneys for their pursuit of the case. Petersen also indicated that he had now begun to understand his dealings with the President during March and April. The Administration got in some last words for itself on September 26 when Patrick Buchanan slashed the committee for its excessive leaks and its treatment of witnesses. Buchanan boldly attacked the committee, but John Dean's image and testimony persisted in the nation's consciousness, not the mauling tactics of club-fighter Buchanan. During the next phases of the hearings, in October and November, the committee heard from several dozen witnesses who testified on the need for legislation regulating campaign practices and finances. That subject, after all, was the committee's *raison d'être*.

For nearly three months, television had given Watergate an immediacy and a familiarity that could not fail to capture widespread attention. How had the revelations affected Americans? Public-opinion polls can offer only a snapshot captured through a particular lens at a given moment. Questions shape responses; a slightly reworded question may sharply shift an answer. That kind of variation appeared throughout the polling in the summer of 1973. In general, polls reflected a nation with increasing doubts and misgivings about its President, yet uncertain as to how to deal with him. Richard Nixon had lost the confidence of the American people, and with it, probably, the capacity to govern effectively. Paradoxically, only the special nature of the American constitutional system kept him in office.

At the conclusion of Dean's testimony in late June, the Gallup poll showed Americans equally divided in their approval of Nixon's job performance; 46 percent of Gallup's respondents said they would still vote for Nixon against McGovern, down some 16 points since the November election. (McGovern, however, had gained only 2 percent.) A few weeks later, an overwhelming 62 percent of those surveyed opposed forcing the President to leave, with only 24 percent favoring such action. But following testimony by Nixon's chief aides, the polls for the first time showed that a majority of Americans regarded Watergate as a "serious matter"; in October 1972, by a 62–36 margin, respondents had considered the affair "just politics."

Questions also could blur answers. One poll showed that 50 percent of Americans believed John Dean, 30 percent did not, and 20 percent were unsure. Yet when told that Nixon had denied Dean's charges, the respondents said that they would believe Nixon as opposed to Dean by 38–37 percent, with 25 percent unsure. In early August, by a margin of 56–35, respondents said that the President should have "the benefit of the doubt," and by nearly the same spread (54–38) they agreed with the President's announced determination to spend more time working for the country than trying to figure out who was to blame for Watergate. That same Harris poll of August 5, however, showed that by a 55–32 margin the President did not "inspire confidence as a President should." Ten days later, the Gallup poll gave the President only a 31 percent approval rating, down 9 points in four weeks and 37 points since January. Congressmen matched the public sentiments. A *Christian Science Monitor* poll of nearly two hundred congressmen in mid-August 1973 found an overwhelming number believing that the President had not adequately changed his staff and operations and that he would be unable to govern effectively. Yet by an equally overwhelming margin, congressmen opposed impeachment and resignation.

Americans evinced some ambivalence toward the press in the polls regarding Watergate. In a Harris survey early in July only 17 percent of those polled believed that the press was out "to get President Nixon on Watergate," while 61 percent disagreed. Yet 40 percent thought that the media had devoted more attention to Watergate than the case warranted. The polls showed that Americans watched the Watergate proceedings in steadily growing numbers, rather evenly spread across sections, age groups, and educational backgrounds. The Senate Select Committee earned high marks. In September, a Gallup poll found that 57 percent of those questioned believed that the committee was more interested in gaining facts than in discrediting the Nixon Administration, while only 28 percent criticized it. The committee's approval rating was the inverse of the President's, again indicating that the Administration had taken a public-relations drubbing. Worse yet, Americans in increasing numbers simply did not believe the President. A Gallup telephone poll showed that 77 percent of the nation heard his televised defense on August 15, but only a little over one-fourth of the audience believed him. Forty-four percent considered him "not at all convincing."[54] The problem was more than public relations.

The summer of 1973 marked a sharp shift in Nixon's fortunes. More verifiable proof than polls demonstrated his declining powers. Since 1966, congressional doves had failed in more than a hundred roll-call votes to reduce the Vietnam conflict either by cutting off funds or imposing bombing halts. But by July 1, Nixon confronted legislation stipulating a cutoff in funds for the bombing of Cambodia. He had successfully resisted such demands before, but now he had to accept the proviso in order to secure other defense appropriations. From Nixon's other flank, conservative critics stepped up charges that the President had appeased liberals in the hope of stifling the Watergate investigation. The signs were apparent: the "liberal" Elliot Richardson had succeeded Richard Kleindienst, the "liberal" Frank Carlucci had been appointed to a high government position, and a new Director of the Office of Economic Opportunity promised to revitalize the agency, which was thought to have a liberal charge. Too, Nixon had allowed Archibald Cox to establish a "Kennedyite" beachhead in the government; the President had been unable to resist expensive increases in farm subsidies, Social Security benefits, and minimum wages; and finally, his giving in on the Cambodian bombing halt amounted to the "largest and most gratuitous concession" in the history of American foreign policy.[55] The President's declining authority in foreign affairs, coupled with the growing disenchantment of his conservative supporters, ominously exhibited the reality of his deteriorating position.

* * *

Save for the discovery of the White House tapes, the Senate Select Committee's efforts mainly replicated what the Watergate prosecutors in the Justice Department already knew. The committee's investigators neither discovered John Dean nor led him to his disclosures about the President. Dean and his lawyer already had seriously discussed "Mr. P." with the federal prosecutors. Still, the hearings kindled public interest in Watergate. Witnesses marched across the television landscape, alternately disillusioned, contrite, defiant, obsequious, stonewalling, disenchanted, and steadfastly loyal. Some had photographic memories and others brilliantly practiced ignorance and absent-mindedness. A fascinated viewing public gleaned lessons in political behavior not usually found in textbooks. Most important, the committee's conduct and the information yielded by the hearings stood in stark contrast to the image and information conveyed by the Nixon White House.

XV

"LET OTHERS WALLOW IN WATERGATE."

AGNEW, THE TAPES,
AND THE SATURDAY NIGHT MASSACRE
AUGUST–OCTOBER 1973

After Alexander Butterfield's startling revelations, the White House tapes took on a life of their own and became the center of attention. Their very existence gave a new lease to the notion that wrongdoing had occurred in high places, and they became the most contested terrain of the Watergate imbroglio. Richard Nixon could fight for or abandon key aides and yet survive himself, but the tapes imperiled him as did nothing else. The struggle to control them consumed the President for one full year, at what cost to his functioning in his office will never be known. But his tenacious battle only confirmed the importance of the tapes. That struggle precipitated the President's dramatic conflict with the Special Prosecutor, ruptured his Administration, exacerbated his relations with Congress (particularly with members of his own party), and most decisively, confirmed the swelling, unshakeable image of Nixon as a man who had something to hide.

As the most prominent figures in the Administration ended their Senate testimony, President Nixon and his staff launched a brief but extensive counterattack in mid-August. In an evening address to the nation on the fifteenth, he again insisted that he had no prior knowledge of the break-in; that he neither authorized nor encouraged subordinates to engage in improper campaign tactics; and that he "neither took part in nor knew" about any of the subsequent cover-up activities. "That," he insisted, "was and that is the simple truth." He alluded to John Dean as "a witness who offered no evidence beyond his own impressions'' and who had been contradicted by every other witness ''in a position to know the facts.'' As for the September 15, 1972 meeting, the President said that Dean had given him ''no reason whatever to believe that any others were guilty.'' Of course, he could not reveal the true nature of that meeting, in which he and Haldeman had discussed the management of the cover-up with Dean.

Nixon said he had been determined throughout ''to get out the facts about Watergate, not to cover them up.'' But he warned that that effort could not include any revelations from the White House tapes, arguing that they might ''irreparably'' harm the ''confidentiality'' of the presidency. Even if the tapes contained conversations that related to illegal acts, that still did not justify making them public. With that twist of Nixonian logic, the President maintained that to release the tapes, even those involving illegal actions alone, ''would risk exposing private Presidential conversations, involving the whole range of official duties.'' Throughout his August 15 speech, he mixed his own taping activities up with official wiretapping by the Department of Justice. He acknowledged a willingness to abide by the limitations that the Supreme Court had set on wiretapping in 1972, but he typically noted that the Kennedy Administration had authorized more than twice as many wiretaps as his own.

Above all, Nixon pleaded for an end to Watergate, seeking to justify his Administration's alleged misdeeds on the grounds of self-defense. ''We must recognize that one excess begets another,'' he told the nation, ''and that the extremes of violence and discord in the 1960s contributed to the extremes of Watergate.'' But the cure, he said, might be worse than the disease. Twelve weeks of televised testimony had brought the nation to the point ''at which a continued, backward-looking obsession with Watergate is causing this Nation to neglect matters of far greater importance to all of the American people.''

A week later the President held a rare news conference (his first in five months and the first to be televised in fourteen), reiterating the themes of his speech. He assailed those who exploited Watergate for their own political advantage, but he maintained that his enemies would not dislodge him. He would not consider resigning, even if he believed that his capacity to govern had been seriously weakened. ''[H]ad I been running the campaign,'' the President lamented, ''other than trying to run the country, particularly the foreign policy of this country, . . . [Watergate] would never have happened. But that's water under the bridge,'' he concluded.[1]

Whatever the force of the President's words, they paled beside the possibility that his deeds and words had been recorded. His credibility, too, showed no signs of recovering. His approval rating rose after the televised speech, but polls showed that more than two-thirds of Americans thought that Nixon had failed to offer "convincing proof" that he was not part of the cover-up, and more than 70 percent thought that he continued to with-hold important information. The President's lawyers thought his press con-ference was "superb" and that it would "go far to put Watergate to bed." They believed he had provided them with "the frosting on the cake" for their briefs defending the President's right to withhold the tapes. California Governor Ronald Reagan said that Nixon represented "the voice of reason," but Senator Barry Goldwater remarked that nothing in the speech, or in other speeches, tended "to divert suspicion" from the President. Equally omi-nous, William Ruckelshaus, who had moved from the FBI to the Justice Department as Deputy Attorney General, said that the speech lacked spec-ificity and would not satisfy Nixon's critics.

The growing controversy over the tapes heightened suspicions on the Republican Right that the "Watergate millstone" had forced Nixon into "preventive appeasement," both at home and abroad, in order that he be able to present the nation with "accomplishments." *National Review* edito-rialized that the tapes "could probably clear up" many of the problems, but the magazine recognized that Nixon's instant refusal to release them signified more controversy and more compromising. Watergate, the editor-ial concluded, had drained the President's "political sinew, his moral au-thority, and his credibility."[2]

When Nixon left Bethesda Naval Hospital on July 20 after his bout with viral pneumonia, he offered the first public hints that Watergate had begun to paralyze his presidency. To White House workers gathered in the Rose Garden, the President spoke movingly of the little time he had left to finish the tasks before him. He noted that there were those who suggested he resign because the burdens of the office had become intolerable—that, he said, was "plain poppycock." He would press forward. "And what we were elected to do, we are going to do," he exclaimed, "and let others wallow in Wa-tergate, we are going to do our job." Spiro Agnew thought the President had the look of a "frightened man" and that he was fearful the tapes would embarrass him and affect his place in history.

Before he left the hospital, however, the President had expressed a thought he could not divulge to the nation: "Should have destroyed the tapes after April 30, 1973," he wrote while in his hospital bed. With some bitterness, he complained that their discovery had unduly affected his Counsel, Leonard Garment, and other staff members. "We must be strong and competent. We must go ahead," the President wrote, as if to spur himself. Raymond Moley, once FDR's chief aide, pleaded with Nixon to do just that. A psychiatrist, long known to Nixon, offered counsel on how the President should deal with the "emotional undertone" of Watergate and how people "perceived [it] by their psyche."[3]

* * *

The discovery that the President had taped conversations astonished and fascinated the nation. In time, Americans would hear that previous presidents, from Franklin Roosevelt to Lyndon Johnson, had also taped conversations, but in that summer of 1973, Richard Nixon had few defenders.

"God bless the blunderers at the Watergate," labor leader George Meany said when he learned about the tapes on July 17. "If they hadn't been so clumsy, America would never have known this was going on." For Meany, the secret taping was "almost beyond belief." Goldwater was not surprised, but he thought that individuals should have been told they were being taped. The President's former protégé Robert Finch was "literally astonished . . . [and] incredulous." Speaker Carl Albert thought the practice outrageous, but Senate Democratic leader Mike Mansfield typically covered all the options: "I am not surprised but I don't like it. I wouldn't have minded if they told me," said Mansfield. Some could not resist the ready quip. Congressman Wilbur Mills (D–AR) said that if he had known he was being recorded in his meetings with Nixon, his English would have been better. And Senator Robert Dole (R–KA) added that he was glad he always nodded when talking to the President. Sam Ervin, now a prosecutor of sorts, appropriately thought the news nothing less than "providential." Republican House leader Gerald Ford was the exception that proved the rule, as he found nothing wrong in the practice of recording presidential conversations and solemnly insisted that "I have never said anything to the President that could not be a matter of public record."

Melvin Laird, the former Secretary of Defense, who had returned to the White House as a presidential aide after Haldeman and Ehrlichman departed, had been told by Counsel J. Fred Buzhardt that the tapes showed the President's involvement in the cover-up. Laird felt betrayed. His recent appointment reflected the President's need to stroke his Republican congressional constituency, with whom Laird had strong ties. In fact, the two men had little liking and much distrust for one another. Laird claimed that when he visited the President in May, he asked him point-blank if he had taken part in the cover-up. The President, Laird said, stated "absolutely, positively" that he had not been involved.[4]

The most important immediate reaction to the exposé of the tapes was the President's decision not to destroy them. Of the numerous imponderables about Watergate, Nixon's failure to destroy the White House tapes is one of the most bewildering and confusing, and yet perhaps it is quite simply explained. Nixon believed that the tapes, selectively exploited, would exonerate him. Beyond that, he regarded them as politically and historically invaluable—again, if used in a selective fashion. Finally, he had every reason to think that executive privilege offered adequate protection against any judicial or legislative demands for the tapes.

Richard Nixon's own memory of that decision was marked by confusion, obfuscation, and above all, regret: "If I had indeed been the knowing Watergate conspirator that I was charged as being," he wrote in his memoirs, "I would have recognized in 1973 that the tapes contained conversations that would be fatally damaging. I would have seen that if I were to survive they would have to be destroyed."

The President acknowledged that the tapes were a "mixed bag," filled with politically embarrassing talk and ambiguities. Yet, years later, he still maintained that they "indisputably disproved" Dean's contention of presidential obstruction of justice since September 1972. Long after the fact, Nixon seemed anxious to hold his advisers accountable for the decision to retain the tapes. According to Nixon's memoirs, Haldeman had assured him that they could explain the March 21 meeting—the tape of which his former Chief of Staff had heard, although Nixon had told his August 22 press conference that Haldeman had listened only to the September 15, 1972 tape. When the two men had met on April 26, they talked about the tapes' references to hush-money payments, Thomas Pappas's role as a money raiser, and other "politically embarrassing" items. Yet the President believed that the tapes would save him, for they could be used to point out Dean's minor inaccuracies and inconsistencies and thereby discredit him.[5]

Alexander Haig reasoned that destroying the tapes would only enhance suspicions of presidential guilt. Nixon concurred, realizing that actual revelations of wrongdoing would be less crippling than the taint of having destroyed evidence. Yet for all his evasiveness on the meaning of the tapes, Nixon later realized what their existence meant: "my presidency had little chance of surviving to the end of its term." The struggle for the tapes aroused the nation, and as the President realized, the fight to keep them private would "paralyze the presidency."[6]

Nixon later blamed his decision not to destroy the tapes on "well-intentioned lawyers who had the cockeyed notion that I would be destroying evidence." Leonard Garment acknowledged his role in persuading the President of that position. Despite the lack of a subpoena, Garment believed that the Senate's demand and the Special Prosecutor's intention to move for the tapes constituted public knowledge of and public demand for the evidence. Once Butterfield had revealed the tapes' existence, Garment argued, destruction would have been an obstruction of justice. Curiously, Nixon's longtime adversary, Washington attorney Edward Bennett Williams, who represented the *Washington Post* and the Democratic National Committee in its 1972 civil suit against CREEP, said he would have advised Nixon to destroy the tapes and make the action public, as long as they were not under subpoena. Williams believed that the President could have said he would not risk compromising conversations with heads of state and foreign ambassadors, not to mention his own aides.[7]

Pat Nixon could not understand her husband's decision. But his daughter Tricia sensed how threatening the tapes were. Her father repeatedly had told her that the tapes could be taken either way, that they contained nothing damaging, yet he might be impeached because of their content. "Because he has said the latter," she wrote, "knowing Daddy, the latter is the way he really feels."[8]

In a remarkably tantalizing, yet blunt and dark, passage in his memoirs, Nixon unveiled probably the most deep-seated of his motives in preserving the White House tapes: the tapes, he wrote, "were my best insurance against the unforeseeable future. I was prepared to believe that others, even people close to me, would turn against me just as Dean had done, and in that case the tapes would give me at least some protection."

Henry Kissinger, a somber observer of that lonely side of Nixon, described how the President might also have taped conversations for devious purposes. Just before Nixon was scheduled to sign the order for the Christmas bombing of North Vietnam in 1972, he summoned Kissinger to his office. There, Haldeman confronted the National Security Adviser, and proceeded to argue vehemently against the measure—even though Kissinger and Nixon had carefully determined their course of action beforehand. Kissinger reflexively defended the decision. Meanwhile, the President remained silent and ultimately signed the order. In all probability, Kissinger believed, Nixon had used the secret recording system in that instance to set up Kissinger as the perpetrator of the deed, in the event anything went wrong.[9]

What is often unsaid in the backward-looking interpretations of Nixon's decision by himself and others is that the President and many around him confidently believed that no one could force him to divulge the tapes. Few knowing students of constitutional law would have anticipated the unanimous decision of the Supreme Court in 1974 forcing Nixon to surrender some of his tapes. However imprecise and vague the standing of executive privilege as constitutional doctrine, mere presidential assertion of the prerogative had historically been enough to sustain it. Common sense, too, dictated that presidential conversations required an important element of confidentiality, generally not to be violated. The conflict here was between the practical problems of governance on the one side and both the demands of criminal justice and the necessity for cleansing the Augean stables of political corruption on the other. Political and public sentiment eventually propelled a resolution of the dilemma; but time, in that sense, was not Nixon's ally.

Sam Ervin and his fellow Senate Select Committee members responded to the Butterfield revelation with an appeal to the President that he surrender all relevant tapes and documents. On July 23 Nixon emphatically rejected the plea, again insisting that he needed to preserve the principle of confidentiality for the presidency. In a separate letter sent that day, he marked his growing estrangement from Congress by refusing a private meeting with Ervin and Baker. The committee promptly issued a subpoena for the tapes. Ervin contended that no writ of executive privilege extended to "either alleged illegal activities or political campaign activities." Never before had a congressional committee served a subpoena on the President, and not since 1807 had a president received a subpoena from any source. Nixon's two-front war heated up. On that same day, his lawyers rejected a similar request for the tapes from Special Prosecutor Cox. One lawyer pointedly reminded Cox that he was part of the executive branch and therefore subject to presidential orders—"and can have access to presidential papers only as and if the President sees fit to make them available to you." Cox was unimpressed, and he, too, similarly secured a subpoena.

The President "respectfully" rejected the Senate's subpoena on July 26. Executive privilege, he insisted in reply to Ervin, was at stake. He had invoked it, Nixon said, "only with regard to documents and recordings that cannot be made public consistent with the confidentiality essential to the functioning of the office of the President." In short, the President would decide the priority between "confidentiality" and "alleged illegal activities," as Ervin described them. The day before, Nixon informed Judge John Sirica that he would "decline" Cox's subpoena, contending that historical precedents demonstrated that presidents could not be subjected to compulsory process from the courts. Responding to a motion by Cox, Sirica directed the President's lawyers to appear for arguments on August 7 and show cause for declining to produce the tapes. As the judge set down his order, the White House announced that the President "would abide by a definitive decision of the highest court," a remark Nixon repeated at his August 22 news conference.

Cox and a presidential lawyer, Charles Alan Wright, clashed in Sirica's courtroom on August 22. Both men touched on sensitive propositions. Wright maintained that the constitutional provision for impeachment provided the only remedy for checking and balancing the President in cases like the one at hand. Cox not so obliquely challenged the President to comply with a subpoena or "dismiss the case"—presumably by firing the Special Prosecutor. But then, Cox noted, "the people will know where the responsibility lies." A week later, Sirica ordered Nixon to turn over some tapes for his personal examination. Citing Chief Justice John Marshall's ruling in a case involving Thomas Jefferson, Sirica held that there could be "no exception whatever" to the compulsory process of the courts. In a brief statement issued at San Clemente on that day, the President announced he would appeal. Perhaps he would have preferred simply to refuse and "let Judge Sirica enforce his order," to paraphrase President Andrew Jackson's alleged reaction to another John Marshall ruling. But Nixon later acknowledged that he "recognized the political reality," and instead of defying Sirica, he decided to observe regular appellate procedures.[10]

Cox's actions, despite his public disavowals of personal antagonism toward the President, reinforced Nixon's convictions that he had given Attorney General Elliot Richardson too much latitude and that Cox spearheaded a Kennedy vendetta. A month before Butterfield's revelations, Cox had requested a tape Nixon had mentioned to Henry Petersen in April. Buzhardt refused. Because of Richardson's generous charter to Cox, the President thought the Special Prosecutor "was so powerful" that a clash "was inevitable." By then, Richardson clearly had lost favor in the White House. In June he had urged the President to be more forthcoming about Watergate, in an "open forum." When Nixon's tactics did not change, Richardson thought it merely an error of judgment. Eventually he "realized that Richard Nixon was more likely to be guilty than stupid."

At the time, Richardson's administrative assistant sensed that the White House had little interest in the Attorney General's advice. The President "and his beleaguered lieutenants," the aide warned, were bent on survival. They were likely to regard Richardson's concerns for integrity and credibility "as either bullshit or dissembling" and to meet them with "suspicion and distrust." Richardson would have to walk a tightrope between the survival concerns of the White House and the enforcement demands of the criminal-justice system. "[A]t some point," the aide continued, "you'll have to [be] ready to draw the line (we once talked about there being worse things than resigning or being fired)"—that line being the Attorney General's willingness to stand by his deputy, Ruckelshaus, his support of Cox, his continuing the investigation of Vice President Agnew, and his refusal to defend the break-in of Ellsberg's psychiatrist on national-security grounds. At this early point—July 9—Richardson's inner circle knew that Archibald Cox represented the fighting ground. Richardson could reassure Haig that he would put certain restraints on Cox's jurisdiction, but in the end, he would "necessarily have to come back to the very broad guidelines announced and endorsed by the Senate." As the controversy over the tapes intensified, Richardson told the American Bar Association in August that he would "forswear politics" for himself in order to counter the suspicion of political influence in the Justice Department.

Richardson, however, occasionally waffled between his loyalty and obligations to the President and his public responsibilities to the Special Prosecutor. In late July he was reported as saying that he did not believe Cox had a clear right to the tapes. Cox's "investigation of a crime doesn't by itself confer a right of access" to confidential presidential papers, he remarked. But Richardson, too, sensed a long court struggle, even envisioning Solicitor General Robert Bork's arguing the question in the Supreme Court. Richardson walked a fine line. He believed that Cox had been acting "in full accord with the requirements of his job." Yet he knew it was important to find a practical means for reconciling the competing public interests of confidentiality for the President and the need to uncover criminal evidence. In fact, that was the nature of Richardson's role in the three remaining months of his tenure.[11]

It was a stressful time for the President. Flying to New Orleans on August 20 to address the Veterans of Foreign Wars, Nixon heard that a threat had been made on his life. Arriving at the convention hall, he suddenly turned on Press Secretary Ziegler, grabbed him, angrily pushed him toward pursuing reporters, and shouted that he did not want the press with him. The White House insisted that the incident never happened, but CBS had captured it on film and played it twice. There was heightened speculation that the President was mentally breaking down, drinking to excess, or both. He believed that his August 15 address had struck a responsive chord; he was certain that "people were tired of Watergate." If so, his New Orleans behavior raised to a different level questions of his competency. Watergate preoccupied Nixon as the fight over the tapes gathered momentum, and there were other signs of the strain. On October 20 his longtime patron and supporter Norman Chandler, publisher of the *Los Angeles Times,* died of cancer. Just prior to this, when the President had been staying in San Clemente, he had twice failed to carry out scheduled visits with Chandler.[12]

Nixon first heard that Vice President Agnew had legal problems of his own at a meeting with Haldeman and Ehrlichman on April 14, 1973. Haldeman reported that a Baltimore grand jury had been investigating bribery and "kickback" charges against Agnew when he was governor of Maryland, and allegations that he continued to accept illegal payments as Vice President. Those charges also led to an investigation of Agnew for income-tax evasion. According to Haldeman, Agnew was "absolutely scared shitless." Nixon was preoccupied with his own troubles; "he's just got to ride that through—what the hell—" the President remarked.

When Richardson assumed office in May, he immediately was preoccupied with the selection of a Special Prosecutor. But he also learned that the U.S. Attorney's office in Baltimore had Agnew under investigation and realized he eventually would have to confront the situation himself. In July Richardson's aide suggested that the time had come to inform the President. "I am worried about the matter surfacing and it developing that you knew about it and hadn't told him," the aide wrote. As Richardson briefed Nixon, he was struck by the President's lack of surprise. Nixon, typically, was well informed about the various compartments of his Administration.[13]

From the moment of his selection as Nixon's running mate in 1968, Agnew had been a focal point of controversy. In large part, this stemmed from Nixon's desire to use Agnew to attack his favorite targets, the media and liberals, a role that made Agnew the "household word" that he had not previously been. Those who regarded him as an ethnic Throttlebottom soon recognized his talents as an effective political voice on the hustings. Suave, distinguished-looking, and articulate, the Vice President represented a storybook tale of ethnic success. As Maryland's governor, he faced down black leaders of the Baltimore riots in 1968, a moment that made him an instant celebrity with conservatives and the Nixon organization. In fact, Agnew's momentary fame obscured what later came to be recognized: that he was a commonplace man, who, as a Nixon speechwriter wrote, merely said what good Republicans "say on commuter trains when their thoughts turn from moneymaking to politics." Moneymaking—before, during, and after his tenure as Vice President—seemed to be the thing that excited Agnew most. When asked if he was happy to be selected as Nixon's running mate, Agnew replied: "The ability to be happy is directly proportional to the ability to suffer, and as you grow older you feel everything less."[14]

After his Des Moines assault on the media in November 1969, Agnew became not only a household word but, to the consternation of some Administration insiders, a growing power within Republican circles. He appealed to and comforted that Silent Majority who deplored the constant stream of protest and demonstrations against authority. In his June 1969 commencement address at Ohio State University, Agnew said that a society that feared its children was "effete." The "tough guy"—from Wyatt Earp to Dirty Harry—who stands up in contrast to a weak society is the stuff of American myth and legend. Agnew did not disappoint. "A sniveling, hand-wringing power structure deserves the violent rebellion it encourages. If my generation doesn't stop cringing, yours," he told his young audience, "will inherit a lawless society where emotion and muscle displace reason." After American Indian militants demonstrated in Washington, Agnew urged the President to press criminal charges, contending that the Administration would look "McGovernish" if it in any way condoned the action.[15]

The institutional limits of the office of Vice President frustrated Agnew, and his relationship with the President was marred by distrust and antipathy, as has often been the case, given the nature of the two offices. Nixon added feelings of contempt. According to Henry Kissinger, the President had referred to Agnew as his insurance policy against assassination attempts. When asked by a newspaper columnist whether he had briefed Agnew on Henry Kissinger's contact with the Chinese in 1971, Nixon seemed incredulous.

"Oh, of course not," the President replied. The two men rarely saw each other and rarely exchanged views, a situation that only added to the Vice President's frustration. "I had long desired to be his close partner, but he preferred to work with a controlled staff," Agnew noted. He knew, according to one of his aides, that Haldeman and Ehrlichman, as well as other White House staffers, "looked at him with disdain and didn't pay any attention to him."

Agnew bitterly remembered that he never engaged the President in a substantive conversation. He claimed that Haldeman had told him that the President did not appreciate it if he said anything that could be "construed to be mildly not in accord with his thinking." Unlike most Vice Presidents (including Nixon during the Eisenhower years), who publicly insisted that they shared in decision making, Agnew refreshingly acknowledged that he never participated directly in any decision. When the two would talk, the President generally embarked on "a rambling, time-consuming monologue," successfully avoiding subjects not to his liking. "I was not of the inner circle," Agnew candidly admitted. Privately, he told his own aides that the Administration was "intellectually bankrupt." He disagreed passionately with the China move but muted his criticism. His contempt for the President's staff was boundless; he considered them "mere technicians," utterly lacking in principles. Those who admired Agnew praised his intellectual honesty and his loyalty to his friends, a source of both weakness and strength but "a problem Nixon never had," according to one of Agnew's more cynical aides.[16]

After the 1972 election, Agnew believed that the President, now a lame duck, resented Agnew's growing political stature and was miffed as well at his failure to put John Connally in Agnew's place. But at that time Nixon told Haldeman that while he did not wish Agnew to appear as his heir apparent, he had no desire to push him down. Agnew, he said, was not the ideal choice as a successor, but Nixon thought he might be the best of a bad lot.[17]

By the summer of 1973, the *Wall Street Journal* had been investigating rumors of Agnew's illegal activities for more than a year and had learned of the Baltimore grand-jury inquiry. The newspaper advised Agnew on August 6 that it would publish the story the next day, mainly fearing that it would be scooped by another newspaper. Agnew immediately informed reporters that he had learned he was under investigation for extortion, bribery, and tax evasion—all of which he actually had known since April. He insisted he was innocent and was confident that the criminal-justice system would vindicate him. Two days later he appeared at a televised news conference to denounce the allegations as "damned lies." Agnew said he had nothing to hide, that he had no expectation of being indicted, and that he certainly would not resign.

Agnew visited the President on August 7 for nearly two hours. He reported that Nixon had "unequivocally" supported him, but Agnew added that he was not "looking around to see who's supporting me. I'm defending myself." The next day the President expressed "confidence" in Agnew. At his August 22 news conference, Nixon again asserted "confidence in [Agnew's] integrity" and praised his "courageous conduct and ability." He joined the Vice President in denouncing leaks from the Department of Justice, the Baltimore prosecutors, and the grand jury. The two men saw each other again on September 1, and four days later at his news conference, the President once more denounced the charges against Agnew as "innuendo and otherwise," but he properly refused to discuss the substance of those charges.[18]

During the next several weeks, Agnew and his staff realized that the President's support was lukewarm, given Nixon's own calendar of woes. The Agnew camp channeled its hostility toward Attorney General Richardson, who, Agnew believed, was engaged in nothing less than a plot to discredit and remove him in order to further his own presidential ambitions. Richardson had written to Agnew on August 1, informing him of the investigation; meanwhile he had told Nixon, through Haig, that he had never seen such a "cut-and-dried" case. Richardson advised the President of his appraisal on August 6—before Nixon met Agnew. Presidential counselors Buzhardt and Garment supported Richardson's assessment. The President's own evaluation of the situation was coldly realistic. He knew the charges were serious and persuasive; he also realized that Agnew's denials had aroused a sympathetic constituency. Yet if the President actively defended Agnew, and the charges were substantiated, he would only impair what he described as his "own already dwindling credibility." If he adopted a neutral stance, however, he knew he would enrage Agnew's supporters. The President wisely chose the second course, stoically willing "to bear the brunt of the criticism that was to come."[19]

For his part, Agnew later claimed to have warned the President that the investigation was merely an attempt to embarrass the Administration and that it was foolish to believe it would divert attention from Watergate. He understood, to some extent, that his removal would make it easier for the "left-wingers who despised us both" to force the President from office. Later, Agnew came to believe that Nixon sought to pacify Richardson because he was preparing to move against Cox. "I was treated like a pawn in the game—the game of the Watergate cover-up," Agnew wrote. He did not realize at the time the President's own vulnerability and weakness; otherwise, he claimed, he "might have fought it out." Conspiracy notions had fueled Agnew's most successful political rhetoric during his first term; quite naturally, he believed that again he had been victimized by what he undoubtedly regarded as an "elite, effete" cabal—this time led by Attorney General Richardson.

Agnew and his staff felt that Richardson "was out to get" him. He later added the touch of Zionist conspiracy: Richardson wanted someone in the line of presidential succession who, like Nixon, "would defend Israel, whatever the risk to the United States." Agnew was convinced that Richardson sensed the President was "cracking" under the Watergate strain, and "so I must be knocked out of the line of succession before it was too late."

Curiously, three years after he left the White House, Nixon lent some credence to Agnew's darkest suspicions when he noted Richardson's presidential ambitions for 1976 and worried that the Attorney General might have had some political motivation. The charges against Richardson, of course, were absurd. He had inherited the Agnew case; moreover, the evidence against Agnew readily persuaded such varied White House advisers as Haig, Buzhardt, and Garment. Henry Petersen had only the highest regard for Richardson's professionalism in the affair; "I never met a man who was so careful," Petersen recalled. Richardson, he thought, was "one of the best, if not *the* best" Attorney General he had ever served. Melvin Laird learned of the Agnew case from Buzhardt. Buzhardt's advice prompted Laird to tell his Republican congressional friends "not to get too far out in front in defense of the Vice President." Ironically, a few days after Agnew's resignation, and as Richardson prepared for his own, the Attorney General noted that rather than proving his independence, the Agnew affair had reinforced the convictions of some that he had merely served the President's interests.[20]

Agnew's felonies had no relation whatsoever to the mounting catalogue of Watergate crimes. But the Vice President's situation and eventual departure from office worsened Nixon's deteriorating position. After Petersen became involved for the Justice Department, the President called him on numerous occasions, expressing opinions that the case against Agnew would not lead to impeachment and that somehow Petersen might "handle" the Baltimore prosecutors. A New York lawyer, a warm Nixon admirer, urged the President to ask Agnew to suspend himself if indicted; if he refused, the President himself should request Agnew to vacate his office in the Executive Office Building. The lawyer claimed—without knowing them—that the liberal New York attorneys representing Agnew were motivated by "the continued distress the internal feuding" caused the President. Apparently, she appreciated what Nixon liked to hear.

As early as September 1, Agnew advised Nixon that he wanted to take his case to the House of Representatives, claiming that a sitting Vice President, like the President, could not be indicted and must be judged by the House. According to Agnew (probably correctly), Haig and Buzhardt reacted with alarm, for the investigation could well result in impeachment and thereby offer a dangerous precedent. Haig pressed Agnew at this point to resign, but the Vice President refused. "I was to be a living demonstration that the President spurned cover-ups . . .—this was the whole idea behind the White House move to make me quit." He detected the fine hand of Laird's lobbying on Capitol Hill when Haig told him that Speaker Carl Albert was not interested in pursuing the case.[21]

Despite White House opposition, Agnew wrote to Albert on September 25, asking that the House inquire into the charges formulated by the U.S. Attorney in Baltimore. His lawyers prepared a memorandum contending that he could not be indicted, although Vice President Aaron Burr had been indicted for the murder of Alexander Hamilton following their famous duel in 1804. (Burr was never tried.) Agnew based his claim on an 1826 precedent established when Vice President John C. Calhoun demanded a similar investigation of charges that he had improperly profited from a military contract when he was Secretary of War. The accusations apparently had been inspired by Calhoun's break with President John Quincy Adams. The House exonerated the Vice President after a forty-day investigation. Calhoun established several interesting precedents. He was re-elected in 1828 with Andrew Jackson at the head of the ticket, and thus became the first Vice President to serve under two different presidents. But then he was also the only man to resign the vice presidency—until 1973.

Despite Agnew's plea, Carl Albert and the House Democrats were reluctant to intervene. Judiciary Committee Chairman Peter Rodino (D–NJ) told the Speaker the matter ought to be left to the courts. Agnew had complained to Albert that the "White House" was behind the campaign against him, "harassing him to death." When Richardson later went to the grand jury, he notified the Speaker, in a move that Albert interpreted as an Administration message, that Congress should let the judicial process run.[22]

Agnew had his defenders. The ranking Republican on the Judiciary Committee, Edward Hutchinson (MI), and thirteen committee colleagues introduced a resolution contending that the House had a "constitutional duty" to honor Agnew's request. Hamilton Fish (R–NY) also sympathized with Agnew's desire for a hearing. Columnist William White criticized the House leadership for a "cop-out" in the Agnew case and asserted that the House would have to face the issue, because Agnew "is simply not going to resign" even if indicted. He also chastised the Justice Department, which was anxious to "sanitize" its poor showing in the Watergate case. House Minority Leader Gerald Ford called Albert's decision "political [and] unfortunate." But Ford had been advised by Richardson and by Nixon of the extent of the evidence against Agnew—a vain attempt, as it turned out, to keep Ford from playing partisan politics or looking foolish. Agnew later sent Ford a note of "gratitude and affection."[23]

Speaking in Los Angeles on September 29, Agnew seemed to brim with confidence and determination. He denounced the Justice Department for the leaks and innuendoes against him and also charged that some of its officials were anxious to recoup their reputations. "I'm a big trophy," the Vice President told his cheering supporters, who waved "Spiro Is My Hero" placards.

The vise tightened. On September 21, Petersen prepared for Agnew a draft resignation statement admitting that as governor, he had received payments from contractors doing business with the State of Maryland. Nixon remained wary. At his October 3 news conference, he defended Justice Department officials but added that Agnew's determination to remain in office "should be respected." He noted that Agnew repeatedly had denied the charges to him personally; still, the President acknowledged that they were "serious and not frivolous." He scored the leaks and their publication and pleaded that Agnew not be "convicted in advance." The Vice President's years of distinguished service should, he added, give him the "presumption of innocence." As so often, Richard Nixon's remarks reflected his own problems. Meanwhile, the President's men—Richardson, Haig, Buzhardt, and to some extent, Garment—persisted in trying to persuade Agnew and his lawyers that the Vice President must resign. According to Agnew, Haig passed word that the signature of the Vice President's wife had been noted on Agnew's purportedly false income-tax returns.[24]

Without effective support in Congress, with the President's aides increasingly hostile and demanding his resignation, and with public support deteriorating as details of the charges emerged, Agnew and his lawyers turned to plea-bargaining. The unspoken assumption on both sides was that the Vice President would resign. That would afford some comfort for the Administration, but it appears that for its own ulterior reasons the White House was equally anxious to avoid a public spectacle. Shame and humiliation would cover the Vice President, to be sure; but he had enough leverage to avoid prosecution and penal punishment. On October 10 Agnew made a dramatic appearance in the federal courtroom in Baltimore and pleaded *nolo contendere* to a charge of income-tax evasion. The Vice President contended that a trial would be lengthy and costly, and would unduly "distract public attention from important national problems." (He later told an attorney that he could not go to trial before a jury of blacks.) Richardson acknowledged that he received less than he wanted in Agnew's subsequent plea, but the government managed to file a more complete summary of its evidence.

The court imposed a suspended sentence of three years' imprisonment and a $10,000 fine. Richardson's plea for leniency proved "so great and so compelling," the judge said, that he made an exception to his usual requirement that tax evaders serve prison time. Several hours earlier, the Vice President delivered a message to the Secretary of State: "I hereby resign the Office of Vice President of the United States effective immediately." The

President's aides drafted a letter to the resigning Agnew, stating: "I have been deeply saddened by this whole course of events." Nixon scrawled "excellent letter" on the draft.[25]

Spiro Agnew's troubles offer a run-of-the-mill chapter in the melancholy history of political corruption and greed, distinguished of course by the fact that he was Vice President of the United States and not merely Baltimore County Executive or Maryland Governor. The heightening sense of the importance of ethical propriety and political morality in part dictated Agnew's fate; more simply, the practical bind that ensnared Nixon made the resignation inevitable. Although disgraced, Agnew had one special contribution to make to the Watergate saga: his forced resignation removed a significant obstacle to unseating the President of the United States. Agnew's presence as Nixon's constitutional successor acted as a brake on impeachment. *Time* magazine publisher Hedley Donovan believed in July that Nixon had committed impeachable offenses and had lost his legitimacy. "But the apparent alternative was Spiro Agnew"—evidently an unthinkable one.

Nixon recognized Agnew's resignation as a "very serious blow," for it opened pressure on him to resign as well. The lesson learned was that he could not accommodate his opponents and that Agnew's resignation only whetted their appetites. The President and his advisers, however, had maneuvered that resignation largely because they chose not to follow the path of impeachment. Solicitor General Bork diligently prepared an argument distinguishing the propriety of indicting a vice president from that of indicting a president. Bork's brief was intended precisely to avoid the possibility of impeaching Agnew. Bork recalled that Buzhardt and the President argued against the case he and Richardson advanced in favor of keeping Agnew in the courts, but finally Nixon agreed that the Justice Department had to proceed. Bork found Nixon impressive and "very sharp"; Richardson told him he had seen the President at his best. Agnew's lawyers believed that Nixon never really wanted impeachment.[26]

The decision to move for a criminal indictment of Agnew might have been a lost opportunity for Nixon. Impeachment might have become dangerously popular, to be sure; but it also would have consumed enormous time and energy, perhaps enough so that following an Agnew impeachment, Congress and the nation might have had neither the inclination nor the will to move against the President. For five years, the President had treated Agnew as a pawn. But when the Vice President resigned, Richard Nixon lost his queen.

At the same time Nixon fought his Watergate war, he had his constitutional responsibilities to attend to, not the least of which involved foreign affairs.

Generally, the Watergate affair ran in a separate ring as the Administration busily carried out its disengagement from Vietnam, its rapprochement with China, and its attempts at détente with the Soviet Union. But in October 1973, with the Watergate crisis heightening, the weight of domestic scandal combined with a new war in the Middle East to bring excruciating burdens to the President and to renew skepticism regarding his integrity. Watergate had become inextricably linked to foreign affairs.

On Saturday, October 6, as the President prepared to meet the embattled Agnew, he received word that Egypt and Syria were about to launch an attack upon Israel. Nixon firmly believed that the Soviets had encouraged their Arab clients, heightening the danger of a superpower clash in the region. The Arab attacks caught the Israelis by surprise in the so-called Yom Kippur War, and in the first few days of the war, the Egyptian and Syrian armies made notable gains. By the fourth day, the Israelis had suffered significant casualties and territorial losses. Just prior to Nixon's meeting with Agnew that day, in which the latter informed him that he would resign, the President ordered a resupply of war matériel for the Israelis. Nixon's bold decision ensured Israeli the recovery and their ability to carry the war to their enemies. Within weeks, Israeli troops could have easily marched to Cairo and Damascus, but the consequences would have been dubious at best. The President recognized the virtues of a battlefield stalemate: the Soviets would have no reason to intervene in behalf of their clients, and the Arab states would have avoided another military humiliation that could further embitter their relations with the United States. The diplomatic shoals were hazardous to navigate; that Nixon and his aides did so amid the fallout from Watergate made the achievement all the more remarkable.

The Joint Chiefs of Staff had some misgivings over the President's decision to resupply the Israelis and stalled in executing the President's order, until Nixon spoke directly to Admiral Thomas Moorer, their Chairman and an outspoken antagonist of Israel. In the short run, the President's actions on behalf of Israel led directly to the Arab oil embargo of 1973, causing the nation no end of domestic woe. But his stalemate policy had the effect of bringing an end to the war, however uneasy the truce. The real fruits came five years later in the Camp David Accords, which witnessed the first public Arab-Israeli negotiations and settlements since 1949. Egyptian President Anwar Sadat was in no position in 1973 to express public admiration for Nixon, but Israeli Prime Minister Golda Meir had no such compunctions. Throughout Watergate and before the Yom Kippur War, she sent messages of warm "sympathy and understanding" to the President. In later years, when Richard Nixon's veracity had little public standing, Golda Meir recorded "that he did not break a single one of the promises he made to us."[27]

* * *

The calm, reasoned foresight that characterized the President's behavior throughout the Middle East crisis deserted him when he confronted his personal crisis. For the Middle East, Nixon worked as a mediating lawyer, carefully serving the interests of all parties in order to obtain some acceptable result. On the other front, he had himself as a client, and the results were predictably disastrous.

As the Agnew affair wound down, the President told Richardson, "Now that we have disposed of that matter, we can go ahead and get rid of Cox." Richardson wavered between a belief that this was an offhand remark arising from wishful thinking and a judgment that it reflected settled policy. Two days after Agnew's resignation, the Circuit Court of Appeals, ruling on Cox's subpoena in a five-to-two decision, concluded that the President must turn over the relevant tapes to Judge Sirica, who would examine them *in camera* and decide which parts to release to the grand jury. The appellate judges firmly held that Nixon was "not above the law's commands" but also pleaded for him and the prosecutors to reach an out-of-court settlement. Historically, courts had avoided direct confrontations with presidents. The "least dangerous branch" had "neither force nor will" of its own, as Alexander Hamilton wrote in *Federalist* 78. But the majority in this case confronted presidential claims in a spirited manner, denying Nixon's theories of presidential immunity, sovereignty, and executive privilege. The President's arguments were stacked against the common-sense notion that no man should judge his own case.

All along, Special Prosecutor Cox had worried about the possibility that the President might not comply with a court order. Some of his staff urged sending a phalanx of U.S. marshals to the White House, conjuring up visions of resistance by Marine guards. Cox himself had visions of Gilbert and Sullivan operettas. During his argument, he told the appeals court that the nation had been "blessed" by a historical pattern of presidential acquiescence in court orders, and he was confident that "the same spirit . . . would prevail here." In their opinion, the judges pointedly appealed for such support, noting that courts always "assume that their orders will be obeyed, especially when addressed to responsible government officials." On October 17 the President scored a rare court victory when Sirica asserted that he lacked authority to support the Senate Select Committee's subpoena for the tapes.[28]

The appellate court earlier had urged the lawyers for the committee and the President to chart their own compromise. In a September 13 memorandum, the judges suggested that the President, along with Cox and Charles Wright, examine the tapes and agree as to what material in them was privileged. If any materials remained in dispute, the court said it would "discharge its duty" and decide the matter. Clearly, the judges sought to avoid a constitutional crisis. A week later, however, the lawyers told the court that they could not agree on any compromise. Suspicion and ill will were rife. Wright believed that Cox had violated the lawyers' ethics code stipulating that attorneys should not give an opinion of the merits of the claims or defenses of the other party. On July 26 Cox had said that he personally "did not doubt the bona fides of the President's position but that his people had researched it and were persuaded it was without merit."[29]

After the arguments in October, an ebullient Leonard Garment had told the President that the situation seemed promising. Wright had been "in fine form" and had won "obvious respect" from the judges. Garment worried because two judges who could be counted as presidential supporters had recused themselves. Still, he believed that the judges, the "Watergate bar," and even the press had begun to understand how "mischievous" it would be to order the President to open his most intimate records. But the court found a different, overriding issue, and held Nixon accountable. On October 13, the day after the court's ruling, Garment and Buzhardt met and spoke by telephone with Wright, who urged them to press ahead with a notice of appeal to the Supreme Court. Wright remained confident that the President still would win. But Nixon (and probably Haig) decided otherwise. They would not risk an adverse ruling in the highest court, one which Nixon had promised to respect. With that, the White House started down a path that within a week left the nation in shock and the Nixon Administration in shambles. Cox, Nixon's advisers told him, had to go. Murray Chotiner, Nixon's veteran political mentor, put it succinctly: "This guy Cox will use anything and everybody," he told the President. "It has to be taken away from him."[30]

Nixon's problem was practical as well as legal. He had to comply somehow with the judicial ruling (unless he appealed) and deliver the tapes to Judge Sirica, yet he had also to prevent them from incriminating him in any way. Cox, of course, was at the heart of the issue for the White House. But day by day, and then hour by hour, the dispute increasingly focused on Richardson and his relationship to the President. Richardson described himself as the "lawyer for the situation," a role that would enable Cox to carry on his responsibilities and yet somehow preserve the President's authority and independence. Richardson told Deputy Attorney General William Ruckelshaus that he had "no desire to be a martyr." Even if Richardson eventually had to leave because of some principle, he must, he said, do everything now to avoid a confrontation. What Richardson did not—and could not—appreciate was the value of the stakes: any compromise served only to compromise the President.

Richardson met Haig and Buzhardt on Monday, October 15, and learned that Nixon would prepare an "authenticated" version of the subpoenaed tapes for Sirica but would fire Cox, thus disposing of his petition for access to the tapes and rendering the case moot. The Attorney General said he would have to resign himself if Cox were fired. A few hours later, Haig again spoke to Richardson and raised the idea of using Senator John Stennis (D–MS) to verify Nixon's summaries. After several more calls, Richardson agreed to present the proposal to Cox, which he did that evening and again the next morning. Haig told the Attorney General that "this was it" as far as access to presidential materials was concerned and that the President expected Richardson's support in the event of a future showdown with Cox. Richardson later claimed that he never committed himself to any agreement beyond a means of authenticating the tapes.[31]

"Judge" Stennis (as Nixon publicly referred to him that week), seventy-two, had only recently returned to his Senate duties following a long illness. He had been hospitalized during many of the dramatic Watergate disclosures, and a colleague told him that he had "come back to a very different world." Stennis claimed that the White House had asked him to verify the accuracy of transcripts and said that only "personal talk" would be deleted. For his part, he insisted that he never would have agreed to be a party to submitting authenticated tapes to a court of law. "I was once a judge," he said, "and the courts can ask for what they want." If Stennis was truthful, then he never saw the "verifier proposal," for it clearly stated that he would furnish "a complete and accurate" record to the court and the grand jury. Stennis had no direct dealings with Richardson concerning the matter.[32]

On October 16 Richardson prepared a proposal for releasing edited transcripts of the tapes, but Buzhardt delayed it in the White House until the next day, when it was transmitted to Cox in the late afternoon. The proposal essentially provided that the President would select a "verifier" to compare the subpoenaed tapes with pertinent transcripts. The verifier was authorized to substitute language in sections of the tapes that covered national-security matters and other areas that he judged embarrassing to the President. Richardson and Cox discussed the proposal twice on the seventeenth and again the next day. On October 18, Cox submitted written comments on the proposal, and Richardson discussed them with the President's lawyers and Haig in the White House that evening. Cox told Richardson that the idea of using Stennis as a verifier was unacceptable, first because Cox could not rely on such a "unilateral" determination of the evidence, and second, because the proposal only allowed for the release of material relating to the break-in and cover-up and omitted the tapes relevant to other areas under investigation. Cox reminded Richardson that the Attorney General had "pledged that I would not be turned aside."

Slowly but surely, events had put Richardson in an untenable position. The White House staff interpreted Cox's letter as a rejection and agreed that he should be fired if he would not accept the proposal. They believed that the President could persuade the nation that his action was correct. Richardson disagreed with both judgments. If Cox were dismissed, Richardson understood that the Justice Department once again would have control of the case, a situation that certainly would not be acceptable to Congress. He urged Wright to speak directly to Cox and persuade him of the merits of involving Stennis.

In a letter to Cox on October 18, Wright warned that "we could not accede" to his demands "in any form." He maintained that the proposal to use Stennis would "put to rest any possible thought that the President might himself have been involved in the Watergate break-in or cover-up." (Wright, however, had never listened to the tapes, as Nixon had barred him from doing so.) He spoke to Cox Thursday evening. At one point, according to Cox, Wright added a stipulation that he "categorically agree not to subpoena any other White House tape, paper or document." Both Cox and Richardson interpreted that message as an attempt to trap Cox into rejecting the President's proposal, this forcing his own resignation or justifying his removal. Cox grimly stated that the prohibition against any further pursuit of evidence required him to violate his pledge to the Senate Judiciary Committee. "I cannot," he stated emphatically, "break my promise now." But Wright left his paper trail—"in the unhappy event that our correspondence should see the light of day." He said that Cox had exaggerated: the President had no intention of denying all tapes; only "private Presidential papers" would be excluded. He praised Richardson's "very reasonable" and generous proposal involving Senator Stennis. Clearly, any further communication was futile. "We will be forced to take the actions that the President deems appropriate in these circumstances," stated Wright.

That same evening Richardson prepared notes outlining reasons for his own resignation. When Haig told him the next morning that the Wright–Cox negotiations had failed, Richardson asked to see the President, expecting to resign immediately. But when he arrived at the White House on Friday morning, Haig told him that firing Cox was not necessarily linked to rejection of the Stennis proposal. Richardson momentarily thought he would not have to resign. He then told Haig and the President's lawyers that the prohibition against Cox's seeking additional materials was not part of the original agreement and should be withdrawn. By this time, however, Nixon apparently had irrevocably linked using Stennis with such a prohibition. Haig misinformed Richardson that Stennis had agreed to serve, that Howard Baker endorsed the idea, and that Sam Ervin would be consulted that afternoon.

Richardson meanwhile met with his advisers, who pressed him to oppose the "linked proposal." He spoke again to Haig, and to Buzhardt, arguing that he could not support it and that it served the President ill. But someone—the President or Haig or the lawyers, or all of them—remained adamant. Haig called Richardson that evening and read him a letter from Nixon instructing the Attorney General to direct Cox to make no further attempts to secure presidential materials by subpoena. The President apologized for his "limited" intrusion on Richardson's promised independence in dealing with the Special Prosecutor. But the fault, he insisted, was Cox's. If Cox had "agreed to the very reasonable proposal," there would have been no confrontation. Samuel Dash, Counsel to the Senate Select Committee, thought that the President was "determined" to dismiss Cox; Garment, however, later "categorically" denied that the Stennis proposal was designed to force Cox into open rebellion. Although the Stennis plan might have been unacceptable to Cox, the White House hoped that it would be sufficient for Richardson to remain in the Administration.

Richardson balked, because he knew that the prohibition on Cox could not work and that the Special Prosecutor would resist it. He told Cox of the President's decision but made clear that he was not relaying the instruction. He prepared a statement (never released) noting that the Stennis plan represented a "significant and sensible" compromise but that the prohibition linkage was "inconsistent" with the original understandings regarding the Special Prosecutor's charge. Richardson always prided himself on being a "loyal team player." On Friday, October 19, he allowed himself a rare moment of judgment when he wrote that the President had been unduly hostile toward Cox. "Many problems and headaches could have been avoided by cooperating with him more and fighting him less," Richardson noted.

Nixon summoned Ervin from North Carolina to meet him and Baker that same Friday afternoon. He informed them of his idea for using Stennis, and they agreed to discuss it with the Senate Watergate Committee. Although Nixon asked them not to talk to the press, that evening the White House announced that Ervin and Baker had agreed to accept Stennis's verification of White House summaries. Ervin spoke to Stennis, who understood he would have custody of the tapes and make verbatim transcripts. For his part, Ervin claimed that he considered the proposal "spurious" from the start and said he never knew of the proposal to prohibit access to tapes unrelated to the break-in and cover-up. He later realized, as Lowell Weicker told him, that he had been "zonked" by Nixon.

On Saturday morning, Richardson informed the President of his opposition, and once more broached a compromise that would not have barred Cox from using the judicial process. Sirica had to be persuaded to accept the Stennis verifier idea, he said, adding that Cox had agreed to abide by Sirica's decision. In lieu of the prohibition proposal, Richardson suggested that the President offer the verifier idea as a precedent in the event Cox sought more material. But clearly the White House projected the use of Stennis as a one-time expedient designed to avoid total humiliation and damaging revelations on the part of the President. What Richardson only later realized was that finally the White House no longer could accept an "independent" Special Prosecutor—or even an Attorney General who felt obligated to keep his public promises of independence.[33]

Archibald Cox had been mainly a spectator—an informed one, to be sure—of the maneuvers between the White House and Richardson. He had been in touch with the Attorney General as well as with Wright, however, and had made his own views forcefully known. For an hour or so on Saturday, October 20, Cox occupied center stage and in a press conference tripped the charge wires carefully laid out by the White House. He offered a masterful professorial performance, designed to explain the legal and constitutional confrontation in terms that struck at the core of layman's treasured values essential to the American system.

"I'm certainly not out to get the President of the United States," Cox disarmingly said at the outset. But he believed it necessary to demonstrate that Nixon had failed to comply with the court order for release of the White House tapes. Cox realized that he had to overcome the Administration's strategy of presenting the use of Stennis as a reasonable alternative. He skirted any question of Stennis's integrity but stressed the dangerous precedent of bypassing established institutions and procedures for evaluating evidence. Cox simply did not believe that tape summaries could be submitted as evidence in a trial. Finally, Cox contended that the prohibition on further subpoenas irreparably damaged his ability to carry out his mandate and that it violated the guidelines set forth by the Attorney General for the Senate in May. Although he maintained that the Stennis proposal was inadequate, the Special Prosecutor said he believed that he and Richardson had been negotiating some compromise in good faith. Wright's phone call on Thursday evening, however, made it clear to Cox that he was being "confronted with things that were drawn in such a way that I could not accept them."

Responding to questions, Cox at first insisted that only Richardson could fire him but later acknowledged that the President "can always work his will." The tenor of the questions, and Cox's answers, left little doubt about the coming course of events. The Special Prosecutor would not—could not—desist from carrying out his appointed functions, yet to do so would only invite the wrath of the President and Cox's dismissal.

"I did not have to wait long for Haig's call telling me that the President wanted me to fire Cox," Richardson recalled. He then asked Haig for an appointment with the President that afternoon. Richardson knew his only honorable alternative.[34]

In Richardson's public letter of resignation, he reminded the President that he had pledged independence for the Special Prosecutor. Still, he offered a note of civility, more in regret than in defiance, stating that he fully respected the President's reasons for discharging Cox.

The moment of resignation was unpleasant. Meeting Richardson that Saturday afternoon, the President urged him to delay his departure because of the Middle East crisis. Nixon accused him of putting his "personal commitments ahead of the public interest." Richardson retorted: "I can only say that I believe my resignation is in the public interest." Nixon later bitterly recalled the meeting and blamed Richardson's resignation chiefly on his unwillingness to support the proposal linking access to some tapes and denial of access to others. Supported only by Haig, Nixon claimed that Richardson himself had formulated the prohibition idea. Ruckelshaus had reason to believe that Haig had misjudged Richardson and assured the President that the Attorney General would remain with them. More than a decade later, Richardson claimed that Haig had "dangled the prospect of White House support" for the 1976 Republican presidential nomination, implying that the Administration could do him "a lot of good." For his part, Haig angrily believed that Richardson had "made him look bad in front of the President." Early in November, Richardson gave Nixon the benefit of the doubt. He told the Senate Judiciary Committee that he thought the President had made "a reasonable effort"—though a "wrongheaded" one—to compromise. Eventually, in May 1974, Richardson recognized that Nixon had determined that Cox must go and that somehow Richardson must be "induced" to go along with the President's wishes.[35]

The events of October 20 moved swiftly and decisively, and with results precisely opposite to what the President and his lawyers had anticipated. Instead of simply removing Archibald Cox's probing lance, they raised a "firestorm" of protest that permanently scarred Nixon's credibility with the public, and, most damaging, with congressional Republicans and Southern Democrats. The news and televised images of FBI agents, following a White House directive, sealing the Special Prosecutor's office and barring access by Cox's staff, shocked and frightened the nation. The ominous action raised talk of a coup and prompted comparisons to the Reichstag fire that prepared Germany for the rise of Hitler. Leon Jaworski, viewing events from Texas, thought the FBI's actions resembled those of the Gestapo.

A decade and a half later, the reverberations from those events still influenced the American political landscape, including the confirmation hearings of a Supreme Court nominee. The "Saturday Night Massacre"—a name appropriate to the bloody political hemorrhaging—of October 20, 1973, was one more irretrievable blunder by the President.

Several incidents are indisputable: Elliot Richardson refused to fire Archibald Cox and resigned; when his deputy, William Ruckelshaus, similarly refused Haig's command ("this is an order from your Commander-in-Chief"), Ruckelshaus resigned—although that evening the White House insisted he had been fired. Haig told Ruckelshaus that Cox had embarrassed the President during the Middle East crisis, and he insisted it was necessary for the Administration to close ranks. Ruckelshaus suggested that the President should postpone firing Cox if he had such a problem. The Justice Department's third-in-command, Solicitor General Robert H. Bork, then agreed to carry out the President's order, to a significant extent because of the urging of Richardson. Why Bork acted as he did, exactly how he acted, and what were the consequences of his acts, became matters of some dispute.

Richardson and Ruckelshaus urged Bork to carry out the President's order to ensure continuity in the Department. At first, Bork was surprised, having convinced himself the night before that Richardson had worked out a satisfactory arrangement with Cox respecting access to the tapes. Bork expressed some anger, according to Ruckelshaus, claiming that he had come to Washington to be the Supreme Court's lawyer, and now, for the third time in eight months, he had to consider resigning. He told Richardson and Ruckelshaus that he would carry out the order but then would resign so that he would not be perceived as an *apparatchik*. Bork then decided—following the theory of his former colleague Yale Law School Professor Alexander Bickel—that in firing Cox he would merely be the instrument of the President's proper power to do so. All three understood that if Bork did not carry out the order, the White House would send someone else to do it—presumably Buzhardt. That, they believed, would only threaten departmental morale and continuity even more seriously. When Bork told Haig he would carry out the order but had been considering resigning immediately afterward, he had "the distinct impression that [Haig] didn't really much care about the second part of my quandary."[36]

Bork shortly afterward went to the White House, where he received his commission and had a chat with the President. Nixon told him that he wanted a "prosecution and not a persecution." That evening, Bork announced Cox's dismissal. Bork believed that Haig somehow understood that following Cox's dismissal the Special Prosecutor's office would have to continue in some form, but both the President and his Chief of Staff "seemed to think that if they got a professional prosecutor life would be easier. As a matter of fact," Bork observed, "life was tougher."

Meanwhile, life was certainly tough for Bork. The next day, he met with Cox's assistants and with Henry Petersen. Cox's staff, obviously shaken, viewed Bork with distrust, particularly when they learned that the Special Prosecutor's office would come under the jurisdiction of Petersen's Criminal

Division of the Justice Department. Bork told the prosecutors to continue with their court appearances and pursuit of subpoenas—and that, he remembered, did not please the White House.

Unfortunately for his own reputation, Bork had failed to co-opt the press at the outset. He did not call in reporters to explain his actions and promise a continuing investigation, because, as he contended, he was "new to Washington." He also bitterly remembered that Richardson offered no satisfactory public explanation for what had occurred between himself and Bork. When Bork accompanied Richardson to a press conference after the Attorney General's resignation, Richardson promised to explain the matter if it were raised. No reporter questioned Bork's role.[37]

Henry Ruth, Cox's deputy, told reporters about the Sunday meeting with Bork and Petersen and said that he had been assured the investigation would be vigorously pursued. Bork publicly repeated the President's instructions: "It is my expectation that the Department of Justice will continue with full vigor the investigations and prosecutions that had been entrusted to the Watergate Special Prosecution Force." He assured reporters on October 22 that he would follow those orders, as well as implementing the President's desire to fold the prosecutors' functions into the Justice Department. As Acting Attorney General, Bork said, he had "ultimate authority and responsibility." Significantly, Bork announced he would support Cox's proposal to extend the Watergate grand jury for another six months. Despite rumors of mass resignations, there were no major defections in either the Justice Department or the Special Prosecutor's office following Cox's departure.

At an October 24 press conference, Bork recognized storm signals and stated: "We will go wherever we need to get the evidence for this prosecution." Bork knew his reputation was on the line; he would not leave Washington, he said, as the man who compromised the Watergate investigations. Finally, he acknowledged that he had been considering reinstatement of the Special Prosecutor. The idea, he admitted playfully, "has crossed my mind." Two days later, the President grimly announced that he would appoint a new Special Prosecutor but insisted that this individual would not be given access to confidential presidential documents, although Nixon promised to make summaries available.

In his October 26 press conference, Nixon denounced the media in words reminiscent of his famous "last press conference" in 1962. The reporting, he said, had been the most "outrageous, vicious, [and] distorted" he had witnessed in twenty-seven years of public life. Although the nation had been "pounded night after night with . . . frantic, hysterical reporting," he assured reporters and his audience that they had not affected him or his job performance. Asked if he felt any stress because of the pressure of both domestic and foreign crises, the President smiled wanly and said, "The tougher it gets, the cooler I get." Reporters were puzzled by his statement that he did "not blame anybody" for the distorted news coverage and asked for specifics. The reply was vintage Nixon: "Don't get the impression that you arouse my anger. . . . You see," he said with a nervous grin, "one can only be angry with those he respects."[38]

On October 23, Bork signed an order abolishing the Special Prosecutor's office effective October 21, and incorporating its functions into the Justice Department. Undoubtedly, at that moment, before the White House fully understood the national mood, there was every intention of giving the Attorney General—and hence the President—greater control over the Watergate prosecutors. Yet, from the moment Bork assumed office until he named a new Special Prosecutor on November 1, Cox's Watergate Special Prosecution Force experienced no significant interruption in its work. The staff carried out its functions, had the FBI and the IRS continue their authorized investigations, and most important, encountered no interference whatsoever with their duties from Bork, Petersen, or any White House officials. The prosecutors neither were dismissed nor did they have any compelling cause for principled resignation. Whatever the original White House intent in challenging the Special Prosecutor, its only accomplishment had been to get Archibald Cox out of office.

Subsequently, Robert H. Bork's critics charged him with being "irrelevant" and "passive." Those descriptions were of a later vintage, designed to discredit Bork's 1987 nomination to the Supreme Court. In fact, however, Bork was neither the passive instrument his detractors portrayed, nor was he any kind of hero in the affair, as his supporters—including Elliot Richardson—later testified.[39]

On October 23, Judge Sirica asked the President's lawyers if they were prepared to respond to his August 29 order for the White House tapes, as modified by the appellate court. Charles Alan Wright, who had eagerly and somewhat confidently anticipated a Supreme Court review, shocked spectators when he announced in Sirica's court that the "President of the United States would comply in all respects" with that order. Wright said Nixon believed that his offer of summaries was adequate but realized that even if the court agreed, he would have been accused of defying the law. Dramatically and firmly, Wright said that "this President does not defy the law," and he intended to comply fully with the order. When Wright appeared as the President's representative before Sirica, he confronted eleven former Cox aides at the prosecution table, anticipating the need to argue for compliance. Bork did nothing to prevent their appearance. The Special Prosecutor's functions remained intact, and the President had been stymied in his effort to rid himself of his persecutors.

The forty-eight hours following Cox's dismissal witnessed an extraordinary outburst of official and public indignation, instantly and dramatically reported on television. NBC's anchorman solemnly suggested that "the country tonight is in the midst of what may be the most serious constitutional crisis in its history." Opponents and even supporters of the President appeared on television to denounce his "reckless act" and his "Gestapo tactics." Outside the White House, marchers held signs proclaiming, "Honk for Impeachment." Nixon bitterly criticized the "apocalyptic" reporting that "painted the night's events in terms of an administration coup aimed at suppressing opposition." But subsequent surveys of the television scripts sharply disagreed with his assessment. Most of the material, the surveys revealed, was "pretty bland, pretty straight and pretty sketchy in detail." Still, the images of outrage and protest conveyed a harsh message.

The Administration was mesmerized. Leonard Garment remembered thinking about little in those days except to marvel "over the mischief we had wrought and the public relations disaster we had brought upon ourselves." The resignations and dismissals created a public reaction that surprised and dismayed the White House, as Haig admitted. The normally voluble Chief of Staff seemed stunned by events. The Washington Western Union telegraph office received nearly half a million telegrams, a record that dwarfed the response to any prior event. The White House hurriedly summoned Wright back from his classes in Texas and announced that Ruckelshaus had resigned and had not been dismissed as earlier stated. The Administration was in disarray and confused—"like being in the belly of the whale," Garment noted—and had no sense of how to respond. A White House "talking paper" gamely tried to stanch the flow of negative comment, but the hostility toward Cox or any independent investigation undermined the veneer of the President's readiness to compromise. Periodically, Nixon's supporters claimed he had wide support for his dismissal of Cox, but their pronouncements seemed pallid.[40]

The responses of Washington political figures and media commentators were predictable, but new voices were also heard. Chesterfield Smith, the President of the American Bar Association, told his group that Nixon's actions had threatened the "rule of law and . . . the administration of justice." He charged that the President had taken "overt" action to "abort" established processes and had instituted an "intolerable" assault on the courts. Smith backed Cox's contention that the President could not choose the nature of evidence essential to criminal proceedings. Finally, he praised "three great lawyers"—Richardson, Ruckelshaus, and Cox—who "honor and cherish the tradition of the legal profession" and who had placed "ethics and professional honor before public office."

Former Nixon speechwriter William Safire urged Congress to "raise the rumpus it is entitled to raise as a result of the Richardson confirmation double-cross." Somewhat cryptically, Safire urged Congress and the grand jury to "find out what lies behind the tapes." Shortly afterward, Senator James Buckley and three of the most conservative Republicans in the House reported that their mail was running 90 percent in favor of impeachment. One of the congressmen insisted that the protest was "not organized" and was a "grassroots" phenomenon. More predictably, the AFL-CIO on October 22 called for the President to resign and for the House to impeach him if he did not.[41]

Retreat was inevitable all along the line. The "firestorm" following Cox's dismissal and his superiors' resignations had given a new momentum to events, a momentum that influenced Wright and Bork and ensured that Nixon could not thwart any investigation of his actions.

In the early morning hours of October 25, the President reportedly had ordered a worldwide military alert of American forces, both conventional and nuclear. The move reflected the Administration's perception of Soviet intentions to intervene in the Middle East to enforce the precarious cease-fire between Israeli and Arab armies. Several hours later, Nixon briefed congressional leaders, who promptly gave him full support. A careful reading of the Nixon and Kissinger memoirs reveals that the Secretary of State and Haig ordered the alert, not the President, who by then was deeply jolted by the aftershocks of the Cox dismissal. Certainly, Kissinger's ostentatious public diplomacy and posturing left Nixon's role only dimly perceived. The President's passion for control began to focus almost exclusively on Watergate.

When Henry Kissinger faced reporters that day, he displayed surprise and dismay at questions suggesting that the alert was designed to divert attention from Watergate and the events of the past weekend. Bitterly, disdainfully, Kissinger told the media representatives that "it is a symptom of what is happening to our country that it could even be suggested that the United States would alert its forces for domestic reasons." He assailed the "Watergate bloodhounds," as he later described them, flatly accused the media of creating "a crisis of confidence" in foreign policy, and warned that there had to be "a minimum of confidence that the . . . American government [is] not playing with the lives of the American people." *Newsweek* nevertheless suggested sinister Administration designs, and it quoted an "Administration source" as saying that "we had a problem and we decided to make the most of it." In an editorial, the *Washington Post* responded to Kissinger, sharply reminding him that "our crisis at home was created by the President."[42]

If Nixon still seemed master of foreign events, he could react only passively, even submissively, to the domestic storms that battered his Administration. In late October, his speechwriters prepared a text for a television appearance, but Nixon canceled it. The draft bitterly denounced Cox for alone opposing the President's offer to provide verified summaries of the tapes. The statement also deplored the "national shock wave" that fostered "cynicism and suspicion," making difficult the task of governance. Most significantly, the planned talk promised that Stennis would carry out the assignment of preparing verified summaries for Judge Sirica, and that the President would not appoint a new Special Prosecutor. "Experience" had shown that the position was an "inherently . . . unworkable arrangement" that should not again be attempted.[43] The decision to cancel the speech underlined the uncertainty within the White House.

At his October 26 press conference two days later, Nixon announced his intention to appoint a new Special Prosecutor, one with "independence" and "total cooperation" from the executive branch. Bork's confusion and ambivalence in the Department of Justice during the past five days reflected the twists and turns of the White House's strategy. Nixon pleaded that it was time to prosecute the guilty and clear the innocent. The President thought it would be unnecessary for a new prosecutor to use the judicial process against him. The compromise of tape summaries that he had offered to Cox, he believed, would be adequate. But the words were hollow, betrayed by Wright's announcement that the President would comply with existing court orders. Nixon reiterated his familiar arguments on behalf of confidentiality, but again he seemed to be going through the motions. Worse yet, he badly misgauged the temper of Congress when he asserted that he did not think that legislators would have to develop new guidelines for the new Special Prosecutor's independence. The old fight, however, was there when he blasted Cox as uncooperative and "more interested in the issue than he was in the settlement." Indeed, Cox was loath to let go. He wrote to Sirica on October 22, reminding him that as "an officer of the Court," he still could be of some service. "[A]lthough I am reluctant to intrude myself, I wish not to shrink from any obligations," Cox told the judge—in words that Sirica interpreted as an offer to be counsel to the grand jury. Sirica took no action.[44]

The time had come to watch congressmen's feet, not their mouths. Within days, House members had introduced over twenty impeachment or impeachment-inquiry resolutions. Despite the President's yielding on the tapes, House Judiciary Committee Chairman Peter Rodino announced that his committee would proceed to organize an inquiry. Speaker Carl Albert the same day said that the House must lay "this thing to rest one way or the other." The full House committee met on October 30 and empowered the Chairman to secure subpoenas without a committee vote. Rodino promised to consult with the Judiciary Committee's ranking Republican, Edward Hutchinson. His gesture was the first of many to foster a spirit of bipartisanship. A number of Republicans and several Southern Democrats in the House admitted candidly that the events of the past ten days had raised questions regarding the President's truthfulness. Walter Flowers (D-AL), generally a warm, conservative supporter of the President, was "thoroughly turned off," especially by Nixon's obsequious references to "Judge Stennis." Some of Stennis's intimates called him that, but Flowers thought the President's doing it was "just a dirty trick" and an obvious "ploy" to elevate Stennis's status for Nixon's advantage.

The "firestorm" had ignited Congress. Ray Thornton (D-AR) and Tom Railsback (R-IL) of the House Judiciary Committee remembered the "storm of mail" after the Cox dismissal. Thornton realized how suddenly "Watergate" was at the center of the committee's attention, given Agnew's resignation and the need to confirm a vice-presidential successor, arrive at new guidelines for a Special Prosecutor, and consider impeachment resolutions. Nobody, Thornton said, could have anticipated "judging these extraordinary questions."[45]

By month's end, newspapers across the land and across the political spectrum had called for the President's resignation or his impeachment. The *Atlanta Constitution*, the *Salt Lake City Tribune*, the *Boston Globe*, the *Honolulu Star-Bulletin*, and the *Detroit News* joined the growing chorus, demanding action against the President. Most wrote more in sorrow than in anger; nearly all had supported Nixon's re-election in 1972. More startling, on November 12, *Time* published the first editorial in its history, calling upon the President to resign. The editorial catalogued Nixon's succession of lies and his defiance of court orders and agreements with Congress. He had passed the limits of "permissible" offenses, he had betrayed the constitutional system, his oath, and his "informal compact with the people." The "nightmare of uncertainty," *Time* concluded, "must be ended."

Sam Ervin received a staggering amount of mail following the Cox dismissal. To his constituents, both those supporting and those opposing the President, he said that the events constituted "a great tragedy for America." Ervin thought Cox had no reasonable alternative but to oppose the Stennis verification scheme. Some of his correspondents urged him to "Remember Chappaquiddick" and suggested that the smears against the President smacked of a "very strong Communist conspiracy." Ervin stood his ground, but added that he "fervently hope[d] that past and future events do not give cause for impeachment of the President."[46]

The events of the last days of October numbed and galvanized. Bork's predecessor as Solicitor General, Erwin Griswold, was shocked. Cox, Richardson, and Ruckelshaus had been his students—and all were "honorable men." Griswold had "lost faith" in the President by April; October's events only confirmed his misgivings. For recently appointed FBI Director Clarence Kelley, the "Saturday Night Massacre" was a turning point. He no longer thought the Administration could be saved. Kelley's "emotions," and those of others in the top echelon of the Bureau, "all shifted into neutral," for he recognized that the President "had indeed something to hide on those White House tapes." During the firings, Haig directed Kelley to seal the offices of Richardson and Cox, as well as those of the Special Prosecutor's staff. But Kelley already was wary, and he ordered his subordinates to maintain contact with Henry Petersen and avoid any appearance of participating in anyone's cover-up enterprise. Richardson warned Kelley to be careful in his future dealings with the White House. For Richardson, the FBI action was the most blatant exercise of presidential power in the "whole sordid history" of Watergate. "A government of laws was on the verge of becoming a government of one man," was Richardson's perception, a strikingly pointed observation from this most accommodating of men.[47]

In the Saturday Night Massacre, Nixon attempted to flush out his demons from the Watergate thicket. But there were legions more in the undergrowth. The Watergate affair had not yet matured into the "greatest constitutional crisis," but the full glare of publicity made it clear that matters had escalated to a new level. The unfolding crisis was of a house divided with regard to the fate of its president. Whether the nation would support or reject him now was the question on the table. The fractures, the divisions would have to cease; in one way or another, Richard Nixon would have to "bring us together."

XVI

"SINISTER FORCES"

FORD, JAWORSKI, TAPE GAPS, AND TAXES:
NOVEMBER–DECEMBER 1973

The Nixon Administration was floundering amid the scattered debris. The President had to choose a new Vice President and a new Watergate Special Prosecutor, and he had also to confront the new challenge from the House Judiciary Committee. His two-front war persisted; now, however, he faced fresh adversaries determined to contest his continued right to his political domain. Meanwhile, the demands for his tapes and papers persisted, as the Cox firing heightened suspicions of his conduct.

The assaults on the Administration had matured into criminal indictments for prized (or formerly prized) subordinates. John Dean pleaded guilty on October 19 to one count of conspiracy to obstruct justice, but the charge encompassed a collection of nefarious activities: raising money for the Watergate defendants, suborning Jeb Magruder's perjury, and gaining access to FBI reports from L. Patrick Gray. Judge John Sirica delayed Dean's sentencing pending his cooperation in forthcoming criminal trials, a move that promised the President more difficulties in the days ahead. Donald Segretti pleaded guilty on November 1 to distributing false campaign literature and five weeks later was sentenced to six months in prison. At the end of November, the grand jury indicted Dwight Chapin, the President's former appointments secretary, on four counts of perjury in connection with his dealings with Segretti.

The President was filled with sympathy, if not remorse, for his people. He told Chapin to "keep your balance and eventually this will all be seen in perspective. Your service to the nation will be remembered long after this unfortunate episode is forgotten." He had his secretary pass word to Charles Colson that he was confident Colson would get "off" in the end. He uttered a familiar refrain: "The irony is that Ellsberg is a hero and those who tried to protect the nation's security are now under attack."[1]

Egil Krogh, one of the directors of the Plumbers, was indicted on October 11, the first fruits of Archibald Cox's five-month tenure. The charges consisted of two perjury counts in connection with the burglary of the office of Daniel Ellsberg's psychiatrist. By the time of the charges, Krogh had admitted in a sworn affidavit to Judge Matthew Byrne (presiding in Ellsberg's criminal trial) that he had authorized burglars "to engage in covert activity" to secure Ellsberg's psychiatric history, contrary to his earlier testimony. Several days before the indictment, Nixon confidently assured Krogh that he would be vindicated. "The situation is really topsy-turvy when a man who stole hundreds of top secret documents goes free on a technicality and those who were trying to expose him are prosecuted. Your courage—under great stress—inspires us all." Nixon seemed genuinely fond of Krogh—"a superior property," he once labeled him. But when Krogh pleaded guilty on November 30, his statement to the court devastated the foundations of the Administration's defenses.

Krogh told Judge Gerhard Gesell of the D.C. District Court that he had intended to invoke "national security" as the basis for his defense. In earlier motions, his attorneys had argued that Krogh had merely been protecting official secrets "classified by the highest security office in the government of the United States, the President himself." But Krogh, an earnest, devout man, had a change of heart. "I now feel," he stated, "that the sincerity of my motivation cannot justify what was done and that I cannot in conscience assert national security as a defense." Whatever his motivations, he added, they could not surmount "the transcendent importance of the rule of law." No Nixon "enemy" struck so hard at the Administration's behavior and its rationalizations as that "superior property," Egil Krogh: "I simply feel that what was done in the Ellsberg operation was in violation of what I perceive to be a fundamental idea in the character of this country—the paramount importance of the rights of the individual—I don't want to be associated with that violation any longer by attempting to defend it." John Ehrlichman had unsuccessfully—and unwisely—defended that same violation in his testy exchange with Herman Talmadge during the Senate Select Committee hearings three months earlier. Richard Nixon's persistent comparisons of his subordinates' deeds to the wrongs of Daniel Ellsberg made it doubtful whether he understood the distinction.[2]

The same day Krogh appeared in court, the President signed a bill extending the Watergate grand jury until June 4, 1974, with a provision for an additional six months if requested. The bill was humiliating; more, it was dangerous. Krogh's painful, yet eloquent, admission pointedly revealed that the Nixon Administration had abused power; the question now was whether the President himself had been complicit.

For the tenth time in its history, the United States was without a vice president. At other times the office had simply remained vacant and, as variously provided by law, different officials, including the Secretary of State, the President *pro tempore* of the Senate, and the Speaker of the House of Representatives, had formed in varying order the line of succession to the presidency. Following Lyndon Johnson's assumption of the presidency after John F. Kennedy's assassination, Congress moved to alter the system and passed the Twenty-fifth Amendment in July 1965. The amendment was ratified in February 1967. It attempted to deal with the thorny problem of determining presidential disability in addition to ordering the succession. It provided that the president nominate a vice president in the event of a vacancy, who then would take office following a favorable majority vote in both houses.[3] The Constitution had served for 180 years without such a provision, but now events would dictate its use twice in one year.

Less than a year after Richard Nixon had been re-elected by a landslide, his maneuvers to select a Vice President exposed his diminished authority. The Democratic-controlled Congress had been the President's nemesis since he had assumed office in 1969. He had ignored it, spurned it, and fought it—at all times, he believed, for personal political advantage. Battling Congress undoubtedly had value on the hustings, but reality and the political system required cooperation. The Democratic congressional dominance alone dictated the need for compromise. But after five years of studied contempt, Nixon could have no realistic expectation that Congress would extend him a free hand in the selection of the Vice President. The Constitution gave Congress an equal voice; that provision in the current context of political reality in effect gave Congress a veto.

Lord Bryce, the shrewd British observer of American institutions in the late nineteenth century, was fascinated by why the "best men" did not become presidents. Given a choice between a "brilliant man and a safe man," the latter, he noted, was preferred. The eminent men naturally made more enemies and gave their enemies "more assailable points" than obscure men. They were, Bryce remarked, therefore far less desirable candidates. Considering the undistinguished models of nineteenth-century presidents whom Bryce viewed, he concluded that "the only thing remarkable about them is that being so commonplace they should have climbed so high."

Gerald Ford confirmed Bryce's theory; in his own words, he stood out as the " 'safest' choice." Ford also correctly believed that Nixon preferred John B. Connally, Lyndon Johnson's protégé, an ex-Democrat, and his own former Secretary of the Treasury. Although Nixon did not drop Agnew in

1972, as he and his advisers had considered, the White House maintained an interest in grooming Connally for the election of 1976. Haldeman met Connally in early January 1973, and his "talking paper" on the meeting contained the notation: "When is he going to move? It's important to develop another horse [before] . . . time will run out. It would be helpful to know what his plans are." Nixon warmly admired the Texan. He also had to realize that while Connally provoked sharp reactions, both from Democrats who despised his trace-jumping and from Republicans who remained skeptical about his commitment, such controversy could divert attention from Watergate.

Speaker Carl Albert warned Nixon that Connally would never be confirmed. The President himself indicated to Connally that he was his first choice, but after several days both men realized that the nomination was too controversial to have any real chance for success. Dwight Chapin (then facing a criminal indictment) passed word that Ford would be "sensational," because he was a team player with strong ties to the party and Congress. But Chapin, too, preferred Connally, although he knew that "the fight would have been rough."[4]

The President asked Republican members of Congress for suggestions. Nixon later said that Ford was their first choice, but congressional responses showed very strong support for Nelson Rockefeller and William Rogers. Connally and Ronald Reagan attracted scattered but significant support as well, as did Barry Goldwater. Many of the responses indicated that Ford would have the least difficulty in being confirmed. Liberal Republican Paul McCloskey (CA) endorsed Ford and Rockefeller, among others. He then added that he had omitted Elliot Richardson only because he thought it more important that Richardson restore "professional integrity" to the Department of Justice. As his first choices, Ford himself listed Connally, former Congressman Melvin Laird, Rockefeller, and Reagan. Ford undoubtedly realized that either the President or Congress had profound objections to all these men; the Republican leader, however, was a master in covering all bases.[5]

Laird, currently a White House aide, who had been a minor player in congressional maneuvers during his lengthy tenure as a representative from Wisconsin, actively promoted Ford's candidacy. He had been disenchanted with the White House since he had joined the staff in May, but he stayed on, because he thought he could serve his friends and also play "an important role in the use of the Twenty-fifth Amendment," once he realized that Agnew had to go.

Laird asked Ford to make himself available. Ford, always a bit wary of Laird's machinations, agreed when he realized that Laird also spoke for others. Ford insisted that he would not promote himself. Laird told the President he would leave the White House if Connally's name went forward.

He urged leading Democrats, including Senate Majority Leader Mike Mansfield, to oppose Connally and favor Ford. Laird thought the Texan was simply "too controversial" to be confirmed; at bottom, however, he preferred Ford and disliked Connally. Not surprisingly, Nixon summoned Ford. The Congressman said he had no ambitions to serve beyond January 1977 and no expectations to be the party's presidential nominee in 1976. Nixon, he reported, was pleased, because, he told Ford, he preferred Connally in 1976, a point he also made to Kissinger. Reportedly, the President mocked Ford to Nelson Rockefeller: "Can you imagine Jerry Ford sitting in this chair?" He sent one of the pens he used to sign Ford's nomination to Fred Buzhardt, with a note: "Here is the damn pen I signed Jerry Ford's nomination with."[6]

With his penchant for surprises, the President trotted out Ford in a nationally televised White House ceremony on the evening of November 12. Mrs. Ford told Nixon she did not know whether congratulations or condolences were in order. "Oh, well," the President replied, "the pay is better." Whatever the President's personal feelings, the event exuded goodwill. Spiro Agnew, for the moment, was the national villain. Five years later, he complained that Nixon had not consulted him on the choice of a successor. Worse yet, he lamented that at Ford's swearing-in ceremony, "my name was not even mentioned once. It was like the Soviet Union where the deposed leaders become nonpersons. It was just as though the previous five years had simply ceased to exist."[7] As the years passed, Agnew would prove to have no monopoly on inability or unwillingness to understand what he had done wrong.

Nixon's pique and displeasure might well have reflected an objective dissatisfaction with the qualities of his nominee or a frustration with his inability to have his real preference. Perhaps too, the dissatisfaction betrayed his sense of danger and concern. The President's low opinion of Ford and his vexation at the need to nominate him further betrayed Nixon's weakness. Agnew's resignation may have removed an obstacle for those seeking to replace Richard Nixon; by nominating Ford, the President handed his enemies a real alternative. For himself, that alternative unquestionably was dangerous. Ford's presence as Vice President spurred *Time*'s call for the President's resignation. The unprecedented editorial described Ford as an "unmistakable improvement over the grievously wounded Nixon." It viewed Ford as free from corruption, with a "solid if unimaginative" domestic-policy record, a man of the center, liked and respected in Congress, and though he was without experience in foreign affairs, he could be relied on to have Kissinger continue Nixon's basically sound policies.[8] The nation had Lord Bryce's "safe man."

If Gerald Ford had any sure qualification to be Richard Nixon's Vice President, it was loyalty, even blind loyalty, some thought. A friendly aide and biographer realized the potential liability of such loyalty, knowing that

Ford had been perceived as a "knee-jerk" supporter of Nixon. In Congress, he had done a number of shadowy chores for the Administration, ranging from supporting the impeachment of Supreme Court Justice William O. Douglas to seeking a contempt citation against CBS for its refusal to release research material relating to a controversial documentary hostile to the Administration. John Ehrlichman reputedly summed up White House disdain for its messenger boy: "What a jerk Jerry is," Ehrlichman is supposed to have said. Ford supported the President on 83 percent of House votes. No one designated such loyalty as a qualification for the presidency, and yet the prospect of a Ford presidency was not far from the minds of the congressmen who voted to confirm him.[9]

Ford's Michigan colleague, Edward Hutchinson, the ranking minority member of the House Judiciary Committee, accused the Democrats of stalling on the confirmation of the new Vice President, despite their leaders' favorable disposition toward Ford. Hutchinson's charge had no basis; if anything, the Democrats were anxious to confirm Ford. But the responsibility of doing so was theirs, and they had to offer both the reality and appearance of a careful scrutiny of Ford's record. The ever-cautious Peter Rodino decided to allow the Senate to act first, perhaps hoping to defuse the more militant liberals on his Judiciary Committee.

In the House committee, Ford faced three factions: his uncritical supporters, led by Hutchinson; a second group, which fed him questions designed to display his integrity, talents, and political folksiness; and finally, his opponents, openly antagonistic, looking for vulnerabilities. Ford played heavily on the chords of honesty and openness. Yes, he was loyal, he acknowledged, but added: "I am my own man and that [sic] the only pledge by which I bound myself in accepting the President's trust and his confidence is that by which we are all bound before God and before the Constitution, to do our best for America." When a Republican member asked him about the financing of his Colorado condominium, Ford delivered a folksy response invoking the fact that he had borrowed money from his children—at interest.

Some congressmen posed questions related to Watergate, but Ford used them to distance himself from events and any possible involvement on his part. When another member reminded him that he had severely criticized President Kennedy for his use of executive privilege after the Bay of Pigs fiasco, Ford retreated and said that some circumstances might dictate the use of the privilege. Generally, Ford managed to disarm his foes. His apparent ease and openness appeared in sharp contrast to the furtive bearing of the President. Whenever flaws appeared in his record—such as his questionable commitment to civil rights for blacks and his subservient role in the Douglas impeachment affair—they were treated as within the bounds of acceptable political behavior. After all, Gerald Ford was not unique in such actions. His critics thus found themselves isolated as excessively partisan and moralistic. Ford moved easily into the center.

John Conyers (D–MI) and Charles Rangel (D–NY) made no secret of their hostility, however. They argued that the House should deal first with impeachment, then move to confirming a Vice President. If Nixon were removed, they contended, the nation would not be saddled with his choice as a successor. Ford calmly responded that the President had the right and duty to nominate a Vice President and to choose someone philosophically compatible with him, given his 1972 electoral mandate. Robert Drinan (D–MA) and Elizabeth Holtzman (D–NY) pressed Ford on his knowledge of the secret Cambodian bombing. Holtzman argued that the President had lied publicly on the issue, and Ford admitted that Nixon had not been "100 per cent truthful." But, he insisted, all presidents had given false and deceptive statements. Holtzman sharply retorted that there was a difference between keeping a secret and falsifying information. "I think all of us understand that difference very well," she said.

Eight committee members voted against the nomination on November 26. The next day, the Senate endorsed Ford by a 92–3 count. The House followed with an overwhelming 387–35 favorable vote on December 6, and Ford immediately was sworn in as the nation's fortieth Vice President.[10]

A close congressional ally of Ford told him shortly after he became Vice President that he was in a powerful position. Nixon needed him more than Ford needed the President. The friend advised Ford to stay away from the White House, travel a good deal, and not listen to the tapes. Ford apparently did not take the advice to heart at first, for, typically, he gave uncritical loyalty to Nixon. Still, his mere presence constituted danger for the President. The day of Ford's inauguration, Senator Jacob Javits, a New York Republican, said that Ford had provided "a new situation concerning any call on the President to resign in the interest of the country. . . . I and others will have to give every thoughtful consideration to that possibility." Even Ford acknowledged that whatever momentary goodwill Nixon had fostered by nominating him had been neutralized by the Saturday Night Massacre.

Two months after Ford's confirmation, a Democrat captured his House seat, the first Democrat since 1910 to represent Michigan's Fifth District. Watergate was the issue, and the result was interpreted as a referendum on the President himself. The Democratic candidate had circulated an appeal: "Our President must stand beyond the shadow of a doubt. Our President must be Gerald Ford." Nixon told Ford that the inflation issue had defeated the Republican candidate.[11] Reality had taken flight.

The vice presidency plagued Richard Nixon in a curious way. His own tenure in that office had catapulted him to fame, but it was an unhappy, frustrating experience, tethered as he was to a President who in truth neither liked nor trusted him. Henry Cabot Lodge, Nixon's 1960 running mate,

preferred afternoon naps to campaign appearances. The candidate who
shared the ticket with him in 1968 and 1972 resigned in disgrace. Finally,
his last Vice President hovered over the White House in 1974, a conspicuous
alternative to the agony of the President and the nation.

As Nixon faced mounting legal and political challenges, he found himself
increasingly outmanned, outgunned, and isolated. For months the Justice
Department had been useless to him in his Watergate battles. In practice,
the department consciously severed itself from the President and his problems. Before the creation of the Special Prosecutor, the department had been
an antagonist, despite the President's concerted efforts to co-opt its leaders
and thwart their investigation. The events of October, beginning with the
Agnew negotiations and the dealings with Cox, further demonstrated that
the department remained an independent power center. Among the many
paradoxes of Watergate was that the President of the United States—the
"Most Powerful Leader of the Free World"—could muster only the most
meager resources against an array of legal talent commanding the full range
of public agencies.

Leonard Garment had joined J. Fred Buzhardt as the President's Counsel
after John Dean had been dismissed in April. Neither man was well versed
in criminal or constitutional issues. Alexander Haig asked Solicitor General
Robert Bork in July to be the President's chief defense counsel. According
to Bork, Haig characteristically framed his request with emotional appeals
to patriotism. "The Republic is going down the drain and only you can save
it"—or words to that effect, Bork recalled. Haig told Bork about Agnew's
difficulties, and for some reason raised the 1971 spying activities of the Joint
Chiefs of Staff as if they were current matters. Bork considered the proposal
for several days and said he would have to listen to the tapes. Haig heatedly
told him that "nobody" could hear them, and that the President would burn
them and resign to protect the presidency if forced to turn them over. Bork
sensed the problems. When he asked what Haig meant by "chief defense
counsel," Haig told him he would have exclusive access to the President.
"Until I give some advice that isn't appreciated, and then I'll sit there and
the phone won't ring," Bork observed. "That's very perceptive of you,"
Haig admitted. They finally agreed that the job was not for Bork.[12]

Buzhardt had come to the White House in 1973 after nearly three years as
General Counsel in the Department of Defense. He had good political ties;
he had been a protégé of Senator J. Strom Thurmond and had developed a
close relationship with Melvin Laird. As a practicing lawyer, Buzhardt had
confined his work to small-town civil matters in his native South Carolina.
He was known as a man who could keep secrets. No wonder, then, that
among Nixon's numerous lawyers, only Buzhardt had access to the tapes.

Given the President's special reliance on him, coupled with an inability to delegate any of his responsibilities, Buzhardt was badly overworked, a situation that only aggravated his deteriorating heart condition.[13]

Garment contrasted sharply with Buzhardt. Friendly and gregarious, he had had a substantial legal career in New York. A close observer of Richard Nixon since 1965, he was familiar with the labyrinths of the President's mind and his Byzantine methods of running the White House. Richard Nixon himself was Garment's cause and fascination. Buzhardt was devoted to conservative politics; Garment promoted himself as the "house liberal." Haldeman at one point had asked Garment to represent the White House at the Senate Select Committee hearings, but with Dean falling out of favor, Ehrlichman approached Garment in April to act as Counsel. Garment, however, insisted that the President personally ask him. He discussed the question of accessibility with Nixon, but the talk was an exercise in futility. Serving the President, Garment understood, "ultimately is something special." Nixon himself considered his lawyers not in a traditional lawyer-client relationship, but as staff workers. A lawyer did not deal with the President directly as he would with an ordinary client. After May, Garment and the other lawyers worked through Haig, and thus Nixon preserved his method of staff dealings, despite the fact that he was coping with a legal, and not a political or policy, situation. Nixon's promise of accessibility "was more honored in the breach," Garment recalled. But he knew Nixon. He "took it as a given who he [Nixon] was, what he was, and what he wasn't."

The work was frustrating for the lawyers: "We are a little bit in the position of having to tie fishing lines with boxing gloves on," Garment told his secretary in June. By midsummer, he felt "overwhelmed" and "frustrated," chiefly because he had no access to the tapes, despite repeated pleas to the President and Haig. Garment also understood his limitations as a criminal lawyer. He feared Nixon's lawyers would be the "patsy" for the President. By November, he had come to realize that he should have removed himself from the case earlier, but he could not stay away from it—he operated with a kind of obsessiveness; protecting the President in the Watergate affair was "like feeling a sore tooth." Yet he worried that he might find himself in trouble, for he was learning too much and might have to disclose what he knew. In December, Garment received an anonymous letter from a fellow staff member expressing concern over Garment's involvement. Garment's loyalty to the President was commendable, but the writer feared that Garment had been drawn into a web of lies and cosmetic face-saving. He told Garment that it was time for "self-respect and dignity" to supersede loyalty.

Throughout his time in the White House, Garment spent long hours talking to journalists. Early on, he perceived the game of prosecutorial politics and believed that it had to be countered with public-relations volleys from

the White House—to put, as it were, the Administration's "spin," or interpretation, on events. His calendar listed regular visits with prominent reporters, including Bob Woodward, J. Anthony Lukas, Theodore White, John
Osborne, and Elizabeth Drew. He would discuss imminent revelations with
frankness, hoping to defuse their impact. By mid-November Garment saw
the President growing more desperate, now realizing that he should have
appealed the tapes order to the Supreme Court. Wearily, he told his secretary
that Nixon would not or could not "trust" his own lawyers and that it was
increasingly difficult to help him.[14]

As the President's case increasingly centered on the control of the tapes,
his need for constitutional expertise became all the more apparent. After
failing to persuade Bork to handle the case, Haig enticed Charles Alan Wright
to join the President's defense team. Wright taught constitutional law and
was an active litigator with substantial Supreme Court experience.

Nixon's hiring of Wright dripped with irony. In 1951, as a young professor
at the University of Minnesota Law School, Wright had published a book
review favorable to Alger Hiss. Senator Richard Nixon fumed and wrote to
a Minneapolis friend, urging him to bring the matter of Wright's beliefs to
the attention of the University's board of regents. Nixon thought Wright had
an "obvious left wing bent," that he was educationally deficient, and that
he should not remain on the faculty.

A year later, the *Saturday Review of Literature* published two reviews of
Whittaker Chambers's book on the Hiss case, one by Nixon and the other
by Wright. Wright's review was entitled "A Long Work of Fiction." In 1953
Wright scathingly attacked Federal Judge Harold Medina for his behavior
toward the lawyers defending leading Communist Party officials, and he
attacked the Supreme Court for upholding the lawyers' contempt citations.
He recognized that Medina's attacks on the lawyers undermined the ideal of
the rule of law that the government purported to defend.[15] But time brings
strange alliances. Nixon's Minneapolis friend, who apparently failed to have
Wright fired, turned out to be George MacKinnon, whom Nixon appointed
to the federal bench and who was one of two judges who supported Wright's
argument in the appeal of the tapes order. MacKinnon considered the balance between the public good in disclosure and the public good in presidential confidentiality and found the greater weight always to be on the side of
confidentiality.

Wright encountered the same frustrations as Garment in defending Nixon.
The President ordered him not to meet with Cox or to listen to any of the
tapes; the tapes remained Buzhardt's domain. Like Garment, Wright recognized that a case "was different when your client was the President of the
United States." Still, his inability to deal with the most material evidence
left him dissatisfied and even embarrassed. Following Alexander Butterfield's revelation of the taping system, Wright and Garment were asked how

they could adequately represent the President without listening to the tapes. Wright finessed the question: "We certainly feel that we wouldn't be here if we didn't hope that we were adequately representing the President, [and] if we didn't think we have had access to everything we need to adequately represent the President." Reporters failed to press the point. Four days later, on July 30, Wright was "appalled" to discover that Haldeman had been listening to the tapes, realizing that this undermined Nixon's own case for confidentiality. Meanwhile, Buzhardt wrote to Haldeman and his lawyers, asking them not to discuss the matter. The Senate Select Committee nevertheless elicited the information.[16]

After the October controversies, Wright lost some of his passion. His secretary regarded him as in a "state of shock," and unenthusiastic about continuing as Nixon's defense counsel. Like Garment, Wright had some ambivalence about being involved in the case. Later, he remembered the work as "demanding," with "more than its share of frustrations." He recalled the physical and emotional strains of his White House role, but in the end he had no regrets. Oliver Wendell Holmes's dictum that a man should share the passion and action of his time "at a peril of being judged not to have lived," summed up Wright's feelings.[17] Considering the constraints of his position, Wright served his client with distinction and fervor, if not success.

Some lawyers refused to accept the conditions the President placed on their service to him. Justice John Sullivan of the Illinois Court of Appeals, whose friendship with Nixon went back to Navy days in the South Pacific, came to the White House in November to join the defense team, mainly because Garment and Wright had begun to withdraw. Sullivan was a highly regarded trial lawyer, but within a few weeks he returned to Illinois, claiming that he had no direct communications with the President and had to see Haig at every turn. Sullivan may also have left because Illinois officials questioned the propriety of a sitting judge's serving as the President's lawyer.

Whatever the reason, Sullivan realized unhappily that the White House saw the case not in lawyer's terms but as a public-relations operation. In a letter to Haig, Sullivan stressed his lack of communication with the Chief of Staff, his dissatisfaction with the quality of Buzhardt's work, and the fact that Buzhardt in fact was not his subordinate, as had been promised. Sullivan apparently never was told directly whether he did or did not have a job; instead, he seemed to drift away, frustrated by his inability to receive direct answers. The White House offered the post of defense counsel to Erwin Griswold in December, but the former Solicitor General declined, mainly because he had lost faith in the President. There was a genuine concern at this time that Nixon could fall simply for lack of a proper, effective legal defense.[18]

* * *

The draconian dismissal of Archibald Cox assured the appointment of a new Special Prosecutor, one with even more ironclad guarantees of independence than Cox had had. With those considerations, and with far more sense of direction than had characterized the charging of the first Special Prosecutor in the spring, the selection process became much simpler. Apparently, the first choice of Bork and the White House was Leon Jaworski, a Houston lawyer and a confidant of Lyndon Johnson. Elliot Richardson had approached Jaworski about the position in the spring, but he had declined because of inadequate assurances of independence. On November 1 the President announced that Senator William Saxbe (R–OH) would be the new Attorney General, a move denounced by conservatives as "appeasement." Bork followed Nixon's announcement to report the Jaworski selection— apparently a matter on which Nixon could not bring himself to speak. Bork said that Jaworski would have no restraints on his freedom to pursue presidential documents, marking a clear retreat from the position Nixon had laid down in his October 26 statement. Jaworski held a press conference in Houston later that day. He said that the nation was "entitled to have some answers without waiting forever, and I intend to get those answers." He had virtually no knowledge of the staff or office he had inherited. He knew only Cox's deputy, Henry Ruth, but he quickly determined that the staff was of "crackerjack" quality.

Leonidas Jaworski was born in 1905 to parents who had recently emigrated from Poland and Austria. He graduated from Baylor University Law School in 1925, established a substantial reputation as a trial lawyer, and eventually became a partner in a leading law firm in Houston. As a young lawyer, Jaworski had lost a black man's murder case because of a coerced confession, but he later disapproved of the Supreme Court's *Miranda* ruling, believing that it had a "very, very . . . disenchanting . . . impact upon law-enforcement officials." After World War II he served at the Nuremberg War Crimes trials, with special responsibility for supervising the investigation of the Dachau concentration camp. He prosecuted numerous SS officials for their Dachau crimes, and later carefully distinguished his work (favorably, of course) from the more political trials of the leading Nazis.

Jaworski returned to Texas and cultivated important political contacts, including Lyndon Johnson, for whom he handled a number of legal matters. Later, he worked for both Johnson and John F. Kennedy in the contests over irregularities in the 1960 presidential balloting in Texas. Attorney General Robert Kennedy commissioned Jaworski to represent the government when Mississippi Governor Ross Barnett defied federal court desegregation rulings in 1962. Jaworski served on several presidential commissions for Johnson, and he enjoyed the reputation of being one of the President's intimate advisers. Jaworski was president of the American Bar Association in 1971–72, and in 1972 he actively supported Richard Nixon's re-election.[19]

Archibald Cox always remained the hero to most members of the Water-gate Special Prosecution Force and to much of the media. But Jaworski's appointment truly was a disaster for Richard Nixon. Jaworski's political and professional reputation denied the President the chance to portray him as a partisan or ideological enemy. The Texas lawyer had enormous prestige, with currency in a world apart, even alien, from that of Cox. That could only result in aligning yet another constituency against the President.

When Jaworski left for Washington, he did not believe that the President had any criminal involvement in Watergate. He recalled that Haig told him at the time of the appointment that "matters are just revolutionary—almost revolutionary. Something has to be done and has to be done quickly about it." At first, Jaworski told Haig that he saw no sense in talking about the Special Prosecutor's position, given the Administration's recent behavior. Haig replied that this was not "an ordinary tender," and assured Jaworski that "we can arrange a situation that would be acceptable to you." At the time of his appointment, Jaworski found Haig "tremendously articulate" and "absolutely sincere." The new prosecutor had confidence in the men in the Administration who negotiated with him over his status—Bork, Laird, Garment, and Bryce Harlow. But there were other signals. The day after Jaworski accepted the Special Prosecutor's job, Haig told him that Cox's staff had acted irresponsibly and advised him to "take a good, close look" at the prosecutors. Incidentally, Jaworski declined an opportunity to visit the President.[20]

Bork formally reinstituted the Special Prosecutor's office on November 2, noting that the specific listing of its functions was "not intended to limit in any manner authority to carry out his functions and responsibilities." A lengthy appendix to the Special Prosecutor's charter spelled out the office's power. Another document, dated November 19, amended the charter to en-sure that the Special Prosecutor would not be removed "except for extraor-dinary improprieties" and then only after the President consulted the Majority and Minority leaders of Congress as well as the ranking members of the two Judiciary Committees to determine "that their consensus is in accord with his proposed actions." The charter went on to stipulate that the Special Prosecutor's authority could not be limited without similar consul-tation. The revamped charter was intended, Bork told Jaworski, as a "safe-guard" to "all aspects" of his independence.[21] The President had completely succumbed to the demands for a truly independent prosecutor.

In the days just preceding Jaworski's appointment, the Senate Judiciary Committee conducted several days of public hearings on the Cox dismissal and heard proposals for insulating the Special Prosecutor from presidential interference. In his appearances before the committee, Cox received enthu-siastic support from the Democrats (his removal was "an insult to this com-mittee," Senator Birch Bayh (D–IN) said). Even Republican leader Hugh

Scott praised Cox. But the partisan fires burned brightly. Senator Strom Thurmond charged that Cox had supported anti-Nixon demonstrations at Harvard and had been the "dean" of John F. Kennedy's "brain trust," while Senator Edward Kennedy thanked Cox for mentioning "those marvelous things you did for my brother."

Cox's service, however, was history; most of the Judiciary Committee's attention focused on a bill that would require senatorial agreement for the President to remove the new Special Prosecutor. Senatorial consent to presidential appointments often is required by the Constitution; since 1789, Congress had debated whether the Senate similarly might have to concur in the dismissal of such officers. Generally, Congress had followed James Madison's advice and agreed that it had no such role. Periodically, however, congressmen have renewed the debate, and in 1867 they passed the Tenure of Office Act, stipulating Senate consent to dismissal in certain cases—a law that Andrew Johnson deliberately violated, resulting in impeachment charges against him in 1868. Cox thought that in certain cases the President's power of removal "could be circumscribed." Sam Ervin promptly and sharply disagreed. By November 1—the day Nixon appointed Jaworski—the committee apparently had struck its bargain with the President whereby he would consult with congressional leaders before dismissing the new Special Prosecutor. Senator Roman Hruska thought the assurances sufficient to make it unnecessary to legislate on a matter of dubious constitutionality. Senator Adlai Stevenson III (D–IL), however, believed it foolish to accept any assurances from Richard Nixon and thought Jaworski naive for doing so.

Two considerations finally produced a consensus in the Senate Judiciary Committee that the President would deal with Jaworski in good faith and not dismiss him without congressional consultation. First, the committee understood the differences between Cox and Jaworski. Bork spelled it out for them: "Mr. Jaworski is a man far on in a very distinguished career. Mr. Jaworski is not going to pull any punches or do anything that would in any way tarnish what is a magnificent career." Some senators refused to believe that Nixon was devoted to "discovering the truth," but they realized that the President could not challenge someone as formidable as Jaworski. Jaworski himself, on November 20, told the committee he was satisfied with the safeguards for his independence. But equally important, Judge Sirica informed Committee Chairman James O. Eastland that the judges wanted no part of appointing a Special Prosecutor such as the committee's liberal Democrats had proposed. The consensus, however informal, was public enough to cloak Jaworski with sufficient independence to make unlikely another Saturday Night Massacre. Months later, during confirmation hearings for Lawrence Silberman, Nixon's nominee for Deputy Attorney General, Senator Kennedy questioned Silberman closely on Jaworski's latitude. While Silberman would not explicitly define "extreme improprieties" as a cause for dismissal, he specifically stated that he would not fire Jaworski for going to court to force the President to turn over tapes or other documents. For Richard Nixon, the Saturday Night Massacre had been in vain, and Jaworski was in a position that Archibald Cox could only envy.[22]

The Democratic-controlled Congress pressed the President on his removal power in another area. After Cox's dismissal, it voted to abolish the offices of Director and Deputy Director of the Office of Management and Budget. The purpose here simply was to remove two Nixon appointees and subject future nominees to a confirmation process. Nixon vetoed the bill, calling it an infringement on his removal power with "an unconstitutional procedure." The President mustered enough support to sustain the veto, but Congress passed subsequent legislation simply requiring confirmation of future nominees.[23] The incident demonstrated the President's residual power and his ability to appeal to constitutional forms, but it also revealed the boldness of the opposition.

As the "firestorm" engulfed the White House following the events of October 20, the President's problems with the courts and the tapes intensified. On October 30, Buzhardt informed Judge Sirica that several subpoenaed conversations had never been recorded. The next day, the media referred to "the two missing tapes," a description that reinforced perceptions of sinister deeds. Nixon complained, because Buzhardt had told the truth. Earlier, however, the President himself had deceived his lawyers. Before Cox learned of the taping system, Henry Petersen had told him about Nixon's remark that he had recorded an April 15 meeting with John Dean. Cox requested a tape of that conversation, but in order not to expose the taping system, Nixon instructed Buzhardt to tell Cox that the President had made a summary of the meeting on a Dictabelt and that the summary was personal. When Buzhardt searched the tape inventories in November, he discovered that no such Dictabelt existed. Chagrined, Garment and Buzhardt visited the President in Florida a few days later to report on the situation. At this meeting, they presented various options, including resignation. Garment also urged Nixon to secure a new, outside lawyer. It was a time for distance.[24]

The President, however, already knew of another bombshell about to explode. Rose Mary Woods, his personal secretary, told him on October 1 that she "might have caused a small gap" in a Haldeman–Nixon conversation of June 20. According to the President, Woods offered a convoluted explanation of reaching for the telephone while transcribing the tape and inadvertently hitting the recorder's delete button "for about four or five minutes." Nixon said that he was not concerned, because he was sure that the subpoena had been in error and the June 20 tape had in fact not been requested. But on November 15 Haig informed the President that Buzhardt

had incorrectly interpreted the subpoena and that the June 20 tape indeed
had been included. And the bad news grew worse: the four- or five-minute
gap actually ran to 18½ minutes. Nixon blithely announced to the press
earlier that day that there would be no more "bombshells"; the same newspaper stories contained Judge Sirica's announcement that Buzhardt had informed him of the 18½-minute gap.[25]

Nixon later recalled exact details of his secretary's alleged mistake, but at
the time, Haig publicly disparaged Woods's description and quoted the President as having complained of her being "imprecise." Haig scoffed at
Woods's contention that at the time of the mysterious erasure she had talked
on the telephone for only five minutes, as she originally reported. Typical
of a woman, Haig said: she did not know the difference between five minutes
and one hour of talking. Haig fairly brimmed with explanations at the time.
Perhaps, he testified, "some sinister force" had applied "the other energy
source and taken care of the information on the tape." Garment reportedly
was "tired and obviously troubled" over the tape gap and thought it would
"destroy everything and everyone before it is all over." During a hearing
in Sirica's courtroom on the tape in question, Rose Mary Woods seemed
confused as to whether the White House lawyers really represented her. For
her December testimony in Judge Sirica's court, Charles Rhyne, a former
President of the American Bar Association and an old law school friend of
Nixon's, appeared with her. "Believers in the accidental theory could gather
for lunch in a phone booth," said the conservative *National Review.*

The Special Prosecutor's office went to elaborate lengths to consider the
possibility of charging Woods with obstruction of justice, mutilation of public documents, and contempt of a court order. But the lawyers realized that
if she claimed the erasure was accidental, Woods could not be charged with
any crime unless the prosecution could show her acts were willful, an unlikely prospect.[26]

The White House and Jaworski's office jointly selected a six-man panel of
experts on November 21 to study the damaged June 20 tape. Within three
weeks Sirica announced that the panel had informed him that neither Woods's
typewriter nor her high-intensity lamp could have caused the constant buzz-
ing sounds heard on the tape gap, as the White House earlier had announced.

Meanwhile, opinion polls showed a continuing deterioration in the President's standing. By late December, a Louis Harris survey reported that by
a 73–21 margin, Americans believed that Nixon had lost so much credibility
that it would be difficult to accept him as President. But when the same
sample was asked whether Nixon should resign for the good of the country,
a 45–44 vote was recorded in the negative. Then, a month later, Harris
found that by a 48–40 plurality, Americans favored Nixon's impeachment if
he should be found to have been "negligent" in the care of the White House
tapes.

The panel examining the erased June 20 tape reported to Sirica on January 15, 1974. It unanimously found that at least five, and possibly as many as nine, "separate and contiguous" erasures had been made by hand-operated controls. When one of the Watergate prosecutors asked if the erasures had been accidental, an expert testified that "it would have to be an accident that was repeated at least five times." Assistant Press Secretary Gerald Warren told reporters on January 16 that the President could in no way be implicated in the tape gap, basing his conclusion "on many discussions" he had held with Nixon. The common defense for the President centered on his vaunted mechanical incompetence. Gerald Ford, for example, knew that the President "wasn't adroit mechanically." The President's new lawyer, James St. Clair, told one of the experts that he would have to talk to "his own experts"—apparently forgetting that the panel had been selected with White House cooperation.[27]

Jaworski attempted to continue the investigation of the tape gap, but both he and the FBI met determined White House resistance. Buzhardt at first consented to a brief FBI interview but then refused further discussions. Repeated efforts by FBI agents to interview Woods, Haig, Ziegler, and Stephen Bull—those with access to the tapes—met with repeated refusals. By March it was clear: the President no longer would tolerate any intra-branch investigations of himself and his staff. It should have been a warning to Jaworski.[28]

James Kilpatrick, a prominent conservative columnist and Nixon loyalist, was satisfied, if St. Clair was not. Nixon's supporters, Kilpatrick wrote, had to confront the "monstrous idea . . . that their President is indeed a crook." The expert testimony could not be "blinked away"; the erasures were deliberate. Kilpatrick had "blinked away" a variety of charges against the President—the Cambodian bombing, the alleged cover-up of Watergate, the overtures to Judge Byrne, the "extortion" of campaign contributions—but the erasures were different: evidence had been knowingly destroyed, and if Nixon could be implicated in any way, "he is done for." The President alone was responsible for the preservation of the evidence; he would have to answer for its destruction. "I want to believe my President is not a crook— but only Richard Nixon himself can dispel the idea now," Kilpatrick concluded. For his part, Jaworski saw the tape-gap incident as a blessing of sorts, for he thought it made the White House realize it could not afford more such hostile public reactions toward tampering with evidence.[29]

The President quickly realized around the same time that "something worse" than the tape gap had happened. Public questions about Nixon's taxes that surfaced in the fall of 1973 prompted IRS Commissioner Donald Alexander to order an audit of his tax forms. The tax payments showed striking changes.

In 1969 Nixon paid more than $72,000, but in the next three years, while serving as President, he paid taxes of $792.81, $878.03, and $4,298.17, respectively. His income had dropped sharply after he left his law practice, it was true, but his reduced payments primarily resulted from a gift of his vice-presidential papers to the National Archives. The problem here was a simple one: the President and his lawyers had falsified dates on the deed of gift to comply with changed laws. The tampering was costly, for the IRS determined in April 1974 that Nixon owed $476,431 in back taxes and interest.[30] The political costs were incalculable.

When Nixon first met Donald Alexander in May 1973, shortly after appointing him Commissioner of Internal Revenue, he told him to do his job "well, and do it honestly." The President never discussed the tax system, or any individual's taxes, with Alexander—but Haig "bawled out" Alexander for some of his actions. Alexander knew that Nixon had tried to fire him on several occasions, although Secretary of the Treasury George Shultz firmly supported him.[31] Alexander was a loyal Republican and an admirer of the President; he was not, however, the kind of IRS Commissioner that President Nixon and his aides often discussed in private, fantasizing an official who would blindly follow Nixon's bidding to settle old political scores.

On December 31, 1969, Congress passed a tax-reform act, following the Administration's wishes. On its own, Congress included a provision eliminating deductions for gifts of private papers. Lyndon Johnson's Commissioner of Internal Revenue alerted the former President's staff and urged that Congress be persuaded to delete the provision. The effort failed, but a compromise provided that gifts made before July 25, 1969 still could be deducted. Nixon had completed a lawful transfer of papers to the National Archives by December 30, 1968. The papers were hurriedly appraised and valued at $80,000, almost all of which Nixon deducted for the tax year 1968. Early in 1969, John Ehrlichman told the President that he should continue to take deductions for more papers. "Good," the President replied on the memo.

Nixon's vice-presidential papers were sent to the Archives on March 26–27, 1969. Of the 1,200 boxes containing the papers, more than 200 contained only invitations to speaking engagements and social affairs. Nixon's lawyer later claimed that he and an appraiser met on April 8 and visited the Archives to make an appraisal. The lawyers executed a deed of gift, supposedly dated April 21, 1969, the day the President sent his tax-reform message to Congress. But in fact the lawyers and the appraiser had not met at that time—indeed, the appraiser never viewed the papers until November 3, 1969. After a few brief visits to survey the material, he established a value of $2 million for Nixon's papers. In the meantime, Congress had eliminated the deduction, but one of the President's lawyers decided that the papers effectively had been given in March 1969, and therefore qualified for

Watergate Special Prosecutor Archibald Cox with reporters just hours before his dismissal, October 1973. (*Washington Star*)

Leon Jaworski, Cox's successor. (*Washington Star*)

Presidential lawyer Charles Alan Wright, Senator Ervin, Nixon, Senator Baker, and Haig, just prior to Cox's firing. (National Archives)

Newly appointed Attorney General William Saxbe (left), Nixon, and Solicitor General Robert Bork after the "Saturday Night Massacre." (National Archives)

House Judiciary Committee Chairman Peter Rodino (left) and Committee Counsel John Doar, May 1974. (*Washington Star*)

James St. Clair, Nixon's lawyer during the impeachment process, May 1974. (National Archives)

Nixon and Anwar Sadat in Egypt, June 1974, just after passing beneath banner proclaiming "We Trust Nixon." (National Archives)

Senators Hugh Scott and Barry Goldwater and House Republican leader John Rhodes, after discussing impeachment and resignation with the President, August 7, 1974. (National Archives)

Pro- and anti-Nixon demonstrators in front of the White House on the night of Nixon's resignation announcement, August 8, 1974. (*Washington Star*)

Rose Mary Woods, the "fifth Nixon" and the President's personal secretary, on the day of Nixon's resignation. (National Archives)

Nixon and family at the East Room farewell ceremony, August 9, 1974. (National Archives)

Nixon's departure. (National Archives)

Vice President and Mrs. Gerald Ford return to the White House after Nixon's departure, August 9, 1974. (National Archives)

the deduction. He consulted with the appraiser, and they now established the papers' net worth at $576,000.

In April 1970, the lawyers prepared a new schedule of valuation to accompany a deed of gift for the papers, and back-dated both to March 27, 1969. The President was shown the forms, reputedly said, "That's fine," and signed the documents. There is no evidence that he knew of the back-dating. But later a Republican staff member of the House Judiciary Committee informed his superiors that Nixon unquestionably attended to details of his own tax returns: he had discussed deductions for donated documents with Lyndon Johnson; his law partner had written him a lengthy memo about the matter; he had signed the deed in 1969 for such a 1968 deduction. In addition, Ehrlichman had relayed instructions in June 1969 regarding Nixon's desire for more deductions for his papers, and the President had met the appraiser to discuss their value. While congressmen focused on whether or not Nixon had violated the tax laws, they carefully skirted the more fundamental question of treating public papers as private property.

Questions regarding the President's taxes dovetailed with discussions of government expenditures for his houses in San Clemente, California, and Key Biscayne, Florida. The General Services Administration had spent more than $1.2 million on house and ground "improvements" at the two estates. Nixon initially claimed that the work had been done for security reasons. But subsequent investigations showed that he himself, not the Secret Service, had requested the work and that a large part of the cost had no security justification, including money spent on a fireplace exhaust fan, a new shuffleboard court, a sewage system, brass lanterns, and a gazebo. Modern presidents are away from the White House a good deal of the time, and Nixon may have established the most extraordinary record of all. Between 1969 and 1972, he spent 195 days in California and 157 in Florida—nearly one-fourth of his first term. When reports of the expenditures on his retreats were first made public, Ron Ziegler denounced them as unjust, unfair, and irrelevant "to our way of life in this country."

Pressure increased for a public accounting of Nixon's taxes and expenditures. On July 29, 1973, Tax Analysts and Advocates, a public-interest law organization, apparently received information on the deed of papers and demanded an investigation. News also leaked regarding the President's home improvements and small tax payments. Finally, on December 8, Nixon disclosed his tax returns for 1969–72 and an audit of his private finances since 1969. During that time, he had become a millionaire. He admitted that the gift of his papers and the sale of some California property raised questions, and he agreed to submit the matter to a Joint Committee on Internal Revenue Taxation, a group of senior members from the House and Senate tax committees. He also announced that he and Mrs. Nixon would contribute their San Clemente home to the nation after their deaths. Finally, he said that he would give the committee full access to all documents and, if necessary, "I will pay whatever tax may be due."

Several weeks earlier, speaking to newspaper editors at Disney World in Florida, the President admitted that he had made some mistakes but insisted that he had never profited from his years of public service. "I have never obstructed justice," he claimed. He welcomed a public scrutiny of his records, because "people have got to know whether their President is a crook." With no hesitation, he quickly and forcefully responded: "Well, I am not a crook. I earned everything I got." These words would haunt him the rest of his days.

The Joint Committee on Internal Revenue Taxation's staff report appeared in April 1974 and included the finding that the President owed nearly $500,000 in back taxes and interest. The staff copiously documented Nixon's tax affairs and subjected them to such scrutiny that they even found he had a right to take another $1,007 deduction for sales taxes and an additional $10 for gasoline taxes in 1972. The impact of the staff report further humiliated and disgraced the President, particularly as charges of personal corruption had stalked him before and because he had so moralistically preached against the chicanery of others.

In a statement issued on April 3, Nixon contended that his tax lawyers could make a successful case in his behalf, but since he had agreed to abide by the tax committee's judgment, he had ordered that payment be put through. Any errors in his returns, the statement concluded, were made by those to whom he had "delegated the responsibility for preparing his returns and were made without his knowledge and without his approval." "In law school I majored in tax law," Nixon had said in June 22, 1972 press conference, and he had added that as a lawyer, he did quite a bit of tax work. Neither remark was true, but once again Nixon implied that if only he had personally controlled matters, the results would have been different.

The President paid $284,000 in April 1974, but he did not pay the 1969 deficiency of nearly $150,000, because the statute of limitations had run out. Despite his promise to make it a gift to the nation, Nixon sold the San Clemente property in 1979 and shortly thereafter demanded that the government bear the cost of removing the Secret Service's "security improvements." Patriotism was his refuge, as he sent the General Services Administration a check for $2,300 to cover the cost of a flagpole he wished to retain on the estate. Richard Nixon bitterly recalled that the attacks on his "financial probity and integrity . . . hurt Pat most of all."[32]

Several days prior to the Cox dismissal, the Special Prosecutor's office had begun to move against corporations that had made illegal campaign contributions and engaged in other illegal activities on behalf of the President.

Much of this material had been developed in the later stages of the Senate Select Committee's investigation. On October 17, 1973, American Airlines pled guilty to a violation of the U.S. code on campaign contributions and was fined $5,000. The same day, the 3M Corporation similarly was fined $3,000, and a corporate officer was fined an additional $500. Before the year was out, Goodyear Tire & Rubber, Braniff Airways, Gulf Oil, Ashland Petroleum, Phillips Petroleum, and the Carnation Company submitted guilty pleas, as did a number of their officials, and all were duly fined. During the next year, another ten companies followed the same pattern. The most prominent was the American Ship Building Company, which was fined $20,000 in August 1974; its chairman, George M. Steinbrenner, received a $15,000 fine, the highest for any corporate official. Steinbrenner originally had been charged with five counts of illegal campaign contributions and four counts of obstruction of justice.

Steinbrenner, a longtime Republican, had switched to the Democrats in the early 1960s. By 1972, however, he was complaining to House Democratic leader Thomas O'Neill that Republican campaign officials had pressed him hard to contribute to the Nixon cause. Steinbrenner claimed that Maurice Stans pressured him to head up the Democrats for Nixon in Ohio, while Herbert Kalmbach suggested a formula according to which Steinbrenner wrote thirty-three separate checks for $3,000, each to be sent to a different Nixon campaign committee. In addition to his fines, Steinbrenner was suspended for two years from his presidency of the New York Yankees by baseball Commissioner Bowie Kuhn. Around the same time, a baseball player convicted of manslaughter received no penalty from the Commissioner; that activity, Kuhn noted, had happened in the off-season.[33] Apparently, Steinbrenner had written his checks between April and October.

Nixon's resiliency in the face of the Watergate crisis is difficult to measure. Outwardly, he appeared like King Canute, vainly sweeping back the sea. On May 5, 1974, Alexander Haig appeared on ABC's *Issues and Answers* and brashly asserted that for the past year, the President "has run this country and its business. . . . [H]e has done it successfully and I am confident that he will continue to." The work of the presidency went on, in ironic, but certainly unintended, confirmation of Nixon's earlier adage that the nation did not need a President for domestic affairs. Melvin Laird admitted that the President was "consumed with this other matter, but we functioned." Laird and his staff worked on the budget process and domestic legislation. Joint Chiefs of Staff Chairman Admiral Thomas Moorer thought little was different. The President had always been uninterested and lackadaisical about domestic affairs. In an emergency, however, Moorer thought the President was "decisive."

Other observers, however, saw a presidency adrift. Henry Kissinger later referred to the "collapse of executive authority due to Watergate." On a more personal note, he thought that Watergate had so affected the President's behavior as almost to undermine Kissinger's diplomatic efforts with Syria. Those efforts, of course, succeeded, making Kissinger's retrospective view altogether self-enhancing.

As early as April 1973, Kissinger thought that Watergate had grown "into bewilderment and frustration for those seeking to keep the government operating and into panic for those directly involved." He undoubtedly had a special frustration of his own. At that very time, Nixon had told Haldeman and Ehrlichman that William Rogers's resignation as Secretary of State must be delayed, despite Kissinger's eagerness for Rogers's departure and his own accession to the office. "[T]he hell with Henry on that," the President said; Kissinger had to be told that "there are bigger things here."

Kissinger's memoirs are ambiguous on the question of presidential paralysis during the period. At times, he portrays a president still in full command of his powers, determined to exercise the full range of his authority and expertise in foreign-policy matters. And yet, Kissinger also depicts a president who was bored by the most calamitous or momentous of international events, and who, to Kissinger's mind, often threatened to upset carefully balanced negotiating postures.[34]

After the Arabs instituted an oil embargo in late 1973, threatening America's supply of essential petroleum products, new confusion and distress swept the nation. Garment thought that the latest crisis might present an opportunity for the President to demonstrate leadership. The country needed, Garment told Nixon, "a sense of direction, [to know] that someone is in control, taking care of people's basic needs in a bewildering, even frightening time. . . . It's up to you to give people the feeling that someone's in charge." Nixon could not afford the appearance of excessive delegation of power, he declared. But Garment also realized that Watergate handicapped the President, and despite his clarion call for action, the President's lawyer remained pessimistic: "If you can make it through the next few months, you may be able to weather Watergate. I honestly don't know."

Garment urged the President to be "exceptionally tough," and to establish national priorities for allocation of scarce oil—even if doing so meant offending people by banning Sunday driving. He linked the energy crisis and Watergate by contending that the President's actions would determine his ultimate fate. If he did not act decisively, Garment warned Nixon, his critics would "say you were brooding over Watergate, paralyzed, unable to control your advisors, when you should have been thinking of the people's need, planning ahead, acting." In response to the Arab oil embargo, the President secured a lowered national speed limit and an extension of daylight savings time, traveled to California on a commercial jet, and reduced the number of lights on the national Christmas tree. He also delivered a nationwide address on the oil embargo. At the end of the talk, Nixon reiterated his intention of not resigning. He would, he said, continue to work sixteen to eighteen hours a day and make every effort to erase any doubts as to his integrity.[35] But he did little to allay the fears of an energy shortage—or to dissipate the increasing concern that Watergate had sorely crippled his presidency.

Up close, Garment and others saw Nixon as possessing an uncanny ability to compartmentalize, to segregate his responsibilities from his personal turmoil and anxieties over Watergate. Yet the brooding and paralysis that Garment had feared were exactly what some perceived—even such admirers as the new FBI Director, Clarence Kelley. Late in 1973, Kelley received a summons to the White House. It was his first meeting with Nixon since his appointment nearly six months earlier. He noted that the President appeared haggard and tired, but his most vivid impressions were of an empty desk and a small statue of Abraham Lincoln, as if, Kelley noted, to signify Nixon's identification with the integrity of a great president who, like him, was constantly under attack. Kelley remembered other meetings with Nixon, marked by crisp, concise conversation. Now, Nixon rambled and digressed. Abruptly, at one point, the President mentioned his taping, contending that his predecessors had done it extensively. Kelley was convinced that the President was "breaking down under enormous strain." Nixon raised the Watergate investigation periodically, but never in any probing way. Finally, the President asked Kelley if he enjoyed his position and then expressed great pleasure with his work. Kelley never understood the purpose of the meeting, their last.[36]

Mordechai Gazit, the Director General of the Israeli Foreign Ministry, accompanied Israeli Premier Golda Meir to the White House following the Yom Kippur War in the fall of 1973. Nixon reminded them that he had resupplied the Israeli army during the war, sent a new aid request for Israel to Congress, and declared a military alert to keep the Russians out of the Middle East. He then told his visitors that he would not be able to do so again. At first, Gazit thought that Nixon intended to project a toughness to the Israelis in order to stimulate the negotiating process. But Gazit eventually understood that the President simply meant that he no longer had the political power to act so decisively, clearly recognizing his deteriorating situation.[37]

After mid-1973 the news summaries prepared daily for the President no longer evoked his elaborate annotations. Kissinger noted their absence as well as the lack of comments on memoranda he addressed to the President. Once the President returned a memo with every option box checked, defeating the purpose of the paper.[38] Nixon's presidential papers, so filled with multiple daily memoranda to Haldeman, Ehrlichman, Colson, and others from 1969–72, only rarely provide similar documents as the Watergate phenomenon gripped the White House after May 1973. Richard Nixon himself seems to disappear from his presidential papers.

Armand Hammer, a prominent businessman with longstanding ties to Kremlin leaders, met Soviet President Leonid Brezhnev in Moscow on November 17, 1973. Hammer reported that Brezhnev was concerned about Nixon's Watergate problems. The Soviet leader could not understand the fuss. "You have your own ways and, speaking confidentially, I must confess I don't understand them," Brezhnev said. He told Hammer he was worried about Nixon: "A man can only stand so much and then he's bound to break down." Brezhnev sanctimoniously promised not to take advantage of Nixon; he would not "jump on him, as others are."[39]

Brezhnev's admiration for Nixon may or may not have been genuine, but foreign powers, friend and foe alike, prefer a known quantity. The Soviets had found that they could do business with Nixon, in large part operating on the theory that a Republican president had less need to concern himself with right-wing reactions to any overtures to Russia. Now, as a British television report in May 1973 noted, the Soviets and China might welcome a scandal in "capitalism's high place," but like Britain, they preferred a strong government in the United States. The Japanese similarly worried that Nixon's undoing would be "most unfortunate" for the "world at large." An Austrian commentator saw the growing impasse in the American government as upsetting the world balance of power. Worse, he said, the preoccupation with domestic affairs only meant an abandonment of concern for American world responsibilities. The President's foreign admirers gloomily predicted more "foreign political consequences of [his] dwindling of power." After the events of October and November, the U.S. Information Service post in London reported to Washington in its "psychological assessment" that Nixon's credibility had dropped sharply as the Watergate situation "became ever more muddled."[40]

The President's political standing with Congress had eroded to such an extent that the legislative branch now boldly asserted itself in foreign-policy matters. Congress ordered a cutoff of the Cambodian bombing effective in August 1973, and in November passed the War Powers Act. That law obligated the president to notify Congress of armed action within forty-eight hours of its onset, and further required him to withdraw military forces within sixty days unless Congress provided an extension. In Richard Nixon's version of history, the War Powers Act and the limitation on the Cambodian bombing sent a clear signal to the Vietnamese enemy and directly led to the Communist takeover of Indochina by April 1975. Beyond Vietnam, he complained that the act made it "impossible" for a president to act "swiftly and secretly." Nixon blamed Congress, the media, and the "peace movement" for harnessing the president to "Marquis of Queensberry rules in a world where good manners are potentially fatal hindrances."[41]

Watergate indubitably fostered a favorable legislative climate for longtime critics of the Vietnam war and of broad presidential military powers. The House approved the War Powers resolution just one day after Nixon again claimed executive privilege for his tapes. Two days later, the Senate concurred, on the heels of Nixon's statement that he would not "wallow in Watergate." Nixon promptly vetoed the bill, charging that Congress had wiped out nearly two hundred years of precedents justifying presidential initiatives. Between the first House vote on October 12, and the veto override on November 7, thirty-three members switched their votes. The Saturday Night Massacre was very much on their minds. House Democratic floor leader Clement Zablocki (D-WI) said that the "time was ripe," and he pointedly acknowledged the influence of the Cox firing and the tapes question. Zablocki also offered a powerful defense of the War Powers Act's constitutionality. Senator John Tower (R-TX) underlined the same point, when he recognized that Congress found itself swept up "in the hysteria of Watergate and desire to punish . . . this President." Tower warned Congress not to "make the power of the President . . . a victim of our emotions on Watergate."[42] Tower's distinction between "this" President and "the" President was an interesting one. Richard Nixon repeatedly tried—without success—to save himself through the same distinction.

The inability of Henry Kissinger and many foreign observers to make the linkage between domestic confidence in the President and the strength of American foreign policy is striking. Nearly a century earlier, Lord Bryce had made the connection. Americans needed to know, he said, the worst as well as the best of themselves—and it was important that all the world should know. Bryce perceived the enormous confidence Americans had in their ability to deal openly with their flaws. He recognized that Americans believed in such procedures to the extent that they thought it would be impossible ever to mistake their own true interests; to believe otherwise, he noted, "seems to them a sort of blasphemy against the human intelligence and its Creator."

But there were limits to what Bryce labeled the "peculiar buoyancy" and "airy hopefulness" of Americans. The conflict surrounding the President began to resemble a civil war. While ordinary citizens were not on the verge of marching to Bull Run, powerful institutions—the presidency, Congress, the courts, the media—fought like scorpions in a bottle. But the combatants settled on one adversary. Events in the late fall of 1973 unleashed powerful tides against the President. When *Time* called for Nixon's resignation on

November 12, the effect was startling. Henry Luce, the founder of *Time*, had regarded Nixon as his special protégé, his hope for the vibrant leader so desperately needed by the Republican Party. The magazine's editors now thought that Nixon and the nation had "passed a tragic point of no return." Alexander Haig complained that the *Time* editorial was like "being hit in the face with a cold fish."[43]

The real danger for the President came not from self-appointed public spokesmen, however, but from the nation's elected representatives. For the second time in the republic's history, Congress prepared for the impeachment of a sitting president. A curious consensus for action began to emerge. Vice President Ford had told reporters on December 12 that if the House failed to vote impeachment by the end of April, then clearly the move to impeach the President was "partisan." Laird announced his White House resignation on December 19. He urged a House vote by March 15—it "would be a healthy thing," he said—in order to clear the way for the fall elections. Ford and Laird, ever the party loyalists, had their own cause; they didn't want congressional Republicans running for election to be in the shadow of Watergate. The senior members of the House Judiciary Committee in both parties had a similar understanding of political needs, as they announced plans for reporting the results of their inquiry to the full House in April.[44]

Doubtless, an early decision by the committee served a variety of political purposes. But the existence of the tapes generated an external influence that neither side could ignore. The case for or against the President in the arena of public opinion hinged on what the tapes could show he did or did not say. In that sense, the House Committee had no control over the calendar of Nixon's ultimate fate.

When the House launched its impeachment inquiry against Andrew Johnson in 1868, it appointed a select committee to consider the matter. In 1973 the Democratic leadership left the matter to the Judiciary Committee. A variety of explanations have been offered, but the most consistent seems to have been a reluctance to circumvent the normal lines of jurisdiction—in other words, entrenched interests. The most simple reason was that Speaker Carl Albert was in a bind. He could not afford to appoint a special committee that might have made him the beneficiary of its deliberations, since Albert, as Speaker of the House, was in the line of presidential succession, and the nation at the time was without a Vice President.

In truth, the House Judiciary Committee was not highly regarded by the Democratic leadership. For years it had been the fiefdom of its longtime Chairman, Emanuel Celler (D-NY). Celler had a reputation—extending from Democratic leader Thomas O'Neill to the Justice Department's Henry Petersen—of being excessively cautious, even obstructionist. According to Petersen, Celler consistently had been an obstacle to needed legislative reforms. Peter Rodino, his successor, may have been even less respected. Rodino had first been elected in 1948, and his primary legislative achievement had been to establish Columbus Day as a national holiday. Although chairman of a major committee, Rodino was not an insider among House leaders; further- more, he never developed the influence or power of Celler. At the outset of the committee's hearings, according to O'Neill, Rodino "needed prodding, and on more than one occasion I had to light a fire under his seat."[45] Iron- ically, Rodino's innate caution created a drift and inertia in the committee's proceedings which prevented the early decision sought by others. That de- velopment undoubtedly was unintended; nevertheless, the passage of time beyond the intended spring vote, and the introduction of decisive evidence, made for a case that eventually proved irresistible.

In the beginning, the regular Judiciary Committee staff assumed the bur- den of organizing and preparing materials for the inquiry. Soon, however, new people were added to work exclusively on the impeachment project. In early November, Rodino solicited law schools for suggestions for additional staff. Richard Cates, a former prosecutor then teaching part-time at the Uni- versity of Wisconsin Law School and highly regarded as a trial lawyer, responded, and through Robert Kastenmeier (D–WI) received an interview with the committee's Chief Counsel and then with Rodino. He was hired in late November. Cates's role was to "evaluate the evidence," as Rodino wished, and determine whether a case could be made for impeachment. Within several weeks, working largely from the findings of the Senate Select Committee, Cates had focused the questions regarding the President's al- leged "high crimes and misdemeanors" and reported that a case could be made. A onetime legislator himself, Cates impressed the members and the regular staff of the Rodino Committee with his integrity and his lawyering skill. He eventually captured the respect and esteem of most members of the committee, cutting across party and ideological lines. But he lacked national stature, and at the outset he had been identified with the committee's liberal wing.

When President Nixon twice selected a Special Prosecutor, he found it imperative to appoint Democrats, whether the liberal Cox or the more con- servative Jaworski. Appearances, as well as substance, dictated those choices. Rodino found himself in a similar position. On December 19 he announced the selection of John M. Doar as Chief Counsel for the committee's majority. Doar, a Republican originally from Wisconsin but then practicing in New York, had served in the Civil Rights Division of the Justice Department in the Kennedy and Johnson Administrations. He seemed ideal: a Republican who had worked with Democrats in nonpartisan causes. Typically, Rodino procrastinated on the appointment, finally yielding to O'Neill's "order" to act before Christmas.[46]

The President's lawyers, already besieged by numerous subpoenas and hampered by the inadequacy of their support staff—to say nothing of their uncooperative client—had little time or inclination to consider the prospect of impeachment, which seemed at that juncture politically and constitutionally remote. Their "real world" centered on court orders, briefs, and relations with the new Special Prosecutor. But one important quarter of the government began to think seriously about the unthinkable.

Robert Dixon, Assistant Attorney General, Office of Legal Counsel in the Department of Justice—a position once occupied by William Rehnquist— was an especially thoughtful man. Widely respected in and out of the Justice Department, Dixon was a consummate professional. Elliot Richardson had called on him for advice when confronted with the legal question of whether the President could dismiss Cox. (Dixon advised him in the affirmative.) Now, he found himself thinking about the President's legal position, and especially about his defense. Dixon and his staff puzzled over the problem of which side the Attorney General should appear for if the President were impeached. Did the Justice Department, or any part of the government, have to provide Nixon's legal defense? Good lawyering required good anticipation. Dixon had to—and did—consider the possibility of impeachment by late 1973.[47]

Following Andrew Johnson's one-vote acquittal in his impeachment trial in the Senate in May 1868, contemporary politicians and subsequent historians alike condemned the impeachment proceeding as brutally partisan and thus cast opprobrium over the constitutional mandate for the public questioning and removal of presidents. The framers of the Constitution, however, had carefully crafted safeguards against executive tyranny. After all, their colonial and revolutionary experience justified suspicion of executive power. The ultimate protection, for the Framers, lay in the time-honored English practice of impeaching executive officers—that is, holding a public inquest into their conduct of public office, as Alexander Hamilton wrote in *Federalist* 65. Yet impeachment had a slender history in the United States. The first great impeachment trial, that of Supreme Court Justice Samuel Chase in 1807, appeared designed more to satisfy the partisanship of the Jeffersonians than to examine Chase's improprieties. The Johnson and Chase trials historically had been treated as aberrations, not models.[48] In early 1973, impeachment was perceived as analogous to nuclear weapons: available, yet too dangerous to use. But the ultimate weapon suddenly proved alive and well in Washington as 1973 drew to a close.

XVII

"FIGHT"

TAPES AND INDICTMENTS,
JANUARY–MAY 1974

For Richard Nixon, the opening of the new year heralded the "campaign of my life." The passing of the old year kindled introspection in him, as it had a year earlier. "Do I fight all out or do I now begin the long process to prepare for a change, meaning, in effect, resignation?" he asked himself. The President reflected not just on his personal fate but on his obligations, as he saw them, to constitutional government. A resignation, he believed, would establish a dangerous precedent that later Congresses might use as leverage against presidents. That path conveniently would relieve Congress of its constitutional responsibility for impeachment. The course was obvious: *"fight."* Fight, otherwise the media and Congress would become overly dominant, and "our foreign policy initiatives" would collapse, Nixon thought. But characteristically, the President exposed his personal motives; resignation, he realized, "admits guilt."

Nixon was determined to conduct the Watergate war with style and substance. "Above all else: Dignity, command, faith, head high, no fear, build a new spirit, drive, act like a President, act like a winner," he wrote. "Opponents are savage destroyers, haters. Time to use full power of the President to fight overwhelming forces arrayed against us."[1]

But Nixon also realized that he must absolve himself of guilt. And most immediately, that involved his dealings with the Special Prosecutor, who continued to demand presidential tapes and documents. The tapes had become the tarbaby of the confrontation. For one side, they loomed large as evidence of criminality and, more important, as authority for legitimating the growing assault on the President's standing. For Nixon's cause, those very reasons made it imperative to resist the demands.

The President's combativeness surfaced in his State of the Union message on January 30, 1974. He sounded the incumbent's familiar chord: America was better off after five years of his Administration. He painted a dismal picture of the state of the nation in 1968: at war in Southeast Asia, alienated from China, its cities burning, its college campuses like battlegrounds for political rather than intellectual encounter, crime and drugs on the increase—all in sharp contrast, the President proudly noted, to where he had led the nation since. But what was at stake was the future—and the present. Nixon offered the standard prescriptions for ensuring national greatness, but he also inserted a "personal word" regarding the lingering issue of the day. It was time, he said, to bring the matter to an end. "One year of Watergate is enough."

Nixon claimed that he had given the Special Prosecutor "all the material that he needs to conclude his investigations and to proceed to prosecute the guilty and to clear the innocent." He promised to cooperate with the House Judiciary Committee, consistent with his "responsibilities to the Office of the Presidency of the United States." He would not, he insisted, do anything to weaken the office for his successors; moreover, he had "no intention whatever of ever walking away from the job that the people elected me to do for the people of the United States."

Two days later, Mike Mansfield delivered an extraordinary reply from the Democrats and Congress. Often criticized for his low-key, nonconfrontational, at times even passive style, Mansfield uncharacteristically challenged the President. He noted that the Democrats had increased their majority in 1972 but shrewdly avoided claiming a partisan mandate; instead, he focused on institutional conflicts and institutional prerogatives. The *congressional* majority reflected a mandate, he said, "to reinforce the nation's system of checks and balances" and to reverse longstanding trends. Specifically, he cited evidence of "an ominous shift to one-branch government"; executive secrecy in the name of national security; executive impoundment of appropriated funds; executive assaults on the media; executive preemption of authority over the federal budget; multiplying expressions of executive contempt for Congress, and thus, by extension, for the people; executive usurpation of changes in basic organizational structure; and illegal invasions of personal privacy by executive agents.

Mansfield's charges were reminiscent of such historic constitutional conflicts as those in 1868 against Andrew Johnson as well as of seventeenth-century British struggles involving royal prerogatives and the role of Parliament. Mansfield conceded that Nixon must decide on resignation by himself, but impeachment belonged to Congress, and he insisted that Congress would handle its responsibility "properly, fully, and deliberately." He praised the work of the Special Prosecutor and the courts, but the Majority Leader challenged the President's call for a quick settlement: "there are no judicial shortcuts," he said. Mansfield's rejoinder sharply reminded the President of the constitutional dictates for separation of powers and functions in the American system of governance.

Meanwhile, the new Special Prosecutor had begun to listen to the President's taped conversations and soon concluded that Nixon had been involved in the cover-up of the widening scandal. Leon Jaworski heard how Richard Nixon schooled his aides to commit perjury and how he moved people around as "chessmen," "to cover this thing up." Jaworski was "stunned" as he realized that he was in "an entirely different affair" from what he had anticipated.[2]

On January 30, the same day that President Nixon declared that "one year of Watergate is enough," the grand jury requested an opportunity to meet with him. Empaneled on June 5, 1972, the jurors had had nearly eighteen months of living with Watergate. They had listened to the evidence that various prosecutors had compiled; they had heard the President's men, from Haldeman to Dean, testify regarding their own culpability—and also that of the President. The jurors had heard the case prepared by the U.S. Attorney's office against the Watergate burglars. They had developed some intimacy in that early relationship, an intimacy not quite matched by the more elaborate structure of the Special Prosecution Force. The jurors knew in January 1974 that the new prosecutors were about to make recommendations; yet, they felt some frustration, because one man—the President of the United States—might have information "highly relevant" to their inquiry. Aided by the prosecutors, the foreman wrote to the President requesting that he appear before the grand jury—in any appropriate place.

The request was no surprise to the White House. Jaworski had already suggested the possibility to James St. Clair, the newly arrived special counsel to the President, who immediately rejected it. Instead, St. Clair recommended that the grand jurors submit written questions. When the jurors rejected his advice, St. Clair replied that the President would not see the jury, citing the independence of his office and the press of his duties. He could not resist a final jab at the proceedings, expressing satisfaction that the jurors were "in the closing stages" of an investigation that had so far consumed more than eighteen months.[3]

The grand jury request was but a pinprick amid the legal challenges assaulting the White House and its new counsel, St. Clair. For the next eight months, he directed a small staff of fifteen lawyers, digesting massive amounts of materials from the Special Prosecutor, from the defense attorneys in the various pending trials, from the House Judiciary Committee, and from such investigative agencies as the FBI. St. Clair and his group confronted a disparity of more than twenty-five to one in the number of lawyers arrayed against them. He saw himself as "engaged to represent the presidency, not the President." It was, of course, a distinction that fit the legal and political strategy the President himself had dictated for nearly a year.[4]

St. Clair had served in 1954 as an assistant to Joseph Welch, the lawyer who represented the U.S. Army in its notorious controversy with Senator Joseph McCarthy. Years later, by then a senior partner in a distinguished Boston law firm, St. Clair represented the Reverend William Sloan Coffin when the government tried Coffin and famed pediatrician Dr. Benjamin Spock for their anti–Vietnam war activities. By some, St. Clair was seen as "all case and no cause." It was a description intended as pejorative, but it came as flattery to those who preferred a lawyer committed to the work at hand rather than to philosophy. Later, the President described St. Clair as a man who did not understand the public-relations aspects of the case; Jaworski, however, complained that St. Clair was too much a public-relations man. The competing views left St. Clair satisfied that the truth lay in between and showed that he had done his work. He believed there was a certain futility in attempting to cultivate the media; trying to co-opt them, he thought, often provided the opposite result. "My role was as a lawyer. It was not as a media representative." In fact, however, St. Clair did hold press conferences, in which he sought to explain the President's legal and constitutional positions.[5]

St. Clair fared as poorly as his predecessors in his access to the President. According to the President's appointments secretary and the logs, he rarely saw Nixon alone. When the two met, Haig usually was present. Haig indeed supervised St. Clair closely; according to St. Clair, he saw the Chief of Staff "perhaps on an hourly basis." Most crucial, St. Clair had no regular access to the White House tapes, the most important evidence in the case. This remained Buzhardt's area. Some in the Special Prosecutor's office believed that St. Clair did not listen to tapes in order to protect his deniability. But that may be off the mark. In June, an aide to Haig wrote to him that St. Clair had called, contending that Haig had approved access for St. Clair's staff people to listen to a tape. "[C]an I therefore deliver these tapes?" the aide queried. "Disapprove," Haig curtly responded.[6]

Publicly, the White House stated that St. Clair had replaced Buzhardt, who had been promoted to Counsel to the President. In fact, however, Buzhardt continued to work closely on Watergate matters, especially auditing and safeguarding the tapes. Nixon trusted him for that work more than any other lawyer; in that sense, Buzhardt was irreplaceable. But Buzhardt had his frustration with the President, sometimes requesting an appointment a dozen times in a day and then failing to gain one. His wife remembered that Buzhardt would work fifteen to nineteen hours, preparing transcripts which he would submit to Nixon, who would then make changes. Charles Lichenstein, a White House aide at the time, watched Buzhardt at work and thought him honest but incompetent, overworked yet incapable of delegating tasks. Nixon undoubtedly had the man he wanted. Jaworski believed that Buzhardt served "the purpose of delaying, and he was pretty good at it." Early in 1973, Sam Ervin grudgingly praised Buzhardt for his work in another area, saying that if he had commanded Robert E. Lee's armies, the Civil War "would still be lasting" because Buzhardt was so "very skillful in the art of obstruction."[7]

In November 1973, the President had indicated to friendly congressmen that he might release some tape summaries. He assigned Pat Buchanan to review the transcripts, particularly with an eye to refuting John Dean. Buchanan's report, the President remembered, reassured him that Dean "had lied" about Nixon's role in the cover-up. Nixon knew that the March 21 tape concerning the cover-up "would cause an uproar," yet he believed that the nation ultimately would remember that he had acted decisively after that meeting, and what he had said would prove unimportant. Other White House aides disagreed, notably Ziegler, Garment, Ken Clawson, Bryce Harlow, and Richard Moore. Pity, Nixon wrote, that they could not hear all the tapes, for surely then they would be convinced of his rectitude. Significantly, the President claimed that the concern of his advisers over the possible political reaction to the tapes clinched his decision. Sometime in December Nixon decided not to release any tapes. His notes for December 23 were headed by his own question: "Last Christmas here?"[8]

On December 19 the Senate Select Committee issued three subpoenas for additional presidential materials. The committee's anxiety for tapes stemmed from a desire to publish as complete a report as possible, but pride also was at stake. Committee interrogators had uncovered the existence of the tapes; Chief Counsel Sam Dash bristled when the House Judiciary Committee refused to share the tapes it had obtained—although he had turned over all of his work product to John Doar and the House committee. The President promptly rejected the Senate committee's subpoenas, arguing in his familiar fashion that he must protect the confidentiality of the executive against incursions by another branch. Federal judges subsequently rejected the Senate subpoena, provoking Ervin to complain about judicial interference with proper legislative processes.[9]

After several delays, including revelations of the missing tapes and the 18½-minute gap, Buzhardt delivered seven tapes to Judge Sirica on November 26, one month after the President's lawyer had agreed to comply with the subpoena. The Special Prosecutor's office was pleased with this progress, and after Sirica listened to the tapes *in camera*, the prosecutors received them on December 21. Before releasing the material to the Special Prosecutor, the judge withheld some tapes, thus sustaining some of the President's claims of executive privilege. Jaworski and his staff immediately realized that the tapes had strengthened their evidence against the President's men; what was more, they believed they now had a case against Nixon—and it was in the tapes. Jaworski himself told Haig around Christmas that he believed Nixon guilty, a remark that left Haig "surprised" and also "visibly shaken," according to Jaworski. Haig tried to dissuade Jaworski from his conclusion, but the Special Prosecutor told him that was impossible. After this, Jaworski recalled, Nixon "got tremendously jittery," and much of the earlier spirit of cooperation dissipated.

Jaworski conducted his White House negotiations exclusively with Haig. Under Haldeman, the paper flow made it clear that the Chief of Staff executed the President's wishes. Haldeman usually carried out those orders while exercising a minimum of discretion. No similar documentary record has been made available for Haig's service. But some of the President's onetime collaborators and longtime friends, such as John Mitchell, believed that Haig operated with far less constraint and much more discretionary room than his predecessor. Several years after the events, when Jaworski read Nixon's memoirs, he was uncertain whether Haig had always fully conveyed his views and messages to the President.[10]

Jaworski and Haig met in the White House on December 21. Haig told the Special Prosecutor that the March 21 tape of Nixon's conversation with Dean was "terrible beyond description." Jaworski concurred, adding that he found it "unbelievable." But Haig insisted that "the White House lawyers" believed no criminality attached to the President's behavior. Jaworski disagreed and suggested that the White House hire a good criminal lawyer. Shortly afterward, Haig called Jaworski at his Houston home, again reporting that Buzhardt found no criminality involved because there was no overt act following the meeting of March 21. Haig and Buzhardt may have invented their own version of criminal law; nevertheless Jaworski again warned the Chief of Staff to get a criminal lawyer. Jaworski, no stranger to criminal wrongdoing, was appalled at the stupidity of maintaining the taping system when such "an evil approach and wrongful conduct by the President" had been taking place. "I would have turned off the system," Jaworski thought.

The Special Prosecutor returned for a secret White House meeting on December 27. Haig now told him that the President had selected St. Clair as his special counsel. Haig again raised the question of the March 21 transcript, giving Jaworski a White House version as well as Nixon's interpretation of that conversation. When Jaworski told the Chief of Staff that the tape would be played to the grand jury, Haig expressed deep concern over its effect. Apparently Haig's confidence had begun to evaporate. Earlier, when the President told him in a taped June 4, 1973 meeting (heard by Jaworski) that "that damn conversation of March 21st" presented a problem, Haig, faintly audible, apparently said, "I think we can handle that."[11]

The President's surrender of the seven tapes on November 26 convinced the Watergate Special Prosecution Force of his guilt. The tapes indicated the probability that other presidential conversations might substantially increase the evidence against Nixon and his colleagues. Accordingly, in January 1974, the prosecutors requested twenty-five more taped conversations from the White House. When Jaworski met St. Clair on January 22, the President's lawyer gave no definitive answer to that request, but within a few days, Haig told Jaworski that Nixon had decided not to release any more documents or tapes. St. Clair's formal answer on February 4 flatly stated "the President's view" that he had furnished sufficient material. St. Clair suggested that Jaworski, rather than demand the tapes themselves, submit written interrog- atories concerning their contents, a tactic designed to forestall further litigation.

The State of the Union message spelled out Nixon's position: He had complied with the court order, and the Special Prosecutor had sufficient material. Further requests, he suggested, reflected only partisan and per- sonal enmities. Again, he had demonstrated his willingness that the affair be ended, and he had provided the means. The public posture served the private stonewalling. The President was in the fighting mood he had char- acterized in his New Year's notes. He knew he had to stop the flow of evidence. "I wanted to stop it. In the past I had made the grievous mistake of saying I was going to stop it but failing to do so. Then, after paying the political price for refusing, we would cave [in] when the pressure started to build. I regretted not having followed my instincts about this in the past and wanted to begin following them right away," he wrote. The moment was critical: "I even talked about destroying the tapes."[12]

Before Jaworski received the formal word from St. Clair of the Adminis- tration's refusal to release more tapes, Haig summoned him to the Executive Office Building on February 1. Haig told him that a "political" decision had been made to reject Jaworski's request—political in the sense that the President had to focus on the impeachment proceedings, which the White House apparently believed took precedence over the Special Prosecutor's work. It is not clear whether Nixon knew of the meeting; Jaworski's account of it emphasized Haig's concern that Jaworski not publicly state that the White House—and, in particular, Alexander Haig—had reneged on earlier promises of cooperation. After St. Clair had appeared in court in May to oppose Jaworski's claims for more tapes, Haig called Jaworski and said cryp- tically, "I needed to know where they were going and they needed to know where I was going." The two met on May 22 in the White House map room, and Haig reiterated how much he wanted Jaworski "to believe that no agreement had been broken by him."[13] Haig had begun to worry about his own future.

The real threat to the President's new defensive position came from the developing inquiry by the House Judiciary Committee. The majority and minority special counsels for the committee met St. Clair on February 11 to discuss access to evidentiary material. Two weeks later the committee requested forty-two tape recordings. A confrontation between Nixon and the committee was quite different from one with the Special Prosecutor. The House had an absolute constitutional right to consider impeachment; how far could the President interfere with, or fail to cooperate with, that process? Edward Hutchinson and Charles Wiggins (R–CA), the President's most ardent partisans within the House committee, had said in January that Nixon should comply with the committee's request for evidence. "Political reality," Wiggins said, would persuade the President not to resist a subpoena. At a press conference on February 25, the day the committee made its request, Nixon underlined his own dilemma: he realized that he must cooperate with the House, but he resorted again to citing his responsibilities to maintain the integrity of "the presidency."[14]

Jaworski made a rare blunder in a *New York Times* interview published on February 27, when he said that his office knew the full story of Watergate. In fact, Jaworski had said similar things before, and St. Clair had used the remarks to justify the President's rejection of additional tape requests. The grand-jury indictments on March 1 apparently reinforced the conviction at the White House that the Special Prosecutor no longer was a threat. In a March 6 press conference, Nixon noted Jaworski's public contention that he had the complete picture; in the meantime, the President would cooperate with the House committee by turning over all evidence he had provided the Special Prosecutor—ignoring the fact that the grand jury itself already had made such a provision. St. Clair pointedly made no reference to Jaworski's repeated requests for access to more material.[15]

The President expanded his public appearances and reiterated his position that the Special Prosecutor's and the House committee's requests amounted to fishing expeditions. Within a week in mid-March, he traveled to Chicago, Nashville, and Houston, where he spoke to business groups, attended the Grand Ole Opry, and tried to project a happy, confident mood. He played the piano, praised his wife, and handled a yo-yo; in the meantime, in response to a question at a broadcasters' convention, he refused to say whether he would comply with the House committee's request. At that meeting, Dan Rather, the CBS White House correspondent, rose to ask a question. The media executives greeted him with cheers and catcalls. "Are you running for something?" the President mischievously inquired. With impudence to match, Rather responded: "No sir, Mr. President, are you?"

* * *

Right-wing conservatives, long uncomfortable with Nixon on ideological grounds, began to assert themselves against him around this time. On March 19, Senator James Buckley (R-NY), one of their most prominent leaders, called for the President's resignation. Buckley's fellow congressional Republicans publicly criticized him; privately they harbored similar doubts. In his announcement, Buckley stole a march on Nixon's traditional defensive position. The Senator argued that a resignation would halt the "agonizing inch-by-inch . . . attrition" of presidential authority. Unless Nixon resigned, the President's power, Buckley said, would succumb "to the death of a thousand cuts"—a phrase that had become commonplace among Nixon's advisers. People had lost faith in the President's "credibility and moral authority," a loss "beyond repair," Buckley said. The President must sacrifice himself to save the presidency, an ironic twist of the very goal Nixon had established for himself. Later that day, the President mechanically insisted that he would not "run away" from the job he had been elected to do; to resign, he argued, might be "good politics but it would be bad statesmanship."[16] Buckley lost the point—that day.

Buckley's remarks affected other wings of the Republican Party. Five days later, Howard Baker urged the President to cooperate with the House committee. House Republican leader John Rhodes (AZ) told Nixon that his party's congressmen could not afford to defend him if he refused to submit evidence. Institutional loyalty and political common sense motivated both Baker and Rhodes. On March 28 the White House announced that ten of the forty-two tapes requested by the House committee did not exist, a remark that seemed to signal a change in posture. The President stopped making public appearances and issuing public rejections of the requests for the tapes; if impeachment were a real possibility, he could ill afford to lose the support of such key Republicans as Buckley, Baker, and Rhodes. The times were perilous: it was a week later that the Joint Congressional Committee on Internal Revenue Taxation revealed that Nixon owed nearly half a million dollars in back taxes and that he had made illegal, even fraudulent, deductions. The Judiciary Committee on April 4 demanded a reply to its request within five days. As the time expired, St. Clair wrote to the committee's Majority Counsel, John Doar, requesting more time and complaining about excessive demands. What seems clear is that during the last ten days of March and the first ten days of April, the President and his advisers made a decision to release new tape transcripts.

The Judiciary Committee may have spurred that decision when it voted 33–3 on April 11 to subpoena the requested material. Peter Rodino complained that St. Clair had been dilatory in cooperating, despite the President's promises that his special counsel would help the committee. Rodino also warned Nixon that he alone could not decide what evidence must be

produced. Five days later, Jaworski appeared before Sirica, seeking an order
to deliver sixty-four more taped conversations, and the judge issued a subpoena on April 18. St. Clair again requested more time: White House secretaries were frantically transcribing tapes. The task was a tedious one:
transcription, then a check by Buzhardt and St. Clair, and then one by Ziegler's aide, Diane Sawyer, who would look for "non-substantive problems,"
such as might be posed by the presence of obscenities. Finally, the President
himself examined the transcripts.[17] "Damage control" was the orthodox
jargon for the procedure. Somehow, in some way, Nixon and his advisers
believed, the manner of releasing the tapes still might serve their purpose.

Richard Nixon knew that his fate rested on the tapes. Perhaps he felt a bit
buoyed by the news, arriving the day before he announced the release of the
tapes, that his friends John Mitchell and Maurice Stans had been acquitted
in New York on charges that they had solicited illegal campaign contributions
and had attempted to block Securities and Exchange Commission investigation of the fugitive Robert Vesco. But that verdict could have afforded only
small comfort, considering the task before him.

As always, legal problems became political ones and thus required a special public-relations twist to ensure favorable understanding. Nixon spoke
on national television on April 29 to announce his decision to release the
tape transcripts. He appeared with a stack of blue notebooks allegedly containing tape transcripts but in fact amounting only to a stage prop, part of
the carefully contrived scenery for presidential appearances which also included, from time to time, family pictures and Lincoln busts, all designed
to foster a favorable illusion on behalf of the President.

Nixon's elaborate speech seemed tailored to establish his interpretation of
the tapes and to anticipate any negative reactions. What eventually appeared
was a 1,200-page book, liberally spaced, of fragmented conversations which
at times seemed incomprehensible or nonsensical when read in abstracted
form. The transcripts occasionally included the phrase "Material Unrelated
to Presidential Action Deleted." This material referred to judgments made
at the time solely by the White House, judgments which eventually proved
to have resulted in the omission of significant material. Unfortunately for
the President, however, the transcripts also contained some clearly repro-
duced unfavorable conversations and introduced the catch phrase "expletive
deleted."

In his speech, Nixon again said that the material now available would
"tell it all," a hardly veiled hint that he would resist demands for further
disclosures. He warned that the transcripts had rough edges, that they would
at first glance appear to make prophets of his critics. He had been reluctant
to release the materials, "not just because they will embarrass me and those

with whom I have talked—which they will—and not just because they will become the subject of speculation and even ridicule—which they will—and not just because certain parts of them will be seized upon by political and journalistic opponents—which they will." He worried most, he claimed, that the tapes threatened the degree of confidentiality so vital to the functioning of the presidency. Almost sheepishly, he also admitted that the transcripts were at odds with previous sworn testimony.

Nixon nevertheless insisted that the transcripts showed he had no prior knowledge of the Watergate break-in and that he was not aware of the cover-up until March 21, 1973. Again, he warned that Watergate kept him from more important tasks: "Every day absorbed by Watergate is a day lost from the work that must be done." Jaworski noted the President's eagerness to adopt the "good-guy attitude." With that, Nixon staked his "trust in the basic fairness of the American people," confident that they would see the records as only "fragmentary" remnants from a distant time, a time when the President had to cope with information he did not understand and which threatened his "hopes, goals, and plans for the people who had elected him as their leader." He knew he had only been "trying in that period to discover what was right and to do what was right."[18]

In a letter accompanying the transcripts, the President emphasized to the House Judiciary Committee that John Dean had withheld information from him until March 21, 1973. He glossed over the account of his September 15, 1972 meeting with Dean, in which he congratulated his aide for his work in containing revelations about the break-in. That interview, Nixon said, referred to Dean's dealings with the Democrats' civil suit and their attempts to exploit the burglary politically. The President's letter, in general, sought to establish the White House interpretation of the documents in the hope of creating a favorable climate of opinion.[19] But the transcripts were not an arcane bit of legislation requiring a lawyer's skill in interpretation. They were about to be public; their words—and their deletions—conveyed a meaning that lay citizens could develop for themselves.

In the long run for President Nixon, the devil was in the details of the transcripts; most immediately, however, their overall flavor and import further devastated his public standing and left him naked to the winds of criticism. The October firestorm left burning embers; the release of the tape transcripts in April and May rekindled the flames. It was another disaster.

The transcripts soon appeared as a paperback book and sold widely. Newspapers reprinted excerpts, usually depicting the seamier parts of presidential conversations. The television networks offered lengthy reports on the contents of the tapes. Several re-enacted the scenes of taped conversations, using the words of the transcripts. Eric Sevareid of CBS labeled the conversations a "moral indictment without known precedent." Even members of the President's party expressed outrage. Hugh Scott called the transcripts "shabby, disgusting, immoral." Senator Robert Packwood (R–OR) deplored the lack in the taped conversations of "even any token clichés about what is good for the people." Representative William Steiger (R–WI) deplored the President's lack "of any sense of moral outrage." Other Republicans thought that the disclosures represented a disaster for the President and the party. Elliot Richardson, referring to a White House appeal for Republican loyalty, bitingly called it "a prescription for suicide on the part of most Congressional candidates." Vice President Ford, although he still thought the President was innocent of any wrongdoing, was "a little disappointed" by the transcripts. Indeed, what could a Republican loyalist think when the September 15, 1972 transcript described the ranking Republican member of the House Banking and Currency Committee as an incompetent and a fool?

Some of the President's closest friends in the media were sorely perplexed. *New York Times* columnist William Safire thought that the transcripts revealed a man "guilty of conduct unbecoming a President." The transcripts illuminated Nixon's "dark side," his "sleazy" acts, his "fear" of personal confrontations—traits painfully familiar to Safire. Now, Safire thought, the President might save his position, but only because Congress would be satisfied with his "personal humiliation." Safire had responded with a measure of hope to Nixon's willingness to be forthcoming in releasing all the White House tapes; but alas, "the reaction after reading the poisonous fruit of his eavesdropping tree is (expletive deleted)!" Columnist Joseph Alsop, too, found the material "repellent"—but quickly added that crudeness was not an impeachable offense. Alsop thought that the nation must rise above any distaste for Nixon's character and language; the real question was whether he had engaged in criminal acts. He firmly believed that the tapes would exonerate the President.

But the President's loss of friends was more ominous. The *Los Angeles Times,* a longtime supporter, thought that "nothing short of impeachment . . . and trial" could resolve the question of Nixon's fitness to remain in office. Six months earlier, when demands for impeachment had first been made, the newspaper had believed the evidence insufficient. But the transcripts had changed everything, the *Times* editorialized on May 10: "Justice for the President and the nation now requires his impeachment."

The White House found ways to excuse even the character and language of the transcripts. White House speechwriter Father John McLaughlin criticized any notion that the tapes were amoral or immoral as "erroneous, unjust [with] elements of hypocrisy." He thought the President's language in the tapes constituted "good, valid, sound . . . emotional drainage." McLaughlin ecstatically celebrated the President's suffering as "beautiful," and insisted that "the more he suffers the more he becomes believable to me." Such feelings were not shared by all clergymen. Billy Graham, more in sadness than in anger, could not "but deplore the moral tone implied in these papers." He was dismayed that the prevailing school of "situational ethics" had infected the highest levels of government. Later, Graham sadly reflected that perhaps he had been "used" to bolster the President's moralistic image.[20]

Nixon himself realized the damage the tapes might inflict on his carefully nourished image as a moral, upstanding leader. The first drafts of the typed transcripts came to him for editing, and he deleted references to Jesus Christ, changed "god damn" to "damn," and made marginal notes by way of explanation. For example, at one point in an April 14, 1973 conversation, Ehrlichman said, "pardon?" Clearly, the aide meant "pardon me," and was not asking about pardon for Watergate offenders, but Nixon himself wrote in the interpretation. Nixon later received some help in expurgating the transcripts from an unexpected quarter when House Judiciary Chairman Peter Rodino deleted scurrilous references to Italians and Jews.[21]

In the midst of his travail, some old friends held fast for the President. One told him that he remained loyal "100% rain or shine" and offered two prescriptions: plenty of rest and daily exercise. A law-school friend, Rose Mary Woods's lawyer, sent word that the Judiciary Committee would be "afraid" to vote for impeachment. Clare Boothe Luce, a prominent and vocal Republican partisan, thought Nixon "should hang on." She complained that Kissinger received credit for anything good that happened, while Nixon had responsibility for anything that went wrong.[22]

Editorial opinion widely condemned the President and weighed heavily in the growing coalition ranged against him. The *Chicago Tribune,* the conservative authority in the nation's heartland and an ardent Nixon supporter, in a May 9 editorial captured the anger directed against a president who had lowered the dignity and standards of his office. "He is humorless to the point of being inhumane. He is devious. He is vacillating. He is profane. He is willing to be led. He displays dismaying gaps in his knowledge." This was no liberal media conspiracy assaulting the President; it was his own people, painfully expressing their outrage and sense of betrayal. No liberal media conspiracy wrote the words heard on television and printed in the newspapers; they were the President's own.

The tapes released at this point did not yet provide a "smoking gun" irrefutably linking Nixon with an impeachable crime—at least not for his band of loyalists. But they certainly revealed a sleazy, troubled White House. Things had come to such a point that the burden of proof shifted. The legal and constitutional case for impeachment still had to be made, yet the tapes unleashed a chain reaction of public opinion that increased pressure for Nixon either to prove his innocence, or resign, or suffer the consequences of impeachment.

As the House Judiciary Committee met on May 9 to consider the impeachment resolutions, Congressman John Anderson (IL), chairman of the House Republican Policy Conference, called for the President's resignation. John Rhodes too thought Nixon should consider that option. Melvin Laird again warned his Republican friends to be "careful" and "cautious" in their support of the President, anxious as he was that they not be embarrassed. For Caldwell Butler (R–VA), a conservative member of the Judiciary Committee, the tapes demonstrated that Nixon had to bear responsibility for his actions. Butler found the President to be "a pretty tough-minded thinker," one who knew the right direction and considered the right options. Yet, Butler said, "he missed the boat; quite obviously, he missed the boat." The President's family believed that the tapes showed how he had been manipulated by his aides, who controlled every situation. But Butler in his own mind had specifically rejected any notion that Nixon had been victimized by unscrupulous supporters.[23]

Alexander Haig appeared on several news programs following the release of the tapes. On ABC's *Issues and Answers* on May 5, he emphasized the need to quell criticism and bring Watergate to an end. He signalled that the House Judiciary Committee had sufficient evidence to bring their inquiry to a conclusion. But the committee did not agree. On May 15 it issued subpoenas for yet more tapes and presidential diaries, and those materials, Rodino told St. Clair, would be the basis for even more demands. In a May 22 letter to Rodino, Nixon firmly refused to comply, although he again offered to accept written interrogatories and to be examined under oath by Rodino and Hutchinson. Rodino declined on May 30. The House alone, he said, had the power to conduct an inquiry and determine what evidence was relevant. Now, he said, the committee had to decide whether to draw "adverse inferences" from the President's refusal and whether that action itself constituted an impeachable offense.[24]

After releasing the tape transcripts, the White House issued fewer denials of presidential involvement and instead sought to direct public attention toward the question of whether Nixon's actions justified impeachment. The President's support among loyal House Republicans greatly depended on how he responded to the impeachment inquiry. Julie Nixon Eisenhower visited some House members and received hard lessons in institutional loyalty, a loyalty that rivaled, perhaps exceeded, any that House members might have for her father. The congressmen urged the President to comply with the Judiciary Committee subpoenas and to make more material available to the ranking members and the Chief Counsel for both parties. Julie Eisenhower understood that the representatives would have little basis for supporting her father in an impeachment vote "unless they see all the evidence which they feel fits in the category of a legitimate area of inquiry." They emphasized to her that the issue transcended partisan lines—"even Republicans," she noted, "sincerely believe compliance necessary, above and beyond politics.''[25] The President had heard from his most trustworthy source: the issue had transcended partisan lines; the "enemies" were no longer just the familiar ones.

Senator James Buckley's defection underscored the President's serious problems with his conservative constituents. The Republican conservative wing devoutly believed that the nation preferred a rightward course; with equal fervor, many of them believed that Richard Nixon had betrayed what they called the conservative "mandate of 1968." His rapprochement with the Chinese Communists, his imposition of wage-and-price controls in 1971, his support for détente with the Soviet Union, and his consequent reduction in military spending, periodically sparked revolts on the part of the conservatives. In the summer of 1971, twelve leading conservatives had announced an indefinite "suspension of support" for the President. This led to Congressman John Ashbrook's insurgency in the 1972 primary campaign. But little else had happened, other than bitter attacks by conservative ideologues on their own leaders, including Barry Goldwater and Ronald Reagan, for steadfastly supporting the President.

As Nixon's Watergate troubles deepened, conservatives began boldly to express their contempt. In December 1973, *Human Events,* a leading spokesman for the cause, referred to the President as "our ceremonial chief of state." Conservatives cared little about Nixon personally, it seemed; he disturbed them deeply, however, with his attempts to appease liberal critics by supporting their programs. Thus Goldwater in March 1974 publicly warned that such efforts were futile; in the meantime, the Senator thought that Nixon's budget only contributed to the current inflationary spiral.[26]

The President's own conservative advisers grew disenchanted. Patrick Buchanan recalled that he disagreed with more than half of Nixon's program. In foreign policy, the conservatives believed that Henry Kissinger had filled a vacuum of power while the President found himself distracted by Watergate. Suspicions that Kissinger was really a Soviet agent, under the *nom de guerre* of "Colonel Boar," floated throughout right-wing circles and eventually into the higher echelons of the intelligence community. James Jesus Angleton, head of counterespionage in the CIA, reportedly "objectively" believed Kissinger to be a Soviet spy. Admiral Elmo Zumwalt, who resigned from the Joint Chiefs of Staff because of his dissatisfaction with the Administration, thought that Kissinger, true to the "dynamics of history," believed that the Soviet Union eventually would surpass the United States and that it was best for the U.S. government now to arrange the best deal it could. Zumwalt specifically referred to the "deliberate, systematic, and unfortunately, extremely successful efforts" of Nixon and Kissinger to conceal their "real policies about the most critical matters of national security." Others heaped scorn on Kissinger's grasp of the issues. "The master delusion of our time," columnist M. Stanton Evans wrote in March 1972, "is the idea that Henry Kissinger actually knows what he's doing."

As such beliefs gathered momentum, the President found little help from conservative quarters. Conservative organizer Howard Phillips charged in April 1974 that Nixon's main "ambition had been toward becoming a President and not being one." At the same time, other conservatives anticipated the Buckley announcement, anxious for the preservation of the "mandate of 1972," which they felt was endangered unless Nixon resigned. The President also threatened the conservatives' moral self-image and commitments; James Kilpatrick, for example, denounced the "record of cynicism and amorality" demonstrated in the tapes. Shortly after the release of the transcripts, Nixon prepared for a summit in the Soviet Union. For conservative writer William F. Buckley, Jr., the prospect was too much. He quoted liberal Republican Senator Jacob Javits, who accused the President of playing "impeachment politics." Buckley believed that Nixon had been "morally fleeced" by the Soviets; now, he was so anxious to bolster his image, Buckley thought, that he might be ready to give the Russians the U.S. Marine Band.

Occasionally, however, Nixon still received some comfort from the Right. As late as May 1974, William Buckley believed that Nixon should destroy tapes to protect his office. Even if the nation concluded that such action proved guilt, and even if it resulted in impeachment, Buckley thought, it would save the presidency. Besides, with no tapes, the charges would remain inconclusive.[27] (The President's moral critics apparently claimed no monopoly on morality.) Still, by May 1974, a good part of the conservative establishment had abandoned the President.

The publication of the tape transcripts coincided with that of advance excerpts from a long-awaited book by two *Washington Post* reporters, Bob Woodward and Carl Bernstein, who had written extensively on Watergate since the June 17, 1972 break-in. Early in April 1974, *Playboy* magazine published the first excerpts from *All the President's Men*, nearly two months prior to the appearance of the book. The *Playboy* excerpts were widely reported throughout the media.

After the book appeared in June, it received extensive attention, generally gaining good notices for the reporters' role (and the *Washington Post*'s) in ferreting out and publishing the Watergate story for nearly two years. Some prominent reviewers criticized the authors' tendency to favor the style of a detective story rather than seeking the introspective level of historical analysis, and critics questioned as well Woodward and Bernstein's failure to address any of the ethical deficiencies of their investigative reporting, including any disclosure of attempts to bribe them, illegally gaining access to

telephone numbers, and talking to members of the grand jury. One reviewer
lamented the barrenness of ideas and essentially boring quality of the reporters' narrative; still, he somehow praised the work as "authoritative."[28]

All the President's Men certainly had its shortcomings, but in a sense they
became virtues that promoted the book, dramatized the story, and compounded the perils of Richard Nixon. The authors' purported reliance upon
an unnamed individual cleverly tagged as "Deep Throat" for information
on the inner workings of the Nixon Administration, as well as the attribution
of pungent, salty observations to unidentified Administration officials, gave
the work a special intimacy and appeal. However self-serving or exaggerated
the work, it undeniably gave an added impetus to the growing understanding
and awareness of Watergate. Newspapers throughout the nation serialized
the book, giving it an enormous audience. Within weeks of its publication
in June, *All the President's Men* was a best-seller, and it remained so
throughout most of the summer. In an important sense, the book offered a
journalistic brief to the nation as it prepared to understand and judge for
itself the impending formal bill of particulars against the President of the
United States.

As John Dean recounted his story to the prosecutors in April 1973, Assistant
U.S. Attorney Earl Silbert realized that he must consider the possibility of
indicting the President of the United States. He asked an aide to research
the constitutional issues involved in that step. The conclusion: "practical
reasons" suggested that no president should be indicted without first allowing the process of impeachment to run. Silbert's aide contended that a president might forbid any government attorney from signing an indictment (an
argument that anticipated those who believed that the Special Prosecutor, as
an executive officer, was subject to presidential command). Furthermore, a
president might pardon himself pending trial. In any case, an indictment
could devastate the nation, especially if a president insisted on maintaining
office—and he could be convicted and still sit pending impeachment. Finally, the precedent of indicting the Chief Executive might be capriciously
invoked by "irresponsible or politically motivated" prosecutors. Instead of
indictment, the report to Silbert suggested naming President Nixon as an
unindicted co-conspirator or having the grand jury make its report and the
evidence available to the public and the House of Representatives. With the
advent of the Special Prosecutor, Silbert left the case, but transmitted the
report to Archibald Cox.[29] The possible scenarios may have been exaggerated, but again, such were the times.

The report to Silbert chiefly relied on practical considerations; after all,
no precedents existed for prosecuting a sitting president. In early January
1974, researchers in the Special Prosecutor's office came to substantially

similar conclusions. But in this office the staff and senior officials were not as sanguine that the House of Representatives would carry out its responsibilities for impeachment. Indeed, references to the "ponderous nature of impeachment proceedings," the "painfully slow rumination of impeachment allegations," and the "tortuous course inherent in impeachment" reflected a belief in the Special Prosecutor's office that the criminal-justice course provided the quicker, more practical method of dealing with presidential misbehavior. Philip Lacovara, a Jaworski aide, concluded that the Special Prosecutor's office could not "totally abstain from coming to grips" with the possibility of presidential involvement—either through providing evidence to the House of Representatives or in a criminal proceeding.

But the prosecutors had practical problems of their own. Henry Ruth, deputy to both Cox and Jaworski, noted that the Special Prosecutor's evidence and witnesses would be involved in any House proceeding, thus presenting "the possibility of interference with our own investigations and trials." Ruth believed that if they did not immediately aid the then-forming House Judiciary Committee staff with evidence, they could find that pending criminal cases might preclude any assistance to the impeachment process. Ruth took seriously recent assertions by both Nixon and Haig that the President never would resign; he thought decisions had to be made on that basis, "and we must face the choices of action immediately." He was convinced that the White House intended to exclude the Judiciary Committee from evidence provided to the Special Prosecutor. Indeed, St. Clair had forwarded tape transcripts with the understanding that the material would remain secret to all but the grand jurors and the Special Prosecutor. Jaworski thought that furnishing information to the House committee might violate a defendant's constitutional right to a fair trial. Yet withholding the evidence would effectively throttle the impeachment inquiry. Coupled with a decision not to indict, the result would be to subject subordinates to the criminal process while permitting "the boss," as Ruth described Nixon, "to walk free among us with undisturbed wealth and dignity." No impeachment, no indictment, Ruth concluded, offered damaging precedents for the future of presidential accountability.[30]

By February 12 Jaworski had received what his staff called the "clear and compelling prima facie evidence of the President's participation in a conspiracy to obstruct justice." The staff now moved more aggressively for a grand-jury indictment or presentment. Those making the recommendation to Jaworski believed that the Special Prosecutor had "overwhelming public support for committing the decision of the President's criminal guilt or innocence to the traditional processes of law enforcement." By their oath, the grand jury, too, had an obligation not to allow anyone to go free out of "fear, favor, affection, reward or hope of reward." Finally, the staff urged the preservation of the rule of law and the necessity for maintaining the longstanding principle that "no man in this country is so high that he is above the law." The Special Prosecutor's staff concluded that the responsibilities and character of impeachment were utterly unique and independent from those of the criminal process. They no longer would accept the "responsibility" for leaving the determination of the President's guilt or innocence exclusively to the "political" process in a judgment of impeachment. The advocates of divorcing the criminal proceeding against the President from the impeachment proceedings forcefully stated their conclusion: "We and the Grand Jury do not exist merely for the purpose of assuring that debate on impeachment is fully informed." In other words, merely transmitting the evidence to Congress no longer was adequate. Prosecutors prosecute.

The report brusquely swept aside the "practical" matters previously thought to militate against indictment—"in essence, political considerations," the staff declared rather disdainfully. It saw such a course as "formulating public policy in private," a role for which they claimed a lack of "expertise," as if prosecutorial discretion was an art or science beyond their ken. Certainly, it was one they quickly mastered. The staff itself disagreed on the indictability of a president but unanimously believed it should recommend a grand-jury presentment that would state the determination of Nixon's culpability and the conclusion that he would have been indicted had he not been president. Having rejected "practical" and "political" considerations, the staff then offered just such reasons for recommending a grand-jury presentment: it would avoid the spectacle of a presidential trial and possible imprisonment; it would not disable the President or automatically remove him from office without an impeachment; it would focus issues for Congress, if Congress were to consider impeachment, and "responsibility for further action would be placed squarely upon Congress." The contest was for winning public opinion. Presentment, the staff concluded, would enable a "primary truth" to emerge: "but for the fact that he is President, Richard Nixon would have been indicted."[31]

The day before, February 11, 1974, Judge Sirica expressed concern to Jaworski that the grand jury might do something irresponsible. Sirica now was convinced that the House was the proper body for dealing with the President. Jaworski agreed in part, but suggested that the grand jury might request that it be authorized to refer its findings to the Judiciary Committee.[32]

The primary Watergate grand jury had been assembled on June 5, 1972 and had soon found itself absorbed, if not overtaken, by events. Twenty-three citizens of the District of Columbia made up the jury, with blacks outnumbering whites almost three to one, reflecting the racial make-up of the area's population. Eleven of the jurors worked for the government and continued to draw their salaries, in addition to their $20 *per diem* remuneration as jurors (later raised, but not retroactively, to $25). The U.S. Attorney's office selected the foreman, Vladimir Pregelj, a Yugoslavian refugee who worked in the Legislative Reference Service in the Library of Congress as an economic analyst.

The jurors immediately developed a comfortable, friendly relationship with the original U.S. Attorney's team of Earl Silbert, Seymour Glanzer, and Donald Campbell. They readily asked questions of witnesses and freely discussed matters with the prosecutors afterward. The relationship was informal and friendly—"we were all kind of buddies," the foreman recalled.

That ambience changed after Cox's team took over, replacing Silbert and his colleagues. The jurors at first resented the new prosecutors. Similarly, one of the prosecutors became upset when the jurors posed questions of their own to witnesses without clearing them with the prosecutors. Another thought the jurors often were too eager to act and were not always mindful of the fact that the prosecutors knew more than they. In time, however, the jurors and the new team reached an accommodation, and the work proceeded smoothly. The Watergate defendants and their lawyers viewed the grand jurors with hostility—convinced that they could not get a fair trial. But Jaworski praised the jurors as "very objective, very constructive, and very sensible"; their questions, he said, showed their "deep concern, their abiding determination to do what was right."

The jurors sat for thirty months. Judge George Hart discharged them in December 1974, noting that they had served longer than any other federal jury. For their part, the jurors did not seem to mind the ordeal and appreciated the historic importance of their role.[33]

On February 25, 1974, Jaworski faced the grand jurors for the first time. Since mid-December, he had believed that Nixon had been "criminally involved" in the cover-up. Early in January, his staff compiled a 128-page report documenting the President's role. Jaworski realized the prevailing strong sentiment for an indictment of Nixon, particularly on the part of the grand jury's most articulate members. A straw poll of the jurors present showed a 19–0 vote in favor of an indictment—although they recognized that the evidence might not yet be sufficient for a successful prosecution. They bristled at the thought of being a "rubber stamp." The growing hostility of Jaworski's staff toward the President, now buttressed by the growing evidence of Nixon's apparent complicity in the cover-up, made the Special Prosecutor's task all the more lonely. He knew, as he told the jurors, that of all the evidence presented, the President's conversations undoubtedly had made the most enormous impact on their minds.

But Jaworski pursued his course in his own fashion: cautious and respectful of the President and the presidency, he argued strenuously against indictment. The constitutional doubts, he maintained, were substantial, and undoubtedly an indictment's constitutionality would be litigated, leaving, Jaworski said, "trauma" within the nation and "scars" on the presidency. Jaworski rankled some of the jurors by focusing on the constitutional issue, and he disappointed some of them by his refusal to deal with the weight of the evidence. Left unspoken was the possibility that a presidential indictment might jeopardize other indictments and, most significantly, the damage to the credibility of the Special Prosecutor should he lose a case against the President for lack of conclusive evidence.

As a compromise gesture, Jaworski told the grand jurors that they could give a report of the evidence and their views about the President to Judge Sirica for eventual transmittal to the House Judiciary Committee. Several jurors expressed their disagreement with Jaworski: they were, he later noted, "appalled by what they [had] heard." Foreman Pregelj, in particular, challenged Jaworski; Jaworski thought him genuinely "shocked." The jurors eventually followed the Special Prosecutor's recommendation—no indictment, but a report to the House. In addition, they secretly named the President as an unindicted co-conspirator. The prosecution believed it essential to name Nixon in order to make his tape recordings admissible as trial evidence. Yet Jaworski feared that a public revelation of Nixon's status as unindicted co-conspirator would give the President an opportunity to claim that the action had prejudiced his case in the House.[34]

That same evening, February 25, Nixon held his first televised press conference in four months. Immediately, reporters raised the issue of impeachment. Nixon said he believed that the Constitution precisely defined an impeachable offense and meant, according to his lawyers, that he had to be guilty of a criminal offense. As if to affirm his innocence to the grand jurors, the President doggedly stated that "I do not expect to be impeached." He reiterated that he would cooperate with the House, "consistent with my constitutional responsibility" to defend the office of the presidency against any attempts to weaken it and also to safeguard the ability of future presidents to carry out their responsibilities.

The inevitable question came when a reporter asked if the President would resign to avoid a political disaster for his party. The question well served Nixon, for it enabled him to raise the issue of "the presidency" above mere partisan concerns. "The stability of this office, the ability of the President to continue to govern, the ability, for example, of this President to continue the great initiatives which have led to a more peaceful world," all were more important than the success of a political party, he insisted. The "presidency" must not be "hostage" to the momentary "popularity" of any incumbent. The work must be continued, he concluded, "and I'm going to stay here till I get it done."[35]

Two months later, in early May, Jaworski informed Haig that the President had been named an unindicted co-conspirator. Jaworski had been pleased that the news had not leaked; it was staggering to think of newspaper headlines broadcasting the President's "indictment." The news "visibly perturbed" the President and his aides, Jaworski learned. Nixon thought that the Special Prosecutor had deceived Haig, for allegedly Jaworski had told the Chief of Staff that no one in the White House had been indicted. The President accused Jaworski of blackmail by threatening to reveal the grand jury's action unless more tapes were produced. Jaworski, of course, had in fact *prevented* the President's indictment—a fact known to the White House at the time. Nixon thought he knew the real object of Jaworski's threat: the Special Prosecutor had demanded incriminating tapes, including the crucial June 23, 1972, conversation with Haldeman, a conversation which the President undoubtedly had listened to, and in which he and Haldeman had concocted the plan for using the CIA to thwart the FBI's investigation of the Watergate burglary. Haig probably knew the contents of that tape; the same day he met Jaworski, he provided a copy to the President. Haig later claimed that Nixon told him the next day that he was too busy trying to run the country and would not listen to any more tapes. But Nixon later admitted that he had heard the June 23 tape.

According to Nixon, St. Clair opposed any further release of material, and at various times, the President attempted to blame his advisers for urging him to resist the House committee and the Special Prosecutor. St. Clair never directly responded to that criticism except to note that if Nixon did not like the advice, he could always replace his lawyer. For his part, St. Clair claimed never to have known the contents of the June 23, 1972 tape until August 1974. Had he known, he said, he would have urged an early release instead of delaying until the tape had to be pried loose by a Supreme Court order—and following an impeachment vote in the Judiciary Committee. Nixon's own memory and records provide ample evidence of his conviction that he had to withhold the additional tapes. He knew he could not compromise on these particular tapes by providing only excerpts. "[H]ow we handle the 23rd tape is a very difficult call because I don't know how it could be excerpted properly," he noted in a July diary entry. For good reason: the tape segment, eventually made public in August, became famous as the "smoking gun."[36]

* * *

The unindicted co-conspirator charge had overshadowed the grand jury's proceedings. The jurors had also returned indictments against a former Attorney General and the President's three closest aides, as well as others. The indictments came down on March 1. The counts ranged from conspiracy and obstruction of justice to perjury and false declarations to the FBI. The jury listed forty-five overt acts of conspiracy to cover up the true nature of the involvement of the Administration and the re-election committee with the break-in.

The defendants—Mitchell, Haldeman, Ehrlichman, Colson, Robert Mardian, Kenneth Parkinson, and Gordon Strachan—pled not guilty before Judge Sirica on Saturday morning, March 9. (Jaworski had opposed indicting Mardian and Parkinson, but he could not be "too oppressive to suit" his staff, he remembered. Assistant Attorney General Mardian's subsequent conviction was overturned, and CREEP counsel Parkinson was acquitted, much to Jaworski's satisfaction.) The court released the accused on their own recognizance; first, however, they had to be fingerprinted and photographed at FBI offices. The Special Prosecutor found himself moved by the proceedings—and pained in his pride of profession, since all the defendants but Haldeman were lawyers. Jaworski saw Mitchell as a "broken-down old man" and the once-ruthless Colson as "a frightened man"; while Haldeman and Ehrlichman "tried to maintain their bravado." When Jaworski entered the court, Mitchell rose and greeted him. "You must be very busy these days," Mitchell said. "Yes," Jaworski responded, "more so than I wish." He found the moment "heartrending"; he "had always liked John Mitchell."[37]

Jaworski's conservative Texas friends had great difficulty comprehending his role. Shortly after the indictments came down, several of them telegraphed the Special Prosecutor, acknowledging that Watergate "was a most stupid thing," but that the President's success in foreign policy made it important that he remain in office. Jaworski gently replied that the telegram should properly have gone to the House Judiciary Committee, but he also insisted that Watergate involved "not stupid, but serious offenses." He had been charged *"by law"* to investigate serious law violations and "other matters," he told his friends.[38]

The day after the indictments, Vice President Ford said that the grand jury's sealed report should be sent to the House Judiciary Committee—the "proper place," he said, to determine President Nixon's role in the Watergate affair. Increasingly since late 1973, the committee had become the focal point for those determined to end the agony of Watergate. The President's friends and most extreme enemies made for strange bedfellows on this solution. His enemies apparently favored turning to the committee as the launching place for an effort at impeachment; his friends apparently thought that the committee would deem impeachment an undesirable or impractical step.

As the talk about impeachment grew, Archibald Cox, true to the lawman's abiding faith in legal process, warned of the necessity for assuring the public that the President was treated fairly. Speaking in January, he noted that a majority of Americans believed Nixon had been guilty of participating in the cover-up, but a majority also opposed his removal by impeachment. For Cox, this translated into an "intuitive understanding that impeachment is extraordinary, . . . legitimate only upon some equally fundamental wrong," that would make the President's continued service unacceptable to a broad national consensus. If impeachment were to be a serious matter, Cox warned, then the time had come to move away from "the fun of factual disclosures" to the more serious business of creating a "substantive law of impeachment." This, of course, was the domain of the House Judiciary Committee. Its task, Cox concluded, was "to sense the as-yet-unstated moral intuition" of the nation, and formulate it into a code of conduct for judging the President.[39]

But the members of the House Judiciary Committee, particularly the seasoned veterans, preferred the old political maxim *festina lente*—"make haste slowly." They realized they had neither the time nor the moral authority to create Cox's "substantive law of impeachment." Practical imperatives of political action, and not the intellectual symmetry of theory and precedent, dictated the course of the committee's progress. The thorny political thicket of impeachment could be raised only by irrefutable evidence. Now, however, the trickle of material assembled by the staff beginning in late 1973 turned into a flood as the Judiciary Committee received, first, the grand-jury material and then the President's own submission of new tape transcripts.

On the heels of the release of the transcripts, the White House again erupted with rage toward Leon Jaworski and the Special Prosecution Force. Haig called Deputy Attorney General Lawrence Silberman on April 30 to report that St. Clair had noted discrepancies between Dean's Senate testimony and his words as recorded in the tapes. St. Clair believed that Dean had shifted his testimony after discussions with Cox, and he wanted copies of internal memos of the Special Prosecutor's office. "If Leon wants to get rough," Haig said, "we will get rough." He never mentioned the purpose of his call, but Silberman considered it a warning of a growing confrontation—and a hint that the White House expected help from the Justice Department. Silberman later called St. Clair directly to remind him that the Special Prosecutor's charter limited the authority of the Attorney General, emphasizing that he and Attorney General Saxbe considered themselves bound by the charter. St. Clair complained that the Special Prosecutor had to be responsible to someone in the executive branch; Silberman, however, forcefully reminded him that Saxbe had entered into a "compact" with Congress, and that the President must abide by it.

As soon as the call to St. Clair ended, Silberman received one from the President, who wanted to know something about a pending Special Prosecutor investigation of John Connally. After speaking to Henry Petersen and hearing his approval of the inquiry, Silberman called the President back. Nixon promptly demanded that Silberman dismiss Petersen, told him to call Haig in an hour, and hung up. When Saxbe got the news, he suggested his deputy "tell the President to go piss up a rope." Petersen provided Silberman with more information about the Connally case and stated that the Criminal Division fully supported Jaworski. Silberman then called Haig again, said that the President had "misunderstood" the matter, and made it clear that firing Petersen made no sense and that he would not do it. Haig promised to speak to Nixon. He called the Justice Department three hours later, instructing Silberman to take no action against Petersen and declaring that the President never intended to fire him. Haig asked Silberman to keep silent about that issue.[40] Who *was* in charge?

The President's wrath against the Justice Department barely concealed his primary target: the Special Prosecutor. His fury paralleled the release of the tape transcripts, an act he thought should end demands for additional materials. On April 16, two weeks before the release, Leon Jaworski had issued a subpoena for sixty-four additional tapes, claiming that they constituted necessary evidence in the pending criminal trial of the President's aides. Nixon's lawyers appeared in Sirica's court on May 2 to oppose the subpoena. Four of the Watergate defendants, however, filed responses supporting the Special Prosecutor's subpoena, provided that the materials produced be made available in full to them. The White House attorneys resorted to familiar refrains: courts had no authority to rule on the scope of executive privilege, and the dispute was an intra-branch controversy wholly within the jurisdiction of the President to resolve. St. Clair argued *in camera* on May 14, insisting that the President had "a right to balance the public interest involved in exerting executive privilege on the one hand against the right of defendants in a pending case on the other hand." It seemed that the executive-privilege argument had been answered by the Court of Appeals in October, but apparently the matter had not been settled to the satisfaction of the President. His authority over the Special Prosecutor had not been litigated, but supposedly it had been resolved by the creation of Jaworski's charter and the agreement between Saxbe and the Senate Judiciary Committee. Those answers satisfied Sirica. He denied the President's motion on May 20 and ordered compliance by May 31, subject to appellate review.[41]

St. Clair promptly appealed the ruling, thus launching what was to become *United States v. Nixon,* a suit that ended in the Supreme Court and gave the President the "definitive" ruling he had demanded, although not the one he preferred. St. Clair naturally carried the dispute to the Court of Appeals, but Jaworski petitioned the Supreme Court to take immediate jurisdiction. The procedure was unusual but not without precedent. The Supreme Court had taken such a path in the Steel Seizure Case in 1952, the last one that had involved broad considerations of presidential powers. Jaworski argued that the "imperative public importance" of the present issues required that the question be resolved during the Court's present term; the Justices' summer break was near, and they would not convene again until the beginning of the Court's new term in October.

In a brief signed first by Charles Alan Wright and then by St. Clair, the President opposed the move, claiming that it would involve a "rush to judgment," and quoting Chief Justice Warren Burger's criticism of haste in the Pentagon Papers case in 1971: "prompt judicial action does not mean unjudicial haste," the Chief Justice there said, in dissenting from the majority view critical of the government's injunction against several newspapers. In a separate petition several weeks later (signed only by St. Clair), Nixon also asked the Court for a judgment of the grand jury's right to name him as an unindicted co-conspirator. The request was merely a sideshow.⁴²

President Nixon later described himself as wavering in this period, amenable to some compromise. He stressed that St. Clair and Buzhardt had urged him to stand fast. Eventually, he said, he came around to their view— a convenient rationalization, given his own worries about the June 23 tape.

During this period, Jaworski sensed that the growing hostility at the White House might well challenge his position. The President "was in a corner, and he was struggling," Jaworski recalled. Prior to the release of the tapes, the White House acted as if the Judiciary Committee offered the greatest potential danger, and it paid little attention to Jaworski. But Jaworski's initiation of subpoenas and court proceedings energized Nixon and his staff to confront the new challenge. The House committee, in the President's mind, constituted chiefly a political threat, an arena in which he thought he could battle on equal terms, but the possibility of an unfavorable Supreme Court decision, one that projected finality, constituted a major danger. Nixon simply could not ignore the Court's prestige and authority in constitutional matters.

Jaworski, for his part, did not treat lightly any signs of challenge to his authority. He reported to Senate Judiciary Committee Chairman James Eastland on May 20 that St. Clair had argued in Sirica's court that Jaworski had no standing because the dispute was "an intra-executive dispute"—in short, Jaworski had no right to take the President to court. Jaworski reminded Eastland that he had taken the Special Prosecutor's position with the understanding that the President would impose no such restrictions on him—an understanding accepted, he said, by Haig, Buzhardt, Bork, and the members of the Senate Judiciary Committee. Jaworski carefully noted that he did not challenge the President's right to raise any other defenses, such as executive privilege. But St. Clair had recently told him that the "fact that the President has chosen to resolve this issue by judicial determination and not by a uni-lateral exercise of his constitutional powers, is evidence of the President's good faith." For Jaworski, that position ominously suggested that in spite of all agreements, the President retained an absolute right to thwart the Special Prosecutor.

Jaworski was in a combative mood. Saxbe and Bork wrote to him on June 5, assuring him that their guarantees of independence remained intact but that they thought St. Clair had reason to pursue the question of Jaworski's jurisdiction. They urged him and St. Clair to work out an agreement for handling the jurisdictional problem. Jaworski responded with lengthy quo-tations from the Special Prosecutor's charter which defined his authority. Compromise? "A highly significant principle is involved, as I see it, one that involves not only the integrity of others but mine as well—and accord-ingly, there is no room for compromise." He suggested that St. Clair join "us" in agreeing that jurisdiction was present and that the Special Prose-cutor had authority to act independent of the President. Privately, Bork be-lieved that Jaworski's threatening to resign over a jurisdictional dispute would have been "ridiculous."[43]

Jaworski continued to raise the issue well into June, as he and St. Clair engaged in an acrimonious exchange of letters. St. Clair insisted that he had done his "duty" by challenging Jaworski's jurisdiction. For the Special Pros-ecutor, however, that move had violated the letter and spirit of his agree-ments with the executive branch and had also violated his charter. Jaworski accused the President's special counsel of "sophistry"—a lawyer's euphe-mism for lying and deception. St. Clair firmly denied that he had tried to "hoodwink" anyone. He later asserted that he was merely protecting the "presidency"; a clear run for Jaworski, he thought, would have been "an irretrievable inroad into the authority of the President of the United States."

The dispute perhaps raised Jaworski's ire more than any single event in his tenure. Clearly, he viewed St. Clair's words and actions as those of St. Clair's master, and therefore as especially sinister in their implications. By raising the jurisdictional issue, St. Clair invited judicial intervention against the Special Prosecutor. After all, the Supreme Court had neither a vested interest in the Special Prosecutor nor had it made a commitment guarantee-ing his independence. If the Court ruled that the Special Prosecutor had no jurisdiction, then to whom would he appeal for the preservation of his existence?

Leon Jaworski was unwilling to be fired on behalf of a vaguely defined principle of jurisdiction; for him, that principle no longer was in dispute, as it had been at the time of Cox's dismissal. He believed that he had ironclad guarantees of independence. "If I had agreed to serve on any other basis, after what happened to Archibald Cox," he told St. Clair, "I should have had my head examined."[44] Was the White House position on Jaworski's jurisdiction its ultimate fallback to prevent further disclosures? Nixon knew of the dispute, according to St. Clair; his subsequent silence on the motive for raising the matter was rare.

After some sharp disagreement, the Supreme Court on May 31 granted Jaworski's petition for a writ of certiorari. The House Judiciary Committee had begun its hearings; the Special Prosecutor remained intact; and now the President faced a formidable third front in the Supreme Court. A year earlier, the favorite White House metaphor consisted of circled wagons under assault from savages. Now, staffers referred to the slow, painful "death of a thousand cuts"; now, too, they had to deal with the "smoking gun," the taped conversation of June 23, 1972, with all its potential for creating a mortal self-inflicted wound.

Nixon told a friendly interviewer at the time that he slept well, he had no "tingling nerves" or "churning stomach." He offered a brave front, standing on his indispensability if the country were to seize "this moment." If we did not, he said, "the world will inevitably move to a conflagration that will destroy everything that we've made—everything that this civilization has produced." Meanwhile, Philip Buchen, a close adviser to Vice President Ford, put together a group to plan for a transition in the event that Nixon were removed or resigned.[45] For the President, his advice to himself at the beginning of the year was all the more imperative: *fight*.

XVIII

"WELL, AL, THERE GOES THE PRESIDENCY."

THE HOUSE JUDICIARY COMMITTEE: JUNE–JULY 1974

The time had come to think the unthinkable. Impeachment was an idea that slowly moved from absurdity to reality. Long shunned, even taboo in the minds of some, the very word triggered waves of shock and indignation. When President Nixon's troubles mounted in April 1973, highly regarded liberal Senator Philip Hart raised the possibility of impeachment. *New York Times* columnist James Reston was alarmed that such an "eminently rational" man could be "smitten by the spring madness." Reston castigated the President and his detractors alike for their idle threats, their chip-on-the-shoulder attitude.

Just a week earlier, Attorney General Richard Kleindienst had contemptuously challenged senators to impeach the President when they had questioned Nixon's interpretation of executive privilege. "You do not need evidence to impeach a President," he said; Congress is the sole judge, and "that is the end, with or without facts," he added. Kleindienst's recklessness shocked Senator J. William Fulbright. "Politically," he thought impeachment "disastrous," and added that "nothing, I hope ever gets so far . . . that we would even consider using that course."

Slightly more than a year later, however, the House Judiciary Committee turned its attention to that very consideration. Committee member Hamilton Fish remembered impeachment as "about the most difficult thing to imagine." But for Fish's colleague Ray Thornton, it was not unthinkable; he viewed impeachment as the system's "safety valve." Shortly after the Saturday Night Massacre, Thornton told his conservative constituents, most of

whom had supported Nixon, that he hoped impeachment would not be necessary, yet he emphasized that he would "not hesitate to vote my convictions" if he believed the President had violated the Constitution. "The
preservation of our system of government is more important to me than any
man's continuance in office, including my own," Thornton said.[1]

Tradition, custom, and practicality strongly militated against impeachment. President Andrew Johnson's acquittal by one vote discredited the process; the acquittal seemed so burnished in the American mind as to make
impeachment irrelevant, a curiosity, at times even laughable. Twenty years
after the Johnson trial, Lord Bryce described impeachment as "the heaviest
piece of machinery in the constitutional arsenal," and "unfit for ordinary
use." In 1960 a prominent presidential scholar thought that the next impeachment would involve not a high political crime but rather "a low personal" one, such as shooting a senator.[2] No wonder, then, that Kleindienst
so freely challenged the senators.

On a practical basis, impeachment was hard for congressmen to consider,
given the President's ability to influence vital events. During a lengthy impeachment proceeding, the President might pursue popular legislative goals,
appealing to diverse interest groups; or he might pursue an activist role in
foreign affairs and achieve a major diplomatic breakthrough. If he did, congressmen considering impeachment risked appearing as petty assassins bent
on obstructing cherished programs and ideals. Still, the history of the Constitution, as well as practical considerations, provided some compelling reasons for considering the impeachment of Richard Nixon.

The Constitution boldly experimented in its delegation of governmental authority, and in no area more so than that of executive power. Republican
governments had a checkered, even sordid, history prior to 1787. They had
floundered and collapsed, largely as a result of executive mismanagement
or tyranny. The "president" designed by the framers offered a bold, innovative approach for establishing an equilibrium between power and restraint.
Presidential power to "execute" the laws, to operate as "commander-in-
chief" of the armed forces, and "to make treaties" offered the basis for
a broad, generous construction of executive authority. Given the Framers'
recent experience with George III, however, neither they nor their constituents conceded "all sail and no anchor" to the office or the man. James
Madison pointedly reminded Americans in *Federalist* 48 of the dangers to
liberty "from the overgrown and all-grasping prerogative of an hereditary
magistrate."

The basic constitutional formula for presidential accountability lay with
the prescribed mechanisms of checks and balances, such as congressional
authority over appropriations, the Congress's confirmation of executive of-

ficers and consent to treaties, and its ability to override a presidential veto. But the provision for impeachment perhaps best reinforced accountability, as it implicitly rejected the traditional English doctrine that "the king could do no wrong." William Blackstone had summed up that tradition when he wrote in the eighteenth century that the "king cannot misuse his power without the advice of evil counsellors, and the assistance of wicked ministers." Those counsellors and ministers might be impeached, but not the king himself.

The history of English impeachment is the story of the drive against absolutist pretensions, the corresponding rise of parliamentary supremacy, and the eventual discarding of the practice. Parliament used impeachment to remove the king's "wicked ministers" throughout the protracted seventeenth-century struggles with the Crown, but the rise of cabinet government, serviced by members of Parliament, made the device unnecessary, as Parliament's own majorities could repudiate "wicked ministers." When the conflict between royal power and Parliament abated by the early eighteenth century, Parliament had established the principle that the king "could not assume responsibility for the unpopular and unsuccessful actions of his ministers." The king might do no wrong, but those who acted in his name were accountable. Ironically, as Americans incorporated their impeachment formula into the 1787 Constitution, Parliament launched what was to be its last great impeachment trial—an eight-year proceeding to remove Warren Hastings as Governor-General of the East India Company.[3]

The American constitutional formula for separation of powers ran precisely counter to the English development of the fusion of powers and parliamentary supremacy. The Constitution's framers rejected executive participation in the legislative branch, thus ensuring separation and providing, in Congress, a way for impeachment to begin and proceed. Combining their senses of history as well as their experiences, the Framers and the state ratifying conventions constructed a careful impeachment procedure and a substantial body of commentary on its justification and meaning. Article II, Section 4 of the Constitution provided that the President and all civil officers might be removed following impeachment and conviction for "treason, bribery, or other high crimes and misdemeanors." The House had the sole power of impeachment; the Senate had the sole power to try the impeached; and the Chief Justice presided over the Senate in the event of a presidential impeachment trial. The constitutional reference to "high crimes and misdemeanors" is not language historically vague in source or meaning. Its origins can be traced to an impeachment proceeding in England in 1386 and amounted to a catalogue of *political* crime. The language has been best described as "words of art confined to impeachments, without roots in the ordinary criminal law."[4]

Unlike later generations, the Framers had no difficulty in recognizing the political nature of the process. They viewed tyranny and abuses of power as familiar political phenomena, to be treated accordingly. Political crimes required political solutions. From the outset, the Framers advocated impeachment as the most effective means for limiting presidential power and for removal; it was the ultimate peaceful defense against executive tyranny. The evidence overwhelmingly points to the conclusion that the framers provided future generations with a powerful, flexible tool for determining malfeasance and abuses by officials. An impeachment inquiry did not (or need not) presume guilt and removal; the audit of executive power simply counted as another form of vigilance for maintaining liberty. To read the Constitution's words in any other way would be to transform historical context and meaning into semantic theorizing and legal abstraction. It also would miss the point that the Framers were practical and realistic politicians. Human nature being as it is, Patrick Henry reminded his fellow Virginians, we could not always expect to be governed by "good" presidents. "Without real checks," Henry said, "it will not suffice that some of them are good."⁵

Benjamin Franklin whimsically offered impeachment as a practical alternative to assassination. As usual, Madison best blended the historical and practical imperatives. He thought impeachment "indispensable" to protect the nation against the President's "incapacity, negligence or perfidy." He might suffer diminished capacities; he might betray the nation to foreign powers; or, Madison added, "he might pervert his administration into a scheme of peculation or oppression." The last caution against "oppression" encapsulated four centuries of English constitutional experience with impeachment and the political meaning of "high crimes and misdemeanors." Madison's fellow Virginian George Mason feared that the President might "subvert the Constitution," and proposed adding "maladministration" to the catalogue of impeachable offenses. Madison thought the idea a bit vague, however, and as the Constitutional Convention ended, he proposed that impeachment be reserved for "high crimes and misdemeanors"—words familiar and understandable to the convention.⁶

The rejection of Mason's suggestion seemed to rule out impeaching a president for "petty misconduct" or for want of judgment. In the North Carolina ratifying convention, James Iredell (a future Supreme Court Justice) thought that impeachment "must be for an error of the heart, and not of the head." Iredell's dictum became, in time, the standard for requiring evil motives as a basic criterion for impeachment. In South Carolina, Charles Cotesworth Pinckney thought that impeachment could lie for those "who behave amiss, or betray their public trust." In the Virginia convention, Madison lent his authority to the proposition that "if the President be connected, in any suspicious manner with any person, and there be grounds to believe that he will shelter him, then he might be impeached." Madison, it should be remembered, had thought Mason's "maladministration" notion too vague. Quite simply, in all their debates, the Framers acknowledged the subjectivity of impeachment proceedings.[7]

The men of 1787 recognized the dangers of executive authority—and they meant to scrutinize that power closely. Determining whether it had been abused ultimately posed questions of allocating power—in other words, it posed *political* questions. In matters of state, political and legal causes may well be indistinguishable. The Framers frankly acknowledged the political quality of impeachments—and their potential for abuse—but they willingly assumed the risk. The grounds for impeachment, Alexander Hamilton wrote in *Federalist* 65, "are those offenses which proceed from the misconduct of public men, or, in other words, from the abuse or violation of some public trust. They are of a nature which may with peculiar propriety be denominated *political,* as they relate chiefly to injuries done immediately to the society itself." Such proceedings, Hamilton acknowledged, would "seldom fail to agitate the passions of the whole community," carrying the danger that the decision to impeach might be made on the strengths of competing interests or factions.

The Framers incorporated impeachment into the Constitution as a means for questioning the President's general conduct as well as of exposing his violations of specific laws or constitutional provisions—in short, impeachment was their formal means for ensuring accountability to the limitations of power. Presidents might, as Madison noted, develop schemes of "peculation or oppression." But what indeed is "oppressive"? Neither dusty statute books nor criminal codes nor the Constitution offers a clear *legal* answer. Accordingly, Hamilton concluded that an impeachment or trial was an appropriate "method of *national inquest* into the conduct of public men." The Framers knew that men are not angels; they had no reason to bet differently on presidents.

Whatever the promise and intent of impeachment, by 1819 Thomas Jefferson thought the process cumbersome and archaic. Experience had shown, he wrote, that impeachment was "not even a scare-crow." Certainly, Jefferson did not believe that any president who had served thus far (Washington, John Adams, Madison, Monroe, and, of course, himself) deserved impeachment. But by that date, Jefferson had come to distrust the federal judiciary and its aggrandizing behavior. In 1803 the House impeached and the Senate convicted Federal Judge John Pickering, notorious for his fits of insanity and drunkenness—hardly much of a precedent. The next year, Jefferson and his congressional lieutenants brought proceedings against Supreme Court Justice Samuel Chase. The House impeached Chase, but the Senate acquitted him.

For a variety of reasons, Jefferson did not vigorously support the action, but in later years, his memory of Chase's behavior undoubtedly contributed to his bias against the judiciary.

Chase showed blatant partisanship when he presided in the trial of a prominent Jeffersonian for violation of the Sedition Act of 1798. This episode was at the heart of the impeachment proceeding against the jurist. Among the eight impeachment articles, the House charged him with "an indecent solicitude . . . for the conviction of the accused, . . . highly disgraceful to the character of a judge, as it was subversive." The Chase impeachment occurred amidst highly rancorous partisan wrangling. The Federalists, still very much alive, thought—with reason—that the attack upon Chase was but an overture to a full-scale assault upon the Supreme Court by their political adversaries, and that Jefferson's particular target was his kinsman Chief Justice John Marshall. Chase's defense counsel and Federalist senators staked some of their case on the partisan issue. The situation was ironic. The Federalists had passed the Sedition Act in large part to quash partisan opposition; now, they conveniently appealed to the legitimacy of political division. For their part, many of the Jeffersonians realized the desirability, even the necessity, for a "new libertarianism" that would insulate political criticism from official reprisal. Both sides thus acknowledged that repression inevitably was circular and contagious. Tolerance served ephemeral majorities and minorities equally well.

Chase's defense substantially argued that impeachment required the commission of an indictable crime, a proposition that would effectively narrow the scope of impeachment. The insistence on proof of a crime carried the day; of eight impeachment articles, the managers' greatest success came on a 19–15 vote against Chase on one count, still short of the two-thirds majority required for conviction. The historical evidence, however, is impressive in showing that neither English practice nor the framers of the American Constitution required an indictable crime as a basis for impeachment. Furthermore, by the standards of any day, Chase's personal conduct toward the defendant had been oppressive and deserved punishment.[8] But the reality is that the Senate acquitted the Justice and severely circumscribed the reach of impeachment. Chase's trial, nevertheless, resulted in a political retreat of the judiciary, and judges following him have generally accepted a cloistered political life. Jefferson was too harsh: impeachment did have some value as a "scarecrow."

The impeachment and trial of Andrew Johnson underlined the hazards of impeachment as a partisan process. Partisanship, of course, is a two-way street. In 1804 no Federalist voted to condemn Chase; similarly, in 1868 no Democrat voted for the impeachment or conviction of Johnson. Indeed, the Senate would have convicted Johnson had the vote been strictly along party lines; Johnson's survival depended on the acquittal votes of seven "recusant" Republican senators.

But if the fires of partisanship had not been banked in the 1860s, Congress had learned something from the Chase proceeding: ten of the eleven articles voted against Johnson alleged indictable offenses. The exception—Article X—comfortably fit Hamilton's category of political crimes. Congress charged in that article that the President had designed and intended "to set aside the rightful authority and powers of Congress, [and] did attempt to bring into disgrace, ridicule, hatred, contempt, and reproach, the Congress of the United States, [and] to impair and destroy the regard and respect . . . for the Congress." The President's speeches, the House charged, were "intemperate, inflammatory, and scandalous," and had brought his office into "contempt, ridicule, and disgrace." The Senate never voted on that proposition.[9]

As the House Judiciary Committee approached its impeachment inquiry a little more than a century later, both sides appealed to a usable past. President Nixon and his defenders found comfort in the partisanship of the Chase and Johnson impeachments, but primarily they turned to the narrow interpretation requiring the charge of a crime. That interpretation's fairness and its simplicity offered an understandable doctrine for politicians and laymen alike. Alexander Hamilton's lofty rhetoric about "political crimes" and "political" proceedings had little chance of resonating in a society that often used "political" as a pejorative word. Republican partisans conveniently forgot Gerald Ford's 1970 assault on Justice Douglas and his contention that the House alone could identify an impeachable crime. With similar ease, Democratic partisans forgot the arguments advanced by Douglas's lawyers, ones Democrats had confirmed, which turned on a narrow restriction of the House's powers. Impeachment, the Democratic-dominated committee concluded in 1970, was for criminal offenses only and was not a "general inquest" into the behavior of judges.

The Judiciary Committee staff, controlled by the Democratic majority, submitted its appeal to history on February 21, 1974. The report argued that the framers had included impeachment as a means of protecting the Constitution from unforeseen presidential abuses. "Impeachment," it noted, "is a constitutional safety valve; to fulfill this function, it must be flexible enough to cope with exigencies not now foreseeable." The report repudiated the criminal-indictability doctrine and closely approximated Ford's 1970 position.

James St. Clair and the White House lawyers dutifully provided the committee with their version of history and constitutional law. An indictable crime was a necessary prerequisite for impeachment, St. Clair argued; any other conclusion placed "a subjective gloss on the history of impeachment that results in permitting the Congress to do whatever it deems most politic." Nixon appeared at a March 6 press conference and took comfort in his lawyers' report. But he did not want people to believe that he favored "a narrow view" of impeachment. That, he feared, "might leave in the minds of some of our viewers and listeners a connotation which would be inaccurate. It is the constitutional view," he insisted, not just a narrow one. The President apparently knew something others did not, for he added: "The Constitution is very precise." Nixon noted that Senator Ervin agreed with the indictability doctrine; but he ignored Ervin's pointed restraint from commenting on the factual question, whether the President had committed an indictable offense.

After nearly two hundred years of constitutional exegesis, the meaning of the impeachment power remained debatable. Representative William Hungate (D–MO) later complimented the House committee's staff on its presentation, but he added that no one could tell "a freely elected Member of this Congress how to define impeachment." The profusion of reports and views unexpectedly confirmed Gerald Ford's basic proposition: the House alone would decide what constituted a basis for impeachment.[10]

The first impeachment resolution was introduced in the Congress by Representative Robert Drinan (D–MA) on July 31, 1973, not coincidentally, it seemed, just after Alexander Butterfield revealed the presidential taping system. Perhaps the suspicions regarding the President might be confirmed after all. Drinan, a Catholic priest and constitutional-law professor, called for an inquiry into the Watergate scandals, the secret bombing of Cambodia, impoundment of allocated funds, the unauthorized taping of conversations, and the development of a "super-secret security force" in the White House.[11]

William Cohen (R–ME) respected Drinan as a man in the forefront on issues yet realized that he had little support at the outset. But following the Saturday Night Massacre in October 1973, four impeachment bills appeared in the House hopper, including one from California Republican Paul McCloskey. The new resolutions repeated Drinan's charges but added others denouncing the President for breaking his trust with Congress when he dismissed Archibald Cox. Edward Hutchinson of the Judiciary Committee told a political lieutenant that it was not likely the House would impeach, despite the "very vocal minority to the contrary." House Majority Leader Thomas O'Neill later believed that the Republicans made a tactical blunder by not calling up a vote on Drinan's resolution, for it surely would have been defeated, affording Nixon some measure of vindication and leaving the impression that only a cranky, partisan few favored impeachment. But Gerald

Ford told O'Neill that the White House did not want a vote, fearing that people would mistake smoke for fire.[12]

The Judiciary Committee faithfully mirrored the House. The membership represented a broad geographical spread, with a proportional share of activists and back-benchers and an ethnic and racial mixture, and reflected a variety of ideological commitments. The leadership was undistinguished. Committee members rarely criticized the two ranking members, both of whom were known for their party loyalty. But Chairman Rodino carefully refrained from partisan or judgmental comments during the inquiry period. He had his ear to the ground within his committee, as well as outside. One Southern Democrat remarked that if O'Neill's aggressiveness had prevailed, Rodino "would have lost the necessary middle of the roaders that shaped [impeachment] in the final analysis." He added that Rodino's style "really paid off in the long run." Ranking Republican Hutchinson, on the other hand, made his loyalty to Nixon clear yet occasionally obliquely criticized the White House. In March he stated that he would advise the President that executive privilege could not stand in the way of an impeachment inquiry. Earlier, Hutchinson had told one of his constituents, baby-food manufacturer Dan Gerber, that he considered the White House's handling of the situation incompetent and "incredible."[13]

For Hutchinson, intelligent but not very energetic, leadership essentially consisted of a passive and feckless faith that no Republican would vote to impeach the President. Consequently, he had little understanding, let alone sympathy, for colleagues who demanded a greater measure of cooperation from Nixon. Hutchinson had become the ranking minority member as a result of a coin-flip with Congressman Robert McClory, and he often deferred to the greater activism of his colleague. Nonetheless, when McClory informed his fellow Republicans in a party caucus that he had begun to believe the President had "technically" violated the Constitution, Hutchinson shot back: "Come on now, there's no *nice* way you can impeach a President of the United States." Hutchinson thought that the Nixon-haters and "some very influential groups" had determined to oust the President at any cost. Yet for months he contrarily asserted that the Democrats had a cynical desire, not to impeach Nixon but instead to stretch the proceeding out in order to fuel a useful political issue.[14]

Most Democrats on the Judiciary Committee generally identified with the party's liberal wing, including Harold D. Donohue (MA), Jack Brooks (TX), Robert W. Kastenmeier (WI), Don Edwards (CA), John Conyers, Jr. (MI), Joshua Eilberg (PA), Jerome R. Waldie (CA), Robert F. Drinan (MA), Charles B. Rangel (NY), Barbara Jordan (TX), Elizabeth Holtzman (NY), and Edward Mezvinsky (IA). A more centrist northern and western group included William L. Hungate (MO), Paul S. Sarbanes (MD), John F. Seiberling (OH), George E. Danielson (CA), and Wayne Owens (UT). Southerners Walter Flowers (AL), James R. Mann (SC), and Ray Thornton (AR) rounded out the Democratic majority.

Two Republican Judiciary Committee centrists from Illinois, Robert McClory and Tom Railsback, had feuded for years. They competed throughout the inquiry for leadership within the minority, and particularly among those Republicans willing to consider impeachment. Several Republicans labored to champion the President's cause. Charles E. Wiggins (CA), who represented part of Nixon's old congressional district, quickly emerged as the President's most able defender on the committee and clearly became the leader of the loyalists. He generally could count on support from Henry P. Smith III (NY), Charles W. Sandman, Jr. (NJ), David W. Dennis (IN), Wiley Mayne (IA), Lawrence J. Hogan (MD), Trent Lott (MS), Harold V. Froehlich (WI), Carlos J. Moorhead (CA), Joseph J. Maraziti (NJ), and Delbert L. Latta (OH). Hamilton Fish, Jr. (NY), M. Caldwell Butler (VA), and William S. Cohen (ME) displayed some independence from the outset, asking pointed questions and sometimes straying from a party-line vote.

John Doar, the House committee's special counsel, had begun to organize his own staff at the end of 1973. He thus bypassed the committee's existing structure, as well as the members' own staff workers, a decision that resulted in unnecessary rivalries and eventually colored the relationship between Doar and the congressmen. At first, Doar seemed inclined not to use Richard Cates, who already had done much to persuade Rodino that a case for impeachment could be made. Cates had established substantial rapport with the members, a relationship that spanned ideologies and parties. Doar apparently sensed Cates's standing, as well as his ability, and retained him as Senior Associate General Counsel, along with Bernard Nussbaum.

By March 1974 Doar had hired a staff that numbered more than 100 persons, almost half of them lawyers. The staff, Democrats and Republicans alike, had no views on impeachment when hired—at least for the record. Forty-three lawyers worked on impeachment matters; eighteen were from Harvard, Yale, and Columbia; and only four came from law schools west of the Mississippi—statistics that undoubtedly reinforced the President's hostility toward East Coast elites. At the same time, St. Clair directed a White House legal staff of approximately fifteen—while busily engaged on another front with Leon Jaworski and the Watergate Special Prosecution Force.

In the committee, Doar divided his staff into two groups: one provided legal support for him and directed research into constitutional issues, while the other (largely headed by Cates) conducted various investigations of allegations involving the Plumbers, the Watergate break-in and cover-up, Nixon's personal finances, White House use of federal agencies for improper political purposes, and other alleged instances of misconduct such as the Cambodia bombing and the impoundment of funds.[15]

By most accounts, Chairman Rodino found in John Doar a man who matched his own caution. Committee members and staff were at sea for months trying to understand Doar's direction and intent. Congressman Butler, who eventually voted to impeach the President, thought Doar to be like John Foster Dulles: "dull, duller, dulles." He also believed that Doar favored impeachment; for Doar to enter the contest without ending in impeachment, Butler said, "would be like playing in the World Series and not hitting a home run." Butler conceded that the staff had struggled to maintain objectivity, yet some observers, then and later, insisted that Doar was committed from the start to carrying out impeachment. One staffer, who claimed a place in Doar's inner circle, wrote that Doar and this group never had any doubt about impeachment and would proceed to recommend it unless the President somehow presented overwhelming evidence of his innocence. She admitted some uncertainty as to when Doar "made his decision" to recommend impeachment, whether in March or July. Whatever Doar's true feelings, he left behind him a wake of conflicting testimony as to his intelligence and ability. Fish praised him as a "giant," while Flowers considered his work "tedious" and his performance like a "shaggy-dog joke."[16]

Members complained that Doar treated them like dull-witted schoolchildren, and veteran staff people found him oblivious to the sensibilities of the members. A prominent staffer thought it symbolic that when Doar made his presentations to the committee, he usually occupied the chair reserved for witnesses. In the meantime, the members indicated that they were wary of Doar by consulting with the regular staff while he spoke. At times, the procedure resulted in the committee staff's directing questions at members of the inquiry staff. For some, the contest eventually appeared as Doar *vs.* St. Clair, with the committee sitting as a jury.[17]

Much of the criticism of Doar centered on his desire to treat the committee as a grand jury, with himself as the members' lawyer and mentor, much like the relation of the Special Prosecutor to the Watergate grand jury. Doar rejected any opportunity for the Nixon defense and its lawyers to make a case. The strategy eventually led Doar to deny St. Clair the right to cross-examine any witnesses that appeared before the committee, or to make any presentment of his own. This approach virtually dictated an impeachment, allowing the Senate then to evaluate the guilt or innocence of the accused. Doar betrayed his insensitivity to the political calculus: no member dared vote for impeachment without effective certainty of the President's guilt. The consequences would have been disastrous. The Republicans naturally objected to Doar's procedure—although their own lead counsel supported

Doar—but longtime committee staff members and liberals joined in opposing him. Rodino at first backed Doar, but in the face of a joint challenge by Edwards and Wiggins, he retreated. Edwards reminded Rodino that in 1970 counsel for Justice Douglas had exercised the right of participating and cross-examining. Edwards, a longtime liberal, realized the basic unfairness of Doar's position; on a more practical level, he knew that it would only polarize the committee and give credence to the charges that the inquiry was partisan.[18]

A more serious criticism came from Leon Jaworski, who found Doar almost incapable of understanding the case. Jaworski remembered that lawyers on his staff had Doar in their office night after night, "coaching him, as poor John didn't know which way was front." Jaworski's relationship with Rodino and Doar apparently was somewhat strained, as is typical of competitive agencies each anxious for a lion's share of the credit. Rodino at one point had complained that Jaworski was withholding material, but the Special Prosecutor dismissed the allegation as a cover for Rodino and Doar's own dilatoriness.[19]

In May 1974, Doar began to read to restless, bored, and confused members of the House committee a multivolume "Statement of Information," a series of books compiled to illustrate the case against the President. During these presentations, Doar had instructed the staff not to offer any conclusions or intepretations, reflecting his determination to maintain the appearance of fairness. Yet the members craved understanding, particularly an understanding of how numerous, isolated incidents demonstrated a consistent pattern of presidential abuse of power, obstruction of justice, or failure to faithfully execute the laws.[20]

Democrats chafed at Doar for being dilatory and insensitive to their needs. Republicans, however, had a different and more serious problem: they believed that their Chief Counsel was unsympathetic to the President and supported Doar's every move. The minority had named Albert Jenner, a Chicago lawyer, their Chief Counsel in January. Jenner had a reputation as a formidable litigator. He had been senior counsel to the Warren Commission, which had investigated President Kennedy's assassination, and had played a prominent role some years earlier in challenging the authority of the House Committee on Un-American Activities. Railsback had sponsored Jenner's appointment. But Republicans may well have had cause for concern from the outset, when Jenner praised Doar and spoke about their "joint effort."

A week after his appointment, Jenner publicly stated that the President might be impeached for the actions of his aides, even if he were unaware of them. Attorney General Saxbe called this a "bizarre theory," while Wiggins furiously criticized Jenner, asking whether he had "appreciated the significance" of his remarks, and urged him to recant. Jenner's deputy, Sam Garrison, clearly more devoted than his chief to the partisan concerns of the

Republicans, complained to Hutchinson that Jenner's cooperation with Doar had undercut the Republican position on numerous matters, particularly on St. Clair's participation. Garrison contended that Jenner considered himself answerable primarily to Doar, not to the Republican members. He feared that Jenner might say publicly that he was obligated to voice the minority's position although he disagreed with it. Jenner's role was a "farce," Garrison told Hutchinson; the Chicago lawyer was acting as if he had a "vested right" to his position. The minority tensions became public, and a columnist accused Hutchinson of instructing Garrison to obstruct the proceedings. But the real issue was whether the divided Republicans on the committee could have a single counsel to advocate their views.[21]

Republican staffers saw Jenner as caught between the conflicting ambitions of Railsback and Wiggins. Yet they knew that Jenner had not devoted much energy to the problem, as he was constantly worrying about the time it was taking and the drain it had imposed on his Chicago practice. His warmest defenders, such as Cohen, recognized that Jenner had alienated many Republican colleagues. Butler, almost desperate to find an advocate for the President, realized by spring that Jenner was not "speaking for us." Even Railsback, his sponsor, acknowledged that Jenner had forgotten his role as adviser and instead had become an advocate for impeachment. Some more conservative Republicans, such as Latta, attacked Jenner for his earlier defense of the civil liberties of prostitutes and complained that he had chaired the American Bar Association Section on Individual Rights and Responsibilities—a liberal bastion within the ABA, according to Latta. By February Garrison criticized Jenner for his support of the committee staff's broad interpretation of the House's impeachment authority.

In May Hogan urged Hutchinson to dismiss Jenner—labeling him the "Assistant Majority Counsel." Hogan charged Jenner with impeding the Republican effort and having been "derelict in serving our needs." As matters moved to a climax in July, the Republicans—including those leaning toward impeachment, such as Hogan and McClory—voted to inform Rodino that Garrison was their Chief Counsel but that Rodino could consider Jenner as an Associate Committee Counsel. They requested, and Rodino agreed, that Jenner sit at the table with Doar. Thus the anomaly developed that the evidence converted the Minority Counsel to the majority position. By then, according to his later testimony, Jenner had been convinced that Nixon "was and is a liar of the most vicious kind." He also disparaged committee Republicans who had sought to rush the inquiry in the hopes of gaining an early acquittal before all the evidence had been developed.[22]

The issue of secrecy plagued the House committee during much of the inquiry. The matter concerned both White House lawyers, who supplied material, and the Special Prosecutor, who worried that premature revelations might impair future prosecutions. The issue touched the members' sensibilities, because security requirements prevented their unlimited access to evidentiary material. More fundamentally, Doar and Jenner perceived the inquiry as a grand-jury proceeding, an interpretation that, by giving the committee's work the secrecy of a grand jury, would severely restrict the President's defense efforts. The majority and minority counsels met with St. Clair early in February and, in effect, told him how the inquiry would proceed. St. Clair strenuously objected and persuaded congressmen from both parties to reject the grand-jury approach, a rare victory for him.[23]

The committee's assertiveness on the grand-jury issue led to open sniping by members who feared a too-independent staff. Early in March, Railsback and Dennis complained that Doar's letters to St. Clair had not been circulated to the committee. A month later, Latta, an outspoken Nixon partisan, demanded to know "who is directing this inquiry, whether it is the staff or whether it is this committee." Latta had support from other Republicans—and in time, from liberal Democrats who objected to Doar's aloofness. After April, the staff tended, at least on the record, to defer more to the committee, and Rodino seemed particularly sensitive to his colleagues' complaints that the committee did not control its own inquiry. Latta persisted in attacking the staff for its bias against the President. When Doar discussed illegal campaign contributions, Latta pressed him about similar offenses in Lyndon Johnson's campaigns. In June, Latta openly mocked his colleagues who agreed with Doar that the committee should hear only a few witnesses and deny St. Clair the right to call his own. Doar had asked for a July 12 cutoff date for testimony; by then, Nixon's supporters no longer favored a quick end to the inquiry, instead believing that lengthy debate and testimony served their cause best.[24]

The committee's dealings with the President over its requests for tapes sharpened the internal conflict. When the White House submitted its first batch of materials in mid-March, Rodino complained about the lack of cooperation and White House attempts to characterize the committee's work as a fishing expedition. Brooks called the Administration tactic "White House hucksterism," but Sandman said that he had heard enough personal attacks on the President and vigorously supported him. Rodino, determined both to defend Doar and to maintain amicable relations among members and staff, replied that the staff had done an excellent job and thanked Sandman for this thoughts and concerns. Again, the grand-jury analogy raised rancor, as some members saw that model as diminishing their role and making them merely the clients of the staff. Mezvinsky had no problem with the theory, however, and argued that St. Clair would have his opportunity to demonstrate "his own renowned trial techniques" in the Senate. But other Democrats realized that theory counted for nothing compared to the necessity for fairness. That need dictated something other than an abstract application of a grand-jury style.[25]

The committee's pursuit of the tapes provoked passionate attacks from the White House. Presidential adviser Father John McLaughlin appeared at the Harvard Law School Republican Club on March 29 and compared the Judiciary Committee proceedings to Joseph Stalin's purge trials. He singled out his fellow Jesuit, Congressman Drinan, for his most vitriolic attacks: "No jury in the country would tolerate this man sitting in judgment. . . . He has all the openmindedness of the Sanhedrin judging Christ," McLaughlin complained.[26]

Throughout April, the committee had bristled at the White House's delay in releasing more tapes. After extensive wrangling, it approved a bipartisan compromise subpoena on April 11. Two weeks later, St. Clair requested and received an additional five days to comply, a deadline he met when the President released the tape transcripts on April 30. The next day, Doar informed the committee that his staff had reason to believe the edited transcripts they had received (the tapes and Dictabelts had not yet arrived) had numerous inaccuracies and omissions that could be rectified with better listening equipment. Clearly, at this point, the majority considered the President in contempt of the subpoena. Rodino, in a rare display of combativeness, contended that the House, and not the President, must determine the relevance of evidence.

The White House and the committee repeatedly clashed over the President's claims to executive privilege and the House's constitutional authorization for "the sole power to impeach." What limits could Nixon impose on the inquiry? More than a century earlier, President James K. Polk had promised that the House would receive "all the archives, public or private" and would have "every facility in the power of the Executive afforded them" if the House believed "that there had been malversation in office." Considerations of confidentiality and national security did, however, constitute a fair qualification on Polk's generosity. In that regard, the committee had to offer Richard Nixon some running room on his claims of executive privilege and give some credence to his fear that "the institution of the Presidency itself would be fatally compromised." But the President's problem was that for every such claim he made, he reinforced assumptions that he was an obstructionist and had something to hide.[27]

The committee eventually voted 20–18 to authorize Rodino to write Nixon, informing him that he had failed to comply with the subpoena of April 11. Republican Cohen broke ranks; otherwise the vote followed straight party lines. But that partisanship masked some growing disquiet among Republicans and conservative southerners. Just prior to the vote, Cohen proposed a more conciliatory letter than the Democrats preferred, renewing a plea for the President's cooperation. The Democrats and Nixon's hard-line supporters opposed Cohen's motion, but he picked up eleven votes, including those of Democrats Flowers and Mann and Republicans Railsback, Fish, and Butler. It was a moment that foreshadowed future developments.[28]

The committee moved to executive session on May 9, and Doar began his presentation of the "Statement of Information." During his readings, Doar complained about the inaccuracies his staff had discovered in the few available transcripts of tapes. He also objected to the insertion of the transcripts' recurrent phrase, "Material unrelated to Presidential action deleted." "I do not know what that word or those words mean," Doar told the members; "I do not know what the test is. I do not know whether it is inaction that is covered, [or] is knowledge covered, [or] is lack of knowledge covered." Doar's position increased demands for renewed pressure on the White House. At the May 30 meeting, Flowers offered a draft of a letter informing the President that the committee considered his acts a "grave matter"; more ominously, the letter warned Nixon that his actions required members to draw a "negative inference," and that his refusal to cooperate might itself constitute a ground for impeachment. Flowers's view reflected the maturation of his suspicions at the time of Cox's dismissal that President Nixon had something to hide. His motion passed overwhelmingly, 28–10.

A coalition of the President's defenders and wavering committee members suggested that the courts decide whether Nixon had complied with the committee's subpoena. "[I]t is imperative that we not act alone," Froehlich told the Chairman. Froehlich thought that the House might find itself in the position of having to vote impeachment on what he called "nonsubstantive," or procedural, grounds, and he apparently believed that it might be easier to cloak the House's action with judicial support. McClory, as well as Doar and Jenner, however, successfully argued the impropriety of judicial involvement in the responsibilities of the House. Waldie, perhaps the President's most outspoken opponent, then proposed that the House order its Sergeant-at-Arms to summon Nixon before the House and show cause why he should not be held in contempt. Republicans objected, and Rodino sustained them. But more ominous words came from staunch Nixon loyalists. When the committee issued the subpoena in March that the White House denounced as a "fishing expedition," Hutchinson thought the subpoena was "not excessive and it's right on target." For Hutchinson, that was equivalent to a denunciation of the President. Vice President Ford later claimed he told Nixon in May that he could no longer support the stonewalling and that the House had a right to the information. "We're handling it this way because we think we're right," the President told Ford.[29] Publicly, the Vice President maintained his steadfast support of Nixon.

Meanwhile, numerous members had become restless with Doar's presentation of the evidence. The information books covered a variety of subjects, with the cover-up being the largest and most important, yet they seemed aimless. The materials were presented chronologically; thus, if numerous calls or conversations occurred in a three-day period, they were set down chronologically. But they related to multiple subjects, and the chronology had to be keyed to the different subjects. Doar's presentation did not attempt to do that. About July 1, several members turned to Richard Cates and other staff members for succinct summaries of the evidence and some clues as to the reasonable conclusions that could be drawn from it. Cates notified the entire committee of his intention to analyze the material. The first two meetings dedicated to that task lasted three hours each, with only Democratic members in attendance, although some Republican staff workers appeared. Essentially, Cates disentangled the material from its rigid chronological setting to offer a coherent theory of presidential involvement in the cover-up. Following this, Cates held smaller breakfast meetings for a variety of Republicans and Southern Democrats, some hitherto identified as Nixon loyalists. Perhaps his most important meetings occurred during the week of July 12, when Cates met exclusively with a group of undecided Republicans. Hamilton Fish had initiated these meetings, but again, representatives of different factions attended.

Fish later testified that Cates, "a highly trained trial lawyer who had done exhaustive work," gave them "a very sensible, rational theory." Fish found it "convincing"; his colleague, William Cohen, similarly was "very impressed" with Cates's briefings. Flowers, the Southern conservative, found Cates always available, always helpful, and always "the facts man"—truly, a lawyer's lawyer.[30]

Material began to leak from the committee, much to the consternation of the President and his supporters, but the leaks made little difference, since the major evidence—the tape transcripts—had become a matter of public record. That being the case, members concerned with the appearances of justice and fairness—members from both sides, it must be remembered—had a valid objection to the continuance of executive sessions.

St. Clair requested that the House committee hearings be open and televised, claiming that the selective leaks of evidence unfairly damaged the President. But Republican staff members sensed a shrewder reason. St. Clair himself had seen how passively the members listened to Doar, their boredom apparent to all. A television spectacle could either discredit the committee or make the members more active, questioning Doar incessantly and dragging the process on indefinitely. The White House now understood that time was on its side and could create a backlash in its favor, as the nation might grow bored with the inquiry. Reluctantly, committee Republicans opposed St. Clair's move. With elections only months away, they had no interest in prolonging the work. McClory reported to an ailing Hutchinson that the inquiry was proceeding "in a most satisfactory manner."[31] As Doar's presentation wound down, the questions became more desultory, more obviously partisan. For his part, Rodino persistently restricted the members' questions and comments to keep the proceedings moving. Finally, on June 21, Doar concluded his presentation of the evidence, six weeks and eighteen closed sessions after he had started.

News releases and deliberate leaks from the committee generated a crescendo of charges and implications of presidential wrongdoing. The President's popularity continued to plunge. In June and early July, Nixon journeyed to the Mideast, traveling where no American President had before, and then to the Soviet Union for another summit. The televised images of the President riding by train through Egypt, cheered by enthusiastic crowds; continuing on to the long-forbidden and malevolent Syria, leader of the so-called radical bloc of Arab states; receiving a warm, emotional reception in Israel; and finally basking in the glow of an apparently enhanced détente with the Soviets, contrasted jarringly with the steady revelations regarding his behavior at home. Cynics saw Nixon's foreign activities as an attempt to distract attention from Watergate, of course; and lay analysts had a field day when the President's physician revealed that Nixon had suffered from phlebitis and a blood clot during the Mideast journey.

While Nixon regarded his trips as an attempt to "restore some respect for the office as well as the man," he had few illusions about their effectiveness in distracting attention from the "merciless onslaught" besieging him. Secretary of State Henry Kissinger, however, dramatically sought to mark Watergate's corrosive effects on foreign policy when he threatened to resign because of a *New York Times* editorial charging that he had lied to congressional investigators about his role in authorizing wiretaps of his aides. In a stopover in Salzburg, Austria, on June 11, Kissinger said he would not have his "public honor" discussed. With his credibility in question, he found it impossible to conduct foreign policy. If the matter were not cleared up, he warned, "I will resign." The President apparently dismissed Kissinger's predicament as an amusing ploy. "A *Times* editorial is not a charge," he told Haig. He nevertheless assured Kissinger of his support. He also reinforced himself during the journey to the Mideast, convinced that his "terrible battering" over Watergate was "really pygmy-sized" compared to what he had done for world peace.[32]

The President's journey came on the heels of a cease-fire arrangement between Israel and Syria. The Gallup poll showed a three-point rise in Nixon's approval rating, and by the end of June, support for his removal had declined from 48 to 44 percent of polled respondents, with 41 percent opposing such action.

The Mideast visit also rekindled some optimism in Nixon. Banking on the euphoria of the trip, the President and his supporters believed that a combination of Republicans and Southern Democrats could stave off impeachment in the House. Haldeman and Haig both conveyed a buoyant confidence to the President. Joe Waggoner (D–LA), a longtime congressional supporter, told Nixon he would not be impeached as long as the Supreme Court did not hold him in contempt. According to Nixon's memoirs, his family's confrontations with the media over Watergate troubled him most. He ignored the fact, however, that his attempts to use his family in his defense put them at risk.[33]

At the end of June, Nixon flew to Moscow to meet with Leonid Brezhnev. Criticism from conservatives in both parties mounted, fearful as they were that the President would fail to bargain effectively because of his political weakness, even desperation. Critics deplored his willingness to engage in further arms agreements with the Soviets and also prodded him to press Moscow for the release of Soviet Jews who wished to emigrate. Secretary of Defense James Schlesinger insulted the President at a National Security Council meeting, when he proposed a SALT agreement that assured overwhelming American nuclear superiority.

The effect of Watergate on other affairs of state is elusive; even the President had his moments of confusion. At one point he said that his domestic problems severely damaged his ability "to defuse, or at least to circumvent" the opponents of détente. Yet at other times he readily denied the effects of Watergate and thought that limiting détente might serve his domestic political needs. Nixon did not secure any agreement on offensive nuclear weapons, but he carefully refrained from blaming that on Watergate. "I think that it came out about right," he remembered. It was just as well that we had not reached any agreement on nuclear weapons, he wrote, because an agreement would invite opposition from "some of our best friends prior to the impeachment vote."

By the time Nixon returned from the Soviet Union on July 4, he realized that he had serious problems in the House of Representatives. The President discounted his aides' optimism. He canceled a speech that would have summarized the development of détente. Was Nixon afraid of alienating his right-wing supporters? Certainly, his well-honed political instincts told him that "on some subsurface level, the political tide was flowing fast, and flowing against me."[34]

James St. Clair finally appeared before the House Judiciary Committee on behalf of the President in late June. Members desperately trying to find a way to support the President had eagerly anticipated the lawyer's appearance. Flowers expected St. Clair to contrast sharply with the tedious performances of Doar and Jenner, and Cohen thought that St. Clair opened with a skillful presentation. But both quickly realized that St. Clair made a damning mistake in his first appearance when he introduced a partial tape transcript that the committee long had sought without success. The tape had been subpoenaed, but the President had not complied. Outraged, Cohen thought that in one brief moment St. Clair had totally nullified his earlier effectiveness. Butler was equally annoyed. He thought that St. Clair had been "trifling with us. When he has the things in his safe and just dribbles them out, . . . it's just unprofessional." Flowers deplored the tactic but acknowledged that St. Clair was handicapped by lack of cooperation from the White House. The President's most ardent liberal antagonists, such as Waldie and Elizabeth Holtzman, openly assailed St. Clair. A broader array of Democrats argued that his presentation had gone beyond the factual and had provided conclusions, contrary to the committee's rules.

From another perspective, Richard Cates thought that St. Clair had failed to grasp what may have been the last opportunity to save the President. In no way did St. Clair appeal to sympathy or humanity in pleading Nixon's cause, nor did he attempt to elicit any responses of compassion and understanding—responses that might have kindled latent support for the President. St. Clair's reputation for "all case and no cause" haunted him. Overall, among committee members, especially Republicans, the feeling was that he had offered many conclusions, but little in the way of exculpatory evidence.[35]

During St. Clair's presentation, Rodino conducted the proceedings with his customary calmness and evenhandedness; indeed, for many of the liberals he may have been too evenhanded. But Rodino perhaps sensed that St. Clair had done the President little good and might even have clinched the case against him. Following St. Clair's appearance on June 27, Rodino said in the presence of reporters that all twenty-one Democrats would vote for impeachment. The remark touched the raw nerves of conservative Southern Democrats who were not yet ready to commit themselves, either in or out of the committee. Rodino took the floor to deny his statement. Interestingly, Hutchinson, sensitive to the courtesies of the House, promptly defended Rodino, while committee member Hogan, one of the most politically calculating of the Republicans, who had his eye on the Maryland gubernatorial race and who later voted for impeachment, denounced the entire inquiry as "biased" and "unfair." Rodino, in predicting a partisan vote to impeach, also may have been guilty of simple inattention or of unwillingness to confront reality, for some of his Democratic colleagues, including Flowers, Jordan, Mann, and Thornton, complained that the case against Nixon had not been made and criticized Doar's "slow movement."[36]

After extended discussions with Doar and St. Clair, and among themselves, the committee members finally agreed in July to hear additional testimony from nine witnesses. Alexander Butterfield appeared to discuss the President's work habits. He portrayed Nixon as the man in charge; Haldeman and other aides did nothing without the President's knowledge, and Haldeman himself was nothing more than "an implementer." St. Clair tried to discredit Butterfield, but the testimony fit the image the President himself had fashioned in his various image-building efforts. Nixon's lawyers had more success in insulating the President when Fred LaRue testified that John Mitchell knew money had been paid to the burglary defendants. St. Clair and several Republican congressmen focused on the President's knowledge of events, something LaRue knew, or would admit to knowing, nothing of. The procedural limitations of the committee hearings were all too apparent. When Cohen questioned LaRue about raising money from Thomas Pappas, LaRue denied doing so but acknowledged that he had seen Pappas for other reasons. Cohen's time for questioning then expired, and no one else pursued the question of why LaRue met with the shadowy Pappas—"the Greek bearing gifts," as Dean and Mitchell had described him.[37]

Mitchell, then preparing for his own trial, appeared, but his lawyer warned the committee that Mitchell would have to be selective in his answers. Mitchell's' most important revelation involved a February 1973 visit from Richard Moore, then a White House special assistant, who was personally close to Mitchell. Moore had been deputized—by whom specifically was never revealed—to visit Mitchell, discuss the forthcoming Senate Select Committee hearings, and request his aid in raising money for the Watergate burglars. Mitchell refused, according to his own version of events.[38]

Once again, John Dean provided the most interest and generated the most heat. For more than a year Nixon's defenders had argued that Dean was a loose cannon, that he had instigated and carried out the cover-up on his own, to protect himself and a few others—but not the President. Charles Colson later testified that Dean ran the cover-up, even exerting pressure on Colson to cooperate in the effort. Dean admitted to St. Clair that Nixon did not specifically instruct him in the cover-up, but the former aide insisted that his conversations with Haldeman and Ehrlichman demonstrated both "concern and instructions" regarding the cover-up; "it was not quite willy-nilly, as you have tried to portray," Dean retorted to a hostile questioner. After he returned to the White House from a Far East trip just after the break-in, he investigated matters for Haldeman and determined that Haldeman, Ehrlichman, Mitchell, Magruder, and Strachan all were "vulnerable and I felt that it was my responsibility to assist." Congressman Butler had been trying to determine the moment of "conception" of the cover-up; for himself, Dean said that had he stayed in Manila, he might not have been "raped."[39]

Dean's appearance provided dramatic evidence pointing to the erosion of the President's public standing. After Dean testified for the Ervin Committee in July 1973, opinion-poll respondents narrowly expressed a belief that Nixon had been more truthful. A year later, by a 46–29 margin, they found Dean to be the more credible.

Henry Petersen vigorously defended the early stage of the Watergate investigation by the Justice Department, and, for the record, noted the U.S. Attorneys' role in exposing the cover-up. Petersen's most devastating remarks centered on his trust in the President and his willingness to share privileged information with him. The tapes, of course, revealed that Nixon had improperly provided his aides with Petersen's reports; the President's own words, together with Petersen's testimony, offered a substantial case for obstruction of justice.[40]

Under St. Clair's prodding, Charles Colson said that the President had no advance knowledge of the break-in of Ellsberg's psychiatrist. He cited a tape transcript of his telephone conversation with John Ehrlichman in which he had recommended that executive privilege be waived and that the President appoint a Special Prosecutor, recommendations that Colson claimed Ehrlichman had not relayed to Nixon. He also claimed that Dean opposed a Special Prosecutor unless the new appointee reported directly to him.

Colson revived the finger-pointing that had characterized Oval Office discussions in early 1973. He claimed he told the President to urge Mitchell—"the guy who was responsible"—to come forward "and take the consequences." At that point—mid-February 1973—Colson said, Nixon responded angrily, insisting that "I am not about to take an innocent person [Mitchell] and make him a scapegoat."

Colson also raised what came to be another favorite White House explanation of events: the CIA had played a decisive role in the events of Watergate. By December 1973, Colson believed that the CIA and the Hughes Tool Company had "unexplained connections" to the affair. He discussed his theory with the President and then talked to Haig about it. As they concluded their conversation, Haig phoned Nixon and relayed the message to Colson that his chief would not harm the nation's foreign policy, yet the President encouraged Colson to dig further and "be careful to get the facts first." Colson concluded that the White House would do nothing. He remembered Haig saying, "Chuck, we may [g]o down and be impeached, but we simply can't drag down the Government of the United States with us." That remark apparently confirmed Colson's faith in the CIA conspiracy theories, but he did not question Haig's shadowy role. In later years, he described Haig as "loyal" to the President, but "never unmindful of his military background."

Colson's hints tantalized. He reminded the committee that the Joint Chiefs of Staff had spied on the President; why not then believe the CIA had undermined Nixon? (Colson eventually acknowledged that internal spying was widespread: Nixon had used both Haig and Colson to spy on Kissinger.) The President, furthermore, could not "crack down" on the military, "because of what they knew and what they had taken"—a dark hint, never really pursued by the committee. It was not Colson's last attempt to till revisionist soil.[41]

The House Judiciary Committee Democrats, supported by Hutchinson and Lott, two of the President's most committed defenders, decided to hear the witnesses in executive session, ostensibly because their testimony might jeopardize pending cases. Most Republican members objected to closing the proceedings, with McClory reminding the Democrats that many people believed they could not impeach the President in the open.[42] But the secret testimony proved rather tepid, except for that provided by Colson and Butterfield. Much of it reiterated what had been tendered to the Senate Select Committee the previous summer. Unlike the Select Committee's senators, the House members had little opportunity to develop any line of inquiry in depth; moreover, the committee and its staff had no inclination for further investigation. A year earlier, Howard Baker had established the basic criteria for determining the meaning of events: what did the President know, and when did he know it? The answers—for some, at least—lay embedded in the tapes, and they had been dissected and analyzed in microscopic detail by the staff. By then, Richard Nixon was the most relevant witness.

As the witnesses testified, the committee released more than 4,000 pages of evidence, including St. Clair's rebuttal. The staff also issued a separate document detailing its corrections and additions to the White House transcripts. In his June 27 presentation to the committee, St. Clair repeatedly remarked that different people would make different transcriptions, given the poor quality of the tapes. As if anticipating some difficulty, St. Clair stressed that transcribing the tapes had become "quite an art." He also gave the impression that the White House had been overly severe in its rendition, as he noted that the committee's transcripts "are more favorable to the President than our own." But the committee found significant discrepancies in the Administration's transcripts; the White House versions had not in fact been less favorable. For example, the committee found a clear indication in the March 13, 1973 tape that Nixon had rejected the "hang-out road"—that is, a full revelation of the truth—in a conversation with Dean. Again, in his March 22, 1973 talk with Mitchell, the President repudiated Eisenhower's scrupulous standards for the conduct of subordinates; more important, in this exchange, he told Mitchell to "stonewall" and to take the Fifth Amendment. In other ways, it is true, the committee's transcripts spared the President. Specifically, Rodino and Hutchinson agreed to delete some of the President's racial and ethnic slurs, although leaks eventually made many of them public. The arbitrary omissions troubled members from different parts of the political spectrum.[43]

The release of the committee's version of the tapes resulted in another publicity disaster for the White House. One staff member, who assisted Buzhardt in listening to the tapes, gave Haig a detailed rebuttal. He admitted that few of his changes had significance, but he contended that the committee's decision to offer its own version was "terribly prejudicial" in itself. He also knew that the White House could not quibble with the transcripts so long as Nixon refused to release tapes and let the public itself judge. The President himself knew the meaning of his predicament: "this innocent discrepancy," he realized, made him "look both sinister and foolish."

One presidential speechwriter complained to Haig that the White House had permitted the public to believe that the committee's transcripts amounted to "the King James version of the tapes—infallible and devinely [sic] inspired." Altogether, he lamented, the White House had been playing "catchup ball, leading with our chin, and letting the opposition shape the news." The President needed a more vigorous "political defense," otherwise his legal defense was meaningless. The glory days of 1972 offered instruction: "we waxed McGovern," by repeating over and over the attacks on the Democratic candidate's vulnerabilities; the same was needed for Nixon's enemies within the committee. The pliable "enemy," as always, was the media: convince the public that coverage was excessive and that consequently any impeachment or trial would be unfair. A " 'sick and tired of Watergate' " theme, the aide believed, might be the most powerful weapon for the Administration. White House publicists and legislative-liaison staff played that message hard in the materials they transmitted to friendly members of the committee. But, above all, the speechwriter concluded, Nixon himself must lead the charge; only his personal leadership could provide the people with "a reason to believe in and trust the President." He had to win both respect and sympathy. It was not to be: by now, Richard Nixon had abandoned the field to surrogates.[44]

Vice President Ford remained dutiful, despite warnings from his aides to maintain distance between himself and the President. On July 12, a day after the House committee made its evidence public, Ford stated that the "new evidence as well as the old evidence" exonerated Nixon. Ford may have been obtuse, as some critics charged, but he apparently had no knowledge of the extent to which the White House had played with the evidence. For example, the White House and the Special Prosecutor both furnished the committee with copies of Ehrlichman's handwritten notes. But the White House compilation included nearly double the number of blank pages, including ones that in the other copies of the same notes described the conversations between Nixon and Ehrlichman respecting the Ellsberg prosecution.[45]

* * *

Whatever shackles had been imposed on St. Clair during the lengthy proceedings before the House Judiciary Committee, they dissolved on July 18 as he presented his closing defense of the President. He spoke for nearly one and a half hours, finally gaining an opportunity to display his reputed skills. St. Clair sensed the decisiveness and the solemnity of the occasion. His argument was impressive: organized, articulate, unyielding in behalf of his client, totally skeptical of the adversarial positions—and selective. At the outset, he called the committee members to account, insisting that they must hold evidence to a "clear and convincing" standard in order to impeach the President. "Inferences," St. Clair said, would not do—a clear attack upon Butterfield's testimony that Haldeman, like any aide, was an extension of the President and merely an "implementer." What Ehrlichman did by way of the break-in at Dr. Fielding's offices, and what he did in his approach to Judge Byrne in the Ellsberg trial, could not be traced to Nixon in a "clear and convincing" manner. How far, St. Clair in effect asked, must the President answer for his aides? After all, he had dismissed them when he realized they might be implicated.

Much of St. Clair's argument came down to Nixon's need to take decisive action on behalf of the national interest. Thus, as Daniel Ellsberg used the national media to justify his conduct, so, too, the President could disseminate derogatory information. "[I]t happens every day. . . . That is the American way of life." Yes, Nixon had ordered Henry Petersen to stay away from any investigation into "very sensitive matter[s]," such as spying by the Joint Chiefs of Staff. The President, his lawyer argued, must be judged on his conduct, not on what he said in frustration or anger; he was imperfect, as we all are. "But it would take a great deal of imperfection, and we have argued to this committee it has to be of serious criminal nature," to justify impeachment.

The cover-up, St. Clair realized, was at the heart of the matter and that, as always, required the President's defenders to impugn John Dean's credibility—the credibility that had earned Dean the grudging respect of the U.S. Attorneys, the Senate Select Committee, and the Special Prosecutor. But St. Clair argued that Dean operated on his own to maintain the cover-up and that Nixon never had approved payments to the Watergate burglary defendants. He thought the record already offered ample support for the President, but at this point he again produced a hitherto undisclosed portion of a tape transcript, this time from March 22, 1973, when Nixon told Haldeman: "I don't mean to be blackmailed by Hunt. That goes too far." That was the "evidence," St. Clair announced, that was the "fact" that the President did not deliberately plot to obstruct justice. Others stood accused for their deeds; they would stand trial, but the President himself had no culpability. The whole affair, St. Clair said, would be resolved because of Nixon's "cooperation and . . . contribution to the end result." Again, he reminded the committee that the American people demanded "clear evidence or justification" for impeachment. "And I submit that does not exist in this case," concluded St. Clair.

St. Clair's dramatic introduction of a new transcript backfired. Chairman Rodino dropped his customary aplomb, furious that once again St. Clair had used subpoenaed material that the White House had denied to the committee. Several Republican moderates demanded to see the entire transcript in order to evaluate the remark in context. Nixon's lawyer sheepishly admitted that he had no power to produce the whole transcript: "There is only one person that can. . . . It is the President's view that this portion relates to the blackmail allegation." St. Clair had offered a rude reminder that Nixon intended to dictate the ground rules. More in sadness than in anger, Railsback complimented St. Clair on his "forceful" and "fair" presentation, but he urged him to relay to the President the committee's insistence that he must comply with their subpoenas if the members were to judge him fairly. Privately, Railsback and other Republican moderates were furious, convinced that Nixon simply had not been as forthcoming as he had promised. St. Clair had quickly negated any pluses he had earned.

Flowers thought that St. Clair's performance was "the most disappointing final act" he had ever seen—nothing "substantive," no "new twist." Indeed, for Flowers, St. Clair's appearance had turned the tide against the President, not so much because of the counsel's lack of ability as because he had a client who had not given him full cooperation and had again unnecessarily challenged the committee's authority. The new tape disclosure, Flowers, thought, amounted to a "bad show," an insult to other lawyers.[46]

Doar's presentation began on July 19 and concluded the next day. By way of contrast with St. Clair, Doar embraced all the matters at issue. His argument lacked St. Clair's succinctness and dramatic impact, however, and his diffuse approach became apparent at the outset. Doar distributed five sets of proposed articles of impeachment, but he told the members that he offered them only for discussion purposes; he and Albert Jenner would listen to the members' views and rework the draft articles prior to the public debates scheduled for the following week. The drafts prepared by Doar and his staff proved unsatisfactory for those members still undecided or still searching for a proper rationale for impeaching the President. But Doar finally gave the committee his conclusion: the evidence justified impeachment.

Doar described his own anguish, assuring members that he had "not the slightest bias" against the President and would not willingly do him "the smallest, slightest injury." But he was sensitive to abuses of power and the subversion of the Constitution—actions that he would require any president to explain. What was at stake, Doar contended, was how one viewed presidential powers. For him, St. Clair's argument had the case "upside down"—St. Clair's concepts excused too much and allowed too much latitude. Doar was struck by St. Clair's omissions of incidents and evidence, as much as he was impressed by the symmetry and logic of his argument. St. Clair had argued that being president justified some of Nixon's actions; Doar turned that proposition inside out. In the ordinary course of affairs, concealing one's mistake might be understandable, but "this was not done by a private citizen." The President of the United States, Doar contended, had used the Department of Justice, the FBI, the CIA, the Secret Service, and his aides to obstruct justice. "It required perjury, destruction of evidence, obstruction of justice, all crimes. But, most important," Doar concluded, "it required deliberate, contrived, continued, and continuing deception of the American people." That evidence, Doar assured his listeners, would "help and reason with you" to reach a verdict.[47]

Two days later, Sam Garrison, the committee minority's Deputy Counsel, made the case for most committee Republicans. Butler, who knew Garrison as "Hanging Sam" from his prosecution work in Roanoke, Virginia, thought it amusing that Garrison urged the members to be "prudent prosecutors." Like St. Clair, Garrison emphasized the President's cooperation and the overriding consideration that he had acted in pursuance of his proper constitutional duties. More than St. Clair, however, Garrison insisted on holding the committee to the narrow interpretation of impeachment, one that required showing the commission of an indictable crime. In Garrison's summary, Nixon had not participated in the cover-up of the Watergate affair and so had no liability for any obstruction of justice. The President admittedly had had subordinates who acted inappropriately, Garrison conceded. But Nixon himself was oblivious of their machinations. "I was sitting there like a dumb turkey," Nixon said to Ron Ziegler in a tape transcript of June 4, 1973. "[Y]ou might every well consider that fact to be of critical importance" in determining whether the President should be impeached, Garrison told the members.[48]

On July 23, the day after Garrison's summation, Hogan became the first Republican to announce that he would vote for impeachment. The President had abused power, and he had obstructed justice, Hogan contended; he was guilty "beyond a reasonable doubt of having committed these impeachable offenses." The White House denounced Hogan's "defection," and noted that he was a candidate for the Maryland Republican gubernatorial nomination. That same day the committee met late in the afternoon to agree on procedures for its public debate, scheduled to begin the next evening.

Flowers moved that the committee hold ten hours of debate "on whether sufficient grounds exist for the House of Representatives to exercise its constitutional power to impeach Richard M. Nixon, President of the United States." Following this, the committee might consider a resolution, together with articles of impeachment, to report to the full House. Hutchinson and other Nixon loyalists challenged Flowers, querying how they could debate without specific articles to consider. Flowers thought that Doar's drafts of impeachment articles offered some foundation for debate. His motives reflected his own political concerns. He had decided to vote for impeachment; still, he had to justify his decision in a convincing manner to his conservative Alabama constituents. Flowers preferred a lengthy debate on the merits of impeachment, its viability, and its applicability to Richard Nixon, followed by a general resolution in which the members simply would vote once, up or down, on the President. This procedure would, he apparently believed, go over better in his district—"one big gusto," he called it. These were games, Flowers conceded privately, "but they were very important games."

Flowers believed that Rodino would deliver Democratic votes for his motion. But Kastenmeier, a leader of the liberal bloc, prepared a substitute motion providing that the committee debate a resolution of impeachment, together with specific articles, and that each article be voted on separately. The committee approved the substitute by a narrow 21–16 vote. Most liberals as well as presidential loyalists supported the Kastenmeier motion, while the Chairman, Southern Democrats, moderate Republicans, and a few scattered liberals opposed it. The vote reflected Rodino's willingness to accommodate the Republicans and southerners who had decided to impeach the President. According to Flowers and Fish, however, that budding coalition for impeachment almost came asunder, since they themselves considered Kastenmeier's resolution a betrayal. The difference certainly measured the very real limits of Rodino's influence.[49]

The committee scheduled the opening of its debate for the next evening, July 24. The nationally televised spectacle was about to begin; first, however, a truly dramatic development unfolded behind the scenes. Despite the procedural fuss, the Democrats were about to gain their crucial bipartisan coalition, and the President was about to lose preciously needed political and moral support. The months of the staff's labors, as well as some careful cultivation by committee members, finally secured the most desired prize of all: votes for impeachment by Republicans and Southern Democrats who also happened to constitute a rainbow of ideological commitments. Much to its consternation, the group was known popularly as the "fragile coalition." They saw nothing fragile at all about themselves. Cohen, for example, needed no comfort from a group, for after St. Clair's final argument, Cohen had known his own mind.

For months, these men had realized that they might have a special role, whether it would be played out for or against the President. They had "this thing" in their hands, as they liked to say, but the prospect neither pleased them nor made them flinch. They did not like some of the surrounding company—including the contentious partisans defending the President, the liberals who hated Richard Nixon and smelled blood, and even the President and his stonewalling. They were self-conscious. But why not? The agony and burdens of decision surely heighten an awareness of the stakes.

Ignoring earlier signals that he might suffer some defections, Hutchinson spoke out in caucuses of Republican committee members on July 10 and again on the eighteenth, telling his colleagues that he did not believe any of them would desert the President. He demanded to know if any intended to do so. Railsback felt that Hutchinson here sought to embarrass Cohen, who had joined the Democrats on several key votes and who many suspected would vote for impeachment. Fish was "amazed" by Hutchinson's unswerving loyalty; seven months of revelations apparently had not touched him at all. But by July 24, Rhodes and House Whip Leslie Arends (IL) advised Republicans "to keep their own counsel" until all evidence was in and arguments concluded. The House leadership understood the committee's growing restlessness.[50]

The coalition emerged rather haphazardly, and only after each of the men had come to a decision on his own. Among the Democrats, Walter Flowers represented Alabama's Seventh District, one that contained the largest percentage of blacks in the state at a time when blacks were beginning to vote in ever-larger numbers. In 1968 George Wallace had captured 61 percent of the district's vote, while Nixon received only 10 percent. Flowers had a reputation as a rising Southern star; a prominent committee liberal remembered him as an "elegant guy," who gave the liberals votes when they needed him. James Mann represented a district in South Carolina that was dominated by textile-management executives who usually voted Republican. Conservative rating groups gave him a 90 percent approval in 1972, while the AFL-CIO put him at zero. Ray Thornton of Arkansas, like Flowers, represented his state's largest concentration of blacks, but his was a district that gave Wallace 46 percent of its vote in 1968. Thornton received barely a majority in his first race, the 1972 primary. In 1973, the Americans for Democratic Action (ADA) gave him a 48-percent rating.

The Republican group, too, varied widely. Virginian Caldwell Butler received a zero rating from both the ADA and labor in 1973, and a 78-percent approval rating from conservatives. He had succeeded Richard Poff, a leader of House Republican conservatives. William Cohen represented a Maine district evenly split between blue-collar and service-industry workers; appropriately, labor gave him a 64-percent rating in 1973. Like Thornton and Butler, Cohen was in his first term. Hamilton Fish may have had the most interesting history. His Hudson River Valley constituency had been a long-time conservative-Republican bastion. Democrats were a forgotten species there, perhaps best remembered (though hardly with approval) for electing Franklin D. Roosevelt to the state senate in 1910, largely because of a split in the Republican Party. Fish's father, Hamilton Fish, Sr., had served as a Congressman in the 1930s and 1940s and often was a particular target of FDR's wrath. The elder Fish must have been certain that his son was pursuing the wrong president. During the impeachment controversy, Fish, Senior, signed public advertisements supporting the President and regularly implored his son to remain loyal to Nixon. But the younger Fish had supported the President on less than half the congressional roll calls prior to 1974. In 1968, he narrowly won election because the state Conservative Party had fielded a candidate who took away much of the traditional Republican vote. The candidate, Gordon Liddy, agreed not to campaign too hard, and in 1969 Fish helped him secure a position in the Treasury Department.

Tom Railsback, of Illinois, had significant personal and political ties to the President. His first race in 1966 had benefited from Nixon's vigorous campaigning that year, and his election marked the Republican revival following the debacle of 1964. Railsback's district contained the strong union towns of Rock Island and Moline, yet he had only a 22-percent rating from labor.[51]

Perhaps most striking of all, the seven congressmen of the "fragile coalition" came from districts that had delivered impressive majorities for Richard Nixon in 1972:

	1972 VOTE%	NIXON'S 1968%	NIXON'S 1972%
FLOWERS	86	10	66
MANN	66	47	80
THORNTON	UNOPPOSED	22	69
BUTLER	55	53	75
COHEN	54	43	62
FISH	66	55	70
RAILSBACK	UNOPPOSED	53	62

Each of the seven took his own path in considering impeachment. In recollecting their decisions, all stressed the weight of evidence, giving surprisingly little attention to any concern about whether impeachment would reduce the President's capability to govern effectively, but they varied in how to calculate the sentiments of their constituents. Most had been impressed by presidential lawyer Herbert Kalmbach's testimony to the committee in

July and by the callous fashion in which the White House had involved him in the hush-money payments. But such presidential friends and supporters as Mitchell and LaRue did not strike the seven congressmen as very credible. For Railsback, committee Counsel Richard Cates's July 20 briefing had been decisive, while he thought St. Clair had failed to make a case for the President. On July 21, Railsback concluded that Nixon's lies constituted a serious obstruction of justice, that he was directly involved in the cover-up, and that he had abused power.[52]

Butler could trace his concerns back much earlier. He had predicted in March that there would be "an explosion" in Republican ranks. He had decided then that he would vote regardless of the political consequences; "the job's not that good anyway," he told a friend. Cates's summaries impressed Butler as well; equally important, he was shocked by the closed-minded and abusive approach taken by such Republican partisans as Hutchinson and Latta. During this time, Butler resisted several White House invitations for special briefings. Butler admittedly had never particularly liked Nixon. He considered the President "cold-blooded"; for him, the tapes revealed an "accumulated effect of the [lack of] Nixon credibility"; they also displayed Nixon as the "man in charge." Butler's decision that Richard Nixon must be impeached preceded his adoption of any theory of impeachment, although he eventually subscribed to Gerald Ford's 1970 latitudinarian view of the House's power to define the grounds for impeachment. Butler had started with a rather narrow construction of grounds for impeachment, but he gradually came to believe that the role of the House was simply to file charges before the Senate if it believed that "clear and convincing evidence" had been established. He did not think that presidential actions must be criminally indictable to merit impeachment.

Railsback, on the other hand, had strong ties to the President. He liked him personally and remembered that Nixon had campaigned on his behalf. At one point, he told Julie Nixon Eisenhower that if her father produced the requested materials, he still had a chance. Railsback gave the same message to Republican National Committee Chairman George Bush. Railsback recalled bitterly that the only reply was more stonewalling. He found the President's defense efforts disturbing, especially the tampering with tape transcripts. But he also criticized the committee's staff for failing to do much original investigation on its own.

Mann, like Butler, had entertained doubts about Nixon since he had arrived in the House in 1969. He thought the President's war and fiscal policies, and his explanations in the Watergate affair, had been "calculated to mislead, or at least were not candid." He considered Nixon "so political," "so partisan," that he would engage in any type of manipulation to further his own ends. But Mann, certainly conscious of the President's strong support in his district, remained publicly undecided until early July. At that point, Doar began to visit Mann to discuss proposed articles of impeachment. In time, the two developed mutual admiration, alternately flattering and using one another.

Thornton believed that Nixon had damaged "the system" with his abuses of power. He saw the White House itself—apart from the executive agencies—as a virtual fourth branch of government, checked by no one. The President's lack of cooperation with the impeachment inquiry buttressed Thornton's conviction that the arrogant pattern of abuse was endemic. "Ford brought his life to the Judiciary Committee," he said, "whereas Nixon brought his lawyers." As for his constituents, Thornton believed that they trusted him to make a "serious and judicious" decision.

Flowers spent a great deal of time nursing sentiment in his constituency. For example, in Alabama he described the Fielding break-in as a threat to all Americans. Thinking as a lawyer, Flowers found Nixon's discussions with Haldeman and Ehrlichman, and his use of grand-jury information, to constitute a particularly striking obstruction of justice. An IRS investigation of Governor Wallace and his brother struck Flowers as "arrogant" and an attempt to manipulate Alabama politics. For him, that was a specific enough abuse of power to warrant impeachment. But Flowers also was very much a man of the House. Nixon's rejection of the committee's subpoena "jolted my blood-warmer," he said. He thought that the President had improperly thwarted the committee's role and angrily told his colleagues in March that Nixon had "to stop playing games with the Constitution." The next day, he heard the March 21, 1973 tape of the meeting in which Dean revealed the cover-up to Nixon—"disgusting," he called it—and became convinced that the President must be impeached. At that point, however, Flowers had a tough primary fight on his hands, and he kept his silence, aware that many of his constituents purportedly believed George McGovern would become president if Nixon were impeached.

Cohen had been dramatically affected by the Saturday Night Massacre (as had Butler). He and Elliot Richardson lived near each other and had a thriving friendship. Cohen had clashed with the Republican leadership as far back as Ford's confirmation hearings, when he objected to Ford's cavalier dismissal of the approach to Judge Byrne in the Ellsberg case. Cohen asked probing and well-prepared questions, but he was limited by time constraints. At one point Hutchinson refused the normal courtesy of granting Cohen some of Butler's time, indicating how much the Republican leadership distrusted him. Cohen criticized some of his colleagues, particularly Railsback, who deplored in private what the President had done but held back on any public commitment or action, such as voting to subpoena presidential tapes. Unlike others, Cohen had no problem defining the criterion for impeachment. As Robert Frost had said of love, the reason to impeach was indefinable but unmistakable, and he would know it when he saw it. Cohen confronted significant opposition in his district, and he realized that a majority of his constituents opposed impeachment. His mail was vicious, obscene, and—Cohen's father was Jewish—anti-Semitic.

By Christmas 1973, Fish believed that impeachment existed as a real possibility but could not be decided by "a poll and popular sentiment." Impeachment involved a "very, very defined constitutional responsibility" that popularity or party could not affect. Yet he realized the importance of giving "the people understanding [of] what you are doing." Fish did not believe that the committee would find "the smoking gun," but he thought enough evidence existed "to spell out the pattern of events in which you could draw conclusions and inference[s]" sufficient to impeach. Before July 22, Fish remembered, the time was "a very lonely thing"; he did not discuss evidence with Republican colleagues, only political implications. Unlike Cohen, Fish had no desire to operate on his own: "I was perfectly willing to confess that I did want company."

Railsback recalled that the inquiry was not "all roses," that at times it became "very antagonistic," "disputatious," and "impassionate." The words and actions of Nixon's partisan enemies aroused Railsback's personal and party loyalties, but he also knew that House Republican leaders had sensed his doubts and had grown wary of him. One GOP committee staff member remembered that many Republicans disliked Railsback and thought that he, and others in the group, were "weak men" who easily succumbed to popular pressures. For the Republican stalwarts, impeachment was a partisan matter, like voting for the Speaker.

The coalition itself had divisions. Fish praised Railsback for his courage; Butler, however, found him too preoccupied with "politics." Railsback's longstanding rivalry with McClory may well have animated his drive for leadership within the coalition. McClory had expressed doubts about Nixon's innocence, and his position as the second-ranking Republican gave him great credibility.[53] Yet McClory, along with Hogan and Froehlich, who had some misgivings about the President's conduct, were excluded from the coalition's deliberations. "I don't think any of those folks would have contributed anything," Butler remarked.

The seven congressmen later agreed that their coming together had an inevitability about it. They had been singled out in the media for some time as the undecided votes on the committee—"undecided" meaning, of course, "unknown." Cohen rejected any allegations of manipulation by the House leadership. Neither O'Neill's pressures, Rodino's patience, nor Doar's maneuvers, he said, had influenced formation of the coalition. At bottom, he insisted, with support from the others, "each member ultimately came . . . to his [own] conclusion."

On July 22, all the coalition's members had their first look at Doar's draft articles of impeachment. They later agreed that the "ambiguous and vague and arbitrary" language galvanized them into action. That evening, Flowers told Railsback to "get your guys together and I'll get mine and let's sit down and visit about this." Flowers then spoke to Mann and Thornton, who agreed to meet with the others. The next morning the seven gathered in Railsback's office. Fish was surprised to find the Southern Democrats. At the outset, Railsback asked whether they could find an alternative route to impeachment, such as censure of the President. Flowers pointed out that the committee had responsibility only for deciding the issue of impeachment. They were in the "driver's seat," Flowers remembers; the "thing" was "in their hands," and they realized their power. What was "fragile" was not the coalition members' attachment to one another; rather, it was their link to the nominal liberal majority, who now found themselves "at the mercy of seven swing votes." Prospects for bipartisanship on the committee had been dim at the outset, but the coalition, which was truly bipartisan, now found itself with the extraordinary ability to determine the nature and outcome of the impeachment hearings. Without them, impeachment would be a partisan contrivance and forever tarnished.

During these months Nixon's moods swung between optimism and gloom. He thought in June that the Democrats feared being held accountable for the disruptions in domestic and foreign policies that impeachment might cause. He also believed that they did not relish Ford as his successor, or the prospect of confronting a united Republican Party. (Later Nixon contended that the Democrats, by contrast, wanted Ford, because he would be easier to defeat in 1976 than any other Republican.) In early July, Nixon looked forward to the 1974 elections, and then beyond, ambitiously anticipating his last chance to impose the "conservative viewpoint" over the McGovernite "radical leftist viewpoint." He envisioned a day when he would look back over recent events "and see that we shouldn't have been worried about things all along." Several weeks later, as the Judiciary Committee prepared to vote and as he awaited the Supreme Court's ruling on the Special Prosecutor's subpoena of tapes, the President shifted to a more existential posture: "I intend to live the next week without dying the death of a thousand cuts. . . . Cowards die a thousand deaths, brave men die only once." It was, he wrote in his diary, his "Seventh Crisis in spades"; he could only "hope for the best and plan for the worst." Publicly, Nixon was defiant. He assured supporters on July 18 that he would leave office "in 1977 when I shall have finished my term of office to which I was elected."

On July 12 a California jury found John Ehrlichman guilty of perjury and of conspiring to violate Daniel Ellsberg's civil rights. At the end of the month, the court imposed a twenty-month-to-five-year sentence. Nixon uttered an old refrain. It was a "tragic irony" that Ehrlichman went to jail and Ellsberg went free. Ehrlichman saw it as much more. Shocked, he learned that Fred Buzhardt had signed an affidavit stating that the White House documents contained nothing material to Ehrlichman's defense. Ehrlichman believed then and in later years that he had been betrayed and went to jail for a crime the President had authorized.[54]

Old California friends entertained the President in Bel Air on July 21. It was a pleasant evening, but Nixon later remembered that it was the last time he felt any real hope. He compared his situation to being in the eye of a hurricane. He knew that the political consensus to impeach had been reached. Two days later, he called Governor George Wallace from San Clemente, desperately seeking to enlist Wallace's help in dissuading Walter Flowers from voting for impeachment. But Wallace told Nixon that it would be improper. The conversation lasted only six minutes. When it ended, the President turned to Haig and said: "Well, Al, there goes the presidency."[55]

XIX

JUDGMENT DAYS

THE SUPREME COURT
AND THE JUDICIARY COMMITTEE:
JULY 1974

The Watergate spotlight briefly moved from the House Judiciary Committee
to the Supreme Court on July 8 as Leon Jaworski and James St. Clair presented their arguments to the Justices. The year-long controversy over the
tapes had reached the Court, draped in the constitutional finery that masks
American political disputes. The President's insistence that the immunity of
his office justified defying the Special Prosecutor's demands and the orders
of the lower court had remained constant throughout the year. The conflict
was one of high drama; sadly, the confrontation had escalated to the point
that it offered scant chance for compromise.

"Scarcely any question arises in the United States that is not resolved, sooner
or later, into a judicial question," noted Alexis de Tocqueville in 1837. By
1974 Tocqueville's brilliant insight had metamorphosed into an unwritten
constitutional corollary. Americans preferred legions of lawyers to battalions
of soldiers, and they looked to the Supreme Court as the ultimate locale for
the peaceful resolution of political and policy disputes. However contradictory the Court and its power were to democratic theory and impulses, its
role had served the nation well for nearly two hundred years. From the time
of John Marshall, the Court frequently has fallen afoul of particular interests,
yet it has displayed resilience, and its authority has steadily grown. Except
in periods of emotional assault upon the institution from those momentarily

aggrieved by a decision, the Court's prestige consistently has remained high among the American people.

In 1857, the Supreme Court, dominated by a majority of slaveholders, attempted to impress pro-slavery doctrines on constitutional law in the Dred Scott Case. Chief Justice Roger B. Taney's decision upholding Scott's master provoked protests throughout the North and the West. The vituperative denunciations of the Court at the time have attracted a great deal of historical attention—at the cost of ignoring a powerful current of opinion that deplored the Dred Scott decision yet recognized the need for maintaining the authority of the Court. "We are a lost people when the supreme tribunal of the law has lost our respect," ran a typical comment that urged Americans to maintain faith in the efficacy of the Court, despite its momentary lapse. Following the Supreme Court's desegregation decision in 1954, segregation advocates regularly denounced the Court, yet they persisted in pursuing judicial solutions. So, too, antiabortion activists, infuriated by *Roe v. Wade* (1973), nevertheless have pressed for a new judicial determination of the question.

Political battle cries for judicial restraint generally amount to little more than convenient appeals to rally the faithful. "What would we do without the Supreme Court?" asked those who stood between the defenders and root-and-branch critics of the Supreme Court following the Dred Scott decision. The Court had long before firmly established itself as an indispensable component of the American governmental apparatus. "Without some arbiter whose decision should be final the whole system would have collapsed," Judge Learned Hand once observed.[1]

Despite the Supreme Court's popular image as the ultimate constitutional arbiter, only rarely has it been called upon to consider the limitations of presidential power. The modern benchmark for such judicial determination was made in 1952 when the Justices rejected President Harry Truman's claim of "inherent powers" to justify his seizure of steel mills to prevent a strike that he believed would impair the Korean War effort. When the steel companies sued to regain control of their property, six of the nine Justices ruled that in the absence of congressional authorization, the President had no such power. In a concurring opinion, Justice Robert H. Jackson eloquently underlined the rule of law: "With all its defects, delays and inconveniences, men have discovered no technique for long preserving free government except that the Executive be under the law, and the law be made by parliamentary deliberations."

William Rehnquist, a Jackson clerk at the time of the Steel Seizure Case, later recalled it as "one of those celebrated constitutional cases where what might be called the tide of public opinion suddenly began to run against the government, for a number of reasons, and . . . this tide of public opinion had a considerable influence on the Court.'' In 1974 Rehnquist implicitly applied that observation to his eight sitting colleagues who considered President Nixon's appeals that they legitimate his efforts to retain control of the remaining White House tapes. Rehnquist recused himself in the case, citing his past association with the Nixon Administration. Ironically, as Jackson's clerk he had listened to the arguments in the steel case; as an Associate Justice, he never heard those in U.S. v. Nixon lest he give the appearance of secret participation. Instead, he assigned seats to the Justices' families, members of Congress, clerks and other Court personnel, the press, and finally, members of the public who would have access to twenty-seven seats, rotated on a five-minute basis.[2]

While the Judiciary Committee weighed the President's political future, the Supreme Court dealt only with his claims of executive privilege to keep his tapes from the Special Prosecutor. The issue was not literally framed as deciding Nixon's ultimate fate, but the reality was plain. The constitutional process concurrently playing in the House inevitably had the burden of ''politics'' or ''partisanship.'' On the other hand, despite the political bearing of the Court's role, the public to a large extent perceived the Justices as being above politics and parties—serving as disinterested constitutional arbiters. As the Court listened to arguments in U.S. v. Nixon, the editorial writers of the Wall Street Journal asserted that the President's fate should not be resolved ''by a unilateral assertion'' of the impeachment power; ''only the courts can draw an ongoing body of standards, that is, a body of law, to balance executive privilege against other necessary principles.'' Richard Nixon himself had said in 1969 that ''Respect for law in a nation is the most priceless asset a free people can have, and the Chief Justice and his associates are the ultimate custodians and guardians of that priceless asset.''[3]

The Justices acknowledged the need to give the President his day in court by allowing three hours of argument instead of the normal one hour. As St. Clair began his presentation on July 8, he recognized the Court's potential for damaging the President's credibility. He told Chief Justice Warren Burger that ''no one could stand here and argue with any candor that a decision of this Court would have no impact whatsoever on the pending inquiry before the House of Representatives concerning the impeachment of the President.'' St. Clair sought to persuade the Court to deny the justiciability of the case and so to leave Nixon's fate to the House alone. The White House much preferred Congress as an adversary. For his part, Jaworski appealed to the Justices to invoke the most sacred phrases in the Court's constitutional liturgy. John Marshall had written in Marbury v. Madison (1803) that ''[i]t is emphatically the province and duty of the judicial department to say what the law is.'' Protecting and interpreting the Constitution, said Marshall, was ''of the very essence of judicial duty.'' St. Clair to the contrary, that is also what the nation looked for in July 1974.[4]

The opposing lawyers publicly exposed the debate that had raged between them for months regarding Jaworski's independence and St. Clair's right to defend the President. But St. Clair now moved beyond those arguments and asked the Justices to dismiss the suit because of "the co-pendency of impeachment proceedings." One Justice interrupted St. Clair, suggesting that this was not the Court's problem. St. Clair thought otherwise. The Court, he insisted, had a long tradition of not deciding "political questions," a doctrine that generally provided an escape route from deciding questions best determined by the political branches of government. St. Clair acknowledged that when it had decided "political" matters, as, for example, the legislative reapportionment cases of the 1960s, the Court had acted to strengthen individual rights and the democratic process. But no such consideration was involved in this case, he argued; instead, a decision would affect the proper duties of Congress. Furthermore, St. Clair went on, a decision against Nixon would "diminish" the democratic process, for it would limit the ability of the President to hold confidential discussions with his aides and thus deprive him of the power, duties, and responsibilities given to other presidents.

St. Clair came perilously close to suggesting that his client stood above the law—a claim that a zealous government lawyer had advanced on behalf of President Truman in the steel controversy in 1952 much to Truman's embarrassment and the annoyance of the Justices. St. Clair conceded that the President was not above the law, yet argued that he had a constitutional standing within the law different from anyone else's. He might be impeached while in office, but not indicted—and by implication, he might not be forced to diminish his authority. Meanwhile, St. Clair squared the circle: the President alone might decide what material would go to the House; if a court examined any of that material, it would infringe on the separation of powers, for only the House might impeach. Justice William Brennan was mystified. How did judicial consideration of taped conversations held for purposes of criminal actions interfere with impeachment? St. Clair replied only that an unfavorable verdict in the criminal proceedings would unduly influence the House. Justice William O. Douglas neatly turned the tables, countering that the material might well help the defendants in various Watergate-related trials now pending. The President's counsel found himself arguing for naked official power as opposed to the rights of individuals.

Defending Nixon's control of the tapes also left St. Clair in the uncomfortable position of protecting matters which the President preferred to hide. Another Justice pressed the counsel to the point that St. Clair admitted that Nixon might claim privilege over any Watergate conversation. What, demanded Justice Thurgood Marshall, was the constitutional authorization for that position? "Well," St. Clair responded, "I would suggest you should find it in the Constitution. And it need not be explicit. It can well be implied." Throughout, St. Clair sought to persuade the Court that the Constitution granted a body of privileges to the executive, just as it did to Congress. The difference, of course, was that the privileges of Congress were enumerated, while those of the President were implicit.

The constitutional privileges and rights of "the presidency" were central to St. Clair's argument—and they proved his Achilles' heel. He contended that the preservation of candor in presidential conversations represented an overriding public interest; such materials could be released only at the President's discretion. But what public interest was there in preserving secrecy regarding a criminal conspiracy, Justice Lewis Powell asked? St. Clair could only beg the question: "The answer, sir, is that a criminal conspiracy is criminal only after it's proven to be criminal." Another questioner posed the hypothetical situation of a soon-to-be-appointed judge who negotiated a deal in which he would give the President money. No, St. Clair said, the conversation remained privileged; the only clear remedy would be to impeach the President. Almost in exasperation, Marshall homed in: "How are you going to impeach him if you don't know about it?" Then there would be no case, St. Clair responded. "So there you are," Marshall said. "You're on the prongs of a dilemma, huh? . . . You lose me some place along there."

Jaworski's deputy, Philip A. Lacovara, followed St. Clair to close the Special Prosecutor's arguments. His task was simpler and less abstract. Lacovara dismissed St. Clair's "co-pendency" argument, requiring the Court to subordinate the criminal case to the impeachment process, as unsupported by "sound constitutional law" or by history. He appealed to the Court's independence and courage, and to its history. The Court had only rarely taken refuge in the doctrine barring decisions of "political questions." Instead, it had regularly decided "political" matters, as in cases concerning reapportionment, civil rights, and the procedural rights of the criminally accused. The Court had understood "its duty to interpret the Constitution"; "that's all we ask for today," Lacovara concluded.

Arrows rained on the President's defenses from unexpected quarters. On the day that Jaworski and St. Clair dueled in the Supreme Court, the United States Customs Court in New York struck sharply at generally conceded presidential powers. That court's docket consists of specialized cases usually confined to technical issues and well-defined legal rules. Constitutional power rarely generates controversy, let alone scrutiny, in such arenas. But in 1971 a Japanese zipper-importing firm in New York challenged a presidential proclamation of August 15, 1971 that had imposed a supplemental 10 percent duty on imports. Nixon's order was part of a broad program designed to cope with inflationary pressures. A three-judge court, however, sharply rebuked the President, ruling that he had assumed power not specifically delegated by congressional statutes.

Although John Locke's seventeenth-century contention that the legislative branch may not delegate its powers lies at the heart of separation-of-powers doctrine, American courts rarely have struck down either legislation or executive action violative of that maxim. In the zipper company case, the court flatly repudiated the President's action, finding no statutory intent to grant him such "unrestrained unilateral authority"; his proclamation "arrogated unto the President a power" simply not delegated to him by Congress. The court conceded that broad and expansive authority over trade matters had in fact been granted for some years to the executive branch, but Nixon had "exceeded" any such precedents.[5] The President had committed a "crime of the head," not "of the heart"; on this score, he had no reason to fear retribution. Still, the case spoke to the times. Nixon may have thought (if he had heard about the case) that he had been rebuked for what "everyone else did."

St. Clair "lost" the Justices while Jaworski and Lacovara successfully persuaded them of the "very essence of judicial duty." As Rehnquist had noted, the Justices did not live in a vacuum. Watergate had captured their attention, as it had that of the nation. The Justices and their clerks avidly followed the Senate hearings, and the daily revelations of Administration wrongdoing had been a frequent topic of conversation. As they absorbed the Jaworski and St. Clair briefs, a consensus emerged: the President might not enjoy an absolute privilege over the tapes. The Special Prosecutor's arguments had provided the Court with compelling reasons to order Nixon to release the tapes in question. Since the Justices differed as to the scope of their ruling, St. Clair might perhaps have been able to exploit those differences and produce a divided opinion, rather than the "definitive" pronouncement that Nixon said he would obey. But St. Clair did not.[6]

William Brennan, a Democrat appointed by Eisenhower, had operated as a major force within the Warren Court, infusing liberal values into jerry-built coalitions. Some of that influence had declined under Chief Justice Burger, but Brennan now sensed an opportunity to revitalize his old role. When he learned that Potter Stewart, Lewis Powell, and Harry Blackmun had decided to vote against the President, Brennan realized the importance of uniting the Court behind one opinion. He suggested a strategy similar to the Court's 1958 response to southern attempts to resist court orders in desegregation cases. In *Cooper v. Aaron,* the Court had sharply rebuked the Arkansas governor, the Little Rock school board, and state courts, and rendered a single opinion signed by all the Justices.

Burger, however, assigned the opinion to himself. He was in a bind as he confronted a case affecting the future political well-being of the man who appointed him. White House gossip in 1973 and 1974 reported that he "had assured the President that the tapes would not be taken away." Burger's closeness to Nixon and the Administration was well known—a situation riddled with irony since the Senate had rejected Lyndon Johnson's nomination of Abe Fortas to be Chief Justice, in part because of charges of cronyism. "The C.J. needs to talk with you *urgently*," the President's Appointments Secretary told Nixon in May 1969. John Ehrlichman recorded in 1971 that Burger had "met periodically" with the President, Mitchell, and himself "to discuss issues of the day and to join a general discussion of current events." Just after the Court took the tapes case in 1974, the *Washington Post* disclosed correspondence between Burger and John Mitchell, indicating a close, "confidential" relationship between the Chief Justice and the Administration.[7]

Burger's decision to write the opinion raised numerous questions. Would he soften the decision? Did he not face a conflict, given his constitutional responsibility as Chief Justice to preside in an impeachment trial? Indeed, for some time Burger had had clerks secretly researching impeachment trials, so that he would be prepared for that contingency. Perhaps he saw the opportunity to establish his independence from the Administration. Whatever his motives, a great deal of ego was involved—as it undoubtedly was for those colleagues who wanted the opinion for themselves. After the Justices assembled in conference the morning after the oral arguments, they quickly revealed their unanimity of judgment; deciding the scope of the opinion proved far more difficult.

Later that day Brennan visited Earl Warren, hospitalized after a series of heart attacks, and told him about the developments. Warren had long disliked and distrusted Nixon, and had been dismayed as the President sniped at Warren Court decisions. Several hours after Brennan's visit, Warren suffered a fatal heart attack. Brennan nonetheless was certain that his news had comforted his old comrade.

The Court's opinion emerged after several weeks of editorial emendation and intensive lobbying among the Justices. Douglas, still resentful over the Nixon Administration's support for his impeachment in 1970, pressed Burger whenever it appeared that he might be willing to assert a too-permissive view of presidential powers. The Chief Justice at one point had suggested that the federal rule allowing courts to subpoena evidence considered potentially relevant and admissible, must be applied more strictly for issuing a subpoena against the President. Douglas would have none of it: "My difficulty is that when the President is discussing crimes to be committed and/or crimes already committed with and/or by him or by his orders, he stands no higher than the Mafia with respect to those confidences." Justice

Stewart eventually provided a draft of the key section that satisfactorily maneuvered between the constitutional rights of the various Watergate defendants and the President's demands for privileged communications.

In the end, Brennan and the others certainly had the input they had wanted all along; meanwhile, Burger alone had his name on an opinion that united the Court: the President must surrender the tapes. The Court met for its final conference on July 23, and the Chief Justice issued a press release noting that it would convene the next morning. Leon Jaworski had some trepidations; he knew the decision was about to come down. He also knew that if the Court ruled in the President's favor, he would have "to close shop." St. Clair was in San Clemente with his client.[8]

The next morning Alexander Haig called the President to report that he had the complete text of the Supreme Court's decision. "Unanimous?" the President asked. "Unanimous. There's no air in it at all." "None at all?" the President persisted. "It's as tight as a drum," said Haig.

The Supreme Court had preoccupied the President for several weeks. St. Clair had tried to create an appearance of optimism; he had written to Jaworski on July 10 that he thought he had won the Court over. Fred Buzhardt had told a White House defense group, chaired by former FCC Chairman Dean Burch, that he thought the President would win unanimously. One of the group remembered thinking that he was "in a madhouse."

Richard Nixon's fatalistic sense came closer to understanding the truth. He knew he could not defy the Court; perhaps he could still devise a plan for deleting some material. But the June 23, 1972, tape "worried" him ceaselessly; it could not be "excerpted properly," he confided to his diary. While St. Clair made the President's case to the Judiciary Committee on July 18, Nixon admitted that his greatest concern was "the Supreme Court thing." On July 23 he talked to Haig and Ziegler about resigning. That night, Nixon stayed up late, reviewing a speech draft on economic matters. At midnight, he wrote: "Lowest point in the presidency, and Supreme Court still to come."[9]

The immediate reaction to the Court's ruling in *U.S. v. Nixon* focused on the Court's order that the President surrender the tapes. Although Nixon had lost the battle, the "presidency" had survived the war. In fact, the misty concepts of executive privilege Nixon and St. Clair had battled to protect finally received the Supreme Court's imprimatur. The Justices did not concede privilege enough to protect President Nixon in this case, but they did provide some precedent and underpinning for future claims. The Court's opinion—a much fairer way to characterize it than to label it "Burger's opinion,'' although the Chief Justice issued the decision—clearly revealed that the criminal implications in the case, and the pressing political confrontation it had produced, forced the outcome. The Court recognized presidential rights to some confidentiality, but it found in the present case "a sufficient preliminary showing that each of the subpoenaed tapes contains evidence admissible with respect to the offenses charged in the indictment."[10]

U.S. v. Nixon is another milestone marking the unique power of the Supreme Court. The heart of the opinion confronted St. Clair's contention that separation-of-powers doctrine precluded judicial review of presidential claims of privilege—that the case, in short, was nonjusticiable. Politely but firmly, the Court invoked John Marshall's 170-year-old dictum that the judiciary's duty was "to say what the law is."

In its partial vindication of the President, the Court agreed that confidentiality had validity—it could be "constitutionally based"; indeed, the opinion noted, the framers of the Constitution had met in secret. But the Justices refused to concede that the President's claims completely insulated him from the judicial process. They would grant him great deference in the exercise of executive privilege, but when his claim depended "solely on the broad, undifferentiated claim of public interest in the confidentiality of such conversations, a confrontation with other values arises." The case did not present a military or national-security matter; hence the Justices contended that confidentiality would not be "significantly diminished" if the President produced the tapes for an *in camera* scrutiny by the judiciary.

In practice, separation of powers, the Court noted, depended greatly on "interdependence," on what Justice Jackson had called in the Steel Seizure Case the need to ensure a "workable government." Nixon's "undifferentiated" claims for confidentiality would "upset the constitutional balance" needed for a "workable government" and, not incidentally, "gravely impair" the judiciary's role under Article III of the Constitution.

The Court conceded a "presumptive privilege" of confidentiality to the President, but the Justices insisted on a balance with the commitment to the rule of law. Here the Court followed the path suggested by Justice Douglas and turned the case against the President into one on behalf of the claims of those criminally indicted—Mitchell, Haldeman, Ehrlichman, and the others: "The generalized assertion for privilege must yield to the demonstrated, specific need for evidence in a pending criminal trial."

The "President's men" had a victory of sorts—but one that cost the President dearly. There is irony, too, in the doctrinal result. Richard Nixon had pressed the cause of "executive privilege" as had none of his predecessors. While the Court denied his desired goal, it established the legitimacy of executive privilege. Insofar as confidentiality was necessary for the effective exercise of the President's powers, the Court held, "it is Constitutionally based." Executive privilege was a myth no more. When Representative Richard Nixon had angrily denounced President Harry Truman for withholding information from Congress in the Hiss case a quarter-century earlier, he ironically anticipated the other side of the coin of *U.S. v. Nixon.* Truman's action, Nixon said in 1948, "cannot stand from a Constitutional standpoint or on the basis of the merits," for it would enable the President arbitrarily to deny Congress its lawful right to investigate wrongdoing in the executive branch.[11]

Typically, Nixon interpreted the decision as a setback for the "presidency," something the Supreme Court had carefully attempted to ensure it was not. After he learned of the Court's action, Nixon closeted himself with Haig and St. Clair. For how long and just how far the President considered resistance to the Court's decision, remains somewhat cloudy. That morning, on July 24, St. Clair had been advised by his White House aides that the Court's decision was imminent. Fifteen minutes later, the wire services carried the news, but Haig did not inform the President for another forty-five minutes. At noon, Ron Ziegler told reporters that St. Clair would make a statement later in the day. The President's lawyer appeared before the press at 4:00 P.M., approximately eight hours after the Supreme Court's decision. Nixon may have been in a Truman-analogy mode at the time, but if so he did not recognize that in 1952 Truman promptly dispatched a letter to his Secretary of Commerce ordering him to return the confiscated steel mills to the owners. The President complied less than thirty minutes after the Justices finished reading their opinions in the Steel Seizure Case.[12]

Nixon had "counted on some air in the Court's ruling"—at least, he thought, the Justices would give him a provision for exempting national-security materials from subpoena. What he had in mind, of course, was the June 23, 1972 discussion with Haldeman concerning the use of the CIA in the cover-up. The notion that such a conversation could be insulated with a national-security blanket indicated the depth of his desperation. The Court, in fact, had provided "air" for such material; Nixon's problem now was that too many in the White House had knowledge of the contents of that particular tape.

Nixon discussed the option of "abiding" by the decision while continuing to withhold materials, thinking that there was some Jeffersonian precedent for doing so. He dropped the idea after some supporters warned that "full compliance was the only option." St. Clair always thought that even now the President "didn't have to turn over the tapes, maybe. I don't know." That "maybe" was predicated on St. Clair's belief that the presidency and the judiciary were two equal and separate branches, a belief traceable to Jefferson and to Andrew Jackson's notion of concurrent powers, under which some actions of the judiciary were not necessarily binding on the executive. During oral arguments before the Supreme Court, when one of the Justices had approached the question of compliance, St. Clair had carefully avoided committing the President. Nixon "was good at dissembling," St. Clair remembered.[13]

The White House's public-relations men had tried to anticipate strategy for reaction to the Supreme Court. "If" the President complied, an aide suggested, then he also should announce that the tapes at issue here would be the last evidence he would submit; clearly, his enemies wanted "not evidence but blood." "If" the President did not comply, or if he "shape[d] his compliance differently than asked for," then speed would be essential. He must keep his enemies "off guard." But late in the day of the decision, the President had touch with the reality that prevailed in Washington. Eight Republican congressmen dispatched a telegram urging him to comply. "We have confidence that your affirmative response to this order will be consistent with the unparalleled significance of this development." That afternoon, Nixon put on a brave front, trying to salvage some victory from the ashes. "I am gratified," he said, "to note that the Court reaffirmed both the validity and the importance of the principle of executive privilege, the principle I had sought to maintain."[14]

The nation barely had time to absorb the impact of the Supreme Court's decision, for that same evening, July 24, the House Judiciary Committee reassembled to continue its impeachment inquiry. Now its debates would be aired on prime-time television. Nixon had fought throughout his presidency to control the media, to use it to his advantage. Whether in unveiling his Cabinet or in announcing his China visit or his selection of Gerald Ford, he had tried to persuade the nation that he was the right man doing the right thing. It was fitting, then, that following his repudiation by the Supreme Court, his "enemies" mounted their own television spectacular, as choreographed in its production and as emotional in its impact as anything that Richard Nixon might have imagined doing.

As the debate opened, Chairman Peter Rodino waited, gavel poised in midair, for the television prompter to signal the start of the proceedings, just as if he were officiating at an athletic event. The air was thick with real drama. For so long, impeachment had been unimaginable; now, the nation was to be a witness to proceedings that might lead to that very end. The Supreme Court news did not overshadow the evening's events in the Judiciary Committee, yet it was pervasive. Moreover, the Court's opinion neutralized contentions that partisan Democrats alone opposed the President, as Nixon's own Chief Justice had rendered the opinion. And some on the committee knew that there would be an unusual outcome to the impeachment inquiry, since at least six Republicans and three Southern Democrats had determined to vote against the President. The "fragile coalition" had met for nearly six hours in Tom Railsback's office that day, mapping strategy to control the language of the outcome that now was cast. Rodino's apparent calm and dignity masked the behind-the-scenes activity that surrounded the coalition's efforts to draft resolutions to be introduced that evening by the Democrats.

The Chairman's speech had been carefully crafted by his aides. It spoke for fairness and education, with a sense of the occasion. "Make no mistake about it," Rodino said. "This is a turning point, whatever we decide." He at once broadened and narrowed the problem before the committee. The House inquiry was not that of a court of law, he told the audience. Quoting Edmund Burke's 1788 definition of impeachment, Rodino said that the inquiry involved accusation and judgment by statesmen of other statesmen who had abused power, and it was not dependent "upon the niceties of a narrow jurisprudence, but upon the enlarged and solid principles of state morality." The narrow question centered on whether the President had told the truth when he said he had been deceived by subordinates, and whether or not he himself had participated in a design systematically to cover up the role of his agents and associates in an illegal political-intelligence operation, together with related activities—whether he, in short, had engaged in a course of conduct that had impeded his faithful execution of the laws and had done this for his own political interest and protection. Finally, Rodino pointedly underlined the constitutional nature of the proceeding. No one welcomed such a test of constitutional practices, he said; still, "our own public trust, our own commitment to the Constitution," were at stake.[15]

Edward Hutchinson briefly responded. His educational homily for the audience focused on the "political" nature of impeachment. He revealed that the committee had not even agreed on the nature and scope of an impeachable crime, as if to discredit impeachment itself as well as the process at hand. Taking his assignment one step further, Hutchinson reflected on the awesome burden of impeachment; conviction allowed for no discretion to fit the punishment to the crime: removal was the only course. Evidence of a serious offense might exist, yet such an offense, he suggested, might not warrant so extreme a measure. He warned his colleagues—and the public— that the offense should be of "sufficient gravity" to justify removal. Finally, Hutchinson took note of the day's events in the Supreme Court and suggested that the Chairman consider postponement until the President yielded additional evidence. Rodino ignored him and instead turned to the committee's senior Democrat, Harold D. Donohue, who introduced a resolution and two articles of charges against Nixon. For the first time in more than a century, Congress confronted the President of the United States with the very real possibility of impeachment.[16]

The first article of impeachment charged that the President, by obstructing and impeding the administration of justice, had violated his constitutional duty "to take care that the laws be faithfully executed." Nixon personally, or through his agents, had pursued a policy to delay or impede the investigation of the Watergate "illegal entry," to cover up the identity of those responsible for the action, and to cover up and conceal "related unlawful covert activities." A list of specific items followed, including misusing the CIA to impede the investigation, interfering with the conduct of the FBI and the Department of Justice, "approving, condoning, acquiescing in, and counseling" others to give false testimony, and suppressing or withholding evidence.

The proposed Article II charged that Nixon had, directly or through subordinates, "abused the powers vested in him." This abuse included the misuse of such various agencies as the FBI, the IRS, and the Secret Service to violate the constitutional rights of citizens; the creation of the Special Investigative Unit (the "Plumbers") to engage in unlawful covert activities; and the exercise of the President's position to impede lawful inquiries into the conduct of his office. At the end of the article, the drafters stated a number of charges centering on Nixon's dealings with Congress, including providing misleading information; refusing to honor congressional subpoenas designed to pursue an impeachment inquiry; and personally or through his agents, seeking to undermine the legitimacy of congressional inquiries into his conduct. Finally, it was charged, his conduct included making "false and deceptive statements" regarding his knowledge of and actions related to matters under investigation.

Donohue did nothing more than introduce the resolutions bearing his name. Article I resulted from feverish drafting efforts during the previous two days by members of the coalition and committee staffers. Responding to the members' wishes for something concrete to debate, John Doar hastily assembled his draft articles and presented them on July 19. Several members of the coalition, including Caldwell Butler, met with Richard Cates on Saturday morning, July 20, and again had been impressed with Cates's tight summary of the evidence and its inexorable conclusion. No such precision appeared in the Doar drafts, which struck the coalition members as vague, rambling, and altogether "a sloppy piece of work." Butler considered them "incompetent" and "shocking" in their inaccuracies. Dissatisfaction with the drafts galvanized the coalition into collective action, and led to their July 23 meeting in Railsback's office. Rodino was well aware of the coalition's activity, and he urged James Mann to rework the articles in consultation with his allies and present them to the whole committee before debate began on July 24. Some language had to be on the table, and as late as the afternoon of the twenty-fourth, Rodino continued to press Mann for "something" to present. The Donohue resolutions were the result. But even after they were introduced, Mann remained busy, refining them and consulting with his coalition partners, as well as with Doar.[17]

The Southern Democrats had caucused among themselves and agreed upon "obstruction of justice" and "abuse of power" as the unifying themes for any articles of impeachment. Ray Thornton drafted one article containing charges of obstruction of justice, abuse of power, and defiance of congressional subpoenas. But, sensitive to the egos of others, Thornton did not lay the draft before the entire group. Meanwhile, Mann prepared a draft article enumerating the President's use of the IRS, the attempt to use the CIA to scuttle the FBI's investigation, the framing of the Huston Plan, the use of the Plumbers, the failure to comply with committee subpoenas, and the making of misleading statements to the public. Walter Flowers, still grasping for some alternative to impeachment, now suggested that censure might be easier. Flowers pushed hard on this point throughout that evening and the next day, but the others prevailed, arguing that censure was not a fitting punishment for the offenses (a position that Flowers would conveniently adopt as his own during the public debates). That same evening, Tom Mooney, a Judiciary Committee staffer with close links to Railsback, armed with copies of the Doar, Mann, and Thornton drafts, also began to compose articles on his own.

When the coalition reconvened at 8:00 A.M. on July 23, Mooney offered a draft article focusing on the President's obstruction of justice. Working through the afternoon, periodically meeting with Mann and other members, Mooney assembled four other drafts before producing one for circulation. Five of the members met the next morning and developed two more drafts. They realized that their articles had to be drawn with the severity of any indictment, charging Nixon only with what could be proven. Nothing troubled them more than linking the President to actions of his subordinates. They knew, as Mooney said, that they must "not attribute something to the President that was done by one of his agents." The acts may not have been Nixon's, the members concluded, but they could link him to "approving, condoning, and acquiescing" in unlawful activities, as Butler suggested. The coalition also carefully avoided attributing motives to Nixon that could not be substantiated, such as the charge that he had considered executive clemency to gain silence and false testimony from the Watergate burglars. Meanwhile, Mooney learned that Robert McClory had instructed Franklin Polk, another minority staff member, to draft an article on abuse of power.

Mann carried his draft to Rodino a few hours before the opening of the public debate. Just prior to that, the group wrote important changes, particularly one designed to make it unnecessary to prove that the President succeeded in accomplishing the purposes of his unlawful activities. At the beginning of specific charges, they now inserted the words "endeavoring to misuse," or "endeavoring to cause" to describe Nixon's action. Flowers and others demanded that any reference to Daniel Ellsberg be deleted, because they believed him to be a "traitor." The resultant language stipulated that the President had concealed "the existence of related unlawful covert activities." Even after Donohue introduced the resolution, the coalition continued to fine-tune the obstruction-of-justice article, the one which they considered the most basic and understandable for impeachment. At a dinner meeting on July 25, with the debate already underway, they changed such words as "burglary" and "illegal entry" to describe the events of June 17, 1972 at the Watergate, replacing them with "unlawful entry," words taken from the D.C. Criminal Code; the members of the coalition, after all, were lawyers.

The coalition had the Mann and Thornton drafts of the charges in Article II on July 23. Meanwhile, McClory, aided by Jenner and Polk, had developed a similar article. Like Mann, McClory planned to incorporate the President's refusal to comply with committee subpoenas as part of his charge, but he agreed to submit it as a separate article when some members of the coalition refused to support it. In the haste to provide material for Donohue's introduction, however, the drafters did not have time to separate the subpoena charges; that refinement would have to wait for substitute motions during the debate of the whole committee. Significantly, the coalition failed to delete any reference to Ellsberg and the Fielding break-in. Article II simply did not bind together all the members of the coalition with the same passionate commitment to its principles that characterized the Democratic majority of the committee.

Each member of the full committee had fifteen minutes during the opening debate for his remarks. The proceedings carried through the afternoon and the evening of the second day, July 25. Most of the remarks were predictable. Liberal Democrats made it clear that they had heard enough over the past months. They were ready to "fulfill their constitutional obligation." The President, Don Edwards declared, had engaged in "serious misdeeds," he had "corrupted and subverted" political and governmental processes, and he "should be impeached." The President's defenders were equally predictable, demanding that impeachment proceedings meet the standards of a criminal legal trial, attacking the paucity and flimsiness of the evidence and the partisan political character of the proceedings, and stressing the relative morality of political behavior. Mayne charged that the case consisted only of "inferences," while Dennis insisted that the Nixon Administration was "not the first to be guilty of shoddy practices."

Attention focused on those "undecided" members, that coalition of Republicans and Southern Democrats who might provide a special stamp of legitimacy and bipartisanship for an impeachment vote. The politics of impeachment involved more than simple arithmetic. Those supposedly uncommitted congressmen had, in fact, determined their course, and had drafted the resolutions on the table. As they began to reveal their positions publicly, their remarks ranged from embarrassment to outrage and even to expressions of faint hope that the President still might rescue himself. And they all spoke directly to their own constituencies—districts, it will be recalled, which had given the President substantial support in the past.

Railsback rambled with a confusing, even maudlin presentation of his own position. He had "agonized" throughout the inquiry, for Richard Nixon twice had campaigned for him, and Railsback regarded him as a "friend." He offered high praise for the President's record, but he had "problems" and "concerns" to share with his colleagues and constituents. He then outlined his views of how Nixon had abused power and obstructed justice in the cover-up of White House involvement in political-intelligence activities.

The next morning, Hamilton Fish ignored Richard Nixon and spoke instead of his own duties as a member of the House and of the nature of impeachment. The evidence "deeply troubled" Fish. Hinting at his course, he concluded that "if the evidence is clear, then our constitutional duty is no less clear." William Cohen was less elusive and made his position quite plain. He had prepared for his remarks by reading the *Federalist Papers*, and thought, "how in the world did we ever get from the *Federalist Papers* to the edited transcripts?" Cohen distinguished between impeachment and a criminal accusation, noting that impeachment involved a determination of "those acts which strike at the very core of our constitutional and political system." Furthermore, he disabused his audience of the popular notion that circumstantial evidence had no validity. Finally, he dismissed any allegations of a conspiracy against Richard Nixon. The President's wounds had been self-inflicted, Cohen declared, and he had invoked "valuable and viable" doctrines such as national security and executive privilege for the wrong reasons and had dangerously weakened their future credibility. "I think," Cohen concluded, "that no man should be able to bind up our destiny, our perpetuation, our success, with the chains of his personal destiny."

Flowers spoke most clearly to his constituents. He enumerated the reasons for impeachment, as well as some of the President's alleged offenses. Still, he promised, he would listen to the debates and then decide—"based on the Constitution and the evidence." His fellow southerner, James Mann, had diligently worked with Republican staff members to draft the articles of impeachment, yet he, too, refused to commit himself publicly. Mann deplored those who questioned the committee's motives or who dismissed the inquiry with the casual observation that "it is just politics" or that political morality was relative. "Are we so morally bankrupt that we would accept a past course of wrongdoing or that we would decide that the system that we have is incapable of sustaining a system of law because we aren't perfect?"

He asked for understanding from his constituents, an understanding that he must fulfill his oath and duty as he saw fit. He also asked for help from Richard Nixon: he was ready, he said, to receive additional evidence. "It is not too late. . . . I am starving for it but I will do the best I can with what I have."

Caldwell Butler's Virginia district had supported Nixon overwhelmingly. Flowers regularly teased Butler about the pickup trucks filled with armed constituents that would visit him if he opposed the President. But Butler's dismay with Nixon and his annoyance at the narrow partisanship of the President's defenders on the committee finally burst forth in a wave of passion and anger that belied his usual calm. Although Butler had to confront a skeptical district, he seemed to focus his public remarks on his fellow House committee Republicans. Watergate, he reminded them, "is our shame," a scandal for a party that had campaigned so often against corruption and misconduct. "We cannot indulge ourselves in the luxury of patronizing or excusing the misconduct of our own people." He challenged the loyalists' analogy of a criminal trial and their rationalization of the relativism of corruption. Butler found such standards "frightening," for they in effect condoned and left unpunished presidential conduct designed to subvert the processes he had sworn to uphold. We, Butler said, will then have said to the nation: "These mistakes are inconsequential and unimportant." The evidence was "clear, direct, and convincing"—St. Clair's words—that Richard Nixon had abused power and that he had engaged in a "pattern of misrepresentation and half-truths" to explain his conduct in the Watergate affair, a policy "cynically based on the premise that the truth itself is negotiable."

The combination of Mann and Butler left no doubt as to the outcome. Together, they offered a bipartisan conservative condemnation of the President. Together, they combined the sadness and fury that must have flowed through all but the most committed Nixon-haters and loyalists alike. Mann's voice broke at the end of his remarks; Butler, his passion spent, quietly said that his "present inclination" was to support impeachment, but "there will be no joy in it for me."[18]

When debate opened at noon on July 26, McClory moved to postpone consideration of the impeachment articles for ten days, if the President assured the committee within twenty-four hours that he would provide the House with the tapes which the Supreme Court had ordered him to submit to Judge Sirica. McClory had no expectation that Nixon would make the materials available. Apparently, he simply wanted to demonstrate that the committee had treated the President fairly and with proper deference. At the same time, he announced his intention to introduce a separate article of impeachment, charging Nixon with contempt of Congress, for his failure to comply with earlier subpoenas. Brooks, Railsback, and Sandman, representing the three major factions in the committee, rejected the gesture as meaningless and opposed it. McClory's motion failed, 27-11. By now the President commanded virtually no trust. A Gallup poll released that same day revealed that his disapproval rating had risen to 63 percent, while his support had fallen to 24 percent.[19]

At this point, Paul Sarbanes introduced a substitute Article I which had been drafted largely by Mann, Butler, and Mooney. Why Sarbanes? Mann had presented the substitute to the committee's Democratic caucus. "I just looked around the room and picked out Paul Sarbanes and said [he] is the best man to do it," Mann said. "And like a good soldier, he didn't flinch." Sarbanes had little opportunity to study the changes he would propose, but Mann credited him with a "remarkable job" of presentation. Mann admitted that he "just didn't care to be that far out front." After all, he had said at the outset of debate that he still had reservations on how he would vote. Meanwhile, he noted that the Democratic liberals carefully worked to be "helpful rather than wanting to impose their thoughts."[20]

Hutchinson attacked Sarbanes for the lack of "specific detail" in the charges. Railsback, in the style of what members call a "planned colloquy," tried to help Sarbanes frame an answer, suggesting that the committee could provide the entire House with supporting information. But Wiggins and Sandman would have none of that. For Wiggins, obstruction of justice was a criminal offense, and any article of impeachment had to contain specific evidence of such acts on the part of the President. Sandman's attack on Sarbanes's article bordered on the abusive. He taunted Sarbanes with demands for specificity. "I want answers, and this is what I am entitled to," Sandman said. "This is a charge against the President of the United States, [and] he is entitled to know specifically what he did wrong. . . . Do you or do you not believe, and you can say yes or no, that the President is entitled to know in the articles of impeachment specifically, on what day he did that thing for which you say he should be removed from office?" Sandman's gusts of passion seemed calculated to extinguish whatever lights of reason could be culled from the evidence. His onslaught was emotional, but it was effective in planting seeds of doubt—and in shaking some of the resolve of the "fragile coalition."

By late afternoon the Democrats had recovered somewhat and had begun to reply effectively to Wiggins and Sandman. Rodino read a staff member's hurried note citing previous impeachment proceedings in which a body of evidence was provided apart from the articles themselves. Sarbanes reviewed the documentary evidence, to provide the members with "some appreciation" of the details behind the charges. None of them was unfamiliar. Hungate scoffed at Sandman and Wiggins. If someone brought an elephant through the door, and a member called it an elephant, he suggested that others would consider it "a mouse with a glandular condition." Still, the President's supporters persisted, alternating between Wiggins's demands for specificity and Sandman's denunciations of the proceedings. "Isn't it amazing? They are willing to do anything except make these articles specific," Sandman said with mordant glee. Even McClory, clearly willing to impeach the President on other grounds, charged that the allegations in Sarbanes's article were "weak" and "fuzzy."[21]

The counterassault by Wiggins and Sandman blistered the pro-impeachment forces. The Republican loyalists had little hope of moving those Democrats who had been firmly convinced by the evidence to vote against the President. Their target was the tenuous, uneasy bloc of approximately six Republicans and three Southern Democrats. Their shock tactics momentarily stunned the coalition and severely tested its mettle. The Sarbanes substitute motion was properly their responsibility; yet, when Wiggins and Sandman demanded specificity, none of them seemed able to respond with the data that had been carefully assembled since October. Cohen, certainly the Republican most solidly persuaded against Nixon, thought "the whole thing" was in danger at that point. The opposition to the President was on the verge of public and national embarrassment. During the nine-month investigation, Sandman had said virtually nothing. Suddenly, he asked: "Well, where's the evidence?" It *was* embarrassing.

That night, Democrats Mann and Flowers, and Republicans Cohen, Railsback, Butler, and Hogan met for dinner and a post-mortem at the Capitol Hill Club. Some blamed Doar and poor staff communication for their own weak reply to Wiggins and Sandman. Flowers complained that the Democratic majority had not made the case. Cohen disagreed. "The members had got stung and they didn't really know what to do," he later recalled. The specificity that Wiggins and Sandman had demanded was readily available. Cohen told his colleagues that they could stay up all night, redraft the articles, and enumerate the specifics. He then proceeded to tick off all the lawyerlike "to wits" and "et ceteras." But he had no takers.

Butler and Mooney remembered the "state of panic" and chaos that pervaded the group that evening. Flowers said that Sandman was the biggest hero in his Alabama district. The "specificators" had "licked us," he complained. Meanwhile, ever politic, he suggested that the group maintain its image of neutrality. But the time for neutrality had passed. The coalition only bent; it did not break. The members had decided, and they were committed. Cohen deplored the label "fragile coalition." He had reached the point where it didn't really matter to him whether others "stayed in or stayed out," as he had made his resolve. And so had his colleagues. The bloc remained intact, and despite Flowers, a number of them eagerly responded to the challenge of the President's defenders.

* * *

When the coalition members returned for the evening session, they held their own against the loyalists' attacks. They "talked facts" in response to the demands of Wiggins and Sandman. Barbara Jordan dismissed the calls for specificity as "phantom arguments, bottomless arguments." She rebuked any claims that the President had not been given due process, pointing out the role the committee had granted St. Clair. "Due process? Due process tripled. Due process quadrupled," she said with solemn dignity. Sandman, however, was not through, and he moved to strike the first paragraph of the article Sarbanes had proposed, on obstruction—the very heart of the charge. Coalition members Railsback, Cohen, Fish, Thornton, and Flowers joined the Democrats to reinforce the points made late that afternoon regarding a full report, as well as citing specific instances of presidential wrongdoing. The debate became increasingly rancorous, as Nixon's supporters barely disguised their contempt for Republicans who opposed him. At the end of the evening, Harold Froehlich signalled another Republican defection when he suggested that the committee provide evidentiary facts in its report to the House rather than in its articles of impeachment. With that, Sandman's motion was rejected 27-11.

Sandman sometimes appeared a man who could not put the trees together to form a forest, but by Saturday afternoon, July 26, he knew the count. He saw no need to "bore the American public with a rehashing" of material and acknowledged that the votes were there to pass the article. Wiggins, too, sensed the futility of the situation. The glue holding together the coalition—in Wiggins's opinion, self-interest and an erroneous understanding of constitutional responsibility—proved strong enough.[22]

But some members, including Flowers, still believed that their constituents needed more justification for the step the committee was about to take. Although the outcome was apparent, at the late afternoon session Flowers moved to strike individual paragraphs from Article I, making his motions one at a time, mainly to give his fellow coalition members an opportunity to recite the specific evidence they had absorbed Friday night and Saturday morning. Each motion was defeated by the predictable majority, and with one exception, Flowers simply recorded himself as "present" in voting on his motions. Sandman would have none of such sham and pointedly rebuked Flowers. Rodino, however, continued to pamper his Alabama colleague, even providing him a final opportunity to justify his vote. Flowers then briefly yielded to allow Fish to speak to his "friends and supporters" in New York who supported Nixon. "There was no smoking gun," Fish noted. "The whole room was filled with smoke."

Suddenly, dramatically, Rodino asked for a vote on the Sarbanes substitute Article I that the coalition had prepared. Choruses of "ayes" and "noes" responded. But Rodino called the roll, and thirty-eight members recorded their vote. The afternoon pattern held firm, and by a 27–11 vote, the committee adopted one article of impeachment against Richard Nixon. Six Republicans—Butler, Cohen, Fish, Froehlich, Hogan, and Railsback—joined the twenty-one Democrats.[23] The bipartisan vote, transcending ideological alliances as it did, belied charges that the committee's proceedings were a partisan vendetta. Richard Nixon had brought the committee together, as he was to bring the nation together—though clearly not the way he had intended in 1968. It was fourteen years to the day since he had first been nominated for the presidency.

XX

"I HEREBY RESIGN."

AUGUST 1974

Richard Nixon received the news of his own "Saturday Night Massacre" in his San Clemente beach trailer; it was, he said, "exactly" what he had "feared." He realized a sense of historical shame—the "first President in 106 years to be recommended for impeachment." Not the kind of first on which he usually prided himself. Compounding his anguish, the June 23 tape, in which he had discussed using the CIA to cover up the Watergate break-in, was, he knew, "like slow-fused dynamite," waiting to explode. He expected his lawyer and aides to soon tell him that the situation was no longer manageable. The President had conceded impeachment in his own mind and was resigned to a six-month Senate trial. But according to his account, that weekend he considered the risks to the nation of a crippled presidency. He also worried about his own financial future, aware that if impeached and convicted, he would lose all government benefits.

Returning to Washington on July 29, Nixon found the White House "cloaked in gloom," the staff's confidence "shattered." St. Clair had returned from a long weekend at Cape Cod and learned the contents of the June 23 tape. According to Nixon, his "breezy optimism" had evaporated. Now, St. Clair expressed concern for his own liability as a party to obstruction of justice.[1]

The House Judiciary Committee resumed deliberations on July 29. In three sessions that day, and three the following day, the members considered four more articles of impeachment. The debates seemed anticlimactic, considering that one article of impeachment had already been approved. Many of the issues raised during the debate over Article I remained apparent when the members discussed the abuses of power charged in Article II. Because they were so similar, the outcome of the debate on Article II never was in doubt, particularly since the "fragile coalition" saw the two articles as different sides of the same coin. But the members seemed anxious to conclude the proceedings and to allow the fate of the President to run into other channels.

At the opening session, William Hungate offered a substitute for Harold Donohue's second article. The language had been refined, but the most important changes involved the deletion, both of the section on presidential defiance of the committee's subpoenas and of the various clauses charging Nixon with impeding and interfering with the power of the House to conduct an impeachment inquiry. Removed, too, was the clause accusing the President of "making false and deceptive statements to the American people" regarding his role in unlawful events. The Hungate substitute catalogued presidential abuses of power similar to those mentioned in the original resolution, but it pointedly avoided the phrase "abuse of power." The new article cited Nixon's misdeeds, in a passage following the statement that he had disregarded his constitutional duty "to take care that the laws be faithfully executed." The President, Hungate's article said, had "repeatedly" engaged in conduct that violated constitutional rights, impaired the proper administration of justice and the conduct of lawful inquiries, or contravened laws and purposes governing executive-branch agencies. Finally, the article stated that Nixon had acted "in a manner contrary to his trust as President and subversive of constitutional government, to the great prejudice of the cause of law and justice and to the manifest injury of the people of the United States."[2]

Charles Wiggins insisted that abuse of power did not fall within the meaning of "high crimes and misdemeanors" and again argued that the only impeachable crimes were indictable ones. Edward Hutchinson admitted some of the President's actions had been questionable but found no evidence that they involved "unconstitutional conduct." Robert McClory, who had voted against Article I, now answered his fellow Republicans. Abuse of power, he said, "really gets at the crux of our responsibilities here for it directed attention toward the President's oath and his constitutional obligations." The Plumbers' actions, and the misuse of such agencies as the FBI, the CIA, and the IRS, constituted "clear acts of misconduct." It was essential, McClory argued, that Congress define a standard of constitutional behavior and establish a precedent for other presidents. Setting that standard and enforcing the Constitution, he thought, made the second article paramount. "I realize that there is no nice way to impeach a President of the United

States," he concluded, almost mocking Hutchinson's same words to the Republican caucus earlier in the month.[3]

The Republican loyalists proposed various motions to strike Hungate's substitute article, but this time their opponents were better prepared. For example, when Wiley Mayne insisted that the Plumbers had a national-security purpose, Hamilton Fish had Albert Jenner read the relevant evidence pointing to the conclusion that the Plumbers' goal was to cultivate public relations, not to protect national security. The President's supporters repeatedly emphasized his need to maintain national security and domestic order, but to no avail. Walter Flowers, for one, frankly acknowledged that he considered the abuses of power more important as a charge than obstruction of justice—an "abuse of public trust," he said, implying that if actions of this kind were left unchecked, no restraint on executive power would be possible. James Mann warned that if presidents were unaccountable, they would be free to do whatever they chose. "But, the next time there may be no watchman in the night," he warned. The voting lines held. McClory crossed over to the majority, and the committee approved Article II, 28–10.[4]

A sense of overkill pervaded the final day of debate. First, McClory presented Article III, accusing the President, "without lawful cause or excuse," of having failed on three occasions to produce materials duly subpoenaed by the committee and thereby having acted "in derogation of the power of impeachment," vested solely in the House. He saw the issue as proper for impeachment, for it involved a violation of constitutional duty and lack of respect for the constitutional powers of the legislative branch. Further, he thought that the article could provide an important precedent for defining the proper role of the executive.

Given the dislike of McClory on the part of some members of the coalition, it may have been a combination of personal pique and skepticism that animated their reaction to McClory's article. Ray Thornton alone of their number supported the article. Tom Railsback thought it might alienate House Republicans who would vote for articles I and II. For all the talk of legislative prerogatives, it is ironic that Railsback also opposed the article because the committee had not challenged the President's defiance in court. McClory picked up only one Republican vote (Hogan's) and lost two southerners; nevertheless, the article passed, 21–17.[5]

The committee had approached the point of diminishing returns. Mann originally had included the subpoena issue in his draft of Article I, but contended that Doar insisted the topic be treated separately. Perhaps Doar reasoned that it might be best to have another article in reserve for a House vote—even one for members to oppose, in order to appear more fair-minded. But Mann and the other conservatives had exposed themselves enough on two votes; now, it seemed, it was time to demonstrate mercy. William Cohen refused to support Article III because the entire House had not voted the President in contempt, and he did not think it fair to raise the issue to an impeachable charge. Fish at first agreed with Cohen, but later events caused him to regret his action.[6]

Except for the final votes, the remainder of the day belonged to the Democratic liberals. First, John Conyers introduced an article condemning the President for his taking "unilateral" military actions against Cambodia without informing Congress and for insisting that he had not done so. Edward Mezvinsky then submitted a fifth article, charging the President with willfully evading income taxes and with receiving compensation in the form of excessive government expenditures for his estates. Both articles failed, 26–12.

Mann thought that he had an agreement with Peter Rodino that these articles would not be introduced, but he realized that the liberals "had to do it." Later, he graciously said that Conyers and others had restrained themselves so as not to overstate the committee's case against the President. In the first vote, Rodino and seven other Democrats joined a solid Republican opposition; in the second, such liberal stalwarts as Hungate, Waldie, and Drinan refused to support the motion. On the Cambodian issue, Cohen pointed out that the President's action followed congressional "sloth and default"; correctly, he noted that far too many members of Congress knew about the bombing and both explicitly and implicitly supported it. The tax issue presented complications of factual interpretations and the expiration of the statutes of limitation, as well as sensitive matters that touched closely on the members' own behavior. Cohen saw the charge as "blatant partisanship," while Jack Brooks considered it an issue of "fairness," understandable to all Americans. This time, Charles Sandman may have won some sympathy for the President when he complained that "any least little thing that Richard does is a crime."[7]

In the wake of the votes, unfounded reports circulated of an impending *kamikaze* attack on the Capitol by military units loyal to the President. Rodino and other Democrats supposedly reacted tearfully to the results of the final voting. Cohen, who had courageously exposed himself for months, found such emotions "disgusting," and thought some of the "hired partisans" were feigning their sadness. He knew there "wasn't too much room for sympathy or empathy or anything else for Richard Nixon." Politics was on the minds of some. After the vote, Flowers retreated to his office and discussed the ramifications of his votes with his staff. "Let's figure out how we are not going to get burned in the next election based upon this," he told them. Party feeling in his native Maine left Cohen somewhat embittered. Shortly after the vote, he appeared in the state, and a hostile questioner reminded him of Maine's great Civil War senator, William Pitt Fessenden, who had opposed the impeachment of Andrew Johnson. Cohen cleverly reminded her that Fessenden had broken party ranks to do so. Mann castigated the Republican loyalists for their partisanship, blaming them for inspiring a flood of hostile mail and telegrams from his district.

At this point, Senate Republican leader Hugh Scott told Vice President Ford that he considered the case lost, with impeachment and conviction virtual certainties. But Nixon loyalist Senator Carl Curtis (R–NB) urged Hutchinson to "drive home the point over and over again" that no hard evidence existed for "a legal basis for impeachment." On the other side, Congressman Wright Patman had a long memory and now understood, he thought, how and why his committee had blocked his proposed Watergate inquiry in October 1972. He urged Judiciary Committee members to cite the event as further obstruction of justice on the part of the President.[8]

The President had not only lost in the Judiciary Committee, but his public support had plummeted. Whatever one's sentiments about impeachment, the prevailing view was that the televised proceedings had conveyed an image of congressional conscientiousness, intelligence, and fair-mindedness. Those images nourished a public confidence that lent some legitimacy and calm to the eventual outcome of events.[9]

Television ratings services gave the White House advance information on their findings. On July 30, as the committee debate ended, the Nielsen Company informed White House aides that the debate had an estimated audience of 35–40 million—extraordinarily high numbers. A few days later, Nielsen reported that the average household watched 1.9 days of a possible four of the debates, for an average of 3 hours and 43 minutes. The viewing audience translated into double the American population of 1868, the year the House impeached Andrew Johnson. Only 10 percent of U.S. adults heard *none* of the House committee proceedings on television or radio. A Louis Harris poll taken on August 2, a week after the first vote, showed public opinion favoring impeachment 66–27 percent. Pro-impeachment sentiment had risen 13 percent in one week.[10]

Public opinion in the Watergate affair amounted to an extraconstitutional check and balance not envisioned by the framers of the Constitution. Little could they imagine an impeachment process in full view of the American population—"live," to use an ahistorical term. Perhaps public opinion eventually perceived the blatant and petty partisanship on both sides that characterized the Andrew Johnson affair, but its influence in 1868 is hard to measure. In 1974, on the other hand, the committee members went to great lengths to make sure that the public understood how and why they acted as they did. That was not a formal constitutional check, but it fulfilled James

Madison's anticipation of the "second sense of the community" as a restraining and validating influence on government.

After the final committee vote, the President spent a restless night. Early the next morning, he wrote out his options: resign immediately; resign if the full House voted impeachment; or fight through the Senate trial. Nixon's "natural instinct" prevailed over any reasoned approach to the options, for at the end of his notes, he wrote: "End career as a fighter." The only other real alternative was to set a precedent for resignation—and that was "far worse," he thought. But hours later, according to Nixon, Haig read the June 23, 1972, tape transcript "for the first time" and agreed with Buzhardt and St. Clair: "I just don't see how we can survive this one," Haig told the President. The next day, August 1, Nixon told Haig that he intended to resign.[11]

Life went on around the President, however. He still had the power to do favors for friends, although White House aides recommended that in the light of the Chinese "internal situation," Ambassador George Bush not ask the Peking government to allow comedian Bob Hope to tape a television special there. More important, Nixon's political and public-relations advisers carried on the resistance. As he and Haig discussed the most incriminating tape transcripts, an aide told the General that the White House must not concede the outcome of an ultimate vote on impeachment in the House. He urged that House Republicans get the message that they had "no easy loophole," that impeachment was bad for the country and destructive of the presidency. "We should say flatly," the aide wrote, "that no politician is going to get off the hook or shirk his duty in this matter." Meanwhile, other advisers offered recommendations to St. Clair of lawyers to assist him in the Senate trial, including Wiggins and Senator John Sherman Cooper (R–KY).[12]

Dean Burch, the former Federal Communications Commission Chairman, had come to the White House in March 1974 to coordinate political and public-relations defenses. Burch suspected he had been chosen because the President and Haig believed that Burch could "tame" his friend Barry Goldwater. That prospect was rather unlikely; nevertheless, Burch could not resist the offer. Burch, his chief aide, Charles Lichenstein, and others met daily to decide on tactics and strategy. Like St. Clair, Burch and his group suffered a great handicap in having no direct access to their "client." Haig had absolute control over their activities; moreover, unlike similar groups who had worked with Haldeman, they did not have the benefit of even indirect presidential orders. The result was a vacuum, as Haig orchestrated efforts of which the President had no knowledge, and which, if he had known of them, he would have realized the futility of pursuing. Meanwhile, Haig prepared Nixon's "talking papers" for meetings with Burch and other counselors. The defense effort also suffered from faulty intelligence. In June Burch informed the President that House Republican leader John Rhodes assured him that no Republicans would vote to impeach.

Burch's group coordinated Watergate strategy; it did not formulate it. Lichenstein particularly remembered the frustration of dealing with Buzhardt, who seemed oblivious to the seriousness of the President's problems. Even after the ominous questions St. Clair encountered at the Supreme Court hearing on July 8, Buzhardt told the Burch group that he expected a unanimous opinion in the President's favor. The group, in fact, believed that St. Clair had performed dreadfully. Burch and Lichenstein also could not understand why Buzhardt did nothing to enhance the quality of his tape machine after Burch heard one tape and said that he could understand nothing. Similarly, they thought Buzhardt responsible for the inaccurate transcriptions and the consequent embarrassment they suffered from facing corrections by the Judiciary Committee. Distrust between Burch and his aides on the one hand, and between Haig and Buzhardt on the other, extended back to the President's release of the tapes in late April. Burch told Lichenstein that Haig and Buzhardt had assured him that Watergate would be resolved in the President's favor, a statement which Burch incorporated in a speech he was to make—much to his later embarrassment and regret.[13]

In the aftermath of the House committee vote, Nixon and his supporters struggled to maintain an outward calm. Press Secretary Ron Ziegler gamely told reporters that the President was "confident" that the charges had no substance and that he would not be impeached. Ziegler added that Nixon knew he had "committed no impeachable offense." Haig typically covered all contingencies, admitting that the President had suffered "very severe losses," but asserting that he remained certain Nixon would be "vindicated." Meanwhile, Wiggins and Rhodes talked about the forthcoming battle in the House, thereby dousing a suggestion by Pat Buchanan that the House quickly and unanimously vote impeachment in order to get on with a Senate trial. Ford dutifully echoed his former House colleagues when he complained about the lack of specificity in the charges; he, too, remained convinced of the President's innocence. For Ford, the Democrats' unanimity only proved the partisanship of the affair; as for the six Republicans who joined them, he said only that he was "disappointed."

Nixon's traditional support eroded. On July 29 Howard Phillips called for the President's removal, either by resignation or impeachment. He announced the creation of "CREEP 2"—Conservatives for the Removal of the President. Phillips expressed a growing fear on the part of conservatives that Nixon would sacrifice any policy to remain in power. Just after the impeachment vote, Federal Judge Gerhard Gesell sentenced John Ehrlichman to a twenty-month-to-five-year jail term for his role in the Fielding break-in, and two days later, John Dean received a one-to-four-year sentence for obstructing justice. The emergence of new enemies and painful reminders of "White House horrors" only reinforced the image of a totally discredited Administration.[14]

Ford's enduring faith must have shattered on August 1 when Haig told him that the situation had so deteriorated that "the ball game" might be over, and Ford should start "thinking about a change" in his life. New transcripts, he said, would refute the President's story of his role in the cover-up and demonstrate his culpability. Ford remembered that both he and Haig were "angry" at the President's deceit.[15] In fact, Haig had known for some time about that June 23 tape; it was, however, time for him to build new bridges.

Anger was a mild word to describe the feelings of presidential supporters four days later when the President released the June 23, 1972 tape transcript, destined to be known as the "smoking gun." At the President's first meeting that day, more than two years earlier, Haldeman told the President that "we're back in the problem area," because Pat Gray did not have the FBI under control. The FBI's investigation had led into some "productive areas," where "we don't want it to go," he said. Haldeman had talked to Mitchell and Dean, who agreed on the need to maintain a cover-up of the Administration's role in the Watergate break-in. Mitchell's recommendation that Deputy CIA Director Vernon Walters call Gray and tell him to "stay the hell out of this" was the fateful instruction. Didn't Gray want to stay out of it? the President asked. Yes, Haldeman responded, but he needed a reason, and the CIA could provide him with one. Haldeman thought the story might be plausible, because the FBI investigation allegedly had been tracing money to some CIA connections.

The tape revealed more of the seamy side of the White House. Did Mitchell know? the President asked. "I think so," Haldeman responded. Had Mitchell pressured that "asshole" Liddy—Liddy who "must be a little nuts!" Nixon rambled. Than, rather cryptically: "Thank God it wasn't Colson." Regarding FBI questioning of White House people, the President ordered: "Play it tough. That's the way they play it and that's the way we are going to play it." The conversation shifted to various legislative and policy matters. But abruptly, Nixon returned to the Watergate problem. Call in the CIA people, he said, and tell them that further inquiry might lead to "the whole Bay of Pigs thing"; "don't lie to them to the extent to say there is no involvement, but just say this is a comedy of errors," Nixon said. The CIA should call in the FBI and say, 'Don't go further into this case[,] period' !"

Again, the President shifted the talk, now to politics, then to aides (Herbert Klein "just doesn't have his head screwed on. . . . He's not our guy at all[,] is he?''), then to his own book, *Six Crises* ("damned good book, and the [unintelligible] story reads like a novel''), and finally, to baseball.

When the two men resumed their conversation later that afternoon, the President urged caution lest the CIA and FBI leaders have "any ideas we're doing it because our concern is political." Instead, he underlined an anxiety that any revelations might "blow the whole, uh, Bay of Pigs thing." Haldeman informed Nixon that he had spoken to Walters and that Gray had informed CIA Director Richard Helms that the FBI had run into a CIA operation. Walters had agreed to call Gray, as Haldeman had suggested, but apparently he told Haldeman that Helms did not understand Gray's call. At this point, Haldeman and the President engaged in a bitter discussion of the Bay of Pigs and an alleged slight to Nixon by former Director Allen Dulles. Perilous moments generally seemed to arouse Nixon's various festering resentments.[16]

The June 23 tape offered a definitive answer to Howard Baker's question, put just over a year earlier: the President knew. He knew that he had instigated a cover-up and thus had participated in an obstruction of justice almost from the outset of events.

When Nixon surrendered this evidence, he no longer had the ability to act as prosecutor, judge, and jury in his own cause; now, he stood alone as the accused, self-anointed, as it were. Even at this painful moment of confronting the truth of his involvement, however, the President could not be wholly forthcoming. He told the nation that the subject of the June 23 tape related to government business as distinguished from politics, a fiction that must have taxed the imagination of his most devoted speechwriters. He took "full responsibility" for not providing complete information to those arguing his case, an act "which I deeply regret," he said. He admitted that he had known of the taped conversation for some time (though he never acknowledged remembering the actual conversation), and he "recognized that [it] presented problems." Still, Nixon insisted that he "did not realize the extent of the implications which these conversations might now appear to have." In his defense, he pointed to other statements and actions that embodied the "basic truth": he had insisted "on a full investigation and prosecution of those guilty."[17]

Haig and St. Clair promptly called Leon Jaworski, insisting that they had not known of the existence of the June 23 tape. Haig, it must be remembered, had provided the President with that particular tape in May 1974. Given Haig's temperament, it is almost unimaginable that he did not know the contents of the tape at that time. Furthermore, Fred Buzhardt undoubtedly gave Haig the tape, but Buzhardt carefully covered his tracks by telling interviewers later that he did not handle the June 23 tape until the day of the Supreme Court decision respecting subpoenaed materials in July 1974. "No way" that Haig alone was aware of that tape, recalled St. Clair. Leonard Garment regarded Buzhardt as a careful lawyer and would have been "surprised" if he had not known the contents of the June 23 tape for some time. Melvin Laird claimed that Buzhardt told him about the particular tape as early as June 1974. When Jaworski described Haig's protestations of ignorance, he interestingly connected their conversation to an observation that "Deep Throat," the alleged source of information on the White House for *Washington Post* writers Bob Woodward and Carl Bernstein, was, according to Jaworski, "somebody who was trying to cover his own tracks in the White House and wanted to make sure that he wasn't going to be under suspicion."

At times, Nixon himself wondered about "strange alliances" surrounding him. John Connally called him in May to relay a message from Jaworski: "The President has no friends in the White House" was Nixon's memory of the Special Prosecutor's warning. Mitchell had no doubts about the lack of loyalty in the President's house, and in time became convinced that Haig and Buzhardt served not the President, but the interests of the military and perhaps the CIA.[18]

Nixon's announcement and release of the "smoking gun" tape produced another "firestorm." One television commentator said, "Let him go." Let the President have his pension, his secretaries, and his office; "give him amnesty," he added, "and draw a curtain over this scene, not for his sake— for ours." For months, Nixon had resisted pressures that he leave office. As far back as the aftermath of the Saturday Night Massacre, in November 1973, he cautioned House Republicans against demands for his impeachment or resignation. "If you cut off the legs of the President, America is going to lose," he said. He invoked a variation of a familiar threat: American allies, he warned, would consider "leaning toward the Soviet Union if domestic issues diminished the authority of the Presidency." After repeated remarks that he would not resign, White House aides counseled that reiteration would "only be counter-productive."[19]

But after they learned of the June 23 tape, Republicans, like cuckolded mates, refused to accept Nixon's expressions of regret for withholding the information. Some wanted him simply to resign; others wished to vent their fury on him. As the news spread through Washington, House Republicans reacted with dismay, sorrow, or anger; whether by impeachment or by resignation, they concluded, the President had to go. Democrat Don Edwards of the Judiciary Committee had anticipated some trouble in the House and Senate on the impeachment issue, but "this thunderbolt," he realized, meant "we had him cold."

One Republican House member urged Edward Hutchinson to move for immediate action on the first impeachment article. The tape revelation had "exacerbated the Executive leadership crisis," he said. He thought that resignation might be in the best interest of the nation, but Congress nevertheless should immediately proceed to fulfill its legal and constitutional responsibilities. Congressman Barber Conable (R–NY) angrily charged that the President had abused the trust given to him. Conable had slowly, but painfully, realized how Nixon had deceived his supporters. Earlier, he privately chided himself for accompanying the President on a Potomac cruise, feeling as though he had been "a party to jury-tampering." The only issue remaining, Conable said, was how to effect an orderly transition of power to Gerald Ford.

Charles Wiggins would have one more moment in the limelight. St. Clair invited him to the White House on August 2 to read the June 23, 1972 transcript. At first, Wiggins persisted in his faith. The words provided "some evidence of obstruction," he admitted, but "the words as used in their context [did] not drive you inevitably to that conclusion." Wiggins felt no sense of betrayal by the President, only sadness. But after the release of the tape, Wiggins sensed the political winds and announced that he would support Article I. He, too, wanted the process to run: the "magnificent public career of Richard Nixon must be terminated involuntarily," Wiggins said.

The President desperately tried to insert exculpatory material into his August 5 statement on his release of the tape. At the last moment, he drafted a notation that he had told Pat Gray to press forward two weeks *after* the June 23 conversation, once he had determined that there was no national-security matter at stake. But the statement would have to wait for his memoirs. Haig told him that St. Clair and the lawyers would leave unless the prepared statement remained intact. "The hell with it," Nixon said. "Let them put out anything they want. My decision has already been made." He knew that Washington had been "whipped into a frenzy"; Haig reported further desertions. "[F]ew, if any," Nixon realized, "would want to be found standing with me."[20]

Et tu, Brute. That evening Gerald Ford also announced that he could better contribute to the orderly conduct of government by "not involving myself daily in the impeachment debate, in which I have no constitutional role." At last, Ford's staff prevailed in their advice that he distance himself from the President. The Vice President's words must have been the unkindest cut of all for Richard Nixon: "I have come to the conclusion," Ford stated, "that the public interest is no longer served by repetition of my previously expressed belief that on the basis of all the evidence known to me and to the American people, the President is not guilty of an impeachable offense."[21] However convoluted the statement, Ford was saying nothing less than that the President was guilty.

Five months earlier, Nixon himself had stated that "the crime of obstruction of justice is a serious crime and would be an impeachable offense, and I do not expect that the House Committee will find that the President is guilty of any of these crimes." But when he released the June 23 transcript, he argued that the information itself did not warrant impeachment. He urged congressmen to consider his comments in the larger perspective of his demands for a full investigation. St. Clair thought it a pity that the transcript had not come out earlier. He believed that if it had been considered along with Nixon's March 21 conversation with Dean, "you could live with those [together] in my view." It "would have been just another difficult tape for the President." Coming as it did, however, the inflamed environment of August following the House committee vote "enhanced its individual importance," St. Clair acknowledged.[22]

When the Judiciary Committee Republicans attached their supplemental views to the committee's report to the full House later in August, they took the President at his word and held him impeachable for the "serious crime" of obstruction of justice. The President, they said, had "effectively admitted guilt of one impeachable offense." Led by Hutchinson, ten Republicans reluctantly, even grudgingly, conceded that Nixon—by his own words—stood guilty under Article I. Hutchinson, however, was not too far from St. Clair. In a separate statement, he contended that the "timing of the disclosure," not the contents itself, damaged the President beyond repair. "Those who had been defending the President were left without a defense and without time to build a new defense," said Hutchinson—a lament for the defenders, hardly for their client. Hutchinson, an aide remembered, remained unconvinced that Nixon was guilty.

Wiley Mayne most vividly displayed the Republicans' dismay. Mayne had been a devoted Nixon admirer for years. As the evidence of the last several months accumulated, a law school friend called Mayne, telling him that people in Iowa no longer believed the President and urging Mayne to reconsider his steadfast loyalty. But Mayne persisted in his allegiance. When he filed his supplemental views, however, the Iowan must have heard footsteps in his district, for he went beyond his Republican colleagues and declared he would vote impeachment under Article II. Nixon's August 5 statement gave him no choice on Article I, he declared; but now he thought the evidence also sufficiently proved the President's abuse of powers with his uses of the IRS, the CIA, and the FBI. Somehow, Mayne thought that the June 23 tape amplified the existing evidence.[23]

Dean Burch knew that he could no longer defend the President. He could only hope to assist Nixon in finding the right resolution of the crisis. On August 5, Burch called Senator Goldwater and told him that the President had been lying. Burch had shown him what was to be the explanation of the June 23 tape transcript. Goldwater was furious: "It was the same old Nixon, confessing ambiguously, in enigmatic language, still refusing to accept accountability. It was, above all, an insincere statement, as duplicitous as the man himself.'' The Senator's contempt was boundless, for Nixon again had tried to blame others, even his friends.[24]

William Timmons, the White House congressional liaison, reported that Republican congressmen had suggested that the President ask Goldwater for a frank assessment of the political reality. At a meeting of Senate Republican leaders on August 6, Goldwater admitted that he ''blew my top'' when he learned that Ford had informed colleagues that more disclosures would magnify Nixon's deception. The President, with some urging from Burch, called in the Republican leaders on August 7. Goldwater's presence was a measure of his untitled stature within the Republican Party and the nation. Burch knew his friend would be blunt and honest. Given the Senator's significant national constituency, and the growing respect of old adversaries, Burch also realized that Nixon could not lightly reject any counsel Goldwater gave him.[25]

Ford had already had what he called Goldwater's ''characteristically blunt'' advice. The Senator thought the situation ''totally out of hand.'' The President's supporters had been ''lied to'' repeatedly. ''The best thing he [Nixon] can do for the country is to get the hell out of the White House, and get out this afternoon,'' Goldwater told his Senate colleagues. Accompanied by Hugh Scott and John Rhodes, Goldwater met the President. According to several accounts, including his own, he never directly told Nixon to resign, indicating instead that he had no significant support in Congress. He informed Nixon that he had at most ten supporters in the Senate, six of whom really were undecided, including himself. Goldwater left the meeting with no doubt as to the outcome: the President ''would resign.''

When the three met reporters late in the afternoon of August 7, Goldwater told them that no decision had been made and that they had visited the President to describe the situation in Congress. Rhodes said that ''four old friends'' discussed a ''painful situation.'' Scott admitted that they told Nixon that the outlook was ''very gloomy'' and ''distressing.'' Goldwater denied that the men had discussed immunity for the President if he resigned. Nixon remembered Goldwater's telling him that he leaned toward voting for Article II. He also recalled saying to Scott as they ended their discussion: ''Now that old Harry Truman is gone, I won't have anybody to pal around with.'' Truman had had monumental contempt for Nixon, and the President knew it. Nixon's remarks to Scott displayed his typical awkwardness and perhaps offered some indication of a momentary flight from reality.

Reporters finally came to the question the leaders obviously wanted to answer. When asked to assess the possibilities for impeachment and conviction, they were a bit circular, but clear. Rhodes said that impeachment ''is really a foregone conclusion''; Scott simply said that there had been ''some erosion of support in the Senate.'' The leaders had told that to Nixon; clearly, they had a public purpose to fulfill as well. Dealing with the media must have entailed its measure of exasperation at such a moment. One reporter actually asked if the House would forgo impeachment, and the Senate similarly forgo a trial, if Nixon resigned. Rhodes seemed stunned; still the reporter persisted: did the President ask that question? Private Citizen Richard Nixon, of course, could not be impeached.[26]

Life in the Nixon White House was winding down. The President told his private secretary that he had decided to resign, and he began to work out notes for a speech. He had some reminder of his latent power, however. Haig informed him that Haldeman had called, urging pardons for all involved and amnesty for Vietnam war draft resisters. Later, Haldeman personally pleaded with the President.[27]

Gerald Ford had had more than Goldwater's advice to prepare him for his new role. For more than three months, some of his staff and old confidants had begun to prepare for his transition to the presidency. As early as May, a reporter asked Ford whether rumors to that effect were true. Ford denied them, saying if anyone were doing so, it was without his knowledge or consent. For Ford's people that remark translated to an expression of the Vice President's hope that "somebody was doing it but he didn't want to know about it." Philip Buchen, a Ford adviser for more than a quarter-century, along with Clay Whitehead, who had served as head of the White House Office of Telecommunications Policy for Nixon, formed a team to develop transition plans. The group became known as "The Ford Foundation." According to Ford, Buchen never told him about the activities until Nixon indicated he would resign—"a real surprise," Ford called it. Had he known, he claimed, he would have asked the group to cease. "It was," he said, "a dangerous and questionable undertaking." The last thing Ford wanted was any accusation of disloyalty.[28]

"Loyalty" by itself inadequately described Ford's behavior as Vice President. Some would have added "dogged"; others would have called it "blind." But Ford had built a career on the principle of not offending anyone. It seemed that he did nothing as Vice President except to travel the land in defense of Nixon. "Somebody ought to do Jerry Ford a favor and take his airplane away from him," a *Wall Street Journal* reporter remarked in June. *Time* called him the "zigzagging missionary," while *Newsweek* labeled him the "zigzag Veep." After a North Carolina speech in which he lamented the "expletives deleted" of the presidential tapes, he added that he thought the President had not lost his sense of morality. "A zigzagger makes touchdowns," he later told reporters. But a conservative Michigan newspaper said he had fumbled the ball.

Meanwhile, Ford delivered Agnew-style speeches—written in the White House—assailing the President's critics and blithely assuring his audience of

Nixon's innocence. "Throughout my political life, I always believed what I was told," Ford later wrote. And he believed that Nixon had told him the truth. When he saw the experts' report on the 18½-minute tape gap, he began to suspect he was being used, yet he dutifully continued to defend the President for months to come. The day before the Judiciary Committee voted the first article of impeachment, Ford told an Indiana crowd: "I can say from the bottom of my heart that the President of the United States is innocent. . . . He is right!"[29]

Ford had his troubles. Nixon's staff, from Haig down, reflected the President's well-known disdain for the Vice President. After Ford told a national television audience in January 1974 that he thought a compromise possible on the tapes, he perceived a "chill" in his relations with the White House. Ford's staff resented the White House's self-serving use of the Vice President and its intrusions on their own efforts. At times, Ford revealed that he "damn near blew my stack." After Ford had assured an Ohio Republican audience in June that "the preponderance of the evidence" demonstrated Nixon's innocence, the news flashed that the President had been named as an unindicted co-conspirator. Ford's press secretary later wrote that Ford never forgave Nixon for lying to him. Ford always described other presidents he had known by their first names or nicknames; when he mentioned his predecessor, it simply was "Nixon."[30]

The days between the Judiciary Committee votes and the release of the "smoking gun" transcripts witnessed steadily growing pressure on the President. Ford, of course, was not oblivious to this. Ford's close friend and political ally Senator Robert Griffin warned Nixon that unless he resigned, he would be impeached and convicted, and that Griffin expected to vote against him. After delivering the letter, Griffin reached Ford in Mississippi through a White House operator. St. Clair gave the Vice President advance information of the June 23 transcript, but the President's lawyer did not yet know whether Nixon would resign or fight. Significantly, St. Clair denied any knowledge whether Nixon was considering granting pardons, a subject that Haig had raised with Ford that same day. Now, in these crucial days, Ford studiously avoided any direct dealings with the President or comments on his course.[31]

President Nixon appeared for his last Cabinet meeting on Tuesday, August 6. As usual, the staff prepared "talking points" for him. Whatever decisions had been reached—tentatively or firmly—the President dealt with the group as he always had: as subordinates whom he needed to exhort to do their best in behalf of the Administration. He had, nevertheless, to confront the impeachment issue and give the Cabinet officers some indication of his course. He reminded his lieutenants that the presidency had experienced enormous trauma in the past decade, with the assassination of Kennedy and with John-son "literally hounded from office." The institution, he said, must not sus-tain another "hammer blow" without a defense. Consequently, he would not resign, and would let the constitutional process run. This, he insisted, would be in the "best interests of the Nation"; he would not "desert the principles which give our government legitimacy." To do otherwise, he con-tinued, "would be a regrettable departure from American historical princi-ples." He offered nothing in the way of personal defense aside from past diplomatic triumphs; instead, he wrapped himself in the mantle of the pres-idency—claiming that he had no choice but to continue the route designed in the Constitution.

With that, Nixon turned to a discussion of economic problems, projecting policies for six months in the future. Attorney General William Saxbe was dumbfounded by Nixon's bravado. "Mr. President, don't you think we should be talking about next week, not next year?" he asked. According to Saxbe, Nixon looked around the table, no one said a word, and with that he picked up his papers and left the room.[32]

The President's line was familiar. He had said in his January 1974 State of the Union message that he never would resign. He had told himself on numerous occasions that resignation could only be equated with guilt. In an interview with columnist James Kilpatrick in May, Nixon vehemently denied any intention of resigning. To do so, he said, would be to fatally weaken the presidency. Future presidents, he warned, would constantly be looking over their shoulders at Congress. Resignation or impeachment, he continued, would destabilize the nation and the world. Either path "would have the traumatic effect of destroying that sense of stability and leadership. And as far as this particular President is concerned, I will not be a party under any circumstances to any action which would set that kind of precedent."

Nixon thought then that he must let the impeachment process run its course because it would be "best for the country, our system of government, and the constitutional process." Two months later, Representative Caldwell Butler came to the same conclusion. Resignation offered only short-term benefits, Butler thought; more important, he did not want to establish a precedent "for harassment out of office, which is what would be claimed." He, too, wanted to follow the constitutional process: "It's a pretty good system." The President at that time gave every appearance of continuing in office. He asked an old friend to "leisurely" prepare a speech on world law and peace. Nixon wanted it as a radio address but then proposed a wide mail distribution. He planned the talk for August or September, and he emphasized there was no need for urgency.[33]

Old friends weighed in with encouraging words. A New York lawyer ex-horted Nixon not to resign and bitterly assailed "gutless Republicans" who had suggested such a course. She urged him to have the "courage and fortitude" to go through the constitutional process. Some religious supporters urged the same course but with a different twist which apparently received no consideration. The Reverend Norman Vincent Peale relayed and endorsed a message from the prominent Jewish Orthodox leader Rabbi Samuel Silver, of Cincinnati. The nation, Silver believed, wanted to "love" its President. "All he needs to say is that he is sorry for the whole thing, that he admits he didn't handle it too well, that he is only human and he regrets the bad habit of swearing, etc.; that he should have cracked down on any wrongdoing immediately, that he hates to hurt people; that all he asks is the forgiveness of the people." Silver added that the President need not act like a "worm." But he must offer "a good, honest, humble attitude of contrition."

Even after the revelations of the June 23, 1972, tape, the President received extraordinary gestures of support. A California restaurateur, who had sent the President $10,000 to help him pay his income taxes, offered to turn over his interest in twenty-nine restaurants to finance a defense. "I love Richard Nixon—he is the greatest President this country has ever had," he declared. An Indiana Republican Congressman offered the same sentiments on the *Today* television show on August 8. "Don't confuse me with the facts. I've got a closed mind," Representative Earl Landgrebe said in response to the question whether he would vote to impeach the President. He would "stick with" Nixon, even if "I have to be taken out of this building and shot. . . . President Nixon has been the greatest President this country has had." But after the "smoking gun" tape became public, James Kilpatrick could take no more. "I am close to tears," he wrote. "Nixon's duplicity is almost beyond bearing." Had he told the truth from the outset, Kilpatrick declared, Watergate would have been a nine-day wonder, Nixon would have been re-elected, and no more would have been heard of the affair. Kilpatrick had believed the President when he said he knew nothing of the cover-up and that he was not a crook. Now, he sadly concluded, "it no longer really matters. . . . My President is a liar. I wish he were a crook instead."[34]

But Richard Nixon was nothing if not a seasoned political hand. He had heard rumors for months that congressional Republicans might view his resignation as a relief from the terrible onus of voting on impeachment and as the way to remove the President as a political albatross for the party. Nixon undoubtedly had put his personal concerns above those of his party; yet, for all his disdain, he knew that he still had to reckon with it as a force of political life. He knew that winning was everything, and he offered a political twist to the sports metaphors he often favored when he noted that generosity or magnanimity had little to do with the outcome of events: "[T]he burden of the wounded must be removed in order for the rest to survive."[35] He knew that either he must remove that burden himself, or others would do it.

Resistance to the legal process, faith in the President, and contempt for their opponents characterized Nixon's inner circle almost to the end. Preventing the "death of a thousand cuts" seemed to be the rallying cry for the President's men. Haig complained, however, that to some White House aides the slogan meant that Nixon should resign rather than suffer such a painful ordeal—the "pussy fire group," he contemptuously called them, comparing them to Vietnamese who would not stand and fight. Some in the White House felt besieged: "It was us against the world." Every day, it seemed, brought what Stephen Bull called the "Oh, Shit Syndrome," meaning another revelation, another disclosure, another indictment. Some left, "either under handcuffs, [or] running for the hills," another aide recalled. But some, like Bull, believed the President would extricate himself—until Bull learned of the June 23 tape.

Still, Bull knew that the White House atmosphere was different; "things just were not happening," he recalled, and the blank pages of the presidential logs offer mute testimony to that fact. For some, like Richard Moore, there was now little to do aside from "long lunch hours." For Moore, it was a time of fear that his friends would go to prison or that he himself would be indicted. Others, like Alan Greenspan, saw the final days as a time to help the President, and, more important, as a time to serve the republic. Greenspan had consistently rejected offers of Administration positions, but near the end he became Chairman of the Council of Economic Advisers, fearing that "the normal process of government would deteriorate or even collapse" unless firm action were taken. Such advisers as Leonard Garment were "amazed" that the President continued to function as well as he did. Nixon, he remembered, "took it right to the end." Finally, for the President's family, of course, it was a mournful time, all the more difficult, apparently, because he could not bring himself to discuss the situation with them. "[W]e never sat down as a family to talk about Watergate," Julie Eisenhower wrote. For Nixon himself, it was a "nightmare" time.[36]

Richard Nixon should be taken at his word. When he learned that Republicans and Southern Democrats had banded together to support impeachment, he knew he could not finish his second term. Thereafter, the only question concerned the manner of his leaving. He later wrote that he decided to resign just before the Judiciary Committee voted, meaning, of course, that his talk to his Cabinet on August 6 was pure sham. Other accounts suggest greater uncertainty in his decision. In these versions, Haig is a hero of sorts, a man who kept the President on the course of resignation, sparing the nation more agony. Haig himself may have been the source of such tales; John Mitchell thought that Haig need not write any account of Watergate: "Haig has already gilded the history. I don't think he has to write any more."[37] Such accounts add a measure of drama, to be sure; yet they betray the history of a man who measured his career by a careful calculation of what was best for him. In all probability, Richard Nixon needed little push from others.

The President may have heard a favorable signal on August 7, when Robert McClory told the White House congressional-liaison man that Rodino had asked him to communicate his view that he had "absolutely no interest in pursuing any kind of criminal action against the President should he elect to resign." According to McClory, Rodino promised to end the impeachment inquiry as well if Nixon stepped down. Speaker Carl Albert concurred, although he added that he had no influence over the Special Prosecutor's course of action. The news from McClory undoubtedly had some appeal. If Nixon learned of that development, then he would have done so just prior to his meeting with Goldwater, Rhodes, and Scott. That conversation, taken together with the news from Rodino, might well have been influential. Rodino later proved to be as good as his word: he promptly closed down the inquiry after the resignation. Democrats were off the hook of carrying out the formal, irrevocable act of impeachment; moreover, any further action on their part would have reeked of vindictiveness and easily generated a counter-reaction of sympathy for the fallen President.[38]

That evening Nixon began to work in earnest on his resignation speech and arranged to meet Vice President Ford the next day to discuss a transition. In that meeting, the President recommended that Ford retain Haig; the rest of the meeting was awkward, as both men seemed to understand, yet were unable to express, what was required of each.

The following night, Nixon saw more than forty longtime, steadfast supporters. "I just hope I haven't let you down," he told them. But he said later that he knew he had—as he had "let down the country . . . our system of government and the dreams of all those young people that ought to get into government. . . . I . . . let the American people down, and I have to carry that burden with me for the rest of my life." Earlier, he met with congressional leaders from both parties. He told them what he would say to the nation that evening: he had "lost his base" in Congress, and he believed the outcome of the impeachment process to be inevitable. Speaker Albert best remembered that Nixon never discussed the question of whether he had done wrong. Perhaps that was asking too much. Instead, the President broke down in tears.[39]

Nixon's last full day in office proceeded routinely. He vetoed annual appropriations bills for the Agriculture Department and the Environmental Protection Agency on the grounds that they were inflationary. On a lesser, but far more symbolic note, he nominated a judge to fill a federal court seat in Wisconsin which had been vacant for three years. Nixon had sought unsuccessfully to appoint an old friend, Republican Representative Glenn Davis, but the American Bar Association, as well as state groups, had mounted an intense campaign in opposition. The new appointment on August 8 painfully measured the President's decline and powerlessness.

Later that day, Nixon addressed his simple letter of resignation to the keeper of the seals, the Secretary of State: "I hereby resign the Office of President of the United States." Richard Nixon had raised Henry Kissinger—the immigrant, the Harvard outsider, the Rockefeller retainer—to a point where he received almost exclusive credit for achievements that properly belonged to the President, and where he far outstripped Nixon in public esteem. Now, Kissinger received a letter unprecedented in American history. Nixon's gods of fortune mocked him.

As the President prepared to resign, groundless rumors surfaced that the White House might use military force to maintain power. The reports were fueled by the curious behavior of Secretary of Defense James Schlesinger. According to later reports given by the ever-elusive unnamed "senior Pentagon official," Schlesinger had requested that General George S. Brown, Chairman of the Joint Chiefs of Staff, monitor all orders from any source to military units. Schlesinger was supposedly concerned that Nixon or his aides might attempt to reach military units outside Pentagon channels, to order action that would block the "constitutional process." Apparently, some believed that the Air Force might assist the President because of his efforts in securing the return of prisoners of war from North Vietnam. Some thought that Marine units or the Eighty-second Airborne Division would stage a coup. On a more practical level, Schlesinger may have feared that a hostile foreign power might attempt to take advantage of the domestic crisis. His suspicions of the Soviets, particularly as his views differed greatly from Nixon's and Kissinger's were a matter of public record. Kissinger, in a July 3 Moscow news conference, had blamed internal factions within the United States and the Soviet Union for the failure to achieve more substantial arms agreements—a clear reference to what Kissinger viewed as Schlesinger's obstructionism.[40]

General Brown sent a message on August 8 to various American military commanders in the United States and abroad, advising increased vigilance. Yet he also urged them not to be overly ambitious in implementing the order. The next day, two other messages went to the same commanders over Schlesinger's name. The first conveyed remarks of President Ford: "I know that I can count on the unswerving loyalty and dedication to duty that have always characterized the men and women of the Department of Defense. The country joins me in appreciation for your steadfast service." The other communique, signed by Schlesinger, stated: "Mr. Ford will have, consistent with our best traditions, the fullest support, dedication, and loyalty of all members of the Department of Defense."[41]

Military men reacted sharply to Schlesinger's personal message. Former Joint Chiefs Chairman Thomas Moorer at the time thought that Schlesinger's communique was "ridiculous," for no military officer could take action outside "the form of command." An adjutant at the Readiness Command in Florida thought that the Ford message was "redundant" and "stated the obvious." The second message from Schlesinger, he believed, was "of little interest," since it stated "what the military do without prodding throughout their careers." General Bruce Palmer, formerly second-in-command in Vietnam, and then head of the Readiness Command, reacted sharply. He was "irritated" and "resented" the message. Palmer thought it "not only unnecessary but insulting to our uniformed men and women," and he blamed it on the overactive imagination of Pentagon staff assistants. "Civilian supremacy was bred into me," Palmer later said—although he worried about "a bloated civilian establishment" and a breed of younger officers with little knowledge and understanding of the American Constitution.

Haig himself pointed with pride to the orderly transition of power, strongly implying that he had a role in ensuring that process. "There were no tanks," he told senators during his confirmation hearing as Secretary of State in 1981. "No troops were drawn up. There were not any sandbags around the White House. There may have [been fears] inside where you were, but there were not outside. There was no indication that anything was amiss at all. It was quiet. The lights were on. It was beautiful. . . . And that was the transfer of power in our system, because I think, at least in part, of this shared responsibility that we have." But Haig, typically, could also say precisely the opposite, in other remarks largely designed to preserve an air of mystery about events, an air that he alone understood. In 1979 he referred to Watergate as one of the "most dangerous periods in American history, [one in which] change occurred within the provisions of our Constitution and established rule of law. This was not a foregone conclusion during those difficult days." Did this refer to the difficulty of securing Nixon's resignation? Haig was asked. "I'll stick to what I told you," he cryptically remarked. Haig's religious and military training gave him a special blend of the mysterious and the mundane, qualities that he exploited and parlayed throughout his career.[42]

The President spent the afternoon of August 8 correcting and memorizing his resignation speech, to be broadcast that evening. "One thing, Ron, old boy," he feebly joked to Ziegler, "we won't have to have any more press conferences, and we won't even have to tell them that[,] either!" Of course, he had said a similar thing a dozen years earlier in California. He also said that he looked forward to writing, noting that it might be done in prison. "Some of the best writing in history has been done in prison. Think of Lenin and Gandhi," he said.

At 9:00 P.M. the thirty-seventh President addressed the nation from the White House for the thirty-seventh time. Comparatively little of his talk had to do with Watergate and his resignation. If Richard Nixon were indeed to write from prison, first he would broadcast his own apologia. Watergate had been "a long and difficult period." He wished to carry on and persevere in the presidency, but events of the past few days convinced him that "I no longer have a strong enough political base in the Congress to justify continuing that effort." He wanted to "see the constitutional process through," but with the loss of his political base, he said, the process had been served, and there was no need to prolong it. Because of the Watergate situation, he contended, Congress would not give him the necessary support to govern effectively. With a hint of defiance, he asserted that he had never been a quitter. To resign was "abhorrent to every instinct" within him. But he would put "the interests of America first." America, he said, needed a full-time President and a full-time Congress; an impeachment battle would only drain both the institutions and the nation. "Therefore, I shall resign the Presidency effective at noon tomorrow," he added.

Nixon seemed sincere as he expressed hope that his act would heal the nation's wounds. And he offered what apparently he had not told the congressional leaders who had conferred with him: "I regret deeply any injuries that may have been done in the course of the events that led to this decision. I would say only that if some of my judgments were wrong—and some were wrong—they were made in what I believed at the time to be the best interest of the Nation." It was Richard Nixon's only moment that approximated contrition.

The rest of the talk focused on his achievements—the end of the Vietnam war, the opening to China, the conciliatory responses of the Arab nations to his diplomatic efforts, and the agreements with the Soviet Union. Nothing was said of any gains toward that domestic peace which Nixon had promised more than five years earlier. Finally, he insisted that resignation would not be his St. Helena; rather, he promised that the nation would see more of him in the years to come.

The networks followed the President's resignation speech with the "instant analysis" that Nixon and Agnew had so bitterly assailed. Nixon undoubtedly savored the irony. Now, the commentators treated him generously—"a touch of class," "conciliatory," "few things in his presidency became him as much as his manner of leaving." He also would have heard more familiar chords. One commentator remarked: "From the viewpoint of Congress, that wasn't a very satisfactory speech."[43] Nixon had expressed "regret," to be sure; but finally, the reason he gave for resigning was that Congress had deprived him of a "political base," making it impossible for him to continue in office. It was the opening salvo in his campaign for history.

Six years earlier, to the day, Nixon had delivered perhaps the best speech of his career as he accepted the Republican presidential nomination. He had told the nation that he would restore respect for the law. "Time is running out," he said at that time, "for the merchants of crime and corruption in American society."

The morning after his resignation announcement, the President gave another speech, a "spontaneous thing," he called it, as he spoke in the East Room of the White House to an assembled group of White House and Administration workers. As often before in his career, Nixon was anxious to bare his soul—never more so than in this, his darkest hour, and perhaps the darkest hour of the American presidency. But it was the wrong time. Now, the time was more appropriate for a quiet fade-out—unless he had another goal in mind. Perhaps he did. The Friday morning talk marked the flip side of the speech the night before—different words, yet all part of the same album designed to impress indelibly the image of Richard Nixon as a man grievously wronged and a man not about to leave the public stage forever. It was, he said, "a beginning."

In the open society of America, the most private of moments often become the most public of spectacles. When a president embraces his family, visits the Lincoln Memorial, or receives a foreign visitor, we know the probing eye of the television camera will accompany him not only to give us "news," but to allow us vicariously to experience the event itself. Richard Nixon's last appearance before White House workers and Administration loyalists seemed, by its nature, a private event. The President could have conducted it in private, had he preferred. His family, he admitted, protested that "after all the agony television had caused us, its prying eye should [not] be allowed to intrude on this last and most intimate moment of all." But he sensed an opportunity to serve himself and seized the moment. "That's the way it has to be," he told them, adding that he owed it to his supporters and to the people. His daughter dutifully found her name mark on the floor.[44] Clearly, Nixon would persist in his unceasing quest for gaining love and understanding from America. Spontaneous? In all likelihood, the occasion had all the spontaneity of a pointillist painting.

Nixon had borne adversity through the years, sometimes with grace, other times with petulance, but always with verve. As he prepared to depart from office, he was reconciled to the inevitability of his punishment. The moment presented him with the opportunity to display a rarely seen introspective side of himself. Whether wallowing in the banality of self-pity or reciting his achievements with a feisty grit and pride, he remained a compelling phenomenon to admirers and adversaries alike.

Nixon appeared that day as he had so often before: the solitary man, fully exposed, with only a microphone and his family as stage props to shield him; the blatant self-consciousness, the twitching smile, the beaded perspiration, the eyes riveted to the red-lighted television camera, almost oblivious to the live audience before him—all that had become so familiar over more than a quarter-century. Familiarity itself gave reality to the moment; it also, on the surface at least, belied rampant rumors of the President's drinking, drug use, and depression. Yet, for Nixon, the reality was failure, pain, and shame. Somehow, he steeled himself against such agony.

Nixon rambled through memories and aphorisms. The advice for others, as so often, was autobiographical. "[T]hose who hate you don't win unless you hate them, and then you destroy yourself." He joked—awkwardly, as usual—that he had to find a way to pay his taxes, and that he read books although he was "not educated." He urged his supporters to be proud of their work and the milestones of the Administration. His "old man" was "a great man because he did his job," and every job counted to the hilt, regardless of what happened. His mother, too, was remembered. No books would be written about her, "but she was a saint," he said, as tears welled up in his eyes.

And then, as he had the night before, Nixon sought to identify with Theodore Roosevelt, a patron saint for presidential toughness. In that first talk, he had quoted Roosevelt's praise for the "man in the arena," the man who fought valiantly and ceaselessly for what he believed, and the man who knew the heights of achievement and who, if he failed, failed while "daring greatly." For his "intimate" gathering, Nixon identified with still another side of Roosevelt—a tender, passionate, loving man obscured behind the image of walking tall with a big stick. The young Roosevelt's beloved first wife had died of Bright's disease when she was a mere twenty-three years old (and on the same day as Roosevelt's mother). Nixon quoted a delicate, moving passage from Roosevelt's autobiography that described her death and his enduring love for her. With her death, Roosevelt wrote, "the light went out from my life forever." How strange that Nixon should have identified with Teddy Roosevelt's lament for his inexplicable loss. For after all, Richard Nixon's cause for grief was all too explainable.

THE IMPACT AND MEANING OF WATERGATE

BOOK FIVE

THE IMPACT AND
MEANING OF WATERGATE

XXI

THE "BURDEN I SHALL BEAR FOR EVERY DAY."

THE PARDON: SEPTEMBER 1974

On Sunday morning, September 8, President Gerald R. Ford attended St. John's Church, across from Lafayette Park. Afterward, he invited a pool of reporters and photographers into the Oval Office, where he read a brief statement and then signed a proclamation granting Richard Nixon a "full, free, and absolute pardon" for any crimes "which he, Richard Nixon, has committed or may have committed" during his presidency. The time had come, the President said, to end this "American tragedy" and restore "tranquility."

Ford had no precedents, of course—the situation of his predecessor was unique. But significantly, he gave as his first reason for the pardon the "common knowledge" that the "allegations and accusations" against Nixon threatened his health. He thought that Nixon and his family had suffered long enough, but added that they would suffer no matter what Ford did. Then he turned to the considerations of "equal justice," contending that Nixon would be "cruelly and excessively penalized either in preserving the presumption of his innocence or in obtaining a speedy determination of his guilt in order to repay a legal debt to society." Ford anticipated long delays in the legal process and endless litigation, circumstances, he said, which would only exacerbate "ugly passions" and challenge the "credibility of our free institutions." Interestingly, Ford noted that the former President might win his freedom on due-process grounds, with the result that the "verdict of history" might be "even more inconclusive" as to his guilt or innocence. At the end, however, Ford returned to his theme of "ending"

Watergate and restoring "tranquility"; the nation could not afford to "prolong the bad dreams that continue to reopen a chapter that is closed."

With that, Ford signed the proclamation and released a statement of acceptance from the former President, who acknowledged his "mistakes and misjudgments." The news of Nixon's pardon erupted across the country, and the new President of the United States found that he had ignited a firestorm of his own.[1]

Among the enumerated powers granted to the President in Article II of the Constitution, few are more absolute than the "power to grant reprieves and pardons for offenses against the United States, except in cases of impeachment." The framers frankly acknowledged the "political" purposes of a pardon. Alexander Hamilton in *Federalist* 74 warmly endorsed its discretionary aspect. There would be, he said, "seasons of insurrection or rebellion," or "critical moments, when a well-timed offer of pardon . . . may restore the tranquility of the commonwealth; and which, if suffered to pass unimproved, it may never be possible afterwards to recall."

When or what was that "critical moment" in 1974, that moment that might "restore the tranquility of the commonwealth?" Gerald Ford assumed the presidency on the crest of a wave of popularity and goodwill. "Our long national nightmare of Watergate" was over, he said as he took his oath of office. The change was cause for celebration: "Our Constitution works," and here "the people rule," he told the country. It was time to return to the nation's business. Three days later, he promised Congress that controlling inflation had his top priority; moreover, he pledged he would not tolerate "illegal tappings, eavesdropping, buggings, or break-ins." The new President and his imagemakers worked strenuously to protect the appearance of an "open presidency." Ford's simple earnestness appeared so credible; people seemed desperately eager to again believe their leaders.

Perhaps the nightmare was over. What remained of Watergate seemed to be a mopping-up operation, one for the Special Prosecutor to conduct through the orderly processes of the legal system. Peter Rodino had closed down the House Judiciary Committee's impeachment inquiry; the days of ever-more-dramatic political bombshells appeared over. Congress would pass the inevitable spate of "reform" legislation to rectify the certified abuses of power. True enough, the future fate of the former President appeared clouded. Would he be a witness at the forthcoming trials of his former aides? Would he find himself "in the dock," the focus of his own criminal trial? That prospect undoubtedly haunted Richard Nixon and certainly worried his former associates.

But did Watergate or Nixon's personal fate impair Ford's ability to carry out his functions? Did they prevent a return to the "tranquility" that had eluded the nation for nearly two years? We cannot portray national moods and conditions precisely; their fleeting elements can be captured only through the perceptions of beholders, each, of course, with his own interest at stake. It is clear, however, that Ford believed the nightmare still haunted the nation, and that he had an antidote. The new President's cure had substantial merit; unfortunately, he fumbled its application, with costly short-run effects for him and for the nation.

At Ford's confirmation hearings in November 1973, a senator asked the nominee whether a new president might terminate any investigation or criminal prosecution against the president he had succeeded. "I do not think the public would stand for it," Ford replied.[2] One year later, President Ford journeyed to Capitol Hill to explain his decision to grant a pardon to Richard Nixon on September 8. So much of the affair of the past two years had been extraordinary; its dénouement was no exception.

We have differing versions of when a pardon for Richard Nixon first received serious consideration. Seymour Hersh's 1983 article on the subject in the *Atlantic* contended that Nixon selected Ford as his Vice President in October 1973 because "he thought that he could rely on Ford to pardon him." Ford himself testified that on August 1, 1974, Haig told him that a pardon for Nixon, if he resigned, should be a possibility. J. Fred Buzhardt later insisted that he and his aides only had considered the contingency of Nixon pardoning himself and suggested that if Haig had indeed raised the idea of a Ford pardon, he had done so at Nixon's behest.

Buzhardt and his staff had been considering Watergate-related presidential pardons for some time in 1974. When the Supreme Court ruled that Nixon must surrender tapes subpoenaed by the Special Prosecutor, Buzhardt knew that the June 23, 1972 tape was "devastating" and undoubtedly would have a "terminal effect." He called Haig and St. Clair that same day, suggesting that the President pardon all the defendants and himself, and then resign. Buzhardt had researched the problem and was satisfied that Nixon had the authority to pardon himself, and to do so against prospective charges relating to acts committed while he was President. Buzhardt repeated that suggestion to Haig on August 1, when he knew that Haig was about to inform Ford of the crucial tape transcript. Buzhardt later insisted that he never proposed any discussion of a Ford pardon of Nixon, yet he drafted a pardon proclamation in Gerald Ford's name, dated August 6, 1974, three days before Nixon's eventual resignation. Within a few days of the transition, Haig informed Ford that "a White House lawyer" had determined that the President could pardon individuals even before a "criminal action" had been initiated.[3]

Haig remained at his post after August 9—much to the consternation of

Ford's longtime retainers. At this critical juncture, Ford found himself surrounded with Nixon's aides, notably Haig, Buzhardt, and Leonard Garment.
Haig apparently had persuaded Ford that he had been running the government for the past ten months and that he was indispensable. The Chief of
Staff quickly established himself in Ford's mind as a man who did things,
and thus he made the President somewhat dependent on him, according to
Clay Whitehead, who served both Nixon and Ford. Sharing in the typical
desire to manage Ford, Henry Kissinger "vetoed" a presidential meeting
with the Joint Chiefs of Staff on Ford's first day in office, but the President
ignored him. In his anxiety to avoid appearances of a "Stalin-like purge,"
and to avoid tarring innocent people with the Watergate brush, Ford kept
much of the Nixon staff in place for several months. Many of Ford's friends
thought it his biggest mistake and that it demonstrated, once again, his
excessive loyalty to Nixon.[4]

Less than a week after Nixon returned to San Clemente, John Ehrlichman's
lawyers subpoenaed the former President as a witness in the forthcoming
trial of Nixon's former aides. The day before, the Special Prosecutor's office
had said that no decision had been made regarding any prosecution of Nixon.
But Nixon had some momentary good news. Ford's press aide announced
that all Nixon tapes and documents not subpoenaed would be returned to
Nixon. Ford had agreed to release the material, the spokesman said, on
advice from Buzhardt and James St. Clair. They had cited no formal authority, and instead had relied on tradition. But pressure from Jaworski and
from Ford's aides on newly appointed White House Counsel Philip Buchen
resulted in a reversal of Ford's decision. Buchen said that the White House
would retain the materials pending the settlement of certain legal issues
raised by Jaworski and "others." Near the end of the month, Nixon received
a subpoena to give a deposition for a pending civil trial related to Watergate.
From his San Clemente exile, the law's long arm seemed menacing to Richard Nixon. "Do you think the people want to pick the carcass?" he said in
a telephone call to a Republican congressman on August 26, adding that
"We've got problems with that fellow . . ."—meaning Jaworski.[5]

As Nixon prepared to resign on August 7, the leading members of the
Special Prosecution Force considered the question of his immunity, his avail-
ability as a witness, the feasibility of gaining a "confession of guilt" from
him, and the prospect of obtaining a promise that he would not pardon
anyone. Much of this discussion recognized the inevitability of Nixon's resignation. James Neal, who later prosecuted the leading White House aides,
stressed the importance of a confession, remembering the Agnew situation
in October 1973. Another Jaworski aide warned that "it would be wrong to
allow [a] deal that would forgo prosecution while allowing President [Nixon]

to go around . . . proclaiming innocence.'' The prosecutors recognized the importance of bringing the congressional leadership into any "deal.''

The next day, Haig informed Jaworski of Nixon's intention to resign and not to pardon any former aides. He also told Jaworski that Nixon would plead the Fifth Amendment if called as a witness in their trials and that he would be taking his presidential papers with him. According to Jaworski, Haig admitted that the tapes had been tampered with but said he did not know who had done so.

Jaworski's staff began earnestly to consider the question of an indictment against Nixon on August 9. The issues emerged quickly: that resignation had been sufficient punishment, obtaining a fair trial would be difficult, and prosecution would aggravate political divisions were all factors which militated against any further pursuit of the case; considerations of equal justice under law, the danger of persistent political division until charges against Nixon reached a final disposition, and the possible appearance of a deal's having been made to exchange resignation for immunity, were all elements which mandated indictment and prosecution. At a meeting later that day, Jaworski insisted that nothing be done in the present context. One of his aides perceptively realized that the prosecutors were in a "no-win" situation, as a decision either way would be criticized.[6]

Jaworski aide Philip Lacovara urged him to seek an indictment of Nixon and join his case with that of the other defendants. But other staff members divided on the issue. Neal, perhaps the most experienced prosecutor and political figure in the group, acknowledged that a *prima facie* case existed against Nixon but argued that "it would not be in the country's best interest to prosecute him.'' He then suggested that Jaworski leave the actual decision to the grand jury. Still another prosecutor urged that the case against Nixon be developed, then presented to President Ford to see if he preferred clemency. He added that if Jaworski chose not to prosecute, then the indictments against the other defendants should be dismissed. But the preponderance of opinion expressed to Jaworski firmly favored prosecution of the former President.[7]

Nixon nevertheless had support from many quarters. The day he resigned, Senator J. William Fulbright said that Nixon's contributions to foreign policy merited the nation's "gratitude and approbation.'' Fulbright suggested both a pardon for Nixon and amnesty for draft resisters, in order to surmount the twin traumas of Watergate and Vietnam. On August 20, Ford nominated Nelson A. Rockefeller, Nixon's old rival, for the vice-presidency. Reporters questioned the former New York governor regarding Nixon's future. He already had been "hung,'' Rockefeller said, and added that he need not "be drawn and quartered.'' He proposed that Nixon be given "immunity from prosecution.'' That same day, by a 412–3 vote, the House of Representatives accepted the Judiciary Committee's report on its impeachment inquiry.[8]

Clare Boothe Luce, in a *New York Times* essay, called for a pardon less than a week after Nixon resigned. She dismissed Nixon as simply "one more crime statistic," and observed that his offenses were far less horrifying than murder, rape, or treason ("Nobody was drowned at Watergate," she said, in an obvious swipe at Senator Edward Kennedy). For that, Nixon already had suffered "cruel and unusual punishment;" he had been "stripped" of the presidency and had "lost all that made his life rich and meaningful." "Booking . . . Citizen Nixon," Luce wrote, would satisfy only revenge. She urged Ford to use his constitutional power for clemency— "if His Majesty, the public, so wills." But public sentiment was skeptical: a Gallup poll, conducted between August 16 and 19, showed that 56 percent of the respondents favored a criminal trial for the ex-president.[9]

Republican Congressman David C. Treen (LA) spoke for most of his party when he urged Leon Jaworski not to prosecute Nixon. Treen believed that it would be "extremely divisive and counter-productive." More important, Treen urged Jaworski to consider mitigating factors: Nixon had rendered the nation a great service by resigning and not extending the impeachment battle; he had not destroyed the tapes; and his resignation alone constituted "punishment of indescribable magnitude." Many Americans thought that the price already had been too high; many others, Treen contended, believed any further penalty altogether unjustified.[10]

On August 27, Leonard Garment talked to several reporters who, he claimed, thought that the time had come for Ford to issue a pardon. Vengeance offered no rewards to the nation, they agreed, and Nixon himself was destroyed. Garment thought that Ford had to act before "institutional momentum" made it impossible for him to do so. Working with Raymond Price, Nixon's chief speechwriter, he drafted a memorandum and a pardon announcement for Ford. Garment presented the documents to Buchen the next morning at the senior staff meeting, and provided a copy to Haig.

The quiet, informal pressures on Ford that had been building throughout the month now came to a focus in Garment's memorandum. Garment warned that demands to punish Nixon would increase, not diminish. Jaworski confronted irresistible pressures to prosecute from his staff, the media, and Sam Dash of the Senate Select Committee. Soon, Garment believed, matters would pass from Ford's control: the national mood of conciliation would dissipate, the President would find it increasingly difficult politically to intervene, "and the whole miserable tragedy will be played out to God knows what ugly and wounding conclusion." On the other hand, Garment argued that after an initial negative reaction to a pardon, the nation would be relieved. He thought prompt action would relieve Ford of Nixon as a distracting issue in both the upcoming congressional elections and the President's efforts to forge a new economic policy. He confidently argued that the nation thirsted for direction and crystallization of its feelings toward the ex-president; Ford, he insisted, had an opportunity to lead and to inspire.[11]

Conveniently—perhaps too conveniently—the first question raised at Ford's press conference that day, August 28, was whether he agreed with Rockefeller on immunity for Nixon and whether he would use his pardon authority. Ford thought that Rockefeller's statement "coincided" with the "general view" of the American people. A bit elliptically, he added that "in this situation I am the final authority," and then pointedly declared that a pardon was a "proper option." For most commentators, Ford left no doubt that he thought the former President had suffered enough. He clearly indicated that he would pardon Nixon—he later admitted that this was his implication— but he also added that he would not take precipitate action: "There have been no charges made, there has been no action by the courts, there has been no action by any jury. And until any legal process has been undertaken, I think it is unwise and untimely for me to make any commitment." The President's Press Secretary, for one, believed that Ford had made a solemn promise not to interfere until the process had run its course.

Ford, of course, knew that the pardon issue would inevitably be raised. He later described that press conference with some bitterness, because reporters had concentrated so on the fate of the ex-president that they failed to raise the substantive national policy issues that Ford faced. "I thought they had wasted my time," he wrote. Further, he thought that similar questions would go on endlessly and his answers be subjected to various, and even irresponsible, interpretations. He admitted that he had some concern over Nixon's personal health, and his own belief was that the country did not want to see him behind bars. But he insisted that the nation's health most concerned him, and he quoted one of his military aides: "We're all Watergate junkies. Some of us are mainlining, some are sniffing, some are lacing it with something else, but all of us are addicted. This will go on and on unless someone steps in and says that we, as a nation, must go cold turkey. Otherwise, we'll die of an overdose."

Immediately after the press conference, Ford told his aides to prepare the necessary pardon documents. Buchen, however, claimed that the President did not order him to proceed until August 30. He, of course, was not unfamiliar with the issue—having read Garment's pardon memorandum as well as having discussed the matter with Haig. And Buchen undoubtedly had shared the material and conversations with the President.[12]

The Special Prosecutor's staff made its own assessment of Ford's August 28 press conference. Lacovara thought that Ford opposed any prosecution of Nixon, and that he had signalled Jaworski accordingly so he would not have to pardon Nixon. Lacovara urged Jaworski to ask the White House (offering to do so himself) if the President intended to pardon Nixon. He apparently hoped to force Ford to act to head off any pending indictment.[13]

On September 4, Jaworski told Buchen that Nixon could not be tried for at least nine months to two years. He added that the forthcoming trial of Mitchell, Haldeman, and Ehrlichman would generate unfavorable, prejudicial publicity, precluding any fair trial for Nixon. Jaworski also had no intention of including Nixon as a co-defendant, believing that the former President's condemnation in the impeachment process might well prejudice the cases of the other defendants. On that same date, Nixon's lawyers delivered a lengthy memorandum to Jaworski, demonstrating "conclusively" that the former President could not receive a fair trial and should not be indicted. The prosecutors themselves never came to a specific conclusion on the fair-trial issue.

Jaworski had a healthy respect for Nixon's new lawyer, as well as a keen memory of the former President's determination to delay and impede legal proceedings. He attached a memorandum of his own to one he had received from his deputy, Henry Ruth, stating that the staff was investigating ten possible criminal violations by Nixon aside from his role in obstructing justice in the Watergate affair. "None of these matters at the moment rises to the level of our ability to prove even a probable criminal violation," Ruth wrote; yet, he thought the investigations proper as the prosecutors fully pursued their duties. Ruth told Jaworski that, if he intended to seek an indictment of the former President, it would be "fair and proper" to notify the White House "sufficiently in advance so that pardon action could be taken before indictment." He believed that good arguments could be made for leniency, but if Ford were to pardon Nixon, "I think he ought to do it early rather than late." Ford claimed that Ruth's remark clinched his decision. The President had his own political calculus to follow; the prosecutors, for their part, found important considerations at stake involving the integrity and viability of the legal system.[14]

Ford had made his decision firm by September 4, perhaps sooner. But for the next few days, he carried out a bargaining charade with his predecessor. At the same time, in this crucial period between his decision and his announcement of the pardon, he failed to do the things that might have made his action more acceptable; instead, his attention focused on fruitless negotiations between his emissary and the Nixon entourage in San Clemente.

On September 4, Philip Buchen met with Nixon's new lawyer, Herbert J. Miller, and Benton Becker, a young attorney who had worked for Ford in Congress. Buchen told Miller that Ford was considering a pardon and that he hoped Miller might be able to help extract a statement of contrition from Nixon. Ford admitted that the idea of such a statement had been broached, but he later added that he had not "demanded" it. In fact, the President was concerned about Nixon's response. He shared Jaworski's fear that Nixon might act as Spiro Agnew had when he offered a *nolo contendere* plea in October 1973 and then publicly insisted he had done no wrong.[15]

Ford dispatched Becker to San Clemente the next day. Becker's mission was threefold: he was to negotiate a statement of Nixon's response to a pardon, conclude an agreement regarding the possession and control of Nixon's papers and tapes, and make some determination of the former President's mental and physical condition. As Becker left the White House, Haig told him Nixon would never surrender his papers and tapes. When Becker arrived in San Clemente, Ronald Ziegler, Nixon's principal aide, greeted him rather belligerently, as Becker recalled, and said that President Nixon would noᴵ admit anything to "Jerry Ford," and he would not give up his papers and tapes. "If you're out here for any of that, you're wasting your time," Ziegler said. Ziegler's knowledge of Benton's mission was not the only indication that Haig may have had his own two-track process, and that he—and perhaps Ford—had spoken to Nixon or to the former President's aides in San Clemente.

Becker believed that Ford had instructed him to get a statement of contrition in Nixon's response to the pardon. But during his second day in San Clemente, Ziegler said the subject was a waste of time, since Ford was not insisting on such a statement. Ford later admitted as much, but only he or Haig could have relayed that information to the Nixon camp. When Becker returned to Washington, he told the President of his suspicions, but Ford responded rather calmly.

Becker's negotiations had an element of the surreal about them. Ford had the upper hand yet seemed to end up at a disadvantage. The San Clemente proceedings resembled a poker game, a pastime that Richard Nixon liked and supposedly had mastered in his Navy years. Perhaps Nixon had an advantage, using Haig to signal Gerald Ford's playing hand; perhaps he simply outbluffed his successor. Becker certainly did not get any statement of contrition, and the agreement on Nixon's presidential materials was so one-sided as to provoke an unprecedented response by Congress.

Nixon and his staff knew that Ford had decided on a pardon, founded in the realization that only in that manner could he end the national obsession with Watergate. Becker had a draft pardon with him, as well as the draft of an agreement on the presidential records. If Ford had been serious about the statement of contrition, Becker might well have carried an advance statement of that as well. He did not. Becker acknowledged that Ford probably was not altogether interested in such a statement, apparently believing that the "Nixon-haters" would object to a pardon under any conditions. The pardon and the materials agreement were linked to some extent, according to Becker, yet the final result in both areas proved beneficial only to Richard Nixon.

Becker spent much of his time in San Clemente working with Miller and Ziegler (who regularly consulted with Nixon) on the language of a statement that the former President would make upon receipt of the pardon. That statement, Becker knew, was not to be one of contrition; it was, he admitted, merely "antiseptic," and he did "not think it [said] very much." The statement went through at least four drafts before all parties settled on its final language.

When he accepted the pardon, Nixon expressed the "hope" that Ford's "compassionate act" would lift "the burden of Watergate" from the nation. Looking back on "the complex and confusing" events of the past two years and more, he acknowledged that he had been "wrong in not acting more decisively and more forthrightly"—but he admitted to no obstruction of justice regarding the Watergate affair itself, and he admitted to none of the abuses of power cited by the House Judiciary Committee. Nixon did leave one small opening for recognizing an obstruction of justice, when he stated that he might have been more forthright after Watergate had "reached the stage of judicial proceedings." Others, he said, believed that his action had been illegal and self-serving. But, quietly defiant, Nixon simply stated that he now understood how his "own mistakes and misjudgments . . . seemed to support" that belief. Those "mistakes and misjudgments," he concluded, amounted to the "wrong way" to deal with Watergate—and that was the "burden I shall bear for every day of the life that is left to me." Watergate thus was merely a blunder, a mistake of the head, not the heart. For Nixon, his actions only "appeared" to cast him as a wrongdoer.

After all the hard bargaining, bargaining in which Nixon did not deal personally with Ford's emissary, Benton Becker had a brief audience with Nixon. He claimed that he told Nixon the White House would stand by prevailing legal doctrine that acceptance of a pardon acknowledged guilt. Nixon seemed uninterested. Becker remembered the conversation as unfocused and depressing. He found Nixon to be "an absolute candidate for suicide; the most depressed human being I have ever met, and I didn't think it was an act." Becker duly conveyed that impression to President Ford. Whatever Nixon's mood when he met with Becker, less than three weeks later he signed a contract for a two-million-dollar advance for his forthcoming memoirs.[16]

Nixon and his advisers apparently decided that they did not need to give Ford any statement of contrition. They believed—and probably knew—that Ford had determined to grant the pardon in any event, in order to get on with the nation's business. Politically, they saw themselves in command of the situation. Melvin Laird later suggested that Ford believed he would get a statement of contrition from Nixon out of gratitude, if for no other reason. Philip Buchen told reporters that Ford had made no effort to secure any acknowledgment of guilt from Nixon; instead, Buchen concentrated on persuading the media that Nixon's acceptance of the pardon itself offered that acknowledgment.

Ford had the best playing hand, had he chosen to use it. Although Nixon had an advantage in knowing Ford's intentions on the pardon, if Ford had really wanted that statement of contrition—if he had realized how important it would have been to soothe the inevitable public reaction—he simply could have issued the pardon, pointing out that its acceptance acknowledged guilt and that he knew Nixon deeply regretted his wrongdoing. How could Nixon have denied that statement?[17]

When Becker went to San Clemente, the disposition of presidential materials was at issue within the White House, amid reports that Nixon had sought to burn documents or remove his personal papers to San Clemente. According to Becker, Buzhardt had attempted, apparently with Haig's full knowledge, to have the records flown to the former President. Becker understood that he was to link an agreement on that subject with the pardon. But, again, he suspected that Haig might have leaked that connection to Nixon's staff and persuaded them to yield somewhat on the records. The "give" was slight, at best.

Becker brought back an agreement on the Nixon records subsequently known as the Nixon-Sampson Agreement, named after the Administrator of the General Services Administration, and announced the same day as the pardon. The agreement required the former President to deposit his papers in the National Archives, yet gave him "all legal and equitable title" to those materials, as well as the right to control access and to withdraw any of them after three years. Nixon was also assured that his tape recordings would be destroyed upon his death or in 1984, whichever came first. Buchen later defended the agreement because he considered the recordings as "so offensive and contrary" to personal privacy. For his part, Becker claimed that Ford was not going to be a party to the "final cover-up" of Watergate by giving Nixon possession of his papers—a statement that somehow ignored the fact that giving him unequivocal control over their use was a complete victory for Nixon.

Within weeks, Congress abrogated the Nixon-Sampson Agreement when it passed the Presidential Recordings and Materials Preservation Act of 1974, giving the National Archives custody of the Nixon records and the authority to determine their use. Specifically, Congress recognized the need "to provide the public with the full truth, at the earliest reasonable date, of the abuses of governmental power popularly identified under the generic term 'Watergate.'" For thirteen years thereafter, Richard Nixon fought to prevent implementation of that law, seeking, as always, to control the understanding of himself and his presidency. Finally, in 1987, the National Archives opened the first batch of papers of his Administration.[18]

The President felt the first shock of reaction to the pardon from within his inner circle, when Press Secretary Jerald F. terHorst resigned in anger on the day Ford announced the pardon. "The mere fact that Ford could throw away the new national mood of trust for the sake of Richard Nixon" left him wondering about Ford's judgment. Ford's pardon *without getting in return a signed 'confession' "* was most shocking of all. TerHorst could not understand Ford's miscalculation. The President believed that he had offered an act of mercy; instead, terHorst thought, what he had done had all the earmarks of a secret deal and a denial of any principles of equal justice. Ford had healed nothing; to terHorst, he had reopened the "Watergate wound and rubbed salt into the public nerve ends." TerHorst complained that Ford had not consulted with his advisers in pardoning Nixon. But in fact he had. Some in the White House agreed, and some disagreed, both among his own aides as well as among the Nixon holdovers. In any event, terHorst concluded that he could not do anything for the President; "my loyalty," he told another reporter, "was pledged to the United States."[19]

The news of the pardon produced a good deal of popular protest. The consummate grassroots politician had previously operated in the friendly confines of his Grand Rapids, Michigan, constituency, and he had faithfully reflected its wishes. Perhaps national soundings were out of Gerald Ford's depth. Yet if he was determined to act as he did, and for the reasons he gave, he had no choice but to accept and then surmount the fickleness of public opinion. Logic compelled a general pardon for all those involved in Watergate if the principal culprit went free; but the political storm generated by the pardon of Nixon ended any such possibility.

The White House received nearly 270,000 written communications following the pardon, almost 200,000 of which opposed Ford's act. Public officials, both high and low, expressed their feelings. A member of the Kansas House of Representatives congratulated Ford for doing "exactly the right thing." An Alabama Democratic judge commended his "courageous and prompt action." A California Assemblyman was "both astonished and appalled," while an Arkansas state legislator warned Ford that he would always be perceived as a "caretaker, cleaning the dirty Nixon dishes he left behind."

The widow of a prominent football coach applauded Ford for his "generous, courageous and compassionate decision," but a popular husband-and-wife acting couple was outraged. Earlier, Paul Newman and Joanne Woodward had telegraphed the new President, extending their good wishes and support in the euphoric days of August. Now, while they could not "cancel" that message, they offered "a scream of protest and a plea to exercise wisdom." The pardon, they thought, was "poorly advised and imperialistic"; it was "stupid," and it made them more "nervous" than "mere political criminality."

A District of Columbia judge, an old New Dealer, warmly supported the President. He dismissed the clamor of the media, given its longtime infection with a bias against Nixon. He scored the federal judges in the District for their refusal to grant venue changes for Watergate-related trials, contending that a typical local jury would "have been about as fair as the one convened by Cromwell to pass upon the fate of Charles I." Rabbi Baruch Korff, who had valiantly defended Nixon during the waning months of his presidency, thought that the pardon "furthered the kinship between God and man." Armand Hammer, a man equally adept at cutting deals with Richard Nixon, Ronald Reagan, Leonid Brezhnev, and Nikita Khrushchev, praised Ford's "compassionate and well-reasoned action." He urged further pardons, "so we can leave this unhappy episode." Good businessman that he was, Hammer offered a quid pro quo: the President should extend amnesty to "those misguided youths" who had evaded military service during the Vietnam war. That equation, which had become commonplace, enraged those who saw no comparison.[20]

The immediate congressional reaction to Nixon's pardon undoubtedly startled the White House. In the Senate, Mike Mansfield remarked that "all men are created equal under law"—including "presidents and plumbers." Robert C. Byrd seconded him, as did most congressional liberals across both parties. The responses reflected the state of Nixon's support throughout the Watergate affair, as most Southern Democrats and Republicans approved the pardon. But the exceptions were revealing. Walter Flowers thought the pardon premature; and Wiley Mayne, who, given his long support of Nixon, had felt so betrayed by the "smoking gun" revelation, believed that Ford should have waited until Jaworski had decided on a course of action.

Representative Albert Quie (R–MN), a Ford crony in the Republican leadership, worried about the divisiveness of the pardon and urged the President not to grant further pardons until the trials of indicted presidential aides ended. House Democrat John Dingell (MI) bitterly assailed his old rival in a lengthy letter. He charged that the President had "whitewashed" the affair and had "gravely impaired" the idea of equal treatment under law. Dingell thought it best to spare the nation the "unseemly spectacle" of seeing Nixon in jail, for it would "greatly demean" the country and the office, but he believed that a "proper prosecution" was necessary to expose all the facts. Republican Paul McCloskey similarly believed that the legal process should have run its course before Ford pardoned the former President. The pardon, and the apparent willingness of the White House to give Nixon his tapes and papers, only enhanced "public suspicion" that the Ford Administration now had "joined in the Watergate coverup."

More seriously, Hugh Scott reported that Republican senators "bitterly" opposed pardons to those awaiting trial. Across the Republican spectrum, from Jesse Helms to James Buckley to Robert Packwood, the senators urged Ford "to go very slow on this volatile issue." Many believed that the Nixon pardon would not hurt too much but that Ford's timing would be very bad—given the approaching elections—if he issued a blanket pardon. It "just kills us," Ford's congressional liaison reported. A week later, that aide assured Republican congressmen that the President contemplated no further action. Charles Colson later claimed Nixon had promised him that he would not leave office "without wiping the slate clear" for everyone, and that there had been a deal for Ford to pardon all Administration defendants until the subsequent storm over the Nixon pardon.[21]

Nixon telephoned Ford about a week after the pardon, apologizing for the political embarrassment he had caused and expressing his gratitude. It was small comfort for Ford, however. The image of goodwill and honesty he had so assiduously fostered now dissipated. The President's Gallup poll approval rating plunged in a month from 71 percent to 49 percent, and would eventually drop even more. Within two days, the White House reported that mail and telegrams ran five to one against Ford, an extraordinary admission.

Perhaps most revealingly, the pardon gave Republican conservatives who had abandoned Nixon cause to dismiss Ford as merely another immoral political *apparatchik*. Months later, when conservative activists attempted to replace Ford with Ronald Reagan for the 1976 election, Richard Viguerie, a leading conservative fundraiser, attacked Ford for the pardon (among other things), claiming it demonstrated that he was not "an honest and forthright" Republican. In a completely cynical vein, William Buckley's *National Review* stated that conservatives were happy with the pardon, for, at last, it had exposed Ford to liberal criticism. The President, the magazine remarked, had "burned his bridges to the great organs of liberal opinion," preparing the way for "the real battle" in American politics. Charles Colson, now a "born-again" Christian, delivered his own innuendoes, and denied the President any comfort in his struggle with conservatives, when he reiterated that Nixon never would have resigned unless he had reason to believe Ford would pardon him. To Colson, it followed that if Ford won the nomination (which Colson obviously opposed), Democrats would campaign on the theme that he and Nixon had struck a corrupt bargain.[22]

Key Watergate figures divided on the pardon. Sam Ervin instinctively turned to a Biblical quotation and then contended that the pardon was "inexpedient, incompatible with good government, and sets a bad precedent for the future." Ervin made it clear that the pardon settled nothing. Pardons, he insisted, "are for the guilty—not for those who profess their innocence." Elliot Richardson, however, thought that Nixon's distinguished service and the humiliation of resignation justified the pardon, although he thought that the President could simply have quashed any indictment of Nixon by using his prosecutorial discretion as Chief Executive. Apparently, Richardson—of all people—did not understand the extent of the independence Jaworski enjoyed on this issue. In defending the pardon, Richardson emphasized most of all the desirability of avoiding the "embarrassment of a protracted trial."[23]

The White House worked desperately to douse the flames. Dean Burch had remained at his post under Ford, still conducting political defenses. With presidential aide Anne Armstrong, he pressed Buchen for explanations to satisfy the media clamor. While congressmen warned Ford not to grant pardons to others, reporters raised a question that readily came to the public mind: why try Nixon's aides, and not Nixon himself? The White House spokesman replied that the former President was "unique" because the House Judiciary Committee had judged him guilty, and that his punishment of resignation was "very severe." Another Ford aide urged the President to plead that the country should not suspect his motives when it disagreed with his decisions. But Ford could not shake such suspicions. Author Larry L. King pithily summed up the situation: the manner and timing of the pardon appeared as if Mr. Clean had suddenly dealt a dirty card from the bottom of the deck.

Without conclusive evidence—such as a tape recording or document sealing a bargain between Nixon and Ford—there is little evidence of a conspiracy leading to the pardon. To be sure, Haig, Garment, and other Nixon White House holdovers pressed for a pardon, undoubtedly in part for selfish and personal reasons, yet also perhaps moved by some degree of altruism. After all, in arguing for pardon they only did what was expected of loyal retainers. The pardon, too, may have been necessary if Ford was to get on with the business of running the government. Watergate, in some measure, continued to be a distracting force after Nixon's resignation.

What went wrong was that Ford failed to prepare the country for what he must have known he would do, certainly as early as the end of August. He apparently consulted with no political leaders; furthermore, his lack of desire—or his inability—to get that measure of contrition from Richard Nixon that the national mood may well have demanded was a serious miscalculation. In deciding to pardon Nixon, Ford relied on only a few advisers. Given his congressional experience, Ford must certainly have understood the virtue and indispensability of consultation. Yet he made no effort to touch the necessary political bases in this momentous case.

Ford made a brave decision; he need not have made one amid such "splendid isolation." As he prepared for his announcement, he telephoned congressional leaders and claimed that they registered no objections. But they confronted a *fait accompli;* their reactions to the President were one thing, to the media, another. Imagine if Ford had asked former congressional colleagues from across the political spectrum—Mansfield, Scott, Goldwater, Albert, Rhodes, and O'Neill—to stand with him as he delivered his announcement. Melvin Laird believed that Ford made a mistake "by surprising people." Laird maintained that the President in a short time might have persuaded congressmen to publicly support the pardon.[24]

Ford's position had logic on more than one level as a means to end the Watergate "nightmare." Lost in the welter of suspicions and charges of corruption was the very practical consideration that the pardon may have spared the legal process from mockery and embarrassment. If Nixon had been indicted and tried, he and his lawyers undoubtedly would have spent years warding off, contesting, and appealing any charges. In time, that spectacle would probably have repelled the nation. Ford also recognized the possibility that Nixon would eventually go free on technical grounds—and that might well have cast a shadow on Ford's legitimacy as President.

"Few people want to see the President in jail," Vice President-designate Rockefeller told a Senate committee in September. Leon Jaworski, by his own account, had no desire to try Nixon. A month after the pardon, Jaworski told a reporter that he found nothing wrong in Ford's action. Although Nixon would not be indicted and tried, Jaworski firmly believed that the existing and forthcoming evidence would "show he's guilty, just as much as a guilty plea." He defended Ford, including the granting of a pardon prior to any indictment; it was wrong, he argued, to believe that a trial would have produced even more evidence. Jaworski refused, however, to engage in "hypotheticals," when asked if he would have sought an indictment and trial had there been no pardon. He insisted that the pardon signified guilt: "A pardon isn't just a beautiful document to frame and hang on the wall. You are offered a pardon only because it is believed you can be charged and convicted."[25]

Jaworski's pointed views reflected his reaction to several months of often heated debate among his subordinates in the Special Prosecutor's office, first over whether to grant President Richard Nixon immunity, and then over how to deal with his pardon. Lacovara pressed Jaworski on confronting Ford, following his earlier suggestion with one outlining a "conditional pardon," contingent upon Nixon's acknowledgment of his complicity and the prosecutors' continued access to his files. Jaworski replied rather sharply, noting that Ford had not sought his advice on the matter: "I believe it would be highly presumptuous, in fact improper, for me to impose my thoughts on his action," he continued. "The President has not undertaken to tell us how to prosecute and I do not regard it proper to tell him how to pardon, if he has this in mind." Lacovara hastily apologized, but he explained that his recent review of new presidential tape transcripts led him to conclude that "Mr. Nixon's role was even more serious" than previously understood, and he was concerned that these revelations should become a matter of public record. Lacovara told an interviewer that the pardon left him dissatisfied, because Nixon had failed to give a statement of contrition and because of the inadequate arrangement for custody of and access to the presidential materials. By this time, according to Jaworski, his deputies were engaged in their own struggles for prosecutorial assignments.[26]

Some prosecutors considered challenging the pardon, with a few even suggesting that the Special Prosecutor's charter precluded presidential interference by means of a pardon. They argued also that the pardon suffered from technical defects, particularly for its failure to specify Nixon's alleged crimes. But Jaworski did not share such concerns. When he resigned in October, he told Attorney General Saxbe that he would neither seek an indictment nor would he question the pardon. As if to refute many of his staff workers, Jaworski thought a challenge to Ford's pardon "would constitute a spurious proceeding in which I had no faith" and would be tantamount to unprofessional conduct.[27]

Watergate presented many extraordinary constitutional issues. The pardon itself provided one; the aftermath another, as President Ford appeared in person before a congressional committee in October to answer questions about his decision. The President had once said he was a Ford, not a Lincoln; but his only predecessor to take similar action in fact was Abraham Lincoln. On September 16 Congresswoman Bella Abzug (D–NY) introduced a resolution requesting that the President respond to ten questions relating to the pardon. A week earlier, she had written to Jaworski, contending that the pardon was unconstitutional and that he should proceed with an indictment. No reply was sent.[28]

Abzug's resolution went to William Hungate's Subcommittee on Criminal Justice. The next day, John Conyers introduced another resolution focused on four specific inquiries and a broad question concerning the possibility of future pardons for individuals involved in Watergate. At first, the White House replied that the pardon documents, subsequent briefings, and a September 18 presidential press conference covered the relevant matters. That proved unsatisfactory, however, and the subcommittee moved to obtain testimony from Buchen, or someone else who had extensive knowledge of the pardon—a prospect that threatened to ignite still-smouldering questions of executive privilege. The White House reply came on September 30 with dramatic suddenness: the President himself would appear to answer questions.

Ford's decision was shrewd. If the subcommittee had insisted on calling Buchen and Haig, then, whether they refused or cooperated, the outcome would have cast doubt on Ford's veracity. But the President's appearance helped to restore his image of honesty and openness. When he testified on October 17, Elizabeth Holtzman carried the burden of the questioning, mainly repeating the questions that Abzug and Conyers had stipulated in their resolutions. But she launched them in rapid-fire succession, hardly allowing Ford time to answer. Finally, he interrupted: '[T]here was no deal, period, under no circumstances.''

Holtzman felt betrayed by her fellow Democrats. She was dismayed that none of them pursued her inquiry into whether Ford would surrender tapes of his conversations with Nixon. She also complained that the subcommittee had not accumulated sufficient staff or taken the time to prepare adequately. Finally, she demanded that Buchen and Haig testify, as well. Holtzman was right: the other members, to be sure, wanted to believe Ford. In the end, they really had no choice. They had not prepared for his appearance, and having questioned the President, they could not logically call Buchen and Haig. Most had voted to confirm Ford in 1973, knew him as a Congressman, and had little desire to pursue the matter. After he testified, the subcommittee had nowhere to go short of a full-scale investigation. Representative Charles Sandman had warned the President not to provide another media opportunity for a liberal vendetta, and now he hastily congratulated Ford on his appearance and his "magnificent job."

William Hungate was a witty, shrewd man, as he had demonstrated throughout the impeachment inquiry. He also had keen political antennae, and he sensed, as he told his staff, that the resolutions of Abzug and Conyers amounted to a fishing expedition. Despite some chagrin and dissatisfaction with Ford's manner of issuing the pardon, Hungate was ready to accept it. He believed that the nation was in no mood to witness another large political inquiry with a full-blown staff—nor, he added, was Congress.

Henry Ruth tried to persuade Holtzman that no one had evidence of any corrupt bargain. She contended that a pardon was invalid if given under fraudulent conditions. But Ruth responded: "You do not challenge every Presidential Act on the idea that it is illegal, you have to have some indication [of wrongdoing], I would think." Covering all contingencies, however, he added: "Unless Watergate has gone further than I thought."

The subcommittee met on November 22 to pass judgment on Ford's version of events. Holtzman sought to continue and expand the inquiry, but the group rejected her request by a 6–3 vote. Hungate and James Mann joined four Republicans in opposition.[29]

Still, the question of a corrupt bargain leading to Nixon's pardon would not die. The *Washington Post's* Bob Woodward and Carl Bernstein published a story more than a year later contending that Haig had actively campaigned for a pardon during August 1974. Holtzman renewed her demand that Buchen and Haig testify on their roles in the pardon. The *Post's* story revolved around technicalities of timing and language, and may have been planted by Haig to embarrass Ford.

Hungate's staff prepared a report and again questioned whether Congress and the nation would tolerate a large-scale investigation; moreover, they believed that the lack of substance to the new charges would only expose the Democrats to accusations of political motivation. The staff report proved decisive, and the subcommittee voted not to reopen the investigation. Holtzman was isolated—and enraged.[30]

The investigations of the Subcommittee on Criminal Justice nevertheless served the Democrats quite well. They could raise the spectre of a corrupt bargain and berate Ford for having granted the pardon without any expression of contrition from Nixon. Meanwhile, the pardon conveniently ended the affair for them while allowing the Republicans to stew in their own juice. But a prolonged pursuit of the matter might have raised a backlash against the seeming Democratic vindictiveness. The lack of will and the lack of evidence operated in a cycle; the task of wisdom was to end the affair.

Sir Edward Coke, the great English jurist of the seventeenth century, defined a pardon as "a work of mercy." In a similar vein, Alexander Hamilton in *Federalist* 74 thought that the pardoning power tempered justice that might be "too sanguinary and cruel" in cases of "unfortunate guilt." In 1915 the Supreme Court concluded that a pardon "carries an imputation of guilt; acceptance a confession of it." In his first full day of office, President Jimmy Carter, who in the campaign of 1976 slyly exploited the nation's memory of Nixon's pardon, granted a pardon to Vietnam draft resisters who had not committed violent acts. During the campaign, he told military veterans that amnesty meant that what you did was right; a pardon, however, only provided forgiveness. Nixon could not escape such judgment; in that sense, President Ford secured for the nation what only a lengthy trial *might* have gained.[31] Jaworski was right: the pardon was no diploma for proud display. Indeed, it became a subject which Richard Nixon always took special pains to avoid, omitting any mention of it whatsoever in his memoirs.

And yet, Ford himself could not ever wholly escape a perception that he might have participated in a corrupt bargain, a perception that only rekindled cynicism about professed ideals of equal justice and the rule of law. One month after the pardon, the White House issued an extraordinary document detailing the chronology of the relevant events, in an attempt to refute any speculation regarding a possible deal. In the years following the pardon, various observers have impugned Ford's motives and put unfavorable interpretations on the unfolding events of August and September 1974. Suggestions have been made that Ford promised Nixon a pardon as early as the time of his vice-presidential nomination, and Seymour Hersh has contended that in a September 7, 1974 telephone conversation, Nixon threatened Ford with a public revelation of Ford's earlier promises of a pardon unless he delivered one.[32]

After fifteen years, hearsay alone supports such notions; no documentary evidence has appeared, and no participant close to the event has gone on record with a story of a corrupt bargain. Still, doubts linger; conspiracy hypotheses have an allure for which students of events can devise only the most tenuous of explanations. However refuted, they persist, and however groundless, they always appeal. What people think *may* be true is often as true as the truth itself. Nixon later acknowledged that he did not use the pardon power himself, because he knew "it would inflame the situation and would obviously look like the ultimate cover-up." Ford learned that as a painful lesson. For many, his action made a mockery of any notion of equal justice. Representative John Anderson, echoing Ruth's admonition to Holtzman, criticized the media inclination to view political decisions "under the lenses of suspicion and doubt," emphasizing ulterior motives and secret deals. Inevitably, he believed, such notions became self-fulfilling prophecies. Small comfort that in an obscure legal challenge to the pardon, a judge praised Ford's action as "a prudent public policy judgment."[33]

Ford pardoned Richard Nixon to rid himself of Watergate's lingering presence; yet in doing so he hampered his credibility as a leader and contributed substantially to his electoral defeat in 1976. The pardon issue constituted the largest "polling negative" against the President. For the remainder of Ford's presidency, Nixon was an albatross seemingly determined to hang on the neck of his benefactor. Nixon insisted on weekly briefings from the Ford White House, covering topics from foreign policy to economic matters. In addition, Ford and his advisers had to answer for Nixon's allegedly lavish furnishing of his offices. The normally mild-mannered Brent Scowcroft, Ford's National Security Adviser, snapped, "Nixon is a shit," when the former President embarked on a trip to China, much to the consternation of the White House.[34]

Ford himself never expressed any doubts as to the correctness of his action; yet he realized exactly what Nixon had cost him. He waffled badly in 1974 on the issue of the former President's contrition. Later, he remembered how Nixon had dodged the real issue of his responsibility. If Nixon had only been more contrite, Ford believed, the pardon might have been more acceptable. But as Ford tartly (disappointedly?) noted: Nixon "couldn't take that final step." It was an old Nixon skill, one aide remembered, to protect himself at the expense of others. The framers of the Constitution debated granting pardon only after conviction. They decided otherwise, in the belief that a pardon might be used as a means of obtaining cooperation from an accused individual. But Richard Nixon provided nothing toward resolving Watergate.[35]

However much the pardon can be rationalized or explained from a distant perspective, Ford's action precipitated a convulsive reaction that once again seared the nation. That great body of undecided Americans, who decisively weighed against Richard Nixon as the evidence mounted against him, must have wondered, following his pardon, about the nation's vaunted concern for equal justice. The energy moving from their doubt was not to be readily dissolved. To acknowledge all that fury, all those assaults against established authority and venerated tradition that had marked the months preceding Nixon's resignation—and then one month later to dismiss the entire experience saying, "Your nightmare is over"—asked too much of the public. A people roused to such a fever pitch could not easily slide from rage to compassion. In time they might—but not then.

XXII

IN THE SHADOW
OF WATERGATE

The pardon no more sounded the last echo from Watergate than it marked Richard Nixon's permanent departure from the public scene. "Watergate" etched itself into public memory, and sustained itself long after August 1974. "History has a unity and continuity; the present needs the past to explain it; and local history must be read as a part of world history," historian Frederick Jackson Turner wrote a century ago. Watergate had been conditioned by the traumas of the 1960s; eventually, it influenced domestic and foreign policies in subsequent years, and resonated throughout public life.

Watergate served as a prescription for attempts to alter the political and legal landscape in the United States, and it became a standard for analyzing political behavior. It did not halt or decisively reverse the long-term trend toward greater executive power and responsibility. Eight years after Nixon's resignation, the Supreme Court upheld presidential immunity in civil cases, and warned against the "dangers of intrusion" on presidential authority and functions. But the perceived abuses of power during the Nixon presidency led to a variety of "reforms" ranging from attempts to institutionalize the special prosecutor, to curbs on presidential manipulation of executive agencies for personal political gain, to new campaign-financing laws. Watergate had a substantial influence on the political parties and political ideology. The wars of Watergate certainly had some effect on the foreign policy of the Nixon Administration, with consequences for the future as well.

As much as anything, however, as a symbol and memory, Watergate shaped public discourse even when distorted or exaggerated. In the campaign of 1980, Ronald Reagan attacked a federal court ruling against abortion restrictions as "an abuse of power" as bad as Watergate. Senator Edward Kennedy criticized President Reagan in 1987 for reaching into the "muck of Watergate" to nominate Judge Robert H. Bork to the Supreme Court. Bork never was able to shake his image as a bloody accomplice in the events of October 1973; he had, Kennedy charged, executed "the unconscionable assignment" of firing Archibald Cox, "one of the darkest chapters for the rule of law in American history." In 1986, Richard Nixon, serenely confident that he had been "rehabilitated," suddenly found Watergate alive and well, hauntingly compared to the Iran-Contra affair that erupted that fall. Watergate proved to be more than the "dim and distant curiosity" that one historian described.[1]

President Ford's decision not to pardon President Nixon's indicted aides enabled the Watergate Special Prosecution Force to proceed with the criminal trials. The WGSPF already had secured a number of convictions during the previous twelve months, often resorting to plea-bargaining arrangements—with "bargain basement abandon," wrote one critic. As early as August 1973, Special Prosecutor Archibald Cox told his staff to connect the recommended length of Magruder's sentence to "the extent of his cooperation."

Donald Segretti pleaded guilty on October 1, 1973, to three counts of distributing illegal campaign literature and eventually served four months. Dwight Chapin was indicted on November 29, 1973, on four counts of perjury relating to his ties to Segretti. After a five-day trial, he was convicted on two counts on April 5, 1974, and sentenced to ten to thirty months in prison. John Dean pleaded guilty on October 19, 1973, to one count of obstructing justice, but the court delayed his sentence until August 2, 1974, to ensure his continuing cooperation. Judge John Sirica ordered a jail term of one to four years, but Dean served only four months, as Sirica ordered him released following the conviction of Nixon's closest associates. Dean spent the entire time at Fort Holabird in Maryland, conveniently available for almost daily questioning in preparation for the Mitchell-Haldeman-Ehrlichman trials, in which he appeared as the principal witness for the prosecution.

Jeb Magruder offered a guilty plea in August 1973 and received a penal term of one to four years. He, too, appeared as a witness against his former associates and had his sentence reduced. Herbert Kalmbach pleaded guilty in February 1974 to several campaign violations, and in return for his testimony, all other charges were dropped. Richard Kleindienst did not contest a one-count misdemeanor charge for refusing to answer Senate questioners when queried about his role in the ITT antitrust suit. The decision not to press criminal charges against Kleindienst alienated many of Jaworski's subordinates from the Special Prosecutor. Kleindienst received a thirty-day sentence and a $100 fine, both of which were suspended.

Charles Colson pleaded guilty to a charge of obstructing justice by scheming to defame and destroy the reputation of Daniel Ellsberg and thereby influence Ellsberg's trial. Other charges for his role in obstructing justice in the Watergate burglary were dropped, and on June 3, 1974, Judge Gerhard Gesell sentenced Colson to one to three years. Egil Krogh earlier had received a two-to-six-year sentence for his role in planning the break-in of Ellsberg's psychiatrist's office; all but six months of the sentence were suspended in exchange for Krogh's testimony against the others. After a two-week trial, a jury convicted Ehrlichman, Liddy, and two Cuban burglars for violating Dr. Fielding's civil rights as a result of the break-in; in addition, the jury found Ehrlichman guilty on three counts of perjury. Ehrlichman was sentenced to concurrent prison terms of twenty months to five years. Liddy received a jail sentence to run simultaneously with the one he was then serving in connection with the Watergate burglary.

The trial of Mitchell, Haldeman, Ehrlichman, Robert Mardian, and Kenneth Parkinson for various charges of conspiracy, obstruction of justice, and perjury began on October 1, 1974. After three months, the jury returned guilty verdicts against all but Parkinson. The appellate court subsequently overturned Mardian's conviction, ruling that his case should have been severed from the others because of his lawyer's illness. On February 21, 1975, Richard Nixon's closest advisers—Mitchell, Haldeman, and Ehrlichman—received sentences of 2½–8 years for their crimes. For many, the verdict represented a conviction of the former president *in absentia*.[2]

Watergate profoundly affected struggles for the leadership and ideological control of the major political parties. Richard Nixon's fall from grace strengthened the claims of Republican conservative ideologues, who had gained control of the party in 1964 only to find their goals frustrated by the rise of the "pragmatic" Nixon. At the same time, Watergate spurred the elections of Democrats bent on an agenda of reform for the political process who, however, had virtually no cohesive program for national policies. Perceived at first as a Democratic triumph and a Republican debacle, Watergate in reality facilitated the conservative takeover that reinvigorated the Republican Party, and although the Democrats temporarily profited, they left unattended the fissures in their old coalition and ignored the need for fashioning programs that would reverse the crumbling of that coalition.

The 1964 rout of Barry Goldwater left the Republican conservatives no alternative but Nixon. Yet even before Watergate, as President Nixon reached out for rapprochement with China and as his domestic programs mounted deficits and produced inflation, conservatives found themselves politically estranged. Watergate discredited Nixon personally; it also dealt a blow to the "middle ground" in the Republican Party that Nixon had preempted in the 1960s between the liberal Rockefeller forces and the Goldwater Right. With Nixon's departure, and Ford's defeat in 1976, the conservative movement captured the field against the relatively feeble challenges from its intra-party foes.

Except for the brief Ashbrook insurrection in the 1972 primaries, conservatives had muted their criticism of Nixon, confining it to occasional attacks on isolated policies. But with Nixon's resignation, conservatives dropped their restraints, launched an ideological assault on his overall policies, and excoriated Ford for maintaining them. William Buckley assailed Nixon for the "humiliating defeat" in Vietnam, for a budget deficit "larger than any Democrat ever dared to endorse," and for the "baptism of détente" with its attendant talk of the "peace-loving intentions of the Communist superpowers." Howard Phillips blamed Nixon for passing strategic superiority to the Soviets, for sowing the seeds of economic destruction because of his inability to make difficult choices, for dismantling the American Navy, and for expanding the Great Society contrary to his campaign promises. Foolishly, according to Phillips and others, Nixon believed that if he appeased the Left on policy matters, he would have a respite from his Watergate difficulties. Barber Conable, though a leader of House Republicans and a more traditional Republican conservative, found that many policies he favored which had been endorsed by Nixon had become discredited because of their association with Nixon.

As President Ford continued the same policies, conservatives refused to submit to party loyalty and offer affection for an incumbent they had once admired. In May 1975 Ronald Reagan condemned Ford for a projected $51-million budget deficit. *Conservative Digest* reported a poll in June 1975 claiming that 71 percent of its readers thought Ford was doing a "poor" job, and 91 percent opposed his nomination for the 1976 election.[3]

The conservative fury against Nixon and his successor nearly resulted in denying the 1976 Republican nomination to Ford, an event that would have been unprecedented in the twentieth century. Senator James Buckley and Pat Buchanan called for an "open convention." The conservatives massed behind a Reagan candidacy and failed to carry it through only by a scant margin; many believed that a second ballot would have given the nod to the former California governor. When Reagan spoke to the 1975 Conservative Political Action Conference, he invoked the sacred appeal of the "Mandate of 1972," a mandate that conservatives believed had been given to them to implement their political and social agenda, and not to Nixon personally. The election, they claimed, had emphatically repudiated the ideology of "radicalism" and "social permissiveness" that had captured the Democratic Party. "The mandate of 1972 still exists," Reagan proclaimed. "The people of America have been confused and disturbed by events since that election, but they hold an unchanged philosophy." Reagan and his advisers held to that faith. In the 1980 campaign, they used the conservative indictment against Nixon and Ford to telling effect against a Democratic President. Ironically, as President Reagan concluded his second term in 1988, conservative spokesmen, such as Buchanan, once more assailed the nation's continued "leftward drift."[4]

Richard Nixon's Republican opponents finally enjoyed a measure of revenge. Fifteen years after he left the presidency, Nixon found himself out of the mainstream of his own party. Periodically, he invoked conservative slogans and labels, but he remained a distrusted and embarrassing figure. The former President had the unique distinction of not appearing at the four presidential nominating conventions of his party that followed his leaving the White House.

Watergate was chiefly responsible for swelling the ranks of congressional Democrats in the 1974 and 1976 elections. In 1974, at the height of interest in the scandal, the Democrats added seventy-five new members to the House. Many of the newcomers were elected on promises of electoral reform. In the meantime, however, the attention to procedural reforms ignored the growing schisms in the Democratic Party, schisms that reflected changing social and economic concerns among the electorate. The 1972 election pointed to the growing strains within the party; Watergate, however, obscured, then postponed, any real understanding or reckoning with the party's dilemmas. "The Real Majority," political analysts warned, no longer consisted of the "have-nots" who had formed the basis for Democratic coalitions for more than forty years. The "haves" had new concerns, which made the Democratic Party's "politics of inclusion" paradoxical, even contradictory.[5]

Many of the new Democrats represented marginal districts, often suburban, middle-class, and domesticated to the politics of affluence. The programmatic concerns of the AFL-CIO, minority coalitions, and women's groups had limited appeal in such districts. The reform-minded new representatives struck a Faustian bargain: the Democratic leadership gave them their "reform" proposals but demanded that they toe the line on policy concerns originating in the party's traditional constituencies. The newcomers' support for the leadership's desired social and economic policies only aroused organized opposition in their local districts from pro-business organizations, as well as from ideological groups demanding a reduced welfare state and support for antiabortion measures.

Jimmy Carter rode to victory in 1976 on promises of greater morality and efficiency in government. "We were responsible for Jimmy Carter," Richard Nixon admitted in 1977.[6] The historical accident of Watergate produced

President Carter, but unlike the Great Depression, Watergate by itself was not an issue that could sustain power. Carter seemed to offer little in the way of a program that would broadly appeal to the nation, his seeming aimlessness reflecting the Democrats' lack of cohesiveness and purpose. Altogether, the situation was a prescription for disaster. Meanwhile, the Republicans united behind Ronald Reagan, a candidate who attractively expressed the conservative ideology which had been dominant in the party since 1964 but which had always lacked a charismatic leader. Reagan led his party to two presidential triumphs and a six-year control of the Senate, and he successfully transferred his aura and image to George Bush in 1988. Three consecutive presidential defeats left the Democrats floundering in search of their identity as a party. Perhaps that identity might have been found nearly two decades earlier, had Watergate not diverted the party from the quest.

Watergate spurred demands for "reform" to prevent future abuses of power, as scandals inevitably do, but, paradoxically, the affair also produced assertions that "the system worked." In the spring of 1974, a distinguished academic panel headed by Yale Law School professors Alexander Bickel and Ralph Winter warned that Watergate was a "poor vehicle" for addressing major reforms. The panel's report contended that both existing law and legal institutions had responded adequately to the crisis. The failures had been those of an individual and not of the political-legal system itself. Yet the panelists warned that reducing presidential power required Congress to reform itself and to accept its proper responsibilities for shared governance, rather than damaging the institution of the presidency. Watergate, they concluded, might result in "history less in danger of being ignored than misunderstood."[7]

Still, the temptation to rectify lawbreaking with more law was irresistible. Ethical standards, guidelines for institutional behavior, restraints on power, and the enforcement of the new rules flowed from Congress in the aftermath of Watergate. The results produced years of bickering over the meaning of the reforms and the willingness to follow them. Samuel Johnson once characterized patriotism as the last refuge of a scoundrel. Roscoe Conkling, a scandal-plagued nineteenth-century Senator, added that Johnson had "underestimated the potential of reform."

The Federal Election Campaign Act of 1971, establishing limits on campaign contributions and forcing more detailed public disclosure of those contributions, had provided the opening wedge for the Senate Select Committee's investigation of the conduct of the 1972 campaign. The findings of the committee and the Special Prosecutor inevitably produced demands for further reforms. Senate Republican Leader Hugh Scott deplored the "deviousness" of CREEP and President Nixon's fundraisers, and he agreed that the disclosure provisions of the 1971 law had proven inadequate. Politicians also piously railed against the excesses of campaign spending. Senator Walter Mondale thought that the Senate hearings had demonstrated that "Government and Government decisions [were] up for sale to the highest bidder." Senator Edward Kennedy vigorously promoted public financing.

The Senate and the House hammered out different legislative proposals in 1974. Public financing was supported by some congressional Democrats aided by a variety of public-interest organizations, as they believed that it could offer them some parity against Republicans and special-interest groups. Other House members, including Republicans, who allied with incumbent Democrats from "safe" districts, had no desire to create opponents with financial parity. The opposition successfully prevented public funding of congressional elections, although it conceded such support for presidential candidacies. President Nixon strongly denounced public financing in March 1974, but his position probably helped the proposal.

If the purpose of the campaign-reform legislation was to curb extravagant fundraising and spending by political candidates, then failure is an inadequate description of its later history. The law limited political action committees (PACs) to a contribution of $5,000 per candidate, but it invited a proliferation of subsidiary PACs created expressly to circumvent the law. An interest group such as the American Medical Association, for example, could by law establish only one PAC per candidate; but its state and local affiliates could duplicate support throughout the nation. Since 1974, the number of corporations and interest groups establishing PACs has grown enormously. Sophisticated computer facilities created a major industry of political fundraising, one that proved particularly fertile for well-organized religious and conservative groups. Liberal Democrats had once profited from the energetic PACs of organized labor, but the decline of the house of labor substantially reduced its political clout. Incumbents particularly fostered and encouraged PACs, which provided a treasure trove for campaigning. No doubt the new financing laws augmented the natural advantages of incumbency.

The 1974 law regulated both contributions and expenditures. But in *Buckley v. Valeo* (1976), the Supreme Court held that expenditure limits violated the First Amendment, except for those imposed on grants of public funds. The Court ruled nine years later that PAC expenditures, if made independently of the candidate, could not be constitutionally limited. The net effect of the judicial decisions was to stimulate the flow of special-interest money. Increased use of the media, involving legions of "creative and support" staff, as well as expanded roles for pollsters and political consultants, made campaigning more expensive, which made the demands for increased campaign funds circular and even more extravagant. The 1974 legislation most clearly changed the fundraising pattern (such as that of CREEP), by substituting for the large individual contributor PAC dollars and large numbers of medium-amount contributors. But loopholes in the law still enabled individual, wealthy contributors to give extravagantly, using family and friends as conduits for individual contributions. Accounts of 1988 contributions indicated that the "fat cats" were back in force, with 130 Michael Dukakis supporters and 267 George Bush backers providing more than $100,000 each.[8]

Sociologist Robert Nisbet observed that "unethical" might well be the most difficult word to define in the American language. Ethical standards for public officials are subject to the whims of "ins" and "outs"; one man's sense of opportunity is another man's grasp of greed. Definitions are debatable; enforcing their applicability compounds the conundrum.

The reality of divided government in 1973 forced Richard Nixon to accept the idea of a Special Prosecutor, who was to be independent of the apparatus of the Justice Department, free to carry on his own investigations, and able to act at his own prosecutorial discretion. After the President summarily dismissed Archibald Cox, Congress and Leon Jaworski pushed for firmer guarantees of independence for the Special Prosecutor. When the Administration raised substantial constitutional objections centering on separation-of-powers doctrine, the move seemed to some observers merely a ploy to limit the authority of the Special Prosecutor.[9]

One year after the House Judiciary Committee had voted to impeach Nixon, Congress first considered institutionalizing the office of special prosecutor and codifying ethical standards. In 1978 it passed the Ethics in Government Act, a law that perhaps more than any other symbolized the lingering concerns of Watergate. When Congress first considered the bill in 1975, Senator Abraham Ribicoff (D–CT) declared that it had the responsibility to prevent future Watergates. In a subsequent hearing, a Justice Department official acknowledged, "in the shadow of Watergate, . . . the appearance of justice is almost as important as justice itself."

The 1978 ethics law required financial disclosures by office-holders in all branches of government. The law restrained the "revolving door" through which public officials readily moved into the private sector and immediately used knowledge and contacts gained in their previous positions for private gain. The act established the Office of Government Ethics to monitor its financial-disclosure and conflict-of-interest provisions.

Demands for such reforms antedated Watergate. But Watergate specifically inspired the creation of mechanisms for judicial appointment of a special prosecutor to investigate allegations of wrongdoing by executive-branch officials. The 1978 law first required the Attorney General to investigate such allegations and then to report to a three-judge panel within ninety days on whether the charges were unfounded or whether the judges should appoint a special prosecutor. The judges defined the prosecutor's jurisdiction. Once selected, the prosecutor had authority to perform the investigative and prosecutorial functions of Justice Department officials. Finally, the prosecutor could not be removed, except by impeachment or conviction of a crime, or by the Attorney General in the event of extraordinary impropriety or physical incapacity. The Attorney General must justify such action to the Senate Judiciary Committee; moreover, the prosecutor might appeal to the courts for review. The Ethics Act institutionalized the memory of the Saturday Night Massacre.

The measure passed both houses overwhelmingly. Congressman Charles Wiggins, however, sounding what some viewed as irrelevant sour notes from the past, led a corporals' guard of resistance in the House (joined, interestingly enough, by Robert McClory and Caldwell Butler, both of whom had voted to impeach Nixon). The minority contended that the government's prosecutorial machinery had not broken down, that Watergate was exceptional and did not justify the creation of a new mechanism. "If an attorney general cannot be trusted to enforce the law against the executive," the minority contended, "the remedy is impeachment and not the cloning of an additional attorney general to do the job of the first." The responsibility, in short, rested with Congress. Henry Petersen, who regretted his "slowness" in recognizing the necessity for a special prosecutor in 1973, nevertheless opposed the bill as well, believing that "political safety" too often would result in narrowing prosecutorial discretion, with unfair consequences to the accused.[10]

Two Carter Administration officials became the first targets of the Ethics in Government Act, as a result of allegations of drug use and conflicts of interest. The lengthy, predictably sensational investigations resulted in no charges. Doubtless, their ordeals impaired the reputations and undermined the effectiveness of both men. When Congress reviewed the operation of the law in 1981, disenchantment was apparent. There were, especially, complaints that the special-prosecutor provisions were too easily triggered. Former Attorney General Benjamin Civiletti, who had served under Carter, warned that "we have selected a weapon which must be used with greater care." He argued that the Justice Department could have conducted the necessary investigations of Carter's men, and that applying the law against 480 executive-branch officials was simply too broad and expensive.

The Reagan Administration opposed the Ethics in Government Act, as well, and focused on constitutional and cost objections. Judicial appointments of prosecutors, the Justice Department contended, involved executive functions but did not allow executive control, an unconstitutional arrangement. But the need for a special prosecutor to provide the "appearance of justice" still had a powerful appeal. The Administration eventually dropped its opposition, although it proposed a wider latitude for removal of the prosecutor. (Interestingly, the Justice Department suggested adding the President's friends and family as objects of attention of a special prosecutor.) Two years of wrangling produced a series of amendments to the Ethics Act in 1983. The changes renamed the Special Prosecutor an "Independent Counsel" (a less "inflammatory" title, one Senator suggested), gave the Attorney General more discretion in the decision to name a counsel, reduced the list of officials who might be investigated, provided for reimbursement of attorney's fees for the subject of an investigation if no indictment were brought, and allowed the Attorney General to remove the counsel for "good cause."[11]

Four years later, the legislation again had to be revised. By then more than half a dozen independent-counsel investigations had been launched. Now the Reagan Administration openly battled continuation of the office. William French Smith, Reagan's first Attorney General, assailed the independent-counsel process as "probably unconstitutional." He believed it negated the ends of justice and that it was "cruel and devastating in its application to individuals—falsely destroying reputations and requiring the incurring of great personal costs." The investigations, he contended, resulted in media circuses and had yielded little at high cost to the taxpayers. Democratic senators accused the Administration of "re-interpreting" and weakening the law when it refused to apply the act on several occasions. For its part, the Administration stressed the unconstitutionality of the system. But pending investigations only strengthened the opposition to changes. Meanwhile, the Administration offered regular Justice Department appointments to the then-acting independent counsels on a dual basis, pending the settlement of court challenges to the constitutionality of the position.

Watergate reverberated as Congress debated extending the Ethics Act in 1987. The bill's chief Senate sponsor, Carl Levin (D–MI), had no illusions about the Reagan Administration's real attitudes. The Reagan Justice Department, he complained, "would have us return to the days of Watergate and Nixon's 'Saturday night massacre' when public trust in our criminal justice system hung in the balance. We don't want to go to the brink again." On June 17—the fifteenth anniversary of the Watergate break-in—the Justice Department reiterated its opinion that all prosecutors must be responsible to the President. During the Senate debate in October, Levin reminded his colleagues that Watergate had raised doubts about the integrity and independence of criminal investigations directed at the President and his entourage. Since then, the statutory arrangements for an independent counsel, Levin insisted, had won wide acceptance from the American people. The ready

support for an independent counsel in the pending Iran-Contra affair contrasted sharply with the "public's consternation over the Watergate investigation," demonstrating that the arrangement had restored "public confidence
in the integrity" of the criminal-justice system. "That is an invaluable
achievement," Levin concluded.

The renewal measure passed overwhelmingly—by a margin making it veto-
proof—and Reagan signed it on December 15, despite Justice Department
opposition. Given four pending investigations of the President's actions as
well as those of his advisers, the "appearance of justice" compelled him to
sign the bill. Coincidentally, one day later, an independent counsel secured
the first conviction under the Ethics Act when a jury found guilty of perjury
Michael Deaver, a former White House aide who had close personal ties to
President Reagan and his wife. After Deaver's conviction, Independent
Counsel Whitney North Seymour complained that the Ethics in Government
Act had too many loopholes and exemptions. Whatever its inadequacies, the
law nevertheless remained imperative, he said, because there was "too much
loose money and too little concern in Washington about ethics in government." Seymour struck particularly at the Reagan Administration's failure
to instill an ethical sense throughout the government. Critics from another
direction used the occasion to chastise Congress again for having immunized
its members from outside investigations for violations of ethical standards.[12]

With the open support of the Reagan Administration, individuals under
investigation pursued a constitutional challenge to the office of independent
counsel. Three former Attorneys General and the Solicitor General lent their
considerable prestige to the campaign. The issue boiled down to differences
over the power of the executive branch to conduct all criminal prosecutions,
on the one hand, and on the other the significance of constitutional language
authorizing Congress to vest in the judiciary the appointment of "inferior
officers." Left largely unspoken in the formal briefs was any recognition of
the importance of the "appearance of justice."

In January 1988 the Court of Appeals, dividing two-to-one, invalidated
the independent-counsel provision as an unwarranted intrusion on executive
authority. Speaking for the majority, Judge Lawrence Silberman articulated
a strict construction of separation of powers. The decision came down amid
growing doubts whether the independent-counsel statute was workable. Critics charged that the counsels' investigations had become at times outright
harassment of public officials. Predictably, former Nixon aides assailed what
one called an "orgy of investigation" and "prosecutorial politics." But even
former members of the Cox and Jaworski staffs noted that the independent-
counsel operations had become elephantine, given the large expenditures and
resources required for investigations, maintenance, and security. Still, public
support for the probe of the Iran-Contra affair remained strong. And in the
meantime, independent counsels secured convictions of two more former

Reagan aides, lending some weight to the idea that only a disinterested prosecutor could proceed against the executive branch.

The Supreme Court put its imprimatur on the independent-counsel statute in a surprisingly firm and broad decision. Reversing the appellate court, Chief Justice William Rehnquist led the Court in rebuffing the Administration. The Justices found no violation of separation-of-powers doctrine. The Court held that the Ethics Act in no way inhibited the President from performing his constitutionally assigned duties. Further, unlike the lower court, Rehnquist rejected any notion that the law constituted "Congressional usurpation" of executive functions. In a lone dissent, Justice Antonin Scalia bitingly referred to "our former constitutional system," as he lamented the Court's refusal to uphold what he believed to be a proper and absolute scheme of separation of powers.[13]

The charges that President Nixon had abused his office by improperly using such powerful executive agencies as the FBI, the CIA, and the IRS produced a sharp reaction in Congress and in the nation. Loosening presidential controls, however, conceivably could enlarge the independence of those same groups, a prospect that gave pause to those who had watched the practically unbridled power of the bureaucracies.

The Watergate years brought into sharp relief the practices and behavior of almost sacrosanct institutions. Questions and challenges to authority invariably raised the issue of accountability. In the years following Nixon's resignation, Congress periodically wrestled with that problem, but it often backed away from fundamental reforms affecting the structure or the role of the FBI, CIA, and IRS. That reluctance reflected the prevailing views, either that the abuses discovered in the Watergate years were mere aberrations, or that later transgressions were so minor that reform might do more harm than good.

Clarence Kelley, who became FBI Director following the Gray fiasco, thought that the Watergate "nightmare" had served "as a much needed cleansing agent for the Bureau," one that enabled him to initiate "long overdue reforms." Responding to criticisms of the FBI counterintelligence program of the late 1960s and early 1970s, as well as to other allegations of misconduct often sanctioned by J. Edgar Hoover, Kelley supposedly reduced the Bureau's role in domestic intelligence probes and instituted wide-ranging organizational changes. Kelley and the Carter Administration also sought a posthumous verdict against the practices of the previous era when they brought criminal indictments for unauthorized burglaries against two high-ranking Hoover aides. The FBI officials were convicted and fined in December 1980, but they appealed the decision, and Reagan pardoned them. The President contended that the officials had acted in the belief that their actions had been authorized at "the highest levels of government," and cited Carter's "unconditional pardon" of those who had violated the Selective Service laws during the Vietnam war.

Congress, in its fashion, sought to retaliate against Hoover when in 1976 it established a ten-year term for future FBI directors. The impetus for the limitation came from congressional concern both over Hoover's excessive independence, developed over his nearly fifty-year reign, and over the cooperation which Gray had given to Nixon's blatant political manipulation of the Bureau. The conflicting motives for imposing the limited term passed almost unnoticed.[14]

Congressional investigations in 1975 had dramatically illustrated the extent of FBI abuses of power and had demonstrated Hoover's willingness to serve the political goals of different presidents, to ingratiate himself, and to augment his power. But Congress failed to develop a legislative charter defining proper FBI activities. Instead, in March 1976, Attorney General Edward Levi established a series of guidelines to restrain FBI domestic security investigations and prevent questionable activities.

Less than a decade later, the nation learned that the more things changed, the more they remained the same. Attorney General William French Smith announced that he had relaxed rules governing domestic spying by the Bureau and claimed that the changes had enabled the government to successfully combat domestic terrorism. A special American Bar Association committee, composed of lawyers who had served various intelligence agencies, praised Smith's revisions of the Levi guidelines for their "healthy degree of balance" between First Amendment rights and the demands of domestic security. Yet it recommended some changes in Smith's rules to "ensure that while the security goals . . . are met, the civil liberties of all of our citizens are protected." In a pointed eulogy, the report praised Levi's work. Smith brushed off any implied criticism, claiming that the ABA report merely reflected "issues of policy and style rather than fundamental disagreements on matters of law." His assessment probably was correct. The American Civil Liberties Union, however, thought that the Administration's interpretation of the guidelines granted "overly broad authority" to the FBI.[15]

In December 1974, Seymour Hersh's *New York Times* articles accused the CIA of wholesale violations of its charter and of the law, as a result of its massive involvement in domestic political-intelligence activities. Hersh based his disclosures on the CIA's internal inquiry into some questionable operations, an inquiry ordered by Director James Schlesinger in 1973. Those activities, subsequently dubbed the "Family Jewels," included not only domestic intelligence activities, but also such questionable legal and moral policies as the assassination of foreign leaders.

The Hersh revelations were eagerly seized upon by the newly elected members of the Ninety-fourth Congress, who felt they were committed to restoring an ethical compass to governmental affairs in the wake of Watergate. Many of the new congressional members, as well as the veterans, had campaigned against abuses of official power and had promised a new direction. William Colby, Schlesinger's successor, perceived that the "radically altered nature of the Congress" gave focus to increasing demands to harness and control his agency. President Ford attempted to pre-empt Congress when he appointed a commission, chaired by Vice President Rockefeller, to investigate CIA activities. But three weeks later, the Senate and the House each authorized a select committee to conduct an investigation of CIA operations.

"The Year of Intelligence had begun," a Senate staffer wrote, and the long, cozy relationship between Congress and the CIA came to a halt. "All the tensions and suspicions and hostilities that had been building about the CIA since the Bay of Pigs, and had risen to a combustible level during the Vietnam and Watergate years, now exploded," Colby remarked.[16]

Years later, in seeming innocence, Nixon praised Richard Helms, the CIA Director he had so summarily sacked. He deplored Helms's subsequent criminal conviction for lying to Congress—a "great injustice," Nixon called it—for Helms, he said, simply had been carrying out a presidential assignment. Nixon went on to denounce the "attempt to castrate the C.I.A. in the mid-seventies [as] a national tragedy." But Helms dismissed Nixon's lament as hypocritical and misguided, for he had "no doubt that the whole Watergate business fueled" the CIA's difficulty with Congress. Nixon's attempt to entangle the CIA in Watergate, Helms contended, had been "the battering ram" for the subsequent congressional inquiry.[17]

The Rockefeller Commission, the Senate investigation headed by Senator Frank Church (D–ID), and the House inquiry chaired by Otis Pike (D–NY), highlighted the "black" side of CIA activities. But the image that most clearly emerged in the public eye was that of the CIA as a "rogue elephant," in Howard Baker's phrase, an agency that had operated without authorization or audit, either by Congress or the President. Baker's characterization seemed innocent; yet to put all the blame on the Agency masked the reality that if neither Congress nor the President knew what the CIA was doing, it was because neither wanted to know.

The resulting uproar over the revelations led to two results. First, the CIA itself now had an excuse to institute an internal housecleaning. Both Colby and his successor, Admiral Stansfield Turner, forced the resignation and retirement of bureaucratic barons who had built great power bases of their own, often independent of the Director. Second, Congress developed a greater interest in oversight and established the institutional means to that end.

Hersh's reports spurred Congress to pass the Hughes-Ryan Amendment at the end of 1975, requiring the President to approve and report all covert operations to Congress. Two years later the Senate formalized the procedure by establishing a standing committee for oversight of the intelligence agencies, and the House followed a year later. Executive orders by President Carter tightened the guidelines on domestic intelligence activities, including a requirement that the CIA obtain warrants from the Attorney General to carry on surveillance activities within the United States. In October 1978, Congress enacted the Foreign Intelligence Surveillance Law, which among other things required that the CIA obtain court orders to wiretap. Two years later, the Intelligence Oversight Act provided new requirements that the CIA report to Congress on its covert activities.

Executive orders are subject to new executive orders, however; relations between the CIA and the Attorney General are subject to the compatibility of their interests; and congressional oversight is dependent, first, on what information the CIA or the President chooses to provide, and second, on the extent of Congress's own vigilance and interest. President Reagan's Executive Order 12333 of December 4, 1981, substantially weakened Carter's 1978 directives and restored a large measure of discretion to CIA activities. (That order also upset the Levi guidelines on the FBI and, in general, "unleashed" the intelligence agencies, as the President noted.) The Iran-Contra affair in 1986–87 demonstrated that the CIA and the Administration had acted without congressional consultation and hence lacked that degree of consent that might have provided some cover of legitimacy to what clearly was a dubious enterprise. The result was predictable; renewed demands to force full CIA disclosure of its activities were followed by expressions of concern that the CIA not be inhibited or compromised in its activities.

When FBI Director William H. Webster moved to head the CIA in March 1987, he remarked wistfully that the "post-Watergate period . . . included some very searching and at times devastating inquiries that affected not only us [the FBI] but the other components of the intelligence community." Reagan's CIA Director, William Casey, undoubtedly agreed, and when he proceeded to act on the premise that congressional oversight inquiries and their conclusions mattered not a whit, no one effectively challenged him. During his tenure, Casey readily secured presidential authorization for aggressive covert operations, and he consistently proved uncooperative with congressional oversight committees. Only the Iran-Contra fiasco and Casey's death emboldened critics to demand more effective control—again.[18]

The charges leveled against President Nixon's misuse of executive agencies touched developing concerns for the right of privacy. Interest in the problem erupted in the 1960s, partly in response to a concern over the government's increasing surveillance of the civil rights movement and of opponents of the Vietnam war, and partly in recognition that sophisticated new technology—including computers and the establishment of centralized computer data banks—threatened freedom of private activities and information. In 1964 the House Government Operations Committee established a special subcommittee to probe the investigative activities of federal agencies. Later, the Fair Credit and Reporting Act (1970) attempted to restrict the gathering and use of credit information. In the early 1970s, several congressional committees pursued a variety of privacy issues.

President Nixon could not afford to leave the championing of the right of privacy to congressional Democrats, who seemed exclusively concerned. In his 1974 State of the Union message, Nixon warned that technology had encroached on the right of personal privacy, citing modern information systems, data banks, credit records, mailing-list abuses, and electronic snooping. The time had come, he told Congress, "for a major initiative to define the nature and extent of the basic rights of privacy and to erect new safeguards to ensure that those rights are respected."

Congress readily responded, but a committee report grasped the irony inherent in its efforts when it credited the "additional impetus" from the "recent revelations connected with Watergate-related investigations, indictments, trials, and convictions." That report cited the White House "enemies list," the misuse of Daniel Ellsberg's CIA profiles, the break-in of his psychiatrist's offices, and the Administration's widespread wiretapping activities. The result was the Privacy Act of 1974, passed four months after Nixon resigned. The new law permitted individuals to see information in their federal agency files and to correct or amend the information. Agencies were prohibited from making files available to other agencies without permission. They also could not maintain records describing a person's exercise of First Amendment rights unless the action fell within the scope of official law-enforcement activities—a loophole that specifically exempted the FBI, the CIA, the Secret Service, and other agencies from the law.[19]

Nowhere was the privacy issue more sensitive than with regard to tax information. Revelations that Nixon and his advisers had used IRS data sensationalized the White House's war against its "enemies." John Caulfield's testimony to the Ervin Committee in 1973, and Nixon's well-known searches for a politically pliable IRS Commissioner, made prophets of the Nixon Administration's critics. The White House and the IRS legal staff had rationalized the President's right to free access to information within the executive branch. Perhaps no other subject more alarmed Nixon's adversaries, however; tax information offered enormous potential for harassing political opponents. Members of Congress ostensibly rose to the defense of the right to privacy, but undoubtedly concerns for their own interests lent a special urgency to their actions. Six weeks after taking office, President Ford signed Executive Order 11805, establishing strict guidelines for presidential access to tax returns. Presidential requests in the future must be signed by the President, who must specify what returns were to be inspected, and by whom.

Congress apparently was not content to leave compliance entirely to presidential and IRS discretion. As part of the Tax Reform Act of 1976, it provided that presidential requests for information must specify the reason for any request and that the President must submit a quarterly report to the Joint Congressional Committee on Taxation, describing the returns requested and the reasons for seeking them. Two years later, Congress passed the Financial Privacy Act of 1978, a law designed to bar government agencies from gaining bank records without knowledge of the person under investigation, except in rare circumstances.[20]

In 1986, Attorney General Edwin Meese III proposed repeal of the Financial Privacy Act. On the surface, Meese's proposal reflected the Reagan Administration's general aversion to Watergate reforms. But his position probably reflected institutional as well as partisan concerns. Once out of office, Benjamin Civiletti, Carter's last Attorney General, wasted little time in attacking the privacy reforms for unduly restricting the investigative functions of the Justice Department. Civiletti complained that the Justice Department was unable to examine tax records unless it could demonstrate that the records were relevant to some chain of evidence that might show illegality. He contended that the 1978 Finance Act similarly hampered criminal investigations, as financial institutions often would not cooperate, despite the department's adherence to ordinary criminal procedures. Civiletti urged that the department have access to bank records and that notification to the individuals involved be delayed until after the relevant investigations.[21]

It would have been naive to expect that Watergate-inspired reform legislation could end official abuses of power. Presidents Carter and Reagan differed dramatically in the freedom they extended to their intelligence agencies; their attitudes filtered down the chain of command through their Attorneys General, as well as FBI and CIA directors. Typically, Congress only reacted to events, rarely anticipating them, and its efforts at control were often inadequate, as in its failure to provide a legislative charter for the FBI.

The Iran–Contra affair, as well as periodic new revelations of FBI and CIA wrongdoing, reminded the nation that such activities did not end (just as they did not begin) with Watergate. The realization that government wrongdoing is not exceptional obviously heightens a diminution of the trust the public should accord the conduct of officials. Yet the Watergate era also tended to reinforce a healthy element in the nation's constitutional tradition, which emphasized that no center of official power should be without some check external to itself, including the check of informed public opinion. The post-Watergate reforms to curb such behavior certainly have shortcomings of their own; yet they provide legitimate weapons for questioning and punishing abuses of official power. The lack of will to use the laws, or to protest such unwillingness, in no measure detracts from their value.

The move toward statutory protection of private information that followed Watergate contrasted sharply with a powerful surge of similar law demanding public disclosure of government business. Watergate at times threatened to become a parody of the "open society," as media, print and electronic, vied with one another for new revelations of official wrongdoing. That enterprise, combined with the Watergate environment, fostered substantial additions to the Freedom of Information Act (FOIA) of 1966, the landmark law that provided an opportunity to scrutinize behind-the-scenes activity in the executive branch (if not the legislative). To comply with the law, agencies established their own FOIA units and made records available with disparate degrees of generosity and reluctance. In effect, there was no one FOIA; the reality was that different standards operated according to the whims of different agencies. In the experience of some researchers, the Defense Department proved one of the most cooperative in furnishing information, while the Criminal Division of the Justice Department quickly acquired a reputation for being the most dilatory. The CIA notoriously released only what it wanted, also using the law as a fig leaf for calculated, self-serving leaks. At times, researchers found that in operation the FOIA was a bonanza for Xerox machines and Magic Marker pens, as agencies duplicated hundreds of thousands of pages studded with deletions.

Enterprising attempts to burrow deeper into bureaucratic and White House behavior revealed the shortcomings of the FOIA. When the Supreme Court ruled in 1973 that the original law did not give courts the right to review bureaucratic decisions, the Watergate context inspired a congressional movement to revise the law. The House passed new provisions in March 1974, followed by Senate action in May. A conference version finally emerged in November.

The bill enhanced judicial-review procedures, stipulated time limits for responses to requests for information and to appeals of denials, authorized courts to award attorney fees in the event individuals successfully sued, narrowed national-security and law-enforcement exemptions from the law, and required all agencies to report to Congress annually on decisions to withhold information. The provision for judicial intervention attracted significant opposition, providing as it did a measure of superintendence of bureaucratic action. But it was the loosening of national-security exemptions that provided the focus for floor opposition to the FOIA. Senator Roman Hruska complained that the bill would "open confidential files to any person who requested them at the expense of our nation's interest in foreign relations and defense and every individual's interest in law enforcement." The day, however, still belonged to the spirit of Watergate. Edward Kennedy thought that FOIA reform was an appropriate response to the abuses of governmental institutions and the corruption of the political processes that had characterized Watergate. Ford vetoed the bill, causing Kennedy to charge that the President had "yielded to the pressures of his bureaucracy to keep the doors shut tight against public access in many areas." The appeal was irresistible, and Congress comfortably overrode the veto.

The Reagan Administration made no secret of its hostility to the FOIA, and it nearly succeeded in 1984 in securing a broad range of restrictions on its application. Congress, however, only provided new exemptions for the CIA which enabled the Agency to skirt search and review requirements. The reality of bureaucratic caprice persisted; the release of information depended more on the predisposition of agencies and individuals than on provisions of the statute.[22]

In what had the appearance of being part of a bargain surrounding the pardon, the Ford Administration had negotiated an agreement with Nixon on September 8, 1974, stipulating the ex-president's "total control over all the materials and records of his Administration," including restricting public access to documents and the right to destroy all tape recordings within a certain time. In agreeing, Ford undoubtedly had acted in terms of his own long-term interest, as well as from pressure by his predecessor and the Nixon loyalists who remained in the White House. William Saxbe, the Attorney General, had provided an opinion that presidential ownership of White House materials had been settled practice and did not violate any law or constitutional provision. Nevertheless, Congress reacted vehemently against the arrangement and within months passed the Presidential Recordings and Materials Preservation Act of 1974 (PRMPA), nullifying the September agreement. The law directed the National Archives to take possession and control of the Nixon materials and to regulate public access.

The PRMPA specifically addressed itself to the problem of Watergate. It noted that the Archives regulations should recognize "the need to provide the public with the full truth, at the earliest reasonable date, of the abuses of governmental power popularly identified under the generic term 'Watergate.' "

Nixon challenged the new law, contending that the delegation of authority to archivists violated his constitutional right of executive privilege. Past practice, however, showed that presidential-library archivists long had exercised discretion over access to materials, and in 1977, the Supreme Court decisively repudiated Nixon's extravagant claims. The Court contended that Nixon "constituted a legitimate class of one" and could be singled out for special treatment in the disposition of his records. Furthermore, the Justices noted that "the expectation of the confidentiality of executive communications . . . has always been limited and subject to erosion" after a president left office. Nixon must yield, the Court concluded, to the legitimate and desirable congressional purpose of "preserving the materials and maintaining access to them for lawful governmental and historical purposes." In a concurring opinion, Justice John Paul Stevens argued that Nixon's behavior properly placed him in a different class from all other presidents; that behavior, he said, justified the 1974 law that "implicitly condemns [Nixon] as an unreliable custodian of his papers." The decision marked the first in a steady line over the next decade that continually frustrated Nixon's demands for total control over his presidential papers and for their treatment as his private property.

The Presidential Records Act of 1978 reversed what Saxbe had declared to be settled historical practice and stipulated that presidential records became public property at the end of a presidential term. The new law exempted personal diaries, private political materials, and materials connected with presidential elections—substantial exemptions, to be sure. Foreign and defense matters, confidential advice from aides or executive officers, personnel files, and trade secrets, would be restricted for twelve years after a president left office.

Following the mandate of the 1974 law regarding Watergate, the National Archives processed more than two million Watergate documents. By 1986, the Archives had, pursuant to the PRMPA, promulgated five sets of regulations governing the use of the documents, each challenged by Nixon or his aides, or by Congress, or by the courts.[23]

The National Archives prepared new regulations in 1986, similar to the previous ones, minus the one-house congressional veto proviso, which violated constitutional standards. But in February, the office of Legal Counsel in the Justice Department attached an "understanding" to the regulations, allowing former President Nixon to invoke executive privilege and prevent disclosure of documents. The unspoken purpose was to protect Reagan and his aides, apparently in the expectation that future presidents would extend the same courtesy to them. In 1988, the Circuit Court of Appeals ruled (in an opinion written by Judge Lawrence Silberman, formerly Nixon's Deputy Attorney General) that executive privilege belongs only to incumbents; no maps chart the doctrine for those in retirement, forced or otherwise. "Ronald Reagan, not Richard Nixon, is the constitutional superior of the Archivist," Silberman wrote. "Ronald Reagan has the constitutional power to direct the Archivist, not Richard Nixon." Just prior to leaving office, however, Reagan revealed his self-concern by issuing an executive order that ignored Silberman's ruling and passed executive privilege on to former presidents.[24]

Despite the controversy over executive privilege, the National Archives opened the Nixon Papers in 1987, first with assorted materials pertaining to policy matters, and then with successive releases of the Watergate "Special Files." The 1974 law had provided that the Archives do so "at the earliest reasonable date." By 1978, the archivists had complied with that dictate, but Nixon's resistance prevented public access to these files for nearly a decade. Meanwhile, Ford and Carter cooperated with the Archives, followed the 1978 law (although it did not apply to either of them), and encouraged a liberal release policy for their own papers. Former presidents retained access to their materials (as Nixon did) in order to write memoirs, but the law upheld the public's interest in those materials, thus preventing any exclusive control of the historical record.

Richard Nixon always realized the stakes, knowing that the documentary and audiotaped record would shape history's final judgments of him and his presidency. Perhaps, too, he knew the Orwellian dictum: "To control the present is to control the past. To control the past is to control the future."

Watergate nourished and mobilized the drive of Congress to expand its activities. The assault against presidential power that erupted with the Vietnam war eventually resulted in various attempts to limit executive authority and, at the same time, it expanded congressional power. Congressional oversight required more eyes and hands: committee staff personnel increased threefold between 1957 and 1975, and the Congressional Research Service and the General Accounting Office grew enormously during the same period. Such important new offices as the Office of Technology Assessment (1972) and the Congressional Budget Office (1974) added both numbers and a new layer of congressional authority. These new entities, along with the expanded staff system, moved Congress toward inevitable alliance to the permanent bureaucracy, thus compounding presidential frustration over inability to secure bureaucratic compliance with policy.[25] The sense of drift and inertia in the Carter Administration stemmed in part from that frustration and arose from a bureaucratic gridlock that had nothing to do with government divided along partisan lines, as in the Nixon Administration or the second Reagan term.

The Budget and Impoundment Act of 1974 represented an attempt of Congress to assert its rightful powers, and at the same time to respond to perceived excesses of the Nixon Administration. The law reflected in equal measures the Democrats' concern that Nixon had excessively impounded appropriated funds, especially as an instrument of his own policy preferences, and the concerns of Republicans to reform the budget process in order to get spending under control, and so lessen the need for impoundment. The act established budget committees in both houses, a Congressional Budget Office with experts to analyze the budget, and authority to enact a budget resolution to guide, yet not bind, the appropriations process.

The impoundment features of the Budget Act included a proviso forcing the president to release funds if either house passed a resolution requiring him to do so, a proviso later invalidated when the Supreme Court struck down the one-house legislative veto. The act also provided that, for any impoundment that cut total spending or abolished programs, a president might be forced to spend the money unless both houses passed a rescission bill within forty-five days. If he ignored the action, the Comptroller General might obtain a court order requiring that the funds be spent. Apparently, the legislators thought they would curb executive impoundments. Nonetheless, Ford requested 330 spending deferrals and 150 rescissions. Carter continued the practice, albeit on a reduced scale. After nine years, Congress had passed, under the Budget Act, eighty-three resolutions disapproving presidential attempts to defer spending allocations.

In signing the legislation on July 12, 1974, Richard Nixon proclaimed it the "most significant reform of budget procedures" in the nation's history; in his memoirs, he strangely called the law "a personal and national triumph." But, given his preoccupation at the time, it is unlikely that he involved himself in the legislation. Nixon always insisted that impoundment was his means of fighting lavish congressional spending; his critics, however, viewed his actions as further proof of an imperious rule. Earlier, he had been forced to accept the principle of Senate confirmation for future OMB directors, a measure clearly reflecting a general desire for greater congressional influence on the budgetary process.

Whatever the institutional and political drives behind the Budget Act, the consensus a decade later was that the legislation had neither substantially facilitated the budget process nor reduced spending. The consistent executive/legislative impasses of the Reagan years reflected differing institutional and partisan agendas, as well as growing intra-institutional conflicts, both among congressional committees and within components of the executive branch. The resultant compromises were derided as "blue smoke and mirrors," and budget deficits continued to mount, with a corresponding crescendo of partisan and institutional recrimination. Still, the impoundment features of the 1974 legislation were used, subject to congressional will, it is true, but apparently effectively enough to stifle the constitutional controversies that characterized the clashes between Nixon and Congress.[26]

Domestic considerations invariably affect foreign policy. The unrest generated by the Vietnam war unquestionably influenced the nature and extent of American involvement. Watergate also influenced the conduct of Richard Nixon's foreign policy, particularly in regard to America's role in Southeast

Asia and relations with the Soviet Union. As Watergate moved from a public perception of a political "dirty trick" to a crisis involving the integrity of the presidency and the tenure of Nixon himself, it inevitably preoccupied the President. Whether that preoccupation distracted him, or emboldened adversaries, so as to alter what would have been the President's course in policy, is a subject of some controversy over the Nixon Administration's reputation for achievements abroad.

Vietnam and Watergate intersected in many ways, especially during those delicate years when the U.S. was winding down its involvement in South Vietnam, and that nation was assuming increasing responsibility for its own defense. The two events played on one another. In 1968 Richard Nixon had promised a "secret plan" to end the war, but his actions in his first term only confirmed for his critics the familiar image of a trickster. Others, of course, believed that his policies fulfilled his promises of "peace with honor." Whatever the perception, protests and congressional criticism of the war escalated as the President entered his second term. Antiwar sentiment existed apart from Watergate; yet Nixon's ruinous involvement in Watergate, with the consequent diversion of his attention and erosion of power, emboldened his critics at home, as well as his adversaries abroad.

To say that the war and the domestic crisis fed each other is a very different thing from saying that one determined the other. But Richard Nixon and Henry Kissinger made exactly that judgment, in order to justify their policies and to belittle the Watergate affair. "We won the war in Vietnam, but lost the peace. All that we had achieved in twelve years of fighting was thrown away in a spasm of congressional irresponsibility," the former President wrote, as he linked Watergate and the collapse of South Vietnam. "As a matter of fact, the Congress lost it," he said in a television interview, implying that Congress proved to be irresponsible in using the power newly gained at executive expense. On occasion, too, Nixon turned the argument around, blaming his preoccupation with the war for the negligence that allowed Watergate to happen.

For Henry Kissinger, the historical stakes were equally great, for as a result of Watergate, he said, "I, a foreign-born American, wound up in the extraordinary position of holding together our foreign policy and reassuring our public." Even some Kissinger critics acknowledged that he was "nearly the sole figure who legitimized or redeemed the government." But Kissinger offered his own maze of contradictions, as he admitted that Nixon resented his Nobel Prize and the adulation of the media for his role in the peace process. "Had Watergate not soon overwhelmed [Nixon], I doubt whether I could have maintained my position in his Administration," Kissinger wrote, taking a position opposite to his usual disdain toward Watergate.

"The debacle of Watergate," Kissinger said, "finally sealed the fate of South Vietnam by the erosion of Executive authority, strangulation of South

Vietnam by wholesale reductions of aid, and [by] legislated prohibitions against enforcing the peace agreement in the face of unprovoked North Vietnamese violations.'' Ten years after the fall of Saigon, Kissinger suggested that Nixon's ''peace with honor'' goals fell afoul of ''liberal critics'' and the ''peace movement.'' Watergate, he added, had destroyed executive power and prevented Nixon and Ford from protecting South Vietnam. Finally, in 1987, Kissinger stated that ''Southeast Asia'' would be ''free'' had it not been for Watergate.[27]

Such arguments usefully condemned Watergate, exonerated the President and his foreign-policy adviser from any blame for the ''loss'' of Indochina, and discredited any notion that the Paris Peace Accords merely had provided the United States with a ''decent interval'' for withdrawal and eventual abandonment of the area to the Communists. Nixon and Kissinger alike argued that Watergate thwarted both the presidential and national resolve to achieve ''freedom and democracy'' in South Vietnam and to protect American national interests. But in fact the options that might have brought the war to a successful conclusion—such as an invasion or blockade of the North—had been foreclosed long before by Lyndon Johnson, whose refusal to take such steps was confirmed by Nixon. In March 1968 Nixon privately acknowledged that the war was not ''winnable,'' and whatever plan he had for ending it underlined American disengagement as the *sine qua non* of any ''peace'' arrangement. Neither Johnson nor Nixon had the will to press any plan for ''victory'' on the American people.

U.S. participation in Vietnam and the fate of South Vietnam eventually confronted glaring realities: the American people had lost faith in the adventure; more important, the United States confronted a determined fighting force, conditioned by a thirty-year struggle, a time span that dwarfed America's longest war. The Nixon-Kissinger search for a scapegoat in the loss of Vietnam had a sinister resemblance to the Nazi revisionism that blamed Germany's defeat in 1918 on a ''stab in the back'' delivered by domestic subversives. Most of all, their argument had the convenient virtue of writing off the President's responsibility for Watergate. Both men scored the climate of dissent, confrontation, and disunity that prevailed during the Watergate affair; but they offered no accounting for the official misdeeds or misdirected policies that had created the poisoned environment they so deplored.

More than a decade of American political history lay behind the end of the Vietnam war, a history that included the deceptions of the Gulf of Tonkin Resolution, Johnson's dishonest campaign utterances in 1964, and the unwillingness of both Johnson and Nixon to work effectively with Congress and defuse the growing criticism of the war. The accumulation of those circumstances, combined with weakened presidential authority, certainly hampered Ford's ability to provide any substantial economic aid to the Saigon regime after he assumed the presidency. Within days of Nixon's resignation, the U.S. Embassy in Saigon warned that congressional cuts in appropriations for the South Vietnamese encouraged the North Vietnamese to increase their offensive operations. The North believed that the presidency had been emasculated, according to Wolf Lehmann, the Deputy Chief of Mission in Saigon, and that assessment sealed the North's determination to launch a decisive offensive. While Lehmann stressed Hanoi's perception of "the great uncertainty" in the United States, however, he also knew that Watergate alone could not explain the fall of the Thieu government in South Vietnam.

Ironically, the North Vietnamese paid a peculiar price for the impaired presidency that gave them an opportunity for total victory in 1975. That very weakness, combined with the aggressiveness and assertiveness of Congress, barred any American move to implement Nixon's promises of American economic aid for "postwar reconstruction" in Vietnam.

By April 1975 Congress undoubtedly reflected a national belief that Vietnam was a hopeless quagmire and that the South Vietnamese government had squandered military equipment and financial aid. When Ford asked Congress for $722 million in emergency aid in April 1975, he invoked the familiar argument that a failure to comply would only undermine America's honor and respect for its commitments abroad. Now, however, that shopworn proposition fell on deaf ears. What is more significant than Congress's reluctance is that neither Ford nor Kissinger seriously considered the use of American naval or air power to interdict the North Vietnamese final offensive. The last, vain request to Congress for aid was a gesture, designed perhaps to lift South Vietnamese morale, but more importantly to exculpate the executive branch from any responsibility for Saigon's fate.[28]

General Bruce Palmer, who has usefully analyzed the intersection of political, military, and diplomatic aspects of the war, acknowledged that Watergate made impossible any response to the renewed North Vietnamese assault in 1975. But he recognized that the more fundamental fault lay within the nature of the peace agreements themselves, and Palmer excoriated Kissinger for his role in concluding those agreements. The "peripatetic" Kissinger, Palmer claimed, was out of his element in dealing with the Vietnamese, mainly because he had so overextended his involvement in numerous diplomatic processes at the time. Kissinger simply failed to give his "undivided attention, skills, and energy" to negotiating a more favorable cease-fire arrangement, Palmer wrote.[29]

The Paris Accords of January 1973 in every respect denied any realistic prospect for peace and independence for South Vietnam. Nixon proclaimed that they had secured "peace with honor," and he gained the release of the American prisoners of war in Vietnam. For his part, Kissinger had his Nobel Prize, but he hardly had a policy. Instead, the American leaders offered illusion and paradox: the United States remained committed to South Vietnam but had withdrawn its military capability to enforce that commitment. The public lost interest, and Congress followed the election returns. The charade was apparent to all—and most of all to Hanoi, which acted accordingly and imposed its will throughout Vietnam in 1975. Thus Nixon had "ended" the war, but after being driven from office, he was spared "losing" it. Later, he could reflect and blame others and such events as Watergate. Kissinger did likewise, but in the minds of many Republican right-wing critics, he had "lost" the war; and for that, among them he remained a pariah, with little chance for the continuing public service and adulation he craved.

Nixon and Kissinger had signed an agreement that provided for the maintenance of North Vietnamese troops in the South and political legitimacy for the Viet Cong. No wonder, then, that South Vietnam's President Thieu balked. He acquiesced to the Paris Accords only after securing President Nixon's secret promise of "full economic and military aid" in the event of North Vietnamese violations of the agreement. According to Nixon, the congressional fury over Watergate prevented him from honoring that commitment. But his undertaking a secret obligation to a course of military action short-circuited both constitutional and political processes. His failure to consult with Congress before promising to come to Thieu's aid marked a dangerous course at any time, but particularly when he served a divided government, with the other half legitimately entitled to a share in such decision making, involving as it did the appropriations process.

Defense Secretary James Schlesinger later complained that he had no knowledge of such commitments; if he had, he insisted, he would have used them as bargaining leverage with Congress. When he learned of them, he at first thought the United States had "welched" on its promises; on reflection, however, he realized that "if you don't know that the commitments have been entered into, you don't know that the country has welched." In later years, Schlesinger deplored the "stab-in-the-back argument," barely disguising his contempt for Nixon's and Kissinger's views: "Congress knew nothing of these [commitments] . . . , when it started bugging out of Vietnam in the summer of 1973."

President Thieu believed Nixon's pledges. While he sensed that Nixon was preoccupied during their January 1973 meeting, his skimpy knowledge of the American political system left him with the conclusion that Watergate was trivial; he apparently could not imagine that the President could be driven from power. Kissinger later offered Thieu his persistent view that Watergate had destroyed the Administration's ability to defend South Vietnam. Belatedly, Kissinger conceded that Thieu had been right about the Paris Peace Accords, but in a curiously obtuse statement he added that Watergate would have been even more catastrophic for South Vietnam if there had been no agreement. In exile and disgrace, Thieu ignored Kissinger's rationalization; perhaps he asked himself what could have been more cata-strophic for him or his fellow citizens.[30]

Watergate undeniably undermined Nixon's prestige at home and his ability to carry through unpopular policies. That, he and Kissinger later argued, is central to understanding the failure to carry through the commitment to defend South Vietnam. The reasoning is labored and tortured. From the time that Kissinger signed the Paris Accords, he and Nixon promised the nation only relief and extrication from the struggle that they well knew would continue in South Vietnam. A stronger president, free of congressional re-straints and criticisms, they implied, would have interdicted the North Viet-namese 1975 offensive by air strikes and once again inflicted heavy losses on the enemy. They obviously ignored the uncomfortable fact that the Amer-ican air attacks since 1965 had hurt, but not thwarted, the Communists. Nixon's problem was the limits of his political influence to exhort the nation to continue the war; and that limitation had little or nothing to do with Watergate. At the time of the January 1973 peace agreements, with his power and popularity still unaffected by Watergate, he never alerted the nation to the possibility that American military operations might continue, with the risk of continuing casualties.

The inability to conclude the war had frustrated Nixon throughout his first term. Could he, after 1972, have summoned a national will to retaliate—a retaliation that might well have resulted in more domestic upheaval, as well as in the North's refusal to return the American prisoners of war? The Pres-ident never prepared for such a contingency; to have made that promise would have negated all the interpretive gloss that he and Kissinger had im-posed on the peace agreement. With or without Watergate, the nation wanted an end to its involvement. "My God, we're all tired of it, we're sick to death of it," wrote an Oregonian. "55,000 dead and $100 billion spent and for what?"[31]

Watergate to some extent had dogged Nixon throughout the Paris negotia-tions in the fall of 1972. But almost total distraction set in after his meeting with Thieu in San Clemente in January 1973. The cover-up began to unravel shortly afterward, and within two months, the President's top aides prepared to resign. But Congress had not yet imposed restraints on Nixon's ability to carry on the war. Enforced bombing pauses and the War Powers Act came later in the year. "I needed desperately to get my mind on other things," Nixon remembered—but he could not or would not do so.[32] If Watergate was a distraction, the President himself allowed it to be. Only he under-stood the dimensions and dangers of Watergate at the time; appropriately, he bent his energies to "lancing the boil." The tortuous taped conversations offer ample testimony to his distraction, but the President himself made Watergate a priority; only later did we understand that he had little choice.

* * *

Watergate and Richard Nixon contributed to the passage of the War Powers Act. The measure had its roots in the frustration of Congress with the Johnson Administration. But the Vietnam War had only exacerbated executive-legislative tension over war making and foreign policy that could be traced back to the beginnings of the republic. President Nixon's inability (or refusal) to end that war promptly enough, combined with a Congress emboldened and aggressive because of his weakness, set the stage for the War Powers Act, which passed over Nixon's veto in November 1973. Johnson's actions provided the inspiration; Nixon's behavior and subsequent vulnerability provoked the occasion.

Alexander Hamilton wrote in *Federalist* 75 that "the history of human conduct does not warrant that exalted opinion of human virtue which would make it wise in a nation to commit interests of so delicate and momentous a kind, as those which concern its intercourse with the rest of the world, to the sole disposal of . . . a President of the United States." The framers had an unhappy, uneasy memory of executive power. "The constitution supposes, what the history of all Gov[ernment]s demonstrates, that the Ex[ecutive] is the branch of power most interested in war, & most prone to it," Madison wrote to Jefferson in 1798. "It has accordingly with studied care vested the question of war in the Legisl[ature]." A half-century later, Lincoln confidently expressed the framers' "original intent" when he told his law partner that they knew that when kings involved their nations in war, it was "the most oppressive of all kingly oppressions, and they resolved to frame the Constitution that *no one man* should hold the power of bringing this oppression upon us."[33]

American presidents have regularly committed combat personnel despite the absence of formal war declarations; the congressional role at best has been consultative. The shared-governance arrangement has worked most effectively as a means for mobilizing national will to endorse executive innovations in foreign policy—as, for example, with the Truman Doctrine in 1947 or Eisenhower's response to the Formosa Strait situation in 1954–55.

The War Powers Act stipulated that a president must notify Congress of any troop deployment abroad within forty-eight hours and required him to withdraw those troops within sixty days unless Congress explicitly authorized their continued use. The legislation passed Congress during the "firestorm" following the dismissal of Archibald Cox. The same weakness that forced Nixon to choose Gerald Ford as Spiro Agnew's successor, and Leon Jaworski as Cox's, made him incapable of persuading enough members of his own party to sustain his veto. But his weakness resulting from the dismissals was of less consequence than the national mood of disgust over the Vietnam war. Symbolically, the War Powers Act may have constituted the most significant attempt to restrict presidential power since Congress passed the Tenure of Office Act in 1867, which limited a president's ability to dismiss cabinet officers confirmed by the Senate. The President then was Andrew Johnson, a man almost bereft of party and interest-group constituencies and a man who confronted a nation tired of conflict and division. When Nixon vetoed the War Powers legislation, he made extravagant claims for executive prerogative, a provocation that might explain why fifteen House members—a mixture of liberals and conservatives—who originally opposed the legislation then voted to override his veto. (Senator Sam Ervin opposed the legislation throughout the voting.)[34]

Subsequent events, however, amply demonstrated that for all its symbolic qualities, the act did not significantly alter the practical power of the presidency. From the *Mayaguez* to the Gulf of Sidra incidents, the lesson was clear: presidents will shoot first and consult Congress later. Limits on a president's military initiative are defined in large part by the extent of his popularity and prestige. A chastened Henry Kissinger noted in 1975 that "comity" between the two branches was "the only possible basis for national action." He conceded that the decade-long struggle over executive dominance in foreign affairs had ended. Kissinger may have been dissembling or speaking as an overeager supplicant, yet there was no gainsaying the reality that Congress must participate in some way: "foreign policy," he acknowledged, "must be a shared enterprise."

Congressional inertia and indifference, however, still offered presidents broad authority to maneuver on their own in foreign policy, as when Jimmy Carter terminated the Taiwan defense treaty and froze Iranian assets, and when Ronald Reagan took action in Grenada, the Mediterranean, and Central America. Congress invoked the War Powers Act for the first time in 1983 after Reagan sent troops to Lebanon. Still, the legislative branch dealt gingerly with the popular President, giving him eighteen months, rather than sixty days, to withdraw troops. Reagan did so before the expiration of the deadline.[35]

The War Powers Act probably is moot if a President will show an appearance of shared governance. In April 1988, President Reagan used American forces to retaliate when Iranian mines imperiled U.S. vessels in the Persian Gulf. Reports then indicated that congressional leaders had no intention of pressing the Administration to invoke the act; instead, those leaders expressed satisfaction that they had been consulted in advance. For nearly two terms, the Reagan Administration and Congress had disputed the efficacy of the law; after the Persian Gulf attacks, a White House official said: "Maybe after eight years we've finally gotten it right."

A month later, however, prominent congressmen admitted that the formal machinery of the War Powers Act never had worked, probably was unworkable, and perhaps was unwise. Senator George Mitchell (D–ME), a vocal critic of Reagan's adventurist foreign and military policies, acknowledged that the law had "failed." Senator Sam Nunn (D–GA) criticized the time constraints of the act, contending that it offered foreign governments a lever for influencing policy debates in the United States. Finally, Democratic Majority Leader Byrd frankly conceded that "if I were president, I would thumb my nose" at the law. "Reform" proposals circulated to institutionalize congressional consultations and abrogate the automatic troop-recall proviso, substituting instead a stipulation that troops would be removed if a majority of Congress so demanded.[36]

Whatever the mechanism, there is no substitute for political will. Well before the passage of the War Powers Act, Richard Nixon realized that Congress would no longer support the Vietnam war. Congress's shared powers are inherent in the governmental apparatus, and the choice to use them rests largely with that body.

Foreign-policy achievements are the historical touchstone for Nixon Administration partisans and will doubtless attract the attention of future historians. Henry Kissinger argued that the Administration attempted to strike a balance between the extremes of crusading and escapism—a "symmetry between the twin pillars of containment and cooexistence." Kissinger conceded failure, but he insisted the fault was in the stars: "History will forever debate," he wrote, "whether without Watergate Nixon could have achieved this goal." The necessary discipline and calculation for such a course, Kissinger contended, "fell prey to the passions of the Watergate era."

Clearly, Kissinger believed that Watergate had prevented that balance in Indochina. In addition, however, beyond the "bitter divisions" engendered by Vietnam, Kissinger complained that "the ugly suspicions" of the "Watergate purgatory" corroded the Administration's pursuit of détente with the Soviet Union. A "rare convergence" of conservatives who despised the Soviet Union and liberals who equally despised Nixon combined, Kissinger lamented, "to dismantle" policies that sought a relaxation of tensions between the United States and the Soviet Union.[37] Watergate's role in aborting détente is more subtle, more complex, and more consequential than its connection to the outcome of the Vietnam war; but like Vietnam, détente aroused opposition for reasons that had nothing to do with Watergate.

Nixon's first inaugural address set the stage for a new era in superpower relations, emphasizing peaceful negotiations: "Let us take as our goal: Where peace is unknown, make it welcome; where peace is fragile, make it strong; where peace is temporary, make it permanent. After a period of confrontation, we are entering an era of negotiation." Remembering his roots and the need to maintain his traditional constituency, the new President also emphasized the need to maintain national strength. In the speech that

Nixon did not deliver in March 1968 when Johnson withdrew from the presidential race, he described "a new era in our relations with the Soviets, a new round of summit meetings and other negotiations."

Nixon himself first used the word "détente" in a 1970 address to the United Nations. But evidence abounds, as Raymond Garthoff has demonstrated, that détente always remained a strategy, not an objective; a means, not a goal, of the Nixon Administration. Another scholar found détente "ambiguous," a characteristic that led to the breakdown of a domestic consensus for its support. The policy essentially spelled *ad hoc* actions and was often subservient to other aims, as witnessed by Nixon's willingness to sacrifice a summit conference and a strategic arms limitation (SALT) agreement rather than halt the bombing of North Vietnam.[38]

By 1973 the Administration's relations with the Soviets had made enormous strides in the direction Nixon had promised, from expanded trade dealings to the 1972 SALT agreement. That agreement produced both a limitation on antiballistic weapons and a more limited deal to contain the number of strategic offensive missile launchers and weapons. Nixon and Soviet leader Brezhnev held summit meetings in 1972 and 1973. The second produced the Prevention of Nuclear War Agreement, but more notably it resounded with chords of amicability and presented images of warm embrace. That meeting occurred during the Senate investigation of Watergate, just prior to John Dean's testimony. Richard Nixon was at the pinnacle of his power and prestige in his dealings with foreign adversaries. But his vulnerability over Watergate soon chipped away at that lofty status.

The traumatic moments of October 1973 are crucial to an understanding of the decline, or what one writer has called the "stall," of détente. That month, of course, was Nixon's cruelest. The Agnew resignation and the dismissal of Cox combined to focus the Watergate crisis on him personally and gave impetus to an impeachment inquiry. Amid those mishaps, the President confronted the Yom Kippur War and the ambiguous competitive policies of the Soviets. Those events sparked the first congressional rejection of détente and laid the groundwork for a decade-long challenge to that policy.

Assaults on the policy had begun earlier. Senator Henry Jackson (D–WA) was a traditional liberal Democrat on domestic issues, but a hard-liner toward the Soviets and an advocate of new weapons systems. Jackson pushed for legislation conditioning the Soviet Union's access to most-favored-nation trading status with the United States on its willingness to ease its restraints on emigration, particularly of Soviet Jews. Détente had emboldened Soviet dissidents. Brezhnev and the Kremlin leaders found no linkage between maintaining détente and internal policies toward their own citizens, but American opponents of détente insisted on that connection. The bill Jackson advocated (with Charles Vanik [D–OH]) finally passed the House in December and the Senate several months later.

Perceptions of Soviet machinations during the Yom Kippur War significantly enhanced Jackson's appeal. Jackson raised public and private doubts as to Kissinger's real motives toward Israel. His attacks cut several ways. For some, his concerns provoked a haunting specter of a U.S.–Soviet condominium that would impose a settlement on the Middle East contrary to the interests of the immediate parties. More important, Jackson accused the Soviets of undermining détente, as he characterized Brezhnev's suggestion to dispatch a Soviet-American combat team to the Suez Canal as "brutal" and "threatening." For Jackson and other foreign-policy conservatives, Soviet diplomacy in the Middle East amounted to an attempt to expand their influence among the Arab nations. Competition, the critics contended, not détente, remained at the center of Soviet intentions. The Administration's rather dubious staging of a military alert at the time of the Yom Kippur War offered its own contribution to the heightening of suspicions toward the Soviets—an action that had its own tenuous links to the Watergate situation.[39]

After 1973 the Center/Right in the Democratic Party converged with the Republican conservative Right in open alliance against the President's policies. Emboldened by Nixon's deteriorating strength, Defense Secretary James Schlesinger and the Joint Chiefs of Staff worked closely with Jackson, his aides, and the sympathetic staff on the Senate Armed Services Committee. Nixon's pursuit of détente increasingly aroused the ire of precisely those elements most likely to support his struggle to preserve his presidency; he could not afford to alienate them. At the same time, if he appeased the Right by backing away from détente, he ran the risk of alienating J. William Fulbright and liberals on the Senate Foreign Relations Committee, who generally supported the Nixon-Kissinger global designs once the Vietnam war was ended. Watergate certainly complicated Nixon's task.[40]

Kissinger acidly assailed Jackson in later years, accusing him of implementing legislative obstacles that "gradually paralyzed" policy toward the Soviet Union. According to Kissinger, Jackson's staff was one of the "ablest—and most ruthless" he had encountered, ascribing invidious interpretations to Administration motives and masterfully leaking information. Jackson and the opposition to détente, Kissinger concluded, elevated "confrontation into a principle of policy," and they did so during the nation's "worst domestic crisis" in a century and against the "most hobbled Chief Executive" since World War II. In Kissinger's ultimate estimation, Jackson "sought to destroy our policy, not to ameliorate it."

The President himself thought that Jackson was "in the pocket of Jews." He considered going public against Jackson, charging that he and "professional Jews" would "torpedo" chances for disarmament agreements with the Soviets. Nixon believed that "a storm" would hit American Jews once he exposed what he saw as their position.⁴¹

By 1974 Nixon's position had deteriorated rapidly, and détente was embroiled in the maelstrom of ideological politics. The President seemed to have little interest in the SALT negotiations; Kissinger meanwhile was overwhelmed by the technical complexities of arms-control problems and by the determined opponents of agreements with the Soviets. For Nixon, the June 1974 summit in Moscow was little more than ceremonial. Jackson and the congressional opposition charged that secret deals had been made in SALT I negotiations and that the Soviets had cheated. He also made clear his determination to thwart the Administration's attempts to expand East–West trade. The President and his entourage were so wary of the attacks from the Right that his spokesmen insisted Nixon had *not* visited Yalta, a place that conjured so much negative symbolism, but rather Oreanda, a nearby area. During the summit meeting, Admiral Elmo Zumwalt, Chief of Naval Operations, resigned and denounced the Administration's policies. Despite explicit orders from Haig, Schlesinger attended Zumwalt's retirement ceremonies and presented him with a medal.⁴² Richard Nixon had lost control of his Administration.

In subsequent years, Soviet commentators noted the Watergate affair, acknowledging belatedly that the President fell victim to his own abuses of power—after long insisting (when they were not ignoring it) that Watergate was a right-wing plot. Interestingly, they blamed the collapse of détente on the counteroffensive of the military-industrial complex, rightist forces, and Zionist groups. Another Soviet diplomat lamented that Watergate had so preoccupied liberals that the urgent problems of foreign policy and arms control eluded them.

At the end of his presidency, Nixon proudly noted his association with détente: "This, more than anything," he said on the night preceding his resignation, "is what I hope will be my legacy to you, to our country, as I leave the presidency." But in a diary entry approximately one month earlier, he cynically noted that the Moscow Summit had come out "about right." To have gone further would have alienated "good conservative supporters, and we did just about what the traffic would bear." He would not do anything to antagonize "some of our best friends prior to the impeachment vote." (Thirteen years later, Nixon in his elder-statesman role still appeased those friends, as he and Kissinger attacked the Reagan Administration for its proposed nuclear-weapons treaty with the Soviet Union.)

Did Watergate abort the full flowering of that legacy of détente that Nixon so proudly hailed as he took his leave? In his memoirs, a more reflective Richard Nixon thought not: "domestic political fluctuations," preceding and apart from Watergate, had impaired his ability to deliver fully on détente. The opposition of Henry Jackson on trade and Soviet emigration, Nixon believed, had undermined Brezhnev's credibility with Jackson's conservatives. Finally, "the military establishments of both countries" bridled at the prospect of real arms control. "These problems," Nixon concluded, "would have existed regardless of Watergate." Even without Watergate, Gerald Ford later ordered his aides to delete "détente" from the White House political vocabulary, as he sought to neutralize the Right in 1976. In truth, the opposition had swung the pendulum away from détente, almost wholly without help from Watergate.[43]

In an immediate sense, Watergate altered public perception of the presidency and the relationship between the executive and other institutions. How much of those changes has endured, however, is questionable. Watergate transformed and reshaped American attitudes toward government, and especially the presidency, more than any single event since the Great Depression of the 1930s, when Americans looked to the President as a Moses to lead them out of the economic wilderness. World War II and the Cold War, with all their attendant dangers to the physical and ideological security of the nation, only exalted that faith. Professor Woodrow Wilson, who often expressed his low opinion of Congress, wrote in 1908 that the presidency "must always, henceforth, be one of the great powers of the world. . . . We have but begun to see the presidential office in this light; but it is the light which will more and more beat upon it."

Intellectuals, liberal and conservative alike, celebrated Wilson's prophecy. "The President is not a Gulliver immobilized by ten thousand tiny cords, nor even a Prometheus chained to a rock of frustration," political scientist Clinton Rossiter wrote in the late 1950s. "He is rather a kind of magnificent lion, who can roam widely and do great deeds, so long as he does not try to break loose from his broad reservation. . . . He will feel few checks upon his power if he uses that power as he should." John F. Kennedy's election in 1960 made that a canonical doctrine of the liberal faith. But by the end of the decade, such glorifications of the presidency seemed embarrassing (when they were not forgotten), and Rossiter's restraints, largely written in as an afterthought, became the new gospel.[44]

Watergate bestowed a new vulnerability on the presidency. Americans alternately inflicted anger and derision on the office and the man. Ford's pardon of Nixon added an element of cynicism. Slander and malice toward presidents, of course, was not new. Washington suffered his share, as did Jefferson, Lincoln, and Franklin D. Roosevelt. But the invective now appeared on a massive scale. Once peerless and invincible, presidential majesty seemed diminished, and Nixon and his immediate successors served as easy prey for cruel, even contemptuous, humor. The media criticism of the presidency, and the preoccupation with presidential sins of omission or commission, had gathered such momentum in the Nixon years that it seemed impossible to turn off the spigot. Jimmy Carter fared no better; indeed, his self-avowed status as an outsider, his mannerisms, and his alternating shifts between doubt and assured faith provided tailor-made targets for equally biting humor and criticism. The Ford and Carter Administrations, especially, offered the spectacle of president as victim.

Clinton Rossiter notwithstanding, the President of the United States now appeared to be an immobilized Gulliver—or worse yet, a Lilliputian. "A feeble Executive implies a feeble execution of the government," Hamilton wrote in *Federalist* 70. "A feeble execution is but another phrase for a bad execution; and a government ill executed, whatever it may be in theory, must be, in practice, a bad government." By the end of the 1970s, the nation seemed to view its government as "feeble," and hence "bad."

Although Watergate gave rise to the criticism of the "imperial presidency," the *leitmotif* in the early Reagan years was that the nation could ill afford a crippled Chief Executive. Ford spoke of an "imperiled presidency." Yet power and authority were not so much at issue during the Watergate years as were responsibility and accountability. Richard Nixon endlessly stressed the importance, the infallibility, and the uniqueness of the "presidency"—reiteration designed, it seemed, to insulate the President from accountability. Nothing in the historical traditions of executive power, nothing in the Constitution, nothing even in the modern celebrations of executive authority justified Nixon's rationalizations. Indeed, had he acknowledged responsibility for Watergate, Nixon might have had a different fate. The President's foes—and the nation—needed more than he offered. Nixon had underestimated the historical tradition of skepticism toward unrestrained power.[45]

In subsequent years, references to Nixon's deeds and the Watergate controversy became a shorthand for amorality, abuse of power, and official criminality. "Watergate" provided a ready suffix to tag onto a range of public scandals. Some such titles stuck, such as "Koreagate," involving illegal lobbying activities, and some did not, such as "Debategate," the controversy over purloined Carter campaign materials in the 1980 election. The language became global when the Japanese used "Recruitgate" to describe a government scandal in the late 1980s. Watergate encouraged a routinized—some would argue a trivialized—response to official breaches of public law and confidence. A succession of congressional investigations, special prosecutors, and media pressures followed the various allegations, some well founded, some not.

Watergate established historical traces as standards for future political behavior. For those who thought the scandal a "dim and distant curiosity," the Iran-Contra affair in 1986–87 offered a rude reminder. The Reagan Administration's secret shipment of weapons to Iran, clearly intended as ransom for American hostages held there, and the diversion of profits to the Contra rebels in Nicaragua vividly revived the memories, the lessons, and even the language of Watergate, sometimes inappropriately so. Almost instantaneously, the media raised the familiar Howard Baker question: "What did the President know, and when did he know it?"

Watergate veterans weighed in with experienced advice. Alexander Haig urged President Reagan to take responsibility for the scandal and immediately dismiss underlings suspected of violating the laws. The President, he continued, should refuse to appoint a special prosecutor, nor should he allow congressional hearings (as if it were in his power to bar them). Finally, Haig thought Reagan should tell the American people: "And if you don't like it, impeach me!" He later lamented that Reagan did not follow his advice and instead "went along with a six-month orgy" of independent-counsel investigations and congressional hearings. Richard Nixon merely told Reagan that the affair would not be "another Watergate, as long as you stay ahead of the curve." More familiar language: thirteen years earlier, he had told Henry Petersen that he wanted "to stay one step ahead of the curve."[46]

Reagan and his advisers had learned a great deal from the Watergate experience. The President appointed the Tower Commission to investigate the Iran-Contra affair. He generally cooperated—and, more important—gave the appearance of cooperation (if not of truthfulness). He never asserted executive privilege; he instructed relevant agencies and individuals to cooperate with Congress and with the independent counsel he appointed (ignoring Haig), and even made available to the congressional committee material held by his designated biographer as well as extracts from his personal diaries. One Congressman, however, was unimpressed and thought that the Reagan Administration had learned a different lesson from Watergate: "they learned to destroy as much evidence as possible and to appear cooperative." The next perpetrators of misdeeds, he thought, would do "even better" at covering their tracks.

The Iran-Contra affair perhaps represented a greater threat to the American constitutional order than had Watergate, yet its dénouement was not nearly as dramatic. Reagan undoubtedly suffered a loss of credibility, but unlike Nixon he retained a substantial measure of public trust. For some, nevertheless, there was a sinister aspect in what was perceived as the privatization of foreign policy by the White House and the adventurism of presidential subordinates; more than anything, perhaps, the affair revealed the shortcomings of Reagan's careless management style. But the congressional inquiry demonstrated that the constitutional arrangements for shared governance remained contested ground in the American system. And within those conflicts, as within that system, "trust," as Secretary of State George Shultz admitted, "is the coin of the realm."[47] Watergate sounded its haunting tones throughout the episode.

Watergate became a permanent part of American political language after 1972, but its meaning could be easily forgotten. At a press conference in December 1978, a reporter asked President Jimmy Carter if he would consider reducing or withholding federal revenue-sharing funds from those cities or states that did not follow his wage guidelines. "I think this would be illegal under the present law," the President said. The reporter, as if oblivious to Nixon's extra-legal policies, persisted and repeated the question. "No," Carter responded very firmly, "we could not do that under the present law." Yet for others, Watergate was more instructive. In 1983, revelations indicated that the Solicitor General's office had covered up important evidence that might have helped the cause of the Japanese-Americans when the Supreme Court heard arguments in 1944 regarding the constitutionality of their wartime internment. A Justice Department attorney, who later went on to a distinguished career as a civil libertarian, was asked some forty years later why he had not publicly exposed the alleged chicanery when he found himself tormented between conscience and loyalty to superiors in 1944. "Watergate," he responded, "hadn't happened yet."[48]

Watergate, on the whole, has lingered in public memory. The public traditionally has been disposed to expect the worst of legislators "and at the same time believe in high virtues of the President and his entourage."[49] But for a while, at least, the situation has been reversed. When the expectation of executive virtue is disappointed, the weight of such disappointment almost inevitably produces a massive response which, however naively, attempts to ensure against any repetition of executive offenses. Some of the resulting measures succeed; some amount to little more than an exercise in futility or wrongheadedness. And so, the judgment of the effectiveness of post-Watergate reforms results in a mixed verdict.

Perhaps above all, however, Watergate revitalized and nourished the tradition of constitutional responsibility. It also elevated moral considerations in the judgment of public officers and in the conduct of public business. Whether involving limitations on campaign funds, ethical standards for elected and appointed officials, governmental intervention in the private sphere, or the conduct of foreign policy, a national consciousness of the need of checks on powerholders was sparked by Watergate. That concern has remained vital in the years since, prompting and rationalizing both legislation and criticism that reflected some standards for the proper conduct of political leaders and governmental officials. However excessive, faulty, or even misguided the character of the responses to Watergate, they reflected an understanding that public officials must themselves adhere to the same rule of law they so piously demand that the governed obey. Richard Nixon's most ardent and passionate defenders, those who most readily assail his persecutors, must either agree, or defend the alien proposition that a president is above the law.

XXIII

RICHARD NIXON, WATERGATE, AND HISTORY

We cannot escape history.
ABRAHAM LINCOLN
Second Annual Address

"In the past few days," Richard Nixon told the nation on the evening of August 8, 1974, he had realized that he no longer had "a strong enough political base in the Congress" to maintain himself in office. The President's contention that he had to resign merely because he had lost his political base sounded the *leitmotif* for his last campaign—his struggle for the grace and favor of history. That political base was Nixon's to lose, yet his remarks implied that he had been the victim of a political conspiracy. He mentioned the Watergate "matter" only once.

Nixon's apologia alarmed his old nemesis Wright Patman, Chairman of the House Banking Committee. The morning after the speech, he wrote to House Judiciary Committee Chairman Peter Rodino, urging that the committee complete its investigation into Nixon's presidential conduct. Patman told Rodino it was imperative to preserve all the documents and tapes and to ensure that nothing was lost as a result of the presidential transition.

Patman understood the stakes. He suspected that "in the coming weeks and months, there will be some who will attempt to distort the record, [to] misconstrue events and to cloud the real issues." Watergate had been a "wrenching experience," he told Rodino, but nothing would be learned if the record were incomplete or distorted. He urged that the committee secure additional White House tapes and publish them. Patman had correctly complained on other occasions that the available tape transcripts revealed nothing of White House discussions between September 15, 1972, and February 28, 1973.

The thought of remaining in the limelight apparently was too much for Rodino. He had been a reluctant warrior from the outset. Now, with almost unseemly haste, he retreated to his familiar obscurity—and shut down the House impeachment inquiry. No one challenged him; Patman again found himself abandoned and isolated. Meanwhile, Rodino had given aid and comfort to Nixon's embarrassed supporters, one of whom had begged Leon Jaworski to put an "immediate end" to this "mess," and allow everyone to "quickly forget about it and go on about their business."[1]

Nixon himself was more than ready to go about the business of refurbishing his historical reputation. What he said when he resigned, and what he did after that, signaled his campaign to capture the soul of history. Gerald Ford, never known for stern judgments of his contemporaries, remarked that Nixon's resignation-eve statement on his loss of political support dodged the real issue. Nixon, he complained, had failed to offer any note of contrition, refusing to "take that final step." Surely, Nixon had no desire for such finality. A contentious man, so self-consciously struggling to emulate Theodore Roosevelt's "man in the arena," Nixon simply could not couple the shame of resignation with the obscurity that public penance might bring. Wright Patman could but ponder the future implications of Rodino's decision to bow out. What, indeed, would history say?

Before and after his resignation, Nixon and his supporters either minimized Watergate or ignored it altogether. In May 1974 Nixon told Rabbi Baruch Korff that Watergate was the "thinnest scandal" in American history. Although embattled by that scandal near the end of his tenure, Nixon suggested to Alexander Haig that a failure to respond to a North Korean attack on an American reconnaissance plane in 1969 "was the most serious misjudgment of my Presidency, including Watergate." He assured his fallen aide, Charles Colson, that Colson's "dedicated service" to the nation would be remembered after Watergate had "become only a footnote in history." At an October 1973 press conference, Nixon anticipated his theme of victimization when he denounced his congressional and media opponents as spiteful enemies who sought to reverse "the mandate of 1972." Just after the resignation, David Eisenhower, the former President's son-in-law, said that in fifteen years, Watergate would "look pretty small." The President, Eisenhower said, had "simply acquiesced in the non-prosecution of aides who covered up a little operation into the opposition's political headquarters"— hardly something to be taken seriously. In an April 1988 television appearance, Nixon repeated the "footnote" thesis but added that his delay in bombing North Vietnam was the biggest mistake of his presidency.

If he could not reduce Watergate to banality, to something commonplace, Nixon's fallback position always was to insist that no wrong had occurred.

"When the President does it, that means that it is not illegal," he told television interviewer David Frost in May 1977, in the first of many self-orchestrated "comebacks." He referred to the "political" (not criminal) activities that led to his resignation. Following the broadcast of the Frost interviews, a Gallup poll found that 44 percent of those who watched were more sympathetic toward Nixon than they had been, while 28 percent felt less so. Yet Nixon's early venture into revisionism and vindication failed dismally. Nearly three-quarters of the viewing audience believed he had been guilty of an obstruction of justice, and nearly as many thought he had lied during the Frost interviews themselves.[2]

Fifteen years after the Watergate break-in, Nixon loyalists faithfully echoed their leader's interpretation. At a 1987 conference, H. R. Haldeman resurrected the "third-rate burglary" pronouncement of June 1972, calling it the work of "stupid" Nixon supporters. If the problem had been "handled within the White House staff structure from the outset," he said, the matter would have been contained—as if John Dean had ever worked for someone other than H. R. Haldeman. In a televised 1984 memoir, one which Nixon and his staff carefully controlled, the former President called the break-in a "botched" job, a "misdemeanor" that his enemies had turned into the "crime of the century." In 1988, Patrick Buchanan dismissed the Watergate events as "Mickey Mouse misdemeanors," evidently forgetting that felonies, as well as stupidity, followed the Watergate break-in. "A child of ten would have been able to figure out that it wasn't a sensible thing for [Nixon] to do, to try that cover-up," observed Richard Helms, no stranger to clandestine affairs. It was "one of the stupidest things that anybody could have done."

Those who would minimize or dismiss Watergate focused on the break-in of Democratic headquarters, an event of which the President and his closest staff members pled total ignorance, and at the same time avoided any discussion of the abuses of power that preceded the burglary and the obstruction of justice that followed it. Those acts, which are part of the Watergate story, run like a seamless web throughout the Nixon presidency, and while they constituted the focus of the impeachment proceedings, they were ignored in the interpretation imposed by the former President. William Ruckelshaus, a victim of the Saturday Night Massacre, had a different stake in the interpretation of Watergate, but one more in accord with the facts: "[T]he break-in was trivial but what happened afterwards was not trivial. It was profound." And Leon Jaworski, who perhaps understood Nixon's stonewalling better than anyone, brusquely noted: "To deny impeachable acts and criminal wrongdoing is untruthful. . . . They cannot be erased by the belated efforts of the man who created them."[3] Jaworski had enthusiastically supported Nixon's re-election bid in 1972; his later judgment gave the lie to Nixon's bald claim that he had been undone by political enemies.

* * *

Revisionism perhaps is as inevitable as death and taxes, and the Watergate affair deserves some, to be sure. Contemporary commentator Nicholas von Hoffman, for example, shrewdly warned of the dangers of history written only from the perspective of the winners. The uncritical fascination with Judge John Sirica and his transformation into a neo-folk idol; the press's excessive claims for its role; the lynch-mob mentality of what von Hoffman called the "monotone" media; and some questionable prosecutorial tactics suggest topics that deserve more critical scrutiny. But that kind of revisionism is quite different from one that proceeds from the premise that "everyone" had engaged in abuses of power, that obstruction of justice was a matter of "national security," and that Nixon's actions pale into insignificance against the achievements of his Administration. Such attitudes come close to validating Voltaire's dictum that history is a pack of tricks the living play upon the dead.[4]

How shall we remember Richard Nixon?

The movie is Woody Allen's *Sleeper* (1973); the scene is set in the year 2073; several people, apparently anthropologists, are watching old videotapes of Richard Nixon:

> DOCTOR: Some of us have a theory that he might once have been President of the United States, but that he did something horrendous. So that all records—everything was wiped out about him. There is nothing in the history books, there are no pictures on stamps, on money. . . .
>
> MILES MONROE: He actually was President of the United States but I know whenever he used to leave the White House, the Secret Service would count the silverware.

That, of course, was at the height of the Watergate affair. In the years that followed, Nixon regularly presented himself as an elder statesman and as a knowing political handicapper; still, for many, he remained a comic figure, a butt of derision, constantly forced back into private retreat as the barbs and jokes resonated. But the *Sleeper* lines about forgetting have a ring of painful reality. We are, to some extent, in danger of forgetting—not forgetting Richard Nixon, but forgetting what he did and what he symbolized to his contemporaries. History, after all, is not just what the present wishes to make of the past for its own purposes; present-mindedness has its own alphabet of sins. Historians are entitled to weigh the past by the measure of the evidence of long-term consequences, and they must weigh by the standards of that past, not those of their own time. Yet as Leon Jaworski cautioned, they must not uncritically accept the judgments of the actors themselves.

Memories proved short in some cases. The upper echelon of the so-called media "lynch mob," the American Society of Newspaper Editors, who had heard Nixon proclaim "I am not a crook" in 1973, welcomed him to their annual meeting in 1984 with a standing ovation. The former President expressed surprise that he had been asked so few Watergate questions. Two years later, *Newsweek* reported that when asked what he considered Watergate's greatest lesson, Nixon replied: "Just destroy all the tapes." Yet two weeks afterward, the same periodical proclaimed Nixon "rehabilitated," and featured him on its cover over the caption, "He's back." One scholar argued that Nixon might be the greatest domestic president of the twentieth century—a notion first advanced by John Ehrlichman—and described Watergate as only a "dim and distant curiosity" which eventually would be seen as "a relatively insignificant event." Worse yet, treatment of Watergate ran the danger of trivialization, as when the *Today* television show interviewed Gordon Liddy for his views on the Soviet Union or when Jeb Magruder was selected to chair an ethics commission. Typically, media fascination with personality rather than with substance served to keep "the slippery former president" alive as a public figure, political writer David Broder noted, "when he ought to be living out his life in private and in disgrace."

The Nixon revisionism attempted to inflict a collective national amnesia on historians, the media, and our political leadership regarding Watergate. Watergate at times seemed lost in the mists of history, an odd fate for an event that consumed and convulsed the nation and tested the constitutional and political system as it had not been tested since the Civil War. But, in truth, once out of the White House, Richard Nixon commanded attention precisely because of his indissoluble links to Watergate, a connection indelibly engraved on our history. When asked in 1968 how he envisioned the first line of his *New York Times* obituary, Nixon replied: " 'He made a great contribution to the peace of the world.' " Twenty years later, he told reporters: "History will treat me fairly. Historians probably won't[,] because most historians are on the left, and I understand that"—resorting to a familiar refrain and technique. Then he asked that he be remembered most for his China initiative.

Nixon certainly will be remembered for his role in world affairs. He will receive heavy measures of both praise and criticism, and historians of both the Right and the Left probably will cross sides in unpredictable ways. It might never have occurred to Richard Nixon that so-called leftist historians helped rehabilitate Herbert Hoover. Whatever historians do, however, no "fair" history of the Nixon era can overlook the centrality of Watergate. Textbooks a century from now will inevitably speak of Richard Nixon as the first president to resign because of scandals. His achievements will get their due, as different generations weigh them, favorably or unfavorably, but they probably will not rival Watergate for historical attention.[5]

Henry Kissinger contemptuously dismissed the political and media assault on the Nixon Administration as an "American extravaganza," something profoundly distasteful to him as a longtime admirer of the ordered past of nineteenth-century Europe. "Extravaganza," indeed; not every president has stood in danger of impeachment. Neither Nixon nor we can escape Watergate. Its history demands our serious attention; it was neither trivial nor insignificant. It raised important, painful questions about American political behavior and the American political system, questions that speak to the traditions and structure of American life. Whether the actors in the drama of Watergate confronted those questions successfully or unsuccessfully, directly or passively, honestly or conveniently, will be the subject for history. That is the significant, inescapable importance of Watergate.

The wars of Watergate are rooted in the lifelong political personality of Richard Nixon. His well-documented record of political paranoia, his determination to wreak vengeance on his enemies, and his overweening concern with winning his own elections, rather than with the fortunes of his colleagues or with the substance of policy, animated the thoughts and actions of his aides, who fulfilled his wishes.

The period is also bounded by much more than a burglary in 1972 and a resignation in 1974. The fall of Richard Nixon was the last act in a decade-long political melodrama that haunted the American stage, beginning with the civil rights movement and John F. Kennedy's assassination. War and unprecedented social protest about the war and other complex problems in American life followed and eventually culminated in Watergate. To that extent, Richard Nixon was the last casualty.

Richard Nixon cannot be separated from Watergate, however valiant his efforts. In time, Haldeman, Ehrlichman, Mitchell, Colson, Dean, Butterfield, Haig, and the other supporting players in the Watergate drama will fade into the same well-deserved obscurity as have their counterparts in other historical scandals. Ultimately, we leave behind the spear carriers, what the poet Coleridge called the Ancient Mariner's "strange and ghastly crew." But Nixon himself will remain as the one indisputably unforgettable and responsable actor.

President Nixon and his defenders have claimed that in the Watergate affair he behaved no differently from other presidents. Watergate emerged "exactly how the other side would have played it," Nixon said in 1977. It was all "politics pure and simple." With even less plausibility, he justified the crimes of Watergate as an outgrowth of the "end-justifies-the-means mentality of the 1960s." The long answer to all that is that *not* everyone did it. The short answer is that others' behavior is beside the point. Sam Ervin impatiently dismissed Nixon's plea: "Murder and theft have been committed since the earliest history of mankind, but that fact has not made murder meritorious or larceny legal.''[6] The Nixon rationalization rested on a claim that he was an unfortunate victim of time and place and deserves to be considered entirely apart from Watergate. Still, there is no dodging the fact that Watergate happened and he was found culpable.

Egil Krogh, who engineered an illegal break-in on Nixon's behalf, confessed that his work, ''as official Government action, . . . struck at the heart of what the Government was established to protect, which is the . . . rights of each individual.'' His mission had not been designed to protect national security but to gain material to discredit Daniel Ellsburg. Charles Colson similarly later admitted that ''the official threats'' to individual rights were wrong and had to be stopped. Yet the President himself repeatedly had initiated and encouraged those threats, and then had sacrificed his closest political subordinates to conceal his own involvement in their abuses of power and obstructions of justice. ''I abdicated my moral judgments and turned them over to someone else,'' Ehrlichman confessed to Judge Sirica. Watergate gives us cause to ponder anew Alexander Hamilton's query in *Federalist* I whether in this nation, men would establish ''good government from reflection and choice, or whether they are forever destined to depend for their political constitutions, on accident and force.''

Richard Nixon discovered that the nation would tolerate an imperial president, but not an imperious one. Centuries of British and American constitutional experience have dictated limitations on executive power. However necessarily powerful the presidency may be in a fragile, dangerous world, however indispensable presidential action may seem for the nation's security and well-being, the practiced traditions of constitutionalism and the rule of law still count for much.

The Watergate wars offered eloquent testimony that the nation had a serious commitment to the rule of law. Our tradition has been that of a nation of laws, not of men only; a nation of orderly means and processes, not of burglars or imperious executives and their compliant servants. That tradition is the essence of American constitutionalism. John Ehrlichman—and Richard Nixon—suffered irreparable damage when Ehrlichman so cavalierly brushed aside Senator Herman Talmadge's concern for the security of home and person. Men are not angels, Madison said, and we wisely have fenced them in with constitutional prescriptions for the restraint of power. The legal order, as Alexander Bickel wrote at the time of Watergate, required ''not a presumed, theoretical consent, but a continuous actual one, born of continuous responsibility.'' Rulers cannot legitimately impose a rule of law on the ruled unless they themselves will submit to it.[7]

''[L]et us begin by committing ourselves to the truth, to see it like it is and tell it like it is, to find the truth, to speak the truth and to live the truth.

That's what we will do," Richard Nixon told his fellow Republicans when they nominated him for the presidency in 1968. "Truth will become the hallmark of the Nixon Administration," Herbert Klein told reporters several weeks after the election. But lies became the quicksand that engulfed Nixon, estranged him from his natural political allies, and eventually snapped the fragile bond of trust between leaders and led that binds government and the people. Nixon's lies brought him to the dock and cost him his presidency. "I have impeached myself," he confessed in 1977.[8]

Political language can conceal the truth, as George Orwell and others have noted. Often truth is concealed with a knowing wink between the political leader and his audience, and much of it is concealed in the language of symbolic politics. Richard Whalen, a one-time Nixon adviser and speechwriter, described how Nixon confined his conservative instincts to private company, while publicly positioning himself to the left—where, he believed, the votes were. "You don't know how to lie," Nixon told an early political associate. "If you can't lie, you'll never go anywhere." But for Nixon, lies led ultimately to a disgraceful resignation. At Republican leadership meetings throughout 1973 and 1974, Nixon's allies pleaded with him to "get it all out on the table." Nixon would say there was no more. But with repeated new disclosures, even those most steadfast among his supporters reached the point where, Congressman Barber Conable recalled, "you didn't believe anything." And still Nixon would insist, "it's all out there." The President informed Republican National Chairman George Bush, "George, I'm telling the truth." But the tape revelations reportedly devastated Bush; lying, a friend said, just was "not in George Bush's book."[9]

Nixon confronted Democratic majorities in Congress throughout his presidency, a fact which doubtless contributed mightily to his sense of peril. But a numerical majority dictates organizational control, not necessarily ideological dominance. Friendly Southern Democrats and Republican loyalists regularly eased Nixon's path through his first term. Conflicts existed, to be sure, but he was not a President denied. The domestic achievements that Nixon and Ehrlichman claimed with such pride offer ample testimony to the President's success with Congress. The unfolding events in 1973 and 1974 weakened Nixon's support base in Congress, and the President's lies, deceit, "stonewalling"—to use the popular phrase of Watergate—eventually destroyed it.

The Saturday Night Massacre convinced many that Nixon had something to hide. The exposure of the taping system betrayed a sinister side to the White House. The 18½-minute tape gap, the incorrect transcripts, and the President's shifting explanations inexorably chipped away at his credibility. The Republican and Southern Democratic members of the House Judiciary Committee watched the President descend the slippery slope away from truth, convinced that he had lied. Repeated sentiments such as he expressed in August 1973—"That was and that is the simple truth"—were seen as hollow and perverse. The Republican loyalists on the House Judiciary Committee realized the irreparable damage of Nixon's lying. After the release of the "smoking gun" transcripts, they expressed amazement and dismay that for so long he had suppressed the truth about his role in Watergate; consequently, they sadly noted, the truth "could not be unleashed without destroying his presidency."

William Buckley thought that presidents must on occasion violate laws, but he judged that Nixon's denials of his actions magnified the violations. For Buckley, the denials, not Nixon's lawbreaking, constituted the President's "real" crimes. Nixon repeatedly promised the "truth," an old refrain that echoed the "Checkers" speech of 1952 when he said that the "best thing is to tell the truth." Barry Goldwater did not share Buckley's brief for moral relativism. "Truth is the foundation of a stable society," he insisted. "Its absence was the crux of Nixon's failure." With biting contempt, Goldwater read the indictment: Nixon had lied to his family, his friends, his political supporters in and out of Congress, the nation, and the world. "Tell the truth," Goldwater told Nixon when he visited the former President in his San Clemente exile in 1975. When he wrote his memoirs thirteen years later, Goldwater was still waiting for the truth from Richard Nixon.[10]

Because he lied, Richard Nixon lost his political base. That deceit was intended to obscure the overwhelming evidence that he *had* abused power and he *had* obstructed justice. The actions of the President and his men were serious. More than seventy persons were convicted or offered guilty pleas as a consequence of the Age of Watergate. These included several Cabinet officers, two Oval Office aides, and numerous presidential assistants. Revisionism, to be whole, must produce more than pardons at the bar of history; it must produce the necessary exculpatory evidence.

Nixon's deeds as well as his own words, on tape, in public, and in his memoirs, convicted him. "I brought myself down. I gave them a sword. And they stuck it in," he bitterly observed. But he reminded us of what he was: "And, I guess, if I'd been in their position, I'd have done the same thing." Resignation, he once said, meant that he was guilty, and it would weaken the presidency he so cherished.[11] For two years, he had resisted cooperation in the name of "preserving the presidency"—meaning, of course, himself. But in the end, he willingly sacrificed the presidency in order to save the President.

Political philosophers since the ancient Greeks have sought to understand the links between politics and ethical behavior—"virtue," as eighteenth-century men were fond of calling it. They agreed at least, Dwight Macdonald once wrote, "that there is some connection between ethics and politics and there is a problem involved." They all, he observed, rejected the "simplistic" view, so congenial to the "pragmatic" American mind, that there was no connection and no problem.[12]

The eagerness of Nixon and his supporters to dismiss his misdeeds because "everyone does it" perversely twisted the conservative political tradition to which they subscribed, a tradition that rests upon virtue and morality. As the impeachment inquiry reached its climax, Congressman William Cohen recognized that perversion as he wondered how we had moved from the *Federalist Papers* of the 1780s to the Nixon tapes of the 1970s. Alexander Hamilton and James Madison, who had few illusions about human nature, nevertheless understood that leadership must rest on something other than covering up crimes or scheming to punish alleged enemies.

Americans idealize their presidents and hence expect them to meet the highest moral standards. People demand leaders better than themselves; such is the stuff of "heroes." Nixon's "tricky" image was one he never escaped. Watergate reinforced, and then confirmed, that image.

Competence and expertise were not enough to protect Richard Nixon. The President symbolizes "legitimacy, continuity, and morality"; Nixon tarnished the symbol, and it cost him dearly. What is clear, above all, is that the country had come together on the fundamental proposition that virtue mattered, that some ethical standard applied in political life. Thomas Jefferson once remarked that the whole art of government consists in being honest. George Washington, who gave a "Farewell Address" in 1796 far different from Nixon's, said that virtue and morality formed the "necessary spring of government" and were "indispensable supports" for political prosperity. "The mere politician," Washington insisted, "ought to respect and cherish them." Washington and the cherry tree myth are deeply ingrained in American civil religion. Richard Nixon never understood. Nearly a decade after he resigned, he wrote: "Virtue is not what lifts great leaders above others."[13] But even those words of self-incrimination pale next to the most fateful ones he ever uttered: "I hereby resign."

A NOTE ON SOURCES

Thanks to congressional vigilance in 1974, the National Archives has preserved most of the Watergate-related paper materials in the Nixon Papers.
The Presidential Recordings and Materials Preservation Act of 1974 mandated that the National Archives "provide the public with the full truth, at
the earliest reasonable date, of the abuses of governmental power popularly
identified under the generic name 'Watergate.' " That law prevented Richard Nixon, despite the support of President Gerald Ford and his staff, from
removing the former President's papers to California; the law also stipulated
that the National Archives, and not Nixon, should retain control of the
papers.

The Archives' staff has done its work: those papers, as well as ones documenting other Nixon Administration activities, have been processed and
made ready for research use. But Richard Nixon, his lawyers, and his past
and present aides repeatedly have intervened to thwart the implementation
of the rules governing the use of the papers. After thirteen years of legal
and bureaucratic battles, the Archives in 1987 opened the first of the "Watergate Special Files." The former President, however, objected to the release of approximately 150,000 documents, and more than two years later,
the Archives was still reviewing appeals against those objections. The materials in question range from such items as a memorandum on the Save the
Seals Campaign, a comment on the Davis Cup tennis team, and a copy of
Mrs. Nixon's schedule, to tantalizing documents giving Kissinger's views on
the Joint Chiefs of Staff after it was revealed they had spied on him, comments on Chief Justice Burger's beliefs, and H. R. Haldeman's files for the
1972 presidential campaign, all of which Nixon's lawyers have insisted are
"personal" or "third-party" protected documents.

The Archives holds several thousand hours of presidential tape recordings
of conversations with aides and whoever else walked into Nixon's various
offices and retreats. The Nixon Archives' staff carefully listened to the tapes
for more than nine years, edited them to accommodate national-security and
family considerations, and prepared a 27,000-page "finding aid" indexing

each conversation. But fifteen years after Congress provided that the material be made available as soon as possible, those tapes remain closed, because of the former President's objections as well as from an apparent reluctance on the part of the administrators at the National Archives to challenge him. For now, we can surmise the tapes' contents by following the elaborate daily notes of H. R. Haldeman and John Ehrlichman as they talked to Nixon. Ehrlichman, incidentally, has predicted that new tapes will reveal an "un-admirable," "petty," and "small" side to Nixon. The disclosures, Ehrlichman added, would mark a major setback in Nixon's struggle for history. Given Nixon's lengthy struggle to suppress the tapes, we can be reasonably certain they will not exonerate him.

The currently available Nixon Papers in the National Archives are invaluable. The President's Personal Files, different topical subjects contained in the Nixon Central Files, the Staff Secretary's Files, and the collections of Haldeman, Ehrlichman, Charles Colson, John Dean, Egil Krogh, and David Young provide important documents for Watergate and the Nixon presidency. No doubt, as more material is released in future years, we will have an even more focused picture. The tape recordings and transcripts of materials used in *United States v. Mitchell* are also housed in these collections.

It is worth noting that the records of Richard Nixon himself significantly diminish after the dismissal of Haldeman and Ehrlichman in April 1973. Memoranda between the President and his aides flowed freely prior to that date, and are crucial for understanding the ideas and style of Nixon. After Alexander Haig became Chief of Staff, however, we have precious few documents passing between Nixon and his aides; the quantity undoubtedly decreased as the President found himself preoccupied with Watergate. Haig, contrary to the letter and spirit of the 1974 law, managed to remove most of his papers from the White House, as did Henry Kissinger. They remain sealed and unprocessed in the Library of Congress. Presumably, Haig will use them in his promised memoir; one hopes he will then allow access to others. If Kissinger's tight control of his records offers any kind of precedent, however, it is unlikely Haig will do so.

The Gerald Ford Library in Ann Arbor has relevant papers in the "Pardon" materials of the White House Central Files. The Philip Buchen, Alexander Butterfield, and Ron Nessen collections were of some use, but the materials of Congressman Edward Hutchinson, ranking Republican member of the House Judiciary Committee, proved exceptionally valuable. The Library of Congress Manuscript Division has the papers of Joseph Alsop, William J. Brennan, Leonard Garment, Fred Graham, and Elliot Richardson. Leon Jaworski's papers and videotaped interviews of him are in the Texas Collection at Baylor University. The Sam Ervin Papers in the Southern Historical Collections of the University of North Carolina at Chapel Hill are useful for sampling the Senator's mail for sentiments of his constituents. Earl Silbert graciously shared his personal diary with me.

The Civil Reference Branch of the Archives has custody of the papers of the Watergate Special Prosecution Force. Previously unreleased material, however, had to be obtained through the Freedom of Information process. The Senate Select Committee Records are in the Legislative Records Section of the Archives. The Federal Bureau of Investigation has opened some 16,000 pages of investigative materials. The FBI records are essential for understanding the early "leaks" to journalists.

The Freedom of Information Act provided access to a number of collections and files in various agencies, but in the past decade, bureaucrats have become increasingly adept at reducing many of the documents to nullities. Indeed, the Act, as I have suggested, at times appears as a conspiracy on behalf of the Xerox Corporation and Magic Marker pens, given the promiscuous deletions and copies of meaningless materials passed on to researchers.

Interviews provide mixed results. Generally, I chose not to interview anyone who had written his own account unless I determined that the subject wished to add to the existing record. Time and different conditions alter memory and the perception of truth. Reliability is elusive. One prominent presidential aide has given at least three different versions of his role in the decision not to destroy presidential tapes.

Richard Nixon has not allowed scholars to interview him about Watergate, and he will not permit taping, according to one historian who has interviewed him. Those ground rules—among other reasons, to be sure—disqualified me. I am satisfied, however, that Nixon has left an adequate historical record.

Transcripts of my interviews will be deposited in the State Historical Society of Wisconsin, in Madison. I also intend to make them available to the Nixon Archives. My copies of the 1975 interviews with members of the "Fragile Coalition" also will be deposited there.

The history of Richard Nixon is a growth industry. Books by Stephen Ambrose, Roger Morris, and Herbert Parmet are the latest entries, and more are promised. Nixon historians will have to confront Watergate. The existing executive, legislative, judicial, and prosecutorial records will serve well, but more primary sources eventually will see the light of day and perhaps offer new perspectives and revelations. The contemporary reportage will remain valuable as a source for understanding the unfolding of the story and the national reaction to it. Bob Woodward and Carl Bernstein, *All the President's Men* and *The Final Days;* Elizabeth Drew, *Washington Journal: The Events of 1973–1974;* John Osborne, *The Nixon Watch;* and J. Anthony Lukas, *Nightmare,* are the most important accounts from the time. But there is nothing quite like *RN: The Memoirs of Richard Nixon*. It is filled, to be sure, with evasions, half-truths, and self-serving explanations. Still, Nixon provides—almost in spite of himself—extraordinary insights into his thoughts and behavior. Without question, it is one of the most useful of presidential memoirs.

INTERVIEWS

Spiro T. Agnew, Palm Springs, California, January 14, 1989
Donald Alexander, Washington, D.C., May 8, 1987
Scott Armstrong, Washington, D.C., February 9, 1987
Benton Becker, Miami, Florida, December 5, 1985
Robert Bork, Washington, D.C., June 17, 1987
Garry Brown, Washington, D.C., October 7, 1987
Stephen Bull, Washington, D.C., May 5, 1987
Dean Burch, Washington, D.C., May 5, 1987
Mrs. J. Fred Buzhardt, Columbia, South Carolina, September 25, 1986
Richard Cates, Madison, Wisconsin, February 6, 1988
William Colby, Washington, D.C., October 9, 1987
Barber Conable, Washington, D.C., May 28, 1985
Samuel Dash, Washington, D.C., February 5, 1986
John Dean, Beverly Hills, California, April 16, 1988
Elias Demetracopoulos, Washington, D.C., June 25, 1985; May 5, 1987
Harry Dent, August 31, 1986 (telephone), Columbia, South Carolina, September 24, 1986
William Dixon, Madison, Wisconsin, November 20, 1985
Don Edwards, Washington, D.C., July 15, 1986
Robert Finch, Pasadena, California, March 4, 1987
Zane Finklestein, Alexandria, Virginia, May 30, 1985
Leonard Garment, Washington, D.C., May 29, 1985; June 26, 1985; April 12, 1988
Mordechai Gazit, Tel Aviv, Israel, December 29, 1985
Kenneth Geller, Washington, D.C., May 26, 1988
Ernest Griswold, Washington, D.C., May 4, 1987
John Hart, New York, February 18, 1986
Richard Helms, Washington, D.C., July 14, September 23, 1988
Bernard Hollander (telephone), August 7, 1986
Elizabeth Holtzman, New York, April 11, 1986
Tom Charles Huston, Indianapolis, Indiana, September 1, 1988

David Keene, Madison, Wisconsin, August 14, 1985
Egil Krogh, Seattle, Washington, August 20, 1986
Melvin Laird, Washington, D.C., June 27, 1985
Wolfgang Lehmann, Washington, D.C., May 8, 1987
Jake Lewis, Washington, D.C., July 22, 1985; July 14, 1986
Charles Lichenstein, Washington, D.C., November 22, 1985; February 7, 1986; July 16, 1986
Morris Liebman, Chicago, June 14, 1988
Steven Lynch, Washington, D.C., October 10, 1985
Robert McClory, Washington, D.C., May 8, 1987
John Mitchell, Washington, D.C., December 30, 1987; February 9, April 11, 1988
Tom Mooney, Washington, D.C., July 14, 1986
Richard Moore, Washington, D.C., December 5, 1987
Thomas Moorer, Washington, D.C., June 25, 1985
Jack Nelson, Washington, D.C., August 22, 1985
Allen Otten, Washington, D.C., October 10, 1985
Henry Petersen, Sunderland, Maryland, August 23, 1985
Howard Phillips, Vienna, Virginia, August 23, 1985
Franklin Polk, Washington, D.C., December 18, 1986
Vladimir Pregelj, Washington, D.C., February 11, 1988
Henry Reuss, Washington, D.C., May 15, 1985
Elliot Richardson, Washington, D.C., May 14, 30, 1985
William Ruckelshaus, Seattle, Washington, August 21, 1986
William Safire, Washington, D.C., February 6, 1986
James St. Clair, Boston, April 10, 1987
Donald Santarelli, Washington, D.C., August 26, 1987
Father Don Shea, Washington, D.C., May 15, 1986
David Shepard, Madison, Wisconsin, April 4, 1988
Earl Silbert, Washington, D.C., February 10, September 30, 1988; February 23, 1989
John Stennis, Washington, D.C., June 25, 1985; June 27, 1985 (telephone)
Robert Stripling (telephone), March 24, 1989
Mike Wallace, New York, December 12, 1986
Clay Whitehead, McLean, Virginia, May 25, 1988
Charles Wiggins, Los Angeles, February 5, 1985
Tim Wyngaard, Washington, D.C., May 15, 1985
Jerome Ziefman, Washington, D.C., February 5, 1986

ABBREVIATIONS

FBI Federal Bureau of Investigation Papers
FL Gerald R. Ford Library, University of Michigan, Ann Arbor
HBC House Banking and Currency Committee Papers
HJC House Judiciary Committee
H.R. House of Representatives
LC Library of Congress, Manuscript Division
NA National Archives
NCF Nixon Central File
NP Nixon Papers
NPF Nixon Personal Files
NTSB National Transportation Safety Board Papers
NYT New York Times
PPPUS:GF Personal Papers of the President of the United States: Gerald R. Ford
PPPUS:LBJ Personal Papers of the President of the United States: Lyndon B. Johnson
PPPUS:RN Personal Papers of the President of the United States: Richard M. Nixon
SJC Senate Judiciary Committee
SSC Senate Select Committee to Investigate Presidential Campaign Activities
SSF Staff Secretary Files (Ford and Nixon Papers)
U.S.S. United States Senate
TT Tape Transcript
U.S. v. M United States v. Mitchell, et al.
WGSPF Watergate Special Prosecution Force
WHCF White House Central Files (Ford and Nixon Papers)
WHT White House Transcript
WP Washington Post
WSJ Wall Street Journal

NOTES

PROLOGUE: TRIUMPH AND FOREBODING: ELECTION NIGHT 1972

1. Haldeman Notes, September 11, 1972, Haldeman Papers, Box 46, NP; Richard Nixon, *RN: The Memoirs of Richard Nixon* (paperback ed., New York, 1979), 2:218-22.
2. David Frost, *"I Gave Them a Sword": Behind the Scenes of the Nixon Interviews* (New York, 1978), 183.
3. TT, President, Dean, and Haldeman, September 15, 1972 (5:24 P.M.-6:17 P.M.), *U.S. v. M*, NA.
4. *PPPUS: RN, 1973*, Speech, April 30, 1973, 333; Buchanan to Nixon, December 8, 1972, Haldeman Papers, Box 230, NP; Garment to Haldeman, January 19, 1973, Garment MS, LC; Garment Interview, May 29, 1985.

I: BREAKING FAITH: THE 1960s

1. Kim McQuaid, *The Anxious Years: America in the Vietnam-Watergate Era* (New York, 1989), offers an insightful synthesis of the period.
2. *PPPUS: LBJ, 1963-1964*, April 21, 1964, 1:513; Eric F. Goldman, *The Tragedy of Lyndon Johnson* (New York, 1969), 334, 335-37; Louis Heren, *No Hail, No Farewell* (New York, 1970), 253. Paul K. Conkin, *Big Daddy from the Pedernales: Lyndon Baines Johnson* (Boston, 1986), offers a recent sensitive portrayal of Johnson.
3. Allen J. Matusow, *The Unraveling of America: A History of Liberalism in the 1960s* (New York, 1984), 144; George Reedy, *Lyndon B. Johnson: A Memoir* (New York, 1982), 123. See Robert A. Caro, *The Path to Power* (New York, 1982), for a lengthy discussion of the negative aspects of Johnson's earlier career.
4. *NYT*, May 27, 1964, July 18, 1964.
5. Rowland Evans and Robert Novak, *Lyndon B. Johnson: The Exercise of Power* (Signet ed., New York, 1968), 502; Goldman, *Tragedy of Johnson*, 228; Matusow, *Unraveling of America*, 143.
6. Lloyd A. Free and Hadley Cantril, *The Political Beliefs of Americans* (New Brunswick, 1967), 173.
7. Reedy, *Johnson*, 138.
8. *PPPUS: LBJ, 1963-1964*, September 25, 1964, 2:1126.
9. Lyndon B. Johnson, *The Vantage Point: Perspectives of the Presidency, 1963-1969* (New York, 1971), 68; John M. Orman, *Presidential Secrecy and Deception* (Westport, CT, 1980), 98; William C. Berman, *William Fulbright and the Vietnam War: The Dissent of a Political Realist* (Kent, OH, 1988), 29. Also see *The Pentagon Papers* (New York, Bantam Books, 1971). In June, Bundy had told the President that the "defense of U.S. interests is

possible, within these [i.e., the current] limits, over the next six months." In other words, the war was not to be widened during the campaign. Matusow, *Unraveling of America*, 149, citing *Pentagon Papers*.

10. Berman, *Fulbright*, Chapters 2, 3; Goldman, *Tragedy of Johnson*, 176.

11. Berman, *Fulbright*, 23-26, 69-70; David Halberstam, *The Best and the Brightest* (Penguin ed., New York, 1983), 496-503, 510.

12. Berman, *Fulbright*, 24, 26-27; Goldman, *Tragedy of Johnson*, 182-83; Halberstam, *Best and the Brightest*, 509. In his memoirs, Johnson cited the Fulbright-Cooper exchange, in effect blaming Congress for its future failure to withdraw consent for widening the war. But he never mentioned Nelson's challenge. Johnson, *Vantage Point*, 118-19. Fulbright later publicly apologized to the Wisconsin senator. AP dispatch (FBI spying), *Madison (Wisconsin) Capital Times*, July 17, 1988.

13. *New York Herald Tribune*, May 23, 1965.

14. Matusow, *Unraveling of America*, 154; Kathryn J. Turner, *Lyndon Johnson's Dual War: Vietnam and the Press* (Chicago, 1985), 176-77.

15. Ronald Steel, *Walter Lippmann and the American Century* (Boston, 1980), 578; Michael Davie, *LBJ: A Foreign Observer's Viewpoint* (New York, 1966), 36-37; John Tebbel and Sarah Miles Watts, *The Press and the Presidency: From George Washington to Ronald Reagan* (New York, 1985), 493.

16. Goldman, *Tragedy of Johnson*, 439.

17. Halberstam, *Best and the Brightest*, 778.

18. David Halberstam, *The Powers That Be* (New York, 1979), 6. Johnson, *Vantage Point*, 530; Eugene McCarthy, *Up 'Til Now* (Orlando, FL,1987), 178; *PPPUS: LBJ, 1967*, June 27, 1967, 1:656; Doris Kearns, *Lyndon Johnson and the American Dream* (New York, 1976), 315-16. Henry Kissinger, *Years of Upheaval* (Boston, 1982), 86-87, presented a concise condemnation of the treason of the intellectuals—according to Kissinger.

19. Kearns, *Lyndon Johnson*, 8; Tebbel and Watts, *Press and the Presidency*, 490; *PPPUS: LBJ, 1968-1969*, January 17, 1969, 2:51; Harry McPherson, *A Political Education* (Boston, 1972), 261.

20. Turner, *Johnson's Dual War*, 181-82, 179. The fickleness of the press sometimes was inexplicable. During Johnson's January 17, 1967, press conference, reporters raised no questions regarding Vietnam.

21. Reedy, *LBJ*, 140; Richard Whalen, *Catch the Falling Flag: A Republican's Challenge to His Party* (Boston, 1972), 100-01.

22. Orman, *Presidential Secrecy*, 108; Kearns, *Lyndon Johnson*, 393; Goldman, *Tragedy of Johnson*, 159-60, 201-02, 523-24.

23. *PPPUS: LBJ, 1963-1964*, October 9, 1964, 2:1266.

24. Kearns, *Lyndon Johnson*, 251; Chalmers M. Roberts, *First Rough Draft: A Journalist's Journal of Our Times* (New York, 1973), 252; Valenti, *Human President*, 367.

25. Heren, *No Hail, No Farewell*, 209-10.

26. Johnson, *Vantage Point*, 148; *PPPUS: LBJ, 1966*, May 17, 1966, 1:519.

27. Kearns, *Lyndon Johnson*, 20-21; Berman, *Fulbright*, 15.

28. George Herring, "The War in Vietnam," in Robert A. Divine (ed.), *Exploring the Johnson Years* (Austin, TX, 1981), 39-40; Peter W. Sperlich and William L. Lunch, "American Public Opinion and the War in Vietnam," *Western Political Quarterly*, March 1979, 32:21-24.

29. *Congressional Record*, 89 Cong., 1 Sess. (September 2, 1965), 22761-63. Two years later, Nixon persisted in his belief that China pulled the strings in Vietnam but then dropped hints that perhaps the United States should "change" China. "Taking the long view, we simply cannot afford to leave China forever outside the family of nations. . . . The world

cannot be safe until China changes." Richard M. Nixon, "Asia After Viet Nam," *Foreign Affairs*, October 1967, 46:111, 121.

30. Orman, *Presidential Secrecy*, 106.

31. Philip Geyelin, *Lyndon B. Johnson and the World* (New York, 1966), 306; Valenti, *Human President*, 134; Herring, "The War in Vietnam," in Divine (ed.), *Johnson Years*, 55.

32. McPherson, *Political Education*, 271-72; Goldman, *Tragedy of Johnson*, 511.

33. Larry Berman, *Planning a Tragedy* (New York, 1982), 128; Herring, "The War in Vietnam," in Divine (ed.), *Johnson Years*, 37-38; Valenti, *Human President*, 300-01; Moorer Interview, June 25, 1985; Turner, *Johnson's Dual War*, 182; McPherson, *Political Education*, 420-21; *NYT*, February 6, 1968.

34. Geyelin, *LBJ and the World*, 15.

35. Edward S. Corwin, *The President: Office and Powers* (New York, 1957), 29-30; Fred I. Greenstein, "A President Is Forced to Resign: Watergate, White House Organization, and Nixon's Personality," in Allan P. Sindler (ed.), *American Politics in the Seventies* (Boston, 1977), 68-70.

36. Richard Neustadt, *Presidential Power* (New York, 1960), 212-13; Fred I. Greenstein, "Political Psychology: A Pluralistic Universe," in Jeanne N. Knutson (ed.) *Handbook of Political Psychology* (San Francisco, 1973), 458.

37. Robert Sherrill, *The Accidental President* (New York, 1967), 221-23; *PPPUS: LBJ, 1965*, June 17, 1965, 2:680.

38. Kearns, *Lyndon Johnson*, 399-400; Geoffrey Hodgson, *All Things to All Men: The False Promise of the Modern American Presidency* (New York, 1980), 73.

39. Johnson, *Vantage Point*, 532-33; *Washington Star*, April 27, 1964.

40. Matusow, *Unraveling of America*, 391.

41. Peter Braestrup, *Big Story: How the American Press and Television Reported and Interpreted the Crisis of Tet in Vietnam and Washington* (paperback ed., Garden City, 1978), 508; Herring, "The War in Vietnam," in Divine (ed.), *Johnson Years*, 50-51; Culbert, "Johnson and the Media," *ibid.*, 233-34.

42. Herring, "The War in Vietnam," *ibid.*, 50-51.

43. Matusow, *Unraveling of America*, 392; William O'Neill, *Coming Apart* (Chicago, 1971), 375-76.

44. McCarthy Speech, March 23, 1968, Milwaukee, Wisconsin, *Madison (Wisconsin) Capital Times*, March 24, 1968.

45. *PPPUS: LBJ, 1968-1969*, March 31, 1968, 1:469-76; *ibid.*, April 1, 1968, 1:476-81; Kearns, *Lyndon Johnson*, 395.

46. *PPPUS: LBJ, 1968-1969*, April 1, 1968, 1:482-86.

47. Goldman, *Tragedy of Johnson*, 520; Turner, *Johnson's Dual War*, 248.

II: MAKING MANY NIXONS: 1913-1965

1. Earl Mazo, *Richard Nixon: A Political and Personal Portrait* (New York, 1959), 10.

2. H. R. Haldeman, *The Ends of Power* (New York, 1978), 76; Ronald Steel, *Walter Lippmann and the American Century* (Boston, 1980), 483, 589, 597; Fawn Brodie, *Richard Nixon: The Shaping of His Character* (New York, 1981), 353.

3. Compare, for example, Mazo and Brodie. A detailed and balanced account of Nixon's life prior to his presidency is in the first volume of Stephen E. Ambrose's projected trilogy: *Nixon: The Education of a Politician, 1913-1962* (New York, 1987). Garry Wills, *Nixon Agonistes: The Crisis of the Self-Made Man* (New York, 1970) is especially insightful.

4. Richard Nixon, *RN: The Memoirs of Richard Nixon* (paperback ed., New York, 1979), 1:25.

5. Nixon, *Memoirs*, 1:17–24.

6. Nixon, *Memoirs*, 1:24–26.

7. Brodie, *Nixon*, 133–39.

8. Nixon, *Memoirs*, 1:30–31.

9. Nixon, *Memoirs*, 1:31–33.

10. Nixon, *Memoirs*, 1:33–36.

11. Nixon, *Memoirs*, 1:39–42.

12. William Costello, *The Facts About Nixon: An Unauthorized Biography* (New York, 1960), 38.

13. Mazo, *Nixon*, 48.

14. Earl Mazo and Stephen Hess, *Nixon: A Political Portrait* (New York, 1968), 38–42.

15. Costello, *The Facts About Nixon*, 38–58, *passim*. The 1946 campaign repelled Nixon's old girlfriend, who also said that she followed his later career with great dismay. Brodie, *Nixon*, 125.

16. Nixon, *Memoirs*, 1:53–54.

17. Nixon, *Memoirs*, 1:57–63.

18. Russell Lynes, *The Lively Audience* (New York, 1985), 421.

19. Allen Weinstein, *Perjury: The Hiss-Chambers Case* (New York, 1978), 557; Weinstein, "Nixon vs. Hiss," *Esquire*, November 1975, 74. Stripling Interview, March 24, 1989, confirmed details of Nixon's own exaggerated role in the Hiss affair. Nixon has admitted to only one mistake: his failure to pursue Mrs. Hiss. Chambers had told him she was the "red hot" of the couple, and that often wives of Communists were the more extreme. Nixon added his own gloss: "[I]t has been my observation that in the political arena, men often tend to be pragmatic; they are willing to compromise. . . . Women seldom will do so. They tend to be total idealist, true believers, whether the cause is on the left or the right." Richard Nixon, "Lessons of the Hiss Case," Address to the Pumpkin Papers Irregulars, October 31, 1985, typescript, 9. Courtesy of Mr. Nixon.

20. *Testimony of Witnesses*, Hearings, Committee on the Judiciary, House of Representatives, 93 Cong., 2 Sess. (July 15, 1974), 3:44. Hereafter cited as HJC, *Testimony of Witnesses*.

21. Costello, *Facts about Nixon*, 68–72; Mazo, *Nixon*, 64–75. Mazo wrote that Marcantonio actually hated Douglas, often referring to her with an obscene five-letter word. After he heard that Boddy had linked her to him, Marcantonio chuckled and reputedly told a Nixon friend: "Tell Nicky to get on this thing because it is a good idea." *Ibid.*, 74n. Marcantonio apparently was familiar enough to call Nixon "Nicky."

22. Mazo, *Nixon*, 84–85.

23. Mazo, *Nixon*, 65–66; Piers Brendon, *Ike: His Life and Times* (New York, 1986), 217.

24. Costello, *Facts about Nixon*, 118; Mazo, *Nixon*, 7, 67–68; Kenneth Davis, *The Politics of Honor: A Biography of Adlai E. Stevenson* (New York, 1967), 282, 300; John Bartlow Martin, *Adlai Stevenson of Illinois* (New York, 1976), 693; Stephen Whitfield, "Richard Nixon as a Comic Figure," *American Quarterly*, Spring 1985, 37:125.

25. Nixon, *Memoirs*, 1:112–33, is essentially a distillation of the account he gave earlier in *Six Crises*. Cf. Costello, *Facts About Nixon*, 103–12; Mazo, *Nixon*, 131–36; Ambrose, *Nixon*, 286–95. Mazo also suggested that without the speech, "Eisenhower might have lost." Such hyperbole can be matched to Hollywood producer Darryl Zanuck's remark to Nixon after his speech: "The most tremendous performance I've ever seen." John E. Hollitz, "Eisenhower and the Admen: The Television 'Spot' Campaign of 1952," *Wisconsin Magazine of History*, Fall 1982, 66:25–39.

26. Nixon, *Memoirs*, 1:120. "Controlling his temper with difficulty, Ike refused to be stampeded by such rudeness into such incontinence." Brendon, *Ike*, 223. Either the story changed through the years, or the standard for acceptable language did. Traditionally, Nixon was reported to have told Eisenhower "to fish or cut bait." Costello, *Facts About Nixon*, 105-06.

27. Nixon's remark on his relationship with Eisenhower is from an undated interview with Joseph Alsop, quoted in Michael R. Beschloss, *Mayday: The U-2 Affair*, (New York, 1986), 154.

28. Mazo, *Nixon*, 150; William B. Ewald, Jr., *Eisenhower the President: Crucial Days, 1951-1960* (Englewood Cliffs, N.J., 1981), 185-87; Beschloss, *Mayday*, 114.

29. *NYT*, October 18, 1956, November 6, 1956. See Mazo, *Nixon*, 152, 157, for Nixon's 1954 talk of leaving politics. The Eisenhower letter to Nixon on the succession is in Eisenhower to Nixon, February 5, 1958, Eisenhower Library, and Dulles Memorandum, February 8, 1958, Dulles MSS, Seeley Library, Princeton University. Also see Stephen E. Ambrose, *Eisenhower: The President* (New York, 1984), 272-73, 275.

30. Beschloss, *Mayday*, 178-81; Ambrose, *Nixon*, 520-28; Nixon, *Memoirs*, 1:250-63; Charles Mohr, "Remembrances of the Great 'Kitchen Debate,' " *NYT*, July 25, 1984. Mohr reported that reporters recognized Nixon's domestic political purposes, as they sang on their plane to the tune of "California, Here I Come": "Moscow Kremlin, here I come. What a place to campaign from."

31. Beschloss, *Mayday*, 183.

32. Nixon, *Memoirs*, 1:264.

33. Ambrose, *Eisenhower: The President*, 319-20, 512, 601; Robert Griffith, "Dwight D. Eisenhower and the Corporate Commonwealth," *American Historical Review*, 1982, 87:122.

34. Ambrose, *Eisenhower: The President*, 559-60.

35. *PPPUS: Eisenhower, 1960-1961*, August 24, 1960, Press Conference, 658.

36. Ambrose, *Eisenhower: The President*, 593-94. Ambrose concludes: "The result of all these structural difficulties, and of Eisenhower's ambiguity toward Nixon, was that Eisenhower's contribution to Nixon's campaign was worse than unhelpful—it actually cost Nixon votes, and probably the election." *Ibid.*, 594. Alsop's report is in Beschloss, *Mayday*, 154. Eisenhower's remark is in Ewald, *Eisenhower the President*, 312. Nixon asked Eisenhower to raise the question of Kennedy's health. Ike's Press Secretary, James Hagerty, denounced this as a "cheap, lousy, stinking political trick." Brendon, *Ike*, 398.

37. Marshall McLuhan, *Understanding Media* (New York, 1964).

38. Richard Nixon, *Six Crises* (New York, 1962), 340.

39. Sidney Kraus (ed.), *The Great Debates* (Bloomington, 1962), 391-93; 417.

40. Kraus, *Great Debates*, 396-97.

41. Edmund F. Kallina, Jr., *Court-House over White House* (Orlando, 1988), is a substantial scholarly study challenging the notion that Daley "stole" the election. Ambrose, *Nixon*, 605-08, praises Nixon's behavior following the election and has high praise for the conduct of his campaign. Also see Nixon, *Six Crises*, 397; Nixon, *Memoirs*, 1:278; Beschloss, *Mayday*, 341. A friend told Nixon shortly after the election that if it hadn't been for the Hiss case, he would have been nominated. Nixon replied that without that case, he probably would not have been nominated. Richard Nixon, "Lessons of the Hiss Case," 10. Daley's remark is in Ben Bradlee, *Conversations with Kennedy* (New York, 1975), 33. Nixon told a friendly writer that Eisenhower urged him not to challenge the election, but the writer sadly noted that "this was the first time I ever caught Nixon in a lie." Brodie, *Nixon*, 433. Timothy Crouse, a journalist hostile to Nixon, conceded that Nixon had valid complaints about the press. *The Boys on the Bus* (paperback ed., New York, 1974), 194. Helms Interview, September 23, 1988.

42. Nixon, *Memoirs*, 1:285–92; Nixon, *Six Crises*, 416. Hubert Humphrey had the same opportunity to announce Nixon's election in January 1969, but Johnson sent him to Norway to represent the United States at the funeral of former UN Secretary General Trygve Lie.

43. Years later, Nixon revealed that Whittaker Chambers had been among the most persuasive of those who favored his candidacy. "I do not believe for a moment that because you have been cruelly checked in the employment of what is best in you, what is most yourself, that that check is final. It cannot be," Chambers said. He conceded that the Democrats probably would control the White House for some time. If so, he observed, "that changes your routing and precise destination. It does not change the nature of your journey. You have years in which to serve. Service is your life. You must serve. You must, therefore, have a base from which to serve." Nixon, "Lessons of the Hiss Case," 11.

44. Haldeman, *Ends of Power*, 76.

45. *NYT*, December 22, 1963.

46. *Time, Inc. v. Hill*, 385 U.S. 374 (1966); Garment Interview, May 29, 1985; *NYT*, April 28, 1966; Leonard Garment, "The Hill Case," *New Yorker*, April 17, 1989, 104.

47. Nixon's remark on Ike reported by William Ewald, an Eisenhower speechwriter, quoted in Brendon, *Ike*, 409. In the extraordinary post-mortem rambling on the Hiss case that Nixon offered in 1985, he also noted that if he had not run for governor in 1962, he "very possibly" would have run for the presidency in 1964, been defeated, and permanently condemned as a two-time loser. Nixon, "Lessons of the Hiss Case," 12. Nixon to Johnson, November 5, 1964; Johnson to Nixon, November 12, 1964, LBJ Library, "Famous Names File."

III: "BRING US TOGETHER": 1965–1968

1. Mike Wallace, *Close Encounters* (New York, 1984), 101–02.

2. Memorandum, Fred Panzer to Jake Jacobsen, November 6, 1966; Jake Jacobsen to George Christian, November 4, 1966, LBJ Library, "Famous Names File."

3. *Washington Star*, October 30, 1966; Stephen E. Ambrose, *Eisenhower: The President* (New York, 1984), 666–67.

4. *WP*, April 1, 1968.

5. Harry McPherson, *Political Education* (Boston, 1972), 449–50; Louis Heren, *No Hail, No Farewell* (New York, 1970), 254; Alexander Bickel, "Watergate and the Legal Order," in Lawrence M. Friedman and Stewart Macauley (eds.), *Law and Behavioral Sciences* (New York, 1977), 221.

6. Richard Whalen, *Catch the Falling Flag: A Republican's Challenge to His Party* (Boston, 1972), 8, 43, has some perceptive observations on this development.

7. *NYT*, May 9, 1968.

8. Whalen, *Catch the Falling Flag*, 148–49. The near-contemporary accounts of the 1968 campaign are quite good, especially Lewis Chester, Godfrey Hodgson, and Bruce Page, *An American Melodrama: The Presidential Campaign of 1969* (Dell ed., New York, 1969); Theodore H. White, *The Making of the President, 1968* (New York, 1969), is far less satisfactory.

9. Edward L. Schapsmeier and Frederick H. Schapsmeier, *Dirksen of Illinois* (Urbana, IL, 1985), 214; Ambrose, *Eisenhower: The President*, 671–72.

10. Robert Dallek, *Ronald Reagan: The Politics of Symbolism* (Cambridge, 1984); Lou Cannon, *Reagan* (New York, 1982).

11. Robert Finch, "Remarks at Monticello" (1986), transcript; Finch Interview, March 4, 1987.

12. See Chester, et al., *An American Melodrama*, 477–560, for a superb account of the convention's proceedings. Harry Dent, *The Prodigal South Returns to Power* (New York,

1978), 82, 207, 93. Dent's account of the "Southern Strategy," admittedly self-serving, is nevertheless the most complete account of the idea and generally is very perceptive about the political scene. Dent Interview, October 31, 1986.

13. Carl Solberg, *Hubert Humphrey: A Biography* (New York, 1984), 323; Solberg's chapters 30–34 describe Humphrey's problems with Johnson.

14. Chester, et al., *An American Melodrama*; Todd Gitlin, *The Whole World Is Watching: Mass Media in the Making and Unmaking of the New Left* (Berkeley, 1980); William O'Neill, *Coming Apart: An Informal History of America in the 1960s* (Chicago, 1971); Stephen Whitfield, "Richard Nixon as a Comic Figure," *American Quarterly*, Spring 1985, 37:116.

15. Hart Interview, September 18, 1986.

16. *WP*, Editorials, August 9, 10, 1968.

17. John C. Whitaker to John D. Ehrlichman, June 14, 1971, Ehrlichman Papers, Box 57, NP; Joseph C. Spear, *Presidents and the Press* (Cambridge, 1984), 60; Marshall McLuhan, *Understanding Media* (New York, 1964), 330–31.

18. Joe McGinniss, *The Selling of the President 1968* (paperback ed., New York, 1970), 78, 117, 27–28, 30–32, *et passim;* Timothy Crouse, *The Boys on the Bus* (paperback ed., New York, 1974), 185–88. McGinniss noted that television and Humphrey were incompatible. The medium magnified his excesses of lengthy and too-fervent rhetoric. For television, McGinniss said, the "performer" comes into the living room as a guest. "It is improper for him to shout. Humphrey vomited on the rug." *Selling of the President*, 66–67. McGinniss's revelations later upset Nixon tremendously. He wanted the "full story" on McGinniss, he told White House aides, and John Ehrlichman assigned his personal investigators to the task. The investigator described McGinniss as "cunning, deceitful and disarming," words that Ehrlichman passed to Nixon. Butterfield to Ehrlichman, July 21, 1969, Caulfield to Ehrlichman, c. August 7, 1969, Ehrlichman to the President, September 3, 1969, Ehrlichman Papers, Box 30, NP.

19. Wallace, *Close Encounters*, 104, 106; Crouse, *Boys on the Bus*, 271–72; McLuhan, *Understanding Media*, 309; Whitfield, "Comic Figure," 118; O'Neill, *Coming Apart*, 380; McGinniss, *Selling of the President*, 66–67.

20. Phillips Statement, July 30, 1974; McGinniss, *Selling of the President*, 192–93.

21. *NYT*, March 6, 1968; Whalen, *Catch the Falling Flag*, 137–38. The speech is printed in Whalen's book, 283–94. Whalen hardly disguised his distaste for Nixon's obvious cynicism. He thought that Nixon in effect had signalled the White House that he would make no trouble for the President. "Thus was laid the groundwork for a nonaggression pact between incumbent and challenger that would become increasingly apparent in the months ahead." *Ibid.*, 143–44. Also see Allen J. Matusow, *The Unraveling of America* (New York, 1984), 402.

22. *NYT*, August 9, September 30, 20, 1968; Solberg, *Humphrey*, 387–88.

23. Hart Interview, September 18, 1986; Jules Witcover, *The Resurrection of Richard Nixon* (New York, 1970), 151–52. Hart remembered that Nixon aide Ron Ziegler got angry at him when Hart failed to attend a party aboard a yacht in Key Biscayne. Richard Nixon, *RN: The Memoirs of Richard Nixon* (paperback ed., New York, 1979), 1:369. Nixon Statement, ABC News, "45/85." September 18, 1985.

24. *NYT*, October 1, 1968; Solberg, *Humphrey*, 380–85; Transcript, *Face the Nation*, October 27, 1968; Kathryn J. Turner, *Lyndon Johnson's Dual War: Vietnam and the Press* (Chicago, 1985), 251. Also see Terry Dietz, *Republicans and Vietnam, 1961–1968* (Westport, CT, 1986), 138–41.

25. Billy Graham Notes, in "Transition File," LBJ Library.

26. *PPPUS: LBJ, 1963–1964*, October 27, 1964, 2:1477; Solberg, *Humphrey*, 407; Joseph Alsop, "Oral History," May 28, 1969, for LBJ Library, in Alsop MS, LC.

27. Matusow, *Unraveling of America*, 438–39.

Notes for Chapter IV

28. White, *Making of the President, 1968*, 396, and Rowland Evans, Jr. and Robert D. Novak, *Nixon in the White House* (New York, 1971), 33–34, tell the contemporary story of Nixon's talk. But see Chester, et al., *An American Melodrama*, 746–47, for a deeper probe.

29. John Bartlow Martin, *It Seems Like Only Yesterday* (New York, 1986), 309; Chester, et al., *An American Melodrama*, 858.

IV: ''THE MAN ON TOP'': 1965–1968

1. Richard Nixon, *RN: The Memoirs of Richard Nixon* (paperback ed., New York, 1979), 1:447–48. Ehrlichman Notes, June 27, 1972, Box 12, Ehrlichman Papers, NP; Alexander M. Bickel, ''Watergate and the Legal Order,'' in Lawrence M. Friedman and Stewart Macauley (eds.), *Law and Behavioral Sciences* (New York, 1971), 223.

2. Ehrlichman Testimony, *Presidential Campaign Activities of 1972*, Hearings, Select Committee on Presidential Campaign Activities, U.S. Senate, 93 Cong., 1 Sess., 6:2512–13. Hereafter cited as SSC, *Hearings;* Magruder's testimony in *ibid.*, 2:854–55; Moorer Interview, June 25, 1985, Nixon in *Newsweek*, April 16, 1984, 37; Ruckelshaus Interview, August 21, 1986.

3. *U.S. News & World Report*, August 13, 1984, 56–59, including remarks by historians; *Newsweek*, May 19, 1986, cover story.

4. *Weekly Compilation of Presidential Documents*, December 13, 1971; Charles A. Moser, *Promise and Hope: The Ashbrook Presidential Campaign of 1972* (Washington, D.C., 1985), 11–13; Nixon, *Memoirs*, 1:541, 527–30, 638–47.

5. Nixon Remarks, Chinese Embassy, Washington, February 27, 1987, Transcript courtesy of Mr. Nixon. See Hung Nguyen Tien and Jerrold L. Schecter, *The Palace File* (New York, 1986); Frank Snepp, *Decent Interval: An Insider's Account of Saigon's Indecent End* (New York, 1977); and Arnold R. Isaacs, *Without Honor: Defeat in Vietnam and Cambodia* (Baltimore, 1983).

6. J. Anthony Lukas's *Nightmare: The Underside of the Nixon Years* (New York, 1976; new ed., 1988) was the first systematic attempt to understand the Watergate story as a persistent thread of the Nixon Administration.

7. George Reedy, *The Twilight of the Presidency* (New York, 1970), 18, *et passim*. Harry Dent characterized Haldeman's aides as the ''Beaver Patrol.'' Harry Dent, *The Prodigal South Returns to Power* (New York, 1978), 239.

8. Edward L. Schapsmeier and Frederick H. Schapsmeier, *Dirksen of Illinois* (Urbana, IL, 1985), 222; Gerald R. Ford, *A Time to Heal: The Autobiography of Gerald R. Ford* (New York, 1979), 88, 150.

9. Joe McGinniss, *The Selling of the President 1968* (paperback ed., New York, 1970); Theodore H. White, *Breach of Faith* (paperback ed., New York, 1978), 128.

10. H. R. Haldeman, *The Ends of Power* (New York, 1978); *Current Biography* (1978), 185–89; John Ehrlichman, *Witness to Power: The Nixon Years* (New York, 1982).

11. n.d., Haldeman Notes, Box 48, NP; *WP*, August 24, 1972; Lou Cannon, ''The Siege Psychology and How It Grew,'' *WP*, July 29, 1973; Richard Whalen, *Catch the Falling Flag: A Republican's Challenge to His Party* (Boston, 1972), 197, 213, 255–57, 277–78; Herbert G. Klein, *Making It Perfectly Clear* (New York, 1980), 320*ff;* Helms Interview, July 14, 1988.

12. Haldeman, quoted in *Newsday*, November 20, 1987; Finch Interview, March 4, 1987; Dent Telephone Interview, August 31, 1986; Krogh Interview, August 20, 1986; Lichenstein Interview, February 7, 1986. Lichenstein expressed the contempt of older Nixon aides, noting that he would not have asked for the advice of Haldeman and Ehrlichman, convinced as he was that it would have been either wrong or self-serving. William Safire, *Before the Fall*

(Paperback ed., New York, 1975), 283–85; Haldeman Memo, "Presidential Objectives Planning Group," October 10, 1969, Dent Papers, Box 1, NP; Julie Nixon Eisenhower, *Pat Nixon: The Untold Story* (New York, 1986), 361–62; Alsop Interview with Nixon, undated, cited in Michael R. Beschloss, *Mayday: The U-2 Affair* (New York, 1986), 154; Jeb Stuart Magruder, *An American Life: One Man's Road to Watergate* (New York, 1974), 61; Samuel Kernell and Samuel Popkin, *Chief of Staff: Twenty-five Years of Managing the Presidency* (Berkeley, 1986), 52.

13. Haldeman Notes, September 19, 1971; Haldeman Memo, September 20, 1971, Haldeman Papers, Box 44, NP.

14. Nixon to Haldeman, June 16, 1969, NPF, Box 1, NP: *ibid.*, Box 3, March 31, 1971.

15. HJC, *Testimony of Witnesses* (July 2, 1974), 1:28–66. Butterfield to SSC Staff, July 13, 1973, Butterfield Papers, FL.

16. Nixon to Rose Mary Woods, March 31, 1971, NPF, Box 3, NP; Nixon to Ehrlichman, July 9, 1969, and Nixon to Haldeman, July 9, 1969, NPF, Box 1, NP; Nixon to Butterfield, April 16, 1972, Haldeman Papers, Box 161, NP; Nixon to Haldeman, April 17, 1972, *ibid.*; Nixon to Haldeman, August 6, 1971, NPF, Box 3, NP; Nixon to Chapin, June 16, 1969, NPF, Box 1, NP; Nixon to Haldeman, November 24, 1969, NPF, Box 1, and Nixon to Price, December 28, 1971, NPF, Box 4, NP; Nixon to Haldeman, May 13, 1972, Haldeman Papers, Box 161, NP; Haldeman to Chapin, May 15, 1971, *ibid.*

17. Dent Interview, October 31, 1986; Dent, *Prodigal South*, 238–39. In Dent's book, the secretary is described as male.

18. HJC, *Testimony of Witnesses*, 1:69–70; Butterfield to SSC Staff, July 13, 1973, Butterfield Papers, FL; Eisenhower, *Pat Nixon*, 361; Lichenstein Interview, February 7, 1986; Agnew Interview, January 14, 1989; Keane Interview, August 14, 1985; Dent Interview, October 31, 1986; Bull Interview, May 7, 1987; Klein, *Making It Perfectly Clear*, 335; Kernell and Popkins, *Chief of Staff*, 21–23.

19. Haldeman, *Ends of Power*, 61; Ehrlichman, *Witness to Power*, 342; John Dean, *Blind Ambition* (New York, 1976), 22–23; Henry A. Kissinger, *Years of Upheaval* (Boston, 1982), 808; Dent Interview, October 31, 1986.

20. Garment to Kissinger, March 21, 1971, Garment MS, LC; Garment Interview, June 26, 1985; Kissinger, *Years of Upheaval*, 73–74.

21. *NYT*, December 12, 1968; Ehrlichman, *Witness to Power*, 297; Carl Brauer, *Presidential Transitions: Eisenhower to Reagan* (New York, 1986), 143–44, 147; Thomas E. Cronin, *The State of the Presidency* (Boston, 1975), 187.

22. Dent to Ehrlichman, January 23, 1969, Box 1, Dent Papers, NP; Aaron Wildavsky, a political scientist, suggested in 1966 that the United States has "two presidencies," one for foreign and defense policy, the other for domestic affairs. Godfrey Hodgson, *All Things to All Men: The False Promise of the Modern American Presidency* (New York, 1980), 73–74. Rowland Evans, Jr., and Robert Novak, *Nixon in the White House* (New York, 1974), 11; Magruder, *An American Life*, 110; Cronin, *State of the Presidency*, 169.

23. Walter Hickel, *Who Owns America?* (Englewood Cliffs, NJ, 1971), 221–22; Magruder, *An American Life*, 11; Ehrlichman, *Witness to Power*, 100–01; Finch Interview, March 4, 1987. John Dean's memo of October 3, 1970, has reference to an internal investigation of Hickel. Dean Papers, Box 39, NP.

24. Henry Kissinger, *White House Years* (Boston, 1979), 47.

25. James Keogh to the President, March 31, 1969, Buchanan to the President, April 1, 1969, both FG-6-11-1, NCF, NP; Cole to Ehrlichman, March 31, 1969, JL-3-1, NP.

26. Nixon, *Memoirs*, 1:435–38; Safire, *Before the Fall*, 284; Evans and Novak, *Nixon*, 35; Safire to Nixon, November 11, 1970, copy in Garment MS, LC.

27. Nixon, *Memoirs*, 1:447–48, 423; Moynihan to Nixon, January 3, 1969, Box 163, Haldeman Papers, NP; Magruder, *An American Life*, 78–81; Kenneth Cole to White House

Staff, July 11, 1969, Krogh Papers, Box 63, NP; Nixon to Haldeman, June 16, 1969, Box 1, NPF, NP.

28. Butterfield to Klein and Bryce Harlow, June 11, 1969, Krogh Papers, Box 63, NP.

29. John C. Whitaker to Ehrlichman, June 14, 1971; Ken Cole to Ehrlichman, June 15, 1971; Ehrlichman to Haldeman, July 8, 1971, Ehrlichman Papers, Box 57, NP.

30. Safire, *Before the Fall*, 219-20.

31. Haldeman Notes, October 6, 1971, Haldeman Papers, Box 44, NP. Memos in NPF, NP: Nixon to Haldeman, January 18, 1971, Box 3; *ibid.*, June 28, 1971, Box 3; *ibid.*, March 2, 1970, Box 2; memos of January 14, 1971, to Haldeman and Ehrlichman, Box 3; Nixon to Haldeman, November 24, 1969, Box 1; *ibid.*, December 1, 1970, Box 2; Nixon to Ehrlichman, February 4, 1969, Box 1; *ibid.*, January 14, 1971, Box 3; Nixon to Haldeman, January 18, 1971, Box 3; *ibid.*, June 1, 1971, Box 3.

32. Nixon to Haldeman, March 1, 1971, NPF, Box 3, NP; Colson to Haldeman, March 8, 1971, Haldeman Papers, Box 169, NP; President's Staff Dinner, Blair House, March 8, 1971, Audio Tape, White House Communications Agency Collection, NP.

33. Garment to Ehrlichman, April 1, 1971, Garment MS, LC.

34. Haldeman Notes, October 5, 1971, Haldeman Papers, Box 44, NP; TT, the President, Ehrlichman, and Shultz, April 19, 1971, (3:03 P.M.-3:34 P.M.), *Statement of Information*, Hearings, Committee on the Judiciary, H.R., 93 Cong., 2 Sess. (May–June 1974), 5:330-31. Hereafter cited as HJC, *Statement of Information*. Ehrlichman Notes, March 9, 1973, Box 14, Ehrlichman Papers, NP; Earl Mazo, *Richard Nixon: A Political and Personal Portrait* (New York, 1959), 36; Nixon, *Memoirs*, 1:31-33; William Costello, *The Facts About Nixon: An Unauthorized Biography* (New York, 1960), 30. In his 1973 conversation with Ehrlichman, Nixon was speaking of a Small Business Administration official who had mishandled a project and subsequently was demoted. But the remarks also occurred in the context of the President's determination to thwart the policies of the Anti-Trust Division for his own political purposes.

35. Dent, *The Prodigal South*, 188-89; Richard Nathan, *The Plot That Failed* (New York, 1975), 83; Arthur M. Schlesinger, Jr., *A Thousand Days: John F. Kennedy in the White House* (Boston, 1966), 413, 415, 431, 681, 683.

36. *Washington Star-News*, August 2, 1973; Haig to John Brown, May 13, 1970, Clark Mollenhoff to Nixon, May 8, 1970, Box 116, SSF, NP; Nixon to Haldeman, Kissinger, Ehrlichman, and Shultz, February 8, 1971, NPF, Box 3, NP.

37. Ehrlichman to Nixon, February 16, 1972, NPF, Box 3, NP.

38. Hodgson, *All Things to All Men*, 103-04, 106-07.

39. The basic story of the Huston Plan is in *Intelligence Activities, Volume 2, Huston Plan*, Hearings, Select Committee to Study Governmental Operations with Respect to Intelligence Activities, U.S.S., 94 Cong., 1 Sess. (September 23-25, 1975). Richard Gid Powers, *Secrecy and Power: The Life of J. Edgar Hoover* (New York, 1986), Ch. 13, has an excellent account of the Nixon–Hoover relationship, and specifically discusses the Huston Plan, 450-64, as do Athan G. Theoharis and John Stuart Cox, *The Boss: J. Edgar Hoover and the Great American Inquisition* (Philadelphia, 1988), 417-22. Nixon, *Memoirs*, 1:583-89; Ehrlichman, *Witness to Power*, 156-67; Dean, *Blind Ambition*, 37.

40. Helms Interview, July 14, 1988; Huston to Krogh, February 20, 1970; Krogh to Haldeman, February 23, 1970; Huston to Krogh, March 25, April 2, 3, 1970, Krogh Papers, Box 14, NP; Huston Interview, September 2, 1988.

41. SSC, *Hearings*, 3:937; Huston Interview, September 1, 1988; Helms Interview, July 14, 1988.

42. Ehrlichman to Hoover, April 14, 1969, Hoover to Ehrlichman, April 28, 1969. Chotiner File, FBI.

43. Loch K. Johnson, *A Season of Inquiry: The Senate Intelligence Investigation* (Lexing-

ton, KY, 1985), 85; William C. Sullivan, *The Bureau: My Thirty Years in Hoover's FBI* (New York, 1979), 211–16; Neil J. Welch and David W. Marston, *Inside Hoover's FBI: The Top Field Chief Reports* (New York, 1984), 153; Dean, *Blind Ambition*, 37.

44. Helms Interview, July 14, 1988; Huston Interview, September 1, 1988; Liddy to Krogh, October 22, 1971, Young Papers, Box 21, NP; Ehrlichman Notes, December 18, 1972, Box 13, Ehrlichman Papers, NP; Nixon's version of his presidential relationship and dealings with Hoover are in his *Memoirs*, 2:70–76; Carl Stern Report (based on Nixon Papers), NBC News, February 12, 1987; Johnson, *Season of Inquiry*, 293. Sullivan, *The Bureau*, 199, raises the possibility of Hoover's blackmailing of Nixon. Nixon's concern for Sullivan's silence is in Ehrlichman Notes, October 25, 1971, Box 5, Ehrlichman Papers, NP.

45. Ehrlichman, *Witness to Power*, 167–68.

46. Sullivan, *The Bureau*, 217; Senate Select Committee on Intelligence Activities, *Hearings*, 2:32, 45; Ovid Demaris, *The Director: An Oral Biography of J. Edgar Hoover* (New York, 1975), 251, 304; Johnson, *Season of Inquiry*, 86.

47. TT, the President and Dean, February 28, 1973 (9:12 A.M.–10:23 A.M.), *Transcripts of Eight Recorded Presidential Conversations*, Committee on the Judiciary, H.R., 93 Cong., 2 Sess. (May–June 1974), 28.

V: "I WANT IT DONE, WHATEVER THE COST":
ENEMIES, PLUMBERS, TAPS, AND SPIES

1. Nixon Notes, November 28, 1970, December 6, 1970, NPF, Box 186, NP.

2. "Six Month Compilation of Activities," Caulfield to Ehrlichman, October 8, 1969, Krogh Papers, Box 6, NP; Caulfield to Ehrlichman, September 10, 1969, Ehrlichman Papers, Box 20, NP; Ehrlichman to Dent, April 17, 1969, Dent Papers, Box 1, NP; John D. Ehrlichman, *Witness to Power* (New York, 1982), 292. Caulfield himself described his extensive activities in a series of interviews with the Special Prosecutor in 1973. Interviews, July 2, 18, 25, October 17, November 29, 1973, Caulfield Witness File and Henry Ruth Files, WGSPF Records, NA.

3. Dean Memorandum, "Dealing With Our Political Enemies," August 16, 1971; Colson to Dean, September 9, 1971; Dean to Larry Higby, September 14, 1971, in SSC, *Hearings*, 4:1689–98; Dean Testimony, *ibid.* (June 28, 1973), 4:1527, 1529. Butterfield to Dean, October 6, 1972, Dean Papers, Box 6, NP.

4. Colson in HJC, *Testimony of Witnesses* (July 16, 1974), 3:453; "Blacklist," Box 38, Colson Papers, NP; see, for example, memoranda of Lyn Nofziger (April 21, 1971), Joan Gordon (March 9, 1971), Tom Huston (January 25, 1971), Colson (August 27, 1970, December 17, 1970).

5. J. Anthony Lukas, *Nightmare: The Underside of the Nixon Years* (New York, 1976), 12–18; Dean Testimony, SSC *Hearings;* 3:1073–74, 4:1529; John Dean, *Blind Ambition* (New York, 1976), 316; Robert Pack, *Edward Bennett Williams: For the Defense* (New York, 1983), 14–15; Nixon in *Newsweek*, April 16, 1984, 37. "I want Moe Annenberg for dinner," FDR told his Treasury Secretary, regarding an income-tax prosecution of an unfriendly newspaper publisher. Ted Morgan, *FDR: A Biography* (New York, 1985), 555–56.

6. *Final Report*, Select Committee on Presidential Campaign Activities, U.S. Senate, 93 Cong., 2 Sess., 135–43. Hereafter cited as SSC, *Final Report*. Dean and Colson's various notes on the subject are in Dean Papers, Box 30, NP; Caulfield to Dean, September 30, 1971, *ibid.;* Clark Mollenhoff Interview, November 27, 1973, Plumbers Task Force, WGSPF Records, NA.

7. Fred Fielding to Dean, September 9, 1971, Dean Papers, Box 30, NP; IRS Talking Paper, prepared by Dean for Haldeman, SSC, *Hearings*, 4:1382, Exhibit 44, 1682–85.

8. Ehrlichman Notes, August 3, 1972, Ehrlichman Papers, Box 12, *ibid.*, December 7, 1972, Box 13, NP.

9. TT, The President and Haldeman, May 5, 1971, printed in *NYT*, September 24, 1981 (story by Seymour Hersh). The transcript is an apparently rough one, but points very clearly to a much seamier conversation on the full tape recording.

10. Richard Nixon, *RN: The Memoirs of Richard Nixon* (paperback ed., New York, 1979), 1:478; H. R. Haldeman, *The Ends of Power* (New York, 1978), 11-12; Colson's remark is in Lukas, *Nightmare*, 71.

11. Caulfield to Haldeman, February 11, 1971, Ehrlichman Papers, Box 30, NP.

12. Colson to Ehrlichman, July 22, 1971, Ehrlichman Papers, Box 17, NP; Colson to Ehrlichman, July 16, 1971, Colson Papers, Box 7, NP.

13. Haldeman Notes, September 18, 1971, Haldeman Papers, Box 44, NP; Nixon, *Memoirs*, 1:629; Sanford Ungar, *The Papers and the Papers* (New York, 1975), 27; Laird's and Nixon's comments are in Ehrlichman's Handwritten Notes, HJC, *Statement of Information*, Appendix III:106, 108; Leslie H. Gelb, "Today's Lessons from the Pentagon Papers," *Life*, September 17, 1971; *NYT*, January 17, 1971.

14. Nixon, *Memoirs*, 629-34; Henry Kissinger, *Years of Upheaval* (Boston, 1979), 116-17; Ehrlichman Notes, August 11, 1971, Ehrlichman Papers, Box 12, NP.

15. *New York Times Co. v. U.S.*, 403 U.S. 713 (1971); Griswold Interview, May 4, 1987.

16. Caulfield Testimony, SSC, *Hearings*, 22:10356-61; Dean, *Blind Ambition*, 44-49; Ehrlichman, *Witness to Power*, 403; Dean to Krogh, July 27, 1971, Dean Papers, Box 30, NP.

17. Nixon, *Memoirs*, 1:635-36; Kissinger, *Years of Upheaval*, 115-16; Nixon to Ehrlichman in Haldeman, *Ends of Power*, 112; Dent Interview, September 24, 1986; Krogh Statement to the Court, January 24, 1974; Krogh Interview, August 20, 1986.

18. *WP*, December 8, 1972; Krogh Testimony, *Nominations: January 1973*, Hearings, Committee on Commerce, U.S. Senate, 93 Cong., 1 Sess. (January 11, 1973), 74-90; Ehrlichman Testimony, SSC, *Hearings*, 6:2529.

19. Colson to Ehrlichman, July 22, 1971, Ehrlichman Papers, Box 17, NP.

20. Helms Interview, July 14, 1988; Krogh's affidavit is discussed in *Nomination of Elliot L. Richardson to be Attorney General*, Hearings, Committee on the Judiciary, U.S. Senate, 93 Cong., 1 Sess. (May 22, 1973), 244-46; Krogh's more formal statement to the District Court came on January 24, 1974. Krogh Interview, August 20, 1986. Ehrlichman, *Witness to Power*, 399-407; Haldeman, *Ends of Power*, 114, raises the distinct possibility that the President authorized the break-in. Ehrlichman Notes, May 2, 1973, Ehrlichman Papers, Box 14, NP; HJC, *Testimony of Witnesses*, 3:54; Nixon's versions of events can be found in Nixon, *Memoirs*, 1:637, and in the account of his 1977 television interviews, described by David Frost, *"I Gave Them a Sword": Behind the Scenes of the Nixon Interviews* (New York, 1978), 281ff.

21. Jaworski Memoir, 5:936-37, Jaworski MS, Baylor University; William Merrill to Edward Soden, December 17, 1973, *ibid.* (re Krogh and Liddy); Ehrlichman-Richardson Telephone Conversation, April 30, 1973, Summary in Richardson MS, LC; Young's statements and Richardson's conclusions are in Elliot Richardson's Notes, May 1, 1973, Administrative Files, WGSPF, NA; Richardson to Assistant Attorney General Petersen, April 25, 1973, Richardson MS, LC; Ehrlichman to Colson, August 27, 1971, Ehrlichman Papers, Box 57, NP. Howard Hunt's grand jury testimony was released on May 4, 1973, and detailed the operational side of events; *NYT*, May 5, 1973. General Robert Cushman's testimony described the CIA's connection: SSC, *Hearings*, 8:3289-3311.

22. Jim Hougan, *Secret Agenda: Watergate, Deep Throat and the CIA* (New York, 1984), 65-76, attached significant importance to the affair.

23. Athan G. Theoharis and John Cox, *The Boss: J. Edgar Hoover and the Great American Inquisition* (Philadelphia, 1988), 417; Krogh Interview, August 20, 1986.

24. Moorer Interview, June 25, 1985; Elmo R. Zumwalt, Jr., *On Watch* (New York, 1976), xiv.

25. *Transmittal of Documents from the National Security Council to the Chairman of the Joint Chiefs of Staff,* Hearings, Committee on Armed Services, U.S. Senate, 93 Cong., 2 Sess. (February 6, 20, 21 March 7, 1974); Moorer Interview, June 25, 1985; Welander "Confession," in Ehrlichman Papers, Box 6, NP; Laird Interview, June 27, 1985; Nixon, *Memoirs,* 1:660; Ehrlichman, *Witness to Power,* 302–08; Raymond L. Garthoff, *Detente and Confrontation: American-Soviet Relations from Nixon to Reagan* (Washington, D.C., 1985), 410; Ehrlichman Notes, January 5, 6, 1972, Ehrlichman Papers, Box 6, NP; Nixon to Kissinger, November 12, 1971, Haldeman Papers, Box 140, NP. (The President preferred to talk about national-defense matters to Moorer without Laird present.)

26. Mitchell Interview, April 11, 1988; Ehrlichman Notes, December 23, 1971, January 5, 6, 1972, Ehrlichman Papers, Box 6, NP; Henry Ruth to Carl Feldbaum, October 7, 1975, SP Files: Jack Anderson, WGSPF Records, NA; Symington in Committee on Armed Services, *Transmittal of Documents,* 6; Hougan, *Secret Agenda,* xviii; Joseph C. Spear, *Presidents and the Press: The Nixon Legacy* (Cambridge, MA, 1984), 135; Ehrlichman, *Witness to Power,* 305; Kissinger, *Years of Upheaval,* 807–09. The "blackmail" incident is described in a memo, Richard Tufaro to Leonard Garment, May 14, 1973, and other memos, furnished by Mr. Garment. Nixon later expressed outright contempt for the Pentagon's handling of the Vietnam war. Richard Nixon, *No More Vietnams* (New York, 1985).

27. *NYT,* May 11, 1973, 1, 18, 19; Nixon, *Memoirs,* 1:478–479; Kissinger, *Years of Upheaval,* 115–16.

28. William Sullivan to J. Edgar Hoover, Gray/Wiretap Investigation, Martin Files, WGSPF Records, NA. Transcripts exist of a Kissinger "spy" reporting on Haig's activities.

29. Martin to the Files, October 10, 1975, WGSPF Records, NA; Sullivan to Hoover, May 20, 1969, Gray/Wiretap Investigation, Young Witness File, Plumbers Task Force, WGSPF Records, NA; Powers, *Secrecy and Power,* 444–48; *NYT,* May 15, 16, 17, 1973; Nixon, *Memoirs,* 1:481; Clarence M. Kelley, *The Story of an FBI Director* (Kansas City, 1987), 155; *WP,* August 6, 1977.

30. Dent to Mitchell, June 17, 1969, Dent Papers, Box 1, NP; Caulfield to Ehrlichman, June 20, 1969, Krogh Papers, Box 66, NP; Butterfield to Krogh, June 6, 1970, Krogh Papers, Box 14, NP.

31. Christopher Pyle, "Military Surveillance of Civilian Politics, 1967–1970." Ph.D. Dissertation, Columbia University, 1974.

32. *Federal Data Banks, Computers, and the Bill of Rights,* Hearings, Committee on the Judiciary, U.S. Senate, 92 Cong., 1 Sess. (February–March 1971), 597–624, 849–914; *ibid.,* Army Regulation No. 381-115 (Delimitations Agreement), July 2, 1969, 1172–75.

33. *Laird v. Tatum,* 408 U.S. 1 (1972). Rehnquist's refusal to disqualify himself is in 409 U.S. 829 (1972). The later revelations of Rehnquist's role, and its ethical implications, are discussed in the *Los Angeles Times,* September 5, 1986, and in a letter from Yale Law Professor Geoffrey C. Hazard, Jr., to Senator Charles Mathias, September 8, 1986. Copy provided by Professor Hazard.

34. John T. Eliff, *Crime, Dissent, and the Attorney General: The Justice Department in the 1960's* (Beverly Hills, CA, 1971), 206–37.

35. *United States v. United States District Court for the Eastern District of Michigan,* 407 U.S. 297 (1972). Arguments are in Records and Briefs. The Circuit Court's ruling is in 444 F. 2d 651 (6th Circ. 1971). Griswold Interview, May 4, 1987. The lead defense lawyer, Arthur Kinoy, has written an invaluable account of the proceedings: *Rights on Trial: Odyssey*

of a People's Lawyer (Cambridge, 1983), Ch. 1. Ehrlichman Notes, June 20, 1972, Ehrlichman Papers, Box 6, NP. Attorney General Kleindienst claimed that he promptly terminated all wiretaps that conflicted with the Court's ruling. He also said that similarly unauthorized programs had existed for twenty-six years. *NYT,* June 20, 22, 1972. Judge Keith rendered a landmark school-desegregation decision involving housing patterns: *Davis v. School District of Pontiac,* 309 F. Supp. 734 (E. D. Mich. 1970).

VI: THE POLITICS OF DEADLOCK: NIXON AND CONGRESS

1. Arthur M. Schlesinger, Jr., *A Thousand Days: John F. Kennedy in the White House* (Boston, 1965), 712; Rowland Evans, Jr., and Robert D. Novak, *Nixon in the White House* (New York, 1971), 105–110.

2. Richard Nixon, *RN: The Memoirs of Richard Nixon* (paperback ed., New York, 1979), 1:512.

3. Dwight D. Eisenhower, *Mandate for Change, 1953–1956* (New York, 1963), 565; Nixon, *Memoirs,* 1:515–17.

4. Dwight D. Eisenhower, *Waging Peace, 1956–1961* (New York, 1965), 479, 37, 45, 272; Nixon, *Memoirs,* 1:559.

5. Nixon to Colson and Haldeman, January 28, 1972, NPF, Box 3, NP; Richard J. Whalen, *Catch the Falling Flag: A Republican's Challenge to His Party* (Boston, 1972), 254.

6. James MacGregor Burns, *The Deadlock of Democracy* (Englewood Cliffs, NJ, 1963).

7. Richard Nixon, *A New Road for America* (New York, 1972), 519–46.

8. *Ibid.,* 519–20; *NYT,* September 11, 1970, Nixon, *Memoirs,* 1:608.

9. Alexander Bickel, "Watergate and the Legal Order," in Lawrence M. Friedman and Stewart Macauley (eds.), *Law and Behavioral Sciences* (2d ed., New York, 1977), 227.

10. Nixon to Ehrlichman, March 13, 1969, NPF, Box 1, NP; Butterfield to Charles Wilkinson, July 16, 1969, Dent Papers, Box 1, NP.

11. The best historical survey of impoundment is in Louis Fisher, "Impoundment of Funds: Uses and Abuses," 23 Buffalo Law Review 141–70 (1973). Also useful for many of the official quotations that follow is the compilation prepared by the House Judiciary Committee during the Impeachment Inquiry: HJC, *Statement of Information,* Book 12.

12. Louis Fisher, *Constitutional Conflicts Between Congress and the President* (Princeton, NJ, 1985), 236; *Opinions of Attorneys General* (February 25, 1967), 42:347–56.

13. James L. Sundquist, *The Decline and Resurgence of Congress* (Washington, D.C., 1981), 204–06.

14. Dapray Muir to John Dean, June 23, 1971, Dean Papers, Box 39, NP.

15. Sundquist, *Decline and Resurgence of Congress,* 206–07. See *Executive Impoundment of Appropriated Funds,* Hearings, Subcommittee on Separations of Powers, Committee on the Judiciary, U.S. Senate, 92 Cong., 1 Sess. (March 1971).

16. Ehrlichman Notes, October 18, 1972, Ehrlichman Papers, Box 13, NP; "Impoundment of Appropriated Funds," Ad Hoc Subcommittee of Government Operations and Judiciary Committees, U.S. Senate, 93 Cong., 1 Sess. (January 30, 1973), 363, 369, 381, 839–841 (Sneed).

17. Ehrlichman Notes, February 28, 1973, Ehrlichman Papers, Box 28, NP.

18. HJC, *Statement of Information,* 12:88–91. The Supreme Court unanimously held some impoundments improper in *Train v. City of New York,* 420 U.S. 35 (1975). The Congressional Budget and Impoundment Control Act of 1974 is discussed in Chapter XXI, *infra.*

19. Peri Arnold, *Making the Managerial Presidency* (Princeton, 1986), 272–73. Richard P. Nathan, *The Plot That Failed: Nixon and the Administrative Presidency* (New York, 1975),

offered a shrewd assessment by a scholar-participant of Nixon's plans to weaken the decision-making power of the bureaucracy and correspondingly to focus it in the White House or in state and local governments.

20. Advisory Council on Executive Organization to Nixon, August 20, 1969, File Group PACEO, NCF, NP.

21. William Safire, *Before the Fall* (New York, 1975), 261–62; Garment Interview, May 29, 1985; Ken Cole to John Ehrlichman, June 15, 1971, Ehrlichman Papers, Box 57, NP; Cabinet Meeting, January 18, 1971, Executive Reorganization File, NCF, Box 34, NP.

22. *Reorganization Plan No. 2 of 1970,* Hearings, U.S. Senate, Committee on Government Operations, U.S. Senate, 91 Cong., 2 Sess.; Evans and Novak, *Nixon in the White House,* 240; Harold Seidman, *Politics, Position, and Power: The Dynamics of Federal Organization* (New York, 1975), 74; A. James Reichley, *Conservatives in an Age of Change* (Washington, D.C., 1981), 239; Arnold, *Making the Managerial Presidency,* 283. The Nixon Central Files have the extensive working and final papers of the Ash Commission, some of which appear in public documents.

23. Arnold, *Making the Managerial Presidency,* 285–86; Reichley, *Conservatives in an Age of Change,* 238–41; Nathan, *The Plot That Failed, passim.*

24. Arnold, *Making the Managerial Presidency,* 300.

25. Charles L. Clapp to Egil Krogh, March 4, 1971, PACEO, NCF, NP.

26. Barry D. Karl, "The Nixon Fault," *Reviews in American History* (June 1979), 7:143, 151; Arnold, *Making the Managerial Presidency,* 301–02; Joel D. Aberbach and Bert A. Rockman, "Clashing Beliefs Within the Executive Branch," *American Political Science Review,* July 1976, 70:456–68.

27. Roy P. Basler (ed.), *The Collected Works of Abraham Lincoln* (New Brunswick, NJ, 1953), 2:495.

28. Fortas Interview, April 27, 1967, Fred Graham MS, LC; Bruce Allen Murphy, *Fortas: The Rise and Ruin of a Supreme Court Justice* (New York, 1988); Robert Shogan, *A Question of Judgment: The Fortas Case and the Struggle for the Supreme Court* (Indianapolis, IN, 1972).

29. Lyndon B. Johnson, *The Vantage Point: Perspectives of the Presidency, 1963–1969* (New York, 1971), 545–46; Murphy, *Fortas,* 234–304.

30. Warren Interview, September 23, 1968, Fred Graham MS, LC; Nixon, *Memoirs,* 1:518.

31. Stewart Interview, April 18, 1970, Fred Graham MS, LC.

32. James F. Simon, *In His Own Image: The Supreme Court in Richard Nixon's America* (New York, 1973), 76–92, has a good summary of Burger's court and public writings before 1969; Nixon, *Memoirs,* 1:519.

33. *PPPUS:RN, 1969,* 391–96; *NYT,* July 1, 1972. The idea of broad construction has its roots in Madison's *Federalist* 44: "No axiom is more clearly established in law, or in reason, that whenever a general power to do a thing is given, every particular power necessary for doing it is included." The principle gave a cue for John Marshall.

34. Murphy, *Fortas,* 568–71; Petersen Interview, December 24, 1969, Fred Graham MS, LC; Petersen Telephone Interview, May 6, 1987; Burger to Nixon, May 8, 1969, Executive FG-51, Supreme Court, NCF, NP.

35. Buchanan to Nixon, May 6, 1969, Executive FG-51, Supreme Court, NCF, NP.

36. Dent to Tom Charles Huston, June 16, 1969, Dent Papers, Box 5, NP. Simon, *In His Own Image,* 105–12, offers a fair summary of Haynesworth's voting record.

37. Nyle Jackson to Dent, October 24, Dent Papers, Box 6, NP; Nixon to Brooke, October 2, 1969, FG-51, Supreme Court, NCF, NP; Nixon, *Memoirs,* 521.

38. Kirk to Nixon, May 31, 1969, NPF, Box 188, NP; "Tentative Plan: Carswell Nomination," March 18, 1970, Dent Papers, Box 11, NP.

39. *George Harrold Carswell*, Hearings, Committee on the Judiciary, U.S. Senate, 91 Cong., 2 Sess. (January 29, February 2, 1970), 114, 238–39, 240–42; *PPPUS:RN, 1970*, January 30, 1970, 39; Ehrlichman Notes, March 26, 1970, Ehrlichman Papers, Box 10, NP.

40. *PPPPUS:RN, 1970*, 345; Simon, *In His Own Image*, 99–101; Evans and Novak, *Nixon*, 165–72. Safire, *Before the Fall*, 269–71, has an interesting account of the President's reaction, crediting him with adding the inflammatory language about the Senate. On June 30, 1987, President Reagan's Chief of Staff and Attorney General met with four senators to discuss a list of possible nominees for a Supreme Court vacancy.

41. Dole to Nixon, April 14, 1970, FG-51, Supreme Court, NCF, NP; Nixon to Haldeman, April 13, 1970, NPF, Box 2, NP; Stewart Interview, April 18, 1970, Fred Graham MS, LC.

42. Jerald F. terHorst, *Gerald Ford and the Future of the Presidency* (New York, 1974), 123–25; *Nomination of Gerald R. Ford to be Vice President*, Hearings, Committee on the Judiciary, House of Representatives, 93 Cong., 1 Sess. (November 15–26, 1973), 619; Becker Interview, December 5, 1985, and Becker to Author, March 28, 1986; Harlow to William Timmons, June 2, 1970, Executive FG-51, Supreme Court, NCF, NP; Murphy, *Fortas*, 579; Athan G. Theoharis and John Stuart Cox, *The Boss: J. Edgar Hoover and the Great American Inquisition* (Philadelphia, 1988), 406; Hoover to Mitchell, August 17, 1970, Douglas Impeachment, FBI Files.

43. *Congressional Record* (April 15, 1970), 116:11912–17; *Legal Materials on Impeachment*, Committee on the Judiciary, House of Representatives, 91 Cong., 2 Sess. (August 11, 1970).

44. Krogh to Ehrlichman, September 24, 1971, Young Papers, Box 17, NP; questionnaire dated October 13, 1971, in FG-51, Supreme Court, NCF, NP. John Ehrlichman, *Witness to Power* (New York, 1982), 122–39, discussed Supreme Court appointments and stated that the President wanted Ehrlichman to supervise nominations—to take on "the added burden of being Mitchell's keeper," as Ehrlichman sarcastically stated. Given the way the Nixon White House worked, Ehrlichman had Krogh devise a plan that Ehrlichman probably then presented to the President—as if it were Nixon's own idea.

45. Julie Nixon Eisenhower, *Pat Nixon: The Untold Story* (New York, 1986), 132.

46. Buchanan to Nixon, September 29, 1971, Garment to Nixon, September 30, 1971, Kleindienst to Lawrence Walsh, September 29, 1971, FG-51, Supreme Court, NCF, NP.

47. Dent to Mitchell, June 17, 1969, Dent Papers, Box 1, NP; Nixon to Ehrlichman, June 18, 1969, NPF, Box 1, NP; Simon, *In His Own Image*, 237; Ehrlichman Notes, Ehrlichman Papers, Box 15, NP; Mitchell Interview, February 9, 1988.

48. Bayh to Nixon, November 4, 1971, FG-51/A, Supreme Court, NCF, NP; William Rehnquist, "The Making of a Supreme Court Justice," *Harvard Law Record*, October 8, 1959, 29:10; Ehrlichman Notes, December 18, 1972, Ehrlichman Papers, Box 13, NP. During Rehnquist's 1986 Chief Justice confirmation hearings, senators learned that Rehnquist had proposed a constitutional amendment to validate "freedom of choice" and antibusing schemes to skirt desegregation. He also had denounced the proposed Equal Rights Amendment on the grounds that it would "hasten the dissolution of the family." *NYT*, September 9, 19, 1986.

49. Ehrlichman Notes, November 22, 1972, Box 13, NP; March 6, 1973, Ehrlichman Papers, Box 14, NP. Burger remained as Chief Justice until 1986, when he decided—or was prevailed upon—to retire. The Reagan Administration found more government service for him as head of the Bicentennial Commission for the Constitution.

50. Louis Fisher, *Constitutional Conflicts Between the President and Congress* (Princeton, NJ, 1985), 26; also see Theodore J. Lowi, *The Personal President: Power Invested, Promise Unfulfilled* (Ithaca, NY, 1985).

51. Henry Kissinger, *Years of Upheaval* (Boston, 1982), 88–89; Ehrlichman Notes, March 16, 1973, Ehrlichman Papers, Box 13, NP.

52. Nixon, *Memoirs*, 1:511.

53. See Safire, *Before the Fall*, 212–20, for an account of the Lincoln Memorial incident.

54. Nixon to Haldeman, March 2, 1970, NPF, Box 2, NP; *Congressional Quarterly Almanac* (1969), 25:177–78; *ibid.* (1970), 26:970.

55. Butterfield to the Cabinet, May 7, 1970, Dent Papers, Box 4, NP.

56. Fisher, *Constitutional Conflicts*, 157.

57. Nixon to Colson and Haldeman, January 28, 1972, NPF, Box 3, NP; Ehrlichman Notes, December 2, 1972, Ehrlichman Papers, Box 13, NP.

58. *Congressional Quarterly Almanac* (1973), 29:908.

59. Arthur M. Schlesinger, Jr., *The Imperial Presidency* (Boston, 1973), 207; Fisher, *Conflicts Between Congress and the Presidency*, 115.

60. Nixon to Haldeman, March 12, 1973, NPF, Box 4, NP. Some months later, Treasury Secretary George Shultz indicated his reluctance to carry out such a program. Shultz to Rose Mary Woods, August 16, 1973, NPF, Box 186, NP. Ehrlichman Notes, January 4, 5, 1973, Ehrlichman Papers, Box 14, NP. Nixon, *Memoirs*, 2:275.

VII: MEDIA WARS

1. William Safire, *Before the Fall* (New York, 1975), 466; Ehrlichman Notes, March 16, 1973, Ehrlichman Papers, Box 13, NP; Richard M. Nixon, *Six Crises* (New York, 1962), 69.

2. Herbert G. Klein, *Making It Perfectly Clear* (New York, 1980), 39–42, 213.

3. Nixon to Haldeman, November 30, 1970, Nixon Papers, Box 2, NP.

4. Michael R. Beschloss, *Mayday: The U-2 Affair* (New York, 1986), 342; Ron Ziegler and Larry Higby to Nixon and Haldeman, March 14, 1970, Nixon Papers, Box 185, NP; Nixon to Haldeman, March 2, 1970 (two memoranda), NPF, Box 2, NP; Nixon to Haldeman, April 14, 1972, *ibid.*, Box 3; Nixon to Herb Kaplow, July 16, 1972, Nixon Papers, Box 10, NP; Transcript, telephone conversation, Haldeman and James Shepley, January 18, 1971, Haldeman Papers, Box 177, NP.

5. Nixon to Haldeman, January 14, 1971, June 15, 1971, April 14, 1972, NPF, Box 3, NP; Haldeman Notes, September 25, 1971, Haldeman Papers, Box 44, NP.

6. Ben H. Bagdikian, *The Media Monopoly* (Boston, 1983), 97–102; Nixon to Peter Flanigan, September 22, 1969, NPF, Box 1, NP.

7. Rowland Evans, Jr. and Robert D. Novak, *Nixon in the White House* (New York, 1971), 409; Ehrlichman Notes, December 8, 1972, Ehrlichman Papers, Box 13, NP; William J. Small, *Political Power and the Press* (New York, 1972), 90–91.

8. Jules Witcover, *The Resurrection of Richard Nixon* (New York, 1971), 151–52; Timothy Crouse, *The Boys on the Bus* (New York, 1973), 192, 195; Hart Interview, September 11, 1986; Stephen E. Ambrose, *Nixon: The Education of a Politician, 1913–1962* (New York, 1987), 671–74.

9. Joseph C. Spear, *Presidents and the Press: The Nixon Legacy* (Cambridge, 1984), 89; Nixon to Haldeman, March 1, 1971, NPF, Box 3, NP.

10. Nixon to Ehrlichman, January 25, 1969, February 4, 1969, February 5, 1969; to Haldeman, February 13, 1969, November 24, 1969; to Ehrlichman, March 11, 1969, NPF, Box 1, NP; Nixon to Haldeman, March 2, 1970, NPF, Box 2, NP.

11. Stanley Karnow, "The Chinese Sayings of President Richard Nixon," *WP*, February

29, 1972; Spear, *Presidents and the Press*, 99–100; *NYT*, September 10, 1987, for Nixon's attempt to explain the context of his remarks.

12. Haldeman to Krogh, July 1, 1970, Haldeman Papers, Box 273, NP; Samuel Kernell and Samuel Popkin, *Chief of Staff: Twenty-five Years of Managing the Presidency* (Berkeley, CA, 1986), 83.

13. Nixon to Haldeman, January 31, 1970, NPF, Box 2, NP; Nixon to Ehrlichman, March 11, 1969, NPF, Box 1, NP; Klein, *Making It Perfectly Clear*, 126.

14. Robert C. Hilderbrand, *The Papers of Woodrow Wilson: The Complete Press Conferences, 1913–1919*, vol. 50 (Princeton, 1985), 3, 5, ix–x, xiii.

15. Kenneth S. Davis, *FDR: The New Deal Years, 1933–1937* (New York, 1986), 35, 43–46, 186–87.

16. Robert J. Donovan, *Conflict and Crisis: The Presidency of Harry S Truman, 1945–1948* (New York, 1977), 118–19, 132–33, 163, 165, 175–76.

17. Stephen E. Ambrose, *Eisenhower: The President* (New York, 1984), 52–54.

18. Arthur M. Schlesinger, Jr., *A Thousand Days: John F. Kennedy in the White House* (Boston, 1965), 716–19.

19. Nixon to Haldeman, January 14, 1971, NPF, Box 3, NP; Nixon to Buchanan, August 23, 1973, NPF, Box 6, NP.

20. Spear, *Presidents and the Press*, 83–84.

21. Nixon to Ehrlichman, June 16, 1969, NPF, Box 1, NP; Safire, *Before the Fall*, 353; Spear, *Presidents and the Press*, 154.

22. Robert H. Ferrell and Howard H. Quint (eds.), *The Talkative President: The Off-the-Record Press Conferences of Calvin Coolidge* (Amherst, 1964), 28.

23. Nixon to Haldeman, October 1, 1969, November 24, 1969, NPF, Box 1, January 6, 1970, January 31, 1970, March 2, 1970, NPF, Box 2, NP. The "friendlies list" is dated January 6, 1971: Strachan Papers, Box 3, NP. See Klein, *Making It Perfectly Clear*, 125–28, for a Higby/Haldeman memo to Klein, September 16, 1970, that directly used remarks contained in the President's memos to Haldeman. The homosexual story was discovered by a scholar researching FBI files: *WP*, December 23, 1987.

24. Jeb Stuart Magruder, *An American Life: One Man's Road to Watergate* (New York, 1974), 1–56, 97, 90. The memo is published in SSC, *Final Report*, 267–68.

25. Safire, *Before the Fall*, 352; Klein, *Making It Perfectly Clear*, 169–73.

26. Evans and Novak, *Nixon*, 315–17; Klein, *Making It Perfectly Clear*, 171–73, Spear, *Presidents and the Press*, 120–21; Safire, *Before the Fall*, 353; Haldeman to Nixon, December 1, 1970, Haldeman Papers, Box 48, NP; Price to Nixon, November 13, 1970, NPF, Box 185, NP; Julie Nixon Eisenhower, *Pat Nixon: The Untold Story* (New York, 1986), 277; Colson to Haldeman, May 20, 1971, Colson Papers, Box 2, NP; *Broadcasting*, November 20, 1972, 8:2.

27. Spear, *Presidents and the Press*, 116–17; Klein, *Making It Perfectly Clear*, 172–75.

28. Spear, *Presidents and the Press*, 140–43; Klein, *Making It Perfectly Clear*, 335; Nixon to Haldeman, March 8, 1970, Haldeman Papers, Box 48, NP.

29. Ziegler to Schorr, August 14, 1972, J. Edgar Hoover to Senator Sam Ervin, January 27, 1972, Dean Papers, Box 65, NP; Bob Haynes to Ehrlichman [?], December 17, 1971, Ehrlichman Papers, Box 26, NP; TT, the President and Ziegler, June 4, 1973, HJC, *Statement of Information*, 9:203–04 (commenting about the March 13, 1973, tape recording); Daniel Schorr, *Clearing the Air* (Boston, 1977), 80–87.

30. Nixon to Haldeman, March 10, 1973, NPF, Box 4, NP. Shakespeare to Hart, October 16, 1972, Hart to Shakespeare, October 18, 1972, Shakespeare to Hart, November 1, 1972, Salant to Shakespeare, October 19, 1972, Internal Revenue Service to Hart, October 16, 1972. (Materials courtesy of John Hart.) Also Hart Interviews, September 11, 18, 1986. Joe McGinniss, *The Selling of the President* (paperback ed., New York, 1970), 42–43, 56, dis-

cusses Shakespeare's 1968 comments. Frank Stanton, President of CBS, and Shakespeare had a friendly relationship. Stanton to Senate Foreign Relations Committee, April 28, 1972, USIA Files.

31. John J. O'Connor, "The TV Antitrust Suits," *NYT*, April 17, 1972; *Broadcasting*, April 17, 1972, 82:21; *U.S. v. National Broadcasting Company, et al.*, U.S. District Court, Central District of California, November 26, 1974; *Broadcasting*, December 16, 1974, 87:24; *ibid.* May 12, 1980, 98:29; Klein, *Making It Perfectly Clear*, 215–16. Hollander Telephone Interview, August 7, 1986. Hollander was a longtime lawyer in the Anti-Trust Division and had served through numerous administrations.

32. Ehrlichman Notes, October 16, 1972, Ehrlichman Papers, Box 13, NP; Spear, *Presidents and the Press*, 150–51.

33. Safire, *Before the Fall*, 341; Nixon to Haldeman, November 15, 1972, Haldeman Papers, Box 179, NP; Nixon to Gary Hart, May 11, 1987, in *NYT*, July 15, 1987.

VIII: "WE SHOULD COME UP WITH . . . IMAGINATIVE DIRTY TRICKS." THE WATERGATE BREAK-IN

1. The FBI's Watergate investigation records contain over 16,000 pages. I have used the Washington Field Office's first week-reports to follow the Bureau's activity and the unfolding of salient facts. Jim Hougan, *Secret Agenda* (New York, 1984), offers the best account of the break-in and a careful reading of the FBI record. The newspaper accounts clearly indicate that reporters had almost immediate access to the FBI reports. The *Post's* reporting is ably summarized in Bob Woodward and Carl Bernstein, *All The President's Men* (New York, 1974).

2. President's Daily Diary, NP; Dent Interviews, September 24, October 31, 1986; Jaworski Oral History, Texas Collection, Baylor University, 2:441–43; *WP*, June 18, 1972.

3. Richard Nixon, *RN: The Memoirs of Richard Nixon* (paperback ed., New York, 1979), 2:113; Keating to Gray, June 19, 1972, Gray to Keating, June 22, 1972, FBI Watergate Papers.

4. TT, the President and Colson, June 20, 1972, *WP*, May 1, 1977; TT, the President and Colson, January 8, 1973 (4:05 P.M.–5:34 P.M.), *US v. M*, NA. Magruder had a transcript of a tapped telephone call between someone at CREEP and someone else at Democratic headquarters. It is likely that Nixon heard of this. Jeb Stuart Magruder, *An American Life* (New York, 1974), 229.

5. TT, the President, Haldeman, and Mitchell, June 30, 1971, HJC, *Statement of Information*, 2:514–16; TT, Dictabelt of President's recollections of telephone conversation with Mitchell, June 20, 1972, HJC Transcript, William Dixon Collection, SUNY–Buffalo Law Library; Harry Dent, *The Prodigal South Returns to Power* (New York, 1978), 242. Former Cabinet member George Romney said in 1984 that Martha Mitchell had persuaded John Mitchell to resign because she had learned that CREEP was spending money to help McGovern win the primaries. *People*, August 6, 1984.

6. James J. Kilpatrick, *Washington Star*, May 14, 1974; Butterfield Testimony, July 2, 1974, HJC, *Testimony of Witnesses*, 1:52–53.

7. Nixon to Buchanan, June 10, 1972, Haldeman Papers, Box 162, NP; Haldeman Background Memo (summarizing notes of meeting with Nixon), October 15, 1972, Haldeman Papers, Box 48, NP; Ray Price to Ehrlichman, July 25, 1972 (Nixon comment on draft evaders) Haldeman Papers, Box 48, NP; Haldeman Notes (special-interest groups), July 21, 1972, Haldeman Papers, Box 46, NP.

8. Nixon to Mitchell, February 15, 1972, NPF, Box 12, NP; Haldeman Memo, Haldeman

Papers, Box 112, NP. Haldeman's notes for his meetings with the President during the campaign are in Boxes 46 and 47. His separate files on the campaign remain closed.

9. Dent Interviews, September 24, October 31, 1986; Mitchell Interview, December 30, 1987.

10. Haldeman Memos, June 10, June 20, July 24, July 26, July 24, September 14, June 25, July 26, August 17, September 16, November 6, 1972, Haldeman Papers, Box 112, NP; Haldeman Notes, September 19, October 15, 1972, Haldeman Papers, Box 46, NP; Ehrlichman Notes, July 5, 1972, Ehrlichman Papers, Box 6, NP. Also see Haldeman Papers, Box 179 for "Presidential Tape Copy of Memos" that link Nixon's instructions to Haldeman's memos. For the President's attention to details, see Haldeman Notes, August 23, 1972, Haldeman Papers, Box 46, NP; Ehrlichman Notes, July 5, 1972, Ehrlichman Papers, Box 12, NP. Nixon, *Memoirs*, 2:213.

11. Ehrlichman Notes, July 26, 1972, Ehrlichman Papers, Box 6, NP; Nixon, *Memoirs*, 2:144.

12. Nixon to Haldeman and Colson, June 6, 1972, Colson Papers, Box 19, NP.

13. Haldeman Notes, July 10, August 17, September 6, 1972, Haldeman Papers, Box 46, NP; Ehrlichman Notes, July 6, July 11, July 20, 1972, Ehrlichman Notes, Box 12, NP; TT, Telephone Conversation, Shultz and Ehrlichman, August 25, 1972, Ehrlichman Papers, Box 28, NP. Nixon to Connally, July 24, 1972, Haldeman Papers, Box 162, NP.

14. Haldeman Notes, July 20, August 16, September 11, October 29, October 30, November 1, 1972, Haldeman Papers, Box 46, NP; Ehrlichman Notes (re Rose Mary Woods and Baker), August 7, 1972, Ehrlichman Papers, Box 12, NP; Haldeman Notes, August 16, 1972, Box 46, NP. Theodore White had thanked Nixon for contributing to his book on the 1968 campaign and pledged full support to the President. White to Nixon, June 27, 1969, NPF, Box 188, NP.

15. Joseph C. Spear, *Presidents and the Press: The Nixon Legacy* (Cambridge, MA, 1984), 178–183, 186; Timothy Crouse, *The Boys on the Bus* (paperback ed., New York, 1974), 272–73, 238–39, 270–71.

16. Haldeman Memo, October 5, 1972, Haldeman Papers, Box 112, NP.

17. Haldeman Notes, August 11, October 28, 1972, Haldeman Papers, Box 46, NP; Spear, *Presidents and the Press*, 179, 149–50; *Broadcasting*, October 30, 1972.

18. Nixon, *Memoirs*, 2:292; 1:614–15.

19. *Los Angeles Times*, May 1, 1973, October 19, 1962; *WP*, August 20, 1973.

20. The Senate Select Committee hearings exposed these operations. The best summary can be found in J. Anthony Lukas, *Nightmare: The Underside of the Nixon Years* (New York, 1976), Chs. 5 and 6. Gordon Strachan Interview, June 18, 1973, SSC Executive Records, NA.

21. SSC, *Final Report*, 240–45.

22. Donald Freed, "Gemstone—the Bottom Line," in Steve Weissman (ed.), *Big Brother and the Holding Company* (Palo Alto, CA, 1974), 91–105.

23. Arthur Kinoy, *Rights on Trial* (Cambridge, MA, 1983), Ch. 1; see Chapter V, *supra*.

24. Helms Interview, July 14, 1988; H. R. Haldeman, *The Ends of Power* (New York, 1978), 109, 25–27. Baker's questions to Director Helms are in SSC, *Hearings*, 8:3266ff.

25. Nixon to Haldeman, May 18, 1972, Haldeman Papers, Box 162, NP.

26. Haldeman, *Ends of Power*, 109, 133–35, 144–47, 159–60, 126.

27. Hougan, *Secret Agenda*, 10–11, 18–19, 168–78, 211–12, 117–19, 220–23, 264. J. Anthony Lukas dissected and analyzed Hougan's assumptions and hypotheses in a lengthy review: *NYT Book Review*, November 11, 1984, 7. When Charles Colson pled guilty on June 3, 1974, he charged that the CIA had "deliberately planted stories" accusing him of criminal involvement.

28. Helms Interview, July 14, 1988; Vernon A. Walters, *Silent Missions* (New York, 1978),

588–89; Colby Interview, October 9, 1987; William Colby, *Honorable Men: My Life in the CIA* (New York, 1978), 321–28; Silbert Telephone Interview, September 30, 1988. Helms was unhappy with Walters's implication that he himself had led the way in blocking White House efforts to have the CIA continue to hamper the FBI investigation when, in fact, he operated under clear orders from Helms. Dean corroborated this in SSC, *Hearings*, 3:945–49. Ironically, Mitchell, whom Nixon, Haldeman, and Ehrlichman had designated as the "fall guy," believed that the CIA had some role in undermining the Administration in the Watergate affair. Mitchell Interview, December 30, 1987. See Chapter IX, *infra*, for a discussion of the CIA role in the cover-up.

29. Colson Papers, Box 97, NP; Haldeman, *Ends of Power*, 19–20, 153–56; *NYT*, January 24, 1972; Haldeman Notes, July 31, 1972, Haldeman Papers, Box 46, NP; Ehrlichman Notes, August 7, 30, 1972, Ehrlichman Papers, Box 13, NP; Nixon to Haldeman, January 14, 1971, NPF, Box 3, NP; Haldeman to Dean, January 18, 1971, Haldeman Papers, Box 196, NP; John Dean, *Blind Ambition* (New York, 1976), 66; Lukas, *Nightmare* (1988 reprint), vii; Magruder Telephone Interview, December 16, 1987.

30. Dean, *Blind Ambition*, 88, 97; Herbert Klein, *Making It Perfectly Clear* (New York, 1980), 329–30; Noah Dietrich and Bob Thomas, *Howard, The Amazing Mr. Hughes* (Greenwich, CT, 1977), 286; Michael Drosin, *Citizen Hughes* (New York, 1985), 417–34.

31. Nixon to Haldeman, August 9, 1972, Haldeman Papers, Box 179, NP.

32. G. Gordon Liddy, *Will* (New York, 1980), 237; McCord Testimony, SSC, *Hearings*, 1:164; Agnew remarks, National Press Club Transcript; Louise Gore to Elias Demetracopoulos, September 27, 1968 (courtesy of Mr. Demetracopoulos); Agnew Interview, January 14, 1989; Democratic National Committee, news release, October 31, 1968: "Nixon-Agnew-Pappas Relationships"; *Boston Globe*, October 31, 1968; *NYT*, October 16, 1968; *New York Daily News*, August 9, 1968; *London Sunday Times*, September 29, 1968. The KYP–CIA connection is discussed most recently in Christopher Simpson, *Blowback: The First Full Account of America's Recruitment of Nazis, and its Disastrous Effect on Our Domestic and Foreign Policy* (New York, 1988), 280. Demetracopoulos Interview, May 5, 1987; Helms Interview, July 14, 1988; Kostas Tsimas, then Deputy Director, KYP, to Author, telephone conversation, January 5, 1987. "I have worked for the CIA anytime my help was requested," Pappas told a Greek interviewer in 1968: Evans and Novak column, *Baltimore Sun*, July 16, 1975.

33. FBI Director William Webster to Representative Don Edwards (D-CA), April 11, 1984 (courtesy of Mr. Demetracopoulos); Eliot Janeway, *Prescriptions for Prosperity* (New York, 1984), 42–43; Evans and Novak, quoting the Greek Ambassador, *WP*, September 3, 1979; Demetracopoulos Interview, May 5, 1987.

34. Caulfield to Ehrlichman, October 3, 1969, Ehrlichman Papers, Box 30, NP; *Greece, Spain, and the Southern NATO Strategy*, Hearings, Subcommittee on Europe, Committee on Foreign Affairs, House of Representatives, 92 Cong., 1 Sess., 64–71, 459–63; *Boston Globe*, November 13, 1971; Tasca to Rogers and Mitchell, July 26, 1971, State Department Files, Internal Security Division Memo, August 10, 1971, DOJ; Abshire to Senate Foreign Relations Committee Staff, November 3, 1971, Abshire to John Dean, December 29, 1971, with enclosures. (All documents courtesy of Mr. Demetracopoulos.)

35. Demetracopoulos Interview, May 5, 1987; Jack Anderson, *WP*, February 12, 1975; Louise Gore to Demetracopoulos, January 24, 1972 (courtesy of Mr. Demetracopoulos).

36. TT, the President and Haldeman, April 26, 1973 (8:55 A.M.–10:04 A.M.), *WP*, May 1, 1977; Raymond Bonner, *Waltzing with a Dictator: The Marcoses and the Making of American Foreign Policy* (New York, 1987), 14; *Washington Times*, January 19, 1988; Testimony of Dean, SSC, *Hearings*, 4:1402; TT, the President, Haldeman, and Dean, April 26, 1973, *WP*, May 1, 1977; HJC, *Testimony of Witnesses*, 2:48; TT, the President and Dean, March 21, 1973 (10:12 A.M.–11:55 A.M.), *U.S. v. M*, NA; Pappas File, WGSPF, NA, Feb-

ruary 7, 22, 1974. These documents, supplied by the Author, also have been used by Christopher Hitchens, *Prepared for the Worst* (New York, 1988), 287–96, reprinting his essay "Watergate—the Greek Connection," *The Nation*, May 31, 1986, 242:745, an account that offers the best extended treatment of this whole affair. Dean, *Blind Ambition*, 173–174.

37. See Seymour Hersh, *The Price of Power* (New York, 1983), 138, for Tasca's testimony; the transcript remains classified. Pappas and the Cyprus invasion are discussed in General Gregorios Bonanos, *The Truth* (Athens, 1986), 218. Kilpatrick in *Washington Star*, July 30, August 10, 1972.

38. Nixon, *Memoirs*, 2:346–47, 363–64.

39. See, for example, Sam Ervin, *The Whole Truth* (New York, 1980), 12; Silbert Diary; *Nomination of Earl J. Silbert to be United States Attorney*, Hearings, Committee on the Judiciary, U.S. Senate, 93 Cong., 2 Sess. (April 23, 1974), 1:5–55.

40. Office of Planning and Evaluation, "FBI Watergate Investigation," 10–11, 13–19, 23–24, 41–45, 52–55, FBI Watergate Papers, offers a review of investigative events following the break-in. The report largely is self-serving, but nevertheless it is valuable as a guide to the investigative process. Other sources for this summary are in WFO to Gray, July 3, 1972; C. Bolz to Assistant Director Bates, July 3, 1972, FBI Watergate Papers; Richard Kleindienst, *Justice: The Memoirs of an Attorney General* (Ottawa, IL, 1985), 46.

IX: "WHAT REALLY HURTS IS IF YOU TRY TO COVER IT UP."
WATERGATE AND THE CAMPAIGN OF 1972

1. Haldeman Notes, September 11, 1972, Haldeman Papers, Box 46, NP; *WP*, September 16, 1972; Ehrlichman Notes, September 14, 1972, Ehrlichman Papers, Box 13, NP; TT, the President, Dean, and Haldeman, September 15, 1972 (5:24 P.M.–6:17 P.M.), HJC, *Statement of Information*, 3:370–71. The opening remarks between Nixon and Haldeman are taken from the House Judiciary Committee version; otherwise, I have followed the transcript prepared by the Special Prosecutor for use in *U.S. v. Mitchell*.

2. John Dean, *Blind Ambition* (New York, 1976), Ch. 1; William Safire, *Before the Fall* (New York, 1975), 471–72; Jeb Stuart Magruder, *An American Life* (New York, 1974), 108.

3. Dean, *Blind Ambition*, 134; John Sirica, *To Set the Record Straight* (New York, 1979), 271; Richard Kleindienst, *Justice: The Memoirs of an Attorney General* (Ottawa, IL, 1985), 142–44; John D. Ehrlichman, *Witness to Power* (New York, 1982), 34–35. Dean ignored his firing by the law firm in *Lost Honor* (New York, 1982), 55.

4. Griswold Interview, May 4, 1987; Clark R. Mollenhoff, *Game Plan for Disaster: An Ombudsman's Report on the Nixon Years* (New York, 1976), 234; Santarelli Interview, August 26, 1987.

5. Dean to Higby and Strachan, May 11, 1972, Dean Papers, Box 84, NP; Colson to Dean, September 1, 1971, Dean to Colson, September 8, 1971, Fred Fielding to Dean, November 16, 1971, Dean to Buchanan, November 16, 1971, Dean Papers, Box 97, NP; Dean, *Blind Ambition*, 38; Dean to Dell Publishing Company, November 27, 1972, Dean Papers, Box 6, NP; Dean to Elmer B. Staats, November 20, 1972, in *Executive Privilege, Secrecy in Government, Freedom of Information*, Hearings, Subcommittees on Separation of Powers and Administrative Practice and Procedure of the Committee on the Judiciary, U.S. Senate, 93 Cong., 1 Sess. (April–May 1973), 1:129. Not without irony, the dust cover of Haldeman's memoirs depicted the presidential seal.

6. Dean, *Blind Ambition*, Ch. 2; Haldeman Interview, May 4, 1973, SSC Records, NA.

7. Magruder Testimony, SSC, *Hearings* (June 14, 1973), 2:816; Magruder Talk, Hofstra Nixon Conference, November 20, 1987.

8. Dean, *Blind Ambition*, Ch. 4; H. R. Haldeman, *The Ends of Power* (New York, 1978),

28-29; Gray Interview, July 18, 1973, Gray Witness File, WGSPF Records, NA; TT, Telephone Conversation, Ehrlichman to Robert Novak, August 28, 1972, and Melvin Laird, September 23, 1971, Ehrlichman Papers, Box 28, NP; Moore Interview, December 5, 1987; Mitchell Interview, April 11, 1988.

9. Gray Interview, July 18, 1973, Gray Witness File, WGSPF Records, NA; Petersen Interview, August 23, 1985; Petersen Testimony, SSC, *Hearings*, 9:3613-15.

10. Haldeman Notes, HJC, *Statement of Information*, 2:246; Haldeman, *Ends of Power*, 217-18, 17-18, 23.

11. TT, the President and Haldeman, June 23, 1972 (10:04 A.M.-11:39 A.M.), *U.S. v. M*, NA; HJC, *Statement of Information*, Appendix III, 56, 65, 67.

12. TT, the President and Haldeman, June 23, 1972 (1:04 P.M.-1:13 P.M.), *U.S. v. M*, NA; Haldeman, *Ends of Power*, 31-32; Richard Nixon, *RN: The Memoirs of Richard Nixon* (paperback ed., New York, 1979), 2:129.

13. TT, the President and Haldeman June 23, 1972 (2:20 P.M.-2:45 P.M.), *U.S. v. M*, NA; *ibid.*, HJC, *Statement of Information*, Appendix III, 83. At General Walters's confirmation hearings after his nomination as United Nations Ambassador during the Reagan Administration, the members of the Senate Foreign Relations Committee raised no questions regarding his CIA connections or the Watergate episode.

14. Helms Interview, July 14, 1988; Gray Interview, July 18, 1973, Gray Witness File, WGSPF Records, NA.

15. Ehrlichman Notes, June 23, 1972, Ehrlichman Papers, Box 12, NP.

16. "CIA Chronology," Statement of Patrick Gray, Gray Witness File, WGSPF Records, NA; Dean Testimony, SSC, *Hearings*, 3:945-48; *Inquiry into the Alleged Involvement of the Central Intelligence Agency in the Watergate and Ellsberg Matters*, Hearings, Special Subcommittee on Intelligence of the Committee on Armed Services, House of Representatives, 93 Cong., 1 Sess. (October 23, 1973), 15-17; SSC, *Final Report*, 39; Memorandum, Gerald Goldman to Richard Ben-Veniste (January 10, 1974), "Evidence of Haldeman's Participation in the Conspiracy to Obstruct Justice," Haldeman Witness File, WGSPF Records, NA; Ehrlichman Notes, July 6, 7, 8, 1972, Ehrlichman Papers, Box 12, NP; David Frost, *"I Gave Them a Sword": Behind the Scenes of the Nixon Interviews* (New York, 1978), 226.

17. Frost, *"I Gave Them a Sword"*, 223, 254; Nixon, *Memoirs*, 2:135.

18. Helms Interview, July 14, 1988; Helms to Author, July 28, 1988.

19. Ehrlichman Notes, July 10, 1972, Ehrlichman Papers, Box 12, NP.

20. Dean to John Nesbit, April 19, 1973, SSF, Box 113; *PPPUS:RN, 1972*, Press Conference, August 29, 1972, 872.

21. Ehrlichman Notes, July 31, August 3, 1972, Ehrlichman Papers, Box 12, NP; August 11, September 2, 5, 7, 14, 1972, *ibid.*, Box 13, NP.

22. Nixon, *Memoirs*, 2:176-77; Haldeman Notes, September 15, 1971, Haldeman Papers, Box 46, NP; Haldeman Interview, May 4, 1973, SSC Records, NA.

23. The transcript prepared by the Special Prosecutor has this reference to Democratic senators. Curiously, it was omitted in the House Judiciary Committee's version.

24. TT, the President, Dean, and Haldeman, September 15, 1972 (5:27 P.M.-6:17 P.M.), *U.S. v. M*, NA. For Dean's account, see *Blind Ambition*, 135-39, 143.

25. *NYT*, September 15, 26, 1972; Gladys Engel Lang and Kurt Lang, *The Battle for Public Opinion: The President, the Press, and the Polls During Watergate* (New York, 1983), 27-29.

26. U.S. Capitol Historical Society, Albert Interview (October 5, 1976), 37-38.

27. Lewis Interview, July 14, 1986.

28. "Chronology," HBC Papers. Maurice Stans, *The Terrors of Justice* (Chicago, 1984), 194-95; for Brown's role, see SSC, *Hearings*, 5:2182-2207.

29. *WP*, September 2, 6, 9, 1972.

30. Patman to Kenneth Parkinson, September 11, 1972, HBC Papers.

31. Patman to Committee, September 12, 1972; "Chronology," HBC Papers; Stans, *Terrors of Justice,* 196.

32. Mollenhoff, *Game Plan for Disaster,* 229.

33. Minutes, October 3, 1972, HBC Papers.

34. Reuss Interview, May 15, 1985; Lewis Interview, July 14, 1986; SSC, *Hearings,* 3:1183-89, 5:2199-2204.

35. Minutes, October 3, 1972, HBC Papers; Reuss Interview, May 15, 1985; Lewis Interview, July 14, 1986.

36. Marjorie Boyd, "The Watergate Story: Why Congress Didn't Investigate Until After the Election," *Washington Monthly,* April 1973, 37, 41-45; Lewis Interview, July 14, 1986.

37. Will Wilson to J. Edgar Hoover, November 16, 1970, Hoover to Henry Petersen, December 9, 1970, *ibid.,* January 27, 1972, Brasco File, FBI Papers; *New York Daily News,* December 3, 1973; *NYT,* March 22, 1978; Lewis Interview, July 14, 1986.

38. *WP,* October 3, 4, 1973; Reuss Interview, May 15, 1985; *Grand Rapids Press,* June 21, 1973; Brown's statement in SSC, *Hearings,* 5:2182-87; Brown Interview, October 7, 1987; Jerald F. terHorst, *Gerald Ford and the Future of the Presidency* (New York, 1974), 167; *Frankfort State Journal,* June 3, 1973.

39. Demetracopoulos Interview, July 16, 1988. FBI Director William Webster to Congressman Benjamin Rosenthal, June 8, August 2, 1982; Rosenthal to Vincent Burke (Riggs National Bank), April 19, 1982; Thomas Wren (Riggs National Bank) to Demetracopoulos, September 16, 1985; documents courtesy of Demetracopoulos. FBI reports in Demetracopoulos's possession, released in 1986, demonstrate that twelve general indexes in the New York Field Office file on Wright Patman and Demetracopoulos had been "destroyed." Congressman Rosenthal's investigation in 1982 was in effect the last congressional investigation of the Watergate affair.

40. *Los Angeles Times,* October 20, 1976; Mollenhoff, *Game Plan for Disaster,* 236; terHorst, *Gerald Ford,* 163, 166; Holtzman to Levi, October 18, 1976, Levi to Holtzman, October 20, 1976, Lynch Papers (courtesy of Stephen Lynch); Gerald Ford, *A Time to Heal: The Autobiography of Gerald R. Ford* (New York, 1979), 427.

41. Patman to Elmer B. Staats, October 4, 1972; Patman to Sirica, October 5, 1972, HBC Papers.

42. Minutes, October 12, 13, 1972, HBC Papers.

43. Dean, *Blind Ambition,* 144; Nixon, *Memoirs,* 2:212.

44. Lewis Interview, July 23, 1985; Ervin to Patman, June 25, 1973, HBC Papers.

45. Stans to Nixon, October 5, 1972, NPF, Box 15, NP.

46. *WP,* October 29, 1972. David Halberstam, *The Powers That Be* (New York, 1979), has an excellent account of the *Post*'s coverage, including the charge that publisher Katherine Graham worried about the paper's reputation at the time of the election (676).

47. Ehrlichman Notes, July 20, 1972, Ehrlichman Papers, Box 6, NP.

48. Ehrlichman Notes, November 20, 1972, Ehrlichman Papers, Box 13, NP; *ibid.,* November 29, 1971, Box 6, NP; Nixon to Connally, July 24, 1972, Haldeman Papers, Box 162, NP.

49. Haldeman Notes, October 4, 1972, Haldeman Papers, Box 46, NP; Dent Interview, September 24, 1986; Mitchell to Nixon, November 27, 1972, NPF, Box 12, NP. Theodore H. White, *The Making of the President, 1972* (New York, 1973), 341-47, has some useful electoral data.

50. Haldeman Notes, October 11, 14, 15, *et passim,* Haldeman Papers, Box 46, NP; Nixon to Haldeman, November 15, 1972, Haldeman Papers, Box 179, NP.

51. George McGovern, *An American Journey: The Presidential Campaign Speeches of George McGovern* (New York, 1974), 232-33.

52. Haldeman Talking Paper to Colson, March 7, 1973, Haldeman Papers, Box 179, NP; Ehrlichman Notes, December 18, 1972, Ehrlichman Papers, Box 13, NP. Stans, *Terrors of Justice*, 198, typically blamed Dean for the cover-up. The same line was pursued with greater venom in Ehrlichman's and Kleindienst's memoirs.

53. Dean to Haldeman, December 1, 1972, with marginal notes of May 2, 1973, done by Bruce Kehrli or Kenneth Cole, SSF, Box 113, NP; Haldeman Interview, May 4, 1973, SSC Papers, NA.

54. Bull Interview, May 7, 1987.

55. TT, Telephone Conversation, the President and Colson, March 21, 1973 (7:35 P.M.– 8:24 P.M.), *WP*, May 1, 1977; *FBI Watergate Investigation: OPE Analysis* (July 5, 1974), 61, FBI Papers.

X: "THE COVER-UP IS THE MAIN INGREDIENT."
A BLACKMAILER, A SENATOR, AND A JUDGE:
NOVEMBER 1972–MARCH 1973

1. NPF, n.d., Box 187, NP; *PPPUS:RN*, April 30, 1973, 328–33. The inadequacy of press coverage of Watergate was first publicized in Ben H. Bagdikian, "Election Coverage '72: The Fruits of Agnewism," *Columbia Journalism Review*, January/February 1973, 9:23.

2. Buchanan to Nixon, December 8, 1972, Haldeman Papers, Box 230, NP; H. R. Haldeman, *The Ends of Power* (New York, 1978), 230; Garment to Haldeman, January 19, 1973, Garment MS, LC; Garment Interview, May 29, 1985.

3. Nixon to Ehrlichman/Ken Cole, December 28, 1972, Haldeman Papers, Box 162, NP; Haldeman Notes ("exhausted volcano"), September 16, 1972, Haldeman Papers, Box 46, NP.

4. Haldeman Notes, November 8, 1972, Haldeman Papers, Box 46, NP; Richard Nathan, *The Plot That Failed* (New York, 1975), 8, 63, 68–69; Vernon Walters, *Silent Missions* (New York, 1978), 604; Thomas Powers, *The Man Who Kept the Secrets: Richard Helms and the CIA* (New York, 1979); Helms Interview, July 14, 1988. The White House view is reflected in Haldeman, *Ends of Power*, 169–80, and John D. Ehrlichman, *Witness to Power* (New York, 1982), 363. Ehrlichman, whose own power would have been greatly aggrandized if Nixon had been successful, is uncharacteristically reticent and perfunctory on the subject.

5. Richard Nixon, *RN: The Memoirs of Richard Nixon* (paperback ed., New York, 1979), 2:275–79.

6. Colson to Ehrlichman, November 29, 1972, Colson Papers, Box 7, NP; Colson to Nixon, November 27, 1972, Haldeman Papers, Box 14, NP.

7. "The New Majority," c. March 8, 1973, Ehrlichman Papers, Box 68, NP. The document appears to be the product of White House aide Ken Clawson or Ehrlichman.

8. Haldeman Notes, November 17, 1972, Haldeman Papers, Box 46, NP; Nixon, *Memoirs*, 2:285.

9. Ehrlichman Notes, August 3, 1972, Box 6, NP; Haldeman Notes, November 13, 1972, Haldeman Papers, Box 46, NP; Ehrlichman to Nixon, December 7, 1972, Haldeman Papers, Box 14, NP; Webster to Author (telephone conversation), August 4, 1987.

10. Haldeman Notes, November 13, 16, 1972, Haldeman Papers, Box 46, NP; February 10, 1973, *ibid.*, Box 47, NP; Ehrlichman Notes, November 27, December 8, 1972, Ehrlichman Papers, Box 13, NP.

11. Ehrlichman Notes, November 14, 16, 17, 22, 24, 30, December 7, 13, 18, 1972, Ehrlichman Papers, Box 13, NP.

12. Ehrlichman Notes, January 4, 1974, Ehrlichman Papers, Box 14, NP; Haldeman Notes,

January 16, February 8, 13, 1973, Haldeman Papers, Box 47, NP; Ehrlichman, *Witness to Power,* 156.

13. Ehrlichman Notes, December 11, 1972, Ehrlichman Papers, Box 13, NP; TT, the President and Dean, February 28, 1973 (9:12 A.M.–10:23 A.M.), HJC, *Transcripts of Eight Recorded Presidential Conversations,* 41.

14. Haldeman Notes, January 27, 1973, Haldeman Papers, Box 47, NP.

15. Haldeman Notes, January 8, 9, 12, February 10, 1973, Haldeman Papers, Box 47, NP; Johnson to Nixon, November 8, 1972, "Post-Presidential Name File," LBJ Library.

16. TT, Dictabelt Recording of Howard Hunt and Charles Colson, November 1972, *U. S. v. M,* NA; John Dean, *Blind Ambition* (New York, 1976), 146.

17. Memorandum, November 14, 1972, copy in Jaworski MS, Baylor University (also exhibit in *U. S. v. Mitchell); NYT,* November 4, 1974; Dean, *Blind Ambition,* 181.

18. Haldeman Notes, November 15, 1972, Haldeman Papers, Box 46, NP; Moore Interview, December 5, 1987; Dent Interview, September 24, 1986; Herbert G. Klein, *Making It Perfectly Clear* (New York, 1980), 278–79.

19. Silbert to WFO, December 10, 1972, SA, Chicago to Acting Director, December 11, 1972, FBI Watergate Files; Chicago Field Office to Ruckelshaus, June 6, 1973, FBI United Airlines Crash Files; NTSB Report, NTSB Papers, United Airlines Crash; TT, the President, Dean, and Haldeman, March 21, 1973 (10:12 A.M.–11:55 A.M.), *U.S. v. M,* NA.

20. TT, the President and Colson, January 8, 1973 (4:05 P.M.–5:43 P.M.), *U.S. v. M,* NA, with additional material quoted in *WP,* May 1, 1977; TTs, February 13, 14, 1973, quoted in David Frost, *"I Gave Them a Sword": Behind the Scenes of the Nixon Interviews* (New York, 1978), 232–34, 248; *WP,* January 7, 1973; Haldeman Notes, March 9, 1973, Haldeman Papers, Box 47, NP.

21. TT, Nixon and John Dean, February 28, 1973 (9:12 A.M.–10:23 A.M.), HJC, *Transcripts of Eight Recorded Presidential Conversations,* 19–46; Haldeman Notes, February 5, 25, March 9, 1973, Haldeman Papers, Box 47, NP.

22. George V. Higgins, "The Judge Who Tried Harder," *Atlantic,* April 1974, 90.

23. John J. Sirica, *To Set the Record Straight* (New York, 1979), 61–90.

24. Petersen to Patman, January 11, 1973, HBC Papers.

25. Harry McPherson, *A Political Education* (Boston, 1972), 34.

26. Sam Ervin, *The Whole Truth: The Watergate Conspiracy* (New York, 1980), 19.

27. *Congressional Record,* 93 Cong., 1 Sess. (February 6, 7, 1973), 3550–3851, *et passim.*

28. Haldeman Notes, February 11, 1973, March 12, 1973, Box 47, NP.

29. SSC, *Hearings* (June 25, 1973), 3:984.

30. *Minutes,* May 9, 1974, SSC Records, NA.

31. Higby to Haldeman, February 10, 1973, Haldeman Papers, Box 110, NP; Haldeman Notes, February 26, 1973, *ibid.,* Box 47, NP.

32. John J. Sirica, *To Set the Record Straight* (New York, 1979), 17–41.

33. Harvey Katz, "Some Call It Justice," *Washingtonian,* September 1973, 128–29; *WP,* December 24, 1972; *NYT,* December 20, 1972.

34. *Houston Chronicle,* July 20, 1986, citing Sirica's remarks in preparation for his retirement.

35. SSC, *Hearings,* 1:196.

36. Sirica, *To Set the Record Straight,* 91–116; TT, the President and Haldeman, March 20, 1973 (6:00 P.M.–7:10 P.M.), *U.S. v. M,* NA; Dean, *Blind Ambition,* 212; Petersen Interview, August 23, 1985; TT, Telephone Conversation, Ehrlichman and Kleindienst, March 28, 1973, HJC, *Statement of Information,* 4 (Part I): 406–08.

37. Sirica, *To Set the Record Straight,* 117–27.

38. Sirica, *To Set the Record Straight,* 116, 108; Richard Kleindienst, *Justice* (Ottawa, IL, 1985), 154; Silbert Diary.

39. *U.S.* v. *Garcia* (9th Circuit), 427 F. 2d 658 (1970); *U.S.* v. *Sweig* (2nd Circuit), 454 F. 2d 181 (1972); Samuel Dash, *Chief Counsel* (New York, 1976), 26–30; *NYT*, October 7, 1973; Joseph Rauh, Book Review, *The New Republic*, May 26, 1979, 36–38; Higgins, "The Judge Who Tried Harder," 90, 94; TT, Telephone Conversation, Kleindienst and Ehrlichman, March 28, 1973, HJC, *Statement of Information*, 4 (Part I): 406–08.

40. TT, the President and Haldeman, March 22, 1973 (9:11 A.M.–10:35 A.M.), *U.S.* v. *M*, NA; Nixon, *Memoirs*, 2:312–24; Sirica, *To Set the Record Straight*, 119.

41. Nixon, *Memoirs*, 2:328, 330, 332.

42. TT, the President, Haldeman, Ehrlichman, Dean, and Mitchell, March 22, 1973 (1:57 P.M.–3:43 P.M.), *U.S.* v. *M*, NA; Nixon, *Memoirs*, 2:326.

43. Haldeman Notes, January 12, 1973, Haldeman Papers, Box 47, NP; Ehrlichman, *Witness to Power*, 368.

XI: "WE HAVE A CANCER WITHIN, CLOSE TO THE PRESIDENCY."
COVERING UP THE COVER-UP, JANUARY–MARCH 1973

1. John Dean to Files, March 5, 1973, SSC, *Hearings*, 3:1251; Moore Interview, December 5, 1987; John Dean, *Blind Ambition* (New York, 1976), 195–96; TT, the President, Dean, and Haldeman, March 21, 1973 (10:12 A.M–11:55 A.M.), *U.S.* v. *M*, NA.

2. Dean, *Blind Ambition*, 184; Dean Interview, April 16, 1988.

3. *NYT*, August 6, 1973; Lichenstein Interview, November 22, 1985.

4. Martin to the Files, Gray/Wiretap Investigation, Francis Martin Files, WGSPF Records, NA.

5. Patrick O'Donnell to Gray, June 13, 1972, Clark Mollenhoff Papers, Box 59, State Historical Society of Wisconsin; Lichenstein Interview, November 22, 1985; Neil Welch and David W. Marston, *Inside Hoover's FBI* (New York, 1984), 198.

6. *Louis Patrick Gray III*, Hearings, Committee on the Judiciary, U.S. Senate, 93 Cong., 1 Sess. (February 28, March 1–22, 1973).

7. *PPPUS:RN*, March 2, 1973, 160; *ibid.*, March 15, 1973, 272; "Statement by the President on Executive Privilege," *Weekly Compilation of Presidential Documents* (March 12, 1973), 9:253–54; Richard Nixon, *RN: The Memoirs of Richard Nixon* (paperback ed., New York, 1979), 2:303 (italics in original).

8. TT, Telephone Conversation, Ehrlichman and Gray, March 7 or 8, 1973, HJC, *Statement of Information*, 3:768; Ehrlichman Notes, March 8, 1973, Ehrlichman Papers, Box 28, NP; Lichenstein Interview, November 22, 1985; Gray Interview, July 18, 1973, Gray Witness File, July 18, 1973, WGSPF Records, NA.

9. TT, Telephone Conversation, Ehrlichman and Dean, March 7 or 8, 1973, HJC, *Statement of Information*, 3:768–69; TT, the President, Dean, and Haldeman, March 13, 1973 (12:42 P.M.–2:00 P.M.), HJC, *Transcripts of Eight Recorded Presidential Conversations*, 61.

10. TT, the President, Dean, and Haldeman, March 21, 1973 (10:12 A.M.–11:55 A.M.), *U.S.* v. *M*, NA.

11. Lichenstein Interview, November 22, 1985; *Gray Hearings*, 100–44, 309–19, 323–43, 661–94.

12. Ehrlichman Notes, March 27, April 5, April 11, 1973, Ehrlichman Papers, Box 14, NP; Telephone Conversation Summary, William Timmons to Ehrlichman, April 4, 1973, Ehrlichman Papers, Box 65, NP; "Statement About Intention to Withdraw the Nomination of L. Patrick Gray III," *PPPUS:RN*, 1973 (April 9, 1973), 257; Telephone Conversation Summary, Louis Nichols to Rose Mary Woods, May 8, 1973, NPF, Box 19, NP.

13. John D. Ehrlichman, *Witness to Power* (New York, 1982), 374–75; Richard Klein-

dienst, *Justice* (Ottawa, IL, 1985), 158; Ehrlichman Notes, April 4, 1973, Ehrlichman Papers, Box 14, NP.

14. Joseph Spear, *President and the Press: The Nixon Legacy* (Cambridge, MA, 1984), 194.

15. *PPPUS:RN, 1973*, March 12, 1973, 184–87.

16. TT, the President, Dean, and Haldeman, March 13, 1973 (12:42 P.M.–2:00 P.M.), HJC, *Transcripts of Eight Recorded Presidential Conversations*, 47–48.

17. TT, the President, Dean, and Haldeman, March 17, 1973 (1:25 P.M.–2:10 P.M.), *U.S. v. M*, NA. For the CIA interest in the Ellsberg matter, Colby Interview, October 9, 1987, was useful.

18. TT, the President, Dean, and Haldeman, March 21, 1973 (10:12 A.M.–11:55 A.M.), *U. S. v. M*, NA; Colby Interview, October 9, 1987.

19. Dean, *Blind Ambition*, 226–30.

20. TT, the President, Dean, Haldeman, and Ehrlichman, March 21, 1973 (5:20 P.M.–6:01 P.M.), *U. S. v. M*, NA; Moore Interview, December 5, 1987; Fielding Interview, July 12, 1973, SSC Records, NA.

21. TT, Telephone Conversation, the President and Colson, March 21, 1973 (7:53 P.M.–8:34 P.M.), Nixon Papers, Box 172, NP. Some of this transcript appeared as part of the record in *U.S. v. M*, NA, and additional pages subsequently were published in the *WP*, May 1, 1977.

22. TT, Dictabelt Recording, President's Recollection of March 21 Conversation, HJC, *Statement of Information*, 3:1245–49. Again, the President ignored the fact that he had learned of the psychiatrist's-office break-in on March 17—at the very latest. The Dictabelt "diary" recordings are widely used in the President's memoirs, but many of them may never be subjected to independent scrutiny.

23. TT, the President and Haldeman, March 20, 1973 (6:00 P.M.–7:10 P.M.), *U.S. v. M*, NA.

24. TT, the President and Haldeman, March 22, 1983 (9:11 A.M.–10:35 A.M.), *U.S. v. M*, NA.

25. TT, the President, Dean, Ehrlichman, Haldeman, and Mitchell, March 22, 1973, (1:57 P.M.–3:43 P.M.), *U.S. v. M*, NA.

26. *NYT*, March 26, 1973; TT, the President, Haldeman, Ehrlichman, and Ziegler, March 27, 1973 (11:10 A.M.–1:30 P.M.), *U.S. v. M*, NA; Bob Woodward and Carl Bernstein, *All the President's Men* (New York, 1974), 278.

27. Dean Testimony, HJC, *Testimony of Witnesses* (July 11, 1974), 2:252, 275.

28. TT, the President, Haldeman, Ehrlichman, and Ziegler, March 27, 1973 (11:10 A.M.–1:30 P.M.), *U. S. v. M*, NA; *ibid.*, J. Fred Buzhardt Notes, courtesy of Mrs. Buzhardt; Garment Interview, June 26, 1985.

29. H. R. Haldeman, *The Ends of Power* (New York, 1978), 224; Dean, *Blind Ambition*, 222–25; Ehrlichman Notes, March 23, 1973, Ehrlichman Papers, Box 14, NP.

30. Goldwater to Nixon, March 29, 1973, NPF, Box 8, NP.

XII: ''WE HAVE TO PRICK THE GODDAM BOIL AND TAKE THE HEAT.''
CUTTING LOOSE: APRIL 1973

1. Ehrlichman Notes, April 2, 1973, April 4, 1974, Ehrlichman Papers, Box 14, NP.

2. TT, Telephone Conversation, the President and Ehrlichman, April 8, 1973 (7:33 A.M.–7:37 A.M.), *Submission of Recorded Presidential Conversations to the Committee on the Judiciary of the House of Representatives*, Richard Nixon, April 30, 1974. Hereafter cited as *WHT*.

3. TT, Telephone Conversation, Larry Higby and Jeb Magruder, April 13, 1973, HJC,

Statement of Information, 4 (Part 2):612–55; Jeb Stuart Magruder, *An American Life* (New York, 1974), 319–26.

4. Ehrlichman's report is in Ehrlichman Papers, Box 214, NP, and reprinted in part in his memoir.

5. Haldeman has given and published various versions of the origins of the taping system, most recently in "The Nixon White House Tapes: The Decision to Record Presidential Conversations," *Prologue* (Summer 1988), 20:79–87.

6. TT, the President, Haldeman, and Ehrlichman, April 14, 1973, Executive Office Building (8:55 A.M.–11:31 A.M.), *U.S. v. M,* NA. The Agnew information is in the draft transcript of this meeting, Nixon Papers, Box 172, NP; Agnew Interview, January 14, 1989; Agnew to Author, February 1, 1989.

7. TT, the President, Haldeman, and Ehrlichman, April 14, 1973, Executive Office Building (8:55 A.M.–11:31 A.M.), *U.S. v. M,* NA; TT, Telephone Conversation, Ehrlichman and Mitchell, April 11, 1973, Ehrlichman Papers, Box 213, NP.

8. TT, the President, Haldeman, and Ehrlichman, April 14, 1973, Executive Office Building (8:55 A.M.–11:31 A.M.), *U.S. v. M,* NA; Haldeman Notes, April 8, 13, 1973, Haldeman Papers, Box 47, NP.

9. TT, the President and Haldeman, April 14, 1973 (1:55 P.M.–2:13 P.M.), HJC, *Statement of Information,* 4 (Part 2):773–76.

10. TT, Ehrlichman and Mitchell, April 14, 1973, HJC, *Statement of Information,* 4 (Part 2):725–68; TT, the President, Haldeman, and Ehrlichman, April 14, 1973 (2:24 P.M.–3:55 P.M.), *U.S. v. M,* NA; Richard Nixon, *RN: The Memoirs of Richard Nixon* (paperback ed., New York, 1979), 2:349; John Ehrlichman, *Witness to Power* (New York, 1982), 380.

11. TT, the President, Haldeman, and Ehrlichman, April 14, 1973 (2:24 P.M.–3:55 P.M.), *U.S. v. M,* NA.

12. TT, the President, Haldeman, and Ehrlichman, April 14, 1973 (5:15 P.M.–6:45 P.M.), *U.S. v. M,* NA.

13. Richard Kleindienst, *Justice* (Ottawa, IL, 1985), 158–60; Nixon, *Memoirs,* 2:350.

14. Nixon, *Memoirs,* 2:350–54.

15. TT, Telephone Conversation, the President and Haldeman, April 14, 1973 (11:02 P.M.–11:16 P.M.), *U.S. v. M,* NA.

16. TT, Telephone Conversation, the President and Ehrlichman, April 14, 1973 (11:22 P.M.–11:53 P.M.), *U.S. v. M,* NA. President's edited copy in Nixon Papers, Box 172, NP. Nixon, *Memoirs,* 2:355.

17. Silbert to Cox, May 31, 1973, courtesy of Mr. Silbert; Silbert Diary.

18. Silbert Diary; Petersen Testimony, HJC, *Testimony of Witnesses* (July 12, 1974), 3:114; Kleindienst, *Justice,* 160–61.

19. TT, the President and Ehrlichman, April 15, 1973 (10:35 A.M.–11:15 A.M.), *U.S. v. M,* NA.

20. TT, the President and Kleindienst, April 15, 1973 (1:12 P.M.–2:22 P.M.), *WHT;* Kleindienst, *Justice,* 162; Petersen Testimony, HJC, *Testimony of Witnesses* (July 12, 1974), 3:82; Petersen Interview, August 23, 1985.

21. TT, Telephone Conversation, the President and Haldeman, April 15, 1973 (3:27 P.M.–3:44 P.M.), *WHT.*

22. TT, Telephone Conversation, Higby and Haldeman, April 15, 1973, *WHT;* Transcript of Fred Buzhardt Tape No. 3, Buzhardt MS, Courtesy of Mrs. J. F. Buzhardt.

23. TT, Telephone Conversations, the President and Henry Petersen, April 15, 1973 (8:14 P.M.–8:18 P.M.; 8:25 P.M.–8:26 P.M.; 9:39 P.M.–9:41 P.M.; 11:45 P.M.–11:53 P.M.), *WHT;* Dean, *Blind Ambition,* 261–63. Dean Testimony, SSC, *Hearings,* 4:1576–77.

24. TT, the President, Ehrlichman and Haldeman, April 16, 1973 (9:50 A.M.–9:59 A.M.), *U.S. v. M,* NA; Ehrlichman Notes, April 16, 1973, Ehrlichman Papers, Box 13, NP.

25. TT, the President and Dean, April 16, 1973 (10:00 A.M.–10:40 A.M.), *U.S. v. M*, NA; TT, the President, Haldeman, and Ehrlichman, April 16, 1973 (10:50 A.M.–11:04 A.M.), *U.S. v. M*, NA.

26. TT, the President and Haldeman, April 16, 1973 (12:00 P.M.–12:31 P.M.), *WHT*.

27. Garment to the President, undated, c. April 1973, Garment MS, LC.

28. Phillips to Haldeman, April 16, 1973, Haldeman Papers, Box 110, NP.

29. William C. Berman, *William Fulbright and the Vietnam War: The Dissent of a Political Realist* (Kent, OH, 1988), 172.

30. TT, the President and Henry Petersen, April 16, 1973 (1:30 P.M.–3:25 P.M.), *WHT;* Petersen Interview, August 23, 1985.

31. TT, the President and Dean, April 16, 1973 (4:07 P.M.–4:35 P.M.), HJC, *Transcripts of Eight Recorded Presidential Conversations*, 209–18.

32. TT, Telephone Conversation Between the President and Petersen, April 16, 1973 (8:58 P.M.–9:14 P.M.), *WHT;* TT, the President and Dean, March 21, 1973 (10:12 A.M.–11:55 A.M.), *U.S. v. M*, NA.

33. Dennis V. N. McCarthy, *Protecting the President: The Inside Story of a Secret Service Agent* (New York, 1985), 21; *WP*, April 18, 1973.

34. TT, the President, Haldeman, Ehrlichman, and Ziegler, April 17, 1973 (12:35 P.M.–2:20 P.M.), *U.S. v. M*, NA. Ehrlichman Notes, April 17, 1973, Box 14, Ehrlichman Papers, NP.

35. TT, Telephone Conversation, the President and Ehrlichman, April 17, 1973 (2:39 P.M.–2:40 P.M.), *WHT*.

36. TT, the President and Petersen, April 17, 1973 (2:46 P.M.–3:49 P.M.), *WHT*. Nixon later told Haldeman that his failure to give Dean immunity in April was a key moment. H. R. Haldeman, *The Ends of Power* (New York, 1978), 309.

37. TT, the President, Haldeman, Ehrlichman, and Ziegler, April 17, 1973 (3:50 P.M.–4:35 P.M.), *WHT*.

38. TT, the President, Rogers, Haldeman, and Ehrlichman, April 17, 1973 (5:20 P.M.–7:14 P.M.), *WHT*.

39. TT, Telephone Conversation, the President and Petersen, April 18, 1973 (2:50 P.M.–2:56 P.M.), *WHT*.

40. TT, the President and Ehrlichman, April 19, 1973 (1:03 P.M.–1:30 P.M.), *U.S. v. M*, NA.

41. TT, the President and Moore, April 19, 1973 (3:45 P.M.–5:00 P.M.), Jaworski Papers, Texas Collection, Baylor University; TT, Telephone Conversation, Ehrlichman and Kalmbach, April 19, 1973, *U.S. v. M*, NA; TT, the President, Haldeman, and Ehrlichman, April 19, 1973, (8:31 A.M.–10:12 A.M.), quoted in Haldeman, *Ends of Power*, 263.

42. TT, the President, Haldeman, and Ehrlichman, April 19, 1973 (9:31 A.M.–10:12 A.M.), quoted in Haldeman, *Ends of Power*, 264–65; TT, the President, Wilson, and Strickler, April 19, 1973 (8:26 P.M.–9:32 P.M.), *WHT*.

43. TT, the President, Haldeman, and Ehrlichman, April 25, 1973 (11:06 A.M.–11:55 A.M.), *U.S. v. M*, NA. Additional fragments quoted in Haldeman, *Ends of Power*, 267–71; Leon Jaworski, *Confession and Avoidance: A Memoir* (New York, 1979), 214–15. The derogatory remarks about Petersen are in Ehrlichman Notes, April 25, 1973, Ehrlichman Papers, Box 14, NP; TT, the President and Haldeman, April 26, 1973, *WP*, May 1, 1977.

44. TT, the President and Haldeman, April 25, 1973 (4:40 P.M.–5:30 P.M.), *U.S. v. M*, NA; TT, Telephone Conversation between the President and Haldeman, April 25, 1973 (7:46 P.M.–7:53 P.M.), *U.S. v. M*, NA; TT, the President and Haldeman, April 26, 1973 (8:55 A.M.–10:20 A.M.), *WP*, May 1, 1977.

45. TT, Telephone Conversations Between the President and Ehrlichman, April 25, 1973 (7:17 P.M.–7:19 P.M., 7:25 P.M.–7:39 P.M.), Haldeman, *Ends of Power*, 278–79; TT, the

President, Haldeman, and Ehrlichman, April 26, 1973, Haldeman, *ibid.*, 282-87, and reprinted in *WP*, May 1, 1977; Petersen Testimony, HJC, *Testimony of Witnesses* (July 12, 1974), 3:98, 99-100.

46. Silbert Diary.

47. TT, the President, Petersen and Ziegler (partial), April 27, 1973 (5:37 P.M.–5:43 P.M.; 6:04 P.M.–6:48 P.M.), *WHT;* Petersen Interview, August 23, 1985; Petersen Testimony, HJC, *Testimony of Witnesses* (July 12, 1974), 3:138. Petersen bluntly summed up his dealings with the President: "You are looking at a guy who was, if you will excuse the expression, screwed." Petersen Interview, August 23, 1985.

48. Ehrlichman Notes, April 27, 1973, Ehrlichman Papers, Box 14, NP.

49. Ehrlichman Notes, April 27, 1973, Ehrlichman Papers, Box 14, NP; Petersen Testimony, HJC, *Testimony of Witnesses* (July 12, 1974), 3:76.

50. Ruckelshaus Interview, August 21, 1986; Neil Welch and David W. Marston, *Inside Hoover's FBI* (New York, 1984), 196-97; Telephone Conversation Summary, Louis Nichols to Rose Mary Woods, May 8, 1973, NPF, Box 19, NP.

51. Ruckelshaus Interview, August 21, 1986.

52. The accounts of the Camp David meeting vary somewhat. See Nixon, *Memoirs*, 2:381-85, 354; Haldeman, *Ends of Power*, 288-94; Ehrlichman, *Witness to Power*, 389-91; Kleindienst, *Justice*, 167-69. Haldeman Notes, April 29, 1973, Haldeman Papers, Box 47, NP; Elliot Richardson Notes, April 29, 1973, Richardson MS, LC; Henry A. Kissinger, *Years of Upheaval* (Boston, 1982), 102-03.

53. Nixon, *Memoirs*, 2:386-88.

54. Kissinger, *Years of Upheaval*, 104; Nixon, *Memoirs*, 2:384; Emmett John Hughes, *New York Times Magazine*, June 9, 1974, 70, cited in Fawn Brodie, *Richard Nixon: The Shaping of His Character* (New York, 1981), 28-29; Moynihan to Nixon, April 22, 1973, NPF, Box 12, NP.

55. Silbert Diary; Silbert to Author, February 26, 1988.

XIII: NEW ENEMIES: THE SPECIAL PROSECUTOR AND THE SENATE COMMITTEE: MAY 1973

1. TT, Telephone Conversation, Ehrlichman and Krogh, May 2, 1973, Ehrlichman Papers, Box 14, NP; Buchanan to the President, May 3, 1973, NPF, Box 6, NP; Kevin Phillips, *The American Political Report*, May 7, 1973.

2. James Kilpatrick Interview with Nixon, May 14, 1974, *Washington Star; NYT*, May 2, 1973; Richard Kleindienst, *Justice* (Ottawa, IL, 1985), 169-70; Garment to the President, May 1, 1973, Garment MS, LC; Bob Woodward and Carl Bernstein, *All the President's Men* (New York, 1974), 311.

3. TT, Telephone Conversation, the President and Haldeman, June 4, 1973, in H. R. Haldeman, *The Ends of Power* (New York, 1978), 198-200; TT, the President, Haig, and Ziegler, June 4, 1973, HJC, *Statement of Information*, 9:177-236, and additional excerpt in *WP*, May 1, 1977; Henry Kissinger, *Years of Upheaval* (Boston, 1982), 110; "Tapes Chronology," Memo in Graham MS, LC. Ehrlichman also remained, drafting statements for Ziegler and generally expressing contempt for the new staff: TT, Telephone Conversation, Ehrlichman and Ziegler, April 30, 1973, Ehrlichman Papers, Box 28, NP.

4. Congressman John Moss (D-CA) to Elmer B. Staats (Comptroller General), June 7, 1973; to Elliot Richardson, June 21, 1973; to Archibald Cox, July 30, 1973; and replies, all in Haig Witness File, WGSPF Records, NA; St. Clair Interview, April 10, 1987; Garment Interview, April 12, 1988; Whitehead Interview, May 25, 1988.

5. Agnew Interview, January 14, 1989; Spiro Agnew, *Go Quietly . . . Or Else* (New York,

1980), 190–91; Garment Interview, April 12, 1988; Haig to Haldeman, April 26, 1971, Haldeman Papers, Box 273, NP.

6. General Bruce Palmer, Jr., *The 25-Year War: America's Military Role in Vietnam* (Lexington, KY, 1984), 98, 135–36.

7. See Chapter V, *supra;* Haldeman Talking Paper to Haig, January 8, 1973, Haldeman Papers, Box 179, NP.

8. Agnew Interview, January 14, 1989; Bull Interviews, May 7, July 20, 1987; Richardson Interviews, May 14, 30, 1985; Nguyen Tien Hung and Jerrold L. Schechter, *The Palace File* (New York, 1986), 139; Kissinger, *Years of Upheaval,* 107.

9. Ehrlichman Notes, June 16, 1972, Ehrlichman Papers, Box 6, NP.

10. Richardson Interviews, May 14, 30, 1985; Richardson to Nixon, January 8, 1973, Haldeman Papers, Box 110, NP; Richardson Notes, April 29, 1973, Richardson MS, LC.

11. Richardson Interviews, May 14, 30, 1985; Elliot L. Richardson, *The Creative Balance* (New York, 1976), 3, 5.

12. Richardson Notes, April 29, 1973, Richardson MS, LC.

13. TT, Telephone Conversation, Ehrlichman and Richardson, April 30, 1973, Richardson MS, LC. Richardson's extensive notes of his briefings and inquiries during the first week in May are in the WGSPF Records, Administrative Files, NA, as well as in the Richardson MS, LC.

14. Richardson Notes, April 29, 1973, Richardson MS, LC; TT, April 14, 1973, NP.

15. WRH [Wilmot Hastings] to Richardson, May 4, 1973; Memo to Richardson, May 9, 1973; Griswold to Richardson, undated memo, Richardson MS, LC; Richardson Interview, May 30, 1985; Leon Jaworski, *The Right and the Power* (New York, 1976), 2; Tyler to Author, August 21, 1987.

16. Richardson Memo, October 19, 1973; Titus, et al. to Richardson, April 30, 1973, Richardson MS, LC; Silbert Diary.

17. *Nomination of Elliot L. Richardson to be Attorney General,* Hearings, Committee on the Judiciary, U.S. Senate, 93 Cong., 1 Sess. (May 21, 1973), 146–225.

18. Richard Nixon, *RN: The Memoirs of Richard Nixon* (paperback ed., New York, 1979), 2:461–64, 486; Bork Interview, June 17, 1987; Lukas Interview, November 20, 1987; Garment Interview, April 12, 1988; *Human Events,* August 4, 1973, 611.

19. Richardson Testimony, *Special Prosecutor,* Hearings, Committee on the Judiciary, U.S. Senate, 93 Cong., 1 Sess., 405–07.

20. Petersen Interview, August 23, 1985; Petersen Testimony, SSC, *Hearings* (August 9, 1973), 9:3639; Griswold Interview, May 4, 1987.

21. Ruckelshaus Interview, August 21, 1986; Agnew, *Go Quietly,* 60; Richardson Interviews, May 14, 30, 1985; Richardson Memo, October 19, 1973, Richardson MS, LC.

22. Archibald Cox, *The Court and the Constitution* (Boston, 1987), 2; Sam Ervin, *The Whole Truth* (New York, 1980), 94, 118; Bork Interview, June 17, 1987.

23. *Los Angeles Times,* January 28, 1973; Ervin, *The Whole Truth,* 12, 98–99; Jack Anderson Column in *WP,* May 25, 1973; Titus to Richardson, April 30, 1973, Richardson MS, LC; Silbert Interview, November 20, 1987. Two accounts, reflecting the point of view of the Special Prosecutor's office, give some credit to the U.S. Attorney's office, but somewhat grudgingly: Richard Ben-Veniste and George Frampton, Jr., *Stonewall: The Real Story of the Watergate Prosecution* (New York, 1977), 24; James Doyle, *Not Above the Law: The Battle of Watergate Prosecutors Cox and Jaworski* (New York, 1977), 51–52, 80–81. A more detached and balanced assessment is in George V. Higgins, "The Judge Who Tried Harder," *Atlantic,* April 1974, 102–03.

24. Silbert Interviews, September 30, 1988, February 23, 1989; Titus to Richardson, May 15, 1973; Richardson to Titus, May 17, 1973; Titus to Richardson, May 18, 1973, Richardson MS, LC; Silbert Diary.

25. Samuel Dash, *Chief Counsel* (New York, 1976), 71-73, 152; Armstrong Interview, February 9, 1987; Silbert Diary; Cox, *The Court and the Constitution*, 3.

26. Silbert Diary.

27. Silbert to Cox, June 7, 1973, WGSPF Records, NA. This extraordinary memo is summarily acknowledged in the Special Prosecutor's *Final Report*, October 1975, 193. It is treated with other data as reflecting the attempt of Silbert and his colleagues to stay in the case or to get Cox to accept their theories—altogether, a wrong, ungracious, and territorial interpretation. Dash, *Chief Counsel*, 143.

28. Silbert, Glanzer, and Campbell to Cox, June 29, 1973; Cox to Silbert, et al., June 29, 1973, WGSPF Records, NA.

29. L. M. Walters to Cox, May 29, 1973; Phil Heymann to Cox and Vorenberg, June 18, 1973; Jim Doyle to Senior Staff, June 25, 1973 and August 15, 1973, WGSPF Records, Administrative Files, NA.

30. Dash, *Chief Counsel*, 141-46; Dash Interview, February 5, 1986; Minutes, February 7, 1973, SSC Records, NA; Cox to Ervin, June 4, 1973, Richardson MS, LC; Minutes, June 5, 1973, SSC Records, NA; Ervin, *The Whole Truth*, 116-17.

31. Dean Testimony, SSC, *Hearings* (June 25, 1973), 3:983-89, 1243-1246, including White House agendas for Baker meeting; Ehrlichman Notes, February 23, 24, March 13, 16, 20, 23, 29, 30, April 8, 11, 14, 1973, Ehrlichman Papers, Box 14, NP.

32. TT, Telephone Conversations, Ehrlichman and Colson, March 30, April 20, 1973; Ehrlichman and Mitchell, April 11, 1973; Ehrlichman and Baker, April 2, 13, 16, 1973, Ehrlichman Papers, Box 28, NP.

33. Ehrlichman Notes, April 4, 17, Ehrlichman Papers, Box 14, NP; TT, the President, Haldeman, and Ehrlichman, March 27, 1973, *WHT;* TT, Telephone Conversation, Ehrlichman and Gray, March 27, 1973, Ehrlichman Papers, Box 28, NP; TT, Telephone Conversation, Ehrlichman and Kleindienst, March 28, 1973, *WHT.*

34. TT, Telephone Conversation, Ehrlichman and Gray, March 27, 1973, Ehrlichman Papers, Box 28, NP; Khachigian Memo, April 14, 1973, and Khachigian to Higby, April 16, 1973, Haldeman Papers, Box 181, NP.

35. William Timmons to Haldeman, March 29, 1973, Haldeman Papers, Box 47, NP; "Potential Matters for Discussion with Senator Baker," n.d., John Dean File, NPF, Box 7, NP; Dash, *Chief Counsel*, 112, 153-54; TT, Telephone Conversation, Colson and Nixon, March 21, 1973, *WP,* May 1, 1977; TT, the President, Haldeman, and Ehrlichman, April 14, 1973 (8:55 A.M.-11:31 A.M.), Nixon Papers, Box 172, NP; Ehrlichman Notes, March 29, 30, April 6, 16, 1973, Ehrlichman Papers, Box 14, NP; TT, Telephone Conversation, Ehrlichman and Baker, April 16, 1973, Ehrlichman Papers, Box 28, NP; Bull Interview, May 7, 1987.

36. Dash, *Chief Counsel*, 89, 95-98, 101-03, 118; Ervin, *The Whole Truth*, 25, 115; Fred D. Thompson, *At That Point in Time* (New York, 1975), 43; Minutes, May 2, 8, 1973, SSC Records, NA.

37. Buchanan to Nixon, May 4, 1973, NPF, Box 6, NP.

38. Minutes, February 21, 1973, SSC Records, NA.

39. Higgins, "Judge Who Tried Harder," 100.

40. Thompson, *At That Point in Time*, 25-26, 46-48; Dash, *Chief Counsel*, 46-47, 55-56; Higgins, "Judge Who Tried Harder," 99-100.

41. Higgins, "Judge Who Tried Harder," 99-100.

42. Ehrlichman Notes, November 29, 1972, Ehrlichman Papers, Box 7, NP; Transcript, Telephone Conversation, Ehrlichman and Ervin, January 8, 1973, Ehrlichman Papers, Box 28, NP; Ehrlichman Notes, February 16, 1973, Ehrlichman Papers, Box 114, NP; Ervin, *The Whole Truth*, 25-26.

43. Dash, *Chief Counsel*, 87.

44. *NYT,* May 11, 17, 25, 26, 1973; *WP,* May 18, 19, 1973.

45. *WP,* May 22, 1973; *PPPUS:RN, 1973,* "Statements about the Watergate Investigation," (May 22, 1973), 547-55; (April 17, 1973), 298-99.

46. Ehrlichman Notes, February 5, 1973, Ehrlichman Papers, Box 14, NP; Ehrlichman to Dean, March 22, 1973, Dean Papers, Box 7, NP; *Executive Privilege,* Hearings, Subcommittee on Intergovernmental Relations and Subcommittee on Separation of Powers, U.S. Senate, 93 Cong., 1 Sess. (April 10, 1973), 18-52.

XIV: "WHAT DID THE PRESIDENT KNOW AND WHEN DID HE KNOW IT?"
THE SENATE COMMITTEE: SUMMER 1973

1. Minutes, June 5, 1973, SSC Records, NA. Various participants have described the hearings from their perspectives, including Ervin, Dash, Thompson, Dean, Haldeman, Ehrlichman, Magruder, Stans, and Kleindienst. Mary McCarthy, *The Mask of State* (New York, 1975) has some vivid characterizations, as does the novelist and former prosecutor George V. Higgins, "The Judge Who Tried Harder," *Atlantic,* April 1974, 83-106. Higgins (106) summed up the hearings as a "lame imitation" of the work of the U.S. Attorney, the FBI, and the grand jury; "it was not a good job," he concluded.

2. SSC, *Hearings,* 1:1-9, 8:3181.

3. SSC, *Hearings,* 1:27, 82.

4. SSC, *Hearings,* 1:128-243.

5. SSC, *Hearings,* 1:267-91.

6. SSC, *Hearings,* 1:159-60, 167, 128-33.

7. SSC, *Hearings,* 1:358-72.

8. Ruckelshaus Address, Columbus, Ohio, June 8, 1973, Department of Justice Press Release.

9. SSC, *Hearings,* 2:568-85.

10. SSC, *Hearings,* 2:632-78.

11. SSC, *Hearings,* 2:726-81.

12. SSC, *Hearings,* 2:489-530.

13. SSC, *Hearings,* 2:818.

14. SSC, *Hearings,* 2:785-875.

15. Minutes, June 5, 1973, SSC Records, NA; *WP,* June 17, 1973.

16. SSC, *Hearings,* 4:1434-35.

17. SSC, *Hearings,* 3:991-1020. Higby Interviews, May 11, June 24, 1973, SSC Records, NA; Bull Interview, May 7, 1987; Henry Kissinger, *Years of Upheaval* (Boston, 1982) 113; Richard Nixon, *RN: The Memoirs of Richard Nixon* (paperback ed., New York, 1979), 2:336-40.

18. SSC, *Hearings,* 3:914, 1030.

19. SSC, *Hearings,* 4:1389, 1407-08, 1460-61.

20. Larry Speakes, *Speaking Out: Inside the Reagan White House* (New York, 1988), 40; SSC, *Hearings,* 4:1412-51. A few weeks later, White House lawyers prepared a memo, popularly known as "Golden Boy," again attempting to discredit Dean's testimony. Garment MS, LC.

21. SSC, *Hearings,* 4:1466-67, 1469, 1488, 1493-94, 1507-08.

22. SSC, *Hearings,* 4:1496-1505.

23. SSC, *Hearings,* 3:1085-86; 4:1515, 1518-19, 1599.

24. *WP,* July 5, May 19, June 7, 13, 1973.

25. Nixon to Haig, July 7, 1973, NPF, Box 4, NP.

26. *PPPUS:RN, 1973,* 636–39; SSC, *Hearings,* 5:1937–38; Minutes, July 12, 1973, SSC Records, NA.

27. Rowland Evans, Jr., and Robert D. Novak, *Nixon in the White House* (New York, 1971), 28; Ehrlichman Notes, April 24, 1973, Ehrlichman Papers, Box 14, NP; SSC, *Hearings,* 3:1050; *ibid.,* 4:1754; *WP,* June 29, 1973. Years later, Mitchell remained troubled by the origins of the memo. Mitchell Interview, December 30, 1987.

28. SSC, *Hearings,* 4:1653–55; 5:1856.

29. SSC, *Hearings,* 4:1606–19.

30. SSC, *Hearings,* 4:1625–26, 1653. Magruder Telephone Interview, December 2, 1987; Dent Interview, October 31, 1986.

31. SSC, *Hearings,* 4:1666, 1678, 5:1817, 1829, 1835, 1895.

32. Higby Interview, May 11, 1973, SSC Records, NA; Washington Field Office to Acting Director, FBI, June 17, 1972, FBI Watergate Papers; Hoopes to Ehrlichman, September 14, 1972; Todd Hullin to Hoopes, September 19, 1972; Butterfield to Hullin, September 19, 1972, Ehrlichman Papers, Box 13, NP.

33. Interview Report, with Addendum: Alexander P. Butterfield, July 13, 16, 1973, SSC Records, NA, corrected copies in Butterfield Papers, FL; original report in SSC Records, NA; Armstrong Interview, February 9, 1987. The Secret Service version of the origins of the taping system is in the WGSPF Raymond Zumwalt Interview, October 31, 1973, copy in Buzhardt MS, courtesy of Mrs. J. F. Buzhardt.

34. SSC, *Hearings,* 5:2090; Dash Interview, February 5, 1986; John Dean, *Blind Ambition* (New York, 1976), 332; Nixon, *Memoirs,* 2:449.

35. Fred D. Thompson, *At That Point in Time* (New York, 1975), 84; Helms Interview, July 14, 1988; TT, the President and Haldeman, April 26, 1973 (8:55 A.M.–10:20 A.M.), *WP,* May 1, 1977.

36. Nixon to Shultz, July 16, 1973, SSC Records, NA; SSC, *Hearings,* 5:2136–37, 6:2478–82, 2486, 7:2657–61; Minutes, November 6, 1973, SSC Records, NA; Sam Ervin, *The Whole Truth* (New York, 1980), 258. The White House's legal strategy was outlined in a memorandum from Buzhardt, Garment, and Wright to the President, July 24, 1973, Garment MS, LC.

37. SSC, *Hearings,* 5:2092, 2107–17, 2167–70, 2122–23, 2127, 2130–31, 2153–56, 2172–75.

38. SSC, *Hearings,* 5:2277–88, 3106–11, 3126–38 (LaRue); 5:2224, 2226, 2247–48, 2263 (Ulasewicz).

39. SSC, *Hearings,* 6:2438–39, 2488–89, 2477–78.

40. SSC, *Hearings,* 6:2450–51, 2503, 2491.

41. Krogh Interview, August 20, 1986; *Manchester Guardian,* June 4, 1987. For some examples of Ehrlichman's clashes with Dash, Ervin, Inouye, and Weicker, see SSC, *Hearings,* 6:2537–38, 2624–25, 2632–33, 7:2671–72.

42. "Witness Estimates," n.d., Buzhardt MS, courtesy of Mrs. J. F. Buzhardt.

43. SSC, *Hearings,* 6:2529–30.

44. SSC, *Hearings,* 6:2541–43, 2545–47, 2643–45.

45. SSC, *Hearings,* 6, 2600–01. Ervin subsequently noted William Pitt the Elder's precise remark: "The poorest man in his cottage may bid defiance to all the forces of the crown. It may be frail, its roof may shake, the wind may blow through it, the storm may enter, the rain may enter, but the King of England cannot enter. All his force dares not cross the threshold of the ruined tenements." 6:2631.

46. SSC, *Hearings,* 6:2608, 2613, 2619–22, 2746–47.

47. SSC, *Hearings,* 7:2864–66.

48. SSC, *Hearings,* 7:2867, 3021.

49. SSC, *Hearings,* 7:2868-69. See Chapter IV, *supra.*

50. SSC, *Hearings,* 7:2874-82; 8:3079-81, 3171-74, 3189-90, 3151-53.

51. SSC, *Hearings,* 7:2893-94; 8:3050-61, 3065-67, 3082-87, 3090, 3107-09, 3122-23, 3114-15, 3164-65, 3207-08. Samuel Dash, *Chief Counsel* (New York, 1976), 197.

52. SSC, *Hearings,* 8:3130-32, 3227. Haldeman's 1987 view was quoted in *Newsday,* November 20, 1987. "The answers to the unanswered Watergate questions lie in other directions [than Haldeman's papers]—and I do hope you are able to find out where because so far no one else seems to have done so." Haldeman to Author, September 17, 1985.

53. SSC, *Hearings,* 8:3198, 3181, 3169-71, 3200-01, 3227-29, 3231-32; *NYT,* July 26, August 2, 3, 1973.

54. The poll data are taken from corresponding dates in the *New York Times* or the *Washington Post.* Gladys Engel Lang and Kurt Lang, *The Battle for Public Opinion: The President, the Press, and the Polls During Watergate* (New York, 1983), 53-90, offers some analysis of the surveys.

55. William C. Berman, *William Fulbright and the Vietnam War: The Dissent of a Realist* (Kent, OH, 1988), 176-78; *National Review,* August 17, 1973.

XV: "LET OTHERS WALLOW IN WATERGATE." AGNEW, THE TAPES, AND THE SATURDAY NIGHT MASSACRE: AUGUST–OCTOBER 1973

1. *PPPUS:RN, 1973,* August 15, 1973, televised speech and additional written statement, 690-703; *ibid.,* August 22, 1973 News Conference, 710-25.

2. Buzhardt, Garment, and Wright to the President, August 22, 1973, Garment MS, LC; *NYT,* August 18, 1973; *National Review,* August 3, 1973.

3. Richard Nixon, *RN: The Memoirs of Richard Nixon* (paperback ed., New York, 1979), 2:451-52; Agnew Interview, January 14, 1989; Agnew to Author, February 1, 1989; Moley to Rose Mary Woods, July 16, 1973, NPF, Box 12, NP; Dr. Arnold A. Hutschneker to Nixon, July 3, 1973, NPF, Box 188, NP.

4. *WP,* July 17, 1973; Samuel Dash, *Chief Counsel* (New York, 1976), 179-80; Laird Interview, June 27, 1985.

5. Nixon, *Memoirs,* 2:452; TT, Nixon and Haldeman, April 26, 1973, in *WP,* May 1, 1977.

6. Nixon, *Memoirs,* 2:452-55.

7. Spiro Agnew, *Go Quietly . . . Or Else* (New York, 1980), 87; Nixon quoted in *Newsweek,* April 16, 1985, 37; Garment Interview, April 29, 1986; Robert Pack, *Edward Bennett Williams: For the Defense* (New York, 1983), 19. The leading precedent at that time indicating that destruction of the tapes would have constituted an obstruction of justice was *U.S. v. Solow,* 138 F. Supp. 812 (S.D.N.Y., 1956).

8. Julie Nixon Eisenhower, *Pat Nixon: The Untold Story* (New York, 1986), 380; Nixon, *Memoirs,* 2:545-46.

9. Nixon, *Memoirs,* 2:452; Henry Kissinger, *Years of Upheaval* (Boston, 1982), 111-13. Nixon and Haldeman offered various explanations in their memoirs for why they created the taping system. Haldeman later offered another version: "The Nixon White House Tapes: The Decision to Record Presidential Conversations," *Prologue* (Summer 1988), 20:79-87.

10. Ervin to Nixon, July 23, 1973, Nixon to Ervin, July 26, 1973, SSC Records, NA; *NYT* and *WP,* July 18, 24, 26, 27, August 23, 30, 1973; *In re Grand Jury Subpoena to Nixon,* 360 F. Supp. 1 (1973); Nixon, *Memoirs,* 2:460-61.

11. Nixon, *Memoirs,* 2:461-65; Jonathan Moore to Richardson, July 9, 1973, Richardson MS, LC; Richardson Interview, May 14, 1985; Elliot Richardson, *The Creative Balance:*

Government, Politics, and the Individual in America's Third Century (New York, 1976), 16, 26-27; *WP*, July 25, 1973.

12. Joseph Spear, *Presidents and the Press: The Nixon Legacy* (Cambridge, MA, 1984), 193; Nixon, *Memoirs*, 2:456. In his memoirs, Nixon berated CBS for its repetition of the film but never said why the network found it necessary. *Ibid.*, 528.

13. TT, the President, Haldeman, and Ehrlichman, April 14, 1973 (8:55 A.M.–11:31 A.M.), Nixon Papers, Box 172, NP; Jonathan Moore to Richardson, July 9, 1973, Richardson MS, LC; Richardson Interview, May 14, 1985.

14. Richard Whalen, *Catch the Falling Flag: A Republican's Challenge to His Party* (Boston, 1972), 241-42; Joe McGinniss, *The Selling of the President 1968* (paperback ed., New York, 1970), 50.

15. Agnew to Nixon, November 10, 1972, Ehrlichman Papers, Box 13, NP.

16. Henry Kissinger, *Years of Upheaval* (Boston, 1982), 92; James Kilpatrick column, *Washington Star*, May 14, 1974; Agnew, *Go Quietly*, 26, 31, 34; Agnew Interview, January 14, 1989; Keene Interview, August 14, 1985.

17. Agnew, *Go Quietly*, 40; Haldeman Notes, November 14, 1972, Haldeman Papers, Box 46, NP.

18. Keene Interview, August 14, 1985; Otten Interview, October 10, 1985; *WSJ*, August 7, 1973; *NYT*, August 7, 8, 1973; NYT, August 22, September 5, 1973; *PPPUS:RN, 1973*, August 22, 1973 Press Conference, 710-725; *ibid.*, September 5, 1973 Press Conference, 732-43. For an account of the investigation and the detailed charges, see Richard M. Cohen and Jules Witcover, *A Heartbeat Away* (paperback ed., New York, 1974).

19. Nixon, *Memoirs*, 2:465-68; Richardson Interview, May 14, 1985.

20. Agnew, *Go Quietly*, 30, 58, 150, 195, 102, 191, 78, 116, 60; David Frost, *"I Gave Them a Sword: Behind the Scenes of the Nixon Interviews"* (New York, 1978), 290-92; Keene Interview, August 14, 1985; Richardson Interview, May 14, 1985; "Chronology," August 20, September 1, 1973, in Leonard Garment MS, LC; Garment Interview, June 26, 1985; Petersen Interview, August 23, 1985; Laird Interview, June 27, 1985; Richardson Memo, October 19, 1973, Richardson MS, LC.

21. Petersen Interview, August 23, 1985; Rita Hauser to Nixon, October 9, 1973, NPF, Box 9, NP; Agnew, *Go Quietly*, 140-43, 146, 151.

22. The Agnew letter is in Agnew, *Go Quietly*, 165-67; Albert Interview, Capitol Hill Historical Society, 25, 29, 30; Keene Interview, August 14, 1985. Memorandum in Support of Motion [to Dismiss Criminal Indictment Against Agnew], September 28, U.S.D.C. (Md.), courtesy of Jay H. Topkis.

23. Hutchinson Speech, September 27, 1973, Hutchinson Papers, FL; Fish Interview, June 26, 1975; *WP*, September 29, 1973; Richard Reeves, *A Ford, Not a Lincoln* (New York, 1975), 32; Gerald R. Ford, *A Time to Heal* (New York, 1979), 103.

24. Nixon, *Memoirs*, 2:471; Keene Interview, August 14, 1985; Petersen Draft, September 21, 1973, in Buzhardt MS, courtesy of Mrs. J. F. Buzhardt; "Chronology," August 7, 20, September 1, 1973, Garment MS, LC; Agnew, *Go Quietly*, 95, 187-89. Agnew said that he had written his memoirs because he was "innocent."

25. *NYT*, October 11, 1973; Pack, *Edward Bennett Williams*, 324; Richardson, *Creative Balance*, 102-03; Nixon to Agnew, October 10, 1973, NPF, Box 5, NP.

26. Hedley Donovan, *Roosevelt to Reagan: A Reporter's Encounters with Nine Presidents* (New York, 1985), 123; Nixon, *Memoirs*, 2:582; Bork Interview, June 17, 1987; Jay H. Topkis to Author, June 10, 1988, January 25, 1989.

27. Nixon, *Memoirs*, 2:475-78, 479-80, 484, 487-88, 494-504; Roger Morris, *Uncertain Greatness* (New York, 1977), 251-56; Kissinger, *Years of Upheaval*, 450-667; Golda Meir, *My Life* (New York, 1975), 362; Garment to Nixon, May 31, 1973, Garment MS, LC; Moorer

Interview, June 25, 1985; Finklestein Interview, May 30, 1985; Gazit Interview, December 29, 1985. The resupply question touched off a contemporary and running historiographical feud between Kissinger and Defense Secretary Schlesinger, longstanding antagonists. Compare, for example, Bernard and Marvin Kalb, *Kissinger* (Boston, 1974), 471–75, as well as the supplement of Kissinger's memoirs, to the account Schlesinger dictated for *Time*, July 1, 1974, 33. In contrast to Middle East developments later in the month, the President seemed actively involved at this time.

28. Richardson, *Creative Balance*, 38; *Nixon v. Sirica*, 487 F.2d 700 (1973); *Senate Select Committee v. Nixon*, 366 F. Supp. 51 (1973); Archibald Cox, *The Court and the Constitution* (Boston, 1987), 11–13.

29. Wright to Fred Graham, March 22, 1974, Graham MS, LC.

30. Garment to Richard Nixon, September 11, 1973, Garment MS, LC; "Chronology," October 13, 1973, *ibid.*; Rose Mary Woods to Nixon, October 10, 1973, NPF, Box 9, NP.

31. Ruckelshaus Interview, August 21, 1986; "Summary Chronology," Richardson MS, LC. This paper was prepared by Richardson on December 10, 1973. Some of Richardson's papers and related documents are collected in the John F. Kennedy Institute of Politics' case study "The Saturday Night Massacre."

32. Stennis Telephone Interview, June 27, 1985; *WP*, December 4, 1973.

33. "A Proposal," #4, October 17, 1973, Richardson MS, LC; "Summary Chronology"; Cox to Richardson, October 18, 1973; Wright to Cox, October 18, 1973; Cox to Wright, October 19, 1973; Wright to Cox, October 19, 1973; Nixon to Richardson, October 19, 1973; Richardson Statement, October 19, 1973; Richardson Memo, October 19, 1973; Richardson to Nixon, October 20, 1973, *ibid.*; Garment Interview, May 29, 1985; Dash, *Chief Counsel*, 267–72; Ervin Interview, John Stennis Project, June 9, 1976, Stennis MS, Mississippi State University; Richardson, *Creative Balance*, 37; "Chronology," October 18–19, 1973, Garment MS, LC. Cox interpreted his telephone conversation with Wright on the evening of October 28 as an attempt to force his resignation; Wright has refused to dispute or confirm that interpretation, courteously maintaining his vow of silence on his role. Wright to Author, June 13, 1985, July 28, November 16, 1987, and the Preface to his father's account, *Legal Eagle* (privately published).

34. Cox News Conference, *NYT*, October 21, 1973; Richardson, *Creative Balance*, 44.

35. Richardson to the President, October 20, 1973, Richardson MS, LC; "Chronology," October 20, 1973, Garment MS, LC; Richardson, *Creative Balance*, 44, 39; Nixon, *Memoirs*, 2:491–92; Richardson in *Boston Globe*, September 9, 1984; Ruckelshaus Interview, August 21, 1986; *Special Prosecutor*, Hearings, Committee on the Judiciary, U.S. Senate, 93 Cong., 1 Sess., 237–318, 383–426.

36. The accounts of Saturday night's events in the Department of Justice are based on interviews with Bork, June 17, 1987, Ruckelshaus, August 21, 1986, and Richardson, May 14, 30, 1985; Richardson, *Creative Balance*, 44–45. The interviews are remarkable for their agreement on facts and language. Cox, *The Court and the Constitution*, 16–25, offers Cox's version of events. Jaworski Oral History, Baylor University, 3:706.

37. Bork Interview, June 17, 1987; *WP*, October 22, 1973.

38. *WP*, October 22, 23, 25, 1973; *PPPUS:RN, 1973*, Press Conference, October 26, 1973, 896–906.

39. *Federal Register*, 38:29466 (October 25, 1973); *Impeachment Inquiry*, Hearings, Committee on the Judiciary, House of Representatives, 93 Cong., 2 Sess., 2:1401. Hereafter cited as HJC, *Impeachment Inquiry*. *WP*, July 2, 27, 1987; *NYT*, September 30, 1987; Bork Interview, June 17, July 18, 1987; *NYT*, July 1, 1987. Bork's acquiescence in the ongoing functions of the WGSPF was acknowledged by the House Judiciary Committee in 1974. HJC, *Impeachment Inquiry* (June 19, 1974), 2:1401.

40. Nixon, *Memoirs*, 2:493; Spear, *Presidents and the Press*, 230–32; Garment Interview,

May 29, 1985; Garment to Author, September 4, 1987; Wright to Author, July 28, 1987; *WP*, October 9, 1987; Watergate "Talking Paper," c. October 21-23, 1973, SSF, Box 113, NP; Strom Thurmond to Bill Timmons, November 15, 1973, Nixon Papers, Box 16, NP. The White House claimed that after four days, it had received approximately 7,000 negative telegrams to 4,600 favorable ones—an unusual admission.

41. Smith Statement, October 22, 1973, in Jaworski MS, Baylor University; William Safire in *NYT*, October 22, 1973; *Human Events*, November 3, 1973.

42. Raymond L. Garthoff, *Detente and Confrontation: American-Soviet Relations from Nixon to Reagan* (Washington, 1985), 374-85, offered the most detailed, least self-serving account of the alert; also see Nixon, *Memoirs*, 2:498-500; Kissinger, *Years of Upheaval*, 583-613; Morris, *Uncertain Greatness*, 245-49; *Newsweek*, November 5, 1973; *WP*, October 26, 1973.

43. Draft Speech, October 24, 1973, with Garment-to-Price memorandum of October 23, 1973, in NPF, Box 114, NP.

44. John J. Sirica, *To Set the Record Straight* (New York, 1979), 175-76. Public advocate Ralph Nader and several liberal Democratic congressmen filed suit against Bork, contending that Cox's dismissal had been illegal. Cox did not join the suit, sensing that his day had passed and that any claims he made to be restored to his position "would only divert attention from getting the real job done." The district court found that Bork had violated the guidelines for his job, but the appellate court vacated the judgment on the ground that the case was moot. *Nader v. Bork*, 366 F. Supp. 104 (D.D.C. 1973); Watergate Special Prosecution Force, *Report* (October 1975), 11-12; *NYT*, November 15, 1973; Nancy Kassop, "President Nixon's Dismissal of Special Prosecutor Archibald Cox," unpublished paper.

45. *NYT*, October 24, 31, 1973; Flowers Interview, June [12?,] 1975; Thornton Interview, June 13, 1975; Railsback Interview, June 11, 1975.

46. Ervin to Ira G. Shamel, November 7, 1973, Box 360, Ervin MS, Southern Historical Collections, University of North Carolina Library, for the Senator's mail following Cox's dismissal. J. H. Hexter, "Firestorm," offered a useful analysis of the Ervin correspondence (unpublished paper, courtesy of the author).

47. Griswold Interview, May 4, 1987; Clarence Kelley, *Kelley: The Story of an FBI Director* (Kansas City, 1987), 123, 131-34, 140; Richardson, *Creative Balance*, 46-47; Jaworski Oral History, Baylor University, 2:537-38.

XVI: "SINISTER FORCES": FORD, JAWORSKI, TAPE GAPS, AND TAXES: NOVEMBER-DECEMBER 1973

1. Nixon to Chapin, October 7, 1973, NPF, Box 6, NP; Nixon to Rose Mary Woods, September 13, 1973, NPF, Box 10, NP.

2. Ehrlichman Notes, November [day?] 1972 meeting, Ehrlichman Papers, Box 13, NP; Nixon to Krogh, October 7, 1973, NPF, Box 10, NP; Leon Jaworski to Stephen N. Shulman (Krogh's attorney), November 30, 1973; Indictment, *U.S. v. Krogh*, Dist. Ct., DC (October 11, 1973); Statement of Krogh to Judge Gesell, November 30, 1973, U.S. District Court Records, *U.S. v. Krogh*, NA; Richard Nixon, *RN: The Memoirs of Richard Nixon* (paperback ed., New York, 1979), 1:637; Krogh Interview, August 20, 1986.

3. John D. Feerick, *The Twenty-fifth Amendment* (New York, 1976); Birch Bayh, *One Heartbeat Away* (Indianapolis, 1968).

4. Haldeman "Talking Paper," January 8, 1973, Haldeman Papers, Box 179, NP; Gerald R. Ford, *A Time to Heal* (New York, 1979), 107-08; Nixon, *Memoirs*, 2:481-82; Chapin to Rose Mary Woods, October 15, 1973, NPF, Box 6, NP; Albert Interview, Capitol Hill Historical Society, 42-45; John D. Ehrlichman, *Witness to Power* (New York, 1982), 257.

5. Larry Winn, Jr. to Nixon, McCloskey to Nixon, Ford to Nixon, October 11, 1973, Nixon Papers, Box 168, NP.

6. Laird Interview, June 27, 1985; Ford, *A Time to Heal*, 103–04, 105; Henry A. Kissinger, *Years of Upheaval* (Boston, 1982), 514; Robert Sam Anson, *Exile: The Unquiet Oblivion of Richard Nixon* (New York, 1984), 39; Richard Reeves, *A Ford, Not a Lincoln* (New York, 1975), 42, 58.

7. Ron Nessen, *It Sure Looks Different from the Inside* (New York, 1978), 4; David Frost, *"I Gave Them a Sword": Behind the Scenes of the Nixon Interviews* (New York, 1978), 78.

8. *Time*, November 12, 1973.

9. Jerald F. terHorst, *Gerald Ford and the Future of the Presidency* (New York, 1974), 127–28; Reeves, *Ford*, 31; Becker Interview, December 5, 1985; Dixon Interview, November 20, 1985.

10. Hutchinson to Stephen Nisbet, October 29, 1973, Hutchinson to Mrs. Robert Beckwith, November 9, 1973, Hutchinson MS, FL; Dixon Interviews, November 20, 1985, January 24, 1986; *Nomination of Gerald R. Ford to be the Vice President of the United States*, Hearings, Committee on the Judiciary, House of Representatives, 93 Cong., 1 Sess. (November 15, 16, 19–21, 26, 1973), 1–2, 5, 45, 49, 57–58, 91, 185–86, 329–67. Miscellaneous House Judiciary Committee documents courtesy of Steven Lynch, a former staff member.

11. Reeves, *Ford*, 44; *NYT*, December 6, 1973; Ford, *A Time to Heal*, 108, 117.

12. Bork Interview, June 17, 1987.

13. "Chronology," December 28, 1973, Garment MS, LC; Dent Interview, September 24, 1986; Mrs. J. F. Buzhardt Interview, September 25, 1986.

14. Garment Interviews, May 29, June 26, 1985; Garment Notes for April 9, 10, 1973, prepared April 16, 1974 for the Special Prosecutor, Garment MS, LC; "Chronology," June 28, November 14, 28, December 14, 27, 28, 1973, *ibid.*; Anonymous to Garment, December 7, 1973, *ibid.*

15. Stephen E. Ambrose, *Nixon: The Education of a Politician, 1913–1962* (New York, 1962), 236–37; Stanley I. Kutler, *The American Inquisition: Justice and Injustice in the Cold War* (New York, 1982), Ch. 6; Charles Alan Wright, "Right to Counsel and Counsels' Rights," *The Nation*, November 21, 1953, 426–28. Fawn Brodie speculated that Nixon may have believed that if the gifted Wright could be persuaded that Hiss had not lied, then he might similarly be persuaded about the President. *Richard Nixon: The Shaping of His Character* (New York, 1981), 199.

16. "Chronology," July 30, August 1, September 15, 1973, Garment MS, LC; Fred Graham Interview with Wright, October 20, 1973, Graham MS, LC; Press Conference, July 26, 1973, Garment MS, LC.

17. "Chronology," December 19, 1973, Garment MS, LC; Wright's Preface, June 9, 1977, to his father's privately published account of his role, *Legal Eagle*, courtesy of Professor Wright.

18. "Chronology," November 10, December 4, 1973, Garment MS, LC; David C. Hoopes to Haig (summarizing Sullivan letter of March 18, 1974), March 19, 1974, Hoopes Papers, NP; St. Clair Interview, April 10, 1987; Griswold Interview, May 4, 1987; Liebman Interview, June 14, 1988.

19. *Human Events*, November 10, 1973; *NYT*, November 2, 1973; Leon Jaworski, *The Right and the Power: The Prosecution of Watergate* (New York, 1976); Leon Jaworski, *Confession and Avoidance: A Memoir* (New York, 1979); Leon Jaworski Oral History, The Texas Collection, Baylor University, 1:210–22, 263–66, 336–41; 2:475–76; 5:897, 906; Bork Interview, June 17, 1987. When Jaworski had met Nixon on earlier occasions, he had been baffled by some of the strange sides of the President's personality: Oral History Memoir, 2:488–90.

20. Jaworski Oral History, 2:529.

21. *Federal Register* (November 7, 1973), 30738–39; *ibid.* (November 19, 1973), 32805; Bork to Jaworski, November 21, 1973, Administrative Files, WGSPF Records, NA; Jaworski Oral History, 2:447, 451–55.

22. *Special Prosecutor,* Hearings, Committee on the Judiciary, U.S. Senate, 93 Cong., 1 Sess. (October 29–November 1, November 5–8, November 14–15, November 20), 2–22, 40–45, 51–61, 147–63, 320–24, 354–55, 451–69, 556, 580–85; *WP,* February 21, 1973. In 1988, Circuit Court Judge Silberman wrote a majority opinion declaring a judicially appointed "Independent Counsel"—the legislative successor to the Special Prosecutor—unconstitutional.

23. Louis Fisher, *Constitutional Conflicts Between Congress and the President* (Princeton, NJ, 1985), 90–91.

24. Nixon, *Memoirs,* 2:507–08; "Chronology," June 16, 27, 1973, Garment MS, LC; Buzhardt to Cox, June 16, 1973, *ibid.*

25. Nixon, *Memoirs,* 2:473–74, 510–15; *NYT,* November 21, 1973.

26. "Chronology," December 5, 1973, Garment MS, LC; *NYT,* December 7, 1973; *National Review,* December 21, 1973; Sidney Glazer, *et al.* to Henry Ruth, November 25, 1973, "18½ Minute Investigation," WGSPF Records, NA.

27. *NYT,* January 16, 17, 1973; Ford, *A Time to Heal,* 115.

28. FBI Director to Jaworski, March 13, 1974; Jaworski to St. Clair, January 15, 1974; St. Clair to Jaworski, March 19, 1974, Jaworski MS, The Texas Collection, Baylor University.

29. *Washington Star,* January 24, 1974; Jaworski Oral History, 2:578–81.

30. Nixon, *Memoirs,* 2:515; "Chronology," May 17, 1973, Garment MS, LC; Garment Interview, May 8, 1987; HJC, *Statement of Information,* "Tax Deduction for Gift of Papers," 10:1–3.

31. Alexander Interview, May 8, 1987.

32. *Examination of President Nixon's Tax Returns for 1969 Through 1972,* Report, Joint Committee on Internal Revenue Taxation, 93 Cong., 2 Sess. (April 3, 1974); HJC, *Statement of Information,* 10:1–19, 12:2–82; Mildred Stegall to Lyndon Johnson, November 5, 1969, "Post-Presidential Names File," Lyndon B. Johnson Papers, LBJ Library; Michael Bloomer to Edward Hutchinson, July 12, 1974, Hutchinson MS, FL; *PPPUS:RN, 1974,* 1005–08; *NYT,* July 24, 30, 1973, May 2, 1976, May 25, September 7, November 18, 1979; *PPPUS:RN, 1973,* November 17, 1973, 956; Nixon, *Memoirs,* 2:515–27; *PPPUS:RN, 1972,* June 22, 1972, 529–30. The story of how the National Archives official discovered the illegal back dating is recounted in Transcript, *U.S. v. DeMarco,* September 25, 1975, 1021–68, WGSPF Records, NA. For an example of skirting the issue of treating presidential papers as private property, see the exchange between Senator Inouye and Gordon Strachan during the earlier Select Committee proceedings: SSC, *Hearings,* 6:2487–88.

33. WGSPF, *Final Report, 1977* (Washington, 1977), 43–62; Thomas O'Neill (with William Novak), *Man of the House: The Life and Political Memoirs of Speaker Tip O'Neill* (New York, 1987), 235–38. President Reagan pardoned Steinbrenner in 1989.

34. Laird Interview, June 27, 1985; Moorer Interview, June 25, 1985; Kissinger, *Years of Upheaval,* 1078, 100, 77–78, 105, 535, 536, 1071, *et passim;* TT, the President, Haldeman, and Ehrlichman, April 14, 1973 (8:55 A.M.–11:31 A.M.), Nixon Papers, Box 172, NP; *Milwaukee Journal,* April 7, 1985.

35. Garment to the President, November 24, 1973, Garment MS, LC; *PPPUS:RN, 1973,* "Address to the Nation About Policies to Deal with the Energy Shortage" (November 7, 1973), 916–22.

36. Garment Interview, May 29, 1985; Clarence Kelley, *Kelley: The Story of an FBI Director* (Kansas City, 1987), 117–20.

37. Gazit Interview, December 29, 1985.

38. Kissinger, *Years of Upheaval*, 77–78.

39. Armand Hammer and Neil Lyndon, *Hammer* (New York, 1987), 409.

40. USIA, *Digest of Foreign Newspaper Comment:* British Commercial Television, May 2, 1973; [London] *Times*, May 14, 1973; *Japan Times*, May 2, 1973; [Rotterdam] *Handelsblad*, May 2, 1973; [Vienna] *Die Presse*, July 30, 1973; [Hamburg] *Die Zeit*, August 3, 1973; [Oslo] *Aftenposten*, August 10, 1973. "Psychological Assessment," London to Washington, December 7, 1973, USIA Papers.

41. Nixon, *Memoirs*, 2:435; Richard M. Nixon, *No More Vietnams* (New York, 1985). See Chapter XXII, *infra*.

42. Nixon, *Memoirs*, 2:535–36; *Congressional Quarterly Almanac, 1973* (Washington, 1974), 906.

43. Kissinger, *Years of Upheaval*, 255; James Bryce, *The American Commonwealth* (paperback ed., New York, 1961), 91; *Time*, November 12, 1973; Hedley Donovan, *Roosevelt to Reagan* (New York, 1985), 127.

44. *NYT*, December 13, 20, 1973.

45. O'Neill, *Man of the House*, 249–52; Petersen Interview, August 23, 1985.

46. Zeifman Interview, February 5, 1986; Cates Interview, February 6, 1988; Franklin Polk to Edward Hutchinson, October 26, November 20, 1973, Hutchinson MS, FL, offered a Republican view of Cates's appointment; O'Neill, *Man of the House*, 256.

47. "Impeachment" File, Dixon MS, Washington University Library; additional Dixon materials are in the files of the Office of Legal Counsel, Department of Justice; J. Woodford Howard, Jr., to Author, June 29, 1987. On January 15, 1974, Howard met with Dixon, who reported that he and his staff had been working on the problem.

48. Coincidentally, as Congress moved into the impeachment inquiry, two scholarly works appeared to question the received wisdom on the Johnson and Chase trials. See Michael Les Benedict, *The Impeachment and Trial of Andrew Johnson* (New York, 1973); Raoul Berger, *Impeachment: The Constitutional Problems* (Cambridge, 1973). Berger justified the Chase impeachment, believing he deserved conviction, but curiously repeated the traditional accounts condemning Johnson's trial.

XVII: "FIGHT": TAPES AND INDICTMENTS: JANUARY–MAY 1974

1. Richard Nixon, *RN: The Memoirs of Richard Nixon* (paperback ed., New York, 1979), 2:537–40.

2. *PPPUS:RN, 1974*, "State of the Union Address" (January 30, 1974), 47–55; *NYT*, February 1, 1974. Twelve years later, Senator Mansfield stated that he would "let my public statements stand." Mansfield to Author, March 8, 1986. Leon Jaworski, Oral History Memoir, The Texas Collection, Baylor University, 2:551.

3. Vladimir N. Pregelj (Foreman) to Richard Nixon, January 30, 1974; St. Clair to Pregelj, January 31, 1974, Jaworski MS, Texas Collection, Baylor University; Pregelj Interview, February 10, 1988.

4. St. Clair Interview, April 10, 1987; *NYT*, January 5, 1974.

5. Jessica Mitford, *The Trial of Dr. Spock* (New York, 1979), 77; Nixon, *Memoirs*, 2:563; Leon Jaworski, *The Right and the Power* (New York, 1976), 84; St. Clair Interview, April 10, 1987; Liebman Interview, June 14, 1988.

6. Bull Interview, May 7, 1987; Kelley to Jaworski, March 13, 1974, Jaworski MS, Baylor University; James Doyle, *Not Above the Law* (New York, 1977), 341–43; Jerry Jones to Haig, June 24, 1974, SSF, Box 157, NP.

7. Garment Interviews, May 29, 1985, April 12, 1988; Bull Interview, May 7, 1987; Dent Interview, September 24, 1986; Mrs. J. Fred Buzhardt Interview, September 25, 1986; Lich-

enstein Interviews, February 7, July 16, 1986; "Chronology," December 12, 1973, Garment MS, LC; Jaworski Oral History Memoir, 2:572-73; *Executive Privilege, Secrecy in Government, Freedom of Information*, Hearings, Subcommittees . . . of the Committee on the Judiciary, U.S. Senate, 93 Cong., 1 Sess. (April 10, 1973), 2.

8. Nixon, *Memoirs*, 2:535-36.

9. Samuel Dash, *Chief Counsel* (New York, 1976), 256-57; *PPPUS:RN, 1974*, 5-7; Sam Ervin, *The Whole Truth* (New York, 1980), 222.

10. Jaworski Oral History Memoir, 2:555; Jaworski, "Observations on the 'Memoirs' of Richard Nixon," undated typescript, Jaworski Papers; Mitchell Interview, February 9, 1988.

11. Jaworski Oral History Memoir, 2:483; "Memorandum," Jaworski to Watergate File, January 15, 1974, Jaworski MS.

12. Nixon, *Memoirs*, 2:544-45; Jaworski to St. Clair, January 9, 22, February 1, 27, March 12, 1974; St. Clair to Jaworski, February 4, 27, 1974, Jaworski MS; Jaworski, *The Right and the Power*, 87-94; Richard Ben-Veniste and George Frampton, *Stonewall: The Real Story of the Watergate Prosecution* (New York, 1977), 216-17; Doyle, *Not Above the Law*, 314.

13. Undated memoranda, regarding February and May meetings with Haig, Jaworski MS.

14. *PPPUS:RN, 1974*, Press Conference, February 25, 1974, 109; *NYT*, January 30, 1974.

15. *NYT*, February 27, 1974; St. Clair to Jaworski, February 4, 1974, Jaworski MS; *PPPUS:RN, 1974*, March 6, 1974, 229-40; Ben-Veniste and Frampton, *Stonewall*, 264; Jaworski to St. Clair, April 11, 1974, Jaworski MS.

16. *NYT*, March 20, 1974; *PPPUS:RN, 1974*, 295.

17. Nixon, *Memoirs*, 2:566-67; St. Clair to Doar, April 9, 1974; Rodino to Nixon, April 11, 1974, Hutchinson MS, FL; Geller to the Files, Haig Interview, July 3, 1975, Bluebook Investigation, WGSPF Records, National Archives.

18. *PPPUS:RN, 1974*, 389-97; Jaworski, Oral History Memoir, 2:482.

19. *Weekly Compilation of Presidential Documents* (April-June 1974), 6:460; *Congressional Record*, 93 Cong., 2 Sess. (April 30, 1974), 12270ff.

20. *NYT*, May 2 (Safire), 4, 29 (Graham), 1974; *WSJ*, May 6, 1974; *WP*, May 2, 1974 (Alsop); *Los Angeles Times*, May 10, 1974; *Detroit News*, May 17, 1974; Joseph Spear, *Presidents and the Press* (Cambridge, 1984), 206-07, 211, 213; Gladys Engel Lang and Kurt Lang, *The Battle for Public Opinion: The President, the Press, and the Polls During Watergate* (New York, 1983), 123-26; *Los Angeles Times*, January 1, 1975 (Graham).

21. TT (Drafts), April 14, April 17, 1973, NPF, Boxes 170, 171, NP; Jimmy Breslin, *How the Good Guys Finally Won* (paperback ed., New York, 1975), 143; Dixon Interview, January 24, 1985.

22. George Allen to Nixon, May 10, 1974; Woods to Nixon, May 13, 1974, NPF, Box 8, NP; Luce to Nixon, May 22, 1974, NPF, Box 19, NP.

23. Bull Interview, May 7, 1987; *NYT*, May 10, 1974; Laird Interview, June 27, 1985; *Roanoke Times*, July 27, 1975; Julie Nixon Eisenhower, *Pat Nixon: The Untold Story* (New York, 1986), 409.

24. Nixon to Rodino, May 22, 1974; Rodino to Nixon, May 30, 1974, Hutchinson MS, FL.

25. Julie Eisenhower to Nixon, May 15, 1974, NPF, Box 8, NP.

26. Keene Interview, August 14, 1985; Phillips Interview, August 23, 1985; Philip Crane, *The Conservative Mandate* (Washington, 1968); "The Leaders Change Sides," *Battle Line* (April 1972), 1-2; *Human Events*, December 29, 1973, February 23, March 9, 1974. See Charles A. Moser, *Promise and Hope: The Ashbrook Presidential Campaign of 1972* (Washington, D.C., 1985), for an account of Ashbrook's revolt and a keen insight into the conservatives' suspicions of Nixon.

27. *Conservative Digest*, June/July 1985, 22; Jim Hougan, *Secret Agenda* (New York,

1984), 75, 63*ff*; Elmo Zumwalt, *On Watch* (New York, 1976), xiv; Phillips Interview, August 23, 1985; *Human Events*, March 30, April 27, May 25, 1974; *National Review*, May 10, 24, 1974.

28. *Playboy* (May 1974); Doris Kearns in *New York Times Book Review*, June 9, 1974; Richard Rovere, *New Yorker*, June 17, 1974, 107–08. Sissela Bok, *Lying: Moral Choice in Public and Private Life* (New York, 1978), 107–22, is particularly critical of the reporters' methods and deceptions.

29. Paul L. Friedman to Earl Silbert, June 7, 1973; Silbert Diary; Silbert to Cox, June 7, 1973, Jaworski Papers, Texas Collection, Baylor University. William Rehnquist and John Mitchell decided in 1969 that Justice Abe Fortas could be indicted without waiting for impeachment proceedings. Robert Shogan, *A Question of Judgment: The Fortas Case and the Struggle for the Supreme Court* (Indianapolis, 1972), 232–33.

30. Ruth to Jaworski, January 2, 1974; Jaworski to Ruth, January 8, 1974; Ruth to Jaworski, January 14, 1974, Jaworski MS.

31. Weinberg to Lacovara, December 26, 1973, Lacovara to Jaworski, January 21, 1974, February 15, 1974, Nixon File #11, WGSPF Records, NA; Feldbaum, Frampton, Goldman, and Rient to Jaworski, February 12, 1974, Nixon File #8, *ibid.*; Ben-Veniste to Jaworski, February 23, 1974, Litigative Memoranda, *ibid.*; Doyle to Barker, March 11, 1974, Nixon File #6a, *ibid.*; Jaworski Oral History Memoir, 2:607–12, 623–31; Jaworski, *The Right and the Power*, 176–90. See *U.S. v. Lee*, 106 U.S. 196, 220 (1882).

32. "Confidential" Memorandum, February 12, 1974, Jaworski MS.

33. Jaworski Oral History Memoir, 2:622–23, 3:729; John Sirica, *To Set the Record Straight* (New York, 1979), 140; Ben-Veniste and Frampton, *Stonewall*, 70–71; *Time*, January 28, 1974, 12; Pregelj Interview, February 10, 1988; *WP*, December 5, 1974; Geller Interview, May 26, 1988.

34. "Jury Materials," Box 13, Jaworski MS; Jaworski Oral History Memoir, 2:623–32, 3:726, 728, 6:1075, 1078–1143; Pregelj Interview, February 10, 1988; Jaworski, *The Right and the Power*, 99–102; Ben-Veniste and Frampton, *Stonewall*, 211–53; Doyle, *Not Above the Law*, 289–309.

35. *PPPUS:RN*, 1974, Press Conference, February 25, 1974, 201–02, 204–09; *NYT*, February 27, 1974.

36. Nixon, *Memoirs*, 2:574–77, 630; Jaworski Oral History Memoir, 2:651–52; Geller to Files, Haig Interview, July 3, 1975, WGSPF Records, NA; St. Clair Interview, April 10, 1987. Sirica announced that Nixon was an unindicted co-conspirator on June 7, a day after St. Clair had given the news to reporters.

37. "Lamentations of a Prosecutor," n.d., Jaworski MS; Jaworski Oral History Memoir, 2:569–71, 3:709–13; Watergate Task Force, "Prosecutive Report," February 7, 1974 (draft), Nixon File #4, WGSPF Records, NA.

38. Earl Hankamer, et al. to Jaworski, March 26, 1974, Jaworski to Hankamer, March 26, 1974, Jaworski MS.

39. Walter Ehrlich, *Presidential Impeachment* (St. Louis, 1974), 130–34.

40. Silberman to the File, April 30, 1974, Special Prosecutor's Files, "Sensitive Investigations," WGSPF Records, NA.

41. The documents relating to the various stages of *U.S. v. Nixon* conveniently are collected in Leon Friedman (ed.), *United States v. Nixon* (New York, 1974). Sirica's opinion is at 162–68. St. Clair's argument is from later unsealed portions of the transcript, filed with *U.S. v. Mitchell* materials in the WGSPF Records, NA.

42. Friedman (ed.), *United States v. Nixon*, 169–87.

43. Jaworski Oral History Memoir, 2:656; Jaworski to Eastland, May 20, 1974; St. Clair to Jaworski, May 17, 1974; Saxbe and Bork to Jaworski, June 5, 1974; Jaworski to Saxbe, June 12, 1974, Jaworski MS; Bork Interview, June 17, 1987.

44. Jaworski to St. Clair, May 24, 1974; St. Clair to Jaworski, May 31, 1974; Jaworski to St. Clair, June 3, 1974; St. Clair to Jaworski, June 13, 1974; Jaworski to St. Clair, June 14, 1974; St. Clair to Jaworski, June 20, 1974, Jaworski MS; St. Clair Interview, April 10, 1987.

45. James Kilpatrick Interview, *Washington Star*, May 14, 1974; Whitehead Interview, May 25, 1988.

XVIII: "WELL, AL, THERE GOES THE PRESIDENCY." THE HOUSE JUDICIARY COMMITTEE: JUNE–JULY 1974

1. *NYT*, April 8, 1973; *Executive Privilege*, Hearings, Subcommittee on Intergovernmental Relations and Subcommittee on Separation of Powers, U.S. Senate, 93 Cong., 1 Sess. (April 10, 1973), 45, 51–52, 81; [Hamilton Fish], "Interview," *Hudson Valley Magazine*, November 1974, 19; Thornton Interview, June 13, 1975.

2. Erwin C. Hargrove and Michael Nelson, *Presidents, Politics, and Policy* (Baltimore, 1984), 35.

3. Clayton Roberts, *The Growth of Responsible Government in Stuart England* (Cambridge, 1966), 435, 23–28, *et passim;* Raoul Berger, *Impeachment: The Constitutional Problems* (Cambridge, 1973), 1–6; Walter Ehrlich, *Presidential Impeachment: An American Dilemma* (St. Louis, 1974).

4. Berger, *Impeachment*, 59–62.

5. Jonathan Elliot (ed.), *Debates on the Federal Constitution* (Philadelphia, 1901), 3:165.

6. Max Farrand (ed.), *The Records of the Federal Convention of 1787* (New Haven, CT, 1911), 2:64–69 (July 20, 1787), 551–52 (September 8, 1787).

7. Elliot, *Debates on the Federal Constitution*, 4:126 (Iredell); 3:498 (Madison).

8. Jefferson to Spencer Roane, September 6, 1819, Merrill Peterson (ed.), *Thomas Jefferson: Writings* (New York, 1983), 1426; Berger, *Impeachment*, 224–51, offers a substantial case against Chase and against the Senate's interpretation of the indictability issue. Leonard W. Levy has eloquently described the emergence of a "new libertarianism" in numerous works, most recently in his *Emergence of a Free Press* (New York, 1985), 282–350. Finally, see Richard E. Ellis, *The Jeffersonian Crisis: Courts and Politics in the Young Republic* (New York, 1971) for the best account of the Chase affair in the larger context of maintaining political accountability of the judiciary.

9. Michael Les Benedict, *The Impeachment and Trial of Andrew Johnson* (New York, 1973), is a revisionist account of the Johnson impeachment, effectively neutralizing the traditional denunciations of the proceedings. Berger, *Impeachment*, 252–96, adhered to the latter.

10. *Constitutional Grounds for Presidential Impeachment*, Report, Committee on the Judiciary, House of Representatives, 93 Cong., 1 Sess. (February 1974); *PPPUS:RN, 1974*, Press Conference, February 25, 1974, 202; *ibid.*, March 6, 1974, 236; "An Analysis . . . of Presidential Impeachment," by the Special Counsel to the President, *Brief on Behalf of the President*, Hearings, Committee on the Judiciary, House of Representatives, 93 Cong., 2 Sess. (July 18, 1974), 60, 102–03; Sam Ervin, *The Whole Truth* (New York, 1980), 265; HJC, *Impeachment Inquiry*, 1:299.

11. *Congressional Record*, 93 Cong., 1 Sess. (July 31, 1973), H7049–51.

12. Cohen Interview, June 17, 1975; Hutchinson to Mrs. Robert Beckwith, November 9, 1973, Hutchinson MS, FL; Thomas O'Neill, *Man of the House: The Life and Political Memoirs of Speaker Tip O'Neill*, with William Novak (New York, 1987), 248–49.

13. *NYT*, March 2, 1974; C. K. Beahm to Hutchinson, February 26, 1974; Hutchinson to Gerber, January 28, 1974, Hutchinson MS, FL.

14. O'Neill, *Man of the House,* 251-52, 255-56; Jimmy Breslin, *How the Good Guys Finally Won* (New York, 1975); Flowers Interview, June [17], 1975; Polk Interview, December 18, 1986; Robert McClory, "Memoirs," 45 (unpublished transcript, courtesy of the author); Hutchinson to Gerber, January 28, 1974, Hutchinson MS, FL.

15. *Work of the Impeachment Inquiry Staff as of February 5, 1974,* Report, Committee on the Judiciary, House of Representatives, 93 Cong., 2 Sess. (February 1974); Renata Adler, "Searching for the Real Nixon Scandal," *Atlantic,* December 1976, 78; Polk Interview, December 18, 1986; Dixon Interview, November 29, 1985; Ziefman Interview, February 5, 1986; Edwards Interview, July 15, 1986; Cates Interview, February 6, 1988.

16. Butler Interview, *Roanoke Times,* July 27, 1975; Adler, "Searching for the Real Nixon Scandal," 79; Fish Interview, June 26, 1975; Flowers Interview, June [17], 1975; Dixon Interview, January 24, November 20, 1985. Father Don Shea, who worked with the committee Republicans, provided me with copies of the 1975 interviews of the House members.

17. David Dennis to Republican Members of the Committee, March 18, 1974, Hutchinson MS, FL; Polk Interview, December 18, 1986; Dixon Interview, January 24, 1985, November 20, 1985; Zeifman Interview, February 5, 1986; Cates Interview, February 6, 1988.

18. Jerome Zeifman, "Chickens and Eagles: The Politics of Their Impeachment of Richard Nixon," unpublished speech, Lynch MS, courtesy of Mr. Steven Lynch; Edwards Interview, July 15, 1986; Cates Interview, February 6, 1988.

19. Jaworski Oral History Memoir, The Texas Collection, Baylor University, 2:559-60, 561.

20. Fish Interview, June 25, 1975; Cohen Interview, June 17, 1975; Butler Interview, June 19, 1975; Railsback Interview, June 11, 1975; Thornton Interview, June 13, 1975; Flowers Interview, June [17], 1975.

21. *NYT,* January 8, 1974; *Washington Star,* January 15, 1974; Wiggins Interview, February 5, 1985; Railsback Interview, June 11, 1975; Garrison to Hutchinson, March 21, 1974, April 9, 1974, Hutchinson MS, FL; Polk Interview, December 18, 1986; Mooney Interview, July 14, 1986; Jack Anderson column, *WP,* February 26, 1974; Garrison to Inquiry Staff, February 26, 1974, Hutchinson MS, FL.

22. Cohen Interview, June 17, 1975; Fish Interview, June 25, 1975; Butler Interview, June 19, 1975; Butler Interview, *Roanoke Times,* July 27, 1975; Railsback Interview, June 11, 1975; Wiggins Interview, February 5, 1985; Polk Interview, December 18, 1986; Mooney Interview, July 14, 1986; Garrison to Hutchinson, February 21, 1974, Hogan to Hutchinson, May 6, 1974, McClory to Hutchinson, July 19, 1974, Hutchinson MS, FL; *Chicago Tribune,* May 3, 1975.

23. HJC, *Impeachment Inquiry,* 1:81-83, 86-88, 93-100, 119-24.

24. HJC, *Impeachment Inquiry,* 1:171-72, 299-302; 2:774; 3:1653-65.

25. HJC, *Impeachment Inquiry,* 1:191-96, 209-13, 227-47.

26. Taped speech, March 29, 1974, White House Communication Agency, NP, NA.

27. *Executive Privilege,* Hearings (April 10, 1973), 47; St. Clair to Rodino, April 9, 1974, Rodino to Nixon, April 11, 1974, Nixon to Rodino, May 22, 1974, Rodino to Nixon, May 30, 1974, Hutchinson MS, FL; Nixon to House Judiciary Committee, June 10, 1974, *PPPUS:RN 1974,* 475-81.

28. HJC, *Impeachment Inquiry,* 1:414-21, 438-58, 545-49.

29. HJC, *Impeachment Inquiry,* 2:844-45, 905-12, 915-20, 939-45; Froehlich to Rodino, May 20, 1974; McClory to Hutchinson, May 31, 1974, Hutchinson MS, FL; *Detroit Free Press,* March 14, 1974; Gerald R. Ford, *A Time to Heal* (New York, 1979), 121.

30. Cates to Author, November 29, 1988; Fish Interview, June 25, 1975; Cohen Interview, June 17, 1975; Butler Interview, June 19, 1975; Railsback Interview, June 11, 1975; Thornton Interview, June 13, 1975; Flowers Interview, June [17], 1975.

31. Polk to Hutchinson, May 20, 1974; McClory to Hutchinson, May 31, 1974, Hutchinson MS, FL.

32. Richard Nixon, *RN: The Memoirs of Richard Nixon* (paperback ed., New York, 1979), 2:586–87, 588–98; Henry Kissinger, *Years of Upheaval* (Boston, 1982), 1118–23.

33. Nixon, *Memoirs,* 2:600–05.

34. Canceled speech, July 3, 1974, NPF, Box 94, NP; Nixon, *Memoirs,* 2:606, 620–21, 628–29. See Chapter XXII, *infra.*

35. Cohen Interview, June 17, 1975; Flowers Interview, June [17], 1975; Butler Interview, June 19, 1975; Butler Interview, *Roanoke Times,* July 27, 1975; HJC, *Impeachment Inquiry,* 3:1731–35, 1864–75; Cates Interview, March 7, 1986.

36. *Los Angeles Times,* June 28, 1974; Nelson Interview, August 22, 1985; *WP,* June 29, 1974; Flowers Interview, June [17], 1975; Thornton Interview, June 13, 1975.

37. HJC, *Testimony of Witnesses,* 1:69–80, 230–44, 262.

38. HJC, *Testimony of Witnesses,* 2:135.

39. HJC, *Testimony of Witnesses,* 2:256–64, 284, 328–29; 3:275–87.

40. HJC, *Testimony of Witnesses,* 3:82–83, 96–104.

41. HJC, *Testimony of Witnesses,* 3:360–62; 412–42, 320, 361–62, 508–09. Colson's later views are contained in Colson to Author, November 16, 1988.

42. HJC, *Impeachment Inquiry,* 3:1868–71.

43. HJC, *Impeachment Inquiry,* 3:1723, 1732, 1885–87; HJC, *Transcripts of Eight Recorded Presidential Conversations;* Franklin Polk to Hutchinson, May 31, 1974, Hutchinson MS, FL.

44. Geoff Shepard to Haig, July 15, 1974, SSF, Box 157, NP; Nixon, *Memoirs,* 2:574; Ken Khachigian to Haig and Ziegler, July 16, 1974, Haig Papers, Box 36, NP; Max L. Friedersdorf to Hutchinson, June 19, 1974, Hutchinson MS, FL. The Special Prosecutor's transcription of the March 22 tape is identical to the House's version.

45. *NYT,* July 13, 1974.

46. HJC, *Impeachment Inquiry,* 3:1889–1908; Railsback Interview, June 11, 1975; Flowers Interview, June [17], 1975.

47. HJC, *Impeachment Inquiry,* 3:1926–36.

48. Butler Interview, June 19, 1975; HJC, *Impeachment Inquiry,* 3:2035–93; *Minority Memorandum on Facts and Law,* Committee on the Judiciary, House of Representatives, 93 Cong., 2 Sess. (July 22, 1974). The committee allowed Jenner to make a response to Garrison's presentation.

49. HJC, *Impeachment Inquiry,* 3:2105–28. Flowers Interview, June [17], 1975; Fish Interview, June 25, 1975.

50. Cohen Interview, June 20, 17, 1975; Railsback Interview, June 11, 1975; Fish Interview, June 27, 1975; Rhodes and Arends to House Republicans, July 24, 1974, Hutchinson MS, FL.

51. Michael Barone, Grant Ujifusa, Douglas Matthews, *The Almanac of American Politics, 1974* (Boston, 1973); Edwards Interview, July 15, 1986; George V. Higgins, "The Judge Who Tried Harder," *Atlantic,* April 1974, 88.

52. Unless otherwise noted, the remarks of the coalition are taken from the tape transcripts of their 1975 interviews with Father Don Shea and Tom Mooney, which they made available to the Author.

53. Polk Interview, December 18, 1986; Mooney Interview, July 14, 1986; McClory Interview, May 8, 1987.

54. Nixon, *Memoirs,* 2:636; *PPPUS:RN, 1974,* 596; John Ehrlichman, *Witness to Power* (New York, 1982), 395–96, 399–407.

55. Nixon *Memoirs,* 2:580, 633, 636, 638–39.

XIX: JUDGMENT DAYS: THE SUPREME COURT AND THE
JUDICIARY COMMITTEE: JULY 1974

1. Stanley I. Kutler, *Judicial Power and Reconstruction Politics* (Chicago, 1968), Ch.2; Learned Hand, *The Bill of Rights* (Cambridge, 1958), 29.

2. *Youngstown Sheet and Tube Co. v. Sawyer*, 343 U.S. 579, 655 (1952); William H. Rehnquist, *The Supreme Court* (New York, 1987, 94, 95, 89–90; Rehnquist to the Conference, William Brennan MS, Box 329, LC.

3. *WSJ*, July 8, 1974; *PPPUS: RN, 1969*, "Remarks Announcing the Nomination of Judge Warren Earl Burger to be Chief Justice of the United States" (May 21, 1969), 388.

4. The oral arguments, as well as the complete briefs for both sides and the American Civil Liberties Union, are reprinted in Leon Friedman (ed.), *United States v. Nixon* (New York, 1974), 523–96. The transcript is taken from audio tapes. My account also benefited from St. Clair Interview, April 10, 1987, and from examination of materials in the Leon Jaworski Oral History Memoir, Texas Collection, Baylor University.

5. *Yoshida International, Inc. v. United States*, 378 F. Supp. 1155 (1974).

6. Bob Woodward and Scott Armstrong, *The Brethren: Inside the Supreme Court* (New York, 1979), 285–347, revealed some of the inner workings of the Court during the case, largely through interviews with former clerks. Much of the complex maneuvering during the drafting of the opinion can be confirmed in the memoranda and draft opinions in the William J. Brennan and William O. Douglas Papers, LC. The following account is based on the book and the materials. Howard Ball, *"United States v. Nixon Re-Examined,"* a paper delivered at the 1987 Nixon Conference at Hofstra University, offers a useful analysis of the Court's development of the opinion.

7. Dent Interview, September 24, 1986; Chapin to Nixon, May 14, 1969; Ehrlichman to Nixon, December 16, 1970, January 18, 1971, FG-51, Box 1, NP; *WP*, June 13, 1974.

8. Douglas to Burger, July 12, 1974, William Brennan Papers, LC; Woodward and Armstrong, *The Brethren*, 339–43; Leon Jaworski Oral History, Texas Collection, Baylor University, 2:641; Presidential Logs, NP.

9. Richard Nixon, *RN: The Memoirs of Richard Nixon* (paperback ed., New York, 1979), 2:629–40; St. Clair to Jaworski, July 10, 1974, Jaworski MS, Texas Collection, Baylor University; Lichenstein Interview, July 16, 1986.

10. *United States v. Nixon*, 418 U.S. 683 (1974).

11. Raoul Berger, *Executive Privilege: A Constitutional Myth* (Cambridge, 1974); *U.S. v. Nixon*, 418 U.S. 683, 712 (1974); "Executive Privilege," *Presidential Studies Quarterly* (Spring 1986), 16:237–246. Ball, *"United States v. Nixon Re-Examined,"* *op. cit.*, and Mark J. Rozell, "President Nixon's Conception of Executive Privilege," both unpublished papers from the 1987 Nixon Conference at Hofstra University, offer valuable commentaries on the decision. Does the Court follow election returns? The next day, the Justices rejected a comprehensive busing plan for Detroit schools. *Milliken v. Bradley*, 418 U.S. 717 (1974).

12. Nixon, *Memoirs*, 2:640–41; *Los Angeles Times*, July 25, 1974; *NYT*, June 3, 1952.

13. Nixon, *Memoirs*, 2:649; St. Clair Interview, April 10, 1987; St. Clair to Author, May 5, 1987.

14. Ken Khachigian to Haig, July 16, 1974, Haig Papers, Box 36, NP; Congressmen Abdnor, Lagomarsino, Martin, Regula, Shuster, Towell, Steelman, and Gilman to Nixon, FG-51, NP.

15. *Debate on Articles of Impeachment*, Committee on the Judiciary, House of Representatives, 93 Cong., 2 Sess. (July 24, 25, 26, 27, 29, and 30, 1974), 1–4. Hereafter cited as HJC, *Debate*.

16. HJC, *Debate*, 4–6.

17. The following account is reconstructed from a taped conversation between Representative M. Caldwell Butler and Thomas Mooney of the House Judiciary Committee staff, July 31, 1974, and from draft copies of the Articles of Impeachment. Material courtesy of Mr. Mooney. Additional material is based on McClory Interview, May 8, 1987, and on interviews with members of the "fragile coalition" done in 1975. Some of this material was made available to the *New York Times* team that described the existence of the "Fragile Centrist Bloc," *NYT*, August 5, 1974.

18. HJC, *Debate*, 23-28, 46-49, 75-80, 57-61, 66-68, 68-71; Railsback Interview, June 11, 1975; Fish Interview, June 25, 1975; Cohen Interview, June 17, 1975; Flowers Interview, June [17], 1975; Mann Interview, June 19, 1975; Butler Interview, June 19, 1975.

19. HJC, *Debate*, 137-49; McClory Interview, May 8, 1987; McClory unpublished memoir, 39.

20. Mann Interview, June 19, 1975.

21. HJC, *Debate*, 149-203.

22. HJC, *Debate*, 204-50. Wiggins to Author, July 18, 1985; Cates to Author, November 29, 1988.

23. HJC, *Debate*, 251-331. Fish notes with Father Don F. Shea's "fragile coalition" Interviews.

XX: "I HEREBY RESIGN." AUGUST 1974

1. Richard Nixon, *RN: The Memoirs of Richard Nixon* (paperback ed., New York, 1979), 2:642-45. Bob Woodward and Carl Bernstein, *The Final Days* (New York, 1976), dramatically portrayed the tensions of the last two weeks of the Nixon presidency. But their depiction of the Administration and the nation as dependent at the time upon Alexander Haig and Henry Kissinger is overdrawn. After the manuscript was written, Haig insisted that he refused to talk to Woodward. Haig told Buzhardt that Woodward wanted to check facts, not because they "might be in error, but because he wanted to be sure that he was being fair to me!" Haig to Buzhardt, February 12, 1973, copy furnished by Mrs. J. F. Buzhardt.

2. HJC, *Debate*, 334-35.

3. HJC, *Debate*, 335-36, 340-42.

4. HJC, *Debate*, 357-71, 385-93, 427-28, 445-47.

5. HJC, *Debate*, 449-50, 454, 455, 473, 488-89; Polk Interview, December 18, 1986.

6. Mann Interview, June 19, 1975; Cohen Interview, June 20, 1975; Fish Interview, June 25, 1975.

7. HJC, *Debate*, 491, 495, 500, 516-17, 517-21, 522-24, 525-26, 531, 553-54; Mann Interview, June 19, 1975; Cohen Interview, June 17, 1975; Dixon Interview, January 24, 1985; Edward Mezvinsky, *A Term to Remember* (New York, 1977).

8. Theodore White, *Breach of Faith* (New York, 1975), 407; Cohen Interview, June 20, 1975; Flowers Interview, June [17], 1975; Mann Interview, June 19, 1975; Gerald Ford, *A Time to Heal* (New York, 1979), 12; Curtis to Hutchinson, August 2, 1974, Hutchinson MS, FL; Patman to Danielson, Mezvinsky, and Rangel, August 5, 1974, HBC Papers.

9. Austin Ranney, *Channels of Power: The Impact of Television on American Politics* (New York, 1985), 167.

10. Alvin Snyder to Ron Ziegler, July 30, 1974, Haig Papers, Box 38, NP; Henry Rahmel to Alvin Snyder, July 31, 1974, August 7, 1974, *ibid.*, Boxes 38, 39; Gladys Engel Lang and Kurt Lang, *The Battle for Public Opinion: The President, the Press, and the Polls During Watergate* (New York, 1983), 168; *NYT*, August 5, 1974.

11. Nixon, *Memoirs*, 2:645-47. Nixon's memoirs imply that St. Clair read the transcript before Haig—a highly unlikely situation. Nixon also emphasized it was the first time Haig

had read a "transcript." But Haig had handled the tape before and he was in regular contact with Buzhardt, his close friend.

12. General Brent Scowcroft to Haig, July 30, 1974, Haig Papers, Box 37, NP; Ken Clawson to Haig, July 31, 1974, *ibid.*, Box 36, NP; William Timmons to St. Clair, August 2, 1974, *ibid.*, Box 39, NP.

13. Burch Interview, May 6, 1987; Burch to Nixon, June 6, 1974, and Haig to Nixon, July 8, 1974, WHSF/WHCF, Confidential Files, Box 12, NP; Bull Interview, May 6, 1987; Lichenstein Interview, July 16, 1986.

14. *NYT*, July 28, 29, 31, August 1, 3, 1974; Phillips Interview, August 23, 1985.

15. Ford, *A Time to Heal*, 2-3.

16. TT, the President and Haldeman, June 23, 1972 (10:04 A.M.-11:39 A.M.; 1:04 P.M.-1:13 P.M.; 2:20 P.M.-2:45 P.M.), *U.S. v. M*, NA.

17. *PPPUS:RN, 1974*, 621-23; Nixon, *Memoirs*, 2:630, 641.

18. Jaworski Oral History, 2:683; Geller to Files, Haig Interview, July 3, 1975, WGSPF Records, NA; Woodward and Bernstein, *The Final Days*, 263; St. Clair Interview, April 10, 1987; Garment Interview, April 12, 1988; Laird Interview, June 27, 1985; Nixon, *Memoirs*, 2:578; Mitchell Interview, April 11, 1988.

19. Harry Reasoner, ABC News, Commentary, August 6, 1974; *NYT*, November 15, 1973; Flanigan to Haig, February 6, 1974, WHCF Confidential Files, Box 12, NP.

20. Nixon, *Memoirs*, 2:654-59; Conable Interview, May 28, 1985 (quoting his diary).

21. Edwards Interview, July 15, 1986; Gilbert Gude (R-MD) to Hutchinson, August 6, 1974, Hutchinson MS, FL; Conable Interview, May 28, 1985; St. Clair Interview, April 10, 1987; Wiggins Interview, February 5, 1985; *NYT*, August 5, 1974; Ford, *A Time to Heal*, 17.

22. *PPPUS:RN, 1974*, March 6, 1974, 236; St. Clair Interview, April 10, 1987.

23. *Impeachment of Richard M. Nixon, President of the United States*, Report, Committee on the Judiciary, House of Representatives (August 20, 1974), 93 Cong., 2 Sess., 359-493, 495-502, 511-14; Polk Interview, December 18, 1986; Shepard Interview, April 4, 1988.

24. Barry M. Goldwater with Jack Casserly, *Goldwater* (New York, 1988), 275.

25. Lichenstein Interview, July 16, 1986; Burch Interview, May 6, 1987; Goldwater, *Goldwater*, 275-76.

26. Ford, *A Time to Heal*, 22; Nixon, *Memoirs*, 2:666-68; Goldwater, *Goldwater*, 277-79; Woodward and Bernstein, *The Final Days*, 413-17; *Weekly Compilation of Presidential Documents: Richard Nixon, 1974* (August 7, 1974), 10:1010-12.

27. Nixon, *Memoirs*, 2:659-60; H. R. Haldeman, *The Ends of Power* (New York, 1978), 311-13; John Ehrlichman, *Witness to Power* (New York, 1982), 409-10, differ in their rendition of the sequence and content of the calls.

28. Whitehead Interview, May 25, 1988; Jerald F. terHorst, *Gerald Ford and the Future of the Presidency* (New York, 1974), 181-81; Ford, *A Time to Heal*, 24; *NYT*, August 26, 1974, has an extensive account of the transition process.

29. Richard Reeves, *A Ford, Not a Lincoln* (New York, 1975), 11-12; terHorst, *Gerald Ford*, 177-78; Ford, *A Time to Heal*, 5, 115-16; *NYT*, July 28, 1974.

30. Robert T. Hartmann, *Palace Politics: An Inside Account of the Ford Years* (New York, 1980), 30-40, 80-88, 97, 106-07, 116-17, 122-52; Ford, *A Time to Heal*, 140, 122; Ron Nessen, *It Sure Looks Different from the Inside* (Chicago, 1978), 36.

31. Ford, *A Time to Heal*, 10-15.

32. David Parker, Background Paper for Cabinet Meeting, August 6, 1974, Hoopes Papers, Box 20, NP; Saxbe to Author, May 15, 1987. Nixon said that the meeting continued; Dean Burch confirmed the Saxbe story: Burch Interview, May 6, 1987. Also see Ford, *A Time to Heal*, 19-21; Henry Kissinger, *Years of Upheaval* (Boston, 1982), 1202-04.

33. James Kilpatrick Interview, *Washington Star*, May 14, 1974; Butler Interview, *Roanoke Times*, July 27, 1975; Nixon to Rose Mary Woods, June 8, 1974, NPF, Box 4, NP.

34. Rose Mary Woods to Nixon, May 11, 1974, NPF, Box 8, NP; Norman Vincent Peale to Rose Mary Woods, May 13, 1974, *ibid.;* Jesus Monrow Telephone Communication, August 7, 1974, *ibid.*, Box 19; Kilpatrick, *Washington Star*, August 10, 1974.

35. Nixon, *Memoirs*, 1:23–24; 2:548.

36. Haldeman, *Ends of Power*, 309; Kenneth Khachigian to Haig, July 14, 1974, Haig Papers, Box 36, NP (the phrase was used by Pat Buchanan in a memo to Nixon, May 3, 1973, NPF, Box 6, NP); Bull Interview, May 7, 1987; Moore Interview, December 5, 1987; Greenspan quoted in *International Herald Tribune*, June 3, 1987; Julie Nixon Eisenhower, *Pat Nixon: The Untold Story* (New York, 1986), 408–09; Nixon, *Memoirs*, 2:661–65.

37. David Frost, *"I Gave Them a Sword": Behind the Scenes of the Nixon Interviews* (New York, 1978), 96; Woodward and Bernstein, *The Final Days*, 384–425; Mitchell Interview, April 11, 1988. Various presidential aides at the time, such as Stephen Bull, Bruce Herschensohn, and Pat Buchanan, have complained that they were misquoted or that contrary evidence they offered Woodward and Bernstein was ignored. Victor Lasky, "The Woodstein Ripoff," *AIM Report*, October 1976. Buzhardt complained about numerous errors, many of which involved him as a source, in an unsent letter to Woodward: copy furnished by Mrs. J. F. Buzhardt. John Dean has made a substantial case for Haig as "Deep Throat," the alleged White House source for Woodward. John Dean, *Lost Honor* (Los Angeles, 1982), 326–54. For Goldwater's autobiography, Haig obligingly described Goldwater as "one of the good guys" of the resignation moment; at the same time, Goldwater painted Haig in heroic terms. Goldwater, *Goldwater*, 281.

38. William Timmons to Haig, August 7, 1974, Haig Papers, Box 39, NP; Timmons to Author, August 7, 1987; Robert McClory, "Was the Fix in Between Ford and Nixon?," *National Review*, October 14, 1983, 1264–66; McClory Interview, May 8, 1987.

39. Frost, *"I Gave Them a Sword,"* 272; Albert Interview, United States Capitol Historical Society, 37–38; Nixon, *Memoirs*, 2:678–79.

40. *NYT*, August 25, 1974; *WP*, August 24, 1974; *NYT*, July 4, 1974.

41. The relevant messages were furnished by the Office of the Assistant Secretary of Defense.

42. Moorer Interview, June 25, 1985; Major General John S. Lekson to Author, May 6, 1986; General Bruce Palmer, *The 25-Year War: America's Military Role in Vietnam* (Lexington, KY, 1984), 140; Palmer Telephone Interview, December 17, 1986 (Palmer's references to later events reflected his criticism of Secretary of the Navy John Lehman, Lieutenant-Colonel Oliver North, and Admiral John Poindexter); *Nomination of Alexander M. Haig, Jr., to be Secretary of State*, Hearings, Committee on Foreign Relations, U.S. Senate, 97 Cong., 1 Sess. (January 14, 1981) 2:69; *Newsweek*, July 16, 1979, 54. General Brown's legal aide did not believe that major military commanders would have responded to extraordinary orders from Haig, considering their personal contempt and animosity toward him. Finklestein Interview, May 30, 1985. Garment Interview, April 11, 1988, provided some special insight into Haig, given Garment's vantage point in the Nixon White House and as a writer and consultant for Haig in 1981–82.

43. Joseph Spear, *Presidents and the Press* (Cambridge, MA, 1984), 235.

44. Nixon, *Memoirs*, 2:685–86.

XXI: THE "BURDEN I SHALL BEAR FOR EVERY DAY." THE PARDON:
SEPTEMBER 1974

1. Gerald R. Ford, *A Time to Heal* (New York, 1979), 4.

2. *Nomination of Gerald R. Ford to be Vice President of the United States*, Committee on Rules and Administration, U.S. Senate, 93 Cong., 1 Sess. (November 5, 1973), 124.

3. Seymour Hersh, "The Pardon," *Atlantic*, August 1983, 55; *Pardon of Richard M. Nixon and Related Matters*, Hearings, Subcommittee on Criminal Justice of the Committee on the Judiciary, House of Representatives, 93 Cong., 2 Sess. (October 17, 1974), 94; Walter Pincus, "Origin of Pardon Idea in Question," *WP*, February 1, 1976; Buzhardt Draft in Buzhardt MS, Courtesy of Mrs. J. Fred Buzhardt; Ford, *A Time to Heal*, 148.

4. Whitehead Interview, May 25, 1988; Richard Reeves, *A Ford, Not a Lincoln* (New York, 1975), 73; Jerald F. terHorst, *Gerald Ford and the Future of the Presidency* (New York, 1974), 217; Benton Becker to Author, March 3, 1986. Robert T. Hartmann, *Palace Politics: An Inside Account of the Ford Years* (New York, 1980), is useful for the conflict between the Nixon and Ford retainers.

5. *NYT*, August 16, 14, 15, 17, 27, 1974; Becker Interview, December 5, 1985.

6. Meeting Notes, August 7, 8, 1974, Nixon File #11, WGSPF Records, NA.

7. Lacovara to Jaworski, August 16, 1974; Richard J. Davis to Jaworski, August 19, 1974; Richard Ben-Veniste to Jaworski, August 19, 1974; Neal to Jaworski, August 27, 1974; Charles R. Breyer to Jaworski, August 27, 1974; Jay Horowitz to Jaworski, August 29, 1974; Nick Akerman to Jaworski, August 29, 1974; Frank Martin to Jaworski, August 29, 1974; Richard Weinberg to Jaworski, September 4, 1974; Thomas P. Ruane to Jaworski, September 4, 1974; Phil Bakes to Jaworski, September 3, 1974; Kenneth Geller to Jaworski, September 5, 1974; Sidney M. Glazer to Jaworski, September 4, 1974; Stephen Haberfield to Jaworski, September 6, 1974, Special Prosecutor's Files, Nixon File #11, WGSPF Records, NA.

8. William C. Berman, *William Fulbright and the Vietnam War: The Dissent of a Political Realist* (Kent, OH, 1988), 193–94; *NYT*, August 24, 1974.

9. *NYT*, August 13, September 2, 1974.

10. Treen to Jaworski, August 22, 1974, Edward Hutchinson MS, FL.

11. Garment to Buchen, August 28, 1974, Garment MS, LC.

12. *PPPUS:GF, 1974*, Press Conference, August 28, 1974, 57; Ford, *A Time to Heal*, 158–61; Hersh, "The Pardon," 55–62; Reeves, *A Ford, Not a Lincoln*, 110; Buchen to William Greener, December 19, 1975, Buchen MS, Box 32, FL.

13. Lacovara to Jaworski, August 29, 1974, Nixon File #11, WGSPF Records, NA.

14. Ford, *A Time to Heal*, 167–68; Jaworski to Buchen, September 4, 1974 (with Ruth memorandum to Jaworski, September 3, 1974), Nixon File #11, WGSPF Records, NA; Herbert J. Miller, Jr., to Jaworski, September 4, 1974, *ibid.;* Peter Kreindler to Lacovara, and Lacovara to Jaworski, September 5, 1974, Legal Memos, *ibid.;* Jaworski Oral History Memoir, The Texas Collection, Baylor University, 2:663–64; Becker Interview, December 5, 1985.

15. Ford, *A Time to Heal*, 165–66; Becker Interview, December 5, 1985; Hersh, "The Pardon," 55–62. See Chapter XV, *supra.*

16. Ford, *A Time to Heal*, 168–70; Becker Interviews, December 5, 7, 1985. Becker claimed that paper burning occurred regularly in the first days of the Ford Administration, but after complaints to the President, the number of burnings declined. Becker to Author, March 28, 1986.

17. Laird Interview, June 27, 1985; Becker Interview, December 5, 1985; *NYT*, September 9, 1974.

18. Becker Interview, December 5, 7, 1985; Buchen to James B. Rhoads (Archivist of the U.S.), September 20, 1974, WHCF, Box 16, FL; *Presidential Recordings and Materials Preservation Act*, Report, Committee on House Administration, 93 Cong., 2 Sess. (November 24, 1974).

19. TerHorst, *Ford and the Future of the Presidency*, 216-40; Reeves, *A Ford, Not a Lincoln*, 92, 110-11; Hartmann, *Palace Politics*, 257-62, indicates that some of the staff members knew, especially Buchen, of course; Ford acknowledged that Hartmann and Jack Marsh on his staff had reservations about the matter, indicating their knowledge: *A Time to Heal*, 161-62.

20. Vertical File, Richard Nixon: Pardon, FL; Earl D. Ward to Ford, September 11, 1974, J. Edgar Bowron to Ford, September 10, 1974, Leroy F. Green to Ford, September 10, 1974, Gayle Windsor, Jr., to Ford, September 11, 1974; Marie Lombardi to Ford, September 29, 1974; Paul Newman and Joanne Woodward to Ford, September 11, 1974; Judge Gerard D. Reilly to Ford, September 12, 1974; Rabbi Baruch Korff to Ford, September 9, 1974; Armand Hammer to Ford, September 10, 1974, WHCF, Amnesties/Pardons: Nixon, Boxes 4 and 5, FL.

21. *NYT*, September 9, 10, 1974; Quie to Ford, September 12, 1974; Dingell to Ford, September 11, 1974; McCloskey to Ford, September 11, 1974; William Timmons to Ford, September 10, 1974; Max Friedersdorf to Representative Pierre S. du Pont, September 17, 1974, WHCF, Amnesties/Pardons: Nixon, Box 4, FL; *Boston Herald American*, March 23, 1976.

22. Ford, *A Time to Heal*, 180-81; Box 16, Nessen MS, FL; *Conservative Digest*, May 1976 (Viguerie), June 1976 (Colson); *National Review*, September 27, 1974.

23. Ervin Statement, September 9, 1974, Box 384, Ervin Papers, Chapel Hill; Richardson to the *WP*, September 20, 1974, Richardson Papers, LC.

24. Conable Interview, May 28, 1985; Ford, *A Time to Heal*, 175; Laird Interview, June 27, 1985.

25. *WP*, September 25, 1974; *WSJ*, October 16, 1974; Dash Interview, February 5, 1986.

26. Lacovara to Jaworski, September 5, 1974, Jaworski to Lacovara, September 6, 1974, Lacovara to Jaworski, September 6, 1974, Lacovara Files, WGSPF Records, NA; Lacovara to Jaworski, September 9, 1974, Nixon File #6a, *ibid.;* Jaworski to Lacovara, September 14, 1974, Nixon File #11, *ibid.* Leon Jaworski, *The Right and the Power* (New York, 1976), 242-46; George Frampton and Richard Ben-Veniste, *Stonewall: The Real Story of the Watergate Prosecution* (New York, 1977), 300-11; Leon Jaworski Oral History Memoir, The Texas Collection, Baylor University, 1:219; 2:644-46.

27. Jaworski to Ruth, undated, Jaworski Subject File, WGSPF Records, NA; Lacovara to Jaworski (with Palmer to Lacovara, September 27, 1974), September 27, 1974, Nixon File #11, *ibid.;* Jaworski to Saxbe, October 12, 1974, Nixon File #6a, *ibid.*

28. Abzug to Jaworski, September 10, 1974, Jaworski Subject Files, WGSPF Records, NA; Lacovara to Jaworski, September 13, 1974, Nixon File #11, *ibid.*

29. "Record of the Subcommittee's Action on H. Res. 1367 and 1370"; Hungate to Ford, September 17, 1974; Ford to Hungate, September 20, 1974; Buchen to Hungate, September 24, 1974; Hungate to Ford, September 25, 1974; Ford to Hungate, September 30, 1974, documents furnished by subcommittee aide Steven Lynch. Sandman to Ford, October 1, 1974; Ford to Sandman, October 4, 1974; Sandman to Ford, October 18, 1974, WHCF, Box 5, FL; Lynch Interview, October 10, 1985; Holtzman Interview, April 11, 1986; "Subcommittee Minutes," November 22, 1974, courtesy of Steven Lynch; *Pardon of Richard M. Nixon and Related Matters*, Subcommittee on Criminal Justice of the Committee on the Judiciary, House of Representatives, 93 Cong., 2 Sess. (October 17, 1974), 107-08.

30. *WP*, December 18, 1975. Compare a story in *The Nation*, November 9, 1974, for its

similarities. Holtzman to Hungate, December 18, 1975; Lynch to Hungate, December 19, 1975; Staff to Hungate, February 17, 1976; "Subcommittee Minutes," February 19, 1976, documents courtesy of Steven Lynch; Holtzman Interview, April 11, 1986.

31. *Burdick v. U.S.*, 236 U.S. 83, 94 (1915); "Does a Pardon Blot Out Guilt?" *Harvard Law Review*, (May 1915) 28:647; Edward S. Corwin, *The Constitution and What It Means Today* (Princeton, NJ, 1978), 167–68.

32. White House Summary, October 6, 1974, Ron Nessen MS, Box 16, FL; Hersh, "The Pardon"; Robert McClory, "Was the Fix in Between Ford and Nixon?" *National Review*, October 14, 1983, 1264–72. Alexander Haig's role, shadowy as always, is very much at the center of the conspiracy ideas. He publicly testified that he never told Ford that Nixon would resign if the Vice President promised a pardon. Senate Foreign Relations Committee, *Nomination of Alexander M. Haig, Jr., to be Secretary of State*, Hearings, Committee on Foreign Relations, U.S. Senate, 97 Cong., 1 Sess. (January 9, 1981), 27. See Frank Fox and Stephen Parker, "Is the Pardon Explained by the Ford-Nixon Tapes?" *New York*, October 14, 1974, 7:41–45, suggests that Nixon's recordings of Ford's loyal service during the Watergate affair gave Nixon leverage in gaining a pardon. John Ehrlichman, *Witness to Power* (New York, 1982), 410.

33. David Frost, *"I Gave Them a Sword"* (New York, 1978), 301; Anderson Press Release, September 17, 1974, Edward Hutchinson MS, FL; *Murphy v. Fox* (W.D.Mi., 390 F. Supp. 1372 [1975]).

34. Ron Nessen, *It Sure Looks Different from the Inside* (Chicago, 1978), 196, 198; John Moss to Buchen, February 18, 1975, Buchen to Richard Cheyney, February 4, 1975, Jerry Jones to Donald Rumsfeld, January 7, 1975, F. Lynn May to Buchen, October 30, 1974, Buchen Papers, Box 28, FL.

35. Ford, *A Time to Heal*, 172; Dent Interview, September 24, 1986; Edward S. Corwin, *The President: Office and Powers, 1787–1984* (5th ed., New York, 1984), 181.

XXII: IN THE SHADOW OF WATERGATE

1. Frederick Jackson Turner, "The Significance of History," *Wisconsin Journal of Education* (October 1891), 21:232; *Nixon v. Fitzgerald*, 457 U.S. 731, 754 (1982); *NYT*, February 22, 1980; *Congressional Record* (July 1, 1987), 133:9188–89; *U.S. News & World Report*, August 13, 1984, 59.

2. WGSPF, *Final Report* (Washington, 1977), 65–73, offered a status report of the various cases. Richard Harris, "Reflections: The Watergate Prosecutions," *The New Yorker*, June 10, 1974, 46–63, discussed the plea bargains. For a typical discussion within the WGSPF, see Cox to James Sharp and James Bierbower, August 16, 1973, WGSPF Records, NA, on the Magruder plea.

3. William Buckley, *National Review*, September 12, 1975, 1008; *Human Events*, December 7, 1974, 14; Phillips Interview, August 23, 1985; Conable Interview, May 28, 1985; *Conservative Digest*, May 1975, 3, June 1975, 39.

4. *Human Events*, June 21, 1975, 4, July 19, 1975, 7, November 24, 1974, 3, March 1, 1975, 5; Keene Interview, August 14, 1985; Buchanan, "A Long March Unfulfilled," *Washington Times*, April 4, 1988.

5. Richard Scammon and Benjamin J. Wattenberg, *The Real Majority* (New York, 1970), Kevin P. Phillips, *Post-Conservative America* (New York, 1982); James L. Sundquist, *Dynamics of the Party System* (Washington, D.C., 1983), and especially, Thomas Byrne Edsall, *The New Politics of Equality* (New York, 1984), offered useful insights into the dilemmas of the Democrats.

6. David Frost, *"I Gave Them a Sword": Behind the Scenes of the Nixon Interviews* (New York, 1978), 62.

7. Ralph Winter, Jr. (ed.), *Watergate and the Law: Political Campaigns and Presidential Power* (Washington, 1974), 1–4, 83–85.

8. *Public Financing of Federal Elections,* Hearings, Subcommittee on Privileges and Elections of the Committee on Rules and Administration, U.S.S., 93 Cong., 1 Sess., 23, 33, 35; "Congress Clears Campaign Finance Reform," *Congressional Quarterly Almanac* (1974), 30:611–33; Herbert E. Alexander, *Financing the 1972 Election* (Lexington, KY, 1976); Gillian Peele, *Revival and Reaction: The Right in Contemporary America* (New York, 1984), 60; *Buckley v. Valeo*, 424 U.S. 1 (1976); *Federal Election Commission v. National Conservative Political Action Committee*, 470 U.S. 480 (1985); Gregg Easterbrook, "What's Wrong with Congress?" *The Atlantic*, December 1984, 254:70. See Paul Huston's account of "fat cat" contributions in the 1988 campaign: *Los Angeles Times*, December 9, 1988. The disclosure requirements of the 1974 legislation have remained largely intact and have provided useful information as to the source of campaign funds.

9. Robert Nisbet, *The Present Age: Progress and Anarchy in Modern America* (New York, 1988), 105–06; Jaworski, Oral History Memoir, The Texas Collection, Baylor University, 5:764–65.

10. *Watergate Reorganization and Reform Act of 1975,* Hearings, Committee on Government Operations, U.S.S., 94 CONG., 1 Sess. (July 29–31, 1975); *Public Officials Integrity Act of 1977,* Hearings, Committee on Government Affairs, U.S.S., 95 Cong., 1 Sess. (May 3–5, July 7–9, 1977); "Carter Signs Government-Wide Ethics Bill," *Congressional Quarterly Almanac* (1978), 34:833–43; Petersen Interview, August 23, 1975.

11. *Special Prosecutor Provisions of Ethics in Government Act of 1978,* Hearings, Subcommittee on Oversight of Government Management of the Committee on Governmental Affairs, U.S.S., 97 Cong., 1 Sess. (May 20, 22, 1981), 2–12, 93–97; *Ethics in Government Act Amendments of 1982,* Hearings, Subcommittee on Oversight of Government Management of the Committee on Governmental Affairs, U.S.S. (April 28, 1972), 97 Cong., 2 Sess., 2–8, 45–47; "Revision of Special Prosecutor Law Cleared," *Congressional Quarterly Almanac* (1982), 38:386–89.

12. *NYT*, March 13, 1987; *Oversight of the Independent Counsel Statute,* Hearings, Subcommittee on Oversight of Government Management of the Committee on Governmental Affairs, U.S.S., 100 Cong., 1 Sess. (March 19–20, 1987), 3–5, 8–10; *Independent Counsel Reauthorization Act of 1987,* Report, Committee on Governmental Affairs, U.S.S., 100 Cong., 1 Sess. (July 24, 1987), 9–14; *WP*, June 17, 1987; *Congressional Record*, U.S.S. (October 16, 1987), 100 Cong., 1 Sess., 14439; "Balky Reagan Signs Extension of Independent-Counsel Law," *Congressional Quarterly Weekly Report* (December 19, 1987), 45:3166; *Los Angeles Times*, December 18, 1987; *WSJ*, October 21, 1987. The most substantial criticism of the ethics legislation is in "Ethics-in-Government Laws: Are They Too 'Ethical'?" (American Enterprise Institute, 1984). In November 1988, President Reagan pocket-vetoed a bill imposing tighter restrictions on lobbying efforts of former government employees.

13. *Morrison, Independent Counsel v. Olson, et al.* (U.S. Sup. Ct., slip opinion, No. 87–1279); *In re Sealed Case*, 838 F.2d 476 (D.C. Cir. 1988). Leonard Garment, "Does America Really Need This Orgy of Investigation?" *WP*, May 10, 1987; Leonard Garment, "The Guns of Watergate," *Commentary*, April 1987, 20–23; L. Gordon Krovitz, "Independent Counsels: Quo Warranto?" *WSJ* (February 9, 1988) and Andrew L. Frey and Kenneth S. Geller, "Better Than Independent Counsels," *WP National Weekly Edition* (February 22–28, 1988), criticized the lack of accountability and excesses of the Independent Counsel; Lovida H. Coleman, Jr., "The Case for the Independent Counsel," *WP National Weekly Edition* (February 29–March 6, 1988), responded.

14. Athan Theoharis, *Spying on Americans: Political Surveillance from Hoover to the Huston Plan* (Philadelphia, 1978), is the best account of the FBI's abuses of power; Clarence Kelley, *Kelley: The Story of an FBI Director* (Kansas City, 1987), 152–53; Mark Felt, one of the indicted agents, bitterly assailed Kelley and the reformist spirit, in *The FBI Pyramid: From the Inside* (New York, 1979), 345–51: "The FBI wouldn't be in this predicament if Clarence Kelley were alive," was, according to Felt, a favorite observation among FBI personnel; Reagan pardon, *NYT*, April 16, 1981; Richard Gid Power, *Secrecy and Power: The Life of J. Edgar Hoover* (New York, 1987), 487; "Watergate Revisited: A Legislative Legacy," *Congressional Quarterly Almanac* (1982), 38:387.

15. *Surveillance Technology*, Staff Report, Committee on the Judiciary, U.S.S., 94 Cong., 2 Sess., 383–402, reprints the Levi Guidelines; Athan G. Theoharis and John Stuart Cox, *The Boss: J. Edgar Hoover and the Great American Inquisition* (Philadelphia, 1988), 431–35; AP Dispatch, in *Wisconsin State Journal*, October 14, 1984; *NYT*, January 14, 1985.

16. Hersh's articles first appeared in the *Times* on December 22, 1974. The best account of the politics of the Senate hearings, and the Senate's findings, is in Loch K. Johnson, *A Season of Inquiry: The Senate Intelligence Investigation* (Lexington, KY, 1985), 9–11, *et passim;* Colby Interview, October 9, 1987.

17. Nixon to Helms, October 24, 1983, courtesy of Ambassador Helms; Helms Interview, July 14, September 23, 1988.

18. Johnson, *A Season of Inquiry*, 195–96, 252–56, 263; Stansfield Turner, *Secrecy and Democracy* (Boston, 1985); Turner, Op-Ed, *NYT*, March 13, 1987; *Los Angeles Times*, March 4, 1987.

19. *PPPUS:RN, 1974* (January 30, 1974), 78–79; *Privacy Act of 1974*, Report, Committee on Government Operations, H.R., 93 Cong., 2 Sess., 5–9; "Privacy Act," *Congressional Quarterly Almanac* (1974); 30:292–293.

20. *Tax Revision Issues 1976*, Joint Committee on Internal Revenue Taxation, 94 Cong., 2 Sess. (April 14, 1976), 32–33, 46; *Summary of the Conference Agreement on the Tax Reform Act of 1976*, Report, Committee on Ways and Means, H.R. (September 29, 1976), 94 Cong., 2 Sess., 44.

21. Christopher Hitchens, "Minority Report," *The Nation*, January 11, 1986, 6; Jack Anderson, *WP*, December 20, 1985; Benjamin R. Civiletti, "Post-Watergate Legislation in Retrospect," *Southwestern Law Journal*, February 1981, 34:1049–51, 1056–59.

22. "Freedom of Information Veto Overridden," *Congressional Quarterly Almanac* (1974), 30:648–54; *Congressional Record* (November 21, 1974), 93 Cong., 2 Sess., 120:36865; "One FOIA Bill Clears, But Overhaul Bill Stalls," *Congressional Quarterly Almanac* (1984), 40:181–85.

23. *Presidential Records Act of 1978*, Hearings, Subcommittee of the Committee on Government Operations, H.R., 95 Cong., 2 Sess. (February 23, 28, March 2, 7, 1978); *Nixon v. General Services Administration*, 433 U.S. 425 (1976); *Allen v. Carmen*, 578 F. Supp. 951 (D.D.C. 1983).

24. *Review of Nixon Presidential Materials: Access Regulations*, Hearings, Subcommittee on Government Operations, H.R., 99 Cong., 2 Sess. (April 29, 1986); *Public Citizen, et al. v. Richard M. Nixon*, No. 87-5215 (D.C. Cir., 1988); also see *Nixon v. Freeman*, 670 F. 2d 346 (D.C. Cir.); *ibid.*, certiorari denied, 459 U.S. 1035 (1982); Jack Anderson, *WP*, November 10, 1988; Executive Order 12667, "Presidential Records," *Federal Register*, January 23, 1989.

25. Samuel P. Huntington, *American Politics: The Promise of Disharmony* (Cambridge, 1981), 203–09.

26. Louis Fisher, *Constitutional Conflicts Between Congress and the President* (Princeton, 1985), 237–39; *Congressional Quarterly Almanac* (1973), 29:252–59; *ibid.* (1974), 30:145–53; *PPPUS:RN, 1974* (July 12, 1974), 588; Richard Nixon, *RN: The Memoirs of Richard*

Nixon (paperback ed., New York, 1979), 2:628-29; Easterbrook, "What's Wrong With Congress," *Atlantic*, December 1984, 254:60-61; Robert Rothman, "Congress's Long Conflict with President Led to 1974 Impoundment Control Act," *Congressional Quarterly Weekly Report* (July 2, 1983), 41:1332-33.

27. Richard Nixon, *No More Vietnams* (New York, 1985), 165; Frost, *"I Gave Them a Sword"*, 139; Henry Kissinger, *Years of Upheaval* (Boston, 1982), 125-26, 414-16, 1122; Henry Kissinger, *White House Years* (Boston, 1979), 986n; Roger Morris, *Uncertain Greatness: Henry Kissinger and American Foreign Policy* (New York, 1977), 252; *Milwaukee Journal*, April 7, 1985; Kissinger remarks at Hofstra Conference on Nixon Presidency, November 19, 1987. Paul Johnson, *Modern Times* (New York, 1985), 654, 658, follows Nixon and Kissinger in blaming Watergate for the fall of Vietnam.

28. Frank Snepp, *Decent Interval: An Insider's Account of Saigon's Indecent End* (New York, 1977); Lehmann to Secretary of State, August 13, 1975, Telegram, courtesy of Mr. Lehmann; Lehmann, Letter to Editor, *NYT Book Review*, February 22, 1987; Lehmann Interview, May 8, 1987; Nayan Chanda, *Brother Enemy: The War After the War* (New York, 1986), 153, 157, 273; George C. Herring, *America's Longest War: The United States and Vietnam, 1950-1975* (2nd ed., New York, 1986), 266. William Hammond, "The American Withdrawal from Vietnam: Some Military and Political Considerations," Hofstra Conference on the Nixon Presidency, November 19, 1987.

29. Bruce Palmer, Jr., *The Twenty-five-Year War: America's Military Role in Vietnam* (Lexington, KY, 1984), 186-87.

30. Herring, *America's Longest War*, 259; Hung Nguyen Tien and Jerrold L. Schecter, *The Palace File* (New York, 1986), 307-308, 354, 163, 363.

31. Herring, *America's Longest War*, 265-66.

32. Seymour M. Hersh, *The Price of Power: Kissinger in the Nixon White House* (New York, 1983), 561ff., tracks the Vietnam negotiations with Watergate events; Nixon, *Memoirs*, 2:306.

33. Nisbet, *The Present Age*, 82; Madison to Jefferson, May 13, 1798, in Saul K. Padover (ed.), *The Complete Madison: His Basic Writings* (New York, 1953), 257-58; Lincoln to Herndon, February 15, 1848, quoted in Arthur M. Schlesinger, Jr., *The Imperial Presidency* (Boston, 1973), 43. Leonard W. Levy, *Original Intent and the Framers' Constitution* (New York, 1988), 30-53, offers a convincing argument for shared powers on foreign policy. Nixon's behavior was not new, as a distinguished line of his predecessors did not approve of congressional intrusions, whatever the original intention of the Constitution's framers: "The necessary secrecy of diplomacy gave to every President the power to involve the country without its knowledge in dangers which would not afterwards be escaped, and the [original] Republican party neither invented nor suggested means by which this old evil of irresponsible politics could be cured; but of all Presidents, none used these arbitrary powers with more freedom and secrecy than Jefferson. His ideas of Presidential authority in foreign affairs were little short of royal. He loved the sense of power and the freedom from oversight which diplomacy gave, and thought with reason that as his knowledge of Europe was greater than that of other Americans, so he should be left to carry out his policy undisturbed." Henry Adams, *History of the United States During the Administration of Thomas Jefferson* (New York, 1889), 2:245.

34. Harold M. Hyman, "Quiet Past and Stormy Present? War Powers in American History" (American Historical Association, 1986), 52-61; Philip J. Briggs, "Nixon versus the Congress: The War Powers Resolution, 1973," Hofstra Conference on the Nixon Presidency, November 20, 1987; Fisher, *Constitutional Conflicts*, 309-10.

35. Department of State Bulletin (1975), 72:562, quoted in Fisher, *Constitutional Conflicts*, 323-24.

36. *NYT*, April 19, 1988. Harold H. Koh, "Comment: The War Powers Resolution,"

Hofstra Conference on the Nixon Presidency, November 20, 1987, offered an insightful critique of the limitations of the War Powers Act; *NYT,* May 20, 1988; *Madison (Wisconsin) Capital Times,* May 20, 1988. Francis D. Wormuth and Edwin B. Firmage, *To Chain the Dogs of War: The War Power of Congress in History and Law* (Dallas, 1986).

37. Kissinger, *Years of Upheaval,* 245-46, 979, 981-84.

38. Raymond L. Garthoff, *Detente and Confrontation: American-Soviet Relations from Nixon to Reagan* (Washington, 1985), 25-29; Robert D. Schulzinger, "The Rise and Stall of Detente, 1969-1974," Hofstra Conference on the Nixon Presidency, November 20, 1987. Also see Harvey Starr, *Henry Kissinger: Perceptions of International Politics* (Lexington, KY, 1984); Robert S. Litwak, *Detente and the Nixon Doctrine: American Foreign Policy and the Pursuit of Stability, 1969-1976* (New York, 1984); Richard W. Stevenson, *The Rise and Fall of Detente* (Urbana, IL, 1980).

39. Garthoff, *Detente and Confrontation,* 356-59, 385-86, 405-08; Richard Pipes, *U.S.- Soviet Relations in the Era of Detente* (Boulder, CO, 1981), xiii, *et passim.* Pipes traces Jackson's "almost solitary campaign" against Nixon's Soviet policy to late 1970 (xv). See Chapter XV, *supra.*

40. Garthoff, *Detente and Confrontation,* 409-13; William C. Berman, *William Fulbright and the Vietnam War: The Dissent of a Political Realist* (Kent, OH, 1988), 175-88.

41. Kissinger, *Years of Upheaval,* 253-54, 983-85, 991, 1030; Ehrlichman Notes, March 6, April 18, 20, 1973, Ehrlichman Papers, NP, NA.

42. Garthoff, *Detente and Confrontation,* 425-31; Schulzinger, "Rise and Stall of Detente"; Nixon, *Memoirs,* 2:610, 612-13.

43. Garthoff, *Detente and Confrontation,* 434-35; Strobe Talbott, *The Master of the Game: Paul Nitze and the Nuclear Peace* (New York, 1988), 136-38; Nixon, *Memoirs,* 2:610, 621; Nixon and Kissinger, "To Withdraw Missiles We Must Add Conditions," *Los Angeles Times,* April 26, 1987. In a 1986 speech, Nixon said: "The policy of detente cannot be resurrected": "The Pillars of Peace," Address, March 6, 1986, copy courtesy of Richard M. Nixon.

44. Woodrow Wilson, *Constitutional Government in the United States* (New York, 1908), 78; Godfrey Hodgson, *All Things to All Men: The False Promise of the Modern American Presidency* (New York, 1980), 71, 76.

45. Fisher, *Constitutional Conflicts,* 21; Philippa Strum, "A Symbolic Attack upon the Presidency," in Thomas Cronin and Rexford G. Tugwell, *The Presidency Reappraised* (New York, 1974), 249-63, has many useful insights in qualifying the criticism of the "Imperial Presidency."

46. "Nineteen eighty-eight, in Washington, at least, was the year of the pig. Not since the Watergate scandal and its aftermath has concern with the ethics of public officials reached such a feverish pitch," Terrence Moran, "The New Breed of Ethics Scandal," *Legal Times,* December 19, 1988; *WP,* January 30, 1988; *Newsweek,* December 22, 1986, 17; TT, the President and Petersen, April 15, 1973, *U.S. v. M,* NA.

47. *Report of the Congressional Committees Investigating the Iran-Contra Affair,* H. Rep. No. 100-33, S. Rep. No. 100-216 (November 1987), 100 Cong., 1 Sess.; Elizabeth Drew, "Letter from Washington," *The New Yorker,* August 31, 1987, 89; Theodore Draper's articles on the Iran-Contra affair in *The New York Review of Books,* October 8, 22, December 17, 1987, are especially insightful. The literature is growing on the Iran-Contra controversy. *Harper's,* February and April 1988, offered some interesting critiques and debates on the congressional report. A thoughtful analysis is Harold Hongju Koh, "Why the President (Almost) Always Wins in Foreign Affairs: Lessons of the Iran-Contra Affair," *Yale Law Journal,* June 1988, 97:1255-1341.

48. *PPPUS:JC, 1978* (December 12, 1978), 2224; Peter Irons, *Justice at War* (New York, 1983), 351.

49. Louis Fisher, *Constitutional Conflicts Between Congress and the President* (Princeton, 1985), 333.

XXIII: RICHARD NIXON, WATERGATE, AND HISTORY

1. Patman to Rodino, August 9, 1974, HBC Papers; Lewis Interview, July 14, 1986. Representative Hamilton Fish deplored Rodino's action, noting that House members were anxious to learn more about the evidence. Fish Interview, June 25, 1975. DeWitt Ray to Jaworski, August 19, 1974, Jaworski Papers.

2. Taped conversation, Nixon and Korff, May 13, 1974, *WP*, September 3, 1986; Hung Nguyen Tien and Jerrold L. Schecter, *The Palace File* (New York, 1986), 31-32; *Weekly Compilation of Presidential Documents*, "News Conference of October 26, 1973," 9:1291; Nixon to Colson, NPF, June 3, 1974, NP; Eisenhower quote in Fawn M. Brodie, *Richard Nixon: The Shaping of His Character* (New York, 1981), 18-19; *Meet the Press*, NBC, April 10, 1988; *Newsweek*, May 16, 1977. A day after the David Frost interview, Ronald Reagan endorsed the Nixon Doctrine: "When the Commander in Chief of a nation finds it necessary to order employees of the government or agencies of the government to do things that would technically break the law, he has to be able to declare it legal in order for them to do that." Irving Louis Horowitz, "When the President Does It: What the Tapes Really Reveal," *The Nation*, June 18, 1977, 224:753.

3. *Newsday*, November 20, 1987 (account of Haldeman's comments during conference on the Nixon Presidency, Hofstra University); Samuel Kernell and Samuel Popkin, *Chief of Staff: Twenty-five Years of Managing the Presidency* (Berkeley, CA, 1986), 65-67; *60 Minutes*, April 6, 1984; *NYT*, April 6, 1984; *People*, August 29, 1988; Helms Interview, July 14, 1988; Ruckelshaus Interview, August 21, 1986; *Newsweek*, May 16, 1977.

4. Nicholas von Hoffman, "How Nixon Got Strung Up," *The New Republic*, June 23, 1982, 24-27; James A. Nuechterlein, "Watergate: Toward a Revisionist View," *Commentary*, August 1979, 38-45; compare, however, Paul Johnson, *Modern Times* (New York, 1983), 649-53, and "In Praise of Richard Nixon," *Commentary*, October 1988, 50-53, for the view that Watergate was of no consequence and that Nixon's enemies were the real enemies of freedom and constitutionalism. Both Bob Woodward and Lewis Lapham ably dissected the Nixon-imposed revisionism, as well as those of Johnson and others: *WP*, October 2, 1988; *Toronto Globe and Mail*, July 11, 1988.

5. *WP*, May 10, 1984; *Newsweek*, May 5, 1986; *ibid.*, May 19, 1986; David Broder in *WP*, April 5, 1989, citing Marie Shear, "Nixon Rises Again (and it's YOUR fault, you fools!)", *Washington Journalism Review*, April 1989, 44-45; *U.S. News & World Report*, August 13, 1984; see David Frost, *The Presidential Debate* (New York, 1968), 22; *Meet the Press*, NBC, April 10, 1988. Nixon announced in 1985 that he would surrender Secret Service protection. The wire-service story read: "The 72-year-old Nixon, who resigned in 1974 because of the Watergate scandal . . ." *Miami Herald*, March 13, 1985.

6. Victor Lasky, *It Didn't Start with Watergate* (New York, 1977); David Frost, *"I Gave Them a Sword": Behind the Scenes of the Nixon Interviews* (New York, 1978), 270; Richard Nixon, *RN: The Memoirs of Richard Nixon* (paperback ed., New York, 1979), 2:387; Sam Ervin, *The Whole Truth: The Watergate Conspiracy* (New York, 1980), 30. In 1969, the Supreme Court noted that because "an unconstitutional action has been taken before surely does not render that same action any less unconstitutional at a later date." *Powell v. McCormack*, 395 U.S. 486, 546-47 (1969).

7. Alexander M. Bickel, "Watergate and the Legal Order," *Commentary*, January 1974, 21; E. P. Thompson, *Whigs and Hunters: The Origin of the Black Act* (New York, 1975), 263.

8. *NYT*, August 9, 1986; *ibid.*, November 26, 1968; Frost, *"I Gave Them a Sword"*, 646.

9. Richard Whalen, *Catch the Falling Flag: A Republican's Challenge to His Party* (Boston, 1972), 267; David Abrahamsen, *Nixon vs. Nixon: A Psychological Inquest* (New York, 1976), 194; Conable Interview, May 28, 1985; *Newsweek*, October 10, 1987, 36. Sissela Bok, *Lying: Moral Choice in Public and Private Life* (New York, 1978), 173–75.

10. *PPPUS:RN*, 1973, August 15, 1973, 692; *Impeachment of Richard M. Nixon, President of the United States*. Report, Committee on the Judiciary, H.R., 93 Cong., 2 Sess., 361; *National Review*, August 30, 1974, 996; Barry M. Goldwater, *Goldwater* (New York, 1988), 255, 282–83.

11. Frost, *"I Gave Them a Sword,"* 268–269. There is no greater political "heresy than that the office sanctifies the holder of it." Lord Acton, *Essays in the Study and Writing of History* (Liberty Classics ed., Indianapolis, 1985), 2:383.

12. *Politics* (December 1946), 3:402.

13. George Reedy, *Twilight of the Presidency* (New York, 1970), 60; Richard Nixon, *Leaders* (New York, 1982), 334. James Madison thought that impeachment was necessary to protect people against the "perfidy" of presidents.

INDEX

Freedom of Information Act (FOIA, 1966), 591

1974 amendments, 591-2

Freund, Paul, 330

Friday, Herschel, 153, 154

Friendly, Henry, 329

Froehlich, Harold V., 480, 486, 503, 525, 526

Frost, David, 614

Fulbright, J. William, 15, 16, 23, 156, 245, 306, 471, 557, 605

Gallup polls:
Ford approval ratio, 566
Nixon approval ratios: 1972, 226; 1973, 323, 380-1; 1974, 488, 523; after Frost interview (1977), 614; Nixon trial, pro and contra, 588

Garment, Leonard, 5, 56, 61, 67, 85, 87, 90, 93-4, 138, 152-3, 544
assessment of Nixon's effectiveness during crisis, 436-7
Counsel to the President, 325, 422, 423-4, 425, 427; comment on Buzhardt, 536; under Ford, 556, 558; and Nixon pardon, 558-9, 567; urges resignation, 429
and tapes, 385, 423, 447, 536; in Cox crisis, 401, 410; destruction opposed by, 387; erased tape, 430; lack of access, 423, 424-5, 447
view of Agnew case, 394, 395, 397
and Watergate, 217, 243, 313; Haldeman resignation urged, 305-6, 308

Garrison, Sam, 482-3, 497

Garthoff, Raymond, 604

Gazit, Mordecai, 437

Gelb, Leslie, 111

Gelb-Halperin papers, 111

Gemstone, Operation, 199, 200
destruction of file, 210, 216

General Accounting Office, 215, 228, 234, 594

General Services Administration, 433, 434

Gerber, Dan, 479

Gesell, Judge Gerhard, 416, 533, 576

Gladstone, William, 243, 288

Glanzer, Seymour, 209, 300, 330, 368, 462

Goldberg, Arthur, 330

Goldwater, Barry, 32, 51, 58, 94, 195, 223, 385, 386, 577

1964 presidential candidate, 13-14, 15, 16, 17, 56, 63, 73, 104, 576; bombing position, 13, 24
Nixon and, 457, 532, 545, 620; and "smoking gun" tape, 538-9; Watergate concern expressed, 289, 385, 539
possible vice-presidential choice, 1973, 418

Goodell, Charles, 148

Goodyear Tire & Rubber, 435

Graham, Billy, 72, 105, 106, 454-5

grand jury, Watergate, 262, 265, 281, 295, 301, 337, 461-5
favoring indictment of Nixon, 460-1, 462
foreman, 462, 463
indictments by, 336; in early trial (Sept. 15, 1972), 210, 212-13, 222-3, 253; in fall of 1973, 415-16; March 1, 1974, 450, 465; of major figures, 465
investigation of Nixon's criminal involvement, 445, 459-61, 462-3; constitutional issue, 460-1, 463; report submitted to House Judiciary Committee, 461, 463, 465-6; unindicted co-conspirator charge, 459, 463, 464, 465, 468
issue of immunity, 278, 336
Nixon's improper use of secret information, 307, 492, 502
perjury in, 288; admitted in Watergate hearings, 355, 357
request to meet with President denied, 445
subpoena to CREEP personnel, 210
tapes played for, 448-9, 450
term extended, 408, 416
transcripts obtained by White House, 275

Gray, L. Patrick, 101, 252, 294, 308, 341, 344, 586
background of, 266-7
FBI director appointment and hearings, 246-7, 261, 262, 265-71, 272-3, 277, 279, 317
resignation, 317, 318
and Watergate investigation, 189-90, 209, 210, 217, 218-20, 223, 261, 317, 347, 534-5; FBI reports given to White House, 210, 267-8, 415; Hunt evidence received and destroyed, 210, 216, 268, 270, 315, 317, 376; Watergate hearings testimony, 379

impeachment, 348, 389, 450, 471-7
  Agnew's discussions for, 395-6, 398
  of Andrew Jackson, 332, 428, 440, 442,
    472, 476-7, 531
  attempt against Justice Douglas, 149-50,
    477, 482, 512
  of Chase, 442, 475-6, 477
  constitutional provisions for, 442, 473-5;
    "high crimes and misdemeanors"
    phrase, 473-4, 528
  Cox quoted on, 466
  definition by Burke, 517
  history and examples of: English, 442,
    473, 474, 476; United States, 442,
    472, 475-7
  impeachable offenses, political vs. crimi-
    nal, 150, 472, 473-5, 476-8, 495, 519;
    Ford on House as arbiter of, 150, 477,
    478, 501
  vs. indictment, 316, 335, 338, 395-6, 398,
    459-61, 463, 508-10; "co-pendency"
    argument of St. Clair, 509-10
  of Nixon (proposed), 313, 316, 348-9,
    363, 388, 398, 471; calls for, 411,
    412-13, 454, 455; congressional poll,
    381; public poll, 430
  of Nixon, inquiry, 440-2, 444, 450, 463,
    465-6, 486-93, 516-32, 614, 619-20;
    Article I, Obstruction of Justice, 518-
    20, 523-6, 528, 536-7, 538; Article
    II, Abuse of Powers, 518-20, 528,
    538; Article III, Defiance of Commit-
    tee Subpoenas, 529-30; articles IV
    and V rejected, 530; bipartisan results,
    504, 517, 522, 526, 528-30; certainty
    of, after "smoking gun" disclosure,
    536-8, 539; charges discussed, 478,
    481, 497, 518-30; claims of executive
    privilege in, 479, 485; "clear and con-
    vincing evidence" standard, 495, 501;
    closed down after resignation, 545,
    554, 612-13; "fragile coalition" in,
    499-504, 517, 518-22, 523-5, 528-9,
    544; grand-jury approach rejected,
    481-2, 484-5; hearings, 85, 470, 486-8,
    489-93; impeachable offenses issue in,
    150, 463, 477-8, 495, 497, 501, 520;
    impoundment as topic for, 136-7, 478,
    481; issue of timing, 440-1, 479, 487;
    leaks, 487, 488, 493; obstruction of jus-
    tice as topic for, 234, 492, 495, 497,

502, 518-19, 523-6, 538; partisanship
    specter, 440-1, 479, 482, 483, 485,
    487-8, 490, 503, 504, 520, 522, 530-1;
    public debate, 496, 498, 516-17, 520-6,
    527-30; public opinion on, after hear-
    ings, 531; questions of fairness, 481-2,
    484-5, 487; records of Senate Select
    Committee made available, 441, 447; re-
    port of grand jury made available, 460-
    1, 463, 465-6; report to full House, 538,
    557; requests and subpoenas for tapes,
    450, 451, 456, 484-5, 490, 496; resolu-
    tions, 412-13, 455-6, 478-9; specificity
    dispute, 523-5; "Statement of Informa-
    tion," 482, 486-8; St. Clair's rebuttal
    and closing argument, 489-90, 493,
    495-6; substantiation of charges, 519,
    521; transcripts released for, 453, 466,
    484-5, 494; transcript discrepancies,
    485, 486, 493-4, 501; transcript sur-
    prises by St. Clair, 490, 495-6; votes,
    526, 529, 530; Watergate cover-up as
    topic, 481, 486-7, 490-3, 495, 518; wit-
    ness testimony, 490-3
  political nature of, 461, 466, 473-5, 517;
    and partisanship, 476-7, 479
  process, 460, 473; House vs. Senate
    roles, 473
  vs. resignation, 443, 444, 451, 532,
    542-4
  trial and conviction provisions, 473, 476
  of vice presidents, history of, 395-6, 398
  see also House Judiciary Committee
impoundment, 306, 444
  Budget Act controls against, 594-5
  Ford and Carter, 595
  history of, 133-4, 136
  by Nixon, 126, 133-7, 444, 594-5; Ervin
    criticism of, 351, 376; impeachment
    inquiry topic, 136-7, 478, 481
  one-house legislative veto invalidated,
    595
Independent Counsel (*formerly* Special
    Prosecutor) provisions, 583-5
  Supreme Court imprimatur, 585
  used for Iran-Contra cases, 609-10
Indochina, 23, 80, 128, 156
  Communist takeover of, 438, 597-600
  inherent powers issue, 123-5, 201, 374-5,
    376, 507, 509-10
  Truman's assertion, 124, 134, 507

21-2, 25, 60, 130; Gulf of Tonkin Resolution, 15-17, 155, 157; impoundment of funds, 133, 134; and leaks,
108; 1965 State of the Union message,
24; 1967 State of the Union message,
24; press relations, 14, 18-21, 30,
162, 166, 173, 175; public standing of,
13-14, 17-18, 20-1, 24, 28, 30, 57,
59; Supreme Court nominations, 141-
2, 512; taping of conversations by,
386; and Vietnam War, 12-13, 15-16,
17-18, 21-5, 26-8, 30, 59, 71, 112,
114, 155, 597, 601
  quoted, on Nixon, 57, 72
  relationship with Humphrey, 72, 224
  as U.S. Senator, 21, 127-8; maiden
    speech, on power of the president, 26;
    Majority Leader, 11
  White House, 81, 83
  wiretapping alleged, 224, 248
  withdrawal from 1968 race, 32, 58-9, 62,
    542
Joint Chiefs of Staff, 399, 422, 457, 605
  spying on NSC (Radford affair), 116-19,
    326, 492, 495
Joint Congressional Committee on Internal
    Revenue Taxation, 433-4, 451
Joint Congressional Committee on Taxa-
    tion, 590
Jordan, Barbara, 479, 490, 525
journalists:
  Nixon's vindictiveness against, 163-4
  "enemies" list, 104, 118, 163-4, 180-2,
    245
  "friendlies" list,
  wiretapping of, 119-21
judicial branch, 514
  and executive branch, concurrent powers
    doctrine, 515-16
  Jefferson's distrust of, 475-6
  Nixon's contempt shown, 154, 410
  review of FOIA decisions by, 591
  role in special prosecutor provisions,
    581-2, 584
judicial restraint, 507
Justice Department, 246, 422, 446-7
  and activist groups and protests, 97-8, 267
  and Agnew corruption case, 390, 391-2,
    394-5, 396-8, 422
  Anti-Trust Division, 164-5, 176-7, 182
  and "enemies," 106, 107, 150, 176-7

and FOIA, 591
and "Greek Connection," 206-7, 208
hampered by privacy reform provisions,
  590
Nixon's misuse of, as grounds for impeachment, 497, 518
political influence in, 390
role in impeachment process pondered,
  442
Saturday Night Massacre at, and aftermath, 406-11
and Special Prosecutor provisions, 582-3
and Supreme Court Justices, 144-5, 147,
  148, 150-1, 153
too independent for Nixon's purposes,
  422
Watergate break-in investigation of, 189,
  209, 212, 217, 228, 234, 254, 290;
  and Patman Committee investigation,
  228-9, 230-4
Watergate cover-up investigation by, 300-
  8, 315-17, 320, 330, 333, 334-5, 337,
  379, 381, 396, 422, 492; after Cox
  dismissal, 408-9, 412, 466-7

Kalmbach, Herbert W., 235, 253, 273,
  275, 279, 315, 355, 435
prosecution of, 575
testimony of: to House Judiciary Com-
  mittee, 500-1; in Watergate hearings,
  357, 371
Kastenmeier, Robert W., 441, 479, 498
Katzenbach, Nicholas, 330
Kearns, Doris, 30
Keating, Kenneth, 33
Keating, William J., 190
Kefauver Crime Hearings, 346, 351
Kehrli, Bruce, 352
Keith, Judge Damon J., 123-5, 201
Kelley, Clarence, 120, 413-14, 437, 585
Kennedy, Edward, 65, 163, 195-6, 245,
  257, 332, 345, 428, 558, 575, 580
  as "enemy," 103-4, 158, 247, 252, 354,
  358
  and FOIA, 592
Kennedy, Ethel, 332
Kennedy, John F., 10-11, 17, 26, 40, 56,
  90, 131, 134, 203, 420, 426, 428, 607
  assassination of, 10-11, 21, 200, 223,
  417, 482, 542, 617
  and the bureaucracy, 94-5

on Watergate, 189, 190-2, 209, 221,
222, 228, 263-4, 268, 304, 347, 360,
383-4; on Watergate as "thinnest
scandal," 613; on Watergate War,
408-9, 443; *see also subentry* Watergate statements
resignation, 9-10, 80, 532, 540, 544-5,
547-50, 620; calls and pressure for,
398, 411, 413, 429, 439-40, 451, 456,
533, 536-9; congressional poll on,
381; considered in mid-1973, 362-3;
considered in early 1974, 443; considered in summer 1974, 513, 532, 542-
4; public poll on, 430; rejection of
thoughts of, 384, 385, 437, 443-4,
451, 460, 463-4, 504, 536, 542;
speech, 547-9, 612, 613; as sufficient
punishment, 557-8, 567
search for rehabilitation after resignation,
87, 549, 575, 612-18
and Special Prosecutor: calls for Prosecutor considered, 278, 296, 301-2, 323,
329; Cox appointment, 332-3, 338,
381; Cox challenge to Nixon over
tapes, 339, 389-91, 400-5; Nixon vendetta against Cox, 363, 400, 405; Saturday Night Massacre, 406-11, 413-
14, 429; surrender to independent
prosecutor, with Jaworski appointment, 426-7
subpoenaed as witness in aides' trials,
554, 556
and Supreme Court decision on tapes,
513-16
and tapes, 287, 314-15, 324-5, 368-9,
383, 447; defense lawyers denied access to, 423, 424-5, 446-7, 464, 535;
failure to destroy, 386-8, 449, 458;
failure to see full significance, 447,
452-3, 535; listening, 325, 360, 464;
question of possession and control after resignation, 556-7, 561, 563-4,
566; refusals to surrender, 315, 370-1,
378, 384, 385, 388-9, 400-6, 447,
449-50, 456, 464, 467-70, 508; summaries offered, 408, 409, 412, 447;
surrender of some, 447-9, 453, 466,
484-5, 494; tape erasure episode, 429-
31; tape of June 23, 1972 ("smoking
gun" tape), 464, 468, 513, 515, 534-
8; tape of Sept. 15, 1972, 453; tape of

March 21, 1973, 314, 447, 448-9,
453; transcript changes made, 447, 455
tax problems and delinquency, 431-4,
451; as impeachment topic, 481, 530
"Tricky Dick" label, 43, 621
use of his family for PR, 489, 549
varied images of, 33-4, 40; New Nixon,
33, 34, 67-8, 81, 162; Old Nixon, 68,
81
and Vietnam War, 112; in 1968 campaign, 25, 60, 67, 69, 71; peace plan
("peace with honor"), 69, 71, 78, 80,
156, 248, 596-7, 598; pre-1968 views
and statements, 23, 58; during presidency, 3, 78-9, 80, 91, 108, 109, 155-
9, 238, 301, 381, 399, 595-9, 604;
Watergate burden made scapegoat for
loss of, 596-600
and Watergate affair, 42, 190-1, 196-7,
203-5, 208-9, 212-13, 223-6, 268,
323-4; attempts to belittle it, 613-14,
617-18; attempts to turn culpability
into "breaking-the-case" merit, 304-
5, 307; basic defense line from May
1973 onward, 347, 373; basic strategy,
348; blackmail discussions, 276-9,
284, 309, 314, 495-6; clemency discussions, 251, 253, 277-9, 297, 304,
347, 354, 359, 376, 519; cover-up involvement, 189, 196, 200, 213, 217-
18, 223-6, 233-5, 240-1, 251-3, 257-
9, 263-4, 273-89, 291-302, 313-15,
384, 386, 445; cover-up testimony on,
in congressional hearings, 357, 359,
492; criminal involvement, 308, 338,
460-1, 462-3, 497; defense counsel,
325, 422-5, 431, 441-2, 445-7, 448,
480; defense counsel hampered and
deceived by Nixon, 423-5, 429, 442,
446-7, 464, 496; denials of awareness
of cover-up until March 21, 1973, 303,
319, 453, 543; denials of criminal conduct, 338, 347; denials of having encouraged or authorized illegal
campaign tactics, 337, 383; denials of
knowledge of offers of executive clemency, 347, 376; denials of participation
in cover-up, 319, 337-8, 347, 357,
360, 383, 386, 453, 497; denials of
prior knowledge of break-in, 209, 277,
347, 383, 453; finger-pointing against

A NOTE ABOUT THE AUTHOR

Stanley I. Kutler is the E. Gordon Fox Professor of American Institutions at the University of Wisconsin, where he has been teaching since 1964. He is also the founder and editor of the journal *Reviews in American History*. His previously published books include *The American Inquisition* (1982), *Privilege & Creative Destruction: The Charles River Bridge Case* (1971), *Judicial Power & Reconstruction Politics* (1968), *The Supreme Court and the Constitution* (3rd ed., 1984), and *Looking for America* (2nd ed., 1982). He regularly contributes to the *Washington Post*, the *Wall Street Journal*, the *Los Angeles Times*, and the *Christian Science Monitor*. For his book, *The American Inquisition*, he won the Silver Gavel Award of the American Bar Association. He is a Guggenheim Fellow, and he has lectured widely abroad.